ENCYCLOPEDIA OF
Erotic Literature

ENCYCLOPEDIA OF
Erotic Literature

2
L–Z
INDEX

Gaëtan Brulotte
John Phillips

EDITORS

 Routledge
Taylor & Francis Group
New York   London

Routledge is an imprint of the
Taylor & Francis Group, an informa business

Routledge
Taylor & Francis Group
270 Madison Avenue
New York, NY 10016

Routledge
Taylor & Francis Group
2 Park Square
Milton Park, Abingdon
Oxon OX14 4RN

© 2006 by Taylor & Francis Group, LLC
Routledge is an imprint of Taylor & Francis Group, an Informa business

Printed in the United States of America on acid-free paper
10 9 8 7 6 5 4 3 2 1

International Standard Book Number-10: 1-57958-441-1 (Hardcover)
International Standard Book Number-13: 978-1-57958-441-2 (Hardcover)

Library of Congress Cataloging-in-Publication Data

Encyclopedia of erotic literature / Gaëtan Brulotte, John Phillips, editors.
    p. cm.
  ISBN-13: 978-1-57958-441-2 (alk. paper)
  ISBN-10: 1-57958-441-1 (alk. paper)
  1. Erotic literature--Encyclopedias. I. Brulotte, Gaëtan. II. Phillips, John. 1950-

PN56.E7E53 2006
809'.9353803--dc22   2006040224

Visit the Taylor & Francis Web site at
http://www.taylorandfrancis.com

and the Routledge Web site at
http://www.routledge-ny.com

TABLE OF CONTENTS

ADVISORS

Sarane Alexandrian
Superieur Inconnu

Peter Brown
Trinity College, Oxford

Peter Cryle
University of Queensland

Joan DeJean
University of Pennsylvania

Michel Delon
Université de Paris-Sorbonne (Paris IV)

Eve Fishburn
University of North London

Lucienne Frappier-Mazur
University of Pennsylvania

Jay A. Gertzman
University of Bradford

Owen Heathcote
University of Bradford

Maxim Jakubowski
University of Colorado at Boulder

Patrick J. Kearney
University of Colorado at Boulder

Peter Michelson
University of Colorado at Boulder

Jane Mills
Australian Film Television and Radio School

Michael Perkins
University of Essex

Ken Plummer
University of Essex

Gerald Prince
University of Pennsylvania

Everett K. Rowson
New York University

Clifford J. Scheiner
Institute for Advanced Study of Human Sexuality

Joseph Slade III
Ohio University

Douglas Wile
CUNY–Brooklyn College

INTRODUCTION

'I authorize the publication and sale of all libertine books and immoral works; for I esteem them most essential to human felicity and welfare, instrumental to the progress of philosophy, indispensable to the eradication of prejudices, and in every sense conducive to the increase of human knowledge and understanding.' (Marquis de Sade, *Juliette*)

Erotic literature is a global cultural expression represented in nearly all literary forms from the ancient world to the present. Recognizing its rich scope and cultural importance, scholars from around the world are drawn to the genre and the study of erotic literature is now a vast and emerging field. In these two volumes, the *Encyclopedia of Erotic Literature* invites the reader to embark on the scholarly exploration of a genre that traverses the horizon of human sexual experience, transforming our understanding of such experience and the experience of literature as well.

In an interview in 2002, the late French philosopher, Jacques Derrida was asked, if he were to watch a documentary about a philosopher—Heidegger, Kant, or Hegel—what would he wish to see in it. He replied 'Their sex-lives... because it is not something they talk about.'[1] The intellectual tradition of the Judeo-Christian West has repressed its sex-life in much the same way as the philosophers Derrida had in mind, and yet, the poets and story-tellers of West and East alike have never stopped talking about sex. This encyclopedia is the first of its kind: a comprehensive discussion and scholarly analysis of those innumerable works, written in many different languages throughout our known history, in which 'sex-talk' is the dominant discourse. The history of this discourse is as old as the history of writing itself.

During the six years since its inception, this project has attracted considerable intellectual interest from all over the globe. Leading scholars in the world's most renowned universities have acted as advisors from an early stage, as well as contributing many of the 546 entries that make up the two volumes of the work. The total number of contributors exceeds 400.

The conceptual framework determining the general organization of contents prior to its distribution in alphabetical order was divided into four categories: Historical Overviews, Topics and Themes, Literary Surveys, Writers and Works. Historical Overviews are categorized by language/geographical or cultural area and ideally include all literary genres (e.g. the Ancient World or French Canadian Literature); Topics and Themes focus on a predominant or general subject in the field (e.g. Libertinism or Necrophilia) or a critical approach (such as Feminism or Queer Theory); Literary Surveys address genres, or publication issues (Pulp Fiction or Bibliographies, for instance), Writers and Works include individual entries on authors or works —whether attributed or anonymous—(D.H. Lawrence or *Jin Ping Mei*, for example), which address their relation to the history of the genre as a whole, and evaluate their contribution to it. Each entry offers a set of bibliographical references and suggested further readings. With very few exceptions, the length of entries varies from a minimum of 1000 words to a maximum of 8000 words, according to the relative importance of the subject-matter.

We have tried to be as inclusive as possible, but as with all undertakings of this size and scope, there are inevitable omissions. Limitations of space regrettably dictate that lines have constantly to be drawn. Audio-visual works (paintings, photos, films), for example, have not been included, since this is an encyclopedia of the erotic *in literature*. On the other hand, if there are a larger number of entries relating to literature in French, it is because French and Francophone writers have contributed more than any other linguistic culture to the development of the erotic genre. The eminent author and publisher, Jean-Jacques Pauvert has called this phenomenon 'l'exception française'[2], the French exception.

Nonetheless, the *Encyclopedia of Erotic Literature* aims to be universal in scope, both geographically and historically, and to reflect current research in the field. The work is principally intended as a valuable resource for all those studying, researching, or teaching any aspect of erotic literature and/or the history of sexuality. Eschewing technical language wherever possible, it will also appeal to the general reader with an interest in exploring this subject.

QUESTIONS OF DEFINITION

Our definition of erotic literature is a universal one, not a judgmental one, encompassing all fictional genres (the novel, poetry, the short-story, drama and some Eastern forms) but also essays, autobiographies, treatises, and sex manuals from a wide range of cultures. Erotic literature is defined here as works in which sexuality and/or sexual desire has a dominant presence. All types of sexuality are included in this definition. When consulting existing reference works and dictionaries on the subject, and the very few specialized histories of the genre, one is struck by the difficulty scholars have encountered in differentiating erotic literature from pornography or from love stories containing sexually explicit passages. Neither of the existing terms, erotic or pornographic, is neutral. But generally speaking the former is usually taken to refer to an acceptable form of sexual representation, while the latter designates a form that is socially or politically unacceptable. Both terms are therefore infected with a degree of judgmentalism that we sought to avoid in an attempt to provide the richest and widest range of literatures to the reader that reflect the abundant diversity within the genre. The distinction between the erotic and the pornographic depends on arguments and stereotypes that are fundamentally subjective, and that are psychological, ethical, feminist, or aesthetic in nature. Legal rulings are themselves influenced and determined by such arguments which are always culturally and temporally relative.

The psychological point of view is wholly related to reader response. According to this point of view, erotica arouses the individual reader, while pornography does not. This distinction is clearly confusing, since pornography can arouse a reader as much as so-called erotica. Webster's English Dictionary defines 'pornography' as 'a portrayal of erotic behavior designed to cause sexual excitement.' Homosexual literature will not arouse everyone but is part of what we call erotic literature. Literary depictions of necrophilia may not arouse most readers but belong to the erotic tradition. The consensus of scholarship during the last quarter century is that such a literary genre cannot be defined according to the individual reader's desire, since each person has his/her own 'sexual template' as modern psychology calls it. Indeed, many erotic texts do not seek to arouse at all.

From an ethical viewpoint, pornography is what other people find erotic, presupposing the existence of a sexual norm according to which one group of persons judge and reject what they dislike. This argument raises the delicate question of 'perversion', since pornography has frequently been associated with 'perverted' sexuality, i.e. with a sexuality or sexual orientation that is different from one's own. The psychoanalytical concept of 'perversion' tends to construct a sexual norm from the standpoint of which there are deviations. Freud defined 'perversion' as any sexual activity that is not intercourse: hence oral sex is 'perverted', so is masturbation, and so forth. In this view most human sexual habits and erotic inclinations turn out to be 'perverted'. However, the notion of 'perversion' has been revisited by modern anthropologists and historians who have demonstrated the temporal and cultural relativity of the concept. When Pierre Klossowski in twentieth century France writes of a husband who enjoys giving his wife to other men, some may consider this gesture 'perverted'. For the Inuit, on the other hand, such behavior is simply the expression of conventions of hospitality.

The sociological perspective defines eroticism as the pornography of the dominant social class. In this view, eroticism has aristocratic associations, while pornography is a lower-class activity. Thus, pornography but not eroticism may represent a threat to the status quo. Yet, as numerous entries demonstrate, the eroticism of 'high literature' is just as capable of subversion as more popular forms of writing about sex. Erotic works by philosophers during the French Enlightenment, for example, arguably helped to pave the way for the French Revolution. Throughout history, in fact, erotic writings generally can be said to have had a socially leveling influence.

The gender of the author is another spurious yardstick, by which the pornography/eroticism distinction is sometimes measured. In this perspective, men produce pornography while women 'write the erotic'. This argument falters when confronted with anonymity, or the extensive use of pseudonyms. Moreover, some authors employ strategies to make believe that the narrator is male or female, creating confusion as to the author's sex or gender. And what are we to think of the many novels by women in contemporary France that are as explicit or as sexually violent as anything authored by a man? Pro-censorship feminists regard any depiction of sexual behavior which degrades and abuses women as pornographic. Such views are highly subjective, and beg the question of what constitutes degradation or abuse, but if the author of the text or image is male, his gender is itself grounds to condemn him in their eyes. Andrea Dworkin, for example, suggests that 'Male power is the *raison d'être* of pornography: the degradation of the female is the means of achieving this power.'[3] A recent ruling by the Canadian Supreme Court, masterminded by Dworkin and her fellow anti-pornographer campaigner, Catherine MacKinnon, defines the related concept of obscenity according to the harm it does to women's pursuit of equality.[4] Yet, much extreme sexual material, such as gay male 'porn', does not represent women at all.

Legal definitions are no more helpful, as they tend to depend on aesthetic norms which vary from culture to culture, and from period to period. In particular, the way in which obscenity is defined has changed considerably over the centuries. Concepts of obscenity are central to anti-pornography legislation in Britain and the USA, as well as in France. In Britain, the law currently defines obscenity as 'anything that may deprave or corrupt persons who are likely to read, see or hear the matter contained or embodied in it'[5]. In the USA, the so-called 'Miller Test' is still the predominant legal definition of obscenity. According to this test, which originated in a 1973 case tried before the American Supreme Court, Miller v. California, there are three criteria: 1) does a work as a whole appeal to 'prurient interest'?; 2) does it depict or describe sexual conduct in a 'patently offensive way'?; 3) does it lack serious literary, artistic, political or scientific value'?[6]

These definitions of obscenity are dangerously vague, since they all depend upon the inescapable subjectivity and cultural relativity of other terms, such as 'indecent', 'deprave', 'corrupt', 'prurient', 'offensive', 'value', 'harm', 'equality', embedded in them. In the French law of the last two centuries, the concept of 'bonnes moeurs' (which roughly translates as 'public decency') is equally vague and culturally relative, as the history of censorship clearly shows — how many of us would consider Flaubert's *Madame Bovary* or the racier pieces in Baudelaire's best known collection of poems, *Les fleurs du mal* (*The Flowers of Evil*), a threat to public morals now?

All of the above arguments fail to produce a satisfactory distinction between the erotic and the pornographic. In antiquity, the word 'pornographos' bore little relation to our contemporary notion of pornography as writing or images that aim to arouse sexually, since it merely denoted a type of biography, 'the lives of the courtesans', which was not necessarily obscene in content.[7] In fact, it was not until the nineteenth century that the dictionary definition of the word was widened to include 'the expression or suggestion of obscene or unchaste subjects in literature or art'[8], and began, therefore, to assume a pejorative meaning.

The etymology of the word, 'obscenity', by contrast, is dubious. Its modern definition of 'indecent' or 'lewd' is preceded by the archaic meaning of 'repulsive' or 'filthy' (OED). Some recent commentators have suggested that the word originally meant 'off the scene', referring, in other words, to actions in the classical theatre that were too shocking to take place 'on stage' in full view of the audience.[9] What all of these definitions have in common is their subjective basis, for what is 'repulsive' or 'shocking' to some will not be so to others. When used in a sexual context, moreover, the word reveals a profoundly negative attitude to the sexual functions and to sexual pleasure. For Susan Sontag,

'It's just these assumptions that are challenged by the French tradition represented by Sade, Lautréamont, Bataille, and the authors of *Story of O* and *The Image*. Their assumption seems to be that 'the obscene' is a primal notion of human consciousness, something much more profound than the backwash of a sick society's aversion to the body.'[10]

Like 'pornography', then, 'obscenity' has acquired a negative charge in a Western culture, conditioned by the puritanism of Christianity, a negativity which legal definitions have reinforced. For Jacques Derrida, each term of such binaries as 'eroticism' and 'pornography', or 'eroticism' and 'obscenity' is already infected with its opposite, and so becomes ultimately undecidable, a signifier whose signified cannot be finally fixed. In view of these linguistic and conceptual slippages, then, and while accepting that even the word 'eroticism' can never be entirely neutral, the decision was taken at an early stage to discourage the use of 'pornography' and 'obscenity' as terms most likely to convey negative impressions. Thus, they are employed sparingly, and always within a clear historical and cultural context. The term 'erotic literature' also benefits from a more stable meaning throughout history and is more inclusive of the variety of works this encyclopedia covers.

One last point on this issue of definition: the dangers of too broad a definition of eroticism were apparent from the outset, and it was thought that to define any work containing sexual scenes as erotic would be to invite entries on practically the whole of World literature.

CORPUS AND CONTENT

Our selected corpus reveals above all a remarkable diversity in the types of sexuality represented (heterosexuality, homosexuality, sado-masochism, fetishism, incest, etc). This sexual diversity is equally matched by the diversity of literary forms in which these sexualities are represented, from pure dialogue to classical narrative, from the epistolary novel to prose poetry. Style too ranges from the highly metaphorical to the extremely crude. Thus, eroticism is found as much in literary masterpieces as in pulp fiction. This diversity may surprise some readers, since it has often been argued that erotic texts are mediocre in quality and repetitive in form and subject-matter. On the contrary, readers will discover here that erotic literature is far more diverse

than generally believed. Indeed, much erotic writing belongs to the literary avant-garde, thanks to a readiness to experiment and innovate on formal levels. Many of the works discussed are also of considerable philosophical and socio-historical interest, conveying a wealth of fascinating information about the history and evolution of intimacy and the social mores surrounding it, offering insights on rites and taboos, on the history of attitudes to the body, and many other cultural practices.

As for the familiar charge that this is a literature aimed only at the male voyeur, erotic texts frequently appeal to all of the senses, from the evocation of the sensation of bodily touch, taste and smells to the screams, whispers and silences that can accompany the sex-act. Such descriptions speak as much to women as to men. This is a literature that is more likely to undermine than to reinforce conventional thinking and social stereotypes. The traditional unity of the person and the body that our western culture has constructed over the centuries is, for example, repeatedly put into question by a writing that foregrounds bodily pleasure.[11] Erotic writing constantly renews itself, finding new ways of staging and figuring desire. Differences of race or ethnicity tend to be effaced in pursuit of the solitary goal of sexual satisfaction.

Erotic works do sometimes project a utopian vision of the world, which they picture as liberated from all its current limitations. But in doing so, they point to the difficulties associated with such idealism, and raise important philosophical questions in relation to concepts of freedom and the other.

It will have become clear by now that the aims of erotic literature cannot be reduced to sexual arousal alone. Indeed, these texts are inspired by a multiplicity of objectives, social, political, and moral, embracing themes and forms that are just as diverse as those of any other literary genre. The literary depiction of sexuality offers essential insights into every aspect of the human condition. Although eroticism is ostensibly linked to materialist views of life, the body has served throughout history as the central focus of a search that ever seeks to transcend it, reaching out to mythical, metaphysical and spiritual dimensions. In this sense, all erotic texts address issues of both life and death—orgasm in French is popularly described as 'la petite mort'—since, as Freud demonstrated, Eros (the life force) and

Thanatos (the death drive) are inextricably bound up with each other... which amounts to saying that the sexual impulse is a fundamental expression of the human story in all its facets.

The twentieth century authors and thinkers, Georges Bataille and Michel Foucault both believed that sexuality was *the* major problem facing mankind, and yet, for mainly political and religious reasons, the study of erotic expression has largely been suppressed, as much in the academy as in society generally. It is true that the recent rise of 'Sexuality and Gender Studies' in universities has given academics permission to read and teach erotic works, but only within the politically correct context of feminism or queer theory. The two volumes of this encyclopedia represent a much wider critical interest on the part of the hundreds of scholars, men and women, of all ethnicities, genders, and sexualities, teaching and researching in universities on every continent, and under every kind of political regime. Others will hopefully follow the lead that they have taken here.

How to Use This Book

The *Encyclopedia of Erotic Literature* is composed of over 500 signed scholarly essays of 1000 to 8000 words in length. Researchers will find the encyclopedia's **A to Z format** easily navigable. Scholars seeking multiple entries within a specific area of inquiry will find the **thematic table of contents** of great value. There one can browse all of the entries concerning authors and works employing a specific *language* (i.e. Indian languages), *historical overviews* of specific nations, regions and periods (i.e. German: twentieth and twenty-first centuries), *literary surveys* of specific genres and trends (i.e. science fiction and fantasy) and entries exploring discrete concepts (i.e. prostitution) grouped as *topics and themes*. Nearly all of the entries concerning individual works or an entire body of work will be followed by a **capsule biography** of the author. Major articles contain a list of **References and Further Reading**, including sources used by the writer and editor as well as additional items that may be of interest to the reader. And a thorough, **analytical index** will instantly open the work up to every reader.

Gaëtan Brulotte
John Phillips

Biographical note on editors:

Gaëtan Brulotte is Distinguished University Professor of French and Francophone Literature at the University of South Florida in Tampa, U.S.A. He has published extensively on the subject of erotic literature, including a critically acclaimed book *Oeuvres de chair. Figures du discours érotique.*

John Phillips is Professor of French Literature and Culture at London Metropolitan University. He has published extensively on eighteenth and twentieth century French literature and on twentieth century film. His latest books are *The Marquis de Sade: A Very Short Introduction* and *Transgender on Screen.*

Notes

1 *Derrida*, a documentary by Kirby Dick and Ziering Kofman (Jane Doe Films Inc, 2002)
2 Pauvert, Jean-Jacques. *L'Amour à la française ou l'exception étrange.* Editions du Rocher, 1997.
3 *Pornography: Men Possessing Women.* New York: Perigee Books, 1981, p. 32.
4 See ibid., p. 54.
5 The Obscene Publications Act, 1959.
6 See Linda Williams, 'Second Thoughts on Hard Core. American Obscenity Law and the Scapegoating of Deviance' in *Dirty Looks. Women, Pornography, Power* (BFI Publishing, 1993), pp. 46–61; this reference, pp. 48–9.
7 See Linda Williams, 'A Provoking Agent. The Pornography and Performance Art of Annie Sprinkle' in Gibson & Gibson (eds), *Dirty Looks. Women, Pornography, Power* (BFI Publishing, 1993), pp. 176–91; this ref., pp. 181–2.
8 Quoted by Stephen Heath, *The Sexual Fix* (London & Basingstoke: MacMillan, 1982), pp. 105–6.
9 See Linda Williams, 'Second Thoughts on Hard Core. American Obscenity Law and the Scapegoating of Deviance' in Roma Gibson & Pamela Church Gibson (eds), *Dirty Looks. Women, Pornography, Power* (BFI Publishing, 1993), pp. 46–61; this ref., p. 47, n. 1.
10 Susan Sontag, 'The Pornographic Imagination' in Douglas A. Hughes (ed.), *Perspectives on Pornography* (New York: MacMillan, St. Martin's Press, 1970), pp. 131–69; this ref., pp. 153–54.
11 This unity is typically cerebral rather than physical, as Descartes's famous 'Cogito ergo sum' illustrates. The modern French critic and semiologist, Roland Barthes has drawn attention to the relative lack of philosophers of pleasure in the Western tradition and dreamed of writing a history of all the pleasures that societies have resisted, as well as of a history of desire (*Oeuvres complètes.* Paris, Seuil, 1995–2002: IV, 244, 255; V, 555)

LIST OF CONTRIBUTORS

Ivan Adamovic Independent Scholar

Jad Adams Independent Scholar

Jon Adams University of California at Riverside

Jonathan Alexander University of Cincinnati

Sarane Alexandrian Superieur Inconnu

Karen Alkalay-Gut Tel Aviv University

Evangelia Anagnostou-Laoutides University of Reading

Eric Annandale Independent Scholar

Sinan Antoon Dartmouth College

Brian James Baer Kent State University

Roger W. Baines University of East Anglia

Scott Bates University of the South

Hervé Baudry Coimbra University

Heike Bauer Independent Scholar

Gerd Bayer Case Western Reserve University

Edith J. Benkov San Diego State University

Juda Charles Bennett College of New Jersey

Patricia Berney Independent Scholar

Marc-André Bernier Université du Québec à Trois Rivières

LIST OF CONTRIBUTORS

Sarah Berry University of Hull

Anne Berthelot University of Connecticut

David Biale University of California at Davis

Lawrence J. Birken Ball State University

Caroline Blinder Goldsmiths College

Eliot Borenstein New York University

Serge Bourjea Centre d'étude du XXème siècle

Pablo Brescia Independent Scholar

Pollie Bromilow University of Liverpool

Diane Brown Macalaster College

Gaëtan Brulotte University of South Florida

Vern L. Bullough Independent Scholar

Gerald J. Butler San Diego State University

Madeline Camara University of South Florida

Rebecca Chalker Independent Scholar

Anthony H. Chambers Arizona State University

Philippe Che Université de Provence

Pamela Cheek University of New Mexico

Margaret Childs Independent Scholar

William J. Cloonan Florida State University

Peter Cogman University of Southampton

Paul Cooke University of Exeter

Michael G. Cornelius Wilson College

Jordi Cornellà-Detrell Lancaster University

Sébastien Côté Université de Montréal

Maurice Couturier Université de Nice-Sophia Antipolis

David Coward University of Leeds

Linda Craig University of East London

Michael Cronin Dublin City University

Ivan Crozier University College London

Peter Cryle University of Queensland

Louise Curth University of Exeter

Monica S. Cyrino University of New Mexico

Mark Darlow University of Nottingham

Ann Davies University of Newcastle

Dick Davis Independent Scholar

Herbert De Ley University of Illinois at Urbana-Champaign

Philip Deacon University of Sheffield

Sara Munson Deats University of South Florida

Camilla Decarnin Independent Scholar

Laura Desmond University of Chicago

Alexandra Destais Caen's University

James Diedrick Albion College

Sarah Donachie University of Newcastle upon Tyne

Wendy Doniger University of Chicago

David Dorais Independent Scholar

Florence W. Dore Kent State University

Lisa Downing Queen Mary, University of London

LIST OF CONTRIBUTORS

Nathalie Dumas Université d'Ottawa

Ted Emery Dickinson College

Michel Erman Université de Bourgogne

Matt Escobar Independent Scholar

Graham Falconer University of Toronto

Tracy Ferrell University of Colorado at Boulder

Alexandra Fitts University of Alaska Fairbanks

Charles Forsdick University of Liverpool

Claude Fouillade New Mexico State University

David O. Frantz Ohio State University

Lucienne Frappier-Mazur Independent Scholar

Patrick Paul Garlinger Northwestern University

Daniel Garrison Northwestern University

Tom Genrich Independent Scholar

Jay A. Gertzman Independent Scholar

Ruth Gilbert University of Southampton

James R. Giles Northern Illinois University

Bernadette Ginestet Independent Scholar

Philippe R. Girard McNeese State University

René Godenne Independent Scholar

S.E. Gontarski Florida State University

Sarah Gordon Utah State University

Robert E. Goss Metropolitan Community Church in the Valley

Nancy M. Grace College of Wooster

Mark Graybill Widener University

Mary Green University of Manchester

Susan Griffiths University of Cambridge

Terry Hale University of Hull

L. Grant Hamby Independent Scholar

Joseph Harris St Catharine's College-University of Cambridge

Jennifer Harrison College of William and Mary

Owen Heathcote University of Bradford

Rosmarin Heidenreich University of Manitoba

Leon-Francois Hoffman Princeton University

Earl Ingersoll SUNY at Brockport

Ben Jacob Independent Scholar

Karla Jay Pace University

Dominique Jeannerod University College Dublin

Toni Johnson-Woods University of Queensland

Dafydd Johnston University of Wales, Swansea

Jean Jonassaint Duke University

David Houston Jones University of Bristol

Miriam Jones University of New Brunswick, Saint John

Pierre Kaser Université de Provence

Thomas Kavanagh Independent Scholar

Michael Kearney Independent Scholar

Patrick J. Kearney Independent Scholar

Debra Kelly University of Westminster

LIST OF CONTRIBUTORS

Hubert Kennedy Independent Scholar

Brian Gordon Kennelly Webster University

R. Brandon Kershner Independent Scholar

Angela Kimyongür University of Hull

Faye Kleeman University of Colorado at Boulder

Jesse R. Knutson University of Chicago

Marc Kober Independent Scholar

Arne Koch University of Kansas

Adam Carl Komisaruk West Virginia University

Max D. Kramer Columbia University

Ricardo Krauel Princeton University

Selim S. Kuru University of Washington, Seattle

Christophe Lagier California State University Los Angeles

E.M. Langille St. Francis Xavier University

Patrick Wald Lasowski Université de Paris VIII

Evelyne Ledoux-Beaugrand Université de Montréal

Judith Yaross Lee Ohio University

Inger Leemans University of Utrecht

Gwendolyn Leick Chelsea College of Art and Design, University of the Arts, London

L. Scott Lerner Franklin & Marshall College

Alain Lescart University of Connecticut

André Lévy Université de Bordeaux

Darby Lewes Lycoming College

Tod Linafelt Georgetown University

Mark Llewellyn University of Wales

Loïc L. Lominé Cheltenham and Gloucester College of Higher Education

Thomas L. Long Thomas Nelson Community College

Edward Lucie-Smith Independent Scholar

Jean Mainil Northwestern University

Merja Makinen Middlesex University

Trina R. Mamoon University of Alaska Fairbanks

Lou Marinoff City College of New York

Chad Martin University of Natal

Diane E. Marting University of Mississippi

Ulrich Marzolph Enzyklopädie des Märchens

Sophia A. McClennen The Pennsylvania State University

Mark McHarry Independent Scholar

Becky R. McLaughlin University of South Alabama

Mark McLelland University of Queensland

Natania Meeker University of Southern California

Nola Merckel University of East Anglia

Jason A. Merrill Michigan State University

Peter Michelson University of Colorado at Boulder

Olivia Milburn University of London

Meredith Miller Independent Scholar

Carolina Miranda University of Hull

Katia Mitova Independent Scholar

Dominic Montserrat Open University

Ian Moulton Arizona State University West

Bradford Mudge University of Colorado at Denver

Mihaela Mudure Babes-Bolyai University

Elizabeth Newton Independent Scholar

Dany Nobus Brunel University

Scott B. Noegel University of Washington

Benedict O'Donohoe University of the West of England

Francis O'Gorman University of Leeds

Efstratia Oktapoda-Lu Independent Scholar

Dominique Paquet Independent Scholar

Julie Paquet University of Ottawa

Lizabeth Paravisini-Gebert Vassar College

John Parkin University of Bristol

Imogen Parsons Independent Scholar

Julie Peakman University College London

Dominique Péloquin Université Laval

Victor Peppard University of South Florida

John Perivolaris University of Manchester

Michael Perkins Independent Scholar

Chris Perriam University of Manchester

Ina Pfitzner Independent Scholar

John Phillips London Metropolitan University

Patrick Pollard Birkbeck College, University of London

Elizabeth Porges Watson Independent Scholar

Karl Posso The University of Edinburgh

Carrie A. Prettiman Cedar Crest College

Mark Pritchard Independent Scholar

Kirsten Pullen Independent Scholar

Walter P. Rankin George Mason University

Ajay Rao University of Chicago

Kokila Ravi Atlanta Metropolitan College

Mireille Ribiere Independent Scholar

Doug Rice California State University, Sacramento

Keith Richards Wake Forest University

Lee Anne Richardson Georgia State University

Michael Richardson Waseda University

Santiago Rodríguez Guerrero-Strachan Independent Scholar

Leyla Rouhi Williams College

Everett K. Rowson New York University

Cristina Ruiz Serrano The University College of the Cariboo

Frank A. Runcie Université de Montréal

Lorena Russell University of North Carolina at Asheville

Elizabeth Sabiston Independent Scholar

Pierre Saint-Amand Brown University

Lori Saint-Martin Independent Scholar

Elise Salaün Independent Scholar

Sarah Salih University of East Anglia

Tilde Sankovitch Independent Scholar

Angels Santa Universidad de Lleida

Chittaranjan Satapathy Independent Scholar

Andrew Schonebaum Barnard College

Paul A. Scott University of Kansas

Renée Scott University of North Florida

Paul A. Scott University of Kansas

Laurence Senelick Independent Scholar

Dorothy Severin University of Liverpool

Namascar Shaktini Florida Atlantic University

Sachie Shioya Independent Scholar

Debra Shostak College of Wooster

Gérard Siary University of Montpellier

Lisa Sigel DePaul University

Anne Simon Independent Scholar

Abigail Lee Six Royal Holloway, University of London

Joseph Slade III Ohio University

Marie-Agnès Sourieau Independent Scholar

Paul Sprachman Rutgers University

Philip Stewart Duke University

Julie Taddeo Independent Scholar

Jill Terry Independent Scholar

Morten Thing Roskilde Universitetsbibliotek

Lyn Thomas London Metropolitan University

Hannah Thompson University of London

Michael Tilby Selwyn College, Cambridge

Steven Totosy de Zepetnek Independent Scholar

Adrian Tudor University of Hull

James Turner University of California, Berkeley

Richard van Leeuwen Independent Scholar

Agnès Vannouvong Université de Marne-la-Vallée

Dimitris Vardoulakis Independent Scholar

Helen Vassallo University of Exeter

Sage Vivant Custom Erotica Source

Radu Voinescu Independent Scholar

Geoffrey Wall University of York

Ruth Wallach University of Southern California

Keith E. Welsh Webster University

Seth Whidden Villanova University

Frederick H. White Memorial Univerity

Barbara White Advanced Studies in English

Douglas Wile Brooklyn College CUNY

Terry J. Wilfong University of Michigan

Gordon Williams University of Wales, Lampeter

Jane Winston Northwestern University

Gina Wisker Anglia Polytechnic University

Gregory Woods Nottingham Trent University

Derek Wright Independent Scholar

I-Hsien Wu Columbia University

Markus Wust University of Alberta

Marilyn Yalom Independent Scholar

A TO Z LIST OF ENTRIES

THEMATIC TABLE OF CONTENTS

Africa

Djebar, Assia
Egyptian: Love Poetry, Ancient
Hainteny (Madagascar)
Nedjma, L'Amande

Ancient: Greek, Latin

Apuleius
Catullus
Entries
Gilgamesh
Greek: Anthology
Ovid
Petronius Arbiter
Song of Songs, The
Theocritus

Arabic and Persian

Abu Nuwas, al-Hasan
Ibn al-Hajjaj
Ibn Hazm
Jahiz, al-
Nafzâwî, al-
Obayd-e Zakani
Persian: Verse Romance
Suyūtī, Jalāl al-Dīn al-
Thousand and One Nights, The
Tifashi, al-

Caribbean

Laferrière, Dany

Chinese languages

Admirable Discourses of the Plain Girl
Art of the Bedchamber Literature
Bai, Xingjian
Ban, Jieyu
Bi Yu Lou [*The Jades Pavilion*]
Book of Odes [*Shih-Ching*]
Cao Xueqin
Collected Writings of Fragrant Elegance
Deng Xixian
Dengcao Heshang Zhuan [*The Candlewick Monk*]
Ge Hong
Huang
Jin Ping Mei [*Plum in the Golden Vase*] and *Gelian Huaying* [*Flower Shadows behind the Curtain*]
Jingu qiguan [*The Oil Vendor Who Conquers the Queen of Beauty*]
Li Yu
Lü Dongbin
Lü T'ian-chêng
Mao Xiang
Sexual Alchemy Literature, Chinese
Shanqing Huangshu Guuoduyi [*Yellow Book Salvation Ritual of Highest Purity*]
Sun Wei
Szû-ma Hsiang-ju
Tang Yin
Yaohu Yanshi [*The Voluptuous History of Fox Demons*]
Zhang Zu
Zhaoyang Qu Shi
Zhulin Yeshi [*Unofficial History of the Bamboo Grove*]

Eastern European languages

Eliade, Mircea
Eminescu, Mihail

THEMATIC TABLE OF CONTENTS

Topics and Themes

Turkish

L

L. ERECTUS MENTULUS (LUPTON ALLEMONG WILKINSON)

c. 1900–1993
British-American poet, journalist, and publicist

The Identity of L. Erectus Mentulus

In 1935, Lupton Allemong Wilkinson began writing erotica on commission for Roy Mellisandre Johnson, a jaded Ardmore, Oklahoma oil millionaire, by creating "L[ongus]. Erectus Mentulus, Ph.D." (Long Erect Member), the narrator and protagonist of the stories collectively known as the "Oxford Professor" series, in which a lascivious academic dispenses outrageous sexual advice. Gershon Legman says that Wilkinson also wrote poems and parodies using the pseudonyms J. Sumner Radclyffe and Seeley Wilcox ("Erotic Songs," pp. 500–501), but no one has corroborated those claims. In 1938, Wilkinson gathered his Mentulus stories, ran off mimeographed copies, solicited erotic photographs from friends, bound photos and pages into a volume he called *An Oxford Thesis on Love*, and persuaded a match factory to manufacture slip cases for an edition of about a hundred (Scheiner, II, 140–141). These copies circulated until Grove Press published the manuscript in 1971.

An Oxford Thesis on Love

Wilkinson's *An Oxford Thesis on Love*, set in a booth in Dave's Soft-Drink Emporium in an unidentified small American town, opens abruptly. Mentulus (here informally called "Lee") holds forth to a barber, a salesman, and a druggist, a naive trio who have gathered to hear ribald adventures that celebrate but also mock sexual diversity. On the one hand, Mentulus insists that every woman reacts differently to sexual stimulation; that is the book's "thesis," illustrated by eight yarns named after the professor's conquests around the world. Even so, he says, universal "scientific" principles govern all forms of intercourse, and in revealing these *An Oxford Thesis on Love* panders to male fantasy that seduction is a rational enterprise. On the other hand, the book's appeal is clearly anti-intellectual. The professor decries outlandish sexual myths only to replace them with academic pretense; the humor derives from the credulity with which his absurd "research" is accepted. In this regard the stories parody the ponderous quasi-anthropological studies that constituted a species of erotica in the early twentieth century. Sometimes known as "the *National Geographic* syndrome" after the double standard manifest in that staid's magazine's fondness for photographing bare-breasted tribeswomen, the approach justified prurience in the guise of ethnographic scholarship on the sexual habits of "primitive" peoples.

Mentulus cites silly theories such as "Professor Vollmer's," for example, to the effect that "the diameter of the distended vagina is a quadratic function of the length of the mouth and the cube root of the volume of one buttock" (1971, p. 42). Mentulus claims to have invented a "tumescencegraph" to calibrate an erection (a send up of the real penile plethysmograph invented by Karl Freund); classifies women according to four breast types; and pontificates on the alleged causes of fetishes. The stories unfold as responses to questions from the three listeners, each of whom has met resistance from a woman. To the druggist, thwarted by a shopgirl who permits only fondling, Mentulus observes that the shape of her breasts indicates a tendency toward the nymphomania that she fears. He advises tearing a hole in her clothing rather than trying to remove it, which allows her too much time to think. For the professor, guile is key: since all women secretly desire intercourse, the seducer must analyze his prey, find her secret stimulus, and encourage the illusion that she is in control. When deception fails, however, force may be necessary, though here the professor's listeners balk (as may modern readers), when he suggests that violence can unleash a lesbian's latent heterosexuality. "'You advise me to beat and rape the girl?' asked the salesman dubiously. 'If she is the type you have described,' said the professor" (1971, p. 96), observing preposterously in "Liza the Lesbian" that some kinds of lesbianism result from a schoolteacher's compelling a left-handed girl to use her right hand.

Most of the episodes graphically describe intercourse once inhibitions have disappeared, when the "natural" inclinations of the female make her more aggressive than the male.

"Mobile Miriam" smoothly adjusts her motion to her lover's, so that they reach orgasms symphonically, while the screaming gyrations of "Jane of the Bouncing Bottom" trigger geysers of sperm. Hints of a serious gender divide linger, however. The virtuoso muscular control of "Bella of the Clutching Clitoris" reinforces male fears of dominant women, and "Rachel of the Spiralling Venus" sports a sinister vagina dentata borrowed from classic folklore. The gymnastics of "The Tumbling Twins," a pair of acrobats performing in Vienna, are less interesting than the telepathic bond between them, which enables Lorine to feel the professor's penis as it penetrates Lorette. The sisters also figure in "The Better Hole," in which the professor finds that he enjoys anal intercourse with Lorette but not with Lorine, an anomaly he claims has been documented by the fictitious Professor Carr-Saunders. But eventually the professor's assurance gives way to a bewilderment that humor can not mask. Having roughly bedded a reluctant woman, an event he has depicted in Hemingwayesque terms ("Flora the Fridge"), he is astonished when she complains. "The world had been cleft in two and put together again, and this unbelievable wench, lying there with my juice still wet on her cunt hair, looked at me and said, 'It hurt'" (1971, p. 120).

A Further Oxford Thesis on Love and *A Later Oxford Thesis on Love*

According to Legman, Wilkinson quickly tired of the Oxford stories and asked Legman and others in the "Organization," the network of writers furnishing erotica for Johnson, to take over ("Introduction," *Private Case*, pp. 52ff). The "Organization" included Robert Sewall, Caresse Crosby, Robert Bragg, Anaïs Nin, Clement Wood, Robert De Niro, Sr., Gene Fowler, Virginia Admiral, Robert Duncan, and Jack Hanley, among others. By now, the authors-for-hire had learned to keep copies of the stories they sold to Johnson. Individual stories (e.g., "Pussy Bumping"), bound as pamphlets under variant titles, could be sold or rented from drugstores and bookstores to Depression audiences eager for them (Gertzman, pp. 93–101). Legman apparently assembled the mimeographed volumes called *A Further Oxford Thesis on Love* (1938) and *A Later Oxford Thesis on Love* (1939) from stories anonymously written by himself and members of the Organization. (Copies of each of these volumes are now in the Kinsey Institute.) The individual stories follow Wilkinson's format and "thesis"; in each the professor recalls an interlude in which a woman of singular prowess demonstrates a new position or practice.

The Passionate Pedant

Legman himself wrote the four tales of *The Passionate Pedant* (1939). A genuine scholar of sexual customs, Legman here somewhat wearily parodies his own knowledge of cultural variations. The stories also occasionally serve as platforms for Legman to criticize Western imperialism, which leads "Dave," the owner of the Soft-Drink Emporium, who by now resembles a bootlegger, to caution the Professor against "communist talk." Legman's flagging interest is evident in the carelessness with which he renames the protagonist "Professor Martin," and the impatience with which he concludes the tales. Asked if Japanese vaginas are slanted, Martin corrects the falsehood by citing a fabricated *The Alleged Obliquity of the Sino-Japanese Cunt*, then by recounting in "Ochre Osukina" his affair with a geisha whose labia are quite conventional. Borrowing from *Madame Butterfly*, the professor seems perversely proud that Osukina becomes so dependent on his erotic skill that she commits suicide when he leaves Japan. The narrator also kills off the heroine of "Coffee-Colored Cobouti." Cobouti is a Malaysian princess reserved for a high priest, whose annual sacred intercourse with her ensures the land's fertility. Visiting Sumatra to study Australasian languages, Martin clandestinely meets her in the ruins of a temple deep in the jungle, where Cobouti introduces him to toe-sucking as foreplay to their intercourse. The Dutch later execute her for leading a revolution. In "Murky Mwamba," set in Mozambique, Martin decries racism even as he endorses the myth of large black penises. He also argues for the superiority of oral sex, which does not preclude his engaging in rough anal sex with his "dusky" lover. In the final story, "Multimethodical Marise," the Professor enjoys a Hungarian on the Vienna-Bucharest Express. Marise encourages him to ejaculate between her breasts, in the crook of her elbow, and in her armpits, and finally treats him to analingus. His imagination

seemingly depleted, the professor then pleads an engagement with a young lady to avoid telling more tales.

The Oxford Professor

Legman attributed the fourth volume in the series, called *The Oxford Professor*, entirely to Robert Sewall (*Horn Book*, p. 36), but may have written part of it himself (see Scheiner, *Compendium*, item 1322). The mimeographed volume appeared around 1948, but the stories were probably written earlier. Stylistically superior to earlier installments, the six stories here are "The Choir Loft," "Alpine Annie," "Tenacious Theresa," "Dipsomaniacal Daisy," "Jacinthe," and "Leslie." Dave now serves wine in the soft-drink parlor, while the druggist, salesman, and barber have been given individual names. The jumble of comic folklore and spurious "authorities," however, remains central. Typical is "Jacinthe," told to rebut the druggist's observation that intercourse underwater is impossible. The story takes place in Paris, where Mentulus has been studying the theories of "Yatumani Norashashu Hirosata," whose lecture before the "Catalonian Society for the Classification, Glorification and Continuation of Cunt" asserted that masculine ears, properly trained, can detect from the timbre of a woman's voice the exact degree of her readiness for sex. By the time Mentulus meets Jacinthe, a Javanese living near the Sorbonne, he can decipher her signals of passion, although her eagerness, as he describes it, would be hard to miss. Jacinthe's expertise includes special ointments that seal orifices tightly enough for sex in a pool, an experience the professor calls unique. Thus edified, the listeners trot out another canard, so that the professor can begin another story: "'You know, Joe [the barber],' the salesman said seriously, 'the Eskimo women have their cunts under their left armpits'" (1968, p. 199).

Torrid Tales

The series guttered out with *Torrid Tales* (c. 1950), two inferior tales written by an unknown writer aiming at a literary style. In the first, "South of the Border," "Professor Martin" relays a memoir by Jan Sumner, a correspondent for *The New York Evening Times* expelled from Mexico for articles critical of President Cardenas.

Speaking in first person, Jan recalls a Mexico City menage a trois involving herself, a prostitute called Juana, and an Amerian prize-fighter named Johnny Blair. When their sexual excess threatens to ruin Blair as a boxer, Jan resolves to send Juana and Johnny away, but finds to her chagrin, that they have decamped before she can make her grand gesture. The second story, "The Court of Kings," is curiously romantic, and, measured against the graphic standards of the series, sexually reticent. Here the barber dreams of traveling with the professor to exotic places as he listens to the tale of yet another princess, an Indian named Ahdali, who couples with Martin in yet another ruined temple. The tale ends on a note that makes explicit the appeal of the *Oxford Professor* series: "'Gosh,' said the barber, 'I can't get over it. A real princess!'" (*Oxford Professor Returns*, p. 182).

Biography

Lupton Wilkinson was probably born in England about 1902. In the United States, after publishing two volumes of poetry (*Interludes*, 1925, and *Blood and Silver*, 1928), he wrote articles, poems, and short stories for the *North American Review* and the *Saturday Evening Post*, and sensational fiction (e.g., "Blonde Alibi," 1931) for pulp magazines such as *Thrilling Detective* and *Detective Story Magazine*. During the early 1930s, he worked as a publicist for the Motion Picture Producers and Distributors Association, often acting as an emissary of Will Hays; Wilkinson's association with the Hays Office lent substance to the legend that censors themselves secretly produce erotica. During the 1940s Wilkinson promoted the careers of Clark Gable, Katherine Hepburn, and Alfred Hitchcock for Metro-Goldwyn-Mayer Studios. He died in St. Louis on June 4, 1993.

JOSEPH SLADE III

Selected Works

A Further Oxford Thesis on Love. Wherein Longus Erectus Mentulus, Ph.D., late fellow of Oxford College, proposes numerous incidents in his experience tending to demonstrate the proposition that in time of stress the unregenerate soul seeks not its own salvation but rather its propagation, the whole cast in the form of amusing but instructive reminiscences and appended by factual sidelights and critical observations on various subjects but more especially on the dominant factor of their [sic] eternal cunt. Done by the hand of the author into a manuscript at Onancock, Virginisa [sic] [New York] 1939; rpt. *The Further Adventures of the Oxford Professor: A Continuation of the Famed Professor's Exploits on Beds Around the World*, by L. Erectus Mentulus. Atlanta: Pendulum Books, 1968. [By Gershon Legman? et al.].

A Later Oxford Thesis on Love. Wherein the author, L. Erectus Mentulus, proves that the waging of the pubic war is a distinct and separate art form in which the participants, through the manner whereby they conduct themselves on its battlefields, may express themselves with more exactness than in any other; this theorem established, examined and restated in the form of narrative and the whole being an inspirational document on the sexual forms as well as a study. Done by the hand of the author into a manuscript at Sopchoppy, Florida, [New York] 1938. [By Gershon Legman et al.].

The Oxford Professor. In which L. Erectus Mentulus, Ph.D., late of Oxford College, is taken further in the narration of his adventures and misadventures, erotic, alcoholic, and otherwise; not to mention a choice accompaniment of drolleries, notes and excursi of one sort or another, metaphysical & also miscellaneously edifying and entertaining. Done by the Hand of the Author Into a Manuscript at Natchitoches, Louisiana [New York, Shomer, c1948]; The Oxford Professor, by L. Erectus Mentulus, Ph.D., Atlanta: Pendulum Books, 1968; The Professor's Tale, Industry, CA: Collectors Publications, 1968. [By Robert Sewall and (possibly) Gershon Legman.].

An Oxford Thesis on Love. In which L. Erectus Mentulus, Ph.D., late fellow of Oxford College, draws from his various experiences for the instruction, entertainment and greater zest of his colleagues, friends and admirers. One Hundred [mimeographed] Copies Done Into A Book By The Hand Of The Author, Taos New Mexico [New York], May 1938; An Oxford Thesis on Love, In which L. Erectus Mentulus, Ph. D., late fellow of Oxford College, draws from his various experiences for the instruction, entertainment and greater zest of his colleagues, friends and admirers. New York: Grove Press, 1971. [By Lupton A. Wilkinson.].

The Passionate Pedant: Being A New Oxford Thesis on Love, wherein L. Erectus Mentulus, late of Oxford, establishes incontrovertibly that the sexual enjoyment of women of divers races is evocative of distinctly different types and degrees of pleasure, through narratives of his own experience, with particular emphasis upon pyschophysiological adumbrations et cetera, for the entertainment as well as the enlightenment of his friends. In Cunnis diversis–voluptates diversae. Done By The Hand of The Author Into A Manuscript At Oshkosh, Wisconsin [New York] September 1939. [By Gershon Legman.] Rpt. with Torrid Tales as The Oxford Professor Returns, New York: Grove Press/Venus Library, 1971.

Pussy Bumping, by L. Erectus Mentulus, n. p.: Privately printed, c. 1940. [Attributed to Robert Sewall (Kinsey Institute).].

Torrid Tales, or, South of the Border, [New York]: Varoni Publications [Miller Brothers?], 1950? (two mimeographed versions). [Author unknown.] Rpt. with *The Passionate Pedant* in *The Oxford Professor Returns*. New York: Grove Press/Venus Library, 1971.

Attributed to Wilkinson

"Radclyffe, Sumner J." trans. *The Imitation of Sappho*, by "Ibykos de Rhodi." "Bruxelles: Privately Printed" [New York: Gotham Book Mart], c. 1930.

"Wilcox, Seeley." *Les Oraisons et Chansons de Marianne de Bon Coeur* (and) *La Vierge Montagne*, manuscript with erotic illustrations signed "José del Castillio." New York, c. 1935.

Unpublished erotic parodies and verse in English with French titles, mimeograph. New York: P. Shostac, 1935.

Further Reading

Cook, Michael L., and Stephen T. Miller, comps. *Mystery, Detective, and Espionage Fiction: A Checklist of Fiction in U.S. Pulp Magazines, 1915–1974.* 2 vols. New York: Garland Publishing, 1988.

Gertzman, Jay A. *Bookleggers amd Smuthounds: The Trade in Erotica 1920–1940.* Philadelphia, PA: University of Pennsylvania Press, 1999.

Legman, Gershon. "Erotic Folksongs and Ballads: An International Bibliography," *Journal of American Folklore*, 103 (October/December 1990): 417–501.

———. *The Horn Book: Studies in Erotic Folklore and Bibliography.* New York: University Books, 1964.

———. "Introduction," *The Private Case: An Annotated Bibliography of the Erotica Collection in the British (Museum) Library*, by Patrick J. Kearney. London: Landesman, 1981.

Scheiner, Clifford J. *Compendium: Being a List of All the Books (Erotica, Curiosa, & Sexology) Listed in Our Catalogs 1–6 (1978–1988).* Brooklyn, NY: C.J. Scheiner, Books, 1989.

———. *Encyclopedia of Erotic Literature.* 2 vols. New York: Barricade Publishing, 1996.

Walsh, Frank. *Sin and Censorship: The Catholic Church and the Motion Picture Industry.* New Haven, CT: Yale Univerrsity Press, 1996.

LA FONTAINE, JEAN DE

1621–1695
French poet

Contes et nouvelles

As something like the Woody Allen of the seventeenth century, La Fontaine rarely wrote anything that was not clearly and visibly an adaptation of an earlier source. His ribald *Contes* are based mainly on such Renaissance writers as Ariosto, the *Cent nouvelles*, the *Heptaméron*, and, most especially, Boccaccio.

Adapting such conventional rowdy stories posed special problems in the classicist 1660s–1670s, when *bienséance* was an essential rule of the classicist aesthetic. In a preface La Fontaine reacts defensively to possible suggestions that his stories were licentious or that they were hard on women. He denies any intention of attacking good morals, and he argues that true *biénseance* just means saying things in a way that fits the subject. Anyone who might want to make Boccaccio as modest as Virgil would surely do nothing worthwhile. It is neither the true nor the *vraisemblable* that make the beauty of such stories, he says. It is simply "la manière de les conter."

Perhaps the most striking example of such tightrope walking is La Fontaine's very first tale, *Joconde*, adapted from Ariosto.

At the court of Lombardy, its especially handsome prince is fatigued by all the attention he receives from court women (La Fontaine never says just what is so fatiguing). He decides he needs an assistant, as handsome or handsomer than is he. One of the courtiers sends for his brother, Joconde. Joconde's wife pleads with him not to go. She will die if he goes to court. But he rides off anyway. Having forgotten something, however, he retraces his steps—and finds his wife asleep in the arms of a gross valet. Joconde doesn't wake them, since in such a case he would be obliged to kill them both:

```
. . . il n'en fit rien;
    Et mon avis est qu'il fit bien.
    Le moins de bruit que l'on peut faire
        En telle affaire
.Est le plus sûr de la moitié
[    . . . he did nothing.
    And my opinion is that he did well.
    The less noise you make
        In such a business
    Is the safest by at least half.]
```

Joconde's good looks fade. He is somewhat consoled, however, when he discovers the prince's wife has taken a dwarf as her lover. After many preambles ("Il ne faut à la cour ni trop voir ni trop dire") he tells the prince. The prince is devastated:

```
Mais bientôt il le prit en homme de courage,
    En galant homme, et, pour le faire court,
        En véritable homme de cour.
[But soon he took it as a man of courage,
    As a worldly man, and, to be brief,
        As a true courtier.]
```

The two of them, thoroughly disillusioned, decide to travel all over Italy seducing other people's wives. After a while, though, they think about settling down. They find a servant girl. To ensure her fidelity she will sleep between them. One night, however, the girl's boyfriend won't take no for an answer. He climbs on top of her, between the two princes, has his way with her, and as each prince wakes up he finds she is busy with someone else (presumably the other prince). The next morning each prince accuses the other of monopolizing her favors. When the girl confesses, they are disillusioned once again. They decide to go home and forget the whole thing. As is typical in classicist narrative, after some aberration, everything becomes normal again. Everything is just as it was before:

```
Ainsi que bons bourgeois achevons notre vie,
Chacun près de sa femme, et demeurons-en là
[Just like good bourgeois let's finish our lives
Each one close to his wife, and let's leave it at that.]
```

The prince and Joconde start out as handsome, superior beings. They end up being just like everybody else. The eroticism of this story consists in the racy situations—but also in La Fontaine's sly, ironic, cynical, elbow-in-the-ribs commentary:

```
Vous autres, bonnes gens, eussiez cru que la dame
    Une heure après eût rendu l'âme.
```

```
Moi qui sais ce que c'est que l'esprit d'une femme
    Je m'en serais à bon droit douté.
[You other naïve people would have thought that the
    lady
    Would have given up the ghost within an hour.
I, who know the heart of a woman, with good reason
    Would have doubted.]
```

Other La Fontaine tales treat *L'Oraison de Saint Julien*, in which a traveler is attacked by robbers and more or less left to die. He finds his way, however, to the house of a merry widow, who rescues and entertains him. In the *Fiancée du roi de Garbe* a princess sets out to become the bride of the king of a far off country. On the way, though, she is kidnapped, seduced, and has eight different adventures (or misadventures), before being delivered as a virgin to the king. La Fontaine writes, "Je me suis écarté de mon original . . ."

Possibly the most striking piece, typically printed with the *Contes*, is La Fontaine's *Clymène*. In this closet comedy the god Apollo complains to the nine muses that there are no more good poems about love:

```
Le siècle, disait-il, a gâté cette affaire:
Lui nous parler d'amour! Il ne le sait pas faire.
Ce qu'on n'a pas au coeur l'a-t-on dans ses écrits?
[Worldly things have spoiled all that:
Talk to us about love! They don't know how to do it.
What they don't have in their hearts, how can they
    write about it?]
```

Apollo expresses sympathy for a certain Acante, very much in love with Clymène. The various muses try out different well known poetic styles—the eclogue, the pathetic, the comical. They pastiche the style of Clement Marot, they do the ode, they do *dizains*, all without melting the heart of Clymène.

Finally the god of love, grateful for so much poetry in his honor, decides to intervene. He whispers to Acante: "Baisez-la hardiment;/ Je lui tiendrai les mains, vous n'aurez point d'obstacle" ["Take her; don't hesitate; I'll hold her hands; you won't have any obstacle"] The rest, says Acante, is a miracle.

Biography

La Fontaine was born in 1621 in the east-of-Paris provincial town of Chateau-Thierry. He is best known as the author of *Fables* (1668 and after), said to be the bestselling book of the seventeenth century, and four books of *Contes* (1664 and after), which readers clamored for, but for which he occasionally had to apologize, and which held up his entrance into the French Academy.

HERBERT DE LEY

Editions

La Fontaine, Jean de. *Oeuvres*, Grands écrivains, 10 vols., 1883–1892.
———. *Oeuvres complètes* I, ed. J.-P. Collinet, Pléiade, 1991.

Further Reading

De Ley, Herbert. *Fixing up Reality. La Fontaine and Lévi-Strauss*. Paris, Seattle, Tübingen: Biblio 17, 1996.
Fumaroli, Marc. *Le poète et le roi. Jean de La Fontaine et son siècle*. Paris: Fallois, 1997.
Giraudoux, Jean. *Les cinq tentations de La Fontaine*. Paris: Grasset, 1938.
Lapp, John C. *The Aesthetics of Negligence: La Fontaine's* Contes. Cambridge: The University Press, 1971.
Lesage, Clare, ed. *Jean de La Fontaine*. Paris: B.N.F. and Seuil, 1995.

LA METTRIE, JULIEN OFFRAY DE

1709–1751
French doctor, essayist, and philosopher

As an author of erotic texts, Julien Offray de la Mettrie is perhaps best known for his influence on the Marquis de Sade, who famously misquotes his *Discourse on Happiness*. "La Mettrie was right," Sade writes, "when he said that it was necessary to wallow in filth like pigs; and that we should find pleasure, as the latter do, in the highest degree of corruption." La Mettrie's writing on erotic love was indeed scandalous, in the eyes of his eighteenth-century readers, for its participation in a form of libertine materialism influenced by a heterodox (and often hedonist) Epicurean tradition of atheist critique. With his commitment to a scepticism inherited in part from Montaigne and the seventeenth-century French libertines, La Mettrie aimed to strip both religious and philosophical orthodoxies of their pretensions to an absolute and incontrovertible truth. In their place, he set a voluptuous image of philosophical inquiry as sensual pleasure. For La Mettrie, "learning has its ecstasies, just as love does."

In his most famous essay, *Machine Man*, La Mettrie argues in favor of an understanding of bodily processes (rather than spiritual or intellectual ones) as determining factors in human behavior. In La Mettrie's words, "The human body is a machine which winds itself up, a living picture of perpetual motion," and sexual desire is a crucial part of this naturally occurring mechanism. Yet La Mettrie does not share Sade's attachment to violence as a mode of sensual and philosophical purification. Nor does his thorough-going materialism depend on a conception of human existence as that of a coldly mechanical community of cyborgs lacking in imaginative ability. Instead, La Mettrie's emphasis, in both his scientific works and his excurses on the joys of erotic experience, remains firmly on the extraordinary delight to be taken in the development of an innately human capacity for sensuousness (or "volupté").

In fact, La Mettrie sees this capacity for erotic experience both as a kind of sensation—the ability to feel erotic pleasure—and as a mode of imaginative perception that he ultimately defines as the mainspring of thought itself. Not only does La Mettrie portray the quest of the philosopher for knowledge as fundamentally sensuous—a kind of intercourse with the natural world—but, in his writings on erotic pleasure (*Sensuousness* and *The Art of Pleasure*), he sees the potential for sensuousness as making access to genuine philosophical knowledge possible: "all nature is in the heart of he who feels sensuousness." Intellectual and sexual delight are intimately conjoined in La Mettrie's work, since erotic feeling can function as a means of linking poetry to science, literary writing to medical discourse. All are expressions of a creative, sensual impulse which produces a commingling of human subjects and the world that surrounds them.

La Mettrie's most widely read work is unquestionably his treatise *Machine Man*, published while he was in exile in Holland. To a certain extent, the implicit mechanical determinism of the title of this essay has overshadowed its author's consistent interest in the connections between erotic delight and imaginative philosophical reflection. His first writing focused on this topic, the short essay initially published under the title *Sensuousness* (and later under *The School of Sensuousness*), predates *Machine Man* by about two years.

Sensuousness begins with a series of literary portraits in which La Mettrie distinguishes carefully between writers who are "obscene and dissolute" and those who are the "masters of the purest sensuousness." While this categorization resembles the modern distinction between pornography and erotica, La Mettrie makes use of his taxonomy, not to extol the virtues of a more muted erotic sensibility, but to demonstrate the multifarious perceptiveness characteristic of the sensuous nature. For La Mettrie, "obscene" writers, who subscribe to a kind of fantasy of objectivity in their almost scientific portrayals of bodies, evince a limited view of human experience. "They wish to see everything and to imagine nothing," he writes. La Mettrie's Epicurean voluptuary, on the contrary, cultivates a state of permanently heightened sensation that renders the very act of reflection a highly pleasurable one; as a result, "to be happy, he has only to wish to be so." The faculty most privileged by this voluptuary is thus not reason, which strips objects of the pleasure to be taken in them, but imagination, which multiplies the possibilities for delight.

These themes—as well as an emphasis on the crucial role played by the imagination—reappear in *Machine Man*, in the dedication to which La Mettrie claims that "nature is the nourishment of sensuousness, and the imagination its triumph." However, in the *Discourse on Happiness*, published a year later, he seems to retreat somewhat from the avid sensualism of his earlier works. "I do not pretend to make happiness consist only in sensuousness," he writes. Nonetheless, he affirms, towards the end of the essay, "It is in any case still plaisir, sensuousness, or any other agreeable sensation which is the necessary cause of our actions."

Despite the hesitations visible in *Discourse on Happiness*, La Mettrie reaffirmed his youthful attachment to an erotic, libidinous philosophy of pleasure before his premature death. Towards the end of his life, he reworked his *School of Sensuousness* as *The Art of Pleasure* and embraced anew (in both *The Art of Pleasure* and *The Systeme of Epicurus*) a vision of materialist philosophy as an *ars erotica*— in which, in the words of Michel Foucault, "sex serves as the basis for an initiation into knowledge"—rather than as a *scientia sexualis* aiming to dissect and discipline human sexual desire under the light of reason.

While La Mettrie's erotic philosophy has been seen as a stepping stone on the way to the more intensely transgressive Sadean *oeuvre*, La Mettrie's work represents in its own right an important contribution to theories of pleasure as a motive force in human existence. His understanding of sensuousness as ideally a kind of "sixth sense" at work in intellection—from memory to scientific reasoning—as well as in bodily experience stands as a significant contribution to materialist philosophy as a source, not of a gloomy determinism, but of hope and transformative possibility for humankind.

Biography

Born in Saint-Malo, 23 November 1709. Attended colleges of Coutance and Caen before enrolling at the Collège du Plessis, Paris; began studies in natural science and philosophy at the Collège d'Harcourt, 1725. Student of medicine at the Faculty of Paris, 1727–1731; received medical degree from University of Reims, 1733. Continued medical studies in Leiden, 1733–1734. Returned to Saint-Malo to begin medical practice, 1734. Married in 1739; one daughter and one son, who dies in 1748. Left Brittany to return to Paris, falling in with libertine and free-thinking circles, 1742. Served as physician to the Duke de Grammont and to a regiment of the French Guards during a series of military campaigns, 1742–1745; placed in charge of military hospitals in Flanders, 1745. Fled to Holland after his

Natural History of the Soul was condemned and burned by the Parliament of Paris, 1746. Obliged to leave Holland for Potsdam after 1747 publication of *Machine Man*, 1748. Served as "lecteur" and doctor, as well as a member of the Berlin Academy of Sciences, in the court of Frederick II, 1748–1751. Died, of "indigestion," at Frederick's court, 11 November 1751.

NATANIA MEEKER

Selected Works

La Volupté. 1745(?).

L'École de la volupté. 1746.

L'Homme machine. Leiden, 1747; as *Man a machine*, translated by Richrad A. Watson and Maya Rybalka in *Man a machine and, Man a plant*, edited by Justin Leiber, 1994; as *Machine Man*, translated and edited by Ann Thomson in *Machine Man and Other Writings*, 1996.

Traité de la vie heureuse, par Sénèque, avec un Discours du traducteur sur le même sujet. Potsdam: Voss, 1748; first part as *Anti-Seneca or the Sovereign Good*, translated and edited by Ann Thomson in *Machine Man and Other Writings*, 1996.

L'Art de jouir. Berlin, 1751.

Système d'Épicure in *Oeuvres philosophiques.* Berlin, 1751; as *The System of Epicurus*, translated and edited by Ann Thomson in *Machine Man and Other Writings*, 1996.

Further Readings

Falvey, John. "Women and Sexuality in the Thought of La Mettrie" in *Women and Society in 18th-Century France: Essays in Honour of J.S. Spink*, edited by Eva Jacobs et al, London: The Athlone Press, 1979.

Jauch, Ursula Pia. *Jenseits der Maschine: Philosophie, Ironie und Ästhetik bei Julien Offray de La Mettrie (1709–1751).* Munich and Vienna: Carl Hanser Verlag, 1998.

Liu, Catherine. *Copying Machines: Taking Notes for the Automaton*, Minneapolis: University of Minnesota Press, 2000.

Rosenfield, Leonore Cohen. *From Beast Machine to Man-Machine: Animal Soul in French Letters from Descartes to La Mettrie*, New Haven: Yale University Press, 1968.

Thomson, Ann. *Materialism and Society in the Mid-Eighteenth Century: La Mettrie's "Discours préliminaire,"* Geneva: Librairie Droz, 1981.

Tiffany, Daniel. "The Lyric Automaton" in *Toy Medium: Materialism and Modern Lyric*, Berkeley: University of California Press, 2000.

Vartanian, Aram. "La Mettrie, Diderot, and Sexology in the Enlightenment" in *Essays on the Age of Enlightenment in Honor of Ira O. Wade*, edited by Jean Macary, Geneva: Librairie Drox, 1977.

Ibid. *La Mettrie's "L'Homme machine": A Study in the Origins of an Idea*, Princeton: Princeton University Press, 1960.

Wellman, Kathleen. *La Mettrie: Medicine, Philosophy, and Enlightenment*, Durham, North Carolina: Duke University Press, 1992.

LA MORLIÈRE, JACQUES ROCHETTE DE

1719–1785
French Novelist

La Morlière's libertine novel *Angola, histoire indienne* (1746) uses the device of the oriental fairytale to provide both a portrait of French court society at the middle of the eighteenth century and a fascinating glimpse at how people actually read and responded to erotic novels. The novel opens with the story of how, at Angola's birth, all the fairies of the earth were invited by his father, King Erzeb-can, to give him gifts. As it happened, the supremely ugly Mutine, offended by the father's indelicate gift to her of a mirror, bestows on the baby the dubious gift of patience, a patience to be exercised when he comes to see his eventual beloved pass first through the arms of a rival. Appalled at what Mutine has done, the queen of the fairies, Lumineuse, a female version of Louis XV, proposes to unravel the curse by having Angola come to her court at puberty. There, the reigning spirit of *libertinage* and its serial conquests forestalling any enslavement to love will surely provide an effective remedy to the fate that threatens.

When the young Angola arrives at this thinly disguised version of Versailles, the fairytale motif is dropped and the novel becomes a witty satire of Queen Lumineuse's utopia of *libertinage*. She makes clear to the young man that his goal is not to avoid passion, but to remain its master. More than any other, it is the passion of love that must be carefully modulated. Guided by his friend Almaïr and his thoroughly non-possessive relation with his mistress, Aménis, Angola must learn never to confuse the joy of seduction with any one of the changing configurations of partners that occur as its results. To confuse coupling with one particular couple is to set oneself against the forces of change and movement that preside over the human condition. When the timid Angola finds himself infatuated with Zobéide, a close friend of Aménis and someone Almaïr also desires, the perfect occasion has arisen for Angola to learn the libertine's version of patience, a patience that will undo Mutine's curse by insulating him from jealousy and suffering. Recognizing that moving apart is just as integral a stage within the process of coupling as coming together, Almaïr explains that he feels no jealousy toward Zobéide's obvious preference for the recently arrived Angola.

The fact that tomorrow will be unlike today, that he and Zobéide may one day be just as probable a couple as Angola and Aménis, endows all involved in such displacements, the women no less than the men, with a lucidity beyond possessiveness and suffering. Serial seductions are the best prophylaxis to the self-inflicted suffering of passionate love. *Angola* does not, however, become either a guidebook for masculine seduction (Crébillon's abiding temptation) or an illustration of feminine resistance and control (Marivaux's abiding temptation).

La Morlière subsumes both these options within a larger and more fundamental dynamic proper to the couple as a mutually defining duality. *Angola* is a story of coupling itself, of coupling as a form of conviviality redefining those who enact its rituals and run its risks. La Morlière lays bare a protocol of social and sexual exchange that lies outside the traditional

options represented by the libertine's celebration of deception and the idealist's solipsism of passion.

Angola's story also tells us something otherwise unnoticed about Enlightenment reading practices, about how and why people so voraciously consumed the scenarios of desire making up the libertine novel. The chapters describing Angola's sexual initiation by none other than Lumineuse foreground the reading together of an erotic novel as a practice that allows Angola finally to overcome the timidity that has so far been his lot. Swept up by this reading as a couple, Angola is able to raise his eyes from the page and complete with Lumineuse the transition from the novel's third person to the first and second person of their own coming together. Emphasizing the contagious desire flowing between the novel his characters read and the scene they enact, La Morlière's staccato alternation between excerpts from their reading and descriptions of their actions breaks down the separation between reading and acting in such a way that life becomes the perfect imitation of art. With this open passage between *reading as a couple* and *coupling while reading* as the structural and semantic center of his novel, La Morlière raises to the power of two the "mirror effect" so frequent in libertine novels of a character who enacts a scene that has been read.

The last stage of Angola's story begins when, having given in to the dangerous powers of the imagination, he falls in love with a woman he knows only through the portrait of her he has happened to come upon in a jewel box belonging to Lumineuse. When he actually meets and falls in love with Luzéide, whom Lumineuse has thoughtfully summoned to her court, he becomes a man enslaved to full-blown passion. Discovering that passion and patience are both rooted in the Latin *patior*, to suffer, Angola's proposal of marriage may be accepted by Luzéide, but, returning to the fairytale motif, she is first stolen away from Lumineuse's court by Angola's rival, the evil genie Makis. Angola may, with the help of a magic coach, find her and bring her back to court, but not before he has fallen under the spell of Makis's talisman which has the power to make him fall soundly asleep at the very moment he is about to make love. The novel's darkest scene comes when, as Angola nods off, Makis takes his place in the newlyweds' bed. The next morning, when

Angola awakens, Luzéide is more than a bit perplexed by his lament that he is now certain his only hope of overcoming his syncopated ardor lies in the reputed powers of a magic brew available only from King Moka.

Angola may end with a marriage; but it is a marriage parodied even before it is consumed. Substituting Makis for the dozing groom reasserts the trope of coupling as a challenge to the exclusivity of passion. Rather than ending his novel with a pious allegiance to marital monogamy, La Morlière keeps it centered on the polymorphous mobility of couples animated by a contagious mimesis of the erotic inspired by its novelistic representation.

Biography

Born in Grenoble, France, on 22 April 1719. Studies in Grenoble after which he is placed by his father in apprenticeship for a crown office. A propensity for brawls and indelicate seductions forced his father to send him to Paris in the Musketeer corps from which he was soon discharged for dishonorable conduct. Began writing novels for money, but his only real success in that genre was *Angola, histoire indienne* published in 1746. Briefly expelled from Paris and later imprisoned for various seductions and swindles of young married women. Became a figure of intimidation and braggadocio in the venal underworld of pamphleteers while pimping actresses and working as a police spy. From 1750 to 1761 he headed up the most powerful theatrical claque in Paris, making and breaking playwrights' reputations at the Comédie Française and Théâtre des Italiens with the hired applause and boos he could provide. From 1761 on, his swindles, forgeries, and pandering were punctuated by expulsions from Paris and stays in jail. Lived in progressively

more dire circumstances under a series of assumed names that kept him one step ahead of the police until his death in a rented room in Paris on 9 February 1785.

THOMAS M. KAVANAGH

Selected Works

Angola, histoire indienne. Paris, 1746; Paris: Éditions Desjonquères, 1991; as *Angola: an Eastern Tale*, translated by Vyvyen Beresford Holland, London: Chapman & Hill, 1926.
Les Lauriers ecclésiastiques ou les Campagnes de l'abbé de T. Paris, 1747.
Mylord Stanley, ou le Criminel vertueux. Paris, 1747.
Mirza-Nadir, ou Mémoires et aventures du marquis de Saint-T. The Hague, 1749.

Further Reading

Démoris, René. "Esthétique et libertinage: amour de l'art et art d'aimer." In *Eros Philosophique*, edited by François Moureau and Alain-Marc Rieu, Paris: Champion, 1984, pp. 149–161.
Goulemot, Jean-Marie. *Forbidden Texts: Erotic Literature and Its Readers in Eighteenth-Century France*. Translated by James Simpson. Philadelphia, PA: University of Pennsylvania Press, 1995.
Huet, Marie-Hélène, "Roman libertin et réaction aristocratique." In *Dix-Huitième Siècle*, 6 (1974), pp. 129–141.
Kavanagh, Thomas M. "Coupling the Novel: Reading Bodies in La Morlière's Angola." In *Eighteenth-Century Fiction*, 13 (2–3), 2001, pp. 389–413.
Laroch, Philippe. *Petits-Maîtres et roués: évolution de la notion de libertinage dans le roman français du XVIIIe siècle*. Quebec: Presses de l'Université Laval, 1979.
Mauzi, Robert. *L'Idée du bonheur dans la littérature et la pensée française au XVIIIe siècle*. Paris: Armand Colin, 1965.
Trousson, Raymond. "Le Chevalier de La Morlière: Un aventurier des lettres au XVIIIe siècle." In *Bulletin de l'Académie royale de langue et de littérature française*, 68, 1990, pp. 218—299.
Versini, Laurent. "Néologie et tours à la mode dans *Angola*." In *Travaux de linguistique et de littérature*, 13, 1975, pp. 505—525.

LA PUTTANA ERRANTE

La Puttana Errante, the title of two sixteenth-century Venetian works, one in verse, one in prose, both probably products of sometime secretaries and imitators of Pietro Aretino. The title, attributed to the pen of Aretino without specifying which of the works was meant, became proverbial in Renaissance England as an *exemplum of* erotic/obscene writing characteristic of libertine Italy (Donne, Guilpin, Harvey, and Marston, among others, make this point).

The verse version of *La Puttana Errante* was written by Lorenzo Veniero (1510–1556), a Venetian aristocrat and follower of Aretino. In a poem written after the appearance of his *Puttana* entitled *La Zaffetta,* (a poem which details a trent-uno, or gang-bang of Angela Zaffetta, a noted Venetian courtesan), Veniero claims that he wrote *La Zaffetta* in order to demonstrate that he, and not Aretino, was the author of the verse *Puttana.* Scholars have accepted this claim. The poem is a mock epic in four long cantos of ottava rima, delivering an account of a true wandering and transgressive whore. The whore of the poem is an unnamed figure who is an embodiment of extraordinary female lust. Scholars have claimed that the whore is based on one Elena Ballarina, a Venetian courtesan against whom Veniero is reported to have developed a strong antipathy. Some scholars have seen the poem as a commentary on Italy's political, social, and literary scene as well as noting what seems to be an exceptionally misogynistic tone in the poem. The whore is certainly a parody of the conquering female warrior of Italian epic, in this instance we have a heroine who battles with her cunt and ass, fucking all comers, whether Christian or infidel, king or commoner, pope or animal. All are serviced in this poem.

The poem imitates one characteristic of erotic writing established by Aretino by insisting upon using vulgar language. Indeed, the poem begins by invoking Aretino as the inspiration for the verse. The poem differs from Aretino's dialogues by its very form (cantos, ottava rima) that clearly conjures up the epics of Boiardo, Ariosto, and Pulci; sometimes the connection is direct (e.g., here is a filthy whore "who did more with her cunt than Orlando/Did with his sword and lance"). The whore makes progress through Italy, conquering with her cunt and ass everyone (and everything) along the way, including the armies of France and Germany (thus providing ammunition for Erasmi's view of the poem as an allegory "amara e irose delle sventure d'Italia"). At one point the whore is awarded a degree in whoredom from the University of Siena and holds forth in a disputation about cocks. The poem concludes with her triumph in Rome (seen as a parody of Petrarch's *Trionfi),* a procession of all of the men she has fucked, among others, and a huge representation of a cock. The procession ends at the Ponte Sisto, the traditional workplace for whores in Rome. The power of the wandering whore is, on the whole, depicted in a negative fashion; the aim of the poem is certainly not the arousal of the reader.

Exactly the opposite claim might be made of the prose version of *La Puttana Errante.* This work cannot be conclusively attributed. Some scholars have argued for Aretino himself as the author; others favor Nicolo Franco (1515–1570). Franco, it should be noted, began as one of Aretino's secretaries but became a notorious enemy, with his most virulent attacks against Aretino appearing in his *Priapea,* an updating of the classical anthology of the same name. Franco was executed by the Inquisition in Rome in 1570. The prose *Puttana Errante* is regarded as one of the most influential models for pornographic works of succeeding centuries. The work comes closest to providing what Steven Marcus has called a pornotopia, especially in two characteristics: the single intention of the author (arousal of the reader) and the extensive use of taboo words. It is also characteristic of much Renaissance pornographic writing in its obsession with sexual positions, a strong anti-clerical bent, and a "how to" section on pleasing men. The work begins in an Aretine mode as a dialogue between Maddalena and Giulia in which Maddalena recounts her life's story to the younger woman. There is some attempt at a plot line, but it is the barest kind of business, concocted merely to allow one copulation scene after another. What is remarkable about the work is the author's attempt at what might be seen as psychological realism as he describes events from Maddalena's point of view at the time she experiences each event, especially in her early years as she gets initiated successively into progressive modes of sexuality: masturbation, same-sex sex, and heterosexual sex.

There is increasingly less dialogue, much extended first-person narration, extensive use of voyeurism, many details of living arrangements—all in the service of providing one scene of sexual activity after another. And so we get scenes of Maddalena copulating with her first boyfriend, Roberto, in a number of positions, most of them of the standing or sitting variety, because of the living arrangements. Such details might cause us to think "realism," but in fact these details are all in the service of the Renaissance obsession with positions; what the author would convince us of is that at any place, at any time, under any conditions, people will engage in sex. Metaphors for sexual organs and acts are used occasionally, but this is a work primarily about cocks, cunts, and fucking. Maddalena's progress moves to her profession as a courtesan, with negative views of her interactions with the clergy, and it concludes with a recapping and

naming by Giulia of the thirty-five positions for sexual intercourse that Maddalena has described (up to fifty-two in the Galderisi version).

DAVID O. FRANTZ

Selected Works

All editions of these two works are problematic in terms of attribution and availability. Most easily accessible for the general reader are, for the verse version:

Veniero, Lorenzo. *La Puttana Errante*, Paris: Liseux, 1883 (but note this work is sometimes catalogued under Aretino).

———. *La Zaffetta*. Paris, 1861. for the prose version, found catalogued under Aretino in a modern edition: *Il Piacevol Ragionamento del'Aretino*, ed. Claudio Galderisi, Rome: Salerno, 1987 (in this version the roles of Maddalena and Giulia are reversed).

Further Reading

Erasmi, Gabriele. "La Puttana Errante: Parodia epica Ispirata all' Aretino," in *Pietro Aretino nel cinquecentenario della nascita*, 2 vols. Rome: Salerno, 1995, 2:875–895.

Foxon, David. *Libertine Literature in England, 1660–1745*. New Hyde Park, NY: University Books, 1965.

Frantz, David. *Festum Voluptatis: A Study of Renaissance Erotica*, Columbus, OH: Ohio State UP, 1989.

Grendler, Paul. *Critics of the Italian World, 1530–1560: Anton Francesco Doni, Nicolo Franco and Ortensio Lando*. Madison, WI: University of Wisconsin Press, 1969.

Moulton, Ian. *Before Pornography. Erotic Writing in Early Modern England*. Oxford: Oxford University Press, 2000.

LA SOURICIÈRE; OR THE MOUSE-TRAP

La Souricière; or The Mouse-Trap was first published in London under the pseudonym of 'Timothy Touchit, Esq.' The subtitle declares it, 'A facetious and sentimental excursion through part of Austrian Flanders and France being a divertiement [sic] for both sexes,' an oblique reference to Laurence Sterne's *A Sentimental Journey though France and Italy*. The story is about a gentleman and his observations of his

fellow passengers while traveling from Dover to Bruges. The book is in two volumes, and is in keeping with a genre of erotic skits on popular travel writing of the day.

The preface lays out the tone of the book offering hints as to the nature of its sexual and jocular content; 'The following extraordinary Performance, was written by a gentleman well known in the *Republic of Letters:* and it displays much wit, good-sense, and fertility of invention, particularly in ludicrous parts, where his allusions and illustrations are peculiar to himself, and have a singular title to originality.' These comments pertain to the type of analogies he employs when making reference to sex.

The main principal of the narrator's work is to provide the reader with a survey of his fellow travelers. The author's intentions are explained in the Advertisement: 'the governing principle throughout this performance is, to exhibit the imperfections and indiscretions of mankind, not for *imitation* but *admonition:* to display the perverseness and frailty of human nature, in the commission of errors repugnant to repeated conviction; and to enforce this great moral principle, that repenting for past offences, and a change of life, are indispensable duties to secure terrestrial happiness.'

The traits and sexual activities of the principal characters are described through *double-entendres*, all italicised to ensure readers do not miss the joke or are left unaware of its true meaning. The first section opens with the narrator's declaration of his plan to travel the Continent in search of novelty. He plans, with his 'Mouse-Trap' to *'catch the manners as they rise.'* The dialogue is steeped in metaphors about the penis as a tree of life, a mouse-trap, and a barometer. The term 'mouse' was traditionally used as a term of endearment for the vagina, the mouse-trap evolving from this usage.

The narrator attacks the state of the prostitutes, "—******, a plague take all *stars;*—-aye, and *garters* too. They are become cheap trash of late days. The venerable Oak is slow of growth; but Mushrooms are of quicker vegetation. Pluck them from the bed of Honour. Return them to their native soil. To the dunghill, away,— away__Foh! how they stink.' He blames the condition of the prostitutes for his sluggish sexual response and attributes to them the causes of fungal growth. The implication is that whores are responsible for the spread of venereal disease. He recalls an earlier experience when 'passing along the *Strand* one evening, I was accosted by a fair lady, who, though I was a perfect stranger, professed great affection, in the most endearing manner, invited me to her place of abode. I was shocked at her familiarity, and wishing to get rid of her, declared myself a married man. It did not abate her importunities;—she continued to solicit my intimacy.

I have no money, child, said I.—'Go to the devil,' said she, and departed—How dreadful! that inclination, or necessity, should *blur the grace and blush of modesty,''* The author uses displays of disingenuous shock to satirize the moral standards of the day.

The narrator takes off in his post-chaise but chastises the post-boy who is driving it for his cruelty in flogging the horse too vehemently. A keen eye for detail allows for colorful vignettes of the characters he meets. On board ship from Dover to Ostend, he meets a fat woman with her young daughter and young gentleman, Mr. Lustring, en route to Bruges. Although the gentleman is elegant, he is foppishly dressed, yet has a 'certain *Je-ne-sçai-quoi.* Because of his effeminate dress, he supposes him to be a dancing master but, during a *tête-à-tête* between the young lady and the fop, he discovers that 'the *distinguishing characteristics* was not in his heels__,'' an allusion to his sexual prowess.

The narrator derides his own 'mouse-trap' (a euphemism for the penis) since it does not respond to the charms of the older woman, "I wish'd the *Mouse-Trap* at the devil, not *having all the good gifts of nature* then at my command.' He describes the state, not only of his own sexual ardour, but that of the younger woman, whose '*empyrosis* was ardent in the extreme.' Within the work, the author manages to satirize the experiments of the Royal Society, in keeping with some of the other erotic writings of the eighteenth century: 'Had that learned body of philosophers, the *Royal Society*, been present, it might have given rise to a tedious debate, to have investigated, whether *something* more simple in its construction than a *fire-engine*, would not have distinguished the young lady's conflagration.''

The older woman's search for pleasure is mocked by her daughter who declares, 'How can you talk as you do? It is time for one of your years to give pleasures up and to think of more serious matters.' Her mother retorts that old folks have a right to some enjoyment. Her daughter, Miss Polly, is escorted by a waiter of nineteen or twenty years old called Jemmy, the 'abundance of his endowments' being his 'particular qualifications.' The narrator recognizes that both the older and younger woman are sexually adventurous and there is an implication that lasciviousness is an inherited quality: 'What is bred in the bone will never be out of the flesh.'

The daughter displays her mother's carnal appetites and is caught in bed with Jemmy who agrees to marry her but only on condition that her mother settles £10,000 on him as a dowry. He declares he must provide for the Fille de Chambre since he has already seduced her. Polly and Jemmy marry. The women meet up with their female cousin. At this stage our narrator leaves the boat and goes on to Bruges.

Continuing his journey, he boards another ship en route to Bruges. He continues with his descriptions of the passengers, this time making use of pelagic analogies. Again, this was a common eighteenth-century technique to describe sex in couched terminology: "On a cursory view round the Cabbin, I was convinced many of the passengers could display *Latitude* as well as *Longitude;* and that the various methods of sailing, and arts of navigation, were perfectly known to them; for some were come booming, having *crowded all the sail* they could, by making the most of *their canvas.* Some had a *reef or two* in their *fore-sail,* and some were *furled.* Some were *ready to traverse,* and others prepared to go *right before the wind.* Some were *booms;* some *cross-jacks;* some were defective in their *bolt-spirits* and some *disabled* in their *rudders.*"

On a passenger boat to Ghent, he meets a mendicant friar who advises him to take up with a pretty Fille de Chambre at a certain hotel, at which he later shares dinner with four gentleman. After becoming inebriated, the young men attack one of the waiters for which the narrator berates them for displaying behavior unbefitting of a gentleman. He ensures they make amends to the waiter and pay damages to the host. Meanwhile, the protagonist enjoys himself with the Fille de Chambre who creeps into his room. He describes his erection as a barometer at full level: "On this she *prepared what I wanted,* and by *collision* effected a *deliquation* which produced a *happy crisis;* and after *repeating the application* three or four times, *pro re mata,* as physicians say, the *elevation of the Barometer* fell down to *changeable,* and I became relieved and composed."

In the following section, 'The Jaunt to Brussels,' he engages a male guide, Francis, who is unemployed. The guide is a modest fellow who plays sweet music on his mandolin. Leaving Brussels they come across two female fellow passengers of eighteen and twenty-five years old. Once more, his barometer grows, upon which he compares his mouse-trap to Francis's Mandelin [sic]. Although one of the young ladies is attracted to Francis, she ends up in bed with our narrator, such is the 'magnitude of the Maypole of love.' The story ends in Paris, where the narrator finds a willing female companion who understands 'the *necessary arts* of bringing the *point-principal* to *its proper bearing.*'

JULIE PEAKMAN

Edition

Anon. *La Souricière; or The Mouse-trap.* (Printed in London for J. Parsons of Pasternoster-Row, 1794).

LABÉ, LOUISE

1520/24–1564
French poet

How did Louise Labé, the daughter of a rope maker, become so famous, or perhaps more accurately, infamous by the 1550s? So famous, indeed, that John Calvin would refer to her as a "common whore" while the poet Jean Antoine de Baïf nicknamed her "belle rebelle" [beautiful rebel]. The answer to these questions relies on understanding of both the poetic traditions of the era and of Labé's environment. In sixteenth century France, the silk industry made Lyons a wealthy city. Trade, proximity to Italy, and major publishing houses, established Lyons as a clear rival to Paris as a site of literature and culture. Poets flourished and literary salons began to form. It is in this atmosphere that

Louise Labé, a bourgeois, was exposed to the world of letters. Yet the role of women in that society curtailed: they were the subject of poetry, not its creator. The beloved stood on a pedestal, an object of longing, yet unattainable. The poetic dialectics were built on the repeated rejection of an erotic relationship and unsatisfied desire.

It might be more accurate to say that there are three Louise Labés: the woman who lived in Lyon and about whom we have only sketchy verifiable biographical information; the myth of Louise Labé, a literary creation, existing in the poetry and the reflections of her contemporaries and of countless later writers; and finally the ground-breaking poet. The real Labé appears to have led a life that pushed the limits of the norm for a sixteenth-century woman of the middle-class. Speculations and rumors about her private life—Did she have lovers? How many? Who?—fed the legends that followed Labé through the centuries. The fictionalized Labé tells us much about how women, and more particularly, a woman who broke with traditions, was viewed by her contemporaries and has continued to occupy the literary imagination of both men and women. Both of these figures depend for their fame on the writer. Labé's consciousness of her role as a writer and her creation of a female poetic voice that rejected the Petrarchan/Neo-platonic ideal of love in favor a reciprocal emotional and physical relationship make her one of the most original writers of the French Renaissance.

Œuvres [*Works*], 1555

Labé's complete works, *Œuvres,* first published in 1555, consisted of a dedicatory epistle, a debate between Love and Folly, three elegies, twenty-four sonnets, and twenty-four poems written about her, presented anonymously. The collection itself was innovative, combining genres and positioning Labé both as subject and as object. Labé dedicated her edition to Clémence de Bourges, a young noblewoman. The letter reads as a proto-feminist manifesto and also reveals Labé's sense of irony. Labé calls for women to become writers and views writing as an access to pleasure and a way of displaying their talents. Nonetheless, she knows that women should not "show themselves alone in public" so Labé invokes Clémence as her guide.

That love dominates the collection is evident in *Le débat d'amour et de folie* [*The Debate of Love and Folly*]. This prose text, written in a style that blends the medieval debate genre, with a theatrical presentation, explores the conceit "Love is blind." When the debate begins, Love (Cupid) has been blinded by Folly, as a result of arguments between them over which one is greater. Although Venus calls for Folly's summary punishment, Jupiter orders a trial. Apollo serves as the advocate for Cupid, while Mercury is spokesman for Folly. Apollo argues that Cupid must have his sight returned and stresses that disasters in Love have always been the fault of Folly, not Cupid. Mercury takes the more cynical position, saying that Folly's blinding of Cupid was justified and, in fact, will do him little harm. Folly has always been the source of Love's greatness. While both speakers present long defenses, Mercury's description of a woman in love, rejected by her lover, announces the main theme of the *Elegies* and the *Sonnets*. In the end, the decision on the dispute is postponed, and Folly is ordered to serve as Cupid's guide until the question is resolved.

The *Débat* is followed by three *Elégies* that introduce the poet and her coming to writing. The tripartite structure of the elegies forms its own narrative. Central to "Elegy I," addressed to women readers, is the notion of the poet as "everywoman" who has been betrayed by her love. Love plays a dual role: it/he functions as both the source of her earlier happiness and now, of her lament. Apollo has filled her heart with "poetic fury," allowing her to write of her joys and miseries. "Elegy II," which speaks to her absent lover, foregrounds the themes of separation and abandonment, exploring the poet's refusal to believe that she has been deserted. She affirms that none could love as she does but beyond that, she emphasizes her worth and how many others desire her. Thus, although speaking from an apparent position of weakness, the poet never truly betrays herself. The elegy ends ironically with an epitaph for the poet, her body consumed by the fires of her love, yet the spark of love lives on in her ashes, and can only be quenched by the tears of her beloved. "Elegy III," turns to the women of Lyons, asking that they not condemn her "foolishness." The poet describes her character, showing that despite her efforts she was conquered by love and that love has endured.

She ends with a request that Love inspire a passion as strong, or even stronger, in her beloved so that together they could better bear its burdens. Thus, the cycle both reprises some of the themes of the *Debate* and leads to the *Sonnets*.

The *Sonnets*, by far Labé's most famous works, develop the love scenario sketched in the *Elegies*. Athough the poems do not follow a strict chronological order, the main elements of the poet's love affair all appear. What makes this series stand out from the typical Renaissance love sonnets is the overt sensuality and emphasis on physical love. As a signal of her rejection of the Petrachan tradition, "Non havria Ulysse ne qualqun'altro mai [Never would Ulysses nor anyone else]," the first sonnet in the cycle, is written in Italian, a language she abandons for the following twenty-three. Fire and water appears again and provide the central metaphors of the sonnets. Love is associated with burning, with flames, with the sun, while the poet's tears provide the counterpoint. In an echo of Elegy II, her love does not grow cold despite her tears, nor are they sufficient to remedy the pain. The poet's corporality, "I am the body," plays with the convention of woman as body and man as soul/spirit. Sonnet 18 makes clear the poet rejects the model of the cold woman, epitomized by the goddess Diana, rather she is like a nymph who has succumbed a man she meets along the road. Sonnet 13, "Oh si j'estois en ce beau sein ravie" ["Oh if I were held to that handsome breast and ravished"] and Sonnet 17, "Baise m'encor, rebaise et baise" ["Kiss me again, kiss again, kiss"] suggest that the end to the poet's suffering is to be found through a sexual relationship. The erotic desire expressed is predicated reciprocity: "Give me one of your most loving [kisses]/I'll give back four more, hotter than coals." Nonetheless, these episodes are the fantasies of the poet who rebukes her short-lived love and hope that he now suffers as much as she. The closing sonnet, "Ne reprenez Dames si j'ay aymez" ["Ladies, do not blame me if I have loved"] ends the cycle with the theme of everywoman, and a cautionary note against suffering much for love as Labé has.

When read together, Labe's *Oeuvres* (Works) form a coherent whole, expressing views on theories of love, on women's role in society, and revealing one woman's transformation of the poetic conventions of her era.

Biography

Born in Lyon, probably between 1520 and 1524, daughter of Pierre Charly, a rope maker, and Etiennette Roybet. Received a private education including reading and writing Latin, Italian, possibly Spanish, horsebackriding, possibly fencing, and later music. Meets poet Clément Marot, 1536. In 1542 (according to a contemporary source), may have fallen in love with a soldier. In 1542 or 1543, married to Ennemond Perrin, also a rope maker, some twenty-five years her elder. In 1545, holds her own literary salon frequented by Lyons' leading poets, humanists, wealthy French and Italians, and others. 1548, first public criticism of Labé, followed by other attacks over a ten-year period. Possible liaison with the poet Olivier de Magny, 1553. Publication of Works in 1555, followed by three more editions in 1556. Husband dies sometime between 1555 and 1557. Died in Parcieux, at her country home outside Lyon, in 1564.

EDITH J. BENKOV

Selected Works

Œuvres. Lyon: 1555.
Louise Labé. *Oeuvres complètes de Louise Labé*. François Rigolot, ed. Paris: Garnier-Flammrion: 1986.
Louise Labe's Complete Works. Translated and edited by Edith R. Farrell; with an introduction by C. Frederick Farrell, Jr. and Edith R. Farrell. Troy, NY: Whitston Publishing Company, 1986.

Further Reading

Baker, Deborah Lesko. *The Subject of Desire: Petrarchan Poetics and the Female Voice in Louise Labe; With a Foreword by Tom Conley* (Purdue studies in Romance Literatures; v. 11). West Lafayette, IN: Purdue University Press, 1996.
Cameron, Keith. *Louise Labé: Renaissance Poet and Feminist*. New York: Berg, 1990.
Rigolot, François. *Louise Labé Lyonnaise, ou la Renaissance au féminin*. Paris: Honoré Champion, 1997.

LACLOS, PIERRE CHODERLOS DE

1741–1803
French novelist

Les liaisons dangereuses

One of the most famous and superbly crafted of all eighteenth-century novels, *Les liaisons dangereuses,* is constructed with all the rigor of a piece of military engineering. The two principal characters, the Vicomte de Valmont and the Marquise de Merteuil, vaunt to each other, in a long series of letters that furnish the novel its backbone, complex amorous exploits they could not confide to anyone else.

Basically, there are two interlocking plots. The first, initiated by Merteuil, is the corruption of innocent Cécile de Volanges by way of a personal vengeance against Gercourt, whom Cécile is to marry, in which she enlists Valmont's help. The second is the seduction of the virtuous and angelic Mme de Tourvel by Valmont. Valmont and Merteuil make a sort of contract by which, after each succeeds separately, they will renew their own earlier liaison. In the unfolding of these separate and combined processes they demonstrate their ability to manipulate numerous simultaneous affairs without the marquise compromising her reputation for wisdom and virtue, and without Valmont losing his for glamour and desirability. A number of different axes of correspondence offer multiple perspectives on the unfolding events, but always, until near the end, their own dominates and steers the reader, who thus shares in their kind of godlike knowledge of everything that is going on. The virtuosity of the two protagonists as shrewd and witty letter-writers has always been recognized; another notable aspect of Laclos's originality is the differentiated styles lent to the numerous correspondents of the 175 letters that make up the novel.

Valmont and Merteuil have a system which they share, and which must remain their own secret: "I am tempted to believe that you and I are the only people in society who are really worth something" ['je suis tenté croire qu'il n'y que vous et moi dans le monde qui valions quelque chose'] (letter 100). It is crucial to their game that one never fall in love, and thereby perhaps (it is a matter of interpretation) comes their downfall.

All the dangerous liaisons in this book are sexual ones, even though they have broader implications for a society where predators find easy victims, and all the more so that its rules harbor and protect them. Valmont's reputation is known to all, yet civility requires he be treated with the same politeness as anyone else of his rank; and even Madame de Tourvel, alerted early to her peril, is unable to undo the effects of his consummate acting when he claims to have reformed.

Critics have virtually all agreed that Merteuil is the stronger, and more intriguing, character of the two: not necessarily better drawn from a novelistic perspective, but endowed with the greater force. This fact she herself asserts and explains in terms of the social structure in her long, autobiographical letter 81: "born to avenge my sex and to master yours, I was able to create means previously unknown." This imbalance is the necessary result of their unequal social positions; the conventions of womanhood are in themselves formidable obstacles for her to overcome. Precisely because a man can be a rake openly whereas a woman's reputation would be undone by the same conduct, she has had to erect a superior level of understanding and dissimulation into a system in order to indulge herself the way Valmont can with much less effort. Their methodical strategic and psychological machine grinds inexorably forward, the conclusions being pretty much the logical working out of the original ingredients, which is indeed how these two characters imagine things—except that at some point their own complicity degenerates suddenly into war.

The ultimate breakdown of their relations admits of more than one explanation. One is that Valmont—despite himself—falls in love with Tourvel; this unavowed and, on his part, perhaps unrecognized passion undermines all his former principles, and because of this he cannot prevent his own destruction at the hands of Merteuil, before whom he cannot bear to lose face. Another is that he is fundamentally in love with Merteuil and always has been, and when finally spurned by her cannot resist, out of ire and frustration, defying her to the perilous limit. A third is that from the outset their own emulation coupled with rivalry, and finally antagonism, ultimately makes any truce between them, let alone a loving and constant relationship, totally impossible. Or one can hypothesize some combination of these factors, which are not mutually exclusive.

It is another aspect of the elegance and brilliant language of Merteuil and Valmont that for all their erotic preoccupations, nothing vulgar ever escapes their pens. Except for one letter of Valmont's written in the presence of a prostitute (letter 48), which is an explicit parody based on the conflation of sexual and amorous terminology, the designation of sexual acts is always more allusive than direct. Despite Valmont's allusion to the "technical terms" he teaches Cécile, no instruction in the mechanics of sex can be obtained from reading *Les liaisons dangereuses*, outside of the fact that it is often performed in bed and often at night; one cannot read this text to learn how to do it, as one can with many novels of sexual initiation such as *L'École des filles* or *Histoire de Dom Bougre*. Cécile and her beau Danceny are in a sense initiated along the way, but this is not a novel of sexual initiation: the main protagonists are not neophytes but veterans. The work has been subjected to a number of quite different interpretations, but Laclos's intentions, which are sufficiently indicated by both its title and epigraph (taken from Rousseau's *Julie*: "I have seen the morals of my time, and I have published these letters") are not in doubt. Perhaps not a moral novel, and certainly not a moralistic one, *Les liaisons dangereuses* depicts a society in serious crisis, morally rudderless and endlessly repeating is own errors, unable to regenerate itself. The fact that the reader shares the privileged perspective of the most morally deplorable characters, however, imposes a certain sympathetic empathy with them and thereby a degree of investment in their successes. Its posture thus has appeared to many ultimately ambiguous, as has its overall meaning.

Biography

Born in Amiens into a recently ennobled family of moderate means, Pierre François Ambroise Choderlos de Laclos was a career military officer, stationed notably in Grenoble, where he spent six years, and later in La Rochelle. Amidst several other writings and theatrical attempts, only his novel, which created a great and lasting sensation, has been broadly remembered, and he never had a full-fledged literary career. He entered the service of the Duke d'Orléans in 1788 and, though he became an active Jacobin and returned to the army as brigadeer artillary general in 1791, narrowly escaped being guillotined with the duke (now Philippe Égalité) in 1793. He ended his career a general, commander of artillery in Naples under Napoleon, and died during military operations in that region.

PHILIP STEWART

Editions

The perduring *Liaisons dangereuses* has rarely been out of print, and since there are few textual problems almost any of the many available editions in French can be considered reliable. The reference standard is Laurent Versini's edition of Laclos's *Œuvres complètes* (Paris: Pléiade, 1979), which superseded that of Maurice Allem (1932) in the same series.

It has been translated many times, the first in 1784, anonymously, under the title *Dangerous Connections*. Ernest Dowson's translation of 1898 was entitled *Les Liaisons dangereuses* but became *Dangerous Acquaintances* in a 1940 reprint (London: Nonesuch). The title *Dangerous Acquaintances* was the one used by Richard Aldington in 1924, a version re-issued by numerous publishers over time under both that title and those of *Dangerous Liaisons* (Signet) and *Les Liaisons dangereuses* (Pocket Books, Bantam, Knopf, and others). P.W.K. Stone's version was published as *Les Liaisons dangereuses* by Penguin in 1961 and reproduced in 1997 in *The Libertine Reader* (New York: Zone). Other translations are by Lowell Bair (1962), Christopher Hampton (1985), Howard Davies (1986) and Douglas Parmée (1995).

Further Reading

Alexandrian, Sarane. *Les libérateurs de l'amour*. Paris: Seuil, 1977.

Bayard, Pierre. *Le paradoxe du menteur: sur Laclos*. Paris: Minuit, 1993.

Belaval, Yvon. *Choderlos de Laclos*, Paris: Seghers, 1972.

Brinsmead, Ann-Marie. *Strategies of Resistence in "Les liaisons dangereuses": Heroines in Search of "Authority."* Lewiston, NY: Edwin Mellen Press, 1989.

Conroy, Peter V. *Intimate, Intrusive, and Triumphant: readers in the "Liaisons dangereuses."* Amsterdam: J. Benjamins, 1987.

Delon, Michel, P.A. *Choderlos Laclos, "Les Liaisons dangereuses,"* Paris: PUF, 1986.

Cazenobe, Colette. *Le Système du libertinage de Crébillon à Laclos.* SVEC 282 (1991).

DeJean, Joan. *Literary Fortifications: Rousseau, Laclos, Sade.* Princeton University Press, 1984, pp. 208–252.

Diaconoff, Suellen. *Eros and Power in "Les Liaisons dangereuses,"* Geneva: Droz, 1979.

Free, Lloyd R. ed. *Critical Approaches to "Les 'Liaisons dangereuses,"* The Hague: Nijhoff, 1974.

Goldzink, Jean. *Le vice en bas de soie, ou le roman du libertinage.* Paris: José Corti, 2001.

Grapa, Caroline Jacot. *Les "Liaisons dangereuses" de Choderlos de Laclos.* Paris: Gallimard "Folio," 1997.

Kamuf, Peggy. *Fictions of Feminine Desire : disclosures of Heloise.* University of Nebraska Press, 1982.

Laufer, Roger. *Style rococo, style des Lumières.* José Corti, 1963, pp. 134–154.

Poisson, Georges. *Choderlos de Laclos ou l'obstination.* Paris: Grasset, 1985.

Pomeau, René. *Laclos.* Paris: Hatier, 1975.

Pomeau, René. *Laclos ou le paradoxe.* Paris: Hachette, 1993.

Rosbottom, Ronald. *Choderlos de Laclos.* Boston: Twayne, 1978.

Stewart, Philip. *Le Masque et la parole: le langage de l'amour au XVIIIe siècle.* Paris: José Corti, 1973.

Stewart, Philip. *Rereadings.* Birmingham, AL: Summa, 1984.

Therrien, Madeleine. *"Les Liaisons dangereuses": une interprétation psychologique.* Paris: SEDES, 1973.

Versini, Laurent. *Laclos et la tradition: essai sur les sources et la technique des "Liaisons dangereuses."* Paris: Klincksieck, 1968.

LAFERRIÈRE, DANY

1953–

Haitian and Canadian journalist and novelist

With the release in 1985 of *Comment faire l'amour avec un nègre sans se fatiguer*, translated and published in English two years later with an abridged and slightly modified title, *How to Make Love to a Negro*—which suggests a passivity of the black man absent of the original title—Dany Laferrière makes his entrance in literature. At the same time, he gets literary recognition and the reputation of an erotic provocative writer enhanced by his second book *Eroshima* (1987), which, beyond the echo to Duras' title, refers more to the bomb as metaphor of party or explosive woman than death. Moreover, this collection of short narratives is a version of "Paradis du dragueur noir" [Black Cruiser's Paradise] by the anonymous narrator-novelist of *How to Make Love*, nicknamed Vieux [Man] by his roommate, Bouba. Indeed, cut off from the original manuscript on request of the publisher, this fictional novel of *How to Make Love*, never quoted or summarized, becomes a real book, in which the main character-narrator is once again anonymous, but this

time nicknamed Tosei by his mistress of Japanese descent, Hoki and becomes initiated to the erotic and literary Japanese world. Hence, unlike *How to Make Love*, in which Man mostly went around with young white Anglophone girls, in *Eroshima*, the narrator was more often with Asian women. He also shifted from a student world to the North American professional artistic milieu—photographs, mannequins, musicians, and so on—from Montreal to some of the world's capitals. Even though *Eroshima* seems more erotic than *How to Make Love*—the main character having first an erotico-exotic function, the lover or ex-lover of Hoki—each book describes less than ten short erotic scenes, of which some are rather fantasized as those of Man's neighbor Belzebuth, or the lesbians at Puerto Rico's International Airport in *Eroshima*. Like in life, one is talking more about sex than enjoying it.

These two books of the same mood and period—which belong to the so called North American part of Laferrière's works that critics like Dennis F. Essar or Jacques Pelletier contrast to the Haitian universe of novels as *L'Odeur du café* or *Le goût des jeunes filles*, even though this last narrative takes place in both spaces, and in *Eroshima*, some stories are framed in European or Caribbean capitals (Berlin, Port-au-Prince, San Juan, and so on)—are not truly erotic novels at first glance. Sex is rather a pretext, the "open sesame" to the gates of creativity, even fame. The first one, novel of a novel, concerns more the literary discourse or universe than eroticism. The second one, novel of celebration or vanity (as in vanity book), presents a series of real or virtual celebrity: Jean-Michel Basquiat, Denise Bombardier, Norman Mailer, V.S. Naipul, and so on. Moreover, in *How to Make Love* as in *Eroshima*, the status of the women depends on their links to the literary or artistic milieu, for the key women figures are mainly Miz Literature, the Quebec star, Carole Laure of which Man is always carrying a picture, the writer and journalist, Denise Bomabardier, or Hoki, the photograph, friend of Leonard Cohen and John Lennon. Hence, to parody Sherry Simon's title article on *How to Make Love*, in those stories the *geopolitics of sex is sign of the narrator's culture*, at least sign of a quest of culture as *jouissance*.

Not until Laferrière's fourth novel, *Le goût des jeunes filles* (1992)—of which the English title, *Dining with the Dictator*, erases its erotic feature and its Proustian reference—, and especially *La chair du maître* (1997), his eighth book, does one read his true erotic stories, those where sexual initiation, pleasure, and perversion are the main purpose. To some extent, politics is omnipresent in *Dining*, but it is rather the framework of the erotic performance. Indeed, the assumed fear, which push the young male protagonist to stay weekend long in the house of his neighbor, Miki, a den of "sharks," which apparently are looking for him, is pretext to satisfy a very old curiosity—the desire to get into this (erotic) world of girls which fascinates him. Indeed, since the opening of fictional film framed in the novel, the voice over, which is that of the boy named Dany, stated clearly: "Miki's house is on the other side of the street [...] I dream the day when, I, too, will go to heaven, across the street" (*Dining* 36).

The politics is also present in *La Chair*, even in the more erotic stories as "Nice girls do it also," in which a white American girl forces her black lover to have sex with her, while her surprised mother is watching the couple without their knowing. In fact, the politics appears under the mask of sexual confrontation as one can see in the short story entitled, "l'Ange exterminateur," when Tina (a poor misfit girl) assaults Anabelle (a very rich beauty), rapes her with rage, forces her to yap like a dog, and takes her pleasure from the suffering and degradation of her victim. Hence in *La chair*, the *bed* becomes a *field* for race or class struggle. This collection is no doubt Laferrière's book which expresses more intensely what could be considered as his erotic poetics, which is quite different from the *happy eroticism* of his senior compatriot René Depestre, or Alix Renaud, probably the first Haitian to publish an erotic novel, *À corps joie* (1985). Inspired in part by Chester Himes— of which the Remington should be used to write *Paradis du dragueur noir* in *Comment*— Laferrière's eroticism makes each partner a well defined socio-historical type, representative of a group fighting another one, using another for his own aims—which are never simply erotic. Indeed, it is less a matter of orgasm than control to enslave the other, to use him for showing or confirming power (of pleasure or over the pleasure), to gain access to a social status.

Laferrière said it so many times, his books form a whole, an "American autobiography." However his collections of erotic stories (*Comment*, *Eroshima*, *Le goût*, *La chair*), even though they are part of this whole, get off to constitute an even more coherent set. A surprising erotic quartet, in which each piece borrows some features, characters, or even pages from the previous one, we move from literature as obsession (*Comment*) to the frontier of pornography (*La chair*).

Biography

Dany Laferrière, baptized Windsor Kléber Laferrière fils, was born in Port-au-Prince, on April 13, 1953. He attended the Christian Brother Elementary School of Petit-Goâve (1958–1964), a small town in the southeast of Haiti, where he was living after 1957 with his maternal grandmother, Da (Amélie Jean-Marie), which is a key figure in his life and in his novels, *L'Odeur du café* (1991, Prix Carbet de la Caraïbe), and *Le charme des après-midi sans fin* (1997). He went to secondary school until his graduation at the Canado-Haitian Academy (Collège Canado-Haïtien) of Port-au-Prince (1964–1972), a private Catholic

School, but did not attend university. Instead, he jumped in to journalism mainly in two important media, which are central in the struggle for democracy in Haiti in the seventies: the cultural and political weekly magazine, *Le Petit Samedi Soir* (PSS), founded and directed by the well known Haitian writer and publisher Dieudonné Fardin, and Radio Haïti-Inter directed by the late famous Haitian journalist, Jean Dominique. As a reporter, he worked for the *PSS* in 1972–1976, then, from Montreal, as a foreign correspondent from 1976 until November 1980, when the Duvalier regime expelled almost all the independent journalists of Haiti; and he commented on cultural events on Radio Haïti until 1976, when he was forced to leave for Montreal after the assassination of his friend and colleague, Gasner Raymond, which is evoked in his novel, *Le cri des oiseaux fous* (2000). After returning to Haiti for six months in 1978, he decided to stay definitively in Montreal, even though he must often stay in New York where his wife, Margaret Andrée Berrouët (Maggie), was leaving until 1982, and where he wrote in part his first published novel, *Comment faire l'amour avec un nègre sans se fatiguer* (1985). The unprecedented success of this book in part allowed him to be hired as a presenter at the new Quebec TV station, Four Seasons (Les Quatre Saisons) in 1986, then in 1989 as a member of the Band of Six (la Bande des Six), a weekly challenging cultural TV show at Radio Canada. The same year, a film version of *How to Make Love to a Negro*, directed by Jacques W. Benoit on a script co-written by Laferrière and Richard Sadler, was released. It is probably his long involvement, even his mastering of the media world, one of the keys of his popular success, which push him to announce the end of his "American autobiography " with *Je suis fatigué* (2000), which is a farewell and a gift to his readers. Indeed, following a tradition of Haitian writers to freely give their books, this work was not sold. Since, after twelve years in Miami where he moved in 1990 with his family to have time and space to complete his "American autobiography," Laferrière is back to Montreal (September 2002), as a columnist for the Montreal base newspaper *La Presse*, and had published a revised and enlarged edition of *Cette grenade dans la main du jeune nègre est-elle une arme ou un fruit?*, in Paris (Serpent à plume) and in Montreal (Vlb éditeur). In 2003, he shot his first film as director and screenwriter, *Comment*

conquérir l'Amérique en une nuit, released in fall 2004.

JEAN JONASSAINT

Selected Works

Comment faire l'amour avec un Nègre sans se fatiguer. Montréal: Vlb Éditeur, 1985 (*How to Make Love to a Negro*, translated by David Homel, Toronto: Coach House Press, 1987; London: Bloomsbury, 1991).

Éroshima. Montréal, Vlb Éditeur, 1987 (*Eroshima: A Novel.* Translated by David Homel, Toronto: Coach House Press, 1991).

L'Odeur du café. Montréal: Vlb Éditeur, 1991 (*An Aroma of Coffee*, translated by David Homel, Toronto: Coach House Press, 1993).

Le goût des jeunes filles. Montréal: Vlb Éditeur, 1993 (*Dining with the Dictator.* Translated by David Homel, Toronto: Coach House Press, 1994).

Cette grenade dans la main du jeune Nègre est-elle une arme ou un fruit? Montréal: Vlb Éditeur, 1993 (*Why Must a Black Writer Write About Sex?* Translated by David Homel, Toronto: Coach House Press, 1994).

La chair du maître. Montréal: Lanctôt Éditeur, 1997.

Le charme des après-midi sans fin. Montréal: Lanctôt Éditeur, 1997.

Le cri des oiseaux fous. Montréal: Lanctôt Éditeur, 2000.

J'écris comme je vis: entretien avec Bernard Magnier. Genouilleux: La Passe du vent, 2000; Montréal: Lanctôt Éditeur, 2000.

Je suis fatigué. Vincennes: Initiales, 2000; Montréal: Lanctôt Éditeur, 2001.

Cette grenade dans la main du jeune Nègre est-elle une arme ou un fruit? Montréal: Vlb Éditeur, 2002; Paris: Serpent à plumes, 2002.

Further Reading

Bordeleau, Francine. "Dany Laferrière sans arme et dangereux." *Lettres Québécoises* 73 (1994): 9–10.

Coates, Carrol F. "An Interview with Dany Laferrière." *Callaloo.* 22, 4 (1999): 910–921.

Coleman, Daniel. "How to Make Love to a Discursive Genealogy: Dany Laferrière's Metaparody of Racialized Sexuality." in *Masculine Migrations: Reading the Postcolonial Male in 'New Canadian' Narratives.* Toronto: University of Toronto Press, 1998.

Desbiens-Magalios, Caroline. "Bed Companions." *Canadian Literature* 150 (1996):136–38.

Essar, Dennis F. "Time and Space in Dany Laferrière's Autobiographical Haitian Novels." *Callaloo.* 22, 4 (1999): 930–946.

Jonassaint, Jean and Anne Racette. "L'avenir du roman québécois serait-il métis?" *Lettres Québécoises* 41 (1986): 79–80.

Laroche, Maximilien. "Manières de lit: érotique et politique." In *Bizango: Essai de mythologie haïtienne.* Sainte-Foy (Québec): GRELCA (Groupe de Recherche sur les Littératures de la Caraïbe)/ Université Laval, 1997.

Lenoski, Daniel S. "Versions of Vulgar." *Canadian Literature* 120 (1989): 236–38.

Mathis-Moser, Ursula. *Dany Laferrière: la dérive américaine.* Montréal: Vlb éditeur, 2003.

Miraglia, Anne Marie. "Dany Laferrière, l'identité culturelle et l'intertexte afro-américain." *Présence francophone* 54 (2000): 121–139.

Nicolas, Lucienne. "Dany Laferrière." in *Espaces urbains dans le roman de la diaspora haïtienne.* Paris: L'Harmattan, 2002.

Pelletier, Jacques. "Toutes couleurs réunies." *Lettres Québécoises* 73 (1994): 11–12.

Ruprecht, Alvina. "'L'Amérique c'est moi': Dany Laferrière and the Borderless Text." in Alvina Ruprecht and Cecilia Taiana, eds. *The Reordering of Culture: Latin America, the Caribbean and Canada in the Hood.* Carleton (Ontario): Carleton University Press, 1995.

Simon, Sherry. "The Geopolitics of Sex, or Signs of Culture in the Quebec Novel." *Essays on Canadian Writing* 40 (1990): 44–49.

Vassal, Anne. "Lecture savante ou populaire: *Comment faire l'amour avec un nègre sans se fatiguer* de Dany Laferrière." *Discours Social/Social Discourse* 2,4 (1989): 185–202.

LATIN: PROSE FICTION

The Romans used several terms to describe works of prose fiction since there was no generic term for such writing in Classical Antiquity: *fabula* indicated quite generally a fictitious report or entertaining story (the term is recorded in the writings of the orator Cicero, 106–43 BCE); *fictio*, pretence or supposition, is first mentioned as a legal term (Quintilian, *The Institutes of Oratory*, 1st century CE); *historia*, originally from the Greek word meaning a question or enquiry, developed over time to include historical composition, a story or anecdote (factual, legendary, astonishing, or exemplary) and, in a general sense, information (there are examples in Cicero and in the works of the ancient rhetoricians); the designation *historiae eroticae* (from Erōs, the Greek god of love) was applied to love stories, but without the modern connotations of obscenity and lewdness; *narratio* was a story and the setting out of facts in a law speech (Terence, in his play *Andria*, 2nd century BCE); *satura* (or *satira*) meant a miscellany of prose and verse, a type of composition known from the *Menippean Satires* of Varro (116–27 BCE), a vehicle to correct the vices of his age. We meet the word specifically in the title of Petronius's *Satyrica* (less correctly *Satyricon*), a punning play on the use of this medley of styles, combined with an allusion to satyrs, the mythical creatures with unrestrained desires for sex and drink. It seems that our examples of extended Roman prose fiction most probably derive from the Greek romances which became increasingly popular in Latin translation from the 1st century BCE, though there could also have been a tradition of scurrilous native literature from which they may have derived several elements. It should be remembered that their educated readership would have been equally at home in either language. Two major examples survive from Roman times: Petronius's *Satyrica* (1st century CE), of which we possess some substantial fragments being only part of an extensive whole; and Apuleius's *Metamorphoses* (*The Metamorphoses, or The Golden Ass*, mid-2nd century CE), which has come down to us complete. Both seem to depend to a great extent on the traditional model of the Greek novel, only at several points to adapt and subvert it. Both are characterized in their different ways by literary sophistication (allusion, burlesque and parody, irony and rhetorical tropes). Both include material from low life, licentious humor (with an emphasis on voyeuristic scenes), and reference to death, the supernatural, and witchcraft. Both are first person narratives with inserted stories: in the surviving parts of Petronius we can read the tales of 'The Boy from Pergamum' (a homoerotic tale of a boy who increases the stakes when being seduced) and 'The Widow of Ephesus' (on the sexual weakness of women). In Apuleius there are a number of tales which are told by various characters, mainly about witches, murder, jealous husbands, and lustful wives, but the longest and most significant is an allegorical one about the love of Cupid and Psyche: Psyche, despite being forbidden to look on her anonymous lover, yields to feminine curiosity and the advice of ill-disposed women. Her trials and final apotheosis are paralleled in the main narrative by the tribulations and ultimate salvation of Lucius the Ass. But there are significant differences. Petronius, in addition to probably drawing inspiration from popular obscene Roman *Mimes*, which commonly featured whores, catamites, adulterers, and other lowlife subjects, may have had in mind something like the pederastic Greek *Iolaus* novel, of which a few scraps have survived. His work seems to have been built on the mock-heroic depiction of unworthy subjects and it satirises, most probably, the excesses of rhetoric and poetry in the age of the emperor Nero. There are examples of literary parody where scabrous elements are used to subvert the models of Homeric epic: the hero has incurred the wrath of Priapus, rather than of Poseidon; Circe, who is an enchantress in Homer's *Odyssey*, is here overfond of slaves and gladiators. Its characters are unashamedly disreputable: Encolpius and his boyfriend Giton are traveling around southern Italy (Campania) in the company of Ascyltus, a well-hung ex-slave, and Eumolpus, a lecherous poet. There are various erotic imbroglios among the four. Encolpius, Ascyltus, and Giton become involved with the brothel keeper Quartilla; they attend a pretentious banquet given by the vulgar nouveau-riche ex-catamite Trimalchio; Lichas and Tryphaena, who both seem to have enjoyed Giton's and Encolpius's favors in an earlier, now lost, episode discover our heroes as they seek refuge in Lichas's ship and become bent on revenge and sex; Encolpius seeks a cure for impotence from the worn-out priestess Oenothea. The fragments come to an end when the protagonists are in Crotona where legacy hunting is rife and a story is told of the women during the siege of Capua who became cannibals and ate their own children. The plot of Apuleius's *Metamorphoses* centers on the story of Lucius, a young man who meddles with witchcraft and is turned into an ass. The nucleus of the narrative can be found in the Greek *Lucius* attributed to the rhetor and satirical writer Lucian (2nd century CE), which, together with Apuleius's own tale, probably depends on an earlier Greek version. Furthermore, it is thought that some connection may exist with Lollianus's *Phoinikika* (extant in brief fragments), where an episode of fornication and human sacrifice is reminiscent of the description of the robbers' lair in the *Metamorphoses.* After many adventures, in the course of which he is the object of brutality, lust, wonderment, and contempt, Lucius regains his human form and dignity by celebrating the mystic rites of Isis and Osiris. Some of the female characters in the *Metamorphoses* are as full of lust and deceit as those in Petronius, but Apuleius also creates types of virtue and faithfulness, nearer to the ideal featured in the Greek Novel: Psyche, though inquisitive, is not vicious; Charite is an idealistic counterpart to the Widow of Ephesus.

Historians and compliers of historical anecdotes sometimes fleshed out their narrative with sensational details. Such is the case, for example, in the legendary part of the *Roman History* of Livy (59 BCE–17 CE) where the rape of Lucretia is described by telling how Tarquin, the last king of Rome, forced her with his drawn sword to yield as he threatened to slit her slave's throat and place him beside her as a decoy for suspicious relatives. In the first century CE, Valerius Maximus put together his *Memorable Doings and Sayings* [*Facta ac dicta memorabilia*]. Among a mass of material on virtues and vices, often with moralistic comment, there are stories on conjugal love (IV.6: husbands commit suicide on the death of their wives), on incest (V.7: King Seleucus with his stepmother Stratonice), on luxury and lust (IX.1: a certain Ptolemy marries his elder sister and rapes her daughter whom he then marries instead), on continence (IV.3: Drusus keeps his sexual activity confined to his wife—this is obviously seen as exceptional), on chastity (VI.1: the rape of Lucretia—again; a Tribune is accused of having tried to seduce his own son; a Triumvir is sentenced to death for having had sexual intercourse with a freeborn youth, who, he alleges, was in fact a prostitute), and on the fidelity of wives (VI.7). Another case in point is the *Historia Augusta*, a collection of biographies of Roman emperors from 117 to 284 CE (Hadrian to Numerian) probably composed at the end of the 4th century CE but whose authorship and purpose are much disputed. It is a work of fictionalized history which draws on some facts and a great array of false documentation and invented stories. Scholars do not agree as to the extent to which its narrative merits the modern label 'History,' but among several descriptions of excessive behavior it notably includes details of the sexual debauchery of Commodus (Emperor 180–192 CE), 'who defiled every part of his body in his dealings with persons of either sex,' and an exuberant account of the orgiastic feasts and sexual extravagances of the youthful emperor Elagabalus (Heliogabalus, who lived from *circa* 203 to 222 CE). Marius Maximus (3rd century CE) is referred to as an authority in the *Historia Augusta* and elsewhere, but his reputedly inventive and scurrilous series of imperial biographies is unfortunately now reduced to only a few fragments. Parthenius of Nicaea (1st century BCE), who lived in Rome and frequented literary circles there among whom his writings circulated, composed in Greek a collection of prose summaries of thirty-six rather startling love stories (*Erōtika Pathēmata*): there is incest and adultery, girls are forsaken by their young men, and lovers commit suicide or fall victim to murder or accidental death. Another perspective is offered by the Latin mythographers whose collections feature a large number of stories drawn from traditional sources. Among them the name of Hyginus (1st century CE), the supposed author of *Fabulae* and *De Astronomia*, is noteworthy. The first of these is a compilation which survives as an epitome of a larger handbook, designed, in all probability, to elucidate references to mythological subjects in the works of poets and playwrights. The stories recount a number of tales of the Olympian gods and goddesses together with their often strange lusts when they decided to pursue attractive nymphs or couple with human beings. Hyginus provides, for example, a list of the most beautiful men and youths, and gives the names of fathers and daughters who slept with each other unlawfully. He narrates the legend of Europa, who was changed into a cow when she was lustfully pursued by Jupiter, and tells the story of Semele who was consumed by fire when she asked Jupiter to reveal himself to her in all his glory as he came to her to make love. He recounts the rape of Philomela by Tereus who was already married to her sister Procne on account of which sexual violation the latter killed their son Itys and fed the corpse to his father. An incestuous version of this theme is narrated in the story of Harpalyce, daughter of Clymenus, who served up her offspring at a feast. The *De Astronomia* is keyed to the constellations and presents the myths which are connected with them. The section on Cygnus tells how Jupiter tricked Nemesis by changing himself into a swan and then nestled in her bosom, coupling with her while she slept. The chapter on Auriga describes how Vulcan fell in love with the chaste goddess Minerva, but when he tried to rape her she resisted and his sperm fell on the ground instead, engendering a son, Erichthonius. Many ancient scholars included such exemplary tales in the margins of the texts on which they were commenting: these exist as *scholia* and a number can also be found in later general compilations such as those ascribed to the three so-called Latin Vatican Mythographers (probably 9th century CE and later). Rather like the prose *Narrationes* which accompany the text of the Latin poet Ovid's (43 BCE–17 CE) *Metamorphoses*, these post-classical collections are not independent compositions. They do, however, provide us with incidental details of several erotic myths from earlier sources as, for example, the story of the virgin Caenis to whom Neptune, after they had made love, gave the ability to change her sex at will. In these chapters we can also read a retelling of the love story of Leander who swam the Hellespont each night to be with his beloved Hero, only finally to drown and cause her death by grief; a version of the bestial love of Pasiphae for the Cretan bull who mounted her; the legend of the Lemnian women who, all but one, murdered their husbands after being rejected by them because of the repulsive smell inflicted on all the wives by Venus; the story of Nyctimene, who had sexual intercourse with her father as a consequence of which she was transformed into a screech owl.

Of the antecedents to the Latin 'Novel,' however, perhaps the most significant are the so-called *Milesian Tales* [*Milesiaca*] which Apuleius in fact openly refers to and inserts in his work. These were short stories of an obscene nature and constituted a genre which probably originated with the collection of lubricious love stories (no longer extant) written in Greek by Aristides, probably in the late 2nd century BCE and apparently translated into Latin by the historian Lucius Cornelius Sisenna (1st century BCE). The Greek biographer and essayist Plutarch (2nd century CE) reports in his *Life* of the

Roman general Crassus (died 53 BCE) that the Parthians attributed the effeminacy of the Romans whom they defeated at Carrhae to these *Tales* when they found copies of them in the looted baggage. But Latin fiction also owes a great deal to the tradition of rhetoric which was widely practiced in the ancient world. In Rome itself the *Debates* (*Controversiae*) of the Elder Seneca (philosopher and rhetorician, 1st century BCE) and the *Set Speeches* (*Declamationes*) of the rhetorician Quintilian both contain examples of shorter prose narratives which reflect the way in which such pieces could be worked up into longer stories. The Elder Seneca, for example, proposes as one of these rhetorical exercises the case of a woman who, though chaste, has accepted an inheritance from an admirer in her husband's absence: should the husband's plea for adultery succeed? Quintilian's collection presents a variety of situations which correspond well to the stories we find developed in fiction: there are examples of divorce, adultery, dishonor, and so on. They afford a good opportunity for the rhetorician to develop a psychological character study and emotional appeal. They also reflect, no doubt, the nature of contemporary society and the more exotic events familiar to the consumer of romantic tales: in one case a kidnapped virgin is placed in a brothel and is respected by all her clients except for one brutal soldier whom she kills. Is she guilty of murder? Somewhat similar events fill the anonymous Latin prose narrative of the *History of King Apollonius of Tyre* (*Historia Apollonii Regis Tyri*) (5th–6th century CE) which probably derives ultimately from a Greek model. Later it was to provide material for John Gower's *Confessio Amantis*, Shakespeare's *Pericles* and T.S. Eliot's *Marina*. The story is full of events: Antiochus, King of Antioch, lives incestuously with his daughter and beheads her suitors who fail to solve the riddle he sets. Apollonius, who has worked out the answer, is also vulnerable so he escapes and marries the daughter of the King of Cyrene instead. After several adventures he is separated from his wife, who, though apparently dead and therefore disposed of at sea, in fact survives anonymously in the Temple of Diana. A daughter, Tharsia, has been born to Apollonius, but she is captured by pirates and sold to a brothel keeper. She nevertheless preserves her virginity (the section which describes these events is relatively extensive, § 37–44). The

Historia has many twists and climaxes which are familiar from ancient romance: shipwrecks, pirates, virginity in danger, recognition scenes, and so forth. Finally, all the good characters are reunited, the prostitutes are set free, and Apollonius becomes king of Antioch, Tyre, and Cyrene. Another story, the *Acta Pauli et Theclae*, which constitutes part of the apocryphal acts of the Apostles, represents the Christian tradition at work on these basic plot elements. It is extant in Latin, though possibly written originally in Greek, and dates from the 2nd–3rd centuries CE. It has been described as recounting, 'quite in the manner of a novel and probably without any historical foundation' (Altaner), how Thecla was inspired through her love of Saint Paul to devote herself to Christ until she died at the age of 90. The sexual–romantic element here is covert rather than being explicitly revealed. The virgin Thecla has many adventures as she is dedicated to preserving her chastity: she escapes several potential martyrdoms (her pyre is quenched by a thunderstorm, the wild beasts in the arena fawn on her or devour each other, carnivorous seals float up dead to the surface of the water in which she was meant to drown, and so on). The *Res gestae Alexandri Macedonis* (commonly known as the *Alexander Romance*) represents a similar type of popular fictionalized history, full of extraordinary events and fabulous creatures, which circulated widely in antiquity and the middle ages. Julius Valerius (4th century CE) is the author of the extant Latin version of this story which derives from an earlier anonymous Greek version of uncertain date by 'Pseudo-Callisthenes.' There is a complex variety of sources for the narrative, most of which derive in all probability from the Hellenistic period (323–146 BCE). The 'Life' of Alexander the Great is here transformed into a wondrous tale which has only a slim connection with historical reality. Among the many marvels which Alexander witnesses on his travels, for example, is a hairy giant who consumes a naked woman who has been offered to him to test whether he has human feelings or not.

It is probable that the different forms of ancient fiction appealed to different audiences: both the idealized and the lower-life Greek romances were often more accessible than Homer's epics to a mass audience, many of whom could not in fact read; works like those of Petronius and Apuleius appealed to a sophisticated and probably cynical elite with a literary taste for parody and what we would term pornography, but which they would have regarded with quite legitimate amusement; stories like those of Paul and Thecla suited Christians who adapted existing narrative conventions to their religious needs.

PATRICK POLLARD

Selected Works

Acta Pauli et Theclae. English translation in *New Testament Apocrypha*. Edited by W. Schneemelcher and E. Hennecke, vol.2. London: Lutterworth Press, 1965.

The Greek Alexander Romance. Translated with an introduction and notes by Richard Stoneman. London: Penguin, 1991.

Apollonius of Tyre. Translated... by Paul Turner. London: The Golden Cockerel Press, 1956.

Apuleius. *The Golden Ass*, or, *Metamorphoses*. Translated with an introduction and notes by E.J. Kenney. London: Penguin, 1998.

Hyginus. *The Myths* [*Fabulae* and *Poetica astronomia* book I]. Translated and edited by Mary Grant. Lawrence, KS: University of Kansas Press, 1960.

Parthenius. *The Love Romances...* with an English translation by Stephen Gaselee. Cambridge (Mass.) and London: Loeb, 1916 (often reprinted. In the same volume as Longus, translated by George Thornley, revised by J.M. Edmonds).

Petronius. *The Satyricon*. Translated with introduction and explanatory notes by P.G. Walsh. Oxford: Clarendon Press, 1996.

Quintilian. *The Major Declamations...* A translation [by] Lewis A. Sussmann. Frankfurt am Main: Lang, [1987].

The Scriptores Historiae Augustae. With an English translation by David Magie. Cambridge and London: Loeb, 1922–1932.

Valerius Maximus. *Memorable Doings and Sayings*. Edited and translated by D.R. Shackleton Bailey. Cambridge (Mass.) and London: Loeb, 2000.

Further Reading

Bowersock, G.W. *Fiction as History. Nero to Julian.* Berkeley, CA: University of California Press, 1994.

Fantham, E. *Roman Literary Culture. From Cicero to Apuleius.* Baltimore, MD: Johns Hopkins University Press, 1996.

Hägg, T. *The Novel in Antiquity.* Berkeley, CA: University of California Press, 1983.

Harrison, S.J., ed. *Oxford Readings in the Roman Novel.* Oxford: Oxford University Press, 1999.

Hofmann, H., ed. *Latin Fiction.* London: Routledge, 1999.

Perry, B.E. *The Ancient Romances.* Berkeley, CA: University of California Press, 1967.

Santoro L'hoir, F. *The Rhetoric of Gender Terms.* Leiden: E.J. Brill, 1992.

Walsh, P.G. *The Roman Novel. 2nd edition.* London: Bristol Classical Paperbacks, 1995.

LATIN: VERSE

Poetry came to Rome through Livius Andronicus, a schoolteacher who was taken captive when the Romans conquered Tarentum but was set free in 275 BCE to instruct the children of M. Livius Salinator. He translated Homer's *Odyssey* into Latin verse and is known to have composed dramas as well as a hymn to Juno. Although Cicero thought little of his work (Brut.71), Livius impressed the Romans to the extent that they granted permission to poets and stage artists to gather for religious purposes at the Aventine temple of Minerva. Still, the Romans of the third century BCE were too preoccupied with their national security to appreciate poetry,

let alone erotic verse. Only after the destruction of Carthage in 146 BCE and the conquest of their Macedonian allies in 168 BCE could the Romans engage in their literary interests. The winner of the crucial battle of Pydna, P. Cornelius Scipio Aemilianus, seized with enthusiasm the break from military expeditions 'to satisfy his delight in all things Greek' (Mendell, *Latin Poetry: The New Poets and the Augustans*, 1965: 4). He gathered around him the so-called Scipionic Circle of aristocratic friends who shared his interest in literature and their artistic protégés including Terence and Lucilius. When the historian Polybius and later the Stoic philosopher

Panaetius came from Greece, they joined their company and advanced intellectual activity in Rome. In the following pages an overview of the main Roman poets will focus on their treatment of erotic themes.

Early Roman Comedy

Popular Roman literary production in the third and second centuries BCE was dominated by the writings of Quintus Ennius (239–169 BCE), an epic poet who also translated Greek dramas and by the work of Titus Maccius Plautus (250–184) who composed comic plays in the manner of Menander (New Comedy). Although Plautus was often inspired by love affairs and in many of his plays the plot evolves around an erotic relationship, the focus of the dramatization is directed on the numerous misunderstandings that surround the relationship and cause the comic effects. The lives and loves of ordinary Romans shine through his work with all the social oppression that forces the females to conspire in order to achieve their goals. Common misogynistic prejudice, financial worries, class compatibility, and romantic youths that persist in their loves are typical themes repeated in Plautus' plays. The sexual jokes, numerous and often rather coarse, are habitually exchanged between the slaves of the households discussed. Plautian comedies often include a 'rape,' which typically takes place during a night festival under the influence of wine; yet the guilty youth appears always to be sincerely in love with his victim and overcomes all obstacles in order to correct his misbehavior by marrying the girl. Terence (Publius Terence Afer) also wrote comic plays in the tradition of Menander and Plautus most of which were produced in the 160s. Terence, who renders the Greek setting and ambiance of his literary models more convincingly than Plautus, used ingeniously his prologues to reply to the accusations of his critics. His work is also distinguished for the sensitivity with which he depicted the female psyche and their social disparity in Roman society (see his *Hecyra*). Both Plautus and Terence exercised great influence on the depiction of women and love affairs in later Latin elegy, particularly in Ovid's work. The misogynistic stereotypes they ridicule in their poetry seem to undermine the contemporary prejudice of traditionalist Romans.

The Neoterics

The opening of Rome to the material and intellectual wealth of the eastern Mediterranean soon became synonymous with an egotistic infatuation of the Roman elite with Greek literature at the expense of an impoverished proletariat. This soon led to inevitable social unrest which was to overtake the Roman public scene for almost an entire century until Augustus' decisive victory over Antony and Cleopatra at Actium in 31 BC which re-established peace and order amid general exhilaration. During his reign the so-called 'Neoteric poets,' inspired by Callimachus' literary revolution that urged for small, elegant poetic forms and departure from heroic epics, celebrated erotic sentiment most enthusiastically.

The new poets favored from the political preoccupations that kept the Roman elite away from their literary pastimes, set about to render a more personal and authentic expression to Roman eroticism. Valerius Cato, Calvus, Cassius, Cinna, Ticidas, Caecilius, and Catullus for whom we are better informed, were among the pioneers of this new trend that encouraged the composition of erotic poetry in Latin. Lucretius, a contemporary of Catullus, was also a neoteric poet in his own right, although he was mainly inspired by Epicurean philosophy. The immense impact of the neoterics is obvious even on their critics like Horace, while in their steps Propertius, Tibullus, and Ovidius, developed Latin erotic elegy to its most fortunate moments. Vergil, who did not shy from writing his *Aeneid* in epic hexameters, welcomed their innovations which he evidently applied in his work.

Lucretius (97/94 –55/51 BCE) composed his hexametric poem *De Rerum Natura* under the influence of the Epicurean thought around the middle of the first century BCE. His work, probably published by Cicero posthumously (Eusth.Chrn. apud St. Jerome; Cic.QFr.2.10.9), proclaims that sensation is the basis of all knowledge. At the end of the fourth book of the *De Rerum Natura*. Lucretius sets on a vehement attack on romantic love (DRN4.1037–1287). In these lines, Lucretius, who develops a metaphor between sexual desire and injury, stresses the addictive character of sexual intercourse which can be compared with that of thirst or hunger. Sex, food, and drink are seen as major temptations to the self-control of the individual;

however, the fact that hunger can be satiated unlike sexual desire stresses the less urgent nature of this need. Although Lucretius acknowledges the natural and agreeable side of sexual consumption, he is strongly opposed to falling in love. In a misogynistic mood he argues that all women are similar and dismisses melodramatic claims of lovers that they cannot live without the object of their desire. In Epicurean thought sex is a natural function of the body described in very mechanical terms and stripped from any nuances of emotion. In fact, the Epicurean doctrine teaches that love, sex, and friendship should be kept separate and marriage should be avoided at all costs. The danger of becoming emotionally involved and therefore, irrational threatens the core Epicurean vision of tranquility. The decision about whether one should indulge in one's sexual appetite should be determined by an evaluation of the danger involved. For example, daughters of prominent people, women likely to spread rumors, or unwilling women should be avoided. Although early Christianity did not approve of his rejection of gods and St. Jerome perpetuated a tradition according to which Lucretius wrote his verses in breaks of sanity, maddened by a love-potion his wife had given him, his prestige among the writers of the early empire is beyond doubt (e.g., Verg.G.2.490–2). Although Lucretius composed in the tradition of the philosophical poetry of Empedocles (*Peri Physeōs*) and the Hellenistic didactic poetry of Aratus and Nicander, he employed in his work a wide range of Greek and Latin erotic poetry including among others Sappho fr.31 (DRN3.152–8), Callimachus fr.260.41 (DRN6. 753), and Antipater of Sidon Anth.Pal.7.713 (DRN4.181–2).

Catullus (84–54 BCE) came to Rome in 62 BCE, probably under the pretext of undertaking a career in politics, but he soon met Valerius Cato and possibly studied under him. He fell deeply in love, probably with Clodia, sister of Publius Clodius, a sworn opponent of Cicero (*Pro Caelio*), and she became the Muse of his poetry. Clodia appears to have been an extremely cultured and charming, yet dangerous woman, who had been suspected of murdering her husband. In a series of elegant short poems, Catullus addressed her with the pseudonym Lesbia to recall Sappho of Lesbos whose influence on Catullus is ubiquitous; his verses express all the nuances of his obsession with her from early passion and tenderness to the hatred and disillusionment that overwhelmed him when he realized she had been unfaithful. Catullus' erotic visions are tormented by his devastating passion, his mistress' infidelities that fill him with anxiety and despair, and his drunken downfalls in local taverns where he meets underground characters like prostitutes and pimps. He does not hesitate to degrade his enemies with bold sexual insults spiced with all his vehement hatred. He lived the life of a real bohemian lover and was unsurprisingly the real life model of all later elegists. Of the 116 poems attributed to him, three (18–20) are almost certainly spurious. Catullus' work which survived thanks to the fortunate discovery of a manuscript in the early 14th century includes, besides the Lesbia poems, poems addressed to his young friend Juventius and epigrams whose tone ranges from pleasant to irreverent to obscene. He also wrote elegies and a few long poems, notably *Attis* and a nuptial poem honoring *Thetis and Peleus* in resonance of Sapphic bridal songs. Catullus was distinguished for his vigorous satire as well as his ability to render his personal emotions in Latin with such perceptiveness and intensity. He was influenced by the Alexandrian poets and drew much on previous Greek poetry regarding forms and meters, but his genius surpassed all models. His lyricism remains beyond compare (Havelock, *The Lyric Genius of Catullus*, 1967), while the influence of epigram in his poems is also sound (Aul. Gell.Noc.Att.19.9.10–14; Cic.De. nat.deor.1.79, 3.194).

Vergil (70–19 BCE) had become acquainted with the Epicurean philosophy early in his career. Most of his poetry is directed towards a philosophical solution to the trauma of the civil war which had left its ugly mark on the Roman psyche. His first collection of poems, the *Eclogues* (39–38 BCE) and even more so, his Georgics (30 BCE) employ erotic themes only to suggest a different way of channelling passion in the service of the community which will prosper again under the benevolent reign of Augustus. In the *Eclogues*, composed in the spirit of Theocritus' bucolic poetry, the unfortunate lover Daphnis, celebrated along Orpheus and other pastoral figures that naively sing about their erotic pangs and the powerful spells of love, is posthumously transformed into a divine agent of cosmic energy that benefits the whole countryside (Ec.3 and 5.42f.). The futility of wasted erotic energy directed towards solitary objects of desire in comparison with cosmic eros that rules all creation is underlined. Daphnis' transformation into a positive and restorative power is similar to that of the recently assassinated Caesar who was believed to have joined the ranks of the Olympians. In his *Georgics* Vergil promoted the image of the farmer as the symbol of a peaceful yet determined agent of the Augustan era in keeping with the agricultural character of traditional Roman societies (Cato Agr.2; Gale, *Virgil on the Nature of Things: the Georgics, Lucretius and the Didactic Tradition*, 2000: 252–9). In the third book of the *Georgics,* Vergil appears occupied with two kinds of love: the fecundity of the carefully disciplined animals and the blind, passionate love which released violent and uncontrolled energies. The tale of *Hero and Leander*, placed at the end of the third book exemplifies the tragic results of maddening love in humans in truly elegiac mood; in fact, Vergil repeatedly treated in his work elegiac themes with which he was obviously very familiar (cf. Ec.10). The influence of Lucretius on the *Georgics* is pervasive and both poets had strong feelings against civil strife. The fourth book of the *Georgics* features the tragic tale of *Orpheus and Eurydice*, in a version which is often accepted as Vergil's own invention (cf. Ov.Met.10.1–10, Anagnostou-Laoutides, *Eros and Ritual: Singing of Atalanta, Daphnis and Orpheus*, 2005: 321ff.). The tale has been arguably interpreted as a chiastic comparison between pathetic, overemotional poets/lovers represented by Orpheus and Vergil and decisive, resolute leaders like Aristaeus and Augustus in an attempt to illustrate the right course of action for achieving the Roman paligenesis.

For the rest of his life Vergil worked on the *Aeneid,* a national epic in hexameters honoring Rome and foretelling prosperity to come. Vergil made Aeneas the paragon of the most revered Roman virtues such as devotion to family, loyalty to the state, and piety, qualities that Aeneas shares with his distant successor, the emperor Augustus. In twelve books, Vergil tells how Aeneas escaped from Troy and managed after several adventures to establish the beginnings of the Roman state. In book four a storm carries him to the shores of Carthage, where he meets and falls in love with queen Dido. The passion with which the Carthaginian Queen surrenders to Aeneas is narrated in truly elegiac spirit: trapped in the antagonism of Hera and Venus, Dido has no chance of surviving her maddening love and she commits suicide having betrayed her kingdom and the memory of her dead husband (cf. Ov.Her.7). With his swan-song Vergil became the most important and most influential Roman poet and his aura continued to charm audiences through the Middle Ages.

Horace (65–8 BCE) was also affected by the violent era that followed the assassination of Julius Caesar and in fact, served at Philippi on the side of Brutus. His political preferences changed progressively when he launched a most successful poetic career under the benefaction of Maecenas, Augustus' 'Minister of Arts.' Yet his poetry remained particularly preoccupied with the political reality of his days and historical references became gradually more abundant in his poems. His first attempts at writing, named *Iambi/Epodes* witness the sound influence of the lyric poet Archilochus. Several of these poems are written in a strong satirical mood (Ep.4, 6, 10, 12) while others treat elegiac motifs such as the unbearable torture of love (Ep.11) or even elegiac characters such as the ruthless, unfaithful mistress (Neaira, Ep.15) or the dangerous witch who would go at any length in order to prepare a strong love potion (Canidia, Ep.12). In 35 BCE, Horace published his first book of *Sermones* (also known as *Satirae*), which is also distinguished for its satirical approach in the tradition of Lucilius and of Greek comedy, including references to sexual issues (Serm.1). Although Horace was evidently familiar with the elegiac motifs which he occasionally transmuted into Latin lyric verse, he treated love in a rather superficial and playful tone. His second book of the *Sermones* (32 BCE) containing numerous references to the Stoic dogma which Horace had by then embraced, also marked a departure from erotic themes (Serm.2.3, 7). Horace's next project that attracted his fancy for seven whole years was the composition of his lyric poems, published in four volumes under the title *Carmina*. Here and despite his preoccupation with national issues, Horace did not refrain from the occasional erotic composition such as the sensual ode to Pyrrha or the playful ode to Lydia (Carm.1.5, 8). The other three books of his *Carmina* range from discreet to patent support of the Augustan program (cf. Carm.3.1–6, the so-called Roman

Odes). Among his other major compositions Horace also produced in the last years of his life the famous *Ars Poetica*, offering advice to young, ambitious poets of his age on how to achieve the desired dramatic effect. This work enhances the perception that Horace filtered erotic passion through the rules of poetry and viewed love as an amusing and rather complimentary theme to the major historical issues of his time that dominated his poetry. His poems, distinguished for having uniquely reconciled the Epicurean and Stoic philosophical theories, largely refer to passion (including sexual promiscuity) as a sign of emotional imbalance and wickedness, such as his famous ode to Cleopatra (Carm.1.37).

Latin Elegiac Poets

Gallus (69–29 BCE) is a very enigmatic figure for whom scanty information survives, although all elegiac poets acknowledge him as their model and a most influential poet in the transmission of Hellenistic poetry from Alexandria to Rome (Ov.Tr.4.10.53). Gallus is known to have composed four books of elegies, probably under the title *Amores*, addressed to Volumnia Cytheris, a mistress of Mark Antony, under the pseudonym Lycoris. Very few verses of his poems have been recovered from a papyrus found in 1978 in Egyptian Nubia, although Vergil's tenth *Eclogue*, in which Vergil tries to console Gallus for his desertion by Lycoris, offers an insight to the content of Gallus' poetry. He also wrote a poem about the Grynean grove of Apollo in the fashion of Eurphorion (Serv.ap.Ecl. 6.72) and was a friend of Parthenius who had composed in hexameters a short collection of erotic tales with the title *Erotica Pathemata* for the use of his friend. His influence on the character of Latin elegiac poetry as developed in the works of Propertius and Tibullus has been vital; based on Catullus' groundwork, Gallus appears to have created the basic script for the unfortunate relation between a cruel mistress and her enslaved victim.

Tibullus (55/48–19 BCE), a rather good-looking young poet of the provincial nobility and relatively wealthy despite his claims of the opposite (Hor.Epist.1.4), wrote three books of elegies, known as *Corpus Tibullianum*. He had won military awards as a soldier and addressed his poetry to M. Valerius Messalla Corvinus, an eminent Roman statesman. Only the first two books belong to Tibullus himself, while the third was divided into two by Italian scholars of the fifteenth century. Although the dates of publication are uncertain, the poems contain some possible clues. His first book contains ten lengthy elegies dealing with his love for Delia whose name seems to indicate her association with the Apolline light. The structure of the collection has been often debated, yet it is accepted that Horace's *Sermones*, also consisting of ten poems, must have been his model (Littlewood, *The symbolic structure of Tibullus' Book I*, 1970, *Latomus* 29.2: 661–669). Apuleius (Apol.10) verified that Delia actually existed and her real name was Plania, although her erotic persona in Tibullus' poetry appears quite conventional. In fact, it could be argued that despite his technical versatility, Tibullus' representation of love is rather artificial and unconvincing with regards to the depth of his passion. His erotic claims are always permeated by a dose of irony and a playful mood, displayed in his effort to elicit erotic advice from the highly sexed god Priapus (Tib.1.4), and even when the poet imagines himself on the brink of death for the love of his mistress (Tib.1.3). Tibullus remained in reality a lover of the peaceful countryside and he viewed love as the perfect complement to his vision of domestic bliss. His first book began with an abnegation of military career, in favor of an abstemious life in rural felicity (cf. 1.10). This agricultural sense of fulfilment protected by traditional Roman gods, such as the Lares and Pales, is completed when Delia's presence is added (Tib.1.57–8). A gentle dandy dedicated to the tender moments he shared with his mistress, Tibullus justifies the opinion of Quintilian that he was the most refined and elegant of the Roman elegists (Inst.10.1.93). His anger at his mistress' infidelities is but a bitter complaint for his betrayed emotions (Tib.1.5 and 6) and his vengeance takes the form of having an affair with a beautiful boy (Tib.1.8 and 9) or of daydreaming that he dies in a distant land far from her treacherous embrace (Tib.1.3; Campbell, *Tibullus Elegy 1.3*, 1973, *YCS* 23). Tibullus' revels are literary exercises in adapting Alexandrian material (Tib.1.2; cf. Anth. Pal.5.137) and certainly in comparison with Propertius' his verses lack the emotional intensity or the illusion of maddening passion that the latter achieves. His long elegies allowed him to treat numerous themes in each elegy. He combined various patterns with transitions which often were considered too smooth to convince critics of his poems' unity (Lee, *Tibullus Elegies*, 1990).

Many of the motifs he treats are also found in Propertius' poetry such as the witch (Prop.1.19 / Tib.2.41), the vanity of the women's adornment (Prop.2.1 /Tib.8.9), the friend who is envious of the lover's happiness (Prop.5.1 /Tib.2.87), the rich rival (Prop.8a2/Tib.5.47), the komoi outside the beloved's door (Prop.16.17 /Tib.1.56), the love of young boys (Prop.20.6/Tib.4.3), the worthlessness of riches in love (Prop.14.15/ Tib.2.75), the comparison between the lover and the soldier (Prop.4.19/Tib.1.53), the value of poetry in love (Prop.7.5/Tib.4.15), or the role of the *magister amoris* (Prop.10.19/Tib.4. 9f.). Tibullus prefers metaphors of every day life rather than resorting to Greek mythology for his erotic imagery and seems to be closer to a Hesiodic approach of poetry with regards to the fulfilment he finds in simple country life. In addition, his poems are distinguished for their sense of religiosity which rules nature and everyday activities (Tib.1.11–14). His second book celebrates a different mistress, Nemesis (Tib.2.3, 4, 6) whose name as well as her character alludes to the darkness of night. Nemesis is a courtesan of the higher classes and enjoys the attention of many admirers. She is an urban creature fanatically devoted to the pursuit of wealthy lovers and a far outcry from the simple beauty of Delia or the idyllic country-house of Tibullus' erotic happiness. The third book of Tibullus' poems begins with six elegies by Lygdamus; it contains the *Panegyricus Messallae*, five poems on the love of Sulpicia for Cerinthus (known as the *Garland of Sulpicia*) and six short poems by Sulpicia herself. The poems on Sulpicia could be possibly written by Tibullus. The book concludes with an elegy allegedly written by Tibullus, and an anonymous epigram.

Sulpicia who composed poetry under Domitian was mentioned by Martial (10.38.12–14). Apparently she wrote erotic poems for Calenus, her husband of 15 years. Her poetry was distinguished for its sensual tone (Mart.10.35.38) and although we only have one short fragment of hers, Sulpicia is frequently mentioned in later poetry (Auson.218.10; Sidon.Carm.9.261; Fulgent.Myth.1.4). A poem of the late fourth or early fifth century AD, written in her name, is traditionally included in the later collection *Epigrammata Bobiensia*. Here Sulpicia appears as castigating the suppression of philosophers, including Calenus, during the reign of Domitian.

Propertius (54 /47–2 BC) came from a noble family of Perugia and settled in Rome around 34 BC. There he met Hostia, a native of Tibur (Apul.Apol.10) who was to monopolize his poetry under the pseudonym Cynthia. Ovid maintains that Propertius was his senior and that he was third in the sequence of elegiac poets, following Gallus and Tibullus. He wrote four books of elegies and he probably published his first book before October 28 BC. Its publication placed him in the first rank of contemporary poets, and procured his admission to the literary circle of Maecenas (cf. Prop.2.1; 3.9). His poems have been often characterized as difficult, obscure, and full of syntactic inconsistency. Occasionally commentators have doubted even his Latinity and it was only the intensity of his passion that deemed his poetry worth reading (Inst.10.1.93; cf. Plin.Ep.9.22). The structure of his first poetic collection, also known as the *Monobiblos*, was the subject of numerous scholarly exercises (Skutch, *The Structure of the Propertian Monobiblos*, 1963, *CPh* 58; Williams, *Tradition and Originality in Roman Poetry*, 1968; Otis, *Propertius' Single Book*, 1965, *HSCPh* 70; Camps, *Propertius Book 1*, 1961). Characteristic of Propertius' love poetry is the claim that he is enslaved to the charms of his mistress as well as that he is a soldier in the name of love (1.6.29f.). Typical too of his love poetry is his abundant and romantic use of mythological figures who serve as reminiscences of a glorious past to which the poet and Cynthia should aspire to. Book two (which some think is an amalgamation of two books by a later hand), is still largely devoted to love poems. Book three has a greater diversity of subject matter than the first two books and in book four Propertius attempted to write aetiological poetry under the influence of Callimachus' *Aetia* (Prop.3.1; 3.3; 4.1.64). Although some of his poems are fragmentary and several corrupted or disarranged, Propertius' genius shines through his elaborate verses. Propertius is thought to have achieved the most systematic use of erotic motifs from the *Garland of Meleager*, a collection of epigrams that had created a literary fashion in Rome and had also influenced Catullus. Since

Meleager came to be admired for his 'double talent of versatility in treatment and felicity in expression,' we might assume that Propertius' style owes much to the Hellenistic epigrams of his master (Gow-Page, *The Greek Anthology*, 1965: vol.2.592). Meleager, also admired for his skilful turn of expression and his passionate descriptions, had first cultivated the image of the elegiac komastis, who unable to resist his amorous addiction spends his nights on the threshold of his relentless mistress (Prop.1.16. 13–4 and 31–2 /Mel.Anth.Pal.5.191.5–8; 12.23. 3–4), often urged by wine (Prop.1.3.13–6; Mel. Anth.Pal.12.119; 12.85.3–6; 12.117.1–5). The impact of Meleager on Propertius' erotic vision can be distinguished in direct linguistic echoes, in overlapping conceptual complexes in the two authors and in their use of the same topoi. Hence, Meleager's description of the violent attack of Eros who implants his feet on the head of his innocent and inexperienced victims appears in the first verses of Propertius' programmatic elegy of the *Monobiblos* (Mel.Anth. Pal.12.101.3–4; 12.48.1 / Prop.1.1.1–4). Other Meleagrian verses that found their way to Propertius' poetry include the claim that Cynthia was the first woman who touched the poet with her love (Anth.Pal.12.101; 12.23.1–2; cf. Prop.1.12. 20; 1.15.32); in fact, she 'captured' Propertius with her erotic eyes (Anth.Pal.12.101.2; 12.109. 1–2; cf. Anth.Pal.12.144; 12.110.1–4; 12.83.3–4; 12.113). Propertius employs exquisite epithets to describe Love in correspondence to Eros' characterization in Meleager; therefore *amor improbus* (e.g. Prop.1.1.6) matches the shameless nature of Love in Meleager (Anth.Pal.5.57). Love is presented as a feathered archer (Prop.1. 6.23; 1.7.15; 1.9.20–4/ Mel.Anth.Pal.5.177.1–4; 5.178.2–7; 5.179.1–6; Anth.Pal.12.144; 12.76.1–2; 12.48.3; 5.198.6; 12.109.3), who inflicts an erotic wound to his victims like the elegiac mistress (Prop.1.1.9–16/ Mel.Anth.Pal.12.72; 12.80. 1–2; 5.163.3–4). Love is like fire burning the poet's soul (Prop.1.5.5; 1.9.17; 1.13.23 /Mel.Anth. Pal.12.80.4; 12.48.3; 12.76.2; 12.82; 12.83. 1–2; 5.176.6), an obsession (Prop.1.1.7; 1.5.3; 1.13.20/ Mel.Anth.Pal.12.48.3–4; 5.139.6) that moves him to tears (Prop.1.5.15; 1.6.23–4 /Mel.Anth. Pal.12.80.1) and renders him helpless (Prop.1. 15.1–8; 1.8a.13–4/ Mel.Anth.Pal.5.24; 5.178.9–10; 5.179.9–10) to its endless torture (Prop.1. 1.33–4; Mel.Anth.Pal.12.158.5–8; AP5. 112). Propertius also cultivates the idea that love

abolishes logic, often found in Meleager's epigrams (Anth.Pal.12.117.3–5; cf. Anth.Pal.5. 24). Motifs such as the praise of a mistress' beauty (Pr.1.2.1–8 and 27–9/ Mel.Anth.Pal.5. 140; 5.139, 195, 195bis, and 196), especially when asleep and surrendered in unfaithful dreams, as often the poet fears (Prop.1.3.27–36 /Mel.Anth. Pal.5.191; cf. Anth.Pal.12.125; 5.151. 7–8, 152.5–6, 166, 174), the pattern of warning a friend for love's hardship (Prop.1.5.27–30 /Mel.Anth.Pal.12.72.5–6), of being jealous of rivals (Prop.1.11.5–8; 1.16; 1.9.5–8/Mel.Anth. Pal.5.166.1–7; 5.160.1–2; 5.191.5), of a mistress' ability to lie (Prop.1.15.1–8 and 33–42/Mel. Anth.Pal.5.24; 5.175, 184) and her ultimate infidelity (Prop.1.15.1–8/Mel.Anth.Pal.5.175) are also traced in both poets. Love is difficult to bear (Prop.1.6.23/Mel.Anth.Pal.12.132b.1); it reduces the lover to its prisoner (Prop.1.9.20; 1.5.12; Mel.Anth.Pal.12.158.3–4; 12.119; 12.158) crashing his steadfast spirit (Prop.1.9.1–4; 1.1.28; Mel.Anth.Pal.12.141.5–6; 12.119.3–4; AP12.132.1–5; AP12.132 and 132a). Propertius' ingenious adaptation of his models could only add to the superlative quality of his descriptions. His powerful erotic imagery captures the essence of Latin elegiac poetry.

Ovid (43 BC–17 CE) had studied rhetoric at Rome before choosing poetry over a career in politics (Sen.Controv.2.2.8–12; Tr.1.2.77–8; Pont.2.10.21ff.). His early erotic poems, the *Amores*, published for the first time between 25 and 15 BCE, impressed his contemporaries and he eventually attracted the attention of the emperor Augustus. His love poems, composed in elegiac couplets, include the *Amores*, the *Ars Amatoria*, the *Remedia Amoris*, and the *Medicamina Faciei*. Ovid was a keen adherent of the Alexandrian poets and Callimachus' *Aetia* is accepted as a strong influence on his poetry. Ovid is also distinguished for his constant inversion of conventional elegiac motifs and for his sense of irony, which is reminiscent of Catullus' sarcasm. He made extensive use of comic themes in his elegies and his work has been criticized for reducing Roman elegy to unsophisticated ridicule (Quint. Inst.10.1.88, 98). It has also been argued that his excessive dependence on his literary models is indicative of his lack of original inspiration. His *Amores*, initially published in five books, reappeared in three BCE in just three. The poems mainly praise the charms of Corinna, the poet's mistress, who appears to have been a fictional character. The poems rework several motifs introduced in the poetry of Propertius and the comic plays of Plautus. Ovid who is very confident about the fame his work will enjoy in posterity (see Met.15.870–9) is using among other techniques hyperbole and theatrical asides addressed to himself or to his audience in order to convince the reader of the sincerity of his experiences. However, by overstating his elegiac persona Ovid is stressing the incredibility of the elegiac lover as treated in the works of Propertius and Tibullus, where he is given a pretentious, melodramatic, and impossibly romantic character. Unlike previous poetry, in Ovid's verses the lover is often successful and willing to devote himself to love in the comforting notion that it is all a game. In the *Ars Amatoria* (Sen.Controv.3.7.2), a didactic poem on how to be successful in love, Ovid employs explicit erotic imagery. His vivid descriptions allow us an almost realistic glimpse of the social life in Augustan Rome where the newly found peace had led to a relaxation of morality. The *Ars Amatoria* was designed as a sequence to the *Amores*, with which it shares several thematic links. However, here Ovid achieves a more complete comparison of art with love. The *Remedia Amoris* (Rem.155–8), written between the first BCE and the second century CE was conceived as a kind of recantation of the *Ars Amatoria*, which concludes Ovid's early work on elegiac motifs. Still in didactic mood, having taught the readers how to secure the affection of their beloved, Ovid now offers advice on how to escape complicated erotic situations. The *Heroides* is an imaginary series of letters written by ancient mythological heroines to their absent lovers. The authorship of Her.15, written allegedly by the poetess Sappho, is often contested. The letters are distinguished for their use of rhetoric device and of the erotic monologue which had briefly appeared in Propertius (Prop.1.18; 4.3), as well as for their adaptation of the Euripidian analysis of female psychology. Sometime before the composition of the third book of the *Ars Amatoria*, Ovid wrote the *Medicamina Faciei*, yet another didactic poem about the cosmetics for the female (Ars Am.3.205–6). Only a hundred verses survive from this work which follows in the tradition of Nicander's *Theriaca* and *Alexipharmaca*.

Ovid also composed the *Metamorphoses* in fifteen books of hexameters. This most influential poem is a collection of myths that relate miraculous transformations. The narration begins with the creation of the world from chaos and finishes with the posthumous catasterism of Caesar. The rest of the books engage mainly with erotic misconducts of gods and men who are often punished by being transformed into animals or plants. The tales are linked together with a number of thematic associations that render to the work an illusion of cohesion. The idea of collecting metamorphic myths was very popular in the Hellenistic period: Nicander of Colophon, Parthenius and the obscure Boios whose *Ornithogonia* was apparently adapted by Aemilius Macer, a friend and contemporary of Ovid (Tr.4.10.43), had all produced such collections, although none of them survived to this day. His other poems focus on the adversities of living in exile to which Ovid was sent in 8 BC. Through his reworking of elegiac themes from a comical point of view and his bold experimentation with the forms and meters of ancient literary genres, Ovid advanced our appreciation of Latin elegy and its boundaries and firmly set his seal on Latin poetry. His work exercised an overt influence on European literature, more than any other classical author.

Martial (38/41–102/103 CE) settled in Rome around 64 CE, where he allegedly lived a life of poverty and dependence (Ep.10.24; cf. Ep.10. 104). He was born a Roman citizen, but he refers to himself as sprung from Celts and Iberians (Ep.10.65.7). Despite the impression that he used to compose poetry at the local tavern, Martial made many influential friends and patrons, and secured the favor both of Titus and Domitian. His poetry, often obscene, reflects the moral decadence of contemporary Rome. Of his works 33 poems survive from his *Liber Spectaculorum*, published around 80 CE to commemorate the opening of the Colosseum. He also published two collections of short mottoes entitled *Xenia* and *Apophoreta* between 84 and 85 CE and 12 books of *Epigrams*, published between 86–102 CE. His final book of epigrams was written three years after his return to Spain and shortly before his death. In his later years Martial appears tired of the intensity of Roman social life and he even sought refuge temporarily in the countryside (Ep.2.38; 12.57; 4.25; 10.96). However, the attraction of Rome was indeed tantalizing and in his prose epistle at the beginning of his last book of epigrams he already confesses he misses the buzz of the cosmopolis.

He was always preoccupied with maintaining his high friends and thus refrained from the aggressive tone of Juvenal's satire. In fact, his verbal dexterity suffers from servile flattery towards the emperor (Ep.12.6).

Juvenal wrote Roman satires between 100 and 128 CE reprimanding the decadence of morality during his time (Sat.2.6). He lived during the reign of Domitian and appears to have been alive when the empire was ruled by Hadrian. He must have come from a wealthy family as he appeared not to be in need of a patron. He wrote 16 Satires varying from 60 to 660 lines in length. His themes included homosexuality (Sat.1.2), and male prostitution (Sat.3.9). His verse established a model for the satire of indignation, and the biting tone of his poetry remains unequalled. In his poetry he powerfully denounces a permissive Roman society that indulges in luxury and sensual pleasures, in brutal exercise of power and the antagonisms of the imperial court. His expression is often enriched with popular mottoes and his style owes much to the rhetorical form. His contribution to poetry was not recognized during his life time and he was not included in Quintilian's history of satire. Servius in the late fourth century drew attention to his talent.

Ausonius' writings (310–394 CE) form a miscellaneous collection divided into *Occasional Works* and *School Exercises and Fragments*. In the *Parentalia*, eulogies to deceased relatives, written in 379 CE, he occasionally expresses personal sentiment. His *Cupido Crucifixibus* is the description of a painting in a dining room at Trier, representing Cupid as tormented in Hell by the women who pursued him on earth. The second group of his writing includes mnemonic verse. In his erotic verse he praises love as a form of tender friendship. He wrote letters to his friends, and poetry, praising his apples and lamenting his verses with light-hearted gentleness. The wife of his youth died after a few years of marriage, but not before leaving him the comfort of children. He had written her a tender lyric in life, and thirty-six years later was still writing of her. Ausonius was a Christian, forever trapped between his religiosity and his keen interest in pagan antiquity.

EVANGELIA ANAGNOSTOU-LAOUTIDES

Selected Works

Arkins, B. *Sexuality in Catullus*. 1982.

Booth, J. *Catullis to Ovid: Reading Latin Love Elegy: A Literary Commentary with Latin Text*. 1999.

Greene, E. *The Erotics of Domination: Male Desire and the Mistress in Latin Love Poetry*. 1998.

Hallett, J., and M.B. Skinner. *Roman Sexualities*. 1997.

Janan, M. *When the Lamp is Shattered: Desire and Narrative in Catullus*. 1994.

Kennedy, D.F. *The Arts of Love: Five Studies in the Discourse of Roman Love Elegy*. 1992.

Laigneau, S. *La Femme et 1 'amour chez Catulle et les Eligiaques augusteens*. 1999.

Miller, P.A. *Subjecting Verses: Latin Love Elegy and the Emergence of the Real*. 2004.

Further Reading

Coffta, D.J. *The Influence of Callimachean Aesthetics on the Satires and Odes of Horace*. 2001.

DeBrohun, J.B. *Roman Propertius and the Reinvention of Elegy*. 2002.

Dettmer, H. *Love By the Numbers: Form and Meaning in the Poetry of Catullus*. 1997.

Fantham, E. *Roman Literary Culture: From Cicero to Apuleius*. 1996.

Fantuzzi, M., and R. Hunter. *Muse e modelli: La poesia ellenistica da Alessandro Magnoad Augusto*. 2002.

Feeney, D., and A.J. Woodman. *Traditions and Contexts in the Poetry of Horace*. 2002.

Godwin, J. *Lucretius*. 2004.

Holzberg, N. *Catull. Der Dichter und sein erotisches Werk*. 2a ed. 2002.

Jacoff, R., and T. Schnapp. *The Poetry of Allusion: Virgil and Ovid in Dante's* Cornmedia. 1991.

Janan, M. *The Properties of Desire: Propertius IV* 2001.

Maltby, R. *Tibullus: Elegies. Text, Introduction, and Commentary*. 2002.

Nappa, C. *Aspects of Catullus ' Social Fiction*. 2001.

Nussbaum, M.C. *The Therapy of Desire: Theory and Practice in Hellenistic Ethics*. 1994.

Paschalis, M. *Horace and Greek Lyric Poetry*. 2002.

Patterson, A.M. *Pastoral and Ideology: Vergil to Valery*. 1987.

Putnam, M.C.J. *Vergil's Aeneid: Interpretation and Influence*. 1995.

Spentzou, E. *Readers and Writers in Ovid's Heroides: Transgressions of Genre and Gender*. 2002.

Thomas, R.F. *Vergil and His Texts: Studies in Intertextuality*. 2000.

White, P. *Promised Verse: Poets in the Society of Augustan Rome*. 1993.

Wray, D. *Catullus and the Poetics of Roman Manhood*. 2001.

LAURE (COLETTE PEIGNOT)

1903–1938
French thinker and writer

"Histoire d'une petite fille"

Georges Bataille and Michel Leiris published "Histoire d'une petite fille" in 1939. The text was included in a limited edition entitled *Écrits de Laure*, which also included Laure's poems and her unfinished notes on the notion of the sacred. In 1977, her nephew Jérôme Peignot compiled the first public edition of Laure's work, including the previously published material and her correspondence with Bataille, Michel Leiris, and others. Peignot also added his introduction "Ma mère diagonale" ("My Diagonal Mother"), and Bataille's article "La vie de Laure" ("The Life of Laure"). Jeanine Herman's English translation of this edition was published by City Lights Books in 1995.

"Histoire d'une petite fille" is a series of memories from the author's childhood and adolescence, recorded chronologically in the form of a loosely crafted memoir. Bataille and Leiris chose the title from Laure's notes, where she had also suggested the titles "Le triste privilège" ("The Sad Priviledge") and "Une vie de conte de fée" ("A Fairy Tale Life"). In "Histoire d'une petite fille," the narrator seemingly purges herself of her most painful memories. She addresses death and eroticism in a language that is at once brutal and ambiguous. The first memory recounted is of a little girl going to bed in a room full of religious paraphernalia and falling victim to terrifying nightmares. It quickly becomes apparent that the narrator's waking moments were no less frightening than her dreams, and she calls childhood 'the stealer of children.' There is a notable tension throughout "Histoire d'une petite fille," and throughout Laure's writing in general, which is self-consciously influenced by the forces of death, eroticism, and religious oppression.

In "Histoire d'une petite fille," Laure describes events which she would later incorporate in her theory of the sacred. For Laure, the sacred is defined by two dueling components: the 'high' sacred, equated with the exultation she witnesses during religious ritual, and the 'base,' which she associates with issues of sexuality. The sacred experience is also founded on a mysticism maintained by concentrating on the infinite. Its roots are particularly evident in a lyrical passage of "Histoire d'une petite fille," during which the little girl is overcome as she 'discovers' the immensity of the sky. The child protagonist is simultaneously fascinated by and frightened of both types of 'sacred' phenomena. From a very early age Laure is aware of the affinity between religious euphoria and sexual transgression, and she envies anyone who is unrestricted by bourgeois social structure. Such abhorrence of bourgeois ideals is perhaps the strongest current in "Histoire d'une petite fille," and each childhood event is described as an expression of the need to break away from social restriction.

Laure's oppressive life in Paris is all the more striking because juxtaposed with euphoric descriptions of the countryside. Her father teaches her about nature at the family's country home, and the young child is enraptured. Any happiness is ephemeral however, as the Peignot family is devastated by a series of deaths during the first World War. Laure's beloved father enlists in the army, and as the family is seeing him off at the train station the child has what she calls her first real sacred experience: she is part of a crowd whose patriotic fervor causes her to see her father as a willing human sacrifice. The experience makes her physically ill. Soon after this epiphany, Laure witnesses a staggering number of deaths. An uncle is first: having returned from the front with tuberculosis, he dies slowly in Laure's bedroom. During the funeral a sheet of water escapes from the coffin and hits the pallbearers, one of whom swears loudly. Laure is stricken by this throwing together of solemnity and profanity, and is literally overwhelmed. Her father's death follows, and Laure's grief is augmented by what she calls the 'spectacle of mourning': her mother grieves most vehemently when guests are present, her aunt pays attention to her make-up while weeping, and there is a general feeling that her father's death has been romanticized. For a short time Laure becomes attached to the young daughter of a family friend, and this toddler also grows ill and dies. The narrator states that she fully understood death when seeing this child's tiny white coffin lowered into the ground.

At this time, Laure contracts tuberculosis, and after being nursed back to health she begins to lose religious faith. This is encouraged by the death of her godson, a young soldier who had vexed her mother during a previous visit because he had been unwilling to discuss combat. Laure likens this encounter to the day a friend of her brother's sobbed uncontrollably in her mother's presence, annoying her greatly. This boy was also killed.

Laure's first sexual experiences added to her trauma: following the multiple deaths already described, she discovers that the family priest—known to her as *Monsieur l'abbé*—had been sexually molesting her older sister. The priest soon turns his attentions to Laure, and the situation is aggravated by the fact that he has symbolically taken over her father's role within the household. When *Monsieur l'abbé* explains human reproduction to Laure, she is torn by the desire to confess her sexual thoughts to a priest and the knowledge that these thoughts were instigated by the relationship between this same priest and her sister. Confused, Laure guards her secret for quite some time.

As Laure rejects her family more fervently, she becomes increasingly withdrawn from social interaction. When she finally tells her brother about the priest's misconduct, they tell their mother who promptly accuses them of lying. From this point on, Laure is deliberately cold towards her family and begins to express her anger through writing. Returning to school, her behavior is erratic and unpredictable; the only stable force in her life becomes her irreligion. She is briefly attracted to music, but eventually rejects even this as a form of escapism.

"Histoire d'une petite fille" is in no way a sexually explicit text. When read within the context of Laure's other writings however, and in relation to Bataille's theory of the sacred, the juxtaposing of the high and base elements of the sacred already present in Laure's childhood acquires renewed importance. The author of "Histoire d'une petite fille" has expunged her most traumatic childhood experiences and incorporated them in a structured (if chaotic) épistémè of transgression, eroticism, and death.

Biography

Laure's full name was Colette Laure Lucienne Peignot. Born into a Catholic, bourgeois family in Paris on October 8, 1903, she died of tuberculosis on November 8, 1938. Laure was linked to many important intellectual figures and movements during her short life: with the author Jean Bernier she collaborated with the French surrealists, with communist activist Boris Souvarine she contributed articles to *La critique sociale*, and with Georges Bataille she wrote for the political journal *Contre-Attaque* and participated in *Acéphale* (a secret society striving to recreate Dionysian rituals).

PATRICIA BERNEY

Editions and Selected Works

Écrits de Laure. Paris: Hors commerce, 1939.
Écrits de Laure (texte établi par J. Peignot et le Collectif Change). Paris: Société nouvelle des éditions J.-J. Pauvert, 1977.
Laure: The Collected Writings. Translated by Jeanine Herman. San Francisco: City Lights Books, 1995.
Une rupture, 1934: Correspondance croisée de Laure avec Boris Souvarine, sa famille, Georges Bataille, Pierre et Jenny Pascal, Simone Weil (texte établi par J. Peignot et Anne Roche). Paris: Éditions des Cendres, 1999.

Further Reading

Barillé, Élisabeth. *Laure: la sainte de l'abîme*. Paris: Flammarion, 1997.
Black, S.L. *Laure: Life Under a Black Sun.* Doctoral thesis, University of Sussex, 1998.
Devaux, Mandelli-Corinne and Anne Roche. "Simone Weil and Colette Peignot ou Qu'est-ce qu'une conviction non-prouvée?." *Cahiers Simone Weil* (Sept. 1984) 7:3, pp. 243–250.
Maubon, Catherine. "L'expérience 'politique' de Colette Peignot" in *Des Années trente: groupes et ruptures* (textes réunis par Anne Roche et Christian Tarting). Paris: Éditions du Centre National de la recherche scientifique, 1984.
Sahely, Nadia-M. "The Laure-Bataille Exchange: Celebrating the Dissymmetry of the Couple in Interwar French Thought." *Cincinnati Romance Review* (1996) 15, pp. 41–49.

LAWRENCE, D.H.

1885—1930
British novelist, poet, essayist

Works

"I always labor at the same things," David Herbert Lawrence commented while writing *Lady Chatterley's Lover*, "to make the sex relation valid and precious instead of shameful." With some qualification, this comment is a fair description of Lawrence's major work. Generally, the "sex relation" he wrote about is heterosexual and genital—"phallic marriage," as he called it—but not entirely, and the heterosexual relationships he portrayed explore a variety of erotic experiences.

Early Work

Before his elopement with Frieda Weekley and up to the completion of *Sons and Lovers* in 1912, his view of heterosexual relationships was that they are tragic, presumably because of the unhappy marriage of his own parents and his own intense Oedipal conflicts. In his first novel, *The White Peacock*, begun in 1905–6 and published in 1911, the strongly masculine farmer George Saxton is flirted with by Lettie because she feels in him the warm manliness she does not feel in Leslie (the better economic match whom she marries); because the desire she arouses in George cannot be satisfied in his subsequent marriage to the less "spiritual," less educated Meg, he destroys himself with drink. "How much this first novel was written for his mother's approval," Richard Aldington remarked, "may be judged from this Band of Hope portrait of George and from the fact that Heinemann had a single advance copy of the book, printed and bound, for Lawrence to give his mother before he died." The story is told from the point of view of a first-person narrator, Cyril, who feels himself to be a disembodied consciousness, "a pale, erratic fragility." Cyril is very close to his mother and identifies with her middle-class sensibilities and refinement—his derelict father is dead and out of the story. Also present in the novel is a gamekeeper who anticipates the famous gamekeeper in *Lady Chatterley's Lover*, but here the representative of male vitality is killed off in an accident in a quarry. The really positive presentation of erotic feeling is in the attraction that Cyril feels towards George, celebrated in what Jeffrey Meyers calls a "Whitmanesque" chapter, entitled "A Poem of Friendship." Naked, Cyril and George swim together, and afterwards they dry each other:

> ... [H]e knew how I admired the noble, white fruitfulness of his form. As I watched him, he stood in white relief against the mass of green. He polished his arm, holding it straight and solid; he rubbed his hair into curls, while I watched the deep muscles of his shoulders, and the bands stand out in his neck as he held it firm ... [L]aughing he took hold of me and began to rub me briskly, as if I were a child, or rather, a woman he loved and did not fear. I left myself quite limply in his hands, and, to get a better grip of me, he put his arm around me and pressed me against him, and the sweetness of the touch of our naked bodies one against the other was superb. It satisfied in some measure the vague, indecipherable yearning of my soul; and it was the same with him. When he had rubbed me all warm, he let me go, and we looked at each other with eyes of still laughter, and our love was perfect for a moment, more perfect than any love I have known since, either for man or woman.

The tragic view of homosexual passion continues in his second novel, *The Trespasser*, published in 1912. The story of the illicit love affair between Siegmund and Helen and its consequences, treated with more intensity (complete with allusions to *Tristan und Isolde*) than was the love-tragedy of the first novel, and Siegmund rather inexplicably hangs himself. But the lyrical descriptions of nature shown through the lover's eyes are an expression of their passion that lets them see the whole world afresh. It is not, however, till *Sons and Lovers* that heterosexual passion is no longer portrayed as somehow inherently tragic but as made unhappy by Oedipal conflicts. It is the middle-class mother, with her disapproval of the working-class father and his drinking, who exacerbates these conflicts. Frieda, with whom he had eloped to the European continent before finishing this third novel, helped him, with her experience of psychoanalysis, to see the Oedipal outlines of the essentially autobiographical story of Paul Morel's inability to find a satisfying sexual experience with a woman. "A woman of character and refinement goes into the lower class," Lawrence was able to write in 1912 describing his novel to his publisher, and has no satisfaction in her own life. She has had a passion for her husband, so the children are born of passion, and have heaps of vitality. But as her sons grow up, she selects them as lovers ... But when they come to manhood, they can't love, because their mother is the strongest power in their lives, and holds them ... William gives his sex to a fribble, and his mother holds his soul. But the split kills him ... The next son gets a woman who fights for his soul—fights his mother. The son loves the mother—all the sons hate and are jealous of the father ... The son decides to leave his soul in his mother's hands, and, like his elder brother, go for passion. Then the split begins to tell again ... The son casts off his mistress, attends to his mother dying. He is left in the end naked of everything ...

This conception of a "split" in erotic feeling is strikingly parallel to Freud's description of the causes of "psychical impotence" in his 1912 essay "The Most Prevalent Form of Degradation in Erotic Life." Because of the attachment to the mother, the boy cannot feel tenderness and esteem (i.e., cannot give his "soul") to the same woman for whom he feels sensual desire, and *vice versa*. "He was like so many young men of his age," Lawrence's novel tells us. "Sex had become so complicated in him that he would have denied that he ever could want Clara or Miriam or any woman whom he *knew*. Sex desire was a sort of detached thing, that did not belong to a woman." Paul's sexual intercourse with Miriam, who is supposed to be full of spiritual feelings and who gives in to him out of a feeling of obligation and self-sacrifice, is unpleasant to both. But with Clara—a feminist separated from her husband—he can experience a joyous, uninhibited sexual release. Lying with her on a river bank, he

> ... sunk his mouth on her throat, where he felt her heavy pulse beat under his lips. Everything was perfectly still. There was nothing in the afternoon but themselves.
>
> When she arose, he, looking on the ground all the time, saw suddenly sprinkled on the black wet beech-roots many scarlet carnation petals, like splashed drops of blood; and red, small splashes fell from her bosom, streaming down her dress to her feet.
>
> "Your flowers are smashed," he said.

But in the relationship that develops, Clara perceives it is not her that he wants but, as she puts it, merely "it."

The Rainbow

In *Look! We Have Come Through!*, most of which was written in 1912, Lawrence has cast off his tragic view of sex. Though it speaks of the difficulties they encounter in their relationship, this poetic sequence celebrates what he has discovered with Frieda. Now he can sing a "Hymn to Priapus," can assert that everything, from the mountains to the dandelion seeds, "starts from us," the sexually-fulfilled couple, can hope to "spend eternity/With my face down buried between her breasts," for it was by touching "the flank of my wife" that he escaped from solipsistic self-entrapment and rises from a kind of death "to a new earth, a new I, a new knowledge, a new world of time." His new view of sexual experience is expressed in the parable that opens his *Study of Thomas Hardy*. In this parable he derides the view that the red color of the flower can be explained as a lure to bees to effect its pollination; thus he exposes the puritanism at the basis of so-called scientific assumptions that suppose the *purpose* of sexual expression, in poppies or in humans, is reproduction. Though in his subsequent work (most notably in *The Plumed Serpent*) he makes harsh remarks about women who insatiably demand frictional stimulation of the clitoris, nevertheless sexual expression in many forms, apparently in "excess" of any reproductive purpose, is, according to his parable of the poppy, natural, and reproduction merely one of the possible consequences.

But it is his novel *The Rainbow*, written while he and Frieda were back in England during the war years, that gives the fullest and most powerful expression to his discovery. Now characters are not destroyed for following their sexual desires but rather find fulfillment though gratification of these desires. Sex is no longer seen as in some way inherently tragic but only made unhappy through the imposition of modern ideals of education and upward social mobility. When it was published in 1915, reviewers attacked *The Rainbow* with comments like "realistic to the point of brutality," "a monotonous wilderness of phallicism," "spoiled by crude sex details," and these attacks were used to prosecute the publisher, who agreed to the destruction of all copies.

The novel spans three generations and gives us a history of marriage in the Brangwen family under the impact of gradual modernization from the first half of the nineteenth century. to the beginning of the twentieth century. It opens with a poetic evocation of the life of the Brangwens as a well-to-do, English farming family, where the men had "a kind of surety" that came from their close physical connection with the organic rhythms of farm life, "cattle and earth and vegetation and the sky," and that gave them a life without either emotional complexity or torment. But the women "were different" and wanted some higher, greater form of life, as they imagine the vicar enjoys, and set out to educate the children so these children can go "beyond" farm life and its animal physicality. Lawrence now sees the mother as the instigator of sexual troubles. The sufferings of young Tom Brangwen in trying to find a mate are the result of this ambition instilled in him by women—exacerbating his Oedipal conflicts—to rise above peasant instincts. "He had one or two sweethearts, starting with them in the hope of speedy development. But when he had a nice girl, he found that he was incapable of pushing the desired development ... He could not think of her like that, he could not think of her *actual* nakedness." On the other hand, his experience with a woman who is not "nice" in his conventional sense shocks him. "Now when Tom Brangwen, at nineteen, a youth fresh like a plant, rooted in his mother and sister, found that he had lain with a prostitute in a common public house, he was very much startled. For him there was until that time only one kind of woman—that which was like his mother and sister." Like Paul Morel, Tom suffers from what Freud called "psychical impotence," for he can have only "nice" feelings towards "nice girls" and "not-nice," that is to say, sexual, feelings towards "not-nice" girls; in

other words, he cannot *marry* anyone he sexually desires. When he tries to find relief with a prostitute "it was with a paucity he was forced to despise." So he drinks, trying to burn "the youth from his blood." A partial exception to his dilemma—how to feel esteem for a woman he experiences sexually—occurs when at an inn he has a sexual encounter with a "light o' love," as the novel calls her, who is the mistress of an aristocratic foreigner. "Afterwards he glowed with pleasure," and, when the man and woman have departed, he "began to imagine an intimacy with fine-textured, subtle-mannered people such as the foreigner ... and amidst this subtle intimacy was always the satisfaction of a voluptuous woman." He has had a sexual experience with a woman he cannot despise for her sexuality because she comes from a more refined world than his. This experience prefigures his encounter with the aristocratic Lydia, who is the widow of, and has had a daughter by, a Polish patriot. Lydia is the solution to his Oedipal problem, for connection with her would satisfy the drive put in him by his mother to get "beyond" his farm world but without his abandoning his own physicality—indeed, he would go to his "beyond" by means of sexual intercourse. In Lydia's foreign origins and aristocracy he can finally overcome the sense of inferiority his mother's expectations gave him, but it takes two years of marriage before he can really overcome his inhibitions and embrace her without clumsiness. Lawrence expresses in rhapsodic terms the struggle and fulfillment they achieve.

With their discovery, the novel passes on to the next generation, to Lydia's daughter Anna. Anna has suffered through the loss of her father and the subsequent too-close connection with her mother, and the frustrations Tom had felt (and still to some degree feels) create sexual difficulties for her as she matures, especially because he raises her to have lady-like sensibilities. Emotionally entangled with her family as she is, Anna as a young woman can only mate with another Brangwen, and marries Tom's nephew, Will, who is town-bred and works as a lace-designer. After their marriage they almost immediately begin to fight one another until her fulfillment comes in the gestation and birth of a child, and in her pregnancy she does a naked, big-bellied dance alone before a mirror to "the Lord," who for her is the ultimate origin of the child, not her husband. This passage was a special shock to early readers. The novel calls her "Anna Victrix," because in her triumphant fecundity she creates a "little matriarchy" to which Will submits. He submits because, after an encounter which arouses him but which he does not consummate with a young woman in a theater, Anna accepts and provokes extreme sexual excitement in him:

> He would go all day waiting for the night to come, when he could give himself to the enjoyment of some luxurious absolute of beauty in her. The thought of the hidden resources of her, the undiscovered beauties and ecstatic places of delight in her body ... sent him slightly insane ... And she, separate, with a strange, dangerous, glistening look in her eyes received all his activities upon her as if they were expected by her, and provoked him when he was quiet to more, till sometimes he was ready to perish for sheer inability to be satisfied of her ... Their children became mere offspring to them, they lived in the darkness and death of their own sensual activities. Sometimes he felt he was going mad with a sense of Absolute Beauty, perceived by him in her through his senses.

The obscurity a reader may find in such a passage may derive not only from a reticence to name the sexual acts specifically but also from the passage's evocative intensity. The poetic power of *The Rainbow*, especially in its first half, comes from a method that seeks to express inner feelings rather than to depict characters, in the conventional manner, in scene and dialogue. But apparently the intercourse of Will and Anna depend greatly on sexual variations, especially anal eroticism:

> All the shameful things of the body revealed themselves to him with a sort of sinister, tropical beauty. All the shameful, natural and unnatural acts of sensual voluptuousness which he and the woman partook of together, created together, they had their heavy beauty and their delight. Shame, what was it? It was part of extreme delight. It was that part of delight of which man is usually afraid. Why afraid? The secret, shameful things are most terribly beautiful.

With these acts they "accepted shame," but this shame "was a bud that blossomed into beauty and heavy, fundamental gratification." But for their children—the novel's third generation, which has gone another step towards the modern, the urban, and the sophisticated—sexuality will be more conflicted than it was even for Will and Anna. Will has turned towards his daughter Ursula for emotional fulfillment even

more than Tom had towards Anna, and Ursula, a modern young lady who goes to college, can find no satisfaction with the men in the book. Her lover Skrebensky, though attractive, is a soldier willing to submit completely to the purposes of the state and therefore has little feeling at his disposal for a woman. He envies a barge man with three children just because the barge man, in simply looking at Ursula, has an "impudent directness" and is capable of "worship of the woman in Ursula, a worship of body and soul together" of which he is incapable. A modern man, Skrebensky has no "self." In her "hard and fierce" kiss, "her soul crystallized with triumph, and his soul was dissolved in agony and annihilation," as if the aroused sex in a woman somehow can only destroy the modern man who is completely caught in the established order of things. Nevertheless she "caressed and made love to him" and pretends to admire him "in open life" so that "they were lovers, in a young, romantic, almost fantastic way"—lovers as the earlier generations, whose erotic experience occurred only in private, never were. As modern people, they live in public. There is no sexual consummation, and Skrebensky goes off to the army and to war, while Ursula goes to college and enters upon a lesbian relationship with Winifred Inger, described as "a rather beautiful woman of twenty-eight, a fearless-seeming, clean-type of modern girl whose very independence betrays her sorrow." But this relationship dissolves and Ursula becomes a teacher herself, only to be disillusioned with the nature of a system that—in preparing children for the world of modern, industrialized work to which all else must be a "sideshow"—makes any personal relationship with them impossible. She begins to feel she lives in an "inner circle of light ... wherein the trains rushed and the factories ground out their machine-produce and the plants and the animals worked by the light of science and knowledge" that denies "the outer darkness." She yearns for something to come out of that darkness for her. But it is only Skrebensky, returning from war, who comes to her. In the chapter entitled "The Bitterness of Ecstasy" she has a "superb consummation" with Skrebensky, yet for all its excitement it is unfulfilling to her:

> The trouble began at evening. Then a yearning for something unknown came over her, a passion for something she knew not what. She would walk the

foreshore alone after dusk, expecting, expecting something, as if she had gone to a rendezvous. The salt, bitter passion of the sea ... seemed to provoke her to a pitch of madness, tantalizing her with vast suggestions of fulfillment. And then, for personification, would come Skrebensky, whom she knew, whom she was fond of, who was attractive, but whose soul could not contain her in its waves of strength, nor his breast compel her in burning, salty passion.

She kisses him, "pressing in her beaked mouth till she had the heart of him"—the reference to "beaked mouth" anticipating the critique in his later novels of "the beakish will," that is, the woman's exertion of friction by the clitoris in sexual intercourse. Skrebensky then, while she lies motionless, serves her with violent motions that "lasted till it was agony to his soul ... till he gave way as if dead." But in a waiter and a cab driver—two men outside middle-class respectability—she and Skrebensky encounter in London, she glimpses something she yearns for from the "unknown." After her miscarriage and abandonment by Skrebensky, Ursula has a prophetic vision that "the sordid people who crept hard-scaled and separate on the face of the world's corruption were living still, that the rainbow was arched in their blood and would quiver to life in their spirit" and that "the old, brittle corruption of houses and factories" would be swept away.

Women In Love

After the banning of *The Rainbow*, Lawrence begins explaining his vision to a world that had rejected it. He took on the role of prophet. Lawrence expresses these tendencies in Rupert Birkin, the main male character of the novel *Women in Love*, published in 1920. He lectures his friends on the horrors of modern civilization and the necessity to escape from its ideals by means of a marriage founded on some other principle than the "love" that is advanced as the highest motive. These harangues are especially for the benefit of Ursula Brangwen, who has the same name as the character in *The Rainbow* (both novels evolved out of an early manuscript called "The Sisters") but who seems a different person, especially in her higher level of sophistication and in the somewhat elevated social world in which she now has her acquaintance. Her sister, Gudrun, an artist of some

reputation, becomes the lover of Birkin's friend, the handsome and wealthy Gerald Critch, who owns the local collieries. The two couples are shown in contrast—according to Lawrence's developing sexual philosophy, Ursula-Birkin on the right path, Gudrun-Gerald on the wrong. Birkin believes that one should act in terms of spontaneous impulses, but Gerald opposes this view because he believes that would mean "everybody cutting everybody else's throat in five minutes." And in a scene in bohemian London early in the novel we see Gerald's aggressive impulses gratified through a sexual experience with Miss Darrington, also called "Pussums" and "Minette" (as in *faire minette* = perform cunnilingus). She looks at Gerald the morning afterwards with the "inchoate look of a violated slave, whose fulfilment lies in her further and further violation," and this look "made his nerves quiver with acutely desirable sensation." Because he feels he must preserve his social position, Gerald will not have any lasting relationship with "Pussums," though she does gratify his spontaneous desires. Instead he enters into a relationship with Gudrun. She, who was attracted to him on first seeing him, initiates their physical intimacy by suddenly (spontaneously) slapping him in the face. Gerald's habit of exerting power piques her, as in the scene where she and Ursula watch him using his spurs cruelly to force a mare, terrified by a passing train, to stand. Their sexual intercourse begins after the death of his father, when, suffering one night from a terrible sense "of his own nothingness," he stealthily enters the house of Gudrun's parents, slips into her room, and tells he must have her:

> ... She let him hold her in his arms, clasp her close against him. He found in her infinite relief. Into her he poured all his pent-up darkness and corrosive death, and he was whole again. It was wonderful, marvelous, it was a miracle ... And she, subject, received him as a vessel filled with his bitter potion of death. She had no power at this crisis to resist. The terrible frictional violence of death filled her, and she received it in an ecstasy of subjection, in throes of acute, violent sensation.

In gratitude for her allowing him to do this, he "worshipped her, Mother and substance of all life." He sleeps beside her like a child, but she is left in a state of "violent active superconsciousness" and cannot sleep. She feels "an ache like nausea ... a nausea of him." Finally, on a winter excursion to the Alps with him and with the newly-married Birkin and Ursula, she torments Gerald by taking up with a sadistic German sculptor who admits that he had to slap the adolescent girl who was his model so she would remain still, and Gerald reacts to Gudrun's treatment of him by going off into the snow and, by a crucifix half-buried there, allowing himself to freeze to death. But the relationship of Ursula and Birkin, going on simultaneously with the unfolding of this deadly process, is life-affirming. Birkin has pulled himself away from Hermione Roddice, a woman who sees herself as a center of advanced culture. She and Ursula are contrasted later in the novel, after an argument about love, from Hermione's point of view:

> ... Ursula could not understand, never would understand, could never be more than the usual jealous and unreasonable female, with a good deal of powerful female emotion, female attraction, and a fair amount of female understanding, but no mind ... And Rupert—he had now reacted towards the strongly female, healthy, selfish woman ...

Birkin wants Ursula to commit herself to marriage—which for Birkin means the end of the dominance of woman. In his view, marriage should allow an "equilibrium" between the man and woman such as he sees in the play of two cats. The man and woman would relate to each other not in terms of personalities or conventional roles:

> "There is [he tells her] ... a final me which is stark and impersonal and beyond responsibility. So there is a final you. And it is there I would want to meet you—not in the emotional, loving plane—but there beyond, where there is no speech and no terms of agreement. There we are two stark, unknown beings, two utterly strange creatures ... And there could be no obligation, because there is no standard for action there ... It is quite inhuman—so there can be no calling to book, in any form whatsoever—because one is outside the pale of all that is accepted, and nothing known applies. One can only follow the impulse ... only each taking according to the primal desire."

Birkin's view is the denial of traditional notions of the subordination of sex to love and to other purposes that Christianity has promulgated. In so far as these needs are sexual, they are for more than procreation and even genital intercourse, as is illustrated in Ursula's kneeling, putting her arms around his loins, touching the back of his thighs and pressing her face against them and finding "release at last." From "the darkest poles of the body"—his anus—her touch causes "a dark fire of electricity" that "rushed from him to her ... and flooded them both with rich peace, satisfaction."

During the course of Birkin's relationship with Ursula, he tries to save Gerald from disaster, most notably in the scene where the two men wrestle together naked. After they have wrestled to unconsciousness Birkin accidentally touched the hand of Gerald, and "Gerald's hand closed warm and sudden over Birkin's." Birkin wants Gerald to acknowledge that the contact they have had is significant and to commit himself to it, but it is finally too unconventional for Gerald. More than anything else, it is this refusal that gives him no escape from the fatal passion for Gudrun. Seeing the frozen corpse in the end of the novel, Birkin says Gerald was a "denier." The novel ends with Birkin's insistence—in opposition to Ursula's objections—that he wanted a union with a man as "eternal" as the union he has with her: "another kind of love." Significantly, a "Prologue" not published with the novel tells us at length that "although he was always drawn to women, feeling more at home with a woman than with a man, yet it was for men that he felt the hot, flushing, roused attraction which a man is supposed to feel for the other sex," and he is deeply ashamed of his powerful homosexual longings.

Lawrence as Prophet

The two small volumes *Psychoanalysis and the Unconscious* (1921) and *Fantasia of the Unconscious* (1922) are Lawrence's attempts to theorize what, he claims, had so far come more or less unconsciously from his pen. He presents what he calls his "pollyanalytics," but their serious, essential point is to make a correction of Freud. According to Lawrence, the Oedipus complex and other Freudian "horrors" do not express true human depths but are the result of the ideals of Western civilization, especially the ideal of Love, having been forced by education onto the "pristine unconscious." Parents force ideas onto the body of the child instead of helping the child respond to life from its physiological "centres," notably from the "solar plexus."

This theory is a development of what Birkin was preaching to Ursula in his notion of marriage. "Coition" is not some union of minds or personalities but an act in which

> ... the two seas of blood in the two individuals, rocking and surging towards contact, as near as possible, clash into a oneness. A great flash of interchange occurs, like an electrical spark when two currents meet like lightning out of the densely surcharged clouds. There is a lightning flash which passes through the blood of both individuals, there is a thunder of sensation which rolls in diminishing crashes down the nerves of each—and then the tension passes.

The two individuals are separate again. But are they as they were before/ Is the air the same after a thunderstorm as before? No. The air is as it were new, fresh, tingling with newness. So is the blood of man and woman after successful coition. After a false coition, like prostitution, there is not newness but a certain disintegration.

Lawrence insists that *this* —and not some ideal purpose—is the "great psychic experience" from the point of view of a man or a woman. And "after all our experience with poetry and novels we know that the procreative purpose of sex is ... just a sideshow."

Nevertheless, in *Aaron's Rod* (1922), *Kangaroo* (1923), and *The Plumed Serpent* (1926)—called his "leadership" novels—sexual experience is relegated to a subsidiary theme and even, in *Aaron's Rod*, treated as something to avoid. This development seems related to unhappiness in these years in his marriage. Frieda had not been faithful to him even from the start, as is revealed in the long continuation—not published till 1984—of his fictional fragment *Mr. Noon*. In the three "leadership" novels, man–man relationships are primary, but the homosexuality is sublimated into "leader–follower" relationships and political ideas that are sometimes strongly reminiscent of fascism. But it seems clear in *The Plumed Serpent* that basic to the revolution proposed for Mexico, that is supposed to overthrow Western and Christian ideals and restore the worship of Quetzalcoatl, is a new relationship between man and woman. The European heroine Kate is supposed to learn the womanly superiority of the Mexican woman, Theresa, to give up demanding from her husband, General Cipriano, "the old desire for frictional, irritant sensation ... the spasms of frictional voluptuousness ... orgiastic 'satisfaction,' in spasms that made her cry aloud." Instead, Cipriano "in his dark, hot silence, would bring her back the new, soft, heavy, hot flow, when she was like a fountain gushing noiseless and with urgent softness from the volcanic depths." In abandoning her craving for "the beak-like friction of Aphrodite" she can become the woman that Birkin and his prophetic avatars have been wanting. The resulting hot "gushing" would seem to correspond to the vaginal orgasm that Freud and his followers believed they could distinguish from clitoral orgasm. According to Brenda Maddox, Cipriano's deliberate denial of Kate's clitoral orgasm is the passage most offensive to feminist readers in all of Lawrence's writings.

Lady Chatterley's Lover

In his most famous novel he abandons his "leadership" themes and returns to a celebration of the possibilities in the sexual relationship of man and woman, though a source for the novel may have been E.M. Forster's *Maurice*, which seems to be a homosexual version that Forster did not allow published till 1970, though Lawrence may well have known about it in manuscript. *Lady Chatterley's Lover* itself, which pioneered in the use of common spoken language to describe sexual acts and in their graphic depiction in a serious literary context, was not legally printed in the United States till the Grove Press edition of 1959. Lawrence's essay *A Propos of* Lady Chatterley's Lover attempted to defend it from the charge of pornography and made some interesting distinctions; he claimed that pornography—as opposed to writing that simply aroused a reader sexually—did "dirt on sex," and that *Jane Eyre* was closer to being pornographic than was his work or Boccaccio's.

The novel opens with a summary of how his heroine Constance Reid came to be married to Sir Clifford Chatterley, who, shortly after their marriage, was wounded in the war and paralyzed from the waist down. But before their marriage she did not care anyway about physical sex. What mattered to her was "the impassioned interchange of talk" with men. "Love was only a minor accompaniment." Above all, she wants to remain *free*. And however one might sentimentalize it," Connie thinks,

... this sex business was one of the most ancient, sordid connections and subjections ... Women had always known there was something better, something higher and now they knew it more definitely than ever. The beautiful pure freedom of a woman was infinitely more wonderful than any sexual love.

When she and her sister Hilda actually have sexual intercourse with men, in "the actual sex-thrill within the body" they "nearly succumbed to the strange male power." But they are able to treat it as a mere "sensation" and so remain "free." For Clifford, even before he is wounded in the war, sex mattered little:

> ... He had been virgin when he married: and the sex part did not mean much to him. They were so close, he and she, apart from that. And Connie exulted a little in this intimacy which was beyond sex, and beyond a man's "satisfaction." Clifford anyhow was not just keen on his "satisfaction" ...

Thus, when he goes off to war shortly after their honeymoon and returns paralyzed from the waist down, little is changed between them sexually. His paralysis is only a symbolic confirmation of what he already was. In his paralysis, he is meant to symbolize the condition of modern man in general. Indeed, there may be much of Clifford in Lawrence himself. But Clifford is especially meant to symbolize the condition of the cultivated upper classes. After the war, Connie and Clifford try to carry on in their sexless marriage. Clifford—obsessed with success, with the need for making a display of himself that Lawrence tells us is typical of modern men—takes up fiction writing. Clifford even tells Connie she may take a lover. His speech to her minimizing the importance of sexual connection as opposed to their relationship based on "the habit of each other" loses its credibility when he concludes: "we ought to be able to arrange this sex thing, as we arrange going to the dentist." He achieves some success and gathers around him the intellectuals of the day. One of these "cronies," Tommy Dukes, more honest than the others, tells them in her presence of the idiocy and profound hatefulness of their vaunted "mental life," and he becomes Lawrence's spokesman in affirming that what one needs—though Dukes himself cannot claim to have them—is "a good heart, a chirpy penis, and the courage to say 'shit!' in front of a lady." Dukes says his own "penis droops and never lifts his head up ... The penis rouses his head and says:

How do you do? to any really intelligent person. Renoir said he painted his pictures with his penis ... he did too, lovely pictures!"

Being present during the conversations of the "cronies" does not make Connie happy. She tries taking a lover from this circle—Michaelis, a young Irish playwright. But he is far more excited by having her praise his play than he could be in "any sexual orgasm." And in their intercourse "Connie found it impossible to come to her crisis before he had really finished his," so that he has to remain erect in her, "with all his will and self-offering, till she brought about her own crisis, with weird little cries ... [L]ike so many modern men, he was finished almost before he had begun. And that forced the woman to be active." But, sick with disillusion with the life she has chosen, one afternoon she by accident comes upon the gamekeeper Mellors, "naked to the hips," washing himself at a pump. She has a "visionary experience" seeing "the warm, white flame of a single life, revealing itself in contours that one might touch: a body!" Later, by herself, she feels her own body "going opaque" and feels that at twenty-seven she is growing old "through neglect and denial." The "mental life" now seems to her to be a "swindle." She takes to going into the wood, on the excuse of seeing the spring daffodils, and again encounters Mellors. But he "had reached the point where all he wanted on earth was to be left alone." He avoids contact with her, dreading "her female will and her modern female insistency"—his estranged wife had evidently been one of the "beakish" sort. Mellors, though from the working-class, had been an officer during the war, but had chosen afterwards to return to his own class in rejection of the modern mentality of trying to rise socially.

In the meantime, Clifford discovers that what excites him more than literary success is what he can know as owner of his coal mines: *power*. The pursuit of power over potency is—as Mark Shorer explains in his introduction to the Grove Press edition—the modern way, instead of the way Mellors takes. Connie has been looking at the pheasant chicks that Mellors has been raising when she is seized with "the agony of her own female forlornness," and Mellors, seeing a tear drop on her wrist, is overcome with a feeling of compassion for her—*compassion which is the same as sexual desire*. That overpowering feeling is, interestingly, an example of the kind of

LAWRENCE, D.H.

feeling Freud means in his 1912 essay by full sexual potency, where the two streams of erotic feeling—tenderness and sensuality—combine, and, later in the novel, Connie uses terms that could well have come out of Freud's essay to explain to her incredulous sister what it is she and Mellors have together. Lawrence stresses that there is nothing *consciously intended* by either of them in the sexual act that is about to happen and that initiates their relationship — Mellors "stroked the curve of her flank, in the blind instinctive caress." He takes her into the hut and at once must enter "the peace on earth of her soft, quiescent body." The orgasm is all his. She feels "asleep" as it happens, yet, afterwards, feels "it lifted a great cloud from her," yet does not know why and wonders if was "real":

> Her tormented modern-woman's brain still had no rest ... And she knew, if she gave herself to the man, it was real. But if she kept herself to herself, it was nothing ... And at last, she could bear the burden of herself no more. She was to be had for the taking ...

Modern man, but especially modern woman, have for Lawrence to come to this point of despair, where they have really given up trying to achieve happiness for themselves, and, especially, have given up the means that modern society offers (money, power, achievement, amusements) for satisfaction. Then the primal instincts can take over.

What works against all such sexual tenderness is "not woman's fault, nor even love's fault, nor the fault of sex," Lawrence tells us. "The fault lay ... in those evil electric lights and diabolical rattlings of engines"—in "the insentient iron world and the Mammon of mechanized greed" that Sir Clifford manages and serves. Mellors wishes there were other men to fight this evil, but the novel offers no revolutionary hopes as did the "leadership" novels before it. The man and the woman will have to go it alone, hiding and trying to keep the feeling they have for each other. And Connie, with her "modern-woman" sensibility, fights this feeling herself. It disturbs her that it "really wasn't personal, "that she was "only really a female to him." But she realizes that while men had been "very kind to the *person* she was," they had been "rather cruel to the female":

> ... Men were awfully kind to Constance Reid or to Lady Chatterley; but to her womb they weren't kind.

And he took no notice of Constance or of Lady Chatterley; he just softly stroked her loins or her breasts.

Indeed, since Mellors is presented in this novel as a paragon—not who Lawrence himself was but wished to be—Connie is in the position of learning to become what Lawrence thinks is a proper female. She learns through sexual experience. When she had no more heart "to fight for her freedom," and, after he has his "helpless" orgasm, too soon for her though she feels "new strange thrills rippling inside her," can no longer "harden and grip for her own satisfaction upon him," he feels her need and instead of withdrawing is aroused again. Then she has an experience that leaves her "crying in unconscious inarticulate cries." After this she lets "another self" come to life in her, "and with this self she adored him." She still feels she can fight this adoration, can instead be "passionate like a Bacchante" and cling "to the old hard passion," but she chooses the adoration: it was "her treasure." Nevertheless, on another occasion, she can detach herself during the sexual act and "look on from the top of her head" so that "the butting of his haunches seemed ridiculous to her." But when she tells him of her unhappiness afterwards, he takes her in his arms, strokes her "between her soft warm buttocks, coming nearer and nearer to the quick of her." He is roused again and she "yielded with a quiver that was like death" and "went all open to him."

...It might come with the thrust of a sword in her softly-opened body, and that would be death. But it came with a strange slow thrust of peace, the dark thrust of peace and a ponderous, primordial tenderness, such as made the world in the beginning ... She dared to let go everything, all herself, and be gone in the flood.

Finally, "in a soft shuddering convulsion, the quick of all her plasm was touched, she knew herself touched, the consummation was upon her, and she was gone. She was gone, she was not, and she was born: a woman."

From then on, it is the malignancy of the "insentient iron world," particularly through the agency of Clifford and Mellors' former wife, that the two must prevent from destroying them. Mellors tells her about his unhappy past with women and that he believes "in fucking with a warm heart"—that all would go well with the world if men and women could only do that. "It's all this cold-hearted fucking that is death and idiocy." Pregnant, she has to leave him for awhile so that he will not appear to be the father of the child, and her last night with him is "a night of sensual passion, in which she was a little started and almost unwilling." Mellors had always shown special attention to her buttocks and anus—he says she has "the nicest, nicest woman's arse as is." Now she lets him penetrate her anus, and the "piercing thrills of passion, different, sharper, more terrible than the thrills of tenderness ... shook her to her foundations, stripped her to the very last, and made a different woman of her. It was not really love." These thrills burn out "the deepest, oldest shames, in the most secret places. It cost her an effort to let him have his way and will with her. She had to be a passive, consenting thing, like a slave ... "She experiences "all the refinements of passion, the extravagances of sensuality" such as are shown "on the Greek vases, everywhere!" "In the short summer night," the novel tells us, "she learnt so much. She would have thought a woman would have died of shame. Instead of which, the shame died." At the end of the novel, Mellors is away learning farming, preparatory to living a life with her.

Of course, *Lady Chatterley's Lover*, just because it is such a "Pilgrim's Progress," as Wayne Burns calls it, may not be as great a novel when judged by literary criteria as *The Rainbow* or *Women In Love*. Two earlier versions exist. In both, and especially in the first, Mellors is less of a paragon. The second version may be more novelistic than the final version. But the final version gives Lawrence's sexual views in their most evolved, coherent, and explicit form. After remaining underground for decades, these views gained publicity during the Lawrence revival of the 1950s and '60s, especially after the 1959 trial that allowed its publication in the United States. It is not going too far to say that reading Lawrence influenced the youth movements of the '60s—but to what extent his message was understood is open to question.

Biography

Born in Eastwood, Nottinghamshire, September 11, 1885, fourth of five children of a collier whose wife was a former schoolteacher. Attended Beauvale Board School, Nottingham High School. Winter 1901–1902 fell gravely ill with pneumonia. Became teacher in Eastwood, began first novel, attended Nottingham University College. Met Mrs. Frieda Weekley (*née* von Richthofen) in 1912, eloped with her to Metz, returned to England in 1913 and married her after her divorce. *The Rainbow* published in 1915 and ordered destroyed for its sexual content. After that it was difficult for him to earn a living as a writer. Lived with help from friends and patrons, and after the war traveled (Italy, Australia, Mexico, and New Mexico, where Mabel Dodge Luhan gave him a small ranch), wrote fiction, poetry, literary criticism, essays, and, later, painted. *Lady Chatterley's Lover* privately printed in Italy in 1928, banned in the United States until 1959. Died of tuberculosis in Vence in southern France on March 2, 1930.

GERALD BUTLER

Selected Works

The White Peacock. 1911.
Sons and Lovers. 1913.
The Prussian Officer. 1914.
The Rainbow. 1915.
Women In Love. 1920.
Psychoanalysis and the Unconscious. 1921.
Fantasia of the Unconscious. 1922.
Lady Chatterley's Lover. 1928.
A Propos of. Lady Chatterley's Lover. 1930.
The Man Who Died. 1931.
Etruscan Places. 1932.
Foreword to. Women In Love. 1936.
The First Lady Chatterley. 1944.
Sex, Literature and Censorship. 1955.
Complete Poems. 1964.
The Paintings of D.H. Lawrence. 1964.
Mr. Noon. 1984.
Study of Thomas Hardy and Other Essays. Ed. Bruce Steele, Cambridge: Cambridge University Press, 1985.
Letters. (7 vols). 1979–1993.

Further Reading

Aldington, Richard. *D. H. Lawrence: Portrait of a Genius, But...* New York: Duell, Sloan, and Pearce, 1950.
Balbert, Peter. *D.H. Lawrence and the Phallic Imagination: Essays on Sexual Identity and Feminist Misreading*. Houndmills and London: Macmillan Press, 1989.
Burns, Wayne. "*Lady Chatterley's Lover*: A Pilgrim's Progress for Our Time." *Paunch* 26 (1966) 16–33.
Butler, Gerald J. *This Is Carbon: A Defense of Lawrence's* The Rainbow *against his Admirers*. Seattle: Genitron, 1986.
Chambers, Jessie. *The Collected Letters, The D.H. Lawrence Review* 12 (1979).

Clark, Colin. *River of Dissolution: D.H. Lawrence and English Romanticism.* London: Routledge and Kegan Paul, 1969.

Delany, Paul. *D.H. Lawrence's Nightmare: The Writer and His Circle in the Years of the Great War.* New York: Basic Books, 1978.

Draper, R.P. *D.H. Lawrence: The Critical Heritage.* New York: Barnes and Noble, 1970.

Green, Martin. *The von Richthofen Sisters: The Triumphant and the Tragic Modes of Love.* New York: Basic Books, 1974.

Mensch, Barbara. *D.H. Lawrence and the Authoritarian Personality.* New York: St. Martin's Press, 1991.

Meyers, Jeffrey. *D.H. Lawrence: A Biography.* New York: Knopf, 1990.

Maddox, Brenda. *D.H. Lawrence: The Story of a Marriage.* New York: Simon and Schuster, 1994.

Moore, Harry T. *The Priest of Love: A Life of D. H. Lawrence.* Middlesex, England: Penguin, 1974.

LE PETIT, CLAUDE

c. 1638–1662
French libertine poet

Claude Le Petit began his writing career in order to pay for his law studies. When only seventeen years old, he helped correct proofs of the controversial *L'Ecole des filles* and authored its preface, the *Madrigal*. His choice of subject matter and candid detail, together with his forthright views on established religion, were to prove his downfall. When the capital's police commissioner succeeded in having a troupe of prostitutes sent to America, Le Petit was inspired to write *L'Adieu des filles de joye à la ville de Paris* [*Farewells of Paris's Goodtime Girls*] (1657) a 320-verse poem which criticized the political expediency and ultimate futility of the punishment. The passion with which this case was considered reflects Le Petit's affinity with those falling foul of society's norms. He became editor of *La Muse du Coeur,* a weekly gazette, which lasted for eight issues. Contrary to the customary anonymity of this type of publication, he put his name to five out of the eight editions. After returning to Paris in 1661, he began writing satirical pieces such as *La chronique scandaleuse ou Paris ridicule* [*The Scandalous Chronicle* or *Ridiculous Paris*]. The work's title emulated *Rome ridicule* of Saint-Amant and Paris is depicted as 'la cité de merde' [shit city] and the Jesuits are described as 'Foüetteurs de petits enfans' [child-beaters]. Members of the order, as well as the recently deceased Mazarin, are accused of being avid practitioners of sodomy. In doing so, he was projecting a common insult hurled against libertine writers back to the camp of the accusers. He composed the *Apologie de Chausson*—a sonnet inspired by the case of Jacques Chausson who, together with his accomplice Jacques Paulmier, was burnt at the stake on December 29 1661, for the multiple rape of young boys. A novel entitled *L'Heure du Berger* appeared in 1662. This is a fantasy about a young man whose mistress is unfaithful, despite the fact she has always refused him sexual relations, and who spends a night of libidinous abandon with a mysterious woman he encounters.

His collection of poetical works, *Le bordel des muses ou les neuf Pucelles putains, caprices satiriques de Théophile le jeune* [*The Muses' Bordello or the Nine Virginal Whores, Satirical Whims of Théophile the Younger*] (1662), would later secure his conviction for blasphemy. One of the sonnets in this edition, 'Aux Précieuses,' alludes to lesbianism with its mention of a 'godemichi,' or dildo. This poem criticizes the precieuses, an intellectual movement of courtly women, and accuses them of hypocrisy by seeking satisfaction interchangeably in letters and sexuality (both solitary and Sapphic). This was published with the assistance of the two sons of the printer Pierre Rebuffé, and the title indicates that Le Petit saw himself as the literary heir of Théophile de Viau's subversive tradition. The collection contains earlier poems such as *Paris ridicule* as well as new material. The first of the *Bordel*'s dedicatory sonnets is named the 'Sonnet foutatif' [Fucking sonnet] and is a laudatory description of various sexual pleasures, including male and female sodomy. This abrupt opening, and its use of straightforward vocabulary to describe sexual acts with no discrimination between heterosexuality and homosexuality, sets Le Petit's agenda and describes sexuality in a manner that goes beyond his self-proclaimed master, Théophile. Sonnet LIX attacks the cult of the Virgin Mary, though it is primarily a parody of flamboyant and excessive devotion and religious hypocrisy. Such anti-religious satire was an established feature of libertine writers such as Brantôme. While he owed a debt to his parish priest for having tutored him as a child, Le Petit's experiences at the capital's Jesuit college colored his judgement of the clergy. He opined that the Jesuits ran his alma mater 'par pure sodomie' ('out of pure sodomy'). The fact that he also penned a religious work, *Les plus belles pensées de saint Augustin, prince et docteur de l'Église* [*Selected Thoughts of St. Augustine, Prince and Doctor of the Church*] (1666), and took the trouble of having it examined and gaining the approval of three doctors of the Faculty of theology at the Sorbonne on 9 October 1661, demonstrates that he never entirely rejected Catholicism. It is curious that this treatise was not published, nor was it alluded to at his trial as a defence against suspicions of heresy and atheism.

The writer had attracted the attention of the ecclesiastical and civil establishment, and after the authorities got wind of the *Bordel*'s existence, this provided an opportunity to precipitate his downfall. When Daubray, a police official, surprised Le Petit red-handed with a manuscript of work, his fate was sealed. The largely unknown twenty-four-year-old poet lacked the assistance of powerful protectors that had helped Théophile de Viau escape the death penalty, and had the misfortune to be writing during a climate of increasing official anxiety towards a burgeoning genre of obscene-themed literature (already tested to the limits by contemporary writers such as Molière). He came to the attention of the authorities as an ideal candidate for receiving an exemplary punishment. Despite the fact that all copies of the work were destroyed by official order, a clandestine edition was published in Leiden in 1663. Le Petit's principal and dubious distinction, however, lies in the fact that he became the first, and the only, writer to be executed for the cause of censorship in seventeenth-century France.

Biography

Born at Beuvreuil in Normandie, the son of a Parisian tailor, in 1637 or 1638. Educated at the Jesuit Collège de Clermont, Paris and passed first law examinations, 1655. Murdered an Augustinian friar as an act of revenge for the cleric's public disapproval of him, October 1657: fled France to avoid justice, spending time in Spain, Germany, Bohemia, Italy; returned to Paris, February 1661. Arrested for the clandestine publication of a licentious work: condemned for *lèse-majesté* against God and the saints, 26 August 1662; burnt alive after having been strangled beforehand, 1 September, 1662.

PAUL SCOTT

Selected Works

L'Heure du Berger. Paris: Antoine Robinot, 1662.
Les Œuvres libertines de Claude Le Petit. Edited by Frédéric Lachèvre, Paris: Capiomont, 1918.

Further Reading

Alexandrian, Sarane. *Histoire de la littérature érotique.* Paris: Payot et Rivages, 1995.
DeJean, Joan. *The Reinvention of Obscenity: Sex, Lies, and Tabloids in Early Modern France.* Chicago, IL: Chicago University Press, 2002.
Pia, Pascal. *Les Livres de l'Enfer du XVIe siècle à nos jours.* 2 vols, Paris: Coulet et Faure, 1978.
Schoeller, Guy (ed.), *Dictionnaire des œuvres érotiques.* Paris: Laffont, 2001.

LÉAUTAUD, PAUL

1872–1956
French novelist, essayist, theatre critic and diarist

Having resolved to devote himself wholly to writing, Paul Léautaud chose himself as his prime subject matter. His legendary misanthropy, misogyny ("I love woman, I do not like women"), and concern for animal welfare clearly stemmed from his unhappy and solitary childhood as told in *Le Petit Ami* (1903) and *In memoriam* (1905). He was abandoned by his mother, an aspiring actress, only a few days after his birth and it was his father, not an affectionate man, who raised him. Marie Pezée, a former prostitute, was hired to look after the child and acted as surrogate mother until she was dismissed in 1880 after reproaching her employer for setting a bad example to the child with his turbulent love-life. Paul Léautaud's mother rarely visited him and he felt her absence keenly. In 1881, not wishing to see her son in the presence of his father's sixteen-year-old mistress, she had the boy sent to her hotel room. He found her still in bed, barely clothed; it was the first time he had seen a woman "in such intimacy" and was greatly troubled by it. When he saw her again, in 1901, he was a man, and their meeting marked the beginning of a correspondence (*Lettres à ma mère*, 1956) whose incestuous overtones she found increasingly compromising and which she quickly brought to an end. Thirty-six years later, aged sixty-five, Léautaud was still dreaming about his mother: "I found myself with my mother (...) After lunch we made love very passionately, on her part and mine (...). She was completely naked, her face shining with pleasure. I've always had her—in my dreams."

Except for three early autobiographical narratives, collected theater criticism, a few essays, and extracts from his diaries, Paul Léautaud published relatively little during his lifetime. He only came to prominence as a literary figure in his late seventies, when, in 1951, he reluctantly agreed to be interviewed at length for French national radio; his audience, particularly the young, were stunned and charmed by his biting wit and sparkling conversation. The publication of his *Journal littéraire* (*Journal of a Man of Letters*) started the following year, but only three of the nineteen volumes appeared before he died in 1954. He emerged as an erotic writer in 1956 when his editor Marie Dormoy revealed the existence of a personal diary, *Le Journal particulier, 1917–1950*, which she published as a limited edition in what we now know to be an edited version. A second personal diary was published thirty years later, after Marie Dormoy's death and at her request: It included the entries for the year 1933 concerning the beginning of her affair with Léautaud, which lasted until his death and remained secret until her own.

Le Fléau. Journal particulier, 1917–1930

The first personal diary re-edited in 1989 focuses on Léautaud's enduring affair with Anne Cayssac, whom he nicknamed *la Panthère* [The Panther] and later *le Fléau* [The Scourge]. This personal diary is a detailed record of their "sessions," and a lucid, though obsessive account of his sexual dependency on a married woman, several years his senior, that he did not even like. She was a cantankerous, dominating, and possessive person, whose caring love for animals did not extend to the human species: "All my life," Léautaud wrote at the time, "I shall never have any luck where love and tenderness are concerned." It was with her, however, that at the age of forty-two he started enjoying sex to the full. She had a formidable appetite for sex and was never so ardent and attractive to him as after some violent outburst. They were perfectly matched: "She was," he wrote, "the partner I had dreamed of, a being (...) possessing to the highest degree what I call the spirit of love, that is to say extreme licentiousness in word, attitude and gesture." As he explained in *Amour*, a small volume of aphorisms inspired by *le Fléau*, love for him was first and foremost "physical sensual attraction, (...) pleasure given and received, (...) mutual enjoyment, (and) the union of two human beings made for each other sexually." "The rest," he added, "the exaggerations, the sighs, the uplifting of the souls, are jokes, (...) the dreams of minds that are refined and impotent."

Journal particulier, 1933

In contrast to the first personal diary, which misses the entries for the first three years of the relationship with Anne Cayssac lent to her but never returned, the second private diary focuses exclusively on the year 1933 which saw the beginning of his relationship with Marie Dormoy. Léautaud was then, by all accounts, a wrinkled, toothless, shabbily dressed and smelly sixty-one-year old, and Dormoy an elegant and buxom forty-six-year old. The age difference was of concern to him and he was reluctant at first to respond to her advances: The affair with *le Fléau* was not quite over and he worried about the effect the new relationship might have on his health and his work. The diary gives a remarkably egotistic and crude account of the affair, which at first seems to only offer basic sexual gratification: Marie Dormoy's body compared most unfavorably with Anne Cayssac's and did not please him. As time passed, however, Léautaud became undeniably sensitive to her own characteristic beauty, her sexuality, and the way she cared for him. It is this gradual and understated awakening of emotion in a man entering old age that distinguishes this diary from the previous one.

The tone and style of the diaries, however, vary little. Léautaud, who was the epitome of the self-taught man, rejected all forms of literary embellishment. In novels, he insisted, we are never told about the "little wet mess" that follows the lovers' embrace, and the embarrassing moments that ensue. Wary as he was of anything that remotely resembled grand, academic, or literary style, he opted for a spontaneous form of writing, akin in its simplicity to "written conversation": "Anything worthwhile is written straight off, in the almost physical pleasure of writing, in the heat of the mind full of its subject." Léautaud, whose sole purpose in life was to write, used the word "pleasure" to describe both writing and sex. In the personal diaries, the two are inextricably linked, and what he says about experiences being more strongly felt and intensely savored when he wrote about them than when he actually lived through them also applies to the erotic.

Biography

Born in Paris, January 18, 1872. Abandoned by his mother and raised by his father in Paris (1874–1882) and Courbevoie, a suburb of Paris (1882–1887). Left school aged 15 and held various office jobs in Paris, 1887–1908. Published his first essay in *Le Mercure de France* in 1895 and started moving in literary circles; was appointed secretary to *Le Mercure de France*, both a literary journal and a publishing house, in 1908 (dismissed 1941). As "Boissard," was drama critic for *Le Mercure de France*, 1907–1920, *La Nouvelle Revue française*, 1921–1923, and *Les Nouvelles littéraires* in 1923. Never married but had lasting relationships with Jeanne Marié, 1889–1892, Georgette Crozier, 1894–1895, Blanche Blanc, 1898–1912, Anne Cayssac, 1914–1934, and Marie Dormoy from 1933 onwards. Wrote the first entry in his diary on November 3, 1893, and the last one on February 15, 1956. Died in Fontenay-aux-Roses, February 22, 1956.

MIREILLE RIBIÈRE

Selected Works

Le Petit Ami. 1903. *In memoriam*, 1905, *Amours*, 1906 ; reprinted in one volume, 1956; as *The Child of Montmartre*, translated by Humphrey Hare, 1959.
Amour, Aphorismes. 1934.
Journal particulier. 1917–1950, edited by Marie Dormoy, 2 vols., 1956; re-edited as *Le Fléau, Journal particulier 1917–1930*, suivi d'un fragment inédit 1932, edited by Edith Silve, 1989.
Journal particulier de Paul Léautaud, 1933. Edited by Edith Silve, 1986.

Further Reading

Brou, Jacques. *Paul Léautaud: le sexe et la plume.* Paris: La pensée universelle, 1985.
Francq, Henri G. *Portrait of a misanthrope.* Sherbrooke (Québec, Canada): Éditions Naaman, 1987.
Harding, James. *Lost illusions: Paul Léautaud and his world.* London: Allen & Unwin, 1974.

LEDUC, VIOLETTE

1907–1972
French writer

Violette Leduc (1907–1972) has often been called France's greatest unknown writer. Admired by Jean Genêt and championed by Simone de Beauvoir, she had written three novels before she gained any serious critical attention. That attention came not for a work of fiction but for the first volume of her autobiography, *La Bâtarde* (1964). Her illegitimacy and its effect on her relationship with her mother, her poverty, her affairs, and her face, described by Simone de Beauvoir as "brutally ugly and radiantly alive"—all are a part of the fabric of that text. *La Bâtarde* established a dialogue with Leduc's novels; the autobiography doubled as a guide to understanding her earlier fictional texts. When considered in retrospect, Leduc's three earlier novels, *L'Asphyxie (In the Prison of Her Skin)* [1946], *L'Affamée (Ravenous)* [1948], and *Ravages* (1955), can be read as alternate visions of *La Bâtarde*. While such autofiction has become the norm for twentieth century literature (from writers as diverse as André Gide and Annie Ernaux), Leduc's works bring sexuality and sexual relationships, both lesbian and heterosexual, to the fore. Indeed, the originality of a woman writing openly about these topics created the scandal of her writing.

Leduc's works, fiction and autobiography alike, focus nearly exclusively on their female protagonist, her experiences of love and sexuality, and her disappointments. Leduc's sexual and emotional experiences with women and men, her long-term relationships with homosexual writers and intellectuals such as Maurice Sachs, Jacques Guérin, and Jean Genêt find their fictional counterparts in her novels, as most tellingly does her obsessive relationship with Simone de Beauvoir, who in some ways functioned as Leduc's ideal reader, her only intended audience. The erotic nature of the text substitutes for the unfulfilled relationship between Leduc and de Beauvoir. Leduc's fiction illustrates the range of her stylistic experimentation and themes while her style of writing has been likened to a sexualization of the text.

L'Affamée [Ravenous], 1948

Understanding Leduc's relationship with Simone de Beauvoir can serve as key to mapping the complex literary space of her fiction and autobiographical writings. *L'Affamée* presents an hallucinatory vision of the beginnings of the ambiguous relationship with "Madame," the object of the narrator's fixation. Its form is an interior monologue, with no cohesive chronological structure. Hunger and sexual longing define the progression of the narrative. The narrator recounts her struggle to reach "Madame" in a series of unconnected, often violent fantasies. For example, the unrequited, unsatiated hunger inspires images of self-mutilation: "I know you're hungry. Slice your flesh. Eat." (184) Both in form and theme, the text recalls Surrealist literature through its series of random violent images.

Finally, the narrator accepts her separation from "Madame" and realizes that the only way to bridge the chasm is through writing. The novel closes with the revelation: "To love is difficult but to love is a grace." (254) *L'Affamée* overflows the boundaries of fiction and lays bare Leduc's obsession with de Beauvoir. The novel defines their later relationship in terms of a *jouissance* in literary, rather than sexual, terms.

Ravages (1955)

Leduc's third novel originally began with the account of a lesbian relationship between two adolescent girls in a boarding school. This section,"Thérèse et Isabelle," was cut from the original Gallimard edition of the novel because of lesbian sexual acts between the narrator, Thérèse, and another schoolgirl, Isabelle. Gaston Gallimard and the senior staff worried about the potential repercussions from the publication of such a work, including a possible trial for obscenity. The moral climate of 1954, they concluded, would not tolerate such a frank description of lesbianism. After Gallimard's censorship of the novel, Jacques Guérin convinced Leduc to create a fake manuscript version of "Thérèse et Isabelle," which he published privately in a limited collector's edition. Eventually the reception of "Thérèse et Isabelle" elicited enough interest that Gallimard issued a highly edited version separately, in 1966. However, it was not until 2000 that Gallimard published the unexpurgated text.

The erotic scenes of the "Thérèse and Isabelle" episode shocked because of their frankness but Leduc had deliberately set out to challenge literary conventions. No other woman writer had written so explicitly about sex, least of all lesbian sex. The search of a new language for female sexuality leads Leduc to intertwine metaphors "we felt the rustling of taffeta in the hollow of our hands" with graphic details "she ... bruised my pubis with her thigh thrust between mine." Overall the descriptions are lyric and sensual in tone.

Ravages also recounts Thérèse's second relationship with a woman, a schoolteacher named Cécile whom Thérèse meets later in life. Thérèse and Cécile fall into the mold of a same-sex bourgeois couple. Cécile takes on the role of the provider while Thérèse becomes a housewife. Yet a second relationship develops between Thérèse and a weak young man whom she eventually marries. She becomes pregnant, has an abortion, and divorces. The parallels with Leduc's life are obvious. But the novel goes beyond the writing of the self. The complex interplay of the gender roles, traditional and non-traditional, and the tensions they create form the backdrop of each episode. Leduc's language loses much of the previous lyricism of prologue in describing the sexual encounters of her protagonist while retaining its sensuality. The tone becomes harsher, marked by short sentences that echo Thérèse's suffering.

Le Taxi (1971)

Leduc's last novella, *Le Taxi*, explores a different type of taboo, incest between an adolescent brother and sister.

Come inside me!

...

Hurry up ...

I am inside you.
All the way!

Thus begins a series of twelve dialogues that take place in a taxi hired for the purpose of a day of love-making and revelry away from the rest of the world. The brief conversations, punctuated by the young couple's repeated sex acts, trace the progression of the taxi through the city and reveal the long preparation that had gone into this single day. To the question: "are we perverse?" comes the reply "we're privileged," exemplifying the attitude of the youths. The setting recalls both the claustrophobic atmosphere of Cocteau's *Enfants terribles* and Leon and Emma's ride in Flaubert's *Madame Bovary*, while the disembodied voices parallels the works of Marguerite Duras and Nathalie Sarraute. Unlike the lushness of Leduc's erotic language in "Thérèse and Isabelle," here the spareness of text highlights the exuberance of the protagonists. Of all of Leduc's text, this one is unmarked by despair or suffering; rather it exemplifies desire satisfied.

Biography

Born in Arras, 7 April 1907, illegitimate daughter of Berthe Leduc, a maid, and André Debaralle. Educated primarily in boarding schools, 1912–1926; failed baccalaureate in 1927. Moved to Vincennes in 1928, liaison with Denise Hertgès, 1928–1935. Took secretarial job with the publishing firm Plon in Paris, 1928–1932. Scriptwriter for Synops, 1937–1939. Married to Jacques Mercier in 1939; separated; 1941; divorced, 1947. Worked for various magazines during World War II; also engaged in black-market traffic. Traveled extensively from 1951–1955: central and southern France, Italy, Belgium, and the Netherlands, Spain. Hospitalized for a "nervous breakdown" in Versailles for six months, 1956-57. First visit to Faucon, 1961; bought house and settled there in 1965. Died of cancer in Faucon, 28 May 1972.

EDITH J. BENKOV

Selected Works

Fiction

L'Asphyxie. Paris: Gallimard, 1946; translated by Derek Coltman as *In the Prison of Her Skin*. London: Hart-Davis, 1970.

L'Affamée. Paris: Gallimard, 1948.

Ravages. Paris: Gallimard, 1955; translated by Derek Coltman with *Therese and Isabelle*. London: Arthur Baker, 1966.

La Vieille Fille et le mort. Paris: Gallimard, 1958.
Thérèse et Isabelle. Paris: Gallimard, 1966; complete edition 2000.
Trésors à prendre. Paris: Gallimard, 1960.
Le Taxi. Paris: Gallimard, 1971; translated by Helen Weaver, New York: Farrar, Strauss, 1972.

Autobiography

La Bâtarde. Preface by Simone de Beauvoir. Paris: Gallimard, 1964.
La Folie en tête. Paris: Gallimard, 1971.
La Chasse à l'amour. Paris: Gallimard, 1973.

Further Reading

De Courtivon, Isabelle. *Violette Leduc*. Boston: Twayne, 1985.

Hall, Colette Trout. *Violette Leduc la mal-aimée*. Amsterdam, Netherlands: Rodopi, 1999.
Hughes, Alex. "Desire and Its Discontents: Violette Leduc/*La Bâtarde*/The Failure of Love" in *French Erotic Fiction: Women's Desiring Writing, 1880–1990*, Alex Hughes and Kate Ince, eds. Berg. Oxford 1996; 69–92.
————. *Violette Leduc: Mothers, Lovers and Language*. London: Maney, 1994
Lacey, Elizabeth. *The Pleasures of the Text: Violette Leduc and Reader Seduction*. Rowman and Littlefield, 2002.
Marks, Elaine. "Lesbian Intertexturality" in *Homosexualities and French Literature*. George Stambolian and Elaine Marks, eds. Cornell University Press, 1979; 353–377.

LEGMAN, GERSHON (G. LEGMAN, ROGER-MAXE DE LA GLANNEGE)

1917–1999
American folklorist, bibliographer, lexicographer, and fiction writer

A polymath of extraordinary reach, Gershon Legman mapped the margins of popular culture. Over his long career he championed origami (the art of Japanese paper-folding), attacked the initiation rites of the medieval order of the Knights Templar, critiqued the typography of the fifteenth-century printer William Caxton, translated *Ubi Roi* by Alfred Jarry, and compiled a bibliography on the economist David Ricardo, but he devoted himself chiefly to the study of sexual humor and folklore. Personally irascible, he shared his erudition and insights generously; his home on the Riviera, crammed with a lifetime's collection of erotic materials, was the center of research into sexual folklore until the waning of censorship in the late twentieth century emboldened less courageous scholars. That censorship was real, and it prevented formal publication of some of Legman's work; as a result, many items appeared in pamphlets of limited circulation or languish still in manuscript.

Too little is known about his early life (though he claimed that his parents wanted him to be a rabbi) to analyze Legman's personality and achievements with the unrepentant Freudianism he himself used to interpret oral and written expression, but it is evident that he was motivated by a fascination with sexuality, a passion for collecting, and a moral sense that manifested itself in continuous polemic. As a young man, he crusaded for women's rights and for rational population control, but gradually his energies flowed into an increasingly opinionated examination of a culture warped by its refusal to accept sex as a natural part of life. A residual puritanism, however, shaped his concept of the "natural": he often seemed homophobic, despite his advocacy of oral sex for all genders; he claimed that women who wore trousers or depiliated their pubic hair were "neurotic"; he excoriated drugs and rock 'n'roll music, terming the latter fascistic; he sneered at the "sexual revolution" of the 1960s, and called it a sham.

In the 1930s, Legman was one of several New York writers in the "Organization," an informal group writing erotica for a wealthy private patron. Legman composed some of the stories that made up the *Oxford Thesis* series of erotic typescripts originally begun by Lupton Wilkinson, who wrote on commission for Oklahoma millionaire Roy Johnson (see entry on Mentulus, L. Erectus). Legman wrote *The Passionate Pedant* (1939) for Johnson himself, and kept copies to print for clandestine audiences. He probably assembled the volumes called *A Further Oxford Thesis on Love* (1938) and *A Later Oxford Thesis on Love* (1939) from stories anonymously written by himself, Clement Wood, Anaïs Nin, Caresse Crosby, Robert DeNiro, Sr. (father of the actor), and other members of the Organization. He probably helped his boyhood friend Robert Sewall (see entry on Sewall) gather other stories for *The Oxford Professor* (c.1948), and may have written some of that volume. The Kinsey Institute holds several short stories attributed to Legman (e.g., "Chippie Wagon" [1941?]). Writing erotica taught Legman a good deal about narrative and style (among writers, he admired Denis Diderot, Jules Michelet, and Thomas Carlyle) though he tired quickly of this opportunistic enterprise, and turned it over to Henry Miller and Anaïs Nin. Ironically, given his preeminence in underground bibliography, Legman himself never sorted out the provenance of these surreptitious volumes. Failures of memory aside, the reason for his reticence is just as ironic: despite a career of collecting, recording, and analyzing sub-genres, Legman avoided vulgarity in his own work, and actually sanitized the sadistic elements of one edition of Sewall's famous *The Devil's Advocate*. Legman's first book for the general public, *Oragenitalism: An Encyclopaedic Outline of Oral Technique in Genital Excitation Part 1: Cunnilinctus* (1940), written under the anagram Roger-Maxe de La Glannége, was a manual on cunnilingus distinguished not only by his typically exhaustive treatment of technique but also by the careful diction he employed. (He later expanded the work to include fellatio.)

During the early 1940s, Legman's interest in outlaw sub-cultures manifested itself in a lexigraphical essay, "The Language of Homosexuality: An American Glossary" (1941), and in his collaboration with birth control activist Robert Latou Dickinson and with the odd "Kenneth S. Green" (aka Rex King), a pedophile, on the latter's massive diaries on penis size and infant orgasm, which Green sent to Alfred C. Kinsey, who would unwisely use some of Green's statistics in *Sexual Behavior in the Human Male* (1948). Through Dickinson, Legman met Kinsey, who hired him (in 1942?) to build archives for what would become (in 1947) the Institute for Sex Research (ISR) at Indiana University in Bloomington (now the Kinsey Institute for Research in Sex, Gender, and Reproduction). Although his passion for bibliography and folklore blossomed here, Legman left few traces at the ISR or at the prototype of Indiana's Folklore Institute, founded in 1942 by Stith Thompson, who was soon joined by Richard Dorson, to systematize the study of folklore. Thompson devised the tale type index and the motif index to systemize comparative study of folkways, but declined to classify obscene materials. Dorson, also a seminal figure in folklore because of his insistance on the cultural and ethnic context of folk materials, later denied Legman a university instructorship on the grounds that he and Ozark folklorist Vance Randolph were simply "scholar-tramps" (*Roll Me in Your Arms*, 24), because the two were convinced of the value of "obscene" folklore that respectable academics shunned.

During his sojourn at Indiana University, Legman worked on bibliographic projects such as "Toward an Historical Bibliography of Sex Technique," which catalogued photographs in the Kinsey archives by types of sexual behavior. Kinsey fired Legman in 1945, apparently over disputes about purchases and cataloguing of materials (Gathorne-Hardy, 232). A few years later, Legman published "Minority Report on Kinsey," an attack on the sexologist for having used improperly gathered statistics, especially those on homosexuality, to buttress the conclusions of *Sexual Behavior in the Human Male*. Feeling beleaguered, Legman wrote "Sex Censorship in the U.S.A." (1945) to contrast American and European attitudes towards sexual representation.

With financing from Jay Landesman, a St. Louis millionaire, Legman founded the journal *Neurotica* (1947–1951) to publish essays by Allen Ginsberg, Marshall McLuhan, Larry Rivers, Lawrence Durrell, and others. The journal's title suggested its thesis, that society had succumbed to psychic disorder, a syndrome best examined, Legman thought, by focusing on documents of popular culture. Legman's own *Neurotica* essays formed the nucleus of *Love and Death: A Study in Censorship* (1949), rejected by 42 publishers until Legman published it himself. In the volume he developed the argument he would elaborate again and again. For Legman, the "degeneracy" of American culture, as manifest in its choice of representations, was the result of its sublimation of natural sexual desire into preferences for violence and sadism. The more a culture represses sexual representations, said Legman, the more it will embrace violent images as socially acceptable substitutes. Because writers, filmmakers, and artists were forbidden to depict human desire honestly and candidly, audiences became used to seeing guns rather than penises, and aggression rather than affection. Worse, he said, a public fed a steady diet of mediated violence was far more likely to accept violence as a solution to social problems. *Love and Death's* chapter called "Not for Children," a reworking of the *Neurotica* essay "The Psychopathology of the Comics," was an analysis of comic books deformed by sexualized violence; it foreshadowed the celebrated anti-comic book campaign of Frederic Wertham. Other chapters of *Love and Death* targeted writers such as Raymond Chandler, Dashiell Hammett, Ernest Hemingway, and Philip Wylie, all of whom Legman charged with maligning women by casting them either as sadists ("Avatars of the Bitch") or as victims ("Open Season on Women"). Despite praise for the volume from Leslie Fiedler and William Carlos Williams, among others, the Post Office harassed Legman for trying to sell *Love and Death* through the mail.

Relocating to France in 1953 permitted Legman to pursue his career as a "scholar-tramp," albeit an impoverished one. Supporting himself with freelance writing, editing, the compiling of anthologies, and a small inheritance from a relative, he began in earnest his investigation of erotica, its classification, and the bibliographic efforts that recovering prohibited printed texts and oral expression required. Two books established his credentials. The first, *The Horn Book; and Other Bibliographic Problems* (1953, later expanded in 1964 to *The Horn Book: Studies in Erotic Folklore and Bibliography*) grew out of

Legman's tracing of editions of a famous text, *The Horn Book: A Girl's Guide to the Knowledge of Good and Evil* (1899), a guide to sexual technique. Legman's sleuthing revealed the activities of bibliographers such as Henry Spencer Ashbee, Louis Perceau, and Jules Gay, bookdealer-publishers such as Charles Carrington and Eric Dingwall, lexicographer-writers such as J.S. Farmer and William Henley, and collectors such as Bernard de La Monnoye and the Duc de la Vallière. Other chapters dealt with Legman's enthusiasms: Robert Burns's *The Merry Muses of Caledonia*, bawdy songs, limericks, and the need for a motif-index for erotic humor to fill out Thompson's index. Here Legman announced what amounted to his creed: "Sexual folklore is, with the lore of children, the only form of folklore still in uncontaminated and authentic folk transmission in the Western world. It has thumbed its nose for centuries at both censorship and print" (1964, 288). Cranky and colorful, the volume remains indispensable to students of erotica.

The second book, *The Limerick* (also 1953), gathered more than 1700 examples of "the only fixed poetic form original to the English language" (1969, lxxii) under a series of categories (e. g., "Strange Intercourse," "Virginity," "Buggery," "Prostitution"). In his introduction to the volume, Legman traced the limerick from its oral beginnings as nonsensical bawdy and satire to its more recent combination of intellectual ingenuity and obscenity ("the folk-expression" of academics [1969, xlv]), noting that periodic efforts to compose "clean" limericks invariably made them nasty ("the substitution of an allowed sadism for a prohibited sexual normality" [1969, xliii]). In a later second collection, *The New Limerick* (1977), ogranized in categories similar to those in the first volume, Legman tried to distinguish between limericks that qualified as "true folklore" and those that did not. He estimated that only a tenth of those he had collected, those "everyone knows," had actually "entered the authentic stream of orally transmitted folklore" (1980, xxx), but aside from noting the importance of constant repetition he did not shed much light on the dynamics of transmission.

Classifying examples on a scale of anxieties did not serve Legman well in the projects for which he is best known: *The Rationale of the Dirty Joke: An Analysis of Sexual Humor*

(1968) and *Rationale of the Dirty Joke, Second Series* (1975). Critics lauded Legmam for amassing hundreds of jokes, but suggested that his analyses were superficial and sloppy, the result of allowing his thesis that sexual humor masks aggression to foreclose other interpretations. Reviews criticized him for insisting that "a person's favorite joke is the key to that person's character" (1968, 16) on the grounds that the joke reveals the teller's secret fears even as he makes light of his neurosis, and also for claiming that the listener to a joke is the real butt of the humor (1975, 20). Critics also dismissed his attacks on such structural analyses as Vladimir Propp's *Morphology of the Folktale*, observing that it was naive for Legman to claim that content alone determines the meaning of a joke. Folklorists chided him for failing to provide the context of jokes, for classifying jokes according to their hostile motifs, for never providing a promised index to the two volumes, and, above all, for summarizing rather than printing versions verbatim.

Legman deliberately summarized jokes rather than commit them accurately to print in the not so paradoxical hope of preserving their oral ephemerality. Doing so, however, exposed a contradiction in his principal thesis. If western cultures systematically warp sexual discourse into violent language and images, then why does the folklore he so meticulously compiled also exhibit the same aggressive traits? Oral transmissions in a past less given to censorship should have escaped the kinds of sublimation that Legman detects in print and visual media of the twentieth century. Legman's methodoloy exhibits the perils of studying folklore, a discipline that embraces what are at base mysterious forms of communication. Ideally, theories should arise from careful comparative examination of examples, but the sheer volume of jokes, stories, and legends often reverses the process; theory and categorization are invoked from the outset to impose order on the chaos of conflicting examples.

Moreover, Legman's faith in folklore as the primary, universal source of erotic representation led him to make extravagant claims about its vulgar but democratic commonality. "All folklore is erotic," he would insist in "Erotic Folksongs and Ballads: An International Bibliography," an amazing list of samizdat versions, spin-offs, reprints, paperback editions, and other mutations of jokes, stories, songs, ballads, and broadsides that he published in 1990. Folklore is not simply a term used to distinguish venerable stories that contain obscenity from narratives that aspire to literary status: "Folklore," said Legman, "is the voice of those who have no other voice, and would not be listened to if they did." ("Erotic Folksongs," 417).

Despite serious illness, he took on his last massive project. He and Vance Randolph never actually met, but the other aging "scholar-tramp" entrusted Legman with editing those portions of his archive of Ozark folklore long denied publication because of their explicit sexual content. Legman accepted out of a sense of obligation, having worried for years about the ephemerality of the items on which he based his own research. Long subject to seizure, erotic materials, especially those but slightly removed from their original oral expresion, often survive only in single examples that must be hunted for years. Even where he was successful in tracking down fugitive manuscripts and destroyed editions, Legman, ever the careful scholar, was reluctant to publish papers based on examples of which he held the world's only copy, since they were unavailable for others to evaluate. In an essay called "Unprintable Folklore? The Vance Randolph Collection" (1990), Legman settled some scores with Dorson and other folklorists, and promised to do justice to Randolph. Both carefully-edited volumes, *Roll Me in Your Arms: "Unprintable" Ozark Folksongs and Folklore* and *Blow the Candle Out: "Unprintable" Ozark Folklore*, appeared in 1992.

Although his reputation remains legendary, Legman's contributions to the study of erotica may yet be judged by what he left unpublished. He may also eventually receive his due as a writer of erotica. Legman often disparaged his erotic fiction, usually in remarks that imagining sexual scenarios and fabricating desire diminished his own libido. Drawing on his own extensive sexual experience, however, added authority and verisimilitude to personalized tales of erotic encounters. For years Legman worked on an autobiography tentatively titled *Peregrine Penis: An Autobiography of Innocence* (the title is a play on Smollett's picaresque novel, *Peregrine Pickle*). Only one small portion of that memoir, "Trio Amoroso," has been published. "Trio Amoroso" is set during the World War II period in which Legman helped Brussel publish the underground "Medusa" edition of Henry Miller's *Tropic of Cancer*, the first American printing of the novel. This fragment contains glimpses of bookstore owner Frances Steloff, writer William Carlos Williams, artist Alexander King, and magazine magnate Henry Luce, set against a backdrop of work and leisure in New York City. Driving the narrative is the explicitly rendered intercourse of a ménage à trois involving Legman, his lover Magdalena, and their mutual lover, fashion artist Susan [Inez] Aguerra. In its lusty physical exuberance, the memoir superficially resembles those of Henry Miller, but Legman brings to it reflections on the nature of his own youthful sexuality and that of his partners, introspections that acknowledge the fragility of gender and desire.

More important, "Trio Amoroso" underscores significant aspects of Legman's legacy. First, it is an example of erotica written for intellectual sensibilities. In this respect, the maturity of "Trio Amoroso" differs markedly from the sniggering tales of the Oxford Professor. Second, it contains biographical information to be found nowhere else. Legman's portrait of Aguerra is the only account of this largely unknown erotic book illustrator, who drew under the name "Rahngild." If it is ever published, the larger autobiography will doubtless recall other equally fugitive figures in the history of American erotica. Third, "Trio Amoroso" reinforces Legman's conviction that writing erotica and studying it are both passions worthy of admiration. Legman's bibliographic studies and scholarly footnotes, enlivened with tales of real individuals who obsessively wrote and collected erotica, often make the same point: that creating sexual representations and interpreting them are immutably human pursuits. Beyond question such pursuits shaped Legman. Few scholars have given themselves up so completely to what were clearly labors of love.

Biography

Born George Alexander Legman to Julia Friedman and Emil Mendel Legman in Scranton, Pennsylvania on November 2, 1917. Julia's uncle, Friedrich Krauss, was editor of two journals of erotica (1880–1910), *Anthropophytéia* [*The Sexual Relations of Mankind*] and *Kryptádia* [*Secret Things*]; the latter was later edited by Freud. After one quarter at the University of Michigan, Legman educated himself at the New York Public Library, teaching himself several languages in the process. In the 1930s, he began working for the National Committee on Maternal Health, part of the Planned Parenthood Program in New York, where he would be arrested at least once for dispensing birth-control information, then considered a species of obscenity. In 1940, he briefly worked for Jake Brussel, a publisher and distributor of erotica, and otherwise supported himself by ghost-writing books, erotic stories, and radio scripts, and dealing in rare books. In 1953, as a result of what he called continuous persecution by the government, Legman moved to France, where, except for a year as a writer-in-residence at the University of California (1964–65), he remained. Legman was married to Beverly Keith, Christine Conrad (annulled), and Judith Evans. He had four children: Ariëla (1957), with Sima Colcher, and David (1968), Rafaël (1971), and Sarah (1973) with Judith Evans. He died of a stroke in Opio, France, February 23, 1999.

JOSEPH W. SLADE

Selected Works

As author or compiler

"Bawdy Monologues and Rhymed Recitations." *Southern Folklore Quarterly*, 40 (March-June, 1976): 59–123.

"Bibliography of Paper-Folding." Malvern, England: A preprint from the *Journal of Occasional Bibliography*, 1952.

David Ricardo and Ricardian Theory: A Bibliographical Checklist, by Burt Franklin and G. Legman. New York: Burt Franklin, 1949.

"Erotic Folksongs and Ballads: An International Bibliography." *Journal of American Folklore*, 103 (October/December 1990): 417–501.

The Fake Revolt. New York: Breaking Point, 1967.

"The Guilt of the Templars," *The Guilt of the Templars*, by G. Legman et al. New York: Basic Books, 1966.

The Horn Book; and Other Bibliographic Problems. New York: American Aphrodite, 1953; expanded to *The Horn Book: Studies in Erotic Folklore and Bibliography*. New York: University Books, 1964.

"Introduction." *The Mammoth Cod*, and *Address to the Stomach Club*, by Mark Twain. Milwaukee: Maledicta Press, 1976, pp. 2–18.

"Introduction." *The Private Case: An Annotated Bibliography of the Erotica Collection in the British (Museum) Library*, by Patrick J. Kearney. London: Landesman, 1981, pp. 3–34.

"Introduction: The Art of Mahlon Blaine: A Reminiscence." *The Art of Mahlon Blaine*, by Mahlon Blaine. East Lansing MI: Peregrine, 1982.

"Introduction." *Children's Humor: A Joke for Every Occasion*, by Sandra McCosh. London: Panther/Granada, 1979.

"The Language of Homosexuality: An American Glossary," Appendix to *Sex Variants*, ed. George W. Henry. 2 vols. New York: Haeber, 1941, 2: 1149–1179.

The Limerick: 1700 Examples, with Notes, Variants, and Index. Paris: Les Hautes Etudes, 1953; San Diego: Greenleaf Classics, 1967; New York: Brandywine Press, 1970; New York: Bell Publishing, 1964, 1969, 1976; *The Famous Paris Edition of The Limerick: 1700 Entries*. Secaucus NJ: Citadel Press, 1979.

Love and Death: A Study in Censorship. New York: Breaking Point, 1949; New York: Hacker Art Books, 1963.

"The Lure of the Forbidden." *Libraries, Erotica, and Pornography*, ed. Martha Cornog. Phoenix AZ: Oryx Press, 1991, pp. 36–68.

"Minority Report on Kinsey." *The Sexual Conduct of Men and Women*, by Norman Lockridge [Samuel Roth]. New York: Hogarth House, 1948, pp. 13–32.

The New Limerick: 2750 Unpublished Examples, American and British (aka More Limericks: 2750 Unpublished Examples, American and British). New York: Crown Publishers, 1977; rpt. New York: Bell, 1980.

"Misconceptions in Erotica Folklore." *Journal of American Folklore*, 75 (1962): 200–208.

On the Cause of Homosexuality: Two Essays, the Second a Reply to the First, by G. Legman and G.V. Hamilton. New York: privately printed pamphlet, 1964.

"On Sexual Speech and Slang." *Dictionary of Slang and Its Analogues, Past and Present: A Dictionary Historical and Comparative of the Heterodox Speech of All Classes of Society for More Than Three Hundred Years with Synonyms in English, French, German, Italian, etc. Vol. I*, by J.S. Farmer and W.E. Henley. New Hyde Park. NY: University Books, 1966, pp. 375–450.

Oragenitalism: An Encyclopaedic Outline of Oral Technique in Genital Excitation Part 1: Cunnilinctus, by Roger-Maxe de La Glannége [an anagram]. New York: J.R. Brussel, 1940; rep. and exp. (with *Part II: Fellation and the Sixty-Nine*) by Legman under his own name, as *Oragenitalism: Oral Techniques in Genital Excitation*. New York: Julian Press, 1969; rpt. New York: Causeway Books, 1969; rpt. as *The Intimate Kiss*. New York: Paperback Library, 1971; rpt. London: *Oragenitalism: Oral Techniques in Genital Excitation*. Duckworth, 1972; rpt. New York: Bell Publishing Company, 1979.

The Oxford Professor, In which L. Erectus Mentulus, Ph.D., late of Oxford College, is taken further in the narration of his adventures and misadventures, erotic, alcoholic, and otherwise; not to mention a choice accompaniment of drolleries, notes and excursi of one sort or another, metaphysical and also miscellaneously edifying and entertaining. "Done by the Hand of the Author Into a Manuscript at Natchitoches, Louisiana [by Robert Sewall and Gerson Legman, New York, c1948]"; rpt. *The Oxford Professor*, by L. Crectus [sic] Mentulus, Ph.D., Atlanta: Pendulum Books, 1968;

rpt. *The Professor's Tale*, Industry, CA: Collectors Publications, 1968.

The Passionate Pedant, Being a New Oxford Thesis on Love, wherein L. Erectus Mentulus, late of Oxford, establishes incontrovertibly that the sexual enjoyment of women of divers races is evocative of distinctly different types and degrees of pleasure, through narratives of his own experience, with particular emphasis upon psycho-physiological adumbrations et cetera, for the entertainment as well as the enlightenment of his friends. In cunnis diversis–voluptates diversae. Done by the Hand of the Author into a Manuscript at Oshkosh, Wisconsin [New York, 1939]; rpt. with *Torrid Tales* [author unknown] as *The Further Adventures of the Oxford Professor*, by L. Erectus Mentulus, Atlanta: Pendulum Books, 1968; rpt. *The Oxford Professor Returns*, by L. Erectus Mentulus, New York: Venus Library, 1971.

"The Psychopathology of the Comics." *Neurotica*, 1:3 (Autumn 1948): 3–30.

Rationale of the Dirty Joke: An Analysis of Sexual Humor. New York: Grove Press, 1968.

Rationale of the Dirty Joke: An Analysis of Sexual Humor, Second Series. New York: Breaking Point, 1975; rpt. *No Laughing Matter: An Analysis of Sexual Humor*. Bloomington, IN: Indiana University Press, 1982.

"Sex Censorship in the U.S.A." *PLAN: Organization of the British Progressive League* (London), 2:1 (January 1945): 2–9.

"A Summer Reading List to End All Summer Reading Lists," *Fact*, 2:4 (July-August, 1965): 38–43.

"Toward an Historical Bibliography of Sex Technique." Unpublished typescript, Kinsey Institute for Sex, Reproduction, and Gender, Indiana University, Bloomington, Indiana, 1942.

"Toward a Motif-Index of Erotic Humor." *Journal of American Folklore*, 75 (1962): 227–248; rpt. *The Horn Book*, pp. 454–494.

"Trio Amoroso," *Libido: The Journal of Sex and Sensibility*, 1 (1988): 1–10; rpt. in The *Ecstatic Moment: the Best of Libido*, ed. Marianna Beck and Jack Hafferkamp. New York: Delta, 1997, pp. 220–248.

"Unprintable Folklore? The Vance Randolph Collection." *Journal of American Folklore*, 103 (July-September 1990): 259–300.

"A Word on Caxton's 'Dictes' and Sayings of the Philosophers." London: Bibliographical Society, 1948.

As Editor

Burns, Robert. *The Merry Muses of Caledonia, Collected and in Part Written by Robert Burns. A new ed., now reprinted for the first time in type-facsimile of the unique original, with additional songs from the Cunningham manusript and other sources*, edited by G. Legman, New Hyde Park, NY: University Books, [c1965].

Les Chansons de Salle de garde. Paris: R. Deforges, 1972.

Jarry, Alfred. *King Turd [Ubi Roi]*, trans. G. Legman and Beverly Keith. New York: Boar's Head Books, 1953.

Kryptádia: The Journal of Erotic Folklore (1968–?)

Neurotica (1947–1951); collected as *The Compleat Neurotica, 1948–1951*. New York: Hacker Art Books, 1963.

Neurotica: Authentic Voice of the Beat Generation, ed. with Jay Landesman. London: Jay Landesman, 1981.

Randolph, Vance. *Blow the Candle Out: "Unprintable" Ozark Folklore*, Vol. II. Fayetteville AR: University of Arkansas Press, 1992.

Randolph, Vance. *Roll Me in Your Arms: "Unprintable" Ozark Folksongs and Folklore*, Vol. I. Fayetteville AR: University of Arkansas Press, 1992.

Sewall, Robert. *The Devil's Advocate*, by "Wood C. Lamont" [Robert Sewall, as typed and enlarged by Gershon Legman], Chicago [New York]: mimeographed, 1942; see entry on Sewall, Robert.

Further Reading

Brottman, Mikita. *Funny Peculiar: Gershon Legman and the Psychopathology of Humor*. Hillsdale, NJ: Analytic Press, 2004.

Buehler, Richard E. "Rationale of the Dirty Joke: An Analysis of Sexual Humor [review]." *Journal of American Folklore*, 83: 327 (January-March 1970): 87–89.

Dudar, Helen. "Love and Death (and Schmutz): G. Legman's Second Thoughts." *Village Voice*, 1 May 1984, pp. 41–43.

Gathorne-Hardy, Jonathan. *Sex the Measure of All Things: A Life of Alfred C. Kinsey*. Bloomington, IN: Indiana University Press, 1998.

Gertzman, Jay A. *Bookleggers amd Smuthounds: The Trade in Erotica 1920–1940*. Philadelphia, PA: University of Pennsylvania Press, 1999.

"Gershon Legman" [Obituary]. *New York Times*, March 14, 1999, p. 49.

Holmes, John Clellon. "The Last Cause: Gershon Legman," *Evergreen Review*, 44 (December 1966): 28–32, 93–101,

"Legman, Gershon." *Contemporary Authors*, New Revision Series 15: 277–78.

Oring, Elliott. "G. Legman, *Rationale of the Dirty Joke: An Analysis of Sexual Humor, First Series* and *Rationale of the Dirty Joke: An Analysis of Sexual Humor, Second Series*," *Western Folklore*, 38: 4 (October 1977): 365–371.

Vinocur, John. "Gershon Legman Doesn't Tell Dirty Jokes ... But He Has the World's Largest Collection of Them Lying Around His House." *Oui*, 4: 3 (March 1975): 94–96, 126, 130–131.

LELY, GILBERT

1904–1985
French poet and critic

Gilbert Lely is doubly meritorious in the history of erotic literature: as a poet, he is an excellent representative of surrealist eroticism, and as a literary critic he is the greatest expert on the works of the Marquis de Sade, whose correspondence and many unpublished writings he has revealed.

Pierre-Raphaël-Gilbert Lévy (who will take at the age of seventeen the pseudonym Lely) was born on the First of June, 1904, in Paris, at 8, rue Parrot (XIIeme). His mother died when he was five years old, and his father, Adrien Lévy, trader of paper goods, after having remarried, sent him to the Lycée Jeanson-de-Sailly, a boarding school, in 1911, and then to the Lycée Lakanal de Bourg-la-Reine, from 1916 to 1920. When his parents retired in Hyères, in the Var, in 1921,

Gilbert Lely stayed in Paris, worked in the Théâtre de l'Œuvre as a secretary and actor, and published at the Jouve library *Les chefs-d'œuvre des poètes gallants du XVIIIe siècle* [*The Masterpieces of the Gallant Poets of the 18th Century*], an anthology which denoted his precocity. It was exceptional that a man as young as he should show such erudition, presenting in original notices thirty-three poorly known poets.

Subsequently, Gilbert Lely published at nineteen years old his first collection of poems, *Aréthuse ou Elégies* [*Arethusa or Elegies*] (Alphonse Lemerre, 1923) and at twenty-three his second, *Allusions ou poèmes* [*Allusions or Poems*] (Bristol, Douglas Cleverdon, 1927). This was his classical period, when he displayed the influence of André Chénier. Still, he returned to surrealism in 1931, and his amorous lyricism, in *Je ne veux pas qu'on tue cette femme* [*I do not want this woman to be killed*], a eulogy of Mata-Hari, (Editions surrealists, 1936, with a frontispiece by Max Ernst), and in *La sylphide ou l'étoile carnivore* [*The Sylphid or the Carnivorous Star*] (Editions le François, 1938), caused André Breton and Paul Eluard to give him the nickname of "the scabrous lamp." Indeed, he presented himself as a worrying fiancé, Arden, who dreamed of sexual situations of strange sophistication.

Gilbert Lely became the editor-in-chief of the medical journal *Hippocrate* in Paris, from January 1933 to September 1939, and was admitted as a member of the Medical Historical Society because of his works. He wrote a series of brilliant articles on physicians like Philippe Ricord, the syphilis expert, or Philippe Pinel, who revolutionized the treatment of mental illnesses. It was in his office at *Hippocrate* that he met Maurice Heine, who had just edited Sade's *Les 120 journée de Sodom* [*The 120 Days of Sodom*], by Sade, and who would introduce him to the Marquis's works. During the war, Gilbert Lely was stationed as a nurse at the air force base of Tours. At the armistice, he went to join the surrealists in Marseille and prepared in 1942 his first version of *Ma civilisation* [*My civilization*], the book of poems that he would never cease to rework. This clandestine edition, limited to twelve typewritten copies, contained "a graphic of a 10-minute sexual congress," with the chart of excitement and orgasm. Among the seven illustrated panels, there was a collage representing his first wife, Lucienne, whom he married in 1929 and divorced in 1937. *Ma civilisation* was published in 1947 by Maeght, in a deluxe edition illustrated by Lucien Coutaud. Its reprinting in 1949 was accompanied by a lower blurb by Yves Bonnefoy. Gilbert Lely was then working as a radio announcer.

On the 22nd of January, 1948, while visiting the descendants of Sade in Condé-sur-Brie, Lely obtained from Count Xavier de Sade the permission to inventory the two boxes handed down by his ancestor, which no one in the family had opened. In them he found a whole treasure of unpublished writings: letters, plays, notebooks, etc.... He published three collections of these letters: *L'Aigle, Mademoiselle* [*The Eagle, Miss*] (Georges Artigué, 1949), *Le carillon de Vincennes* [*The Bells of Vincennes*] (Arcannes, 1953), Monsieur le 6 [*Mister the 6*] (Julliard, 1956), the *Cahiers personnels* [*Personal Notebooks*] (Corréa,

1953) and the rest, with a critical commentary. Possessing a knowledge of this author that no one had ever possessed before, Gilbert Lely wrote a *Vie du marquis de Sade, écrite sur des données nouvelles, accompagnée de nombreux documents, le plus souvent inédits* [*A Life of the Marquis de Sade, based on new data, accompanied by many, often unpublished, documents*], published by Gallimard in two large volumes, the first in 1952, the second in 1957. He also gave another edition, reviewed, corrected and extended by an examination of the works of Sade, in 1962. He also directed the "definitive edition," at the Cercle du Livre précieux, of *Œuvres complètes du marquis de Sade, établies sur les originaux imprimés ou manuscrits* [*The Complete Works of the Marquis de Sade, Established on Many of the Printed or Manuscript Originals*] (1962–1964), in fifteen volumes with 360 illustrations. He added to the reprinting of 1966 a sixteenth tome of *Mélanges littéraires et Lettres* [*Literary Mixes and Letters*], with six introductions by his own hand. Much of what we know of Sade today we owe to Gilbert Lely. He enriched his *Vie de Sade* with new documents up to his last edition in 1982, at Garnier. His flamboyant style, together with his gift of evocation of the past and his meticulousness of a conscientious exegete, have made this biography an incomparable book. One of his admirers has called him the "prince of Sadiens": nothing is more correct.

In 1977, outside of his *Œuvres poétiques* [*Poetic Works*], of an erotic lyricism, Gilbert Lely published non-commercially *Kidama vivila*, "sotadic poetry," that is, frankly obscene, like *Lady K****, a hymn to a woman copulating with "three libertines, endowed with scandalous members." Its title is derived from a melanesian chant which begins with *kidama vivila ikanupwagega* [let us suppose woman one instant she is lying down, open], that he dedicated to his mistress Betty, concluding, "Hail, sweetness of my soul! The memory of your breasts, of your secret wetness, pierces me through, more acutely than the moans of orgasm, carried by hertzian waves, of all the women in Paris at the same instant."

On the 19th of January, 1979, Gilbert Lely married Marie-Françoise Le Pennec, 46 years his junior, whose presence by his side stimulated him to the end. He died on June 4th, 1985, at his Parisian address, 12 rue Emile-Allez (XVIIe). The centenary of his birth was celebrated in Paris in 2004, at the Sorbonne and at the Bilbiothèque de l'Arsenal, by a cycle of conferences presided by Marie-Françoise Lely.

SARANE ALEXANDRIAN

Selected Works

Kidama vivila, poesies sotadiques, avec 7 dessins de Julio Pomar. Paris, La Différence, 1977.

Vie du marquis de Sade. Liminaire de Philippe Sollers. Paris, Mercure de France, 1989.

Poésies complètes, texte établi et annoté par Jean-Louis Gabin. Tome I (preface d'Yves Bonnefoy) et Tome II: 1996. Tome III: 2000 Paris, Mercure de France.

Further Reading

Gabin, Jean-Louise. *Gilbert Lely, biographie*. Paris, Librairie Séguier, 1991.

Gilbert Lely. Etudes critiques inédites d'Yves Bonnefoy, Thierry Bouchard, Jacques Henric et Claudie Massaloux. Losne, Thierry Bouchard, 1979.

"Hommage à Gilbert Lely." In *L'Infini*, no 18, printempts 1987, Paris.

Pia, Pascal. *Feuilletons littéraires*. Tôme 1, Paris, Fayard, 1999.

Alexandrian, Sarane. "Gilbert Lely dans ses cinq aspects mémorables." In *Supérieur Inconnu*, no 17, janvier-mars 2000.

"Hommage à Gilbert Lely." Catalogue de la Bibliothèque de l'Arsenal, Paris, 2004.

LESBIAN LITERATURE

As a genre, Anglo-American lesbian literature is a phenomenon of the twentieth century. Whilst the literary exploration of lesbian themes had a first heyday in the early twentieth century, the study of lesbian writing in English developed, parallel to lesbian theory, from the 1970s onward. The genre of lesbian literature is polymorphous: it encompasses all literary forms, including novels, short stories, poetry, and so on. The genre has sometimes been divided into two main strands, fictional and autobiographical writings, although the boundaries between the two are fluid.

The first major accumulation of lesbian writing can be found in the modernist literature of the early twentieth century. However, the earliest known lesbian autobiography was written in the eighteenth century by the Yorkshire gentlewoman Anne Lister (published in 1998 as *The Diaries of Anne Lister*). Lister openly documented her lesbian desires, carefully noting how many women she slept with, whereby she referred to the sexual act as "kiss." Her autobiography provides a unique insight into eighteenth-century lesbian experience.

In the nineteenth century, the main strand of writing by women was connected to the feminist movement of the day. Its proponents include in Britain the French-born Vernon Lee (her real name was Violet Paget), Australian-born George Egerton (Mary Chavelita Dunne), the South African Olive Schreiner, and Sarah Grand (Frances Elizabeth Bellenden McFall), who was born in Ireland. Grand coined the term "New Woman" which gave the literature its name. Much New Woman literature concentrated on the moral and sexual development of a female protagonist, often featuring close female friendships and alluding to different forms of female desire. Similarly, in the United States, Kate Chopin, Charlotte Perkins Gilman, and Edith Wharton produced for the time often candid and daring representations of female sexuality. Outside feminist writings, lesbian erotic themes also played a role in the literature of the nineteenth-century Gothic movement. Here, the eroticism of the female vampire featured in a number of texts, such as Sheridan Le Fanu's short story *Carmilla* (1872), which was based on the allure of female same-sex desires. *Carmilla* is exemplary of this kind of writing, which appears simultaneously fascinated and repulsed by lesbian sexuality. A different literary observation on lesbianism can be found in the work of Henry James. In *The Bostonians* (1885) James focused on a woman who is caught between the love for a man and that for another woman. In *The Turn of the Screw* (1898), James more subtly explored female desire in the relationship between an eight-year-old girl and her governess. The religiously infused poetry of "Michael Field" provides a biographically unusual body of lesbian writing in the later nineteenth century. "Michael Field" was the pseudonym of the Englishwomen Katherine Bradley and Edith Cooper, who were aunt and niece—and lovers. As "Michael Field," they published a series of homoerotic poetry volumes, the first of which was entitled *Callirhoë and Fair Rosamund* (1883).

In the first decades of the twentieth century a distinct artistic lesbian subculture emerged, which was connected to the concerns of the feminist movement. Some of the female authors of this period have been grouped together under the label "Sapphic modernism," both for their increasingly open engagement with lesbian themes, and for the lesbianism of the authors themselves. The poetry of Hilda Doolittle, known as H.D., belongs to this group. Her poetry, such as the collections *Sea Garden* (1916) and *Hymen* (1921), subtly engages with erotic female same-sex longing. Her most explicit lesbian work is constituted by the largely autobiographical prose manuscripts *HERmione* (1926–1927), which were unearthed after her death. Here H.D. describes the relationship with her lover Bryher (Annie Winifred Ellerman), also a writer, who wrote under male literary covers. More open explorations of lesbian desire can be found in the short stories of Katherine Mansfield, especially *Bliss* (1920), which revolves around the female narrator's sexual desire for another woman. Mansfield's feminist concerns are similar to that of arguably the best-known woman writer of the period, Virginia Woolf. Women's emancipation and female sexuality play a central role in Woolf's work, much of which depicts lesbian homoeroticism. This is visible in her *Mrs Dalloway* (1925) in the portrayal of the relationship between the protagonist and her daughter's governess, the suggestively named Doris Kilman. Three years later, Woolf published the gender-metamorphosing story of *Orlando* (1928), which intimated notions of same-sex desire through the sex change of the protagonist. *Orlando* was partly inspired by Woolf's lover, Vita Sackville-West. The married Sackville-West was a prominent figure in contemporary Sapphist circles. She had first gained notoriety through her elopement with Violet Trefusius. Sackville-West fictionalized their affair in the novel *Challenge* (1923). Trefusius later wrote a novel entitled *Pirates at Play* (1950), which teems with homoerotic and androgynous themes.

Djuna Barnes was another influential writer loosely linked to the Sapphic modernism. Her novels were influenced by her own life, especially her experiences within the lesbian communities of the early twentieth century. Barnes' erotically explicit *Ladies Almanack* (1928) and *Nightwood* (1936) were inspired by the lesbian communities in Greenwich Village and Paris. Paris attracted many lesbian intellectuals of the day, and Barnes had an affair with one of the central figures of 1920s lesbian Paris, Nathalie Clifford Barney. Barney's other lovers included the writer and music hall star Colette, whose work comprises the erotically charged short story *Nuits Blanches* (1934), and the reflective autobiography *My Apprenticeships* (1936). The Paris circle further included Gertrude Stein, who lived openly with her lover Alice B. Toklas. Stein wrote an account of her lover's life entitled *The Autobiography of Alice B. Toklas* (1933), which is one of the most unapologetic and erotically explicit early twentieth-century lesbian texts.

The Paris circle was fictionally portrayed in what has become the classic of lesbian literature, Radclyffe Hall's *The Well of Loneliness* (1928) [see entry]. Hall's novel was influenced by contemporary medical and psychological theories of female homosexuality. Hall was not the first to draw on the new theories, however. In 1917, Clemence Dane (Winifred Holtby) published *Regiment of Women*, which presented a psychological case study of the relationship between the aptly named sadistic headmistress Clare Hartill and her submissive younger female colleague Alwynne. Arnold Bennett, who had woven the passionate friendship between women into the subplot of his main exploration of the unconventional love between a wealthy bachelor and a French courtesan in *The Pretty Lady* (1918), took a psychological approach in the short novel *Elsie and the Child* (1924). Here he suggested that female homosexual desire was a natural occurrence during puberty. In 1927, Rosamond Lehmann's *Dusty Answer* focused in the central section of the novel on an erotic friendship between two female students at Cambridge, engaging with questions of the naturalness of female homosexuality.

This rich and varied production of lesbian literature came to a halt with the outbreak of the Second World War. In the immediate post-war period, one of the few writers who engaged with lesbian eroticism was Anaïs Nin. Many of her short stories, notably *Ladders to Fire* (1946), and experimental novels explicitly describe lesbian sexual desire. One of the few women writing about lesbianism in the 1950s and 60s was the American Ann Bannon. The repressive political climate of the McCarthy years is reflected in her novels, which portray the fears, but also the support among the gay community in Greenwich Village. Bannon's work was also amongst the first to explore the eroticism of butch–femme relationships, most explicitly in *Beebo Brinker* (1962), the fifth and last novel in a series of related works.

The 1969 Stonewall Riots in New York saw the birth of the lesbian and gay civil rights movement. The lesbian literature of the time influenced and was influenced by the radical lesbian feminist movement. In 1972, John Nestle founded the Lesbian Herstory Archives and Educational Foundation in New York. Like many of the writers of the time, Nestle published both fictional and theoretical works, including *The Persistent Desire: A Femme–Butch Reader* (1992). Among the most influential theorists and writers of the 1970s was Kate Millet, who came to fame with the theoretical milestone *Sexual Politics* (1970). Millet's political belief that the private is always the political informs her autobiographically inspired novel *Sita* (1977), which depicts the destructive sexual–emotional relationship she had had with an older woman. Tied in with radical feminist politics, much of the lesbian literature of the 1970s followed an anti-pornography agenda. However, some books such as Rita Mae Brown's successful *Ruby Fruit Jungle* (1973), contained explicit descriptions of lesbian sex. The celebration of lesbian desire was focal to many works, such as that of the French critic and writer Monique Wittig, whose *Le corps Lesbien* [The Lesbian Body] was published in 1973, or that of the radical lesbian feminist and poet Adrienne Rich. Rich produced a vast and varied number of poetry volumes, which have in common the search for a lesbian poetic voice. Famous for her critical work *Compulsory Heterosexuality and Lesbian Existence* (1981), Rich explores and celebrates lesbian eroticism in her poetry, such as *The*

Twenty-One Love Poems (1977), and she continues to publish at the beginning of the twenty-first century.

In the 1980s, a number of distinct lesbian texts were published. Audre Lorde's autobiographical *Zami, or a New Spelling of My Name* (1982) was rooted in feminist concerns relating to how to express specific female experiences, in this case growing up a black lesbian. The lesbian critic and writer Sara Maitland paid tribute to the lesbian feminists of the 1960s and early 70s, for example in her short story *Lullaby for My Dyke and Her Cat* (1987). A radical break with early feminism can be found in the work of Pat Califia. In 1982, she published *Coming to Power*. Its explicit erotic content caused furore, as it challenged the radical feminist anti-pornography movement of the 1970s. Califia explored lesbian sado-masochism in a series of lesbian leather and vampire writings, including *Macho Sluts* (1988), and the short story "The Vampire" (1988). Erotica entered the lesbian mainstream with the opening of the lesbian sex shop *Sh!* in London in 1992, and the launch of the American erotic magazine *On Our Backs* in 1995.

In 1985, Jeannette Winterson's coming-of age story *Oranges Are Not The Only Fruit* was published, which became one of the most widely-read lesbian novels in Britain. Written in the tradition of lesbian autobiographical novels, the book's depiction of the lesbian protagonist is noteworthy for the way it unapologetically takes for granted lesbian sexuality. In her subsequent books *The Passion* (1987), *Sexing the Cherry* (1989), and *Written on the Body* (1992), Winterson continued to experiment with the narrative form, whilst depicting the often hilarious manifestations of sex.

Lesbian literature of the 1990s is made up of a wide range of different forms and subjects. It includes the haunting poetic voices of the black Scottish poet Jackie Kaye, whose most famous collection of poetry, *The Adoption Papers*, came out in 1991. In the same year the best-selling lesbian American author Katherine V. Forrest published *Flashpoint*, which combines a portrayal of lesbian relationships and contemporary American politics. Contemporary Ireland provided the location for Emma Donaghue's novel *Stir Fry* (1994), which humorously charts a young woman's sexual awakening. Donaghue's second novel *Hood* (1995) engages with issues of love and possessing someone, centerd on the impact of the lesbian protagonist's sudden bereavement. The theorist Judith Halberstam and the queer activist and photographer Del LaGrace Volcano investigate the erotic allure of the drag king in the *Drag King Book* (1998), whilst Patricia Duncker explores the life of the nineteenth-century *James Miranda Barry* (1999), who, born female, lived life as a man to become a doctor, and went undiscovered until her death.

One of the most successful lesbian writers at the beginning of the twenty-first century is Sarah Walters. Her rich and intricate novels are set in Victorian England and follow the emotional and sexual adventures of a variety of lesbian characters. Waters' first publication *Tipping the Velvet* (1998) challenges gender and sexuality stereotypes with the story of the of the Oyster-girl turned music hall star turned tomboy turned activist Nan King. The second novel *Affinity* (1999) charts the mysterious net a female prison inmate draws around her lady visitor. In 2002, Walters published her third novel *Fingersmith*. *Fingersmith* pays a tongue-in-cheek tribute to erotic literature in the figure of a celibate male character who meticulously and obsessively records even the most minor erotic publication to date. The two female heroines, meanwhile, find love and sexual fulfilment with each other.

HEIKE BAUER

Further Reading

Faderman, Lilian. *Surpassing the Love of Men: Romantic Friendship & Love between Women from the Renaissance to the Present*. London: Junction Books, 1984.

Lilly, Mark (ed.). *Lesbian and Gay Writing: An Anthology of Critical Essays*. Basingstoke: Macmillan, 1990.

Hobby, Elaine and Chris White (eds), *What Lesbians Do in Books*. London: The Women's Press, 1991.

Palmer, Paulina. *Contemporary Lesbian Writing: Dreams, Desire, Difference*. Buckingham and Philadelphia, PA: Open University Press, 1993.

Wolfe, Susan J. and Julia Penelope (eds). *Sexual Practice/Textual Theory: Lesbian Cultural Criticism*. Cambridge, MA: Blackwell's, 1993.

De Laurentis, Teresa. *The Practice of Love: Lesbian Sexuality and Perverse Desire*. Bloomington, IN: Indiana University Press, 1994.

Halberstam, Judith. *Female Masculinity*. Durham, NC: Duke University Press, 1998.

Hart, Linda. *Between the Body and the Flesh: Performing Sadomasochism*. New York: Columbian University Press, 1998.

Griffin, Gabriele. *Who's Who in Lesbian and Gay Writing*. London: Taylor and Francis, 2002.

Summers, Claude, J. *The Gay and Lesbian Literary Heritage: A Reader's Companion to the Writers and their Works*. New York: Routledge, 2002.

LÉVEILLÉ, J.R.

1945–
French-Canadian novelist, poet, essayist, visual artist, and television journalist

To date Joseph Roger Léveillé (b. 1945) has published twenty-one books in various genres: novels, short fiction, poetry, and essays. His most unconventional works include assemblages presented as "visual texts" using *collage* that have been published in unusual formats, including a densely printed 40" x 26" poster titled *Extrait*. Léveillé's earliest novels (*Tombeau* and *La disparate*, the latter published under the pseudonym Jesse Janes) and poetry (*Oeuvre de la première mort* and *Le livre des marges*) invoke the polarities of desire and death, artistic creation and latent violence, and while they reveal unmistakably the influence of the French symbolists, notably Rimbaud, they anticipate the qualities that situate his subsequent work in the context of post-modern writing: fragmentation, intertextuality (allusions to other works), and an often playful self-referentiality. Léveillé's early novels share many features with the *nouveau roman* of Michel Butor and Alain Robbe-Grillet, and also with the novels of Samuel Beckett: indeterminacy (the deliberate creation of "blanks" or "gaps" by withholding or contradicting narrative information), abrupt segmentation of plot, and general narrative ambiguity. His later poetry abounds with intertextual references to painting, sculpture, and music as well as literature, while his "visual" works evoke the Dada movements of the 1920s, although Léveillé's texts are much more graphically suggestive and densely scripted. Like his most recent novels, they can be situated in a literature of the extreme, transgressing the framework of literary genre.

Léveillé's eroticism manifests itself in virtually all his works, be it in the sensuality of the narrator's gaze or in the explicit description of sexual experience. It is derived from conceptions of *eros* ranging from Epicure to Zen philosophy, conceptions according to which the erotic is a spiritual practice involving the entire body. Léveillé adopts the Freudian notion that it is the life-affirming erotic impulse (*eros*) that vanquishes *thanatos*, the force of death. Furthermore, *eros*, the force of desire, is inextricably linked to aesthetic creativity, both of which are characterized by a dialectic of presence and absence: the act of writing (rendering present that which is absent) is equated with the fulfillment of erotic desire, in that the author inscribes the "blank page" (an emblem of absence) with the presence of the feminine figure that constitutes at once the subject of the text and the object of desire.

In *Tombeau,* the polarity of *eros* and *thanatos* is thematized in a kind of paradox: the entire narrative is centerd almost obsessively on the female figure whose death (absence) is implicitly overcome by *eros*, the creative act producing the novel itself. In a subsequent novel, *Plage*, the deserted beach and the blank page are metaphors for an absence that is displaced by the virtual presence of the multiplicity of female images that inhabit it. The feminine image is not only the object of the narrator's physical desire, but she also appears as a carrier of cultural meaning: she is compared to a totem, an African statue, an amphora, and as she rises up out of the water, the origin of organic life, she also inspires its aesthetic (re) creation: Botticelli's painting of the birth of Venus comes to mind. *Eros* is thus at once carnal desire and the ultimate source of all life as well as the vehicle for its aesthetic transcendence.

L'Incomparable explodes the borders of literary genre in its assemblage of "fragments" inspired by the Greek poetess Sappho, the

"incomparable" designated in the title. The work can be read both as an essay on the pleasure of the text, echoing French literary theorist Roland Barthes, and as a long lyrical prose poem in which the sensual pleasures of *eros* are inextricably bound up with aesthetic inspiration and the creative act.

Extrait, an enormous poster densely covered in small-print words, some of which appear in primary colors, radicalizes this "poetics of the fragment," both formally and thematically. The words seem to be entirely devoid of context, and there are no syntactic marks such as punctuation. The persistent reader can nevertheless identify a thematic thread in the promise of pleasure and seduction evoked in each one of these decontextualized words, all of which Léveillé has excerpted, collage-style, from advertising. In its exhaustive listing of objects of desire, this mini-inventory of modern day-to-day life parodies and subverts the manipulative strategies of cynically eroticized contemporary advertising while it ironically affirms the timelessness and universality of these objects themselves.

Léveillé takes his exploration of the visual quality of the written text even further in *Montréal poésie*, published in magazine-format, and *Pièces à conviction*. In the preface to the latter, he poses a question that had already been raised by the Dadaists: "Est-il possible d'écrire comme on peint?" In other words, can writing be made to resemble the act (and the effects) of painting? In these densely constructed collage compositions, the signs of language become alienated from their habitual communicative functions. The iconic assumes a significance equal to the semantic, and as in all Léveillé's work, it is charged with erotic signification. In "Corrida," for instance, two roughly parallel, diagonally positioned bars of fragmented text whose shapes resemble the horns of a bull are clearly phallic. In "Prière d'ouvrir grand" [Open wide], the "o" in the center of the page evokes a wide-open eye, but also, due to the text fragments that converge on it, the "opening" that permits penetration and birth.

Léveillé's later poetry, *Les Fêtes de l'infini, Causer l'amour* and *Fastes*, consists for the most part of a joyous celebration of an *eros* grounded in a sensuality negating the rupture between the erotic and emotive and the cognitive and intellectual. Far from constituting an object of sublimation that would undermine erotic desire and its sexual realization, the cultural artefact, be it painting, music, or a work of literature, is closely associated with the love-object and even deliberately confused with it. As in the *chansons des troubadours* of ancient France, cultural emblems become the vehicle that "causes" love in both its erotic and spiritual manifestations. If in these poems it is erotic love and *joie de vivre* that create an "infinite feast" transforming (aestheticizing and eroticizing) everyday life, they are also what inspire their poetic expression.

In his latest prose works, notably in *Nosara*, the sexual act stands at the center of the narrative and is depicted with a rawness and explicitness reminiscent of Henry Miller. Like Miller's Paris novels, the erotic is overlaid with the exploration of cultural alterity, or "otherness," which manifests itself in the choice of setting and in the "other" cultural identity of the narrator's lovers. Unlike Miller's works, however, Léveillé's are characterized by a subtext whose theme is aesthetic perception itself. If the erotic is the union of subject and object of desire, of Self and Other, the aesthetic is the incorporation of the "strange" or unfamiliar with the known, the familiar. Like its erotic counterpart, aesthetic pleasure is not only sensual, but also grounded in the recognition of the Self in the Other. The dialectic of presence and absence found in Léveillé's earlier work here takes the form of oppositional complementarities, expressed in a play of interaction between male and female, yin and yang, light and shadow, figure and ground, in which, in true post-modernist mode, the fictive reality of the narrative is constantly reconstituted.

Biography

Born in Winnipeg, November 10, 1945. Educated at Collège universitaire de St-Boniface, Winnipeg (BA 1966), and University of Manitoba (MA in French literature, 1968). Doctoral studies in French literature, University of Paris (Vincennes) and University of Manitoba (1969–1972). Married Suzanne Corbeil in 1970 (divorced in 1994). Married Christine Gosselin in 2004. Television journalist and producer with Radio-Canada since 1981.

ROSMARIN HEIDENREICH

Selected Works

Parade ou Léveillé sur les autres. Saint-Boniface: Éditions du Blé, 2005.
Nosara. Saint-Boniface: Éditions du Blé, 2003.
Fastes. Ottawa: Bibliothèque canadienne, 2003.
New York trip. Ottawa: L'Interligne, 2003.
Dess(e)ins II Drawings. With Tony Tascona Saint-Boniface: Éditions du Blé, 2001.
Le soleil du lac qui se couche. Saint-Boniface: Éditions du Blé, 2001.
Dess(e)ins avec Tony Tascona. Winnipeg: Éditions Ink Inc., 1999.
Pièces à conviction. Winnipeg: Éditions Ink Inc., 1999.
Une si simple passion. Saint-Boniface: Éditions du Blé, 1997.
Les Fêtes de l'infini. Saint-Boniface: Éditions du Blé, 1996.
Causer l'amour. Paris: Éditions Saint-Germain des Prés, 1993.
Anthologie de la poésie franco-manitobaine. Saint-Boniface: Éditions du Blé, 1990.
Montréal poésie. Saint-Boniface: Éditions du Blé, 1987.
L'incomparable. Saint-Boniface: Éditions du Blé, 1984.
Plage. Saint-Boniface: Éditions du Blé, 1984.
Extrait. Saint-Boniface: Éditions des Plaines, 1984.
Le livre des marges. Saint-Boniface: Éditions des Plaines, 1981.
Oeuvre de la première mort. Saint-Boniface: Éditions du Blé, 1978.
La disparate. Montréal: Éditions du Jour, 1975.
Tombeau. Winnipeg: Canadian Publishers, 1968.

Translated Works

New York Trip. Ottawa/Winnipeg: L'Interligne/Éditions Ink Inc., 2003. *The Setting Lake Sun* [novel], Winnipeg: Signature Editions, 2001.
Dess(e)ins II Drawing(s). With Tony Tascona, St-Boniface: Éditions du Blé, 2001.
Dess(e)ins Drawing(s). With Tony Tascona, Saint-Boniface: Ink Inc, 1999.

References and Further Reading

Annandale, Eric. "La francophonie et l'ouverture à l'Autre: Roger Léveillé, romancier, poète, essayiste." *Cahiers franco-canadiens de l'Ouest.* Vol. 13, No. 2, 2001, pp. 99–108.
Doyon-Gosselin, Benoit. "Autant en emporte les vents: portrait de la Métisse dans *Le soleil du lac qui se couche* de J.R. Léveillé." *Cahiers franco-candiens del'Ouest.* Vol. 14, Nos. 1 and 2, 2002, pp. 243–253.
Dubé, Paul. "Portrait d'auteur: J.R. Léveillé." *Francophonies d'Amérique.* No. 6, 1996, pp.75–84.
Gaboury-Diallo, Lise, Heidenreich, Rosmarin, Valenti, Jean, eds. *Léveillé par les autres.* Saint-Boniface: Les Éditions du Blé, 2005.
Gaboury-Diallo, Lise. "Manifestations du transculturel et du métissage chez Ronald Lavallée et J.R. Léveillé, deux écrivains contemporains du Manitoba

français." *Cahiers franco-candiens de l'Ouest*. Vol. 13, No. 2, 2001, pp. 125–142.

———. "Expression créative et réception critique dans un milieu minoritaire - le cas du Manitoba." In *Toutes les photos finissent-elles par se ressembler? Actes du Forum sur la situation des arts au Canada français*. Sudbury: Prise de parole/l'Institut franco-ontarien, 1999. pp. 123–139.

Hardy, Stéphan. "De la *Genèse* à *Une si simple passion* de Roger Léveillé." *Cahiers franco-canadiens de l'Ouest,* Vol.13, No. 1, pp. 3–35.

Hebert, Raymond. "Essai sur l'identité franco-manitobaine" in *La question identitaire au Canada francophone*. Les Presses de l'Université Laval, 1994, pp. 63–78.

Heidenreich, Rosmarin. *Paysages de désir. L'oeuvre de J.R. Léveillé*. Ottawa: L'Interligne, 2005.

———. "Lecture d'un texte de Roger Léveillé: l'oeuvre littéraire comme objet de consommation." *Les Actes du quatrième colloque du Centre d'études franco-canadiennes de l'Ouest*. Saint-Boniface: CEFCO, 1985, pp. 109–116.

———. "Objet même de son écriture." In *Anthologie de la poésie franco-manitobaine*. Saint-Boniface: Les Éditions du Blé, 1990, pp. 409–415.

———. "Recent Trends in Franco-Manitoban Fiction and Poetry." *Prairie Fire*. Vol. 11, No 1, Spring 1990, pp. 54–63.

———. "Le canon littéraire et les littératures minoritaires: l'exemple franco-manitobain." *Cahiers franco-canadiens de l'Ouest*. Vol. 2, No. 1, printemps 1990, p. 21–29.

———. "Production et réception des littératures minoritaires: le cas des auteurs franco-manitobains." *Francophonies d'Amérique*. No. 1, 1991, pp. 87–97.

———. "Causer l'amour dans le Far-West du Canada: l'oeuvre de J.R. Léveillé." In *Poétiques et Imaginaires (Francopolyphonie littéraire des Amériques)*. Pierre Laurette and Hans-George Ruprecht, eds., Paris: L'Harmattan, 1996, pp. 375–385.

———. "Tout est dans la ligne: *Pièces à conviction* de J.R. Léveillé." In *La francophonie panaméricaine – état des lieux et enjeux. Actes du dix-huitième colloque du Centre d'études franco-canadiennes de l'Ouest*, Presses universitaires de Saint-Boniface, 2000, pp. 137–145.

———. "Nouveaux courants dans la poésie francophone de l'Ouest du Canada." In *Itinéraires de la poésie*. ed. Robert Yergeau, Ottawa: Le Nordir, 2004, pp. 127–141.

Lafontant, Jean. "L'art 'minoritaire': entre les conventions identitaires et l'émancipation." In *Toutes les photos finissent-elles par se ressembler? Actes du Forum sur la situation des arts au Canada français*. Sudbury: Prise de Parole / l'Institut franco-ontarien, 1999. pp. 43–49.

Macdonell, Alan. "Le bon usage dans le roman de l'Ouest" in *Langue et Communication. Actes du 9ᵉ Colloque du Centre d' Études Franco-canadiennes de l'Ouest*. Presses universitaires de Saint-Boniface, 1990, pp. 171–180.

Paré, François. "*Romans. An American in Paris in Montréal: la ville palimpseste de J.R. Léveillé." *University of Toronto Quarterly*. Vol. 70, No. 3, Summer 2001, pp. 727–736.

Roy, Nathalie. "Le religieux dans *Les Fêtes de l'infini* de J.R. Léveillé et *La Beauté de l'affaire* de France Daigle." *Revue internationale d'études canadiennes*. No. 23, Spring 2001, pp. 37–56.

Véron, Laurence. "Entrevue avec J.R. Léveillé, écrivain." *Cahiers franco-canadiens de l'Ouest*. Vol. 13, No. 2, 2001, pp. 159–173.

LEWIS, MATTHEW GREGORY

1775–1818
English novelist, poet, dramatist and legislator

The Monk: A Romance

It was at The Hague in 1794 that Lewis—bored and unable to live within his father's allowance—wrote the novel that earned him the nickname "Monk." Lewis cited as his immediate source the *Santon Barsisa*, a Persian tale published in *The Guardian* in 1713, about a hermit whom Satan tempts to commit rape and murder.

He also drew on German, Danish, and Spanish legends. The strongest inspiration for *The Monk*, however, came from Gothic fiction such as Horace Walpole's *The Castle of Otranto* (1764), William Beckford's *Vathek* (1786), William Godwin's *Caleb Williams* (1794), and especially Ann Radcliffe's *The Mysteries of Udolpho* (1794).

The Monk centers on Ambrosio, a Capuchin abbot in medieval Madrid. Thought to be incorruptible, he succumbs to every imaginable crime, including a lustful affair with Matilda de Villanegas, who has disguised herself as the novice

Rosario; the rape and murder of the beautiful virgin Antonia; the sexually tinged murder of Antonia's mother Elvira Dalfa; and the eventual pledging of his soul to Lucifer, who condemns him to a spectacular death that takes seven days. Lewis interweaves this plot with that of Raymond, the Marquis de las Cisternas, who attempts to rescue his beloved Agnes from her confinement in the convent of St. Clare. Don Lorenzo de Medina, himself smitten with Antonia, assists. Agnes is imprisoned and reported dead by the tyrannical Domina, the public recitation of whose crimes later sparks a riot in which she is torn limb from limb. Agnes is freed to marry Raymond, their child having died in the prison where she gave birth to it; Antonia being dead, Lorenzo marries Virginia de Villa-Franca, another inmate of the convent who has assisted in Agnes's rescue.

The Monk was published anonymously on 12 March 1796 to mostly positive reviews. A second edition came out in July 1796, signed "M.G. Lewis, Esq., M.P." These last two letters scandalized readers, notably Samuel Taylor Coleridge, who shuddered to think that a government representative should have penned such horrors. In a climate dominated by morality police such as William Wilberforce's Proclamation Society, *The Monk* became synonymous with pornography, although today we would not recognize it as such. Threats of prosecution and sales injunctions never materialized—possibly because, for the fourth edition in 1798, Lewis toned down the book's language and deleted a passage in which Ambrosio calls the Bible licentious.

Sexuality in *The Monk* has most commonly been understood in terms of contemporary politics; the Marquis de Sade thought such Gothic enormities clumsy but necessary to express "revolutionary shocks" (*Reflections on the Novel*, 1800). In what appears to be standard French-Revolution anticlericalism, Lewis exposes the monastic repression of healthy sexuality such as Agnes's, and even suggests it has turned Ambrosio and the Domina into deviants. That Ambrosio's crimes include incest—the raped Antonia is his sister, the murdered Elvira his mother—may further allude to the inbred corruption of the *ancien régime*. Others, however, see in Ursula's death the kind of rape-imagery that anti-revolutionary tracts such as Edmund Burke's *Reflections* (1790) employed to express a fear of the mob; or interpret Lewis' Catholic church as symbolic of bourgeois domestic ideology, which similarly subjugates women.

In a more philosophical vein, *The Monk* has been linked to eighteenth-century anxieties about sexual identity and difference. If this period invented sexual dimorphism, as Thomas Laqueur has argued (*Making Sex*, 1990), then *The Monk's* effeminate males, domineering females, and transvestites ("Rosario"/Matilda) imply the instability of the one-sex continuum. Lewis's portrayal of the dangers of sexual desire, moreover, has been read in terms of his all-but-proven homosexuality—something that, unless veiled like *The Monk's* "Rosario"/Ambrosio plot, risked violent persecution by the church, the state, or the mob. Further grounds for *The Monk's* skepticism about sexuality may be found in eighteenth-century theories of the sublime, as advanced by Burke (*Philosophical Enquiry*, 1757) and Immanuel Kant (*Critique of Judgment*, 1790) and reinterpreted by Jacques Derrida (*The Truth in Painting*, 1978). That is, the human body provokes disgust when apprehended as a sensuous object, rather than as a mere doorway to a state—such as death or mutual love—in which subject and object alike are annihilated. Ambrosio's self-aggrandizing lust—beginning with the famous scene in which Matilda exposes her shapely breast and threatens to stab herself if Ambrosio rejects her—consistently turns to loathing; by contrast, the half-dead Agnes remains selflessly devoted to her child even after it putrefies.

The afterlife of *The Monk* has been colorful indeed. In 1798, a parody appeared titled *The New Monk, A Romance*, by "R.S., Esq." The author—possibly Richard Sicklemore—states that his purpose is to ridicule modern immorality and its expression in novels such as Lewis's. *The New Monk* thus relies on humorous substitutions and bawdy innuendo while refraining from the graphic descriptions favored by its predecessor. It takes a topical dig at the alleged erotomania of the Methodists by making its Ambrosio-figure a hellfire preacher, the Rev. Joshua Pentateuch. Rosario/Matilda becomes Peter/Betsy; Antonia, Ann Maria Augusta; Elvira, Olivia; Raymond, Henry Mountfordington; Agnes, Alice; the convent of St. Clare, the boarding school of Mrs. Rod. Having forsworn meat and alcohol, Joshua meets temptation in the form of a talking pork chop. Alice is imprisoned in a wine-cellar, as is Ann, whom Joshua robs rather than rapes. *The Monk* itself crops up in the hands of several characters, including Henry, who notices striking parallels between Raymond's adventures and his own. The tale ends on a cautionary note, however, as Joshua murders both Olivia and Ann before being hanged.

Antonin Artaud hoped to realize *The Monk* as a film but, never getting farther than photographing a series of stills, instead published a novel, *Le moine*, in 1931. Unsure of his command of English, he probably relied on Léon de Wailly's 1840 translation. Artaud's version is, as he himself puts it, "neither a translation nor an adaptation...but a sort of 'copy' in French of the original English text" (17)—or, perhaps more accurately, a drastic abridgement. The erotic passages are substantially identical to Lewis's, although Artaud's brisker pace may be judged either to intensify or to diminish their effect. In one significant departure from Lewis, Artaud adds to Lorenzo's dream of Antonia's demonic abduction a vision of her being "fondled in the most obscene fashion" by a strange man while "she eagerly reciprocate[s]" (37). Generally, Artaud saw *The Monk* as a depiction of what happens when "feeling [is] repressed to its maximum degree"—adding that Lewis exhibits a "sadistic urge" that exceeds Ambrosio's, inasmuch as he erects various "barriers against the natural urges of love" if only to demolish them (17–18). While he found the "shoddy satanism" of its dénouement more "amusing" than compelling, Artaud admired the supernatural elements of Lewis's text for their power to purge "that common residue and excrement of the mind called *reality*" and provide intimations of the eternal (17, 19). The numerous other adaptations of Lewis range from *Zofloya* (1806) by Charlotte Dacre, who used the pseudonym "Rosa Matilda"; to the screenplay *Le moine* (1972) by Luis Buñuel and Jean-Claude Carrière.

Biography

Matthew Gregory Lewis was born in London on 9 July 1775, the eldest of four children from the unhappy marriage of Matthew Lewis and Frances Maria Sewell. Educated at Christ Church College, Oxford, he went to Weimar in 1792–1793, where he met Goethe and became a proficient German scholar. He served as attaché to the British embassy to Holland in 1794; and as M.P. for Hindon, Wiltshire from 1796 to 1802. Lewis inherited his father's sugar plantations in Jamaica upon the latter's death in 1812 and visited there in 1815–1816. A moderate abolitionist, he amended his will in 1816 to finance triennial inspections of his slaves; Percy Shelley, Byron, and Dr. Polidori witnessed the signing at Villa Diodati, Geneva. While returning to England from a second visit to Jamaica in 1818, he contracted yellow fever, from which he died on 14 May. His *oeuvre* of original compositions and translations includes some sixteen works for the stage, half a dozen "romances" and collections of tales, numerous ballads and other poems, and the *Journal of a West India Proprietor*.

ADAM KOMISARUK

Major Editions

The Monk: A Romance. London: J. Bell, 1796.
Ambrosio, or The Monk: A Romance, with Considerable Additions and Alterations. London: J. Bell, 1798.
S[icklemore?], R[ichard?]. *The New Monk: A Romance*. London: Minerva Press, 1798.
The Monk. Ed. Howard Anderson, New York: Oxford University Press, 1973.
Artaud, Antonin. *The Monk*. Trans. John Phillips, New York: Creation Books, 2003.
The Monk: A Romance. Ed. D.L. Macdonald and Kathleen Scherf, Toronto: Broadview Press, 2004.

Other Major Works by Lewis

Village Virtues. 1796.
The Minister. 1797.
The Castle Spectre. 1798.
Rolla; or, The Peruvian Hero. 1799.
The East Indian. 1800.
Adelmorn, the Outlaw. 1801.
Alfonso, King of Castile. 1801.
Tales of Wonder. 1801.
The Bravo of Venice. 1805.
Adelgitha; or, The Fruits of a Single Error. 1806.
Feudal Tyrants; or, The Counts of Carlsheim and Sargans. 1806.
Rugantino; or, The Bravo of Venice. 1806.
The Wood Daemon or "The Clock Has Struck." 1807.
Contributions to Romantic Tales. 1808.
Venoni; or, The Novice of St. Mark's. 1809.
One O'Clock! or, The Knight and the Wood Daemon. 1811.
Timour the Tartar. 1811.
Poems. 1812.
The Harper's Daughter; or, Love and Ambition. 1813.
Rich and Poor. 1814.
Journal of a West India Proprietor. 1815–1817.

Further Reading

Ellis, Kate Ferguson. *The Contested Castle*. Urbana, IL: University of Illinois Press, 1989.

Gamer, Michael. *Romanticism and the Gothic*. New York: Cambridge University Press, 2000.

Hendershot, Cyndy. *The Animal Within: Masculinity and the Gothic*. Ann Arbor, MI: University of Michigan Press, 1998.

Komisaruk, Adam. "Mortal Frames: Desire, Disgust and the Grotesque Body." *Journal of the Association for the Interdisciplinary Study of the Arts* 3.1 (1997): 17–31.

Macdonald, D.L. *Monk Lewis: A Critical Biography*. Toronto: University of Toronto Press, 2000.

Tuite, Clara. "Cloistered Closets: Enlightenment Pornography, the Confessional State, Homosexual Persecution and *The Monk*." *Romanticism on the Net* 8 (November 1997), 6 May 2002 <http://www.erudit.org/revue/ron/1997/v/n8/005766ar.html>.

Paulson, Ronald. *Representations of Revolution 1789–1820*. New Haven, CT: Yale University Press, 1983.

Punter, David. "1789: The Sex of Revolution." *Criticism* 24.3 (1982): 201–217.

LI YU

1611–1680
Chinese novelist

Rou putuan [*The Carnal Prayer Mat*]

Although it was in question for a long time owing to an errroneous dating, attribution of the *Rou putuan* to Li Yu was recently confirmed by the discovery, in Japan, of a manuscript providing its most complete and coherent version, and dating its completion to the year 1657; a period when Li Yu was fully devoting himself to novel-writing. The similarities of the *Rou putuan* with the writings of Li Yu are so numerous that doubt is hardly permitted. That feeling is also strengthened when one reads the commentaries added at the end of each chapter: these confirm that we are here dealing with an author fully mastering his mode of expression, willing to assert his originality and, what is more, willing to tackle the issue of the proper place of sexuality in life from a fresh perspective. In doing so, he displays a stark ability for innovation and a form of imagination which, as he admits in a commentary, "really mocks everything."

During the Zhihe era (1328), a young man of letters by the pseudonym of Vesperus [Weiyangsheng] remains deaf to the advice of a monk called Lone Peak [Gufeng] concerning sexual moderation, and instead gives free rein to a fantasy of his urging him to try and marry the most beautiful woman in the world. Unable to be satisfied with the yet radiant beauty of Jade Scent [Yuxiang], his first wife and the prudish daughter of the austere Confucian greybeard Master Iron Door [Tieshan daoren], Vesperus sets to go hunting again. He is soon assisted by a master bandit and man of genius nicknamed The Knave [Sai-Kunlun], who quickly manages to convince him that the small size of his penis is a bridle to his pretensions. Once he's been surgically transplanted with the penis of a dog, which turns him into a matchless lover, Vesperus moves on to seducing Fragrance [Yanfang], a shopkeeper of ardent nature. Fragrance having eventually become pregnant, Vesperus on the sly conquers Cloud of Scent [Xiangyun], another beauty whom he had spotted long before his operation. The young woman introduces him to three relatives of hers: her aunt, who is a widow, and two "sisters" whose husbands happen to be away at the capital to take part in the official examinations and who have also proved, as husbands, not to be particularly well-gifted for nocturnal jousts. While Vesperus is unrestrainedly carousing with all four women, Fragrance's husband, a merchant by the nickname of Honest Quan [Quan Laoshi], seduces Jade Scent in a bout of revenge and gets her pregnant before selling her to a brothel in the capital, where she rapidly becomes the most sought-after prostitute in the whole Empire. Enticed by her reputation, Vesperus, who by now thinks himself a widower—as his father-in-law was always too ashamed to confess his daughter's elopement,— joins the crowd of patrons who aren't exactly queuing up. But when he finally finds himself ready to get down to the job, the husbands of his various gallant conquests have already had a taste of his legitimate spouse's privileges, and Jade Scent commits suicide to avoid such an embarrassing confrontation with her husband. Realizing, at last, that he's been going astray, Vesperus returns to Lone Peak, the monk who had long ago tried to divert him from his tragic fate. Firmly resolved no longer to follow the winding roads of debauchery, he castrates himself and takes his vows together with a group of new converts, among whom we also find The Knave and Honest Quan.

A summary of the novel may certainly show how subtly Li Yu wove his plot; and in so doing, he actually respected a principle that he would later advocate for playwrighting, namely to build the plot around a key-character and a central action for the story to revolve around [*yi ren yi shi*]. It may also give an idea of the considerable number of saucy scenes that the author managed to accumulate, the effective description of which owes a lot to their variety. However, the strength of the novel lies not as much in what is being narrated as in the way Li Yu chooses to do it. In that regard, any attempt at summarizing eclipses the real innovations of the *Rou putuan*, a novel which continues the tradition of Chinese erotic novels—some of which are duly referred to, such as the *Chi pozi zhuan* [*Biography of a Foolish Woman*], the *Ruyi Jun zhuan* [*The Lord of Perfect Satisfaction*], and the *Xiuta yeshi* [*An Unofficial History of the Embroidered Couch*]—only to better assert its superiority and explore the theme of sexuality even further than they ever did.

The appended commentary pertinently insists not only on the dazzling imagination here at work, but also and above all on the main formal innovations. It has to be conceded that these are indeed sizeable and, as such, amply justify that this novel be considered a masterpiece of Chinese literature in vernacular language.

The first and foremost striking feature of the *Rou putuan* is probably its constantly humorous tone, which naturally resorts to plays on words, but also to learned expressions diverted from their original context. This humorous tone is carried by a remarkably fluid style which puts all the resources of vernacular language to good use. In addition, numerous entertaining metaphors give the narrative texture, such as comparisons between the futile resort to doping by candidates at the mandarin examinations and the illusory use of aphrodisiacs for sexual jousts by mediocre lovers, or between the art of literary composition and the practice of copulation. Li Yu furthermore very skillfully inserts digressions [*yilun*] in the narrative, sometimes even in the very height of a sex scene asides that gives him the opportunity to express his views on a variety of subjects including sexual practices, thereby turning the reader into some cat on a hot tin roof and reinforcing his/her interest in the story, the narration of which eventually resumes as if nothing had happened.

The novel combines such control of the output with perfect mastery in organizing the situations, many of the latter being chosen according to the surprise effect they may be able to trigger. Scenes of that kind are truly surprizing and often comical; an example among others would be when Fragrance has Vesperus's sexual capacities secretly tested by her neighbor, who happens to be an excessively ugly woman. The effect that Li Yu draws from them is all the more powerful since the novel's chapters are all designed as independent episodes further assembled into a methodically organized progression, exactly the way they would in a theater play. Li Yu starts off by putting the reader into the comfortable position of a mere voyeur amused at the doings of a thoughtless young man so as to, later, better have him/her feel the horror of a tragic paroxysm which consummates the ruin of illusions, the latter eventually provoking the final revelation. Behind the novelist concerned with his effects, one feels the mark of the dramatist who presides over the destinies of his characters.

The number of characters is deliberately limited and reduced to a typology which characterizes Li Yu's works and which mainly operates on straight-forward oppositions between characters with clearly marked tempers. Thus, the rigoristic Confucian father who locks his daughter up to protect her from the dangers of the outside world contrasts with the open-minded bandit who frees himself from the barriers of privacy. In that regard, the character of The Knave who, ridding himself of all barriers, offers a forthright viewpoint on the sexual reality of his contemporaries, is a real find. Besides, by providing the hero with the means for his emancipation, The Knave is actually at the origin of Vesperus's career as a great seducer. But the *tour de force* of this moral tale certainly lies in the recourse to surgery—a practice literally poles apart from traditional Chinese medical science—which in the novel enables a young man (of originally mediocre capacities, when all is said and done) to become a top-grade stallion through the transplant of an animal sex organ. As the commentary indicates, it is indeed "complete aberration, which invites us to see the hero's feats as purely bestial acts." And at the same time as he turns his main character into an outstanding lover, the author also warns his reader of the dangers the latter would face were he/she to take the story he/she is so brilliantly being told too literally. "Fiction," the commentary informs us, "is parable."

The lesson to be learned, which could be summed up by the injunction that one should remain moderate in matters of sex, is not only expressed using the allegorical mode and through the commentaries, but also, very surprisingly and in an original way, in a long essay that takes up the entire first chapter of the novel. That essay is in fact the preamble of a far more comprehensive treatise, the elements of which are provided to the reader in the numerous dialogues that punctuate the story, forming a real *ars erotica* that goes much further than a mere introduction and gives the novel a true educational and moral character.

Li Yu used to describe his *Wushengxi* as "a refreshing drink in a house on fire." The *Rou putuan* actually offers all the characteristics of a "silent comedy"; it is namely a book which, under cover of an erotic comedy likely to enthrall even the most *blasé* of readers, brings along original and disturbing views on a hotly debated subject. Of higher moral qualities than it may appear on the first reading, the novel was conceived according to a process that Li Yu unveils in the introduction: the elevated, varied, and sensual narrative, rich in licentious episodes, is supposed to be "like the date wrapped around the bitter olive which, alone, brings each and everyone to eventually experience the flavour of the fruit it conceals." Recourse to this kind of technique proves necessary, according to the

author, in such times of trouble when "moral books" would serve only to "cover winepots or light pipes."

The impact of the *Rou putuan* was tremendous at the time it was first released, and later on as well. Despite quickly becoming the target of a formal ban, the novel nonetheless continued to be circulated under various titles. Its influence on Chinese novel-writing, and mainly on that of erotic novels, was also considerable. Many a pattern, and even whole passages borrowed from it are to be found in other works. Yet, the *savoir-faire* it displays was never equalled, nor even really copied.

The same way as Li Yu's entire work is some sort of comet in the field of Chinese letters, this novel is a constellation of its own in that of Chinese erotic literature.

Biography

Li Yu (1611–1680) is a quite original and astounding figure in the history of Chinese letters. As it is, his work and contribution widely exceed the sole field of literature. After failing three times the examination to what then was the step before last to an official position, the Bachelor's degree, Li Yu soon (probably around 1642) abandoned any hope of making a career in the Imperial administration. He subsequently withdrew from society for a while, before taking up various activities which were to become his only source of income until the end of his lifetime.

Throughout his life, Li Yu mingled with high-level officials; from his early days when he was living in the Jinhua prefecture of Zhejiang province, and later in Hangzhou, where he stayed from the beginning of the 1650's before settling in Nanjing ten years later. He was to return from that city only in the spring of 1677, to spend his last years by the shores of the East Lake in Hangzhou, a place which remains intimately tied to his most famous penname: "The Old Fisherman by the Lakeside" [Hushang liweng].

But although he would often associate with officials, Li Yu nonetheless made a living from what his prolific imagination could yield, much more than from the occasional support that some of these friends would grant him. And being an inveterate hedonist, he always took great care in creating a suitable environment for himself and his large household to live in, often squandering the fruits of his inventiveness as fast as he had earned them.

Proof of Li Yu's ever-fermenting creativity is not only to be found in the field of writing, but also in that of publishing, as he, over the years, set up several publishing studios through which he issued his own works, as well as that of garden design and theater direction. All these activities led him to travel extensively across the Chinese Empire in search of contracts. And while, as a true charmer and captivating narrator gifted with pleasant conversation, he graciously bowed to the necessities of society, he would however never let go of his taste for provocation which, for instance, led him to put several of his very own concubines on stage and direct them as a theater group. Such actions tarnished his reputation for good and definitely draped his name and work with an aura of scandal. As a result, he was truly rediscovered only as late as the end of the Twentieth Century.

Li Yu, it has to be conceded, is a puzzling character: he was as innovative regarding his works as he was regarding daily life. The initiator of an art of living which places the pursuit of pleasure and of harmony above all the constraints of Confucian society, he would always seek to convince others of the validity of his own beliefs and share his tastes. In doing so, he would also unhesitatingly display his loss of affection for right-thinking routine, just as he would often hunt down generally accepted ideas. Put back in the context of a traumatic dynastic shift which ended with the setting up of Mandchu power (1644), his attitude is actually one of unequalled boldness. No longer part of the literati, as he was tuned into the world of business (publishing, design, theater management and direction), and yet not completely a businessman either, since he always kept in touch with literati circles (although his interest led him to the fringe of official culture), he somehow opened a new way which turned out to match his audacity and talent. The fact that he managed to keep his course certainly owes a lot to a strong personality blessed with wily optimism, but also to his fundamental conception according to which "there are no more major genres than there are minor ones; the important question is whether one excels in the genre one has chosen or not."

Li Yu's written production is in the image of the rowdy and bubbling nature of its creator.

It naturally appears profuse and original, but also provocative and laced with constantly underlying humor and irony. In as much as Li Yu would support the whole of it with unvarying fervor and took pleasure in constantly enriching it by implicitly or openly coming to the fore, it is thus difficult to take up one aspect of his work without referring to its entirety, and, even more so, to the author. For ages, Li Yu's work was however reduced to its most acceptable part.

Yet, it would be extremely inaccurate to limit its highlights, as many still often do, only to the two introductory books of his collection of open essays, the *Xianqing ouji* [*Casual Expressions of Idle Feeling*]. Besides this major treatise on dramatic art, the value of which has been prized ever since it was first published in 1671, Li Yu actually left a work covering the whole spectrum of literary genres that were valued at that time, ranging from poetry, an art which he practiced with much liberty and talent, to essay-writing and to theater, the latter genre being his favorite: he left us no less than ten successful comedies that were highly rated in his days.

He, who every single time had brought new life into genres that were being neglected or were losing momentum, could not possibly have avoided getting to grips with the art of writing novels in vernacular language, at some stage. He eventually did so, with consummate aptness and stunning mastery that were crowned with success. Within a period of three to four years, Li Yu thus managed to compose three collections of short stories and one novel in twenty chapters, delivering a work of remarkable coherence, revealing his will to offer a readership fond of novelty some quality entertainment while at the same time developing new forms of expression.

This work starts with the publication of two collections of tales entitled *Wushengxi* [*Silent Comedies*], probably between 1654 and 1656. The second issue, made up of only six fairly developed stories already shows real progress as compared to the first one, which consisted of twelve shorter pieces written in a form that was taking liberties with the traditional *huaben* format. Li Yu's style further evolves into an even more refined form of narrative with the publication of *Shi'er lou* [*Twelve Towers*], (1658) three years later, which offers twelve stories no longer told in one go but now organized in chapters. In these stories, the fading away of the oral form of the tale [*huaben*] inherited from the tradition of public storytellers and taken up by late-Ming literati such as Feng Menglong (1574–1645) and Ling Mengchu (1580–1644) becomes even more obvious, making room for a form of literary expression deliberately meant to be read silently. In addition, this new approach to the genre owes a lot to Li Yu's innate sense of comedy and taste for theater. His choice of uncalled for and sometimes shocking situations, of eccentric characters, of issues viewed from innovative angles, and subject to thematic variations in which humor and irony blend together, gives Li Yu's ever-evolving work a unique flavour. The maturity of its ultimate stage—which Li Yu probably considered impossible to surpass—certainly owes a lot to the practice of novel-writing. To an author seemingly unable to be satisfied with the marginalia and end-of-chapter commentaries which he used to lard his texts with from the early days, the cutting up of the story into chapters, in that respect, allows for even more elbow room to manuever. This way, he could insert his voice in the very narrative, through digressions or racy interventions in which humor vies with mischievousness, nay self-advertising. These two collections, which together total thirty short stories, constitute Li Yu's "official" literary work, and after signing them he incidentally started embodying a new type of literati as he, on several occasions, showed ready to defend his copyright—as author and publisher—before the law, against rather unscrupulous booksellers. Yet, he already ventures to throw in a few saucy stories and scatologic details when he, for instance, wishes to illustrate the superiority of a countrywoman's sense of wit on a highwayman's deceitfulness (W I 5), the love of an effeminate young boy for his friend that leads him to emasculate himself (W I 6), the jealousy of a husband titillated by an impish friend during a drinking binge (W II 10), the sensuality of a naiad (S 4), or the frigidity of a wife in need of attention (S 8). However, the overall tone and content remain formally acceptable and good-mannered, as if care had been taken all along to remain within the limits of correctness. Such self-restraint must certainly have turned out to be extremely frustrating for an author who had repeatedly displayed his will to blow up all barriers, both formal and thematical! These barriers, he eventually did blow up; by writing the *Rou putuan*.

PIERRE KASER
Translated From The French
by Victor Thibaut

Selected Works

Translations

Wushengxi
Li Yu. *A mari jaloux, femme fidèle*. Kaser, Pierre (trans.), Arles: Editions Philippe Picquier, "Picquier Poche" n° 95, (1990) 1998, 268 p.
Li Yu. *Silent Operas*. Hanan, Patrick (ed.), Hong Kong: The University of Hong Kong, "*Renditions* Paperbaks." 1990, xiii+201 p.

Shi'er lou
Li Yu. *A Tower for the Summer Heat*. Hanan, Patrick (trans.), New York: Ballantine Books, 1992, xv + 249 p.

Rou putuan
Li Yu. *The Carnal Prayer Mat* [*Rou Putuan*]. Hanan, Patrick (trans.), New York, Ballantine Books, 1990, xiv +316 p. Reprint: Honolulu: University of Hawai'i Press, 1996, xiv + 317 p.

Further Readings

Hanan, Patrick. *The Invention of Li Yu*. Cambridge, MA: Harvard University Press, 1988, 272 p.
Chang Chun-shu, Chang, Shelley. *Crisis and Transformation in Seventeenth-Century China: Society, Culture and Modernity in Li Yü's World*. Ann Arbor, MI: The University of Michigan Press, 1992, x + 452 p.
Kaser, Pierre. *L'œuvre romanesque de Li Yu (1611–1680). Parcours d'un novateur*. Université de Paris VII, 1994. 588 p. [*Unpublished PhD*]
———. "Présentation et traduction des commentaires du *Rou putuan*." in Dars, Jacques, Chan Hingho, *Comment lire un roman chinois*. Arles: Editions Philippe Picquier, 2001, pp. 182–196.

LIBERTINISM

Historically, the libertine novel is a literary phenomenon of the French eighteenth century. The earliest examples were inspired by the Regency (1715–1723) but written and published under Louis XV, while the last ones were written during the French Revolution, notably by the Marquis de Sade. The end of Louis XIV's reign stood under the influence of the austere and religious Madame de Maintenon, and when the king died the court happily anticipated more joyous times, welcoming the Regency style. Free from Versailles etiquette and the centralized power wielded by the self-proclaimed Sun-King, the aristocracy flocked to Paris in search of renewed pleasures. The libertine novel signals this renewal of exuberant and frivolous attitudes, opposed to the strict morality enforced at Versailles after the Revocation of the Edict of Nantes.

The two main branches of the genre end with the French Revolution. The *mondain* libertine novel, an aristocratic genre *par excellence*, declined when French aristocrats were guillotined or went into exile. At the same time, erotic or obscene libertine novels became political, taking the shape of pro- or anti-revolutionary or anti-royalist pamphlets directed against Louis XVI or against the very unpopular Marie-Antoinette.

The English term "libertine" encompasses the French *libertin* (masculine) and *libertine* (feminine). The type and its associated thought and behavior are not an eighteenth-century invention: there had been libertines in the previous century. However, some contemporary critics insist on a distinction between *libertinage érudit* [erudite libertinism] in the seventeenth century and *libertinage des mœurs* (libertinism of behavior) in the eighteenth century. The erudite libertines were more explicitly anti-religious and more articulate in their philosophical views, although they were also condemned for their sexuality, most notably the practice of sodomy, and their general turpitude. The second-wave libertines appear less concerned with abstract philosophical systems and more directly interested in sexual freedom, but they did have newer systems of beliefs. Theirs was an age that claimed frivolity as a philosophical tenet: far from being avoided or hidden, frivolity was now claimed as a moral and philosophical principle. It was appreciated not only by novelists and writers of fairy tales but also by philosophers who saw in the frivolous an ideal means to practice one of the fundamental tenets of the Enlightenment—didacticism. Jean-Jacques Rousseau, better known for his sentimental *Julie; ou, la nouvelle Héloïse* [*Julie; or, The New Eloise*] (1761) and his political treatises, such as *Du contrat social; ou, principes du droit politique* [*Of the Social Contract; or, Principles of Political Right*] (1762) also wrote a fairy tale, *La reine fantasque* [*The Whimsical Queen*] (1758). Voltaire also wrote dozens of philosophical tales of oriental inspiration, and Denis Diderot, the coeditor of the *Encyclopédie*, wrote a libertine novel in the oriental vein, *Les bijoux indiscrets* [*The Indiscreet Jewels*] (1748). The libertine side of otherwise prestigious Enlightenment philosophers was often erased from official histories of French literature: *The Indiscreet Jewels*, a novel in which a sultan who possesses a magic ring can make women's sex ("the jewels") speak, was ignored for nearly two centuries. Diderot's writing a libertine novel has often been attributed to his dire financial situation, a myth created by the philosopher's daughter and by his friends after his death. It is now universally acknowledged that Diderot's libertine novel in fact makes an important contribution to his political and philosophical program. In his *Histoire de la sexualité* [*History of Sexuality*] (1976) Michel Foucault analyzed Diderot as a key witness to the sudden increase in discourses on sexuality in the eighteenth century, although it has now also been recognized that the sexual discourse provided by the jewels are highly biased, as no male "jewel" ever confessed in eighteenth-century libertine fiction.

But if libertinism is rife among eighteenth-century novelists and philosophers, there is no real consensus about what exactly constitutes the "libertine novel." The word *libertine* refers to a whole range of types: on the one hand, the free-thinking spirit who claims an individual right to knowledge, advocates free inquiry, and refuses the precepts of the Church; and on the other, a person who claims as inalienable the right to individual pleasure and sexual gratification outside the moral norms imposed by society. The expression "libertine novel" is just as problematic: to qualify, does the libertine novel have to be about *libertins and libertines*, or should the text itself be libertine? In other words, does its ideological program have to follow the precepts advocated by libertines themselves? Rather than reading this apparent confusion as a restriction, I will concentrate on the variety and richness of a genre that remains one of the most distinguishable features of a century that is mostly remembered as "philosophical" but that proudly claimed to be at once libertine and frivolous.

The libertine novel is polymorphous: it can be an epistolary novel, a memoir-novel, a novel in dialogue form, in the first or third person, and so on. The genre has often been split into two main categories: the *mondain* novel (also sometimes called the *galant*) and the erotic libertine novel. The *mondain* novel is often associated with the aristocracy, and it takes the form of confession-memoirs relating the coming of age of young male aristocrats. Prominent examples are *Confessions du comte de **** [*The Confession of Count ****] (1741) by Charles Pinot-Duclos and *Les égarements du cœur et de l'esprit* [*The Wayward Head and Heart*] by Crébillon *fils* (not to he confused with his father, Crébillon, a once-famous playwright now mainly forgotten). Other *mondain or galant* libertine novels include such epistolary novels as Claude-Joseph Dorat's *Les sacrifices de l'amour* [*The Sacrifices of Love*], *Les malheurs de l'inconstance* [*The Sorrows of Fickleness*] (1772), and the most popular eighteenth-century French novel, Choderlos de Laclos's *Les liaisons dangereuses* (1782). The epistolary genre was a favorite form of the libertine *mondain* novel as it allowed greater manipulation of characters, the plot unfolding at the same time as the writing of the letter. Better than any other genre, epistolary novels allow libertines to manipulate their prey by controlling not only what they do but ultimately what they read, write, and think. Writing thus becomes the

epistolary libertines' lethal weapon but also the cause of their demise—the Marquise de Merteuil's downfall in *Les Liaisons dangereuses* is brought about by the very same letters that had empowered her.

Erotic libertine novels such as Crébillon *fils*'s *Le sopha* [*The Sofa*], Diderot's *Indiscreet Jewels*, and La Morlière's *Angola* (1746; *Angola: An Eastern Tale*) include more or less thinly veiled sexual allusions. Because of Antoine Galland's translation of *Les mille et une nuits* [*The Arabian Nights*] at the beginning of the eighteenth century, erotic libertine novels often draw on fashionable orientalist themes. They are often dialogues: a *libertin* reads an oriental and salacious tale to the countess he would like to seduce (as in *Angola*), or, in *The Sofa*, an oriental narrator tells a sultan and his sultana of his adventures when, transformed into a sofa, he was able to witness many libertine adventures. These pseudo-oriental novels are often satirical, and the erotic possibilities of the dialogue are never exploited. In fact, the tone is often amused or sarcastic: in Crébillon's novel, the stupidity of the male omnipotent sultan stands in contrast to the refinement of his sultana. La Morlière prefers not to give any clue as to the success of his libertine and leaves the novel unfinished (a libertine characteristic) by declaring that, unfortunately, the editor has not been given the last part of the manuscript.

Still ignored or rejected by some critics, the obscene libertine novel represents at once the most striking and popular genre of the eighteenth century. If some recent critics are still reluctant to attribute any value to these texts of the "second shelf" (as some French critics have referred to them), obscene novels better exemplify those definitions of the word libertine that include a philosophical dimension. As Robert Darnton has shown, these texts were "philosophical" at the time, and orders from the clandestine book trade included, side by side on the same list, works by philosophers (Diderot, Rousseau, Voltaire) and obscene texts, all under the same category of "philosophical texts" (see Darnton, 1995). Even so, historians have preferred to ignore the erotic output to concentrate on the philosophical impact of the eighteenth century on contemporary France. Yet the proliferation of philosophical writings coincides, after 1740, with a sudden increase in obscene texts. The vast production and numerous reprintings of obscene libertine novels throughout the century attest to their undeniable popularity.

While the first obscene novels were usually dialogues—*L'École des filles* [*The School for Girls*] in 1655 and *L'Académie des Dames* (Women's Academy), first in Latin and in French in 1680—the eighteenth-century obscene libertine novel may also be epistolary, written in the first or third person, a memoir-novel, dialogues, or even very close to drama. The first obscene bestseller of the Enlightenment was *Histoire de D[om Bougre], Portier des Chartreux* [*History of Dom Bougre*] (1740) by Gervaise de Latouche, a book which Adélaïde, daughter of Louis XV, appreciated so much that she wanted to share it with her brother. Their father intervened. *Dom Bougre* even spawned an entire obscene dynasty: later in the century, his sister's raunchy confessions were also published as *Mémoires de Suzon, sœur de Dom Bougre* [*Memoirs of Suzon, Sister of Dom Bougre*] (1777) as were his niece's memoirs, *Histoire de Marguerite, fille de Suzon, nièce de Dom Bougre* (1784; History of Marguerite). The most popular obscene novel throughout the eighteenth century, published the same year as John Cleland's *Fanny Hill*, was *Thérèse philosopbe* [*The Philosophical Thérèse*] (1748), attributed to Boyer d'Argens. It tackles the philosophical problems of human nature, temperament, and social organization and is written in an anti-clerical vein. It was reprinted throughout the century, and Sade even calls it the first truly immoral book in his *Juliette* (1797). Then came Fougeret de Monbron's *Margot la ravaudeuse* [*The Amorous Adventures of Margot*], Andréa de Nerciat's *Félicia; ou, Mes fredaines* [*Félicia; or, My Mischief*] and many other scantily dressed confessions.

Contrary to the first (*mondain* or *galant*) or even the second (erotic) *libertinage*, these obscene novels depict characters who either are not of aristocratic origin or do not function in the aristocratic world. And while *libertinage mondain* is interested in male rites of passage organized by more mature women, the obscene *libertinage* focuses mainly, although not exclusively, on female rites of passage (two exceptions include *Dom Bougre* and *Le libertin de qualité* [*The Noble Libertine*], attributed to Honoré Gabriel de Mirabeau, whose young hero becomes a gigolo). In obscene *libertinage*, female protagonists

either end up in prison or lead a happy life enlightened by philosophy, as is the case with Thérèse.

Whether the novels belong to what today we would call pornography (a word first used in the nineteenth century) or to the more prestigious genre of *mondain* boudoir pre-Sadean libertinism, they share with Enlightenment philosophers one common concern—pedagogy. All libertine novels are mainly about the education of young men and women and their entry into the world of conventional aristocracy. Consequently, the moral implications of the erotic component are not only indirect but also sly: working against the grain of morality, the libertine novel deals primarily with the non-oppositional integration of new members into a society whose rules are not to be changed. By its nature and its objective (as a *Bildungsroman*), the libertine novel is faced with a dilemma: how can novels pretend to be at once libertine (i.e., oppositional) and also portray the efforts of heroes and heroines (aristocrats or future prostitutes, male and female) to fit into that particular society? This contradiction is often reflected in the closure of libertine novels: libertine heroes and heroines either eventually find "true love" and live happily ever after, or else they end up disfigured like Laclos's Marquise de Merteuil. Similarly, the heroes and heroines of the obscene branch end up happily married or diseased, locked up or castrated. In other words, they are either completely rejected or just as completely adopted by a society that remains untainted by unruly, but temporary, sexual prowess and practices.

Undoubtedly the most notorious libertine author from the eighteenth century remains the Marquis de Sade, nicknamed the Divine Marquis. While locked up in the infamous Bastille (accused, among other things, of incest and numerous murders), Sade wrote among the most philosophical and most cruel of libertine novels. The libertine tradition culminates in Sade, who united in his work the old (and rather artificial) divide between the libertinism of credo and of behavior: his works are at once philosophical (notably atheist) and they list with a sometimes suspicious complacency endless varieties of sexual practices that usually involve cruelty. In addition to being among the most prolific libertine authors, Sade is the eighteenth-century writer whose work has been the most analyzed by members of the twentieth-century French intelligentsia, from Georges Bataille, Maurice Blanchot, and Pierre Klossowski to Jean Paulhan and Roland Barthes. Sade wrote in many genres, from short stories, *Les crimes de l'amour* [*The Crimes of Love*] (1800) to epistolary fiction, *Aline et Valcour; ou, Le roman philosophique*, 1795. His most famous productions are *Les 120 journées de Sodome* [*The 120 Days of Sodom*], *Justine; ou, les malheurs de la vertu* [*Justine; or, The Misfortunes of Virtue*], (1791) *Histoire de Juliette; ou, les prospérités du vice* (1797) [*Juliette*], and *La philosophie dans le boudoir* [*Philosophy in the Bedroom*] (1795). Sade's novels, still banned in the 1950s, are now being edited for the prestigious Bibliothèque de la Pléiade, a literary Pantheon immortalizing the classics of French literature. After editions causing much publicized lawsuits leading to the condemnation in 1957 of publisher Jean-Jacques Pauvert, this collection, printed on a paper referred to as "Bible paper" because of its thinness, marks an ironically fitting fortune for the "Divine Marquis."

Ultimately, the libertines exemplify the paradoxical relationship between the Enlightenment and new forms of morality and sexual ethics. Both fiercely aristocratic and *mondain*, the libertine novel also found comfort in heroes and heroines who reacted against the strict norms imposed by the Church. Ultimately, however, libertines were not allowed to oppose the state apparatus that had allowed the French aristocracy to survive and dominate for so long. Everyone agreed that changes were necessary, but libertines who did not conform were expelled, imprisoned, or maimed. It is not clear, however, if the reason for such closures was strictly moral or if the power to eliminate opposition so drastically was a case of wishful thinking, the last respite of

an arrogant and refined class that felt its power and authority were already undermined, as the 1789 revolution would soon confirm.

JEAN MAINIL

Further Reading

Brooks, Peter. *The Novel of Worldliness: Crébillon, Marivaux, Laclos, Stendhal.* Princeton, NJ: Princeton University Press, 1969.

Cazenobe, Colette. *Le système du libertinage de Crébillon à Laclos.* Oxford: Voltaire Foundation, 1991.

Cryle, Peter. *Geometry in the Boudoir: Configurations of French Erotic Narrative.* Ithaca, NY: Cornell University Press, 1994.

Darnton, Robert. *The Forbidden Bestsellers of Pre-Revolutionary France.* New York and London: Norton, 1995.

DeJean, Joan. *Libertine Strategies: Freedom and the Novel in Seventeenth-Century France.* Columbus, OH: Ohio State University Press, 1981.

DeJean, Joan. *Literary Fortifications: Rousseau, Laclos, Sade.* Princeton, NJ: Princeton University Press, 1984.

Feber, Michel (editor). *The Libertine Reader: Eroticism and Enlightenment in Eighteenth-Century France.* New York: Zone Books, 1997.

Goulemot, Jean-Marie. *Forbidden Texts: Erotic Literature and Its Readers in Eighteenth-Century France.* Translated by James Simpson, Cambridge: Polity Press, and Philadelphia, PA: University of Pennsylvania Press, 1994.

Hunt, Lynn. *The Family Romance of the French Revolution.* Berkeley, CA: University of California Press, and London: Routledge, 1992.

Hunt, Lynn (editor). *The Invention of Pornography: Obscenity and the Origins of Modernity, 1500–1800.* New York: Zone Books, 1993.

Kearney, Patrick J. *A History of Erotic Literature.* London: Macmillan, 1982.

Laroch, Philippe. *Petits-maitres et roués: Évolution de la notion de libertinage dans le roman français du XVIIIe siècle.* Québec: Presses de l'Université Laval, 1979.

Trousson, Raymond (editor). *Romans libertins du XVIIIe siècle.* Paris: Laffont, 1993.

Wagner, Peter. *Eros Revived: Erotica of the Enlightenment in England and America.* London: Secker and Warburg, 1988.

LIBRARIES

The preservation of many works of erotic literature has frequently depended on the complex interactions not only of booksellers, collectors, and scholars, but also of police and customs agents, all of whom erratically deposited books considered morally questionable and culturally worthless in those few libraries willing to house and even to hide them. Many books never made it into libraries, of course, and have been lost. Those which did remained vulnerable to theft, mutilation, neglect, and removal by censors. Today, archival policies are more enlightened and acquistions of modern examples of popular works are more Catholic, but gaps in the world's erotic heritage are legion.

Major Repositories

Despite a persistent rumor probably started inadvertently by Alfred Kinsey, who joked to a visitor that the Kinsey Institute for Research in Sex, Gender, and Reproduction owned the largest collection of erotic books outside of the Vatican, the Vatican Library has never compiled an archive of erotica, though it does own a few important volumes. The largest and most legendary repositories of classic erotic books, that is, those published in various western (and a much smaller number of oriental) languages prior to the early twentieth century, are in four major institutions: the British Museum Library (London), the Bibliothèque Nationale (Paris), the Library of Congress (Washington), and the Kinsey Institute for Research in Sex, Gender, and Reproduction (University of Indiana, Bloomington). For obvious reasons, these libraries exercise some control over access to erotica collections. Scholars should attempt to ascertain ahead of time the holdings of particular archives by using published guides and bibliographies, beginning perhaps with Deakin's bibliography of bibliographies.

British Museum (BM): The core collection of the British Museum Library, the so-called Private Case, was assembled by Henry Spencer Ashbee, greatest of bibliographers of English erotic literature, then supplemented by the collections of Edward Phelips, once housed in the Guildhall Libary but transferred to the BM in 1950, and Charles Reginald Dawes, part of which was transferred to the BM in 1964. According to Paul Cross, deaccessions and losses had, by 1991, reduced the number of items in the archive to 2,143, of which Patrick J. Kearney's *The Private Case* (1981) lists 1,939 (Cross, 225). Kearney's long-promised second volume of his bibliography will trace those lost and missing. The collection, which boasts such early examples as "Antonia's" *The Crafty Whore* (1658), an English adaptation of Aretino's *Ragionamenti*, is unparalleled, and previously unnoted manuscripts and troves of ballads and bawdy poems turn up from time to time. Students attempting to locate similar English-language items in other libraries should consult Alfred Rose's still useful *Register of Erotic Books* (originally issued under the name Rolf S. Reade in 1936), a bibliography of 5,061 entries compiled from shelflists in the British Museum, with interpolations from the Bodleian Library at Oxford University, the Cambridge University Library, the Vatican, and a few other minor English archives.

Bibliothèque Nationale: The French national library began depositing erotic books in a special "Hell" section during the Napoleonic era. In 1991, according to Cross (225), the L'Enfer collection of the Bibliothèque Nationale contained roughly 1500 books, of which 108 were in English. Most of the rest, though many nationalities are represented, are examples of classic French erotic literature from the seventeenth, eighteenth, and nineteenth centuries. The 1998 revision of Pascal Pia's first (1975) edition of *Les Livres de L'Enfer*, itself an updating of earlier guides, has been supplemented by 200 additions from the Roger Peyrefitte and Michel Simon collections. Digitalization has helped the

Bibliothèque Nationale to integrate books from L'Enfer into its main online catalog, which makes searching much easier.

Library of Congress: Integration is also the practice of the Library of Congress. Where once access to erotic books in the so-called Delta (or Blue) section was limited, the Library now catalogues its items with the main collections. SCORPIO (the LC online catalog) lists them by author, title, and subject. That has been a rational strategy for coping with the flood of erotic books into the Library since the 1960s, when the waning of censorship led publishers of erotic books to apply for copyrights they previously would have not sought out of fear of prosecution; copyrighting a work requires that one copy be deposited at the Library of Congress. On the other hand, dispersal of restricted materials has sometimes meant that scholars have to search more diligently for items considered erotic.

Kinsey Institute: The Kinsey Institute houses the world's most concentrated collection of sexual materials: books, journals, reprints, ephemera, art, artifacts, film, photographs, data, and biographies, many of which are unique. Its erotic fiction sub-collection is replete with manuscripts, folklore, and classic bound volumes in many languages, some from the Dawes Collection, some deaccassioned duplications from the BM's Private Case, some from European collections, notably many volumes spirited away from the library of Berlin's Institut für Sexualwissenschaft before it was destroyed by the Nazis in the early 1930s. American works are impressively represented by imprints from pre-Civil War publishers to modern pulp houses. Especially valuable are the vertical files containing dealer catalogs and flyers; these old and new brochures indicate what sort of materials have circulated over time. The Kinsey's photography archives are the world's largest, with more than 70,000 individual prints, and its erotic film collections, especially strong in stag films, are the world's most historically comprehensive. Rooms hold erotic art and artifacts both Oriental (e.g., a phenomenal group of Japanese erotic woodcuts) and western. The electronic catalog is available on-line. Scholars can use it to locate specific texts, but extensive searches of particular genres of erotica, some of which have not been fully indexed, even under the Kinsey

Library's unique nomenclature and descriptors, require the services of staff that includes anthropologists, sociologists, and psychologists. Research libraries throughout the world own the 120 microfilm reels of the Institute's mostly eighteenth- and nineteenth-century materials (novels, joke collections, woodcuts, scholarly works, etc.), but the microfilm set and its index, *Sex Research*, do not reflect additions deposited since 1983. Staff members, however, continuously revise and update bibliographies available for purchase.

To these four major institutions might in the future be added two others. The first is the Russian State Library (formerly the Lenin Library) in Moscow. Nikolai Skorodumov, deputy director of the Moscow State University Library, assembled 11,000 items of erotica (books, postcards, artwork, articles, pamphlets, and objects), which were moved to the Lenin Library in 1947. These and subsequent additions have never been catalogued, but visitors claim to have seen erotic poems by Lermontov and Pushkin, samizdat versions of erotic novels from the 1920s that were clandestinely circulated in the Soviet Union, and various erotic books from the West, some seized by authorities, others donated by collectors (Schmidt). Strong sub-collections of folk tales, chastushka (short rhymed folk songs), and barkoviana (bawdy burlesque poetry, a Russian version of an eighteenth-century French genre) are also likely. Eventually, these archives may revise the longstanding conviction that Russia and Slavic countries produced no erotica of note.

Second in potential are the erotica collections of the Institute for Advanced Study of Human Sexuality in San Francisco, which has followed an admirable policy of gathering chiefly modern ephemeral publications before they could be lost. The success of the strategy, however, has resulted in prolonged storage of thousands of uncatalogued materials literally in warehouses in widely dispersed locations. Eventually, students at the Institute, which grants graduate degrees in sexology, will get around to identifying and indexing these large, far-flung archives. The Institute's San Francisco library maintains modest collections of fiction and memoirs, mostly contemporary American examples, poetry (in manuscript and published form, much of it local), extensive collections of short stories (again principally contemporary American), erotic periodicals containing fiction, and dissertations by its graduates on erotic genres.

Other Libraries

In Bibliotheca Erótica, a valuable research tool, José Antonio Cerezo has identified and cross-checked titles from the collections of the British Museum, the Bibliothèque Nationale, and the Kinsey Institute against significant holdings by the Biblioteca de Catalunya Barcelona, the Biblioteca Municipal de Madrid, the Biblioteca Nacional (Madrid), the Bodleian Library (Oxford), the Bayerische Stadtsbibliothek (Munich), the Bibliothèque Universitaire (Montpellier), the Cambridge University Library, the Library of Congress, the New York Public Library, and the Wiener Stadt-und-Landesbibliothek (Vienna). Not surprisingly, concentrations in these repositories tend to be heaviest in works written in the languages of their respective countries, so that the Bayerische Stadtsbibliothek, for instance, is a good source for nineteenth-century German examples. For German libraries, the bibliographies compiled by Hayn, Gotendorf, and Englisch and those included in the Bilderlexicon are indispensable.

Two other libraries deserve special mention. The first is that of the American Antiquarian Society of Worcester, Massachusetts, which was founded by Isaiah Thomas, perhaps the most distinguished of early American printers, and one who pirated an American edition of Cleland's *Memoirs of a Woman of Pleasure*. Although the AAS has no particular erotic orientation, its cabinets of books published in America before 1877 contain sensational and risque works, including 42 Indian Captivity narratives and books written by George Thompson (*Venus in Boston*, 1849) and unknown authors (*Confessions of a Washington Belle*, 1863). It is especially rich in "sporting papers" such as *The Whip*, *The Flash*, and *The Libertine*, the scandalous tabloids of the 1840s in whose pages appeared some of the first erotica written by American authors. Available also are period publisher and dealer catalogs. Curators at the AAS, moreover, are familiar with early advertising and printing technologies, traffic in contraband, and the histories of marginal publishers.

Also important is the New York Public Library, whose wide-ranging acquistion policies have garnered both finely-bound classics and extremely cheap editions in many languages. Erotic books were once catalogued within a separate card system under what Gershon Legman called the xxx designation, and older, more fragile items are often still kept in special rooms, but many others can be requested through normal channels, and careful searching will discover English, German, French, Russian, and Slavic works from the eighteenth and nineteenth centuries as well as Oriental examples in both original languages and translations. Cheaper editions tend to be available only on microfilm, a medium adopted by the Library to preserve ephemera and to prevent theft. A scholar searching for erotic stories published during the 1920s and 1930s will find on a single microfilm reel an entire sub-collection of fifty pamphlets published—or in some cases mimeographed—under such imprints as the Erotica Biblion Society of London and New York, the French Modern Art Society of Paris, the London Press, the Parisian Publication Company, the Havana Publishing Company (most of the places of publication are spurious), and many others. The New York Public Library now owns the holdings of the International Gay Information Center, which include fiction by virtually all American writers working in gay erotic genres from the 1960s to the 1980s. Routinely catalogued in CATNYP, the library's digital catalog, individual items are available to patrons in the main reading room.

University libraries also repay investigation. Trinity College (Oxford), for example, holds the Sir Francis Dawson Collection of erotic books, chiefly in the English language. Harvard holds the extremely rare manuscript of Butler's *Dildoides*, and the Magdalene College Library at Cambridge owns a copy of Millot's *Escole des Filles* (1655), the book that so inflamed Samuel Pepys. Determined to build research centers, newer American universities have been more aggressive than their European counterparts in securing significant literary artifacts, often in manuscript form. Given the headstart of older institutions and the expense of acquiring classic texts, newer universities are more likely to cherry-pick singular items when they appear on the market. Dealers and auction houses now sell internationally, so that works may end up far from their countries of origin. Thus, books published by the eighteenth-century English erotica publisher Curll are in the University of Kansas Library; German, French, and Russian erotic titles are available at the Providence Athenaeum (Providence, Rhode Island). Competition among research libraries can be intense, with the result that pieces can be scattered. Henry Miller's prodigious output has been fragmented among the University of California at Los Angeles, the Henry Miller Memorial Library at Big Sur, California, the New York Public Library, the University of Southern Illinois at Carbondale, the University of Texas at Austin, the University of Virginia, and Yale University.

Occasionally writers donate their papers to their alma maters, as in the case of John Colleton (Robert Walter Marks), who left the manuscripts of his erotic and mainstream works to the College of Charleston, in South Carolina, but more celebrated authors may also sell them to the highest bidder. Institutions with the deepest pockets usually prevail. Selected items at the Harry Ramson Humanities Research Center at The University of Texas at Austin (one of the more aggressive acquisitors) include the earliest known poetic fragment of *The Court of Venus*, but also the papers of the British Sexological Society from the 1910s to the 1940s; a collection of Havelock Ellis and another of Frank Harris; unusually broad collections of Radclyffe Hall and James Joyce, the latter including 39 copies of the first edition of Joyce's *Ulysses*, some with annotations by original owners such as Lawrence of Arabia; a large archive of civil rights attorney Morris Ernst, who defended *The Well of Loneliness* and *Ulysses* in America; the papers of Aleister Crowley; the papers of Jean Cocteau (especially his drawings), Pierre Louÿs, and Henri Pierre Roché; and many letters by authors of erotic works.

In recent years, academic interest in issues of gender and sexuality has led libraries and advocates for minority subcultures in most western countries to archive explicit texts. Brown University holds a pulp erotica collection that, with 4,600 gay novels (but only 31 lesbian titles), outstrips that of the New York Public Library. In addition, Brown's Katzoff Collection contains 31,500 mostly literary works relating to gays and lesbians, including the John Preston (author and editor of gay literature) and the Larry Townsend (sadomasochistic fiction and pictorial erotica) subcollections. Brown also supports a truly massive gathering of women's romance novels of varying degrees of explicitness. Guides by Gough and Miller and contributors to Cornog's *Libraries, Erotica, and Pornography* can help locate other such gay and lesbian collections. Scholarship on popular culture genre has fueled acquisitions of demotic literature. In decades past, folklorists compiled folk tales, ballads, broadsides, songs, poems, and chapbooks, depositing them in libraries such as the University of California (both Los Angeles and Berkeley), Indiana University, Harvard, and the Nottingham University Library, as well as in many European institutions. Modern day equivalents are underground comics and erotic graphic novels such as those housed at Bowling Green State University (Ohio), the University of Minnesota, and Michigan State University. French universities now accumulate bandes dessines (comics) just as Japanese institutions purchase manga. In the same spirit, the National Library of Australia has begun to archive sexual materials from the Internet. It has been recording selected Web sites since 1996, including those which feature erotic fiction, and it steadily adds others in an attempt to establish a historical timeline.

Virtually all large public libraries throughout the world have been the recipients of erotic books when donors insisted that they accompany more "desirable" bequests. In today's relatively tolerant climate, librarians may quietly enter the items into catalogs, especially since, as Evelyn Geller points out, legendary "inferno" collections once closeted by public libraries in America usually contained books that are now considered harmless (Geller, 61). Legal records of seizures and prosecutions can be revelatory as well. The papers of the pioneering American anti-censorship attorney Theodore Schroeder, who defended many literary works prosecuted in the early twentieth century, are in the library at Southern Illinois University; the early records of the New York Society for the Suppression of Vice, which seized many books, are in the Library of Congress, while the papers of John Saxton Sumner, Comstock's successor as leader of the Society, are at the State Historical Society of Wisconsin (Madison). The British Museum holds the only surviving copy of the Polunbi Catalog (*Verzeichnis der auf Grund des [section] 184 des Reichstrafgesetzbuches*), which lists books seized by police during the Weimar Republic.

In searching for materials, especially primary texts, students of erotic literature should bear in mind several factors. First, many extensive collections are still in private hands, especially in France. Collections infrequently migrate; the most celebrated was that of J.P. Morgan, whose heirs removed it from his New York library and sold it back to French aficionados. When owners die, heirs may dispose of parcels without publicity, and it can take years for these to find their way into libraries. Second, collections in libraries often reflect the biases of their compilers. Some bibliophiles systematically strove to gather complete runs of authors or genres, while others sought only rare or expensive examples, ignoring cheap, "trashy" but nonetheless historically valuable ephemera. Still other donors obeyed the dictates of their own tastes, so that an assemblage of flagellantia might not be representative of a place or historical period. Similar caveats apply to materials haphazardly seized by police or customs agents, and then seconded to a repository, a practice that has notably contributed to the growth of holdings in the Bibliothèque Nationale, the Library of Congress, and the Kinsey Institute, where readers often find court docket numbers stamped on copies. Third, despite the efforts of the Kinsey Institute to regularize sexual subject headings, many libraries prefer not to use them. Public libraries in particular avoid the heading "erotic literature" for fear that it will act as a flag to censors, and they are even less likely to employ formal terms for fetishes (though they occasionally opt for euphemisms such as "covert cultures" or "alternative literatures") especially now that so many catalogs are available online. Even so, electronic services are a boon, because they make global searches increasingly viable. OCLC, RLIN, and WorldCat often furnish the location of specific editions in particular libraries, and can sometimes be used to request them.

JOSEPH W. SLADE III

Further Reading

[Ashbee, Henry Spencer], pseudonym Pisanus Fraxi. *Index Librorum Prohibitorum; Centuria Librorum Absconditorum; Catena Librorum Tacendorum, Being Notes Bio-Biblio-Iconographical and Critical on Curious, Uncommon and Erotic Books.* 3 vols. London: Privately Printed, 1877, 1879, 1885; rpt. *Index Librorum Prohibitorum; Centuria Librorum Absconditorum; Catena Librorum Tacendorum.* 3 vols. London: Skilton, 1960; rpt. *Bibliography of Forbidden Books.* 3 vols. New York: Jack Brussel, 1962; rpt. *The Encyclopedia of Erotic Literature.* 3 vols. New York: Documentary Books, 1962; *Forbidden Books of the Victorians: Henry Spencer Ashbee's Bibliographies of Erotica*, ed. Peter Fryer. London: Odyssey, 1970.

Bilderlexicon der Erotik. Ein bibliographisches und biographisches Nachschlagewerk, eine Kunst- und Literaturgeschichte für die Gebiete der erotischen Belletristik ... von der Antike zur Gegenwart. 6 vols. Vienna and Hamburg: Verlag für Kulturforschung, 1928–1931, 1963. Edited by Leo Schidrowitz: I: *Kulturgeschichte*; II: *Literatur und Kunst*; III: *Sexualwissenschaft*; IV: *Ergänzungsband*. Edited by Armand Mergen: V and VI: *Sexualforschung: Stichwort und Bild.*

Cerezo, José Antonio. *Bibliotheca Erótica: Sive, Apparatus Ad Catalogum Librorum Eroticorum: (Ad Usum Privatum Tantum) José Antonio Cerezo.* Madrid: Ediciones El Museo Universal, 1993.

Cornog, Martha, ed. *Libraries, Erotica, Pornography.* Phoenix, AZ: Oryx Press, 1991.

Cross, Paul James. "The Private Case: A History," *The Library of the British Museum: Retrospective Essays on the Department of Printed Books*, ed. P. R. Harris. London: The British Library, 1991, pp. 201–240.

Deakin, Terence. *Catalogi Librorum Eroticorum: A Critical Bibliography of Erotic Bibliographies and Book-Catalogues.* London: Cecil & Amelia Woolf, 1964.

Geller, Evelyn. *Forbidden Books in American Public Libraries, 1876–1939: A Study in Cultural Change.* Westport CT: Greenwood Press, 1984.

Gough, Cal, ed. *Gay/Lesbian Archives and Libraries in North America.* Rev. ed. Atlanta: American Library Association Gay and Lesbian Taskforce Clearinghouse, 1989.

Hayn, Hugo, Alfred N. Gotendorf, and Paul Englisch. *Bibliotheca Germanorum Erotica and Curiosa. Verzeichnis der gesamten deutschen erotischen Literatur mit Einschluss der Übersetzungen, nebst Beifügung Originale.* 9 vols. 1912–1914; vol. 9, 1929; rpt. Hanau/München: Verlag Müller & Kiepeneuer, 1968.

Kearney, Patrick J. *The Private Case: An Annotated Bibliography of the Private Case Erotica Collection in the British (Museum) Library.* London: Jay Landesman, 1981.

Kinsey Institute for Research in Sex, Reproduction, and Gender. *Sex Research: Early Literature From Statistics to Erotica: Guide to the Microfilm Collection.* Woodbridge, CT: Research Publications, 1983.

Matusak, Susan, comp. *Bibliography of the Eighteenth-Century Holdings of the Institute for Sex Research.* Bloomington, IN: Institute for Sex Research, 1975.

Miller, Alan V., comp. *Directory of the International Association of Lesbian and Gay Archives and Libraries.* Toronto: International Association of Lesbian and Gay Archives and Libraries, 1987.

Pia, Pascal [J. Durand]. *Les Livres de L'Enfer. Bibliographie critique des ouvrages érotiques dans leurs différente éditions du XVIe siècle à nos jours.* Paris: Librarie Arthème Fayard, 1998.

Reade, Rolf S. [Rose, Alfred]. *Registrum Librorum Eroticorum.* London: Privately printed, 1936; rpt. Rose,

Alfred. *Register of Erotic Books.* 2 vols. New York: Brussel, 1965.

Schmidt, Josephine. "Psst, Comrade: Check Out the Erotica in the Library." *New York Times*, 5 September 2001, p. B2.

Scott, Randall W. *The Comic Art Collection Catalog: An Author, Artist, Title, and Subject Catalog of the Comic Art Collection, Special Collections Division, Michigan State University Libraries.* Westport, CT: Greenwood Press, 1993.

Slade, Joseph W. "Major Research Collections (and the Problems of the Librarian," *Pornography and Sexual Representation: A Reference Guide.* 3 Vols. Westport, CT: Greenwood Press, 2001, I: 317–343.

Verzeichnis der auf Grund des [section] 184 des Reichs-strafgesetzbuches eingezogenen und unbrauchbar zu machenden sowie der als unzüchtig verdächtigen Schriften (Polunbi-Katalog). Berlin: Polizeipräsidium in Berlin, 1926. *Nachtrag,* 1929.

LORRAIN, JEAN

1855–1906
French novelist, journalist, and poet

As a writer, Jean Lorrain spanned the *fin de siècle* spectrum, from Zola's squalid naturalism to Maeterlinck's otherworldly fantasies, but without any sense of proportion or good taste. His novels, short stories, and poetry are a compendium of the decadent fads of the period: Florence and Venice, Medusa and Ophelia ("the charm of a virgin and a perverse boy," "Sur un portrait de Botticelli"), gems and poppies ("a breast-plate studded with amethysts grips his torso and he wears a huge crown of enormous purplish poppies," *Coins de Byzance*); melancholy lilies and irises which "revealed to me my infamous and chaste dishonour," *La forêt bleue*); barbarians and Byzantium ("Yes, let them come, let them burn everything here; let them empty my coffers, let them crush my pearls, let them crucify the steward, let them rape my mother," *Coins de Byzance*); the paintings of Gustave Moreau, Jan Toorop, and James Ensor; Sarah Bernhardt, for whom he wrote unproduced plays, and Yvette Guilbert, for whom he composed lyrics; Wagnerian operas and Arthurian legends, the color mauve and Black Masses, motley masks and necrophiliac orgies, erotic delirium and odors "of sex, of cosmetics, of sweat." All this is described in a lapidary vocabulary, an indigestible mix of *recherché* arcana and the latest slang.

The world of Lorrain's fiction is ruled by women, whose morbid and perverse psychology is expressed in interior decoration, wardrobes, and scents. Madame Litvinoff in *Très russe* (1886), with the "sourire inquiétant de Joconde," dominates feminine men, "doux comme un enfant," and practices chastity as an erotic refinement. Another of Lorrain's heroines concentrates on making half-naked acrobats fall from their trapezes and tightropes. Depravity is common in courtesans like "the pianist" whose expert fingers can rouse enfeebled dotards, or the twelve-year-old "graveyard hooker," who plays the schoolgirl for pedophiles. Even the chlorotic virgin in *Ames d'automne* wants to warm her chilled extremities inside the bosom of a stable-boy. The fashionable blend of Sadic and mystical themes is found *par excellence* in *Princesses d'Ivoire et d'Ivresse* (1902), teeming with enchanted maidens and *femmes fatales.*

An ether addict, perpetually in failing health, Lorrain excelled at portraying physical decrepitude and superannuated desire. For him, love consists of the intimate contact of two solitary and incompatible beings. It can only be expressed in excess, which leads to madness or violence. Characters who long for beauty tend to be repellent lunatics or venial perverts. Near death, impelled partly by patriotism, partly by a sense of waning fashion, Lorrain attacked the idols of his youth in his unfinished novel *Pelléastres*, savagely criticizing aesthetes, Wagner and Maeterlinck. Nor had he any compunction about mocking other's sodomitic penchants, calling Jacques d'Adelsward-Fersen "a petty suburban

Nero," whose taste for Black masses "is better suited to the pink mass (vaseline and essence of Guerlain)."

Monsieur de Bougrelon (1897)

The title character is a flamboyant charlatan, the narrator's guide through Amsterdam. A grandiloquent, impoverished dandy based on Barbey d'Aurevilley, starving to death in his fine linen and laces, he recounts stories of low-life and grotesque passion. There is the Spanish girl, raped fifteen times, who has in expiation had 15 rubies imbedded in her flesh. Another tale tells of a chaste Dutchwoman, who dotes on her she-monkey and her macaw, and insists that her Ethiopian slave, clad only in a pair of leather shorts, help her, nude, into her bath and dress her again. One day the lady is found strangled, her throat cut, and her breast half-devoured.

Vice errant: Les Norontsoff (1902)

Vladimir Norontsoff is a fabulously wealthy Russian prince, who, loaded down with vices like an idol with precious stones, lives on the Riviera in a sumptuous villa. He imposes his mad caprices on his sycophants: dressed in sumptuous robes, he often receives on a *chaise percée*, has two sailors abducted from the port of Nice to spin him yarns, and organizes a fantastic party in honor of Adonis where he goes too far by serving his guests three naked tattooed men on an immense, flower-decked platter. Norontsoff is a Neronian absolutist, a Slavic scion of Byzantium who despises the Tatar hordes of the modern world. His destructive mixture of rage, ennui, and love is so contradictory that he has to kill himself to live out the desires of his delirious imagination.

Lorrain lavished his full talent for description on what he called a "heart-breaking chronicle of a frightful usury of the soul." He considered the book a moral work: "To hypocrisy and human cowardice, to the ferocity of decent people and the decency of social climber, to the acknowledged defenders of virtue [...] I dedicate these pages of sorrow and lust, a great lust whose frightful distress and incurable ennui they cannot conceive."

Monsieur de Phocas (1910)

Subtitled *Astarté*, its protagonist is the young Duc de Fréneuse, alias M. de Phocas, Lorrain's answer to Huysmans's Des Esseintes in *A Rebours* (other major influences are Rachilde, Wilde, Moreau, Whistler, and Toorop). Cherubic in appearance, but icily impotent, owing to his acute cerebralism, he lives in a state of hallucinatory tension. Each sensation is exacerbated, each thought obsessional, each desire magnified in this etiolated sensibility. His morbid desires are vitiated only by a sort of voluptuous somnabulism.

This complete neurotic seeks out extraordinary experiences, moving like a voyeur from drug-fuelled high-society parties to crapulous slums, hoping to grasp in transitory fleshly pleasure a flash of terror or pain, yet tormented by awful visions. These peregrinations are guided by weird characters such as the painter Ethal who catches in a picture the death agony of a young model. Phocas goes to his death seeking a wonderful shade of green he had once glimpsed in a pair of eyes, a certain glaucous gaze of Astarté, goddess of Lust, cold as emeralds and moving as the sea. Phocas's disenchantment makes him a cross between the glacial aesthete and the bestial barbarian, a hybrid of Dorian Gray and Mr. Hyde. Lorrain's matter may be derivative, but the overruling mood, a sort of mournful and sadistic sensuality, is very much his own.

Le tréteau

Written in 1906 and published posthumously, *The Boards* is a highly entertaining novel of theatrical life. Intricately constructed, it concerns the liaison of an actress Linda Monti, based largely on Sarah Bernhardt, and Mario Nérac, a young man come to Paris from the Midi to make a success as a playwright, based partly on Lorrain. They become lovers and the actress imposes her protégé's works on Paris. Rivalries, intrigues, the interference of the actress's lesbian sister, and the malice of a cast-off author lead to a duel. Mario, gravely wounded and partially paralyzed, is taken home by his mother, away from the influence of the fatal actress. (Mothers in Lorrain are always long-suffering saints.) Each character in this backstage comedy of manners is based on a real person, and no one is spared. For all its glamour, literary Paris is portrayed as a charnel house and a jungle, as if the dying Lorrain had poured his disillusionment, bitterness, and rancour about the theater into this novel.

Biography

Martin-Paul-Alexandre Duval, son of a Normandy ship-owner, arrived in Paris in 1881 to make a literary reputation as Jean Lorrain. His first published poems *Le Sang des dieux* (1882), which daringly featured Ganymede, Antinous, "Hylas, his arms polished by Hercules' kisses," and Bathyllus scorching sailors in low dives with his come-hither glances and revealing dances, met with modest sales but major publicity. They reflect Lorrain's own weakness for what he called *Fleurs de boue*, especially fairground pugilists, "those gentlemen of the ring, a tiger skin/About their loins, bare chests, their own skins fine and clear" (*Modernités*). Himself of strapping physique, with the moustache of a Viking, Lorrain painted his face, rimmed his eyes with kohl, and adorned his fluttering hands with bizarre rings.

Lorrain soon won fame as a journalist, in such periodicals as *Le chat noir, La vie moderne,* and *Le courier français,* where his columns were devoured for their colorful reportage and innuendo-saturated gossip. He haunted the galleries and theaters, puffing a painter or slating a star in articles which he signed with names from Sentillana and Salterella to Mimosa and Stendhaletta. "As unctuous as a frosted pastry," Lorrain became known as "the Petronius of the decadence...the best observer of a milieu of which he was also the worst ornament" (Philippe Jullian). An early example of the celebrity homosexual as social and artistic arbiter, a role later played by Andy Warhol and Truman Capote, Lorrain was pilloried in Armory's comedy *Le monsieur aux chrysanthèmes.*

LAURENCE SENELICK

Selected Works

Le sang des dieux. 1882; repr. 1920.
La forêt bleue. 1883.
Les Lépillier. 1885; repr. 1999.
Loreley. 1885; repr.1897.
Modernités. 1885.
Viviane. 1885; repr. as *Brocéliande* in *Théâtre.*
Très russe. 1886; repr. 1913; as *Ville mauresque,* 1942.
Les Griseries. 1887.
Dans l'oratoire. 1888.
Sonyeuse; soirs de province; soirs de Paris. 1891; repr., 1903.
Buveurs d'âmes. 1893; repr. 1929; part one repr. as *Sensualité amoureuse,* 1902. [with Oscar Métenier] *Très russe* [play], 1893.
Yanthis, comédie en 4 actes. 1894.
Sensations et souvenirs. 1895.
Un Démoniaque. 1895.
La petite classe. 1895.
Monsieur de Bougrelon. 1896; repr. 1903, 1927, 1928, 1944, 1993.
Une femme par jour; femmes d'été. 1896.
La princesse sous verre. 1896.
Poussières de Paris. Tome 1. 1896.
L'Ombre ardente; poésies. 1897.
Ma petite ville. 1898.
Ames d'automne. 1898.
La dame turque. 1898; repr. 1903.
Princesse d'Italie. 1898.
Madame Baringhel. 1899.
Heures d'Afrique: chroniques de Naghreb (1893–1898). 1899; repr. 1930, 1994.
La Mandragore. 1899. [with A. Ferdinand Herold] *Prométhée, tragédie-lyrique en trois actes.,* 1900; repr. 1925, 1960.
Vingt femmes. 1900; repr. as *Femmes de 1900,* 1932.
Histoires de masques. 1900; repr., Paris, 1922; 1966; *suivi de Contes d'un buveur d'éther et de textes inédits,* 1987.
Monsieur de Phocas. Astarté. 1901; 1922, 1929, 1966, 1992.
Le vice errant: Coins de Byzance. 1902; repr. 1922, 1926, 1979.
Le vice errant: Les Norontsoff. 1902, repr. 1922, 1979.
Princesses d'ivoire et d'ivresse. 1902.
Poussières de Paris. Tome II. 1902.
Quelques hommes. 1903.
Propos d'âmes simples. 1904; repr. 1931. [with Delphi Fabrice] *Clair de lune,* 1904.
Fards et poisons. 1904.
La maison Philibert. 1904; repr. 1926, 1928, 1932 [with Gustave Coquiot] *Deux heures du matin, quartier Marbeuf. Pièce en deux actes,* 1904. [with Gustave Coquiot] *Hôtel de l'Ouest... Chambre 22,* 1904.[with Gustave Coquiot] *Une Nuit de Grenelle. Pièce en un acte,* 1904.
Quatre femmes en pièces. Paris, 1904.
Le crime des riches. 1905; repr. 1919, 1927, 1996.
L'École des vieilles femmes. 1905; repr. 1930, 1995.
Heures de Corse. 1905; repr. 1997. [with Gustave Coquiot] *Sainte Roulette.* 1905. [with Charles Esquier] *Une Conquête,* 1906.
Madame Monpalou. 1906; repr. 1928.
Le Tréteau. Roman de moeurs théâtrales et littéraires. 1906; repr. 1941.
Théâtre. 1906.
L'Aryenne: gens de mer, bords de Seine, bords de Marne. 1907; repr. 1931.
Hélie garçon d'hôtel. 1908; repr. 1929.
Des belles et des bêtes. 1908.
Maison pour dames. 1908; repr. 1926.

Narkiss. 1908.
Soixante-huit lettres à Édouard Magnier. 1909.
Eros vainqueur. 1909.
Pelléastres. 1910.
Du temps que les bêtes parlaient. 1911; partially repr. as *Portraits littéraires et mondains,* 1926.
La jonque dorée: conte japonais. 1911.
La nostalgie de la beauté. 1912.
Voyages. 1921.
Quelques lettres curieuses et inédites. 1925.
Lettres à ma mère (1864–1906). 1926.
Correspondence de Jean Lorrain... suivies des articles condamnés. 1929.
L'Art d'aimer. 1929.
La ville empoisonnée; Pall-Mall Paris. 1936.
Lettres inédits à Gabriel Mourey et à quelques auteurs (1888–1905). Edited by Jean-Marc Ramos, 1987.
Lettre au docteur Tartarin 28 février 1900. edited by Jean-Louis Lacordaire, 1991.
La poison de la Riviera. Edited by Thibaut d'Anthonay, 1992.
Venise. 1997.
Correspondences et poèmes Jean Lorrain/Gustave Moreau. Edited by Thalie Raquetti, 1998.
La dame aux lèvres rouges. Edited by F. Lacason, 2000.

Further Reading

Anthonay, Thibaut d'. *Jean Lorrain, barbare et esthète.* Paris: Plon, 1991.
Armory, Carle. "The Gentleman of the Chrysanthemums." in *Lovesick. Modernist Plays of Same-sex Love, 1894–1925.* edited and translated by Laurence Senelick, London, Routledge, 1999.
Dalanzac, Joël. "Moreau contre Moro. La monstruosité picturale dans 'Monsieur de Phocas'. *La Licorne* 35 (1995): 113–124.
Fleischmann, Hector. *Le massacre d'une Amazone. Quelques plagiats de Jean Lorrain.* Paris: Genonceaux, 1904.
Gaubert, Ernest. *Jean Lorrain: biographie critique.* Paris: E. Sanset, 1905.
Gauthier, Pierre-Léon. *Jean Lorrain: la vie, l'oeuvre et l'art d'un pessimiste à la fin du XIXe siècle.* Paris: A. Lesot, 1935.
Gauthier, Pierre-Léon. *Jean Lorrain. Un second oratoire: chroniques retrouvées.* Dijon: Jobard, 1935.
Jullian, Philippe. *Jean Lorrain, ou La Satiricon 1900.* Paris: Fayard, 1974.
Kingcaid, Renee A. *Neurosis and Narrative: the Decadent Short Fiction of Proust, Lorrain and Rachilde.* Carbondale, IL: Southern Illinois University Press, 1992.
Kyria, Pierre. *Jean Lorrain.* Paris: Seghers, 1973.
Lucet, Sophie. "Le théâtre statique de Lorrain." In *Statisme et mouvement au théâtre.* edited by Michel Autrand, Poitiers: La Licorne, 1995.
Mourousy, Paul. *Evocations. Jean Lorrain.* Paris: Jacques Lanvin, 1937.
Normandy, Georges. *Jean Lorrain (1855–1906), son enfance, sa vie, son oeuvre.* Paris: Bibliothèque générale d'édition, 1907.
Normandy, Georges. *Jean Lorrain. 20 portraits et documents hors-texte.* Paris: V. Rasmussen, 1927.
Normandy, Georges. *Jean Lorrain, intime.* Paris, 1928.
Paré, Sébastien. "L'érotologie eschatologique. Le mythe obsessional du Fin des Temps chez Lorrain." In *Le Fin des Temps.* edited by Gérard Peylet, Talence: Université Michel de Montaigne, 2000.
Phillip, Winn. *Sexualités décadentes chez Jean Lorrain: l'héros fin de sexe.* Amsterdam, Atlanta, Ga: Rodopi, 1997.
Santos, Rose. *L'Art du récit court chez Jean Lorrain.* Paris: Librairie Nizet, 1995.
Sipala, Carminella. *Mutazioni di fine secolo: i romanzi di Jean Lorrain.* Catania: CUECM, 1998.
Uzanne, Octave. *Jean Lorrain.* Paris, Les Amis d'Édouard, 1913.

LORRIS, GUILLAUME DE AND JEHAN DE MEUNG

Lorris, Guillaume de

c. 1215–c. 1278

Meung, Jehan de

c. 1250–c. 1305

Romance of the Rose

The huge *Romance of the Rose* (almost 22,000 octosyllabic lines) introduces itself as an *ars amandi,* a treatise about love—especially about the methods to win the favors of a lady. The first part, written around 1225 by Guillaume of

Lorris, follows the rules of courtly writing: presented as the first-person retelling of an allegorical dream, that has proven completely true in the narrator's real life, it describes how the young man wanders to the door of the closed garden of the God of Love; on the wall he sees the pictures of those who do not belong with love: Age, Poverty, Envy, Avarice, and so on. Love is an activity reserved for the young, the rich, and the idle. Welcome by the beautiful "Oiseuse" (the personification of Idleness, she spends her time combing her hair and looking at her reflection in a mirror), the young hero then falls in love with a beautiful, budding rose. He makes voluntary homage to the God of Love, who gives him the ten commandments of Love, plus a few practical pieces of advice, and promises he will get his reward if he serves Love well. The allegorical encoding of the text gives the story-line a very abstract tonality; feeling, moral attributes, and qualities are embodied by one-dimensional characters who play their part in the courtly game. With the help of "Bel Accueil" (or "Pleasant Greeting," the young lover succeeds in stealing a kiss from the Rose, but then she is imprisoned in a tower built by the villain "Dangier" ("Shame/Prudence") and Jealousy. Guillaume's poem ends after 4,056 lines in the midst of the desperate narrator's complaint, in the best tradition of the love-stricken *trouvère*. Despite the concrete advice and anecdotes provided by a few characters who try to enlighten the young lover about the real nature of love, this first *Romance of the Rose* is very much a courtly *cansó*, the narrative development of the typical lyrical situation.

Almost fifty years later, a rather famous writer by the name of Jehan de Meung takes over the story of Guillaume and his Rose where the previous author left it (actually, he does not say anything about the change in writers before the middle of the romance, five thousand lines further). However, Jehan's approach is much more pragmatic, or cynical: the goal is certainly not any more to obtain the Rose's love, but to enjoy her ultimate favors in the most straightforward way possible. In order to reach that goal the lover enlists a number of somewhat disreputable characters, like "Faux Semblant" the hypocritical false cleric or "la Vieille" (an old hag who turned a pimp when she could not sell her body anymore); all of them try to give sound advice to the lover, putting the accent on the satisfaction of erotic desire without caring about the so-called noble love. The most impressive change is the replacement of the God of Love by his mother, the Goddess Venus. She embodies feminine sensuality, and through the means of her burning arrows awakens the desire of the Rose, who stops being a passive object of passion to become an active participant in the game of love. Venus does not care overly for courtly discourse, and the text strongly suggests that even when she hides it, woman is "hotter" than man and can barely wait for the satisfaction of her inexhaustible lust. The rise of Venus over her son reveals the fascination and fear of feminine sexuality at the root of Jehan's continuation of the *Romance of the Rose*.

After the Rose has been inflamed by Venus' arrows, the lover-narrator turned pilgrim is able to enter the fortress built by Jealousy. The last sequence of the *Romance* is actually a long metaphor of the sexual act, depicted very graphically as the various steps of a successful pilgrim's quest; precisely when the pilgrim reaches the heart of the sanctuary, however, the dream ends up abruptly, and the dreamer wakes up. Although the second part of the *Romance* was at the root of the so-called "Quarrel of the *Romance of the Rose*," it seems that Jehan of Meung is not primarily interested in the *ars amandi* initiated by his predecessor. Two of his most original characters are Nature and Genius, her chaplain. Both follow the tradition started by Alanus de Insulis in his *De planctu Naturae*, according to which Nature bitterly deplores the various vices developed by mankind, mainly sodomy, to escape its *natural* destination—*crescete et multiplicamini*. The refinements of courtly love, as well as the tricks pertaining to venal love, detract human beings from playing the only serious game intended for them by God, the game of generation. Nature and Genius incite men and women to make love in order to produce offspring, without caring for the niceties of civilization.

Except for this generative duty laid on man by God himself, however, the poem does not have much use for the feminine. The text is deeply misogynistic—although not more than most clerical writings of the time. Sexuality is indeed seen in a rather positive light, as long as it satisfies the requirements of generation, but at the same time the possibility that women do enjoy sex makes them into whores who are not to be trusted. Paradoxically, what starts out as a courtly poem exalting noble love for a lady ends up as an apology for free sexuality disengaged of any reference to love, and as a tacit dismissal of all women as being no ladies at all. Jehan of Meung's *Romance of the Rose* will remain for two centuries the bluebook of misogyny, although it is somehow more concerned about gathering knowledge in all areas pertaining to sexuality, the relationship between man and woman, and what can be loosely called "love"—including a discussion on semantics and the meanings of words.

ANNE BERTHELOT

Editions

Le Roman de la Rose, edition and translation A. Strubel, Paris: Livre de Poche (LGF), Series "Lettres gothiques"; 1992.

Le Roman de la Rose, 2 volumes, ed. F. Lecoy (scholarly edition, no translation), Paris: Champion, Series "les Classiques du Moyen-Age,". 1966 and 1968.

Le Roman de la Rose, ed. D. Poirion (without translation or notes), Paris: Livre de Poche (LGF), 1974.

Frances Horgan's 1994 translation for Oxford World Classics is clear and exact, but with very little notes to help the reader.

Charles Dahlberg's 1971 translation for Princeton Univ. Press is more scholarly. The third Edition, in 1995, corrects a few errors and gives an update of the scholarly publications about the work.

Allen, Peter L. *The Art of Love: Amatory Fiction from Ovid to the Romance of the Rose.* Philadelphia, PA: University of Pennsylvania Press, 1992.

Further Reading

Bloch, R. Howard. *Medieval Misogyny and the Invention of Western Romantic Love.* Chicago, IL: University of Chicago Press, 1991.

John V. Fleming. *The* Roman de la Rose: *A Study in Allegory and Iconography.* Princeton, NJ: Princeton University Press, 1969.

Gunn, Alan M.F. *The Mirror of Love: A Reinterpretation of "The Romance of the Rose."* Lubbock, TX: Texas Tech Press, 1952.

Kristeva, Julia. "Manic Eros, Sublime Eros." In *Tales of Love,* 59–82. New York: Columbia University Press, 1987.

Lewis, C.S. *The Allegory of Love: Studies in a Medieval Tradition.* New York: Oxford University Press, 1936.

LOUŸS, PIERRE

1870–1925
French poet and novelist

Pierre Louÿs (he adopted the archaizing spelling c. 1889) is notable for the quantity and variety of his erotic production and the playfulness and exuberant humor that characterizes much of it. It was written throughout his life, with the same obsessive method that he brought to documenting his active sexual life, to research into and classification of female experiences, including a *Manuel de Gomorrhe* [Manual of Gomorrha] on sodomy, and to erotic photography. It was not a sideline distinct from his published work (three very different novels, stories, prose poems, and Parnassian poetry); it provides the most provocative expression of his unchanging views. The Preface to *Aphrodite* sets up as an ideal the morality of antiquity based on the right of the individual to pursue happiness while respecting that of others. Sexuality and sensuality ("volupté") have a central role in human life and are mankind's *raison de vivre*. Sexual and moral freedom have however been restricted by conventional morality, prudishness, and "Protestantism," against which he constantly campaigned; nudity and sexuality should be seen not as shameful or sinful, but as subjects for contemplation, even worship.

On Louÿs's death some 400 kg of unpublished erotic manuscripts—the figure probably expresses astonishment rather than an accurate estimate—were discovered in his library, and dispersed uncatalogued through specialist booksellers. Some 1,200 pages have subsequently been published, at first clandestinely in limited editions, starting in 1926 with *Trois Filles de leur mère* [*Mother's Three Daughters*] and the *Manuel de civilité* [*Handbook of Good Manners*]; as much again is probably still in private collections. Much of it is incomplete: Louÿs was as capable of abruptly changing his subject of interest as he was of obsessive work developing one idea. All the works conjure up alternative closed worlds given over to sex. Louÿs's erotic work is not the relation of individual experience; it involves all humanity in frenzied consensual sexual activity, free from any coercion or violence, which displaces all other activities and values. The only restriction in his ideal of erotic liberty, which embraces lesbianism, incest, sodomy, coprophilia, and bestiality, is towards male homosexuality, generally ignored or treated as incomprehensible, although it does figure fleetingly in a few works. Louÿs's key idea is summed up in the poem "Philis, il serait bon...": "Rien n'est en soi pervers, ni vil, ni ridicule" [Nothing is in itself perverse, base or ridiculous]: our only guide should be the quest for pleasure.

Louÿs's published work provides a world, a theme, and above all a language to exploit in sexually explicit parallel versions. The sequence of prose poems, *Les Chansons de Bilitis* [*The Songs of Bilitis*], composed in a uniform pattern of four paragraphs that form a prose sonnet, purport to be a translation of the works of a Greek poetess contemporary with Sappho (Louÿs enjoyed practical jokes and hoaxes). They form a "lyrical novel" tracing her awakening sensuality in the natural paradise of Pamphylia, her love for the young Mnasidika on Lesbos, and her life of debauchery as a courtesan on Cyprus. For Louÿs the twin dangers of erotic writing were a Satanic or a smutty presentation of woman and sex. The subversive hedonism of the poems rehabilitates a natural sensuality and tranquilly accepts heterosexual and lesbian sexuality and prostitution. The poems are also bold in their discreet but unambiguous allusions to the clitoris, masturbation, artificial phalluses, sodomy, and fellatio. The volume's index teasingly lists poems that were "not translated," implying the existence of some too audacious to print. These hints are developed by Louÿs in the *Chansons secrètes de Bilitis* [*Secret Songs of Bilitis*]. Some are alternative versions of the published ones: where in the opening poem, "L'Arbre" [The Tree], a young girl sits innocently astride a branch, in the "secret" version she

stimulates herself; in another, Paris sees not "the secret" but "the vulva" of the three goddesses. Sometimes the erotic version makes more sense than the published one and clearly precedes it; in other cases it is clearly a subsequent elaboration. But all keep the same atmosphere of uncomplicated sexuality in an idyllic world.

The same idealized pagan world is found in *Aphrodite*, an evocation of the life of courtesans in 1st-century BCE Alexandria. Through the relationship between the courtesan Chrysis and the sculptor Démétrios the novel demonstrates the danger of passion that enslaves and the paradoxical superiority of art and imagination—here, as Jennifer Birkett has argued, the privilege of the male—over physical reality. Again the published novel was bold in its relaxed presentation of sexuality: in the opening chapter, Chrysis has her pubic hair shaved and masturbates in the bath. Louÿs had to excise one scene of bestiality from the published novel, but planned a series of 172 monologues of seduction for Chrysis, abandoned by Démétrios, not as part of the novel, but existing parallel to it. Ten were completed; in them she conjures up a series of erotic experiences to entice him back from a handsome youth, culminating with coprophagy. They are a linguistic *tour de force*, a set of lyrical variations on a theme exploiting the novel's style: long harmonious sentences and elaborate imagery.

Les Aventures du roi Pausole [*The Adventures of King Pausole*] is in contrast a light-hearted philosophical tale presenting a benign king with two Louÿsian principles: do not harm others, apart from that, do what you will. He rules over a utopia where characters can respond uninhibitedly to all the calls of sensuality. It has its counterparts in two very different works. *Histoire du Roi Gonzalve et des douze princesses* [*The Tale of King Gonzalve and the Twelve Princesses*], part utopia, part fairy tale, traces the gradual sexual initiation of his twelve compliant and enthusiastic daughters, aged from 18 to seven-and-a-half, by the King himself, assisted by his chambermaid. The potential repetitiveness is avoided by Louÿs's inventiveness. Court protocol intrudes incongruously into new areas (it does not permit the King to take the same virgin twice in succession). The daughters are differentiated by their manner and language: Tertia, aggressive and contemptuously vulgar; Septima, cheerfully indecent; Prima, languorous and literary; Puella (nine), impudent and with a taste for sweat and coprophagy... Louÿs plays off the outrageous explicitness of the daughters against the restrained, formal voice of the third-person narrator. The varied incestuous sexual acts are extended by dialogue, as the sisters bicker, boast, and egg each other on, rather than by depiction. The second parallel novel, *L'Ile aux dames* [*The Island of Ladies*], echoing Jules Verne's *L'Ile mystérieuse* [*The Mysterious Island*], exists as little more than an outline for a novel, though it runs to some 120 pages. The utopia of sexual freedom is here all encompassing. The heroine, Fernande, lands on an unknown island where she is guided around the town by Lucienne, gets to know her family, is introduced to court, and finally becomes a prostitute specializing in sodomy. What she discovers with initial surprise, then enthusiastic involvement, is a society, from court to working quarters, solely, openly, and uninhibitedly occupied with sex. The children above all know no obstacles in the form of modesty, family relationships, or class. The island had been discovered in 1623: the expedition's leader, named 'King,' decreed the "licence de foutre" [licence to fuck] which allows total freedom for all male and female subjects to enjoy any sexual activity with consenting women or girls (again, this excludes male homosexuality), in private or in public. Virginity is banned after puberty; abduction and rape however are capital offences. Louÿs's inventive imagination devises local equivalents for the diverse aspects of normal life: the various booths at the fair, the religious festivals, the annual court orgy (by invitation only), the Charity Brothel that raises money for the poor. Above all, Louÿs's classificatory zeal conjures up lists: a delirious catalogue of street names, the titles of the establishments in the Street of Forty Brothels, the program for a concert at the lesbian boarding school. New trades prompt neologisms, like "cunnovate" for the fortune-teller who can read pudenda. These "absurd complications" are conjured up with a sense of bizarre detail, and sometimes teeter into the excessive: theatrical coprophagy, or the brothel of dead women to cater to necrophiliacs. At the same time some ideas have subsequently been overtaken by reality: men putting their penis through a grill to be anonymously fellated; the sex museum (waxworks represent positions); illustrated guides to masturbation; prostitutes behind shop windows.

Louÿs's published work thus stimulated the production of parallel erotic versions; so did parody. In the *Manuel de civilité pour les petites filles à l'usage des maisons d'éducation* [*Handbook of Good Manners for Little Girls, Especially Recommended for Use in Schools*], Louÿs's blithely deadpan guide to "good behavior" offers a series of instructions for behavior in a variety of situations: at home, in class, out shopping, at the theater, or the seaside... The humor calmly takes for granted a defiance of conventional morality, and both the proscribed and the prescribed evoke outlandish situations: partners are masturbated at society balls and priests in the confessional, beggars are offered fellatio, and dildos are given as wedding presents. "If you have used a banana to amuse yourself with alone or to make the chambermaid come, do not replace it in the fruit bowl without having carefully wiped it." "Do not ask a chambermaid to go down on you more than twice a day. You must not tire out the servants." As the work is, again, a stylistic exercise, Louÿs plays with verbal as much as behavioral impropriety. Obscene expressions intrude into the prim instructions: "Do not say: 'When you suck him he comes at once.' Say: 'He is impulsive'." The world predicated is dominated by masturbation, incest, and sodomy, embodying an underlying universal desire for sexual satisfaction on which only hypocrisy, misguided modesty, and a narrow view of virtue impose restraint. "You must understand this truth that everyone present, whatever their age or sex, has the secret desire for you to go down on them, but that most will not dare to say so."

In the known narrative fiction, which includes several abandoned fragments, parody enables Louÿs to adopt a variety of voices for evoking spontaneous and guilt-free sexual encounters. He mimics the Bible in *Au temps des juges* [*In the Time of the Judges*], the Oriental fairy tale in *Farizade* (with spoof learned footnotes), the "Realist" autobiography of a prostitute in *Mémoires de Joséphine* [*The Memoirs of Josephine*], where the atmosphere of squalor is pushed to comic excess and the events plunge into absurdity. The most substantial is *Toinon* [*The Erotic Adventures of Toinon*], a first-person narration by a sexually and linguistically innocent girl joining a boarding school, of her sexual education. As this is substantially complete by the end of the first night and the other girls are equally knowledgeable, Louÿs introduces variety in the form of an English-speaking assistant mistress.

Several works could be grouped under the heading "plays"; they are essentially "armchair theater" designed for reading and the imagination rather than for performance (unlike, say, Maupassant's *A la feuille de rose, maison turque*). Not only would they present problems in staging an action which is both relentlessly sexual and frequently acrobatic; Louÿs uses dialogue to displace performance. On the one hand exchanges between characters, rather than stage directions, evoke acts that they are in the act of performing or about to perform: in *Jeunes filles*, Lucienne describes an elaborate position she has dreamed up, and dictates it to the participants, then Jean as a spectator describes what he can see when it is assembled. But also an exchange between characters can imply the activity they are engaged in, while simultaneously conjuring up another encounter in the past that is stimulating them now as they recall it. In this "double scenario" the narration of events is shifted to the character, foregrounding its essentially linguistic nature. Jean sodomizes Simone, but this present act is evoked simply by her instructions; at the same time she questions him about his activities with the other two girls, Berthe and Lucienne, and this exchange simultaneously conjures up a second, past act.

These theatrical works, though substantial, are all abandoned fragments presenting Louÿs's hedonism in differing conventional settings: parody is ever-present. *Jeunes filles* presents the initiation of Simone as she stays with two sisters. The successive acts represent not so much plot development as the extension of sexual activities as Simone moves from ignorance and distaste to curiosity, then enthusiastic participation (Lucienne conveniently possesses an 8-cm clitoris—one of the recurrent implausibilities of Louÿs's scenarios, where female autonomy goes hand-in-hand with a masculinized portrayal of female sexuality: women get hard and ejaculate). Participants (the maid, her boyfriend, the mother) are added as the play progresses around the house. *Connette et Chloris* hilariously parodies the situations and language of seventeenth-century French theater, introducing the complications of lesbianism and intercourse into the jealousies, betrayals, and unrequited loves of Racinian tragedy. The verbal comedy lies in the contrast between the formality and restraint of Classical

tragedy and the activities evoked. *Filles de ferme* [*Farm Girls*] represents a marathon of cunnilingus and coprophilia by a sexually voracious 14-year-old girl in a caricatural rustic setting reminiscent of Zola's Naturalist fiction.

This "theater" is at its most successful—inventive, ludic, provocative, linguistically varied—in *Douze douzains de dialogues* [*Dialogues of the Courtesans*], a sequence of brief exchanges, all shorter than a page, mostly between female characters, with settings ranging from society balls to street corners, classified under twelve headings: women masturbating or masturbated, phallophores, mothers and daughters... The challenge of a numerical framework prompts a proliferation of varied scenes. The sequence is again triggered by a pre-existing work: Lucian of Samosata's *Dialogues of the Courtesans* that Louÿs had himself translated in 1894. The exchange establishes the context and evokes the action; it frequently relies on the "double scenario": two women masturbate as they talk on the telephone, one arousing her partner by describing another couple observed in mutual cunnilingus, and inviting the telephonist to join in. Louÿs conjures up absurd or bizarre situations: maids gossip about the help they have to give the girls in their houses; concierges encourage sex on the staircase; children play hot cockles, using penises rather than hands. Even conventional situations are enlivened with an exuberant lack of inhibition, or by inventive details: the maid being interviewed by a new mistress takes off her hat to demonstrate her oral skills. The *Dialogues* rely above all on the inventive and ingenious use of language. Louÿs deftly mimics a range of registers, from the invitation to sodomy couched as an invitation to a dance at a ball, to the stream of obscenities proffered by a 10-year-old girl.

Trois filles de leur mère [*Mother's Three Daughters*]

The French title suggests that they take after their mother, probably written *c.* 1913, stands apart from other fictional works, both narrative and theatrical, in its coherence and completeness. It is a freestanding work neither parodying another genre nor complementing one of Louÿs's own works (though there are parallels with the Spanish novel *La femme et le pantin* [*The Woman and the Puppet*], in which an older man trapped in an obsessive relationship with a young woman tells how she repeatedly entices, exploits, then refuses him. The 20-year-old narrator meets in turn, living in an adjacent apartment, Mauricette (aged 14), her mother Teresa (36), and her sisters Lili (10) and Charlotte (20), and is led by them through a varied, increasingly outrageous series of sexual acts, first individually, then jointly. Although he makes his preferences clear to Mauricette at the start: "To make love," this straightforward pleasure is one that they refuse, tricking him either with their agile bodies or by extracting promises into other acts. As the novel progresses, these become more complex, and they are increasingly displaced by mediated representations: first by the women's accounts of their pasts, then by the evocation of future acts and by playlets in which they and the narrator improvise on scenarios the women have devised (prostitute and client, lecher and young girl, classroom scene, catechism). This process is increasingly frustrating for the narrator, so much so that, exactly halfway through the novel, after his first encounter with each, he escapes to visit his friend Margot, exhausted but desperate to make love "in front," and does so to great relief. After this first cycle he is drawn back to the four women, but is increasingly frustrated. On the fourth day Mauricette announces that she will allow herself to be publicly deflowered by him (she is still technically a virgin). Although the act is announced three times, in increasing detail, and even rehearsed with Teresa paying Mauricette's role, it is never carried out; the narrator becomes baffled by the games that the four women are playing with him and their role-playing. The novel ends with an abrupt epilogue: the family leaves, without ever reaching the deflowering of Mauricette; but also with a promise (or threat) of resumption: Teresa leaves a note with the *concierge* saying: "We will meet again."

The novel is in many ways a compendium of Louÿs's erotic writing, both in its insistence on his favorite themes: uninhibited and guiltless sexuality, the dominance of sodomy, masturbation, and incestuous sapphism, and by integrating ideas from other works: Teresa's practical hints about fellatio recall the *Manuel de civilité*, the playlets recall the *Dialogues*, the catechism scene recalls *Histoire du roi Gonzalve*. The action is verbal, not just in the reliance on dialogue to evoke ongoing and to plan future sexual activity,

and on the "double scenario" where narrating about the past accompanies present activities, but also in the foregrounding of language. For once there is a role for the voice of a male narrator (elsewhere Louÿs tends to rely either on dialogue, as in the playlets, or the narrative voice of fictional women in pseudo-memoirs, or an omniscient external narrative voice), which is played off against the voices of the four woman: Teresa, authoritative; Mauricette, defiant; Charlotte, languid and self-deprecating; Lili, playful and impudent. From the beginning the narrator's coy periphrases are met by the provocative frankness of Mauricette, both in what she does (displaying her virginity) and in her language (repeating "I'm wanking" eight times). Restrained, a bit pedantic, he relies on the reader being able to pick up incongruous but deft cultural allusions, from the music of Louÿs's friend Debussy to Catullus or La Fontaine. For the women freedom of language is a source of pleasure just as much as sex is: as Teresa reaches one climax she unleashes on the narrator a torrent of obscenities. Whether as spectator or participant in their scenarios, he is bewildered, recurrently judging them "mad," discomfited by their self-assured quest for their own pleasure, in sodomy (which avoids the dangers of conception), in masturbation (as Charlotte says: "You come when you want"), and increasingly disturbed by his discoveries about them. Teresa has brought up Charlotte so that she has a "vice": to be aroused when insulted; she vainly attempts to get the narrator to insult her as she conjures up for him a series of degrading acts to which she has been subjected, culminating in her relationship with a notable who imposes acts of bestiality. But even then, as she evokes fellating farm animals or being sodomized by a goat, she arouses in the narrator only desire and pity. Nor can he respond to Mauricette's masochism, similarly the product of her mother's "education," inculcated as a conditioned reflex. He submits to their more excessive demands reluctantly and cannot describe certain scenes. The rational, open-minded, even libertine narrator had initially looked forward enthusiastically to the prospect of unlimited sex with his four neighbors. He finds himself trapped in an alternative world of apparent sexual freedom, and used, as spectator or as participant, in acts that they determine and increasingly stage-manage. The language and deeds of the seemingly inexhaustible women frustrate, outrage, and bewilder him. Louÿs's premise is that there are no moral limits: the inhibitions of the "liberated" narrator serve perhaps more forcefully than elsewhere to dissolve any fixed guidelines.

The foregrounding of language is heightened by a constant sense of artifice: both actions and the novel itself are highly self-conscious. The narrator at times thinks himself in a novel that he cannot quite make sense of, plays humorously with psychological and moral paradoxes, and comments on his actual writing (and loses track of what he is saying mid-sentence). He addresses the reader directly, attributing to this "reader" a range of different possible characters: male or female, naïve or experienced, hostile or sympathetic, commenting on potential reactions and assuming a range of different voices, from the ironically moralizing to the flippant. He repeatedly insists that his implausible tale is true as the women's' exploits become increasingly implausible (as in Charlotte's preposterous account of Lili's conception, achieved by transferring sperm from her anus to Teresa's vagina, or Lili's massaging of the narrator's penis from inside Teresa's vagina during anal intercourse), and, as John Phillips has argued, these exploits provoke increasingly astonishment and admiration rather than arousal: this is the comic world of Boccaccio or Rabelais, not that of Sade. The final evening is dominated by play-acting: Lili's performance as a serpent-girl accomplishing oral autoerotic acts is followed by a series of improvised playlets. Sex is an "act" in which the narrator, like the hero of *La Femme et le pantin*, cannot know the true feelings of the others; it is a performance, both in that it increasingly involves gymnastic expertise (the family are double-jointed acrobats) and that it is a display for spectators, as when Mauricette demonstrates her newly-acquired skill at fellatio by executing it "brilliantly" on the narrator before the others. It is also a game, with its combination of rules, improvisation, and pure enjoyment, especially for the younger girls, reinforcing the playfulness of the novel as a whole. And in these areas it is the women, especially Lili, who are the natural performers.

In Louÿs's published erotic poetry, pre-existing works, forms, or characters often provide the challenge to produce a set of variations. He parodies past literature (La Fontaine's fables, the exotic Romanticism of Hugo or Musset) by inserting invitations to sodomy or drunken debauchery, and reworks folk songs and children's game rhymes by introducing sexuality or obscene words. Not all these variations are comic: the reinvented Wagnerian heroines of *Le Trophée des vulves légendaires* [*The Trophy of the Legendary Vulvas*] maintain an appropriately heroic status in their sexually voracious exploits. In *Pybrac* the springboard for invention is the moralizing *Quatrains* of the sixteenth-century Guy du Faur de Pibrac, Louÿs's target the morality campaigner Senator René Béranger. He produces a series of alexandrine quatrains in the manner of the *Manuel de civilité*, mostly starting: "Je n'aime pas à voir..." ["I do not like to see..."], each conjuring up a vivid scenario of some activity contrary to conventional values of decency in family, religion, or society: the schoolboy masturbating behind his mother, then ejaculating over her dress; a soldier raping a girl of 17, then sodomizing her, being fellated, and having his penis bitten off. Not only does the moralizing voice paradoxically evoke what it condemns; Louÿs ironically adopts a tone of mild disapproval for a series of activities that are outlandishly excessive, apparently implying that something just slightly less excessive would be quite acceptable, again undercutting moral guidelines by tut-tutting at a shepherd who sodomizes a 13-year-old shepherdess, then ejaculates in her mouth, on the grounds that "wisdom in love is content with less." 314 of these quatrains have been published; a manuscript of over 500 more was auctioned in 1936 but has disappeared; two other manuscripts exist in private collections. *Pybrac* is perhaps the most extreme demonstration of the fact that a simple idea can lead Louÿs to seemingly endless multiplication: his erotic work is excessive both in its insistent return to key preoccupations and words, and in the proliferation of variations on a single model.

It is in poetry in particular that formal difficulty can serve as a stimulus: Louÿs's friend Paul Valéry defined the poet as someone to whom the inherent difficulty of his art gives ideas. Over one third of the published erotica is rhymed (poetry or verse playlets). There are several examples of extreme ingenuity in rhyme scheme: an acrostic sonnet on lesbians, a poem using the notes of the tonic sol-fa as rhymes. The many non-parodic poems published fall into two main groups. One is of serious and lyrical poems, such

833

as *La Femme*, planned in 1890 as a sequence of twelve groups of twelve sonnets, each celebrating in the manner of the sixteenth-century poetic *blason* a part of the woman's body, a type of woman, or an act. They are Parnassian in their choice of a difficult form, and exploit musicality of line and a traditionally poetic language with rare or archaizing vocabulary and with imagery drawn from nature, precious stones, religious worship, or classical mythology. The emphasis is on delicacy, sensuality, and mystery; the poems seek nobility and intensity, while in no way disguising the physical reality of the activities hymned. The second group consists of brief scenes evoked in a few octosyllabic quatrains. Inside this constraining form, with its short lines and rigid rhyme scheme, Louÿs produces witty, neat, or ironic sketches spiced with realistic detail and displaying an excellent ear for popular language, in the manner of *Douze douzains de dialogues*. Here the language is not conventionally poetic but direct, sometimes obscene. A snatch of dialogue suffices to conjure up a scene—between prostitute and customer, bourgeois woman and servant, mother and daughter—light-hearted, outrageously subversive of conventional morality, and with an undercurrent of disrespect for authority and the establishment. Mothers encourage daughters to masturbate; a maid advises her mistress that incest or sex with domestics is better for her son than going out "to catch the pox in town"; schoolgirls are let off their homework as they were prostituting themselves.

Not all the poems fit into these two categories: there are—for instance—some serious poems that represent sexual acts lyrically but with a direct realism and specifically modern accessories, such as sewing machines or bicycles. "Camille," the verse monologue of a hermaphrodite, first published in 1994, or the novel *L'Ile aux dames*, only published in 1988, are, the one in terms of character, the other in setting and form, very different from Louÿs's previously known erotic work in these genres. His unpublished works may reserve surprises: the revised edition of Jean-Paul Goujon's study (2002) signals their diversity, from spoof news items to erotic dialogues in English, and they include several hundred poems. Louÿs operates with a bewildering variety of forms and tones: a realism that can be satirical or crude; utopian fantasy; idealized antiquity; parody; elevated lyricism.

Two things, nevertheless, remain constant. One is the simple hedonistic message whose very straightforwardness lends itself to countless variations. The other is a limited number of recurrent preoccupations that fill the differing alternative sexual worlds that he creates. Much of the work is anchored in the *Belle époque* that he knew, from brothels and street prostitutes to society balls or gentlemen seeking thrills with the lower classes. Louÿs's permissiveness and individualism have affinities with the literary anarchism of contemporaries like Remy de Gourmont: a hatred for the state's restrictive laws, a mockery of bourgeois respectability, of which the church forms part, are coupled with delight in showing the frank enjoyment of all who defy convention. He never depicts dangerous passion, jealous and obsessive, which (in his published works) leads only to humiliation, enslavement, and death. He may depict characters like Mauricette who enjoy pain, or even coprophilia, but shuns violence and cruelty. Guilt is totally absent. The insistent preoccupations are incest and lesbianism, with a marked tendency to involve young girls in these, especially in the formulaic setting of boarding school (a closed feminine world) or among the working class; Louÿs's fantasy presents them consistently as sexually aware, surpassing the adults in their uninhibitedness, and spontaneously enthusiastic for all manifestations of sexuality, confidently usurping the role of the adults. Sodomy, enjoyed by both participants, is obsessively present and is the subject of nearly half his erotic poems, corresponding to a personal interest (Louÿs kept a file, with dated photos, labelled *Enculées* [*Women sodomized*], covering 1892–1907).

The settings of Louÿs's erotica may seem dated: an idealized antiquity, 1900s Paris, worlds of fantasy that are its double, but it is in some ways modern. The role of formal difficulty and numerical patterns as the trigger anticipates the practices of the OuLiPo writers of the 1960s and later who used formal constraints to prompt literary creation. The exuberant excess of the activities evoked goes hand-in-hand with a verbal excess: Louÿs attacked not just the lack of sexual freedom in his time, but the inability to talk about it, so he repeats forbidden words, rewrites innumerable variations on the same scene in a series of works which remain preeminently linguistic exercises. The self-consciousness and playfulness underline the fictive nature of the text: it is a game, a linguistic construct, in the brief and witty dialogues in prose and verse as much as in the interplay of voices and the ironic teasing of the reader(s) in *Trois Filles de leur mère* or the sequence of *Pybrac*, works both infinitely extensible but equally capable of being abruptly dropped.

Biography

Pierre-Félix Louis was born 10 December 1870 in Ghent, Belgium. After his mother's death in 1879, his upbringing was largely entrusted to his half-brother Georges Louis, who may have been his father. Educated at private establishments in Paris 1879–1882, then Ecole Alsacienne, Paris 1882–1888, Lycée Janson de Sailly, 1888–1889. Registered Faculté des Lettres and Faculté de Droit, Paris, 1889–1892 but att18ended little and failed examinations. Military service 1893–1894, discharged for ill health. Dissipated within three years his inheritance on majority (1892), and extravagance left him in frequent financial difficulty even after the success of his novel *Aphrodite* (1896). Ceased to publish new work after 1901 and increasingly withdrew into private writing and scholarship, his health and eyesight progressively declining (cigarettes, drugs). Traveled notably to England, visiting Oscar Wilde (1892, 1893), Bayreuth (1891, 1892), Belgium (introducing Debussy to Maeterlinck, 1893), Spain (1895, 1896, 1900, 1903) and North Africa (Algeria 1894, 1895 with André Gide, 1896–1897, Egypt 1901). Married Louise de Heredia 1899 (divorced 1913), Aline Steenackers 1923 (one son, two daughters); one son by Marie de Régnier. Died of emphysema, Paris, 4 June 1925.

PETER COGMAN

Selected Works

Les chansons de Bilitis. 1894; as *The Songs of Bilitis*, translated by Alvah C. Bessie, 1926; as *The Songs of Bilitis*, in *Two Erotic Tales*, translated by Mary H. Harrison, 1995.
Aphrodite. 1896; as *Aphrodite*, translated by Frances Keene, 1960; as *Aphrodite*, in *Two Erotic Tales*, translated by Mary H. Harrison, 1995.
La femme et le pantin. 1898; as *The Woman and the Puppet*, translated by Jeremy Moore, 1999.
Les aventures du Roi Pausole. 1901; as *The Adventure of King Pausole*, translated by Charles Hope Lumley, 1919.
Manuel de civilité pour les petites filles à l'usage des maisons d'éducation. Privately printed, 1926; 1976;

as *Handbook of Good Manners for Little Girls, Especially Recommended for Use in Schools*, translated by Sabine d'Estrée, 1971.
Trois filles de leur mère. Privately printed 1926; 1970; as *The She-Devils*, by Peter Lewys, 1958; as *Mother's Three Daughters*, translated by Sabine d'Estrée, 1969. *Histoire du roi Gonzalve et des douze princesses*, privately printed 1927; 1977.
Poésies érotiques de Pierre Louÿs. Privately printed 1927; in *Poésies*, 1988.
Pybrac. Privately printed 1927; in *Poésies*, 1988; as *Pybrac*, translated by Neil Crawford, 1997.
Douze douzains de dialogues, ou petites scènes amoureuses. privately printed 1927; 1976; as *Scènes de Péripatéticiennes*. Privately printed, 1937; 2000; as *Dialogues of the Courtesans*. translated by Guy Daniels, 1973.
Aphrodite. With erotic passages, 3 vols, edited by Pascal Pia, privately printed, 1928; as *Un Chapitre érotique inédit d'Aphrodite*, 1991.
Les chansons secrètes de Bilitis. Privately printed 1929; 1961.
Au temps des juges. Privately printed 1933; in *L'Œuvre érotique*, edited by Jean-Paul Goujon, 1994.
La femme. Privately printed 1938; in *Poésies*, 1988.
Poèmes inédits: poésies libres. Privately printed 1938; in *Poésies*, 1988.
Proses inédites: pièces libres. Privately printed 1940; in *L'Œuvre érotique*. Edited by Jean-Paul Goujon, 1994.
Le trophée des vulves légendaires. Privately printed 1948; in *Poésies*, 1988.
Cydalise. Privately printed 1928; in *Poésies*, 1988.
Jeunes filles. Privately printed 1978; in *L'Œuvre érotique*, edited by Jean-Paul Goujon, 1994.
Pastiches et parodies. Privately printed, 1981; in *L'Œuvre érotique*, edited by Jean-Paul Goujon, 1994.
La soliste. Privately printed,1983; in *L'Œuvre érotique*, edited by Jean-Paul Goujon, 1994.
Farizade ou les vœux innocents (in collaboration with Louis Louviot). Privately printed, 1984; in *L'Œuvre érotique*, edited by Jean-Paul Goujon, 1994.
Les mémoires de Joséphine, suivi de Filles de ferme et de Paroles. Privately printed, 1984; in *L'Œuvre érotique*, edited by Jean-Paul Goujon, 1994.
Petites miettes amoureuses (*Poèmes libres, Deux contes*). Privately printed, 1986; in *L'Œuvre érotique*, edited by Jean-Paul Goujon, 1994.
L'Ile aux dames. 1988.
Poésies. Edited by Jean-Paul Goujon, 1988.
Toinon, 1991. As *the Erotic Adventures of Toinon*. translated by John Phillips, 1999.
L'Œuvre érotique. Edited by Jean-Paul Goujon, 1994.
Manuel de Gomorrhe. 1994.
Le sentiment de la famille. 1996; translated by Wendy Parramore, 1996.

Further Reading

Alexandrian, Sarane. *Histoire de la littérature érotique*. Paris: Seghers, 1985.
Birkett, Jennifer. *The Sins of the Fathers*. London: Quartet, 1986.

Clive, H.P. *Pierre Louÿs: A Biography*. Oxford: Clarendon Press, 1978.

Goujon, Jean-Paul. *Pierre Louÿs: une vie secrète (1870–1925)*. Paris: Seghers/J.-J. Pauvert, 1988; revised edition, Paris: Fayard, 2002.

Goujon, Jean-Paul. "Pierre Louÿs photographe érotique." *Recherche photographique*. no. 5 (1988): 39–47.

Goujon, Jean-Paul. "Pierre Louÿs ou la subversion de la morale." *Europe*. 69, nos 751–752 (1991): 61–69.

Millan, C. Gordon. *Pierre Louÿs ou le culte de l'amitié*. Aix-en-Provence: Pandora, 1979.

Niederauer, David J. *Pierre Louÿs: His Life and Art*. Ottawa: Canadian Foundation for the Humanities, 1981

Phillips, John. "Sexual and Textual Excess: Pierre Louÿs's *Trois Filles de leur mère*." In John Phillips. *Forbidden Fictions: Pornography and Censorship in Twentieth-century French Literature*. London: Pluto Press, 1999.

Venuti, Lawrence. "The Scandal of Translation." *French Literature Series*. 22 (1995): 25–38.

Zinszner, D. "*Pybrac* et *La Perle*." *Histoires Littéraires*. 3 (2002):63–71.

LÜ DONGBIN

c. 755–c. 805
Taoist sexual alchemy

True Classic of the Complete Union, by All-assisting Lord Ch'un-yang

This longish title, *Chunyang yen-cheng fu-yu ti-chün jiji chen-ching*, so translated by Robert van Gulik, is rendered somewhat differently by Douglas Wile: *All-Merciful Lord Chunyang's True Classic of Perfect Union*. The book exists only in compilations, together with another work of Deng Xixian, *Explanation of the Meaning of the Cultivation of Truth, by the Great Immortal of the Purple-gold Splendour* [*Zijin guangyao daxian xiuzhen yanyi*], under the common title of *Baizhan bi sheng* [*Victory assured in every battle*].

The Chinese text, as copied in van Gulik's *Erotic Prints* from a late nineteenth-century Japanese print, is said to be identical to a small Chinese block print of the Wan-li era (1573–1620). According to van Gulik: "Whereas the main text shows many archaic features, the commentary bears the hall mark of a late Taoist sexological text, and seems to date from the early Ming period" (15th century). Wile (p. 114) agrees with this theory and classifies both works among handbooks for householders.

The term *yanyi* (amplifying the meaning) was, since the sixteenth-century, a rather common denomination for popular amplification turning history into romance. Would it be far-fetched to consider the original edition as a late Ming commercial venture caring for a larger public at a time when prohibition of such book was lax? Should it be read as a pleasant pastiche of the battle of love rather than a serious guide to immortality? The following work seems to preclude such a hypothesis.

The main text of the booklet, less than four hundred words, is divided by commentaries in nine sections where the opposition we/ them (the enemy) is to be explained as ego/she. The archaisms, sounding Tang (618–906), are indeed within the reach of any scholar of average competence of that time. The comments, in rather plain language, must not have been out of the reach of an eager though popular readership. Let us submit to the best of our judgment the penultimate paragraph when the description of the final battle turns rather more technical, in the tentative translation below:

> While we slow down, they rouse up, and the situation becomes again momentous. While arms clash, we enter and retire again, sucking anew their supplies and seizing their grains. Tortoise, tiger, snake and dragon: retracting, terrifying, swallowing and absorbing. For sure they will throw up their arms. We shall reap winds and rains. That is what completes victory and lengthen peace for a whole generation. The battle

is over and arms at rest. Stretched in the void, we aspire for rest, lying on the back. Returning the booty to our armoury, we climb the highest point.

Momentous means the intensity of her excitation. Her arousal being complete, one must again enter, deep or shallow, methodically, and retire again a short while. One should **suck** her tongue and **seize** her breasts. When following the previous procedures, her true essence will be entirely shed while one gathers and absorbs it. After this **completion**, the true Yang is to be obtained. A dozen years form a **generation.** By mastering the true Yang after completion it is possible to lengthen one's life by a generation. **Armoury** means the marrow-sea, the brains. The **highest point** is the *niwan* (top of the brain). After the battle, it's time to dismount and rest, lying on the back. By **stretching** the waist and undulating, we ascend the **highest point** in order to return to our primal stock. Then, protected against any disease, we should obtain long life.

What is this true Yang leading to immortality? The preface of Deng Xixian clarifies somewhat what is at stake: "After completion, *jiji* (translated in the title *Complete Union* by van Gulik, *Perfect Union* by Wile), is the name of a hexagram in the *Yijing* (Confucian Classic of Mutations). The upper trigram is called *kan*, the lower *li*. *Li* is the male, but the void (a broken line) in the middle is the true Yin. That is why male is Yang on the outside, but Yin inside. *Kan* is the

female trigram, full male in the middle. That is why female is Yin on the outside, but male inside. In the intercourse of *kan* with *li* true Yin can be absorbed to reinforce true Yang which becomes pure Yang. That is why "after completion" is part of the title of the following book."

Biography

Dongbin is the well-known nickname of Lü Yan who may have lived around 755–805.

ANDRÉ LÉVY

Editions

Gulik, Robert van. *Erotic Colors Prints of the Ming Period, with An Essay on Chinese Sex Life from the Han to the Ch'ing Dynasty, B.C. 206–A.D. 1644. Trois volumes, 210 + 243 + 50 p., privately published, Tokyo 1951, vol. II, p. 91–96.*

Wile, Douglas. *Art of the Bedchamber, The Chinese Sexual Yoga Classics, including Women's Solo Meditation Texts.* State University of New York Press, Albany 1992,). "All-Merciful Savior Lord Ch'un-yang's True Classic of Perfect Union," p.133–136.

Further Reading

Gulik, Robert van. *Sexual Life in Ancient China, A preliminary survey of Chinese sex and society from ca. 1500 B.C. till 1644 A.D.* Leiden: E.J. Brill 1961, p. 277–280.

LÜ TIANCHENG

c. 1580–c. 1620
Chinese novelist

Xiuta Yeshi [*Unofficial History of the Embroidered Couch*]

Xiuta Yeshi [*The Unofficial History of the Embroidered Couch*] is a short novel likely written about 1600, in the flourishing region south of the Yangzi river in China. This work, like many other works of pornography of its time, has limited literary value, and its fame has been tied to its status as pornography rather than as literature. It did not survive the Qing dynasty (1644–1911) censorships and quickly fell out of wide circulation, while erotic novels of greater literary merit like the *Jin Ping Mei* became increasingly famous and now are counted among the masterpieces of Chinese literature. *Xiuta Yeshi* was not singled out by the Qing Imperial code but rather was among many works banned and burned by decrees of 1688, 1702, and 1710 prohibiting all fiction with obscene words. It was later singled out by name and banned by the Prefect of Zhejiang in 1844 and the Governor of Jiangsu in 1868. *Xiuta Yeshi,* was never forgotten, though, since it is mentioned twice by name as an example of pornographic literature in the much more famous and well-regarded novel *Rou Pu Tuan* [*The Carnal Prayer Mat*], and referenced by many other works as epitomizing Ming pornographic fiction.

The plot of *Xiuta Yeshi* is simple, and serves primarily as a framework to recount all manner of sexual acts and to describe them in very coarse, direct language. It concerns a candidate of literature named Yao Tongxin, who goes by the name of "Dongmen" who has a beautiful wife and a homosexual lover who is a younger colleague called Zhao Dali. After Dongmen's wife dies in the first pages of the story, he marries a bawdy young girl named Jin, who at his behest has a liaison with his friend Dali. Dali's mother is a young widow called Mrs. Ma, who is infatuated with Dongmen. Over the course of the novel, these four people engage each other in sexual combat, in all possible combinations and positions; with the young maids of the Dongmen household occasionally joining in. Jin, Mrs. Ma, and Dali all die untimely deaths, and Dongmen repents and enters a monastery.

One of the few remarkable aspects of this novel lies in its vigorous colloquial style, using specific slang, rather than euphemisms, to describe anatomy and sex acts. The poems at the end of each chapter are the only aspect of the work to receive critical praise, in part because they approximate the poetry in more esteemed works of erotic narrative. Much of the value of *Xiuta Yeshi* lies in its cache as the epitome of popular Ming pornography, its citations by later, better works, and its indebtedness to earlier ones. In particular, it is influenced by *Jin Ping Mei.* The protagonists Dongmen ("Eastern Gate) and Jin of *Xiuta Yeshi* are obvious references to Ximen ("Western Gate") and Jinlian, the most notorious characters of *Jin Ping Mei.* There is borrowing of phrases and motifs, for instance the odd situation of a Buddhist monk supplying characters with dangerous sexual aphrodisiacs. As an anthropological text, it is notable for its representation of a much wider spectrum of sexual activity, fellatio, anal sex, cunnilingus, male and female auto-eroticism, and so forth, than is presented in more literary works. Thus it serves primarily as an important work for the study of literati culture and the history of Chinese literature.

There is evidence that *Xiuta Yeshi* was quite popular during the time of its author. Over the last decades of the Ming Dynasty, it was published in no less than three separate editions. In the waning years of the Ming which fell in 1644, the *Xiuta Yeshi* and similar obscene novels were read all over China, and exerted great influence on erotic paintings and picture albums, which frequently featured their poems. Most erotic pictures in Ming Dynasty sexual manuals are also accompanied by an explanation in verse. Additionally, erotic albums often featured poetry alongside their pictures matching the name of the poem's metrical pattern or a line of the poem to a subject or sexual position featured in the plate. Many of the poems in *Xiuta Yeshi* and erotic albums are entirely or practically identical, showing a widespread community of producers of erotic literature and painting that were mutually influential.

Biography

The title page of early editions ascribe the authorship to the "Master of Perverse Desires," but it now appears that *Xiuta Yeshi* was written by Lü Tiancheng (c. 1580–1620), a native of Zhejiang province, who seems to have spent most of his life in Suzhou and Nanjing. Chiefly known as a poet, he may have also written another erotic novel called *Xianqing Bie Zhuan* [*Unofficial Record of Leisurely Passion*]. It has been postulated by Van Gulik that the poems in *Xiuta Yeshi,* its primary literary achievement, were composed by a number of authors. These were likely members of the author's literary group who met regularly and wrote poems while drinking and enjoying the company of courtesans. The famous scholar Li Zhi (1527–1602) added a commentary, and Feng Menglong (died 1644) edited the text.

ANDREW SCHONEBAUM

Editions (and Translations)

Lü Tiancheng. *The Embroidered Couch*, trans. Lenny Hu. Vancouver: Arsenal Pulp Press, 2001.

Xiuta Yeshi [Qingdianzhuren zhu] Minguo sinian Shanghai Tushuguan paiying ben. In *Zhongguo gu yan xi pin cong kan. di 2 ji* reprint Taipei, 1987.

Further Reading

Van Gulik, R.H. *Erotic Color Prints of the Ming Period.* Privately published in fifty copies in Tokyo 1951.

Van Gulik, R.H. *Sexual Life in Ancient China: A Preliminary Survey of Chinese Sex and Society from ca. 1500 B.C. till 1644 A.D.* Leiden: Brill 1961.

See also **Jin Ping Mei Hong Lou Meng Zhulin Yeshi**

LUNCH, LYDIA

1959–
American poet, dramatist, and novelist

The artist Lydia Lunch may best be described as a *confrontationalist*. Whether Lunch is using music, film, photography, poetry, prose, or spoken word, she engages her audience with the apathy and oppression of modern industrialized society: "the ills that obsess" her. Her material is, thus, primarily non-fictional. She marks as influences Henry Miller, Hubert Selby Jr., and Jean Genet: artists she sees as having had no fear in revealing "the truth about their lives."

Many of Lunch's spoken word pieces focuses on human sexuality. In *Oral Fixation* (released in 1988; included on 1996 reissue *The Uncensored Lydia Lunch/Oral Fixation* and on *Crimes Against Nature*, 1994, reissued 1999), sex is presented as "an animal act" that has been convoluted by emotion. Lunch portrays sexuality as a struggle in which "the human animal" vainly attempts to control sexual instinct "in order to ... fit into the *norm* of society." With "the banality of" life becoming "too chronic and depressing a constant to bear," it is only "the threat of constant danger or the imprisonment of incomprehensible pain" that can offer a "suitable distraction" from "dull reality."

Noted among Lunch's musical works for displaying a concern with the erotic are 1989's *Stinkfist* and 1998's *Matrikamantra*. *Stinkfist* is a percussive sexual mantra depicting the "life cycle as practiced in the ritual of coition." Lunch collaborated on the album with Jim

"Foetus" Thirlwell (formerly of the Birthday Party and using the alias Clint Ruin). *Matrikamantra* (Mother of all Mantras; Om; the magical sound that brought forth everything in existence) is a double-CD in what Lunch calls the illustrated word style. Lunch's E.M. Coiran and Baudelaire inspired lyrics are set against the atmospheric musical compositions of Joseph Budenholzer. The album deals with what Lunch calls the "transgenerational orgy" that perpetuates human existence. It opens with the song *Need to Feed*, which includes lines from *Paradoxia: A Predator's Diary* that discuss the void within the self and a search for meaning beyond the cycle of life and death.

Among her films, *Fingered* (1986) and *Visiting Desire* (1996) are noted for their erotic content. *Fingered* was directed by Richard Kern. Lunch scripted and performed in the 25-minute, black-and-white film focusing on the relation between sex and violence (see Bataille's *Eroticism*, for relation between sex and violence). In *Visiting Desire*, director Beth B placed her camera before a bed and had twelve people, including Lunch, interact with each other in attempts to satisfy their sexual desires. The results highlighted the connection between sexuality and identity.

In 1982, *Adulterers Anonymous* (a book of poetry) was released. Lunch collaborated with Exene Cervenka, formerly of the Los Angeles punk band X. Many of the poems present the brutal side of the male/female sexual relationship that is the focus of much of Lunch's work. In 1992, *Incriminating Evidence*, illustrated by

Kristian Hoffman, was released. The book is a collection of some of Lunch's spoken word pieces (*The Beast* and *Daddy Dearest* are on the CD *Crimes Against Nature*; *The Gun is Loaded* has been released on video), essays, stories, and plays. Lunch thrusts upon the reader a challenge to examine the darker side of human existence. This includes frank and vivid considerations of the sex/violence matrix. In the play, *South of Your Border*, Lunch posits that power and control are central to this matrix. Whether it is Captain Leanardo raping, beating, and cutting a bound Lydia Lunch, or Lunch, as a dominatrix, threatening her bound, hooded client, the roles of victim and victimizer are not absolute: they vary between situations dependant upon who controls the sex/violence matrix.

Paradoxia: A Predator's Diary was Lunch's first novel, published in 1997 by Creation Books. The novel is an autobiographical work that chronicles the author's relationships with men. Throughout the book the duplicity of Lunch's character is evident. Her desire to control, abuse, and consume men is matched with her quest for men who are themselves seeking to control, abuse and consume. She is a predator preying on predators.

The novel aptly begins with the first and defining male relationship of her life: her father Lenny. He is portrayed as a small-time hustler and gambler turned door-to-door salesman who thrives on the weak resistance that lonely housewives offer against his sexual advances. Lunch identifies herself as her "father's daughter" in that she has inherited his predatory nature.

Raised under his mental and physical (violent and sexual) abuse, Lunch's psyche is constructed as a copy of the father's, that of the male predator: "So twisted by men, a man, my father that I became like one"(7). She defines males and herself as being ruthless, arrogant, stubborn, distant, and cruel. She admits to adoring these qualities in males but is also cognizant that men despise these same qualities in women. In Lunch's work, the physical male/female binary is maintained while the mental binary is torn asunder. This establishes the role reversal of sexual mentality and ensuing power struggles that underlie Lunch's conflictive relationships with men.

However, there is an affinity between Lunch and her partners: the desire for an excessive behavior that breaks through the boundaries of social constraints. These excesses are manifested in drug and alcohol indulgence, violence, and sexual practices, usually in combination. Propelled by an insatiable thirst, Lunch travels through locals which include New York, Los Angeles, London, San Francisco, and New Orleans, recounting a journey of one-night stands, orgies, and long-term relationships with a cast of sexual partners that includes women, young-boys, musicians, artists, drifters, and criminals. The constant upon which these myriad encounters are tied is Lunch's attempt to "find someone, anyone, something, anything, that could feed into me what I needed" (Lunch uses these lines in *Need to Feed*). Lunch's epiphany comes with the realization of her "vampirism," her understanding that she was trying to steal from others those aspects of their being which reminded her of herself. Of this struggle through mutilation, physical and mental, self-inflicted and received, and her own penchant for using others, Lunch concludes: "I was looking in vain for myself as I willingly disappeared inside of others"(149).

Biography

Born Lydia Koch in Rochester, New York 1959. Ran away from home to New York City at the age of 14. In 1976, started New York "No-Wave" band *Teenage Jesus and the Jerks*. Lunch's career picked up momentum in 1979 when the band was featured on the *No New York* album, conceived of and produced by Brian Eno. In 1984, Lunch founded Widowspeak Productions to facilitate the release of her diversifying art and that of other non-mainstream artists. The labels first release was of spoken word material, *The Uncensored Lydia Lunch* (1984). Co-presented with Matthew Yokobosky, curator of the Whitney Museum, *The History of Underground Film*. Taught a visiting artist workshop in the Performance/Video Department of the San Francisco Art Institute. Coeditor of online magazine called *Sex and Guts* where Lunch contributes essays and reviews on myriad topics and products ranging from the political to the erotic.

MICHAEL KEARNEY

Selected Works

Adulterers Anonymous. With Exene Cervenka, 1982, reissued 1996.
The Gun is Loaded. (Video), 1988.
Bloodsucker. Illustrated by Bob Fingerman. 1992.

Incriminating Evidence. Illustrated by Kristian Hoffman, 1992.

As.fix.e.8. With Nick Cave. Illustrated by Mike Matthews, 1993.

Crimes Against Nature. (Audio), 1994.

Stinkfist + The Crumb. (Audio), 1996.

Paradoxia: A Predator's Diary. 1997.

Matrikamantra. (Audio), 1998.

Adulterers Anonymous II. With Exene Cervenka, 2001.

Further Reading

Bataille, Georges. *Eroticism.* translated by Mary Dalwood, London: Penguin, 2001.

Bockris, Victor. *Beat Punk: New York's Underground Culture from the Beat Generation to the Punk Explosion.* New York: Da Capo Press, 2000.

Hancunt, Maren. *Lady Lazarus: Confronting Lydia Lunch.* Blaenau Ffestiniog UK: Questing Beast, 2000.

Kristeva, Julia. *The Sense and Non-Sense of Revolt.* Translated by Jeanine Herman, New York: Columbia University Press, 2000.

McNeil, Legs. *Please Kill Me: The Uncensored Oral History of Punk.* New York: Penguin, 1997.

Moi, Toril. *Sexual/Textual Politics: Feminist Literary Theory.* London: Routledge, 2002.

Sargent, Jack. *Suture: The Arts Journal.* London: Creation Books, 1998.

Vale, V. *RE/Search #13: Angry Women.* San Francisco, CA: RE/Search Publications, 1992.

LUSTFUL TURK, THE

The Lustful Turk was first published in 1828 in London by John Benjamin Brookes and reprinted later in the century by William Dugdale. The anonymous author of *The Lustful Turk* appears to have also written *Scenes of the Seraglio*, a similar work published first in the 1820s by Brookes that was also reprinted by Dugdale.

An epistolary novel largely composed of letters between Emily and her cousin Silvia, the Dey of Algiers and the Bey of Tunis, it also features a description of convent life in Italy and recollections of abductions and seductions that are loosely bound together by the theme of harem life. *The Lustful Turk* sets out many of the fantasies and tensions in nineteenth-century Orientalist literature by focusing on the "Eastern" predilection for Western women and the sexual decadence of the harem. According to Edward Said, such Western beliefs about the Orient emerged from "a battery of desires, repressions, and investments, and projections." Thus, the novel details a Western libidinal investment in the East, rather than mapping the libido of the East itself. The novel features heterosexual intercourse, deflorative rape as a method of inducing female passion, flagellation, anal intercourse, and anti-clerical allegations. Set against the Greek uprising against the Ottoman Empire,

the story makes use of current anti-Turk accusations laid out in Byron, Gothic motifs, and eighteenth-century libertine works. Thus, the writer demonstrates a familiarity with contemporary literature and with the history of pornography.

The main story of Emily Barlow and her cousin Silvia, begins in 1814 when Emily's parents send her to the marriage market in India. On her voyage, Emily is abducted by Moorish pirates who send her to the Dey's harem where he rapes her, thereby awakening her passions. Little distinction is made in the novel between Moors, Algerians, Arabs, and Turks or between seduction and rape. Throughout the story, virginity is an aphrodisiac to men and a impediment for women; the penis becomes a weapon and an instrument of pleasure a "wonderful instrument of nature—this terror of virgins, but delight of women." (*The Lustful Turk*, 39) As her familiarity with the harem and its inhabitants grows, Emily recounts the histories of its inhabitants which include an Italian, a Greek, and a French woman. The Italian woman, Honoria, married her lover but was afraid to consummate the union. An abduction on the Mediterranean brought Honoria to the Dey's harem where she was flogged for struggling and then raped, introducing her to sensuality.

Honoria informs Emily of the Dey's penchant for anal sex bringing about a stalemate: Emily struggles to use the Dey's affections for her to guarantee his abstinence, whereas the Dey sees it as one of his natural rights to her body. Emily's searches for an ally in the contest and finds that a Greek girl in the harem also dislikes anal intercourse. This leads to another aside: a failed but heroic attempt of Greek resistance told through the Ozman's machinations to steal the Greek girl's virginity. Oddly enough, while the Turks are vilified for murdering her lover and father, the Dey is absolved of all responsibility because of his skills as a lover. The letters then relate Silvia's abduction by the Dey. Interspersed with these harem stories are letters that detail the Dey's own sexual machinations and desires, and "found" letters from priests who supplied the harem with women from Italian convents.

This novel contrasts the hypocrisy of the Western treatments of sexuality with the sensual transparency and sexual pleasures of harem life. The harem stripped away social proscriptions from Western women and encouraged them to realize their supposedly inborn sexual nature. Western convents and marriages impede female sexual pleasure; the harem, in contrast, creates an ambiance for abandoned sexuality as each girl lets go of false modesty and prudery to find sexual pleasure. At the same time, though, the variety of women confined for a single male's pleasure extols the benefits of unrestrained, rampant masculine privilege. The plethora of women and complete sexual control over them allows for an exploration of man's capacities for sexual freedom, but only at the expense of the women's. Attempts to reconcile despotism with natural sensuality lead to a model in which women desire a loss of freedom when controlled by a good master. "The Dey, indeed had soon discovered my folly [chastity], and like a man of sense, took the proper method to subdue me. In this way, in one short night, you see, he put to rout all my pure virgin scruples, rapturously teaching me the nature of love's sacred mysteries, and the great end for which we poor weak females are created." (*The Lustful Turk*, 62–63)

The Lustful Turk illustrates the pleasures of the harem but demonstrates that these pleasures devolve into degeneracy in sexuality as in politics. The Dey is eventually castrated by a harem slave when he "commenced his attack on her second maidenhead." Because he loses all desire as a result of castration, he liberates his harem and the inhabitants return home. Still, the Dey's skills as a lover remain unquestioned: Emily comments that she will never marry until she finds as good a lover as the Dey. The vacillation between admiration for the harem and condemnation for Eastern sexual degeneracy, particularly the Eastern penchant for sodomy, frames the story. *The Lustful Turk* resolves this by showing the Turk to be at once both dominant and subordinate, rampant and castrated.

Although at the time it was published the epistolary novel had gone out of vogue in English literature, *The Lustful Turk* shows its continued efficacy as an erotic medium; the confessional letters create multiple viewpoints allowing for multiple subjectivities and a great deal of indeterminacy. The loose links between letters creates a pastiche-effect rather than a clear narrative structure. The continued representation of women as needing domination, however, creates a model of female sexuality that was outdated, even for nineteenth-century erotic literature, but one that presaged later erotic tales like "The Story of O."

LISA Z. SIGEL

Further Readings

Colligan, Colette. "Obscenity and Empire: England's Obscene Print Culture in the Nineteenth Century." PhD Dissertation, Queen's College, 2002.

Kendrick, Walter. *The Secret Museum: Pornography in Modern Culture.* New York: Viking Press, 1987.

Marcus, Steven. *The Other Victorians.* New York: W.W. Norton & Company, 1985.

Mendes, Peter. *Clandestine Erotic Fiction in English 1800–1930.* London: Scolar Press, 1993.

Said, Edward, *Orientalism.* New York: Vintage Books, 1979.

Sigel, Lisa Z. *Governing Pleasures: Pornography and Social Change in England, 1815–1914.* New Jersey: Rutgers University Press, 2002.

Yeazell, Ruth. *Harems of the Mind: Passages of Western Art and Literature.* Yale University Press, 2000.

M

MACORLAN, PIERRE

1882–1970
French novelist, essayist, journalist, poet, and *chansonnier*

Pierre MacOrlan was a major exponent of post-1918 *inquiétude,* the cultural and intellectual disorientation following World War I. Although he only established himself as a novelist with the pirate novel *Le Chant de l'équipage* (1918) and the major body of his work was produced between the two world wars, his extensive career began before World War I and continued until he was in his eighties. He is best known for his 1927 novel *Le Quai des brumes* following its adaptation into a successful film (1938) directed by Marcel Carné and starring Jean Gabin and Michèle Morgan; nonetheless, other novels, such as *L'Ancre de Miséricorde* (1941), also brought him considerable commercial success. MacOrlan was a member of the prestigious Académie Goncourt and received the Légion d'honneur in 1967 (although reservations about his morality due to the pornographic writing he had published under his own family name before World War I delayed this for two years).

MacOrlan's distinctiveness as a writer resides in his invention of what he calls *le fantastique social,* an unhealthy, threatening presence hidden beneath the surface of modern bourgeois urban society, of which modern technology, satanism, violence, and, in particular, morbid sexual violence are key elements. Within this *fantastique social* he constantly uses techniques and subject matter from German Expressionism to depict the disturbing landscape of the modern city, post-1918 inflation and decadence, prostitutes and gangsters, and doomed adventurers. His bleak, negative view of sex is discernible in some of his essays but is most evident in his established, post-1918 fiction—for example, in the satanism of *Le Nègre Léonard et maître Jean Mullin* (1920) and *Picardie* (1943), in the female espionage fiction of *Filles d'amour et ports d'Europe* (1932) and *La Nuit de Zeebrugge* (1934), in the portrayal of murdered prostitutes in *Quartier réservé* (1932) and *Le Tueur no 2* (1935) and in the unconventionally eroticized poverty of the prostitute character Nelly in *Le Quai des brumes* (1927). The title characters of the apocalyptic novels *La Cavalière Elsa*

(1921) and *La Vénus internationale* (1923) share characteristics with his prostitutes and his female spies in that they are all ultimately portrayed as masochists who are the victims of what, for MacOrlan, is sexually stimulating violent death, whether it be as the dismembered prostitutes in *Quartier réservé*, the female spies hanged or shot by firing squad in *Filles d'amour et ports d'Europe*, or the crucified Claude in *La vénus internationale*.

The eroticization of sexual violence with women as victims links the more mainstream post-1918 fiction described above to MacOrlan's earlier pornography. Many critics, and indeed Mac Orlan himself, claimed that his pornographic writing was merely a way of relieving hunger in what was a period of unremitting poverty for him, but there is evidence which belies this claim. Although his pornographic output was indeed written mostly before World War I, four pornographic novels were also published after the war when he was established, and while MacOrlan did use a variety of pseudonyms for his pornography, he also used his own family name (Dumarchey, possibly in defiance of the "respectable" uncle who had brought him up), and crucially the sadomasochistic preoccupations of his pornography are central to his post-1918 fiction. The pornography is conventional and functional, with undeveloped characters, in particular the females, and for the most part the effect is relatively tame. *La Semaine secrète de Vénus* (1926) is an example of this "soft-core" pornography. Possibly in line with his post-1918 position as an established writer (although published anonymously), this novel is written in a much more highbrow style than some of the earlier pornography. Comprising seven male "confessions" alongside the depiction of sexual acts, it also contains much philosophical reflection. The confessions are variously situated in an office with a "modern" typist; in the street with a member of *les classes dangereuses*, with *une gigolette*, and with a prostitute who will be murderd; in brothels; and at a devil-worship ceremony. These diverse settings reflect MacOrlan's constant interest in "modernity" and in the pulp-fiction categories of gangsters, prostitutes and satanism. However, MacOrlan also wrote a number of pornographic texts which were more "hardcore," focusing almost exclusively on flagellation, which French courts required to be destroyed— *Les Aventures amoureuses de Mademoiselle de*

Sommerange (1910), for example. Some of MacOrlan's pornography has continued to be republished since his death, for example: *La semaine secrete de Vénus*, *Les aventures amoureuses de Mademoiselle de Sommeranges,* and *Petite Dactylo*.

There is no romantic love depicted in MacOrlan's established fiction, and this is not surprising given that his treatment of sex is grounded in his sadomasochistic pornography, with its defining paradigm in Eros and Thanatos, in an obsession with death and particularly the execution of women. In exploiting the pain and suffering of his female characters, MacOrlan draws, again, on the pulp-fiction categories of satanism, espionage, and prostitution and manages to force his readers into the prurient, voyeuristic position of realizing that they are reading pornography, the power of which he has no doubts about. Like the adventure writing he theorizes on in *Le petit manuel du parfait aventurier* (1920), Mac Orlan maintains that erotic writing can have considerable power over a reader and that this is dangerous because it unleashes the imagination.

Biography

Born Péronne, France, February 26. Educated at the Lycée d'Orléans and then the Ecole Normale d'Instititeurs, Rouen (1888–99). Arrived in Paris (Montmartre) in 1899. Spent 1901–5 in Rouen as a copyeditor/proofreader for a publisher before returning to Montmartre. Traveled to London, Le Havre, Knokke, Bruges, and Naples before 1914. Married Marguerite Luc (1913). Invalided out of World War I at Bapaume in 1916. Subsequently traveled to Alsace and the Rhineland, Barcelona, Brest, Tangiers, Tunis, Berlin, and Brighton after the war, often as a journalist. Moved from Paris to Saint-Cyr-sur-Morin in 1927. Elected to the Académie Goncourt (1950). Awarded Légion d'honneur (1967). Died June 27.

ROGER W. BAINES

Editions

Filles d'amour et ports d'Europe. Paris: Editions de France, 1932.
La cavalière Elsa. Paris: Gallimard, 1921.
Le nègre Léonard et maître Jean Mullin. Paris: Editions de la Banderole, 1920.
La nuit de Zeebrugge. Paris: Le Masque, Librairie des Champs Elysées, 1934.

La Vénus internationale. Paris: Gallimard, 1923.

Le Quai des brumes. Paris: Gallimard, 1927.

Le Tueur no 2. Paris: Librairie des Champs Elysées, 1935.

On Board the Morning Star. Translated by Malcom Cowley. New York: Boni, 1924.

"One Floor Up." In *La Tradition de Minuit,* translated by Vyvyan Holland. London: Hamish Hamilton, 1932.

Picardie. Paris: Emile-Paul, 1943.

Quartier réservé. Paris: Gallimard, 1932.

Pseudonymous Works

Anonymous. *La Semaine secrète de Vénus.* Paris: Cotinaud, 1926.

———. *Entrée interdite au public* [?]: Cotinaud, 1926.

"Chevalier de X." *Femmes du monde et du sang bleu.* Hors Commerce, 1908.

"Claude de Saint-Hièble." *L'Instrument des apothicaires.* Paris: Fort, 1920.

"Pierre du Bourdel." *Les Aventures amoureuses de Mademoiselle de Sommerange.* Quebec: Sweetgra's, 1910.

———. *Mademoiselle de Mustelle et ses amies.* Quebec: Sweetgra's, 1911.

"Pierre Dumarchey." *La Comtesse au fouet.* Paris: Fort, 1908.

———. *Les Grandes flagellées de l'histoire.* Paris: Fort, 1909.

———. *Le Masochisme en Amérique.* Paris: Fort, 1910.

———. *Lise fessée.* Paris: Fort, 1910.

"Pierre de Jusange," preface to Docteur Fowler, *Les Flagellants.* Paris: Fort, 1911.

"Sadie Blackeyes." *Baby douce fille.* Paris: Fort, 1912.

———. *Miss.* Paris: Fort, 1912.

———. *Quinze ans.* Paris: Fort, 1913.

———. *Petite dactylo.* Paris: Fort, 1914.

"Sadinet." *Petites cousines* [?]: *A La Folie du Jour,* 1919.

Further Reading

Baines, Roger W. *'Inquiétude' in the work of Pierre Mac Orlan.* Amsterdam: Rodopi, 2000.

Grainville, Patrick. Preface to Mac Orlan, *La Semaine secrète de Vénus.* Paris: Arléa, 1993.

Hewitt, Nicholas. "Montmartre and 'Inquiétude' in the Interwar Novel: Dorgelès and Mac Orlan." *Essays in French Literature* 37 (2000): 45–61.

Lacassin, Francis. Preface to Mac Orlan ("Sadinet" pseud.), *Petites Cousines.* Paris: Ramsay, 1987.

Lamy, Jean-Claude. *Mac Orlan, l'aventurier immobile.* Paris: Albin Michel, 2002.

Pia, Pascal. Preface to *Madmoiselle de Mustelle et ses amies.* Paris: Ramsay, 1980.

MADNESS

The definition of madness has not remained stable and probably never will, for defining madness is primarily a social act, the concept of madness itself a cultural construct. There is no such thing as a transhistorical or universal definition of madness. The term is simply a generic one used to label a wide array of ideas and/or behaviors thought to be abnormal. Because our beliefs and practices change over the centuries and differ across cultures, so too does our perception of what is rational or irrational, what is sane or insane. Beliefs that would have seemed perfectly reasonable to a person living during the Middle Ages might seem rather mad to those of us living in the twenty-first century. In the medieval realm of medicine, for example, it was considered important to keep women under control or subordinate, for medical authorities believed that if a man allowed his wife to move toward any degree of equality, she would be liable to somatic change and apt to challenge him for control. This idea may have gained support from the writings of the tenth-century philosopher and physician Avicenna, who asserted that if a hen fought with and conquered a rooster, she would grow spurs.

Like beliefs, practices that might seem mad to us today were considered perfectly acceptable or even desirable in the past. In 920 CE, during the reign of the Southern Tang dynasty, the ancient Chinese practice of foot binding became popular and remained so until it was formally outlawed in 1911. Despite the fact that the binding of a five-year-old girl's foot resulted in the breaking of bones, the malformation and malodor of the foot, an inability to walk without aid, and in some cases ulceration, paralysis, and gangrene, the practice was considered highly fashionable;

and on an adult woman, the tiny three-inch foot, referred to as the "golden lotus," was considered erotic. Crippling the body for the sake of eroticism was not limited to the East, however. In the 1800s and early 1900s, women in many Western countries wore corsets laced so tightly that a 26-inch waist became a 17-inch waist. And while a corset may have given a woman the S-curve silhouette considered desirable at the time, it also, if laced too tightly, created lower back pain, breathing difficulties, and knee problems. With the rise of the twentieth century's "let it all hang out" attitude, the corset ceased to play a central role in everyday fashion, becoming instead a popular fetish item, the costume of the dominatrix; and for those living in the first decade of the twenty-first century who wish to take their fetishism to what might be called its dramatic and artistic height, it is possible to get a corset piercing: two vertical columns of back surface piercings that mimic corset eyelets through which ribbon can be threaded. Although an erotic attachment to a handkerchief seemed aberrant enough to be labeled a paraphilia in nineteenth-century Vienna, today this fetish would seem quaint indeed, for now there are acrotomophiliacs, or amputee devotees (nicely exemplified by Flannery O'Connor's Manly Pointer, a young Bible salesman who is attracted to a woman because of her wooden leg), and apotemnophiliacs, or amputee wannabes, who wish to have a limb removed in order to feel whole. Clinicians refer to this condition as "body integrity identity disorder." The slide from fashion to fetish is a short one, and although perversion was not assigned its sexological sense by the Oxford English Dictionary until the publication of its 1933 supplement, it has always been easy to draw a vector from the sexual to the perverse to the insane.

Perhaps the most vivid example of this vector, capable of showing in narrative form the vicissitudes of madness, is hysteria, which has a long and venerable history. For centuries, the symptoms of hysteria have been associated with "deviant" sexual conduct and conditions such as masturbation, stimulation by pornography, irregular menstruation, and childlessness. And thus, since the time of Plato, the cure for hysterical abnormality has been the "normality" of marriage and pregnancy. We may be accustomed to thinking of hysteria as a Victorian ailment, but it has been around for centuries, the oldest known record being an Egyptian medical papyrus dating from about 1900 BCE. The Egyptians believed the cause of hysteria to be the dislocation of the uterus, which they conceived of as a mobile organism, capable of shifting up and away from its normal position. Given this explanation for the cause of hysterical disturbances, the cures the Egyptians came up with seem perfectly logical if rather humorous. In order to get the uterus to return to its proper place, one of two approaches could be taken: a woman's genitals could be treated with fragrant substances to attract the uterus from below, or a woman could be given unpleasant-tasting potions to swallow in order to force the uterus back into place from above. In medieval times, hysteria was no longer thought of as an illness but as a form of witchcraft or demonic possession. By the eighteenth century, the explanation for hysteria had become attached to the notion of "sympathies" and the nervous system. Because women were supposed to have a more highly impressionable sensibility than men, they were more frequently attacked by the illness. It is not surprising that in the early nineteenth century, moral and ethical components had been added to hysteria's etiology. By the late nineteenth century, Freud was connecting the medieval theory of possession to his own theories of the foreign body and the splitting of consciousness. And by 1897, his analyses of hysterical patients had convinced him that the "medieval demons" that possessed them were actually close male relatives such as fathers, uncles, brothers, and cousins. If what typically comes to mind when one thinks of the hysteric is something akin to the creature that New York physician E.H. Dixon wrote of in the 1840s:

[a] "patient writhing like a serpent upon the floor, rending her garments to tatters, plucking out handsful of hair, and striking her person with violence—with contorted and swollen countenance and fixed eyes resisting every effort of bystanders to control her

it's no surprise that this is how the hysteric is represented in a literary text such as *Jane Eyre*, which features Bertha Mason, the quintessential madwoman in the attic whose intemperate and unchaste behavior was said to have prematurely developed the germs of insanity.

BECKY MCLAUGHLIN

Further Reading

Foucault, Michel. *Madness and Civilization: A History of Insanity in the Age of Reason*. New York: Vintage, 1988.

Gilman, Sander. *Seeing the Insane*. New York: John Wiley and Sons, 1982.

Goffman, Erving. *Stigma: Notes on the Management of Spoiled Identity*. New York: Touchstone/Simon & Schuster, 1986.

Goldberg, Ann. *Sex, Religion, and the Making of Modern Madness*. New York: Oxford University Press, 1999.

Grob, Gerald N. *The Mad Among Us: A History of the Care of America's Mentally Ill*. New York: Free Press, 1994.

Hacking, Ian. *Mad Travelers: Reflections on the Reality of Transient Mental Illnesses*. Cambridge, MA: Harvard University Press, 2002.

————. *Rewriting the Soul: Multiple Personality and the Sciences of Memory*. Princeton, NJ: Princeton University Press, 1998.

Jimenez, Mary Ann. *Changing Faces of Madness: Early American Attitudes and Treatment of the Insane*. Hanover, NH: University Press of New England, 1987.

Jordanova, Ludmilla. *Nature Displayed: Gender, Science and Medicine, 1760–1820*. London: Pearson Education; New York: Longman, 1999.

Lunbeck, Elizabeth. *The Psychiatric Persuasion: Knowledge, Gender, and Power in Modern America*. Princeton, NJ: Princeton University Press, 1994.

McDonald, Michael. *Mystical Bedlam: Madness, Anxiety, and Healing in Seventeenth Century England*. Cambridge, UK: Cambridge University Press, 1981.

Ng, Vivien W. *Madness in Late Imperial China: From Illness to Deviance*. Norman: University of Oklahoma Press, 1990.

Porter, Roy. *A Social History of Madness: The World Through the Eyes of the Insane*. New York: E.P. Dutton, 1987.

Showalter, Elaine. *Hystories*. New York: Columbia University Press, 1998.

Torrey, E. Fuller, and Judy Miller. *The Invisible Plague: The Rise of Mental Illness from 1750 to the Present*. New Brunswick, NJ: Rutgers University Press, 2002.

Whitaker, Robert. *Mad in America: Bad Science, Bad Medicine, and the Enduring Mistreatment of the Mentally Ill*. Cambridge, MA: Perseus Publishing, 2003.

Wood, Jane. *Passion and Pathology in Victorian Fiction*. Oxford and New York: Oxford University Press, 2001.

MAHABHARATA

Kama as a deified abstraction appears from time to time in the *Mahabharata*, usually accompanied by his twin vice, Krodha (Anger), less often by his wife Rati (Sexual Pleasure). And the *Mahabharata* on occasion refers to, but does not tell, the story of Kama's conquest by Shiva. But *kama* as a force in human life dominates the text, determining major moves in the plots.

The basic problem posed by *kama* in this text is that in generation after generation, kings keep falling in love with the wrong women, thus putting the royal line of success in jeopardy and leading to violent, deadly conflicts. It begins with the inappropriate lust (*kama*) of the great-grandfather of the heroes, King Shantanu, who, first of all, falls in love with an incarnate river goddess (the Ganges). She makes him promise to destroy all of their children at birth, until at last the eighth, Bhishma, survives to be the legitimate son (though the Ganges departs, abandoning him) [1.94]. Shantanu then falls in love with a lower-class woman, Satyavati, a fisherman's daughter and already a woman with a past: she has already given birth to the sage Vyasa after a one-night stand with a sage [1.99]. Satyavati makes Shantanu promise that her son(s) will rule, passing over Bhishma, whom she forces to swear a vow of eternal chastity, and Shantanu, overpowered by *kama,* rashly agrees to this. When Shantanu dies, and his sons by Satyavati die, Bhishma is unable to assume the throne; Vyasa therefore begets sons by Shantanu's widows, but these sons are flawed: Pandu is "pale" (which seems to amount to being functionally impotent) and Dhritarashtra is blind [1.100]. (A parallel quandary appears in the *Ramayana* when Dasharatha falls in love with a woman who demands that her son, rather than Rama, the legitimate heir, assume the throne.)

847

Pandu becomes king but is again undone by *kama*. He kills a sage who took taken the form of a stag to mate with a doe. The dying stag/sage curses Pandu for killing him at such a special moment, when the sage was deluded by *kama*. He therefore curses Pandu to be similarly "deluded by *kama*" and to die at that moment, lying with the woman he loves. And this does happen. Elsewhere in the *Mahabharata* [1.173], another king who has been cursed to become a man-eating demon devours a sage who was making love to his wife (still in human form), and the wife, furious because she had not "finished," curses the king to die if he embraces his own wife. (Again there is a parallel text in the *Ramayana*, though it is composite: Rama's father, king Dasharatha, mistakes a boy for an elephant, kills the boy, and is cursed to lose his own son [2.57–8]; and the author himself, the poet Valmiki, saw a hunter kill the male of a pair of mating cranes, and when the hen grieved, Valmiki cried out, "Hunter, since you killed one of these birds at the height of its passion, you will not live very long" [1.1–2].)

Death and sex are thus closely intertwined in the foundational plot, as they are in countless subplots. The *Kamasutra* (composed in the 3rd century CE, the end of the period of the recension of the *Mahabharata*) warns against the dangers of desire and cites an episode from the *Mahabharata:* "Kichaka with Draupadi ... and many others afterward were seen to fall into the thrall of desire and were destroyed" [1.2.34–36]. Yashodhara, the 13th-century commentator on the *Kamasutra*, tells only part of the story: "Kichaka is said to have been super-powerful because he had the strength of a thousand elephants; but even he was destroyed by desire, for Bhima killed him when he lusted after Draupadi." "Killed him" is putting it mildly: Kichaka demands that Draupadi come to his bed; Bhima, one of Draupadi's five husbands (about whom more later), dressed as a woman, takes Draupadi's place and beats Kichaka to such a pulp that when people find his mangled corpse the next morning they say, "Where is his head?" "Which are his hands?" [4.21.1-67]—yet another example of deadly sex in disguise.

Yashodhara mentions Draupadi again, a bit later, when the *Kamasutra* quotes another scholar who said that any married woman who is known to have had five men can be seduced without moral qualms [1.5.30], and the

commentator adds: "If, besides her own husband, [a woman] has five men as husbands, she is a loose woman and eligible for everyone who has a good reason. Draupadi, however, who had Yudhishthira and the others as her own husbands, was not eligible for other men. How could one woman have several husbands? Ask the authors of the Epic!" Draupadi, the heroine of the *Mahabharata,* indeed has five husbands, the five sons of Pandu (including Bhima and Yudhishthira), under circumstances extenuated in various ways by various texts (both in the original Sanskrit version and in various retellings in Sanskrit and in vernacular languages) but never sufficiently to protect her from frequent slurs against her chastity. So the tradition looks upon them, too, the sons of Pandu, as having made a problematic sexual choice, not with regard to the particular woman but with regard to the practice of polyandry.

The sage Shvetaketu, cited often in the *Kamasutra* as a sexual authority, also has a sexual history, as Yashodhara reminds us:

Once upon a time, there was so much seduction of
    other men's wives in the world that it was said:
Women are all alike,
just like cooked rice, your majesty.
Therefore a man should not get angry with them
nor fall in love with them, but just make love with
    them.
But [Shvetaketu] forbade this state of affairs, and so
    people said:
"[Shvetaketu] forbade common people
to take other peoples' wives."
Then, with his father's permission,
Shvetaketu, who had amassed great ascetic power,
happily composed this text, which distinguishes
those who are eligible or ineligible for sex.

This is told at greater length in the *Mahabharata* [1.113.9–20]:

The great sage named Uddalaka had a son, named Shvetaketu, who became a hermit. Once, right before the eyes of Shvetaketu and his father, a Brahmin grasped his mother by the hand and said, "Let's go!" The sage's son became enraged and could not bear to see his mother being taken away by force like that. But when his father saw that Shvetaketu was angry he said, "Do not be angry, my little son. This is the eternal dharma. The women of all classes on earth are not fenced in; all creatures behave just like cows, my little son, each in its own class." The sage's son could not tolerate that dharma, and made this moral boundary for men and women on earth, for humans, but not for other creatures. And from then on this moral boundary has stood: A woman who is unfaithful to her husband commits a mortal sin that brings great misery, an evil equal to killing an embryo, and a man who seduces another man's wife, when she is a woman who keeps her vow to her husband and is thus a virgin obeying a vow of chastity, that man too commits a mortal sin on earth.

The Epic keeps insisting that this is all hearsay, as if to make us doubt it; the primal scene that it imagines is a vivid, quasi-Freudian narrative, explaining a kind of sexual revulsion. A Brahmin's right to demand the sexual services of any woman he fancies evokes violent protest in ancient Indian texts; a notorious example in the *Mahabharata* is the story of Yavakri, who tried to exert this right on the wife of another Brahmin and died [3.137.1–20].

This basically negative attitude to *kama* is only slightly balanced by stories in which good women love good men and save them (as Savitri saves her husband, Satyavan, when the god of death comes to take him way), or at least wait faithfully for them (as Damayanti waits for Nala) or, finally, follow them through thick and thin, as Draupadi follows her husbands into exile. But the *Mahabharata* is, after all, a tragic text, and in it love, certainly sexual love, is more tragic than romantic.

WENDY DONIGER

Edition

Vyasa. *Mahabharata.* Poona: Bhandarkar Oriental Research Institute, 1933–69.

Further Reading

Bhattacharya, Narendra Nath. *History of Indian Erotic Literature.* New Delhi: Munshiram Manoharlal, 1975.

Doniger, Wendy. *The Bedtrick: Tales of Sex and Masquerade.* Chicago: University of Chicago Press, 2000.

Meyer, Johan Jakob. *Sexual Life in Ancient India.* New York: Barnes and Noble, 1953.

O'Flaherty, Wendy Doniger. *Asceticism and Eroticism in the Mythology of Siva.* Oxford: Oxford University Press, 1973; retitled *Siva: The Erotic Ascetic.* New York: Galaxy, 1981.

———. *Tales of Sex and Violence: Folklore, Sacrifice, and Danger in the Jaiminiya Brahmana.* Chicago: University of Chicago Press, 1985.

———. *Women, Androgynes, and Other Mythical Beasts.* Chicago: University of Chicago Press, 1980.

Schmidt, Richard. *Beiträge zur Indischen Erotik. Das Liebeslebens des Sanskrit Volkes.* Berlin: Verlag von H. Barsdorf, 1911.

———. *Liebe und Ehe im alten und modernen Indien.* Berlin: Verlag von H. Barsdorf, 1904.

Valmiki. *Ramayana.* Baroda: Oriental Institute, 1960–75.

Vatsyayana. *Kamasutra.* With the commentary of Sri Yasodhara. Bombay: Laksmivenkatesvara Steam Press, 1856.

———. *Kamasutra.* Translated by Wendy Doniger and Sudhir Kakar. Oxford World Classics. London and New York: Oxford University Press, 2002.

MANGA

Japanese comic books

Manga are a multimillion-dollar industry and are published in a number of genres and styles on a variety of topics. During the peak period of the manga boom in the early 1990s, manga were estimated to comprise 40 percent of all print publications in Japan, and *Shōnen Jump*, the most popular among boys' manga, routinely sold over five million copies a month. However, manga are not simply for children but have a wide readership among adults as well. *Eromanga*, or so-called erotic manga, are very popular, and many titles exist, aimed at both men and women.

The term *manga* originally meant "random sketches," and antecedents of the genre can be found as far back as the seventh century. However, the origins of modern manga, which are an amalgam of illustrations and text, can be traced to illustrated tales popular during the Edo period (1603–1868). This was a time of increasing urbanization, when literacy was spreading throughout the newly emergent middle classes. The development of woodblock printing technology ensured that books, or at least unbound printed sheets, were available at a sufficiently low price to appeal to a broad audience. *Yomihon,* or "reading books," that employed simplified scripts as well as elaborate illustrations were printed on a variety of topics, of which one of the most popular proved to be *ukiyo-zōshi,* or "floating-world story books." These contained tales about the courtesans of Japan's brothel districts (euphemistically known as the "floating world"). Most of these tales are fairly innocent in nature, but a pornographic genre known as *shunga,* or "spring pictures," developed that explicitly focused on scenes of sexual intercourse involving a wide range of partners in a variety of poses, including autoerotic and homosexual scenes. Trouble with the censors meant that this kind of reading matter was frequently banned, and it remained impossible to reproduce these illustrations uncensored in books or museums in Japan until as recently as the early 1990s.

The depiction of sex in modern erotic manga is constrained by Article 175 of the Japanese penal code, which prohibits the sale of "indecent" material to minors. In actual practice, definitions of indecency where pictures are concerned tend to focus exclusively on depictions of pubic hair and sexual organs. So long as these are not included in the picture, material of an erotic nature is permitted, even in comics aimed at a young audience.

Since the 1980s, the most widespread form of erotic comic aimed at men has been "Lolita complex" stories referred to in Japanese as *rorikon.* It is commonly observed that *seinenshi* (magazines for youths) and *seijinshi* (magazines for adults) often contain at least one *rorikon* story, in which a young girl is featured as a sexual object. However, the very stylized manner in which these girls are drawn, with long legs, blond hair, and big, saucer-like eyes, works against a literalistic reading of these images: they are not meant to depict "real" girls. Since Article 175 is interpreted as prohibiting only realistic depictions of sex, *rorikon* manga can contain a range of paraphilic activities, most commonly sadomasochistic scenarios in which the girls are groped by phallic stand-ins such as alien feelers, tentacles, or machine parts. Extreme versions compose a distinct subgenre known as *hentai* (or "perverted") manga, which are not generally available from kiosks and high-end bookstores.

"Ladies' comics" (*redikomi*) cover the same kind of themes as do comics for men. At their peak in the mid-1990s there were over fifty women's titles published monthly with a combined annual circulation of 120 million. Many of these manga contain at least one erotic story, and some titles, such as *Comic Amour,* the most popular women's *eromanga,* focus exclusively on erotic stories, many of them written and illustrated by women artists like Milk Morizono. The sex depicted is not necessarily softer or more romantic than that featured in men's manga but frequently explores fantasies of rape, anal penetration, pedophilia, bondage, and sex with transvestites, transsexuals, threesomes, foursomes, and in orgies.

One of the most interesting aspects of Japanese comics is the fascination for depicting male homosexual liaisons in *shōjo* manga, or girls' comics. Stories about boys in love with boys date back to the early 1970s, when a newly emergent group of women artists dispensed with the tired boy-meets-girl theme that had previously characterized the genre. Instead, artists such as Moto Hagio and Keiko Takemiya began to depict *bishōnen,* or "beautiful boys" who were in love with each other. Classics of this genre, when collected in book form, can run into several volumes and include Hagio's *Tōma no shinzō* [*The Heart of Thomas*] (1974), which is the tragic tale of a menage à trois that takes place in a German public school at the turn of the twentieth century. The first same-sex bed scene featuring beautiful boys was drawn by Takemiya in her *Ki to kaze no uta* [*The Song of the Wind and the Trees*] (1976). By the end of the decade, stories about the homosexual liaisons of beautiful boys had become as common in girls' manga as *rorikon* stories were to become in men's. In 1978, *June* became the first monthly manga to specialize exclusively in boy-love stories, selling, at its peak, 150,000 copies a month.

Interest in boy-love stories has been stimulated in Japan due to the existence of a vibrant amateur manga movement comprising mainly young women artists and writers who create and distribute their own comic books at *komiketto* (comic markets) and, increasingly, on the Internet. This amateur genre is known as YAOI, an acronym of the Japanese phrase YAmanashi, Ochi nashi, Imi nashi, which means "no climax, no point, no meaning" and refers to the somewhat slender plots that the authors create as a pretext to get their male heroes in bed together. It has many similarities to the "PWP" (Plot? What plot?) genre of slash fiction, popular among Western women, which takes the male leads of popular TV dramas and imagines them in sexual interaction with each other.

New media such as the Internet, computer games, and mobile phones (which in Japan are used to surf the Net) have cut into manga sales in recent years, but there is no sign that erotic manga are about to disappear. Indeed, the development of the Internet has increased the number of amateurs who create their own stories and illustrations and has given wider distribution to extreme *hentai* stories that could not be published in print form because of censorship.

MARK MCLELLAND

Editions

Hagio, Moto. *Tōma no shinzō*. Tokyo: Shogakukan, 1974, 1995.

Takemiya, Keiko. *Ki to kaze no uta*. Tokyo: Hakusensha, originally published 1976, 1995.

Further Reading

Allison, Anne. *Permitted and Prohibited Desires: Mothers, Comics and Censorship in Japan*. Boulder, CO: Westview Press, 1996.

Buckley, Sandra. "Penguin in Bondage: A Tale of Japanese Comic Books." In *Technoculture*, edited by Constance Penley and Andrew Ross. Minneapolis: University of Minnesota Press, 1991.

McLelland, Mark. *Male Homosexuality in Modern Japan: Cultural Myths and Social Realities*. Richmond, VA: Curzon Press, 2000.

———. "No Climax, No Point, No Meaning? Japanese Women's 'Boy-Love' Sites on the Internet." *Journal of Communication Inquiry* 24 (July 2000): 274–91.

Schodt, Frederik. *Dreamland Japan: Writings on Modern Manga*. Berkeley, CA: Stone Bridge Press, 1996

Shiokawa, Kanako, "'The Reads' and 'Yellow Covers': Pre-Modern Predecessors of Comic Books in Japan." *Journal of Asian Pacific Communication* 7 (1996): 19–29.

MANN, THOMAS

1875–1955
German novelist

Thomas Mann's homoerotic writings are remarkable for their simple, honest, and open presentation of raw emotion and genuine passion. These writings also tend to be among Mann's most accessible and personal, reflecting his own nascent and lasting yearnings and appreciation of male beauty. In spite of Mann's apparently stable marriage of 50 years, most biographers acknowledge his bisexual, if not primarily homosexual, orientation, and critics readily interpret his characters as the embodiment of Mann's own sexual frustation. Two works of particularly homoerotic merit balance each other in this theme and context, providing the reader with male heroes, one an awkward adolescent, the other a mature, solitary man, transformed by their devotion to beautiful male figures: *Tonio Kröger*, 1903, and *Death in Venice* [*Tod in Venedig*], 1912.

The eponymous hero of *Tonio Kröger* is, like Mann himself, a physically dark figure who wants to become an artist. He is slight and gangly, and he believes that his hair, eyes, and skin reflect his racially mixed background. Although Tonio's central struggle lies in his coming to terms with his mixed heritage, he also struggles briefly with his initial homosexual feelings. His first true love is the remarkable Hans Hansen, the epitome of an idealized Germanic male: extraordinarily handsome, blond, blue-eyed, well-built, and athletic. He is also, at least to the adolescent Tonio, popular, intelligent, and kind. A simple walk together fills Tonio with palpable joy, and the narrator declares Tonio's intense love for Hans, while noting that it is sexually and emotionally unrequited. Tonio himself believes that his passion is founded in the purity

and harmony with which Hans appears to interact with the world, and the world with him. He
loves Hans for what he is not and for that which
he cannot become. Likewise, he knows that Hans
cannot reciprocate the same desires for someone
so seemingly foreign and out-of-place; tellingly,
Hans will call him by only his German surname,
Kröger, because he is repulsed by Tonio's given,
foreign name.

Mann allows Tonio to experience this intense
crush as little more than a brief phase, quickly
introducing Ingeborg Holm, a blond, blue-eyed
female counterpart to Hans. Tonio's passion for
Ingeborg seems no less intense, but she, like
Hans, remains an unattainable image rather
than a clearly defined character. Tonio leaves
town to become an artist and returns several
years later. The objects of his earlier desire
have become nearly indistinguishable, and it is
no surprise—for neither the reader nor Tonio—
to learn that they are a couple by the conclusion
of the work. Tonio writes to a friend that he feels
stranded between the worlds of the bourgeois
(represented by his father) and the artist (his
mother), and he is not fully at home in either
realm. He declares that his deepest and most
secret love will forever be reserved not for Ingeborg, nor for Hans, but for what they represent:
the blond, the blue-eyed, the happy, and the
commonplace.

Death in Venice could well be considered an
ersatz sequel to *Tonio Kröger*, as Mann introduces Gustave von Aschenbach, a sickly but
respected novelist in his fifties who finds his
passions restored by a beautiful youth. Like
Tonio, he is also physically dark and slight,
and he too is drawn to his opposite. Walking
past a cemetery one day, Aschenbach finds himself struck by an adolescent male with reddish
hair and milky skin. He watches him for a brief
while and then realizes that the young man is
staring back with an unpleasant grimace.
Aschenbach breaks his stare and immediately
feels renewed vigor, deciding to travel at that
instant. He chooses Venice as his destination
(where Mann actually began writing this piece),
and once there, he encounters what he terms the
pure visage of Eros: Tadzio, a young Polish man
of perfect, godlike beauty. Aschenbach marvels
at his ivory skin and blond, curly hair, and he
spends the remainder of his stay obsessively
watching and following Tadzio. Slowly, he
comes to believe that Tadzio is cognizant of his

desires and that the two take pleasure in brief
exchanged glances. Aschenbach contends that
human beings naturally feel respect and love
for one another as long as they do not come to
know each other so well that they can judge the
other's motives. To that end, he appears content
to watch Tadzio from afar, even as he takes
great pains to improve his own appearance by
dying his hair, choosing his ties carefully, and
applying cologne. The work's most passionate
scene alludes to and transforms Aschenbach's
first encounter with the grimacing adolescent at
the cemetery. One evening he unexpectedly happens upon his dear Tadzio (Eros) and believes
that the young man has smiled directly at him, a
smile that is so unexpected and enthralling, he
becomes flush with emotion and must run away.
He collapses from desire on a bench, sighing for
the first time the words, "I love you."

The work ends quietly, as Aschenbach
watches Tadzio swimming alone at dawn. He
enters a dreamlike state and envisions Tadzio
beckoning him to come forward; he collapses
silently in his chair and passes away that evening. It remains unclear whether Tadzio was
ever truly aware of Aschenbach. What is clear,
however, is that Mann affords Aschenbach a
deep, fully realized respect for his homoerotic
feelings that he could not allow Tonio earlier
and, perhaps, himself.

Biography

Born in Lübeck, June 6. Attended elementary
school (*Volksschule*) and high school (*Gymnasium*) in Lübeck; graduated from the *Gymnasium*
with low grades and ceased formal education,
1894. Married Katja Pringsheim, 1905; three
daughters and three sons. Visited Venice, 1911.
Supported the German war effort, 1914; life
spared by German Soviet ruler Ernst Toller at
conclusion of World War I, 1919. Awarded
Nobel Prize for Literature, 1929. Journeyed to
Switzerland, 1933. Moved to Vienna, 1935. Lost
German citizenship and became Czech citizen,
1936. Lectured at Princeton, 1939. Moved with
family to California, 1941; became American
citizen, 1944. Son Klaus committed suicide,
1949. Lectured in both East and West Germany,
1949. Returned to Switzerland, 1952. Died
of arteriosclerosis in Kilchberg, Switzerland,
August 12.

WALTER RANKIN

Selected Works

Buddenbrooks. 1901; translated by John E. Woods, 1993.
Tonio Kröger. 1903; translated by David Luke, 1988.
Tod in Venedig. 1912; as *Death in Venice*, translated by David Luke, 1988.
Der Zauberberg. 1924; as *The Magic Mountain*, translated by John E. Woods, 1996.
Doktor Faustus. 1947; as *Doctor Faustus*, translated by Helen T. Lowe-Porter, 1948.

Further Reading

Apter, T.E. *Thomas Mann: The Devil's Advocate.* New York: New York University Press, 1979.

Hayman, Ronald. *Thomas Mann.* New York: Scribner, 1995.

Heilbut, Anthony. *Thomas Mann: Eros and Literature.* New York: Knopf, 1996.

Izenberg, Gerald N. *Modernism and Masculinity: Mann, Wedekind, Kandinsky through World War I.* Chicago, IL: University of Chicago Press, 2000.

Ritter, Naomi, ed. Death in Venice: *Complete, Authoritative Text with Biographical and Historical Contexts, Critical History, and Essays from Five Contemporary Critical Perspectives.* Boston, MA: Bedford, 1998.

Stock, Irvin. *Ironic out of Love: The Novels of Thomas Mann.* Jefferson, NC: McFarland, 1994.

Wolf, Ernest M. *Magnum Opus: Studies in the Narrative Fiction of Thomas Mann.* New York: Lang, 1989.

MANNOURY D'ECTOT, MARQUISE DE

Nineteenth-century French novelist

Works

There is no longer any debate among scholars about Mannoury d'Ectot's authorship of *Les Cousines de la colonelle* [*The Cousins of the Colonel's Wife*] and *Le Roman de Violette* [*The Novel of Violette*]. The circumstances of publication suggest that she may also be the author of *Mémoires secrets d'un tailleur pour dames* [*Secret Memoirs of a Ladies' Dressmaker*]. All three works appear to have been published in Belgium during the period 1880–85. Her works, like those of other women authors of erotic novels, were frequently attributed by rumor to well-known men, including Théophile Gautier, the elder Dumas, and Maupassant.

Les Cousines de la colonelle (ca. 1880) tells of the sexual development of two sisters who follow divergent paths. One, by accepting a proposal of marriage from a much older man, enters into a situation that occurs regularly in French novels of the late nineteenth century: the wife is young and innocent, while the husband, already worn out by pleasure, is of precarious virility. But the emphasis in Mannoury d'Ectot's novel is not on

dark secrets of debauchery hidden in the man's past. The novel does not indulge at length in the prurient mixture of psychosexuality and moral indignation that is the standard fare of the time. Rather, the emphasis is on the quality of the young woman's pleasure and the expedients which allow her a degree of satisfaction in conjugal sex. Her sister follows a more adventurous path, agreeing to live with her lover, a Polish count, until such time as he can be free of a promise made to an aging aunt. The social risks taken in this case are great, but they are managed with a degree of support from her sister and from her guardian. The novel's tone is never outrageous, as these young women find their pleasure in realistic, pragmatic ways.

Le Roman de Violette (1883) is an interesting thematic hybrid. It has many elements in common with those classical stories of erotic training that abounded in Italian and French in the sixteenth and seventeenth centuries: a girl is initiated into erotic womanhood by being taught the art of pleasure. Before 1700, the teacher was usually a woman, but male characters often played the role in later texts. *Le Roman de Violette* recycles and renovates this basic story by having a young woman, Violette, come under the protection of a man, the narrator-hero, who takes it as his delightful obligation to provide the erotic training. He has a rival for the role, the beautiful lesbian Odette. Odette herself is well aware of the traditional role assigned to women as practical educators in amorous positions and techniques. She sees it as a lesbian prerogative, if only to prepare the way for later heterosexual lovemaking. But her efforts to reestablish the classical role are not so much thwarted as carefully managed, since the hero, Christian, is always one step ahead of her. After deflowering Violette himself, he arranges to hide in order to observe the two women, then intervenes in order to bring Odette to climactic pleasure by stealth. This is in itself a sign of Christian's great skill and sensitivity, since Odette, now widowed, was married in her youth to a much older man who treated her brutally and has become a confirmed man-hater. Christian has one very general advantage as a teacher: he is a professor of medicine. Having medical knowledge about sexuality was not a part of classical initiation stories, but sexual pathology was a prominent concern in France in the last decades of the nineteenth century. *Le Roman de Violette* thus brings together two kinds of teaching: practical instruction in lovemaking, and theoretical lectures about the supposed norms of human sexuality combined with the requirements of sexual hygiene.

Mémoires secrets d'un tailleur pour dames has little in common with these two novels. It is a collection of worldly vignettes with no strong thematic coherence, and indeed some contradictions in narrative point of view. The tone is decidedly more frivolous and more smug than in the two novels. There are allusions in sophisticated language to farcical and obscene events. The stories are often male centered, and there must be considerable doubt, on internal evidence, about the text's authorship.

Biography

Relatively little is known about the life of the Marquise de Mannoury. She appears to have been the granddaughter of a French inventor, Nicolas Le Blanc, whose work went unrewarded by Napoleon III's regime. She married a man much older than she, the Marquis d'Ectot, and was left a widow at a relatively early age. There is no evidence that she regarded her widowed state as an affliction, entertaining artists such as Verlaine and Maupassant at her country estate or at her salon in Paris. She may, however, have fallen victim to men who profited unduly by her generosity, and was reduced in the 1870s to running a matrimonial agency. It is likely that her publication of erotic novels was motivated in part by financial need.

PETER CRYLE

Selected Works

Le Roman de Violette. Paris: Le Serpent à plumes, 2002.
Les Cousines de la colonelle. Paris: Le Grand Livre du mois, 1995.

Further Reading

Lepelletier, Edmond. *Paul Verlaine, sa vie, son œuvre*. Paris: Société du Mercure de France, 1907.
Pauvert, Jean-Jacques. "Présentation" to *Le Roman de Violette*. Paris: La Musardine, 1999.

MANSOUR, JOYCE

1928–1986
French Surrealist writer and poet

Joyce Mansour, widely accepted as the most prominent French woman Surrealist writer, created a magnificent opus of passionate, aggressive, and highly erotic works that questioned bourgeois principles and the patriarchal order through her disruption of preexisting concepts, values, and rules of language. She claimed that writing "came" to her—it was not thought out or developed in any conscious way, but was a natural and inevitable process. Her poetry does not conform to traditional or standardized rules of meter, rhyme, or versification, but instead follows natural impulses.

Greatly influenced by the Marquis de Sade, Mansour's work consequently draws on the ideas of one of history's most notorious erotic writers. Erotic expression was a feature of Surrealist writing in general, but the singular blend of eroticism and humor in Mansour's work is particularly reminiscent of de Sade. Mansour's work displays other qualities typical of Surrealist writing, including a criticism of organized religion, a subversive attack on the patriarchal order and bourgeois values, the devaluation of reason and logic vis-à-vis the valuation of all things wild and natural, and the Surrealist preoccupation with the *femme-enfant* (woman-child). Although not affiliated to the French women's movement, Mansour's work is nonetheless also consistent with many facets of French feminism: the abjection of the female body apparent in her work is comparable to that theorized by Julia Kristeva in 1980, and the way in which she uses irony to comment on the physical and emotional oppression and repression of women is similar to that of many French women writers in the late twentieth century: "La rage la souffrance la jouissance et le crime / Tous enterrés sous le masque de la sérénité féminine" [Madness suffering pleasure crime / All buried beneath the mask of women's serenity] (*Faire signe au machiniste*). Also in accordance with feminist ideals is Mansour's utopian vision of a world in which women would be emancipated. This runs parallel to her argument for the emancipation of the working class and of Nature, suggesting that all these liberations are connected.

Hailed by André Breton as "l'enfant du Conte Oriental" (the child of the Eastern story), Mansour's work is heavily imbued with a sense of her Egyptian origins. Critics have seen in her work references to Hathor, the Egyptian goddess of love, as Mansour rejects the Westernized representation of a male deity who, from a feminist/feminine perspective, perpetuates guilt and division: "Oublie-moi mon Dieu / Que je me souvienne" [Forget me my Lord / That I may remember myself] (*Cris*). Instead, Mansour celebrates a female genealogy with origins outside of Western culture. Her Egyptian heritage, upbringing in England, and position in the

French literary canon lends a unique multicultural aspect to her œuvre that enhances its sense of universality. The themes and ideas in her work are consistent, and certain terms are repeated and echoed throughout (death, silence, tomb, penis, vagina, anus, urine, fecal, excrement). These are indicative of the common themes in Mansour's work (sex, death, abjection) and reinforce the sense that all of her texts combine to form an opus greater than any individual piece. An overall simplicity and the consistency of themes and ideas render her writing accessible, while the Surrealist preoccupations evident in her work still challenge her readers to question existing perceptions of reality: "L'œil doux de la cuisinière / Cuit dans une soupe épaisse" [The sweet eye of the cook / Simmers in a thick broth] (*Déchirures*).

Mansour's work is aggressively erotic, full of black humor and caustic irony. She uses violent and often vampiric sexual imagery and writes with an unsettling frankness of sex, body parts, illness, and death. The linking of sex and death is an important leitmotif of her work, indicating the importance of the "id" (*Ça*), the deepest level of the unconscious, dominated by Eros and Thanatos: "Malgré moi ma charogne fantasise avec ton vieux sexe débusqué / Qui dort" [In spite of myself, my corpse fantasizes about your old sleeping flushed out / penis] ("Rhabdomancies" in *Rapaces*). Many of her references to corporeality depict the body as either dismembered or orgasmic, demonstrating both the oppression of the female body and its ultimate potential for redemption through *jouissance*.

Mansour plays with language, engaging in a "fiery deconstruction" (Bishop, xvi) of words and meanings to subvert traditional rules of grammar and the patriarchal/colonial order they represent. Her verse has been described by David Kelley and Jean Khalfa as "a feminine version of André Breton's (largely masculine) appeal for sexual liberation," and Bishop sees in her writing a "virile liberty," evident in the way in which Mansour challenges preconceptions about women's place and role: "Les vices des hommes / sont mon domaine / Leurs plaies mes doux gâteaux / J'aime mâcher leurs viles pensées / Car leur laideur fait ma beauté" [The vices of men / are my estate / Their wounds my sweet cakes / I like to chew on their vile thoughts / For from their ugliness comes my beauty] (*Cris*). Thus, Mansour's writing can be not only viewed in the context of Surrealism, but also theorized in terms of *écriture féministe/féminine*: like many other French women writers in the latter half of the twentieth century, she uses a "masculine" language and "masculine" devices to subvert the old order from a position of submission. However, as Hubert Nyssen suggests, it is too simplistic to "reduce Joyce Mansour to an erotic and rebellious Surrealist oracle" ("réduire Joyce Mansour à une espèce d'égérie du surréalisme, érotomane et révoltée"), as there is more to her work than a homogeneous "surrealist" or "feminist" label might suggest. For example, her outrageous metaphors are juxtaposed with a relentless lucidity: "Ne mangez pas les fleurs rouges de l'été / Car leur sève est le sang des enfants crucifiés" [Do not eat the red flowers of summer / For their sap is the blood of crucified children] (*Cris*), and her social consciousness is blended with a wicked sense of humor: "Vous qui voulez maigrir rappelez-vous que: *femme qui roule n'amasse pas mousse*" [Women who want to lose weight, remember: *a rolling woman gathers no moss*] ("Rubrique lubrique").

Mansour is an important erotic writer because of her unfettered and uncensored depiction of the human body, in its abject state as well as in its glory. The claim that Mansour is one of the few genuine expressions of the Surrealist voice situates her work within a theoretical framework as well as a philosophical context: she "writes the body" both consciously and unconsciously, opening up the female form to new possibilities through language and reasserting the feminine by using an eroticized, aggressive writing style more traditionally associated with the "masculine." Mansour's individual and provocative work assures her place not only within the Surrealist movement, but also within the French literary canon.

Biography

Born Joyce Patricia Adès in Bowden, England, into a Jewish-Egyptian family. Educated in England, Switzerland, and Egypt. Spent most of her early life in Cairo, where she first became interested in the Surrealist movement. Moved to Paris in 1953, and published there her first collection of poetry (*Cris*, 1953). This attracted the attention of the Surrealists, notably André Breton, and she joined the Surrealist group in Paris in 1954, one of the few women accepted into the Surrealist movement. She is considered one of the most authentic expressions of the Surrealist voice. Greatly influenced by Breton, she later dedicated four of her works to him. After the disintegration of the Paris Surrealist group in 1969, she was one of a majority of adherents who regrouped around the *Bulletin de liaison surréaliste*. Wrote mainly poetry (16 collections), although her bibliography also includes four works of prose, one play, and several journal articles, as well as three poems published posthumously. Wrote primarily in French, but interspersed this with occasional poems or stanzas of poems in English. Many of her literary works were illustrated by prominent Surrealist artists, and several have appeared in English translation. Wrote typically Surrealist "automatic" writings, as well as more controlled works. Died in Paris of breast cancer.

HELEN VASSALLO

Selected Works

Poetry

Carré blanc. Paris: Soleil Noir, 1965.
Cris. Paris: Seghers, 1953; as *Screams*, translated by Serge Gavronsky. Sausalito, CA: Post-Apollo, 1995.
Déchirures. Paris: Minuit, 1955.
Faire signe au machiniste. Paris: Soleil Noir, 1977.
Flammes immobiles. Paris: Fata Morgana, 1985.
Jasmin d'hiver. Paris: Fata Morgana, 1982.
Prose et Poésie: œuvre complète. France: Actes Sud, 1991.
Rapaces. Paris: Seghers, 1960.

Prose

Ça. Paris: Soleil Noir, 1970.
Histoires nocives. Paris: Gallimard, 1973.
Jules César. Paris: Seghers, 1968.
Les Gisants satisfaits. France: Jean-Jacques Pauvert, 1958.
"Rubrique lubrique pour petites bringues." *L'Archibras* 3 (1968): Le Surréalisme en mars 1968.

Theatre

Le Bleu des fonds. Paris: Soleil Noir, 1968.

Further Reading

Balakian, Anna. *Literary Origins of Surrealism: A New Mysticism in French Poetry.* London: University of London Press, 1947.
Bédouin, Jean-Louis. *La Poésie Surréaliste.* Paris: Seghers, 1964.

Bishop, Michael, ed. *Women's Poetry in France, 1965–1995*. Winston-Salem, NC: Wake Forest University Press, 1997.

Bosquet, Alain. *La Poésie Française depuis 1950: Une anthologie*. Paris: La Différence, 1979.

Deforges, Régine. *Poèmes de femmes: Des origines à nos jours*. Paris: Le Cherche Midi Éditeur, 1993.

Deluy, Henri, and Liliane Girandon, eds. *Poésie en France depuis 1960: 29 femmes*. Paris: Stock, 1994.

Dunstan Martin, Graham, ed. *Anthology of Contemporary French Poetry*. Edinburgh: Edinburgh University Press, 1972.

Hackett, C.A., ed. *New French Poetry: An Anthology*. Oxford: Basil Blackwell, 1973.

Hubert, Renée Riese. "Three Women Poets." *Yale French Studies* 21 (1958).

Kelley, David, and Jean Khalfa, eds. *The New French Poetry*. Newcastle upon Tyne: Bloodaxe Books, 1996.

Matthews, J.H. *Toward the Poetics of Surrealism*. Syracuse, NY: Syracuse University Press, 1976.

———. *French Surrealist Poetry*. London: University of London Press, 1966.

Rosemont, Penelope, ed. *Surrealist Women: An International Anthology*. London: Athlone Press, 1998.

Sorrell, Martin. "The Poetry of Joyce Mansour." *In Other Words: The Journal for Literary Translators* 7 (Summer 1996): 29–30.

———. *Modern French Poetry*. London: Forest Books, 1992.

Suleiman, Susan Rubin. *Subversive Intent: Gender, Poitics and the Avant-Garde*. Cambridge, MA: Harvard University Press, 1990.

———. "A Double Margin: Reflections on Women Writers and the Avant-garde in France." *Yale French Studies* 75 (1988).

MAO XIANG

Chinese poet
1611–1693

Yingmeian Yi Yu

Yingmeian Yi Yu [*Reminiscences of the Plum-Shadow Hermitage*] is a biographical account written by the Ming scholar Mao Xiang, after the death of his favorite concubine, Dong Xiaowan, which was popular because of its lyrical, romantic portrayal of love, longing, and loss. It is interesting as a moment in Chinese literary history in part because of its portrayal and perpetuation of the literary ideal of the sick and suffering woman. The ephemeral figure of Dong Xiaowan, often ill and subject to attacks of fever at the slightest emotion, foreshadows the type of very young, fragile, and delicate woman that during the Qing period would become the ideal of feminine beauty. *Yingmeian Yi Yu* is also well known for its concise and beautiful literary style.

Mao Xiang writes that Dong Xiaowan was exceedingly attractive, and though she was once a singer in the pleasure quarters, he writes that once she became his concubine, their affection was never tainted with lasciviousness. Thus, when she inevitably falls ill, it is from the disease of maidens, of passion repressed and not expressed. There no sexual description in Mao's account. In fact, much of his memoir deals with their frequent separation, and particularly her suffering, from hunger, illness, robbers, weather, and so forth while they are apart or while she is trying to reach him. Whatever eros lies in the memoir is derived from this account of female devotion and suffering.

Mao describes Dong Xiaowan as an ideal companion and mentions frequently how much his friends admired her. After becoming his concubine in 1642, she took part in her husband's literary work, copying out texts for him and keeping his books and manuscripts in order. She had a natural gift for poetry and painting, and they would pass entire evenings together talking about the works of the famous Tang poets. She had a great talent for memorizing poetry and amused herself by culling from old literature references to women's dress, personal adornment, dancing, and singing, which she then compiled into a brief treatise entitled *Lianyan* [*The Elegance of the Dowry*].

The memoir moves back and forth in time, with Mao stopping the narration to comment on his present circumstances. He says of her study, where she would have books piled up all around her, and where she would often fall asleep with volumes of poetry by her pillow or under her bedclothes, that it is now locked up and covered with dust, and that he could not bear to enter. He writes that he will do his best to sustain his grief and try to collate her work and have it published.

He details her many habits, what she ate and how, her penchant for placing a lamp in front of a flower so it would cast a shadow on a curtain. He talks about her clever way of learning how to make culinary delicacies and how she could hold her liquor better than he could.

Mao Xiang's romance with Dong Xiaowan happened during a period of great historical turmoil. The Ming dynasty was overthrown by the Manchus in 1644, causing many to lose their households and fortunes. Mao writes that there were rumors that the local garrison had mutinied, and everyone fled their town for the country. As invading forces continued to push south into China, many, including Mao and his family, tried to stay ahead of them. Mao writes of how thoughtful Dong was in preparing for their travels, always displaying her loyalty and resourcefulness. He recounts their fleeing before the invading troops and bandits and the grief it caused them. Such a life on the run took a terrible toll on both Mao and his concubine. At one point, during a severe winter, they had to hide in an empty house in a desolate city. They could not go on because Mao had fallen seriously ill, and Dong Xiaowan tended to him tirelessly.

They were together for nine years. She had always been of delicate health, and when she was twenty-six, she died, presumably of consumption. Tradition has it that Dong Xiaowan did not die in her prime, as Mao Xiang would have liked her to be remembered, but rather was forcibly carried away by the new Qing emperor or one of his relatives and admitted to the palace as imperial consort. This theory, however, is likely fictional, since we have many couplets and verses composed by Mao's friends on the occasion of her death that are available in their respective literary works. Mao Xiang himself lived to an old age, but he could never forget her. The reminiscences he wrote of Dong Xiaowan, in a highly polished literary style, rank among the masterpieces of Qing literature. In addition to being an account and testament to their love, *Yingmeian Yi Yu* is also an important historical document that records personal experiences of the turbulent period during the change of dynasties.

Biography

Mao Xiang was born into a wealthy family in the late Ming dynasty. His family was so well known that in his youth, Mao Xiang was considered one of the "four famous aristocrats," a designation approximately equivalent to "most eligible bachelor."

DOUGLAS WILE

Editions and Translations

Yingmeian Yi Yu. Changsha: Yuelu shushe, 1991.

Mao P'i-chiang. *The Reminiscences of Tung Hsiao-wan.* Translated by Pan Tze-yen. Shanghai: The Commercial Press, 1931.

MARA

1933– ?
French novelist

Journal d'une femme soumise

The Diary of a Submissive Woman is not structured as fiction: it is a seemingly genuine, irregularly dated diary kept between 1958 and 1973. Virtually nothing has been written about this work since the only edition was published by Flammarion in 1979. The pseudonym "Mara" appears to be less a literary persona than an expression of the author's genuine—and successful—attempt to remain anonymous. This is in keeping with Mara's general fascination with the concept of anonymity, a fascination which she explores in some detail in *Journal d'une femme soumise* and pushes even further in *Journal ordinaire,* her subsequent book. *Journal d'une femme soumise* contains a postface by Michèle Causse, in which Causse essentially draws attention to the many literary and theoretical influences on Mara's text, while noting the relevance of the *Journal* for contemporary feminists.

Like much writing not intended for publication, *Journal d'une femme soumise* is written in an extremely disjointed and elliptical style. There is often little or no apparent link between entries, and no background information is given regarding characters or events. The author's passion for and extensive knowledge of literature is obvious throughout the *Journal,* and Mara's personal observations are frequently juxtaposed with references to Baudelaire, Breton, Alphonse Daudet, de Sade, Marguerite Duras, Foucault, Rimbaud, Virginia Woolf, and numerous others. Mara's strongest influence, however, is clearly Georges Bataille. The linking of death with eroticism, the quest to understand existence through transgression and excess, and the questioning of language as conveyor of ultraviolence are all clearly Bataillian themes. Mara incorporates Bataille's ideas deliberately, stating that she wants to write the female equivalent of "Dirty," the lascivious heroine of Bataille's *Le bleu du ciel.* For Mara, however, this is more than a literary exercise: she claims to live these phenomena as well as write them.

Journal d'une femme soumise does not have a distinguishable plot. Rather, the description of "real" events is positioned alongside artistic, emotional, and intellectual impressions, which are in turn punctuated with historical facts. The leitmotif of Mara's diary is her relationship with her husband, N., a man whose near constant physical and psychological absence causes his wife intermittent outbursts of agony and anger. Mara is N.'s willing slave, and she submits herself to numerous acts of degradation at his hands and at the hands of strangers and friends. As N. becomes Mara's pimp, she tries simultaneously to please him through total obedience and to surpass his violent desires with her own sexual excesses. This fundamental ambivalence toward the nature of submission is a forceful undercurrent in the *Journal.* Even as Mara is traded among men as property, is beaten, performs fellatio on large numbers of men in public places, and allows herself to be ejaculated, urinated, and defecated on, her lucidity and ironizing disrespect with regard to her "master(s)" express a paradoxical and masochistic power. Mara's journal is thus a concise playing out of the primordial contradiction that defines masochistic strength, which is by definition precarious and exhausting. More precisely, the narrator is never completely able to decide whether the strength she sees in her deliberate submission—i.e., that of rising above and defeating the violence being inflicted (and the person inflicting it) by welcoming and submitting to it—is communicable and therefore real. More alarmingly, she describes herself as someone who exists only as others see her, an entity that is transparent until seen, and the fear that her strength may pass unnoticed even by the man to whom she submits poses a serious metaphysical problem. Mara blames such issues for her unhappiness, and fears she will go insane or be deemed insane and institutionalized by N. During her worst periods of self-doubt and deprecation, she does in fact write her entries from a psychiatric clinic.

Mara's goal of total submission requires that she allow herself to be violently degraded and mistreated. In prostitution, she finds the ultimate expression of anonymity and obedience. She calls her special breed of "nymphomania" an attempt to shatter her individuality, become invisible (because interchangeable), and thus become what she deems "absolutely a woman." De Sade's influence is extremely apparent here and elsewhere in the *Journal*, as Mara's definition of feminine strength demands absolute submission to and satisfaction of men's physical desires. Despite her underlying condescension toward these "dominant" men, the narrator is incessantly and profoundly afraid that her submission is more a display of cowardice than of strength.

Despite the frank manner in which *Journal d'une femme soumise* addresses the psychology of sadomasochism, the book is anything but a titillating series of sexual adventures. In fact, any sex acts which are described are vastly overshadowed by the reasons behind and reactions to such behavior. This is particularly relevant given Mara's literary goal—to embody the chaotic voice of Bataille's female protagonists, to be "sovereign" (the term is Bataille's), and to obtain through excess a knowledge which is distinctly other compared with the trials of everyday life. In a particularly Bataillian turn, Mara uses the realm of eroticism to confront and meditate on death. Death and eroticism are irrevocably linked for both authors: each views sexual excess as a way of welcoming and describing death. Mara even calls her writing the "autopsy of a suicide." While death-obsessed eroticism is a consciously Bataillian phenomenon, its expression through complete submission and humiliation adds an important twist. Even more notable is the fact that Mara claims to be expressing a uniquely feminine worldview. In a move that takes Bataille's *érotisme* to a more violently personal level, Mara makes herself a willing and conscious human sacrifice in an attempt to welcome the sacred silence of extreme violence and eroticism into her life (and death).

Although not crafted as fiction, *Journal d'une femme soumise* is an extremely self-conscious and auto-representative text. As Mara admittedly prefers literature to life, she defines her diary as the effort to turn her life into a fiction and to structure her existence. She tries to write her life and then examines the effects of this process. She refers to her desire to "vomit" words, and her writing is reminiscent of the bulimia to which she alludes on several occasions. Mara sees literature as the ultimate space of transgression and defines her own writing as an act of violence, robbing dictionaries of their words in order to refurbish language with its original transgressive power. For this reason she forces herself to record in writing even her most violent experiences of humiliation.

Journal d'une femme soumise is a brutally honest discussion of the complicated concepts of submission, domination, death, and eroticism, and it provides a paradoxical and lucid expression of what it can mean to be a woman dealing with these issues. Mara's desire to surpass domination through submission poses serious questions in the domains of literature, sexuality, and feminism, and the form of the nonfictional journal provides a particularly self-reflexive outlet. *Journal d'une femme soumise* is especially interesting given the turn its author will take in *Journal ordinaire:* namely, toward purely lesbian sexual relationships and even greater submission and anonymity.

Biography

The identity of the author known as Mara is not known. When *Journal d'une femme soumise* was published in 1979, Mara claimed to be a woman approaching the age of 40, living in Paris with her husband and two children. The book's title is taken from a journal entry, and there is no indication that it was chosen by the author. Mara did not publish anything (under this name) during the years the journal was kept, but she did publish another text, *Journal ordinaire,* in 1984.

PATRICIA BERNEY

Complete Works

Journal d'une femme soumise. Paris: Textes/Flammarion, 1979.
Journal ordinaire. Paris: Textes/Flammarion, 1984.

MARGUERITE DE NAVARRE

1492–1549

French short story writer, dramatist, and poet

Marguerite's religious writings are not free of erotic motifs, some quite extravagant, though they belong to a religious tradition dating back to the Song of Solomon and express in her case an ardent, devout, and total submission to the power of divine grace. In the *Heptaméron*, as is traditional in the early-modern short story, love, both marital and extramarital, forms a major theme, hence Marguerite's onetime reputation for licentiousness. However, she is particularly original in considering desire, cuckoldry, and illicit affairs more in their psychological consequences and moral dimensions than as mere comic motifs. Eros is also set in contrast with courtly love, Platonic love, and *agape* (spiritual) love, all of which feature in different ways in the stories proper. But Marguerite also orchestrates many of the storytellers' discussions and activities, for a further novel feature of the collection is the way in which these ten characters (who are variously married, widowed, celibate, and/or in love with other group members) both debate and enact different love themes which their tales introduce and which stretch from absolute dedication to God down to fetishism, incest, necrophilia, and rape.

The violence and perversion of these latter topics help emphasize two connected topics: the corruption rife among contemporary clerics and the aggression inherent in male sexuality, themes sufficiently prevalent in the *Heptaméron* to be safely identifiable as preoccupations of the author herself. It is, moreover, notable that she does not present the battle of the sexes at all one-sidedly; hence, for instance, her men attack women's sexual discretion as mere hypocrisy and cruelty. Nor is the status of marriage presented without ambiguity, as Oisille, eldest and most respected of the narrators, imputes reservations concerning marital love to St. Paul, and Marguerite herself chooses to depict marriages which are in most cases failing and whose partners are scarcely ever happy.

Marriage in the sixteenth century was not exclusively based on physical attraction, especially among the wealthy and powerful, hence the prevalent cultural theme of loves, be they adulterous or chaste, defied conjugality. Again, however, Marguerite is not simplistic in her treatment of this subject. One of the happiest marriages described (nouvelle no. 30) is between the (unknowingly) incestuous couple of a brother and a bastard sister whom her husband had (again unwittingly) sired via his own mother. Meanwhile, Parlamente (the character most often identified with Marguerite herself) sees the selfless love of the adoring suitor as outdated, while Dagoucin, a celibate possibly in love with Parlamente, tells a tale (no. 9) in which just such a *parfaite amour* ends only in death.

The reason for this reticence may well once more be religious. Human love, however perfect, can draw one away from God, a message discernible in St John's First Epistle, which Oisille reads to the company in the prologue to the sixth day. Hence courtly love, as displayed in the overlong but deeply significant tenth nouvelle, is corrupted, nay even parodied, in the life of its hero, Amadour. Marguerite's Platonism, which most scholars regard as relatively superficial, is also mitigated by this preoccupation. Unlike the Florentine neo-Platonist Ficino, for whom physical desire could lead to God via a process of sublimation and idealization, Marguerite presents access to sacred love more as the result of catastrophe or disillusionment with profane love, as in the life of Floride, whom Amadour loves devotedly for years but then attempts to rape.

However, it remains vital for an appreciation of Marguerite's work to realize to what extent these and other messages remain implicit and thus debatable. Rather than through dogmatic systems and didactic allegories, her approach operates via allusiveness, dissimulation, and fragmentation, which, speaking generally, scholars have linked both to Renaissance aesthetics and to female susceptibility.

Biography

Born in Angoulême, April 11, daughter of Charles d'Orléans (d. 1496) and Louise de Savoie (d. 1531), who secured her an education which included classical and modern languages. Married Charles, duc d'Alençon, in 1509 and joined the royal court on the accession of her brother (1515), whom she tended during his captivity in Madrid (1525). Widowed in the same year, she then married Henri d'Albret, king of Navarre (1527), by whom she had a daughter, Jeanne (b. 1528), the eventual mother of King Henry IV of France. Having been strongly influenced in the 1520s by the reformist zeal of Bishop Guillaume Briçonnet and his vicar-general, Jacques Lefèvre d'Etaples, Marguerite gave significant support to religious dissidents and may for some years have exerted a moderating effect on Francis's religious policy. However her sway over him declined in the later 1530s, whilst her restrained and pietistic religiosity was outflanked by the Calvinist reform, which she never espoused. Semiretirement to her courts of Pau and Nérac in the remote southwest led to an increase in her literary composition. As the writer of highest social rank in French history, she wrote plays and devotional poetry, some of it condemned by the Catholic censors; but her masterpiece is the *Heptaméron*, a collection of 72 short stories written in imitation of Boccaccio's *Decameron* and intended similarly to number 100. Despite this plan, the book remained incomplete on her death (1549), which came two years after the accession of her nephew Henry II.

JOHN PARKIN

Editions

Heptaméron. Edited by R. Salminen. Textes Littéraires Français, 516. Geneva: Droz, 1999.
The Heptameron / Marguerite de Navarre. Translated with an introduction by P.A. Chilton. London/New York: Penguin Books, 1984.

Further Reading

Cazauran, Nicole. *L'Heptaméron de Marguerite de Navarre*. Paris: Société d'édition d'enseignement supérieur, 1977.
Cholakian, Patricia F. *Rape and Writing in the* Heptaméron. Carbondale, IL: Southern Illinois University Press, 1991.
Déjean, Jean-Luc. *Marguerite de Navarre*. Paris: Fayard, 1987.
Febvre, Lucien. *Amour sacré, amour profane: Autour de l'Heptaméron*. Paris: Gallimard, 1930.
Gelernt, Jules. *World of Many Loves: The* Heptaméron *of Marguerite de Navarre*. Chapel Hill, NC: University of North Carolina Press, 1966.
Jourda, Pierre. *Marguerite d'Angoulême, étude biographique et littéraire*. Paris: Champion, 1930.

MARLOWE, CHRISTOPHER

1564–1593
English poet and playwright

Hero and Leander

Christopher Marlowe's *Hero and Leander* ranks as a singular achievement in 16th-century English verse. Published in 1598, five years after Marlowe's early death, it was immediately recognized as a remarkable work. The two Sestiads composed by Marlowe were completed by George Chapman, who also added a dedication and provided a synopsis of each Sestiad. Within the next half century, there would follow no less than seven editions. Initially thought to be the final work written by Marlowe, some modern scholars have proposed that the poem represents work done during Marlowe's years at Cambridge, though the debate is hardly over.

Hero and Leander has been classified as an "epyllion," after the short narrative verse used by classical authors, most notably Catullus' poem 63. The influence certainly is classical in tone and theme as well as structure. Marlowe infuses his poem with a rich sensuality not seen even in the sensual 16th century. The narrative of the poem recounts the story of two lovers separated by a stretch of sea. In attempting to cross the sea, Leander drowns, and upon the discovery of his body, Hero dramatically takes her own life by throwing herself from her tower. Unfortunately, Marlowe's poem is unfinished. Though Chapman's completed version is not incompetent, it cannot compare to Marlowe's brilliance.

Marlowe's narration begins with a description of Hero and then of Leander. The story had been told in a poem identified by Renaissance scholars as having been by Musaeus, considered the greatest of the Greek lyricists. In recent scholarship, the origins of the story have been shown to be anonymous. Marlowe's other source comes from Ovid's *Heroides*. Ovid's influence on Marlowe is considerable and predominates throughout this poem.

After the descriptive introductory sections, the narrative begins in earnest as a feast at Sestos brings Leander to town, where he spies Hero while she is making sacrifice to Venus. They meet and Leander begins the first of several speeches to persuade Hero to recant her vow of virginity to Venus. Hero resists with tears and platitudes, but Leander persists with all the rapacious force of Marlovian rhetoric. Won already, Hero recounts the story of Hermes and afterward faints. Leander revives her with a kiss. She returns to her room, having made plans to meet with Leander in the evening. The night is given to erotic play. The next day Leander returns home to Abydos. His desire increased by Hero's absence, he swims the Hellespont to see her again. Neptune sees Leander swimming and makes sexual advances to him but is rebuffed. Neptune takes the refusal in stride, but when Leander willfully ignores Neptune's speech in his haste to return to Sestos, Neptune plans revenge. Leander arrives at Sestos, and he and Hero return to her bed, where their love is consummated. Hero leaves their bed and goes for a walk. As she returns, Leander gazes on her nude body, and she feels embarrassment. The poem's narrative breaks off here.

The most striking aspect of the poem is not the narrative itself, but the rich sensuality of the lines and the apparent homoeroticism throughout. Though common in Greek and Roman poetry, the overtly frank assertion of homoerotic male desire is somewhat odd in the 16th century.

One can discern this by comparing Marlowe's description of Hero with his description of Leander. Hero's beauty is limited by a sense of woman's incompleteness. Indeed, a description is commonplace in erotic lyric of the time. The focus is more or less on her clothing and other fetishistic complements. With Leander, however, Marlowe presents us with the full glory of Greek masculine beauty. There are few lines in English poetry to match his description of Leander's neck, "Even as delicious meat is to the tast, / so was his necke in touching" (63–4). The description overflows into erotic ecstasy: "And whose immortall fingars did imprint, / That heavenly path, with many a curious dint, / That runs along his backe" (67–9). Further, there are references to Narcissus that seem to reinforce Leander's own ambiguous sexuality. What is most particular here are the numerous references to the Ganymede myth. Marlowe demonstrated a singular fascination with Ganymede, even devoting the first scene of his play *Dido, Queen of Carthage* to an erotic tryst between Ganymede and Jupiter. This interest in the homoerotic openness of the classical world is continued in *Hero and Leander*.

Aside from the homoerotic content of the poem, it is truly the language of the poem that is so refreshing and powerfully erotic. Marlowe is the first writer in English to beat the Ancients at their own game. The language is light and delicate and flows with graceful fluidity, yet explores the psychology of sexual intimacy. Hero's embrace upon realizing Leander's gaze marks such a moment. This poem contains one of the only lines known to have been borrowed by Shakespeare from one of his contemporaries and remains very well known today, "Who ever lov'd, that lov'd not at first sight?" (176). The language has a visceral quality. Marlowe's description of Hero and Leander's erotic hand play takes the reader into the heart of the sensual feel of seduction to an unprecedented degree in English poetry.

Except for his translations of Ovid, this poem constitutes Marlowe's only extensive contribution to lyric poetry and one in which he could have been justifiably proud. The erotic in Marlowe is an overwhelming force that draws us to itself in an unrelenting and cruel, perhaps even violent, manner. The description of Venus' temple with its depictions of rapes and the Dionysian atmosphere of erotic license serve to illustrate the true power of erotic desire when unleashed.

Biography

Born 1564 in Canterbury, England. Killed in a quarrel in Deptford, England. His first significant play, *Tamburlaine*, was published in 1590. Known principally for his plays and influence on early Shakespeare, Marlowe also wrote poetry and translations from classical authors, especially Ovid. He apparently served in the Elizabethan secret service under Walsingham, for which service the Privy Council ordered the conferring of his MA from Cambridge despite his long absences from university.

GRANT HAMBY

Editions

"Hero and Leander." In *Complete Works of Christopher Marlowe*. Vol. 1. Edited by Roma Gill. Oxford: Oxford University Press, 1987.

Selected Works

Tamburlaine. 1590.
Edward the Second. 1594.
Doctor Faustus. A-text, 1604.
Doctor Faustus. B-text, 1616.
The Jew of Malta. 1633.

Further Reading

Bakeless, John. *Christopher Marlowe: The Man in His Time*. New York: William Morrow, 1937.
Bloom, Harold, ed. *Christopher Marlowe*. New York: Chelsea House, 1986.
Rowse, A.L. *Christopher Marlowe: His Life and Work*. New York: Harper and Row, 1964.
Steane, J.B. *Marlowe: A Critical Study*. Cambridge: Cambridge University Press, 1964.
Tromly, Fred. *Playing with Desire: Christopher Marlowe and the Art of Tantalization*. Toronto: University of Toronto Press, 1998.

MARTIN DU GARD, ROGER

1881–1958
French novelist and dramatist

Roger Martin du Gard's work should not really be included among so-called erotic literature. Political and social preoccupations take pride of place in his work. However, from his first writings (perhaps under Naturalist influence), he showed a concern with problems connected with sex, and this is why his most representative novels explore a certain eroticism. This erotic character is also influenced by the environment in which his work developed. Martin du Gard lived among a circle, headed by André Gide, in which homosexuality was prevalent, and we think that he inclined more closely to this tendency than appears at first sight. His proven discretion made him take refuge in literature, where he found a way to show his deepest desires and his phantoms about sex and eroticism. These composed an essential subject in his work and remained a defining force all his life,

as is proved by his letters, journal, and private papers.

In his most representative work, *Les Thibault*, eroticism is represented in some of the relations between two brothers, Jacques and Antoine. Jacques' first flirtation with the German Lisbeth or his feelings for Gise, Mlle de Waize's favorite, show clearly this tendency. Gise is the erotic dream of his early adolescence, a dream which is completed by prohibition. The phantom of incest turns up because the young lady is considered almost his sister. They never have sexual intercourse, but the dream and the girl's animal sensuality fill Jacques' mind with erotic thoughts and obsessions that are explicit in the story *La Sorellina* and are a sort of catharsis for him. When he returns after his flight at the end of his studies, Lisbeth represents his sexual desires, which are mingled with a certain tenderness. The young German lady likes to think of herself as a leader, and her maternal instinct plays an important role in their relationship. However, neither of these experiences satisfy Jacques. Only Jenny quenches his thirst for the absolute.

The character which best represents eroticism is Rachel, lover of the elder brother, Antoine, who changes his life and leaves an indelible mark on his mind. Because of her Jewish origins and sexual freedom, Rachel symbolizes what is forbidden. Nothing is taboo in her life; lesbian relationships, incest, interracial sex are all embraced. All that is important to her are her personal erotic fulfillment and a happy sex life, untroubled by religious or social complexes. Rachel is born from the writer's erotic mind and represents his extension of femininity to apotheosis. Her flaming head of hair resembles the mane of a lion, an appearance which is emphasized by the pink color of her room. According to Martin du Gard, pink is the color of eroticism. Antoine, a physician, is seduced when Rachel appears by the sickbed of the niece of his father's secretary. While Antoine is trying to save the little girl, Rachel's presence there both disturbs and elates him. After that, the outcome is inevitable. The reward for his medical victory is the possession of Rachel, who shows him what love and sex are. Previously he was used to only hygienic experiences to maintain balanced health. From this moment on, the young doctor lives the most wonderful period of his life and is led by Rachel to destroy all the sexual taboos that conditioned his past behavior. He will have joyous memories of her. Her body, the verses of the *Song of Songs* that show his feelings, and the perfume of the amber from her necklace follow him throughout his life and become deeply identified with his concept of love. His later relationship with Anne de Battaincourt, despite the exciting anxiety it creates, can't be compared to his experience with Rachel. Without a doubt, Rachel represents the erotic ideal of Martin du Gard.

There are other little elements with erotic meanings that are not as powerful as Rachel—in particular Mme de Fontanin's feelings for her husband: even though he is unfaithful to her and abandons her during the worst moments of her life, nevertheless his perfume of cinnamon and verbena trouble her, and she is unable to avoid the fascination that he exercises on her. Jérome fascinates Rinette too, and his personality permeates the whole novel, so he represents Don Juan's myth. Incest features once again, committed this time by two brothers. The determinism of the story cannot erase the memory of the impulse that made the brother and sister, Jacques and Gise, love and enjoy their feelings for each other.

In his latest work, *Maumort*, the writer's old phantoms appear with energy. A great part of the novel deals with the first sexual experiences of the youthful Guy (perhaps a portrait of André Gide), which is observed by Maumort (Martin du Gard?). "La Baignade" is a passage of this story where the eroticism arises. Eros and Thanatos come together again in the writer's work. In the second part, the relationship between Maumort and a young girl from Martinique recall the links between Antoine and Rachel, but less powerfully.

Biography

Roger Martin du Gard was born in 1881 in Neuilly-sur-Seine, outside Paris. In 1906 he graduated from the École des Chartes. His first success as a writer was the novel *Jean Barois*, published in 1913. Martin du Gard spent most of World War I at the front lines. After the war, he devoted most of his time to writing *Les Thibault*. The twelve volumes of the series were published between 1922 and 1940. He won the Nobel Prize for Literature for *Les Thibault* in 1937. In 1940 Martin du Gard fled to Nice, where he spent most of World War II. He was at work on a large novel, *Le Lieutenant-Colonel de Maumort*, when he died in Bellême on August 23.

ÀNGELS SANTA

Editions

Oeuvres completes. Vol. 1 ("Devenir," "Jean Barois," "In Memoriam," "Les Thibault" [*Le Cahier gris, Le pénitencier, La Belle Saison, La Consultation, La Sorellina, La Mort du Père*]); Vol. 2 ("Les Thibault" [*L'Eté 1914, Épilogue*], "Vieille France," "Confidence Africaine," "Le Testament du Père Leleu," "La Gonfle," "Un Taciturne," "Notes sur André Gide"). Paris: Bibliothèque de la Pléiade/Gallimard, 1955.
Le Lieutenant-Colonel de Maumort. Edited by André Daspre. Paris: Pléiade/Gallimard, 1983.

Further Reading

Daspre, A., and J. Schlobach, eds. *Roger Martin du Gard. Etudes sur son oeuvre.* Paris: Klincksieck, 1984.
Emeis, Harald. *L'Oeuvre de Roger Martin du Gard: Sources et signification.* Essen: Verlag Die Blaue Eule, 2003.

Garguilo, René. *La Genèse des* Thibault *de Roger Martín du Gard.* Paris: Klincksieck, 1974.

Santa, Àngels, and Montse Parra, eds. *Relire* L'Été 1914 *et* Épilogue *de Roger Martín du Gard.* Lleida, Spain: Pagès Editors, 2000.

Tassel, Alain, and A. Daspre. *Roger Martín du Gard et les crises de l'histoire (colonialisme, seconde guerre mondiale).* Nice: Presses Universitaires de Nice–Sophia Antipolis, Nice, 2001.

MARTORELL, JOANOT

1410/11–1465
Spanish novelist

Joanot Martorell is the author of *Tirant lo Blanc*, a complex chivalry novel that mixes history and fiction. What makes this novel important in the context of the medieval narrative is its dose of rationality and verosimilitude. The physical and moral qualities of the hero Tirant are described in great detail, so Tirant becomes a realistic and rounded character. Martorell accurately reports the amorous adventures of Tirant in order to describe the knight's proper behavior, and often establishes comparisons between the abilities of Tirant in the battlefield and his abilities in the "siege" and "conquest" of ladies. War and love, therefore, become the two axes of the novel. Eroticism affects the whole work, but it is especially important in the chapters that take place in the court of Constantinople.

Chapters 115–296 are set in the Greek empire, and they contain most of the erotic adventures of the novel. The Empire of Constantinoble is about to be attacked by the Turks, and the emperor asks for the help of Tirant, who accepts the challenge. In Constantinople he meets Carmesina, the princess, and they fall in love. The result is that Tirant feels distressed, which concerns the emperor. Just before an expedition to Cyprus, the princess asks Tirant what worries him. He replies that he is deeply in love with a lady. Carmesina wants to know her name, and Tirant gives her a mirror. Tirant goes on to win several important battles against the Turks. Later on Viuda Reposada, former wet-nurse of Carmesina, falls in love with Tirant and organizes several tricks to make the lovers fall out. Carmesina falls into her traps and rejects Tirant,

and as a result he is distressed. Thanks to Plaerdemavida he breaks into Carmesina's chambers and slips into her bedroom, but he is discovered, and during his escape he jumps from the window, causing him to break his leg. While he is recovering, he and Carmesina they start to exchange love letters. At the same time, the empress falls in love with the knight Hipòlit, who hides for two weeks in her room. Viuda Reposada tries again to separate Tirant and Carmesina by trying to convince him that Carmesina has sexual relations with a gardener. In Chapters 271–2 Tirant and Carmesina get married in secret, but the marriage cannot be consummated, since it would cause a scandal. This leads to several erotic encounters. In the end, all of these tribulations are overcome, and in the final part of the novel the two formalize their marriage.

Martorell deals with love in several forms—for instance, courtly love and its rituals, as well as passionate, direct love that includes lesbianism and erotic fantasies such as fetishism and voyeurism. The writer analyzes a range of topics such as the importance of pleasure, the torture of love, and the idealization of desire. Moreover, he dwells on the language of passion, its codes and double meanings. Sex is described in both methaphorical terms and direct language.

Tirant lo blanc contains many explicit passages in which vital and passionate desire is depicted. These adopt a refined level of eroticism and are often about humorous encounters. In the most famous passage, Plaerdemavida takes Tirant to Carmesina's bed and makes him lie down beside the princess. When Tirant has lain down, the maiden tells him to be still and not to move. Then she places Tirant's hand on the princess's breasts, and he touches her nipples and her belly. The princess complains, and Plaerdemavida says: "You've just come out of the bath, and your skin is so smooth and nice that it makes me feel good just to touch it." The princess replies: "Touch all you like, but don't put your hand so far down." They spend more than an hour at this play, and he does not cease touching her. But the princess begins to wake up, and she asks Plaerdemavida: "What are you doing? Have you gone mad, trying to do what is against your nature?"

The novel places human relationships in an intermediate position between moral virtue and the pursuit of pleasure, although pleasure usually prevails. It is also remarkable that there is no concept of sin in the novel; this has been considered very modern in relation to other chivalric novels. The affair between the knight Hipòlit and the empress is a good example of this, since their adulterous relationship is awarded with marriage and the social ascension of the knight.

The novel is full of jovial situations based on the fears and social constrictions of Tirant and Carmesina. When they finally get married, the wedding night is ironically described as a battle that Tirant wins in less than one hour. Carmesina begs for mercy, but Martorell, using metaphorical language, tells us that Tirant "went in the castle by the force of arms." Tirant, a very brave knight who is also adept at all kinds of diplomatic problems, is in fact extremely shy and lacks confidence when it comes to declaring his love. On the other hand, Carmesina is always concerned about the social gap existing between them, and what is more, she is constrained by religious concerns.

The love between Tirant and Carmesina and other characters is intercalated with Tirant's battles and military campaigns in order to sharpen the attention of the reader. The relationship between the two main characters is both gentle and shameless and has a subtle, spiritual, and refined side, yet it is also tinged by provocation and sensuality. The characters of *Tirant lo Blanc* show different discourses in relation to love. According to Plaerdemavida, it has to be divided in two categories: courtly love, based on fidelity, characteristic of nobles; and gross desire. Estefania divides love into three categories: virtuous (the dame has to love the knight who carries out heroic deeds), profitable (she loves in relation to

the benefits she obtains), and depraved (which only takes into account sexual satisfaction). In the novel there are examples of all these kinds of love, and Martorell offers a wide catalogue of erotic situations: petting, adultery, anal sex, fetishism, carnivalesque scenes, relationships with or without sex, lesbianism, and voyeurism.

Biography

Born in Valencia, Spain. Member of a decadent noble family, had several duels, and was imprisoned for numerous crimes. Martorell lived in England, 1438–39, and often traveled to Naples during the 1440s–50s. In 1452, he became assistant to the Catalan king Alphonse the Magnanimous. In 1460, he started to write *Tirant lo Blanc*, which was first published in Valencia in 1490 and was reprinted in Barcelona in 1497. Martorell probably died in Valencia.

JORDI CORNELLÀ-DETRELL

See also **Catalan**

Editions

Tirant lo Blanc. Translated by David H. Rosenthal. London: Macmillan, 1985; Baltimore: John Hopkins University Press, 1996.
Tirant lo Blanc: The Complete Translation. Translated by Ray La Fontaine. New York: Peter Lang, 1993.
Tirant lo Blanc. Edited by Martí de Riquer. Barcelona: Ariel, 2000.

Further Reading

Badia, Lola. "Tot per a la dona però sens la dona. Notes sobre el punt de vista masculí al Tirant lo Blanc." *Journal of Hispanic Research* 2 (1993–1994): 39–60.
Beltran, Vicenç. "Realismo, coloquialismo y erotismo en Tirant lo Blanc." In *Estudios sobre el* Tirant lo Blanc, edited by Juan Paredes, Enrique Nogueras, and Lourdes Sánchez. Granada: Universidad de Granada, 1995.
Beltran, Rafael, and others. Tirant lo Blanc: *New Approaches.* Edited by Arthur Terry. London: Tamesis Books, 1999.
Cacho Blecua, Juan Manuel. "L'amor en el Tirant lo Blanc: Hipòlit i la Emperadriu." In *Actes del Symposion* Tirant lo Blanc. Barcelona: Quaderns Crema, 1993.
Espadaler, Anton M. "Milícia i sexualitat a la part anglesa del Tirant." *Anuari de Filologia* 20 (1997): 9–23.
Hart, Thomas R. "Comedy and Chivalry in *Tirant lo Blanc.*" In *The Age of the Catholic Monarchs 1474–1516*, edited by Alan Deyermond and Ian Macpherson. Liverpool: Liverpool University Press, 1989.

McNerney, Kathleen. "Elements of Courtly Romance in Tirant lo Blanc." In *Courtly Romance*, edited by Guy Mermier. Detroit: Fifteenth-Century Symposium, 1984.

———. Tirant lo Blanc *Revisited. A Critical Study.* Detroit:"Michigan Consortium for Medieval and Early Modern Studies, 1983.

Miralles, Carles. "La dona és el món." In *Actes del Symposion* Tirant lo Blanc. Barcelona: Quaderns Crema, 1993.

Riquer, Martí de. *Aproximació al Tirant*, Barcelona: Quaderns Crema, 1990.

Yates, Alan. "Tirant lo Blanc: the Ambiguous Hero." In *Hispanic Studies in Honour of Frank Pierce*, edited by John England. Sheffield: University of Sheffield, 1980.

MASTURBATION

Masturbation is one of life's great pleasures, and references to it appear everywhere in all cultures and all societies. Mostly, however, the descriptions of the act are not put in erotic terms, but simply reported, sometimes facetiously. Most of the reports are about males, and the male semen was regarded as especially important. In ancient Egypt, creation itself is associated with masturbation of Atum (Bullough, 62). References to masturbation are common in classical literature, especially in the writings of Martial (died about 104 CE). It was the Romans in fact who gave us the word *masturbation.* Often in the past, the term was said to be derived from a combination of the word *manus* (hand) and *stupro,* meaning to defile. This derivation almost immediately puts a sinful and negative connotation on masturbation, with which the Romans would not have agreed. An equally possible and more likely source is a combination of the word *manus* with the verb *turbo,* meaning to agitate or disturb, which both is descriptive and removes the stigma from such action. Martial implies that it was the custom to masturbate with the left hand, and he calls his left hand a "Ganymede" to serve him (Martial, *Epigrams,* II, 43).

In the Qur'an masturbatory discharges by men are regarded in the same way as a discharge during intercourse, and the male involved (even if they were wet dreams) had to undergo ritual purification, which required that he wash himself all over. Women had to make the same kind of ablutions after their menses. Though the *hadith* (the sayings of Muhammad) hold that those who masturbate are cursed, no such language exists in the Qur'an. In fact, many Islamic commentators justify the practice as a way of relieving lust. The learned Abu Hanifa (c. 700–767) permitted the use of silken cloth to rub the penis in case of emergency. Some commentators have held that to masturbate is a commendable way of honoring beauty in a woman who should not be approached but whose sighting allows the male to have all kinds of erotic fantasies.

In Hinduism, especially the antinomian cults associated with Krishna, masturbation was widely accepted. The ancient Hindu literature describes many devices (*apadravya*) to take the place of the penis (in case of women) or of the vulva (in case of men). One such instrument for men was the *viyoni* (literally "without *yoni*"; *yoni* = vagina), which was made of wood and cloth and shaped like a female, with a *yoni*-like opening. The *Kritrima linga,* or artifical phallus, was used by both men and women. Dildos were made from radishes or other tubers, from eggplants and bananas, and also from candle wax, baked clay, wood, bone, or metal. Many writers on eros urged men to use such devices to stimulate their female partners before intercourse.

Less permissive of masturbation were the ancient Chinese, who believed that such activities would result in the loss of vital essence, and it was condoned only in special circumstances. Probably, however, the most hostile were the Christians, who under the influence of St. Augustine regarded even foreplay as sinful. Augustine stipulated that sexual activity should be engaged in only for the purpose of procreation, with the proper instrument, the penis, and the proper receptacle, the vagina, and with the female on the bottom and the male on the top.

In spite of this Christian hostility, medical writers in the West were far more accepting of masturbation, going so far as to regard it as essential for women in some cases in order to expel accumulated secretions. All of this changed in the eighteenth century, when the concept of homoestasis became the dominant medical doctrine, and both the voluntary and involuntary loss of semen, or of orgasmic expulsions in women, was regarded as harmful to health. The major advocate of this view came to be the physician Samuel Auguste David Tissot, and his influence dominated medical ideas through the end of the nineteenth century. Despite this, however, people continued to masturbate.

In fact the psychiatrist Wilhelm Stekel (1868–1940) claimed that everyone masturbated, consciously or unconsciously, although his definition of masturbation included mannerisms involving the tongue, scratching, finger-boring of the nose, and various tics. Masturbation, according to Stekel and most other writers who dared to openly discuss the topic, was usually accompanied by fantasies of one kind or another. One early study of these fantasies was published by Lukianowicz in 1960, who reported on visual masturbatory experiences as reported to him by 188 patients, 126 of whom were male and 62 female. He classified these erotic fantasies into two basic groups, heterosexual and homosexual, but with subgroups such as transvestism, fetishism, masochism, sadism, zoophilia, etc. He found the heterosexual imaginary partner to be the most common of fantasized love obejcts. Among fantasy themes were kleptomania, gambling, and pyromania. These fantasies occurred very early in the life of the individual and were as much remembered by those who had been child masturbators as they were currently part of the fantasies being reported.

Despite the fact that we know that fantasies and erotic daydreaming are common, it is difficult to find much descriptive literature. For example, we know that Gustave Flaubert (1821–80) found release for his sexual tensions through masturbation, but we know little of what he fantasized. One major testament to the place that fantasy literature plays in masturbation is provided by the oil millionaire Roy Melisander Johnson of Ardmore, Oklahoma. He collected erotic works to read as he masturbated, and in the process gathered together one of the world's largest collections of erotica. Fortunately or unfortunately, he wanted more than he could find, since once he had read a book or saw an illustration, he was no longer aroused. His solution was to commission original erotic works through literary agents. He received two new mansucripts a week, one from an agent in New York City, another from an agent in California. For each of these Johnson paid $200, to be split between the agent and the writer. Gershon Legman, who was writing regularly for him, recruited, among others, Anaïs Nin to do so. On Legman's advice she kept carbon copies of the material she sent him, and after Johnson's death, she published the best of them as *The Delta of Venus* (1977) and *Little Birds* (1979). Nin also recruited some of her friends to write for Johnson, two of whom she later identified in her diaries as Virginia Admiral and Caresse Crosby. Interestingly, Johnson's wife, who knew of his collection, would not let him keep the material in the house. Instead he kept them in his office in old green filing cabinets. After his death in the 1960s, she sold off the collection, which served as the source of many of the printed erotic books hitting the market at the end of that decade.

We also know that when some groups of males get together, masturbation serves as an erotic athletic event, to see who can go the longest or ejaculate the most. Interestingly, one instance of such erotic competition has been recorded in a Scottish sex club of the eighteenth century, known as the Beggars Benison (Stevenson). Members apparently had to publicly masturbate to be admitted, and then at club meetings they often masturbated to sensuous lectures or demonstrations usually dealing with females. It was not just in the eighteenth century that such practices occurred. Following football games in the high school attended by one of my informants in the 1940s, the players on the winning team had ejaculation contests in the showers afterward.

As American obscenity laws relaxed, X-rated movie theaters opened, in which many individuals masturbated to porno movies; and X-rated bookstores, which also sold videotapes, opened special rooms for patrons to masturbate in. Prometheus Books published eight volumes of guides to X-rated movies during the l980s and 1990s, until the market collapsed due to the availability of both information and product on the Internet. In fact, the Internet became so vital a source of erotica that some observers have gone so far as to claim that its rapid success was due to its pornographic websites. Whether this is true or not, the Web has become the great dispenser of erotica and pornography. Those who need visual fantasies to masturbate by can get any type they want. Sex therapists and marriage counselors have often advised both sexually blocked individuals and couples to watch porno films and visit Internet porno sites and learn from them, especially about the importance of what can be called masturbatory foreplay in the couple relationship.

Perhaps inevitably, masturbation became a fictional theme. The number-one best seller in 1969 was Philip Roth's *Portnoy's Complaint,* which the publishers called "the most talked about novel of our time." It certainly broke down the barriers to openly discussing masturbation in fiction, and other writers, while not trying to compete with Roth, have included masturbation since then. Perhaps encouraged by the success of Roth's book, nonfiction accounts of the joys of masturbation also appeared, most notably by

Betty Dodson, whose *Sex for One,* also published as *Selflove and Orgasms,* and *Liberating Masturbation,* appeared first in 1974. She includes sections on romantic images, erotic images, sex art, and genital imagery, as well as masturbatory stories. Even in nonfiction accounts, the eroticism of masturbation is emphasized.

VERN L. BULLOUGH

References and Further Reading

Bullough, Vern L. *Sexual Variance in Society and History.* New York: Wiley, 1976.
Dodson, Betty. *Sex for One: The Joy of SelfLoving.* New York: Crown, 1996.
Fitch, Noel Riley. *The Erotic Life of Anaïs Nin.* Boston: Little, Brown, 1993.
Lukianowicz, Narcyz. "Imaginary Sexual Partner: Visual Masturbatory Fantasies." *Archives of General Psychiatry* 3 (1960): 429–49.
Martial. *Epigrams.* Translated by Walter C.A. Ker. London: William Heinemann, 1958. Some translations of the Epigrams are much more specific than those of the Loeb Library, and the reader is advised to look at them.
Roth, Philip. *Portnoy's Complaint.* New York: Random House, 1969.
Stekel, Wilhelm. *Autoeroticism.* Translated by James S. Van Teslaar. London: Peter Nevill, Ltd., 1951.
Stevenson, David. *The Beggar's Benison.* East Lothian: Tuckwell Press, 2001.

MATSUURA RIEKO

1958–
Japanese novelist and essayist

Yoko, the heroine of *Natural Woman,* is a writer of very morbid mangas, as is her female lover, Hanayo. Matsuura Rieko translates the language of manga into a very precise and lively style. This novel is a *bildungsroman,* a coming-of-age tale, tinged with melancholy. Though it has been read as cocktail pop-pulp, or as belonging to a new pornographic pulp genre and lesbo-feminist literature, Matsuura's style and the story itself are based on delicate sensations alternating with extreme sex. Her style is measured and sober, with a sad tonality, even in the hard sex scenes.

Her themes are first of all lesbianism with a zest for sadomasochism, as a game of master/slave in *Sebastien* and in *Natural Woman.* She writes about sexual relations between lesbian partners, trying to find out wether this is a specific sexuality or not. Mixing the feminine sex drive and the masculine feelings derived from the male supplementary organ will help her exploration through a monstruous organic reality. It can be the octopus met by Yoko and Yuriko in the kitchen of a hotel, or the "Flower Show," an erotic freak show in which all the sexual components are abnormal. Kazumi has a toe penis, Sachie has a vagina dentata, and Tamotsu has two penises, his and that of Shin, his conjoined brother inside of him.

We can link these novels to the Japanese economic boom of the 1980s, when women began to work as much as men, creating turmoil in feminine identity, which was no longer defined in relation to men. Matsuura Rieko may be describing a new female type: neither feminist nor conservative; a hybrid metamorphosis. She also describes a sociological fact: that there is a lack of interest among many young Japanese adults in normal careers or behavior. They are called *moratorium ningen*, "those who wait," or *Kurisutaruzoku*, the "crystal generation," after Tanaka Yasuo's famous 1981 novel of that name. Young Japanese girls experiment in social drifting from school toward violence and prostitution. Matsuura glorifies the margins of society in terms of sexual difference, as do other young Japanese writers. Her work is closely in touch with this behavioral change. For example, Kitahara Minori has created the "Love Piece Club" in Tokyo where women can improve their sex lives with items usually bought by men, and she has created, from Matsuura's novel, a vibrator which can be placed on the groin.

The aim of Matsuura's novels and essays is not only to affirm a lesbian identity. She contributes to the deconstruction of national identity in current Japanese literature. She emphasizes the variety of the notions of sex and gender beyond chromosomal definition. Kazumi, in *Big-Toe Penis,* for instance, is a hybrid girl. She imagines a new human being who is androgyne. Conventions and roles can no longer be thought of as before, and sexual roles especially have to be redefined. It is this phenomenon which is described in her novels.

During her odyssey of sex, Kazumi in her early twenties and her brand-new toe penis lack any kind of mastery, but her way of thinking is extremely fluid, and she is emblematic of a new generation which hesitates between the "Lover Ship" (the name of a love encounter club) and the "Flower show" (erotic showbiz, but also therapy for abnormality, discover of human identity in love sufferance). Finally, what is developed is "skinship"—the physical contact, modeled on the mother/child relationship. It is not surprising in a country where these contacts are said to be deficient, and for a society in

which the langage is gendered and separaters men and women.

Using the trick of Kazumi's big-toe penis enables Matsuura to try to understand masculine pleasure (penetration and masturbation) in all of its phallocratic power, from the feminine point of view, as well as the dysfunctions of male sexuality, especially impotence. It is the end of passive feminine sexuality. The heroine, who relates her adventures to a female writer called M., seeks a sexual and affective happiness which is linked to skinship rather than to mere penetration, active or passive. The ideal sexual act is finally defined as "making love with love" by the transsexual Masami.

In conclusion, sentimental love is back inside free sexuality. Without love, there is no happy sex, whatever that sex can be. Companionship and the importance of family are stressed, as well as the couple, but they cannot be compared to the existing ones. Love is reevaluated through point of view of abnormality and rediscovered as an illimited new emotional field.

Biography

Born in Matsuyama; lives and works at the moment in Tokyo. In 1978, Matsuura received the *Bungakukaishinjichô* (new young writer's prize) for *Sôgi no hi* [*The Funeral Party*]. Since then, she has published an anthology of short stories, three novels, and several essays. *Sebastien* (1987) is often related to the cult of Mishima and she is considered a direct descendant of that writer. She is praised by her contemporaries, such as Nakagami Kenji. *Big-Toe Penis* (1993) was in a few days a best-seller. She had been a cult writer; suddenly, she came to the attention of the mass media. This novel won the *Joryubungakushô* (prize for feminine literature). Since then, she has been regarded as a feminist writer. And indeed, *Natural Woman,* her next novel, dealt with the theme of feminine homosexuality. She almost won the Akutagawa Prize.

MARC KOBER

Selected Works

Novels, Short Stories

Sougi no hi. Tokyo: Bungei shunjuu (now Kawadeshobou Shinsha), 1978.
Sebastien. Tokyo: Bungei shunjuu (now Kawadeshobou Shinsha), 1987.

Oyayubi-P no shugyo jidai. Tokyo: Kawadeshobou Shinsha, 1993.

Nachuraru uman [Natural Woman]. Tokyo: Kawadeshobou Shinsha, 1994.

Essay Collections

Poketto fetisshu [Pocket Fetish]. Tokyo: Hakusuisha, 1994.

Yasashii kyosei no tame ni [For a Gentle Castration]. Tokyo: Chikuma Shobo, 1997

Oboreru jinsei sodan [Advice for a Drowning Life]. Tokyo: Kadokawa Shoten, 1998.

Ura-vajon [Reverse Version]. Tokyo: Chikuma Shobo, 2000.

Translation

Takekurabe. Poems by Higuchi Ichiyou. Tokyo: Kawade Shobo Shinsha, 1996 (translation into modern Japanese; first publication in the review *Bungakukai*, 1985).

Further Reading

Borel, France. *Le Vêtement incarné.* Paris: Pocket, 1998.

Mourthé, Claude. "Matsuura Rieko, grande prêtresse de Lesbos." *Le Magazine littéraire* 352, March 1997.

Nakagami, Shigeki. *What's Happening to Sexuality? Corporeal Sensations in Matsuura Rieko's* Oyayubi-P no Shugyo jidai. In *Love and Sexuality in Japanese Literature*, edited by Eiji Sekine. Vol. 5. Lafayette, IN: Midwest Association for Japanese Literary Studies/Purdue University Press, 1999.

Souzenelle, Annick de. *Le Symbolisme du corps humain.* Paris: Albin Michel, 1991.

MATZNEFF, GABRIEL

1936–

French novelist, essayist, diarist, poet, columnist, and critic

Gabriel Matzneff is no doubt the most controversial living French writer, simultaneously glorified as a literary genius by scores of intelligentsia and villified as a violent sex offender by child protection agencies, parent organizations, and government lobbies on both sides of the political divide. Yet despite the defiant candor with which he relentlessly narrates his sexual adventures, he has never been put into prison, his works have never been censored, and some of the most prestigious French publishers are queuing to reprint his intimate diaries. For obvious reasons, perhaps, his work has not been translated into English, yet in his homeland he remains the undisputable, if not undisputed, *enfant terrible* of letters.

Although Matzneff himself has divided his literary output into novels, diaries, essays, and poetry, the contents of these works are remarkably similar. Almost invariably, they are stories of lust-driven adults who desperately seek to make the acquaintances of, seduce, and love fourteen- and fifteen-year-old boys and girls. Countering the odium associated with the term "pedophilia," Matzneff describes the devouring passion of his protagonists (under whose thinly disguised names and characters he situates his own experiences) as the practice of "philopedia," a mixture of religion (worship) and eroticism (sexual pleasure), with which the aging man can satiate his hunger for eternal youth. In *La passion Francesca*, which details his passionate involvement with a fifteen-year-old girl, Matzneff puts it as follows: "This is how I shall suck your heart and your brains, much like drinking Coca-Cola with a straw. You will never break up with me. I give you too much pleasure. If you break up with me, I will drive you crazy. You are in my power and in order to escape it, your heart will have to bleed liters and liters of blood." The "philopedic" narrator clearly appears as a cruel and selfish predator here, yet in the end (and perhaps inevitably) he also knows that he will be slaughtered on the altar of the young girl's sexual appetite. Time and again, the narrator discovers that his beloved has betrayed him with another (younger) man or that she is not who he thought she was—madly jealous instead of happily indulgent, loudly demanding instead of quietly obsequious. And so he is forced to break off the relationship, yet only in order to woo a new, purer nymph into the realm of his desire, ad infinitum.

If Matzneff designates the acts of his character(s) as "philopedic," he never really endeavors—like André Gide in *Corydon*, for example—to plumb their psychological motives. Matzneff is adamant that they are part and parcel of an irreducible *ars vivendi*, a "way of life" or, as he calls it, "une dietétique." Combined with the aforementioned religious dimension of "philopedia," this principle endows his work with moralistic overtones, yet at the same time Matzneff is rarely inclined to teach or preach, which may explain why he has managed to escape censorship. Rather than elevating his narration to the level of an ethical or philosophical doctrine and developing its exoteric qualities, Matzneff elaborates his discourse in an ultra-intimistic fashion, sharing with his readership thoughts and feelings that few people would want to admit to themselves, and simultaneously recording (the admittedly scandalous) events of his love life in a form that commits them to posterity. Matzneff challenges our erotic codes, but the main challenge for himself as a writer seems to be to capture in writing all the unspoken (and often unspeakable) fragments of an idiosyncratic erotic experience.

Insofar as the fictionalized truth of Matzneff's writings brings to mind the devious acts and assertions of Humbert Humbert, their style is also reminiscent of the outstanding stylistic qualities of Nabokov's *Lolita*. Matzneff is renowned for saying that he has only ever been faithful to the French language and that his writing is primarily an exercise in style, which could also mean that unlike the many boys and girls with whom he has shared his bed, the French language has never let him down. Hence, whatever the reader may experience in the content of his works, their style is extraordinarily persuasive and seductive, so that even if the reader is disgusted by the story line, its purified aesthetics may still exert a strong power of attraction.

Biography

Gabriel Matzneff was born August 12 in Neuilly-sur-Seine of Russian parents who had emigrated to France after the 1917 Russian revolution. The Franco-Russian community in which he grew up conditioned his lifelong allegiance to the Orthodox Church. Educated at the École Tannenberg and the Lycée Carnot, he read classics at the Sorbonne during the 1950s. In 1957 he wrote to Henri de Montherlant, which signals the beginning of a lifelong friendship between the two men. Matzneff started his military service in 1959, which he performed with so much skill and enthusiasm that his brothers-in-arms dubbed him "Gab la Rafale" (Burst-Gab). After he tried to commit suicide, he was discharged from the military and spent two months in a psychiatric hospital. During the early 1960s he devoted most of his time to traveling, writing, and pursuing his passion for (pre)adolescent boys and girls. In 1962 he started writing a weekly column for *Combat*, which gradually earned him a reputation as a new literary stylist. His first collection of essays, *Le défi*, was published in 1965, followed a year later by his first novel, *L'archimandrite*. In 1974, his essay *Les Moins de seize ans* caused a scandal because of its uninhibited celebration of cross-generational sexual relationships. With the publication during the 1970s and 80s of his intimate diaries, containing detailed autobiographical accounts of an endless series of erotic encounters with minors, Matzneff became a thorn in the eye of French law enforcers. In December 1982 his apartment was raided and he was accused of being a member of a notorious pedophile ring, yet three years later he was cleared of all charges. His image tarnished, he lost his acclaimed column in *Le Monde*, but it didn't deter him from his literary and sexual activities. During the 1990s he continued to seduce, write, and publish in the same vein, shamelessly rendering public his most intimate moments of love and hate with (pre)adolescent girls, whilst also appearing on the catwalk for fashion designer Yohji Yamamoto. Matzneff's latest book is a collection of essays entitled *Yogourt et Yoga* (2004), and critics are eagerly awaiting the publication of his post-1987 notebooks.

DANY NOBUS

Selected Works

Cette camisole de flammes—Journal intime, 1953–1962, 1976 (2nd ed., 1989)
Douze poèmes pour Francesca, 1977
Harrison Plaza, 1988
Ivre du vin perdu, 1981.
La diététique de Lord Byron, 1984
La passion Francesca—Journal intime, 1974–1976, 1998
L'Archimandrite, 1966 (2nd ed., 1981)
Le défi, 1965 (4th ed., 2002)
Le taureau de Phalaris, 1987 (2nd ed., 1994)
Les lèvres menteuses, 1992
Les moins de seize ans, 1974 (5th ed., 2005)
Les passions schismatiques, 1977 (3rd ed., 2005)

Mes amours decomposés—Journal intime, 1983–1984, 1990
Yogourt et yoga, 2004

Further Reading

Bulletin de la Société des Amis de Gabriel Matzneff, 1999–2004, 10 issues
Delannoy, Philippe. *Gabriel Matzneff.* Monaco: Editions du Rocher, 1992.
Hocquenghem, Guy. "Les Écrivains de la transgression." *Le Quotidien de Paris,* November 5, 1985.
Lire 218, November 1, 1993.
Roy, Vincent. *Matzneff. L'Exilé absolu.* Paris: Editions Michalon, 2003.

MAUPASSANT, GUY DE

1850–1893
French novelist and author of short stories

In the short stories on which his literary reputation is principally based, Maupassant reveals a pessimistic vision of mankind marked by Schopenhauer's denunciation of love as a mask for the reproductive instinct, of woman as nature's trap to ensure the continuance of the species. In over half of this oeuvre, sexuality is the driving force, with results that can be comic (an ignorant young bride mistakes orgasm as the onset of rabies) or disastrous (when infidelity, repression, or jealousy drive to murder). The prostitute often serves as a figure whose honesty shows up hypocrisy, subverts respectability, or reveals the fragility of social distinctions. Pleasure is totally separate from marriage: indeed it is the social constraints on desire that lead to unhappiness and crime.

Maupassant attacked in his journalism the inability to talk frankly and explicitly about the plain fact of coupling as something natural, useful, and innocent, but the stories inevitably resort to allusion and euphemism. On occasion his directness led to censorship difficulties. The poem "Au bord de l'eau" [At the Water's Edge] links sensual eroticism with a realistic setting in nature: when it was published in a review in 1880, Maupassant was charged with outrage to public morality, though the case was dismissed. His first novel, *Une Vie* [*A Woman's Life*] (1883) was briefly banned from sale in railway bookstalls for its direct evocation of the marital disillusionments of the sexually ignorant and romantic heroine.

Such works attempted to confront certain realities while remaining within the boundaries of what could be published openly. Maupassant's erotic work represents, however, an exaggerated protest against hypocrisy, and an antidote both to sentimental idealizing and to the lyrical disguising of natural instincts, through a blunt insistence on physical reality.

In his journalism Maupassant called for bold and passionate poems celebrating sex, without crude words, lewd jokes, or innuendo. His known erotic poems were written between 1874 and 1878. Three were published in Belgium in 1881; of several others written, some have been lost, and three are in private collections. "Désirs de faune" [A Faun's Desires] fits his prescription, balancing a lyrical evocation of sex with intensity and realism. "Ma Source" [My Spring] less successfully celebrates cunnilingus with an incongruous series of overconventional poetic images coupled with sacrilegious overtones: moss, spring, the rock struck by Moses; it closes with the poet carrying away the woman's odor on his mustache like a censer. Two others are provocatively anti-poetic, exaggerated, and demythificatory. "La Femme à barbe" [The Bearded Lady] describes a sexual encounter with down-to-earth directness. The woman startles the poet by aggressively acting out a male role; there is no pretense of emotional feeling: he is motivated by curiosity, she by the desire for "a good screw." The story "69" desentimentalizes that act even further: the woman in the story is old, ugly, and dirty, the language violent and crude.

During the same period that he wrote these poems, Maupassant devised, together with four boating friends, the one-act play *A la feuille de rose, maison turque* (the untranslatable title suggests a Turkish establishment called "At the Rose Leaf," but is also a slang expression for analingus). He organized private stagings in 1875 and 1877; the audience for the second included Zola, Flaubert, and Maupassant's father. All the roles were played by the group of male friends; the women characters had gaping vaginas painted on their costumes, the men had giant phalluses made of draught excluders. The manager, Miché ("Pimp"), has dressed the three prostitutes in his Parisian brothel in Turkish costumes to attract customers; unfortunately, only one, Raphaële (played by Maupassant), is presentable. One plot line is provided by the arrival of Monsieur Beauflanquet ("Well-endowed"), the mayor of Conville, and his wife, lured to this "hotel" by Léon, who wishes to have intercourse with the wife. This plot is interrupted by a series of clients, all of whom select Raphaële, to the mounting distress of the servant Crête-de-Coq ("Coxcomb," but also a genital growth), the lover of Raphaële and an ex-seminarist. The clients, all acted by the same man, are a series of comic stereotypes: a cesspool emptier whose stammering produces a series of crude puns, a hunchback, an army captain who refuses protection on the grounds that "you don't sheath a sabre when charging" (the servant points out that he will be discharging), a boastful Marseillais who claims to have killed a woman with his member but who fails to reach orgasm, a miltary sapper, an Englishman who thinks it is a museum and copulates with the "waxwork" Raphaële. The farcical plot is enlivened by juvenile jokes and conversations at cross-purposes: Mme Beauflanquet innocently misreads the sexual terms, such as "pussy" and "doggie-style," used by the whores: her "knowledge" astonishes them. The preposterous climax involves a complex exchange of sexual partners in the dark between M. and Mme Beauflanquet and Raphaële and Léon. After a standard recognition scene echoing *The Marriage of Figaro*, the Beauflanquets return to the provinces; Miché, desperate for money, offers to satisfy the cesspool worker himself when the whores refuse; and the servant, spurned by Raphaële, is reduced, as in the seminary, to masturbation.

The playlet represents a series of denigrating male jokes for men (the women in the audience were not amused). The crude realities of sex and money aggressively de-poeticize sentimental illusions; it is not just a "realistic" corrective to idealism, but also an exuberantly gross farcical exaggeration. The (mimed) sexual acts are increasingly performed on stage, before the other characters as well as the audience, blatantly immodest and veering to the scatalogical: the sapper, unable to afford Raphaële, dunks his penis in her urine in compensation. The customers want only sex, but most cannot pay or cannot perform adequately; the whores embody eager availability and lesbianism. It mocks the establishment (the army and religion) and exposes bourgeois hypocrisy: Mme Beauflanquet, the frustrated wife, yields to Léon and then to Raphaële's lesbian advances; her boring husband is ready to make love to the entire harem. The play is a demystifying jape, but one carried off with verve.

Biography

Born at Château de Miromesnil, commune of Tourville-sur-Arques, Normandy, August 5. Educated at Lycée Napoléon, Paris, 1859–60; as boarder at the Institution ecclésiastique, Yvetot, 1863–68; then at Rouen Lycée 1868–69. Attended Faculté de Droit, Paris 1869–70. Mobilized July 1870 and served in the Supply Corps during the Franco-Prussian War. Civil servant in the Ministry for the Navy and the Colonies 1872–78, then Ministry of Education 1878–82 (on extended leave from 1880). The success of his story "Boule de Suif" in 1880 opened up collaboration with major Parisian newspapers, notably the *Gaulois* (1880–88) and *Gil Blas* (1881–91) for both short fiction and journalism; he also published six novels. Already suffering from ill health, Maupassant visited spas in Switzerland and France (1877, 1883, 1888, 1890). Returning frequently to Normandy, he also traveled in mainland France and to the Channel Islands (1879), Corsica (1880), North Africa (1881, 1888, 1890), and England (1886). From 1891 general paralysis affected his mental capacities; after attempting suicide in January 1892 he was interned in Dr Blanche's clinic in Passy. Died of tertiary syphilis, July 6.

PETER COGMAN

Selected Works

"Ma Source," "La Femme à barbe," and "69." In *Nouveau Parnasse satyrique du XIXe siècle*, 1881.
"Mars et Vénus," 1903.
"Désirs de faune," 1927.
"Eglogue bien amoureuse," 1939.
A la feuille de rose, maison turque, 1946.

Œuvres poétiques complètes: 'Des Vers' et autres poèmes. Edited by Emmanuel Vincent. Rouen: Université de Rouen, 2001.

Further Reading

Douchin, Jacques-Louis. *La Vie érotique de Maupassant*. Paris: Suger, 1986.
Ignotus, Paul. *The Paradox of Maupassant*. London: University of London Press, 1966.
Lanoux, Armand. *Maupassant le bel-ami*. Paris: Fayard, 1967.
Leclec, Yvan. *Crimes écrits: La littérature en procès au XIXe siècle*. Paris: Plon, 1991.
———. "Maupassant, poète naturaliste?" *Bulletin Flaubert-Maupassant* 9 (2001): 181–93.
Place-Verghnes, Floriane. "Maupassant pornographe." *Neophilologus* 85 (2001): 501–17.
Steegmuller, Francis. *Maupassant*. London: Collins, 1950.
Stivale, Charles J. "Horny Dudes: Guy de Maupassant and the Masculine *Feuille de rose*." *Esprit Créateur* 43 (2003): 57–67.
Vincent, Emmanuel. "'*Des vers*' et autres poèmes de Maupassant." *Bulletin Flaubert-Maupassant* 9 (2001): 169–80.

MEAKER, MARIJANE (ANN ALDRICH AND VIN PACKER)

1927–
American novelist

It was at the Fawcett publishing house, where she worked as a secretary, that Meaker began, in 1952, to write and publish novels under the first of several pseudonyms she has used throughout her career. When asked about the pseudonyms under which she wrote for Fawcett, Meaker said, "Because I couldn't get an agent, I became my own, using various disguises as my clients" (Lovisi, 18). Although she is now best known for her work writing young adult novels as M.E. Kerr, in the postwar period she wrote a number of very popular mass-market paperbacks for Fawcett as Vin Packer and Ann Aldrich. The Vin Packer novels came primarily under two categories, so-called JD, or juvenile delinquent,

novels and novels featuring lesbian characters which are prized by collectors of lesbian pulp fiction. As Ann Aldrich, Meaker wrote both fiction and nonfiction solely on the lesbian theme.

The Vin Packer and Ann Aldrich books were written for Fawcett's Gold Medal line of paperback originals. The first of these was *Spring Fire*, a novel about lesbian love published in 1952. *Spring Fire* was an instant success. This may be partly due to the fact that it was included on the list of books investigated by the House Select Committee on Current Pornographic Materials in 1952. The novel was introduced into the record as evidence of "books [which] extol by their approbatory language accounts of homosexuality, lesbianism and other sexual aberrations" (US Congress, 14). *Spring Fire* went through five reprintings between 1952 and 1965.

Following the success of *Spring Fire* Meaker wrote JD and lesbian novels as Vin Packer throughout the 1950s. These two themes came together in 1958 in *The Evil Friendship,* a novel based on the Australian Parker-Hulme case of 1954, in which two lesbian lovers were tried for murder. Meaker has said that she and her editor often followed cases in the press and then chose to base novels on them (Lovisi). Two Vin Packer novels *(Dark Don't Catch Me,* 1956, and *3-Day Terror,* 1957) were based on interracial sex and the violence it provoked toward black men in the segregated South. The plots were drawn from the case of Emmet Till and other newspaper reports of the period. *Dark Don't Catch Me* and *3-Day Terror* fall into a category of postwar mass-market fiction which exploited the threatening concept of interracial sex in America. It is clear from comments made by the House Committee on Current Pornographic Materials in 1952 that interracial sex was commonly classed as a perversion. As such it was exploited by paperback houses and no doubt consumed, like lesbian pulp, by those seeking to articulate dissident sexualities.

Meaker began writing under the name Ann Aldrich, a pseudonym specifically attached to a lesbian persona, in 1955. The first of the Ann Aldrich paperbacks was *We Walk Alone (Through Lesbos' Lonely Groves).* This book takes the form of a nonfiction exposé of the imaginary lesbian underworld of the 1950s. Chapter titles include "Who Is She?" "How Did She Get That Way?" "Gay Paris," "Can a Lesbian Be Cured?" and "A Word to Parents." These titles exemplify the complicated pose of being both an agent of voyeuristic pleasure and a socially concerned commentator taken by Aldrich and other writers of lesbian pulp paperbacks. The cover of *We Walk Alone* contains commentary by one "Dr. Richard Hoffman, world famous psychiatrist," who describes Aldrich as "herself a member of the sisterhood."

Following the success of *We Walk Alone,* the Aldrich persona was exploited in four other titles between 1955 and 1963. The most notable of these is *Carol in a Thousand Cities,* an edited collection including European and American literature and medical commentary. Selections in *Carol* include everything from Carol Morgan (Patricia Highsmith)'s contemporary lesbian writing to an essay by Sigmund Freud and extracts from Colette and Guy de Maupassant.

At least five of Meaker's Fawcett Gold Medal titles were published in British editions during the 1960s. *Take a Lesbian to Lunch,* another Aldrich paperback which might be viewed as part of this period, was not published until 1971.

The novels of Vin Packer and Ann Aldrich are often mentioned in life-history accounts by women who lived as lesbians in the postwar era. Meaker's novels are not often remembered with the fondness attached to the works of Ann Bannon and Valerie Taylor. Rather, Ann Aldrich came to exemplify a self-deprecating tone which lesbians sought to distance themselves from in the wake of the feminist and gay liberation movements. She is most often cited as an example of the repression under which lesbian sexuality formed itself in the 1950s and 60s. In her essay "Cruising the Libraries," Lee Lynch mentions *The Evil Friendship* and *Take a Lesbian to Lunch,* describing the characters as "more miserable than Sartre's, and despised as well" (Lynch, 40). Despite this later view of Aldrich as a negative role model, it is clear that many lesbians, including lesbian writers, formed their own ideas and aspirations through the process of reading her novels. Their bold and sensational treatments and massive distribution through Fawcett made them a ready vehicle for lesbian identification, whether women worked with or against their objectifying tone.

Into the 21st century, Marijane Meaker is well known as the writer of young adult novels and teacher of writing M.E. Kerr. Her young adult titles often continue her lifelong preoccupation with sexuality and sexual identity.

Biography

Marijane Meaker was born in Auburn, New York, May 27. She was raised in upstate New York and attended Stuart Hall boarding school in Virginia from 1943, then attended the University of Missouri from 1946 to 1949 as an English literature major. She moved to New York City in 1949 and sold her first story to *Ladies' Home Journal* in 1951. She worked for some time as a journalist and then as a secretary at the Fawcett publishing house.

MEREDITH MILLER

Selected Works

(All Greenwich, CT: Fawcett)

As Vin Packer

Spring Fire, 1952.
Look Back to Love, 1953.
Come Destroy Me, 1954.
Dark Don't Catch Me, 1956.
3-Day Terror, 1957.
The Evil Friendship, 1958.
The Twisted Ones, 1959.
Something in the Shadows, 1961.

As Ann Aldrich

We Walk Alone (Through Lesbos' Lonely Groves), 1955.
We, Too, Must Love, 1958.
Alone at Night, 1963.
We Two Won't Last, 1963.
Editor. *Carol in A Thousand Cities*, 1960.

Further Reading

Danielson, Audrey Marie. "Interview with M.E. Kerr." At http://www.teenreads.com/authors/au-kerr-me.asp. Retrieved March 15, 2006.

Lovisi, Gary. "An Interview with Marijane Meaker, the Woman Behind Vin Packer and Ann Aldrich." *Paperback Parade* 47 (1997).

Lynch, Lee. "Cruising the Libraries." In *Lesbian Texts* and *Contexts: Radical Revisions,* edited by Karla Jay and Joanne Glasgow. London: Onlywomen Press, 1992.

M.E. Kerr website, at http://www.mekerr.com

U.S. Congress. House. Select Committee on Current Pornographic Materials (Senator E.C. Gathings, chairman), 82nd Cong., 2nd session, pursuant to House Resolution 596. Washington: United States Government Printing Office, 1952. Commonly referred to as the Gathings Report.

MECHAIN, GWERFUL

c. 1462–1500
Medieval Welsh poet

"The Female Genitals"

"The Female Genitals" ("Cywydd y Cedor"; cedor is translatable as "cunt") is an attack on those practitioners of Welsh bardic poetry who readily describe a woman's beauty but fail to make reference to the "clear excellence" of that most important aspect of the female anatomy—the vagina itself. The poem begins with an assault on "Every foolish drunken poet" who has ever "declaimed fruitless praise" upon a woman's hair, face, breasts, arms, and hands. Although the speaker credits these poets with good taste in offering their accolades to the hair ("gown of fine love") or breasts ("lovely shape / the smoothness"), the failure to address adequately a woman's sexuality by avoiding the lower body is seen as an affront to the woman's own desires and needs, a snub to her very womanhood. The condemned male poets and their unsatisfactory verse are dismissed with a speed similar to that with which they disregard the female genitalia. After opening with an outcry against other poets, the speaker continues not by a prolongation of the attack on these bards, but by using the remainder of the poem as an ideal opportunity to offer the praise of the female genitals so distinctly lacking in their work.

The poem explores in graphic detail the nature and desires of womanhood that the speaker sees as symbolized by the vagina. The "middle" which is left "without praise" is both "the place where children are conceived, / and the warm quim, clear excellence, / tender and fat, bright fervent broken circle." These lines associate female sexuality on one level with a purely reproductive purpose but counter this by the elaborate description of the "quim below the smock," which means that the reader is left in no doubt that this part of the body is also perceived to be the seat of desire, pleasure, and delight. Particularly interesting is the way in which the possibility that the sex of the speaker is male (Mechain was a woman) is revealed to us through this description of the female genitals. They are described as the place "where I loved, in perfect health, / the quim below the smock," and from this point in the poem the speaker begins her own process of eulogizing (in stark contrast to her fellow bards) about the beauty and attractiveness of the quim.

The speaker cleverly manipulates the poetic language of the bards in the comparisons she makes between the vagina and the natural world, so that the "cunt there by the swelling arse" is also "a valley longer than a spoon or a hand, / a ditch to hold a penis two hands long." The genitals later become a "sour grove," a "very proud forest," and "a girl's thick grove" (in the original Welsh, the meaning is subtly ambiguous because *llwyn* can mean both "grove" and "pubic hair"). But the speaker also falls into the trap of generalizing, to the extent that the object of the speaker's desire—which seemed at first to be specific ("where I loved")—becomes merely a "cunt." The speaker also de-eroticizes the subject of the poem through an ironic reversal of her complaint about other poets. In the other bards' writing, the speaker feels that there is no emphasis on the genitals themselves; in her own poem, the woman is only the genitals.

The daring of Gwerful Mechain's inclusion of references to the church is of interest because this emphasizes the God-given naturalness of female sexuality. These references eroticize the female genitals so as to tempt the men of the cloth. The speaker writes that even "the bright saints, men of the church, / when they get the chance ... don't fail ... to give it a good feel," and this fact is brought into the poem as a justification for the attack on other poets—if even churchmen cannot resist the female genitals, why should poets hold back their own praise? Indeed, as the poem draws to a close, the speaker declares that it is "for this reason, thorough rebuke / all you proud poets / let songs to the quim circulate / without fail to gain reward." The poem concludes with a final call for all to praise the female genitals—"lovely bush, God save it."

The poem's eroticism resides largely in the speaker's open assertion of female sexual desire (as displayed in the luxuriant descriptions of the "cunt") and the subversion of the bardic tradition in descriptions of such lust. Unwilling to fall into line with the traditional poetry of praise, Gwerful Mechain's frank portrayal of female sexuality in "The Female Genitals" continues to mark her out as one of the more interesting, and still controversial, figures of medieval Welsh poetry.

Biography

Little is known of Gwerful Mechain's life apart from the fact that she came from Mechain in Powys (mid-Wales). As a poet she was active in the late fifteenth century (ca.1480–1500), and a relatively large amount of her work survives. Most famous for her salacious verse and her erotic poems (such as "The Female Genitals" and "To Jealous Wives," although her authorship of the first is supposed rather than certain), she also wrote many religious pieces and one of her best poems concerns the passion of Christ. She has been described by Ceridwen Lloyd-Morgan as "the most important and prolific woman poet of the Middle Ages."

MARK LLEWELLYN

Further Reading

Conran, Anthony. "The Lack of the Feminine." *New Welsh Review* 17 (Summer 1992): 28–31.

Johnston, Dafydd, ed. and translator. *Canu Maswedd yr Oesoedd Canol / Medieval Welsh Erotic Poetry.* Bridgend, Wales: Seren, 1991.

Lloyd-Morgan, Ceridwen. "Women and Their Poetry in Medieval Wales." In *Women and Literature in Britain, 1150–1500,* ed. Carol M. Meale. Cambridge Studies in Medieval Literature 17. Cambridge: Cambridge University Press, 1993.

MELÉNDEZ VALDÉS, JUAN

1754–1817
Spanish lawyer and poet

Los besos de amor

Outstanding in Meléndez's poetic output are the pastoral anacreontics which in theme and tone are close to the *Besos de amor*, a group of 23 erotic poems which remained unpublished in the poet's lifetime. Though not printed until 1894, the *Besos* must have circulated in manuscript because they were banned by the Inquisition in 1801, being listed in the 1805 *Suplemento* to the Spanish Index of prohibited books. Described there as anonymous translations of the sixteenth-century, neo-Latin *Basia* of Joannes Secundus (Jan Nicholaus Everaerts), the researches of John Polt have attributed some of Meléndez's *Besos* to other neo-Latin authors, while the remainder could well be original.

The eroticism of the *Besos de amor*, as the title suggests, is principally focused on kissing and the sensual play involved in touching, caressing, and contemplating the loved one. The poems present the thoughts of the unnamed male lover to his female love, who bears various conventional pastoral names: Amarilis, Amarílida, and Filis (all once), Nise (twice), Galatea (four times), and, predominantly, Nisa (twelve times). The tone is refined, with constant use of euphemistic phrases to refer to aspects of the physical relationship. The concentration on the kiss gathers power as the reader advances through the 23 poems. The sensuality seems designed to evoke images of the physicality of kissing but nevertheless achieves erotic intensity because of the cumulative effect of the series of compositions. The poems vary in length from 12 to 95 lines, but most have less than 40. Having examined the vocabulary used by Meléndez, Mario Di Pinto has highlighted the repetition of "dulce" [sweet] and its derivatives, used 45 times. The style of the poems owes much to the anacreontic tradition. Line length is generally short and frequently heptasyllabic, though some poems alternate heptasyllables with hendecasyllables (Odas 12 and 13). The characteristically Spanish light assonantal rhyme is generally preferred, though a few poems have full consonantal rhyme (Odas 12, 13, 21).

The love play is mutual both in its passion and in its emphasis. Oda 3, with antecedents in two poems by Secundus, has Nise as protagonist, initiating the action by kissing her lover and taking him in her arms. Her behavior is termed "lasciva" ("lascivious," perhaps "passionate," used 18 times in all in the collection), and the effect of her kisses leads his hand to caress her "nevado vientre" (snowy stomach). She sighs, moves, speaks haltingly, asks him to stop, but kisses again with a bite, mouthing desire as she moves. Oda 5, which translates an epigram by Muret, is powerfully succinct, centering on eyes and kisses. The passion ascends through three levels resulting from three actions; her look, their kissing, and his being taken to her bed. Yet kisses are at the heart of these poems. Oda 2 evokes the first kiss the implied author gave Nise. Oda 6 climaxes with the combination of Nisa caressing her lover's neck while she kisses him lasciviously, gazing at him and smiling. In Oda 11 the lover wants to kiss Nisa's eyes and hair, and when his flesh is pierced by her nails he kisses her more and tightly embraces her body. Oda 14 extends his kisses over Nisa's cheeks, eyes, lips, neck, and breasts.

Kisses are counted as part of the lovers' ritual in Odas 8, 11, 16, and 21. Oda 20, with antecedents in two *Basia* by Secundus, concerns "besos lascivos" [passionate kisses], compared to the sweetness of honey and the pecking of doves, hovering between sensuality and eroticism. Her trembling tongue and sighing lips in the closing lines make his soul wither (*fallece*, literally "die") with delight. Oda 18, a mere 24 lines, is one of the most intensely erotic compositions in the group. It seems to contain a wish rather than recount a concrete occasion. The poet imagines Filis regaling him with kisses, caresses, and love on her soft bed. She entwines herself around his neck with their mouths joined; her eyes respond as his hand seeks her body and she gives off a gentle murmur, and as passion takes hold she gently sighs. In the final two quatrains her sighing animates him as her tongue bites him; her arms enfold him and her desire increases his urgency; the climax comes, not like death ("muerte"), but transmitting life.

The other poem expressing heightened passion is Oda 13, an erotic fantasy in which the poet dreams of Amarílida. Though comparisons have been made with works by Bonnefons and Propertius, it appears to be an original composition by Meléndez and is ambitious in its length, which contrasts with the surrounding texts of the collection. It is more overtly rhetorical in its reiterated exclamations of wonder and joy which initially look back to the previous night of passion, but then recount a dream the previous day. In some respects it is a summation of most of the elements which appear less comprehensively in other poems; its greater extension allows this fullness, though with its mixture of seven and eleven syllable lines, in strict rhyme, it is less light and concise, less given to suggestion and more to explanation. The first scene of the dream is his gazing at her body, contemplating her arms, her breasts, her waist, before expressing his wish to enjoy her beauty. The poem may be entirely original, revealing Meléndez's mastery of this poetic subgenre.

Biography

Born in Extremadura at Ribera del Fresno on March 11. Meléndez studied law and humanities at Salamanca University, where he taught briefly before entering government service as a lawyer in the provincial capitals of Zaragoza and Valladolid, and later Madrid. An active liberal intellectual, he was memorably painted by Goya, but his principal claim to fame is a substantial body of poetry. His compositions are predominantly philosophical, including a significant reworking of Alexander Pope's "Essay on Man," as well as more socially committed political satires, praise of enlightened figures, and nature poems. He died in Montpelier, France, on May 24.

PHILIP DEACON

Editions

"Los besos de amor. Odas inéditas de D. Juan Meléndez Valdés." Edited by Raymond Foulché-Delbosc. *Revue Hispanique* 1 (1894): 166–95.

"Los besos de amor." In *Obras en verso*, edited by John H.R. Polt and Jorge Demerson, 293–310. Oviedo: Cátedra Feijoo, 1981.

Los besos de amor. Edited by Mario Di Pinto. Naples: Liguori, 1999. Spanish text with accompanying Italian translation.

Further Reading

Cerezo, José Antonio. "Meléndez, Valdés." In *Literatura erótica en España: Repertorio de obras 1519–1936*. Madrid: Ollero y Ramos, 2001.

Di Pinto, Mario, "L'osceno borghese (Note sulla letteratura erotica spagnola nel Settecento)." In *Codici della trasgressività in area ispanica. Atti del Convegno di Verona 12–13–14 giugno 1980*, 177–92. Verona: Istituto de Lingue e Letterature Straniere, 1980.

García Montero, Luis. "Juan Meléndez Valdés y el optimismo de los cuerpos." In *El sexto día. Historia íntima de la poesía española*, 127–47. Madrid: Debate, 2000.

Gies, David T. "Sobre el erotismo rococó en la poesía del siglo XVIII español." In *Luz vital. Estudios de cultura hispánica en memoria de Victor Ouimette*, edited by Ramón F. Llorens and Jesús Pérez Magallón, 85–95. Alicante: McGill University–Caja de Ahorros del Mediterráneo, 1999.

Haidt, Rebecca. *Embodying Enlightenment: Knowing the Body in Eighteenth-Century Spanish Literature and Culture*. New York: St Martin's Press, 1998.

Moreno, J.I. "Notas sobre la poesía del siglo XVIII a propósito de los *Besos de Amor*." In *Estudios sobre literatura y arte dedicados a Emilio Orozco Díaz*. Vol. 2 , 463–71. Granada: Universidad de Granada, 1979.

Polt, J.H.R. "Juan Meléndez Valdés's translations from the Latin." *Dieciocho* 16 (1993): 119–29.

Real Ramos, César. "Meléndez Valdés, poète de l'érotisme." In *Éros volubile. Les Métamorphoses de l'amour du Moyen Âge aux Lumières*, edited by Dolores Jiménez and Jean-Christophe Abramovici, 254–66. París: Desjonquères, 2000.

MELTZER, DAVID

1937–
American novelist and poet

David Meltzer's *The Agency Trilogy* is an outstanding example of how poets influenced erotic writing in the 20th century. In these three novels—*The Agency*, *The Agent*, and *How Many Blocks in the Pile?*—Meltzer conveys his poetic vision in a spare, allusive style, using techniques and elements of science fiction. Meltzer's metaphor for the way we conduct our sex lives is extended according to emotional logic. His trilogy was first published as separate volumes by Essex House in California in 1968, and appeared together in a second edition from Richard Kasak Books in 1994.

The Agency in the novel by that name is a well-organized, self-sufficient sexual underground. In *The Agency* a young man is picked up by sexual agents and spends the rest of the novel being indoctrinated with The Agency's tyrannical precepts. Brainwashed, he becomes an agent himself, ready to propagate the fantasy of The Agency. In *The Agent* the satirical possibilities implied in *The Agency* are applied more broadly. Meltzer's deliberately ambiguous portrayal of two agents who may or may not be working for the same agency is often reminiscent of scenes from the movie *Dr. Strangelove*. But his employment of multiple first-person narrative, voices sliding in and out of focus, confirms that his intention is to address his theme of power and sex in the indirect, allusive manner of poetry.

How Many Blocks in the Pile? only hints at the existence of The Agency. In the concluding volume of his trilogy, Meltzer creates an exaggerated portrait of its customers, a married couple who respond to sexual advertisements. The Agency, according to Meltzer is "both cause and effect of dehumanized sex and its relationship to American society."

The poet's notion that erotic writing expresses the secret sexual life of America is abundantly illustrated by *The Agency Trilogy*, but in his next novel, *Orf* (1968), he not only plumbs the national psyche on a deeper, mythical level, he achieves a fusion of poetic approach and erotic subject matter that beautifully demonstrates how the lessons and concerns of poetry can influence modern erotic writing. The title character Orf is a rock singer, a contemporary incarnation of the poet Orpheus. Orf's agent Schlink is a repulsive character who exploits singers, but he is not a caricature; he personifies Meltzer's theme of exploitation. The poet allows him his own human meaning—in fact, he is the book's strongest character.

Orf rises to national prominence at a concert in which he is literally ripped to pieces by his "Sacred Harlots." Of course the story of *Orf* is a retelling of the myth of Orpheus; the rock singer is a closer equivalent to the mythical figure than the modern poet, if only because of the violent nature of the audience's response to him. Meltzer seems to be saying that in America we use sex and dreams (the rock singer creates the background music for our dreams—and nightmares) to affirm the fact of our existence in an exploitative world.

Meltzer followed *Orf* with his most ambitious project, *The Brain-Plant Tetralogy* (1969), consisting of *Lovely*, *Healer*, *Out*, and *Glue Factory*. In classical Greek drama, a tetralogy is a group of four dramatic pieces, either four tragedies or three tragedies and a satire. Meltzer's *Brain-Plant* novels are not tragedies in the classical sense, but satire is a prominent feature in each of them.

The *Tetralogy* demands study as a whole, before it is possible to grasp the meaning of any one of the four novels. The complexity of Meltzer's design, his fantastic inventiveness, and his large cast of characters are such that it is best to approach a critical reading with a few guidelines. Meltzer's novels are designed according to the imperatives of poetry, not logical prose fiction; his tone is often satirical, but his novels are not satires; and finally, his theme is the exploitation of people through sex, power, and dreams.

The theme of *Star* (1970) is once again exploitation; in this case the users are Hollywood studio bosses, and the used are both the movie stars who people celluloid dreams and the audiences to whom they play. *Star* is after *The Martyr* (1969), Meltzer's most accessible novel. He seems to know as much about the film world as he does about rock music; his satire is controlled and effective, his characters three-dimensional, and his narrative straightforward. His most recent erotic novel, *Under* (1994), is a return to his signature themes.

Meltzer proves in his eleven erotic novels that he was correct to call them "fierce moral tracts." Although his work is crowded with vividly erotic scenes, their effect is more often frightening than arousing. In novels written like poems, eroticism is the physical exploitation of one person by another and is assaultive and outrageous, never loving or tender, never a path to transcendence. In a sense, his erotic work is an indictment of sexuality, challenging and chilling.

Biography

Born in Rochester, New York. He graduated from Los Angeles City College in 1955 and studied at the University of California, Los Angeles, 1955–56. His first book, *Poems*, was published in 1957. His selected poems, *Arrows*, appeared in 1993. He has written eleven erotic novels, criticism, and a biography of the artist Wallace Berman, and edited many anthologies and magazines. He teaches at the New College of California in San Francisco.

MICHAEL PERKINS

Selected Works

The Agency. 1968.
The Agent. 1968.
How Many Blocks in the Pile?
Orf. 1968.
The Martyr. 1969.
Lovely. 1969.
Healer. 1969.
Out. 1969.
Glue Factory. 1969.
Under. 1994.

MÉMOIRES DU BARON JACQUES, LES

Les mémoires du Baron Jacques is a novel told as a first-person account of the life of a rich, young aristocrat, written by Alphonse Gallais under the pseudonym "A. S. Lagail" sometime in the first ten to fifteen years of the 20th century. In October 1913, the book was banned for immorality by a Parisian court. It begins when the four-year-old Jacques is introduced to oral sex by his widowed mother. The sexual initiation lasts until Jacques turns ten and his mother dies while making love with her son. After five years of mourning, Jacques moves from his castle in Tours to Paris, where he settles in a stately mansion. Part diary, part poetry, part apocryphal autobiography, the bulk of the book relates Jacques's sexual exploits during his adult life.

Jacques vows never to have intercourse with women, creatures he accuses of being physically ugly and prone to venereal diseases and declares his passion for men and sodomy (the only notable female character is a lesbian who betrays one of Jacques's male partners). His mother stands out as the one exception to this blanket misogyny. Jacques even recovers her bones so that he can use them for masturbation and foreplay.

Sadism and necrophilia are another major theme. Aside from his posthumous relation with his mother, Jacques regularly has sex with dead, or dying, children, adults, and animals. In one episode, a twelve year old suffocates as he performs oral sex on Jacques. Other children are sacrificed during weekly black masses Jacques organizes for his friends. In one such orgy, one adult kills himself, after which other participants masturbate themselves with, then eat his body parts. Animals ranging from chickens to dogs and a calf, among others, also figure prominently, as Jacques experiments with new sexual practices. Graphic episodes succeed themselves at a brisk pace, with Jacques and his friends ejaculating up to ten times in a few hours. Their priapic tendencies seem to consume most of their lives, for brief references to Jacques's literary works are the only evidence of nonsexual activities.

The characters' indolence illustrates one last, important subtext of the work: social criticism. Contrary to many other erotic writers, Gallais did not write the work to arouse, but to shock and disgust. Subtitled "the diabolical debaucheries of the decadent aristocracy," *Les mémoires du Baron Jacques* criticizes the rich for going to the worst extremes, including murder, in their belief that no law has a right to prevent them from satisfying their degenerate cravings. Tipped by one of Jacques's disgruntled servants, the police finally raid one of his orgies, and Jacques dies shortly thereafter in the Parisian prison of Fresnes, "after delicate surgery on his rectum."

The book's parallels with real-life characters, not its style or literary merit, make it noteworthy. Early-twentieth-century readers familiar with Parisian life would have had no problem identifying Baron Jacques d'Adelsward-Fersen as the real-life aristocrat whose sexual depravities Gallais purported to describe in his work. Adelsward, born in 1880, came from a line of Swedish aristocrats who had settled in France during the Revolution and enriched themselves in the steel industry. Spending most of his early life in Paris, Adelsward started a successful literary career as a novelist and a poet. The title of a poem in *Les mémoires du Baron Jacques,* "Notre-Dame des verges fortes" [Our Lady of the Sturdy Cocks] is a parody of the title of one of Adelsward's novels, *Notre-Dame des mers mortes* [*Our Lady of the Dead Seas*] (1902). Several characters in Gallais's book also have their real-life counterpart in Adelsward's circle of friends, including writers Pierre Loti and Jean Lorrain.

As in Gallais's book, one of Adelsward's valets told the police that his employer was holding private parties in which teenage men drawn from neighboring high schools took part. The ensuing trial, involving boys and adults drawn from the highest circles of Parisian society, attracted tremendous popular and media attention, and many surmised that the parties were of the orgiastic, satanic kind described in Gallais's

portrayal of the Baron's black masses. Court records are still not available, but it seems that the parties were actually more subdued affairs in which scantily clad young men participated in *tableaux vivants* inspired by classic antiquity, as Adelsward recited poetry (a homosexual and a pederast, Adelsward may have had sex with these young men as well). Arrested and condemned for public indecency, Adelsward spent six months in jail at Fresnes and was forced to break up his wedding plans with a wealthy aristocratic lady. He unsuccessfully tried to kill himself, then to enroll in the Foreign Legion.

Contrary to the literary Baron, the real Adelsward survived his judicial ordeal and spent the rest of his life in Capri, Naples, and Nice, and traveling around the Mediterranean and Asia. He wrote numerous other novels and poems, sharing his bed with a succession of male lovers and boys. An opium and cocaine addict, he died in Naples on November 5, 1923, of a drug overdose. Roger Peyrefitte later offered a dramatized version of Adelsward's life, more historically accurate than the apocryphal *Mémoires du Baron Jacques,* in *L'Exilé de Capri* (1959).

Little is known about the life of Alphonse Gallais. Even his birth and death dates are uncertain. He was a French pornographer of the fin-de-siècle. Also writing under the name "Grimaudin d'Echara," Gallais composed a variety of erotic short stories, novels, and songs, along with songs and essays dealing with radicalism and occult sciences. The author Lagail claims that *Les Mémoires du Baron Jacques* was first published in 1904 in Priapeville by the "Librairie Galante" publishing house, which may refer to the publisher Jean Fort, in Paris.

PHILIPPE R. GIRARD

Editions

Lagail, A.S. *Les mémoires du Baron Jacques: Lubricités infernales de la noblesse décadente.* Priapeville [Paris?]: Librairie Galante [Jean Fort?], 1904.

d'Echara Grimaudin. "Les Memoires du Baron Jacques." In *Passions de femmes. Roman vécu de moeurs féminines et autres. Luxures orgiaques et ordurières. Livre III* [c. 1913]; as *The Memoirs of Baron Jacques: The Diabolical Debaucheries of Our Decadent Aristocracy,* translated by Richard West, Vancouver: Ageneios Press, 1988.

"Les Memoires du Baron Jacques." In *Dossier Jacques d'Adelsward-Fersen,* edited by Patrick Cardon, 63–95. Lille: Cahiers Gai-Kitsch-Camp, 1991.

Other Selected Works of Alphonse Gallais, A. S. Lagail, and Grimaudin d'Echara

Mémoires d'une fille de joie, 1902.
Amours d'Apache: Roman de la basse pègre, 1903.
La confession d'un pot de chambre, 1903.
Les paradis charnels, ou, le divin bréviaires des amants: art de jouir purement des 136 extases de la volupté, 1903.
Le roi s'amuse: tirade de Saint-Vallier... corrigée pour l'usage des écoles chrétiennes, 1903.
Tableau de l'amour charnel, ses extases, ses tares, ses vices, ses démences, ses turpitudes et ses crimes, 1905.
En voulez-vous du repos hebdomadaire, 1906.
Refus d'obéisssance: drame social en un acte, 1908.
Aux camarades de l'internationale ouvrière, 1909.
Les mystères de la magie, 1909 (with Léon Roze).
Les enfers lubriques (sadiques et sataniques). Curiosités, excentricités, et monstruosités passionnelles, 1906.
Le véritable trésor des sciences magiques, 1910. (with Léon Roze).
Plaisirs fangeux, 1911.
Cochons d'hommes, 1911.
Cécile Coquerel tailleuse de plumes, 1911.
Orgies à bord d'un yacht, 1911.
Un bordel modern-style, 1911.
Scènes lubriques, 1911.
Les Messalines modernes, 1912.
Blasées en rut, 1912.
Ces dames s'amusent, 1912.
Sadisme sanglant, 1912.
Les mystères de Vermenton ou l'Apache-ivrogne et Sainte-Vipère, 1931.
La muse vermontaise, 1931.
J'attends les soirets! 1934.

Selected Works of Jacques D'Adelsward-Fersen

Conte d'amour, 1898.
Chansons légères, 1900.
Poèmes de l'enfance, chansons légères, 1901.
Ebauches et débauches, 1901.
L'Hymnaire d'Adonis, 1902.
Notre-Dame des Mers Mortes, 1902.
Les Cortèges qui sont passés, 1903.
L'Amour enseveli, 1904.
Lord Lyllian. Messes noires, 1905.
Le danseur aux caresses, 1906.
Une jeunesse, 1906.
Le poison dans les fleurs, 1906.
Ainsi chantait Marsyas, 1907.
Le baiser de Narcisse, 1907.
Et le feu s'éteignit sur la mer, 1910.
Akademos, revue d'art libre et de critique, 1910.
Le sourire aux yeux fermés, 1912.
Paradinya, 1913.
Hei Hsiang, le parfum noir, 1921.
La neuvaine du petit faune (unfinished).

Further Reading

Cardon, Patrick, ed. *Dossier Jacques d'Adelsward-Fersen*. Lille: Cahiers Gai-Kitsch-Camp, 1991.
Lorrain, Jean. *Pelléastres: Le Poison de la littérature*. Paris: A. Méricant, 1910.
Ogrinc, Will H.L. "A Shrine to Love and Sorrow: Jacques d'Adelsward-Fersen (1880–1923)." *Paidika, The Journal of Pedophilia* 3 (1994): 30–58.
Peyrefitte, Roger. *L'Exilé de Capri. Edition définitive* [1959]. Paris: Flammarion, 1974.

MENDÈS, CATULLE

1841–1909
French novelist and short story writer

Catulle Mendès made his first mark on the Parisian literary scene by means of two reviews which he founded in the 1860s and which served as a link between the Romantic and Symbolist generations: *La Revue fantaisiste* (1861) and *Le Parnasse contemporain* (1866, 1871, 1876). In addition to his work as a poet, editor, and critic, the versatile Mendès also enjoyed subsequent success as a prolific author of novels and short story collections, many of which might be described as semi-erotic in intention. These will provide the main focus for the present article. Although academic commentators, perhaps unjustly, have tended to dismiss these later works as trivial and superficial, Mendès must be seen as one of the key architects of fin-de-siècle decadence. He also enjoyed some success as a playwright and librettist.

Mendès's first collection of short stories—*Histoires d'amour* (1868)—set the tone for what would follow. The longest story in the book is a dramatic study of precocious adolescent sexuality caused by prolonged illness; another concerns an adroit scheme hatched by an aging society belle to win a younger lover; while a third features a young dandy who attracts a string of mistresses by affecting such a sense of ennui that it is feared he is constantly on the point of self-destruction. Although Mendès would further refine the writing style, the majority of his short fiction might broadly be seen as the modern (i.e., post-1871) embodiment of the long French tradition of *gauloiserie*. In essence, these are light-hearted stories of sexual misunderstandings and accounts of the clever strategies employed by more experienced lovers to overcome the resistance of the naive or inhibited. In all, Mendès would pen nearly fifty such collections, their very titles clearly signposting the curious blend of elegant sophistication (note the references to bathing or dressing, makeup, and fashion) and decadent symbolism (note the references to religious practices or institutions together with the occasional suggestion of sexual aberration) in which their greatest appeal resides: *Monstres parisiens* (1883), *Jupe courte* (1884), *Le boudoir de verre* (1884), *Pour lire au bain* (1884), *Pour lire au couvent* (1887), *Robe montante* (1887), *Le confessional* (1890), *La messe rose* (1892), *Arc-en-ciel et sourcils rouges* (1897), etc.

The sheer number of titles in this vein issued by Mendès (who was by no means the only author of such works) would tend to suggest that, as in America slightly later, leisure time in France was becoming increasingly bound up with the erotic. This is especially true of those wealthy enough to buy books such as Mendès's *Les iles d'amour* (1886) and *Lila et Colette* (1885). The former consists of twelve short texts, each accompanied by an engraving, and was published in a luxurious edition of 1,040 numbered copies; the latter, which contains ten short stories, in addition to its sumptuous design, has a cover illustration which was hand-painted. Though many collections were more modest in appearance, there is no doubt that these works were aimed mainly at the carriage trade.

Perhaps the most amusing story ("L'Expérience") to be found in *Lila et Colette* concerns a bet made by the two eponymous heroines (one blonde, the other brunette) with the handsome Valentin. If, after spending the night with one of the women in a darkened room, he can correctly identify his lover, he will have the right to make love to both in broad daylight (if he fails, of course, he will never sleep with either again). Valentin, after having undergone this experiment, is confused as to whether he has spent the night with Lila or Colette, and it is only after he returns from a long walk that he manages to figure out the solution to the problem— they were both in the room at the same time and periodically changed places. By modern standards this may seem somewhat ridiculous, but such risqué little narratives obviously struck a chord with well-heeled purchasers in late-nineteenth-century Paris.

Interestingly, both *Les iles d'amour* and *Lila et Colette* were reprinted (in abridged translations) several times in the United States in the 1930s and '40s by publishers known for producing cheap editions of classic literature, including gallantia, for department-store shoppers. Not surprisingly, given the censorship which prevailed in the United States between the world wars, "L'Expérience" was excluded from the various editions of *Lila and Colette* out of New York.

Generally speaking, Mendès's work as a novelist is more somber and pessimistic compared with his short stories. This is particularly true of the novels discussed by Mario Praz (*The Romantic Agony*), who, in a telling phrase, describes Mendès as the belated purveyor of the "more succulent morsels from the Baudelarian table," referring to Mendès's *Zo'har* (1886), *La Première maîtresse* (1887), and *Méphistophéla* (1890). The typical focus of these works includes not only incest and lesbianism, but also relationships in which the woman takes the virile role. This is particularly true of *La première maîtresse*, in which a much older woman seduces a youth hardly out of school, draining his energy (to the point at which he becomes a virtual invalid) by the insistency of her sexual desires. Although some form of vampirism is hinted at, this is presumably intended only as a metaphor for fellatio. Unlike Mendès's shorter fiction, where the tone is mostly polite and urbane, these novels are written in a distinctly overblown and frenzied manner. Similarly Gothic embellishments may be found in other novels by Mendès, such as *La vie et la mort d'un clown* (1879), which deals with the consequences of a wealthy woman's sexual obsession with a member of the criminal subclasses. One memorable passage concerns a jailer being raped by a lunatic during a thunderstorm—though it should be noted again that what is exceptional about this scene is that it is a woman who takes the virile role.

Mendès himself would seem to have enjoyed an active erotic life. In 1866, he married Judith Gautier, daughter of the Romantic writer Théophile Gautier. The marriage was not a success. Subsequently, he lived with the composer Augusta Holmès (with whom he had two daughters, celebrated by a charming painting by Renoir entitled "Les Filles de Catulle Mendès"), Marguerite Moréno, and Jane Mette. If his shorter fiction is typified by Gallic lightness and wit, his longer fiction explores the dark side of the fin-de-siècle imagination, with its fears of virile women and hereditary insanity. In recent years, various works by Mendès have been reprinted in French (though none of his novels are available in English and there is still no standard biography), and it seems that his writing is slowly receiving more recognition in his native country.

Biography

Catulle Mendès was born in Bordeaux on May 22, of Jewish extraction. He founded the *Revue fantaisiste,* contributed to the *Parnasse contemporain,* and wrote many volumes of verse, including *Philoméla* and *La grive des vignes.* When he died, his body was discovered in the railway tunnel of Saint Germain. It is thought that he had left Paris by the midnight train the day before and that he'd opened the door in the night, thinking the momentarily stopped train was in the station.

TERRY HALE

Selected Works

Histoires d'amour. Paris: Lemerre, 1868.
La vie et la mort d'un clown. 2 vols. Paris: Dentu, 1879.
Monstres parisiens. 2 vols. Paris: Chez tous les libraires, 1883.
Jupe courte. Paris: Havard, 1884.
Le boudoir de verre. Paris: Ollendorff, 1884.
Pour lire au bain. With 154 illustrations by Fernand Besnier. Paris: Dentu, 1884.
Lila et Colette. Illustrations by Gambard et Roy. Paris: Monnier, 1885.
Zo'har. Paris: Charpentier, 1886.
Les iles d'amour. Withc 6 etchings and 38 original illustrations by G. Fraipont. Paris: Frinze, 1886.
Pour lire au couvent. With 60 illustrations by Lucien Métivet. Paris: Marpon et Flammarion, 1887.
Robe montante. Paris: Piaget, 1887.
La première maîtresse. Paris: Charpentier, 1887.
Méphistophéla. Paris: Dentu, 1890; repr. ed. Jean de Palacio, Paris: Séguier, 1993.
Le confessional. Paris: Charpentier, 1890.
La messe rose. Paris: Charpentier, 1892.
Arc-en-ciel et sourcils rouges. Paris: Charpentier, 1897.
Lila and Colette. New York: William Faro, 1931; New York: Golden Hind, 1934.
The Isles of Love. Ilion, New York: Privately printed, 1927.
Lila & Colette and The Isles of Love. With Illustrations by Rahnghild and Decorations by Valentin Le Campion. New York: Boar's Head Books, 1949.

Further Reading

Badesco, Luc. *La Géneration poétique de 1860*. 2 vols. Paris: A.-G. Nizet, 1971.
Praz, Mario. *The Romantic Agony*. Translated by Angus Davidson. London and Oxford: Oxford University Press, 1970.

MESOPOTAMIAN, SUMERIAN, AND AKKADIAN

Mesopotamian literary works form but a small percentage of textual sources written on clay tablets in a style known as cuneiform ("wedge shaped"), which was produced by the imprint of a sharp stylus on the damp surface of a tablet. The writing system is composed of word signs, syllabic signs, and vowel signs, all of which can convey different phonetic and/or semantic values. Such multiple readings are the result of using this system to render two distinct languages, Sumerian (not part of any known language groups) and the Semitic Akkadian. The understanding of Sumerian literary texts is hampered by the facts that the writing did not attempt to accurately record all parts of speech and that an oral exegesis most likely accompanied the reading of such compositions in antiquity. Poetic texts and especially erotic passages employ a range of euphemisms and metaphors which are not always obvious to the Western, contemporary scholar. Extant translations of Mesopotamian, especially Sumerian, erotic literature therefore differ widely from one another, with scholars disagreeing fundamentally not only over some minor literary allusion but over the intent and erotic content generally. Akkadian texts are comparatively more straightforward to understand, although badly preserved tablets leave gaps in the texts (see *Gilgamesh Epic*).

Sumerian Erotic Myths

Most of the available copies of Sumerian erotic literature come from the archives of the ancient city of Nippur, a well-known center of cuneiform learning. They were written in the Old Babylonian period (c. 2000–1600 BCE), although some were composed at an earlier date, most likely the time of the Third Dynasty of Ur (c. 2200–2000 BCE). The understanding of such texts is hampered by the fact that Sumerian does not differentiate gender in either verbs or nouns. There was no discernible ancient category for erotic compositions, and modern commentators have variously grouped them into love songs, bridal songs, courtly love poetry, sacred marriage songs, etc. A number of love songs have the Sumerian subtitle *balbal.e,* which points to a particular musical accompaniment, but not all of the known *balbal.es* have erotic contents.

Despite uncertainties as to the categorization of these texts, one can differentiate two major groupings on the basis of the main protagonists and literary form: (1) erotic myths, consisting of narrative texts some several hundred lines long which feature male deities and deal with impregnation and fertilization, and (2) love songs, which, like song in general, are shorter compositions with a refrain and a lack of narrative structure. They deal primarily with a female protagonist (and her bridegroom/lover) and

celebrate female sexuality without privileging conception.

The most important sexually active male protagonist in Sumerian literature is the god Enki, a deity whose center of worship was Eridu, in present-day Iraq. He was the god who presided over the "sweet water ocean" (source of groundwater and rivers), the primary supplier of water and fertility in the rainless alluvial plains of southern Mesopotamia. In Sumerian the word for "water" is synonymous with the word for "sperm," and hence Enki's sperm is said to have filled the Tigris and Euphrates with their life-giving waters, as described in the myth "Enki and the World Order." The same theme occurs in the myth known as "Enki and Ninhursaga," which best exemplifies the genre. Enki presents a city to his bride Ninsikila, who complains that it lacks the most essential commodity, fresh water. In the presence of a goddess called Nintur, the god fills the ditches with semen and "has his phallus glut the reeds with an overflow of sperm." From this perhaps masturbatory action he proceeds to full intercourse by commanding the goddess Damgalnunna (his official wife in the Sumerian pantheon) to lie down in the marshes. She conceives and gives birth to another goddess after a gestation period of nine days. Then follows a section which is repeated verbatim four times, except for the change of the female deity's name. The daughter grows up and ventures into the marshes, where Enki hangs out, and, seeing her, he desires her, and promptly possesses the girl. She likewise conceives and gives birth to another daughter, and so on. Eventually the mother-goddess Ninhursaga warns her granddaughters to demand more from the lusty Enki than presents of "cucumbers, apples and grapes" and advises the young Uttu to resist his advances until he improves his rather mechanical lovemaking. So, Enki now strokes Uttu's thighs and massages her first. Ninhursaga removes Enki's sperm and uses it to grow eight plants. When Enki sees the grown plants, he is filled with desire to consume them, is cursed for his gluttony by Ninhursaga, and becomes pregnant, which makes him very ill. Ninhursaga places him in her vagina to give birth on his behalf and four gods and four goddesses emerge from her womb, who heal the ailing parts of Enki.

The text abounds with puns and allusions, but the primary references are to Enki's ever-lustful member as the source of water, and hence fertility, and the locale of the marshes, which have strong erotic connotations in many other Mesopotamian sources, including potency incantations. The impregnation of the girl is equated with her being "watered by the sperm" of the male—in cosmogonic myths, Sky makes love to Earth in order to trigger the differentiation of the universe, depicted as a series of divine generations. The circumstances of the impregnation of the goddess Ninlil by her husband-to-be Enlil in the myth "Enlil and Ninlil" is essentially similar to the scenario described in the "Enki and Ninhursaga" myth but with much attention to the sociocultural restrictions on sexuality. Both gods are described as "young," and the myth charts the maturition from adolescent and irresponsible lovemaking to social approval as a married couple.

Sumerian Love Poetry

In contrast to these narratives, which focus on impregnation and the fertilizing properties of the phallus, there are compositions which give voice to a uniquely female expression of eroticism. The main protagonist here is the goddess Inanna, whose main cult center was at Uruk (present-day Iraq). Royal inscriptions from the Early Dynastic period (c. 2800–c. 2250 BCE) refer to Inanna's role as the loving "spouse" of the EN, the holder of the highest office at Uruk. Inanna was the patron of libidinous love in all its manifestations and not a mother-goddess; prayers and hymns, as well as myths and other narratives, emphasize her sex appeal and sexual appetite, as well as her ambition for power. In a syncretistic merging with the Semitic deity Eshtar, equated with the planet Venus, she also acquired masculine traits, such as a love for battle.

The erotic texts concerning Inanna comprise several scenarios which relate to the different stages of female sexual development. Firstly, they concern the nubile Inanna who rejoices over her breasts and pubic hair as the outward signs of her ability to consummate marriage (e.g., Alster, "Sumerian": 152). Some texts describe the premarital courtship and trysts between Inanna and her lover, Dumuzi the Shepherd (see Jacobsen: 8–12). She meets the young man in the garden, which becomes a metaphor for her own body: "Into the garden of apple trees he brought joy, for the shepherd the apples in the garden are loaded(?) with attractiveness" (Alster,

"Manchester": 1–7). In most of these texts, Inanna speaks in the first person, describing the caresses of her lover, although other voices, such as those of her female companions, or at times that of the lover, can also be heard. They call each other "brother" and "sister," and the language abounds with allusions and metaphors, which have been variously interpreted. While some of these texts could be taken as traditional wedding songs, with their references to gifts being brought by the groom and banquets held at the brides's house—even the exhortatory refrain "plough my vulva, man of my heart"—others are located in a more exclusively cultic context and mention specific amulet stones and the terminology of priestly titles (see Alster, "Sumerian": 151; Alster, "Manchester": 23; Jacobsen: 6, 21). It has long been proposed that some form of ritualized sexual performance was linked to rites of increase and fertility (notably Kramer). There are no references as to which personages were involved and where and at what times such rites took place. As a literary topic the sexual union between Inanna (and other city goddesses) and the representative of the urban community or, later, the king of the country, had currency especially during the time of the Third Dynasty of Ur and the Isin/Larsa period (c. 2200–1800 BCE). In a royal hymn for King Shulgi, for instance (who reigned c. 2094–47), Inanna declares that since the king, called Dumuzi in this context, "the one lying down by the holy Inanna," had laid his "hands on my pure vulva," she will decree "a good fate" for him (Klein: 153). A similar theme is pursued in the hymns to the Isin ruler Iddin-Dagan (reigned c. 1953–35), where it is stated that Inanna "demands the bed that rejoices the heart," "the bed that makes embrace delicious" (Kramer: 501, see also Reisman).

Sumerian erotic poetry dwells on female sexual enjoyment and concentrates attention on the vulva. Several texts extol the "sweetness" and the moisture of the vulva. It is compared to "the heavenly barge of the moon," "a fallow plot in the desert, a field of ducks, full of ducks, well-watered hilly land" (Alster, "Two Sumerian": 21), "sweet like beer" (Alster, "Sumerian": 134), as well as a garden, where lettuce grows (Alster, "Two Sumerian": 21). Possible metaphors for the clitoris include "barley-corn," "a fruit-tree bearing fruit at the top," "the dubdub-bird in its hole," and the "holy pin"; see Leick: 119–23, 129). Lovemaking ("that which is honey-sweet") takes place on "the honey-flowing bed" (Alster, "Two Sumerian": 22), the male lover is told to "squeeze it there for me," to "pound and pound it in there for me! as (one would) flour into the old dry measuring cup" (ibid.). The lover, referred to as the "honey-man," does "sweet things" and "waters the lettuce" (Jacobsen: 94); he is equated with sensations he brings, his limbs "are honey," and they "make honey flow," as the woman enjoys his "sweet sex appeal," a rather unsatisfactory translation for the complex notion of the Sumerian word *hi.li,* which also means "voluptuousness, attractiveness, libido." The tone of such poems or songs is languorous and seductive, the voice of an experienced woman or courtesan who seeks her pleasure on a perfumed bed. Some poems set in dialogue form have proved particularly difficult to interpret because of the richly allusive language and ambiguity of grammatical gender (see Jacobsen: 97 and Alster, "Sumerian": 3, as well as the discussion in Leick: 126–28 and 153–56).

Akkadian Erotic Literature

The smaller number of Akkadian erotic compositions compared with the Sumerian is likely to have been due to the vagaries of survival of sources; according to a library tablet, 400 titles of songs in Sumerian and Akkadian were recorded, which included such titles as "I smile at the lusty shepherd," "I'll let you stay the night, young man," and "Tonight, this evening," but only one of these has so far been recovered (Black). There are Babylonian hymns to Ishtar which largely echo the Sumerian epithets for Inanna ("She of joy, clothed with love," "adorned with seduction, grace, and sex appeal"; Thureau-Dangin). One poem from the Old Babylonian period is equally influenced by Sumerian examples:

In your delicious lap, the one for lovemaking, your passion is sweet, growing luxuriantly is your "fruit." My bed of incense is ballukku perfumed. Oh by the crown of our heads, the rings of our ears, the hills of our shoulders, the voluptuousness of our breast, the bracelet of our wrists, the belt of our waist, reach out (and) with your left hand touch our vulva, fondle our breasts, enter, I have opened (my) thighs. (Goodnick-Westenholz)

An apparently new genre are love dialogues between divine couples such as Nabu and his wife Tashmetum, which were probably sung to

the statues of the gods during the daily(?) rituals in their temple (Livingstone: 35f). The language of these songs is less earthy and more metaphorical than in the poem quoted above, and abounds with descriptions of jewelry and ornaments; the divine pair are said to delight in each other in "the garden," and there are allusions to "twittering birds" and the "plucking of fruit." The most direct references to sexual activity can be found in the Babylonian potency and love-magic texts, although they cannot be counted as literature in the strict sense (see Biggs). However, there was no such distinction in antiquity, and there are frequent crossovers between omen literature, incantations, spells, and cultic songs with what we perceive as "secular" literature (for the sexual omen texts, see Guinan). The treatment for impotence, diagnosed as the "hand of Ishtar," consisted of a ritual which included spells with graphic descriptions of animals copulating. In severe cases one could tie a she-goat in heat to a bed and have her mounted by a billy.

Other passages recall hymns to Ishtar and her libidinous powers. Love spells for women wanting to seduce particular men and eliminate a rival also include references to sexuality in animals ("the dog is lying down, the boar is lying down. You, lie down again and again on my thighs"; see Scurlock: 108). Such texts address the psychologically distressing aspects of erotic passion: insecurities about male performance and (female) jealousy. They deal with slander and gossip and doubts about a lover's faithfulness:

... ([S]o that) she may not love you, may Ishtar, the queen, strike [her] with blindness; may she, like me, be afflicted with sleeplessness; may she be weary, [and toss around] all night. ... I shall attain victory ... over my gossiping women, and I shall [return] happily to my lover. (Held).

A late Babylonian text deals with female rivalry and jealousy as affecting the great god Marduk, his wife Sarpanitum, and his "slippery girl" Ishtar. The injured wife hurls abuse at her rival, who she says "was preferred to me, so I hear, to make love with" and infers that her husband's lover is but "a little thing one can have for money" and casts spells on her: "Into your vulva, in which you set such great store, I shall make a (guard) dog enter and will tie shut the door." It mentions the "reek of armpits," exhorts the women of Babylon not "to give her a rag to wipe your vulva, to wipe your vagina" (see Edzard; Lambert). Akkadian myths also include erotic episodes. In "Nergal and Ereshkigal," the goddess of the Underworld, Ereshkigal, pines for a male companion and manages to seduce Nergal on a rare visit to her realm. Despite being warned by the wise god Ea not to "do what comes naturally to men and women," Nergal embraces Ereshkigal, who appears before him in a transparent gown (see Dalley: 163–81). The Descent of Ishtar to the Underworld describes the consequences of Ishtar's (temporary) death as the cessation of all copulation, amongst animals and human beings. Ea's solution was to create a being of ambiguous gender (a castrato? a transsexual?), who tricks Ereshkigal, mistress of the Underworld, into rendering up the corpse of Ishtar to be revived by the Waters of Life. Ereshkigal curses the transsexual "with the Shining Face" by condemning him to a life of destitution in the "shade of the city walls" (Dalley: 154–64). A similar imprecation is uttered by Enkidu against the prostitute in the Gilgamesh epic.

GWENDOLYN LEICK

Primary Texts (in translation)

Alster, Bendt. "Enki and Ninhursag." *Ugarit Forschungen* 10 (1978): 15–27.

———. "Sumerian Love Songs." *Revue d'Assyriologie* 79 (1985): 152.

———. "The Manchester Tammuz." *Acta Sumerologica* 14 (1992): 1–7.

———. "Two Sumerian Short Tales and a Love Song Reconsidered." *Zeitschrift für Assyriologie* 82 (1993): 186–201.

Attinger, Pierre. "Enki et Ninhursaga." *Zeitschrift für Assyriologie* 74 (1985): 1–52.

Biggs, Ronald D. *SA.ZI.GA: Ancient Mesopotamian Potency Incantations.* Locust Valley, NY: Augustin, 1967.

Dalley, Stephanie. *Myths from Mesopotamia: Creation, The Flood, Gilgamesh, and Others.* Oxford: Oxford University Press, 1989.

Edzard, Dietz Otto. "Zur Ritualtafel der sogenannten 'Love Lyrics.'" In *Language, Literature and History: Philological Studies Presented to Erica Reiner,* edited by Francesca Rochberg-Halton, 57–70. New Haven, CT: American Oriental Society, 1987.

Foster, Benjamin. *From Distant Days: Myths, Tales and Poetry of Ancient Mesopotamia.* Bethesda, MD: CDL [California Digital Library] Press, 1995.

———. *Before the Muses: An Anthology of Akkadian Literature.* 2 vols. Bethesda, MD: CDL Press, 1996.

George, Andrew. *The Epic of Gilgamesh.* Harmondsworth: Penguin Classics, 2003.

Goodnick-Westenholz, Joan. "A Forgotten Love Song." In Rochberg-Halton, *Language, Literature, and History,* 415–25.

Held, Moshe. "A Faithful Lover in Old Babylonian Dialogue." *Journal of Cuneiform Studies* 1 (1961): 1–26; 2 (1962): 37–39.

Jacobsen, Thorkild. *Harps That Once ... : Sumerian Poetry in Translation.* New Haven, CT: Yale University Press, 1987.

Klein, Jacob. *Three Sulgi Hymns.* Ramat-Gan, Israel: Bar-Ilan University Press, 1981.

Kramer, Samuel Noah. "The Sumerian Sacred Marriage Texts." *Proceedings of the Society of Biblical Archaeology* 107 (1963): 485–525.

Kramer, Samuel Noah, and John Maier. *Myths of Enki, the Crafty God.* Oxford and New York: Oxford University Press, 1989.

Livingstone, Alasdair. *Court Poetry and Literary Miscellenea.* Helsinki: Helsinki University Press, 1989.

Reisman, Daniel D. "Iddin-Dagan's Sacred Marriage Hymn." Journal of Cuneiform Studies 25 (1973): 189–202.

Scurlock, J.A. "Was There a "Love Hungry" Entu Priestess Named Etirtum?" *Archiv für Orientforschung* 36/7 (1989–90): 107–12.

Sefati, Yitschak. *Love Songs in Sumerian Literature: Critical Edition of the Dumuzi-Inanna Songs.* Ramat-Gan: Bar-Ilan University Press, 1998.

Thureau-Dangin, François. "Un Hymne à Ishtar." *Revue d'Assyriologie* 22 (1925): 169–77.

Further Reading

Black, Jeremy. "Babylonian Ballads: A New Genre." *Journal of the American Oriental Society* 103 (1983): 25–34.

Cooper, Jerrold S. "Sacred Marriage and Popular Cult in Early Mesopotamia." In *Official Cult and Popular Religion in the Ancient Near East: Papers of the First Colloquium on the Ancient Near East,* edited by Eiko Matsushima [n.p.] (Winter 1993): 81–96.

Guinan, Ann K. "Auguries of Hegemony: The Sex Omens of Mesopotamia." *Gender and History* 9 (1997): 462–79.

Lambert, Wilfred G. "The Problem of the Love Lyrics." In Unity and Diversity, edited by Hans Goedicke and J.M.Roberts, 104–6. Baltimore: John Hopkins University Press, 1975.

Leick, Gwendolyn. *Sex and Eroticism in Mesopotamian Literature.* London and New York: Routledge 1994.

METAMORPHOSIS

The erotic possibilities of metamorphosis—the change from one physical shape or state to another—have fascinated authors from the earliest times. Ancient stories of metamorphosis stem from the belief that borders between the divine, human, and animal worlds are permeable and fluid. Classical writers, most notably Ovid in his *Metamorphoses* (c. 2 CE) used this idea to examine the relationship between eroticism and marginal states of being, with changing bodies as metaphors for culturally specific desires and fantasies. Christianity's new sexual ideologies brought different literary inflections to metamorphosis. Following the New Testament story of Christ's temptation (Matthew 4:2–3), early Christian and medieval saints' lives are full of eroticized battles between celibate saints and shape-shifting devils who take on various seductive forms to lure the saints into sexual transgression. These human–demon metamorphoses fed into a rich suite of oral literature, from folktales such as *The Frog Prince* and *Beauty and the Beast* to (it might be argued) the stories of erotic shape-shifting preserved in the confessions of women accused of witchcraft. In due course Gothic fiction, with its fascination for boundaries and the links between the supernatural and the erotic, was drawn to metamorphosis, especially in Victorian times. R. L. Stevenson's *The Strange Case of Dr Jekyll and Mr Hyde* (1886) and other tales of humans changing into animals or animal–human hybrids express the bestial and archaic desires that are never far below the surface of acculturated man. Sheridan Le Fanu's *Carmilla* (1869), Oscar Wilde's *The Picture of Dorian Grey* (1891), and Bram Stoker's *Dracula* (1897) are all centered on eroticized bodies metamorphosing between death and life. Sexual comedy has always been a part of literary metamorphoses, too. Shakespeare drew on Apuleius' second-century CE Latin novel of human–animal metamorphosis, *The Golden Ass*, for the love story of Titania and Bottom in *A Midsummer Night's Dream* (c. 1595). In the twentieth century, feminist authors in the postmodern Gothic and magic realist genres reworked metamorphosis stories to interrogate male sexual fantasies about women humorously and ironically.

Myth cycles and hymn cycles preserve the oldest erotic fantasies of metamorphosis, usually based on gods moving between human and animal forms. One Egyptian story relates how the goddess Isis changed from human shape into a bird of prey so that she could alight on the phallus of her dead husband Osiris and be impregnated by him. This was a central episode of a cosmogonic myth, even though the image of a bird-goddess hovering over an aroused corpse may now seem deeply uncanny. Ancient Greek literature, the product of a more patriarchal culture, tends to embed metamorphosis in narratives of sexual pursuit and flight. This was a trope of Greek erotic writing in every genre, because fear of rape was believed to make women more sexually attractive. Typically, Greek metamorphosis stories involve gods pursuing human women (or occasionally vice versa) and the pursued changing shape in order to evade being caught and sexually mastered. Perhaps the most familiar is the story of Daphne, who turns into a laurel tree to avoid being raped by Apollo. In other narratives, metamorphosis is a divine punishment for inappropriate sexual conduct and is connected with other powerful erotic fantasies—voyeurism and sadism. All three are central to the myth of Actaeon, who while out hunting saw the virgin goddess Artemis naked. She changed him into a stag and watched as he was torn apart by his own hounds.

In the first century CE, the myths of Daphne and Actaeon were among many others retold by the Latin poet Ovid in his *Metamorphoses*. Here he drew on the rich pool of Greek mythology to explore the erotic potential of metamorphosis for a sophisticated Roman audience. Many of the metamorphoses Ovid recounts are more sexually aggressive than their Greek originals, since Roman culture relished images of eroticized violence. Stories like that of Tereus and Philomela (*Metamorphoses* 6.411 ff) have disturbingly misogynistic undertones to modern readers. Tereus abducts Philomela and hides her in a cabin in a forest, where he rapes her and cuts out her tongue so that she can never accuse him. But Philomela takes revenge on Tereus by killing his children and serving them to him at a feast, eventually being changed into a nightingale because she no longer deserves to be human. Ovid cleverly ties together Philomela's brutal forest rape, her awful revenge, and ultimate metamorphosis to explore the idea of the beast in man, with all of its sexual implications.

Translations of the *Metamorphoses* were among the first printed books—William Caxton produced a prose version as early as 1480—and they provided Western writers with a fertile resource of erotic narratives, metaphors, and images. Shakespeare, for instance, makes a version of the Philomela myth central to the erotic machinery of *Titus Andronicus* (1594), and the story of Actaeon figures in *Twelfth Night* (1601). This story particularly appealed to Elizabethan poets and dramatists because it reflected the cultural conceit of the queen's own carefully preserved virginity. But perhaps the story from Ovid most frequently retold in explicitly erotic terms is that of Pygmalion (*Metamorphoses* 10.240ff). Where this differs from other metamorphosis stories is that the change is of physical *state* rather than physical *form*, so that there is a transition from inanimate to animate object of desire. According to Ovid, Pygmalion was a sculptor who fell in love with the statue of a beautiful woman he had carved himself. He dressed it up like a mannequin, and watched it obsessively. Eventually Venus took pity on Pygmalion's passion for the statue and made it come to life. This statue-into-woman metamorphosis has been interpreted as a patriarchal sexual fantasy of woman as passive object of male desire. The eroticism of this dynamic underpins the numerous fantasies of male-created female bodies—mummies, marionettes, or automata—that come to life and interact sexually with humans.

One example is Bram Stoker's *The Jewel of Seven Stars* (1903), a narrative of sexual danger featuring a female mummy revealed by male archaeologists. Angela Carter subverted these conventions in her short story *The Loves of Lady Purple* (1974), a feminist reworking of *Pygmalion*. Here Lady Purple, a puppet who performs in a peep show, comes to life, destroys her creator, and becomes a prostitute. Cynthia Ozick's novella *Puttermesser and Xanthippe* (1982) inflects this basic story differently by introducing the traditional Jewish figure of the golem, a dummy animated by occult knowledge to become the servant of its creator. The heroine, Puttermesser, creates a female golem who helps her become the first woman mayor of New York, but the golem develops into a grotesque parody of the monstrously feminine. Her unleashed sexuality soon wrecks Puttermesser's career.

Dominic Montserrat

Further Reading

Bynum, Caroline Walker. *Metamorphosis and Identity.* New York: Zone Books, 2001.

Clarke, Bruce. *Allegories of Writing: The Subject of Metamorphosis.* Albany, NY: State University of New York Press, 1995.

Diaz, Nancy Gray. *The Radical Self: Metamorphosis to Animal Form in Modern Latin American Literature.* Columbia, MO: University of Missouri Press, 1988.

Forbes-Irving, P.M.C. *Metamorphosis in Greek Myth.* Oxford: Oxford University Press, 1988.

Gross, Kenneth. *The Dream of the Moving Statue.* Ithaca, NY: Cornell University Press, 1993.

Hofmann, Michael, ed. *After Ovid: New Metamorphoses.* New York: Farrar, Strauss & Giroux, 1995.

Hughes, Ted. *Tales from Ovid.* London: Faber & Faber, 1997.

Montserrat, Dominic, ed. *Changing Bodies, Changing Meanings: Studies on the Human Body in Antiquity.* London: Routledge, 1998.

Rousselle, Aline. *Porneia: On Desire and the Body in Antiquity.* Oxford: Basil Blackwell, 1988.

Stoneman, Richard. *Daphne into Laurel: Translations of Classical Poetry from Chaucer to the Present.* London: Duckworth, 1982.

MEUSNIER DE QUERLON, ANGE GABRIEL

1702–1780
French novelist, critic, journalist, and essayist

La tourière des Carmélites

The Doorkeeper of the Carmelites, serving as a sequel to "P. des C." [*Portier des Chartreux*] was anonymously published in 1745 and attributed to Meusnier de Querlon by the Marquis de Paulmy. This novel was intended to be the female answer to the adventures of Saturnin, the famous title character in *Le Portier des Chartreux: Histoire de Dom Bougre* (bugger), which was a resounding success in 1741.

Like the *portier* Dom Bugger, Sister Agnès is a doorkeeper (*tourière*), of a community of the Carmelite order, which she has entered at the age of forty-five. By so doing, she has come full circle, having been born in the convent as a result of a clandestine amour of her mother, the prioress, with one of her numerous lovers. Agnès could not but follow in her mother's footsteps, multiplying in her turn the adventures, which have made her pregnant several times. Nicknamed "Sainte Nitouche" because of her innocent looks, as a young woman she trained in the school of *filles du monde* and entered a career of prostitution. On the backdrop of the Parisian demimonde, she experienced all kinds of adventures, from moments of glory to moments of violence to moments of humiliation, having to change her name and residence when the heat was on, finding herself in prison for syphilis, and trying successively lesbian tribadism, Jesuitism, and Jansenism before opening her own house of pleasure. She meets La Duchapt, a Parisian fashion designer who really existed and was well known in the eighteenth century, who tells her her story. The novel thus presents an account of the tribulations of picaresque heroes, whose lives are precarious lives and fates uncertain. The burlesque scenes are lessons of social philosophy.

Anticlerical satire denudes the hypocrisy of priests. The institutions of power all seem to be schools of vice and sources of injustice and humiliation.

Written with less rigor and imagination than *P. des C.* and less ambitious in claiming a philosophy of pleasure, *La Tourière des Carmélites* nevertheless ups the ante by showing us Agnès making love with her father, a line Dom Bougre (though "released from prejudice") had refused to cross when invited to the bed of his mother, sister Monique. The ban on incest was henceforth defeated. Having thus taken up where the *Portier* had left off inchoately, *La Tourière des Carmélites* opened the way for the descendants of the Dom Bougre to redress this omission, as in *Mémoires de Suzon, D.B., portier des chartreux* (1778) and *L'Histoire de Marguerite, fille de Suzon, nièce de D.B.* (1784). The network expands. The Dom's sister and niece spread the fine words that libertinism should be a family affair, and who could doubt it?

The Greek Novels

Meusnier de Querlon is known for his work in the genre of French eighteenth-century writing that focused on the courtesan of classical antiquity. The trend began with the historical *Les Belles Grecques ou l'histoire des plus fameuses courtisanes de Grèce* [Lovely Greek Women, or the History of the Most Famous Greek Courtesans], published by Catherine Bedacier in 1712. Novels then took over in their turn. After the adventures of Boret's *Cythéride* ("a gallant history translated from the Greek") (1743) and of Lycoris (in 1754), and the publication of Godart de Beauchamps's *Hipparchia, histoire galante, traduite du grec, divisée en trois parties* (1748) (another "gallant history"), Meusnier de Querlon joined the vogue (which crosses that of the girl novels; see *Fougeret de Monbron*) and published *La courtisane philosophe ou l'appologie* du P*** (reprinted as *Psaphion ou la courtisane de Smyrne*) [Psaphion, or the Courtesan of Smyrna] (1748). The ancient inspiration also nourishes a part of the *Impostures innocentes*, which in 1761 will gather the collection of light works of Meusnier de Querlon, among which are *Cinname, histoire grecque*.

In *Psaphion ou la courtisane de Smyrne,* Cynare, the most famous courtesan of Ionia, takes care of Psaphion's education: singing, dance, language courses taught by a sophist, reading of the "tender poems" of Sappho and of "soft elegies" of Antimachus—nothing is missing for making the young girl a perfect courtesan. The slave Sussion makes her acquainted with the "amorous ecstasy," before Psaphion imposes herself onto the career as the equal of Aspasia. They nickname her, at the age of sixteen, the "Venus of Smyrna." The story tells of the encounters, debauchery, orgiastic parties, and the successive lovers (vigorous oldsters, dissipated young people) enjoyed by Psaphion, whose main merit is that she knows how "to spiritualize pleasures."

The tale of Cinname is that of a competition between the painter Pausanias and the sculptor Charès: whoever makes the most beautiful image will take away the most beautiful girl of Athens. Charès plans to sculpt the likeness of the fair Cinname. He bribes one of her servants so that while he looks at Cinname behind a divider during her bath, the servant should make her mistress strike the most voluptuous of postures. Apprised of the hidden beauties of his model, Charès takes away the palm leaf before being assassinated. Cinname stays a widow and pure at the end of the story.

In a language loaded with gallant paraphrases, Meusnier de Querlon re-creates a world devoted to pleasure but crowned by Aphrodite's flowers. Erudition and eroticism meet to extol an image of voluptuosity "à l'antique," as opposed to the brutal and cynical energy of the obscene novels. Charles Nodier will thus evoke the effeteness and mannered graces of Meusnier de Querlon, who was a giant to those who would celebrate Greek voluptuousness after him, as, for instance, Pierre Louïs would do.

Designating his story an "erotic fragment" (relative to amour, in the context of Greek literature), Meusnier de Querlon anticipates the familiar meaning that the word "eroticism" will take (in opposition to "pornography") in the second half of the twentieth century.

Biography

Born in Nantes, Meusnier de Querlon was a lawyer in Paris in 1723. Recognized for his erudition, he was attached to the guard of the manuscripts of the Royal Library, whose erudite editions he multiplied as a translator of Greek and Latin. He was also active in early journalism, working with several newspapers, most notably the *Affiches de province*. Devoid of livelihood toward the end of his life, he was given charge of the library of the financier Nicolas Beaujon as a means of support.

Patrick Wald Lasowski

Editions

La tourière des Carmélites, servant de pendant au "P. des C." Constantinople: The mufti's printer, 1745.

Sainte Nitouche, ou l'histoire galante de la tourrière [sic] *des carmélites: Followed by the history of La Duchapt, published for the first time in full in the author's autogroph* [sic] *manuscript, in order to serve as a sequel to the* Portier des Chartreux. London, 1830.

La courtisane philosophe. Cologne, 1748. Reprinted the same year under the title of *Psaphion ou la courtisane de Smirne* [sic], erotic fragment translated from Greek by Mnaseas on a manuscript of Lord B***, where *Les Hommes de Prométhée* by Thomson has been attached; London [Paris].

THE MIDNIGHT RAMBLER: OR, THE ADVENTURES OF TWO NOBLE NIGHT-WALKERS

Eighteenth-century English novel

The anonymous *The Midnight Rambler* is a racy tale in the tradition of eighteenth-century libertinism. Related in 26 pages, the book sold inexpensively for sixpence. The omniscient narrator tells the story of two women, Lady Betty and Mrs. Sprightly, who go out on a "midnight ramble" to trace the ribald escapades of their profligate husbands. Their journey is used to describe the happenings of a night on the town and as a device to make comments on contemporary events.

Taking up the gossip of the day, the story concerns characters referred to as "Persons of Rank and Distinction." Thus the narrator questions, "Who does not know of *Dorimant*, the Son and Heir apparent of a noble *British* Peer?" He explains that due to the extravagance of Dorimant's ancestors, the family estate had been depleted. His father therefore married off his son to a lady of a "very large Fortune" and set them up with an annuity of 2,000 pounds per annum, while procuring him a post with a large salary entailing little work. Already debauched since his early days, Dorimant took off in pursuit of his own pleasures, much to the consternation of his wife, "Lady *Betty* who, as she had been educated in the strictest Principals of Virtue, could not refrain viewing *Dorimant's* dissolute Course of Life, with the utmost Horror and Detestation." He spent his evenings in riotous mirth and licentiousness about the taverns of the town and was frequently found in the arms of a courtesan from a bagnio (a bathhouse doubling as a brothel, in much the way that modern massage parlors are said to do). His wife strove hard to reclaim him from the bottle and his mistresses, but finding her admonitions in vain, she assumed the indifference of a lady of quality.

After this introduction to the history of the couple, the story itself takes off.

Ned Sprightly, a close friend of Dorimant who lives in the same neighborhood, rarely goes to bed before approach of day and then usually intoxicated with liquor. His wife, the daughter of a country baronet, also takes to the distractions of the metropolis, enjoying the masquerades, balls, assemblies, and town life. Mrs. Sprightly and Lady Betty become friends and combine in a plot to uncover their husband's nightly rambles, to find out what they are doing and whose company they are keeping. They make plans over a breakfast of a "Dish of Chocolate." Lady Betty has already ascertained from her drunken husband where they are to go—the Bedford-Arms in Covent Garden Piazza, then on to the Convent Garden playhouse. That night, after fortifying their spirits with a bottle of champagne, the two ladies secretly follow their husbands. They take with them a companion, their milliner, Mrs. Flimm, since she is acquainted with the streets and knows the ways of the town. They spy their husbands in a balcony box with two Town-Misses who frequent the coffeehouses and bagnios. But the night's rambles take a turn as Dorimant and Sprightly make their way to Temple-Bar tavern, and the three women are unable to pursue them because of the rain and lack of coaches in which to follow. The women become entangled in a fight with four streetwalkers they encounter along the Strand and call the night watchman for help. He is in the pay of the whores, but luckily three gallants who have come out of the Crown and Anchor to investigate the commotion leap to their aid. The ladies dine with these gentlemen, a captain of the Foot Guards and two independent gentlemen of small fortunes, and then go on in pursuit of their husbands accompanied by Mrs. Flimm.

They drive on to Temple-Bar, where they expect to find Dorimant and Sprightly, but an accident with their coach, in which a wheel flies off, means they have to trudge on by foot. On the way home, they come across a constable who mistakes them for streetwalkers. Mrs. Flimm has the forbearance to bribe him so he will take them to his own house where they will be safe. From there, they can send for someone who might vouch for their characters. The constable keeps an alehouse and has a wine license, so they refresh themselves as they wait, while Mrs. Flimm sends for a laceman of her acquaintance, who reprimands the constable for causing the ladies such trouble. Making their way home, the two drunken husbands demand that the coach stop to let them get in. Too drunk to recognize the women, the men fall to kissing them. Not until they arrive home do they discover, to their surprise, that it is their own wives whom they have accosted. The husbands promise to mend their ways.

The tale is written as a "Warning to the Female Sex, not to trust themselves abroad on any Frolicks." The women's encounters and adventures are depicted in an atmospheric setting of the town at night, evoking danger, darkness, and difficulties of vision. The moon, rather than street lamps, light their way, highlighting the problems of walking out in the ill-lit alleys and secluded passages of London, which were frequented by robbers and whores.

The four main participants are stock characters—two rakes and their irate wives—who do not have clearly defined individual characteristics. A general sense of confusion is conveyed, as if feeling one's way through the jumbled events of a drunken evening in the dark streets. The characters are less important than the overall story line, which fits with a genre of tales of nights on the town, with their ensuing escapades.

JULIE PEAKMAN

Edition

Anon. *The Midnight Rambler: Or, The Adventures of Two Noble Night-Walkers*. London: B. Dickson on Ludgate-Hill, 1754.

MILLER, HENRY

1891–1980
American novelist

Henry Miller's improbable journey from college dropout to telegram currier for Western Union to struggling writer to banned novelist with a reputation for pornography to an American icon and Nobel Prize nominee is the stuff of literary legend, the quintessential myth of the ribald Romantic artist having leeched into the twentieth century. That journey was finally the subject matter of his quasi-autobiographical novels, what longtime friend Lawrence Durrell called "a single, endless autobiography." While Norman Mailer hailed him as the "Grand Speliologist of the Vagina," Miller saw himself as an advocate of human freedom rather than as champion of the libertine life. His principal preoccupation, like that of all Romantic writers, from Jean-Jacques Rousseau onward, was "the struggle of the human being to emancipate himself, that is, to liberate himself from the prison of his own making." The heroes he revered were those who did not "impose their authority on man; on the contrary, they sought to destroy authority. Their aim and purpose was to open up life, to make man hungry for life, to exalt life—and to refer all questions back to life" (*The Books of My Life*, 1952).

The *Tropics*

While the *Tropics* were published in Paris in 1934 and 1939, they remained banned as obscene and pornographic in the United States and the United Kingdom until 1964. A breakthrough might have come in 1958 when Miller was elected to membership in the American Institute of Arts and Letters, the citation calling him "the veteran author of many books whose originality and richness of technique are matched by the variety and daring of his subject matter." That daring was of course his sexual explicitness in an age of puritan repression. Miller's American publisher, New Directions Press, quickly issued *The Henry Miller Reader*, edited and with an introduction by Lawrence Durrell. The *Reader* included nothing that might have tested American censorship laws, however, and Durrell opened his introduction by calling attention to an irony: "It would be invidious to make extravagant claims for the genius of an author the better part of whose best work is unavailable to his countrymen." Miller would need another champion in the United States to make the *Tropics* freely available to his countrymen and to launch him into the pantheon of American writers. This champion appeared as neophyte publisher and anti-censorship crusader Barney Rosset of the fledgling Grove Press.

Rosset bought his first copy of *Tropic of Cancer* from legendary bookseller Frances Steloff of the Gotham Book Mart in New York City shortly after he matriculated at Swarthmore College in 1940. The only edition then available (and that illegally) was the Paris edition published by Jack Kahane's Obelisk Press. Even Kahane was cautious, however, asking Miller first to write a literary study of D.H. Lawrence to establish his literary legitimacy (finally published as *The World of Lawrence: A Passionate Appreciation* in 1979). For Rosset the appeal of Miller was political not erotic. "I was so naive," he noted of his undergraduate reading: "I didn't even know *Tropic of Cancer* was banned in this country. ... I loved it. I've never felt *Tropic of Cancer* was at all sexy, but I found it exciting because it was anti-American and anti-conformity. ... I came out of [reading Miller] with a loathing for the United States, and I left school. I read it, and it made that big an impression on me. ... I ran away." It would take another 21 years before Rosset had the opportunity to share that experience with his and Miller's countrymen.

While Rosset may not have deemed Miller "at all sexy," certainly a puritanical America did, since Miller's work, at its very core, celebrates the human body performing its most private, intimate activities. In the chapter "A Saturday Afternoon" from *Black Spring*, Miller assaults

propriety that denies the honest consideration of the body: "No more peeping through keyholes! No more masturbating in the dark! ... *Unscrew the doors from their jambs!* I want a world where the vagina is represented by a crude, honest slit. ... I'm sick of looking at cunts tickled up, disguised, deformed, idealized." Miller's work is thus foremost an assault on propriety and authority, a rejection of "creeds and principles. I have nothing to do with the creaking machinery of humanity—I belong to the earth." The earth itself is often represented as a female body in all its glorious eroticism:

> The earth is ... a great sprawling female with velvet torso that swells and heaves with ocean billows; she squirms beneath a diadem of sweat and anguish. Naked and sexed she rolls among the clouds in the violet light of the stars. All of her, from her generous breasts to her gleaming thighs, blazes with furious ardor. (*Tropic of Cancer*)

By April of 1959 Rosset was determined to risk all and publish Miller's most audacious work in the United States, and he traveled to Big Sur, California, to make his first offer to Miller, a $10,000 advance and an agreement that Grove would assume the cost of all litigation involving the book. The following year he upped the ante, proposing a $10,000 overt payment and $40,000 against royalties. Miller refused a second time, with surprising rationale: "Part of my reluctance to wage open combat with our American authorities arises from the fact that I see no evidence of genuine revolt in the people themselves. We have no real radicals, no body of men who have the desire, the courage and the power to initiate a fundamental change in our outlook or in our way of life." Miller feared that if he triumphed it would be as "the king of smut." Rosset had no such reservations, shunning neither "open combat with our American authorities" nor the label "king of smut." Miller finally acquiesced once he realized that Rosset was capable of just such "genuine revolt."

The road to publication of Miller's *Tropics* was paved on July 21, 1959, by Judge Frederick van Pelt Bryan's ruling that *Lady Chatterley's Lover* was a serious work of literature and not, as Postmaster-General Arthur E. Summerfield had claimed, "smutty filth." The decision was upheld on March 25, 1960, and the US attorney general decided not to bring the case before the

Supreme Court. The *Lady Chatterley* decision enjoined the US Postal Service "from denying the mails to this book or to the circular announcing its availability." Thus the *Tropics* too would be allowed through the mails once they were published. The legal battles over them would be in defense of individual booksellers prosecuted by local district attorneys. Such prosecution as a means of censorship had been established in the United States as early as 1930 when a bookseller in Massachusetts was convicted of selling a "lewd and obscene" book, Theodore Dreiser's *An American Tragedy*. To allay the fears of booksellers in 1961, Rosset offered to defend any of them who were prosecuted for selling the books. The result was that Grove fought over 60 separate, local legal cases before the US Supreme Court ruled on June 22, 1964, that the *Tropics* were entitled to constitutional protection under the first amendment.

Part of the legal strategy that finally succeeded was to establish the literary value of the book by soliciting a critical appraisal from Karl Shapiro. In his introduction, Shapiro compared *Tropic of Cancer* to James Joyce's *Ulysses* (a book itself banned in the United States from 1922 to 1933). Shapiro called Miller's achievement "miraculous; he is screamingly funny without making fun of sex." With the publication of the *Tropics*, Miller's international reputation would grow for a decade, and for three years (1975–78) he was nominated for the Nobel Prize. Norman Mailer compiled a massive anthology of Miller's work called *Genius and Lust* (1976), which was perhaps the anthology that *The Hernry Miller Reader* should have been in 1959. The genius that Durrell could not claim for Miller, Mailer could.

Within the next decade the spirit of the erotic revolution that Miller (and Rosset) championed would face another, more formidable challenge. Despite being among the first writers to recognize and celebrate what he called "female writing" (or what would later come to be called *écriture féminine*) in the work of Anaïs Nin, whose writing, he noted, "rearranges the world in terms of female honesty," Miller became a target of rising feminism. The writer who battled Anglo-Saxon Puritanism, who criticized American materialism, who attacked middle-class values, who, in fact, led the sexual and moral revolution we loosely call "the Sixties," was again under attack, but now from the intellectual and political left,

not the moralistic right. The assault was led by Kate Millet, whose *Sexual Politics* (1969) singled out Sigmund Freud, D. H. Lawrence, Norman Mailer, and Henry Miller as writers who dehumanized and so degraded women. For Millet "Miller's ideal woman is a whore." She found the emphasis in the novels not on the erotic, or on intimacy, or on the beauty of the nude body, for instance, but simply on fucking—or on the "disassociated adventures of cunt and prick." Miller's writing represented "[t]he complete depersonalization of woman into cunt," and Miller was a writer "converting the female to a commodity." Such an analysis has had so profound an effect on Miller's reputation that when Erica Jong came to write her memoir/biography of Miller, *The Devil at Large* (1993), she felt it necessary to apologize for his work before celebrating its spirit, "Because of his sexism, his narcissism, his jibes at Jews. ... He treats women horribly and doesn't seem to care." She finally recovers from so scathing an initial critique to celebrate the life force of one of America's most original and revolutionary writers.

Biography

Henry Valentine Miller was born in Brooklyn, New York, on December 26. He grew up the son of a tailor, and much of his formal education served him as negative example. He briefly attended the City University of New York in the fall of 1909, and, as he wrote in *It Stands Still Like a Hummingbird* (1962), the required reading of Edmund Spenser's *The Faerie Queene* turned him toward writing—of a very different sort: "To think that this huge epic is still considered indispensable reading in any college curriculum! ... Let me confess that today it seems even more insane to me than when I was a lad of eighteen. ... What a poor second to Pindar!" Miller went on to become less Pindar than a curious blend of Rabelais and Rimbaud.

In 1917 Miller married Beatrice Sylvas Wickens (a version of whom appears as Maude in *Sexus*), with whom he had a child, but an affair with his mother-in-law upset the first of what became five failed marriages. He soon left his family to live with June Mansfield Smith, a sometime dancer who encouraged his writing and who appears as Mona-Mara in the *Tropics* (1934, 1939), *Black Spring* (1936), and the trilogy *The Rosy Crucifixion* (1965), which includes

Sexus (1949), *Plexus* (1953), and *Nexus* (1960) and deals with the years before the flight to Paris. In 1922 he had written his first and still unpublished book, *Clipped Wings*, and by 1930, his life having become little more than a long, rosy crucifixion, a penniless Miller headed to France for what would become a decade-long, picaresque romp. In Paris he needed the support of new friends like Alfred Perlés and the writer Anaïs Nin, who was instrumental in arranging for the publication of *Tropic of Cancer* with Jack Kahane, for which volume she wrote a laudatory preface. In an essay entitled "Un Etre Etoilique" (written for T. S. Eliot's magazine, *The Criterion,* and collected in *Max and the White Phagocytes,* 1938), Miller returned the favor, placing Nin among the great confessional writers, like St. Augustine and Rousseau—and, by implication, like Miller himself. A portion of those confessions from 1931–2 was excerpted for the best-selling *Henry and June: The Unexpurgated Diary of Anaïs Nin* (1986; film version directed by Philip Kaufman, 1990). Miller himself treated that period in *Quiet Days in Clichy* (1956; film versions by Jens Jorgen Thorsen in 1970 and by Claude Chabrol in 1989) and most magnificently in the *Tropics* diptych, *Tropic of Cancer* (Paris, 1934; New York, 1961) and *Tropic of Capricorn* (Paris, 1939; New York, 1961). In the years since, Miller's principal Paris address, 18 de la Villa Seurat, where much of the *Tropics* was written, has become a literary shrine.

With the prospect of war in Europe, Miller fled Paris in 1940 for Greece and Corfú at the invitation of Lawrence Durrell. The short stay resulted in *The Colossus of Maroussi* (1941) and a lifelong interest in Greece. Miller returned to the United States in 1940, traveling cross-country to take up residence in Big Sur, California, where he spent the next 20 years in semi-seclusion, writing, painting, and becoming an American mystic. The cross-country trip resulted in devastating critiques of American culture, *The Air-Conditioned Nightmare* (1945) and *Remember to Remember* (1947) in particular. The alternative was the harmony Miller finally found in Big Sur and celebrated in *Big Sur and the Oranges of Heironymous Bosch* (1957)—and in his painting, the spirit of which is captured in the titles of two works: *To Paint Is to Love Again* (1960) and *The Paintings of Henry Miller: Paint as You Like and Die Happy* (1982). In 1960, after the breakup of his fifth marriage, Miller moved to Pacific Palisades in southern California, where he devoted more time to painting than writing and where he died on June 7.

S.E. GONTARSKI

Selected Works

Tropic of Cancer. Paris: Obelisk, 1934; New York: Grove, 1961.

What Are You Going to Do About Alf? Paris: Lecram-Servant, 1935; Berkeley: Porter, 1944; London: Turret, 1971.

Aller Retour New York. Paris: Obelisk, 1935.

Black Spring. Paris: Obelisk, 1936; New York: Grove, 1963.

Scenario (A Film with Sound). Paris: Obelisk, 1937.

Money and How It Gets That Way. Paris: Booster, 1938; Berkeley: Porter, 1945.

Max and the White Phagocytes. Paris: Obelisk, 1938.

The Cosmological Eye. Norfolk, CT: New Directions, 1939.

Tropic of Capricorn. Paris: Obelisk, 1939; New York: Grove, 1961.

The World of Sex. Chicago: Abrahamson, 1940; New York: Grove 1965.

The Colossus of Maroussi. San Francisco: Colt, 1941.

The Wisdom of the Heart. Norfolk: New Directions, 1941.

Sunday After the War. Norfolk, CT: New Directions, 1944.

The Air-Conditioned Nightmare. New York: New Directions, 1945.

Maurizius Forever. Waco, TX: Motive, 1946; San Francisco: Colt, 1946.

Remember to Remember. New York: New Directions, 1947.

The Smile at the Foot of the Ladder. New York: Duell, Sloan, and Pearce, 1948.

Sexus. Paris: Obelisk, 1949; New York: Grove, 1965.

The Books of My Life. London: Owen, 1952; Norfolk, CT: New Directions, 1952.

Plexus. Paris: Correa, 1952 (French); Paris: Olympia, 1953: New York: Grove, 1965.

Nights of Love and Laughter. Edited by Kenneth Rexroth. New York: Signet/New American Library, 1955.

The Time of the Assassins: A Story of Rimbaud. Norfolk, CT: New Directions, 1956.

Quiet Days in Clichy. Paris: Olympia, 1956; New York: Grove, 1965.

A Devil in Paradise. New York: Signet/New American Library, 1956.

Big Sur and the Oranges of Hieronymous Bosch. New York: New Directions, 1957.

The Henry Miller Reader. Edited by Lawrence Durrell. New York: New Directions, 1959.

The Intimate Henry Miller. Edited by Lawrence Clark Powell. New York: Signet/New American Library, 1959.

Reunion in Barcelona. Northwood, England: The Scorpion Press, 1959.

Nexus. Paris: Obelisk, 1960; New York: Grove, 1965.

To Paint Is to Love Again. Alhambra, CA: Cambria, 1960.

Stand Still Like Hummingbird. Norfolk, CT: New Directions, 1962.

Just Wild About Harry: A Melo Melo in Seven Scenes. New York: New Directions, 1963.

Henry Miller on Writing. Edited by Thomas H. Moore. New York: New Directions, 1964.

The Rosy Crucifixion: Sexus, Plexus, Nexus. New York: Grove Press, 1965.

Insomnia: Or, the Devil at Large. Albuquerque, NM: Loujon, 1971.

My Life and Times. Chicago: Playboy, 1971.

On Turning Eighty: Journey to an Antique Land: Forward to the "Angel Is My Watermark." Santa Barbara, CA: Capra, 1972.

Reflections on the Death of Mishima. Santa Barbara, CA: Capra, 1972.

First Impressions of Greece. Santa Barbara: Capra, 1973.

Henry Miller's Book of Friends: A Tribute to Friends of Long Ago. Santa Barbara, CA: Capra, 1976.

Genius and Lust. Edited by Norman Mailer. New York: Grove Press, 1976.

Mother, China, and the World Beyond. Santa Barbara, CA: Capra, 1977.

Gliding into the Everglades. Lake Oswego, OR: Lost Pleiade Press, 1977.

My Bike and Other Friends. Santa Barbara: Capra, 1978.

Joey. Santa Barbara, CA: Capra, 1979.

The World of Lawrence: A Passionate Appreciation. Santa Barbara: Capra, 1979; London: John Calder, 1980.

The Paintings of Henry Miller: Paint as You Like and Die Happy. San Francisco, CA: Chronicle Books, 1982.

Opus Pistorum. New York: Grove, 1983.

The Henry Miller Reader. Edited by John Calder. London: John Calder Publishers; New York: Riverrun Press, 1989.

Crazy Cock. New York: Grove Press, 1991.

Moloch: Or This Gentile World. New York: Grove Press, 1992.

Nothing but the Marvelous: Wisdoms of Henry Miller. Edited by Blair Fielding. Santa Barbara: Capra, 1999.

Further Reading

Durrell, Lawrence, and Alfred Perlès. *Art and Outrage: A Correspondence about Henry Miller (With an Intermission by Henry Miller)*, 1959.

Fraenkel, Michael. *The Genesis of "Tropic of Cancer,"* 1946.

Hargraves, Michael. *Henry Miller Bibliography with Discography*, 1980.

Hutchison, E.R. *Tropic of Cancer on Trial: A Case History of Censorship*, 1968

Jong, Erica, *The Devil at Large*, 1993.

Kersnowski, Frank L., and Alice Hughes, eds. *Conversations With Henry Miller*, 1994.

Mailer, Norman. *Genius and Lust: A Journey Through the Major Writings of Henry Miller*, 1976.

Martin, Jay. *Always Merry and Bright: The Life of Henry Miller*, 1978.

Nin, Anaïs. *Henry and June: The Unexpurgated Diary of Anaïs Nin, 1931–1932*, 1986.

Rembar, Charles, Jr. *The End of Obscenity: The Trials of "Lady Chatterley," "Trial of Tropic of Cancer," and "Fanny Hill" by the Lawyer Who Defended Them*, 1968.

MILLET, CATHERINE, AND JACQUES HENRIC

1948–
Contemporary art critic
La vie sexuelle de Catherine M.

Henric, Jacques

1938–
Essayist and novelist
Légendes de Catherine M.

La Vie sexuelle de Catherine M.

Catherine millet's autobiographical text entitled *La vie sexuelle de Catherine M.* was first published in 2001 and is now a best seller, translated into more than thirty languages. It received the "Prix Sade," dedicated to freethinking, awarded to a book that surpasses the boundaries of censorship or political and moral oppression. Her husband, Jacques Henric, also published in 2001 an autobiography entitled *Légendes de Catherine M.*, complemented by essays and 50 photographs depicting his wife in the nude.

La vie sexuelle consists of four chapters, written in a simple, refined and oftentimes crude style, and portrays unashamed Millet's sexuality as uninhibited by cultural taboos. It relates, for instance, many group-sex experiences. The first chapter, entitled "Le nombre" [Numbers], begins, not surprisingly, by highlighting the author's fancy for numbers. During her childhood, the author spent much time partaking in numeric-based activities. Ironically, as an adolescent, in the weeks following the loss of her virginity, seeing no moral conflict, Catherine M. starts a long series of sexual encounters with multiple partners. Millet specifies that at present, she can count 49 men with a name, or in some cases with a basic identity, with whom she has had intercourse. It is impossible, however, for her to put a number "on those that blur into anonymity." This notion of anonymity summarizes exactly the essence of her book. An emissary for a sexual network, it is impossible for Millet to know all of the players. The numerous identities of the men encountered in her sexual activities finish by merging into a long blur of flesh.

The two following chapters, entitled "L'Espace" [Space] and "L'Espace replié" [Confined Space], associate physical love with the conquest of space. The author reveals her need for travel, on geographical terms, in order to access, through a symbolic identity quest, some parts of herself. Millet relates her experiences in the outdoors as well as travel memoirs, then in closed spaces. In "L'Espace replié" Millet relates various sexual episodes where the relationship to pain (caused by headaches, for example) is perceived as another manner through which to disintegrate the Self, just as pleasure, displeasure, and abjection allow her to escape her body's fleshiness and consequently attain a state of well-being. However, the withdrawal into pain does not provide any excitement, whereas an unknown gaze provides the reverse effect. The gaze of the "Other" assumes an important place of protection and security in Millet's narrative.

Her husband, Jacques Henric, always prefers transitional spaces of passage when taking nude photographs of her. For example, Millet describes how, at the Port-Bou train station in Spain, she modeled for her husband wearing an unbuttoned dress despite the masses of people nearby. It is with this same scene that Jacques Henric begins *Légendes de Catherine M.* Over a span of 30 years, Henric took pictures of his wife's body that, despite the years he claims, has not lost any beauty. These photographs, of which Henric emphasizes the banality and repetition, compose a family album with his wife as

the only member. None of those photographs should be considered pornographic, a genre that Henric admits having little use for, his interest tending toward the way in which space and the body interact. For the author, nudity empowers his wife, her sex becoming a source of energy. Throughout Henric's narration, he specifies, on many occasions, how Catherine is the inspiration for his novels's feminine characters. Between the photographs, the author retells, while also alluding to writers such as Georges Bataille, the story behind the snapshots. Despite the photographs, Henric's narrative is less erotic than *La vie sexuelle de Catherine M.*

In Millet's last chapter, "Détails" [Details], the author confesses that pleasure was never considered the motive behind her sexual experiences, further emphasizing that the precise descriptions of her body and her sexual acts in fact created a detachment from the Self; writing a book in the first person thus helps Millet see herself from a third-person perspective. Sexual orgasm procures for the author this same feeling: one of distancing one's self from the body. Catherine Millet talks willingly about her sexuality, establishing nonetheless a distinction between love and sex. Millet only briefly alludes to her conjugal life, while still underlining that her sexual promiscuity diminished with the beginning of this relationship.

After having given her body away to many men, Millet's body is then literally read in *La vie sexuelle de Catherine M.* and left at the disposition of the viewer in *Légendes de Catherine M.* In 2004, Jacques Henric's *Comme si notre amour était une ordure* was even more explicit regarding his wife's sexual life and the aftermath of their book's publication. He also describes what he felt while viewing pornographic videos featuring his wife, Catherine. In its own way, this book attempts to reunite love and sexuality.

Biography

Born in France, Catherine Millet (1948–) is editor and cofounder of the French art magazine *Art Press*. Well known in the art milieu, she has published several books of art criticism, including *L'Art contemporain* (1997). She is married to Parisian Jacques Henric (1938–), a French essayist, novelist, and collaborator on the *Art Press* project.

NATHALIE DUMAS

Editions

La Vie sexuelle de Catherine M. Paris: Seuil, 2001; Paris: Seuil (Points), 2002, as *The Sexual Life of Catherine M.*, translated by Adriana Hunter, New York: Grove Press, 2002.
Légendes de Catherine M., Paris: Denoël, 2001.

Selected Works

Catherine Millet

Textes sur l'art conceptuel. 1972.
Yves Klein. 1982.
L'Art contemporain en France. 1987.
Conversation avec Denise René. 1991.
Roger Tallon, designer. 1993.
De l'objet à l'œuvre, les espaces utopiques de l'art. 1994.
Le critique d'art s'expose. 1995.
L'Art contemporain. 1997.
Riquet à la houpe, Millet à la loupe. 2003.

Jacques Henric

Archées. 1969.
Chasses. 1975.

Paradigme du bleu jaune rouge, Albert Ayme. 1979.
Caroussels. 1980.
La peinture et le mal. 1983.
Car elle s'en va la figure du monde. 1985.
En plein dans tout, Bernard Dufour. 1986.
Walkman. 1988.
Pierre Klossowski. 1989.
Tombeau de Van Gogh, le triomphe d'A.A., 1989.
Le Roman et le sacré. 1990.
Céline. 1991.
Du portrait, Jean Rault. 1991.
L'Homme calculable. 1991.
Adorations perpétuelles. 1994.
Dormez mes bien-aimées, Édouard Manet. 1995.
C'est là que j'entreprendrai des sortes de romans. Fismes 1960–1970. 1996.
L'Habitation des femmes. 1998.
Et si au contrairee du poisson, le XXe siècle pourrissait par la queue. 1999.
Comme si notre amour était une ordure. 2004.

Further Reading

Authier, Christian. *Le nouvel ordre sexuel.* Paris: Bartillat, 2002.

MILLOT, MICHEL, OR JEAN L'ANGE

Mid-seventeenth-century French sex manual writer

L'Ecole des filles (attributed)

One aspect of the development of publishing in the seventeenth century was the appearance of numerous practical manuals on a variety of subjects, from horsemanship to fencing, gaming, agriculture and the like. The earliest books of this type often seemed more interested in quoting literary sources or humanistic knowledge than getting down to business. As the century progressed, however, more and more of these books offered relatively "practical" knowledge of their subject. Instead of quoting Vitruvius, a later book might actually explain how to build a building.

Ovid and Aretino notwithstanding, Millot's (or L'Ange's) *L'École des filles* of 1655 really offers the first practical sex manual published

in France and perhaps in the Occident. The author makes his intentions clear from the beginning:

> Beautiful and curious ladies, here is the School of your wisdom and the collection of the principal things you will want to know to satisfy your husbands when you are married; it is the infallible secret to make yourselves loved by men, even if you are not beautiful.

There follows an Aretino-like dialogue (opinions are divided as to whether the *École des filles* was actually influenced by Aretino or is merely similar to it) between an experienced woman and a young, more naive girl—Suzanne and Fanchon. There follows a sort of anatomy lesson, with vocabulary like "cul, con, vit et couillons" (ass, cunt, dick, and balls). Fanchon is interested in a certain Monsieur Robinet, and Suzanne encourages her to overcome her shyness the next time he comes over. There follows a lengthy and perhaps repetitious recital of sexual encounters—with varying positions, "mignardises" [delicacies], rosebuds and jasmine incense, and the like.

Michel Camus comments that *L'École des filles* is almost exactly contemporary with the very differently inspired *Carte du Tendre,* Madeleine de Scudery's anti-vulgarian précieuse. What the two texts have in common, as mid-seventeenth-century productions, is the way they move in an orderly, progressive fashion, expressing each in its own way this classicist aesthetic.

Indeed, the *École des filles* is curiously and methodically annotated, with over a hundred and fifty subject headings paralleling its explicit, sexy narrative—so that when Suzanne explains:

> This is how it happens: sometimes the boy and the girl are alone in a bedroom or in a garden, it doesn't matter where, and they make small talk; most often it doesn't occur to them to give each other pleasure, because of some other concern they might have; and the boy would merely like to kiss her once before leaving, just to be polite. The girl, who knows about such things, as soon as she feels the boy's mouth press against her own, pushes the point of her tongue little by little into his mouth and rubs it against his lips so energetically that she puts the boy in the mood. He asks her to begin again. Then the girl can take another pleasure and, having looked all around to see if anyone is watching, she puts her tongue in the boy's mouth and kisses him, sliding her hand over his organ, which she takes hold of inside his fly

all the while, the subheadings are indicating soberly: "[23] "Great and different virtues of the hand of a girl to give pleasure to boys ... [24] First virtue. [25] Second virtue," and so on.

In the later parts of their discourses, as the *argument* explains, the two women "investigate and examine everything which relates to love and its game, and do so with such rare and tickling and amusing and new questions, so subtle and so convincing, that they inspire love as they are read" (they get pretty philosophical: Descartes's method prescribed that his inventories should be complete and omit nothing). Actually, the last parts of *L'École des filles* introduce the well-known theory of Platonic love, the reunification of separated souls, the power of feminine beauty, and its resemblance to divine beauty. The author adapts this view to his own ideas opposing conventional morality and favoring all-out sex.

Meanwhile the various editions of *L'École des filles* had a curious history of being found in the bedrooms of various womanizers and aristocratic daughters of the seventeenth and eighteenth centuries—Louis XIV's sometime treasury minister Fouquet, various daughters and ladies in waiting of Louis XV, and the like.

Biography

Not much is known about Michel Millot or Jean L'Ange (but see Lachèvre below). One or both of them presented the manuscript to a Paris printer—who accepted payment and then turned them over to the police. L'Ange was sentenced to five years in the galleys, a sentence later reduced. Millot, who benefited from higher social standing and apparently had friends in high places—possibly the ribald novelist Paul Scarron, or even Scarron's wife, Françoise D'Aubigné, later to marry Louis XIV—was simply burned in effigy with most of the copies of the book, and he himself was allowed to flee. Nowadays there is apparently no known copy of the first (1655) edition, with extant texts based on later publications.

HERBERT DE LEY

Editions

Anon. *L'École des filles.* Edited by Michel Camus. *Oeuvres érotiques du XVIIe siècle.* L'Enfer de la Bibliothèque Nationale. Paris: Fayard, 1988.

Further Reading

De Ley, Herbert. "Dans les reigles du plaisir ...Transformation of Sexual Knowlege in Seventeenth-Century France," edited by W. Leiner. *Onze nouvelles etudes sur l'image de la femme dans la littérature française du dix-septième siècle.* Tübingen: G. Narr, 1984.

Foucault, Michel. *Les mots et les choses.* Paris: Gallimard, 1966.

Lachèvre, Frédéric. "Trois grands procès de libertinage." *Le Libertinage au dix-septième siècle.* Vol. 2. Paris: Champion, 1920.

Larson, Ruth, "Sex and Civility in a Seventeenth-Century Dialogue—*L'Escole des filles.*" *Papers on Seventeenth-Century French Literature* (*PFSCL*) 24 (1997): 475–511.

MINUT, GABRIEL DE

1520–1587
Essayist, humanist

Gabriel de Minut is the author of two medical texts, the first published before 1584, possibly in Toulouse, of which only the title has survived: *Dialogue au soulagement des affligés. Interlocuteurs: Gabriel, malade patient, et Blaise, chirurgien agent.* The second was published in Lyon in 1587, *Morbi Gallos infestantis salubris curatio et sancta medicina, hoc est malorum, quoe intestinum crudeleque Gallorum bellum inflammant, remedium.* Gabriel wrote an unpublished musical treatise with Louis du Pin that discusses the influence of the musical score written by Antoine de Bertrand (c. 1530–1581) for the first book of the "Amours de Cassandre" of Pierre de Ronsard. There also exists in manuscript form a study on astrology by Minut (*Alphabet de l'astrologie judiciaire*).

De la beauté

Gabriel de Minut wrote *De la beauté* [*On Beauty*] but was not able to publish it himself because of his death shortly after he composed the text in 42 nights. He had planned to dedicate it to the queen mother, Catherine de Medici. His sister, Charlotte de Minut, abbess of a Toulouse monastery, took it upon herself, after she found the manuscript among his papers, to write an epistle to the queen mother in order to get it published.

As *De la beauté* points out, Minut's discourse is based on the tenet that "ce qui est naturellement beau, est aussi naturellement bon" [What is naturally beautiful is also naturally good]. He bases this statement on the scriptures, the Greek χαλὸν χάγαθδα, and the Hebrew ברט. The author uses many examples from antiquity to illustrate and corroborate his discourse.

The text recalls first how in antiquity people revered beautiful creatures, so that a beautiful person was worthy of a kingdom. At the same time, it is said that ugly newborns were to be suffocated at birth. It also discusses Theban law as it affected the raising of children (branding for Theban identification, forbidding marriage with foreigners, building of one's tomb before one's house, and killing ugly girls and sacrificing them to the Gods). Minut then offers the argument of the possible metamorphosis of an ugly girl into a beautiful one by changing the milk she drank. Minut recalls that in certain cultures, men allowed their wives to have sex with other men in order to procreate beautiful children, because it was believed then that a better seed would produce a better harvest. Minut condemns this practice. He then tells of women who affect the looks of their child-to-be by looking at the portrait of a beautiful person. This allows an indiscreet married woman to have the child of another man without being found unfaithful because the child will look very much like her husband. Thus it can happen that a common person may look very much like a monarch or a common man—Minut cites the example of Martin Guerre. At this point, Minut introduces a quick story dealing with Nero, leaving it to the reader's discretion to believe it or not: the Roman emperor is reported to have had an anal incision performed on his servant Sporus as an alternative to having sex with the empress Sabine.

If children's beauty does not match that of their parents, the reason may be that they were conceived, for instance, after a time when the parents had been sick. It is quite important to make sure that children are taught to behave properly in their youth so that they will not act lasciviously as adults. It is also suggested to parents that they should be aware of their children's friendships if they wish to keep them away from corruption and vices. Bawdiness is to be put under check especially because humans can perform sexual acts all the time. Bathing in virtue is preferable to wallowing in vice, the author suggests.

A child, Minut advises repeatedly, should not drink the milk of anyone but his mother, to prevent inheriting someone else's bad complexion or ill temper: this is used to explain Caligula's bad temper, as it is recorded that on one occasion he drank the blood of his nurse after she had been stabbed. Nursemaids should be avoided also because of alcoholism. A woman who is addicted to alcohol is also addicted to sex. According to Minut, the planets do not play a role in deciding the beauty or ugliness of a person. Rather, it is God's will that determines such choice.

Beauty can be a dangerous gift: Minut tells the story of one Democles, who decided to throw himself into a cauldron of boiling water rather than accept the advances of a certain Demetrius.

The last important discussion in *De la beauté* centers around three types of beauties in women. The first is the beauty of the body, which is qualified as being seditious or scandalous; the second is the beauty of the mind, which is qualified as soberly ribald; and the third is the beauty of the soul, which is qualified as a religious beauty, holy, chaste, and modest.

De la beauté is followed by a curiously titled text: *La Paulegraphie* [*The Paula-ography*], a detailed description of a cousin of Minut named Paule Viguier. Minut explains that he introduced the three types of beauty as a temple to the glory of *la belle Paule*, a woman without compare from pole to pole. Born around 1518, she was considered to be the epitome of beauty in her days and was ordered by the Toulouse municipal magistrates to appear on her balcony twice a day to avoid riots in the city. When King François I visited Toulouse in April 1533, he received the keys of the city from her hands. She was married twice and died in 1607. It is quite possible that Minut wrote *De la beauté* because, even late in life, he was enamored of his cousin—he is reported to have written poems to her two weeks before his death. Once Minut has lavished his praise upon Paule, he begins a detailed description of her, starting with her hair (a mixture of gold and silver), which is long enough to hide her naked body. He then describes her forehead as a true representation of her personality. Her sky-blue eyes perfectly fit the size of her face. Her eyebrows match so symmetrically well that one could think they were painted. Her straight nose has the shape that surpasses any other. Her lips and her cheeks are of the perfect color. The shape of her ears are an indication of her good, gentle, and generous spirit, just as her earlobes point to her lenient character, free of anger and dissent. Her chin and throat are of a perfect white marble hue. Based on the testimony he has received, Paule's breasts are more beautiful that any others in shape, size, and skin tone. After a description of her arms and hands, her belly is described as small, round, white, and firm. Mentioning the area described as *la porte pour la sortie des enfants* [the gate through which children exit] allows Minut to discuss the chastity of *la belle Paule* as one who should not be touched or mentioned. The same goes for her thighs, although Minut assumes that they are perfect because the rest of her body is. The buttocks are described as small cushions. *La Paulegraphie* concludes with an *envoi* that summarizes the beauty and goodness of *la belle Paule*.

Biography

Gabriel de Minut, baron de Castera, was born in southern France. He spent most of his life in the city of Toulouse, but it is doubtful that this was the place of his birth. His father, Jacques de Minut, died on November 6, 1536, after he had held the prestigious office of first president of the Parliament of Toulouse. At the age of 15, Gabriel started studying law, philosophy, medicine, and theology at the University of Paris. Later, he was the seneschal of Rouergue, an area east of Toulouse that would not become a part of France until 1607. He was attached to the staff of the queen mother and was an ordinary gentleman of the king's chamber. In *De la beauté*, Minut's major work, he digresses in chapter 15 to introduce briefly his ancestors in classical Rome as being one of its most important families, who are even mentioned by Cicero, while another ancestor is introduced as a captain of one of Pompey's legions. He is generally considered one of the most learned scholars of his time, as demonstrated by his best-known work, *De la beauté*.

CLAUDE FOUILLADE

Selected Works

De la beauté; discours divers pris sur deux fort belles façons de parler, desquelles l'hébrieu et le grec usent, l'hébrieu Tob, et le grec Kalon Kagaçon, voulant signifier ce qui est naturellement beau et aussi naturellement bon. Avec La Paule-graphie; ou, Description des beautez d'une dame tholosaine, nommée la belle Paule. Geneva: Slatkine Reprints, 1969.

De la beauté. Brussels: A. Mertens et fils, 1865.

Ruelle, Pierre. *L'Ornement des dames, Ornatus mulierum.* Brussels: Presses universitaires de Bruxelles, 1967.

MIRBEAU, OCTAVE

1848–1917
French writer

Le Journal d'une femme de chambre

According to the preface to *Diary of a Chamber-maid* (1900), it is a genuine diary, written by Célestine R., a real chambermaid, who would have hardly asked Octave Mirbeau for help with editing—but this claim is transparently a literary device enabling the author to write in the first person. Célestine did not have a happy childhood in Brittany: her father died when she was very young, and her violent, alcoholic mother become a low-class prostitute. As a teenager, Célestine left her hometown of Audierne to go to Paris and earn a meager living as a chambermaid (interestingly, Mirbeau himself occasionally worked as a manservant in Paris in the late 1870s).

The diary starts in mid-September 1899 when Célestine arrives at the fictitious village of Mesnil-Roy in Normandy, about to start a new job working for the umpteenth time as a chambermaid—this time for the wealthy but reclusive Lanlaire family at their austere mansion called Le Prieuré. Célestine will keep her diary for several weeks, both chronicling her daily life and service at Le Prieuré and recounting over twenty incidents that happened to her with previous employers in Paris. Without any narrative chronology, all these stories, rich in anecdotes, portraits, and descriptions, intertwine two major themes: the chambermaid's dire life and her employers' decadence, with several minor themes in the background: the hypocrisy of Catholicism, the bourgeoisie's moral decay, nationalism, and social scandals. The perverse nature of the relationship between masters and servants lies at the heart of all the stories, usually with an element of sex, with the maid invited to sleep with a male member of the household (sometimes the father, sometimes the son or even the grandson, or the chief butler) and, without much resistance, Célestine would accept, as a good working girl is expected to do. Calculating but always honest, Célestine explains and justifies her behavior, even when she knows that it was not ethical (for instance, with young Monsieur Georges, who is terribly ill and weak and ends up dying whilst having sex with her).

Whilst narrating all these past stories, Célestine languishes at Le Prieuré, failing to find much interest in local gossip and loathing Madame Lanlaire's despising attitude. Hen-pecked Monsieur Lanlaire (who regularly has sex with the insipid cook Marianne) and poison-tongued neighbor Rose (who proudly shares her employer's bed) are of little interest to Célestine, unlike the mysterious factotum Joseph, who has been working for the Lanlaires for fifteen years. Initially repulsed by his monstrous ugliness, she gradually falls in love with him, even if he is probably a rapist and murderer (though this is never fully clarified), as well as a thief, eventually robbing the Lanlaires of their silver. After some awkward courting, he offers Célestine marriage—she briefly hesitates then accepts, realizing that no man has ever excited her as much as Joseph. The last chapter of the book is almost an epilogue, written eight months later. Célestine briefly narrates how she is now married to Joseph; they have left Le Prieuré and are now happily settled in Cherbourg, where, ironically enough, they have their own domestics. They own a small café called "A l'Armée Française," which is rapidly becoming the favorite meeting point of all local anti-Semite, militarist activists.

Written as a satire of Parisian society in the wake of the Dreyfus affair, this long novel ends up being an excellent sociological and historical documentary about the decadence and hypocrisy of the Parisian upper classes at the turn of the twentieth century and about the condition of chambermaids (and servants in general, be they cooks or footmen). It is a fine piece of social criticism (showing Mirbeau's talents as a radical journalist and cynical social commentator), yet it was dismissed by many critics of the time as pornography and was initially banned in the United States: in 1901, the American anarchist Benjamin Tucker attempted to publish his own translation, but the US Postal Service, under the puritanical guidance of Anthony Comstock, put a stop to it on grounds of obscenity (Tucker later deleted some of the book's best passages and released an abridged edition). All these claims and the subsequent censorship are due to the fact that the book depicts a wide range of sexual acts, from fetishism (the first story, only three pages into the book, is that of an elderly gentleman with a fetish for women's leather boots, Monsieur Rabour, who dies in his bed with one of Célestine's boots in his mouth, having seemingly choked to death) to lesbianism (which Célestine discovered with her friend Cléclé when working in a convent run by exploitative nuns).

Le Journal d'une femme de chambre has inspired two of the best filmmakers of the twentieth century: Jean Renoir (1894–1979) and Luis Buñuel (1900–1983). Renoir's version, released in 1946 with Paulette Goddard and Burgess Meredith (who were both also coproducers), was highly praised, yet less so than Buñuel's 1964 version: with Jeanne Moreau as Célestine, Buñuel's film has become a classic (though it must be said that it took some distance from Mirbeau's original story line). Mirbeau is now becoming fashionable again, with all of his work coming back into print; his play *Les Affaires sont les affaires* [*Business Is Business*] (1904) made a triumphal return to the Paris stage in 1995, and his novels are again being translated and published in English, some for the first time. There is very little in terms of secondary literature about Mirbeau, though; the main specialist is French scholar Pierre Michel, who is the director of the Société Octave Mirbeau.

In terms of erotic imagery, the key element of *Le Journal d'une femme de chambre* is the French maid as object of desire, with her strict uniform: a black dress with long sleeves, a white ribbon tie-back apron, and a lace headpiece, yet a French maid who is not a naive ingénue: Célestine is the French maid who knows how to manipulate men to her advantage. Almost a literary archetype, she is a key character of the commedia dell'arte of erotic literature.

Biography

Octave Mirbeau was a political activist (an anarchist) and a man of letters in the broadest sense; he published widely, as a novelist, playwright, ghostwriter, art critic, and journalist. Yet, nowadays he is remembered mainly for two books: *Le Journal d'une femme de chambre* and *Le Jardin des supplices* [*Torture Garden*] (1899), a bildungsroman about Chinese tortures and sadomasochism that doubles as a political pamphlet denouncing murder and colonialism.

LOYKIE LOÏC LOMINÉ

Editions

Le Journal d'une femme de chambre. Paris: Flammarion, c. 1983.
The Diary of a Chambermaid. Translated by Douglas Jarman, with an introduction by Richard Ings [c. 1966]. Sawtry, UK: Dedalus, 1991.

Further Reading

Michel, P., and J.F. Nivet. *Biographie d'Octave Mirbeau, l'imprécateur au cœur fidèle*. Paris: Séguier, 1990.
Michel, P. *Édition critique de l'oeuvre romanesque de Mirbeau*. 3 vols. Buchet/Chastel: Société Octave Mirbeau, 2000.

MISHIMA, YUKIO

1925–1970
Japanese novelist, dramatist, and essayist

The sexuality, eroticism, and fascination with the body that characterize much of Mishima's literary work are also clearly discernible in his life. He was a vocal critic of the consumerism that he believed had polluted Japan and led to the loss of traditional samurai virtues. Mishima felt that the Japanese "salaryman," the archetypal emblem of postwar masculinity, had become effeminate, and he invested a great deal of effort in bodybuilding in pursuit of his own perfect masculine body. He was later to write about the transformation of his body from that of an effete intellectual to a man of action in the homoerotically charged *Taiyō to tetsu* [*Sun and Steel*] (1968).

Mishima's exhibitionism was notorious; he appeared dressed in a *fundoshi* (traditional loincloth) in several photo albums extolling the beauty of the male form, including *Bara-kei* [*Ordeal by Roses*] (1963) and *Taidō* [*The Way of the Body*] (1967). He also starred in macho roles in a number of gangster movies. Despite marrying and fathering two children, as was expected of a man of his class, Mishima had strong homosexual inclinations. He was attracted to members of the working classes, particularly manual laborers, who feature as objects of desire in several of his novels.

Mishima was not conscripted during the Second World War because of ill health. However, he was nostalgic for the homosocial world of the soldier, and in 1967 he began training with Japan's Self-Defense Forces. In 1968, he founded a paramilitary group known as the Shield Society, which was pledged to protect the emperor and his interests. Mishima invested a great deal of energy training with these men and in designing their uniforms, and he seems to have been attempting to re-create something of the homoerotic ethos of the samurai era. Indeed, at this time he published *Hagakure nyūmon* [*The Way of the Samurai*] (1967), a commentary on a little-known samurai text from the eighteenth century that extolled *nanshoku* (male homoeroticism) and praised the willingness of the samurai to die for his master. In a now-famous maxim, it is argued in *Hagakure* that "[t]he way of the samurai is death," and Mishima clearly saw his own suicide by *seppuku* (ritual disembowelment) as a continuation of this samurai practice. His own death was anticipated by two graphically depicted *seppuku* scenes in the short story *Yūkoku* [*Patriotism*] (1966) and in the novel *Homba* [*Runaway Horses*] (1969).

Mishima was well read in works of Western sexology, and he incorporated in his novels ideas from Freud and Magnus Hirschfeld, along with Eastern themes deriving from Hinduism and Buddhism. The compulsive nature of sexual desire lies at the heart of much of his fiction, where it proves to be a dark, destructive force that cuts through social convention, driving characters from high and low social strata alike to acts of violence and depravity. *Kamen no kokuhaku* [*Confessions of a Mask*] (1949) is a semi-autobiographical work in which Mishima writes of his discovery of masturbation, brought about by his coming across Guido Reni's painting of St. Sebastian pierced by arrows. In the novel he speaks of his incipient desire for the night-soil collector, whose job it was to clean out the latrines, and of his sadistic fantasies where "young Roman gladiators offered up their lives for my amusement" and a naked schoolmate was served up to him on a plate. Scenes of necrophilia were to recur throughout his later fiction.

Images of sex, death, and the body's animal functions are common. *Ai no kawaki* [*Thirst for Love*] (1950) describes the passion a rich young widow feels for a local farmhand. When she observes him cavorting at the local shrine festival clad only in a loincloth, she frenziedly scratches his back with her nails. Yet, when he responds to her advances, she panics and kills him with a scythe. *Gogo no eikō* [*The Sailor Who Fell from Grace with the Sea*] (1963) features another widow, this time besotted with a sailor. In this story, the widow's thirteen-year-old son watches his mother making love to the sailor through a chink in the wall. For the son, the sailor's capitulation to desire for a woman makes him a fallen hero and he hatches a plan to poison and then mutilate him.

In the novels, sex is a demonic force that leads the possessed individual to transgress all rules of etiquette and personal decorum, leading to downfall. This theme is brilliantly explored in *Kinjiki* [*Forbidden Colors*] (1951). In this novel, Yuichi, "an amazingly beautiful young man" whose body "surpassed the sculptures of ancient Greece," brings disaster to the lives of all his lovers, both men and women. Mishima shows how the power of youthful physical beauty can defeat riches, breeding, or education. He shows sexual desire to be a great leveling force that brings all men and women, no matter how rich, well born, or erudite back down to the level of their primal animal natures. For Mishima beauty was something terrible, a force that could consume and annihilate the lover. This theme is dealt with metaphorically in *Kinkakuji* [*The Temple of the Golden Pavilion*] (1956), in which a young priest, driven mad by the beauty of the temple, burns it down.

Beauty does not last in Mishima's novels; most youthful lovers either kill themselves or are murdered. In his last work, the tetralogy *Sea of Fertility* (1965–1970), the original hero of the novel either kills himself (or, in the third volume, *herself*) or dies at the end of each novel and is reincarnated in the next. Honda, the hero's best friend from the first book, survives to reencounter his friend in each subsequent reincarnation; but while his friend lives and then dies at the peak of his/her beauty, Honda lives on to face an old age of senility and decrepitude. *Tennin gosui* [*The Decay of the Angel*] (1970), the title of the final volume, completed the night before Mishima's suicide, is a reference to the Buddhist belief that even the gods, when their store of merit is exhausted, fall from their lofty perches back into the world of human suffering. The obsession with the terrifying nature of beauty and distaste for its inevitable decline dealt with in many of Mishima's novels help explain what was to follow.

On November 25, 1970, Mishima and a group of followers from the Shield Society stormed the office of the commander-in-chief of the Self-Defense Forces in an attempt to convince him to support Mishima's demand for constitutional reform that would allow Japan to rearm and restore the full rights of the emperor. When it became clear that the attempt had failed, Mishima committed ritual suicide by cutting open his belly, while his second in command, reputedly his lover, decapitated him with a samurai sword. Mishima's suicide struck most Japanese as a perversely anachronistic gesture, coming as it did on the eve of Japan's most spectacular period of growth and prosperity.

Today, Mishima remains a controversial and slightly embarrassing figure in Japan. Over thirty years after his suicide, the gruesome circumstances of his death that mirror so closely scenes described in his novels still make it difficult to disentangle Mishima's life from his art.

Biography

Yukio Mishima is the pen name of Kimitake Hiraoka, who was born in Tokyo on January 14. His ancestors on his father's side were of peasant origin, although both his father and his grandfather were government officials; his mother's forebears were of upper-class samurai stock. Mishima was sent to the elite but austere Peers' School, where he showed precocious literary talent, publishing his first short story while still a student. He graduated first in his class in 1944, later attended the prestigious Law Department of Tokyo University, and served a brief stint in the finance ministry. Then he turned to writing full time. His first novel was not well received, but his second, *Confessions of a Mask,* was a critical success which launched him on a literary career that was to result in over thirty books, including novels, short stories, essays, and plays. This prolific career was brought to an abrupt and premature end with Mishima's suicide at the age of forty-five.

MARK MCLELLAND

Selected Works

Kamen no kokuhaku. 1949; as *Confessions of a Mask,* translated by Meredith Weatherby. 1958.
Ai no kawaki. 1950; as *Thirst for Love,* translated by Alfred H. Marks. 1969.
Kinjiki. 1951; as *Forbidden Colors,* translated by Alfred H. Marks. 1968.
Kinkakuji. 1956; as *The Temple of the Golden Pavilion,* translated by Ivan Morris. 1959.

Gogo no eikō, 1963; as *The Sailor Who Fell from Grace with the Sea*, translated by John Nathan. 1965.

Hagakure nyūmon, 1967; as *The Way of the Samurai* translated by Kathryn Sparling. 1977.

Tennin gosui, 1970; as *The Decay of the Angel*, translated by Edward G. Seidensticker. 1974.

Further Reading

Keene, Donald. "Yukio Mishima." In *Kodansha Encyclopedia of Japan*, edited by Gen Itasaka. 9 vols. Tokyo and New York: Kodansha, 1983.

Jackson, Earl, Jr. "Kabuki Narratives of Male Homoerotic Desire in Saikaku and Mishima." *Theatre Journal* 41 (1989): 459–77.

Nakao, Seigo. "Yukio Mishima." In *The Gay and Lesbian Literary Heritage*, edited by Claude J. Summers. New York: Henry Holt, 1995.

Scott Stokes, Henry. *The Life and Death of Yukio Mishima*. New York: Farrar, Straus and Giroux, 1994.

Starrs, Roy. *Deadly Dialectics: Sex, Violence and Nihilism in the World of Yukio Mishima*. Honolulu: University of Hawai'i Press, 1994.

Wolfe, Peter. *Yukio Mishima*. New York: Continuum, 1989.

MISTRAL, GABRIELA

1889–1957

Chilean poet, cultural ambassador, and educational reformer

Gabriela Mistral's writing career began in 1914 when *Sonetos de la muerte* [*Sonnets of Death*] received a commendation during the Juegos Florales de Santiago, one of Chile's most prestigious literary competitions. This was also the first occasion on which she employed the soubriquet Gabriela Mistral, a name derived from that of her two favorite poets: Gabriele D'Annunzio and Frédéric Mistral. She herself thought that her existence was marred by tragedy—the broken home of her own childhood, the suicide of her lover, and her failure to have children of her own. Out of such personal sadness, however, she wove the rich tapestry of her poetry, which is marked by its compassion, warmth, humanity, and love of children.

Treated with hostility in her own country, her talents were first recognized in neighboring Latin American states. Mistral's anti-establishment ideas and left-wing views—both inspired by Christian humanism—made her unpopular with her peers and other members of the teaching profession. This was especially true of the Santiago bourgeoisie, who considered her a *criolla*—an ignorant peasant woman. National newspapers such as *El Mercurio* and *El Diario Ilustrado* refused to publish her articles after she attacked the regime of Gabriel Gonzalez Videla (1949–1952), not only for persecuting Pablo Neruda, the eminent poet and member of the Chilean Senate, but also for first labeling as Communists and then dismissing hundreds of public employees.

In 1922 she accepted the invitation of José Vasconcelos to become Mexico's guest of honor and take part in the plan to establish new secondary schools and libraries—put into effect by the Mexican government after the Revolution (1910–1917). Aged thirty-three, Mistral went into voluntary exile. Except for rare visits to her native country, she would spend the rest of her life outside Chile. Indeed, Chile's failure to recognize her talents as a poet is reflected in her publishing record. Mistral's only volume of poetry to appear in Chile before being brought out elsewhere was the 1954 collection *Lagar* [*Winepress*].

Although Mistral focuses mainly on spiritual rather than physical or erotic love, the language used to describe religious and spiritual passion is very much eroticized. Eroticism is never described as experienced in the flesh; it is all the same enhanced by religious experience, a tendency toward asceticism, unsatisfied maternal yearnings, and a natural communion with the land.

In her *Sonetos de la muerte*, the central theme is grief over the death of a lover. Physical love is portrayed as an elusive goal, achievable only in death, which in turn symbolizes the safe haven where rest can be achieved. Spiritual love, a love that has the power to right all wrongs, is equated with poetry. In *Desolación, Tala,* and *Lagar* Mistral turns a mystic eye on basic elements such as water, light, and earth, as well as salt, maize, and bread, often in relation to indigenous rituals. Mistral's "Pan" [Bread] (from *Poesías completas* 1976: 350) is particularly charged with sexual imagery. The protagonist feels in ecstasy when the smell of freshly baked bread gets to her. The sensual experience continues as she opens it, penetrating the white, warm, soft bun with her fingers, anticipating the joy of pacifying her oral and tactile cravings. This is described in such a way that it clearly evokes carnal pleasure. Water becomes a particularly sensual topic, which Mistral associates with the washing off of sins and compares to a lover. In her poem "El agua" [Water], Mistral tells a little child that fear of water is worth experiencing in anticipation of the exhilarating pleasure the stream will give him. Water is also a source of oral pleasure, as it calms one's thirst. Furthermore, it symbolizes fertility, for it makes nature bloom. For Mistral, physical pleasure is also experienced when in contact with Latin American landscapes and its pre-Columbian cultures. In "América" (*Poesías completas* 1976: 359), maize, central to the culture and diet of the Aztecs, becomes irresistible gold that, when kissed, brings spirits to life. The corn plant becomes a symbol of virility, whose erect fruit seduces gods, humans, and birds alike.

The theme of love is ever-present in Mistral's metaphysical poems *Desolación, Tala* and *Lagar*. Nevertheless, unlike other female postmodern South American writers (such as Delira Agustini, 1886–1914; Juana de Ibarbourou, 1892–1928; and Alfonsina Storni, 1892–1979) Mistral is not concerned with love as an erotic force but with love as a spiritual entity: the love of God, nature, and one's fellow creatures.

During her formative years the Bible was Mistral's main source of moral instruction and poetic inspiration. This would be reflected in her work as a whole, which replicates her religious beliefs, the renunciation of carnal desire, and the insistence of continual self-purification. It is perhaps because of this that her *Cartas de amor* [Love Letters] created such controversy at the time, since they revealed an unknown side of Mistral's persona. Her *Cartas* are addressed to the writer Manuel Magallanes Moure, a renowned writer and public figure at the time. They maintained an intense, though chaste, epistolary relationship; actually Mistral set eyes on Magallanes only once. Although her erotic desire is never addressed, Mistral's letters reveal her need for a perhaps more carnal relationship. Indeed, at times the letters fill the void of carnal love; Mistral confesses to Magallanes that sometimes after reading his letters she has to lie down, physically exhausted, her heart pounding after so much romance, his words so sweet that they actually touch her.

Mistral's correspondence is extremely frank, although inclined to safeguard the "mystery" of her sexuality. As it develops, the reader gains a privileged insight into Mistral's innermost feelings toward herself: she heroically and blatantly confesses being aware of her "rough looks" and lack of femininity. Because of that, she is determined to keep her love affair exclusively to the writing and the reading, to save her platonic lover from having to kiss her and caress and make love to an ugly woman. When Magallanes finally deserts her to marry a wealthy bride from Santiago, Mistral resolves to devote the rest of her life to the poor, the weak, and the downtrodden, to compensate for her lack of romantic attachment by dedicating herself to children, and thus exploiting her maternal drive in her role of devoted teacher.

Biography

Lucila Godoy Alcayana, who wrote under the pen name Gabriela Mistral, was born in Vicuña, Chile, in April. Despite her hostility to the Chilean regime, she represented Chile at the League of Nations (1926), was consul at Naples (1932), Madrid, and Lisbon (both in 1933), and later became plenipotentiary minister responsible for promoting Spanish and American literature and culture. In 1945 she became the first Latin American to receive the Nobel Prize for Literature. Gabriela Mistral died in New York City.

CAROLINA MIRANDA

Editions

Desolación. New York: Instituto de las Españas, 1922.
Tala. Buenos Aires: Sur, 1938.

Lagar. Santiago: Pacífico, 1954.

Cartas de amor de Gabriela Mistral. Edited with introduction by S. Fernández Larrain. Santiago de Chile: Bello, 1978.

Selected Works

Poesia para mujeres. México: Porrúa, 1923.

Ternura. Madrid: Saturnino Calleja, 1924.

Poema de Chile. Edited with preface by Doris Dana. Barcelona: Pmaire, 1967.

Selected Poems of Gabriela Mistral. Edited by Doris Dana. Baltimore MD: Library of Congress/Johns Hopkins University Press, 1971; bilingual edition, 1972.

Crickets and Frogs. Edited by by Doris Dana. New York: Atheneum, 1972.

Poesías completas: Desolación; Ternura; Tala: Lagar I. Madrid: Aguilar, 1976.

Further Reading

Alegría, Fernando. *Genio y figura de Gabriela Mistral*. Buenos Aires: Editorial Universitaria de Buenos Aires, 1966.

Arce de Vazquez, Margot. *G. Mistral, the Poet and Her Work*. Translated by Hélène Masslo Anderson. New York: NYU Press, 1964.

Caimano, Sister Rose Aquin, O.P. *Mysticism in Gabriela Mistral*. New York: Pageant, 1969.

Gazarian-Gautier, Marie-Lise. *Gabriela Mistral: The Teacher from the Valley of Elqui*. Chicago: Franciscan Herald Press, 1975.

Johnson, Harvey L. *Gabriela Mistral's Affiliation with the United States*. Los Ensayistas: Georgia Series of Hispanic Thought (March 1951): 79–83.

Taylor, Martin C. *Gabriela Mistral's Religious Sensibility*. Berkeley and Los Angeles: University of California Press, 1968.

MOGADOR, CÉLESTE

1824–1909
French memoirist

Adieux au monde: Memoires

Adieux au monde, which might more rightly be called *Adieux au demi-monde*, was written with the aid of Mogador's lover, her lawyer Desmarest, and read aloud to the playwright Camille Doucet, the Girardins, and Alexandre Dumas *père*, who put it on a par with the confessions of Rousseau. He puffed the book in *Le Mousquetaire* and Girardin helped draw up new terms with the publisher. The book, which covered Mogador's picaresque career up to her meeting with Chabrillan, was published in five volumes in Paris in 1854; this edition was suppressed. It was republished in 1858 in four volumes, with information added about the romance of Céleste and "Robert," and again confiscated.

The reviews, which appeared while Mogador was in Australia, were severe. Villemessant in *Le Figaro* (April 25, 1854) suggested that certain books, like certain creatures, could turn lending libraries into brothels, and feared that "our daughters and sisters" would learn from them that the shortest road to a social position was prison and prostitution. Although there was a flourishing market for ghostwritten autobiographies of loose women, few were prepared to welcome an ex-prostitute's account of her struggle to establish an identity and pursue personal happiness in a society that overeroticized women. For instance, Mogador's portrait of the poet Alfred de Musset, whom she had entertained in a brothel, gave great offense. He is portrayed as a drunken, petulant lout prone to such boorish behavior as squirting seltzer water at her during a dinner at the Rocher-Cancale.

Mogador displeased with her straightforward language, her candor about sex, her refusal to tittilate, and her contempt for the publicity establishment which had launched her. She complained of the way in which men of letters, short of a better subject, chose to celebrate ugly, stupid tarts.

> Journalists treat women like governments: they invent them; after having invented them, they cry them up and afterward try to unmake them. It used to be there were only one or two public dance halls; why are there ten nowadays? Because of the female

celebrities whom you enjoyed creating in your leisure hours. This tinsel glory has attracted envious women. Thousands of young women are dragged into the public dance halls, lured by this fraudulent renown. Young men go to see these competitions, these onslaughts of legs. (II, 286)

Mogador left some 15 notebooks of reminiscence dealing with the period 1859 to 1907. These passed into the possession of Françoise Moser, whose biography is still the most reliable. It is Moser who declared that although Mogador, in her published memoirs, "arranged" part of the truth and novelized another part, what she says deserves to be believed.

Biography

Élisabeth-Céleste Vénard (Comtesse Lionel de Moreton de Chabrillan), illegitimate daughter of a suicidal laundress, was born near the Boulevard de Temple, Paris, December 27. Her father, a hatter, was affectionate but died when Céleste was six, leaving her feckless mother to drift from one abusive man to another. After a time in Lyon, where mother and daughter had fled to escape the violence of the current lover, the precocious and headstrong girl was apprenticed to an embroidery maker in Paris. Sexually molested at 15 by her mother's latest boyfriend, Céleste ran away and, exhausted and expiring, was given shelter by a prostitute in a brothel on la Cité. A raid landed her in St.-Lazare women's prison, where she received writing lessons; and, at 16, with her mother's consent, she registered with the police as a prostitute. From a high-class bordello, she moved to an apartment provided by a rich admirer and became a fixture in the Parisian *demi-monde*.

Dance-hall managers would promote star dancers for publicity, and Céleste was put forward as a rival to Reine Pomaré at the Bal Mabille. She was given the name Mogador when on September 26, 1844, as she was stormed by would-be partners, her sponsor declared, "I'd have less trouble defending [the North African town of] Mogador than my dancer." Also called the Queen of the Prado, she was a tall, handsome brunette, with arched eyebrows, mildly pockmarked skin and the "bold proportions of Michelangelic caryatids" (*Larousse du XIXème siècle*). At masked balls, she would turn up the sleeves of her stevedore's smock to show off her exquisite arms. From the dance hall, Mogador

moved to the circus, but her career as a bareback rider at the Hippodrome ended when she broke her leg in a chariot race.

Mogador the courtesan, rather than giving her body to the best-paying customer, gave "her soul, her body and her trust to the most loving." This turned out to be Count Paul-Josselin-Lionel de Chabrillan (b. 1818), former attaché to the French legation in Copenhagen, who set her up in a mansion and went bankrupt in his inept attempts to make a fortune by gambling and stock speculation. When he sailed for Australia to try his luck in the gold fields, Mogador tried to cope with his debts by acting under the name Céleste at the Folies-Dramatique (1850), the Variétés (1851–52), and the Théâtre du Luxembourg (1852), where as Cristal in *La Revue* of 1852 she performed a new dance, the "Impériale." She also reluctantly wrote her memoirs (in which Lionel appears as Robert), without telling him. When Céleste and the count married in London, on January 27, 1854, she tried, without success, to prevent the book's publication. Chabrillan had been appointed consul in Melbourne and hoped they could begin afresh; but Mogador's memoirs preceded her to the Antipodes and she was shunned by good society. After a controversial time in office, Cabrillan died in Melbourne, December 29, 1858.

Céleste returned to France, ruined, and was ill for six months. She then set out to improve her literacy through self-education. Her in-laws tried to remove her titled name, but neither their offers of compensation (an annual pension of 12,000 francs for life) nor their lawsuits could force her to give it up. Evidently resolved to be rehabilitated and with the encouragement of Dumas, she churned out sensational novels (*Sapho*, 1858; *Miss Pewel*, 1859; *Est-il fou?* 1860) and in 1862 took over the management of the Petit Théâtre des Champs-Élysées, where, under the pseudonym Mme Lionel, she presented her own plays *Bonheur au vaincu*, *En Australie*, and *En garde*, before turning it over to the actor Montrouge for 15,000 francs. He renamed it the Folies Marigny. Her oeuvre consists of 33 plays and operetta libretti, and a certain number of poems and songs. For a while she managed the Nouveautés and even performed in a music hall in 1865, before returning to writing. Critics commended her valiant struggle to overcome her past but suspected that her notoriety as Mogador would overshadow her literary efforts. The least unreadable of her fictional works are *Les Voleurs d'or* (1864), later dramatized, and *Mémoires d'une honnête fille* (1865). In 1877, drawing on her Australian diaries, she issued a sequel to her memoirs, *Un Deuil au bout du monde*. She died in the asylum of La Providence, Montmartre, February 7.

LAURENCE SENELICK

Editions

Adieux au monde: Mémoires de Céleste Mogador. 5 vols. Paris: Locard-Davi et De Vresse, 1854.

Mémoires de Céleste Mogador. 4 vols., with additions. Paris: Librairie nouvelle, 1858; 2 vols., 1876.

Mémoires de Céleste Mogador, 1824–1854, où une jolie fille raconte sa jeunesse misérable et scandaleuse, comment elle devint la vedette du bal Mabille et de l'Hippodrome, fut entretenue par les plus riches viveurs et se racheta en épousant un jeune comte ruiné, chercheur d'or, puis consul dans l'Australie des convicts. Paris: Les Amis de l'Histoire, 1968.

Memoirs of a Courtesan in Nineteenth-Century Paris. Translated by Monique Fleury Nagem. Lincoln: University of Nebraska Press, 2001.

Un Deuil au bout du monde; suite des Mémoires de Céleste Mogador. Paris: Librairie nouvelle, 1877;

The French Consul's Wife. Memoirs of Céleste de Chabrillan in Gold-Rush Australia. Translated by Patricia Clancy and Jeanne Allen. Carlton South, Victoria, Australia: Miegunyah Press, 1998.

Selected Works

Les Voleurs d'Or. 1857.
Miss Pewell. 1859.
Un miracle à Vichy. 1860.
Est-il fou? 1860; repr. 1879.
Mémoires d'une honnête fille, with Alfred Delvau. 1865.
Un amour terrible (Sapho), 1876.
Émigrantes et déportées, ou Les deux soeurs, 1876; repr. 1887.
Une méchante femme. 1877.
La duchesse de Mers. 1881.
Les forçats de l'amour. 1881.
Marie Baude. 1883.
Un drame sur la Tage. 1885.

Further Reading

Haldane, Charlotte F. *Daughter of Paris: the Life Story of Céleste Mogador, Comtesse Lionel de Moreton de Chabrillan.* London: Hutchinson, 1961.

Larousse, P., ed. *Grand Dictionnaire universel du XIXème siècle.* 17 vols., 1865–1890.

Leclercq, Pierre Robert. *Céleste Mogador: Biographie.* Paris: La Table ronde, 1996.

Moser, Françoise. *Vie et aventures de Céleste Mogador, fille publique, femme de lettres et Comtesse (1824–1909).* Paris: Albin Michel, 1935.

MOIX, TERENCI

1943–
Spanish prose writer

La noche no es hermosa: Textos de Eros

La noche no es hermosa (1994) is a miscellany which unites erotic texts previously published by Terenci Moix in various forms, including short stories, fragments from novels, selections from memoirs, and articles from newspapers and magazines. The number and variety of these pieces (which range from three or four pages to narratives of more than forty pages) provide a very representative account of the multiplicity of registers adopted by Moix's erotic writings up to 1993; samples are given from about fifteen different books. Mirroring a Dante-esque itinerary, the collection is divided into three parts: "Inferno," "Purgatory," and "Paradise," with the addition of a "Stravaganza" and "Finale." The use of irony and a subversive toying with tradition, together with a penchant for "culturalist" re-creation, permeate the texts throughout. Alongside some medieval settings that cannot fail to add meaning to the Dante-esque character of the work, Moix's deeply ingrained Mediterranean cultural sensibility recurrently frames his writings in the pseudo-mythical spaces of ancient Egypt, Greece, and Rome.

These become ideal scenarios for the celebration of hedonism and sexual refinement, but also, in many cases, for the celebration of cruelty and abuse as a means to attain ultimate sexual gratification. Accompanying these journeys into the past, a number of selections have strictly contemporary settings, situating themselves especially in large and modern cities such as Madrid and Barcelona, where the night life is treated as an experience leading to the furthest frontiers of sexuality.

Many of the texts, particularly those published before the end of the sexually repressive Franco dictatorship in 1975, incorporate a palpable component of provocation that nonetheless managed to elude the censorship that was still in force during the last years of Franco's regime. This attitude would earn Moix a reputation as a precocious *enfant terrible* of Spanish letters. With a degree of explicitness perhaps unprecedented in the country's literature, Moix's writings not only delved into what might at the time have been considered conventional sexual taboos (autoeroticism, homoeroticism, transvestism, and oral sex), but they also treated with equal explicitness and detail practices such as sadomasochism, incest, pederasty, bestiality, coprophagy, and even anthropophagy practiced for sexual satisfaction. Witchcraft, torture, and criminal pedagogy of evident de Sadean reminiscence complete the background for this summa of unconventional practices. All of these experiences, of course, are detailed without the least indication of moral condemnation. On the contrary, they are seen as an incentive and stimulus for artistic creation.

Quite frequently, there exists a sense of playfulness that in some way undermines the "drama" arising from the situations depicted and any possibility of tragic implications. In many cases the very excess of exaggeration intentionally strips verisimilitude from the effects inscribed in the texts. If tragedy appears at all, it is as a result of the feeling of loneliness that emerges from many of the selections, a feeling that always seems to coincide with the experience of the subject in contemporary society, no matter how ancient the times dealt with in the texts. In this respect, and despite the meticulous documentation gathered by Moix throughout years of study and travel to the sites of his imaginative incursions, his creative work is one that perhaps can be understood only in terms of the sociocultural context of a young generation of the 1960s and 70s avid for cultural and political change and for the modernization of its country.

Though the selections are very different in conception and realization, as are the original sources from which they are extracted, some recurrent preoccupations and topoi traverse the volume. These include the relation between Eros and death, the interplay between the sacred and the profane, the conception of sex as an illusion or as acting, and the materiality of a desire that ends up leading to frustration, weariness, or dissatisfaction.

Eros and death intertwine in a near obsession with the passage of time and the disfiguration of beauty, a theme which is also manifested in the intermingling of pleasure and pain. Amputations and castrations are not infrequent as components of extreme erotic experiences; vomiting may become a stage of pleasure. As a counterpart, there is a constant celebration of youth, with the exaltation of pederasty of classical inspiration, as well as an assumption of narcissism that acquires a perhaps insuperable expression in the act of masturbation in front of the mirror.

The duality of the sacred and the profane projects itself onto the intersection of the sublime and the abject, and onto the rituality observed in sexual practices related to scenes depicting, for example, crucifixion and martyrdom. In spite of apparently spiritual resonances, such an opposition underscores the carnality and rich sensuality that can be discovered beneath the surface of the most radical religious attitudes.

The pieces set in contemporary times are perhaps the ones that more visibly illustrate the inner emptiness to which the mere material satisfaction of desire may lead. These are the selections that also develop more prominently the challenge to an essentialist conception of sex by playing with changes in identity and roles. The idea of sex as a permanent and proteic performance is perhaps best embodied in the figures of transvestites and transformists that appear in some of these selections.

In general, the multiculturalist perspective that presides over much of the whole collection correlates with the blend of racial, textual, and sexual hybridity manifested therein. It also seems to be naturally in agreement with the combination of high and low culture always found in Moix's works.

One of the best expressions of such a combination is represented by his passion for cinema and his re-creations of the lives and the glamour of Hollywood stars. Perhaps as a result of this influence, many of his writings reveal a deliberate search for visual excess and even artificiality, presenting spaces, characters, and effects that seem to have been drawn from a movie set. As he repeatedly indicates in his memoirs and elsewhere, the cinema provides him with a complement or substitution for the experiences he was deprived of as a child in the very sparse environment of post–civil war Spain. That reservoir of images and stories is constantly present in *La noche no es hermosa*, testifying to his firm inclination toward cultural pastiche. He may re-create the sexual battles between Marc Antony and Cleopatra, or penetrate the intimacy of an opera diva, or present the reader with an adolescent's experiences with sex, alcohol, and drugs in a nightclub in Madrid, but all of this is executed with the same lightness of tone.

A visible icon of Spanish gay culture, Terenci Moix has extensively participated in Spanish media and cultural life, with frequent appearances on TV shows and in collaborations with the most widely circulated newspapers and magazines. Through its combination of personal confessions and fantastic flights of imagination, this volume offers a dual perspective that justly represents a figure who has adopted the permanent vocation of keeping life and literature inextricably intertwined.

Biography

Born Ramón Moix in Barcelona, Spain, January 5. During the second half of the 1960s he began publishing fictional works, primarily in Catalan, and his first collection of stories, *La torre dels vicis capitals,* was awarded the Víctor Català prize in 1967. Around 1980 he adopted Spanish as his primary language for the writing of fiction. Other literary awards include the popular Planeta Prize, which he received in 1986 for his novel *No digas que fue un sueño*, a work that sold more than one million copies.

RICARDO KRAUEL

Editions

The stories and fragments included in *La noche no es hermosa* appeared initially in the following publications (in many cases, the author has modified previous versions of the texts or their translation from the Catalan):

"El demonio" and "Lilí Barcelona." In *La torre del vicis capitals.* Barcelona: Selecta, 1968; as *La torre de los vicios capitales*, translated by Joan Enric Lahosa, Barcelona: Taber, 1969.

"La Adalgisa." In *Onades sobre una roca deserta.* Barcelona: Destino, 1969; as *Olas sobre una roca desierta*, translated by José Miguel Velloso, Barcelona: Destino, 1979.

"La canción del barrio." In *El dia que va morir Marilyn.* Barcelona: Edicions 62, 1969; as *El día que murió Marilyn*, translated by José Miguel Velloso, Barcelona: Plaza y Janés, 1984.

"Boy Hungry." In *Terenci del Nil: Viatge sentimental a Egipte.* Barcelona: Selecta, 1970; as *Terenci del Nilo: Viaje sentimental a Egipto*, translated by the author, Barcelona: Plaza y Janés, 1983.

"Narciso y los espejos de china." In *Siro o ia Increada consciència de la raça*, Barcelona: Edicions 62, 1971; as *Melodrama o la increada conciencia de la raza*, translated by Ana María Moix, Barcelona: Lumen, 1976.

"El banquete" and "La bestia llamada hembra." In *Món mascle.* Barcelona: Aymà, 1971; as *Mundo Macho*, translated by Jaume Pomar, Barcelona: Aymà, 1972; edition by the author, Barcelona: Plaza y Janés, 1986.

"Glorificando a la masturbación europea," "Marcovaldo o el sabor de los obeliscos," and "Minifac Steiman, novelista de orgasmos fallidos." In *La caiguda de l'imperi sodomita i altres històries herètiques.* Barcelona: Aymà, 1976.

"Misterios iniciáticos." In *Nuestro Virgen de los Mártires.* Barcelona: Plaza y Janés, 1983.

"La menstruación de los dioses." In *Amami Alfredo! (Polvo de estrellas).* Barcelona: Plaza y Janés, 1984.

"El misterio del amor." In *Terenci del Atlas*, *El País* [daily newspaper]. Madrid: August 28–30, 1985.

"Lamento de la malquerida" and "Placeres de la reina Cleopatra Séptima." In *No digas que fue un sueño.* Barcelona: Planeta, 1986.

"Yo Cristo, yo rey" and "Domina Brunilda." In *Extraño en el paraíso*, *El País* [daily newspaper]. Madrid: May 1, 1986 through December 10, 1986.

"Fedro o la agonía" and "Damas en subasta." In *El sueño de Alejandría.* Barcelona: Planeta, 1988.

"Flor de onanismo." In *El cine de los sábados (El peso de la paja I).* Barcelona: Plaza y Janés, 1990.

"La noche del Viernes." In *Garras de astracán.* Barcelona: Planeta, 1991.

"El Domingo del joven triste," "La piel amada," and "A un moderno Telémaco." In *Máscaras alejandrinas*, *El País Semanal* [weekly magazine]. Beginning November 1, 1992.

Selected Works

El beso de Peter Pan (El peso de la paja II). Barcelona: Plaza y Janés, 1993.

Venus Bonaparte. Barcelona: Planeta, 1994.

Sufrir de amores. Barcelona: Planeta, 1995.

Mujercísimas. Barcelona: Planeta, 1995.

El amargo don de la belleza. Barcelona: Planeta, 1996.

Extraño en el paraíso (El peso de la paja III). Barcelona: Planeta, 1998.

Chulas y famosas; o bien, La venganza de Eróstrato. Barcelona: Planeta, 1999.

El arpista ciego. Barcelona: Planeta, 2002.

Further Reading

Chávez-Silverman, Susana, and Librada Hernández, eds. *Reading and Writing the "Ambiente."* Madison, WI: University of Wisconsin Press, 2000.

Ellis, Robert Richmond. *The Hispanic Homograph: Gay Self-Representation in Contemporary Spanish Autobiography*. Urbana, IL: University of Illinois Press, 1997.

Forrest, Gene Steven. "El mundo antagónico de Terenci Moix." *Hispania* 60 (1977): 927–35.

Krauel, Ricardo. *Voces desde el silencio: Heterologías genérico-sexuales en la narrativa española moderna (1875–1975)* Madrid: Libertarias, 2001.

Lucio, Francisco. "Aproximación a la narrativa de Terenci Moix." *Cuadernos Hispanoamericanos* 263–64 (1972): 461–75.

Merlo, Philippe. "Terenci Moix, 'enfant terrible' ou 'enfant prodigue' de la littérature espagnole: À propos de *Venus Bonaparte*." In *Postmodernité et écriture narrative dans l'Espagne contemporaine*, edited by George Tyras. Grenoble: Université Stendhal, 1996.

Smith, Paul Julian. *Laws of Desire: Questions of Homosexuality in Spanish Writing and Film 1960–1990*. Oxford: Clarendon Press, 1992.

Sobrer, Josep Miquel. "Ironic Allegory in Terenci Moix's *El sexe dels angels*." *Bulletin of Hispanic Studies* 75 (1998): 339–56.

MOLLOY, SYLVIA

1938–

Argentinean literary critic and novelist

Sylvia Molloy is a central figure in the North American (as well as European and Latin American) literary milieu. In addition to her work on Latin American writers such as Jorge Luis Borges, she has contributed to the growing field of sexuality studies with books and articles about sexuality and difference in the Hispanic world, including the coedited collection *Hispanism and Homosexualities* (1998). While she is an important figure in the academic world because of her work in literary criticism, it is with her first novel, *En breve cárcel* (translated as *Certificate of Absence*) (1981) that she made her mark as a writer of fiction. *En breve cárcel* is one of the first novels by a Latin American woman to deal overtly with lesbian themes, through its presentation of a first-person lesbian protagonist who is in the process of writing her memoirs and subsequently discovering her identity.

Eroticism is presented as a key factor in identity formation both in the dissolution of static binarisms that is necessary in order for the protagonist to find her lesbian identity and in the linking of language and writing with the body and sexuality.

En breve cárcel is first and foremost a novel about the process of writing. The protagonist is in the process of writing the story of her life (and simultaneously writing herself into being) in a room of indeterminate location (at least until the end). Through her writing, we learn of her childhood as well as two dysfunctional (and often abusive) love affairs.

The novel is divided into two parts, each with a unique structure. Part I sets up dualities: between the narrator and each of her ex-lovers, Renata and Vera; between Renata and Vera themselves; between the narrator and her sister Clara; and between the narrator as writer and written self. Structural binaries are presented as well, including the all-important dichotomy of presence and absence, which is encapsulated in the written word. Thus, when the protagonist writes about Renata, she is aware of Renata's presence within the writing at the same time that she is aware of the way in which the writing signals Renata's "real" absence. Finally, a spatial binary is set up through the opposition of the outside world (which the protagonist views through her window panes) and the inside space of the room in which she appears to be trapped (escaping only through the written word).

Part II of the novel serves as a binary to Part I while also beginning to destruct the dualisms hitherto presented. Molloy begins this process of pluralization through triangularization, liminal dissolution, and both mirroring and fragmentation. The doubles set up in Part I are destabilized by the introduction of a triadic structure. Thus, although relationships are presented in pairs in Part I of the novel, Part II focuses on relationships as triangles. The primary Oedipal triangle of mother/father/daughter is shown to be replicated in the relationship of the narrator and her two lovers, Renata and Vera. It is not through dual opposition that the protagonist will be able to carve out her lesbian identity, but rather in the change and space provided by the rupture of this "third" element.

The binaries presented in Part I are also dissolved through the uniting of two apparently disparate entities. This can be seen most clearly in the linking/dissolution of language and writing to/with the body and sexuality. Thus, the novel is not only a text about the writing of a novel, but also a novel about the writing of the body and the expression of sexuality. The act of writing is both violent and pleasurable, an act on and through language, just as sex is a violent and pleasurable act on and through the body. The uniting of these two binary systems comes about in the text through the repeated image of the hand—an instrument of writing, alimentation, violence, and sexual caresses. In addition, the room in which almost the entire novel takes place becomes a space for these binaries to join together as it provides a meeting place for the present tense of linguistic creation and the past tense of the pain and pleasure of sexuality (the protagonist's past love affairs).

Finally, Molloy adopts the theories of both Lacan and Derrida in order to describe her protagonist's journey toward identity. This is seen through a variety of motifs present in the text, including a proliferation of mirrors and mirror images. However, rather than agreeing with Lacan that the subject must enter the ordered world of the symbolic (moving past the "mirror stage") for a full development or maturation,

she rewrites the symbolic (perhaps melding it with the pre-symbolic) and asserts that only with the subject's acceptance of disorder and Derridean fragmentation can she truly transform herself.

En breve cárcel deals with the presentation and destruction of dualities while positing that language can write into being a stable (if not entirely unified) sexual subject. Through a displacement of a traditional view of dichotomies as discrete entities, Molloy creates a novel that simultaneously writes its lesbian subject into existence paradoxically through the questioning of language, space, place, individual identity, and both presence and absence. Not only is language all-important for the protagonist's identity development in the novel, but her sexuality (tacitly defined as "lesbian") becomes intricately linked to that language. Thus, the protagonist must accept a fragmentation of language and sexuality in order to understand herself and arrive at her self-identity at the end of the novel—a lesbian identity, but one that is neither unified nor necessarily coherent.

Biography

Born in Buenos Aires, Argentina. Grew up speaking English, French, and Spanish in a multilingual household. Received a doctorate in literature at the Sorbonne. Has taught in Spanish programs at the State University of New York/ Buffalo, Vassar, Princeton, Yale, and New York University. Received a fellowship from the National Endowment for the Humanities in 1976, a Guggenheim fellowship in 1984–1987, and a doctorate of humane letters from Tulane and has served as the president of both the Institute of Iberamerican Literature and the Modern Language Association. Has written over 84 essays and articles, as well as several books of literary criticism.

TRACY FERRELL

Selected Works

At Face Value: Autobiographical Writing in Spanish America. 1991.
En breve cárcel, 1981; as *Certificate of Absence*, translated by Daniel Balderston and Sylvia Molloy. 1989.
Hispanism and Homosexualities, coedited with Robert Irwin. 1998.

Further Reading

Boling, Becky. "The Gaze, the Body and the Text in Sylvia Molloy's *En breve cárcel*." *Hispanófila* 123 (May 1998): 73–89.

Kaminsky, Amy. *Reading the Body Politic: Feminist Criticism and Latin American Writers*. Minneapolis: University of Minnesota Press, 1993.

Martínez, Elena M. *Lesbian Voices from Latin America: Breaking Ground*. New York: Garland Publishing, 1996.

Norat, Gisela. "Textual/Sexual Inscription of Lesbian Identity in Sylvia Molloy's *En breve cárcel*." *Monographic Review* 11 (1995): 291–301.

MONK, MARIA

1816/17–c. 1850
Canadian memoirist

The Awful Disclosures of Maria Monk was first published in New York in January 1836. The public eagerly awaited it because it had been puffed some months earlier in the *American Protestant Vindicator*. The hyperbolic anti-Catholic book was an immediate success because of its sensational disclosures of sexual defilement, infanticide, and beatings at the Canadian Hotel Dieu Nunnery. It had sold more than 300,000 copies by 1860 and was second only to *Uncle Tom's Cabin* as a best seller. It has remained in print continuously.

Monk's apocryphal tale differs from typical "ecclesiastical erotic" stories, epitomized by Boccaccio's nymphomaniac nuns in *The Decameron*, Denis Diderot's lesbian title character in *The Nun*, and Rosa Matilda's libidinous title character in *Confessions of the Nun of St. Omer*. Monk's story reflects the contemporaneous nativist literature of Bourne, Cuthbertson, de Ricci, Mahony, and Reed.

Monk's disclosures are sexually coy compared with more traditional erotica. For example, she describes her sexual initiation:

> Father Dufresne called me out, saying, he wished to speak to me. I feared what was his intention; but I dared not disobey. In a private apartment, he treated me in a brutal manner; and, from two other priests, I afterward received similar usage that evening. Father Dufresne afterward appeared again; and I was compelled to remain in company with him until morning. (Chapter 6)

Not only did the nuns service the priests in the adjoining seminary; Monk claims that they were also visited by the 350 priests who lived in the Montreal district. In order to not attract attention in such numbers, the priests accessed the convent via a subterranean passage or a sheltered door, where they rang a concealed bell and then made "a peculiar kind of hissing sound" before they could be admitted (Chapter 9). Though the book shies from explicit sexual detail, it revels in sadistic and masochistic detail. Monk describes a number of torture implements, including a belt worn for self-mortification:

> I had my hands drawn behind my back, a leathern band passed first around my thumbs, then round my hands, and then round my waist and fastened. This was drawn so tight that it cut through the flesh of my thumbs, making wounds, the scars of which still remain. A gag was then forced into my mouths [sic], not indeed so violently as it sometimes was but roughly enough. (Chapter 18)

The worst was a leather cap which was "fitted close to the head, and fastened under the chin with a kind of buckle." The wearer experienced "violent and indescribable [sic] sensation ... like that of a blister, only much more insupportable. ... It would produce such an acute pain as to throw us into convulsions" (Chapter 18).

One of the most brutal passages describes the murder of a nun who rebuffed the priests' advances:

> In an instant [a] bed was thrown upon her. One of the priests ... sprung like a fury first upon it, and stamped

upon it, with all his force. He was speedily followed by the nuns, until there were as many on the bed as could find room, and all did what they could, not only to smother, but to bruise her. Some stood up and jumped upon the poor girl with their feet, some with their knees, and others in different ways seemed to seek how they might best beat the breath out of her body, and mangle it, without coming into direct contact with it, or seeing the effects of their violence. (Chapter 11)

Because children resulted from these illicit liaisons, Monk recounts numerous instances of infanticide:

When [the priest] had baptized the children, they were taken, one after another, by one of the old nuns, in the presence of us all. She pressed her hand upon the mouth and nose of the first, so tight that it could not breathe, and in a few minutes, when the hand was removed, it was dead. (Chapter 16)

The bodies were buried in the basement. According to her book, Monk fled the convent when she discovered she was pregnant and told her story to a sympathetic minister in New York—thus conveniently explaining her illegitimate child.

Not surprisingly, the book attracted considerable attention, and Monk's claims were refuted by various people, including Col. William Stone, a Protestant sympathizer and editor of a mildly anti-Catholic publication, *New York Commercial Advertiser*. He visited the convent and compared it with Monk's description, and when the two didn't tally, he printed a pamphlet exposing Monk as a fraud. Maria Monk had never been a nun, she wasn't Catholic, and she had never resided in the Black Convent. Maria Monk has fostered an industry which still survives in books and on Internet sites today.

Biography

Maria Monk was born to a Protestant family in St. Johns, Quebec. She was an uncontrollable child and was admitted to Magdalen Asylum for Wayward Girls in Montreal in an effort to reform her; apparently, at the time, she was working as a prostitute. Her behavior did not improve and she was asked to leave. At 18 and pregnant, she formed an alliance with William K. Hoyte (or Hoyt), an ardent anti-Catholic. She and Hoyte went to New York City, where they associated with a group of Protestant

sympathizers, among whom were Rev. George Bourne, who wrote Monk's *Awful Disclosures* (and had earlier written *Lorette*, another purported nunnery exposé), and Rev. John J. Slocum, author of *Further Disclosures of Maria Monk*. Monk left Hoyte and started a relationship with Slocum. In 1837 she ran away to Philadelphia with an unidentified man. While there she met William Sleigh, author of *An Exposure of Maria Monk*, and gave birth to another illegitimate child. Completely discredited, Monk drifted from man to man and returned to prostitution. She was arrested for pickpocketing her male companion and died in prison on Welfare Island, New York, aged 33.

TONI JOHNSON-WOODS

Editions

The Awful Disclosures of Maria Monk as Exhibited in a Narrative of Her Life and Sufferings during a Residence of Five Years as a Novice and Two Years as a Black Nun in the Hotel Dieu Nunnery in Montreal. New York: Howe & Bates, 1836.

Awful Disclosures by Maria Monk of the Hotel Dieu Nunnery of Montreal. Whitefish, MT: Kessinger Publishing, 2003.

Further Reading

Anon. *Awful exposure of the atrocious plot formed by certain individuals against the clergy and nuns of lower Canada, through the intervention of Maria Monk.* Montreal: Jones and Company, 1836.

Billington, Ray Allen. *The Protestant Crusade, 1800–1860: A Study of the Origins of American Nativism.* New York: Macmillan, 1964.

Bourne, George. *Lorette. The History of Louise, Daughter of a Canadian Nun: Exhibiting the Interior of Female Convent.* New York: Wm. A. Mercein, 1833.

Buntline, Ned. *The Beautiful Nun.* Philadelphia: Paterson, 1866.

Culbertson, Rosamond. *Rosamond; or, A Narrative of the Captivity and Sufferings of an American Female under the Popish Priests.* Introduction and annotation by Samuel B Smith. New York: Leavitt, 1836.

DE Ricci, Scipione. *Female Convents, Secrets of Nunneries Disclosed. Compiled from the autograph manuscripts by [L.J.A.] de Potter.* New York: Appleton, 1834.

Ewens, Mary Ann. *The Role of the Nun in Nineteenth Century America.* New York: Arno, 1978.

Griffin, Susan M. "Awful Disclosures: Women's Evidence in the Escaped Nun's Tale." *PMLA* [Proceedings of the Modern Language Association of America] (1996): 93–107.

McCarthy, Maureen A. *The Rescue of True Womanhood: Convents and Anti-Catholicism in 1830s America.*

Ph.D. thesis, Rutgers University, New Brunswick, NJ, 1996.

Mourão, Manuela. *Altered Habits: Reconsidering the Nun in Fiction*. Gainesville: University Press of Florida, 2002.

Mahony, Dorah. *Six Months in a House of Correction. Or, The narrative of Dorah Mahony, who was under the influence of the Protestants about a year, and an inmate of the house of correction, in Leverett St., Boston, Massachusetts, nearly six months in the year 18–. With some preliminary suggestions by the Committee of Publication*. Boston: Benjamin B. Mussey, 1835.

Matilda, Rosa [Charlotte Dacre]. *Confessions of the Nun of St. Omer*. London: J. F. Hughes, 1805. Reprint, New York: Arno Press, 1972.

Schultz, Nancy Lusignan. *Veil of Fear: Nineteenth-Century Convent Tales by Rebecca Reed and Maria Monk*. West Lafayette, IN: NotaBell, c. 1999.

Reed, Rebecca. *Six Months in a Convent. Or, The Narrative of Rebecca Theresa Reed, who was under the influence of the Roman Catholics about two years, and an inmate of the Ursuline Convent on Mount Benedict, Charlestown, Mass., nearly six months, in the years 1831–2*. Boston: Russell, Odiore and Metcalf, 1835.

Mrs. Sherwood. *The Nun*. Princeton, NJ: M. Baker, 1834.

Sleigh, William Wilcocks. *An exposure of Maria Monks pretended abduction and conveyance to the Catholic asylum, Philadelphia by six priests on the night of August 15, 1837: with numerous extraordinary incidents during her residence of six days in this city*. Philadelphia: T. K. & P. G. Collins Printers, 1837.

Slocum, Rev. J.J. *Further Disclosures by Maria Monk, concerning Hotel Dieu Nunnery of Montreal; also, Her Visit to Nun's island, and Disclosures Concerning that Secret Retreat*. New York: Leavitt Lord and Coy, 1836.

St. John Eckel, L. *Maria Monk's Daughter*. New York: United States Publishing Company, 1874.

Stone, William Leete. *Maria Monk and the Nunnery of the Hotel Dieu, Being an Account of a Visit to the Convents of Montreal, and Refutation of the "Awful Disclosures."* New York: Howe & Bates, 1836.

Sullivan, Rebecca. "A Wayward from the Wilderness: Maria Monk's Awful Disclosures and the Feminization of Lower Canada in the Nineteenth Century." *Essays on Canadian Writing* (1997): 201–22.

Thompson, Ralph. *The Maria Monk Affair*. New York: n.p., 1934.

MONSTERS

When we think of monsters and the erotic, we probably call to mind Fuseli's famous painting *The Nightmare*, which pictures an incubus of medieval European folklore crouching on the bosom of a sleeping woman; or perhaps we call to mind the equally disturbing image of a cannibalistic Donestre inserting a man's forearm into his mouth. But just as the human subject has changed over time, so too have the monsters it creates. In fact, if we were to chart what might be called the vicissitudes of the "I" from the ancient world to the modern, we would necessarily be charting the vicissitudes of our fears and desires or what we find monstrous and what we find erotic.

Although the shape of our fears and desires has altered over time, what has remained constant is the tension that exists or the ambivalence of the relationship between what we fear and what we desire. As early as Hesiod's *Theogony*, for example, we see a poet establishing a causal link between a monstrous act and its erotic result in the story of Aphrodite's birth. As Hesiod tells it, when Great Heaven, desirous of love, spread himself over Earth, his son Kronos ambushed him with a metal reaping hook and cut off his genitals. From the blood that splashed onto the earth came the Great Giants, a race of huge and powerful beings who were, properly speaking, neither men nor gods, and the Furies, hideous creatures who hunted down and exacted retribution from those who spilled kindred blood; and from the castrated genitals, which were flung into the ocean and mingled with sea foam, came the beautiful goddess Aphrodite. Born of Great Heaven's bloody genitals, Aphrodite represents the powerful and often destructive force of sexual desire, the monstrously erotic fruit of mutilation and violence. In Hesiod's geneology of the gods, then, not only do we see the monstrous and the erotic arising from one source and one act, and thus coupled as "twin" siblings, but we also see in narrative form the antecedent of what will later take a theoretical form in the modern psychoanalytic principle whereby castration (or lack) is said to give rise to desire.

In Homer's *Odyssey*, we again find the monstrous and the erotic rubbing elbows, as Odysseus makes his way back from the battlefields of Troy to the island of Ithaca. During his ten-year journey homeward, Odysseus confronts obstacles that take either the monstrous forms of Charybdis, a whirlpool that sucks men to their death, and Scylla, a six-headed monster that chews men up with row upon row of sharp teeth, or the erotic forms of Circê and Calypso, beautiful nymphs who trap Odysseus in their beds. But whether it is the biological "big death" offered by a monster or the metaphorical "little death" offered by a nymph, the monstrous and the erotic are structurally the same in Homer's narrative. That is, both operate as a lure that seduces Odysseus into delaying his return to Ithaca and thus to his duties as husband, father, and king. Perhaps this is why the monstrous and the erotic are often considered taboo, for they distract us from the duties laid out for us as members of a social community.

By the time we reach Sophocles's Theban plays, we see emerging a new type of monster, man himself. While the Sphinx, a hybrid creature often pictured as having the face and torso of a woman, the body of a mountain lion, and the wings of an eagle, is the ostensible monster in Greek myth, under Sophocles's dramatic influence, the city of Thebes is forced to recognize the murderous and incestuous Oedipus as the real threat to its citizens' welfare. Oedipus not only commits regicide in committing parricide, but also couples with his mother, producing "monstrous" offspring who are both his children and his siblings. With Sophocles, then, the causal link between the monstrous and the erotic becomes the inverse of Hesiod's, for in *Oedipus Rex* it is an erotic act that produces monstrous fruit. Because the offspring of Oedipus defy normal classification, falling as they do under two categories that do not generally overlap, they operate just as monsters do, collapsing biological and sociological categories and signaling by their unnatural birth the onslaught of social crisis and civic disarray. This, in any event, is how the ancient world understood the monster.

It was a world less troubled than the modern by the appearance of monsters because monsters were seen as celestial signs or portents, and thus they were always readable, always pregnant with allegorical meaning. In fact, if we look into the etymology of the word *monster,* we find a connection to Latin words such as *monstrare,* meaning to show or expose; *monstrum,* that which teaches; *monere,* to warn; and *demonstrare,* to point out, indicate, show, or prove.

It would be foolish to say that Sophocles betrays a modern sensibility, but he gestures toward a post-Enlightenment understanding of the monster by placing Oedipus at the center of his drama and making only passing reference to the Sphinx. For modernity's monster is no longer a mere prop with which a hero such as Odysseus shows off his prowess but the site around which all energy circulates, especially erotic energy. Modernity's monster is nothing if not sexual, and we have as proof the creatures populating the works of writers such as Coleridge, Keats, Hawthorne, Poe, Le Fanu, and Stevenson. By the time Freud makes use of Sophocles to establish one of the most fundamental concepts of psychoanalysis (the Oedipus complex), Bram Stoker is creating the most erotic of monsters, Count Dracula. Not only is Stoker's vampire more sensual and potent than the men who track him down, but he also liberates and exalts sensuality in the matronly women belonging to his Victorian enemies. It is hardly a coincidence that Stoker's *Dracula* appeared just shortly before Freud's *The Interpretation of Dreams,* for many scholars read the vampire, and the modern monster in general, in psychoanalytic terms: i.e., as a return of the repressed in disguised form. In this respect, monsters operate in much the same way dreams do, allowing us to express unconscious desires that we think are unacceptable while at the same time concealing them.

BECKY MCLAUGHLIN

Further Reading

Brisson, Luc. *Sexual Ambivalence*. Berkeley and Los Angeles, CA: University of California Press, 2002.

Cohen, Jeffrey Jerome, ed. *Monster Theory: Reading Culture*. Minneapolis, MN: University of Minnesota Press, 1996.

———. *Of Giants: Sex, Monsters, and the Middle Ages*. Minneapolis, MN: University of Minnesota Press.

Deutsch, Helen, and Felicity Nussbaum, eds. *Defects: Engendering the Modern Body*. Ann Arbor, MI: University of Michigan Press, 2000.

Foucault, Michel. *Abnormal: Lectures at the College de France 1974–1975*. Paris: Picador, 2003.

Gillmore, David D. *Monsters: Evil Beings, Mythical Beasts, and All Manner of Imaginary Terrors*. Philadelphia, PA: University of Pennsylvania Press, 2002.

Halberstam, Judith. *Skin Shows: Gothic Horror and the Technology of Monsters*. Durham, NC: Duke University Press, 1995.

Ingebretsen, Edward J. *At Stake: Monsters and the Rhetoric of Fear in Public Culture*. Chicago, IL: University of Chicago Press, 2003.

Jones, Michael E. *Monsters from the Id: The Rise of Horror in Fiction and Film*. Dallas, TX: Spense Publishing Company, 2000.

Paré, Ambroise. *On Monsters and Marvels*. Chicago, IL: University of Chicago Press, 1995.

Remshardt, Ralf. *Staging the Savage God: The Grotesque in Performance*. Carbondale, IL: Southern Illinois University Press, 2004.

Shildrick, Magrit. *Embodying the Monster: Encounters with the Vulnerable Self*. Thousand Oaks, CA: Sage Publications, 2004.

Sudan, Rajani. *Fair Exotics: Xenophobic Subjects in English Literature, 1720–1850*. Philadelphia, PA: University of Pennsylvania Press, 2002.

Tiffany, Grace. *Erotic Beasts and Social Monsters: Shakespeare, Jonson, and Comic Androgyny*. Newark, DE: University of Delaware Press, 1995.

Todd, Dennis. *Imagining Monsters: Miscreations of the Self in Eighteenth-Century England*. Chicago, IL: University of Chicago Press, 1995.

MONTERO, MAYRA

1953–

Cuban-born novelist and journalist

As a novelist, Montero is known best for her fascination with pan-Caribbean culture and her erotic writing. Her knowledge of Caribbean history and religion was already evident in her first novel, *La trenza de la hermosa luna* [*The Braid of the Beautiful Moon*] (1987), a beautifully rendered tale of an exile's return to Haiti after twenty years as a wandering sailor and of the transformation that leads him from disillusionment to passionate commitment to action against the Duvalier regime. The novel marked Montero as the talent to watch in Caribbean writing, a promise that she has fulfilled repeatedly in the period since *La trenza de la hermosa luna* first dazzled critics. In *Del rojo de tu sombra* [*The Red of His Shadow*] (1992), she unveils the vicious and corrupt politics and African-derived religious traditions that link the Dominican Republic and Haiti through the disturbing tale of the contest of wills between the leaders of two Vodou societies—Mistress Zulé, an inexperienced but gifted priestess, and Similá Bolesseto, a notoriously violent and devious priest—and the disastrous impact on their religious communities, composed mostly of Haitians who have

crossed the border into the Dominican Republic to cut sugar cane in slavery-like conditions. In *Tú, la oscuridad* [*In the Palm of Darkness*] (1995), Montero tells the story of an American herpetologist who, with the aid of his Haitian guide, is on a quest for an elusive and threatened blood frog, extinct everywhere but on a dangerous, eerie mountain near Port-au-Prince. In the volatile and bloody setting of the Haitian mountains, controlled by violent thugs, through her weaving together the stories and vastly different worldviews of her two protagonists, Montero uncovers a new and haunting postcolonial space built upon the conflict between a scientific and an animistic worldview: the extinction of species due to a collapsing environment; the troubled landscape of Haiti, peopled with zombies and other frightening, otherworldly creatures; political corruption and violence; and religious turmoil.

Montero's concerns with Caribbean spirituality, particularly as represented by the Afro-Caribbean religious practices that have been at the heart of so much of her fiction, maintain their centrality in her 1998 novel *Como un mensajero tuyo* [*As Your Messenger*]. Narrated by a young Cuban woman of Chinese and African ancestry, it relates the secret events that transpired when, during a series of performances in

924

Cuba in 1920, legendary tenor Enrico Caruso fled for his life into the streets of Havana after a bomb exploded in the theater where he was rehearsing Verdi's *Aida*. Montero has also published *El capitán de los dormidos* [*The Captain of the Sleepers*] (2002) and *Vana illusion* [*Vain Illusion*] (2003). *El capitán de los dormidos* builds on the legend of Amelia Earhart through the story, set in 1950, of a young boy growing up in the island of Vieques. His father is fighting against the government in the nationalist insurrection while his mother dies, and he must depend on his friendship with an old American aviator to transcend his reality. *Vana illusion* is the fictionalized account of the life of Puerto Rican concert pianist and composer Narciso Figueroa.

Montero also established herself during the 1990s as the Caribbean's foremost writer of erotic fiction. Her two erotic novels, *La última noche que pasé contigo* [*The Last Night I Spent with You*] (1991) and *Púrpura profundo* [*Deep Purple*] (2000), fuse two deep interests: the nature of erotic desire and its connection to Caribbean classical and popular music. For the former novel, she was a finalist for the 1991 Sonrisa Vertical Prize, given in Barcelona by the prestigious Tusquets Press for the best erotic novel written in Spanish in a given year; for the latter novel, she won the prize in 2000.

La última noche que pasé contigo, a just-so-slightly parodic erotic tale, tells of the encounters of a late-middle-age couple suffering from empty-nest syndrome who look to a Caribbean cruise as a way out of their boredom with each other. Their sexual adventures in the highly eroticized Caribbean of the tourist imagination play against the rhythms and sentimental universe of the Latin American *bolero*, from the classic "La última noche que pasé contigo," which provides the novel's title, to the more contemporary variations of the genre by Dominican star Juan Luis Guerra. The various interwoven narratives grow increasingly explicit in their depictions of erotic behavior, as the main characters penetrate the Caribbean space and shed their inhibitions, bringing themselves as close to sexual ecstasy as to self-destruction. The novel has been praised by critics as much for the rich profusion of its sexual imagery as for the dark humor and subtlety with which it exposes cultural clichés and the often absurd connections between desire and death.

Montero continues to explore the connection between music and eroticism in her award-winning erotic novel *Púrpura profundo*. Its narrator, Agustín Cabán, a music critic who has hoarded the memories of his erotic adventures like a scrupulous miser, is persuaded by his editor to narrate his varied and complex sexual life in vivid detail. Featured prominently in them are Virginia Tuten, a beautiful mulatta from Antigua who handled her violin like an eroticized body, and Clint Verret, a pianist who took him to the verge of homosexual love. *Púrpura profundo* differs from Montero's earlier erotic novel in its single narrative perspective (*La última noche* has multiple points of view and incorporates multiple types of texts, particularly letters), which allows Montero to delve deeper into her narrator's psychology and build a more vivid and more deeply etched main character.

Biography

Mayra Montero was born in Havana, Cuba, in 1952, but has lived in Puerto Rico since the mid-1960s. She studied journalism in Puerto Rico and Mexico and began her writing career as a newspaper correspondent in Central America and the Caribbean. She continues to write for *El Nuevo Día*, a San Juan newspaper. In 1981 she published her first collection of short stories, *Ventitrés y una tortuga* [Twenty-three and a Turtle] and has gained increasing recognition for her fiction ever since.

LIZABETH PARAVISINI-GEBERT

Selected Works

Como un mensajero tuyo. Barcelona: Tusquets, 1998; as *The Messenger*, translated by Edith Grossman, New York: HarperFlamingo, 1999.

El capitán de los dormidos. Barcelona: Tusquets, 2002; as *The Captain of the Sleepers,* translated by Edith Grossman, New York: Farrar, Straus, & Giroux, 2005.

Púrpura profundo. Barcelona: Tusquets, 2000; as *Deep Purple*, translated by Edith Grossman, New York: HarperCollins, 2003.

Del rojo de tu sombra. Barcelona: Tusquets, 1992; as *The Red of His Shadow*, translated by Edith Grossman, New York: HarperCollins, 2001.

Tú, la oscuridad. Barcelona: Tusquets, 1995; as *In the Palm of Darkness*, translated by Edith Grossman, New York: HarperCollins, 1997.

La última noche que pasé contigo. Barcelona: Tusquets, 1991; as *The Last Night I Spent with You*, translated by Edith Grossman, New York: HarperCollins, 2000.

La trenza de la hermosa luna. Barcelona: Anagrama, 1987.

Vana ilusión: Las memorias noveladas de Narciso Figueroa. San Juan: Ediciones Callejón, 2003.

Veintitrés y una tortuga. San Juan: Instituto de Cultura, 1981.

Further Reading

García-Calderón, Myrna. "*La última noche que pasé contigo* y el discurso erótico caribeño." *South Eastern Latin Americanist* 38 (1994): 26–34.

Lauer, A. Robert. "La representación del deseo masculino en *La última noche que pasé contigo* de Mayra Montero." *Entorno* 43 (1997): 45–48.

León-Vera, Antonio. "Mayra Montero: Las islas del deseo." *Torre: Revista de la Universidad de Puerto Rico* 10 (1996): 183–201.

Manzotti, Vilma. "Mayra Montero y su ritual del deseo desterritorializado." *Alba de América* 14 (1996): 363–71.

Piña, Cristina. "Mayra Montero y los topoi de la erótica masculina revisitados por una mujer." *Cuadernos Hispanoamericanos* 659 (2005): 7–15.

Rosario-Vélez, Jorge. "Somos un sueño imposible: Clandestinidad sexual del bolero en *La última noche que pasé contigo* de Mayra Montero?" *Revista Iberoamericana* 68 (2002): 67–77.

MORATÍN, NICOLÁS FERNÁNDEZ DE

1737–1780
Spanish poet and dramatist

The *Arte de putear* or *Arte de las putas*

The *Arte de putear* [*Art of Whoring*] or *Arte de las putas* [*Art of Prostitutes*] is an extensive mock-didactic poem in four cantos probably composed in the early 1770s and, like all erotic poetry in eighteenth-century Spain, not printed at the time due to the Spanish Inquisition, hence the uncertainty concerning the author's preferred title. Though Moratín's poem circulated only in manuscript, it fell into the hands of the Inquisition and was banned in 1777, remaining unpublished until an anonymous edition of 1898. Comprising some 2,000 hendecasyllabic lines, Moratín's work echoes Ovid's *Ars amatoria*, though directed to the impecunious young man who seeks to satisfy his sexual appetite in safety and with the minimum expenditure of money, not the man in pursuit of love. The poem is a curious miscellany centered on eighteenth-century Madrid, providing the reader with a wealth of scientific, cultural, and social information on sexuality at the time. The use of the didactic format allows for multiple digressions and contrasts of tone, features which have provoked a variety of sometimes contradictory interpretations from the work's readers.

In Canto I, Moratín justifies his topic by contrasting the poetic treatment of sexuality with the epic's traditional high-culture topic of war. Taking a sideswipe at Catholic morality, he points out that were the world to heed the Church's admonition to abstain from sex, humanity would come to an end. Moratín claims as his moral starting point that whatever nature ordains must be right, going on to justify brothels and their legalization. He nevertheless claims that there is no pleasure equal to that enjoyed by those in love. Ecclesiastical hypocrisy is exposed by Moratín in the constant examples of clerics who are described seeking sexual pleasure. To those who would condemn his poem he points out that he only provides a mirror to life, insisting that his work serves the purpose of giving useful advice.

Cantos 2 and 3 deal directly with Madrid's prostitutes, and Moratín recommends the use of condoms to avoid sexually transmitted diseases, providing a brief excursus on the condom, its origins and history. Admitting that wealthy men will always manage to attract willing sexual partners, Moratín offers advice to the rest. He lists the parts of Madrid where prostitutes and other women willing to have sex are to be found: the terminus points of provincial carriage routes being among the best. In a manner not dissimilar to published guides in late-eighteenth-century London (cf. *Harris's List of Covent Garden*

Ladies), Moratín names individual prostitutes, their favored haunts and outstanding features. These sometimes involve details of physical characteristics and sexual attributes. The variety of prostitutes is evident, and none is singled out for negative comment. Other likely meeting places are pointed out, such as the public masked balls, theatrical entertainments, bullfights, fairs, and street spectacles. The author seems to know his way around and to be well acquainted with a host of women, some of whom receive his personal seal of approval.

The final, fourth canto treats women who, while not prostitutes, may often prove to be willing sexual partners. At this point the male art of seduction is invoked. Street vendors who come from the countryside to sell their produce in the capital will often lend themselves to sex, as will household servant girls. Moratín, following a standard technique, reviews the characteristics of women from the various regions of Spain, seeming to award the prize to those from Aragon. He suggests that the female sexual appetite is no smaller than the male, but faithful to his male target audience, he offers advice on how to make oneself attractive to women in order to achieve seduction. He argues that women are attracted by various features in a potential lover: an athletic body or fine physique may be no more effective than a fine mind or literary and cultural appeal.

Moratín's poem conveys a festive, playful spirit in spite of the economic imperative to obtain sexual pleasure with the minimum of expense. The variety of sexual pleasure for the young male is emphasized, as are the arts of prostitutes in providing satisfaction. Contemporary descriptions of sexual activity and attitudes are contextualized against the historical record, evoking comparisons with episodes from the Bible, the documentary and literary record of classical Greece and Rome, and more recent European and Spanish history. Traditional moralizing is ridiculed, and the acceptance of an apparently biological imperative with a consequent absence of traditional constraints comes across forcefully.

The Anacreontic "Éramos inocentes"

The anonymous anacreontic ode "We Were Innocent," discovered by Francisco Aguilar Piñal in 1980 in a manuscript collection in Madrid's Historical Municipal Library, can also be reliably attributed to Moratín. The heptasyllabic lines, in assonantal rhyme, allow a light, swift rhythmic pulse to carry the narrative forward. It presents the first sexual experience between the fifteen-year-old narrator and his thirteen-year-old girlfriend in a garden setting, viewed in retrospect. Their initial innocence is evoked as he, affected by the summer heat, falls asleep by a fountain, to be awoken by Dorisa, who has been stung by a bee. She raises her skirt to point out the intimate location of the sting, revealing her genitalia in the process, a sight which the narrator has never before seen. In delicate language (a constant of the poem) he describes what his eyes behold, with the innocence of youth mediated by the experience of maturity, re-creating the novelty of what his body then felt and how his mind reacted. In the hope of reducing the pain, Dorisa asks him to rub the sting, but the sensitivity of the location causes her to become sexually aroused. Not knowing how to proceed, the narrator invokes nature, which encourages him to caress her skin and then kiss her mouth. On his touching her breasts, she reacts with delight, and they proceed to exchange kisses and caresses as their bodies move excitedly, overwhelmed by pleasurable sensations. The poem ends with the narrator recalling that as a consequence of this first sexual encounter, when Dorisa wants to initiate physical intimacy she coyly pretends to have been stung by a bee.

Biography

Born into a family with a tradition of service in the royal household, where he also served, Nicolás Moratín achieved fame during his lifetime as a poet and dramatist. His poetry covers the full range of contemporary genres, among which the anacreontic odes rehabilitated the form for his generation, evoking the sensuality of many of the classical models.

PHILIP DEACON

Editions

Arte de las putas. Poema, Madrid: 1898; edited by Manuel Fernández Nieto, Madrid: Siro, 1977.

Arte de putear. Edited by Isabel Colón Calderón and Gaspar Garrote Bernal. Málaga: Ediciones Aljibe, 1995.

Aguilar Piñal, Francisco. "Moratín y Cadalso." *Revista de Literatura* 42 (1980), 149–50.

Further Reading

Cerezo, José Antonio. "Nicolás Fernández de Moratín." In *Literatura erótica en España: Repertorio de obras 1519–1936*. Madrid: Ollero y Ramos, 2001.

Colón Calderón, Isabel, and Gaspar Garrote Bernal. "Introducción." In Calderón and Bernal, *Arte de putear*, 7–91.

Cristóbal, Vicente. "Nicolás Fernández de Moratín, recreador del *Arte de amar*." *Dicenda* 5 (1986): 73–87.

Deacon, Philip. "El cortejo y Nicolás Fernández de Moratín." *Boletín de la Biblioteca Menéndez Pelayo* 55 (1979): 85–95.

————. "Nicolás Fernández de Moratín: Tradición e innovación." *Revista de Literatura* 42 (1980): 99–120.

Gies, David T. "'El cantor de las doncellas' y las rameras madrileñas. Nicolás Fernández de Moratín en *El arte de las putas*." *Actas del VI Congreso Internacional de Hispanistas*. Roma: Bulzoni, 1980, I: 320–23.

————. *Nicolás Fernández de Moratín*. Boston: Twayne, 1979.

Glendinning, Nigel. *History of Spanish Literature: The Eighteenth Century*. London: Benn, 1972.

Helman, Edith. "The Elder Moratín and Goya." *Hispanic Review* 23 (1955): 219–30; Spanish translation in *Jovellanos y Goya*, 219–35. Madrid: Taurus, 1970.

MORAVIA, ALBERTO

1907–1990
Italian novelist and short story writer

The characters of Moravia are often haunted by a feeling of lassitude which prevents them from living (they doubt whether their actions have any sense), whence their difficulty in transforming and evolving their lives. Moravia's stories are thus not sustained by the logic typical of a *bildungsroman* (or coming-of-age novel) as is common in English-language literature, but by a principal idea (angst, lassitude) dominating the text and expressing the difficulty man has in grasping a reality which escapes him.

In this aesthetic-narrative context, eroticism plays an important role, but it should be noted that the stories are generally not centered around a sexual thematic. Except, perhaps, in *L'uomo che guarda* [*The Voyeur*], a novel which recounts the obsessions of a voyeur haunted by an image from a lesbian poem of Mallarme's describing a vulva as resembling the pale and pink interior of a mollusk. However, for Moravia, sexuality is a fundamental reality which makes an extremely important contribution to man's existence. Because of this, his works were placed on the *Index librorum prohibitorum* by the Roman Catholic Church in 1952 because of their potential content as "lascivious and obscene things." And some critics even think that the erotic dimension of his work prevented him from being awarded the Nobel Prize.

A novelist concerned with existential agitation much like Dostoevsky (whom he admired) and his contemporaries Camus and Sartre, Moravia used eroticism in his early novels as a psychological resource for expressing the reality of the life of his characters (*Gli indifferenti*, 1929; *Agostino*, 1944). This eroticism accounts for much in giving a true-to-life effect to his characters, especially in *La noia* [*Boredom*], a novel in which eroticism symbolizes a vital life force. But nevertheless this life force is susceptible of being turned into a morbid impulse: in *L'attenzione* (as *The Lie*), the protagonist, Francesco, has sex with a prostitute whose body is compared to a corpse.

From the 1970s onward, a special erotic modality, which was already hinted at in earlier works, becomes more and more pronounced in the author's work: scopophilia. One can even affirm that this voyeuristic impulse is the most essential element of Moravia's eroticism. These stories often present male characters who take pleasure in secretly watching naked female bodies as if this sort of contemplation were necessary both to give birth to and to accomplish their desire. The ultimate aim of this attitude is to reveal what is hidden: the vagina, which is often minutely described, e.g., "a cyclamen crack" (*La Cosa e altri racconti* [*The Fetish and Other Stories*]), "a petite vertical mouth with well defined red lips" (*La donna-leopardo* [*The Leopard Woman*]).

Corresponding to masculine voyeurism there is also feminine exhibitionism, which seeks to attract the looks and desires of men. In *L'uomo che guarda*, women voluntarily exhibit their bodies: Silvia, for instance, masturbates in front of her husband in a public bar, bent slightly backward in order to better reveal her vulva, while asking him to give names to her pubic hair, e.g. "a frightened pussy," "a rooster's crest," "the rising sun." In *La donna-leopardo*, Ada doesn't want to betray her husband and is content to display herself before her putative lover; nevertheless, her vulva remains hidden by a large amount of pubic hair. These virtual contacts incontestably symbolize the difficulty of amorous relations between the two parties. If women are the objects of masculine imagination, mixing the real and the imaginary, at the same time their desires are often incomprehensible and their characters often impenetrable. As for their physical appearance, it is often a mixture of voluptuous and underdeveloped attributes: small busts together with large asses or vice-versa. In general, once again Moravia can be placed in a tradition, one deriving from Dante and Beatrice, who makes love a sad quest much more than a reciprocal relationship.

His novel *Il viaggio a Roma* [*Journey to Rome*] gives an explanation of the importance of the voyeuristic regard. The protagonist, Mario, recalls a scene from his childhood when he saw his mother make love with an unknown man and during which their eyes met momentarily. Occasionally he sees this type of maternal look in the eyes of women; but most importantly, the memory of this scene leads him to allow himself to be seduced by his father's mistress, thus to repeat the scene as a simulacrum of incestuous desire.

The fact that seeing, desiring, and having orgasms form a continuity in Moravia's stories is related to the nature of narrative literature, which is often a modality of making us see some things that are hidden. The narrator of *L'uomo che guarda*, a professor of literature, explains this very clearly at the beginning of the novel by referring to the work of Proust: the novelist makes us see what no one could see unless he is really a voyeur.

Biography

Alberto Moravia was born Alberto Pincherle in Rome. He excels at a tight narrative style which, while emphasizing concentrated action more than description, permits a focusing on the intensity of an experience rather than on the orderly unfolding of the plot. Moravia belongs to the Italian narrative tradition, principally consisting of short works, of Buzatti, Pirandello, and Pavese.

MICHEL ERMAN

Selected Works

La noia. Milan: Bompiani, 1960; as *Boredom*, New York: New York Review of Books, 2004.

L'attenzione. Milan: Bompiani, 1965; as *The Lie*, New York: Panther, 1969.

La vita interiore . Milan: Bompiani, 1978; as *The Time of Indifference,* South Royalton, VT: Steerforth Press, 2000.

La Cosa e altri racconti. Milan: Bompiani, 1983; as *The Fetish and Other Stories,* Westport, CT: Greenwood Press, 1976.

L'uomo che guarda. Milan: Bompiani, 1985; as *The Voyeur*, London: Secker and Warburg, 1986.

Il viaggio a Roma. Milan: Bompiani, 1988; as *Journey to Rome*, London: Secker and Warburg, 1990.

La donna-leopardo. Milan: Bompiani, 1991.

MURASAKI SHIKIBU

c. 973–c.1015
Japanese novelist

The Tale of Genji

The Tale of Genji, by Murasaki Shikibu, is the most highly regarded work of narrative fiction in all of Japanese literature. It revolves around the emotional repercussions of the sexual liaisons of several members of the imperial court, but does so without including explicit descriptions of physical intimacy. The work opens with an account of the emperor's unseemly exclusive passion for one woman of rather low rank, Kiritsubo. The jealousy this ignites in the emperor's other consorts is less a matter of personal feeling than a reflection of the fact that the emperor was expected to bestow his affections according to the political value of his various women. Aristocratic families strove to marry their daughters to emperors in the hope of becoming maternally related to the imperial line. In fact, that is what lies behind the creation of the tale itself. Its author, known as Murasaki Shikibu, was invited to live at court in the service of Empress Akiko with a view to making Akiko's quarters the kind of lively and engaging place to which an emperor would be drawn.

Genji, like his father, behaves according to the dictates of his heart rather than out of political ambition. This fact and his physical beauty, many artistic talents, and impeccably good taste signify that he is an admirable character in the world of the text. In his youth Genji seeks out a variety of romantic entanglements and is attracted to a fairly wide range of women, but has only a chilly relationship with his official wife, who is several years older than he. Even in his mature years he is unable to resist the allure of the prospect of surprising beauty and elegance. The last quarter of the work examines the romantic adventures of Genji's putative son and his grandson, and does so in greater depth while focusing on a smaller number of characters. The tale stops without any particular sense of resolution for these troubled figures.

Major themes of *The Tale of Genji* are set forth in chapter 2, when a few young men spend a rainy night discussing the qualities they seek in a wife and describe their expectations of women of the various ranks in their hierarchical society. This is where Genji first gets the notion that there may be hidden beauties tucked away in unexpected places. The stories these young men share also reveal a double standard whereby men may freely engage in several amorous affairs simultaneously, while women are expected to be at least relatively faithful to a man, but may enjoy multiple affairs if they do so sequentially. Another feature of the social system in which these characters operated was that a man tended to marry for the career opportunities available through his wife's father's connections. Thus, women without influential male relatives had dim prospects.

Once Genji is married to the daughter of the Minister of the Right, an event described at the end of chapter 1, his career prospects are secure, even after she dies in childbirth. Genji's relationship with his father-in-law is more important than that between Genji and his wife, and his father-in-law is inclined to tolerate Genji's sexual adventures, as long as Genji treats his daughter with respect. The first such adventure is with Utsusemi, the young wife of a middle-ranking older man. While visiting as a guest of her stepson, Genji sneaks into Utsusemi's quarters and spends the night with her. An attendant considers intervening but acquiesces to avoid attracting attention to a situation that is already embarrassing. While dialogue between Genji and Utsusemi is recounted, their physical actions are left vague. Most scholars suggest that sexual intercourse is to be presumed. Utsusemi is at first frightened, then angry, and finally distressed. Genji tries to win her affection with romantic words, but Utsusemi refuses to be placated. She is described as like bamboo: bent, but unbreakable. This metaphor might plausibly be understood to mean that penetration did not occur, but it might also be taken to refer to her will rather than her body. Afterward Genji longs for another meeting and is frustrated by her reluctance even to correspond with him. She regrets that her marriage makes an affair with Genji inappropriate. As consolation Genji takes her younger brother under his wing, and then into his bed. When Genji attempts another meeting with Utsusemi, he finds himself accidentally alone with a different woman. He suavely seduces this woman instead, partly to avoid an awkward situation, partly because this woman is attractive and he enjoys an adventure.

As a young man Genji is also involved in a relationship with someone of equal rank, the widow of the former crown prince. The text does not describe his courtship of Lady Rokujo; it merely suggests that Genji pursued her largely because she represented a challenge, although he acknowledges that her elegance is very impressive. Lady Rokujo, however, becomes deeply attached to Genji, and when humiliated by his wife and Genji himself, her anger and jealousy are so intense that her spirit, of its own accord, leaves her body and attacks her rivals. One of these rivals is Yugao, a hidden treasure of the sort foreshadowed in the rainy night conversation. Quite unlike his aloof wife, the difficult Rokujo, and the resistant Utsusemi, Yugao is experienced but docile, shy but affectionate. Having fallen deeply in love, Genji neglects his obligations at court to spend uninterrupted time with her at a deserted villa. Vulnerable in this lonely place, Yugao dies by spirit possession, and Genji is devastated. In the course of his recovery from an illness brought on by this shock and grief, Genji discovers the young Murasaki, who strikingly resembles her aunt, Fujitsubo. As adults, men and women of the aristocracy did not mingle freely, but as a child Genji had been able to meet Fujitsubo, the emperor's consort who resembles Genji's mother and replaced her in his father's affections. Unlike Kiritsubo, Fujitsubo has the appropriate rank and family connections to thrive at court and eventually rises to the rank of empress. As a youth Genji falls in love with Fujitsubo and she becomes the standard by which all other women are judged. Ruled by his heart as he is, Genji pursues Fujitsubo and induces her to indulge his passion when, in his despair at her resistance to him, he voices suicidal thoughts. The child that results is passed off as the emperor's progeny, and Fujitsubo never again allows physical intimacy between them, but Genji and Fujitsubo are forever bonded in their concern for their son's well-being.

Meanwhile, Genji kidnaps Murasaki and raises her to become an ideal wife: elegant but dependent, loving but tolerant of his other relationships. She was a child of ten when he found and took charge of her, and a young woman of fourteen when he marries her and consummates their relationship. The evening before Murasaki's first sexual experience Genji is described as impatient to satisfy his long-deferred desire and concerned about Murasaki's potential reaction. The next morning Murasaki is depicted as alienated from him, but there is no description of their sexual intercourse itself. Translators tend to imply that she is angry because Genji forced himself on her, but it is also plausible that Murasaki's anger is inspired by a sense of betrayal. Genji has casually suggested in a poem he leaves by her pillow that he had been dissatisfied with their previous platonic relationship. She might be insulted by the casualness of this note or offended by his dismissal of their prior friendship. Genji's advance concern may have reflected an awareness that the loss of one's virginity is a momentous occasion, especially if one has been left ignorant of sexual matters, as Murasaki seems to have been, since she has been described as naive. In any event, Murasaki's anger dissipates and they enjoy a deep and relatively stable relationship for the rest of their lives.

Another sexual liaison that has major ramifications is Genji's affair with Oborozukiyo, who is both an aunt of, and betrothed to, the new emperor. Although Oborozukiyo flirted with and eagerly accepted Genji as a lover, when Genji is found in Oborozukiyo's room one night, her sister Kokiden, the new emperor's mother, takes Genji's affair with her sister as a brazen affront and uses her political influence to make life miserable for him. Genji chooses to exile himself, hoping that his fortunes might revive in the future.

While in exile, Genji enjoys an apparently fated encounter with the Akashi Lady. Despite the disadvantage posed by her country upbringing, her father, an obscure prince, is intent on finding a prestigious husband for her. He offers her to Genji. The Akashi Lady is sure that a relationship with so high ranking a man is a mismatch that will only lead to grief and resists Genji's advances. Without explaining how he managed to get around or through a locked door, the text next describes Genji's impressions of the lady during their first night together. Genji does not, indeed, treat the Akashi Lady with a great deal of respect, but she tries to make the best of the situation and Genji learns to appreciate her. That it was a fortuitous union eventually becomes apparent when the daughter that the Akashi Lady bears Genji becomes an empress. Although the Akashi Lady had to give her daughter to Murasaki for a proper upbringing, she willingly puts her daughter's future first and ultimately wins respect for her dignity and immense prestige as mother of an empress.

Although Genji loves Murasaki deeply, she lacks social standing because of her deceased mother's obscurity and because her father more or less abandoned her, and Genji never makes her his official wife. While he makes sure she knows she is first in his affections, he continues to court other women. What distinguishes Genji from other men and marks him as a hero is not fidelity, which is neither expected nor widely valued, but his reliability and generosity. When some of the women he had hoped would turn out to be hidden treasures disappoint him, he takes permanent responsibility for their material support. His flirtation with Tamakazura, a long-lost daughter of Yugao's, whom he has adopted, is inappropriate, but she wittily and resolutely rebuffs his advances, and he does not, after all, bed this surrogate daughter.

Late in life, Genji accepts a princess as his official wife, partly because her father asks him to do so, and partly because he is curious. This marriage is a disaster, because Murasaki is genuinely threatened by the princess's high status and Genji finds the young princess impossibly immature. The young courtier Kashiwagi, however, falls in love with her. Intending only to tell her of his love, Kashiwagi manages a nighttime intrusion. The princess is terrified, but he interprets her naive passivity as docility and consummates his desire. Afterward, he becomes desperate for her to acknowledge his love but she is nearly mute in her dismay. Kashiwagi later falls ill and dies because of his guilt at having cuckolded his friend Genji.

While this partial summary has focused on the sexual liaisons of the characters, the text also painstakingly describes music and dance concerts, banquets, and poetry contests as it chronicles the lives of the characters. Romantic encounters and sexual adventures were part of the culture of court life, where the value that linked all activities was the pursuit of beauty and elegance.

Modern adaptations of the work tend to include only the first few chapters and to present the content as a scandalous soap opera. Some twelfth-century readers believed Murasaki Shikibu must have gone to hell for concocting such a tale. The great poet Fujiwara Shunzei (1114–2104), on the other hand, admired Murasaki Shikibu's style and urged any serious poet to become familiar with her work. The scholar Motoori Norinaga (1730–1801) understood the tale as a reflection on the workings of the human heart and admired the author's ability to evoke *mono no aware* [the pathos of things].

Biography

Murasaki Shikibu was a servant of the imperial court during the Heian period. Her mother died when she was a child and she was raised and given a male's education by her father, contrary to tradition. Murasaki was the lady in waiting for Empress Shoshi/Akiko and kept a diary giving a vivid account of court life.

MARGARET H. CHILDS

Translations

Seidensticker, Edward. *The Tale of Genji*. New York: Knopf, 1980.
Tyler, Royal. *The Tale of Genji*. New York: Viking Penguin, 2001.
Waley, Arthur. *The Tale of Genji*. London: George Allen and Unwin, 1935.

Further Reading

Bowring, Richard. *Murasaki Shikibu: The Tale of Genji*. Cambridge, UK: Cambridge University Press, 1988.
Childs, Margaret H. "The Value of Vulnerability: Sexual Coercion and the Nature of Love in Japanese Court Literature." *Journal of Asian Studies* 58 (November 1999): 1059–79.
Field, Norma. *The Splendor of Longing in the* Tale of Genji. Princeton, NJ: Princeton University Press, 1987.
Morris, Ivan. *The World of the Shining Prince*. Oxford, UK: Oxford University Press, 1964.
Shirane, Haruo. *The Bridge of Dreams: A Poetics of the Tale of Genji*. Stanford, CA: Stanford University Press, 1987.

MUSSET, ALFRED DE

1810–1857
French novelist

Gamiani ou deux nuits d'excès (attributed)

Gamiani, a minor pornographic classic of the French Romantic period, is now generally (but by no means universally) attributed to the well-known poet and dramatist Alfred de Musset (1810–1857). The story takes place over "two nights of excess," the first Night and the second Night. The bibliographical history of this brief dialogue novel is extremely complex, and despite a century and a half of specialized research, basic information about its composition, publication, and diffusion is still unavailable, and given the nature of such works, likely to remain so. A lavishly and, at least in its original form, graphically illustrated book which, even in the relatively liberal early years of the July Monarchy, ought have attracted the notice of the police, *Gamiani* is not recorded in the *Bibliographie de la France*, the official listing of all books published in France since 1810. There are no copies of the rare hand-engraved, lithographed first edition (advertised on its title page as "Brussels 1833") in either the Bibliothèque Nationale or the NUC (National Union Catalog). Two copies of the equally rare first typeset (i.e., second) edition, inaccurately labeled "Vénise [*sic*], 1835, par Alcide, baron de M******," no doubt in order to hint at a connection with Musset's ill-starred but at the time celebrated romantic escapade to Venice with George Sand in 1833, were acquired by the Bibliothèque Impériale only in the 1860s thanks to a police raid on a collection of pornographic material. A duodecimo edition appeared in Paris around 1864, backdated "Amsterdam, 1840," with a preface in which Musset is explicitly designated as the author. In several of the many subsequent 19th-century reprints, George Sand is referred to as the author or coauthor of the second Night, or alternatively as a model for the insatiable lesbian heroine; a suggestion that, given what we now know of Sand from her voluminous correspondence and her autobiography, appears quite implausible, and for which there is not a shred of evidence. In 1881, Alcide Bonneau, a specialist in contemporary erotic literature, published a strongly worded refutation of the attribution on stylistic and moral grounds; the notion that the author of *Les Nuits*, those much anthologized poems celebrating spiritual love, could have penned this sulphurous text, in which nuns indulge in unspeakable orgies, and at least three characters copulate with animals, was simply not to be entertained. Yet serious debate about the question of authorship continued for the next hundred years, at least within specialist circles, with Dr. Iwan Bloch, one of the founders of modern sexology, among the yea-sayers and Pascal Pia, both in his own name and behind the pseudonym of "Dr. Fr. Froebel" leading the skeptics, while Louis Perceau, another specialist in erotic literature, took the "plausible but not proven" middle ground. For a discussion of the current state of the debate, the reader is referred to the late Simon Jeune's 1992 edition. However, since *Gamiani* has been neglected by mainstream literary historians and critics, a brief summary of the plot, such as it is, may be in order.

The story opens in the aristocratic apartment of the comtesse Gamiani. The narrator, Baron Alcide, wonders why she has no known attachment, despite her many advantages; and, like Raphaël de Valentin at the beginning of part 2 of Balzac's *La peau de chagrin*, he resolves to spend a night in her bedroom in order to solve the mystery. (A footnote in the first edition compares her to Balzac's Foedora, proving beyond doubt that *Gamiani* could not have been written before August 1831, when *La peau* first appeared). But in Gamiani's case, according to another guest, there is in fact no mystery: "C'est une Tribade!" i.e., a lesbian. Alcide decides nevertheless to observe for himself these forbidden forms of love. (From this opening scene to the melodramatic

933

denouement, voyeurism will constitute one of the basic elements of the plot). Gamiani duly enters, accompanied by her inexperienced (but, as things turn out, all too willing) partner Fanny, whose name may not be entirely coincidental: John Cleland's celebrated *Memoirs* were readily available in both French and English at the time. Gamiani seduces Fanny, and during one of their pauses for recuperation, Alcide joins in the fun. Gamiani confesses that she has "unnatural" desires that can never be satisfied; whether this is because she is a lesbian or a woman is a question frequently addressed, but never satisfactorily answered in the text. The three protagonists then proceed, between bouts of triangular lovemaking, to tell the stories of their respective initiations into the world of sex; these embedded stories take up the balance of the first Night.

Gamiani had been brought up in Italy by a widowed aunt, who used to take her into her bed and embrace her with strangely powerful (and to the heroine incomprehensible) convulsions (readers of Diderot's *La Religieuse* will recognize not only the situation, but the virtually identical words used to describe it: "I thought she was having an epileptic fit"). But since the niece was growing up, she needed to be prepared to suffer for her future sins, as Christ did to redeem ours; consequently, the aunt takes her to a monastery, where she is predictably flogged and then raped by twenty priests, after which, understandably, she vows eternal hatred of men. Fanny's tale is one of typical adolescent longings, with pillows stuffed between her legs and a general incomprehesion of what was happening to her body; words like "love" and "passion" trouble her, but until this evening, she had no idea what lay behind them. As for the narrator Alcide, his initiation takes the form of a sustained daydream, largely inspired by the paintings of Bosch and the younger Breughel, together with images from classical literature, in which visions of fleeting, unattainable virgins alternate with nocturnal bacchanals. The reaction of the three protagonists to this poetic orgy is consistent with their behavior throughout the novel: Fanny is exhausted and wants to sleep; Alcide, a mere man, is used up by the various excesses of the first Night; while Gamiani, as always, wants more, and continues her exercises in an adjacent room with the help of her servant and an obliging dog. After satisfying desires revived by this spectacle, Alcide and Fanny fall asleep.

Next morning, by a curious but significant twist in the story, they resolve to leave this den of vice and give themselves over to more conventional expressions of love.

As the second Night opens, Alcide is discovered once more in his observer's position, but this time contemplating the sleeping Fanny and hoping she is cured of the excessive desires inflamed by Gamiani. When the latter reappears, with servants dismissed and doors locked in the best de Sadean tradition, it becomes clear that this is far from the case, and Alcide witnesses another scene of lesbian love at its most extreme. Most of the second part of *Gamiani* consists of an account of the sequel to the heroine's education, this time in a convent under the dubious, but to readers of 18th-century anticlerical literature, all too familiar tutelage of the Sisters of Redemption, an apprenticeship that culminates in the murder of a male intruder. For a time, Gamiani consoles herself with men, primarily in order to prove their inadequacy. In a final scene, still in search of her goal of a sexual absolute, she gives Fanny a "love potion" and takes some herself. Before Alcide can intervene, both women die; as the heroine had predicted, Eros and Thanatos have finally come together.

From this brief synopsis, it is clear that *Gamiani*, by any standards, is an obscene book. But to dismiss it as a cheap, formulaic imitation of the Marquis de Sade, as Mario Praz does in his influential *The Romantic Agony*, is to do it an injustice; for if we apply to it the question of "redeeming literary merit" raised by judges in every obscenity trial from *Madame Bovary* to *Lady Chatterley's Lover*, the answer must be an unequivocal affirmative. Alcide's lengthy account of his initiation is an imaginative *tour de force* worthy of Nerval. As Simon Jeune has shown, the text is full of linguistic inventiveness. The author makes clever use of embedded stories designed to stimulate both listeners and readers, while the occasional witty aside encourages the latter to keep a critical distance from the appalling events that are being narrated; thus, at the end of Alcide's story, the heroine remarks: "You spin a fine yarn, sir, that was just like something out of a book," to which he demurely replies, echoing Boccaccio or *The Arabian Nights*: "Il faut bien passer la nuit" [It helps to pass the night]. Above all, the heroine's desperate search for a sexual absolute that will satisfy her, and her association of sexual climax with death, is carefully developed throughout the story. Whoever wrote it, *Gamiani* is a somber and disturbing book, one that the pioneer students of sexual pathology in late-19th-century Germany were right to take seriously. Small wonder that Baudelaire, no stranger to the theme of lesbian love and a discerning literary critic in his own right, openly confessed his admiration for the book, while never ceasing to pour scorn on Musset's better-known sentimental works.

GRAHAM FALCONER

Modern Editions

Gamiani. Facsimile of the Paris edition ("Brussels, 1833") with an introduction by Jacques Duprilot. Geneva: Slatkine Reprints, 1980.

Gamiani, ou deux nuits d'excès. Edited by Simon Jeune. Paris: Ramsay/Jean-Jacques Pauvert, 1992. Aside from the question of authorship, no substantial critical study of *Gamiani* exists, but many relevant issues are raised by the critical *notice* in Simon Jeune's edition.

Gamiani. London: Scarlet Library, 2001.

Gamiani, or Two Nights of Excess. London and New York: Tandem Books and Anchor Books, 1968.

MYSTICISM AND MAGIC

Satanism is an extreme form of the occult; however, in terms of erotic literature, it figures prominently. The Devil is often portrayed as sexually alluring, as Mark Twain writes in *The Mysterious Stranger*, "[W]e could only listen to him, and love him, and be his slaves, to do with us as he would. He made us drunk with the joy of being with him, and of looking into the heaven of his eyes, and of feeling the ecstasy that thrilled along our veins from the touch of his hand" (Twain). The Devil as an erotic figure, however, predates the nineteenth century. In 1772, Jacques Cazotte's romance *Le Diable amoureux* portrayed the sultry temptress Biondetta, who ultimately turns out to be the Devil in disguise. Fiction in the Middle Ages often invoked images of an incubus or a succubus—a male or a female demonic figure, respectively, who comes to sleepers in their nightmares to have sex with them. Balzac used the theme in his 1833 story *Le Succube* [*The Succubus*], about "the tragic fate of a beautiful woman, believed by her contemporaries to be a demon who charmed men in order to lead them to their ruin" (Rudwin).

Satanism in the nineteenth century was different from medieval witchcraft and cults that were linked more to ancient beliefs and pagan forms of worship. In medieval times, Satanism was an act of rebellion on the part of the lower and oppressed classes and a means of escape from the tyranny of the Catholic Church. By the nineteenth century, however, Satanism had become adopted in many European capitals and was practiced by cultured socialites. This is described in J.-K. Huysmans' novel *Là-Bas* [*The Damned*] (1891), which focuses on the Parisian underground of black magic and erotic devilry. Its principle character, Durtal, decides to write a biography of Gilles de Rais, a marshal of France and an infamous leader in the French medieval witch cult who confessed to the ritualistic killing and mutilation of hundreds of children in perverse and sadistic acts of diabolism and was executed in 1440. Durtal's involvement with the mysterious Madame Chantelouve enables him to attend a black mass. Afterward, it is described that "[s]he grabbed hold of him, took possession of him and initiated him into obscenities whose existence he had never suspected; she was like a ghoulish fury. But when, eventually, he was in a position to escape, his heart stood still: for he saw that the bed was littered with fragments of the Eucharist" (Huysmans, 230). Indeed, the inclusion of a black mass is unsurprising in erotic literature, as it contains numerous examples of sexual perversion, debauchery, blasphemy, and sacrilege. The spilling of blood in the form of a sacrifice (usually an animal) and the substitution of holy water with urine replaced Christian

935

rituals such as the Eucharist and the sprinkling of holy water. The body of a nude woman was often used as an altar, and the mass would often end in an orgy.

This literary genre of occult fiction was not restricted to France. Toward the latter part of the nineteenth century, an organization for the study of magic and the occult was established in London. Members of the Hermetic Order of the Golden Dawn included A.E. Waite, William Butler Yeats, Arthur Machen, Algernon Blackwood, and Aleister Crowley. Their interest in magic and the occult influenced their works. Machen's novel the *Great God Pan* (1894) portrays the demonic individual Helen Vaughan, a name she uses among many other aliases. "The text hints at a correspondence between Helen's perverse activities and primitive, orgiastic rites said to have been practiced by certain of the ancient Romans, cultists of Pan, who once inhabited Britain" (Hurley).

Aleister Crowley had first experimented with magic as a student at Cambridge, and throughout his life he referred to himself as the Great Beast. His magic focused on blasphemy, sacrilege, and sexual rituals. The most famous of his few novels is *Moonchild*, which was written in 1917 but published later, in 1929. This work describes a "magickal" war between Good and Evil and focuses on the sexual nature of magic rituals: "She saw Cyril and Cybele draw together; they gave a laugh which (once again) she fancied she could hear. It rang demoniac in her very inmost soul. An instant more, and their mouths met in a kiss" (Crowley). This ritual scene continues with the protagonists discarding their robes and "dancing together. It was wild and horrible beyond all imagination; the dancers were locked so closely that they appeared like a single monster of fable, a thing with two heads and four legs, which writhed or leapt in hideous ecstasy" (Crowley).

Finally, it is worth mentioning that there are other, less obvious examples of erotic devilry and black magic—for instance, vampirism. The vampire novel was an already established literary genre before Bram Stoker's *Dracula* (1897). Vampirism had always been portrayed as erotic, where moral, social, and sexual boundaries were pushed to the limits. Indeed, the vampire is a predator for whom race, class, and particularly gender make no difference (Sheridan Le Fanu's *Carmilla* [1871], for example, flirts with the idea of lesbianism). Stoker's text perhaps illustrates the true nature of vampirism and eroticism and conveys its three requisite appeals in erotic fiction, viz., vampirism itself is erotic; it "embodies some form of sexual threat or 'subversive' sexuality; and ... the (male) characters in the text, being 'typical' Victorians, fear vampires because of the threat they pose to orthodox sexuality" (Mighall).

Occult literature was rare in Britain in the nineteenth century, but there was much produced in France that "a blanket term such as 'mysticism' could not hope to cover" (Griffiths). It would be difficult to describe, for example, Barbey D'Aurevilly's *Les Diaboliques* (1874) and various *Contes cruels* by authors such as Villiers de l'Isle-Adam, Charles Baudelaire, or Gérard de Nerval as works of "mysticism." They portray horror and the macabre, focusing on subjects from Gilles de Rais to alchemy. During this period, the French Revolution was, by no means, a distant memory, and poets and writers poured their fears and anxieties into their work. They reacted pessimistically and cynically against Christianity, politics, and primarily materialism, and one of the most extreme crazes born out of this social rebellion was the rise of the occult.

SARAH BERRY

Selected Works

Ashley, Leonard R.N. *The Complete Book of Magic and Witchcraft.* London: Robson Books Ltd., 1996.

Cazotte, Jacques. *Le Diable amoureux.* Paris: Flammarion, 1979.

Crowley, Aleister. *Moonchild.* New York: Samuel Weiser Books, 1970.

D'Aurevilly, Jules Barbey. *Les Diaboliques.* Edited by Michel Crouzet. Paris: Imprimerie nationale, 1989.

Stoker, Bram. *Dracula.* Edited with an introduction and notes by Maurice Hindle. London: Penguin Books Limited, 1993.

Twain, Mark. *The Mysterious Stranger: A Romance.* New York: Harper and Brothers, 1916.

Further Reading

Ashley, Leonard R.N. *The Complete Book of Vampires.* London: Souvenir Press Ltd., 1998.

Griffiths, Richard. *The Reactionary Revolution: The Catholic Revival in French Literature, 1870–1914.* London: Constable, 1966.

Hale, Terry, ed., and Liz Heron, trans. *The Dedalus Book of French Horror: The 19th Century*. Cambs, UK: Dedalus Ltd., 1998.

Hurley, Kelly. *The Gothic Body: Sexuality, Materialism and Degeneration at the Fin-de-Siecle*. Cambridge: Cambridge University Press, 2004.

Huysmans, Joris-Karl. *Là-Bas*. Translated and with an introduction and notes by Terry Hale. London: Penguin Books, 2001.

Lloyd, Christopher. *J.-K Huysmans and the Fin-de-Siècle Novel*. Edinburgh: Edinburgh University Press, 1990.

Mighall, Robert. *A Geography of Victorian Gothic Fiction: Mapping History's Nightmares*. Oxford: Oxford University Press, 2003.

Rudwin, Maximilian. *The Devil in Legend and Literature*. La Salle, IL: Open Court, 1973.

Shepard, Leslie, ed. *Classic Vampire Stories*. New York: Citadel Press, 1995.

N

NABOKOV, VLADIMIR

1899–1977
Russian novelist

Nabokov, who owes his worldwide popularity largely to *Lolita* and the scandal it created, was a prominent novelist, one of the most original in this century with Joyce and Proust, as well as one of the most sexually explicit. In one of his interviews published in *Playboy*, however, he derided sex in the following terms: "Sex as an institution, sex as a general notion, sex as a problem, sex as a platitude—all this is something I find too tedious for words. Let us skip sex." (*Strong Opinions*). There is an element of bad faith, of course, in this statement, for sex plays a prominent role in most of his novels, starting from his second one, *King, Queen, Knave,* a modern version of *Madame Bovary,* in which Franz, the young protagonist, masturbates repeatedly until he becomes the lover of his mature cousin. Already, in this novel, Nabokov avoids using crude words to describe the lovers' sexual behavior: "The rather droll but endearing contrast between his thin body and one cocked part of it, shortish but exceptionally thick, would cause his mistress to croon in praise of his

manhood: 'Fatty is greedy!'" (90). Most of his other novels written in Russian, especially *Glory, Laughter in the Dark* and *Despair*, contain subdued erotic scenes but they never flirt with pornography, with one exception, *The Enchanter,* a short piece which Nabokov wrote in the late thirties but never tried to publish in his lifetime; after the publication of *Lolita* he did mention it to Walter J. Minton of G.P. Putnam's who was willing to consider it for publication but he never sent it, being aware, apparently, that it might hurt his reputation. It is a primitive prefiguration of his masterpiece: the story is more or less the same, with the difference that the nymphet's mother does not die in an accident but as a result of an incurable illness; it ends abruptly with the nympholept's suicide after he ejaculates in front of the girl who has unexpectedly woken up at that critical moment. The sexual fantasy at the root of this short fiction is very much the same as in *Lolita,* but the erotic scenes are a great deal less poetic in comparison.

Most of the novels Nabokov wrote in English, beside *Lolita* and *Ada* which will be analyzed below, contain a number of erotic scenes, especially *Bend Sinister* (Mariette trying to seduce Krug), *Pale Fire* (homosexual King Xavier's funny dealings with women), *Transparent Things* (Person's clumsy sexual commerce with his wife), and *Look at the Harlequins!* (Vadim's strange lovelife with his four women). None of those scenes, however, are as developed and "poerotic" (poetic and erotic) as those described in *Lolita* and *Ada*.

Lolita

Nabokov's pet fantasy as evoked in *The Enchanter,* to wit the seduction of a prepubescent girl by a mature man, was already present in *Laughter in the Dark* and *The Gift*. When he had finished writing *Lolita*, he wrote to Katharine White of *The New Yorker* that it had taken him "five years of monstrous misgivings and diabolical labors" and offered to send her the manuscript "under the rose of silence and the myrtle of secrecy." (*Selected Letters,* 140) He originally planned to publish the novel anonymously to protect his status and reputation at Cornell which had already suffered as a result of his so-called "dirty lit course" in which he taught, among other novels, *Madame Bovary* and *Ulysses.* After four American publishers had turned down the book, he accepted Maurice Girodias's offer to publish it in his Paris-based firm, The Olympia Press, whose catalogue included not only famous or less famous pornographic works but also novels which are now literary classics, such as Beckett's *Watt* or Donleavy's *Ginger Man.* Immediately after its publication, *Lolita* was banned by the French Minister of the Interior at the English government's prompting, along with twenty-four other books published by Girodias. The latter, to save his house, petitioned the *Tribunal Administratif* (Administrative Court) which eventually rescinded the Minister's ban in 1958— a little before the novel was published by Putnam's in the United States to become a best-seller.

The novel tells the story of a thirty-seven-year-old man of letters of Swiss origin, Humbert Humbert, who has always been attracted to prepubescent girls between the age limits of nine and fourteen endowed with special gifts whom he calls nymphets: "Between those age limits, are all girl-children nymphets? Of course not. Otherwise, we who are in the know, we lone voyagers, we nympholepts, would have long gone insane. Neither are good looks any criterion;

and vulgarity, or at least what a given community terms so, does not necessarily impair certain mysterious characteristics, the fey grace, the elusive, shifty, soul-shattering, insidious charm that separates the nymphet from such coeval of hers as are incomparably more dependent on the spatial world of synchronous phenomena than on that intangible island of entranced time where Lolita plays with her likes." (*Lolita,* 19) Fearing for his sanity and safety, he decided to marry Valeria, a woman who gave an imitation of a little girl, but, as he was about to embark with her for the United States, she left him for a Russian taxi-driver. Following a period of mental illness, Humbert retires to a small New England town, Ramsdale, where he takes lodging with a dull but passionate widow, Charlotte Haze, whose only asset, from his perspective, is her twelve-year-old daughter, Lolita, in whom he recognizes a girl he once loved in his youth on the Riviera. Within a few weeks, he manages to attract the girl's attention and even masturbates, fully dressed, against her buttocks one Sunday morning: "The nerves of pleasure had been laid bare. The corpuscles of Krause were entering the phase of frenzy. The least pressure would suffice to set all paradise loose (...). Suspended on the brink of that voluptuous abyss (a nicety of physiological equipoise comparable to certain techniques in the arts) I kept repeating chance words after her—barman, alarmin,' my charmin,' my carmen, ahmen, aha-hamen—as one talking and laughing in his sleep while my happy hand crept up her sunny leg as far as the shadow of decency allowed." (62) Charlotte, though unaware of what is happening between them, sends Lolita to a summer camp and wants her to go to a boarding school after that, firing Humbert with murderous frustration. Providence, indirectly goaded by him, causes her accidental death, which makes of him Lolita's natural guardian. He joins her at the camp and takes her to a hotel where, at the end of a harrowing night when he vainly tries to possess her, she playfully offers to make love with him: "She saw the stark act merely as part of a youngster's furtive world, unknown to adults. What adults did for purposes of procreation was no business of hers. My life was handled by little Lo in an energetic, matter-of-fact manner as if it were an insensate gadget unconnected with me. While eager to impress me with the world of tough kids, she was not quite prepared for certain discrepancies between a kid's life and mine." (135–136) This marks the beginning of a long journey together across the United States during which Humbert becomes more and more possessive and tyrannical, and Lolita moody and uncomplying. When they settle in a college town for a few months, she drifts away and, unbeknown to him, starts an affair with a playwright, Clare Quilty. She guilefully begs Humbert to take her upon a second journey during which Quilty, with her complicity, bedevils the more and more perplexed nympholept who never manages to discover his identity. Finally Lolita elopes with Quilty and disappears from Humbert's life until, years later, she writes him explaining that she has married a young engineer, is pregnant, and needs money. He calls on her and brings her to surrender the name of the man she eloped with, Quilty, whom he murders a few days later. In the concluding lines of the novel, Humbert, who is now in prison and cannot hope ever to live with Lolita, confesses that he truly loves her and says, addressing her beyond death: "One had to choose between him and H. H., and one wanted him to make you live in the minds of later generations." (311)

The erotic element of the novel, important as it is in the first part, gradually disappears in the second part in which Humbert, faced with his nymphet's unwillingness to play his sexual games, becomes more and more tyrannical and cruel. In his first-person narrative, he does not so much try to defend himself as to turn the chronicle of his perversion into a genuine love story and to gain the aesthetic approval of the literary connoisseur.

Ada

Ada, less famous than *Lolita*, is infinitely more erotic though it has never caused a similar scandal. It is a story of incest, the chief characters, Van Veen and his "cousin" Ada Veen, being in fact biological brother and sister. Their idyll begins on a paradisiacal estate, Ardis, on a planet called Antiterra: these two highly educated and supremely sensual children, respectively fourteen and twelve, soon begin to caress each other, uninhibited by any moral laws. In one of the most erotic scenes of the novel, Ada plays with Van's penis until he ejaculates:

"Oh, dear," she said as one child to another. "It's all skinned and raw. Does it hurt? Does it hurt horribly?"

"Touch it quick," he implored.

"Van, poor Van," she went on in the narrow voice the sweet girl used when speaking to cats, caterpillars, pupating puppies, "yes, I'm sure, it smarts, would it help if I'd touch, are you sure?"

"You bet," said Van, "*on n'est pas bête à ce point*" ["there are limits to stupidity," colloquial and rude].

"Relief map," said the primrose prig, "the rivers of Africa." Her index traced the blue Nile down into its jungle and traveled up again. "Now what's this? The cap of the Red Bolete is not half as plushy. In fact" (positively chattering), "I'm reminded of geranium or rather pelargonium bloom."

"God, we all are," said Van.

"Oh, I like this texture, Van, I like it! Really I do!"

"Squeeze, you goose, can't you see I'm dying."

(*Ada*, 119)

After this scene, they start a very active and creative lovelife in every nook and cranny of the estate, without bothering about the servants who spy on them, though their stepsister, Lucette, a nine-year-old nymphet, soon starts to interfere with their idyll. Van leaves Ardis at the end of the summer and comes back four years later: he is still madly in love with Ada who is now surrounded with men; Lucette tries to participate in their sexual games but her stepbrother refuses to make love to her. The summer ends in disaster when Van discovers that Ada has had two lovers. In the following years they see each other at more or less regular intervals until their father finds out that they are lovers and orders them to separate. Ada marries a man she does not love and becomes a film actress; Lucette commits suicide when Van refuses to make love to her; and Ada's husband finally dies. Van and Ada, now respectively fifty-two and fifty, resume their life together, and together, as they are nearing the age of a hundred years, write the present chronicle.

Here again, the erotic scenes, often more poetic and comic than in *Lolita*, are to be found mostly in the first half of the novel. This violates the principles of "pornography" which, in Nabokov's view as expressed in his after-word to *Lolita*:

... connotes mediocrity, commercialism, and certain strict rules of narration. Obscenity must be mated with banality because every kind of aesthetic enjoyment has to be entirely replaced by simple sexual stimulation which demands the traditional word for direct action upon the patient (...). Thus, in pornographic novels, action has to be limited to the copulation of clichés. Style, structure, imagery should never distract the reader from his tepid lust (...). Moreover, the sexual scenes in the book must follow a crescendo line, with new variations, new combinations, new sexes, and a steady increase in the number of participants (in a Sade play they call the gardener in), and therefore the end of the book must be more replete with lewd lore than the first chapters." (*Lolita*, p. 315)

Though he creates erotic scenes often more exciting than many pornographers, Nabokov manages to transmute sexual desire into what he calls "aesthetic bliss" (*Lolita*).

Biography

Vladimir Nabokov, born in Saint Petersburg on April 22 1899 (new style), was the son of a professor of penal law who later became a prominent figure in Paul Milyukov's Kadet movement and participated in the first provisional government after the March 1917 Revolution; he was shot to death in Berlin in 1922 while trying to shield Milyukov. Following the October Revolution, the family moved to Crimea and then to London and Berlin. Vladimir, after graduating from Trinity College, Cambridge, joined his family in Berlin where he started his literary career while giving private lessons in English, Russian, tennis, and even boxing. In 1925, he married Vera Slonim who remained his faithful companion, his secretary, and favorite reader throughout his life. His first novel, *Mary*, written in Russian like all the books he published until 1940 (see the bibliography), came out in Berlin in 1926. His elitism, his aloofness, and lack of involvement in the political debates agitating the Russian community labeled him as an eccentric. Fearing for his Jewish wife and his three-year-old son, he left Germany in 1937 for France where he wrote his first "English" novel, *The Real Life of Sebastian Knight*. In 1940, running away from the Nazis, he went to the United States where Edmund Wilson acted as his mentor and helped him publish fiction and essays. While doing research on butterflies at Harvard's Museum of Comparative Zoology, he started teaching literature at Wellesley College and, after 1948, at Cornell University, having acquired American citizenship three years earlier. *Lolita*, his third novel written in English, came out in France in 1955 and became a bestseller after its publication in the United States in 1958. Having achieved financial security at last, he resigned from Cornell and went back to Europe, settling in Montreux where he remained until his death in 1977. During his European years, he continued to write novels of which *Pale Fire* and *Ada* are the best known, and had his Russian novels translated into English.

MAURICE COUTURIER

Selected Works

Mary. 1926.
King, Queen, Knave. 1928.
The Defense. 1930.
The Eye. 1930.
Laughter in the Dark. 1932.
Glory. 1933.
Despair. 1936.
The Gift. 1937–1938.
Invitation to a Beheading. 1938.
The Real Life of Sebastian Knight. 1941.
Bend Sinister. 1947.
Lolita. 1955.
Pnin. 1957.
Pale Fire. 1962.
Ada. 1969.
Transparent Things. 1972.
Look at the Harlequins!. 1974.
The Enchanter. 1986.

Further Reading

Appel, Alfred. *Nabokov's Dark Cinema*. New York: Oxford University Press, 1974.
Boyd, Brian. *Vladimir Nabokov*. 2 vols., London: Chatto & Windus, 1990 and 1991.
Couturier, Maurice. *Nabokov ou la tyrannie de l'auteur*. Paris: Ed. du Seuil, "Poétique," 1993.
———. *Roman et censure ou la mauvaise foi d'Eros*. Seyssel: Champ Vallon, 1995.
Proffer, Carl R. *Keys to Lolita*. Bloomington, IN: Indiana University Press, 1968.

NAFZÂWÎ, AL-

Early fifteenth century
North African story writer

The Perfumed Garden of Sensual Delight
[*Al-raud al-'âtir fi nuzhat al-khâtir*]

Nafzâwî's *Perfumed Garden,* written around 1411–1433, is a classic of international erotic literature. Following a conventional manner of presenting knowledge to a general audience, the work is written in an entertaining style, offering serious information amidst humorous tales and anecdotes. In general, the author follows the agenda of discussing and presenting all kinds of phenomena he regards as relevant for a contemporary heterosexual Arab male. In a rather loosely arranged program of 21 chapters, the author informs about images and qualities of men and women, about the arts of seduction and sexual stimulation, about aphrodisiacs, contraceptives, and abortion; besides, the narratives he quotes give ample room to sexual fantasies-fantasies.

The chapter headings run as follows: (1) The Man of Quality; (2) The Woman of Quality; (3) The Repulsive Man; (4) The Repulsive Woman; (5) Sexual Intercourse; (6) Sexual Technique; (7) Harmful Effects of Intercourse; (8) Names for the Penis; (9) Names for the Vulva; (10) The Members of Animals; (11) Women's Tricks; (12) Questions and Answers for Men and Women; (13) The Causes and Stimulation of Sexual Desire; (14) Remarks on Female Sterility and Methods of Treatment; (15) Causes of Male Sterility; (16) Ways to Provoke Miscarriage; (17) Treatment for Three Types of Erection Problem; (18) How to Expand and Enlarge a Small Penis; (19) How to Remove Underarm and Vaginal Odour, and How to Tighten the Vagina; (20) The Symptoms of Pregnancy, and How to Determine the Sex of the Unborn Child; (21) The Benefits of Eggs and Sexually Stimulating Beverages.

Both the way of composition and the work's content show it to be a late descendant of a traditional genre of Arabic literature dealing with sexual hygiene from a medical perspective. In contrast to other works of the genre, the *Perfumed Garden* is a compilation with little ambition. It aims at the general reader and is rather intended as a practical guide for the ordinary man. The *Perfumed Garden* might have remained relegated to obscurity, had it not been for French novelist Guy de Maupassant (1850–1893) to "discover" the work and English orientalist scholar and translator of the *Arabian Nights* Sir Richard Burton (1821–1880) to utilize it as a further ingredient in the nineteenth-century European invention of the Orient. These Western renderings of *The Perfumed Garden* have resulted in a distorted perception that had more to do with Western expectations and fantasies than with the original work's intention.

Nafzâwî presents the male individual as unquestionably heterosexual. A man's only goal is to satisfy the lust of women, or rather to use women in order to satisfy his own lust. In contrast to men, women are allowed autoerotic manipulations as well as homoerotic contacts. Besides these digressions, which are, albeit, heavily criticized by the author, Nafzâwî regards women exclusively to serve men, and there is no discernible effort to see female sexuality in its own right. The satisfaction of female sexuality is rather regarded as a social necessity, because otherwise women would strive to satisfy their lust beyond legitimate borders, that is, extramarital, and, consequently, threaten social order. In short, Nafzâwî writes against a male chauvinist and decidely misogynist backdrop. Moreover, by describing his role models joyfully and without a notable degree of reflection, Nafzâwî both accepts them and partakes in passing them on within his own cultural context.

This evaluation of Nafzâwî's work explains to a certain degree why the work was so fascinating for Western male readers. After all, Nafzâwî presents a world in which the male individual is legitimated to devote his activities solely to satisfy his own desire without having to take over social responsibility for his acts. Moreover, the sexual behavior of Nafzâwî's characters contrasts sharply with social reality, as they neglect and contradict social restrictions, enjoying sexual intercourse with a naive lust and total lack of inhibition. With these characteristics, the work offered itself as a matrix for Western sexual fantasies, a fact that furthered its enthusiastic reception in the nineteenth century.

Nafzâwîs's *Perfumed Garden* was first translated by a French army officer in Algeria, who in the French translation achieved in 1850 bashfully mentions his name as "Monsieur le Baron R***, Capitaine d'Etat Major.." A quarter of a century later, four French officers, presenting themselves with the initials J.M.P.Q., printed this translation. It is said that they printed the work on the official lithographic press of the army, and when their activity was discovered by their superior, had to stop. Some 35 copies were printed. The next trace of the work is found in a letter dated August 25, 1884, mailed by Guy de Maupassant from the oasis of Bou Saada to Paris. While the letter's addressee is unknown, shortly after, in 1885, an almost identical reprint of the first edition was published. In addition, the Paris publisher Isidor Liseux, renowned for his interest in exceptional works of literature, had the French text typeset and printed in Paris in 1886, in an edition of 220 copies. This edition, which has been reprinted numerous times, due to its wide availability has served as the basis for several translations. The English translation prepared from the French by Sir Richard Burton is still more influentiual. It was published in two editions in 1886 as the third volume edited by Burton's Kama Shastra Society, following the translations of the Indian erotic classics *Kamasutra* (1883) and *Anangaranga* (1885). Virtually all of the numerous translations of the *Perfumed Garden* prepared in the nineteenth and twentieth centuries rely on either the French or the English translations without taking recourse to an original Arabic text. Only when the critical edition of an old manuscript of the *Perfumed Garden* preserved in Copenhagen was published, a new English translation was prepared, aiming at representing the original text as faithfully as possible without any conscious interference of orientalist imagery, such as Burton's translation.

Nafzâwî's worldview does not differ decisively from the worldview of contemporary Western or Christian authors. This evaluation is corroborated by the fact that several of the tales Nafzâwî quotes appear both in early Oriental as well as medieval Western tradition. The story of *The Lover's Gift Regained*, in which the wise fool Buhlûl tricks the vazier's wife into granting triple intercourse without any recompensation, is widely known in a similar version contained in Italian novelist Boccaccio's *Decamerone* (8,2). Likewise, the story of *The Weeping Bitch*, in which an old woman employs a weeping dog in order to convince a woman to grant her favors to her lover, is of Indian origin; it was transmitted to Europa by the famous *Disciplina Clericalis* of Petrus Alfonsus, who wrote early in the twelfth century, and is met with in a large range of medieval compilations.

Nafzâwî's work remains an important source for the cultural history of the Near East, conveying detailed information about sexual attitudes and fantasies in the fifteenth-century Arab world. The way it deals with sex in an outspoken and uninhibited manner makes it interesting reading, even though at times it is rather amusing than either stimulating or edifying.

Biography

Little is known about the life of Abû 'Abdallâh Muhammad ibn Muhammad al-Nafzâwî. He was born at Nafzawa sometime before 1411 and lived most of his life in Tunis (modern day Tunisia). As evidenced by the medical understanding displayed in his writings it is possible that Nafzawi was trained as a physician.

ULRICH MARZOLPH

Selected Works

The Perfumed Garden of the Shaykh Nezfzawi. Translated by Sir Richard Burton. Edited, with an Introduction and Additional Notes by Alan Hull Walton. London: Neville Spearman 1963 (and numerous reprints in paperback).

The Perfumed Garden of Sensual Delight [...] by Muhammad ibn Muhammad al-Nafzawi. translated from the Arabic with a short introduction and notes by Jim Colville. London, New York: Kegan Paul International 1999 (The Kegan Paul Arabia Library, vol. 7).

Le Jardin parfumé. Manuel d'érotologie arabe du Cheikh Nefzaoui. Traduit par le baron R*** et présenté par Mohamed Lasly. Paris: Philippe Picquier 1999.

Further Reading

Nafzâwî: *Der duftende Garten.* Ein arabisches Liebeshandbuch. Aus dem Arabischen übersetzt und herausgegeben von Ulrich Marzolph. Munic: Beck, 2002.

Bousquet, H.-H. *L'Éthique sexuelle de l'Islam.* Paris: G.-P. Maisonneuve et Larose 1966.

Bouhdiba, A. *La sexualité en Islam.* Paris: PUF 1986.

NASHE, THOMAS

c. 1568–c. 1601
English poet, satirist, and pamphleteer

The Choise of Valentines

This, Nashe's only surviving narrative poem, is likely to have been written around 1594. A number of manuscripts exist, but no early edition. Its extraordinary and highly sophisticated play of allusion, style, and vocabulary indicate that it may well have been originally written for the entertainment of a noble patron and his friends: the Earls of Derby and Southampton have both been suggested as possible intended recipients. It appears to have circulated fairly widely: a number of contemporary writers comment adversely on its lubricity, including Gabriel Hervey, with whom Nashe engaged in a prolonged and vitriolic pamphlet war, in *The Trimming of Thomas Nashe,* Sir John Davies of Hereford in *The Scourge of Folly* and Joseph Hall, Bishop of Exeter and Norwich, in his *Satires.*

The poem takes as its context the old custom of choosing, privately or by lot, a lover, friend, or sweetheart on the fourteenth of February to be one's 'Valentine' for the coming year. The choice was usually marked by a gift. Nashe writes in the first person, in the character of comic anti-hero. His narrative interweaves Ovidian worldliness, Chaucerian farce, even Spenserian epic and lyric registers with touches of the new metaphysical style into a brilliant, burlesque fantasy of his own anticlimatic sexual humiliation. The opening presents a quite misleading evocation of pastoral innocence:

It was the merie month of Februarie,
When yong men, in their iollie rogerie,
Rose earlie in the morne fore breake of daie,
To seeke them valentines soe trimme and gaie...
And goe to som village abbordring neere,
To taste the creame and cakes and such good cheere;
(11. 1–12)

When the poet then begins his own, urban, pilgrimage 'to my ladies shrine' however, this dainty prelude can be seen to be a witty expansion of the same pun on 'country matters' with which Hamlet will later taunt Ophelia. Nashe goes to the lady's lodging only to find that recent enforcement of the town statutes against prostitution,

...had scar'd her from the place;
And now she was compel'd, for Sanctuarie,
To fly unto a house of venerie.
(11. 22–34)

He follows her there, and is welcomed by the brothel-keeper who, on due payment, shows him to...

...a shady loft
Where venus bounsing vestalls skirmish oft,
(11. 47–48)

and offers him 'of prettie Trulls, a paire'. He 'spake them faire,' but insists on having his own, far more expensive, 'gentle mistris Francis' who, as the brothel keeper tells him,

'...in her veluett gounes,
And ruffs and perwigs as fresh as Maye,
Can not be kept with half a croune a daye.'
(11. 64–66)

She is summoned, and welcomes her 'Tho-malin,' with joy. He falls upon her, literally, and sweeps away her skirts, like Donne in *Loves Progress* ascending to his goal;

> First her bare leggs, then creepe up to her kneese,
>
> (1. 102)

only to be foiled by his own inadequacy; literally he cannot rise to the occasion:

> Her armes are spread, and I am all unarm'd (L. 123).

The lady is all sympathy, and her fully detailed professional skills prevail upon his 'silly worme,' to their mutual, graphic but short-lived delight. 'To die' was at this time a common euphemism for orgasm: his is premature, and he laments his failure accordingly in terms of elegiaic pathos:

> The whilst I speake, my soule is fleeting hence,
> And life forsakes her fleshly residence.
> Staie, staie sweete ioye, and leaue me not forlorne
> Wht shouldst thou fade that art but new lie born?
>
> (11. 209–212)

The lady's frustrated distress matches his, but is combined with exasperation:

> Adieu! faint-hearted instrument of lust;
>   That falslie hath betrayed our mutual trust;
>
> (11. 233–234)

She has, after all, a reliable alternative to such masculine fallibility:

> My little dildo shall suply their kinde...
> And plays at peacock twixt my 1eggs right blythe,
> And doth my tickling swage with manie a sighe.
>
> (11. 237–241)

There follows her lover's impassioned and explicit diatribe against 'this woman's secretarie' and all its very varied works. He himself can do no more:

> I am not as was Hercules the stout,
> That to the seaventh iournie could hold out.
>
> (11.299–300)

Aphrodisiacs, 'Druggs and Electuaries of new devise,' might be a solution, but he cannot afford them. He pays the brothel keeper her full price, and leaves, '...as Jeane and lanke as anie ghoste.'

That the whole poem is a virtuoso performance to be relished by the leading actor as well as by his audience is revealed in the conclusion:

> What can be added more to my renoune?
> She lyeth breathlesse; I am taken doune;
> The waves do swell, the tides climb or'e the banks;
> Judge gentlemen! if I deserue not thanks?
> And so, good night! unto you euer'ie one;
> For loe, our thread is spunne, our plaie is donne.
>
> (ll. 309–314)

The Virgilian pastoral reminder that the irrigation channels should be closed at nightfall (Ec. III. 111) plays on the vinous revelry of Nashe's likely audience to provide a neat conclusion: '...sat prata biberunt: the meadows have drunk enough'.

Biography

Born in about 1567, he studied at Cambridge and, like the hero of his picaresque novel *The Unfortunate Traveller*, journeyed briefly in France and Italy. By 1588, he was living in London. He made a living by writing pamphlets, for the most part virulently satirical, on an enormous range of topics, as well as plays, poetry, and his novel, the first of its kind in English. His prose style has been compared to that of Rabelais. He died in or about 1601.

ELIZABETH PORGES WATSON

Editions

The Choise of Valentines, Or the Merie Ballad of Nash his Dildo. Ed. John S. Farmer, London, 1849: Privately printed for Subscribers only.

The Works of Thomas Nashe. Ed. R.B. McKerrow, London, 1910, Vol. III.

Thomas Nashe: The Unfortunate Traveller and other Works. Ed. J.B. Steane, Penguin English Library, 1972 (Modernized text).

Further Reading

Hibbard. G.R. *Thomas Nashe, a Critical Introduction*, London, 1962.

NECROPHILIA

The theme of sexual arousal on contact with a corpse has been a feature of literature since classical antiquity (Achilles is said to have slept with Penthesileia after her death) and continues to occur in the form of the present day Western fascination with sexual transgression, death, and violence. Seemingly regardless of local cultural and historical factors, desire for the dead stands as one of the universal taboos of socio-sexual life, transgressing both the Christian edict which states that the corpse is sacred, and the socially-acquired responses of disgust and fear that the living are taught to feel for the dead. However, the ways in which necrophilia is conceived and represented artistically have undergone important shifts over time.

The naming of sexual typologies in socio-medical discourse and the privileging of perverse sexual subject matter in literature share common historical and ideological roots. The term "necrophilia" (literally, "love of corpses") was coined by the Belgian alienist, Joseph Guislain in 1852, as one of a group of sexological categories in the late-nineteenth century, and was adopted by E. Monneret in his *Treatise on General Pathology* (1861). It was mentioned by Richard von Krafft-Ebing in the first edition of *Psychopathia Sexualis* (1886), the most famous work of nineteenth-century sexology, and filtered into the major European languages via subsequent translations of this work. Probably the first literary work to use the word was Guy de Maupassant's story, "La Chevelure" [The Head of Hair] in 1884. The nineteenth century in Europe saw an efflorescence of necrophilic subject matter, as attested to by Mario Praz in his, now famous, account of the underside of the Romantic literature *The Romantic Agony* (1933). The Modern European fascination with the morbid aesthetic, which elevates corrupt and disturbing subject matter to the status of beauty in the interests of social and aesthetic transgression, can be traced from the Marquis de Sade in the late-eighteenth century, through Edgar A. Poe and Charles Baudelaire in the mid-nineteenth century, to Decadent literature in the 1880s and 1890s. Some examples of necrophilia exist prior to Sade's writing, but within the scope of this article, the intention is primarily to explore necrophilic representations, produced in their heyday, as the symptoms of a recognizably modern phenomenon and, secondly, to cast an eye towards their legacy in the twentieth century.

Sade's *œuvre* features several instances of necrophilia. In the final section of *Les 120 Journées de sodome* [*The Hundred and Twenty Days of Sodom*] (1784–1785), entitled "Murderous Passions," Sade describes several acts of intercourse with corpses, often in scenarios involving other taboos such as incest and blasphemy. Here, necrophilia is of interest primarily as one figure of extremity among many, rather than in and of itself. In *Juliette* (1797), for example, a female libertine, the Abbess Delbène enjoys sex with a living partner on top of the bodies of her murdered victims. Juliette herself is also described using her victims' bones as dildos. In these cases, the corpse itself is less the object of erotic interest than the bizarre and blasphemous use to which the "relics" can be put.

Representations of necrophilia in the nineteenth century run the gamut from subliminal and suggestive to explicit and extreme. "Subliminal" necrophilia, when the deadness of the object desired is expressed by the evocation of states which resemble it, is found in such themes as the sexual violation of an unconscious woman (Heinrich von Kleist's *Die Marquise von O*, 1808) or the libidinal investment in cold, inanimate, pale statues (Théophile Gautier's *Spirite*, 1866). In these cases, the necrophilic impulse finds its manifestation in a gentle passion, an eroticism akin to sleep and dream. In Georges Rodenbach's Belgian novel, *Bruges La Morte* (1892), the wasted, moribund cityscape of Bruges is lovingly and nostalgically described in an allegorical mode which collapses the fashion for the dying/dead female body onto topographical subject matter. Here, necrophilia becomes less a sexual perversion and more a flavor of the aesthetic *Zeitgeist*.

Necrophilia can be understood as the result of the failure of mourning (see Ernest Jones, 1933). The theme of the dead beloved who is reanimated by the strength of erotic memory and desire is common in tales of the supernatural (e.g. Edgar A. Poe's "Ligeia" [1835], "Morella" [1838], and Villiers de l'Isle-Adam's "Véra" [1874]). In other cases, the dead being is transformed into a powerful figure; a sexualized vampire, zombie, or ghost. (See Gautier's *La morte amoureuse* [1836], Bram Stoker's *Dracula* [1897], and Rachilde's *Le grand saigneur* [1922]). These texts offer insight into a common underlying fantasy of necrophilia—the projection of desire by the living being onto the dead other. The epigraph of Heinrich Heine's *Der Doktor Faustus* (1847) offers a particularly good insight into this phenomenon. The first person poem is voiced by a dead woman who has been called back into the world of the living by her grieving partner: "Du hast mich beschworen aus dem Grab / Durch deine Zauberwillen" / "'Thou hast called me from my grave / By thy bewitching will.'" In the closing lines, this relation is neatly turned around, so that it is the dead woman herself who desires an impossible consummation: "Die Toten sind unersättlich!/ The dead can never be sated."

Charles Baudelaire's *Les fleurs du mal* (1855) features more explicit representations of necrophilic desire. "Une martyre" recounts the erotic reactions of a viewer standing before a painting of a decapitated female corpse. The poetic voice starts by describing the dead body, with its gartered leg and artlessly inviting pose, before going on to imagine the sexual murder which led to the creation of the *tableau*. The poem embodies powerfully the imaginative identifications the poet makes with both the imagined killer and the corpse, and invites the reader to collude disturbingly with the poetic persona's fantasy.

The Decadent French female writer Rachilde is responsible for one of the few full-length novelistic explorations of necrophilia in existence, *La tour d'amour* (1899). This work charts the relationship of a lighthouse keeper, who sates himself on the bodies of female shipwreck victims, and his young assistant who, by the end of the novel, admits to his own necrophilic tendencies. It is lyrically written in a style which focuses on a progressive sliding of identity, encroaching

delusion and delirium. The figure of the seabed as joint symbol of birth, death, and nirvana is exploited by Rachilde, as is the idea of family romance: the novel can be read as a perverse oedipal parable.

In Georges Bataille's pornographic writing, death and sexuality are aligned as experiences through which the boundaries of the ego and subjectivity are fatally transgressed. It is not surprising, then, that in works such as *Histoire de l'oeil* [*The Story of the Eye*] (1928) and *Le bleu du ciel* [*The Blue of the Sky*] (1935), scenes of necrophilia and the mutilation of corpses are accorded a particular prominence. In *The Story of the Eye*, it is noteworthy that it is the female protagonist who carries out necrophiliac practices on the body of a priest, skewing the expected gendering of necrophilia as a male perversion.

Indeed, in the twentieth century, the figure of necrophilia has featured increasingly in writing by women. Gabrielle Wittkop's erotic novella *Le Nécrophile*, published by Jean-Jacques Pauvert in 1972 and republished in popular *livre de poche* format in 1998, takes the form of the sexually explicit confessional journal of a necrophile character, Lucien. Similarly, and more recently, the Canadian writer Barbara Gowdy's beautiful and spare short story "We So Seldom Look on Love" (1992) is a first-person narrative which voices the story of a young, female necrophiliac. In both of these stories, medico-legal language and Christian discourse are carefully avoided. The writers' tone is deliberately guilt-free and void of ethical comment. They treat necrophilia as an identity and a form of self-expression, tapping into the cultural and epistemological change which starts to see sexual taste less as a physiological and psychiatric condition and more as an expression of identity politics. The (post)modern texts authored by Wittkop and Gowdy write against the tradition which makes necrophilia a masculine perversion and its aesthetic representation a symptom of misogyny (See Bram Dijkstra, 1986 and Elisabeth Bronfen, 1992). They neutralize the gendered power imbalance (by featuring in one case a bisexual male necrophile and in the other a female necrophile), and make necrophilia the default model of desire in the fictional universes described, rather than an aberrant deviation.

LISA DOWNING

Further Reading

Bronfen, Elisabeth. *Over Her Dead Body*. Manchester: Manchester University Press, 1992.

Dijkstra, Bram. *Idols of Perversity: Fantasies of Feminine Evil in fin-de-siècle Culture*. Oxford: Oxford University Press, 1986.

Downing, Lisa. *Desiring the Dead*. Oxford: Legenda, European Humanities Research Centre, 2003.

Downing, Lisa. "Death and the Maidens: A Century of Necrophilia in Female-Authored Textual Production." *French Cultural Studies*, 14, no. 2, 2003, 157–168.

Epaulard, Alexis. *Nécrophilie, nécrosadisme, nécrophagie*. Lyon: Stock, 1901.

Goodwin, Sarah Webster & Elisabeth Bronfen (eds). *Death and Representation*. Baltimore and London: Johns Hopkins University Press, 1993.

Jones, Ernest. *On the Nightmare*. London: The Hogarth Press and the Institute of Psychoanalysis, 1931.

Praz, Mario. *The Romantic Agony*. Oxford: Oxford University Press, 1933.

Rosario, Vernon A. *The Erotic Imagination: French Histories of Perversity*. Oxford: Oxford University Press, 1997.

NEDJMA

North African novelist

L'Amande

This book is described as "the first erotic narrative to be written by a Muslim woman," however, Nedjma is not the first Moroccan woman to speak of her sexuality. Fatima Mernissi, Soumaya Naamane-Guessous, and Ghita El-Khayat have already unveiled the taboo of the female sexual speech. Nevertheless, Nedjma's intimate narrative gained the most popularity when it first appeared in France with close to 50,000 copies sold. Many other countries have also bought the rights to *L'Amande*.

This intimate narrative, written in the first person, recounts in a crude and sensual manner the weight imposed on a young Arabian woman bearing the many cultural interdicts. *L'Amande* is foremost the testimony of a woman who discovers for the first time her own sexual urges. Nedjma's style is quite liberal—she speaks overtly of sex, however, she has a keen sense of human nature and knows how to punctuate her novel with some much needed mystery which allows the element of erotica to create the desired impact upon the reader. The author allows Badra, the main character, to speak freely since she is perceived by her entourage—husband and family members—as a mere body, an organ responsible for procreation. As the story unfolds, Badra discovers her womanhood and attempts to emancipate herself from the many sexual taboos which plague Morocco in the 1960's. Written with the intent to restore the Arabian woman's once confiscated voice, Nedjma's intimate narrative makes the reader swing from one end of the pendulum to the next, seeing the world through the eyes of the submissive woman and then seeing it through the eyes of the liberated one. The story occurs through short chapters where Badra's past, before she ran away to Tangier, is found in italicized chapters interlacing the course of the main story where the reader can observe the protagonist's sexual and psychological growth.

The heroine, Badra bent Salah ben Hassan el-Fergani, is fifty years old when she decides to tell her story. Wed at 17 years old to Hmed, a forty-year-old notary who had previously repudiated two other women for reasons of infertility, she will suffer the same fate when she will leave him five years into their marriage. Leaving Imchouk, her native village for Tangier, brings a key character in Badra's personal development. She takes refuge with her aunt Selma, a strong, free-thinking woman, who will indicate to Badra the necessary steps to take for her to find herself as a woman. One night, where Selma prepares a reception dinner, Badra meets the man her sex will ever worship. Although her aunt does not approve of Driss, a cardiologist in his thirties, Badra nonetheless indulges in her sexual urges.

Disappointed in her niece's choices, Selma abandons Badra and refuses to offer her any more guidance and counsel. On the other hand, Driss allows Badra some financial security, encouraging her to get an education and eventually a good job; however he refuses to engage himself matrimonially. This encounter with an experienced man, loving and churlish, will teach her to discover her own body and will allow her to achieve her climax. However, Badra will refuse to engage in some sexual transgressions. After being "heart amputated," she therefore decides to break things off with Driss, leaving the only man she has ever loved.

The author begins her story with a long list of well known clichés (such as Arabian and Persian women being more fertile than other races, or Nubians having rounder and firmer buttocks) defied by the narrator by stating openly her belief that her cunt is the most beautiful of all. A strong statement she is allowing herself to openly say because at the moment where the writing takes place, Driss is already deceased. She adds that in spite of her aging body and her menopause, and although she is in her fifties, she is well capable of giving birth. She returns to Imchouk to write her story, having left behind Tangier and all those idiotic women wearing the traditional veil because of their refusal to wear their sex.

Then, Badra reveals how her future mother-in-law, accompanied by her eldest daughter, examine her at the hammam "like a sheep," the human flesh, according to her, having much less value than animal's flesh. Badra also explains how, before her wedding, the family will intentionally make her gain weight and make her skin go pale, as well as how they curtly verify her virginity. In an evocative chapter entitled "La nuit de la défloration" [The Night of the Deflowering], which is a complete opposite to eroticism, Badra recounts the details of her first night with Hmed. Her family tells her she must place a white shirt beneath her in order for them to see the deflowering blood, then her sister advises her to bite her lips and think about something else. Her husband, unfortunately, is unable to perform intercourse with his new wife; the mother-in-law is infuriated and binds Badra's hands and feet. That way, she looses her virginity in front of her mother and sister-in-law's eyes.

Later, her husband's family will not hesitate to track Badra, looking intensively for any sign of pregnancy; none will appear and Badra will be humiliated.

Badra also reveals another key moment of her childhood, which she calls "The Annunciation," where near a river she recalls of a hand caressing her breasts and vagina. This experience introduces her to sex and she links it to the birth of a second heart between her legs. Stemming from this experience, Badra will have a deep desire to explore her sexuality. The tale is as erotic as it is mystic; in fact, the intensity of her relationship with Driss makes her believe that it was him who had first caressed her genitals near the Harrath River. Badra also believes that it was with Driss with whom she lost her "true" virginity, that is the one of the heart. The first real erotic scene comes when they finally have their first sexual intercourse. Through the story, sex and soul become one even after Driss's death, because even angels have a sex.

It is therefore with love, hate, or even laughter that the author attempts to deliver an erotic story, troubling, crude, searching to show the difficult steps to take for a submissive woman towards an impossible attempt of personal liberation. Albeit her separation from Driss, Badra has a hard time controlling her mind, body, and soul. Her vagina remembers all of the penises that have penetrated it, but has no gratitude for them and the memory of all the men vanishes with the years. At the end, only her mind remains.

Biography

Information regarding the author of *L'Amande* is quite limited. For reasons of personal safety, the author writes under the pseudonym of Nedjma referring to Kateb Yacine's famous character. The outside back cover only indicates that the author is in her forties and lives in North Africa.

NATHALIE DUMAS

Editions

L'Amande. Paris: Plon, 2004; as *The Almond: The Sexual Awakening of a Muslim Woman*. Translated by C. Jane Hunter, New York: Grove Press, 2005.

Further Reading

Mernissi, Fatima. *Dreams of Trespass: Tales of a Harem Girlhood*. Massachusetts: Addison Wesley Publishing Company, 1994.

Mernissi, Fatima. *Beyond the Veil: Male–Female Dynamics in Modern Muslim Society*. Bloomington and Indianapolis: Indiana University Press, 1987.

Naamane-Guessous, Soumaya. *Au-delà de toute pudeur: La sexualité féminine au Maroc*. Casablanca: Soden, 1987.

NERCIAT, ANDRÉA DE

(1739–1800)
French novelist

Andréa de Nerciat had theatrical aspirations, but is remembered today mainly for his erotica. A musician, diplomat, soldier, spy, and novelist, Nerciat, a member of France's hereditary aristocracy, harbored Republican tendencies; politically, he might be best described as a constitutional monarchist. He led a tumultuous life during a time of great political and social upheaval. He wrote ten works in all, more than 2,100 pages.

His literary works show greater philosophical cohesion than his chaotic political career. They are uniformly both licentious and aristocratic, and permeated throughout with the *joie de vivre* of the sensualist. They encompass a wide range of genres: some reflect the classical structure of the *roman d'éducation* (*Félicia, Monrose, le Doctorat impromptu, La matinée libertine*); others are written in the picaresque tradition (*Le Diable au corps, Les Aphrodites, Julie philosophe*), and still others are poetic compositions (*Contes polissons, Contes nouveaux*).

In *Félicia ou mes fredaines* (1775), the narrator Félicia, an uninhibited libertine, recounts her escapades. Her sexual curiosity is piqued for the first time when she looks through a keyhole and sees Sylvina amusing herself with Béatin, a debauched priest whose sins, according to Nerciat's ethics, include hypocrisy, scandalmongering and cowardice. Curious and intrigued, Félicia asks Belval, her ballet master, to explain the lovers' actions. Belval agreeably reenacts the scene as she describes it and encourages her to participate in the playacting. Sylvina enters the room unexpectedly, surprising them. She doesn't hold Félicia accountable, but expels Belval from the house.

Félicia and her friends meet at the home of a member of the local bourgeoisie, Madame Dupré, for an evening orchestrated by the local prelate, who is famous for his skill at throwing parties—everything about the evening's atmosphere reflects his careful planning and heightens the sensuality. An ensemble of Italian musicians participate in an assortment of amorous acts; Félicia's antics outdo those of Sylvina, and she wins the right to bed the passionate Géronimo. Another guest, D'Aiglemont, stirs the lust of two young Italian women, but finally chooses Argentine; after much hesitation, Madame Dupré gives in to the knight despite her upcoming marriage to Lambert. The evening turns into an orgy: cries of pleasure and cries of those refusing their importuners are heard throughout the entire neighborhood, but a scandal is avoided with ingenious explanations.

The introduction of a new character, fourteen-year-old Monrose, changes the dynamics between the characters. Monrose recounts his traumatic childhood as an orphan to Félicia and Sylvina. After his abuse at the hands of the regent and principal of his school, Monrise fled the institution, and found himself among the dregs of society. Félicia and Sylvina, moved by his story and seduced by his charming personality, take him under their wing and invite him to Paris. Once again, the adoptive mother and daughter compete for the sexual attentions of the same man. Félicia wins and introduces Monrose, whose experience until now is limited to men, to sexual pleasure with a woman. She insists that he is hers alone, but Sylvina persists in trying to seduce Monrose, and the resulting competition results in almost farcical comedy.

The arrival of Lord Sydney, an Englishman, further complicates the plot. Sydney tells Félicia of the unusual circumstances of his birth and the unexpected ties his family has to Madame de Kerlandec (the woman in the portrait, who is also known as Zéila), ties shared by him and Monrose. The mystery surrounding Monrose is solved, and the novel ends with happy endings for all—marriages, a small fortune won in the lottery, trips to Italy and England—except for the repulsive Béatin, who is finally punished for his hypocrisy and pettiness.

The posthumously published *Le Diable au corps* (The Devil in the Flesh) (1803), is both a celebration of sexual pleasure and a sexually-expressed affirmation of Nerciat's Republicanism. All social classes are mixed together—bodies, regardless of their social origin or standing, pile up on top of each other. The book is essentially a collection of ribald stories connected by the slightest of plots and intertwined like the participants of the orgy which Nerciat describes in the course of the narrative. It opens with a tale that sets the tone for the rest of the book.

The Reverend Boujaron conspires with Bricon, a peddler of erotic paraphernalia, to introduce a Marquise to the pleasures of sodomy. The pair arouses the Marquise with Bricon's assortment of merchandise, such as a dildo made for "*Saint Luc et Saint Noc*" (the names are palindromic puns—in French, *boustrophédon*: spelled backwards, *Luc* and *Noc* spell *cul* and *con*, French slang terms for the female genitalia. The sacrilegious addition of the word 'Saint' increases the shock value of the humour), and she submits to Boujaron and Bricon's advances.

The Marquise and her friend the Countess then collaborate in an elaborate scheme to determine whether the Viscount Molengin deserves his name (another pun from Nerciat—the surname 'Molengin' combines two French words: 'mol,' soft, and 'engin,' penis: thus the Viscount's own name mocks his erectile disfunction). But the Countess will also be duped as the story continues. She complains that her lover, Tournesol, is recently showing less passion in bed. Tournesol tells her about his discovery of a miraculous aphrodisiac, the *immortalita del*

Cazzo. The pair hurries to the Countess' bed-chamber to test the elixir's efficacy, but Tournesol replaces himself with six different men, each of whom in turn bring the countess to such a climax that her extreme pleasure renders her incapable of distinguishing among her partners.

A young girl named Nicole is sexually initiated by the knight Rapignac. Although she does not know by whom she is being deflowered, she gladly participates in the act.

At one point, the Countess, who has contracted smallpox, tells the Marquise that both Dupeville and Rapignac want to marry her. She tells the Marquise that her smallpox may force her to curb her antics, but the Marquise refuses to believe her, especially since the Countess has recovered fully. In the end, the countess opts to keep her freedom and continue her mischievous adventures.

The Marquise and the Countess also arrange an escapade with Félix, a jockey in the Marquise's service, which unfolds like a ribald play. The countess pretends to be asleep with her derrière exposed, and she is sodomized by Félix, who cannot resist her. But as Felix is sodomizing her, she grabs his pants, refusing to let him withdraw. Totally astonished, Félix swoons. When he awakens, he weeps, humiliated at having been fooled by the women. The escapade ends well for everyone—to assuage his feelings, the Marquise announces that henceforth, Félix will serve the Countess.

The Countess reveals to the Marquise and a character named Belamour that her brother, the Baron, once had sex with Nicole while she was still Belamour's mistress. The Baron disguised himself as Cascaret (another name for Belamour) in order to seduce Nicole. Instead of taking offense, Belamour and the Baron reconcile, and the tale ends with the two seducing both Nicole and her mother. Nicole allows Belamour to bed her again, while at the same time and in the same room, the Baron amuses himself with Nicole's mother, Madame Culchaud (another sexual pun. Here Nerciat combines *cul* with *chaud,* French for 'hot'). While copulating with Belamour, Nicole syncs her lovemaking to the rhythm of her mother's, so that the sounds of her own lovemaking will not be heard.

We also learn of Mademoiselle Julie, now Madame de Conbannal, who is in fact Belamour's mother. Before her death, she locates her son in order to leave him her entire fortune, believing that her good deed will help her avoid the fires of Hell. Belamour inherits his mother's fortune, allowing him to leave the Marquise's service. The Countess, disappointed at the loss of a lover, regretfully recounts her adventures with Belamour to the Marquise. The Countess' nymphomania shocks even the Marquise, who feigns prudery and begins spouting moralistic platitudes on licentiousness, but the facade dissolves under the Countess' repeated caresses, and she proposes sexplay with an enormous dildo. Their antics are interrupted by the unexpected arrival of Tréfoncier, who is invited to participate in the festivities. The Countess, always seeking unusual pleasures, attaches the dildo to Trefoncier's face, allowing him to penetrate them both at once.

The book is an exercise in sensual anarchy. All manner of trickery results in countless combinations of characters and sexual acts. Nothing is taboo: homosexual liaisons between prelates and young boys, the Marquise and her servants, and between Nicole and Philippine, a servant girl, abound. At one point, the Countess and Philippine engage in bestiality with a donkey in a series of acts originating in the Countess' fertile imagination.

In *Les Aphrodites* [*The Aphrodites*] (1793), Nerciat writes of a secret society headquartered in a château near Paris, where aristocrats go to indulge in lascivious pleasures in an atmosphere of utter sexual abandon. Madame Durut, the royal go-between who masterfully orchestrates all encounters between the society's members, demands a large sum from the men (the women pay nothing) in exchange for a highly erotic visit. Everything in the castle stimulates lust: the decor, which continually changes according to different needs, is indescribably beautiful; the rituals are orchestrated performances that embellish the numerous unorthodox activities that take place in the different rooms of the castle or in its nearby rotundas. The guests compete in sexual exploits in this paradise, a world devoid of intolerance and restraint. Everyone is young and beautiful and in possession of a perfect body, and is described according to his or her sexual capacities. Certain games organized by the inventive Madame Durut require the participants to race to climax. There is no sadness or heartbreak in this cheerful paradise, and if misfortune arrives, Madame Durut quickly

remedies the situation with various stratagems, each one more amusing than the rest.

Other works, equally engaging and often shorter in length, illustrate similar themes that all expound upon Nerciat's key concept: that sexual pleasure is at the centre of any fully experienced life. Some examples are *Contes nouveaux* (1777), *La matinée libertine ou les moments bien employés* (1787), *Contes polissons (appelés aussi contes saugrenus)* (1799), *Le Doctorat impromptu* (1788), *Julie Philosophe ou Le bon patriote* (1791), *Monrose ou le libertin par fatalité* (1792), *Mon noviciat ou les joies de Lolotte* (1792).

Nerciat's novels, for all their unbridled lewdness, exhibit a surprisingly commonsense and centrist political philosophy, and overflow with a happy and healthy appreciation of human sexuality. This philosophy stands in stark contrast to the cynicism and harshness of the political life of his era, which was particularly corrupt and bloody. If his work is any reflection of his life, Nerciat – a spiritual libertine – must have experienced great personal joy throughout the many vicissitudes of his professional life.

If, however, his work bears no resemblance to the actual events of his life, his imagination is all the more impressive for its elaborate compensation. If so, the contrast is sharp—Nerciat's life was as dangerous as his work is full of joy.

If this question must be resolved, we suggest that Nerciat's work is largely autobiographical and presents a faithful reflection of the very uninhibited morals of the pre-Revolutionary French aristocracy (but without their corruption and violence).

The picture Nerciat presents of his era and its ethos also contrasts sharply with the atmosphere of the post-Napoleonic Restoration era, and the relentless moral repression that accompanied it.

Biography

Andréa de Nerciat was born in 1739 in Dijon and died in Rome in 1800. At the age of twenty, Nerciat became a soldier, in which capacity he traveled to Denmark, Flanders, Germany, and Switzerland. Participation in a conspiracy resulted in his banishment from the court of Hesse-Cassel; he petitioned Frederick II for patronage, but was unsuccessful, even though the Prussian king enjoyed his play *Dorimon ou le Marquis de Clarville*, and abandoned his career as a playwright. Following his expulsion from Hesse-Cassel, Nerciat went to Amsterdam, where, as a lieutenant–colonel, he defended the Republicans against the conservative Stadhouder. He participated in the French Revolution, but apparently served both sides in spite of his clearly Republican inclinations. Following his active participation in the Revolution, the aging Nerciat became a bookseller in Hamburg and Leipzig. In 1796, he became a spy for France while living in Vienna and was expelled from that city. He served Marie Caroline of Naples and was imprisoned by the France's General Berthier in Rome's Castel Sant'Angelo from 1798 to 1800. He died upon his release from prison.

JULIE PAQUET
Translated from the French by
KATHRYN GABINET-KROO

Works

Le doctorat impromptu. Paris, Société Européenne d'Édition et de Diffusion, Collection "*Aphrodite classique*", 1978.

Unexpected love lesson. Translation and introduction by Dudley Leslie, London, Odyssey Press, 1970.

Félicia ou mes fredaines. Editions PA, coll. "*Chefs-d'oeuvre érotique* (sic) *du 19e siècle*", 1980.

Mon noviciat ou les joies de Lolott. Cadeilham, Éditions Zulma, 2001.

Le Diable au corps. (Edité en 1803, mais écrit avant 1775), Préface d'Hubert Juin, Paris, La bibliothèque oblique, 1980, Tomes 1, 2 et 3.

Monrose ou le libertin par fatalité. Paris, Texte intégral d'après l'édition de 1792, Introduction bibliographique par Guillaume Apollinaire, Bibliothèque des curieux, coll. "*Les maîtres de l'amour*", 1912.

Les Aphrodites, fragments thali-priapiques pour servir à l'histoire du plaisir. Paris, Union générale d'édition, 1997.

The Aphrodites. Translation and introduction by Howard Nelson, Los Angeles: Holloway House, 1971.

Contes nouveaux. En vers, Liège, 1777.

Contes polissons dits aussi *Contes saugrenus*. Paris, réimpression de 1891 conforme comme Texte et Gravures à l'édition originale de 1799, 88 p.

La matinée libertine ou les moments bien employés. Suivis de *Vingt ans de la vie d'une jolie femme* par Julia R., Euredif, Paris, Coll. "*Aphrodite*", 1979, ou Paris, Éditions Civilisation nouvelle, coll. "*Civilisation d'Éros*", 1970.

Julie philosophe ou le bon patriote. Tome 1, Paris, Bibliothèque des Curieux (Le coffret du bibliophile. Les romans libertins), 1910.

Julie philosophe ou le bon patriote. Tome second, Paris, Tchou, 1968.

Fragments de *Constance ou L'Heureuse Témérité*, comédie mêlée d'ariettes, sujet, dialogue et musique de la composition de M. Le chevalier de Nerciat. Paris, Bibliothèque Nationale de Paris, Réserve des livres rares, Enfer-6.

Further Reading

Abramovici, Jean-Christophe. Préface de *Félicia*, Andréa de Nerciat, Cadeilham, éditions Zulma. 2002.

———. Préface de *Lolotte*, Andréa de Nerciat, Cadeilham, éditions Zulma. 2001.

Alexandrian, Sarane. *Les libérateurs de l'amour*. Éditions du Seuil, Paris, coll. Points, no 79, Paris. 1977.

Apollinaire, Guillaume. *L'oeuvre du chevalier Andréa de Nerciat*. Paris, Bibliothèque des curieux. 1927.

Goulemot, Jean-Marie. *Ces livres qu'on ne lit que d'une main. Lecture et lecteurs de livres pornographiques au XVIIIe siècle*. Editions Alinéa, Collection de la Pensée, Aix-en-Provence. 1991.

Henriot, Émile. "Le chevalier de Nerciat" dans *Les livres du second rayon irréguliers et libertins*, Paris, Grasset. 1948.

Ivker, Barry. "The parameters of a period-piece pornographer, Andréa de Nerciat", *SVEC*, 97(1972): 199–205.

Juin, Huber. "Un portrait d'Andréa de Nerciat" dans *Chroniques sentimentales*, Paris, Mercure de France. 1962.

———. Préface de *Le Diable au corps* (1803), Paris, La bibliothèque oblique, tome 1. 1980.

———. Postface de *Les Aphrodites, fragments thali-priapiques pour servir à l'histoire du plaisir* (1793), Paris, Union générale d'édition, collection 10/18. 1997.

Laroch, Philippe. *Petits-maîtres et roués. Évolution de la notion de libertinage dans le roman français du XVIIIe siècle*, Québec, P.U.F. 1979.

Scott, S. "Le rôle du narrateur dans *Félicia*", *Australian Journal of French Studies*, vol. XXI, no. 1. 1984.

Toebbens, Marion Luise. *Étude des romans libertins du chevalier de Nerciat (1739-1800)*, University of Alabama Press. 1974.

Trousson, Raymond. *Romans libertins du XVIIIe siècle*, Paris, Laffont (Bouquins). 1993.

Wald Lasowski, Patrick. " Introduction", *Romanciers libertins du XVIIIe siècle*, Paris, Gallimard, "La Pléiade." 2000.

Wilkins, Kay. "*Andréa de Nerciat and the libertine tradition in eighteenth-century France*", in *Studies on Voltaire & the eighteenth-century*, no 256, 1988.

NIN, ANAIS

1903–1977
French diarist and novelist

Anais Nin's early life was spent traveling around Europe with her parents and two brothers during which she was exposed to a variety of artistic and bohemian circles. After the family was abandoned in 1914 by Nin's father, she began what was to become her most notorious piece of writing, namely her diary en route to the United States. From 1914–1922, Nin lived with her family in New York, dropping out of high school at the age of sixteen. In 1923, she married a rich banker, Hugh P. Guiler, in Cuba and in all probability lived there for a number of years. In 1931, Nin returned to Paris with her husband and it was here that she was introduced to a number of influential artists and other seminal influences, which were to color her later writing. While living near Paris in Louveciennes, Nin completed her first book: *D.H. Lawrence: An Unprofessional Study* (1932) and also began psychotherapy with Dr. Rene Allendy and later the famous Jungian disciple: Otto Rank. During this time she also became deeply involved with the American expatriate writer Henry Miller and his wife June, (whom she met through lawyer Edward W. Titus. Titus negotiated the contract for her Lawrence book). Nin eventually went on to support Miller's literary efforts by financing his accommodation and providing him with a typewriter. In 1934, Nin partially paid for the publication of Henry Miller's novel: *Tropic of Cancer* (1934). Together with Miller and a number of other writers, Michael Fraenkel, Walter Lowenfels, Lawrence Durrell, and Alfred Perles, Nin became part of the Villa Seurat Circle, named after the artists' studio that many of them occupied. Through their own publishing ventures Nin's second book *House of Incest* (1936) was published under the imprint Siana (Anais spelled backwards) and later *Winter of Artifice* (1939) under the imprint of Obelisk Press.

During World War II, Nin returned to the United States, establishing her own press: the Gemor Press. Gemor Press reprinted limited editions of *Winter of Artifice* (1942) as well as collections of short stories: *Under A Glass Bell* (1944), *The Hunger* (1945), and a reprint of *House of Incest* (1947). Following an extremely favorable review by the critic Edmund Wilson in The New Yorker, *Under a Glass Bell* was the only selection of Nin's short stories to appear in a second edition within four months of the original publication. In 1946, Nin was offered a contract by E.P. Dutton to publish the five-part series of her 'continuous novel': *Cities of the Interior*. *Ladders of Fire* came out in 1946, followed by *Children of the Albatross* (1947), *The Four Chambered Heart* (1950), *A Spy in the House of Love* (1954), and *Solar Barque* (1958). In the 1960s, another version of *Solar Barque* was eventually published as *Seduction of the Minotaur* (Swallow Press, 1961) as was a collection of short pieces, *Collages* (1964). Most of Nin's time in the 1960s and 70s was spent editing her voluminous diary for publication. According to herself, the diary was over 35,000 pages in 200 manuscript volumes by the time she began editing them. The first volume was published in 1966 and five more volumes were published up through 1976. Nin also published a brief treatise on writing in general: *The Novel of the Future* (1968). In 1977, the year Nin died, a collection of erotica: *Delta of Venus* became a posthumous bestseller. Nin died of ovarian cancer in Los Angeles, January 14, 1977.

While Nin's literary reputation rests largely on the success of her diaries, the novels that precede them introduce her assertively personal style; a mixture of self-actualization described in poetic terms coupled with a firm belief in the value of minute introspection. Nin's first novel *The House of Incest* (1936) and the following three novelettes published under the heading: *Winter of Artifice* (1939) explore the female psyche through a combination of dream analysis and surreal imagery. In these texts, the overall strategy is designed to convey the disjointed life of a women for whom the boundaries between dreams, desire, and actual experience is deliberately left unclear. *The House of Incest*, in particular, represents the style Nin was later to explore to a varying degree in most of her fiction. Through the work of Henry Miller, above all, Nin realized that the exploration of the unconscious, the use of stream of consciousness, and an acceptance of the irrational could lay the foundation for a form of writing dedicated to an exploration of the feminine psyche—for better or for worse.

The majority of Nin's fiction is structured in the form of lengthy prose poems, using a combination of interior monologue, dreams, and psycho-analytical jargon to represent an unnamed narrator in the midst of self-discovery. Although there appears to be no structure for the action per se, the subconsciousness of the character—or rather the development of that subconsciousness into an instrument of poetic intent—constitutes the main narrative.

House of Incest thus contains the basic stylistic ideas and themes that were later to become Nin's hallmark. Nin's writing is characterized by the use of highly symbolic imagery, and above all, a focus on the importance of dreams as a harbinger and symptom of liberating desires.

Seeking to reveal the hidden feelings and emotions of a women hovering on the edge of hysteria, Nin's legacy as a feminist writer is a mixed one. Her style can either be seen as an honest attempt to investigate the unchartered territory of female sexuality in a liberating sense or as a deeply narcissistic exercise in a form of self-revelatory writing that suffers from an obsessive need to be constantly self-revelatory.

Another complicating factor in any reassessment of Nin's work lies in the fact that selections of the material originating in the short stories re-emerges in Nin's diaries, and similarly, the diary often contains material passed off as fictitious in another literary context. Nin, like Henry Miller, believed firmly that the distinction between autobiography and fiction was a fluid one vis-à-vis the intrinsic value of the confessional voice within literature.

Although Nin published her five novels at regular intervals between 1945–1961, she intended for the novels to be interrelated through recurring characters and themes. Under the heading: *Ladders of Fire*, Nin set forth an ideology of writing based on the concept of the continuous novel, what Nin called "a series of novels on various aspects of relationships." From *Ladders of Fire* (1946), *Children of the Albatross* (1947), *The Four Chambered Heart* (1950), *Spy in the House of Love* (1954), and *Seduction of the Minotaur* (1961), a collage of stories emerge chiefly with and about female protagonists.

In the prologue to her continuous novel Nin states: "I have to begin the story of women's development where all things begin: in nature, at the roots. It is necessary to return to the origin of confusion, which is women's struggle to understand her own nature. Man appears only partially, because for the woman at war with herself, she can only appear thus, not as an entity."

Throughout most of her fiction as well as in her diaries, Nin's work walks a tightrope between the liberating stance that enamored her largely female readership in the 1970s, and a rhetoric more reminiscent of largely Francophile libertarianism that owes a great deal to Surrealism. Contrary to much surrealist writing, however, Nin's protagonist is often punished for her sexual indiscretions and remains unfulfilled emotionally and psychologically. This paradoxical stance has puzzled feminist critics who, one the one hand, wish to appropriate Nin into a canon of positive role-models for feminist writing while, on the other hand, have to get to grips with her oftentimes torturous stance on female sexuality and tendency towards biological determinism. Although Nin's work is predominantly read as a burgeoning female modernist voice within a largely male-dominated literary establishment, there is also much to be said for a reading of her, which takes into account the politics of modernism at a time when a feminist voice did not necessarily take the form of a directly liberal and/or leftist response. Instead Nin channels her writing through a form of modernist endeavour that freely embraces the psychoanalytical discourse of the 1910s and '20s. In other words, Nin's introspective heroines are also the mouthpieces for a discourse that unashamedly embraces the value of the irrational and the dreamworld as a creative impetus in itself, without necessarily taking the issue of gender and political correctness into account.

Similarities have nevertheless prompted many to compare Nin to the Surrealists, and indeed Nin's friendship with the famous French actor Antonin Artaud, who operated on the fringes of Surrealist practice, is relatively well documented. Nevertheless, despite attempts to consolidate

Nin's reputation within the context of Surrealism the affiliation remains tenuous. Less so is her literary relationship to Henry Miller, a writer whose early style and diction Nin's own writing mimics to a disturbingly close extent. While much has been written in biographies of Nin on her sexual and personal relationship with Miller, little has been documented on their common attraction to a Spenglerian worldview in which the personal and the erotic is symbolically related to a politics of despair, a sense that would have been augmented by the increasing sense of impending doom just prior to and after World War II. Nin's search for her own body through a process of sexual healing for example, shares a great deal with Miller's use of sexual promiscuity as an analogy for a modernism gone astray, fearful of its own effectiveness and potential neglect of humanism and sensitivity.

In 1961, Nin moved to Los Angeles and began to intensify the reediting of her diaries. The first volume (1931–1934) was published in 1966, at which time she also began to give lectures and interviews around the country on the art of writing fiction and autobiography. Nevertheless, in spite of its relatively late success in terms of Nin's overall career, the diary itself had been a well-known fact since the early 1930s amongst her friends and those sympathetic to her writing. Following an enthusiastic article on Nin's Diary by Henry Miller: 'Un etre etoilique' (1937), the publication of an installment of the diary was actually announced in an issue of the Booster; an Anglo-American journal briefly edited by Miller, Lawrence Durrell, and Alfred Perles in 1937. Nevertheless, the publication never occurred and it was not until a cautious first printing by Harcourt in 1966 that the diary eventually reached the public, by which time it became so popular it was quickly reprinted several times.

Volume I (1931–1934) details Nin's artistic awakening and early collaborations, literary as well as sexual and personal with Henry Miller and his wife June, her encounters with the psychoanalysist Rene Allendy, and her meeting with the actor Antonin Artaud. It also documents the return of her father and finally her meeting with the famous psychoanalyst Otto Rank, whom she ended up working with in New York. This is documented in Volume II of the diary. In Volume II (1934–1939), Nin further explores her oftentimes volatile and stormy relationship with Miller as well as her nurturing of him and other writer/lovers throughout the decade. The supposed disclosure of Nin's sexual liaisons with most of the artists she encountered has, indeed, become one of the mainstays of her work's allegedly risqué content. In this respect, Otto Rank, Henry Miller, a Peruvian Marxist writer Gonzalo, and indeed her own father, figure prominently.

Throughout the diaries, the last and sixth Volume documents the period 1955–1966, Nin's attempts to establish herself as a writer and artist are interspersed with her psychoanalytical sessions and her sexual encounters. Whether these "sessions" are imaginary and/or real is deliberately made unclear in many instances. Other passages in the later diaries detail in slightly more pragmatic terms Nin's return to the United States and how she attempts to get to grips with American mores and morals.

The popularity of the diary elevated Nin, who presents herself as the diary's chief protagonist and dominating persona, to a cult figure for a strengthening feminist movement in the late 1960s and throughout the 1970s. As Nin's life of sexual exploration became a marker for an increasing feminist awareness, Nin herself capitalizecapitalized on this, drawing larger audiences for the increasingly popular college and literary lectures she gave. In critical terms, there was a general agreement that the diaries provided a remarkable sense of the bohemian life of 1930s Paris. Coupled with the sexual life of a young childless and uninhibited woman, the diaries were thus taken by many to be a reflection of an early attempt at feminine self-liberation. Since 1985, however, large amounts of material expurgated from the original diary publications have emerged, prompting a revision of Nin's allegedly liberated sexual life. Hitherto undisclosed facts about Nin's life—such as a possible incestuous relationship with the father she was reunited with at the age of 20, and several unintended abortions—have tended to color the previous "so-called" true accounts in the diaries.

In the wake of these disclosures, two unexpurgated versions of Nin's Diaries: *Henry and June: From the Unexpurgated Diary of Anais Nin* (1986) and *Incest: From 'Journal of Love,' the Unexpurgated diary of Anais Nin* (1992) can be seen as either predominantly commercial attempts by the estates of Nin's work to make money following her death or alternatively further testimony to the honest and passionate disclosure in writing of a women's most private life.

Henry Miller's relationship to Nin likewise stands as an ambiguous testimony to both of their ouvres as it is unclear how much they edited and rewrote each other's work during the 1930s. From a staunchly feminist perspective, Nin's long-term relationship with a writer such as Henry Miller, known for his supposedly male chauvinist agenda, is a troubling reminder that her public persona is possibly very different from the one she advocated the disclosure of in most of her work. As an example, it was through Henry Miller that Nin was introduced to an anonymous collector searching for compliant writers of erotica for private consumption. Nin acquiesced and the following years not only supplied short pieces but became the procurer and middleman for friends wishing to submit. According to Miller, as quoted by Nin in her diary, the stories were to "leave out the poetry and the descriptions of anything but sex. Concentrate on Sex."

In spite of this, Nin's *Delta of Venus* (1977) and *Little Birds* (1979) are still remarkable visions of a sexual landscape set within a no-man's land of dreams and desires. Dealing with such issues as voyeurism, bisexuality, and the elaborate enactment of fantasy and role-playing, Nin's erotica displays a more playful and neurosis-free version of a woman's quest for sexual fulfilment than that oftentimes witnessed in the diaries. Nin's value as a writer of erotica is an issue that has nevertheless fallen by the wayside in most critical assessments of her work.

Towards the latter part of her life, Nin also successfully published a number of books on the art of writing in general: *The Novel of the Future* (1968) and *In Favour of the Sensitive Man and other Essays* (1976). *The Novel of the Future* was published by Macmillan in an attempt to capitalize on the success of the diaries and indeed on Nin's growing reputation as a role model for young aspiring female writers. *The Novel of the Future*, a series of thoughts and commentaries on writing in general, can be seen as an extended exposition on her previous fiction. Reaffirming her interest in the psychological, the use-value of dreams, and symbolism in writing, *The Novel of the Future*, rather than elaborate on her use of sexuality as a guiding principle, returns to Nin's preoccupation with individual empowerment through an acceptance of the irrational and

dreams. *In Favour of the Sensitive Man and other Essays* (1976) briefly deals with the issue of sexuality after the sexual revolution. In typical Nin vein it pays homage to the so-called "sensitive man" whilst simultaneously reminding women that their femininity must be preserved and indeed celebrated in order not to be suppressed.

Biography

Born in Paris, France 21 February 1903, the daughter of Joaquin Nin, a Spanish composer and pianist and Rosa Culmell, a singer of French and Danish ancestry. At age 11 she began keeping the diary for which she became one of the most celebrated diarists in literary history. She died in Los Angeles, California on January 14, 1977. The last volumes of her diaries were published posthumously.

CAROLINE BLINDER

Selected Works

D.H. Lawrence: An Unprofessional Study. 1934.
House of Incest. 1936.
Under A Glass Bell and Other Stories. 1944.
Cities of the Interior (includes *Ladders to Fire, Children of the Albatross, The Four Chambered Heart, A Spy in the House of Love, Solar Barque*). 1959.
Delta of Venus. 1977.
The Little Birds. 1979.
The Journals. 7 vols, 1973; Vol.1 1931–1944, Vol.2 1934–1939, Vol.3 1939–1944, Vol.4 1944–1947, Vol.5 1947–1955, Vol.6 1955–1966, Vol.7 1966–1980, edited by Anais Nin and Günther Stuhlmann, 1973.
Linotte: The Early Diary of Anais Nin 1914–1920. 1986.
A Literate Passion: Letters of Anais Nin and Henry Miller 1932–1953. Edited and introduced by Günther Stuhlmann, 1988.
Incest: From a Journal of Love: The Unexpurgated Diary of Anais Nin, 1932–1934. Introduced by Rupert Pole with biographical notes by Günther Stuhlmann, 1993.

Further Reading

Bair, Deidre. *Anais Nin: A Biography*. New York: Putnam, 1995.
Cutting, Rose Marie. *Anais Nin: A Reference Guide*. Boston, MA: G.K. Hall, 1978.
Duxlor, Margot. *Seduction: A Portrait of Anais Nin*. New York: Edgework, 2002.
Fitch, Noel Riley. *Anais: The Erotic Life of Anais Nin*. New York: Little Brown and Company, 1994.
Hinz, Evelyn J. *Woman Speaks: The Lectures, Seminars and Interviews of Anais Nin*. Ohio: Ohio University Press, 1976.
Spencer, Sharon, ed. *Anais, Art, and Artists: A Collection of Essays*. New York: Penkewill, 1987.

NOËL, BERNARD

1930–
French novelist and poet

Le château de Cène

Bernard Noël's *Le château de Cène* is a classic twentieth-century French erotic novel. First published in 1969 in Paris under the pseudonym of Urbain d'Orlhac, it was immediately banned by the authorities. In 1971, J.-J. Pauvert reissued it under Noël's name. The second edition drove Noël back to court where, in 1973, he was found guilty of obscenity. This may have been one of the last instances of prohibitions of this nature during the Fifth Republic; soon after censorship was abolished in France. Free again to be printed and distributed, *Le château de Cène* was published in 1977 in a paperback series (10–18). In 1985, another edition was released by Éditions Nulle Part and the novel was published by Gallimard in 1990. It coincided with the novel's stage adaptation at the Bataclan in Paris starring Philippe Léotard.

Le château de Cène is a short novel, but a disconcerting one that was obviously influenced by the Surrealist movement. Written in a highly poetic style, it stages an array of characters that are fascinated by the frightening and the unusual and are open to all sorts of excesses, including sadism and zoophilia. The story is about a special kind of apprenticeship, which takes place in two stages. In the first, the hero-narrator runs ashore on a remote island of the South Atlantic. For the local celebration of the equinox, he is chosen to deflower a young woman, Emma, who represents the new moon. This ritual ceremony takes place in public and is similar in its general structure to the famous poetic suite *Amers* by Saint-John Perse, although the analogy stops there. Noël's hero must go through a series of physical suffering before he can make love to the young woman. When he does, he finds a moment of true happiness.

In the second stage, the hero learns that he was chosen for this initiation by a mysterious and extremely beautiful lady from a neighboring island, whom he saw nude during the moon ritual. He decides to go to the island and meet her. Guarded by dogs, Arabs, and armed Black men, this island is dominated by Mona, a mythical countess who resembles the dangerous Hecatus. Before having access to his lady, the narrator is once again put to the test. He has to experience sex with two dogs who are mastered by a cruel Black man—this is one of the episodes for which the novel was censored. He also has to watch the atrocious execution of one of Mona's lovers, who is torn apart by a pack of dogs. Finally, he has to endure the unbearable spectacle of Emma, who is entwined with a snake within a glass prison.

Once he has passed these tests, the hero can have access to Mona, but he soon understands that his initiation is not over. He will still have to submit to the sadistic domination of the countess and her sexual fantasies, which include his being raped by a monkey.

Beyond this erotic calvary of the dark sides of sexuality, the hero will be happy to see the cruel Mona change into the sweet Ora. Further, for his great courage, he will be introduced to an exclusive secret society in which he will experience a new self and have the privilege of becoming the imagination of the group. There he will receive new powers including that of life and death over others.

The *Cène* (the Last Supper) of the title refers to his invitation to join this group and to the principles of sharing and reciprocity that govern the castle of Mona–Ora, a castle that is a hidden paradise of pleasures. The *Cène* also highlights the oral and digestive themes that dominate the sexual representation in the novel. This reaches its peak in an episode in which a black male is castrated and his erect phallus is thrown into a boiling bouillon.

This oneiric novel was followed by *Le château de Hors*, a brief coprophagic narrative, which further explores the oral and digestive dimension of this universe.

The author also added two texts, *L'Outrage aux mots* and *La pornographie,* which serve as commentaries on *Le château de Cène* as well as reflecting on the creative writing. Among other things, Noël draws a political parallel between his novel and the Algerian war, an intellectual interpretation that may also be used as a means of justifying his discursive production of sex by "serious" discourse. This self-interpretation is similar to another major problem that Noël courageously confronts: self-censorship, which may be as important, if not more so, than dealing with official censors. In these texts the reader discovers that the writing of *Le château de Cène* was a liberating experience for its author: this book was not written to sexually arouse the reader but to help the author master his own most intimate fears, thus helping to create the artist he ultimately became. Noël's first victory over his own censorship occurred with the publication of the second edition of the novel in 1971, when he decided to stop using a pseudonym: "[...] the pseudonym was making the censorship last, my signature was voiding it. " (157)

Bernard Noël goes even further by creating a new word, *sensure* ("sensorship") besides the usual *censure* (censorship). The *sensure* is for a new kind of repression in our modern cultures and refers to the deprivation of more than just speech, meaning itself (*sens* in French). The traditional *censure* acts against words, the new *sensure* acts on us with the words. With this in mind, he sees eroticism, when it is elitist and sectarian and has a defined set of rules, as the last resort of a moral order to *sensor* the body of its physical and organic dimensions. He uses the erotic genre against that eroticism as a subversive tool to fight the political blunder and as a means to subvert bourgeois values.

Biography

Born in 1930 in the French Aveyron. His first book of poety, *Extraits du corps,* was published in 1958.

He has written several novels, plays, collections of poetry (for which he won the National Poetry Award in 1992), essays, and art criticism. He contributed to numerous literary magazines, and is currently editor-in-chief of the magazine *Correspondances.*

GAËTAN BRULOTTE

Editions

Le Château de Cène, Paris: Pauvert, 1971; Paris: Gallimard: 1990; as *The Castle of Communion*, translated by Paul Buck and Glenda George, London: Atlas Press, 1993.

Selected Works

Extraits du Corps. 1958.
Dictionnaire de la Commune. 2 vols., 1971.
Le lieu des signes. 1971.
Une Messe Blanche. 1972.
Les premiers Mots. 1973.
Treize Cases du je. 1975.
Le 19 Octobre 1977. 1979.
URSS: Aller-Retour. 1980.
La moitié du geste. 1982.
La Chute des temps et Poèmes 1. 1983.
Le Sens, la Sensure. 1985.
La Rumeur de l'air (poèmes): *farce tragique en neuf scènes*. 1986.
Matisse, 1987. As *Matisse*, translated by Jane Brenton, 1987.
Journal du Regard. 1988.
Onze romans d'œil. 1988.
Portrait du Monde. 1988.
La Reconstitution. 1988.
Arbre, portrait. 1991.
Le Dieu des poètes. 1991.
Géricault. 1991.
La Nuit des Rois (translation and adaptation from Shakespeare). 1991.
Les Peintres du désir. 1992.
André Masson: la chair du regard. 1993.
La Chute des temps (Poèmes 2). 1993.
L'Ombre du double. 1993.
Adam et Ève. 1993.
Le Syndrome de Gramsci. 1994.
L'espace du désir. 1995.
La maladie de la chair. 1995.
Le roman d'Adam et Ève. 1996.
La castration mentale. 1997.
Site transitoire: Jean-Paul Philippe. 1997.
L'Espace du poème: Entretiens avec Dominique Sampiero. 1998.
La langue d'Anna. 1998.
Le tu et le silence. 1999.

Further Reading

Apert, Olivier. *Ecrit de la mer: Bernard Noël*. Xonrupt-Longemer: Ancrages, 1991.
Carn, Hervé. *Bernard Noël*. Paris: Seghers, 1986.
Dhainaut, Pierre. *Bernard Noël*. Rennes: Ubacs, 1977.
Wateau, Patrick. *Bernard Noël; ou, L'Expérience extérieure*. Paris: Corti, 2001.
Winspur, Steven. *Bernard Noël*, Amsterdam: Rodopi, 1991.

NOSAKA AKIYUKI

1930–
Japanese writer

In all his work novelist Nosaka Akiyuki tries to tear down the usual distinction between the *watakushi shosetsu* [the I-novel] and the entertaining novel which deals with relations between men and women. He rejects also the difference made between "popular" and "pure" literature. He loved writing songs, and then subverted the popular detective story as well as the porno novel. *The Pornographers* is not a pornographic novel in the usual sense of the term, as it doesn't oppose a strong male to a weak woman, which is always the case in Japanese literature. On the contrary, he often depicts weak men, and the voyeur–reader at the same time is deceived: there are none of the expected erotic scenes, and the censors have no precedents on which to decry such a tricky masterpiece. The casting is nether convincing and the mise en scène of pleasure is always laborious. What is described is rather the traffic of sexual fantasies organized for "art" and by "philanthropy" by a funny quatuor which is described. This polemical writer was prosecuted in 1974, at a time when he was editor-in-chief for the *Omoshirohambun* review. He published an anonymous short story, *Yojouhanfusuma no shitabari*, attributed to Nagai Kafù in the Taishô period. The trial became an opportunity to open the debate on censorship in Japan. Though he lost the trial, this short story is no longer forbidden.

With *Tomuraishitachi* [*The Funeral Undertakers*], it will be another type of organization, this time turned towards the death industry. The four characters are worried, like the previous pornographers, about how they can take advantage of the emerging capitalist market, and from their own experience of survival during war time. The economical progress is linked to the sex and death profits.

The last opus of the ero-guro-tero" (erotic-grotesque-terrorist) literature, *Tero-Tero* (1971) close a destructive achievement of an "eye-writer," cruel and lucid, who never stops critiquing post-war Japan, and his own destiny. Nosaka is strongly influenced by French naturalism, and he defines himself as a "hakkaisakka" (a writer without pity). The pornographic writer Kakiya that he imagines in *The Pornographers* writes in an old-fashioned way, and only while masturbating. He writes only with his imagination and through his act of writing he masturbates himself. The verb "kaku" means "to write" and onanism simultaneously. This novel is a deep investigation into masculine Japanese mentality. These men who sell sex fantasies, such as false virgins, "live" and natural sex audio tapes, photos and various items, films (which they shoot and direct themselves, before Imamura Shohei made his own version of the whole story in 1965, under the title *Erogoshitachi yori jinruigaku nyûmon* [*Gang bangs*], are charlatans. It is a "cock-novel" ("le roman du zizi," wrote Patrick de Vos) which showed the failure of sexual liberation. Subuyan discovers the main law: onanism. The climax comes when he marries a "poupée gonflable" wearing a girl school uniform. In fact, the main character feels an incestuous desire for his daughter, and then he becomes impotent. The lack of sexual power, associated with masturbation, resumes the main conception of the author. In *Amerika no Hijiki* (1968), Toshio brings the American friend of his wife to witness Japanese sexual power, but the actor, Kitchan, is completely impotent, a circumstance tied to his memories of the war and a shameful sense of inferiority.

Kan [*Viol*] deals with the ritual sexual intercourse between a shintoist temple guardian in a remote southern island and the cadavers of virgins. The ghost of a little dead girl disturbs the sexual and religious intercourse of the guardian who becomes impotent, and dies in the waves still having a holy wooden olisbos on his hips. The guardian refused to have sex with the little girl, because she looked like his sister. Then she became a ghost. Nosaka never stops writing to express his guilt at having survived the Kobe bombing, and to have left behind his mother and his little sister. *Hotaru no haka* [*The Firefly's Grave*] is the basis from which his novels can be understood as a way of asking forgiveness. The last utopy he can imagine is a pornotopy, based on onanism, impotency, and incest, like the collective tribal incest and sacrifice of newborn babies in *Honegami Toge Hotoke-Kazura* [*The Dead Vineyard on the Skinny God's Pass*], just the opposite of the democracy offered by the sexual liberators.

Biography

Born in Kamakura near Tokyo, Nosaka Akiyuki was brought up by adoptive parents in Kobe, as his mother died when he was born. At 14 years old, after the bombing of Kobe, he loses his parents, and his young sister. He survives then in the "yake-ato" time (literally "after burning") of the black market and ruins. His father, vice-governor for the province of Niigata, takes him out of the corrective house where he was placed. He entered Waseda University in Tokyo, but is not keen on studying for a long time. He worked many unusual jobs. In 1957, he writes scripts, commercial songs, and slogans for advertisments on radio and TV. In 1963, he publishes his very first novel, *Erogoshitachi* [*The Pornographers*]. It became a cult novel of the sixties. From 1962 to 1972, he wrote novels, political fiction, and many essays, being involved in the political life of the country first as a member of the United Left Front, then as a senator.

MARC KOBER

Selected Works

Novels, short stories

Erogoshitachi. 1963.
The Pornographers. Translated by M. Gallagher. Tuttle, 1970.
Tomuraishitachi. Kodansha, 1967.
Honegami Toge Hotoke-Kazura. 1967.
Kan. 1967.
Amerika no hijiki. 1968.
Iro Hôshi, Shosetsu shinchô. 1968.
Macchi-Uri no shojo. 1969.
Soudoushitachi. 1969.
Tero Tero. 1971.
1945 natsu Kobe. Chuuou kouron sha, 1979.

Essays

Hikyômono no shisô. 1969.
Pornotopy. 1970.
Otagai no shisô.
Hyôhaku.

Further Reading

Kober, Marc. *La Tombe des lucioles* (interview of Akiyuki Nosaka). *Pris de Peur* N°5, Rafael de surtis Editions, Cherves, 1997.
Kober, Marc. *Nosaka ou le Don Quichotte des lettres japonaises.* *Supérieur Inconnu* N°7, Paris, Juin-Septembre 1997. Translation of *Kan* included under the title "Histoire de Bunkichi gardien sacrilège" by Akira Hamada.
Perol, Jean. *Regards d'encre—Ecrivains japonais (1966–1986).* "Akiyuki Nosaka," La Différence, Paris, 1995.
Vos (de), Patrick. *Cinema et littérature de l'ère Meiji à nos jours au Japon.* "Nosaka Akiyuki," Cinéma/singulier, Centre Georges Pompidou, 1986.
Vos (de), Patrick. *Introduction to Hotaru no haka and Amerika no hijiki.* Picquier, Paris, 1988.
Interview of Akiyuki Nosaka, *Les Voix, Le Magazine franco-japonais,* Kyôto (Japan), printemps 2001.

NOUGARET, PIERRE

1742–1823
French compiler, historian, novelist, and dramatist

Pierre-Jean-Baptiste Nougaret was an indefatigable literary hopeful who left the provinces to make his way as a writer in Paris. Intent on selling books, he tried his hand at nearly every possible literary genre. His more than one hundred published works include heroic poems, geography books for children, libertine novels, patriotic hymns, plays and theatrical criticism, religious history books, pro-monarchy treatises, pro-revolutionary treatises, a history of French prisons, and a collection of amusing stories about monkeys. In short, his unrestrained output reveals an obsession to publish that left him with a reputation for literary metamorphoses and a certain prodigious mediocrity.

Virtually nothing is known about his childhood or family, and his education appears to have been minimal. After staging a one-act play in Toulouse at the age of eighteen, he left the provinces for Paris. There, he attempted to do precisely what an obscure newcomer from the provinces should do—make alliances with the literary establishment. He went about it rather badly, however, and soon was known for his sequels, vaguely disguised copies, and alternate versions of other people's work. He wrote a poem about the Calas affair to ingratiate himself with Voltaire, as well as a supplement to one of Voltaire's more scandalous poems, "La Pucelle." The addition to "La Pucelle" was deemed immoral, and Nougaret was imprisoned in the Bastille. Imprisonment gave him a certain literary cachet; opportunistic booksellers soon encouraged him to compose licentious works, as *livres obscènes* were selling well in 1760s Paris. The result was his first novel, *Lucette, ou les progrès du libertinage*, published in 1765. In 1769, he was imprisoned again for publishing the adventures of a libertine monk, *La Capucinade.*

He was a puppet of the book market, trying to mimic whatever was selling well, as is illustrated by many of his titles, which echo those of other writers: *Les nouvelles liaisons dangereuses,* [*New*

Dangerous Liaisons] after Laclos, and *La paysanne pervertie* [*The Perverted Peasant Girl*], after *Le paysan perverti* [*The Perverted Peasant*] by Rétif de la Bretonne. (Rétif, who hated Nougaret, later published his own *Paysanne pervertie.*) He also increased sales by republishing his own works with new titles, making only minor changes in plot or character names.

Of Nougaret's seventeen or eighteen texts that have at some point been classified as *livres obscènes*, the two most often cited are *Lucette, ou les progrès du libertinage* and *La Capucinade.* Some of his licentious novels were published anonymously, some with the indication N***, still others under the pseudonym Frère P.J. Discret N*.

Lucette, ou les Progrès du libertinage, 1765

Two young lovers, Lucette and Lucas—both peasants from the provinces—end up in Paris where they engage in sexual intrigues throughout the city. He is a lackey who keeps busy entertaining aristocratic women; she is a kept woman who flits from lover to lover: a prince, a bishop, several different merchants. Finally, worn out from their urban exploits, they escape from the city and are married. Cripped with debt and miserable, they soon die penniless. The sexual adventures are recounted within the frame of a cautionary tale in which the narrator helps the reader recognize characters' "false steps," as is illustrated in the narrative of Lucette's lost virginity:

> From that moment—fatal to her virtue—she felt an unknown agitation, and for a long time felt the strong desire in her heart to follow the example of the ladies of the city, persuaded that she could imitate them.

La Capucinade, histoire sans vraisemblance, 1769 [The Capucinade, Story against All Probability]

A young monk discovers the pleasures of love with the young Nanette. From this initiation, he enjoys a series of nights of pleasure with different women. He soon learns that his fellow monks share his inclination for the pleasures of the flesh and they begin to calculate different ways to sneak young women into the monastery. The novel is more anticlerical than erotic. To be sure, many characters have sexual liaisons with many other characters, but details are scant and the narrative seems written to amuse rather than to excite. For example, after seducing a virgin, the narrator offers only this commentary: "A cry announces my victory and lets me know that the gate to pleasure is now open for good." If anything, the narrative offers a diatribe against clerical celibacy: the narrator-monk continually reminds his reader of the natural inevitability of his desire for women.

Biography

Pierre-Jean-Baptiste Nougaret was born in La Rochelle, 16 December 1742. Moved to Toulouse where his first play was staged, 1760; moved to Paris, 1763; published his first novel, 1765; imprisoned in the Bastille for publishing an illicit book, 1765 and 1769; during the French Revolution, worked as an intelligence agent, following an alleged spy throughout southern France, 1792; named head of the office of surveillance in Paris, 1792; after the Terror, lived off the modest revenue from his writing. Died in Paris, June 1823.

DIANE BERRETT BROWN

Selected Libertine Works

Lucette, ou les Progrès du libertinage. 1765; also published, with modifications, as *La Paysanne pervertie ou les moeurs des grandes villes*, *Les Dangers de la séduction et les faux pas de la beauté*, *Juliette, ou les Malheurs d'une vie coupable*, and *Suzette et Pierrin, ou les Progrès du libertinage*.
La Capucinade, histoire sans vraisemblance. 1765.
Ainsi va le monde. 1769; also published as *Les Jolis péchés d'une marchande de modes, ou Ainsi va le monde*.
Les Mille et une folies, contes français. 1771.
Les Faiblesses d'une jolie femme, ou mémoires de Madame de Vilfranc, écrits par elle-même. 1779.
La Folle de Paris ou les extravagances de l'amour et de la crédulité. 1787; reprinted as *Stéphanie, ou les Folies à la mode*.
Les Perfidies à la mode ou l'école du monde. 1808.

Further Reading

Feher, Michael (ed.). *The Libertine Reader: Eroticism and Enlightenment in Eighteenth-century France* / New York: Zone Books; Cambridge, MA: Distributed by MIT Press, 1997.

NOUVEAU PARNASSE SATYRIQUE DU DIX-NEUVIÈME SIÈCLE, LE

In 1864, Auguste Poulet-Malassis, publisher of Baudelaire's *Les Fleurs du Mal*, established in Brussels as a publisher of erotica works after bankruptcy in France, published *Le Parnasse satyrique du dix-neuvième siècle* [*The Satirical Parnassus of the Nineteenth Century*], an anthology of "spicy and ribald verse" (according to its subtitle) by contemporary writers. Poulet-Malassis also assembled the poems for a second anthology, *Le nouveau Parnasse satyrique du dix-neuvième siècle* [*The New Satirical Parnassus*] (1866). (The titles echo the volume of satirical and erotic poems published in 1622 under the name of Théophile de Viau.) Both collections encompass a variety of pieces; their tone ranges from the colloquial and popular (the poems are often monologues or dialogues), to the witty and allusive, and the highly literary.

The collections comprise contemporary satirical poems and epigrams (including Musset's deft review of the members of the Académie française, and Joachim Duflot's "Portraits de femmes" [Portraits of Women], evoking the alleged sexual proclivities of famous actresses); mildly indecent verse that had fallen foul of the censors (risqué popular poems by Pierre-Jean de Béranger, ribald celebrations of sex, food, and drink by Félix Bovie); a facsimile of a letter by George Sand to her seamstress about an overtight corset; humorous pieces such as an innocent drinking song that adapts obscene terms as its rhymes; poems exploiting *double entendre*, like an indecently allusive hymn to a candle; bawdy parodies of contemporary poems and songs from vaudevilles, including "Le Con" [The Cunt] (Albert de La Fizelière), a sustained transposition of Lamartine's idealized recollection of lost love, "Le Lac" [The Lake]; mockheroic verses on themes such as a chambermaid's battle against pubic lice; realistic monologues with a comic flavor, such as Henri Monnier's "La Pierreuse" in which a prostitute addresses her client; outrageously explicit humorous verses, such as a prostitute's jaunty account of her life and chief pleasure ("Minette," i.e., cunnilingus). Many poems are verbally and formally inventive. A subversive element is often present in the celebration of prostitutes, drunkenness, and in antimilitarist and anticlerical mockery. Paul Saunière's "L'Amour" is provocative in its grossly realistic demythification of "love" through insistence on the physicality of sex. Among the more serious poems in the 1864 edition were the six condemned poems from Baudelaire's *Les Fleurs du Mal*, and Théophile Gautier's "Musée secret" [Secret Museum], a celebration of pubic hair through art, literature, history, and legend, which he had withdrawn at the last minute from his volume *Émaux et camées* [Enamels and Cameos], alongside four neatly turned comic poems including a fantasy on a battle between fleas and pubic lice, and an evocation of the column in the place Vendôme as a giant dildo.

The second anthology (1866) included further poems by Baudelaire, including "Les Promesses d'un visage" [Promises of a Face], refused for publication in France because of its closing reference to pubic hair. The Appendix made several corrections and additions to the first collection, and revealed the identity of several authors presented anonymously or disguised in 1864. A third collection, published in Brussels by Henry Kistemackers in 1881, subsumed material from the first two and further included, grouped together, works by the five Naturalist writers associated with Émile Zola in the volume of stories *Les Soirées de Médan* [The Médan Soirées] (1880), but not Zola himself. These demonstrate not the uniformity of a school but variety. Henry Céard's "Ballade des pauvres putains" [Ballad of the Poor Whores] is a sympathetic and realistic portrayal of the plight of street prostitutes in winter; it is coupled with an ironic ballad to the Virgin whose refrain is a plea to preserve the poet from syphilis. Léon Hennique contributed two light-hearted poems, one a Rabelaisian monologue of a monk mixing sex, scatology, food, and drink in pastiche Old French. Paul Alexis's "Le Lit," a Naturalistic evocation (with some squalid touches) of the bed as a place of birth, love-making, illness, and death, is philosophical and lyrical rather than shocking. In contrast, J.-K. Huysmans contributed two dense sonnets: one evokes cunnilingus with a menstruating woman; the other ("Sonnet masculin," with exclusively masculine rhymes) is a graphic description of sodomy. Both push language to extremes in order to shock, but are highly literary in their rare words and elaborate syntax, and combine fascination with physiological revulsion. Maupassant is represented by three erotic poems, one celebrating cunnilingus in conventionally poetic terms, the others provocatively crude. The collection also reprinted several pieces from Jean Richepin's *La Chanson des gueux* [The Song of the Beggars] that had earned the author a year in prison: they exploit popular language and evoke vividly and with sympathy marginal characters and working-class victims (the son of a prostitute turned thief in "Fils de fille").

The first volumes represent a mixture of unpublished material acquired by Poulet-Malassis and his collaborators, previously published but banned material, and pieces contributed by their authors. Stéphane Mallarmé's *Les Lèvres roses* [Pink Lips], a vivid but uncharacteristically explicit and sadistic evocation of a pedophile lesbian negress, animalized and "in the grip of the demon," was written for the 1866 anthology (at the instigation of his friend Albert Glatigny, who contributed several poems). The choice indicates a desire to show reputable authors in a new light, and sometimes to discredit figures now in positions of importance or displaying an ostentatious devoutness under the Second Empire: the 1866 Preface draws a parallel with Ham unveiling Noah's nakedness and the anthologist revealing his contemporaries in questionable poses. The volumes were smuggled into France for clandestine sale. The first volume was condemned in Paris in 1865 for "outrage to public and religious morality," the second in Lille in 1868. The volumes were however widely known; the critic Charles Monselet (whose verse figures in the 1866 anthology) devoted a lengthy article in *L'Événement* (Paris) in 1878, shortly after Poulet-Malassis's death, to the 1864 collection, noting that "everyone is a bit compromised in it, the most famous as well as the most obscure, as everyone has had, in his life, a moment of madness."

PETER COGMAN

Editions

Le Parnasse satyrique du dix-neuvième siècle. 2 vols. Rome [Brussels], À l'enseigne des sept péchés capitaux [Poulet-Malassis], n.d. [1864].

Le Nouveau Parnasse satyrique du dix-neuvième siècle suivi d'un appendice au Parnasse satyrique. 2 vols. Eleutheropolis [Brussels], Aux devantures des libraries, Ailleurs, dans leurs arrière-boutiques [Jules Gay], n.d. [1866].

Le Parnasse satyrique du dix-neuvième siècle, suivi du Nouveau Parnasse satyrique. 3 vols. Brussels, Sous le manteau [Henry Kistemackers], 1881.

Further Reading

Pichois, Claude. *Auguste Poulet-Malassis: l'éditeur de Baudelaire.* Paris, Fayard, 1996.

NUNNERY TALES

Nunnery Tales (printed anonymously from 1866–1868 for the booksellers of London, under its full title of *Nunnery Tales; or Cruising under False Colours: A Tale of Love and Lust*) is one of many such tales set in a convent and part of a genre of anti-religious erotica which became popular during the eighteenth century. By the nineteenth century, these stories have become more explicit and detailed in their description of increasingly varied sexual acts. The narrative takes the simple form of introducing a handful of characters who then go on to describe their own sexual adventures in turn. In order to ensure progressive heightened sexual excitement, a device is followed, whereby the sexual action becomes increasingly outrageous (or what would have been perceived as "abnormal" behavior in the nineteenth century). The stories guide the reader through increasing gradations of sexual fantasy ranging from flagellation and the taking of virginity to sodomy, incest, and bestiality. Flagellation was particularly prevalent in this type of nunnery tale as it assimilated Catholic religious penitence of self-mortification into sexual fetish.

Told in three volumes, this story is essentially that of a young man, Augustus Ermenonville, who hides away in a convent and has sex with many nuns. Augustus's aristocratic father had fled to England to escape the Sans-Culottes. His mother plans to take refuge in a convent of St. Claire, where her sister is abbess. Augustus suggests he should disguise himself and enter the convent alongside her, renaming himself Augustine and passed off as his father's first wife's niece.

Within the convent setting, a space of sexual frenzy is depicted with the introduction of a flagellation scene. A young nun comes forward to receive her punishment from her confessor, Father Eustace. Alongside him is the abbess who proclaims, "But stripped you will have to be, and I think slightly whipped. So you had better begin to undress yourself at once in order to save time." The buffet on which she was to be whipped is described in detail by Augustus: "It was a sort of low divan, provided with pillows and cushions, and covered with black velvet—at each corner moreover it was furnished with leather straps and buckles. On this black velvet altar then, which set off the dazzling whiteness of her skin most charmingly, the beautiful Emile knelt down as a victim for sacrifice, and having deposited the rod between her spread legs, proceeded to her devotions or what we presumed to be such." He admires the lovely naked Emile awaiting her punishment which is due as a result of her being caught masturbating with the extra candle she had been given by the abbess Agatha, Augustus's aunt. The father who has come to inflict the punishment has no breeches and his cassock hung loose exposing his genitalia; "his frock became a little open in front, and a most monstrous standing prick became undisguisedly exposed to view,—it was a powerful machine, with a huge purple knob." He performs "his whispering forgiveness" on her, a euphemism for cunnilingus, and "anoints" her with his "his holy oil" (sperm).

Augustus, still disguised as Augustine, acts as chamber maid to the lovely young nun. He offers to wipe her dry with his handkerchief. She in turn, introduces him to Louise and Adele. The reader is then introduced to incest when Emile warns him he will be expected to sleep with his aunt, who has sex with all the new young nuns, "By the bye [sic] I hope you do not consider it immoral to sleep with your Aunt; for she will most certainly make you do so tonight."

Adele explains how the abbess seduced her. She describes oral sex with details of female ejaculations and a torrent of genital fluids; Adele declares, "my mouth was filled, and my face and throat drenched with a warm oily liquor." Inspections for virginity are frequent in this erotica. The abbess checks on Adele's status by thrusting her fingers inside the young nun. She then declares her intention of taking her maidenhead. The dildo is described, "a curious thing that seemed like a thick ivory ruler, about nine inches long, partly covered with red velvet.—This apparatus had an elastic appendage round-shaped like a ball, which was filled from a phial, and the whole machine was firmly strapped round her front and bottom by a strong bandage." On squeezing the ball, the dildo ejects a milky liquid.

They all have supper together upon which it is noticed by Father Eustace that Augustus is no nun by virtue of the discovery of his great cock. Eustace declares, "He is his Father's own Son" thereby claiming paternity of Augustus, it having been made obvious from the onset that the mother knew Eustace intimately. He agrees that Augustus should have the run of the young nuns but stay dressed as one himself. Agatha, his aunt, protests that she should have him first. Father Eustace facetiously remarks that "con-

nection between relatives so near of kin was not allowed by the Canons of the church!" Father Eustace begins to have sex with Augustus's mother while the son takes up with his aunt. Augustus sums up the situation; "this is rather a strange predicament for a young man!—To find himself in girl's clothes riding the Lady superior of a strict Convent, and which lady is his own Aunt! And at the same time witnessing his Mother being outrageously fucked in the same rim by her Father Confessor whom I firmly believe to be my own bodily Father!"

The Abbess then recounts the tale of her seduction by the monks, Abelard and Eustace, overseen by Beatrice her superior. Both of them inspected her to ensure she has maintained her virginity. The reader is then introduced to anal sex during Agatha's tale, "you had better grease her bottom hole, as well as your infernal machine." Both the men enter her together, one in her vagina, one in her anus. She describes it, "I felt as if my belly and the lower part of my body was complete filled up by two large snakes."

The stories continue along the same lascivious vein; another scene follows with Augustus taking the maidenhead of Louise, assisted by Emile and Adele, and yet another where he takes the virginity of the pious young Agnes who turns out to enjoy it. The other nuns are also involved.

Louise goes on to tell her tale involving bestiality when she stayed at the Chateau of Madame de Fleury who kept numerous extraordinary pets including dogs, birds, and a baboon which masturbates itself. Her grandmother wonders if they could not pay a peasant girl to satisfy the baboon. During one incident, Louise witnesses her respected governess as "she grasped the baboon's ugly stiff red machine and worked it up and down." Her monitor, Madam Herbelot, is then mounted by the baboon, Sylvain. The grandmother buys a peasant girl, Marie, to have sex with the animal while Louise looks on. Louise also described a scene where Jean, Marie, Robert, and Annette watch a bull mounting a heifer.

Emile then tells her story of losing her virginity. The story so excites the listening nuns that they fall upon each other. Adele is sodomized by Augustus, while she in turn, complete with strap-on dildo, thrusts into Aunt Agatha. Emile continues with another story, followed by Eustace who recounts a tale about a woman called Julie, the king's favorite; his mother then tells her tale.

By volume three, we are introduced to Helene, her brother Charles, and her cousin "fucking her rump hole." After a sexual encounter with her dalmation dog, her mother issues her a warning about a girl who had two half-monkeys as a result of having sex with a baboon. She was sent away to the country to deliver "three or four little animals" which she never saw.

Finally, leaving the convent for Bordeaux where Father Eustace has hired them a schooner, Augustus and his mother return to England as the Revolutionaries are nearing. He takes Agnes with him for gratification en route. His mother has sex with Captain Dufour of the ship, who tells of his encounter with Donna Isadora and Donna Isabella. In the post-chasie for London, with his mother watching on, he penetrates Agnes with her bottom in his lap. Further adventures ensue in London.

The book is fairly well-written, although the stories do at times become repetitious.

JULIE PEAKMAN

Editions

London c. 1888; 1890; 1892; 1893; c. 1895; 1896; 1899, 1902; c. 1921.

Further Reading

Kearney, Patrick. *The Private Case. An Annotated Bibliography of the Private Case Erotic Collection in the British (Museum) Library* London: Jay Landesman, 1981.

Mendes, Peter. *Clandestine Erotic Literature in English 1800–1930.* London: Scholar Press, 1993.

Peakman, Julie. *Mighty Lewd Books. The Development of Eighteenth Century Pornography.* London: Palgrave, 2003.

Wagner, Peter. *Eros Revived. Erotica of the Enlightenment in England and America.* London: Secker & Warburg, 1988.

O

OBAYD-E ZAKANI

c. 1300–1371
Persian poet and prose writer

Throughout the fourteenth century, Iran was ruled by various local princes appointed by the Mongols, who had invaded and devastated the country in the previous century. Great wealth existed alongside abject poverty, and changes in the personnel of local government could be abrupt and frequent: the venality and internecine belligerence of most of the country's rulers were proverbial. Obayd-e Zakani came from a family known for its administrative abilities and he appears early in life to have been a functionary at a provincial court (which one is not known), possibly rising to the rank of minister. However, in his poetry he constantly complains of his debts and extreme poverty, as well as his lack of connections with the powerful. Although claims of poverty are conventional for medieval Persian poets, the consistency and vehemence of his remarks implies that for much of his life he lived at or beyond the edge of respectable society, and indeed harbored a deep-seated contempt for those who were successful in it.

His writing clearly reflects the unstable social conditions prevalent throughout Iran during his lifetime, but it is also part of a more local literary tradition. Shiraz had been well-known as a literary haven since the time of the poet Sa'di (thirteenth century) and Obayd's contemporaries and neighbors in Shiraz included two major poets, Hafez, and Jahan Khatun, (who was a daughter of the provincial ruler). A number of themes explored by Obayd, including the recommendation to cultivate a private life of hedonism away from centers of power, skepticism as to the claims of religion, and a sharp eye for the hypocrisy of those who possessed either secular or religious authority, were shared by these and other local writers. What makes Obayd's works distinctive are his highly developed use of irony and parody as literary devices, the intensity of his denunciations of hypocrisy (it is this that chiefly draws his ire), and the obscene language that pervades many of his most famous compositions.

Most of his work is self-consciously literary, often to an extreme degree, delighting in direct and indirect allusions to other works, elaborate parodies, and quotations from well known and obscure sources: (one result of this is that much of it is extremely difficult to translate effectively). In their combination of ironic playfulness, vehement anger, and scatological aggression his writings can remind one of Swift: the glimpses they give of a bohemian life of debts, brawls, drunkenness, and indiscriminate sexual energy can give the impression that the author was a kind of Persian Villon. But the western author Obayd's writings most insistently call to mind is Rabelais; this is due largely to their mixture of parodied learning (Obayd uses Arabic and the literary traditions of medieval Islam much as Rabelais uses Latin and the literary traditions of medieval Christendom) with lewd, hyperbolic fantasy (as for example in his *Book of the Beard* [*Rishnameh*], a mock treatise on the appearance of an adolescent male's beard, which marks the end of his sexual attractiveness).

His chief satirical work is *The Ethics of the Nobility* [*Akhlaq al-Ashraf*]. Parodying serious works on ethics, this is divided into seven chapters each of which defines a virtue. But rather than describing these virtues as timelessly incumbent on all Moslems, as is usual in such works, Obayd describes an old or "abrogated" form of each virtue, and then the new or "preferred" form. The "abrogated" form is the virtue as it is normally understood, the "preferred" form is its moral opposite: thus the "preferred" form of bravery is cowardice, the "preferred" form of chastity is sexual license, the "preferred" form of religious belief is atheism, and so forth. The work is a prosimetrum (a common form for a serious didactic work in medieval Persian) with the prose containing most of the exposition, while the verse passages are usually used as a gnomic summing up of the points being made. In what is perhaps the work's best known passage of verse, an encounter between the greatest Persian epic hero, Rostam, and one of his enemies is described: their combat is not however with swords, instead they alternately sodomize one another.

Obayd wrote a number of other works in prose: among these the best known are *The Treatise of a Hundred Councils* [*Resaleh-ye Sad Pand*, a book of cynical advice], *The Heart Delighting Treatise* [*Resaleh-ye Del-Gosha*, a book of facetiae, jokes, and amusing anecdotes], and *The Treatise in Ten Chapters* [*Resaleh-ye Dah Fasl*]. This last is a kind of a "Devil's Dictionary" in which words are given cynical and derogatory definitions: for example, "A lawyer" is "One who perverts the truth"; "Thought" is "That which uselessly makes men ill"; "A virgin" is "A noun with no referent," and so forth).

Recent writers on Obayd (Javadi, Mahjoub, Sprachman) have seen him mainly as a satirist, and as most of his satire is in prose they have regarded these works as his most important. However he has been traditionally regarded primarily as a poet, and it is the present writer's view that his poetry is at least as significant as his prose. His best known poem is a comic fable with clear political overtones (*Mush o Gorbeh*, [*Mouse and Cat*] about a predatory cat and a horde of mice who unsuccessfully try to destroy it. His other chief, relatively long, poem is a work celebrating masturbation, particularly as practiced by sufis (Moslem mystics, who often claimed to be celibate). Indignation at the sufis' hypocrisy seems to be interwoven with a genuine enthusiasm for the poem's subject. A number of short poems celebrate sex either with women or with adolescent boys: in some the author claims he doesn't have a preference between the two, in others he stages brief mock debates on the relative virtues of their sexual parts. Obayd also wrote a number of serious poems, including panegyrics to local rulers, as well as conventional ghazals (love lyrics) and shorter poems, which are by no means contemptible.

Biography

Obayd-e Zakani was born in the north of Iran, in Qazvin, but spent most of his life in Shiraz, the capital of Fars, the chief province of southern central Iran.

DICK DAVIS

Edition

Kolliyat-e 'Obayd Zakani. Edited by Mohammad-Ja'afar Mahjoub. New York 1999.

Further Reading

Sprachman, Paul. *Suppressed Persian: An Anthology of Forbidden Literature*. Costa Mesa, 1995, pp. 44–75.
Sprachman, Paul. "Persian Satire, Parody and Burlesque," in *Persian Literature*. Ed. Ehsan Yarshater, pp. 226–248, New York, 1988.
Javadi, Hasan. *Satire in Persian Literature*. Fairleigh Dickinson University Press, 1988.
Javadi, Hasan, trans., *Obeyd-e Zakani: The Ethics of the Aristocrats and Other Satirical Works*. Piedmont, CA, 1985.

OCAMPO, SILVINA

1903–1993
Argentine poet and short story writer

Silvina Ocampo's own writings first appeared in the newspaper *La Nación* and Victoria Ocampo's *Sur*. In 1936, Ocampo contributed to the short-lived *Destiempo*, a literary magazine founded by Bioy Casares, and in the following year, published her first collection of short stories, *Viaje Olvidado* [*Forgotten Journey*].

Most of Ocampo's stories and poems are narrated in the first person and are populated by eccentric child-like figures whose intensity of experience belies the ordinariness of their surroundings. Bestiality and same sex relationships are also present in Ocampo's work, and although explicit sexual episodes are never dealt with, sensuality is very much part of her prose and poetry. A good example of this is the autobiographical poem "El caballo Blanco" [The White Horse] (2001), where Ocampo relates her first attempt at drawing and the immense pleasure she experienced after finishing a sketch depicting a white horse. In her recurrent fashion of portraying children as sensitive to sensual and sexual delight, Ocampo vividly recalls 'una profesora francesa cuya cara se ha borrado pero no la mano ni el sexo.' That French teacher whose face she cannot recall but whose hand and sex are clearly imprinted in Ocampo's memory triggers the young girl's physical pleasure for drawing. In this poem Ocampo describes in detail the sensuality and gratification the girl experiences while drawing the animal, particularly the genitalia, which she draws from memory. That precision to detail is what shocks her puritan family and friends. Furthermore, Ocampo hints at a trace of oral sex in her fetish for sketching; the young girl in the poem would happily abandon the delight of sucking her sweets in favor of secretly drawing under the table.

In general, these young narrators are not only ahead of their sexual awakening but also particularly sensitive to any manifestation of desire. In 'Cornelia frente al espejo' (1988), for instance, the mirror with whom Cornelia engages in conversation tells her how he remembers her as a precocious young girl who was eight years old and had twenty orgasms a day (*Cuentos Completos II*). This in itself intensifies the fantastical element in her work as well as justifying an ever-present tendency towards black humor. Hidden behind the over simplistic and innocent titles of individual tales—"La muñeca" [The Doll], "La nube" [The Cloud], "Las fotografías" [The Photographs], and "El cuaderno" [The Notebook]—Ocampo's stories invite a psychoanalytical reading. They present a world in which all manner of crimes, sins, acts of cruelty, and sexual aberrations are hinted at, though never precisely unveiled. In addition, her protagonists, although often very young, also tend to suffer some form of psychological abnormality in their own right. This forces them to behave in a manner which is likewise either anomalous or cruel, especially when they are confronted with rites of passage, unwanted sexual initiation, or even the normal processes of maturation and growth. One of Ocampo's most popular tales, 'El pecado mortal' (Mortal Sin) offers an account on one such passage from innocent childhood to sexual awareness. As in most Western literature, this change is brought about by adult sexual aggression. A woman, who is only identified as the narrator, tells a story rich in erotico-religious symbolism of a young girl who falls victim to a male servant's sexual fantasies but is then forced to take her first Communion without confessing her sin. The text is left deliberately vague as to its interpretation, however. An ideological reading, for example, might attempt to link the themes of sexual exploitation, ritual humiliation, and guilt to one of class conflict, especially given the discrepancy in social status of the woman and her seducer. Yet, as is often the case with Ocampo, the victimizer is often the victim of his or her own inner conflicts too, such that the denouement often entails a psychological reversal. In some stories, for example, male aggression is ultimately explained in terms of a failure of potency or a metaphor of homosocial desire.

Voyeurism is another frequent theme in Ocampo's work. In 'Los mastines del templo de Adriano' [The Mastiffs of Hadrian's Temple], the narrator experiences a form of erotic pleasure by secretly witnessing a sexual encounter. Likewise, in 'The Atonement,' a complex *ménage à trois* establishes itself between Antonio, his wife, and Ruperto, such that Antonio is resentful of Ruperto's obvious fascination with his wife but is only able to perform sexually with her when he is resident in the house. The fantastical denouement of the story involves Ruperto's being blinded by a flock of carefully trained canaries with poisoned beaks. Sometimes Ocampo deliberately conceals the elements needed to offer any meaningful level of interpretation. In 'Miren cómo se aman' [Look How They Love Each Other] the protagonist, Adriana, who works in a circus, has a boyfriend who is very jealous of Plinio whom she has 'trained' and feeds and looks after every day with a passion and devotion she hardly shows for anyone else. Because the author refuses to tell the reader whether Plinio is a baby or an old man, any psychological judgment concerning the boyfriend's jealousy has to remain in abeyance. Ultimately, Adriana returns home one day to find Plinio apparently dead. Having rejected her boyfriend's offer of marriage, Adriana agrees to marry Plinio who, to the reader's surprise, is no longer a monkey but a prince.

Silvina Ocampo's position as one of the principle South American writers of the twentieth century seems assured on her own continent. The recurrent themes she explores in her writing—themes which encompass sexual perversion, cruelty, and sadism—are clearly important ones. However, it also seems likely that her work is too resolutely linked with Argentine mores to appeal easily to English-speaking readers.

Biography

Born into a prosperous Buenos Aires family among whose ancestors were several of the founding fathers of Argentina, Silvina Ocampo's initial education was provided by French and English governesses, combined with annual trips to Europe; later she studied painting and drawing in Paris. In common with many Argentine literati, her early tastes were shaped by French and English models, both in the literary and the artistic domain.

Although a prolific author in her own right, Ocampo is perhaps best known for her ties with many of the most illustrious names on the Argentine literary scene of the period: her husband, Adolfo Bioy Casares (b. 1914), is now an internationally celebrated novelist; Jorge Luis Borges (1899–1986), probably the most outstanding Argentine figure of the twentieth century, was a close friend and best man at her wedding; while her sister, Victoria Ocampo, was the founder of the literary journal *Sur*, the main conduit by which European literature was introduced not only to Argentina but Latin America generally, and the publishing house of the same name.

CAROLINA MIRANDA

Bibliography (Selected Works)

Páginas de Silvina Ocampo, seleccionadas por la autora. Buenos Aires: Editorial Celtia, 1984.
Cuentos Completos II. Buenos Aires: Emecé, 1999.
Poesía inédita y dispersa. Buenos Aires: Emecé, 2001.
Viaje Olvidado. Buenos Aires: Sur, 1937.
Enumeración de la patria y otros poemas. Buenos Aires: Sur, 1942.
Espacios métricos. Buenos Aires: Sur, 1945.
Autobiografía de Irene. Buenos Aires: Sudamericana, 1948.
Sonetos del jardín. Buenos Aires: Colección La Perdiz, 1948.
Poemas de amor desesperado. Buenos Aires: Sudamericana, 1949.
Los nombres. Buenos Aires: Emecé, 1953.
Pequeña antología. Buenos Aires: Ene, 1954.
La furia y otros cuentos. Buenos Aires: Sur, 1959.
La invitadas. Buenos Aires: Losada, 1961.
Lo amargo por dulce. Buenos Aires: Emecé, 1962.
El pecado mortal. Buenos Aires: Universitaria, 1966.
Informe del cielo y el infierno. Caracas: Monte Avila, 1970.
Los días de las noches. Buenos Aires: Sudamericana, 1970.
Amarillo celeste. Buenos Aires: Losada, 1972.
Yasí sucesivamente. Barcelona: Tusquets Editores, 1987.
Cornelia frente al espejo. Barcelona: Tusquets Editores, 1988.

Translations

Balderston, Daniel (ed. and trans.) *Leopoldina's Dream*, London and New York: Penguin, 1988.
Lewald, H. Ernest (ed. and trans.) *The Web: Stories by Argentine Women*. Washington, DC: Three Continents Press, 1983.

Manguel, Alverto (ed.). *Black Water: The Book of the Fantastic Literature*. New York: Clarkson N. Potter, 1983.

——— (ed.). *Other Fires: Short Fiction by Latin American Women*. New York: Clarkson N. Potter, 1986.

Mayer, Doris and Margarite Fernadez (eds.). *Contemporary Women Authors of Latin America: New Translations*. Brooklyn, NY: Brooklyn College Press, 1983.

Further Reading

Corbacho, Belinda. *Le monde féminin dans l'œuvre narrative de Silvina Ocampo*. Paris: L'Harmattan, 1998.

Fishburn, Evelyn (ed). *Short Fiction by Spanish-American Women*. Manchester: Manchester University Press, 1998.

Nisbet Klingenberg, Patricia. *Fantasies of the Feminine: The Short Stories of Silvina Ocampo*. Lewisburg, PA: Bucknell University Press, 1999.

Ulla, Noemí. *Invenciones a dos voces: ficción y poesía en Silvina Ocampo*. Buenos Aires: Emecé: 1992, re-edited and revised 2002.

———. *Silvina Ocampo, una escritora oculta*. Buenos Aires: Emecé, 1999.

OGAWA, YÔKO

1962–
Japanese novelist

Yôko Ogawa's works are restricted to a very intimate sphere, especially the body, reaction, sensually to smells and sounds, closed spaces, such as an old hotel on an island (*Iris Hotel*), an orphan's institution (*Diving pool*), a laboratory for specimens (*The Annular*), or a dormitory. Most of the time, the main character is a young woman who is experiencing an intimate universe of sensations the narrator who is experiencing strange, scandalous relations with peculiar isolated men. Ogawa creates opportunities to draw portraits of perverse male characters far beyond the normal standards, and may be thematically linked to the activity of writing itself, an abnormal activity. The female narrator describes very precisely the reasons for which she is attracted. We can trace back a few of these basic instincts, which can shed light.

The first is related to elegance and to a tidiness of appearance and perfection of physical motion. For example, Ogawa describes the scrutiny of Jun's body by the female character while he performs a dive: she loves his muscles, his technique, and she washes his swimming trunks at night. Through secret viewing, this young voyeur desires to be embraced by him, and she feels caresses from the inside. Jun embodies cleanliness related to water, and ablution for her feelings of guilt and impurity. The story culminates in a brief dialogue with Jun who happens to have known from the beginning that she was looking at him almost every day. They avoid direct contact and maintain that visual relation. In contras, Jun sees her sadistic acts towards an orphaned five-year-old girl, Rie. This is the second aspect of her personality. Her yearning for the kindness of Jun, and for pure elements (like snow or water) is opposed to her deep hatred of her mother. She desires to crush her lips between her fingers. Her homicidal compulsion towards the small Rie, whom she tries to poison with rotten food, seems to be linked to her own suffering. It is revealed she was raised as just one among the many orphans of the Hikari institution run by her parents. She becomes intimately familiar with the cruelty of adults very early in her life and repeats it, taking pleasure in Rie's tears, which she keeps in a jar. These obsessions may not be those of the author, but the sadistic aspects of education, and the rude behavior of mothers in particular towards daughters are a recurring theme in her work; for example, the dysfunctional relationship between Mari and her mother in *Hotel Iris* which leads Mari into a masochistic relationship with an old man. All of her childhood memories are of taboo acts and as a teenager, love seems to be poisoned and out of reach because of her sadistic impulses and obsessions, like decaying food, the flesh of children and a mold she imagines is growing on her skin.

The female main character is attracted to particular aspects of the male body such as fingers, the hands, or the feet, and then they are remembered with tenderness and desire. They are intricately described, in great detail and are isolated them from the rest of the body.

A glimpse of the physical appearance of the director of a dormitory is enough to create an intimate link, because he is a cripple. His erotic beauty is not obvious: he has no arms and only one leg remaining, and he is slowly dying from a strange illness. His sex appeal is not separate from his handicap. The narrator compares the perfect shape of her cousin, an athlete, to the beauty of a perfect hand used skillfully to serve tea. The handicapped man is, likewise, attracted by perfect young men's hands. The example of an isolated aspect of the body as the spark for sensual passion can be found in the sound of the voice. The old man in "Hotel Iris" speaks to a prostitute with a quiet and decisive voice in front of Mari, who will be led to erotic submission. She is also attracted by the tidiness of his clothes, house, and writing.

In the case of "Iced Perfume," the narrator can remembers her late suicidal lover through the perfume he created, but more precisely through the smell of his brother's body. To fall in love, she only needs to smell his hand, and to remember the touch of his finger behind her ear.

Ogawa's novels are not systematically erotic, but they are always based on a very sensitive approach toward space and sound, like the swimming pool where she feels swallowed as if by a monster, or a ringing phone compared to a sensual animal. In "The Annular," we find a good example of that eroticisation of space. The laboratory for specimens of M. Deshimaru is a wide and complex space where the narrator enters as an employee. She once had a growth removed and she imagines this annular floating in a test tube, among other items in that strange laboratory. Deshimaru has a penchant for transforming the suffering objects into classified specimens which he stores away. As a suffering girl, he transforms her into a passive object for his desires, in a sadomasochistic relationship like the one described in "Iris Hotel." The erotic scenes take place in an old bathroom. She strips, and puts on a new pair of shoes in which she feels as if she is floating. She must then walk in the bath, and feel the coldness and the hardness of the tiled floor. The sexual relations she has with the specimen's master seem to transform her into a suffering thing, a specimen. In "Iris Hotel," the strange relations between Mari and the old translator occurs in a pattern of bondage and sadomasochism. At the same time, the female narrator and character can be the source of unconscious sadism as in "Pregnancy," where she encounters a normal couple, and imagines that she can destroy her sister's fetus through chemically treated grapefruits. She feels compassion and disgust towards her pregnant sister's appetite and change of mood.

Erotic and compassionate feelings are very often mixed together with a sensitive and personal worldview in a very detailed and precise manner, which is the charm of these novels.

Biography

Born in 1962, she published her first novel in 1988, and received the Kaien prize for it. In 1991, she received the Akutagawa award for "Ninshin Calendar."

MARC KOBER

Selected Works

Diving Pool. Fukutake Publishing and Co. Tokyo, 1990. Original title in English.
Samenai kocha. Fukutate shoten. 1990. (A tea that never gets cold).
Dormitory. Bungeishunju Ltd. Tokyo, 1991. Original title in English.
Ninshin Calendar. Bungeishunju Ltd. Tokyo, 1991.
Yugure no kyushokushitsu to ame no puru. Bungeishunju Ltd. Tôkyô, 1991.
Kusuriyubi no hyhon. Shincho-sha. Tokyo, 1994.
Hoteru Airisu. Gakken: Tôkyô. 1996.
Koritsuita Kaori. Gentosha: Tôkyô, 1998.

OLESHA, YURY KARLOVICH

1899–1960
Russian novelist, short story writer, newspaper
serial-writer, dramatist, and film scriptwriter

Yury Karlovich Olesha was the author of the
novel *Envy*, a number of short stories, several
plays, and co-author of several film scenarios, as
well as articles and reviews for the press. Olesha
was a writer of immense talent whose total output is modest and who did not realize his full
potential. Nevertheless, *Envy* is a minor classic
that still provokes an active response from
critics, especially in the West; and a handful of
Olesha's short stories, especially "The Chain,"
"Liompa," "Love," 1928, and "The Cherry
Stone," 1929, are among the best of the Soviet
period. Eroticism in Olesha is both heteroerotic
and homoerotic, as may be seen in the first pages
of *Envy*, where the hero Nikolai Kavalerov spies
on Andrei Babichev doing his morning exercises.

When Babichev lies down on the bath mat on
his back and begins to raise his legs one after
another, a button on his trouser snaps, exposing
his crotch, which is magnificent; "A tender spot.
A forbidden nook. The groin of a progenitor. I
saw just such a groin on a male antelope. A
single look from him is probably enough to send
amorous currents flowing through his girls, the
secretaries and office girls" [my translation from
Izbrannoe].

Here, Olesha moves from homoeroticism to
heteroeroticism; one might say he uses the latter
as a cover for the former. This passage is especially effective as an early statement of the novel's profoundly ambiguous sexuality. When the
NEP entrepreneur Babichev, a sausage maker
and proprietor of a communal dining facility
(The Quarter), runs, his breasts bounce up and
down. He also has maternal instincts, as when he
takes waifs like Kavalerov off the street and
replaces motherhood itself with The Quarter.
Andrei's androgyny is symptomatic of the
whole short novel. Valya, supposedly Babichev's
niece adopted from his brother Ivan, is also
androgynous, as she is both a tomboy who

jumps rope with her friend Volodya, the soccer
goalie, and the object of Kavalerov's desire. At
the soccer match, one of the few ostensible
events in *Envy*, the whole crowd is drawn to
her. When the wind blows her dress over her
head, her is on display for all to see. Yet, it is
just this sight that makes Kavalerov realize that
her youthful purity puts her out of his lascivious
reach and that his attraction to her can never be
realized. This pattern of arousal followed by its
denial is characteristic of Olesha's treatment of
eroticism in *Envy* and elsewhere.

Ivan Babichev's all-powerful fantasy machine, Ophelia, is similarly laden with paradox.
Named for Shakespeare's ultra-sensitive heroine, Ophelia impales her creator with a long
proboscis in a drunken dream of Kavalerov
and thus displays her male, phallic side that
complements her machine–like and feminine
qualities. Her maker Ivan's sexuality is only
revealed in the last words of the novel, when it
turns out that he and Kavalerov are living in
a ménage à trois with Annichka Prokopovich,
a repulsive widow who embodies the debased
lasciviousness of the two men.

William Harkins has made a definitive analysis of sexuality in *Envy* in which he finds
that sterility is the dominant theme. Volodya
Makarov, who in soviet fashion takes as his
model the machine, promising (perhaps jocu-
larly) not to kiss Valya for four years. Andrei,
the object of Kavalerov's spying, is never shown
in a relationship with a woman (or a man).
Kavalerov, who likes his blanket and dreams of
Annichka's bed, is largely infantile in his sexuality. Whether or not this sterility is an essential
part of Olesha's depiction of a Soviet dystopia,
everything from erotic impulses to sexual relations in *Envy* seems either unfulfilled or even
degraded.

The film *A Strict Youth* begins with a shot of
the heroine Masha's naked back—she is in a
bathing suit. The hero Grisha Fokin, who soon
appears in a white outfit, is another androgynous
Oleshian hero who could appeal to both men

and women. His friend Kolya, the discus thrower, receives a rub-down that features a vigorous massage of his breasts as some young men and women Komsomol members look on in a room filled with phallic Grecian pillars (Heil.) There is humor here too, as characters run around in their undershorts and a dog spies on Masha getting dressed. Her relations with Fokin are unresolved, as she can not decide between him and her husband. The paradox of this film is that the strict Komsomol members, who mouth empty slogans about fitness for labor and defense, are the vehicle for their authors' ventures into erotic zones that must have given the censor a thrill even as s/he banned it.

In "Love," the hero Shuvalov is so overwhelmed by his infatuation for Lelya that he sees things that do not exist and thinks in images, so that when a wasp flies into the room he cries, "It's a tiger!" He even offers to trade places with a colorblind man to escape the press of his feelings. In the end, however, he tells the man to go eat his blue pears, after putting his head on Lelya's breast. "His head lay on her sweaty breast and he saw her nipple, pink with wrinkles that were delicate like foam on milk" [my translation from *Izbrannoe*]. This is one of the most graphic and certainly the most tender erotic passage in all of Olesha's work.

The mercurial eroticism found in Olesha is an integral part of his poetics, for it lies at the base of the characters' ever–changing, ambiguous identities. With Olesha, we are never sure what the true nature of people and things might be; we never know which version of his story is the "real" one.

Biography

Born in Elizavetgrad, Ukraine, March 3, 1899; grew up in Odessa. Studied at Rishelevsky gymnasium. As a youth played soccer, which he followed all his life. Married to Olga Gustavovna Suok. Wrote jingles under the pseudonym of "The Chisel" for *Gudok* [The Whistle], 1922–1929, where Isaac Babel and Mikhail Bulgakov also worked. Publication of the novel *Envy*, 1927, gave Olesha instant recognition. Published the children's story *Three Fat Men*, his best known work in Russia, 1928. Worked on play *A List of Blessings*, 1931, with Meyerhold. The film *A Strict Youth,* is banned as "ideologically depraved," 1935, and not shown until late 1980s. Worked on other films in 1930s. Returned to serious literature in 1956 with publication of excerpts from his writer's diary named by compilers *No Day Without a Line* posthumously and first published in 1965 after his death in 1960.

VICTOR PEPPARD

Selected Works

Strogii iunosha (A Strict Youth). Film made in 1935, in *Yury Olesha. The Complete Plays*, edited & translated by Michael Green and Jerome Katsell, under the title of *A Stern Young Man*, Ann Arbor: Ardis, 1983.

Yury Olesha. Izbrannoe. Moscow: Khudozhestvennaia literatura, 1974.

Yury Olesha. Complete Stories and Three Fat Men. Translated by Aimee Anderson. Ann Arbor, MI: Ardis, 1979.

Yury Olesha. No Day Without a Line. Translated and edited by Judson Rosengrant, Ann Arbor, MI: Ardis, 1979.

Yury Olesha. The Complete Plays. Edited and translated by Michael Green and Jerome Katsell. Ann Arbor, MI: Ardis, 1983.

Envy. In *The Portable Twentieth Century Russian Reader.* Edited with an introduction and notes by Clarence Brown. New York: Penguin Books, revised and updated, 1993.

Further Reading

Barratt, Andrew. "Yurii Olesha's *Envy*." *Birminigham Slavonic Monographs* 12, Birmingham, 1981.

Beaujour, Elizabeth Klosty. *The Invisible Land: A Study of the Artistic Imagination of Iurii Olesha.* New York: Columbia University Press, 1970.

Harkins, William. "The Theme of Sterility in Olesha's Envy," in *Olesha's* Envy: *A Critical Companion.* Edited by Rimgaila Salys. Evanston, IL: Northwestern University Press / AATSEEL, 1999.

Heil, Jerry. "No List of Political Assets: The Collaboration of Iurii Olesha and Abram Room on *Strogii iunosha* (A Strict Youth)." *Slavistische Beitrage,* Band 248, 1989.

Ingdahl, Kazimiera. *The Artist and the Creative Act: A Study of Jurij Olesha's Novel* Zavist' (Envy): *Stockholm Studies in Russian Literature* 17. Stockholm: Almqvist & Wiksell International, 1982.

Peppard, Victor. *The Poetics of Yury Olesha.* University of Florida Humanities Monograph 63, Gainesville: University of Florida Press, 1989.

Salys, Rimgaila. "Sausage Rococo: The Art of Tiepolo in Olesha's *Envy.* In *Olesha's* Envy. *A Critical Companion.* edited by Rimgaila Salys. Evanston, IL: Northwestern University Press / AATSEEL, 1999.

OLYMPIA PRESS

The Olympia Press, probably the twentieth-century's most celebrated and influential publishing house specializing in English-language erotic literature, began operations at Paris in the Spring of 1953, initially as part of a sort of symbiotic relationship between its founder, Maurice Girodias, and a group of young American and British expatriate writers centered around a literary magazine called Merlin that had itself started only a year earlier.

The Merlinois, as Girodias referred to them, were anxious to begin publishing books, especially English translations of the works of Samuel Beckett, an Irish novelist and playwright who preferred to write in French. Under French law, however, publishing companies run by foreigners were required to have a French manager. Girodias was happy to fill this role, and also provide access to an accommodating printer. In return, members of the Merlin crew would supply him with translations of Sade and Apollinaire, and later with original novels, as will be seen.

Girodias was no stranger to the publishing world, and erotica in particular. His father, the English-born Jack Kahane, had founded the Obelisk Press in Paris in the summer of 1931 with a view to publishing books that for one reason or another were persona non grata in Great Britain or the United States. Among his more celebrated offerings were the first editions of *Tropic of Cancer* (1934) and *Tropic of Capricorn* (1939) by Henry Miller, and *My Life and Loves* (1933, 4 vols.) which had originally been privately printed at Paris (Vol. 1) and Nice (vols. 2–4) by their author, Frank Harris. Two others, *The Young and Evil* (1933) by Parker Tyler and Charles Henri Ford and Lawrence Durrell's *The Black Book* (1938), were to see print again in the 1950's when Girodias dusted them off for the Olympia Press.

Kahane père died the day World War II officially began, leaving his son Maurice to run the business. Having such a Jewish name as Kahane during the Occupation was definitely a liability, and Maurice prudently assumed his mother's maiden name and exchanged his British passport for forged French documents.

Girodias' initial publications under his own steam consisted at first of trifles such as *Paris-Programme*, a periodical listing of the latest films and plays. In 1941, he founded Éditions du Chêne, and for the remainder of the war he published under this imprint a series of books dealing with art, architecture, tapestries, and similarly 'safe' subjects.

With the War over in 1945, Girodias took advantage of the large numbers of Americans and British in Paris by reviving the Obelisk Press and reprinting some of his father's more lucrative titles, including Henry Miller's books. Soon he was able to offer Miller the opportunity of having *Sexus*, the first volume of his 'Rosy Crucifixion' trilogy, published in a handsome, 2-volume limited edition.

Despite the success of the English-language books, the Éditions du Chêne imprint was not abandoned, and one of Girodias' more important coups occurred in 1947 when he acquired the manuscript of Nikos Kazantzakes' novel *Alexis Zorba, ou le Rivage de Crète*, which he published in Yvonne Gauthier's French translation. However, it was another Éditions du Chêne title, *Le Pain de la corruption* (1947) by an ex-resistance fighter named Yves Farge, which gave the first indications of his penchant for butting heads with authority.

Le Pain de la corruption was an exposé of the official protection given to black marketeering, and both its author and publisher were prosecuted for their efforts. The case was eventually dismissed, but Girodias at least was not to get off so lightly, and he was again prosecuted, this time for publishing Jean-Claude Lefaure's French translation of Henry Miller's *Tropic of Capricorn* (1947). That case too was dismissed, but he was nailed for *Sexus* (1949) which was banned in any language. Soon after this disaster he lost control of Éditions du Chêne to the publishing conglomerate Hachette who, having acquired at the same time the Obelisk Press imprint, continued to issue reprints of Henry Miller's 'Paris' books and, ironically, were to publish the first English language edition of Miller's *Nexus* (1960), the final volume of the 'Rosy Crucifixion' trilogy.

For two years or so, Girodias struggled to stay afloat until, as we have seen above, he joined forces with the Merlin editors and contributors and the Olympia Press was founded.

Olympia's first publication, in April 1953, was *Plexus*, the second volume of Henry Miller's Rosy 'Crucifixion' trilogy, which like *Sexus* was issued in two volumes in a limited edition. In May, the first integral English editions of the marquis de Sade's *Justine, ou les Malheurs de la vertu* and *La Philosophie dans le boudoir* were published. The translations had already been done by Austryn Wainhouse and were originally intended to have been issued under the Merlin imprint, but it was felt that they were more in keeping with Olympia's objectives and so appeared there. Later in the same year came English versions of Apollinaire's *Les Onze mille verges* and *Les Exploits d'un jeune Don Juan*, and of Georges Bataille's *Histoire de l'œil*.

The Olympia/Merlin publishing alliance also began in 1953, first with a slim volume of verse by Christopher Logue called *Wand and Quadrant* and with Samuel Beckett's novel *Watt*. Three other titles would appear before Merlin left the scene, a translation by Bernard Frechtman of Jean Genet's *Journal du voleur*, Austryn Wainhouse's novel *Hedyphagetica* and finally, in 1955, James Broughton's *An Almanac for Amorists*.

In 1954, Girodias started the Atlantic Library, the first of several subsidiary imprints. Ten titles in all appeared, including *Helen and Desire*, by 'Frances Lengel,' (Alexander Trocchi) and *An Adult's Story* by 'Robert Desmond' (Robert Desmond Thompson) who, together with 'Marcus van Heller' (John Stevenson), were to become the mainstays of the Olympia stable of writers. The poet Christopher Logue assumed the identity of 'Count Palmiro Vicarion' for a novel called *Lust* that also appeared in the series, and later, under the Olympia Press imprint, edited two volumes of obscene limericks and bawdy ballads.

In February of the following year, the Traveller's Companion series was founded and with its famous green wrappers became the most iconic element of the Olympia Press. The first title to be published was *The Enormous Bed*, a wonderfully comic novel by 'Henry Jones,' a pseudonym of the English journalist John Coleman. This was followed by *Rape*, the first of the 'Marcus van Heller' titles, after which appeared a further ninety or so novels, a number of which have become much sought after in the modern first edition market, including J.P. Donleavy's *The Ginger Man*, William Burroughs' *Naked Lunch*, *The Soft Machine*, and *The Ticket that Exploded*, and Gregory Corso's *American Express*.

The year 1955 also saw the first appearance of Vladimir Nabokov's *Lolita*, a further example of Girodias' ability to spot good writing when he saw it. Although appearing first in two volumes with green wrappers very similar to those of the Traveller's Companion series, it didn't form part of the series until a reprint was published in November 1958.

Many of the titles appearing in the Traveller's Companion series, while certainly unpublishable in the United States and the United Kingdom, were of a distinctly literary tone, or otherwise, not the typical erotic novel sought by foreign visitors to Paris. In part to subsidize them, Girodias started three other series in which more conventional pornographic fare could be found. But even here quality tended to creep in, and among the offerings appearing under the ægis of the Ophelia Press was *The English Governess* by 'Miles Underwood,' a pseudonym of the Canadian poet John Glassco, and an anonymously executed translation of *Trois Filles de leur mère* by Pierre Louÿs, one of the most extraordinary erotic novels of the twentieth century, here rendered as *The She-Devils* by 'Peter Lewys.'

Girodias' early brushes with the authorities following the war resulted in continued tribulations for years afterwards. While other Parisian publishers of pornography at the time remained for the most part untouched, the Olympia Press suffered constant harassment, and title after title was put on a list of proscribed books. Girodias responded to this by reissuing them with different titles and rewritten first pages of text. Thus, *Candy* by 'Maxwell Kenton' (Terry Southern and Mason Hoffenberg) was reborn as *Lollipop*, and *The Woman Thing* by 'Harriet Daimler' (Iris Owens) became simply *Woman*.

This sort of thing can be amusing, but eventually the constant battles in court and with publishers in America and England seeking to relieve him of his less incandescent novels grew burdensome, and in January 1966 the last book to be published by the Olympia Press in Paris rolled off the presses. Curiously, it was a new printing of the third volume of Sade's *120 Days of Sodom*. Shortly afterwards, Girodias moved his business to New York. Censorship, which he had fought so hard against in France, had effectively disappeared in the United States. Strangely, the freedom that this created seemed to act against him; although by comparison with other American erotica publishers he put out many good novels, he was never able to find authors of quite the stature of some of those he published in Paris.

PATRICK J. KEARNEY

References and Further Reading

Girodias, Maurice. *J'arrive! Une Journée sur la terre.* Paris: Stock, 1977.

Girodias, Maurice. [*J'arrive! Une Journée sur la terre.* An anonymous, augmented translation:] *The Frog Prince.* New York: Crown, 1980.

Girodias, Maurice. [*J'arrive! Une Journée sur la terre,* greatly revised and expanded text:] *Une Journée sur la terre. I. J'arrive!* Paris: Editions de la Difference, 1990.

Girodias, Maurice. *Une Journée sur la terre. II. Les Jardins d'Eros.* Paris: Editions de la Difference, 1990.

Kearney, Patrick J. *A Bibliography of the Paris Olympia Press 1953–1966.* London: Black Spring Press, 1987.

Kearney, Patrick J. *A History of Erotic Literature.* London: Macmillan, 1983.

St-Jorre, John de. *The Good Ship Venus. The Erotic Voyage of the Olympia Press.* London: Hutchinson, 1994.

ORGY

In ancient Greece, the *orgia* were religious rites that induced the participants into a sacred delirium where they either worshipped the gods of the material world, Demeter, or Dionysus. The Dionysus cult orgies, dedicated to god of drunkenness and immoderation, could be described as licentious, due to the consumption of wine, their phallophoria or phallic processions, and naked and ecstatically convulsing bacchantes. King Demetrius and Alexander the Great indulged in prodigious orgies (reported by Plutarch and Quintus Curtius), as they considered themselves to be the God Dionysus. The ancient Greeks, who actually invented the orgies in their initial sense, did not leave us with any literary description. However, Pierre Louÿs—a skillful Hellenist—wanted to shed light on this matter. In his novel *Aphrodite*, he describes an orgy at the courtesan Bacchis' residence in Alexandria, where the guests would get drunk and have sex with the female dancers and female slaves during a sumptuous dinner.

The Romans started to desecrate the orgies and transfigured them into pure debauchery, mainly consisting of food excesses. The first orgy described in Latin literature is the banquet of Trimalcion in Petronius' *Satyricon*, during Nero's time. One would find information on the orgies organized by the Roman emperors in the works of historians like Dion Cassius, and mostly by Suetonius, whose *Life of the Twelve Caesars* cited the debaucheries of Caligula, Tiberius, Domitian, Commodus (the latter would even go as far as incorporating coprophilia fecal fetishes). For example, he recounts that Tiberius, in his Capri residence, had a specific hall where he had young girls and ephebes having sexual intercourse in front of him. Lampride dedicated a book to the Emperor Heliogabalus' orgies, who considered himself the son of the Sun. Christianism did not end these pagan customs. Burchard, chaplain of Pope Alexander VI Borgia, relates in his *Diarum* [*Diary*] (1696) the orgies organized by the Duke Borgia, where fifty courtesans had sex with the majority of the male invitees, and where rewards were given to those couples who excelled in their performance. Buchard specifies: "The Pope, the Duke and

Lucrece, his sister, were all present and observed."

The Romantic poet Gérard de Nerval said once that "a good orgy has always two levels: above and below the table." In modern terms, the word orgy designates the paroxystic nature of group sexuality. It does not just imply food excesses, but sexual acts carried out under the effect of the orgy's atmosphere. Some might slide under the table because their legs will no longer support them, having drunk too much; but others would descend to fornicate. The history of orgies is not limited to Europe. Those of Tang Ti, Emperor of China, murdered in 618, were the subject of an anonymous book, *Milow-ki, souvenir du Palais labyrinthe* [Milow-ki, *Memoirs of the Labyrinth Palace*] although European countries were the ones that continued the orgiastic tradition of Greco-Roman antiquity.

The most extraordinary orgies in literature were those depicted in French novels from the eighteenth century that, accordingly, were inspired by true events and expressed an ideal of freedom of behavior, Philippe, Duke of Orléans, being and Regent of France during Louis XV's childhood the main instigator. His dinners at the Royal Palace, accompanied by his favorite aristocrats, ended in bacchanals where he invited expensive prostitutes. The *Philippiques de Lagrange-Chancel* [*Philippics of Lagrange-Chancel*] constitute a series of satirical poems about the orgies of the Regent. As a mere imitation, the Duke of Richelieu and the Duke of Lauzun had "small residences" where they held libertine parties. The orgies became so fashionable that the writings opposing the religious establishment, like *Le portier des Chartreux* [*The Carthusian's Carrier*], sent the most uninhibited women to the convents. The novels written by the marquis of Sade—*Justine* and *Juliette*—depict a series of monstrous orgies where all sorts of wicked instincts are exposed, in order to illustrate his pessimistic philosophy where he would propose that human nature is vicious and that the only purpose of sex is to satisfy its own viciousness. The subject of *120 journées de Sodome* [*120 Days of Sodom*] is the methodical organization of everyday orgies at the Silling castle by four "villains" (as he defines them), indulging in an escalation of depravities. On the other hand, Andrea de Nerciat, describes in *Les Aphrodites* [*The Aphrodites*], and *Le Diable au corps* [*The Devil in the Body*], a series of refined and enjoyable characters who take part in marvelous orgies filled with humor and sensual pleasure (like his friend the Prince of Ligne). In English literature, the most beautiful orgy was depicted by John Cleland in *Memoirs of a Woman of Pleasure,* when Fanny Hill, Emily, and Harriett offer themselves to a baronet and to his friends, customers of Mrs. Cole.

During the nineteenth century, there was an orgy in almost any available erotic novel (one would refer to them in the twentieth century as "*partouze*" or *gangbang*, a French word invented by Victor Margueritte in *Ton corps est à toi* [*Your Body is Yours*]). The novel of Alphonse Belot, *La Canonisation de Jeanne d'Arc* [*The Canonization of Jeanne d'Arc*] (1890), recounts the most sensational orgy of the 3rd Republic, organized by the Duchess of Liancourt and her mother in her Parisian apartment. After a ball, where all the women danced naked, wearing a wolf-styled velvet mask, they would pick the names of that night's lovers from a vase. Nothing compares to this scene, even the one in which the nymphomaniac Régina throws herself into *La bourgeoise pervertie* [*The Perverted Bourgeoisie*] (1930) by André Ibels. In this case, the orgy is a meal that lasts the entire night, and during the event the guests get undressed, and the lights are turned off. Next morning, Régina asks herself: "Who has taken me?"

There has even been a philosopher of orgies, Charles Fourier, the social reformer (whose ideas about sexuality were put into practice by the American Fourierist John Humphrey Noyes). In *Le nouveau monde amoureux* [*The New World of Love*], Fourier described the orgies of the future, when humanity will live in harmony. These will consist of sex combined with art, and harmlessly favoring all the passions. This book is so provocative that the French disciples of Fourier did not dare to publish it even after his death, appearing only in 1966. *Le nouveau monde amoureux* will remain, for a long time to come, a reference book of orgies, containing the theory and the principles that make it attractive and stimulating.

SARANE ALEXANDRIAN

Bibliography

Bagneaux de Villeneuve (pseudonym: VEZE, Raoul): *L'orgie romaine* (The Roman orgy). Paris, Daragon, 1908.

Partridge, Burgo: *Histoire des orgies*. London: Anthony Blond, 1958; Paris, edition. The open eyes, 1962.

Maffesoli, Michel. *L'Ombre de Dionysos, contribution à une sociologie de l'orgie*. Paris: Méridiens Library, Klincksierk and Company, 1985.

"L'element orgiastique dans la religion grecque antique", Kernos, number 5 (1995). *Revue internationale et pluridisciplinaire de la religion antique*, Liège.

Marbeck, Georges. *L'Orgie, voie du sacré, fait du prince, instinct de fête*, Paris: Robert Laffont, 1992.

Orgies, a livre d'images (Orgies, a book in pictures). New York: Ipso Facto, 1999.

OVID

43 BCE–17 CE
Roman poet

Ovid, who referred to himself as 'the poet of tender loves' (Tr.3.3.73–76), is traditionally regarded as 'the fourth and final Roman elegist.' His poems are divided in three groups: erotic, mythological, and poems of exile. With the exception of the *Metamorphoses* and a fragment from *Halieutica* (probably a spurious work), which are written in dactylic hexameter, Ovid composed in elegiac couplets. His love poems comprising the *Amores*, the *Ars Amatoria*, the *Remedia Amoris*, and the *Medicamina Faciei*, indicate the extent to which Ovid occupied himself with the composition of elegy, a genre which he essentially redefined by testing its boundaries to the extreme, in real Alexandrian fashion. His constant experimentation with elegiac themes drove him to meticulously reworking several of the conventional motifs of Latin elegy, often by inserting into the elegiac context well-recognized material from comic playwrights. A balanced approach to this tendency is essential as it lies at the heart of Ovid's humorous approach to elegy and of the negative criticism his work has suffered since antiquity (Quint.Inst.10. 1.88, 98).

Ovid wrote erotic elegies and, although he later favored hexameters, he never ceased narrating in verse tales of erotic passion. The analysis of Ovidian poetry is often preoccupied with the numerous techniques the poet employs in retelling the legendary loves of gods and heroes as well as his own amorous adventures. Despite their pedantry, such analyses indicate in depth Ovid's stance towards love, as a poet and perhaps as an individual. Ovid's *Amores* consists of forty-nine short poems initially arranged in five books and republished in 3 BCE in three volumes, an illustrative demonstration of Ovid's tactic of reworking his own verses. The poems are largely dedicated to extolling the charms of the poet's mistress Corinna. Her character is probably a synthesis of the elegiac mistresses featured in the works of Propertius and Tibullus, Ovid's older contemporaries in elegiac composition, who devoted their poetry to Cynthia and Delia, respectively. The influence of the shadowy figure of Cornelius Gallus, whom Ovid mentions by name (Tr.4.10.53–54), cannot be doubted since he seems to have played an equally important role in inspiring all Roman elegiac writers as well as Vergil (Prop.2.34.91; Verg.Ec.10). In addition, the spirit of Catullus, whose Lesbia can be regarded as the prototype of Roman elegiac women, is also evident (cf. Am.2.6); in particular, Catullus' sarcasm and sharp castigation of Roman social morals seems to have shaped Ovid's familiar sense of irony, omnipresent in the *Amores* as well as the later *Ars Amatoria*. It appears that despite their feigned dedication to the principles of the simple farmers and hardy soldiers of Rome past, the noble Romans, especially after coming in contact with the lustful ways of the Greeks, embarked on endless revels and worship of beauty and love. The Latin elegists captured this Roman celebration of sexual liberation in their poetry, while carefully paying tribute to their Greek models, which inspired them to not only love passionately, but also to write passionate poetry.

The references to Ovid's literary models already foreshadow a major fault of his entire corpus Ovid has been often classified as a representative of the so-called *Silver Age* of Roman poetic production, obviously in contrast to a *Golden Age* epitomized by Vergil's *Aeneid*. Since antiquity, literary criticism viewed Ovid primarily as a reader of classical poetry rather than as a composer; his work was diagnosed with lack of originality because his inspiration was too technical and rested excessively on his literary models. In contrast with Propertius and Tibullus, who often claim to draw their themes from personal experiences, Ovid is accused of borrowing literary patterns by previous literature. Brandt (*Amorum Libri Tres*) remarked that "[t]here is no motive of any importance in the *Amores* to which one cannot point out a literary predecessor," and many studies have repeatedly stressed his imitation of Propertian themes, especially with regards to Propertius' employment of mythological illustrations. It has also been argued that Ovid parodies Propertius' verses to the point where his own poetry becomes burlesque. His imitation of and irreverence toward literary models is considered to expand in parodying, apart from Propertius, the works of Hesiod, Lucretius, and even Vergil. His humorous style seems to encourage the impression that his elegies were superficial reproductions of the poetic flair of unrivalled predecessors. However, this inability to appreciate Ovid's poetry has been the result of constant comparison to the other elegiac poets, and the application of modern literary and aesthetic criteria to his work. Ovid consciously tried to overcome this parallelism by incorporating his predecessors' work into his as explicitly as possible. He exploited the typical elegiac themes over their limits and he even inverted several of them; it appears that through the systematic reversal of his models he hoped to distinguish his own poetic substance. In addition, Ovid's obvious employment of his literary predecessors forces the reader to think of elegiac loves as artistic products of talented creators; although

the erotic claims of Propertius and Tibullus are probably disqualified as poetic exaggerations, they nevertheless retain their value as representations of love in contemporary Rome, a city ruled by its courtesans and their expensive caprices, a city where rich soldiers win the girls over sobbing poets protesting with pathetic serenades. In the *Amores*, Ovid parades through a Rome that has special places where men can access the women such as the hippodrome; it has notorious socialites, and a new class of noble women who do not fear scandal. It is a true cosmopolis surrendered to carnal passions, and its streets witness every night the whimsical desires of its inhabitants.

Elegiac poetry projecting the most memorable urban characters of this era allows for some classification: the constant subversion that Ovid applied to his treatment of the elegiac lover was mainly directed against the established (until then) division between the figures of the learned poet and the ignorant lover. Conversely, Ovid appears as conscious of his poetic pursuits as he is of his erotic ones. He addresses the reader in the first person with an immediacy and frankness that removes the barrier between the poet and the object of his composition. In the *Ars Amatoria* as well, due to the admonitory character of the poem, Ovid reveals himself and his aims openly from the first lines of his work. By creating an epiphasis of personal experience, Ovid is able to convince the reader about the autobiographical character of his poetry, but this is simply his deconstruction of yet another elegiac motif. The poet is often keen to acknowledge the mind games he plays with his audience as this admission allows him to keep uncovering the imperfections of the elegiac lover and of his own poetic persona which he often treats with mockery. Ovid is able to laugh at himself both in the capacity of a poet and a lover, yet this level of detachment, particularly explicit in the *Amores*, indicates Ovid's confidence in the power and versatility of his poetry. In fact, he frequently referred to the sway of his poetry and he did not hide his ambitions for the renown of his work (Am.1.3; 1.15).

In the footsteps of their Hellenistic models, Roman elegists had further cultivated the typical image of an elegiac lover as being poor and endowed only with his art; as suffering the cruelty and infidelity of his mistress in desperation by spending long nights outside her threshold.

Above all, the elegiac lover was not allowed but short spells of happiness in love, doomed to meet with failure at all levels and even at his core quality as a lover. However, in Ovid's elegies the lover is often successful and his mistress easily accessible, almost too easily. Ovid confesses to addressing his poetry to the *admissus amator* and not to the *exclusus* as expected (e.g., Am.1.2). A point missed by modern critics is that Ovid, unsatisfied with regurgitating the conventional elegiac motifs, discovered in the continuous reversal of them, his own unconventional means of claiming his personal contribution to the elegiac genre. His loves are as rebellious as the real Roman lovers of his era who entertained any danger, any doorkeeper, and any social precepts in order to enjoy their mistresses.

Ovid's erotic poetry is characterized by a special ethos which was frequently misjudged. His explicit sexual descriptions were also understood as an effort to portray his personal experience rather than to entertain some established generic conventions of Latin elegy. His lustful descriptions which seem designed to cause the audience's discomfort are effortlessly turned to jokes and Ovid is able to laugh at his skinny figure, the result of being a tireless soldier in the ranks of Love (Am.1.6.1–6; cf. 3.7). Ovid's overstatement of elegiac motifs is in essence the reinvention of a generic rule. His erotic imagery is ruled by a bold and almost sarcastic mood which often renders elegiac passion facetious and even comical. The typical elegiac lover exhibits a tendency for uncontrollable melodramatic reactions. Elegiac poetry is rife with overemotional confessions of unending passion and exaggerations of the hardship the lover must withstand in order to win temporary affection by his pitiless and volatile mistress. Love is painted with the darkest colors as a horrible destiny of vain fighting against the winged god of Love, allotted only to those who can endure divine adversity (e.g., Prop. 1.1, 5, 8a, 9). Ovid's innovation lies in the fact that he shifts the focus of his poetry by emphasizing the detrimental aspects of love as a natural and social phenomenon leaving little space for the romantic overcoat of previous elegiac poetry. The contentment with which Ovid decides to give in to Love is characteristic of his disbelief of pompous statements a propos amorous exclusiveness

(Am.2.11b; 3.8). This light-hearted approach to love is also reflected in the relation that the elegiac couple aspires to achieve: unfaithfulness is no longer a reason for unrelenting misery and tearful suffering, especially as Ovid's Corinna appears to have been already married. Ovid, a lover devoted to lovemaking by his own free will and not because of the torrential yoke of a great passion, argues that the elegiac lover is unfaithful by nature. He knows the rules of the erotic game and expects his mistress to be kind enough to feign her faithfulness for the sake of his fancy (Am.3.3.1–2, 41–48). Cairns chose the term 'generic self-imitation' to describe Ovid's rebellious technique of representing elegiac love. Ovid exaggerates his statements only to prove that they are unrealistic. He follows the rules only to cancel them eventually. Ovid does not simply follow literary principles, but he criticizes them in a double capacity as a poet and reader.

Ovid's tendency toward hyperbole, a technique familiar to Roman writers of comedy such as Plautus and Terence, produces comic effects unparalleled in previous samples of Latin elegiac poetry. Therefore, in Am.1.7 he bitterly regrets being violent to his mistress during an argument. The poet sounds completely desperate and devastated by the boldness of his almost profane deeds, and he even compares himself to Ajax and Orestes, tragic figures of Greek mythology, who were haunted by their sacrilegious crimes. In an effort to exorcise his victim's anger, he praises her beauty, thus employing another typical elegiac motif. However, this mistress, compared here with Atalanta, Ariadne, and Cassandra (ll.1–18) is not beautiful while sleeping or while praying. Ovid's beloved is beautiful because she has been beaten by her lover, apparently in the fashion Greek heroines used to get bruises from their heroic companions. Ovid's wit is to be detected in his comparing himself to Homeric heroes who acted supposedly in the same way as this exasperated lover. His way of securing a place in the pantheon of heroes is not only an example of de-mythologizing classical champions, but a conscious endeavour to shape the character of the 'anti-lover' in Latin elegy. A sudden change in tone at the poem's concluding lines ensures that the audience is aware of Ovid's humorous mood; we are informed that the 'terrible abuse' the poet inflicted upon his mistress was a disarranged hair-do.

Unlike the unbearably sentimental and gentle lover of Propertius and Tibullus, Ovid's lover behaves like a boor. Even in his regret he is able to rationalize the situation and appreciate the triviality of the event.

Ovid's originality is also evident in the treatment of the conventional comparison of the elegiac lover with a soldier; the contrast of the two characters was boisterous in Roman society which would reject by tradition the image of the elegiac lover, always consumed by his erotic troubles, never interested in pressing public affairs. The elegiac lover was typically presented as living effectively in a permanent situation of *otium* (vacation), pursuing predominantly what traditionalist Romans viewed as pastime, unlike the soldier whose excellence in the coordination of his *negotium* (professional activity) secured the glory and prosperity of Rome (Am.1.6.19–30). Although Propertius did try to balance out the disadvantages of being a hopeless lover (1.14.11–16), Ovid succeeds in totally equating the toils of a lover with those of a soldier by redefining the motif of *militia amoris*, the motif of taking up an expedition in love rather than an expedition in war (Am.1.9). The pattern was extensively treated in comic plays, albeit not exclusively (Plaut.Merc.24ff, 62ff; Most.133ff; Trin.646ff; Truc.141ff). However, comic writers adjusted military metaphors predominantly to the *paraclausithyron*, the bitter complaining of the lover by his mistress' threshold, a clue that did not escape Ovid's attention. In the *Amores* the lover is often described as acting like a soldier in peacetime; instead of besieging a hostile city he camps outside his mistress' threshold (Am.1.6.29–30, 57–58; 1.9.1–2, 19–20, 41–42). The motif is a direct borrowing from comic plays where it also enjoyed popularity (Her.2.63ff; Ter.Eun.771; Plaut.Pers.569ff, Bacch.1118; Ter.Ad.88f.). Another variation of the *militia amoris* summoned by Ovid is that of treating the elegiac *puella* as an enemy (Am.1.7.33–34). Although violence against the mistress is not exclusively found in comedy, comic plays use it profoundly. Ovid's celebrated attack on his mistress' hair is reminiscent of Philostratus' *Epistles* and of Terence's *Perikeiromene* (see Am.1.7 above; Phil.16, cf. 61). The representation of *the triumph of Love* in military terms is a third variation of the *militia amoris* motif, inspired perhaps by the Hellenistic idea regarding the cruelty of erotic attacks by a winged Eros

(Mel.12.101; Prop.1.1; Am.1.2.51–52); Ovid compares the triumph of Eros on him with the military triumphs of the emperor Augustus who had allegedly felt himself the power of love (Am.1.2.7–14; cf. Am.1.7.35–40). Although the military metaphor has been employed in comedy extensively this specific image has not been particularly developed (Plaut.Pers.2526; Ter.Eun.59–61). Moreover, by rallying his imagination Ovid enriches once more the motif of *militia amoris* in Am.1.7.36–41 by allowing himself to indulge in a vivid triumphal procession which consists of a single prisoner: his mistress.

An essential feature of Alexandrian and Roman erotic poetry is the *komos*, the wooing of a mistress by singing or complaining on her threshold alone or with a group of drunken revellers. The lover, who typically appears as begging for his admission, is often jealous of a rival whom the lady favored that night instead of him (Am.1.4.61–2). In most *komoi* the lover leaves his mistress' doorstep disappointed by her cruelty. Prior to his sad departure, he is seen shedding tears or leaving his komastic garlands on the steps where the dawn found him cold and lonely. Ovid contributes to the pattern by presenting the lover as addressing his supplications to the doorkeeper, a mean slave. Although, doorkeepers were regarded as the worse kind of slaves, Ovid treats him with flattery and respect, thus amusing his audience and inserting to elegiac imagery another motif of comedies, the only literary scripts in which slaves assumed central roles in the plot.

Ovid admits his indebtness to comedy by openly suggesting Menander as an appropriate reading for the youth of both sexes (Ov. Tr.2.369–370); in the concluding poem of the first book of the *Amores* Ovid seems to indicate clearly which stock characters he has borrowed from the Menandrian tradition, namely the *fallax servus*, the *improba lena,* and the *meretrix blanda* among others (Am.1.15.17–18). Apart from Plautus, Terence, and their Greek models, Ovid was influenced by the mimes of Herodas, especially with regards to the treatment of the *komos* (cf. Pro Rab.Post. 35). Although mimes were considered as 'a trivial sub-literary form of entertainment, far beneath the notice of such highly sophisticated poets as the elegists' (Mckeown), they were apparently appreciated by the Roman elite for their *doctrina*. Rough jokes and adultery appear to have been their major forming parts and they also involved an elementary stage presentation. Mimes represent the low classes' perception of love, and in fact a more realistic image of everyday life and love in Rome, outside the villas of the elite. From this point of view, the introduction of mime scenarios and characters in elegies destined for the noble circles is revolutionary in presenting love as the force that makes a *matrona* act like a courtesan and the other way round. Moreover, Ovid might have been familiar with the mimiambs of Gnaeus Matius who composed his work in the steps of Herodas in the Sullan period (Aul.Gell.10.24.10; 15.25.1–2; 16.7.1; 20.9.1–3), as well as with comical epigrams. Ovid's introductory epigram of his republished *Amores* is comparable in structure and effect to the prologues of Roman comedians.

A well-recognized comic pattern that Ovid incorporated and further developed in his poetry is the so-called *Gebetsparodie,* the habit of addressing ordinary humans or even slaves by adopting the language and forms of prayers to gods (Am.1.3; 1.16; cf. Plaut.Cas. 137; Curc.88, 147f.; Men.Perik.724). The motif is usually included in poetic renderings of the *paraclausithyron.* It appears that liturgical vocabulary would be often transferred in a *komos* included either in an elegy or in a comedy. Ovid as well as Plautus parodies the high style of the prayers to deities, especially the exaggerated worship offered to the oriental deities that swarmed into Rome in the Augustan years. Ovid also largely employed in his verses personification of inanimate things; although not an exclusive feature of comedy, it is typically found in almost every comic play (Am.1.8; cf. Plaut.Curc.15–20, 88–90). Ovid even succeeds a variation of the *Gebetsparodie* by attributing a divine nature to inanimate things.

Another typical comic motif that Ovid seems very fond of is that of the *erotodidaxis* [erotic teaching]. Here again the influence of Plautus and of the mime is evident in the persona of the 'cultus adulter'; this figure comes directly from the so-called adultery-mime which was particularly popular in Ovid's time and involved a love-triangle outlined by McKeown like this: 'a suave lover, a crafty wife and a stupid husband' (Am.1.4.39–40; Am.2.5.29; cf. Plaut.Bacch.918). The scenario appears to suit perfectly the situation of Ovid, Corinna, and her husband, whom she is often encouraged to deceive (Am.1.4). In comedies the *erotodidaxis*

is usually uttered by the *lena,* an old, alcoholic procuress, and a comic stock character which Ovid decides to impersonate himself in his poetry (Am.1.4; 2.5.30; Plaut.Asin.775f., Mil.Glor.123–125, Ter.Haut.372f.). Treachery is a main feature of the *lena* employed by both Ovid and comic writers (Am.1.8.85–86; Plaut. Pers.243f.). The *lena* endowed with such an unpleasant character is often the receiver of curses by the lover; curses which are found abundantly in comic plays, also suit Ovid's humorous and vivacious style nicely (Am.1.8.113–114; Plaut.Asin.46f.; 127; Most.192; Mil.1038; Pers.483; Poen.1055; Ter. Phorm.519). Another comic motif traced in Ovid's erotic poems is that of receiving advice from the 'lena,' normally willing to act as a go-between for a rich client who has fallen in love with a girl or to express cynicism about love, often described as an 'investment' on behalf of the girl for her old age (Am.1.8; 3.3.21ff.; Plaut.Cist. 120, 149; Most.47ff, 157ff., 170f., 196f.; Asin.524ff., Pseud.308, Ter.Hecyr. 67ff.; Herod.Mim.1.37f.61ff.). Herodas' influence in Ovid's employment of the motif is highly probable. Ovid's affinity with the comic themes, especially regarding the *erotodidaxis,* could be also argued indirectly, through the work of later Greek authors of erotic verses. Lucian of Samosata, who has obviously used Menander for his *Dialogue of the Courtesans,* often employs motifs similar to those of Ovid and Plautus (Am.1.8.65f; cf. Plaut.Truc.; Amph.940f; Ter. Andr.555 and Eun.59ff.; also Luc.3 and 6 ad finem).

The unyielding *ianitor,* the doorkeeper of the mistress' house, is also a stock character of comedy which Ovid inserts in his poetry (Am.1.6.41–42; Plat.Curc. 153; Aul.721a; Epid.50; Pers.783f.). In comic plays the doorkeeper is typically presented as the main obstacle between the lover and the object of his desire, although he can usually be bribed or fooled (Am.1.8.77–78; Plaut.Asin. 241f; Pseud.255f.; however cf. Am.1.6.49-50 and Plaut.Curc. 20f.). Moreover, where the lover was usually expected to be tormented by the thought that his beloved is perhaps sleeping with someone else, Ovid implies that the doorkeeper experiences love himself, underlining once more the free man /slave role-reversal, so common in comedy (Plaut.Pers.25).

The *fallax servus* of comic plays, a cunning slave often acting on behalf of the young and inexperienced lover, also appears in Ovidian imagery (Am. 1.8.87–88). The *puella* that attracts the lover's interest is also often accompanied by a loyal servant. Plautus writes about Pardalisca in the *Casina*, Milphidippa in the *Miles Gloriosus*, Astaphium in *Truculentus*. This character appears to correspond to Nape, Corinna's clever hairdresser (Am. 1.11.2; 1.12.4). The old man who decides to find himself a young bride, known as the *senex amator* of numerous comedies also parades in Ovid's verses (Am. 1.9.3–4; cf. Plaut.; Asin.; Bacch.; Cas.; Cist.; Merc.; Stich.). The motif of the *avaricious puella*, a common topos of comedies, appears also in the *Amores* where Ovid implies that the entire family of his mistress is taking advantage of his generosity (Am. 1.8.89–92; Plaut. Asin. 181f; Men. 541f; Trin. 251f).

Amatory fowling and hunting are also two very common images in elegiac poetry and comic scripts, although Ovid excels at it (Am. 1.8.69–70; cf. Plaut. Asin. 215f.). Although a sexist view of love has often been suspected in Latin elegy, the alternate scripts where love now forces the lover, now the beloved, to succumb to his humiliating power, indicate once more the rebellious nature of Aphrodite's suave child. *Servitium amoris*, the enslavement that the lover suffers to his mistress, is again a general topos in Latin elegy freely employed by comic plays as well. Comedy depicted mostly the relations between prostitutes and their clients who are often compared with sheep ready for shearing, a motif also implied in the *Amores* (Am. 1.8.54–56; Plaut. Asin. 540ff; Bacch. 1121aff; Merc. 524ff; Cist. 76–79).

Ovid's vocabulary has also been influenced by comedy. He has famously introduced comic words in elegiac context, some of which were earlier found only in comic plays, usually in Plautus (see Am.1.10.35–36 for 'damnosus' which previously occurs only in Plautus[8] and Terence[1] and Am.1.10.43–44 for 'conducere' meaning 'to hire a prostitute' which is borrowed directly from Plaut.Amph.288, Bacch.1096). Word plays which are plentiful in comic plays, often in scenes of violence or threats of it to the slaves, are also employed in the *Amores* (Am.1.6.19–20, 64; Ter.Haut. 356; Ad.470; Plaut.Men. 978; Truc.112, Poen.446, 509, 1152; Aul.745; Bacch.87–88; Curc.1ff., Most.15f., Ep.121; Men.972f.). It has been argued that Ovid's words have a static function and that

his language is shallow. However, several times Ovid incorporates in his poetry other people's words and he 'pretends' to have a dialogue with them (Am.1.7.73–74) or he even lends them a voice to speak their minds (Am.8.21–24). It could be argued that his vocabulary is in keeping with the social status of his characters (cf. Dipsas in Am.1.8.21–24 and the doorkeeper in Am.1.6) whose phraseology could not have been very lofty. His language is not static but rather colloquial. It might sound from time to time somewhat theatrical, but this is a result of his characters' intense awareness of their conventional quality (Am.1.6.41–42). In several instances Ovid includes in his poetry asides which are obviously the result of his influence from the theatrical performance of comedy or mime. His asides, addressed mainly to himself, give to his speech a dramatic tone (Am.1.4; 1.6; 1.13) and are reminiscent of the stage directions Plautus included in his plays (Bacch.234; Curc.156f.; Men.523; Mil.154; Most.507; Cas.163).

In terms of structure, Ovid mostly favors the linear indication of images and arguments which renders to the poetic result more immediacy. A technique fond to the poet are the numerous rhetorical questions that are interspersed in his poems and can be addressed either to himself or the audience. In each case the queries are answered by the poet and their obvious aim is to dramatize the poetic speech. This technique is used by the other elegiac poets as well, but, not to the extent Ovid does (Am.1.13). Repetition of words or phrases is also employed by Ovid in his effort to create an atmosphere of agony and suspense (Am.1.6). A very interesting method which Ovid rallies for the composition of his work, obviously a remnant from his education in rhetoric, is to treat the same poetic theme from a different point of view in two separate poems which are placed in sequence. This tactic, traced in the other elegiac poets as well, seems to be employed more frequently and more expressly by Ovid (Am.2.7 and 8).

As mentioned already, Ovid also wrote the *Ars Amatoria* (Sen.Controv.3.7.2), a didactic poem in imitation of Alexandrian poetry, in three books, with complete instructions on how to acquire and keep a lover. The first two books, dated around the first century BCE, offer advice to men about winning the affection of women, while the third book attempts with arguable success to address erotic matters from a female point of view or, as the poet puts it in the beginning of this book, to 'provide the Amazons with weapons.' The situations presented in *Ars Amatoria* owe much to previous elegies and the *Amores* to which it was designed as a sequence. In typical Ovidian manner the poet appears to explore the rules of love poetry as much as the rules of love in an attempt to break free from the conventional character of both. In the *Ars Amatoria* Ovid cultivates further the metaphor of love as art; the topoi of love as sport and as military conquest are also employed extensively, while the motif of love as madness leading to bestiality is also worked thoroughly. The sudden change in tone in book three which put emphasis on moderation has given rise to a number of arguments with regards to Ovid's possible literary and political shifts. In addition, much of the novelty of *Ars Amatoria* is achieved through a reversal of the implied roles of the poet and the reader: in the *Amores* the readers are invited to amuse themselves with the erotic adventures of the poet, while in the *Ars Amatoria* the poet appears entertained with the love troubles of the reader to whom he acts as an advisor.

In addition, Ovid is not afraid of depicting the social reality of his time accurately. He lived in the early imperial period and in a society that experienced the grand opening of Rome to the world. This is a society thirsty for power and pleasure, especially after the long and traumatic period of the civil wars. Moreover, the opportunistic character of the era had left its mark on the values of the individual in a time when nobility and class had become the apple of the eye of the unsophisticated rich nouveau. The Ovidian lover cannot ignore the frivolity of the world in which he lives and loves; his *Ars Amatoria* functions as a mirror that he turns towards his audience who can observe themselves for the first time. However, it has been implied that this revolutionary reversal that allows the poet to satirize social phenomena not in relation to himself or distant protagonists, but in relation to his readers might have offended the more sensitive of them. In addition, it could be argued that thus Ovid made himself an easy target for accusations of encouraging debauchery in his works which were put forward more overtly when his relation with the emperor turned sour (Ars Am.1.31–34; Tr.2.245–252). Another important aspect, in which Ovid

marked his progress from the *Amores* and towards his more mature works, is the fact that he chose to write the *Ars Amatoria* in elegiac couplets, against the instructions of tradition that associated didactic poetry exclusively with hexameters. Although his choice reflects the humorous and irreverent style of the *Amores*, especially towards the serious Lucretius (*De Rerum Natura*) and Vergil (*Georgics*), Ovid's didactic models, it also foreshadows his poetic experimentations in the *Metamorphoses*. In addition, in the *Ars Amatoria*, Ovid occasionally digresses from his main theme to narrate at length a mythological tale that serves to some extent only as an illustration of his argument, a technique which he mastered in the complicated structure of the *Metamorphoses*.

Sometime between the first century BCE and the second century CE, Ovid composed the *Remedia Amoris* (Rem.155–158), a kind of recantation of the *Ars Amatoria*. Here, the poet, convinced about the impropriety of falling madly in love, instructs his audience how to avoid passionate affairs and how to extricate themselves from desperate erotic situations. However, once more Ovid adopts a sarcastic mood and mocks pretentious castigation of sexual infatuation by offering long and detailed sexual descriptions. The *Remedia* appropriately concludes Ovid's early career in erotic elegiac experimentation.

The *Epistulae Heroidum*, mentioned as Heroides by Priscian (Gramm.Lat. 2.544) is an imaginary series of letters written by ancient mythological heroines to their absent lovers. The first fourteen letters are known as single in contrast to epistles 16 to 21, which are often referred to as double in the sense that Ovid also composed the replies to the initial letters. The authorship of Her.15, written allegedly by Sappho to Phaon, her mythical lover, is often contested. Although the historical character of Sappho is beyond doubt, apparently the erotic content of her poetry had given rise to several mythic traditions with regards to her love affairs. The letters which are characteristic of their argumentative character serve as a reminiscence of Ovid's rhetorical training. His tendency to give to the letters of his heroines the epiphasis of court cases loaded with the frequent use of legal terms (Her.20 and 21, *Acontius and Cydippe*) led some critics to charge Ovid with plain enumeration that fails to convince the audience about the heroines' emotional sincerity; yet especially in the double epistles the refutation of the accusations that the lonesome heroines typically address to their lovers is necessary for the full appreciation of the dramatic situation between the protagonists. Ovid not only develops to the extreme his sophistic ability of composing on a single theme from two different points of view (and here it could be argued that he is more successful in rendering the feminine thought in comparison with *Ars Amatoria* 3), but he also takes advantage of every opportunity to induce an intertextual dialogue between his epistles and a vast range of ancient literature. Therefore, Penelope, Briseis, Helen, Oenone, and Dido are immediately juxtaposed against their epic profiles in Vergil and Homer. Medea, Phaedra, Hypsipyle, Hermione, Deianera, Hypermestra, and Ariadne recall their tragic personas and momentarily appear as suffering more realistically than the previous heroines, although they are still distant from the immediate experiences of the Roman audience. This gap becomes perhaps smaller with the tales of Laodamia, Phylis, and Canace whose roles as mothers and wives might have been more appealing to Ovid's contemporaries, while the passionate romances of Leander and Hero, as well as of Cydippe with Acontius derive clearly from the Hellenistic background of Latin elegy and celebrate youthful love. The technique of inserting erotic monologues in elegiac context was already employed by Propertius (see 1.18 in imitation of Callimachus), who had also worked on the pattern of lovers exchanging passionate notes (4.3). The motif reappeared briefly in Ovid's *Amores* (Am.11 and 12) but in the *Heroides* Ovid appears very conscious of his effort to establish a new literary genre by raising the Alexandrian dramatic monologue to new heights (Ars Am.3.346). In rendering the most secret thoughts of his inamoratas, Ovid deftly adapted Euripides' psychographic analysis of female emotions and succeeded in incorporating the process of writing in the literary action.

Although the authorship of the double *Heroides* was doubted they are now accepted as Ovid's and it has been suggested that stylistic differences might be explained by a different compositional date (perhaps contemporary with the *Fasti*). The inspiration for these paired letters might have come from Sabinus, Ovid's friend, who is said to have composed replies for the single *Heroides*, possibly written between the two editions of the *Amores* (cf. Am.2.18).

Medicamina Faciei is yet another didactic poem about the cosmetics for the female face which predates the third book of the *Ars Amatoria* (Ars Am.3.205–206). Only a hundred verses survive from this work which is, nevertheless, enough to indicate a strong influence from Nicander's *Theriaca* and *Alexipharmaca*.

The fifteen books of the *Metamorphoses,* the most influential poem of Ovid, belong to the mythological category. Written in hexameters, it is a collection of myths concerned with miraculous transformations linked together with a number of thematic associations that render to the work an illusion of cohesion. The poem was written in the years preceding Ovid's exile and it borrows material from classical and Near Eastern mythological traditions. The idea of collecting metamorphic myths was popular in the Hellenistic years; Nicander of Colophon, Parthenius, and the obscure Boios whose *Ornithogonia* was apparently adapted by Aemilius Macer, a friend and contemporary of Ovid (Tr.4.10.43), had all produced such collections, although none of them survived to this day. Undoubtedly, Ovid's poem exhibits a chronological framework which begins with the genesis of the ordered universe out of a chaotic mass of elements, he employs the Hesiodic myth of the five races which ends with Lycaon's sin and the irrevocable departure of the gods from the earth. Jupiter's disappointment with the human race drives him to the decision to obliterate humanity in an episode similar to the Biblical and the Mesopotamian flood (*Epic of Gilgamesh*). He spares only Deucalion and Pyrrha who are bestowed with the task of restarting the human race. From then on the poet relates unremittingly a great number of tales from Greek mythology starting with Apollo and his amorous adventures. Ovid continues with the love affairs of the gods until the first half of the sixth book, and then he turns his attention to the great heroes of ancient Greece from Jason and Theseus to the protagonists of the Trojan War. The retelling of the conquest of Troy by the Greeks is significant because it offers Ovid the chance to refer to Aeneas, his escape from his blazing city and his eventual arrival at the Italian peninsula. Obviously at this point Ovid reworks the theme of the *Aeneid* regarding the origin of the Romans from the Trojan refugees who established themselves in Lavinium in the area of Rome. Aeneas' son Iulus, the ancestor of the Julian clan, built Alba Longa and united the scattered villages of the area to what would later become Rome. Ovid relates the early traditions of the Romans in the days of the Etruscan kings and concludes his work with the most glorious metamorphosis of all, the apotheosis of Julius Caesar who was transformed into a star, soon after his murder in 44 BCE (Met.15.745–879; Verg.G.1.25f.). This last transformation ensures that Augustus is the son of a god, indeed of divine stock himself. The poem was an obvious tribute to the emperor, and although in a rage Ovid threw it into the fire at the news of his own exile, other copies of his work were already in circulation, thus ensuring the survival of the work.

Although the poem starts with the typical epic invocation to the gods, Ovid certainly does not confine himself in epic themes and in fact a great proportion of the *Metamorphosis* deals with sexual misconduct. According to Otis who detected four main thematic divisions after the prologue to the work, books one to two as well as books six (from line 400 onwards) to eleven is dedicated to the passion of love, divine or heroic. Otis also distinguished the theme of avenging gods in books three to six, while the history of Rome to the deification of Caesar in books twelve to fifteen (Otis, *Ovid as an Epic Poet*). His outline presupposes a thematic movement from gods suffering like humans due to falling in love, to humans suffering divine wrath, to humans tormented by their passion for other humans to the possibility of humans becoming gods in an ongoing questioning of the boundaries between divine and human nature. Each section offers connections for future sections: therefore, the adventures of the Minyads in book four anticipate the third section on doomed love affairs; equally, Hercules' apotheosis in book nine foreshadows those of Aeneas, Romulus, and of Caesar in the last section of the work. Throughout the *Metamorphoses*, Ovid creates a complex chain of interconnecting themes employing various techniques such as having a hero to tell an anecdote or narrate a story for the sake of the company, thus putting a story within a story. On other occasions he follows the same character through different adventures or proceeds from one tale to narrating the story of a friend or a relative of his heroes, or moves geographically from one location to a neighboring one and its traditions. It could even be argued that in the *Metamorphoses* Ovid exploits to perfection his tendency to provide variations of poetic themes within each of his more general thematic sections. The variety of themes and landscapes, of the narrative pace and of the numerous intertextual voices make the *Metamorphoses* an interesting reading, although the thematic links of the text soon surpass any pretext of chronological continuity. The poem's transitions and forced unity have been criticized already since antiquity (Quint.Inst. 4.1.77). In addition, despite the epic facade of the work, Ovid certainly deviated from traditional epic composition by inserting in his poem erotic tales as well as the tastes and techniques of his Hellenistic models. Hence, it could be argued that structurally as well as with regards to its interest in etiological myths, the *Metamorphoses* shares great affinity with the *Aetia* of Callimachus, this great master of Hellenistic poetry, despite the fact that Callimachus utterly rejected epic forms in favor of short, elegant poems. Although Ovid's powerful descriptions of landscapes, peoples, and emotions make the poem a memorable reading, the sheer accumulation of so many mythological details, poetic techniques, and generic inversions give to the whole work a superficial tone and reduce its dramatic effect. As implied, in the course of his work Ovid became more and more interested in the art of poetry than in the art of love: the *Metamorphoses* act as a boundary for his exploration of erotic sentiments since by this time he had covered the passions of everyday people, of heroes, and of gods. Erotic tales in the *Metamorphoses* tend to have didactic messages, above all the unhappiness caused by excessive love, and allow the reader a glimpse of ancient customs and beliefs about marriage and love.

Ovid's other works include the six books of the *Fasti*, a mythological poem relating legends and notable events of the Roman calendar with one book devoted to each month. The work is a syncrasis of the Roman religious calendar, Julian Panegyric, and astronomical material regarding the risings and settings of the stars in relation to the Roman year. At the time of Ovid's exile it was incomplete, and only the first six books (January–June) survive; these show evidence of partial revision at Tomis, perhaps during the years surrounding the death of Augustus in 14 BCE (Fast.1.3, 4.81–84).

Ovid appears to have abandoned any intentions of composing the remaining books, devastated by his sad existence in exile. At some point before Ovid's death in 17 AD the poem was rededicated to Germanicus, Augustus' younger heir, perhaps with renewed hope for his clemency that would allow Ovid's return to Rome. The poem's astronomical details (books 1–2) derive from Aratus' *Phenomena*, a mostly influential work which was translated both by Ovid and by Germanicus in Latin. The poem is also distinguished for its etiological approach to history and religion, especially in the first book, which bears the obvious influence of Callimachus. However, despite the fact that Ovid is openly indebted to his Hellenistic models, the distinctively Roman character of his material, which belongs to the tradition of Varro's lost *Antiquitates*, is not overshadowed. Moreover, the work was given much currency due to Augustus' interest in reestablishing the traditional Roman cults and religious sentiment which included his eminent calendar reform in 46 BCE (Fast.1.13–14). Through the stars Ovid introduces Greek mythic narrative into the Roman calendar so to fulfil the poem's 'elegiac agenda' of celebrating peace rather than war, and, of course, he substantiates the praise of the emperor, the generator of this newly found prosperity. As Gee explains, "Ovid's carelessness about dates is in reality a device calculated to give him the freedom to position his Greek star myths so they challenge the points of view encoded in the Roman material" (Gee, *Ovid, Aratus and Augustus*). The structure of the poem appears restrictive by the subject matter which is characterized by periodic repetition, while the fragmentation of the narrative material, which seems designed to parallel the structure of the *Metamorphoses*, has been given political gravity as a subtle protest on behalf of the poet against the unity which the Augustan calendar promoted (Fantham, *Fasti Book IV*). Ovid appears in his own poem as an enthusiastic antiquarian always eager to embark on a debate regarding etiological and etymological variants.

The five books of *Tristia* conveying the poet's despair in his first five years of exile and his supplications for mercy are dated between 9 and 12 CE. They consist of poems addressed by Ovid to his wife and to various unnamed persons in Rome. The *Tristia*, like the later *Epistulae ex Ponto*, function as open letters in which the poet campaigns from afar for a reconsideration of his sentence. The second book of the *Tristia*, which is addressed to Augustus, differs in format from the other four in that it is a single poem of over 500 lines in which the poet adopts an overtly self-depreciatory tone perhaps under the grim prospect of spending his life in Tomis. In *Tristia*, Ovid attempts a profound self-reflection which allows little space for any colorful descriptions of the places and peoples the poet comes across; the gloomy atmosphere of the poem becomes even heavier with ominous metaphors as everything is turned into a negative sign of what the poet will face in exile. Hence, the ship that takes Ovid into exile is seen as the ship of his fortune (1.5.17–18). It has been suggested that from a post-modern point of view, in the *Tristia,* 'exile' can be read as the intellectual (at least) death of the poet, a notion that appropriates the use of the elegiac meter, initially reserved for funereal laments (Hinds, OCD s.v. Ovid).

In contrast with his tactic in the *Tristia*, Ovid addressed his *Epistulae ex Ponto* in four books, to friends in Rome, whom he tends to name (1.1.17–18). The poet claims that the letters of the first three books were gathered randomly into a single collection in 13 CE (Ep.3.9.51–54). It is likely that the fourth book 4 written in 16 CE, appeared posthumously.

Ibis, an elaborate curse poem in elegiacs, written possibly around 10–11 CE, was inspired by a lost work of Callimachus (Ib.55–62). The poet attacks an enemy whose identity is hidden under the name of a bird of unclean habits. Ovid explains his newly discovered thirst for revenge in dramatic terms as a result of the sudden disaster that befell him. A man broken by the unjust punishment that was imposed on him, he now seeks to achieve a new sense of peace and reconciliation with himself in hating his enemy.

Ovid also wrote a tragedy, *Medea*, from which only two verses survive (Quint.Inst.8.5.6; Sen.Suas.3.7). Equally from his hexametric translation of Aratus' *Phenomena* only two short fragments survived to this day. At last, the poems *Halieutica* and the *Nux* are suspected to be spurious works.

In conclusion, despite the negative criticism that Ovid's work received for his imitative tendency towards his predecessors, Ovid should be given credit for the genius treatment of his material. His comical treatment of the typical elegiac themes also poses as a frequent reason that has led critics in the past to deny Ovid his poetic substance. To these reproaches some enthusiastic supporters of his talent compared him to Callimachus. Although Callimachus has been the initial model of all elegiac poets, Ovid is related more closely to him with regards to his fondness of paradoxical tales and his habit of challenging his poetic persona. Ovid's originality as an elegiac poet can also be argued with reference to his thematic innovations. Ovid attempted an unconventional reversal of the lover's adverse fate by allowing him easy access to his mistress. He interpreted elegy and its conventions through his own spirit and contributed to the understanding of the genre. He adjusted the Hellenistic vision of poetry to the needs of his age and of his temperament and managed to compose amusing and pleasant poems. His bold sexual imagery and sharp social observations deliver a vivid reflection of the social reality of Augustan Rome, while his employment of comic motifs render to his work the immediacy of a street performance.

Ovid exercised an overt influence on European literature, more than any other classical author. Dante, Boccaccio, and Chaucer in the twelfth century were among the first admirers of the *Metamorphoses*, soon to be joined by numerous artists of the Renaissance. Ariosto, Montaigne, Cervantes, La Fontaine, and Camoens were also impressed by his confident and light-hearted treatment of glorious poets of the past, by his energetic versatility and meticulous improvement of his own creations. Ovid devoted most of his career to writing elegy, so by the time of the *Remedia Amoris* he could already boast that 'elegy owes as much to me as epic does to Vergil' (Rem.Am.395–396). In the Anglophone world Ovid was mainly introduced by Dryden and Pope; Shakespeare's familiarity with Ovid's spirit survives in the verses of his *A Midsummer Night's Dream* and Milton was allegedly fond of listening to the tales of the *Metamorphoses*. Later poets such as Keats, Shelley, Byron, and Browning were also acquainted with Ovid's talent.

Biography

Publius Ovidius Naso, for whom our main source of information remains his own poetry, was born on 20 March 43 BCE in the Apennine city of Sulmo in Paeligne (nowadays Sulmona),

approximately 90 Roman miles away from Rome (Am.2.16.1; 3.15.11; Tr. 4.10). His father, a member of the equestrian class, envisaged for his son a future in Roman politics which required the ability of making public speeches. Consequently, Ovid came to Rome and excelled in rhetorical studies under Arellius Fuscus and Porcius Latro, before completing his education with a visit to Athens and possibly Asia Minor (Sen.Controv.2.2.8–12; Tr.1.2.77–78; Pont.2.10.21ff.). After his return to Rome he embarked on a legal career and held some minor judicial posts. However, with the support of M. Valerius Messalla Corvinus, he soon abandoned his political ambitions and joined the literary circles of Rome (Pont.1.7.27–28). His early erotic poems, the *Amores*, published for the first time between 25 and 15 BCE, earned him admiration from established poets like Tibullus and Propertius and he eventually attracted the attention of the emperor Augustus who remained an enthusiast for his poetry for almost twenty years.

However, the relation between Ovid and Augustus was not destined to have a happy ending. In 8 CE, the poet was exiled to Tomis, a Black Sea outpost, on the pretext of offending the moral principles of Augustus by composing the *Ars Amatoria*, a work full of adulterous, debauched imagery. Although the emperor was always keen to be seen as the restorer of Roman traditions and ethical values, the time that he allowed to lapse between the composition of the supposedly insolent Ars Amatoria and the unraveling of his wrath makes the explanation less credible. Ovid also refers in his work to an *error*, an indiscretion (Tr.2.103–108), which appears to have been the real reason behind his exile. It has been assumed that perhaps the poet unintentionally witnessed a scandal regarding Julia, Augustus' granddaughter. Despite his repeated plea to be allowed to return to Rome, Ovid died in Tomis in 17 CE. Several of his elegies from exile are addressed to his third wife back in Rome while there is also mention of a daughter and two grandchildren (Pont.1.2.136). His harsh treatment by Augustus and his successor, Tiberius, gave ground to an already rising belief in Ovid's anti-Augustan feelings. The issue, which is often debated in scholarship, seems to rely partly on Ovid's 'tongue in cheek' style and partly on his financial viability which allowed him independence unlike most other poets who relied on the generosity of Augustus and his confidants.

EVANGELIA ANAGNOSTOU-LAOUTIDES

Bibliography

M. Innes (1995) *Ovid: Metamorphoses* (prose).

J.C. Mckeown (1987).

Ovid: Amores, G. Showerman (²1977, revised by G.P. Goold) *Ovid, Heroides and Amores*.

E.J. Kenney (1961) *P. Ovidi Nasonis Amores / Medicamina faciei / Ars Amatoria / Remedia Amoris*.

A. Barchiesi, P. Hardie and S. Hinds (1999) *Ovidian Transformations: Essays on the Metamorphoses and its Reception*, B. Weiden Boyd (2002) *Companion to Ovid*, ed. B. Weiden.

Boyd, S. Raval (2002) "Cross-Dressing and Gender Trouble in the Ovidian Corpus," *Helios* 29: 149–172, S. Brown (1999) *The Metamorphosis of Ovid: from Chaucer to Ted Hughes*.

J.B. Solodov (1977) "Ovid's Ars Amatoria, The lover as cultural ideal," *Wiener Studien* n.s. 11, 106–127.

J.T. Davis (1981) "Risit Amor, aspects of literary burlesque in Ovid's Amores," *ANRW* II. 31.4, 2460–2506, N.P. Gross (1979) "Rhetorical Wit and Amatory Persuasion in Ovid," *CJ* 74, 305–318.

Further Reading

G.K. Galinsky (1975) *Ovid's Metamorphoses. An Introduction to the Basic Aspects* and ibid. (1989).

"Was Ovid a Silver Latin Poet?," *ICS* 14, 69–88, P. Hardie (2002).

Ovid's Poetics of Illusion and ibid. (2002) *The Cambridge Companion to Ovid*.

E.J. Kenney (1982) 'Ovid' in *The Cambridge History of Classical Literature* vol. II, 420–457, C. Martin (1998).

Ovid in English, C. Martindale (1990) *Ovid Renewed*.

K.S. Myers (1999) 'The metamorphosis of a poet: recent work on Ovid' *JRS* 89, 190–204, S. Wheeler (1999).

A Discourse of Wonders: Audience and Performance in Ovid's Metamorphoses.

L.P. Wilkinson (1955) *Ovid Recalled*.

K. Berkman (1972) "Some Propertian Imitations in Ovid's Amores," *CPh* 67, 107–117, R.O.A.M. Lyne (1980) *The Latin love Poets*, B. Otis (1938) "Ovid and the Augustans," *TAPHA* 69, 188–229.

V.A. Tracy (1978/9) "Ovid's self-portrait in the Amores," *Helios* 6.2, 57–62, E. Thomas (1964) "Variations on a Military Theme in Ovid's Amores," *GR* 11, 151–165, G. Giangrande (1981) "Hellenistic topoi in Ovid's Amores," *MPhL* 4, 25–51.

OVIDIAN VERSE

"Ovidian verse" is an ambiguous expression. Is it merely Latin verse composed by Ovid and later often called "Ovidian elegiac verse," or Ovidian verse understood as a metrical form with an erotic content. Or alternatively, 'Ovidian elegiac verse' as a genre?

It existed in the fifth century BCE Greece, a distich composed of a hexameter followed by a pentameter, itself always ending with two dactyles. The recurrence of the same ending on every second verse conveyed deep rhythmic effect, turning the poem into a gloomy threnody, as if the dynamic move initiated by the hexameter, a complete verse, was broken by a sob echoed by the pentameter, an incomplete verse.

This distich was described as elegiac. The elegy was originally used for gnomic, moral, political, patriotical, philosophical, as well as love poems. Later, from Augustus' reign on, Latin poets associated the elegiac distich with the singing of love. Ovid was preceded by a number of elegiac poets, but he no longer sang of a quiet rural life or revelled in celebrating secular love in Augustean Rome.

As it appears from Ovid's *Amores*—Latin for *erôtika pathèmata*, love's passions, although *amor* does not include any idea of passive love like *pathèma*—the Ovidian elegiac verse is the product of the merging of a metrical form, the elegiac distich, and of an erotic content (s. Anne Videau's analysis).

In the first elegy of *Amores*, Book I, the epigram expresses a shift from equality to unequality, from epic parity to elegiac imparity. The rise of the epic hexameter, associated with the large number of *libelli*, booklets, is opposed by the fall of the pentameter, that asserts that the volume has been reduced to three books:

Qui modo Nasonis fueramus quinque libelli, / tres
  sumus
We who of late numbered five books, are now but
  three

Such an æsthetics of reduction is adapted to the narrative of an elegiac transformation and opts for smallness and lightness, as opposed to the first heavy hexameter and to the poet's epic project:

Arma graui numero uiolentaque bella parabam
edere, materia conueniente modis.
Par erat inferior uersus ; risisse Cupido
dicitur atque unum surripuisse pedem (I.1.1–4)

I was about to sing, in heroic strain, of arms and fierce combats. 'Twas a subject suited to my verse, whose lines were all of equal measure. But Cupid, so 'tis said, began to laugh, and stole away one foot]

This constitutes a mini-*recusatio* of the epic and analogically announces the surreptitious imposition by Cupid of the elegiac distich upon the poet, that is, another imparity and inequality. Cupid's unexpected and parodical interference so confers its mocking tone to the text.

The page's space is also concretely represented as an *inferior uersus*, a new page, *nova pagina*, which arises with the hexameter and then flatly falls back with the pentameter:

Cum bene surrexit uersu nova pagina primo,
attenuat neruos proximus ille meos. (I.1.17)
[Brave was the line that sounded the opening of my
  new poem, but lo!
Love comes and stays my soaring flight.]

The *neruos* symbolize the hero's deflating male energy. Other distichs are still more explicit. An erotic image is underlying Naso's explanation for the passage from the hexameter to the pentameter:

Sex mihi surgat opus numeris, in quinque residat
  (I.1.27)
Now let six feet my book begin, and let it end in five.

The distich imitates the desire's trials, from tumescence to detumescence. The verb *surgere*, which explicitly refers to the erecting organ and expresses love's furtive character, is to be found elsewhere, for example when the ring offered by Naso to her beloved turns into a male member:

Sed, puto, te nuda, mea mebra libidine surgent
et peragam partes anulus ille uiri. (II.15.25–26)

[And yet, methinks, if naked I beheld thee, I should
  be consumed
with desire, and that ring would like a man acquit
  itself]

or when the beloved fails to excite her lover:

Sed postquam nullas consurgere posse per artes
immemoremque sui procubuisse uidet: (III.7.75–76)
[But seeing that all her arts were vain, that my body,
  forgetful of its former
prowess, would give no sign of life]

The elegiac pentameter, deriving from the epic hexameter, was meant to render love's rhythm as it goes, as well as to set a parallel and parodic love's epic against the hexameter, and the social power underlying it. Elegy consequently appears in Book III as a courtesan with one foot longer than the other, a limping woman, a personification of the uneven and unbalanced pentameter. However, epic is not opposed to elegy: *eros* is not to be dissociated from *eris*, struggle, and is integrated and intricated into the community's fate, whose heroes, preys to love, are the champions. That is why Ovid's narrator is also a soldier of love (I.9.1):

Militat omnis amans et habet sua castra Cupido;
[Thy lover is a soldier, and Cupid hath his camp.]

The Ovidian verse is a metrical structure that gives love an intrinsic form, meaning, flavour and consistency, and partakes in Ovid's pervading subversion of poetic genres.

The Ovidian elegiac verse was often imitated in Europe. An example is John Donne's *Elegies* (1611), the opening verses of *Going to Bed*, which renders the elegiac distich's inflating and deflating process, as well as the play upon *eros* and *eris*:

Come, Madam, come, all rest my powers defie
Until I labor, I in labor lie.
The foe oft-times having the foe in sight,
Is tir'd with standing though he never fights.

The Ovidian elegiac verse was held to be an adequate one to sing of love, but that didn't always result in a love's proper poetics, and the Ovidian elegiac verse became more of a stereotyped vehicle to express subversive ideas on love.

One ought not to confuse Ovid's elegiac verse and the Ovidian verse posterity resorted to for its nicety, variety, and dialectical virtue.

GÉRARD SIARY

Further Reading

Boyd, Barbara Weiden. *Brill's Companion to Ovid*. Leiden, Boston, Köln: Brill, 2002.

Grimal, Pierre. *L'Élégie érotique romaine. L'amour, la poésie et l'Occident*. Paris: Seuil, 1983.

Dangel, Jacqueline. "Intertextualité et intergénéricité dans les *Héroïdes* d'Ovide: la métrique à l'œuvre." http://ars-scribendi.ens.lsh.fr

Kennedy, Duncan F. *The Arts of Love. Five Studies in the Discourse of Roman Love Elegy*. Cambridge University Press, 1993.

Sabot, A.F. *Ovide poète de l'amour dans ses œuvres de jeunesse: Amores, Heroïdes, Ars Amatoria, Remedia Amoris, De Medicamine Faciei Femineae*. Paris: Ophrys, 1976.

Videau, Anne. "Le livre I des *Amores* d'Ovide: poétique et parodie." Paper on 'Love's poets' (Montpellier 3, 5.11.2004), ed. in *L'information littéraire*, n°1, 2005.

Videau, Anne. "Les avatars du *pathos erotikon* dans les *Métamorphoses* d'Ovide." http://ars-scribendi.ens-lsh.fr

P

PALLAVICINO, FERRANTE

1615–1644
Italian academician and satirist

La Retorica delle puttane

In Italian literature, where most "pornographic" motifs originate, the prostitute or mistress often fashions herself a higher status by manipulating appearances. This active, self-crafting capacity is most fully explored in Pallavicino's *La Retorica delle puttane* [*The Whores' Rhetoric*] (1642), a mock-didactic satire that instructs the common whore in the arts of rhetoric, gesture, decor, music, and architecture—so that she can create a facade, both literal and figurative. As the old bawd explains to the young recruit, following the rules of this "rhetoric" will lift her above the rough subculture of the brothel and the street.

Pallavicino reveals passion itself as an "art," both in the sense of fraud and in the sense of aesthetic achievement. He gives the courtesan the skill of an artist, able to fabricate sexual identities, even sexual experiences, while remaining coolly aware that they are "chimeras,"

fictions, trickeries, or *furberie*. Her education becomes a university course in rhetoric, the highly specialized technique used by poets and public speakers. Pallavicino follows the subdivisions of Cypriano Soarez's school textbook *De Arte Rhetorica*, recast into 15 lessons that represent the 15-day cycle of the waxing moon. The courtesan must organize her seduction according to a step-by-step plan: the Exordium, in which she snares lovers by demure glances in public, "turning herself into a display apparatus or projection screen"; the Narration, in which she creates an intriguing and affecting home life to involve the client more deeply and render her yielding more plausible; the Confirmation, when the lovers actually go to bed; and the Epilogue, when the lover is sent off with promises of infinite pleasure (Coci: 36, 44, 46–51, 66; all citations are from Coci's edition). The art of memory enables her to keep track of multiple lovers (stowed in a warren of small bedrooms), while Images, in the form of painted nudes and Aretinesque postures, help her to simulate rapture for those dull or repulsive clients who "think every woman melts for them" (83–5). In bed, figures of speech become "corporeal eloquence": metaphor, for example, is created by "translating, not the words, but the member from the proper place to the other improper one—improper with regard to natural laws but not with regard to pleasing the appetite." As in *L'Alcibiade fanciullo a scola*, by Pallavicino's fellow-incognito Antonio Rocco, sodomy is declared the pinnacle of the erotic art, "the most delightful metaphor" (ff. 88, 57).

Fashioning the erotic self in *La Retorica* involves all the arts, musical and plastic as well as verbal. Like a Renaissance sculptor, the whore must transform physical matter to "conform to the idea of Cupid" (93). The perversions constitute a "sublime art" which generates the maximum pleasure from those tastes and orifices that nature has made most disgusting (57). Transvestism and anal intercourse reveal her ability to "transform the serving-dish into the cup" and "feign oneself Ganymede the cupbearer of Jove" (81). The mirrors of her luxurious apartment allow her lovers to "enjoy the representation of those delights they also feel in the actual coupling" (94–5). The erotic painting on her bedroom wall—"the figures of Aretino gathered into a single picture"—serves as a "theatre" and as a musical score for her to play "a toccata on the organ of the senses" (85). Thus she creates "diversity, sole seasoning of earthly delight," by "exquisite" performance and by "mutation of sex to find variety, mother of pleasures" (89).

All this artistry must be concealed, however. No longer the earthy whore, the seductress must simulate a respectable woman swayed by genuine passion. She evolves from a coarse trickster into a proto-novelist, "sweetening her narrative by weaving in fascinating incidents figured in her own person" (44). Gesture, voice, motion, interior decoration, and reading matter should form an "authentic" model that the gullible customer takes as a real person feeling sincere love for him and him alone (62–3). Though the man believes himself the instigator, the courtesan retains controlling power over the script and ownership of the means of seduction: her verbal and pictorial "figures" are the primary reality, her sighs and facial expressions "authenticate the words," and the figures of Aretino "authenticate the force of her persuasion" (91, 84–5).

While the courtesan's exterior is all simulated rapture, inside she must be "dead to the world," like a nun entering the cloister, devoid of any response or feeling except the pleasures of control, security, and profit. Imitating the sex object that men expect, she should paradoxically "not think of herself as being a woman." The greatest danger for the professional seductress, as for the 18th-century libertine typified by Valmont, is to fall in love—Pallavicino's speaker having been reduced to beggary because of such a mistake (86–7, 16, 82).

Where does the author himself stand in all this? Pallavicino gestures toward moralism by claiming to expose rather than condone prostitution, but this failed to convince the papal nuncio in Venice, who denounced the *Retorica*'s trickeries, or *furberie,* and fueled the persecution that soon led to Pallavicino's arrest and execution (137). In his preface and in the "Author's Confession" that follows the lecture, Pallavicino adopts wildly contradictory roles. Sometimes he "abhors" all prostitutes, sometimes he vents his spleen on a few individuals, sometimes he declares himself an "adherent" who has "dedicated his heart" to the whores (9, 126, 116, 4). On the one hand he argues that all sexual desire is "natural" (following the latest materialist philosophy), but on the other hand he exalts the "sublime art" and "nobility" of unnatural sex, in which "the perfection of art has supplemented the simple crudity of mere nature" (118, 22, 95). He claims to follow the golden mean but praises the most extreme kinds of desire: "even the excesses of lasciviousness are signs of glory" (5, 122). His own "lascivious genius" [il mio lascivo genio] likewise achieves "glory" by painting an abject subject so well (117, 6). Even the frauds of the courtesan have something admirable about them, since they resemble the "well-woven texture" of the novelist (8, 64, 87). At moments, erotic literature escapes morality entirely. Pallavicino envisages an almost Flaubertian role for the artist, whose responsibility is not to discriminate against abject and scandalous materials but to render them with supreme aesthetic power and "perfect execution" ["operazione perfettamente eseguita"] (6).

The Whores Rhetorick

La Retorica delle puttane was reissued in 1673, and its influence was not confined to the loose English adaptation, *The Whores Rhetorick,* dedicated "To the most famous University of *London-Courtezans,*" published and prosecuted in 1683. A French imitation appeared in 1771, and Italian echoes have been traced in Laura Coci's scholarly edition (lxxxix–xcii, 215–25). The English playwright William Wycherley followed Pallavicino by dedicating his sardonic comedy *The Plain-Dealer* (1676) to one of "the most famous Courtesans." Like Pallavicino, he begins with a triple parallel of text, painting, and sexual career, and sarcastically praises the honor of a profession officially permitted "in the best governed and most Catholic cities" (Wycherley: 370–1) In Wycherley's version, Pallavicino's demand to "have free entry to [your] pleasures without charge," in exchange for favorable literary treatment, becomes the principle that "a Poet ought to be as free of your Houses, as of the Play-houses."

Wycherley also features in *The Whores Rhetorick* itself, which contains many more topical references than Pallavicino's original. The old bawd—now named as the notorious Mrs. Cresswell, frequently cited in English pornography, drama, and satire—contrasts the hard-nosed courtesan to high-flown "Romantick Ladies" like the idealistic heroines of "*Cleopatra, Cassandra, Pharamond,* and others of that nature" (65–66, 106). The ultimate goal is to marry the rich customer (a possibility only briefly entertained in the original *Retorica*, 34), and such romances come in useful when the courtesan has to simulate a lover pleading for a more legitimate relationship, "torn in pieces" by the conflict of love, shame, and religious guilt. But she must never actually *believe* in these "Romances, where constancy in love is cryed up as a vertue"; instead, she must train herself by reading "Modern Comedies," where "you will find fraud and dissimulation called discretion and prudence, cuckolding Husbands, cheating Lovers, prudently styled Address and Wit" (150). Wycherley's *The Plain-Dealer* and *The Country-Wife* are cited as supreme examples of the kind (189), narrowing the gap between Restoration sex-comedy and pornography.

The Whores Rhetorick breaks up many of Pallavicino's structural devices, such as the systematic naming of rhetorical-sexual "figures" and the 15-part lunar lecture cycle, recasting *La Retorica delle puttane* into the dialogue form of *L'Escole des filles* and *The Wandring Whore*. The "rhetoric" idea becomes just one theme among many. Long stretches of intellectual ingenuity are cut and the space filled with extracts from Aretino's *Ragionamenti*, topical allusions to the London sexual underworld, and satire against the Puritans. Pallavicino had introduced an element of social satire when he encouraged upper-class refinement in the prostitute (she must not sound and move "like a porter"; Coci: 93), but this class awareness is now sharpened by specifically English references: at one end of the social spectrum, the sexual adventures of Charles II and Monmouth; at the other end, the vulgarities of Bartholomew Fair and the dangers of Bridewell, where poor whores were publicly whipped ("Philo-Puttanus": 182, 37). Even vaginal hygiene is treated with local London color, evoking the steps of a Thames boat landing: use a "drying Pessary" after each customer, since "the Stairs will be wet and the Passage slippery" (122–3).

In some ways, *The Whores Rhetorick* paints a broader canvas than the intellectually serious *Retorica delle puttane*, but in some ways it is narrower. The sex is certainly more limited. The "Italian" fascination with sodomy—for Pallavicino the goal and test of erotic art, the instrument on which the courtesan plays her *toccata*, the prime instance of "translation" and self-mutation—is either removed completely or explicitly rejected: the old teacher reverses the recommendation of *La Retorica*, warning that "*Aretin*'s Figures have no place in my Rhetorick; . . . they are calculated for a hot Region a little on this side *Sodom*, and are not necessary to be seen in any Northern Clime" ("Philo-Puttanus": 171). In Pallavicino the courtesan turns herself *into* Ganymede to please the man who secretly desires boys, offering her anus as a "cup" of divine nectar; in the English version she "makes herself Ganymede" in a different sense, imagining a beautiful but fictitious youth—called her "Ganymede"—while pretending to adore her ugly customer (166, 168). With this increasingly heterosexual focus comes a loss of interest in "sublime" perversity.

Having cut out the core of Pallavicino's work, the English author "Philo-Puttanus" [Whore-Lover] stuffs his book with all kinds of sexual lore and humor. Long passages are plagiarized from Aretino's *Ragionamenti*, including the blunt statement "A Whore is a Whore, but a Whore is not a Woman" (144). Political allusions give the satire an up-to-date feel. In the period when the Royal Society was promoting the Scientific Revolution, Mrs. Cresswell often "talks Philosophically," citing Hobbes and theorizing that "the whole series of carnal satisfaction does purely consist in fancy" (71, 85, 167). Medicine inspires an extraordinary parallel between pen and penis, a surreal fantasy on green quills, sheets tinted with syphilitic discharge, and venereal ink flowing with all the hues of the rainbow (ff. A3–v, A6–v). And science provides the metaphor that links the art of the courtesan to the power of the author: "a judicious writer, like an expert Chymist, will so order the most abject, the most indisposed matter, as to extract thence both pleasure and advantage" (f. A8).

Biography

Pallavicino was born March 23 in Parma, a younger son of a major aristocratic family. Took classes at the University of Padua, then the center of radical new ideas in medicine and philosophy. Entered religious orders as a canon of the Lateran in 1632, in Milan, and moved restlessly around Germany, France, and Italy before settling in Venice, where he was welcomed into the freethinking and adventurous Accademia degli Incogniti [Academy of the Unrecognized]. Pallavicino's short life was turbulent but incredibly productive. He published at least 20 books, in many different genres, but his outrageous satires were condemned by the papal authorities (eager to close down the free presses and anti-Vatican sentiments of Venice). He was imprisoned in 1641–2, then released (perhaps with the help of a well-connected courtesan), then again arrested in France. Cardinal Richelieu had recruited him to establish a French Academy for the study of Italian literature, but passing through the papal territory in Avignon he was betrayed by a friend and captured, with a valise full of scandalous manuscripts. Representatives of the papacy particularly condemned *La Retorica delle puttane* and *Il Corriere svaligiato* [*The Postman Robbed of His Mail Bag*]; he was also suspected (probably wrongly) of authoring *Il Divortio celeste*, in which Christ repudiates His Roman spouse. Tried and tortured, Pallavicino was beheaded on March 5, at the age of 28.

The character Ferrante Palla, in Stendhal's *Charterhouse of Parma*, is based on him.

JAMES GRANTHAM TURNER

Editions

Coci, Laura, ed. *La Retorica delle puttane, composta conforme li precetti di Cipriano, dedicata alla Università delle Cortigiane più Celebri* [The Whores' Rhetoric, Composed According to the Precepts of Cypriano (Soarez), Dedicated to the University of the Most Famous Courtesans], 1642, 1673 (the "Villafranca" edition). Parma: Ugo Guanda, 1992. With full biographical and bibliographical details.

"Philo-Puttanus." *The Whores Rhetorick, Calculated to the Meridian of London, and Conformed to the Rules of Art.* London: George Shell, 1683; facsimile edition, introduction by James R. Irvine and G. Jack Gravlee. Delmar, NY: Scholars' Facsimiles and Reprints, 1979.

"V.T.H.S." *La Rhétorique des putains, ou la fameuse maquerelle, ouvrage imité de l'italien.* "Rome" [Paris?], 1771; as *Le Philosophie des courtisanes*, edited by Guillaume Apollinaire, Paris: Bibliothèque des Curieux, 1913.

Opere scelte [Selected Works]. "Villafranca," Amsterdam, 1660, 1666, 1673.

Selected Works

Gildon, Charles, trans. *The Post-Boy Robbed of His Mail, or The Pacquet Broke Open.* London: John Dunton, 1692, 1693, 1706. For similarities between this work and *La Retorica*, see Coci, lxxvi–viii.

Marchi, Armando, ed. *Il Corriere svaligiato* [1641] and *Continuazione* [1644]. Parma: Università di Parma, 1984.

Further Reading

Orr, Bridget. "The Feminine in Restoration Erotica." In *Women, Texts and Histories, 1575–1760*, edited by Clare Brant and Diane Purkiss. London and New York: Routledge, 1992.

Spini, Giorgio. *Ricerca dei libertini: La teoria dell' impostura delle religioni nel Seicento italiano* [1950]. Rev. ed. Florence: Nuova Italia, 1983.

Turner, James Grantham. "*The Whores Rhetorick*: Narrative, Pornography and the Origins of the Novel." *Studies in Eighteenth-Century Culture* 24 (1995): 297–306.

———. *Schooling Sex: Libertine Literature and Erotic Education in Italy, France, and England, 1534–1685*, chaps. 2 and 7. Oxford: Oxford University Press, 2003.

Wycherley, William. *The Plays of William Wycherley*. edited by Arthur Friedman. Oxford: Clarendon Press, 1979.

PANERO, LEOPOLDO MARÍA

1948–
Spanish poet

Leopoldo María Panero belongs to the group of 1970s writers, most of them poets, who began publishing around 1968 and who share an understanding and appreciation of pop culture in its broadest sense. Cinema, pop music, posters, and the sexual revolution are among those features. By no means, however, can it be said that Panero was loyal to all of the main trends of this group. Though he shares many of their sensibilities, he makes a personal use of them, distorting their meanings, images, or aims. Panero was an outcast in a group that was characterized by its nonconformism.

Panero's erotic poetry cannot be dissociated from his poetics. As I have already pointed out, Panero is heterodox, as a poet and as an individual, who holds radical views of life in the tradition of Antonin Artaud, Lautréamont, and Arthur Rimbaud. It is thus that his peculiar use of some literary motifs can be properly understood. They all revolve around the same idea of destruction of the old without a clearly stated interest in the construction of something new. This implies that Panero views them as illusions that people need in order to bear the unbearable reality of life.

Childhood represents the first of these degraded motifs. Generally associated with paradise and innocence, Panero writes of childhood as if it were a lost paradise and a time of cruelty and sadism, as can be read in "Unas palabras para Peter Pan" [A Few Words for Peter Pan]. Childhood foregrounds an elegiac tone. It is closely related to death and to the burial of the treasures of innocence, as reflected in "20000 leguas de viaje submarino" [20,000 Leagues Under the Sea], "Blancanieves se despide de los Siete Enanos" [Snow White Says Farewell to the Seven Dwarfs], and "Deseo de ser piel roja" [I Wish I Were a Redskin] There is also a slight eroticism present in the poems dealing with the topic, as for example in "Unas palabras para Peter Pan" and "Blancanieves se despide de los Siete Enanos."

Another important topic that is violently attacked is the figure of the mother. Panero destroys a mythic figure that in his mind has become a taboo. Never can a positive or indulgent view of the mother be found in his writings. It is Narcissus' reaction to an image he finds in the mirror, since mother and son are not so different. But there is also a Freudian reading in which the womb would be equated to paradise, and consequently to innocence. Thus, birth is the loss of innocence, and the beginning of evil. The figure of the mother is regarded as a sacred, everlasting evil, as can be read in "Ma mère" [My Mother], probably because of the oedipal connotations that the relationship between mother and son has acquired through history.

The other parent, the father, is depicted as a symbol of power, who does not permit the development of the poet as a person. The poet's rejection is absolute. The relationship between father and son is accounted for in terms of sex and death. All social, moral, literary, and cultural codes are broken as the poet writes about incest and pedophilia, while the father changes his gender in the last lines of "Carta al padre" [Letter to Father]. In the end, eros displaces power.

Panero's poetics underlie all his creative writing. For him life is an illusion that is supported by a number of cultural institutions, in the manner of Freud's philosophy. Writing is an illusion, which main task is that of destroying the accepted meanings of society. It is an exercise in coherence if one follows Panero's thought; it is a result of his view of reality, society, and himself. Another obsession is that of naming, related to literature and to life. Not to have a name of one's own means to be free and offers one the possibility of wandering through the mythology of names. A name imposes a fate on a person; it is a sort of sham. Another illusion—or better, another producer of illusion—is cinema, an art form not unlike literature. It represents another escape from life and the possibility of living in the realm of modern mythology. It also presents an erotica of death, symbolized by Marilyn Monroe. Another illusion is Paris, or at least the image people have of it. For Panero it is the the city of Paul Verlaine, Rimbaud, and Baudelaire. It is a city of bohemians, *clochards* [tramps], and marginality. Dreams are also illusions, though it must be said that the poet's dreams have turned into nightmares. Finally, sex is grouped among the illusions. Love is regarded as impossible; besides, sterile love is the only ethical option.

Sex is represented in Panero's poetry as a form of transgression, in close relation to writing. The reader will find incest, coprophilia, homosexuality, necrophilia, sadism, masochism, and all variants of sexual deviations. For Panero the commonly accepted sexual relations reproduce systems of power. His rejection of society makes him choose alternative social codes that exist on the fringe of normality. I have pointed out the Freudian aspect, but we should remember too Marcuse's assertion in *Eros and Civilization* that fantasy is the last realm of childhood, and that it can be enjoyed via sexual perversions. What I have been saying is exemplified by two of Panero's poems. The first one is "Storia," about a love affair with a beggar. The affair is a purification, since the other lover has to overcome nausea, the mechanisms of rejection, and the Manichaean dichotomy of these conflicting concepts. Thus, both lovers can enter paradise, though a degraded one, naturally. The other poem is "Shekina," an ambiguous poem about a child who gives his mother a gift for her love; his own corpse, remarking that freedom comes always after death.

Panero was the author of a few short stories dealing with the same themes, and he translated any writer whom he considered, for any reason, marginal.

Biography

Leopoldo María Panero was born in Madrid, the son of an important Francoist poet. The details of his life are virtually unknown, except that he spent periods in a mental hospital. He is the last of the Spanish marginal poets.

Selected Works

Por el camino de Swan. 1968.
Así se fundó Carnaby Street. 1970.
Teoría. 1973.
Narciso en el acorde último de las flautas. 1979.
Last River Together. 1980.
El último hombre. 1982.
Poesía, 1970–1985. Madrid: Visor, 1986. See the introduction by Eugenio García Fernández.
Poemas del manicomio de Mondragón. 1990.
Contra España y otros poemas no de amor. 1990.
Heroína y otros poemas. 1992.
Agujero llamado Nevermore. (Selección poética, 1968–1992). Madrid: Cátedra, 1992.

Further Reading

Barella Vigal, Julia. "La poesía de Leopoldo María Panero entre Narciso y Edipo." *Estudios Humanísticos. Filología* 492 (1984): 123–28.

Blesa, Túa. "El laberinto de los espejos." *Tropelías* 1 (1991): 43–63.

———. "El silencio y el tumulto." *Cuadernos de Investigación Filológica* 16 (1991): 89–107.

Domínguez, Gustavo. "Leopoldo María Panero." *Diez años de poesía en España, 1970–1980. La moneda de hierro* 3–4: 85–89.

Gimferer, Pedro. "Notas parciales sobre poesía española de posguerra." In *30 años de literatura española*, edited by Pedro Gimferrer and Salvador Clotas. Barcelona: Kairós, 1971.

Mas, Miguel. "Una lectura generacional sobre la destrucción. Notas acerca de Narciso, de Leopoldo María Panero." *Ideologies and Literature* [*I&L*] 1 (1985): 194–206.

Mesquida, Biel. "Leopoldo María Panero nombra y recita los protagosnistas de la revolución." *El viejo topo* 5 (1997).

Miró, Emilio. "Leopoldo María Panero y sus poemas del manicomio de Mondragón." *Ínsula*, 494.

Saldaña Sagredo, Alfredo. "Leopoldo María Panero, poeta vitalista." *Turia* 11 (1989).

Talens, Jenar. "De poesía y su(b)versión. (Reflexiones desde la escritura denotada 'Leopoldo María Panero')." In Panero, *Agujero llamado Nevermore*, 9–62.

PAZ, OCTAVIO

1914–1998
Mexican poet and essayist

One of the collections of Paz's poetry in English is entitled *Configurations*. This word perhaps more than any other indicates the central unifying theme both of his life and of his work: configurations between places—between Mexico and India by way of Europe, in particular—and between people and ideas. And these configurations are founded in eroticism. Paz, perhaps in a more intense way than any poet or thinker since Novalis, experienced the universe as a whole held together and energized by sensual experience. We can see this most clearly in the poem that is probably his finest and indeed may be considered one of the greatest sustained pieces of lyrical writing of our time. This poem, "Piedra de sol" [Sun Stone], based on the Aztec calendar, has a cyclical structure with no beginning or end. Endless transformation through openness to the world of experience is its theme, in which love is the transformative force *par excellence,* transgressive of the restrictions of social life but in accord with universal flow:

> . . . and the world is changed
> if two people shaken by dizziness and enlaced
> are fallen among the grass: the sky descending,
> the trees pointing and climbing upward, and space
> alone among all things is light and silence,
> and pure space opens to the eagle of the eye
> and it sees past the white tribe of the clouds,
> the body's cables snap, the soul sails out,
> now is the moment we lose our names, and float
> along the border-line between blue and green,
> the integrated time when nothing happens
> but the event, belonging, communicating . . .

This theme of the tension between (1) the unbound quality inherent in eroticism and the loved relation and (2) the social need to control both is central to the whole of Paz's work, explored in multifarious ways. Paz's poetic journey took him a long way into the passional ties by which we are bound to other people and to the world; this was a journey of the senses, in which the erotic becomes a kind of moral touchstone for the relation between the person, as a limited entity, and the vastness of the universe. Paz was a poet who took seriously Rimbaud's demand for a poet to "possess truth in one body and soul."

But if Paz is a poet of erotic transformation, he is equally an essayist, the vitality of whose writings is maintained by configurations of place and time. As a Mexican who has lived in Europe and India, he had a cosmopolitan spirit that nevertheless remains rooted in a Mexican sensibility, which he extensively explored in two books, *The Labyrinth of Solitude* (first published in 1950) and *The Other Mexico: Critique of the Pyramid* (1969). The first of these books has been highly influential, and in its final chapter, "The Dialectic of Solitude," Paz first explored the theme of love in relation to identity, something that runs through all of his work.

Paz visited India in 1951; he returned in 1962 as Mexican ambassador, a post he retained until 1968, when he resigned in protest over the massacre of students by Mexican government troops. Meditations of aspects of Indian culture as Paz experienced it provide a central thread in his work, explored in *The Monkey Grammarian* (1974), an account of a journey to the ruined city of Galta, and the more recent *Vislumbres de la India* [*In the Light of India*].

In *The Monkey Grammarian* (in some ways a companion volume to *The Labyrinth of Solitude*), Paz uses the image of the journey to anchor an exploration of perennial themes of solitude and loss and of movement and fixity through India as experienced by a Mexican imbued also with European ideas. It may be said that the sensual image Paz gives us of India is overly exoticized, but it is an India as imagined by a Mexican in a way that may be said to constitute an erotic relation. And this is an important aspect of understanding Paz's work: eroticism is threaded through it as much in the relation between phenomena and ideas as it is through the relation between people.

His most extended meditation on the erotic relation is a late collection of essays, *The Double*

Flame (1993, translated in 1996). Eroticism and love are forces of energy uniting body and soul, heaven and earth, life and death; they are the double flames the title refers to, interrelated through sexuality. In distinguishing among these three elements, Paz emphasizes their indissolubility: "Love and eroticism always return to the primordial source, to Pan and his cry that makes the forest tremble," writes Paz. From out of the primordial fire of sexuality rises the red flame of eroticism, which in turn feeds the blue flame of love.

In *The Double Flame*, Paz quotes Hegel: "Love excludes all oppositions and hence it escapes the realm of reason. . . . It makes objectivity null and void and hence goes beyond reflection. . . . In love, life discovers itself in life, devoid now of any incompleteness." This is a key element to Paz's conception, in which necessity and freedom are held in tension, "love is the involuntary attraction toward a person and the voluntary acceptance of that attraction."

If sexuality is attraction necessary to the life force and differentiation, simultaneously seeking unity and the reproduction of the species, eroticism is specifically human longing that emerges from our awareness of mortality, while love is a passion, born from life itself but transcending it. It is in the tension between these different motivations that, for Paz, our relation to the world is founded.

Biography

Octavio Paz was born in Mexico City. He spent several years living in France and India and also lived in England and the United States. As a young man, he witnessed the Spanish Civil War firsthand; he was a member of the Surrealist group in Paris; he was a poet, diplomat, writer on a vast range of themes, and founder of one of the most important literary journals in Mexico, *Vuelta*, which he edited between 1977 and 1997. Paz was awarded the 1990 Nobel Prize for Literature.

MICHAEL RICHARDSON

Selected Works in English

Poetry

Selected Poems. Translated by Muriel Rukeyser. Bloomington: Indiana University Press, 1963.

Configurations. Various translators. New York: New Directions; London: Cape, 1971.

Renga: A Chain of Poems. Translated by Charles Tomlinson. New York: George Braziller, 1972. A collaborative poem written with Tomlinson, Jacques Roubaud, and Edoardo Sanguineti.

Early Poems: 1935–1955. Various translators. New York: New Directions, 1973; Bloomington: Indiana University Press, 1974.

¿Aguila o sol? Eagle or Sun? Translated by Eliot Weinberger. New York: New Directions, 1976.

A Draft of Shadows and Other Poems. Edited and translated by Eliot Weinberger (with additional translations by Mark Strand and Elizabeth Bishop). New York: New Directions, 1979.

Selected Poems. edited by Charles Tomlinson (various translators). Middlesex, England: Penguin Books, 1979.

Selected Poems. edited by Eliot Weinberger (various translators). New York: New Directions, 1984.

Airborn/Hijos del Aire. Translated by Charles Tomlinson. London: Anvil Press, 1981. Collaborative poem written with Tomlinson.

The Collected Poems of Octavio Paz, 1957–1987. Translated by Elizabeth Bishop. New York: New Directions, 1987.

A Tale of Two Gardens: Poems from India, 1952–1995. Edited and translated by Eliot Weinberger et al. New York: New Directions, 1997.

Essays (Translator)

Marcel Duchamp, or the Castle of Purity. Donald Gardner. London: Cape Goliard; New York: Grossman, 1970.

Claude Lévi-Strauss: An Introduction. J.S. Bernstein and Maxine Bernstein. Ithaca, NY: Cornell University Press, 1970.

The Other Mexico: Critique of the Pyramid. Lysander Kemp. New York: Grove Press, 1972.

Alternating Current. Helen Lane. New York: Viking Press, 1973.

The Bow and the Lyre. Ruth L.C. Simms. Austin: University of Texas Press, 1973.

Children of the Mire: Poetry from Romanticism to the Avant-Garde. Rachel Phillips. Cambridge, MA: Harvard University Press, 1974.

Conjunctions and Disjunctions. Helen Lane. New York: Viking Press, 1974.

The Siren and the Seashell, and Other Essays on Poets and Poetry. Lysander Kemp and Margaret Seyers Peden. Austin: University of Texas Press, 1976.

Marcel Duchamp: Appearance Stripped Bare. Rachel Phillips and Donald Gardner. New York: Viking Press, 1978.

The Monkey Grammarian. Helen Lane. New York: Seaver Books, 1981.

The Labyrinth of Solitude: Life and Thought in Mexico. Lysander Kemp, Yara Milos, and Rachel Phillips Belash. New York: Grove Press, 1985.

One Earth, Four or Five Worlds: Reflections on Contemporary History. Helen Lane. New York: Harcourt Brace Jovanovich, 1985.

On Poets and Others. Michael Schmidt. New York: Seaver Books, 1986.

Convergences: Selected Essays on Art and Literature. Helen Lane. New York: Harcourt Brace Jovanovich, 1987.

Sor Juana Inés de la Cruz or the Traps of Faith. Margaret Seyers Peden. London: Faber & Faber, 1988.

Essays on Mexican Art. Helen Lane. New York: Harcourt Brace, 1993.

The Double Flame: Love and Eroticism. Helen Lane. New York: Harcourt Brace, 1995.

In Light of India. Eliot Weinberger. New York: Harcourt Brace, 1997.

An Erotic Beyond: Sade. Eliot Weinberger. New York: Harcourt Brace, 1998.

Itinerary: An Intellectual Journey. Jason Wilson. New York: Harcourt Brace, 2000.

Figures and Figurations (with Marie José Paz). Eliot Weinberger. New York: New Directions, 2002.

Further Reading

Fein, John M. *Toward Octavio Paz: A Reading of His Major Poems, 1957–1976*. Lexington, KY: University Press of Kentucky, 1986.

Phillips, Rachel. *The Poetic Modes of Octavio Paz*. London: Oxford University Press, 1972.

Stavans, Ilan. *Octavio Paz: A Meditation*. Tempe, AZ: University of Arizona Press, 2002.

Wilson, Jason. *Octavio Paz: A Study of His Poetics*. Cambridge: Cambridge University Press, 1979.

PEDOPHILIA

Alongside matrimony, whether polygamous or monogamous, pederasty is one of the main modes of erotic organization in civilizations dominated by the principle of male superiority. In such societies, segregation of the sexes institutionalizes homoeroticism, but taboos surrounding sexual passivity in adult men reduce the available field to young boys. Relationships between men and boys are rendered safe by being socially sanctioned and, therefore, subject to close inspection. The well-established economy of gift exchange for sexual favors is obviously in need of scrutiny if young male citizens are not to be turned into prostitutes. An erotic etiquette is developed, governed by close attention to facial and bodily hair—that is, to the physical development of the boy.

The institutionalized practice of the love of boys in ancient Greek culture was informed by the precedent of Zeus' relationship with Ganymede. Of mortal human men, Orpheus was said to have been the first to follow the god's example and make love to a boy. The most complete analysis of the Athenian ethics of boy-love was Plato's *Symposium*. In Greek society a pair of lovers were, respectively, the adult inspirer [*eispenelas*] and the adolescent hearer [*aïtas*]. As these two terms suggest, the nature of the relationship was essentially educational, where the social purpose of man–boy love was the leading out (*education*, as it would later be termed in Latin) of (male) children into manhood. Male lovers inducted and initiated the next generation of citizens into their useful participation in the *polis*. Since this process was so clearly central to the security and continuance of the state, love between men and boys was circumscribed by rigorous rules and conventions in ways that woman–girl relationships were not.

The main act of homosexual expression was intercrural intercourse (the insertion of the man's penis between the boy's thighs). That is not to say that other acts were not indulged in and enjoyed, but they were subjected—as they have been since—to stricter taboos. The boy's sexual pleasure was subordinate to the man's; indeed, strictly, the boy was not expected to seek pleasure other than that of giving pleasure. In practice, love was often more mutual in its practices than the rules allowed.

The richest source of Greek pederastic verse is *Mousa Paidiké* [*Pederastic Poems*], compiled by the poet Strato and later absorbed into that incomparable resource of over 6,000 epigrams, *The Greek Anthology*. Most such texts refer to a narrow window of desirability between the first tender shoots of puberty and the more tenacious furze of the beginnings of manhood. Pederastic literature is almost always elegiac, for obvious reasons intensely attuned to the passing of time. Conventionally, the poet courts a boy; the reluctant boy resists him but eventually succumbs, often tempted by promises of gifts; he is teasing and unfaithful, however. When puberty kicks in and the boy becomes hairy, he officially ceases to be desirable. The poet looks elsewhere, and the boy duly turns his attention to younger boys and to women. The poet often expresses the hope that the boy will suffer the same pangs of unrequited longing that he once put the poet through.

Most of the major Roman poets wrote love poems to boys as well as women; none was solely interested in boys. Horace, Catullus, Propertius, Vergil, and Tibullus all manifest a bisexuality which is balanced in terms of their strict understanding of social conventions. Even the epigrams of Martial, which cheerfully celebrate many sorts of sexual desire but show a distinct preference for the masculine boy, include advice to married men to give up boys and attend to their wives. For his own part, Martial says he would prefer any boy to a miserable woman (XII, 75).

The Greek tradition resounded throughout the European Middle Ages and Renaissance, most productively, where literature is concerned, in the unreformed seminaries and monasteries. References to Jove and Ganymede are common in Latin poetry by Christian monks. This may explain why Dante, when seeking the personification of virtue in a child, chose not a boy but a girl, Beatrice. However, not until the concerted campaigns of Victorian sentimentalists was childhood most decisively sanctified. Dickens used the epithet "little" (as in Little Nell and Little Dorrit) to connote not only vulnerability but also an undeveloped physicality that characterized the young person's moral sanctity. He liked to thrust such children into the arms of a personified moral threat: Nell with Quilp, Oliver Twist with Fagin. A similar sentimentality about childhood pervades the work of the British "Uranian" poets of the late 19th and early 20th centuries, who emerged from the public schools into a nostalgic haze of regret for the lost institutions of the male palestra and the Socratic academy.

Anthologies show that there was a market for pederastic literature in other sex-segregating societies: for instance, in China the Ming collection *Records of the Cut Sleeve;* and in 17th-century Japan *The Great Mirror of Male Love.* In Arabic literature in the 13th century, Ahmad al-Tifashi produced *The Delight of Hearts*, which includes works by Abu Nuwas, most famous for his poems celebrating the pleasures of wine (*khamriyyat*) and boys (*mudhakkarat*). Nuwas is especially well known in the West through his appearances in the *Arabian Nights*, where he is generally engaged in either the pursuit of boys or the justification of that pursuit. The *Arabian Nights* and the works of such poets as Hafiz had many translators and imitators in 19th-century Europe. In Victorian times and since, European culture finds its visions of erotic pleasure with the young in the South and the East—that is, in poorer countries, and often in countries where the sexes are segregated as they were in ancient Greece.

In France more than elsewhere, pedophile writers have maintained a position of cultural power. Merely to name André Gide is to cite pederasty close to modern French literature's center of gravity. Gide's *Corydon* is a defense not of homosexuality, as is often claimed, but of pederasty. Henry de Montherlant and Roger Peyrefitte both tried to reconcile a classically based, idealized pederasty with a right-wing, Roman Catholic orthodoxy, the former by cloaking physical desire in claims of spirituality, the latter more willing to adopt a pose of being above scandal, but thereby laying claim to a class-based immunity from scandal's consequences.

Such strategies were superseded by the radicalism of Tony Duvert, whose fiction unashamedly celebrates boys' sexuality from what he constructs as their own point of view. As the cases of Duvert, William Burroughs, and Dennis Cooper confirm, modern fiction about boy-love is at its best when, instead of sentimentally laying claim to an understanding of boys' emotional needs, it deliberately sets out to be transgressive in both content and form.

GREGORY WOODS

Further Reading

Aldrich, Robert. *The Seduction of the Mediterranean: Writing, Art and Homosexual Fantasy.* London: Routledge, 1993.

Tifashi, Ahmad al-. *The Delight of Hearts, or What You Will Not Find in Any Book.* San Francisco: Gay Sunshine Press, 1988.

D'Arch Smith, Timothy. *Love in Earnest: Some Notes on the Lives and Writings of the English 'Uranian' Poets from 1880 to 1910.* London: Routledge & Kegan Paul, 1970.

Duvert, Tony. *L'Enfant au masculin.* Paris: Minuit, 1980.

Foucault, Michel. *The Use of Pleasure: The History of Sexuality, Volume Two.* New York: Random House, 1985.

Geraci, Joseph. *Dares to Speak: Historical and Contemporary Perspectives on Boy-Love.* London: Gay Men's Press, 1997.

Gide, André. *Corydon.* New York: Farrar, Straus, 1950.

Hinsch, Bret. *Passions of the Cut Sleeve: A History of the Male Homosexual Tradition in China.* Berkeley and Los Angeles: University of California Press, 1990.

Kincaid, James R. *Child-Loving: The Erotic Child and Victorian Culture.* London: Routledge, 1992.

Percy, William Armstrong. *Pederasty and Pedagogy in Archaic Greece.* Urbana and Chicago: University of Illinois Press, 1996.

Robinson, Christopher. *Scandal in the Ink: Male and Female Homosexuality in Twentieth-Century French Literature.* London: Cassell, 1995.

Saikaku, Ihara. *The Great Mirror of Male Love.* Stanford, CA: Stanford University Press, 1990.

Watanabe, Tsuneo, and Jun'ichi Iwata. *The Love of the Samurai: A Thousand Years of Japanese Homosexuality.* London: Gay Men's Press, 1989.

Woods, Gregory. *A History of Gay Literature: The Male Tradition.* New Haven, CT: Yale University Press, 1998.

PÉLADAN, JOSÉPHIN

1858–1918
French novelist

This writer—given the nickname of "the Balzac of occultism," due to his epic *La Décadence latine* [*Latin Decadence*]—is the first representative of erotic mystique in modern literature. Never before had a writer had the boldness to display so consistently the powers of sexual magic in his novels and his essays. Having failed as a student in conventional education, Péladan directed was toward the sciences of the occult by his brother, Adrien. Reading Eliphas Lévi's *Dogma et rituel de la haute magie* [*Transcendental Magic: Its Doctrine and Ritual*] had a crucial role in his evolution.

In February 1881, Péladan came to Paris and maintained a relationship with Henriette Miallat, a mystical erotomane that Huysmans wrote about in his satanic novel *Là-bas* [*Over There*], referring to her as Mrs. Chantelouve. Péladan wrote a biography of Marion de Lorme, a courtesan of the reign of Louis XIII; followed by the *Livre du désir* [*Book of Desire*]; he then began *Passionate Studies of Decadence* while he was seeing Barbey d'Autrevilly. At the same time, he created his doctrine aiming at the renewal of Catholicism by introducing notions of Chaldean magic. He later taught his ideology in the seven essays of his *Amphitheater of Dead Sciences,* of which the first two were: *Comment on devient mage, éthique* [*How to Become a Sorcerer, Ethical*], and *Comment on devient fée, érotique* [*How to Become a Fairy, Erotic*]. The sorcerer must follow the example of the sorcerer kings of Chaldea; it is this way that Péladan discovered that he was the descendant of Merodack-Baladan cited in *Livre des rois* [*Book of Kings*]. With respect to the second work, his advice to the woman who wanted to become a fairy was to train on a daily basis so that she could develop her innate powers.

His novel *Le vice suprême* [*The Supreme Vice*], in 1884, made quite an impression because of its main character, the sorcerer Merodack, who, in the Parisian foyer of Léonora d'Este, a virgin and a pervert, enthralls her guests with his words and actions. He has superhuman powers: his science of magnetism allows him to put to sleep an opponent or to push him back with liquid substances coming out of his fingers. He is capable of attending an orgy and remaining impassive, without suffering the contagious nature of the others' sexual delirium. In the first chapter, he recounts how he freed himself from sex: not by depriving himself from the act of sex, like a monk, but by reading erotic books and by admiring naked women, to the point that it no longer had an effect on him. This would be a principle that Péladan would invoke ceaselessly: to become asexual or androgynous by experiencing all forms of sexual excess.

Le Vice suprême enthused the occultist Stanislas de Guaita, who became Péladan's friend; together, they restored the esoteric Order of the Rosicrucians. Soon after, though, he came to a disagreement with Guaita, who attacked Catholicism in the name of the Kabbalah; then, Péladan founded in 1890 the Order of the Catholic Rosy Cross "brotherhood of the intellectual virtue," of which he was the self-acclaimed "secular cardinal." It had its sixth and final salon in March 1897. Péladan became Sar Mérodack J. Péladan (*Sar* means *king* in Assyrian), organized art expositions, theatrical plays, appeared in eccentric outfits (which Léon Bloy mocked), and mostly was " the unrivaled teller of lyrisms and great ideas" (as he says about one of his main characters) of *La Décadence latine.* He wrote his manuscripts on yellow paper—"solar paper"—without pausing, and sometimes without rereading his drafts; this is how certain he was of his thoughts.

La Décadence latine is an *éthopée,* a rhetorical term meaning "drawing of mores and human passions," according to Littré. The title suggests that the Latin countries (France, Italy, Spain, and even Russia, "Latinized Slavic") are in states of decadence, having lost the principles that invigorate esoteric Christianity. Péladan's intention is to describe at the same time the vices of those subject to this degradation and the virtues of the sorcerers and the fairies opposed to the latter. The 21 novels of the La Décadence latine were published in the following order: 1. *Le Vice suprême* (1884); 2. *Curieuse!* [*Curious!*] (1886); 3. *L'Initiation sentimentale* [*The Sentimental Initiation*] (1887); 4. *A coeur perdu* [*In a Lost Heart*] (1887); 5. *Istar* (1888); 6. *La Victoire du mari* [*The Husband's Victory*] (1889); 7. *Coeur en peine* [*Heart in Sorrow*] (1890); 8. *L'Androgyne* [*The Androgyne*] (1891); 9. *Le Gynandre* [*The Gynander*] (1891); 10. *Le Panthée* [*Panthea*] (1892); 11. *Typhonia* (1892); 12. *Le Dernier Bourbon* [*The Last Bourbon*] (1895); 13. *Finis Latinorum* (although set in Rome during the election of a new pope by seven Rosicrucians, it still recounts sexual perversities) (1899); 14. *La Vertu suprême* [*The Supreme Virtue*] (1899);

15. *Pereat!* (1901); 16. *Modestie et Vanité* [*Humbleness and Vanity*] (1902); 17. *Peregrin et Peregrine* (1904); 18. *La Licorne* [*The Unicorn*] (1905); 19. *Le Nimbe noir* [*The Black Nimbus*] (1907); 20. *Pomone* (1904); 21. *La Torche renversée* [*The Knocked-Over Torch*] (1925). Of course, all of these novels are more or less well crafted and of interest to a general erotic readership, but they reflect the ideas of the Order of the Catholic Rosy Cross, and some of them are exceptional testimonials of mystical eroticism.

In the trilogy *Curieuse!, L'Initiation sentimentale,* and *A coeur perdu,* the painter Nebo undertakes to free the Russian princess Paule Riazan from temptations of vulgar love. Nebo takes Paule to cabarets and brothels and to socialite circles of the capital so that she can see vice in all of its forms. He takes her to "The Erotic Office: where men prostitute themselves": a poet sells himself to her for one night. In the next novel, Nebo presents to Paule couples who appear to love each over but whose unions conceal the worst selfish judgments. Pleasure or love, as practiced by the uninitiated, is abominable. Paule believes Nebo to be an archangel and offers herself to him in order to experience sacred eroticism. *A coeur perdu* has the subtitle of "Erotikon," because therein one can see all the rituals employed by the sorcerer to acquire highest pleasures. In his apartment, transformed into temple, dressed in an Adrinople red robe, Nebo subjects Paule to "formidable excitement without satisfaction." Nebo only kisses Paule in the "little salon of kisses, empty of furniture" and seeks only the contact of their skin: "hugging nude made them touch each other's soul." Nebo celebrates an "Erocy" (referring to a ritual of the cult of Eros), by reciting hymns and fumigating. When she begs him to possess her, it happens in a red room, where even the bed has purplish red silk sheets. This very ardent room becomes "a forge where flesh strikes flesh with the breathlessness and the moaning of the pounders." Their sweat forms a "mist of love" over them. This supra-erotic experience takes Paule to the verge of insanity. Nebo asks for the help of Merodack, who plunges the young girl into a hypnotic sleep, so that she forgets this session. Paul Valéry wrote to Pierre Louÿs that *A coeur perdu* was "the masterpiece novel of this era."

Other novels of this cycle carry through Péladan's ideas on transcendental sexuality. In *Istar,* which inspired in Péladan his "platonic flirtation" in Marseille with a married woman, Clémence Couve, novelist Nergal regularly visits Istar Capimont, to whom he says: "In a higher place than sex, well beyond desire, resides a religious sentimentality, and we are both examples of it." Their sexual relationship consists in sitting across from each other "without caresses, without kisses, nothing else than sparks of tenderness." Their connection in "ecstatic love" was not about orgasm: "A kind of euphoria was born, a blissful euphoria with no preoccupation, very close to the seraphic state." On a stormy day, "they glowed onto each other," charged with psychic electricity, when "suddenly drawn from their reverie by loud caterwauls, they saw the cat, intoxicated by their sexual discharges and filled with love, rolling on the carpet, a victim of two nervous streams subjecting it to a flaming emanation."

In *La Victoire du mari*, two newlyweds, Adar and Izel, go to Bayreuth during their honeymoon, where they experience "the correlation of sound wave and erotic wave" by attending Wagner's operas. Izel, daughter of a defrocked abbot, says: "I am a mystic of love. . . I can never have enough of your gaze, of your kisses, of your caresses." After each opera—deeply moved by the music—they hug and become acquainted with "the nirvana of love"; a kind of death from which one returns regenerated: "In one month, they got to the edges of sensation." After Bayreuth, they go to Nuremberg to meet Doctor Sexthenthal, "the maleficent saturnian," who has the power theosophists bragged about: "to exit in astral," meaning that his soul exited his body to visit the other world. Sexthenthal says that he has the power to send his spirit (or astral body) far off to fulfill his desire. While his body is in lethargy before Adar, his spirit rapes Izel, who has stayed in their bedroom. She confesses with desperation to her husband: "I made a temple of my body where only you officiate: it has been desecrated." This case of "sidereal debauchery," where a woman is subject to an elusive rape, is unique in literature.

Coeur en peine, a "symphonic novel" without action, starts off with the reverie of Bêlit, leaning on the balcony of a cabin on the oceanfront. She is under the impression that the sea makes love to itself: "The waves must love each other, given their evanescent embraces. . . . This wave rising and collapsing on the preceding wave, could it

be a spasm ending up breaking on the pebbles?" Bêlit learns from Merodack that she is predestined to be "a lover of charity." In fact, there is a sacred form of prostitution, and the woman practicing it is a saint. In *La Vertu suprême*, one sees Bêlit prostituting herself for noble causes. Deputy Rudenty has to make a speech before the Chamber of Deputies in order to send an expedition to Sou-King, in Indochina, running the risk of slaughtering the local inhabitants. He desires Bêlit, and thus she asks him to meet her in his bed before the (parliament) session; although she finds him repugnant, she lavishes him with such caresses that he forgets time. He does not intervene at the podium and the murderous expedition does not take place.

In his two novels on homosexuality, *L'Androgyne* and *Le Gynandre*, Péladan intends to show that "erotic asceticism" allows for liberation of the self. Samas, the main character of *L'Androgyne* is a student at the high school of Avignon, over whom two boys, Tanis and Agür, fight; the former for a platonic relationship, the latter for a physical relationship. Samas feels troubled, but across from his room a teenage girl undresses herself in front of the window in order to seduce him. Each time, she shows him a different part of her body, until the moment she appears naked: "He becomes initiated to a sexual experience without contact." Samas will never touch this girl, Stelle de Senanques; however, he becomes familiar with the feeling of desire for a woman more effectively than by direct contact: "Samas began eroticism through his eyes. . . . Now eroticism is in his imagination, next it will be in his flesh." Following that, Samas loses his virginity to a virgin girl who is in love with him, and this will be "the death of the androgyne"; in other words, the effeminate that existed once no longer is.

Le Gynandre is the oddest novel ever written on lesbians by a man who associated with them and loved them. Péladan was the only man admitted to the Club of the White Carnation, founded by a painter, Louise Abéma, for the women of the lesbian society of Paris. They considered him their "chaplain" and their "confessor." In this novel, young Tammuz, infatuated with the lesbian princess Simzerla, wants to free her from this sexual preference. In vain, Nergal makes a mockery of his mission of "reformer of deformed love." Tammuz establishes relationships with all kinds of lesbian women without criticizing them: "He sympathizes with these women as a thinker and an emotional doctor." He becomes a regular of the Atelier d'Aril (just as Péladan did of the White Carnation club) and of its friends, Carmente the queen of orchids, Ennar the red-haired, Nundi the diabolic whisperer. Finally, Tammuz disguises himself as a woman in order to board the yacht Sapho, where the homosexual women of the Royal-Maupin are on a cruise, with the intention of converting them to heterosexual love.

In 1900, following his divorce, Péladan fell in love with one of his old admirers who came back to him, Christiana Taylor. He wrote the 136 erotic poems of *Livre secret* [*Secret Book*] for her: "Every day Péladan improvised ardently on a piece of paper that the courier would deliver the following day to the one who had inspired him," wrote Victor-Emile Michelet, adding that those "pages of love" made regrettable the fact that Péladan left unfinished his *Traité de la volupté* [*Treatise of Voluptuousness*]. In poems entitled *Rite d'admiration* [*Ritual of Admiration*], *De la chair à la chair* [*From Flesh to Flesh*], *Tout en toi* [*Everything in You*], *Tu es un monde* [*You Are a World*], etc., he celebrates "the solemn works of hedonism" and claims that "voluptuousness is nothing but music."

Following his marriage to Christiana Taylor in February 1901, he attempted to teach men how to be sure that they were in a good marriage. His novel *Pereat!* presents the story of Maurice Trainel, who finds himself split between two women and marries the one he should have run away from. In 1902, Péladan's treatise on practical magic, *L'Art de choisir sa femme d'après la physionomie* [*The Art of Choosing His Wife Following Physiognomy*], describes with pictures the types of women following the esoteric Tradition, in such a way that the candidate groom will know what to expect from any woman. Soon after, Abbot Mugnier, who advises him "to write for young girls," influences Péladan, who proceeded to write the three novels of *Drames de la conscience* [*Dramas of Conscience*], and the last novels of *La Décadence latine*, less original than the previous ones, with the exception of the Erotikon *Pomone*, a most beautiful book on conjugal eroticism in mature age.

In that book, Claude Tillières, a misunderstood musician at fifty years old, retires to a country house with his wife, Colette, forty

years old (this was the age difference between Péladan and Christiana), thus saying farewell to society. After having surprised his wife in her toilette, he realizes that "she is built to live naked, like a goddess." He decides to compose "the plastic sonata of feminity," on the piano by watching her undressing on the sofa in front of him. For seventeen nights, Colette shows to her husband all of her body, part by part: the arms, the breasts, the legs, the knees, by varying her poses. The musical composition follows, from andante to adagio: "Similar to towers, the thighs, magnificent columns, carry the architrave of the mysterious belly." This sight inspires in Claude "a hieratic largo where powerful notes succeed almost equal notes." The buttocks, "figure of joyful geometry," fascinate him, but he does not want to go further: "I have not backed down. . . . I hesitated before obscenity." Claude resists: "The flesh is sacred because of its splendor, it illuminates our poor ephemeral moments." What follows is a fight between the couple, then a passionate dialogue, where Claude justifies himself: "It has been fifteen years that I have slept with you without obligation, without meditation, superficially. The idea—brilliant, I think—come to me to make of your body a musical score, to become a musician of voluptuousness." Everything he writes on voluptuousness is to be admired: "Voluptuousness, Colette, is not an exact act, it is rather a state where the most indifferent act becomes delicious." Colette, in despair after having disappointed him, climbs one night onto a mossy pedestal in the garden, and the moment he passes by she lets fall the cloth draping her and appears naked: "She is a statue, but a vibrant, trembling statue." He gazes at her, fascinated, and when a ray of moonlight illuminates her sex, he thrusts himself upon her and they make love on the stone. This is the "work of autumn" that lovers can only accomplish in their maturity.

After Péladan's death, his widow Christiana published first of all *Le Livre secret*, in 1920; then in 1921 his novel *Les Dévoles d'Avignon* [*The Winners of Avignon*]. In that book, the writer Ramman, in love with young Emmezinde de Romanil, believes himself to have been bewitched by her and proceeds to effect a counterspell, which works, and she loves him back. Through vows of chastity, Ramman behaves like Emmezinde's dog and lies down in front of her feet. They start kissing and embracing each other under the supervision of Adélazie de Pierrefeu, Ramman's landlady. The synthesis of mysticism and sexuality is pushed to its extreme. In the documents of the Péladan Fund at the Bibliotheque de l'Arsenal in Paris, one can see that *Les Dévoles d'Avignon* should have a sequel. This was the first volume of a trilogy, of which *En paradis* [*In Paradise*] was on marriage, and the third, *Le Grand oeuvre sexuel* [*The Great Sexual Work*], was on procreation. If he had lived longer, Péladan would have continued to glorify sacred eroticism.

Biography

Joséphin Péladan was born on March 2 in Lyon, into a family that intended him for the apostolate (his father, Adrien Péladan, was a Catholic fundamentalist whose works on the prophecies of the saints earned him the appointment of Knight of Saint Sylvester by Pope Leon XIII). During his studies in Nîmes from 1871, Péladan was expelled from three schools due to his lack of discipline, was unable to obtain his baccalaureate, and had to rely on the support of his older brother, Dr. Adrien Péladan Jr., initiator of homeopathy in France.

In 1881, Péladan came to Paris, found a job at the Crédit Français, and married the rich young countess Constance-Joséphine de Barde; in 1899 she accused him of having ruined her with his extravagance, and a divorce was granted in 1900, when Péladan begon a second marriage with to Christiana Taylor. He traveled in Italy, Romania, and Egypt and wrote tragedies such as *Sémiramis* and *Oedipe et le sphinx*. Péladan died of food poisoning in Neuilly, on June 27, 1918.

SARANE ALEXANDRIAN

Selected Works

Histoire et légende de Marion de Lorme. Paris: Privately printed, 1882.

Etrennes aux dames: Le livre du désir. Paris: Librairie des auteurs modernes, 1885.

La Queste du Graal. Proses lyriques de l'Ethopée La Décadence latine. *Avec 10 compositions et un portrait par Alexandre Séon*. Paris: Ollendorf, 1893.

L'Art de choisir sa femme d'après la physionomie. Avec 14 figures d'après les maîtres et de nombreuses têtes historiques. Paris: Per Lamm, 1902.

Le Livre secret, avec un portrait et deux allegories gravées à l'eau-forte par Henry de Groux. Paris: La Connaissance, 1920.

La Science de l'amour. Paris: Messein, 1922.

Les Dévoles d'Avignon. Foreword by Gustave-Louis Tautain. Paris: Editions du Monde Nouveau, 1923.

La Décadence latine. 21 novels in 9 vols. Geneva: Editions Slatkine, 1979.

Further Reading

Alexandrian, Sarane. *La Magie sexuelle* [Sexual Magic]. Paris: La Musardine, 2000.

Aubrun, R.-G. *Péladan*. Paris: Les Célébrités d'aujourd'hui, 1904.

Beaufils, Christophe. *Le Sar Péladan*. Paris, 1986.

———. *Joséphin Péladan, essai sur une maladie du lyrisme*. Grenoble: Jérôme Million, 1993.

Bertholet, Dr. Edmond. *La pensée et les secrets de Joséphin Péladan*. 4 vols. Lausanne: Editions Rosicrusciennes, 1952–58.

Breton, J.-J. *Le Mage dans "la Décadence latine" de Joséphin Péladan*.

Dantinne, Emile. *L'oeuvre et la pensée de Péladan*. Brussels, 1948.

Doyon, René-Louis. *La Douloureuse aventure de Péladan*. Paris, 1946.

Gheusi, P.-B. *Cinquante ans de Paris: Mémoires d'un témoin 1889–1938*. 4 vols. Paris: Plon, 1940.

Nist, Ray. *Un prophète (Péladan)*. Paris: Chamuel, 1893.

Les Péladan. Les Dossiers H. Péladan project developed and directed by Jean-Pierre Laurant and Victor Nguyen. Lausanne: L'Age d'Homme, 1910.

Revue des études Péladanes. Official organ of the Joséphin Péladan Society, Jean-Pierre Bonnerot, director-founder. 15 issues, 1975–78.

PERCEAU, LOUIS

1883–1942
French poet

Louis Perceau was a multifaceted political journalist, well-known newspaperman, songwriter, storyteller, and bibliophile. As a young journalist, he published *Contes de la Pigouille* [*Stories of La Pigouille*], which were ghost and werewolf tales told by a peasant in patois, pertaining to the folklore of Perceau's native Poitou. But Perceau is best remembered by posterity for having become the greatest connoisseur of erotic literature, both ancient and modern, of his day. With Guillaume Apollinaire and Fernand Fleuret, he edited the catalogue of the "Enfer" [Hell, inferno]—the section for forbidden books—of the Bibliothèque Nationale. The catalogue first appeared in 1911 in the *Mercure de France;* and in 1919, after Apollinaire's death, Perceau published a revised edition.

Afterward Perceau collaborated with Fleuret on erudite works of eroticism, which they signed "Chevalier de Percefleur" (a contraction of Perceau and Fleuret) or "Dr. Lodovigo Hernandez" (i.e., Louis Fernand in Spanish). This was a strange association of two authors so unlike each other. Perceau was a leftist, engaged in social action. Fleuret was a right-wing conservative who always wore a handgun, which he fired on the pigeons of Paris (under the pretext of feeding them) and who would end up in the Sainte-Anne psychiatric hospital. However, it was Fleuret, spending whole days sorting through the manuscript cabinet of the Bibliothèque Nationale, who found the most rare and curious artifacts the two published. Thus, in the "Livre du Boudoir" collection (founded by Perceau) (1920) can be found *Les mémoires de l'abbé de Choisy, habillé en femme* [*The Memoirs of the Abbott de Choisy, Dressed as a Woman*], and *Cheveu* [*Hair*] by Simon Coiffier de Moret, with comments by the Knight Percefleur, whom they presented as an embassy attaché in Constantinople who committed suicide in 1855 in the Sultan's harem. According to them, the notes of

those editions were those that the knight, a member of the Ladies' Academy, used to write "in the margins of his favorite books."

Perceau and Fleuret used their real names to publish their critical editions of Ronsard's erotic poems (*Le livret des folastries* [*The Coltishness Booklet*], 1920; *La bouquiniade et autres gaillardises* [*Bookshopping and Other Cheerfulness*], 1921). But it was Dr. Ludovigo Hernandez who published *Le procès inquisitorial de Gilles de Rais, maréchal de France, avec un essai de réhabilitation* [*The Inquisitorial Trial of Gilles de Rais, Marshal of France, with a Rehabilitation Attempt*] (1921); *Le procès de sodomie au XVIe, XVIIe et XVIIIe siècles, publiés d'après des documents judiciaires conservés à la Bibliothèque Nationale* [*Sodomy Trials in the Sixteenth, Seventeenth, and Eighteenth Centuries, Published According to Judicial Documents Preserved at the National Library*] (1923); and *Les procès de bestialité au XVIe et au XVIIe siècles, documents judiciaires inédits* [*Bestiality Trials in Sixteenth and Seventeenth Centuries: Unseen Judicial Documents*] (1929). For the historian of social mores, these are seminal publications.

Perceau flourished following his separation from Fleuret. In 1930 he published two large volumes of his *Bibliographie du roman érotique du XIXe siècle* [*Bibliography of the Nineteenth-Century Erotic Novel*], an unparalleled critical resource which, according to its subtitle, gives "a complete description of all novels, short stories, and other works in prose, published secretly in French, from 1800 to date, and of all their reprintings." He procured most of these books from secondhand booksellers, as these books were in no public library: "Twenty years of research has enabled me to establish a collection that is perhaps unique. . . . My desire is to see it one day reunited with that of the Enfer of the Bibliothèque Nationale." Rectifying the errors of his predecessors, Perceau could flatter himself for having done "the first serous bibliographic essay on erotic works."

Also making an inventory of the erotic writings of the pre-1800 past, Perceau published *Le Cabinet du Parnasse* [*The Cabinet of Parnassus*] (1935), "a collection of free, rare, or obscure poems, serving as a supplement to the so-called complete writings of French poets."

Through a clandestine printer, Maurice Duflou, Perceau published erudite editions of the erotic classics, which were at that time forbidden in bookstores. He signed his introductions and his notes "Helpey, bibliophile from Poitou" (a signature based on the transcription of his initials, L.P.). Among the twenty or so books presented by Helpey, there was *Anti-Justine ou les délices de l'amour* [*Anti-Justine, or the Delights of Love*] by Restif de la Bretonne, in a "new edition founded for the first time on the original text of 1798," and *Histoire de Dom Bougre, portier des Chartreux* [*History of Dom Bougre, Doorkeeper of Chartreux*], also in a "new edition revised from the original text and containing all of the fragments removed in all modern editions." It is impossible to make an accurate study of erotic literature without referring to Louis Perceau. It is he who published 65 erotic letters by Théophile Gautier, in *Lettres à la Présidente et Galanteries poétiques* [*Letters to the President and Poetic Gallantries*] (editions of the Secret Museum, 1927), a book "the annotation of which required several months of thorough research" and which bibliophiles look upon as "the most beautiful volume published secretly in a century."

Besides his works of erudition, Perceau wrote erotic poems under the pseudonym "Alexandre de Vérineau." These collections included *Douze sonnets lascifs* [*Twelve Lascivious Sonnets*] (1925), on the libertine watercolors of Gerda Wegener; *Au bord du lit* [*By the Bedside*] (1927), illustrated leaves by Luc Lafnet; and *Le pisseuses* [*The Females*] (1934), which Perceau would recite once a week at "Lapin Agile" in Montmartre. Being interested in erotic humor, Perceau composed *Le keepsake galant* [*The Gallant Keepsake*] (1924) in the style of the romantic almanacs, with erotic advice for each month. *La redoute des contrepèteries* [*The Treasury of Puns*] (1934) was a book of obscene puns. Finally, in order to celebrate the Gallic spirit,

this time under the guise of "an old journalist," he collected salacious intimate anecdotes in *Histoires raides pour l'instruction des jeunes filles* [*Stiff Tales for the Instruction of Young Girls*] (1938).

During the Nazi occupation of Vichy France, officers of the Wehrmacht came calling on Perceau's widow to confiscate the books of his erotic library, the existence of which they had learned of. However, the collection had been locked away in cases and hidden outside of his apartment. Hence, it remained intact for some time after the war, when it was finally dispersed.

Biography

Son of a tailor and a dressmaker of Coulon, in the Poitou, Louis Perceau was born September 22, 1883. His parents wanted him to be a schoolteacher, but at the age of sixteen, he joined the Socialist Federation of Deux-Sèvres and began devoting himself to poetry. In 1901 he went to Paris, where he joined a group of so-called revolutionary poets and songwriters, and the staff of Jean Jauré's newspaper *L'Humanité*. Perceau died in Paris under the German occupation.

SARANE ALEXANDRIAN

Editions

Au bord du lit. "Erotopolis" [Paris?]: A L'Enseigne des Bacchantes, 1927.
Douze sonnets lascifs. "Erotopolis": A L'Enseigne des Faunes, 1924.
Le Keepsake galant. "Foutropolis" [Paris?]: Privately printed at the expense of Father Dupanloup, 1924.
La Redoute des contrepèteries. Paris: Briffault, 1934.

Further Reading

Cabanel, Jean. "Louis Perceau." *Triptyque* (June-July 1932).
Pauvert, Jean-Jacques. *Anthologie des lectures érotiques, de Guillaume Apollinaire à Philippe Pétain.* Paris: Jean-Claude Simoen, 1979.
Pia, Pascal. *Les Livres de l'Enfer.* 2 vols. Paris: C. Coulet and A. Faure, 1978.
Le Quellec, Jean-Loïc. Préface to Perceau, *Contes de la Pigouille.* Benet, Vendée: Editions du Marais, 1993.

PERI ROSSI, CRISTINA

1941–
Uruguayan poet, novelist, journalist, and essayist

Cristina Peri Rossi's collection of stories *Indicios Pánicos* [*Panic Signs*] (1970) foreshadowed the repressive state that was to govern her country and force her into exile. The government in Uruguay was threatened by a rise in socialist sentiment while its economy continued to decline in the early 1970s. Consequently, the government moved progressively toward a repressive military state, which officially took power in 1973. Peri Rossi was acutely aware of the connections between bourgeois values and authoritarianism in her country. Her narration of these connections did not help her country to avoid full-scale dictatorship; it only caused her to flee into exile. Peri Rossi's early work was openly political, and her notoriety as a political writer would have been enough to lead to her exile. Nevertheless, it was only after personal loss that Peri Rossi decided to flee her country. In March of 1972 Peri Rossi gave refuge to a young student, Ana Luisa Valdés, who was being pursued by the secret police. On the one day that Ana decided to venture out of the house she was picked up and never heard from again. It was then that Peri Rossi began to realize the extent of her dangerous situation and she made plans to leave Uruguay, arriving by boat in Barcelona in October 1972. In 1974, the military government in Uruguay withdrew her citizenship. She left for Paris and later returned as a Spanish citizen to Barcelona, where she continues to reside.

Peri Rossi has published eight collections of short stories, six novels, and a collection of essays, and her work has received numerous awards and prizes. Passion, desire, and the erotic flow throughout her works. From the beginning of her career to her most recent published works, the erotic has been a central element of her writing. While it is possible to mark shifts in her literature, certain common themes run throughout her literary presentation of sexual desire and passion: Peri Rossi is especially interested in producing literature that breaks down traditional gender categories, and her writing challenges the hegemony of patriarchal, heterosexual society. Another common theme is the association of the woman's body with language and of writing with sex.

One of the fundamental strategies that Peri Rossi uses to destabilize gender identities is multiple–gendered narrative voices. She often writes her poetry and short stories from ambiguous gender positions that allow the reader to imagine either a male or a female speaker. Since her poetry clearly has the female body as an object of desire, this ambiguous gender identity allows the reader to receive the poem as an example of either heterosexual or lesbian love. Peri Rossi rarely marks the narrative or poetic voice as female, and it is interesting that she often adopts a male voice. Some critics find this practice to be disturbing, since it may suggest her avoidance of openly lesbian literary representation. Others, of an opposing opinion, caution that the reader is always aware that the author is a woman. According to this position, the practice of adopting a male voice is transgressive, because it destabilizes preestablished notions of gender identity.

One way that Peri Rossi's works challenge traditional gender relations is through the depiction of impotent and/or antipatriarchal male characters. In her novel *La nave de los locos* [*The Ship of Fools*], the protagonist, Ecks (X) is an exile as well as a symbol of all marginalized segments of society. The novel critiques authoritarianism, patriarchal society, Christian ideology, and heterosexism. Each of these is intertwined within the narrative, suggesting that to address only one of these axes of oppression is insufficient. Ultimately, the novel suggests that the end of male domination and of phallocentric control of the symbolic order is the necessary beginning of social change. The protagonist is not only socially marginalized; he is impotent. Ecks dreams that the way in which patriarchy can be destroyed is through men's renunciation of virility as an act of love. If all men gave the women they loved their virility, then patriarchy would be destroyed. Hopeful and pessimistic, celebratory and critical, this novel is full of contradictions and fragments, all of which revolve around the central dilemma of how modernity is predicated upon centralizing systems of power, especially patriarchy and Christianity. The novel demonstrates how Peri Rossi uses literature to destroy phallocentrism and the hegemony of traditional heterosexuality. In a similar vein, *Solitario de amor* [*A Loner in Love*] has an unnamed protagonist, who, while capable of sexual intercourse with the woman he loves, is effectively impotent. He tells the reader that he is a man without a "key" (109). Like Ecks, he is nameless and marginalized. His only identity is his obsession with a woman who has rejected him.

Just as Peri Rossi eschews a stable subject position and critiques patriarchy, she also refuses fixed categories of desire. Desire and identity are fluid and interconnected. Peri Rossi draws attention to the fact that fixing identity and containing desire are ways of controlling and repressing society. Her multiple narrative and poetic voices are combined with myriad forms of sexual desire. Peri Rossi also describes passion and desire as feelings that resist narrow definitions. For instance, her collection of short stories *Una pasión prohibida* [*A Forbidden Passion*] includes many different descriptions of human desire. The theme throughout the collection is that identity and desire are inseparable and that social forces have always tried to limit and control them. Many of the stories focus on the ways that desires have been brutally restricted, causing great suffering. Alternatively, other stories focus on the ways that desire coupled with power often results in the marginalization and oppression of others. Peri Rossi emphasizes that desire almost always relates to issues of power: The one who desires is either powerful or powerless over the object of obsession. While her writing tries to free those whose desires have been repressed, she also challenges the use of power to forcefully control desire. For instance, she often describes lesbian love as a social transgression and even refers to the love between women as wonderfully incestual, in an effort to disrupt social norms and taboos. *Lingüística general* [*General Linguistics*] ends with two

clearly lesbian poems that are celebratory and playful. Both highlight the way that same-sex love simultaneously rejoices in sameness and difference. In contrast with her celebration of lesbian desire, Peri Rossi associates military dictatorships and authoritarianism with rape and the violation of humanity's freedom to desire. Three of her collections of poetry written during exile, *Descripción de un naufragio* [*Description of a Shipwreck*], *Diáspora*, and *Europa después de la lluvia* [*Europe After the Rain*], narrate desire as loss and represent fear as the inability to connect and love. In these collections Eros implies power which can lead to corruption, objectification, and alienation. Yet in other texts, Eros is also about adoration, celebration, pleasure, and harmony. Peri Rossi describes an eroticism unbound and examines the dark as well as the beautiful aspects of desire.

Peri Rossi's only published essays, in the collection, *Fantasías eroticas* [*Erotic Fantasies*], focus on the history and variety of erotic fantasies. She traces a broad array, including bestiality, inflatable sex dolls, rape, prostitution, hermaphrodites, and gender bending. One of her principle interests is in tracing the equation of sexual fantasies with violence. For instance, she describes how members of the military conducting torture during authoritarian regimes reported that they had incredibly intense orgasms. In contrast, she describes lesbian desire as idealistically rejecting the connections between sex and violence (107). The collection is driven by the notion that the saddest confession is to admit the absence of fantasies. Once again, Peri Rossi equates identity and existence with desire, passion, and fantasy.

The images of women that reappear in her poetry and prose are often similar to traditional icons of women. She associates the female body with a utopian refuge (focusing on the womb), and women are connected to nature, especially water. Contrasted to these traditional images in which woman's body occupies the center of desire and is celebrated as a source of passion and pleasure, Peri Rossi also depicts the female body as violated and vulnerable. These images are especially recurrent in *La nave de los locos*. The novel describes the defibulation (splitting of vulval skin in female circumcision) of women and the experiments performed on Jewish women during the Holocaust. The main character (Ecks) watches a movie in which a woman is raped by a machine; he befriends an aging prostitute; and he falls in love with a woman who has a clandestine, painful abortion. In addition to these images, Peri Rossi's writing depicts women who are resistant and who refuse to submit to the system and to be victims of the desires of others. In *Solitario de amor*, for example, the protagonist is in desperate love with a woman named Aída. She is alternatively described as a welcoming, nurturing figure and as a strong and self-sufficient woman who steadfastly rejects the protagonist.

Focusing on language and desire, Peri Rossi equates writing with sex and language with women. In this way she links the aesthetic with language. These themes are particularly noteworthy in her poetry. Her first collection of poetry, *Evohé,* caused a scandal when it was published in Uruguay in 1971. Beginning with a quote from Sappho, the collection is a passionate, sensual series of poems about the female body, at times equating the female body with a temple and love with prayer. Peri Rossi draws on the tie between the collection's title, which comes from Euripedes' play, *Bacchae*, in her exploration of passion unbound. The Bacchae were the female followers of Bacchus (Dionysus), and "Evohé!" was the cry uttered at the end of their celebration of freedom from civilization. Consistent with her critique of Christianity and of confining systems of social organization, this text demonstrates the way in which lesbian love challenges the prevailing system of belief. Woman and word are equal symbols, and the poet/lover interacts with woman through words and the sensuality of language. In *Babel bárbara* [*Barbarous Babel*] Peri Rossi continues to work with sensual, lesbian-oriented poetry. In this collection, the concept of "woman" is likened to the Tower of Babel, where the multiplicity of meaning in language and in the female body are equated. The result is a highly ambiguous fusion and confusion of sex and language. In *Otra vez eros* [*Eros Again*] Peri Rossi continues to explore sensuality, language, pleasure, and the female body. The title, again, refers to Sappho's poetry, in which she describes the untying of desire. The collection continues to exalt lesbian love, passion for the female body, and the ties between sensuality and language, but Peri Rossi also includes relatively newer themes, like the effects of science, technology, and AIDS on contemporary passions.

Biography

Born in Montevideo, Uruguay, November 12. Peri Rossi's mother's side of the family were Italian immigrants, and her father's side is Basque and Canarian. In 1947, at the age of six she began her studies at José Enrique Rodó, a public school named after a famous Uruguayan essayist. At university she studied music and biology, receiving her degree in comparative literature at the Instituto de Profesores Artigas in 1964. During this same time she began teaching at university and writing for the leftist magazine *Marcha.* Peri Rossi has taught at a number of universities, including the Deutscher Akademischer Austauschdients in Berlin in 1980, and the University of Barcelona and the University of San Sebastián in Spain. She has participated in conferences in the United States, Canada, and Europe.

SOPHIA A. MCCLENNEN

Selected Works

Poetry Collections

Evohé. Montevideo: Editorial Girón, 1971.
Descripción de un naufragio. Barcelona: Lumen, 1975.
Diáspora. Barcelona: Editorial Lumen, 1975.
Lingüística general. Valencia: Promoteo, 1979.
Europa después de la lluvia. Madrid: Fundación Banco Exterior de España, 1987.
Babel Bárbara. Caracas: Editorial Angria, 1990.
Otra vez Eros. Barcelona: Editorial Lumen, 1994.
Aquella noche. Barcelona: Editorial Lumen, 1996.
La inmovilidad de los barcos. Vitoria-Gasteiz, Spain: Bassarai, 1997.
Poemas de amor y desamor. Barcelona: Plaza y Janés, 1998.

Short Story Collections

Viviendo: Relatos. Montevideo, Alfa, 1963.
Indicios pánicos. Montevideo: Nuestra América, 1970.
La tarde del dinosaurio. Barcelona: Plaza y Janés, 1980.
El museo de los esfuerzos inútiles. Madrid: Seix Barral, 1983.
Una pasión prohibida. Barcelona: Editorial Seix Barral, 1986.
La rebelión de los niños. Barcelona: Seix Barral, 1988.
Los museos abandonados. Barcelona: Lumen, 1992.
Cosmoagonías. Barcelona: Juventud, 1994.

Novels

El libro de mis primos. [1969]. 2nd ed. Barcelona: Plaza y Janés, 1976.

La nave de los locos. Barcelona: Seix Barral, 1984.

Solitario de amor. Barcelona: Ediciones Grijalbo, 1988.

La última noche de Dostoievski. Madrid: Grijalbo Mondadori, 1992.

Desastres íntimos. Barcelona: Lumen, 1997.

El amor es una droga dura. Barcelona: Editorial Seix Barral, 1999.

Essay Collection

Fantasías eróticas. Madrid: Temas de Hoy, 1991.

Further Reading

Basualdo, Ana. "Cristina Peri Rossi: Apocalipsis y paraíso." *El viejo topo* 56 (1981): 47–49.

Camps, Susana. "La pasión desde la pasión: Entrevista con Cristina Peri-Rossi." *Quimera* 81 (1988): 40–49.

Dejbord, Parizad Tamara. *Cristina Peri Rossi: Escritora del exilio.* Buenos Aires: Editorial Galerna, 1998.

Deredita, John F. "Desde la diáspora: Entrevista con Cristina Peri Rossi." *Texto Crítico* 9 (1978): 131–42.

Feal, Rosemary G. "Cristina Peri Rossi and the Erotic Imagination." *Reinterpreting the Spanish American Essay: Women Writers of the 19th and 20th Century*, edited by Doris Meyer, 215–26. Austin: University of Texas Press, 1995.

Golano, Elena. "Soñar para seducir: Entrevista con Cristina Peri Rossi." *Quimera* 25 (1982): 47–50.

Kaminsky, Amy K. "The Question of Lesbian Presence." *Reading the Body Politic: Feminist Criticism and Latin American Women Writers*, 115–33. Minneapolis: University of Minnesota Press, 1993.

Kantaris, Elia. "The Politics of Desire: Alienation and Identity in the Work of Marta Traba and Cristina Peri Rossi." *Forum for Modern Language Studies* 25 (July 1989): 248–64.

Mántaras, Graciela. "Cristina Peri Rossi en la literatura erótica uruguaya." *Cristina Peri Rossi: Papeles críticos*, edited by Rómulo Cosse, 31–45. Librería Linardi y Risso: Montevideo, 1995.

Narvaez, Carlos Raul. "Eros y Thanatos en *Solitario de amor* de Cristina Peri-Rossi." *Alba de América* 10 (1992): 245–50.

Pertusa, Immaculada. "Revolución e identidad en los poemas lesbianos de Cristina Peri Rossi." *Monographic Review/Revista Monografica* 7 (1991): 236–50.

Rowinsky, Mercedes. *Imagen y discurso: Estudio de las imágenes en la obra de Cristina Peri Rossi.* Barcelona: Editorial Trilce, 1997.

Verani, Hugo J. "La rebelión del cuerpo y el lenguaje." *Cristina Peri Rossi: Papeles criticos*, edited by Rómulo Cosse, 9–21. Librería Linardi y Risso: Montevideo, 1995.

Zeitz, Eileen. "Cristina Peri Rossi: El desafío de la alegoría." Interview. *Chasqui* 9 (1979): 79–101.

PERSIAN

Definitions of Erotica

Erotic literature in classical and modern Persian is not an independent genre. There is no stable term for this type of writing in the language. In his survey of erotic writing, Khaleghi (1996) uses both the neologism *tan-kame-sarai* ["body-gratification composition] and the borrowing *erutik.* In an essay about the romantic epic *Vis-o Ramin* by Fakhr al-Din As'ad Gorgani (11th century), the literary critic M.A. Eslami Nodushan (109) speaks of a *nafkhe-ye kh v ahesh,* or "puff of desire" that "rises ftom its pages." He explains that it is this air of indecency which has given the work its unwholesome reputation. M. San'ati (1: 71) uses the more clinical *havas-kamane* [pleasure-fulfilling] in his analysis of the modern writer Sadeq Hedayat (d. 1951). Regardless of what terms they use, scholars of Persian generally distinguish erotic writing from what is generally called *Aifiye va shaifiye* works. The latter owes its name to a pornographic work (now lost) whose roots lie in Sanskrit sex manuals (Qazvini in J\Te_mi 'AruQi: 178). *Aifiye va shaifiye* works use eroticism to arouse lust, or *shahvat,* which directly violates Islamic legal and moral standards. By contrast, many feel that truly erotic poetry and prose have aesthetic goals that are less morally problematic. This article is a survey of the erotic in Persian in its broadest sense; it includes the high and low ends of the moral spectrum and everything in between.

Persian Anti-Eroticism

To appreciate how poets and other writers approach sexual themes in Persian, one needs to understand why they do so with trepidation. In many cases, the strong sociocultural bias against eroticism influences the ways in which it emerges in Persian literature. Besides the obvious religious prohibitions against explicitly sexual expression, there is a general tendency to negate the physical and dwell on the soul. This tendency is especially strong in works of Sufism or Persian mysticism. According to the Persian commentary to the sayings of the 11th-century mystic Baba Taher 'Oryan, "true ecstasy is the obliteration of bodily preoccupations and attainment of spiritual qualities" (Maq_ud: 775).

Perhaps the most influential theologian of his time, Imam Abu Hamid Ghazali (1058–1111) preached moderation when it came to sexual pleasure in his Persian treatise *The Elixir of Happiness* (2: 55). According to Ghazali, lust has one purpose: the continuation of the species. Accordingly, the Ghazalian threshold for excess in matters of the flesh is very low by Western standards. In his view, any place where men and women can see one another is fertile ground for the "seed of corruption" (2: 61). This horror of *na:plr* or *ne?iir6* [wanton glance, gaze] explains not only the protective artifice of Persian eroticism but also certain features of dress and architecture in places where the language is a medium of literary expression (Iran, Mghanistan, Tajikistan, Pakistan, India). To guard against the stray stare in public places, women spectators wore, and in some places continue to wear, fine masks (Arabic: *neqab;* Persian: *piche*) and veils (l; Jejiib) and to sit behind windows with prophylactic screens made of carved wood or alabaster.

Ghazali's theology also extols procreation and frowns upon physical attractiveness for the lust it may cause. In support of his argument, he appeals to popular wisdom, which says that it is better to marry an ugly but fertile woman than a barren beauty (1: 303). Besides encouraging procreation, the pleasures of intercourse have an otherworldly purpose: they offer a foretaste of heaven's rewards (1: 304). In both cases, sensuality and sexual pleasure are never ends in themselves; they must lead to a greater good. There is no place, then, for eroticism as such in Ghazali's theology.

Classical Erotic Literature

The moralistic tendency to interpret the erotic as mystical was very strong in the classical period of Persian literature (late 9th to 19th centuries) and still influences contemporary criticism and exegesis. "Wine" cannot be wine, but the ecstasy of beholding or joining the divine; "eyebrows" don't merely rim the eyes but indicate divine attributes (Rypka: 86). While these interpretations are often valid, sometimes they are intended to subvert the erotic, to sublimate its earthiness and direct it toward loftier (aesthetic, moral) goals.

One of the most common places to find the erotic in classical Persian literature is the introductory part of the *qa{iide* [ode], known as the *tashbib* [youthfulness; analogous to the idyll], in which poets often demonstrated their mastery of erotic description. These celebrations of spring and love use the same images again and again to describe the lover's beauty: e.g., his/her (Persian pronouns have no gender) lips are ruby or sugar; his/her stature is a cypress tree; his/her face is the brightest, fullest moon set off by the darkest mole; her (most likely) breasts are pomegranates or lemons. The formalism does not please Western critics, who expect originality (Rypka: 85); however, to aficionados the art of the *tashbib* lies in its "conventional" inventiveness.

Rather than singing the praises of particular lovers, court poets competed for patronage by idealizing beauty itself with images that ranged from the conventional to the bizarre. To illustrate this, one need only take a short inventory of hair conceits. Abu al-Hasan of Lavkar (11th century) begins an ode by contrasting the blackness of the lover's curled tresses and the whiteness of his/her body and face: "On jasmine s/he has ring mail of ambergris / On the moon s/he has curls of hyacinth" (Foruzanfar: 35). In a flight of alphabetic imagination, Ma'rufi of Balkh (mid-10th century) uses two Persian letters, *Jim* and *'ayn,* to evoke the look of his lover's hair (Lazard: 134): "Twist on black twist, tresses like *'ayn* upon *'ayn* / Curl on black curl, locks like *Jim* within *Jim*."

The nested letters reproduce the endless folds of hair with their tails, while the cascading letters provide dots that punctuate the cheeks with the requisite moles. Addressing his lover, 'On_ori (d. 1039/40) complains: "Your hair lies as flame on your head, yet I am the one roasted"

(Foruzanfar:121). Finally, Manuchehri (d. ca. 1040) compares the beloved's coiled tresses to "silkworms" (138).

As it developed, the *tashbib* became a vehicle for poets' erotic yearnings. Typically they demand the requisites of passion: *bus* [kissing] and *kenar* [caressing/hugging], and, just as typically, the lover coyly resists. The opening of one of Farrokhi of Sistan's (d. 1037/38) odes expresses the conventional impatience with this reticence. The conceit is Marvell-like ("Had we but world enough, and time / this coyness, lady, were no crime": "Enough excuses, blame no more! / This be not love, my dear, but war" (Farrokhi: 191).

Erotic monologue occasionally blossoms into a full narrative that describes the poet/lover relationship. Sana'i of Ghazni (d. 1130/31) writes of the visit of his lover, a drunken boy (256–8). But, though one might expect a specific debauchery, standard erotic imagery prevails. Black down deposits "camphor" on the boy's face, and his tresses are "disturbed" by "thrice-distilled spirits." The boy is about to bypass the door of the poet, who cries out in despair and love: "Have you no fear of God, forsaking me in this state?" The boy acquiesces, but when the poet caresses his waist [*kenar*], the strong wine foils his plans. In consolation, the poet, like a "parrot," spends the night feeding on the "sugar" produced by "kissing" [*bus*] the unconscious boy's lips.

In the romance about Queen Vis and her lover and brother-in-law Ramin, erotic narrative breaks free from standard *tashbib* imagery. When Vis, who has been imprisoned in a walled garden by her much older husband, learns that Ramin has secretly entered the palace grounds, she cannot contain her passion. Vis's mad dash to her lover is a methodical striptease that, as eroticism for its own sake, offends the Ghazalian standard of modesty and decorum: first, she removes her slippers to scale the large tent that blocks the palace portico; second, the leap from porch to canvas unveils her face; third, her earrings break; fourth, her *chador* catches on something and falls away as she jumps from the wall; fifth, her skirt rips to shreds in the fall; and last, the rope belt that holds up her undergarments breaks, revealing her thighs (Gorgani: 278–9).

When the two lovers finally meet, the narrative becomes less inventive and more predictable, reverting to *tashbib* and other types of received imagery. Exhausted by the ordeal of reaching her lover, Vis falls asleep in the garden. She appears to Ramin as a "newly blossomed flower," with "violet-dark tresses" and "narcissus face." Like the narrator of Sana'i's night of thwarted passion, Ramin takes his dozing lover by the waist and feasts on her sugary lips. The erotic becomes alphabetical when the lovers kiss: "the lips of the two like [the letter] *mim* <r) on *mim*."

Homoeroticism

Homoerotic Persian literature generally features two actors: the poet and a beardless youth, or *amrad*, whose love, like that of the courtesan, is often for sale. The *amrad* is a "mercilessly pretty boy" (Sprachman), on the cusp of puberty with cheeks dusted with fine hair—metaphorically like down, elegant calligraphy, camphor, etc. His cupola-like buttocks are "rounded mounds of silver" (Farrokhi: 4), and with the exception of breasts, he is endowed with all the attributes of feminine beauty. The *amrad* can also be a Ganymede-like figure [*saqi*]: "A cuddly cupbearer, so sleek and coy / No houri ever mothered such a boy." In this line, Anvari (101) refers to the Qur'anic heaven inhabited by .*f1lU*, "female companions with eyes whose whites and pupils are sharply contrasted" (Qur'an 52: 20), and *ghelmiin.*, "handsome boys as precious as pearls" (Qur'an 52: 24).

Homoerotic literature in Persian is often about the *amrad*'s hairy passage from adolescence to adulthood. A few of the stories in the *Go/estan* (chapter 5) of Sa'di (b. ca. 1213–19) and the mock-treatise *Rishnam e [Book of the Beard]* (*rish* = "beard" in Persian) of 'Obeyd-e Zakani (ca. 1300–72) are about that tragic turning point. Zakani's work begins at night, which is eroticized: "when the ashen sighs of lovers befogged the mirror of the sun and the smoldering love in each longing breast inflamed the face of day: They combed the night's long locks so dark. They overwrote the day with sin's black mark" (*Suppressed Persian*: 63). The narrator pines for his boy-love in traditional *tashbib* imagery, complaining that he is "[m]ore twisted than [his love's] coiled hair / More wasted than [his] eyes' hypnotic stare." Coyness is the common topos in the beginning: "Although the age belongs to your sweet face / Beware: past marvels fade without a trace"; "He with no beard has something we could desire / But bearded boys can do nothing but retire." However, the reader soon discovers that this introduction is no ordinary *tashbib*. Instead of the lover, a fabulous creature called Beard—ironically, "father of beauties"—appears. There follows a highly inventive and allusive debate in which the narrator, who is implacably anti-*rish*, trades barbs with and ultimately defeats the intruder. The essay ends by cautioning: "[May] the day never come when your face is seared / With the kind of misery they call the beard."

Zakani not only turns the serious essay (*resale*) into homoerotic pastiche, he also deflates the Persian national epic *Shaname* with sexual wordplay. In his mock moral treatise, *Akhlaq Ashraf* [*The Ethics of the Aristocracy*], the most accomplished warriors of Persian literature, Rostam (also known as Tahmtan) and Human, trade favors:

> As soon as Tahmtan had undid his belt,
> Like smoke Human whipped out his great upright.
> He battered Rostam harder and harder.
> Human then turned and bared a mighty rear.
> He lanced Human with such a rocklike staff: Behold!
> Two champions, their arses worn.
>
> Before Human the noble hero knelt;
> The very way that Godarz ruled he might.
> Till Rostam's rectum smoldered with ardor.
> A lion, fierce, Tahmtan displayed no fear;
> That Human's behind was nearly torn in half
> Became the greatest heroes ever born.
>
> (*Suppressed Persian:* 58)

Zakani's technique of taking serious poetry out of context and providing it with an ironic meaning is common to many forms of classical erotic literature. Just as hair, lips, letters of the alphabet, etc., can be imbued with erotic meanings, so can entire lines of poetry that had been free of such associations when first recited. *Rostam al-tavarikh* [*The Rostam of Histories*] uses the technique to spice a passage about the rampant immorality of early-eighteenth-century Shiraz. The passage (A__ef: 344) describes how Khosrow Khan, the governor of Kurdestan, after a night with a boy of surpassing beauty and knowledge of poetry, reached for his "lithe charmer" in the morning, and the boy awoke and recited this line by Ijafe_: "At dawn when Khosrow of the East [i.e., the sun] planted his banner on the hills / My love knocked on the door of the hopeful with the hand of favor." The boy changes the poem's original intent (i.e., to be a panegyric, Ijafe_: 1: 314): the great king's standard becomes phallic, the landscape erogenous, and the motion of the royal hand foreplay.

Autoeroticism

For the many writers who could not afford to keep costly courtesans and beardless boys, there was a solitary alternative. One of the first masturbatory odes in Persian was known as *jalqname*, or "book of maturbation." This was a poem by Jamal al-Din Kashi (c. 1265–82), whose purpose was essentially literary (al-Jajarmi:2:919–23). He used autoeroticism to deflate the pretensions of the classical Persian poetic form, known as *tarji' band*, which consists of several stanzas, each of which ends with a couplet. In the hands of 'Obeyd-e Zakani, the form becomes socially satirical, a genre in its own right that one might term "onanistic." In his *jalqname*, Zakani adopts the persona of a *rend*, or free spirit, a renegade, which gives him license to say the most outrageous things. For example, he seems to advocate masturbation, which Islam strongly condemns; however, he is actually skewering religious hypocrisy. His targets are mystics (Sufis) and preachers (*khatibs*) who claim that the road to union with God begins with the denial of physical pleasure, vanity, pride, greed, etc., but who at the same time pleasure themselves because they lack the funds to buy love. The Persian language itself abets Zakani's exposure of sanctimonious mystics: *jalq*, or "jerking off," happens to rhyme with *dalq*, the thick woolen cloak worn by novice Sufis. These two words are rhymed in the refrain. Surrounded by the obscenities of Zakani's harsh social criticism, traditional *tashbib* imagery seems wildly out of place. Here is the third stroph:

> We are vulgar toughs from Kalmuk land,
> Bohemian buzzards, a thieving band.
> With beloveds we plot all night and day,
> With lovers months and years we while away.
> For sugar-mouthed darlings we'd gladly die;
> We'd give our souls for boys with jasmine thigh.
> We are the bane of tedious preachers;
> Against two-faced Shaykhlings and false teachers.
> We've given cunt and ass a goodbye kiss,
> Although the both of them we'll sorely miss.
> So listen, brother, if you've half a brain,

You'll heed this onanist's timeless refrain:
Let's masturbate, for jerking off's a ball;
It's fun to whack it 'neath a woolen shawl!

(*Suppressed Persian*: 51)

The fourth strophe is typical of Zakani's three-fold approach: attacks on the cloaked novices' drunkenness and solitary vice, the undermining traditional erotic language, and recapitulation with the *jalq/d£11q-rhyming* couplet:

All night, all day, around the town we go,
Searching for distilleries, high and low.
We're drunken fools, alive and courageous,
Smitten by moon-faced beaus and outrageous!
Their lasso locks have bound our minds and hearts;
Their eyebrows have pierced our body parts.
We are immune to time's unkindly ways,
Exempt from malevolent and wicked days.
No cunt? No ass? No worries or alarms;
For we're bohemians with mighty arms.
So have a seat and pull out that big thing,
And masturbating, we'll happily sing,
Let's masturbate, for jerking off's a ball;
It's fun to whack it 'neath a woolen shawl!

(*Suppressed Persian*: 51–2)

Zakani is a perverse follower of Ghazalian principles. He avoids eroticism for its own sake, using it instead to scourge the hypocrisy of corrupt clerics and self-indulgent seminarians.

Modern Eroticism

One of the most striking differences between modern Persian eroticism (starting in the late 19th century) and the classical is the emergence of women's writing on the topic. Scholars mention one bona fide woman eroticist of the classical period: Mahsati of Ganja (12th century). Though very little is known about the poet (Meier), anthologists and literary biographers attribute to her a cycle of bawdy quatrains (rhyme scheme: a, a, b, a) in which she expresses her needs to her "husband" in the crudest terms:

I'm Mahsati, the fairest of the flock,
O preacher's boy, you good-for-nothing bum,
For beauty famed from Mashhad to Iraq;
We're through if I've no bread or meat or cock!

(*Suppressed Persian*: 3)

Very few other women dared to express their sexual desire so bluntly in Persian until the early 1950s, when Forugh Farrokhzad (1935–1967) wrote "Goniih" [Sinning]:

In arms burning and hot I sinned a sin that utterly pleased me
I sinned in his arms, and burning iron-strong and avenging was he

In that dark and silent meeting
the eyes I saw were full of mysteries
My heart in my breast shook, anxious to answer his hungry eyes' pleas

In that dark and silent meeting
I rested in his arms, undone
From his lips desire poured into mine and my wild heart's gloom was gone

I chanted the story of love in his ear:
I want you, O life of this life of mine
I want you, O life-giving embrace
You—O mad lover of mine!

Passion struck a flame in his eyes
In the cup the wine danced red
Against his breast my own body shivered drunk in the yielding bed

I sinned a sin that pleased me utterly in arms that trembled with ecstasy
In that dark and silent meeting
O God, whatever happened to me?

(Farrokhzad: 127–8)

The difference between the language of lust in this poem and stock *tashbib* imagery of classical eroticism is marked. Instead of the conventional "kissing and embracing" and "sugary lips," the poet speaks of palpably "burning and hot arms" [*agbushi garm-o atashin*]. Farrokhzad also pictures a specific act of passion with a series of prepositions: pouring the story of love *down into* her lover's ears *on* a bed, *within* its yielding softness. The shock of this specificity has not worn off; and the debate about the literary merit of the poem continues (Katouzian). For her open affront to propriety, many critics have classed Farrokhzad with the *A/fiye va shaljiye* authors of old (Langaroodi: 2: 193).

But Farrokhzad was much more imaginative than such a dismissive judgment suggests. She fashioned a vocabulary from nature that was well suited to the expression of her own particular yearnings. In "Union," the narrator's lover is a murky figure, sometimes liquid, sometimes fire:

I saw him breaking over me in waves like the red glow of fire
like a watery reflection
like a cloud tremulant with rains
like a sky breathing summery warmth . . .

The hour flew
The curtain blew off on the wind
I had pressed him
in the aura of the flames
I wanted to speak
but strang_
the shadowing weight of his eyelashes
streamed from the depths of darkness
during that long reach of desire
and the shuddering, that death-tainted shuddering
down to my roots.

(Farrokhzad: 34–5)

Simin Behbehani (b. 1927), Farrokhzad's contemporary, occasionally uses a classical form, the *ghazal* (ode), to explore erotic themes. About the same time as Farrokhzad's "Sinning" (1956), she wrote "Naghme-ye ruspi" [The Prostitute's Song], which is typical of the modern tendency to write erotically from the point of view of the object of affection. The poem approximates the thoughts of Banu Mahvash, a famous entertainer and prostitute (Behbehani: 128):

Pass me the rouge,
so I can add some color to my colorlessness.
Pass me the ointment,
so I may revive my face withered from sorrow.

Pass me the perfume,
to give my flowing hair the scent of musk.
Pass me that tight-fitting dress,
so people may hold me tighter in their embrace.

Pass me that see-through shawl,
to make my nakedness twice as enticing in its folds,
to add to the allure of my breasts and legs. . . .

How tiresome he was, how repulsive, my companion
last night.
But when he asked me, I told him,
I had never seen a man as handsome.

In the short story *Safar-e 'E_mat* [*E_mat's Journey*, or *The Passing of Innocence*] by Ebrahim Golestan (b. 1922), an ironically named prostitute visits one of Shiite Islam's holiest shrines in an attempt to regain her purity. As she prays near the sepulchre of the Imam:

memories of the nights at the house were swept away, the smell of sweat vanished, and the terrible bloodstain at the end of her anguish. The drunkenness and the nausea were dispelled. The man whose breath failed him, the man with a heavy body, the man smelling of manure, the man whose manliness under his round, balloon-tight stomach dangled like the last autumn leaf from the hollow trunk of a tree, panting in useless desire, unable to reach her.
(Golestan: 149)

Another significant trend in modern Persian is the increasing divergence of domestic and expatriate erotica in the language. After the Iranian revolution of 1979, the number of expatriate users of the language increased markedly. Some writers living abroad in relatively uncensored exile have produced a wide variety of works that can be called erotic. There is even a journal called *Shahrzad* that regularly publishes original Persian works and translations that address such taboo topics as clitoridectomy, homosexuality, and pre- and extramarital love. Because the prevailing sociocultural climates of places where Persian is an official language are to one extent or another "anti-erotic," expatriate writing on sexual matters has proliferated in reaction.

Bijan Gheiby, who is also a scholar of classical literature, has produced something quite novel in Persian: erotica for its own sake, without any socially redeeming value. His description of an exotic dancer follows the modern inclination toward specifity, not one eyebrow is bowed, and instead of being pomegranate or citrus, breasts are pneumatic:

Past 11:00 at night, one of the towns of the American west, in a bar. A girl dancer, half naked, half conscious. She says her family on one side goes back to the Indians, and for this reason she brags about her American origins. Her face is young and thin, and doesn't go at all with her tubby figure. She is wearing a strapless, one-piece bathing suit, which has a map-of-the-world pattern on it; the Indian Ocean covers her belly and between her legs, and North America takes up her ass. Sometimes she removes from a rack a large black cowboy hat that, she said, a man from Montana had given her, and places it over her breasts—now bared—and dancing this way, she bends over and straightens up without letting the hat fall off. At the table, in order to make her happy I asked with feigned amazement how she did it. She explained it to me, and with her hand demonstrated how she squeezed her breasts together and stuffed them down into the hat, and then released them so that they pushed in two directions keeping the hat from falling. (Gheiby, *Haft*: 14)

Though such writing was possible in Persian-speaking environments before the neo-puritanism of the Islamic Republic or of the Taliban in Afghanistan, one never encountered it in mainstream publications. The only type of literature in which such erotica might have found a home was social satire, where it might be considered socially redeeming. This makes such writing a throwback to the mock-treatises of 'Obeyd-e Zakani.

Perhaps the best satirical eroticist in the modern era is Iraj Mirza Jal'ul Mamalik (1873–1926), a prince of the Qajar dynasty. His 515-line 'Arefname (1921) begins with a complaint against the famous poet, pederast, and singer 'Aref Qazvini. Iraj became enraged when he learned that the poet was in Mashhad with his lover but failed to pay him a visit and share the boy. This seemingly trivial slight inspired an attack on gender segregation, pederasty, and veiling that is full of obscene and erotic language.

Veiling and gender segregation were deplorable to Iraj because they led to widespread pederasty in Iran. He saw this vice on every level of Iranian society, from the lowly *amm* to his own circle, the *caret*, or "aristocracy" (a pun on his victim's name that Iraj never tires of using):

> O Lord, what this is this pedomania
> That plagues 'Aref and greater Tehrania?
> Why is it only in this commonwealth
> That sodomy takes place with little stealth?
> The European with his lofty bearing
> Knows not the ins and outs of garçon-tearing.
> Since Iran's haven to every donkey buck,
> Who else are these asses going to fuck?
> If anyone with reason knew this score,
> They'd surely yowl with a hearty *cri de coeur:*
> Until our tribe is tied up in the veil,
> This very queerness is bound to prevail.
> The draping of the girl with her throat divine
> Will make the little boy our concubine.
> You see: A cute and cuddly little boy,
> Who's ready to become your fawning toy;
> Not seen: His sister, naked without her wimple,
> So there's no hope of doting on her dimple.
> (*Suppressed Persian:* 82)

The most erotic part of the 'Arefname is its parable about a woman who is seduced but keeps her modesty, because she remains steadfast throughout the ordeal. This poem within a poem plays on the paradoxical nature of the veil. On one hand, as a covering or "curtain," it is intended to preserve modesty, to prevent illicit stares. On the other hand, by cloaking the body, it fuels erotic interest in what is underneath, fetishizing parts of the female body that would not otherwise be erogenous. The prophylactic nature of veiling emerges at the end of the parable when Iraj draws his moral. He accuses women who wear the full covering, or *chador,* and mask of impersonating vegetables:

> Pardon me, but are you some onion-ball,
> A garlic in *chador* or praying shawl?
> You who're the mirror of God's Divine Splendor,
> A turnip sack of undetermined gender?
> Bound at both ends when down the lane you careen,
> Not like a lady—maybe aubergine?
> (*Suppressed Persian:* 89)

But in the parable itself, the *chador* is provocative. The narrator remembers the time when, as a youth, he heard the seductive *khesh-o fish,* or "rustling," of a passing veil. It appears that the partial concealment of a woman's throat, chin, and lips makes the ultimate object of his desire, her *kos* [cunt], even sexier. The seduction also encorporates polite *tashbib* imagery that clashes with the poem's obscenities. It begins:

> Those days when I was still a simple boy,
> I faced the door of a haramsaroy,
> Out came a woman with a rustling sound,
> Who made the blood in my veins jump around.
> I saw a bit of throat under her clip,
> A little chin and hints of lovely lip.
> These peeked out from behind her veil as might
> Slivers of the moon on a cloudy night.
> I approached her and politely salaamed,
> And said that someone had just telegrammed.
> Doubtful, the fairy-face tried to remember,
> Who could the bearer be and who the sender?
> (*Suppressed Persian:* 83–4)

The ruse works, and when the boy finds himself alone with the lady, he marshals every progressive argument he can to get her to *de-lJejab.* But like the courtesans and beardless boys of the classical period, she coyly resists:

> The rascals in this town, I do declare!
> al-LAH al-MIGHty, keep them very rare!
> Tell me to unveil—hardy har, and, HAR!
> The nerve! The brazenness! al-LAH akBAR!
> To hell with you! Am I some kind of whore,
> Who'd appear to the proscribed sans *chador?*
> The aim of this whole thing was my disgrace;
> I see it all now and spit in your face!
> Never would I've experienced husbandhood,
> Unless I had kept hidden to those I should.
> (*Suppressed Persian:* 85)

When the seduction actually occurs, instead of preventing adultery, the veil acts as an aphrodisiac. Because a woman's honor resides in her *chador,* so long as it remains intact during the act of adultery, the lady can pretend that she has not

1021

sinned. Instead of reciting progressive arguments for de-lejabization, the boy woos the lady with crisps. The new tack proves fruitful and, true to the realism of modern erotic writing, he narrates the progress of his love in specific detail:

My hands caressed that beauty with the love
A mullah showers on his rice pilav.
I tossed her on the carpet like a rose;
Frantic, I raced from her heights to her toes.
My nerves had made me clumsy by surprise;
My hands slipped from her ankles to her thighs.
My heart was racing as she'd buck and rear;
She talked and talked but I would hardly hear.
Her hands: clamped across the veil on her face;
My hands: busy exploring another place.
I said, "You guard the heights, keep the coast clear,
I'll get the bunker ready from down here."
Although her thighs were hard to penetrate,
I was soon staring at the pearly gate.
I saw a budding *kos,* new-blossomed red,
A jonquil cunt, half-asleep in its bed;
Outside, the lemon fragrance of Shiraz,
Inside, the honey-soaked dates of Ahwaz;
Brighter than the face of a believer,
Purer than the breed of a retriever.
Not depilated, but a hairless *kos*
That makes mouths water like sour grape juice.
The rarest cunt of cunts, the smallest bore
Against my cock its width engaged in war. . . .
But, since her purity was in her visage,
She kept it tightly veiled from start to finish;
The hold she had was two-fistedly good,
Lest she lose something of her "chastitude."
(*Suppressed Persian:* 87–8)

Despite its inventiveness and message of female emancipation, the *'Arefname* never appeared uncensored in the homeland of its creator, though many know it by heart. The current arbiters of the canon are as anti-erotic as their puritanical forebears. This means that the gap between domestic and expatriate literature will continue to widen until it becomes unbridgeable. Of course this prediction does not merely apply to erotic literature.

PAUL SPRACHMAN

Further Reading

Anvari, Owl.ad ai-Din 'Ali. *Divan* [1352]. Edited by Modarres Ralavi. Tehran: Bonyad-e Tarjome, 1973.

_ef, Mohammad Hashem. *Rostam al-tavarikh* [1352]. edited by Mohammad Moshiri. Tehran: Amir Kabir, 1973.

Behbehani, Simin. *A Cup of Sin.* Edited and translated by Farzaneh Milani and Kaveh Safa. Syracuse, NY: Syracuse University Press, 1999.

Iami Nodushan, Mohammad 'Ali. *Jam-e lahan-bin* [1355]. Tehran: Tus, 1976.

Farrokhi Sistani. *Divan* [1349]. edited by Mohammad Dabir Siaqi. Tehran: Zovvar, 1970.

Farrokhzad, Forugh. *Bride of Acacias.* Translated by Jascha Kessler with Amin Banani. Delmar, NY: Caravan Books, 1982.

Foruzanfar, Badi' ai-Zaman. *Sokhan va sokhanvaran* [1350]. Tehran: Khvarazmi, 1971.

Ghazali, Abu Hamid Imam Mohammad. *Kimia-ye Sa' ada* [1361]. edited by H. Khadivjam. 2 vols. Tehran: Markaz-e Intisharat-e 'Elmi va Farhangi, 1982.

Gheiby, Bijan, "Amrad-bazi dar iran." In *KhordeMaqaIat,* 294–322. Bielefeld, Germany: Nemudar, 1977.

———. *Haft, tarl) va do she'r.* Bielefeld, Germany: Nemudar, 1997.

Golestan, Ebrahim. "'E_mat's Journey." In *Stories from Iran: A Chicago Anthology, 1921–1991,* edited by Heshmat Moayyad, translated by Carter Bryant. Washington, DC: Mage, 1991.

Gorgani, Fakhr ai-Din As'ad. *Vis-o Ramin* [1338]. edited by Mojtaba Minovi. Tehran: Beroukhim, 1959.

Ijafe_, Kh Vaje Shams ai-Din Mohammad. *Divan* [1362]. edited by Parviz Natel Khanlari, Tehran: Sehami, 1983.

al-Jajarmi, Mohammad b. *Badr,Mo'nes al-AI;1rar fi daqa'eq aI-ash'ar.* edited by Mir _aleh. Tabibi, Tehran: Anjoman-e Athar-e Melli, 1958–71.

Katouzian, Homa. "Az Gonahan-e Fomgh Farrokhzad." *Iranshenasi* 12 (Summer 2000): 264–87.

KhaIeghi Motlagh, DjaIal. "Tan-kameh-sarai dar adab-e falsi." *Iranshenasi* 8 (Spring 1996): 15–54.

Langaroodi, Shams. *Tarikh-e TaI;11ili-e She'r-e Now* [1370–77]. Tehran: Nashr-e Markaz, 1991–98.

Lazard, Gilbert. *Les premiers poetes persans IXe–Xe siècles. (siecles): Fragments rassembtes, edites et traduits.* Vol. 2: Textes persans. Paris: Maisonneuve, 1964.

Manuchehri Damghani. *Divan* [1348]. edited by Mohammad Dabir Siaqi. Tehran: Zovvar, 1%9.

Maq_ud, Javad. *Shar};l-e A};lval-e Baba faher 'Oryan* [1354]. Tehran: Athar-e Melli, 1975.

Meier, Fritz. *Die Schone Mahsati: Ein Beitrag zur Geschichte des Persischen Vierzeilers.* Wiesbaden: Franz Steiner, 1963.

Ne_i 'AruQi, _ad b. 'Omar. *ChahiirmaqaJe1.* edited by Mohammad Qazvini. Leiden: E. J. Brill, 1910.

Rypka, Jan. *History of Persian Literature.* edited by Karl Jahn. Dordrecht, Holland: D. Reidel, 1968.

Sana'i Ghaznavi. *Divan* [1354]. edited by Modarres Raqavi. Tehran: Sana'i, 1975.

San'ati, Mohammad, _adeq Hedayat va haras az marg [1380]. Tehran: Nashr-e Markaz, 2001.

Sprachman, Paul. "*Le Beau garçon sans merci:* The Homoerotic Tale in Arabic and Persian." In *Homoeroticism in Classical Arabic Literature.* edited by J.W. Wright and Everett K. Rowson. New York: Columbia University Press, 1997.

———. *Language and Culture in Persian.* Costa Mesa, CA: Mazda, 2002.

Suppressed Persian. Edited and translated by Paul Sprachman. Costa Mesa, CA: Mazda, 1995.

PERSIAN: MEDIEVAL VERSE

A gender/genre distinction exists in medieval Persian poetry: long narrative poems (epics, romances), insofar as they deal with erotic subject matter, are concerned almost exclusively with heterosexual relationships; short poems (lyrics, epigrams) are frequently addressed by an older male speaker to a preteen or teenage male, or refer to a relationship between such a couple. The lack of gender distinction in Persian pronouns renders the addressee/subject of many poems ambiguous, but it is probably safe to assume, unless there is internal evidence to the contrary, that many, and perhaps the majority, of short poems which take sexual desire as their theme are addressed by males to younger males. Long poems which are compendia of short anecdotes (these are often mystical in orientation, e.g, the longer works of Sanai, Attar, and Rumi) include both heterosexual and homosexual anecdotes apparently indiscriminately.

In addition to being a literary topos, pederasty certainly existed as a social phenomenon at the medieval Persian courts, where most poetry of the period was written. It is explicitly referred to, for example, in the *Qabusnameh* [*Mirror for Princes*], an 11th-century text by a local king for his son (the writer recommends that boys are best for the summer, girls for the winter). Attempts to suggest that this was due to the influence of central Asian Turkish mores (by, the Iranian literary historian Zabiholla Safa) seem wide of the mark, as boy-love was a significant element of a number of aristocratic cultures, from the Mediterranean to India, from antiquity to the early medieval period (including ancient Iran; see Herodotus, Book 1, Section 135, who says that the Persians learned the custom from the Greeks), and for considerably longer in some areas (e.g., Safavid Iran).

Although pederasty as a literary topos predates Islam, it was modified by Muslim mores. In the work of the influential Arab poet Abu Nuwas (c. 750–815), for example, it is associated with wine drinking (forbidden by Islam) and a more or less blasphemous/contemptuous attitude toward Islamic orthodoxy. Such associations are also to be found in Persian poetry, and an atmosphere of bibulous pederasty, centered on the beautiful *saqi* [cupbearer/Ganymedean figure] and existing in defiance of Islamic orthodoxy, is a given of much medieval Persian lyric and epigrammatic verse. Suggestions of heterodoxy are increased by the fact that the *saqi* is often a non-Muslim (a Zoroastrian, Christian, or, in Persian poetry written in India, Hindu). Despite this suggestion of interfaith sexual relations, it is never the case in such poetry that a non-Muslim adult male desires a Muslim boy. In keeping with the general ancient and medieval notion of sexual relations as basically power relations (signified by who is penetrating whom), it is always the older, active, speaking partner who is Muslim, and the younger, passive, addressed partner who may be of another faith. Although the poetry can imply the speaker's tangential or contemptuous attitude toward orthodoxy, only relationships that confirm Islam's dominant social position vis-à-vis other faiths are celebrated.

The association of pederasty with religious heterodoxy is also to be found in the considerable amount of mystical poetry (traditionally regarded with some suspicion by the orthodox) which refers to the topos, either literally or as a metaphor, of the soul's longing for God. The praise of Yusuf's (Joseph's) beauty in the Qur'an, and the interpretation by Sufis (Muslim mystics) of this as being emblematic of Divine beauty, gave apparent scriptural authority to mystical justifications for a preoccupation with male beauty. As Sufi literature's other major metaphor for mystical desire and insight is wine drinking and drunkenness, the details of such poems are often virtually indistinguishable from their secular counterparts. Such ambiguity was often deliberately cultivated (e.g., by Hafez, 1325–1389), and it is sometimes virtually impossible to decide whether the wine and the *saqi* of a given poem are meant literally, or as metaphors for spiritual experience, or both. In the same way that pederasty was a reality of medieval courts, it was often assumed to be a reality in the all-male gatherings of Sufis, which were typically organized around a Sufi master in ways reminiscent of a secular court, with similar relationships of authority and subjection. Both detractors of Sufis and Sufis themselves warned of the possibility of the Sufi *pir/morid* (master/ aspirant) relationship turning into a sexual one. The ritual (practiced by some Sufis) of using beautiful male adolescents as the focus of mystical contemplation was particularly frowned upon.

The work and career of the prominent Sufi poet 'Eraqi (1213–1288) may be taken as indicative of pederasty's ambiguous status in Sufi experience and literature. Many of 'Eraqi's poems can be read as declarations of passionate physical desire addressed to adolescent males: however, his *Estelahat-e Sufiyeh* [*Sufi Idioms*] is one of the first of many handbooks explaining the secular imagery, including erotic elements, of Sufi poetry as a series of metaphors for the mystic's longing for God. This might have decided the matter were it not that 'Eraqi's life was shadowed by accusations of inappropriate homoerotic infatuation, suggesting that his poetry's sentiments were not in fact solely metaphors for mystical aspiration. Paradoxically, pederasty was seen both as a scandal of Sufism (whereas it seems to have been accepted with much less anxiety as a part of court culture) and, in its metaphorical form at least, as a mark of spiritual authenticity. This latter association is reminiscent of Platonic (as in the *Phaedrus* and the *Symposium*) and neo-Platonic teaching, although there is scholarly dispute as to whether a direct influence from neo-Platonism on Sufi spirituality is discernible.

In general we can say that pederastic references are common in Persian lyric and epigrammatic poetry during the medieval period and that in a courtly context they were presented as unexceptionable. However, when they occurred in Sufi poetry, they were sometimes viewed as more problematic and in need of an explication that denied their literal import.

DICK DAVIS

Further Reading

'Eraqi. *Majmu'eh-ye asar-e Fakhr alDin 'Eraqi* [1372]. edited by Dr. Nasrin Mohtasham. Tehran, 1993.

Safa, Zabihollah. *Tarikh-e adabiyat dar Iran* [1366]. 5 vols. 7th printing. Tehran, 1987.

Schimmel, Annemarie. *Mystical Dimensions of Islam*. Chapel Hill, NC: University of North Carolina Press, 1975.

———. *As Through a Veil: Mystical Poetry in Islam*. New York: Columbia University Press, 1982.

Southgate, Minoo. "Men, Women, and Boys: Love and Sex in the Works of Sa'di." *Journal of the Society for Iranian Studies* 17 (Autumn 1984): 413–52.

Sprachman, Paul. *Suppressed Persian: An Anthology of Forbidden Literature*. Costa Mesa, CA: Mazda, 1995.

Wright, J.W., and Everett K. Rowson (eds.) *Homoeroticism in Classical Arabic Literature*, New York: Columbia University Press, 1997.

PERSIAN: VERSE ROMANCE

The earliest examples of Persian verse romance were written in the 11th century and draw extensively on pre-Islamic (pre-7th century) material. The most significant is *Vis and Ramin* by Gorgani (c. 1050), a work which shares many features with the Tristan story of western Europe, and for which it may be one source. The most notable pre-Islamic feature of the tale is its countenancing of sexual relations considered incestuous under Islam but meritorious in pre-Islamic Iran (e.g., between a brother and sister; Vis's first husband is her brother, Viru). This provides a frisson of transgressive sexuality for the tale's Islamic audience which was absent for its original, pre-Islamic audience. In Gorgani's work, carnality is represented for its own sake, and his poem refers to corporeal matters, especially as they pertain to women, with an unembarrassed frankness rare in contemporary Islamic poetry. Thus, Vis's menstruation, her defloration, her and her lover's delight in one another's physical charms, and her husband's impotence are all openly represented. Extramarital female sexuality and desire are celebrated rather than demonized.

Nezami (1140–1203) drew extensively on Gorgani's work for the rhetoric with which he presents carnal love, but the origins of three of his four narrative poems are to be found in Ferdowsi's *Shahnameh* (completed in 1010), an epic poem recording the exploits of Iran's pre-Islamic kings. Two of these, *Haft Paykar* [*The Seven Portraits*] and *Khosrow and Shirin*, are romances involving erotic material. Taking a hint from Ferdowsi's Bahram Gur (the hero of Nezami's *Haft Paykar*, who at one point says, "Whether he's a prince or a warrior, a young man finds comfort and happiness with women. They are the foundation of our faith, and they guide young men toward goodness"), erotic love in these two tales is seen largely as an *education sentimentale* for the hero, who is guided by love to become a more chivalrous and ethically aware ruler. Since the emphasis is now on spiritual rather than carnal experience, in Nezami's romances unfulfilled love is as intrinsically interesting as consummated love. An important subplot of *Khosrow and Shirin*, for example, concerns the hopeless and ultimately suicidal passion of the stonemason Farhad, who is Khosrow's rival for Shirin's favors. Unfulfilled love and its attendant mental and spiritual states are also the subject matter of Nezami's one narrative which does not utilize pre-Islamic Persian material, *Leili and Majnun*. This originally Arab story concerns the interdicted love of the children of tribal enemies, and the resulting madness of the hero, Majnun (his name means "maddened," "gone mad"), which leads him, like the similarly maddened French Arthurian hero Yvain, to abandon civilized society for a life among animals in the wild.

The emphasis on the mental state of the male protagonist in Nezami's narratives gives them a didactic, allegorical, and at times mystical tone which is quite absent from the work of his 11th-century predecessors in the field of romance. The propensity for allegory and implied mysticism is clearest in the *Haft Paykar*, considered by most commentators to be Nezami's masterpiece. Although his romances abound in erotic situations and eroticized descriptions of female attractiveness, erotic activity per se is almost always subordinated to ethical and chivalric considerations. Thus in the locus classicus of voyeuristic scenes in Persian poetry, when Khosrow catches sight of Shirin bathing, the poetry leaves us in no doubt of either Shirin's beauty or Khosrow's desire, but Khosrow turns away in order not to embarrass Shirin, and no sexual activity results from the encounter. Despite their male orientation, and the function of women in them primarily as beautiful educators, Nezami's works show a real sympathy with women's possible roles in a male-dominated world. The pervasive tenderness of their female portraits renders them generally free of overt misogyny and obvious women-directed male anxiety.

Matters are otherwise in the works of Nezami's best-known successor, Jami (1414–1492), whose primary concerns were Sufism (mystical and didactic), explicitly allegorizing erotic encounters in mystical terms, and whose works can easily be read as evincing both misogyny and a fascinated horror of female sexuality. His erotic scenes are both more explicit and more prurient than Nezami's (for premodern Iranian schoolchildren his works once had the reputation that Ovid's had for premodern European schoolchildren, as a source in respectable literature for the most excitingly sexy stories). Their baroque rhetoric can be seen primarily as an attempt to surpass Nezami, but the vehemence of their apparent emotional concern can seem neurotic (rather than purely literary) in intensity.

Like Nezami, Jami also wrote a *Leili and Majnun*, but his two best-known romances are *Yusof and Zuleikha* (which tells the story of Joseph and Potiphar's wife as it appears in the Qur'an, which lays great stress on Yusof's [Joseph's] beauty), and *Salaman and Absal*. The erotic scenes in *Yusof and Zuleikha* are among the most sexually graphic in any medieval Persian romance. *Salaman and Absal* is an allegorical fantasy in which the concupiscent female character (Absal) represents the infinitely attractive physical world which the male, Sufi aspirant (Salaman) must renounce in order to attain spiritual insight. In both these works the purity of the beautiful young man is the focus of the author's didactic purpose, and the lust for him felt by the female protagonist is presented as simultaneously carnally arousing and morally questionable. A homoerotic subtext is arguably present in both tales, with the heroine's desire for the beautiful hero standing in for the (male) reader's response: this desire can be seen as both validated (as the reader's, and male) and invalidated (as the heroine's, and female).

In the 400-year history (11th to 15th centuries) of the medieval Persian romance, a number of linked developments can be discerned: from the empirical to the allegorical and didactic; from the celebration of carnal experience to its devaluation except as a prelude to, or metaphor for, spiritual experience; and an increasing suspicion of female sexuality per se.

DICK DAVIS

Further Reading

Burgel, J.C. "The Romance." In *Persian Literature*, edited by Ehsan Yarshater, 161–78. Albany, NY: Bibliotheca Persica, 1988.

Gorgani. *Vis o Ramin* [1337]. edited by Mohammad Ja'far Mahjub. Tehran, 1958; as *Vis and Ramin*, translated by George Morrison, New York: Columbia University Press, 1972.

Jami. *Haft Owrang* [1378]. edited by A. Asahzad and H. A. Tarbiyat. 2 Vols. Tehran, 1999.

Nezami. *Haft Peykar* [1377]. edited by Behruz Servatiyan, 1998; as *The Haft Paykar: A Medieval Persian Romance*, translated by Julie Scott Meisami, Oxford and New York: Oxford University Press, 1995.

———. *Khosrow o Shirin* [1366]. edited by Behruz Servatiyan, 1987.

———. *Leili o Majnun* [1364]. edited by Behruz Servatiyan, 1985.

Meisami, Julie Scott. *Medieval Persian Court Poetry*. Princeton, NJ: Princeton University Press, 1987.

Najmabadi, Afsaneh. "Reading—and Enjoying—'Wiles of Women' Stories as a Feminist." *Iranian Studies* 32 (Spring 1999): 203–22.

Najmabadi, Afsaneh, and Karen Merguerian. "Zulaykha and Yusuf: Whose 'Best Story'?" *International Journal of Middle Eastern Studies* 29 (1997): 485–508.

PETRONIUS ARBITER

d. 66 CE
Roman author

There are several Roman persons of the name Petronius, but most scholars now agree that Petronius Arbiter, a senator at the imperial court of Nero and Master of the Revels (*Arbiter elegantiae*) is the probable author of the *Satyricon* (more correctly *Satyrica*, being possibly a wordplay on the Roman literary genre of satire and the sexual exuberance of satyrs, the unruly and lascivious attendants of the wine god, Bacchus). If this is so, then he can be identified as the pleasure-seeking aristocrat who eventually committed suicide by imperial decree as described by the historian Tacitus (c. 56–120 CE) (*Annals* 16, 18–19). It is highly unlikely that in revenge he intended the *Satyrica* as an unflattering attack on Nero. The *Satyrica*, of which only extensive fragments survive, appears to have been a lengthy novel in prose and verse. A humorous and sophisticated work, it satirizes the excesses of oratory and poetry of the time

of Nero and contains literary parody and burlesque.

Book 15, which was discovered near Belgrade in Dalmatia in about 1650, was first published in Padua (Italy) in 1664. It is virtually complete and constitutes the "Cena Trimalchionis" [Feast of Trimalchio], an extravagant satirical portrait of an ignorant, vulgar upstart, formerly his master's sex toy, who lives in luxury near Naples. The remainder of the extant portions of the novel consists of a series of substantial fragments described from the point of view of Encolpius, one of the major characters. Encolpius is traveling with his boyfriend Giton and two companions, Ascyltus (an ex-slave on the make) and Eumolpus (a lecherous poet and double-dealer). Part of the narrative describes the sexual rivalry between Encolpius and his fellow travelers for the favors of Giton. The rest tells of the encounters and adventures which these disreputable characters have as they wander through southern Italy (Campania and Crotona). Some critics, like Branham and Kinney, see in the novel "a systematic and paradoxical inversion of Roman norms" (*Satyrica*); while others, like Ernout, assert that it is vain to attempt to discover any thematic structure in it at all (*Le Satiricon*). It is frequently asserted that a probable key is the section in the *Satyrica* devoted to the "Wrath of Priapus" (Priapus being the god of fertility, who had an enormous phallus). This would in some way be a subversion of Homer's "Wrath of Achilles" (from the *Iliad*), or the "Anger of Poseidon" (from the *Odyssey*), for our unheroic hero Encolpius seems to have offended against the god in an earlier (lost) chapter and is now being punished by having become impotent.

In addition, it is quite possible that the *Satyrica* constitutes a parody of the standard romantic Greek novel (as, for example, Heliodorus's *Aethiopica* [*Ethiopian Tale*]), in which a pair of heterosexual lovers finally achieve a chaste reunion after many tribulations. But these interpretations remain speculative. The *Satyrica* contains a variety of very lively erotic scenes. The brothelkeeper, Quartilla, obliges Encolpius, Ascyltus, and Giton to perform the rites of Priapus: as Giton consummates his "marriage ceremony" with the seven-year-old Pannychis, Quartilla gets excited while watching through a keyhole (16–26). She is a priestess of Priapus; as is the rather dilapidated Oenothea (134–8), from whom Encolpius will seek a cure for his impotence, only unfortunately to cause the death of her favorite goose, with its suggestively shaped neck. In this later part of the novel the whole of the Circe episode (126–141), which contains another parody of Homer by using the name of the enchantress in the *Odyssey*, centers on Encolpius's ironic inability to service her sexually. Even punishment by whipping with nettles will not do the trick. Circe prefers degraded sexual objects, such as slaves or lovers in rags (she turns men into swine in the *Odyssey*), and this adds a further level to the sexual suggestiveness of the text. Ascyltus, who has lost his cloak in the public baths, is applauded for the size of his member (92); Encolpius, when impotent, castigates his cock for letting him down; Lichas, a sea merchant, who featured earlier in the lost part of the story, reappears and recognizes Encolpius by his genitals. And Lichas, in fact, has a wife, Tryphaena, who seems equally to have shared Encolpius's favors in the past and is now expecting to make up for lost time. This married pair

are bent on sex and revenge, but an untimely storm provides them with a watery grave (103–113). Encolpius and Ascyltus quarrel over Giton (6–11), and later Ascyltus and Giton abandon Encolpius (79–82), with a joyful reunion of Encolpius and Giton to follow. A couple of false suicides satirize the commonplaces of romantic fiction by having rogues enact the parts of young lovers in despair: Encolpius, intending to hang himself, uses a rotten rope, which breaks; Giton threatens to cut his own throat with a blunt razor. Ascyltus eventually comes looking for Giton, who hides under the bed, like Odysseus clinging to the underbelly of a ram to avoid the giant Cyclops Polyphemus (97–99). A bed also features when Encolpius and Eumolpus are in Crotona: they are entrusted with two children by fortune-hunting parents when Eumolpus, posing as a sick but rich old man, has his bed humped up and down by his servant to service the girl, while Encolpius at the keyhole satisfies his own desires with the boy.

Two inserted "Milesian Tales" survive among the fragments. In the first (85–87), Eumolpus tells how a boy from Pergamum (Asia Minor) connives at his own seduction when promised a reward, but as the stakes rise higher and a horse is demanded, the deal falls through. In the second, "The Matron of Ephesus" (111–112), the standard theme of the weakness and lustfulness of women is amusingly exploited (alternatively it could be read as a realistic lesson in taking pleasure as it comes): a widow has vowed to keep watch over her husband's corpse, but when a handsome soldier arrives, she soon recognizes the advantages of a live body. However, the gallows which he is supposed to be guarding is robbed during his assignation in the tomb, and so the husband's corpse is hoisted up instead, as a sacrifice from the dead to the living.

In the past, the *Satyrica* was presented as a satire against vice, but nowadays we can more openly enjoy its realistic portrayal of gay low life.

PATRICK POLLARD

Editions

The Satyricon. Translated by M. Heseltine. London and Cambridge, MA: Loeb Library, 1913 (and reprinted).

Le Satiricon. Troisième édition, corrigée. edited by A. Ernout. Paris: Les Belles Lettres, 1990.

Satyrica. Translated by R.B. Branham and D. Kinney. London: J.M. Dent, 1996. (English text only.)
The Satyricon. Translated and edited with explanatory notes by P.G. Walsh. Oxford: Clarendon Press, 1996.
The Satyricon. Translated by J. P. Sullivan. Harmondsworth: Penguin Books, 1977.

Further Reading

Conte, G.B. *The Hidden Author: An Interpretation of Petronius's Satyricon*. Berkeley and Los Angeles: University of California Press, 1996.
Courtney, E. *A Companion to Petronius*. Oxford: Oxford University Press, 2001.

Konstan, D., *Sexual Symmetry: Love in the Ancient Novel and Related Genres*. Princeton, NJ: Princeton University Press, 1994.
Scobie, A. *Aspects of the Ancient Romance and Its Heritage: Essays on Apuleius, Petronius and the Greek Romances*. Meisenheim am Glan: Hain, 1969.
Slater, N.W. *Reading Petronius*. Baltimore: Johns Hopkins University Press, 1990.
Sullivan, J.P. *The Satyricon of Petronius: A Literary Study*. Bloomington: Indiana University Press, 1968.
Walsh, P.G. *The Roman Novel: The Satyricon of Petronius and the Metamorphoses of Apuleius*. Cambridge: Cambridge University Press, 1970.
Williams, C.A. *Roman Homosexuality*. Oxford: Oxford University Press, 1999.

PHILOSOPHY AND EROTICISM IN LITERATURE

The idea of literature, in the modern sense of written works characterized by both beauty of form and emotional effect, is a category of relatively recent invention. To be precise, the exploration of philosophy and eroticism "in literature" in a Western context dates back to only around the seventeenth century, when the notion of literature began to take on its present significance. Nonetheless, prior to the development of literature per se, philosophical reflections on the meaning, function, and nature of erotic desire have often taken what modern readers would consider to be literary forms. Perhaps the best-known examples of this intermingling of philosophy and literature *avant la lettre* are Plato's dialogues on love, among which the *Symposium* and the *Phaedrus* in particular have served as foundational texts for a Western tradition of the analysis of *erōs* (or erotic love) as playing a crucial role not only in the human experience of beauty but in the quest for philosophical truth.

The *Symposium* (written between 384 and 379 BCE) and the *Phaedrus* (375–365 BCE) examine the relationship between philosophy and *erōs*, a passion most perfectly and consistently expressed, for Plato, in the love of one man for

another (or, indeed, in the love of a man for a beautiful boy). In the *Symposium* as in the *Phaedrus*, the philosophical love of truth is reflected in the erotic love of earthly beauty. Both dialogues, with their imaginative re-creations of historical figures and settings as well as their emphasis on highly suasive speech, draw the reader into fictional spaces in order to illustrate the essential interconnectedness of erotic love and philosophy.

Furthermore, the *Phaedrus* explicitly links the pursuit of beauty and philosophical truth to the more literary art of rhetoric, which Plato reads as ideally enabling audiences to come closer to wisdom (just as erotic love allows the lover to develop a more complete understanding of Form). In a sense, rhetoric and *erōs* play similar roles: both give a privileged access to truth. In addition, both are a source of tremendous pleasure, which, in Plato's terms, "directs the soul."

Other early writings on eroticism investigate the connections between poetry, sexual love, and philosophical or analytic knowledge in more explicitly theological frameworks. The Old Testament Song of Songs, with its provocative imagery evoking the sexual love between bride and bridegroom, has long been read allegorically as an illustration of the ideal relationship between God and the human soul (or the community of believers embodied in the Church). In this sense, the Song of Songs presents a theory of the nature of religious faith as an expression of (erotic) love. In a different context, the *Kamasutra* (written in Sanskrit in the third century CE) describes the cultivation of erotic knowledge as an essential component of experience. Here the poetic depiction of an erotic "art of pleasure" serves to demonstrate the full compatibility of processes of sexual and spiritual development.

What draws such disparate writings together is the way in which each one presents the poetic and philosophical exploration of erotic desire as in some sense profoundly connected to collective or communal truths rather than to the detailed depiction of human sexuality as necessarily private, intimate, or personal. In these early works, the expression of an erotic philosophy takes on poetic or rhetorical forms in order to transmit general or universal truths more effectively to diversely constituted communities of readers.

Around the eighteenth century, the collective or social function of poetic examinations of eroticism was significantly transformed with the development of the literary genre that has remained perhaps more devoted than any other to the intimate, individualized, and above all detailed portrayal of erotic love and sexual desire: the novel. The rise of the Enlightenment in Europe and the West more generally coincided with the heyday of the philosophical novel, which provided a highly malleable and innovative forum for the investigation of theories of material existence, the body, and sexuality. Philosophical novels (a genre which could include frankly pornographic writing) worked to persuade readers of epistemological and ontological truths through the sympathetic presentation of individual characters who solicit readerly identification with their positions (whether intellectual or sexual). John Cleland's *Fanny Hill*, to take one example, is both the sexy tale of the experiences of a "woman of pleasure" and a polemic in defense of materialist philosophy. In *Fanny Hill*, sexual pleasure is portrayed as both natural and rational; a detailed rendering of sexuality sheds light, for Cleland, on the truth of human nature itself in a manner consistent with the tenets of an enlightened empiricism.

While Cleland's work promotes a vision of sexual desire as joyous (and even egalitarian),

the most (in)famous eighteenth-century writer of philosophical novels took a different perspective. The marquis de Sade, also a deeply committed materialist, dedicated himself to the literary portrayal of a philosophical perspective centered around the notion of *erōs* as a destructive, albeit overwhelmingly natural, force. In his novels, de Sade shows with great expertise how the development of rational philosophical knowledge may coincide powerfully with the literary depiction of exemplary scenarios of instruction. His texts thus prevail upon the reader to see the fundamental resemblances between literature and philosophy as means of persuasion. Moreover, the most exquisite expression of his materialist philosophy is in the literary portrayal of the violent act of sexual intercourse as an allegory of universal aggression.

Modern writers of philosophical erotica (including, for instance, Georges Bataille and the surrealists) have often had to confront the lingering authority of the de Sadean oeuvre. Yet it may be the combined influence of the feminist and gay rights movements (whose relationship to de Sadean philosophy is often tenuous) that had the most visible and widespread effects on literary depictions of theories of sexuality in the twentieth century. Writers as varied as Dorothy Allison, Gloria Anzaldúa, Angela Carter, Ana Castillo, Hélène Cixous, Samuel R. Delany, Audre Lorde, Cherríe Moraga, and Edmund White have worked to transfigure readers' understandings of sexuality and desire by examining the relationship between expressions of erotic longing and political, intellectual, and social liberation. In a sense, by illustrating poetically the way in which desires make and move individuals, these modern authors rework and rediscover the Platonic analysis of the pleasures of rhetoric, eroticism, and philosophy as profoundly and potently intertwined.

NATANIA MEEKER

Further Reading

Alexandrian, Sarane. *Histoire de la littérature érotique.* Paris: Seghers, 1989.

Barthes, Roland. *A Lover's Discourse: Fragments.* Translated by Richard Howard. New York: Hill and Wang, 1978.

Bataille, Georges. *Erotism: Death and Sensuality.* San Francisco, CA: City Lights Books, 1986.

Brooks, Peter. *Body Work: Objects of Desire in Modern Narrative.* Cambridge, MA: Harvard University Press, 1993.

Cleland, John. *Fanny Hill, or Memoirs of a Woman of Pleasure.* edited by Gary Gautier. New York: Modern Library, 2001.

Dean, Carolyn J. *Sexuality and Modern Western Culture.* New York: Twayne, 1996.

Hunt, Lynn, ed. *The Invention of Pornography: Obscenity and the Origins of Modernity, 1500–1800.* New York: Zone, 1993.

Lorde, Audre. "Uses of the Erotic: The Erotic as Power." In *Sister Outsider: Essays and Speeches.* Trumansburg, NY: The Crossing Press, 1984.

Plato. *The Symposium and the Phaedrus: Plato's Erotic Dialogues.* Edited and translated by William S. Cobb. Albany: State University of New York Press, 1993.

Reiss, Timothy J. *The Meaning of Literature.* Ithaca, NY: Cornell University Press, 1992.

Rosario, Vernon A. *The Erotic Imagination: French Histories of Perversity.* Oxford: Oxford University Press, 1997.

Solomon, Robert C., and Kathleen M. Higgins, eds. *The Philosophy of (Erotic) Love.* Lawrence: University Press of Kansas, 1991.

The Song of Songs: A New Translation. Translated by Ariel and Chana Bloch. Berkeley and Los Angeles: University of California Press, 1998.

Vatsyayana, Mallanaga. *Kamasutra.* Translated by Wendy Doniger and Sudhir Kakar. Oxford: Oxford University Press, 2002.

PIERRE, JOSÉ

1927–1999
French novelist, dramatist, and art historian

José Pierre arrived in Paris in 1951, very quickly joined André Breton and the Surrealist movement, and began to participate in its activities and assemblies. He thus met Eric Losfeld, the future publisher of *Emmanuelle,* and saw in this encounter a sign of destiny. Pierre began to appear in Surrealist reviews, publishing articles on the history of painting and defending Surrealist theory of graphic art. Around 1965, he undertook his first novel, *Qu'est-ce que Thérèse? C'est les marronniers en fleurs* [*What Is Thérèse? She Is the Blooming Chestnut Trees*], which title is comes directly from the Surrealist game of questions and answers. The fundamental themes that Pierre would explore and extend in his subsequent novels are present in the first: initiation of a group into sensuality and libertinage, fascination for just-nubile girls, absence of sin and guilt, transgression of all familiar bonds, lesbianism. But his main problematic lies in the question of the frontier between love and libertinage. If erotic books and films intend to show that desire and love are the same, Pierre's characters, on the contrary, try to overcome and sublimate the difference between them.

In that first novel, Thérèse organizes initiations and dominations of young boys and girls. A large part of the novel takes place in a castle, a traditional place of orgy, but its originality is in the large space given to philosophical conversations about pleasure and ethics, as in de Sade's novels. Thérèse is the incandescent point at which all desires converge, and her departure to Phnom-Penh at the end of the novel unravels all the relations of the little group. The plot folds in a dreamy, wonderful atmosphere of erotic heroism, each character "challenging destiny constantly without admitting to being overcome by his victories."

Thérèse appears again in *Les adolescences de Thérèse,* the only novel of Pierre's in which the narrator is the heroine. She tells with suavity the story of her deflowering by her father (preceded by mutual masturbation, fellatio, cunnilingus, and a delicious lesbianism) and the gradual techniques she invented to seduce both boys and girls. This narrative form is recurrent in several of Pierre's novels, in which the narrator becomes the initiator of young girls who always fall in love with him, confirming that libertinage cannot do without love.

Blend of Styles

Pierre allowed himself to try a number of different styles. In *Le dernier tableau,* he uses the style of American pulp thrillers of the 1930s–40s; in *La fontaine close,* he chooses the narrative structure of a Gnostic novel; in *Femmes de braise,* he sets the plot in the world of whores and pimps in the south of France. For him, the erotic roman favors these miscellanea, as de Sade did. In *Le dernier tableau*, the fusion is complete between an erotic/existential problem and an aesthetic one, set during the period of abstract expressionism in New York City in 1953. *Gauguin aux Marquises* develops a plot on three levels: the diary of a script girl working on a film about the painter Gauguin; the script, sequence after sequence; and Gauguin himself speaking of love and painting.

Pierre's originality lies in the plastic exploration of the erotic by mixing different types of narration and organizing the plot as a series himself giving up the idea of becoming a painter in the 1960s, the novelist writes as a painter draws, and builds his erotic arrangements of bodies as does a sculptor. His experience as an art critic can be discerned in *La haine des plages,* the plot of which tells of the initiation of a nymphet by the narrator, under the eyes and with the agreement of her mother, who takes pictures of their sexual acts. Then the mother covers up the genitals and breasts by colors or drawings. These photos look like puzzles that both reveal and conceal the tracks of passion between the protagonists, and reveal the jealousy of the mother. In *Les baisers de la femme fidèle,* the frolics unfold according to the 16th-century Mannerist style of the painter Domenico Beccafumi, the novel's wet kisses and caresses echoing of the curves and lushness of the Italian painter.

The writer doesn't deny himself philosophical or psychoanalytic thoughts. Freud is regularly mentioned in support of bisexuality or to explain the heroes' fascination with women smoking before fucking. In his evocation of agricultural and sexual communes in *Les barreaux du coeur,* Pierre refers to Charles Fourier, the French utopian socialist of the 19th century, especially his theory of harmony founded on the alternation of love and work.

Pierre's novelistic work is complemented by a number of plays in which erotic scenes are written as he would like them to happen. *Le vaisseau amiral* (Bordeaux, 1981, directed by Patrick Simon) represents a party involving two men and a woman. *Magdeleine Leclerc* (Paris, 1993, directed by Thomas Lévy) tells of the apprenticeship of reading, writing, and sexuality that constituted de Sade's last love. In this last of his published plays, Pierre wanted to paint the Marquis "in love like a beetle."

Pierre's writing is Precise and tender. He uses refined words and elegant syntax, for erotic novels are for him like fairy tales. He remains a Surrealist writer through his fascination for beauty, especially that of young girls, in which can be seen the future woman emerging from childhood. His characters are always in love and joyously share sensuality and pleasure. Elegant candor and gentle brutality alternate in a constant, and astonishing necessity of each other. As he writes: "Love [can be] anywhere. . . . It's the key to the world."

Biography

Born in the French Landes. Contacted the Surrealist group in 1952 and frequented it until its dissolution in 1969. Published in many reviews. Professor of literature in 1955. Wrote several historical books about painting from 1966 to 1991. Organized many international exhibitions on Surrealism: New York, 1962; Paris, 1967; Cologne and Bari, 1983; Vilamoura, Portugal, 1987. Joined the CNRS (Centre national de la recherche scientifique) and worked on Surrealist flyers and posters. From 1974 to 1996, wrote erotic novels and theatre.

DOMINIQUE PAQUET

Editions

Novels

Qu'est-ce que Thérèse? C'est les marronniers en fleurs. Paris: Le Soleil Noir, 1974.
Eva, Viviane et la fée Morgane. Paris: Galilée, 1980.
La haine des plages. Paris: Galilée, 1980.
La charité commence par un baiser. Paris: Galilée, 1980.
Gauguin aux Marquises. Paris: Flammarion, 1982.
La fontaine close. Paris: L'Instant, 1988.
Femmes de braise. Paris: France Loisirs, 1994.
Le prince de Padoue. Paris: France Loisirs, 1994.
Les adolescences de Thérèse. Cadeilhan: Zulma, 1995.
Le dernier tableau. Grignan: Complicités, 1996.
Les barreaux du cœur. Paris: Cercle Poche, 2004.

Theatre

Le vaisseau amiral ou les Portugais. Paris, Denoël, 1969.
Magdeleine Leclerc (Le Dernier amour du Marquis de Sade). Chambéry: Comp'Act, 1995.

Art (Selected Works)

Le cubisme. Paris: Rencontre, 1966.
Le surréalisme. Paris: Rencontre, 1967.
L'Univers surréaliste. Paris: Somogy, 1983.
André Breton et la peinture. Geneva: L'Age d'homme, 1987.
L'Univers symboliste. Paris: Somogy, 1991.

PIERROT

Pseudonym of author of French novel of seduction

Une séduction [*A Seduction*], an erotic novel signed by "Pierrot," appeared in 1902 and was sold discreetly out of the back of the bookshop of André Hal, a Parisian librarian and publisher. This work was published again, mainly for bibliophiles, in 1908, "sold everywhere and nowhere" and titled *Jeunes amours, au château, à la pension* [*Young Love, at the Castle, at the Boarding House*]. It became a classic of French eroticism during the 20th century. *Une séduction* is a beautiful tale about the initiation into sexual pleasures of a young man and a young woman from high society. The novel's style lacks crude descriptions, and settings and costumes are presented as most exquisite and, above all, extremely stimulating, owing to the intense passions boiling inside the young protagonists.

The story unfolds in Touraine, by the Loire River, at Messange Castle, owned by the marquis André, whose daughters Claire, eighteen years old, and Marguerite, thirteen years old, grew up together with Claude, an orphan adopted by the marquis, now twenty years old. While catching crawfish, Claude, hidden behind a bush, discovers Claire getting undressed. "Believing she was alone in that remote location, she opened wide her blouse to enjoy the wind's touch, and Claude, who had never seen anything more of her than just her face and hands, was able to admire the ravishing breasts of the young woman." He realizes that he loves her and that the goal of his life is to possess her. "The craziness of sexual passion and the intoxication of the flesh went through him like the wind blowing during a storm that sweeps everything out of its way. He felt he was defeated. He needed Claire at any cost. He would not rest until he had satisfied this lust frenzy that drove him, as vertigo anticipates the abyss." Claire loves him too, but her prude upbringing causes her to be scared away by the kisses he is able to snatch from her, and Claude has to seduce her gradually.

All these failed attempts only serve to his ardor, and he would have sickened of sheer frustration without Germaine, the maid, a piquant Parisian who was previously employed by a lady of dubious refinement who had numerous lovers. When Claude discovers Germaine in a barn making love to Jean, the coachman, "It was the wild brutality and superb strength of the coupling of the male and the female." He is obsessed by the desire to enjoy the body of the pretty maid, although he initially resists this obsession, "to avoid profaning his love for Claire," but he gives in to his temptation. In the course of a few nights of love, Germaine initiates him into all known ways of lovemaking. When, at last, Claire finally gives herself to Claude, he knows not only how to take her virginity, but how to teach her sensual pleasures that would transform her into a passionate lover who dares anything.

There are several initiations in this novel. The younger Marguerite is a precocious adolescent who spies on her sister's lovemaking and provokes Germaine and Claude with the sole purpose of discovering its pleasures. Sent to boarding school after summer break, Marguerite imparts sex education to her female companions in an astonishing way. During this time, Germaine, introduced to the delights of sapphism by her previous female boss, seduces Claire. When Claude has to leave for military service, the young woman consoles herself with the maid to avoid being deprived of carnal affection. But one should not forget that "[t]he two lovers proclaimed a touching farewell, by mutually promising to meet again afterward and to love each other forever." Nothing seems too corrupt in this book, either morally or in terms of the insistent beauty of the characters.

The anonymous author of this novel poses a literary enigma. The bibliography by Louis Perceau suggests "Dr. Brennus," who published *L'Art de jouir ou traité pratique des caresses voluptueuses* [*The Art of Enjoyment, or the Practical Compendium of Voluptuous Caresses*]

(1908), as a possible author. It was discovered at the Bibliothèque Nationale that Dr. Brennus was one of the many pseudonyms of Dr. Jean Fauconney, who, under the names of "Dr. Caufeynon" and "Dr. Jaf," published several books on sexuality, such as *Histoire de la femme* [*The History of the Woman*], *L'Amour lesbien* [*Lesbian Love*], *Les Venus impudiques* [*The Indecent Venuses*], and *La Volupté et les parfums* [*Sensual Pleasure and Perfumes*]. In Fauconney's *Scènes d'amour morbide* [*Morbid Love Scenes*] (1903), his heroine Emma is a prostitute whose specialty is the satisfaction of sexual perverts, and publication of the book was restricted by the publisher to "be sold under strict control and to persons of a certain age." In *L'Hermaphrodite au couvent* [*The Hermaphrodite in the Convent*] (1905), Fauconney narrates the adventures of Paula d'Hestier, who becomes Paul, and therefore is able to "enjoy the role of the man and the woman during sexual intercourse." In *L'Amour secret* [*Secret Love*], he teaches us how a man can initiate a woman into pleasure, the same subject as *Une séduction*. One might reasonably assume that Jean Fauconney, before specializing in popular sexology, started with this mundane novel.

However, the Dutel bibliography states: "Pierrot is the pseudonym of Roland Brévannes, who usually signed his works about sexuality under the name of Dr. Brennus." Brévannes's authorship can be equally argued. His collection *Les voluptueuses* [*The Voluptuous Women*] (1903–1910), published by the Parisian publisher Offendstadt, consists of a series of small and comparatively polite novels: *Amante cruelle* [*The Cruel Female Lover*], *Amoureux caprices* [*Amorous Caprices*], *Charmeuse* [*Seductress*], *Corruptrice* [*Corruptress*], and *Courtisane légitime* [*Rightful Courtesan*]. In 1907, Brévannes created the *Almanach du déshabillé* [*Almanac of the Naked*] (with some suggestive illustrations), in which he described "Les 36 positions de la femme du XXe siècle" [The 36 Positions of the Woman of the 20th Century]. But is this enough to prove that Pierrot was Dr. Brennus, who wrote a compendium about premature ejaculation? It remains unclear, since there is no proof. Jean Fauconney and Roland Brévannes have at least one thing in common: they wrote books about black masses (Fauconney in 1905, Brévannes in 1908).

We will probably never know who wrote *Une séduction*. We can only read it as the work of Pierrot—perhaps the real author was thinking of the character of that name from the Commedia del'arte and the *Theater of the Tightrope Walkers,* wearing a black cap and a white collar, a symbol of fantasy for the poets of those times.

SARANE ALEXANDRIAN

Selected Works

Alexandrian, Sarane. *Histoire de la littérature érotique.* Paris: Seghers, 1989.
Dutel, Jean-Pierre. *Bibliographie des ouvrages érotiques publiés clandestinement en français entre 1880 et 1920.* Paris: Privately maintained, 2002.
Perceau, Louis. *Bibliographie du roman érotique au XXe siècle.* Paris: Georges Fourdrinier, 1930.

PIGAULT-LEBRUN, CHARLES

1753–1835
French novelist and dramatist

Although Pigault-Lebrun's first successes were achieved in the theatre, and a number of his novels spawned stage versions penned by others, his name remains identified with an early-neneteenth-century form of comic fiction known as *le roman gai*, a genre of which he was the sole inventor. Composed in the later years of the Revolution and during the first years of the Empire, his risqué productions, which F.C. Green, following Saintsbury, described as "joyous coarse novels of adventure in the manner of

Smollett," exploit a hallowed tradition of Gallic humor that harks back to Rabelais and the prominent carnivalesque strain in French medieval culture. With the partial exception of the sentimental and moralistic *Angélique et Jeanneton* (1799), the title page of which suggested that mothers could safely allow the contents to be read by their daughters, the novels of Pigault-Lebrun's first period are licentious, picaresque fictions featuring episodes of sexual opportunism loosely strung together. The male protagonists, whether sympathetic young foundlings on the make or libidinous members of the clergy, possess an overriding inclination to find happiness through the pleasures of the flesh, while the representatives of the female sex are scarcely less inhibited. Alongside the multiple scenes of private sexual congress, characters regularly find themselves in involuntary states of public undress, to the delight of concupiscent onlookers. At all times, sexual appetite and its satisfaction are the subject of earthy amusement rather than a sophisticated exploration of erotic impulses. Although Pigault-Lebrun, as a man of the eighteenth century, was keen to allege a philosophical purpose, it was undoubtedly the proliferation of salacious and smutty detail that caused the success of his more notorious novels. The strong vein of anticlericalism betrays his Voltairean inheritance, as well as being the motive force behind his widely read assault on the Christian religion, *Le Citateur* (1803).

In his fiction Pigault-Lebrun does not merely delight in a transgression of decorum or in the conspiratorial relationship he establishes with his reader, but overtly relishes the fictionality of his creations. He makes extensive play with the far-fetched nature of the chaotic episodes in which the characters become embroiled and, in a manner reminiscent of Diderot's *Jacques le fataliste* (to which novel *L'Enfant du carnaval* [1796] is explicitly linked through the presence of the term "rhapsodies" in its subtitle), engages in a self-conscious questioning of the activity of novel writing. The tone of his compositions is set by the satirical subtitle of *Les Barons de Felsheim* (1798); by the spurious indication that *L'Enfant du carnaval* was published in Rome at the "Imprimerie du Saint-Père" (or "Papal Press") and *Le Citateur* in Hamburg; and by the title-page epigraph of *L'Enfant du carnaval*: "Valeat res ludicra" [Farewell to the comic stage]. Yet his novels also borrow elements from contemporary Gothic scenarios in which the hero and/or heroine are thwarted by the malevolent actions of those in power.

Although *Monsieur Botte* (1803) has received plaudits for the way its depiction of bourgeois character prefigures the nineteenth-century French realist novel and Pigault-Lebrun's admirers have sometimes singled out *Les Barons de Felsheim* as his masterpiece, it remains *L'Enfant du carnaval* that gives the best idea of his basic formula. Echoing Fielding's *Tom Jones* and the works of Laurence Sterne (amongst other eighteenth-century classics), it depicts, in the first person, the life and adventures of the illegitimate son of a Franciscan monk and an aged clerical housekeeper, who is conceived, without premeditation, on top of a dish of spinach left out on the kitchen table (the omission of this scabrous scene from the third edition apparently aroused mass indignation). After a childhood involving a number of vicissitudes, Jean, or Happy as the character is philosophically renamed on becoming Lord Tillmouth's servant, acquires a social and artistic education. His lasting love for the nobleman's daughter is returned, though it is no obstacle to his enjoying other sexual adventures. The couple face various adversities, including imprisonment during the Revolutionary Terror, before Happy ends up as a prosperous London businessman.

The instant success of Pigault-Lebrun's novels was a striking example of a literary genre creating its audience rather than supplying an already advertised need, but in addition it was enhanced by astute promotion by his publisher, Barba. It has been claimed that the profitability of his writing was the result of a high rate of production rather than exceptional print runs, though the copies acquired by the newly founded lending libraries were instrumental in securing his reputation.

As Thomas Love Peacock observed, Pigault-Lebrun's novels are "impressed with the political changes of the day." The earliest of them represent a response to the desire for unalloyed pleasure that manifested itself in the years following the end of the Terror. The author's archetypal heroes of modest origins (the hero of *Mon oncle Thomas* [1800], a pirate who rules over an island on which marriage is banned, is the son of a prostitute) succeed in making their way to the top through their own initiative and even marry into noble families. Pigault-Lebrun's novels periodically fell foul of the censor, both in the immediate aftermath of their publication and during the more conservative Restoration. A token 50 copies of *La Folie espagnole* (1799) were apparently seized in the year of its publication. In 1825, both *L'Enfant du carnaval* and *Monsieur de Roberville* (1809), which depicts a newly married couple's obsessive dedication to bedroom activity, were banned and Barba's publisher's license withdrawn.

The anonymous and unashamedly pornographic *L'Enfant du bordel* (1800) cannot be attributed to Pigault-Lebrun with certainty, but he is a more plausible author of this short narrative than Mirabeau. (The presence of a lecherous Franciscan friar provides undeniable continuity with *L'Enfant du carnaval*.) The adolescent Chérubin, a superficial echo of Beaumarchais's character in *Le mariage de Figaro*, is the illegitimate son of a sixteen-year-old royal page and a young girl espied by him in a shop doorway, who subsequently dies in childbirth. Chérubin is brought up in a brothel, which he, accompanied by his favorite inmate, Félicité, is later forced to flee in the first in a series of loosely linked burlesque adventures reminiscent of the *roman gai*, in which the threats of death or penury are never remotely real and are brought to an end by his being reunited with his father. The young hero's charms and vigor are found irresistible by the female sex, regardless of their age, class, or marital status. Although sexual deviance is present in the form of homosexual acts (male and Sapphic), troilism, and cross-dressing, these are largely for the sake of a comic "plot" that requires tricks to be played on the unwary (these include the far-fetched attribution to Chérubin successively of hermaphroditism and a giant clitoris). The work is essentially a paean to the delights of unrestrained heterosexual intercourse, though with a notable emphasis being given to reciprocal oral pleasuring and masturbation. If all these activities are directly described (the text includes bawdy songs in which slang terms for the sexual organs are prominent) and the female genitalia the focus of much celebration by the hero, the composition, arguably at least, recognizes equality between the sexes, through due insistence on the female characters' capacity for experiencing correspondingly high levels of sexual pleasure. The pornographic is, nonetheless, subordinated to the comic throughout and represents an attractive broadening of the scope of conventional comic fiction rather than the creation of a specialized, more secretive, or illicit reading experience.

Pigault-Lebrun's novels were much imitated and were the subject of various spurious sequels. Existing bibliographical accounts of his work contain manifest errors of date and attribution, partly owing to the fact that no single library possesses a complete holding. Further, detailed research will be necessary before an authoritative bibliography of his work is possible. Accounts of his life have relied almost exclusively on the racy essay compiled by Barba the year after his death, the claims of which might usefully be checked against such archival evidence as exists.

Pigault-Lebrun's mantle was assumed by the soon equally prolific, but less philosophically or politically inclined, Paul de Kock, who astutely timed his first major assault on the popular market to coincide with Pigault-Lebrun's retirement from the *roman gai*. Balzac, whom Sainte-Beuve scornfully dubbed "the duchesses' Pigault-Lebrun," considered Pigault-Lebrun underrated and imitated his manner in one of his pseudonymous early fictions: *Jean Louis, ou la fille trouvée* (1822). Stendhal was a self-confessed admirer, and in 1821 had one of his fictional personae choose Pigault-Lebrun as his desert-island author. The lack of modern reprints has inhibited more recent appreciation of his work, which has also been the subject of less scholarly attention than it merits, though the poet Paul Valéry may be counted one of his more unexpected admirers.

Biography

Born Charles-Antoine-Guillaume Pigault de l'Epinoy into a family of magistrates, Calais, April 8; educated by Oratorians in Boulogne. Worked for a merchant named Crawford in London before eloping with latter's daughter (who died in a storm at sea), 1769–71; held in prison on *lettre de cachet* obtained by his father, 1771–73; served in *gendarmerie du Roi*, Lunéville, c. 1773–76; imprisoned in attempt by father to thwart marriage to Eugénie Salens, impoverished daughter of a deceased merchant, 1776–78; abetted by jailer's daughter, escaped disguised as a woman. Married Eugénie in Holland, c. 1778; she died several years later. Actor and playwright in Low Countries, 1778–88.

Discovered father had secured annulment of his civil status; adopted name Pigault-Lebrun. Birth of son, Jean-Baptiste-Guillaume Pigault-Le Brun in Tournay, 1785. Returned to Paris, 1788. Success as playwright in Paris, 1788–92, notably with the autobiographical *Charles et Caroline, ou les abus de l'Ancien Régime*, 1790. Enlisted in dragoons; saw active service at Valmy, 1792. Read speech to Société des Amis de la liberté et de l'égalité de Saumur', May 26, 1793. Resumed career as playwright, 1794. Publication of first novel, *L'Enfant du carnaval*, 1796. Appointment as secretary to Madame Murat vetoed by Napoleon, as was his appointment as librarian to his friend Prince Jerome in Westphalia, 1806. *Chef de bureau* in French customs service, 1806–24. Abandoned novel writing for eight-volume history of France, 1823–28. Following the death of his son in a duel, moved to Valence to live with his daughter (married to lawyer Victor Augier; their son would become the playwright Emile Augier). Published *La Sainte Ligue*, an historical novel, 1829. Returned to Paris, 1830. Died at La Celle Saint-Cloud, July 24, survived by second wife, sister of the actor Michot.

MICHAEL TILBY

Selected Works

L'Enfant du carnaval, histoire remarquable et surtout véritable pour servir de supplément aux rhapsodies du jour. 2 vols. Rome: Imprimerie du Saint-Père [sic], 1796; reprinted with a preface by Roland Virolle, Paris: Desjonquères, 1989; as *The Shrove-Tide Child; or the Son of a Monk*, anonymous translation, London, 1797.

Les Barons de Felsheim, histoire allemande qui n'est pas tirée de l'allemand. 4 vols. Paris: Barba et Ouvrier, 1798; as *The Barons of Felsheim*, anonymous translation, London, Lane, Newman & Co [Minerva Press], 1804; as *The History of Tekeli*, a translation of a portion of part II by Catharine B. Thompson, Albany, NY: H. C. Southwick Printers, 1815.

La Folie espagnole. 4 vols. Paris: Barba, 1799; reprint [with *Le Citateur*] edited by B. de Villeneuve [Raoul Vèze], Paris: Bibliothèque des curieux, 1914.

Mon Oncle Thomas. 4 vols. Paris: Barba, 1800; as *My Uncle Thomas*, anonymous translation, London: William Lane [Minerva Press], 1801.

Monsieur Botte. 4 vols. Paris: Barba, 1803; as *Monsieur Botte*, anonymous translation, London: Lane and Newman [Minerva Press], 1803.

Jérôme. 4 vols. Paris: Barba, 1805.

L'Homme à projets. 4 vols. Paris: Barba, 1808.

Monsieur de Roberville. 4 vols. Paris: Barba, 1809.

L'Enfant du bordel. 2 vols. Attributed to Pigault-Lebrun. Paris, 1800; as *Les Aventures de Chérubin, l'enfant du bordel*, Cythère [Paris]: À L'Enseigne de la Volupté [Maurice Duflou, 1924]; reprinted with introduction by Michel Delon, Cadeilhan: Zulma, 2002; and in *L'Erotisme au XIXe siècle*, edited by Sarane Alexandrian, Paris: J. C. Lattès, 1993.

Further Reading

Barba, Jean-Nicolas. *Souvenirs de Jean-Nicolas Barba.* Paris: Ledoyen and Giret, 1846.

Berkovicius, André. "Visages du bourgeois dans le roman populaire (1799–1830)." *Romantisme* 17–18 (1977): 139–55.

Dagen, Jean. "Stendhal à la manière de Pigault-Lebrun. (Un modèle méconnu de *La Chartreuse de Parme*?)." *Littératures* 14 (1986): 59–75.

Girault de Saint-Fargeau, Eusèbe. *Revue des Romans. Recueil d'analyses raisonnées des productions remarquables des plus célèbres romanciers français et étrangers.* Vol. 2, 167–72 (these pages are virtually identical to a section of Barba's *Souvenirs* of 1846). Paris: Firmin-Didot, 1839.

Green, F.C. *French Novelists from the Revolution to Proust.* London and Toronto: J. M. Dent, 1931; new rev. ed., New York: Ungar; London: Constable, 1964.

Grimaldi, E.F. *Hommage à la mémoire de Pigault-Lebrun.* Paris, 1840.

Guise, René. "Le Roman populaire." In *Manuel d'histoire littéraire de la France.* Vol. 4, pt. 2, edited by Pierre Abraham and Roland Desné, 371–74. Paris: Editions sociales, 1973.

Jones, James F., Jr. "Bakhtin, Pigault-Lebrun, and the Ideologies of Two Carnivals." In *Transactions of the Eighth International Congress of the Enlightenment.* Bristol, July 21–27, 1991. Vol. 1, 326–30. Oxford: The Voltaire Foundation, 1992.

Le Breton, André. *Le Roman français au XIXe siècle.* Paris: Société française d'imprimerie et de librairie, 1907.

Ludlow, Gregory. "The Novels of Pigault-Lebrun." Unpublished Ph.D. dissertation, McGill University, 1970.

———. "Pigault-Lebrun and the Satire of the Novel After *Jacques le fataliste*." *French Studies* 27.1 (January 1973): 9–15.

———. "Pigault-Lebrun, a Popular French novelist in the Post-Revolutionary Period." *French Review* 46.5 (April 1973): 946–50.

———. *A Successful Novelist-Tradesman: Pigault-Lebrun*, 117–28. French Literature Series. Columbia: University of South Carolina Press, 1973.

Lyons, Martin. *Le Triomphe du livre. Une histoire sociologique de la lecture dans la France du XIXe siècle.* Paris: Promodis/Editions du cercle de la librairie, 1987.

Nathan, Michel. *Splendeurs et misères du roman populaire.* edited by René-Pierre Colin, René Guise, and Pierre Michel. Lyon: Presses universitaires de Lyon, 1990.

———. "Les Voyages picaresques de Pigault-Lebrun." In *Voies, voyages, voyageurs dans la littérature*, edited by Kasimierz Kupisz. Vol. 2. Lodz: Wydamictwo Uniwersytetu Lodzkiego, 1994.

Olivier-Martin, Yves. *Histoire du roman populaire en France.* Paris: Albin Michel, 1980.

Oppici, Patrizia. *Bambini d'inchiostro. Personaggi infantili e 'sensibilité' nella letteratura francese dell'ultimo Settecento.* Pisa: Goliardica, 1986.

Peacock, Thomas Love. "French Comic Romances" and "The Epicier." In *Memoirs of Shelley and Other Essays and Reviews,* edited by Howard Mills, 207–13 and 217–29. London: Hart-Davis, 1970.

Petitot. "Pigault-Lebrun." With revisions by Ernest Desplaces. In *Biographie universelle ancienne et moderne,* edited by Michaud, new edition, vol. 33, 301–7. Paris: Delagrave, 1870–73.

Rodmell, Graham E. *French Drama of the Revolutionary Years.* London and New York: Routledge, 1990.

Saintsbury, George. *A History of the French Novel.* 2 vols. London: Macmillan, 1917–19.

Serfaty, Anne. "Nouvelles pièces anciennes? Réécritures dramatiques d'un roman de Pigault-Lebrun." In *Réécritures 1700–1820,* edited by Malcolm Cook and Marie-Emmanuelle Plagnol-Diéval, 271–80. Oxford et al: Peter Lang, 2002.

Vareille, Jean-Claude. *Le Roman populaire français (1789–1914). Idéologies et pratiques.* Limoges: PULIM; Quebec City: Nuit blanche, 1994. (See pp. 43–46 for an account of *Jérôme*.)

Vie et aventures de Pigault-Lebrun publiées par J.-N. B [arba]. Paris: Barba, 1836. According to Quérard, this was the work of Horace Raisson and merely based on notes provided by Barba; but Quérard's editors indicated that he later changed his opinion and attributed it to the equally prolific Louis-François Raban (see J.-M. Quérard, *Les Supercheries littéraires,* 2nd ed. enlarged and revised by Gustave Brunet and Pierre Jannet, Vol. 1, 428, Paris: Daffis, 1869).

PIRON, ALEXIS

1689–1773
French poet and playwright

Ode à Priape

Piron's *Ode to Priapus* (1710–11) is dedicated to the Phrygian god of fertility in Greek mythology (son of Dionysus and Aphrodite), who was said to have huge genitals. It consists of a celebration of the sexual act, concentrating upon ejaculation and describing *le foutre* [ejaculate] as both the source of physical pleasure and "la source féconde / Qui rend l'univers éternel" [the fertile spring that makes the universe eternal]. Historical and mythological references abound, and the vocabulary is crude.

Described by Piron in the preface to *La Métromanie* as having been written in a moment of "brief distraction," the *Ode* was circulated in manuscript and seen by the procurer general of Dijon, provoking a scandal which was difficult to suppress and which needed the intervention of Piron's protector, Jean Bouhier, president of the parlement of Dijon. Printed copies of the *Ode* have tended to truncate it, giving only 12 of the 17 stanzas and removing the most salacious.

Described as "le délire et le dérèglement d'une imagination de 18 ans" [the delirium and disturbance of an 18-year-old imagination] by Dufay (*Oeuvres complètes,* x: xvi), this first immature work was regretted by Piron later in his career, and has been seen by some critics as a reason for his unsuccessful campaigns for election to the Académie Française. (On the *Ode,* see Veréb, 81–3.)

Oeuvres badines

First published in 1796, the *Oeuvres badines* collects erotic songs and poetry from throughout Piron's career, as the presence of the much earlier *Ode à Priape* in the collection attests. It is also republished in the edition of Piron's works edited by Pierre Dufay, but has received little critical attention to date.

Different editions of the work present the contents in different orders, increasing the impression of a collection of diverse material, rather than a constructed volume. Some of the poems collected here have also been attributed to Jean-Baptiste Grécourt. One notable feature of the *Oeuvres* is the number of satirical references to Voltaire, which, even if toned down by Piron for publication, are still clear. A note to "L'Anti-*Mondain*" describes it as the counterpart to Voltaire's *Le Mondain* (1736). Similarly in "Le Tirliberly": a young couple is separated when the man is called away to sea; when the young woman asks him to leave his penis ("le tirliberly") as a keepsake, he throws it to shore, and the ensuing description of a passerby searching for it on the ground mocks Voltaire's exaltation of Newton: "Tel un visionnaire / (Mons Arouet, suzerain de Voltaire) / Cherche le jour dans la nuit de Newton! / Ou, si l'on veut, tel un savant breton [Louis Moreau de Maupertuis] / Grand scrutateur de forme planétaire" [Like a visionary / (His Lordship Arouet, Master Voltaire) / Searches for day in Newton's night! / Or, if you wish, like a Breton scholar [Maupertuis] / The great scrutinizer of planetary form].

A few references to the supposed homosexuality of the Jesuits also form part of Piron's comic inclusion of contemporary topics, and the lubricity of the clergy is amply discussed as one of the literary clichés of the day ("Les cinq voyelles" [The Five Vowels], "Le carme et le diable" [The Carmelite and the Devil], "Le port du salut" [The Door of Salvation]). The well-worn theme of the lubricity of monks is developed in a series of "Licentious Epigrams" and in the final piece, "My Testament," where Piron states: "Je veux qu'après ma mort, cent putains toutes nues, / Soient, dessus mon tombeau, cent fois par jour foutues, / Et que les cordeliers, en chantant leurs offices, / Aient tous les vits bandants dans le cul des novices" [After my death, I want a hundred naked whores, / Fucking a hundred times a day on my grave / And Franciscans singing their offices / With their stiff pricks in the cunts of novitiates].

More frequently, Piron's references are to classical antiquity, which lends a ready stock of stereotypes—to mock the non-erotic nature of wives (in "Leçon à ma femme")—along with such borrowed examples as Ulysses and Penelope, Hector and Andromaque, Jupiter and Juno, and Priapus (cf. the *Ode*), as in "Saint-Guignolé." Some pieces are pure galant poetry with far less emphasis on physical sexual pleasure and pornographic description; for example, "Thélème et Maccare" and "Les Misères de l'amour."

Biography

Born in Dijon, Piron was the son of Aimé Piron, an apothecary and writer of satirical poems.

In 1719, after studying law in Besançon, Piron moved to Paris, first working as a copyist, then writing plays for the Théâtre de la Foire, where his *Arlequin-Deucalion*, a dramatic monologue in three acts, was performed in 1722, during a period of intense rivalry with the Comédie Française and increasingly stringent restrictions upon the material forms which the actors of the Fair companies were allowed to employ. His best-known play is a comedy, *La Métromanie*, performed at the Comédie Française in 1738. His literary work is both abundant and varied, comprising tragedies, comedies, comic operas, epigrams, poems, satirical works, and epistles. His rivalry with Voltaire was long-standing, and a number of his works attack the philosophe and his ideas (see Verèb, 13–71).

MARK DARLOW

Editions

Oeuvres complètes illustrées d'Alexis Piron, publiées avec introduction et index par Pierre Dufay. Paris: François Guillot, 1928–31. The most complete and reliable edition of Piron's works.

Selected Works

Oeuvres badines d'Alexis Piron. Paris: Chez les marchands de nouveautés, 1796.
Chansons badines et joyeuses, par Piron, Collé, Panard, Gallet at autres. Paris: Le Bailly, 1862.
Contes érotiques et poésies libres d'Alexis Piron. Amsterdam, 1796. Pascale Verèb notes that the majority of the contents of this work are in fact not by Piron.
Epigrammes licencieuses. N.p.: Privately printed by the Friends of Maki, 1943.
Pironiana érotica. Paris: Chez les marchands de nouveautés, 1809.

Further Reading

Proschwitz, Gunnar von, ed. *Alexis Piron, épistolier: Choix de ses lettres*. Göteburg: Acta Universitatis Gothoburgensis, 1982.
———. "Alexis Piron, un moderne malgré lui: Réflexions sur le vocabulaire de ses lettres." *Le Français moderne: Revue de linguistique française* 49 (1981): 291–98.
Verèb, Pascale. "Alexis Piron, poète ou la difficile condition d'auteur sous Louis XV (1689–1773)." *Studies on Voltaire and the Eighteenth Century* 349 (1997): 632–35 (a list of epigrams and *contes* written by Piron).
———. "Alexis Piron, défenseur des Modernes ou un Episode inédit de la Querelle des Anciens et des Modernes." *Revue d'Histoire Littéraire de la France* 95 (1995): 282–93.

PIZARNIK, ALEJANDRA

1936–1972
Argentinean writer

Alejandra Pizarnik was the author of a large corpus of poetry, as well as selected prose works, letters, and diaries. She is best known for her poetry and her short prose work *La condesa sangrienta*. During her time in Paris she became very familiar with French writers, especially the Surrealists, and her work was highly influenced by such writers as Georges Bataille and Antonin Artaud. The most common themes of her work are language and silence, dichotomy (paradox and contradiction), madness, and death. Many of her poems express a link between eroticism and language, as well as a subtle lesbian sensuality, while her major prose work, *La condesa sangrienta,* deals with sadism and power and their relationship to sexuality.

In Pizarnik's poetry, the body is often related to the word, and eroticism comes alive in and through language. This connection is made clear in the prose poem "The Desire of the Word" from *El infierno musical*, "Ojalá que pudiera vivir solamente en éxtasis, haciendo el cuerpo del poema con mi cuerpo" [Oh God if I might live in ecstasy, making the body of the poem with my body] (*Obras,* 300). This "desire" for and of language can also transform itself into lesbian desire, as in the poem "Tragedy" from the same collection, in which a young girl in her backyard has sexual thoughts about her music teacher. She imagines that "she has nothing on under her red velvet" and that she rides her bicycle nude, squeezing harder and harder on the seat until it disappears inside of her. Such overt sexuality is rather rare in Pizarnik's poems, however, as most deal primarily with the relationship between language and the body and the subtle eroticism at play between the two.

While many of her poems are concerned with eroticism, it is in *La condesa sangrienta* that Pizarnik most explicitly writes of erotic themes while simultaneously expressing all of the themes seen in her other works as well. *La condesa* was first published in Mexico in 1969, but due to unavailability, the most commonly cited reference is the Aquarius Libros edition, published in 1971. In this work, Pizarnik self-consciously rewrites the 19th-century French writer Valentine Penrose's novel *La comtesse sanglante* [The Gory Countess]. In fact, the first lines of the work mention Penrose specifically, "There is a book by Valentine Penrose which documents the life of a real and unusual character: the Countess Bathory. . . . The Countess Bathory's sexual perversion and madness are so obvious that Valentine Penrose disregards them and concentrates instead on the convulsive beauty of the character" (*La condesa,* 71). Both works tell the tale of the 16th-century Hungarian countess Erzebet Bathory (whose story has long fascinated writers such as Georges Bataille and Andrei Codrescu, as well as filmmakers). This real-life "female Dracula" tortured and killed more than 600 virgin girls, peasants from her kingdom, in the belief that the shedding of their blood would keep her forever youthful.

Pizarnik's version of this history is a short text which defies genre—it is broken up into twelve vignettes of poetic prose which detail Bathory's character and her many forms of torture. Each of these vignettes is preceded by an epithet by such male writers as the Marquis de Sade and Jean-Paul Sartre which sheds perspective on the scenes to follow. Throughout these vignettes, madness and death are intermingled with both sexuality and gender. In addition, paradox and contradiction are evident throughout the text in the description of the Countess's horrific acts of torture through a beautifully crafted, lyrical prose poetry.

While death is of primary concern in the Countess's history (she tortures and kills in an attempt to maintain eternal life), in Pizarnik's story the act of killing is explicitly sexualized in the sense of her mentor Georges Bataille's idea of the "continuous." She writes in the fourth vignette, "Classical Torture": "Sexual climax forces us into death-like gestures and expressions. . . . If the sexual act implies a sort of death, Erzebet Bathory needed the visible, elementary, coarse death, to succeed in dying that other phantom death we call orgasm" (76).

Just as death becomes linked to sex, acts of torture also become sexual acts for Pizarnik's Countess. Her torture sessions are described as her "erotic convulsions" and include such acts as placing "burning paper soaked in oil" between the victims legs, burning their breasts with hot pokers, or tearing at them in the "most sensitive places." Pizarnik even writes that the Countess "used to plunge a burning candle into the genitals of the victim" (81). Her victims were generally stripped naked, and the Countess would often bite at their flesh. Even the Countess's words during the tortures demonstrate their sexual nature: "More, ever more, harder, harder!" (75).

In addition, Erzebet's gender and sexuality are foregrounded in *La condesa sangrienta*, and are linked with her cruel acts. The fact that her sexualized acts of torture victimize only young girls marks her as a lesbian, to which Pizarnik alludes: "The rumors concerning her own homosexuality were never confirmed" (79) (a statement that could also be made about Pizarnik's sexuality). Her gender is foregrounded by Pizarnik in the seventh vignette, "The Melancholy Mirror": "She lived deep within an exclusively female world. There were only women during her nights of crime" (79).

Whether or not Pizarnik is condemning the Countess or recognizing and valorizing aspects of herself in this lonely figure has been held open to debate. Some critics have read the text as political allegory, some as autobiography, some as outright condemnation. However, one thing is certain about *La condesa sangrienta*: it is a text in which eroticism is a powerful presence which unites many of the themes treated by Alejandra Pizarnik's oeuvre as a whole. While some of her poems treat issues of eroticism, it is in this short prose poem that female eroticism and its links with death, madness, and contradiction are most fully expressed.

Biography

Born in Buenos Aires, Argentina, April 29. Studied philosophy and letters at the University of Buenos Aires (1954–1957). Left school to study painting under Juan Planas. Lived in Paris from 1960 to 1964, where she worked for the publication *Cuadernos*, as well as several French journals. Translated works by Antonin Artaud, Henri Micheaux, Aimé Cesairé, and Yves Bonnefoy. Studied religious history and contemporary French literature at the Sorbonne. After returning to Buenos Aires, published three of her most important volumes of poetry, *Los trabajos y las noches* (1965), *Extracción de la piedra de la locura* (1968), and *El infierno musical* (1971), as well as her prose work *La condesa sangrienta* (1965, 1971). Won a Guggenheim Fellowship in 1969 and a Fulbright in 1971. Died on September 25 from a self-induced overdose of seconal.

TRACY FARRELL

Selected Works

La condesa sangrienta. Buenos Aires: Aquarius Libros, 1971.
"The Bloody Countess." In *Other Fires: Short Fiction by Latin American Women*, translated by Alberto Manguel. Toronto: L. & O. Dennys, 1986.
El infierno musical, 1971.
La extracción de la piedra de locura y otros poemas, 1993.
Obras completas, 1990.

Further Reading

Bajarlía, Juan Jacob. *Alejandra Pizarnik: Anatomía de un recuerdo*. Buenos Aires: Editorial Almagesto, 1998.
Bassnett, Susan. "Blood and Mirrors: Imagery of Violence in the Writings of Alejandra Pizarnik." In *Latin American Women's Writing: Feminist Readings in Theory and Crisis*, edited by Catherine Davies and Anny Brooksbank Jones. Oxford, UK: Clarendon Press, 1996.
Bordelois, Ivonne. *Correspondencia Pizarnik*. Buenos Aires: Seix Barral, 1998.
Foster, David. "Of Power and Virgins." In *Structures of Power: Essays on Twentieth-Century Spanish-American Fiction*, edited by Terry J. Peavler and Peter Standish. Albany: State University of New York Press, 1996.
Goldberg, Florinda F. *Alejandra Pizarnik: Este espacio que somos*. Gaithersburg, MD: Hispamerica, 1994.
Molloy, Sylvia. "From Sappho to Baffo: Diverting the Sexual in Alejandra Pizarnik." In *Sex and Sexuality in Latin America*, edited by Daniel Balderston and Donna J. Guy. New York: NYU Press, 1997.
Piña, Cristina. *Alejandra Pizarnik*. Buenos Aires: Planeta, 1991.
———. *Poesía y experiencia del límite: Leer a Alejandra Pizarnik*. Buenos Aires: Botella del Mar, 1999.

PLATONOV, ANDREI

1899–1951
Russian novelist

From his earliest years as a journalist, poet, and short story writer in the Russian provinces, Platonov made sexuality one of the dominant themes of his work. Apparently influenced by the writings of Nikolai Fiodorovich Fiodorov (1828–1903), whose *Philosophy of the Common Task* [*Filosofiia obshchego dela*] argued that all sexual feeling and reproductive activity should be sublimated in favor of the physical resurrection of the dead, Platonov wrote a series of articles between 1920 and 1922 arguing that the sexual instinct is a bourgeois holdover: true communists would find fulfillment in comradeship and the construction of socialism rather than in relations with women (for Platonov, the subject was almost always exclusively male). "Communist society," he wrote in 1920, "is essentially a society of men. . . . Humanity is courage (man) and the embodiment of sex (woman). He who desires the truth cannot desire a woman." Platonov's views, though extreme, were very much in the spirit of his times. Although the 1920s in the Soviet Union saw an unprecedented relaxation of both the legal code and sexual mores, as well as an official emphasis on women's equality, this so-called sexual revolution was counterbalanced by revolutionary asceticism, which stressed personal discipline and the careful husbanding of all one's energies in order to create the new Soviet world.

By the mid-1920s, Platonov had retreated from his early revolutionary utopianism and had begun to reevaluate his approach to sex and the family. In 1926, he wrote a satirical sketch entitled "Anti-sexus," which purported to be a brochure for a product designed to rid its user of all sexual feeling. In 1929, he completed his masterpiece, *Chevengur*, a novel that puts his early ideas about gender and sex to the test: twelve men and one woman (clearly the Judas figure) attempt to build socialism in one town, based on male comradeship rather than on the traditional family.

The Chevengurians initially feel that their virtually all-male town will be a comradely paradise, but after the arrival of a contingent of "miscellaneous" people (homeless, leaderless men who have heard that life is good in Chevengur), the men start to demand the importation of women. The women's arrival signals the end of the revolutionary experiment. Not long after, nearly everyone is killed by mysterious invaders.

Even as the protagonists espouse their revolutionary idealism, the novel is pervaded with a strong sense of homoeroticism, as well as necrophilia. One of the men who come to Chevengur toward the end of the novel has sex with a woman on his mother's grave; Sasha Dvanov, the novel's hero, experiences his first orgasm after he is shot and falls to the ground clutching a horse's leg. Here as in the rest of Platonov's work, sexuality's denial is based on an implicit sense of bodily economy: if energy is released through sexual activity, it depletes body and spirit.

Platonov's 1930 short novel *Kotlovan* [*The Foundation Pit*] continues the author's skeptical, yet wistful reassessment of communist utopianism, although the sexual theme is less prominent. The only sensual feelings the male protagonists have toward a female involve a woman who dies early on, leaving behind her young daughter. The novel can be seen as a failed experiment in all-male group parenting: the entire collective of construction workers tries to take care of little Nastia, but the best they can do for her is provide a coffin when she dies. His 1937 short story *Reka Potudan'* [*The Potudan River*] features a young married couple who are able to consummate their relationship only after the husband's failed suicide attempt. In 1946, Platonov once again shocked the censors with his short story *Sem'ia Ivanova* [*Ivanov's Family*]. Also known as *Vozvrashchenie* [*The Return*], this story was premised on the scandalous idea that not all wives remained faithful while their husbands were off at war.

In his complicated transition from being a fierce opponent of sex and the family to having a guardedly positive outlook on matrimony, Platonov provides the reader with an invaluable perspective on sexuality in early Soviet culture.

Biography

Born Andrei Platonovich Klimentov in Voronezh, September 1. In 1914, Platonov was forced to interrupt his formal education to help support his family. He served in the Red Army during the Russian Civil War (1917–1920) as both a soldier and a journalist, and graduated from the Voronezh Railroad Polytechnical Institute in 1921. He joined the Communist Party in 1920 but resigned from it in 1921 for ideological and personal reasons. He worked as an electrical engineer and land reclamation expert while beginning his literary career in the early 1920s. Married Maria Kashintseva in 1922, and had two children: Platon and Maria. By the late 1920s, Platonov was having increasing difficulties getting his work published. During World War II, he was a correspondent for the military newspaper *Krasnaya Zvyezda* [*Red Star*] and had three novels and a collection published; but after the war his publishing difficulties resumed and he found himself vulnerable to official criticism. In 1938, his son had been arrested, dying in 1943, but not before having infected his father with the tuberculosis that eventually killed him, January 5.

ELIOT BORENSTEIN

Selected Works

Chevengur, 1929; translated by Anthony Olcott, 1978.
Sem'ia Ivanova, 1937; as "Homecoming," translated by A. Kiselev in *Collected Works*, Ann Arbor, MI: Ardis, 1978; as "The Return," in *The Return and Other Stories*, translated by Robert and Elizabeth Chandler, London: Harvill Press/Random House, 1999.
Koltlovan [1930]. Translated by Mirra Ginsburg. Evanston, IL: Northwestern University Press, 1994.
"Reka Potudan'" [1937]. In Kiselev et al., trans., *Collected Works.*

Further Reading

Borenstein, Eliot. *Men Without Women: Masculinity and Revolution in Russian Fiction, 1917–1929.* Durham, NC: Duke University Press, 2000.
Naiman, Eric. "Andrej Platonov and the Inadmissability of Desire." *Russian Literature* 23 (1988): 319–67.
———. *Sex in Public: The Incarnation of Early Soviet Ideology.* Princeton, NJ: Princeton University Press, 1997.
Osipovich, Tatiana. "Sex, Love, and Family in the Works of Andrei Platonov." Ph.D. dissertation, University of Pittsburgh, 1988.
Podoroga, Valery. "The Eunuch of the Soul: Positions of Reading and the World of Platonov." In *Late Soviet Culture: From Perestroika to Novostroika*, edited by Thomas Lahusen with Gene Kuperman, 187–231. Durham, NC: Duke University Press, 1993.
Seifrid, Thomas. *Andrei Platonov: Uncertainties of Spirit.* New York: Cambridge University Press, 1992.

POGGIO

1380–1459
Italian humanist

Poggio's pursuits were typical of an early humanist: he was an avid and important collector and noted copier of manuscripts of ancient authors; he was famous for perfecting a clear and elegant italic script; he authored a number of treatiese of his own; he engaged in extensive correspondence with humanists across Europe and published this correspondence, including quarrels with several figures who are noteworthy for the art of obscene invective. To elaborate, Poggio's discoveries were numerous and significant: the first complete copy of Quintilian's *Institutiones;* several orations of Cicero, as well as Asconius's commentary on five orations of Cicero; *De Rerum Naturae* of Lucretius; works of Plautus; and fragments of Petronius and Tacitus; among many others. His own works include treatises such as *De avaritia, De infelicitate principum, Contra hypocrites*; he wrote a *History of Florence* and a treatise often cited as the most important early Renaissance archaeological work on Rome, *De varietate fortunae*, noteworthy for its illuminated initial with a portrait of the author.

Poggio also sent forth volumes of his correspondence. Most of these are marked by the full range of interests of a humanist who traveled throughout Europe (including two years spent in England): sharing with friends the excitement of finding manuscripts, the difficulties of living away from Italy, the charms of the baths at Baden, questions of whether and when to marry, and the difficulties of secretarial employment. However, in other letters, Poggio enjoyed engaging in literary and scholarly controversies which in some instances showed him the master of obscene invective. In a series of attacks on his fellow humanist Filelfo, he characterizes Filelfo's assault on his friend Niccolo Niccoli as coming from the "feculent stores of his putrid mouth." He claims that Filelfo inherited his filthy nature from his mother, who was a whore, that he debauched his wife in order to force marriage, and that he later sold her favors, and he concludes his attack by proposing to crown Filelfo not with the laurel branch but with a pile of shit. And he hurls the ultimate Italian insult at Filelfo, calling him a a cuckold several times over: Filelfo is a "stinking he-goat," a "horned monster," and one whose forehead is adorned with *i corni*. In attacking Filelfo in such terms, Poggio established a pattern in his use of obscenity in literary quarrels that other humanists were to follow, both in Italy and in England.

The *Facetiae*

Poggio deserves attention in this volume chiefly for his compilation of the jokes that make up the *Facetiae* (1450). The jests were written in Latin, and by Poggio's own account they "flooded" all of Europe (in fact, several jests were added to the end of Caxton's edition of *Aesop* in 1484, one of the earliest books printed in England). Poggio claims that the jests were the product of frequent gatherings of the papal secretaries in a group he called the *Bugiale*, the place for telling tall tales. The jokes then are the product of a group of

learned men who enjoyed the combination of wit and bawdiness that is found throughout the jests. Given changing mores, we would certainly not categorize the jests as "dirty jokes," but Gershon Legman in his monumental study *The Rationale of the Dirty Joke*, is certainly right when he claims that Poggio transformed the longer *nouvelle* and *fabliau* into a shorter form, often (but not always) with a punch line. Taken as a whole, both in the context provided for the jests and in the details within them, the *Facetiae* gives us a partial picture of the world of the humanists in early Renaissance Italy.

Jokes have to do with the problems of the papacy; several relate to the Council of Constance (attended by Poggio) and the uncertain place of a humanist in a world governed by preferment. Some number of the 272 jests in the collection are bawdy and reflect typical attitudes of the times. The venality and wiliness of the clergy, especially as sexual predators, are prominent features (see especially 5, 6, 44, 45, and 230; all references are to the Hurwood edition). The stupidity of husbands who allow themselves to be cuckolded is a commonplace (1, 5, 156), as are the cleverness and sexual drive of wives (1, 6, 10, 42, 45, 156, and 230). Especially noteworthy are jests 110 and 111, reflecting as they do what Legman and Keith Thomas would call the anxieties of what was supposed to be a male-dominated society. Both jests turn not on punch lines but on the notion that the "marital act" is the "best remedy for all female disorders" (see 24 as well). With urbane wit and appreciation for the comic in sexual experience the *Facetiae* set the pattern both in form and subject matter for the many collections of jests and jokes that were to follow in Italy and across the continent throughout the Renaissance.

Biography

Giovanni Francesco Poggio Bracciolini was born in Terranuova, near Arezzo, and educated in Florence by the leading figures of the new humanism: Manuel Chrysoloras, Giovanni da Ravenna, and Coluccio Salutati. Poggio served as a papal secretary (chiefly in Rome) from 1403 to 1415 and again from 1423 to 1452. From 1453 to 1458 he held the position of chancellor in Florence, where he died.

DAVID O. FRANTZ

Selected Works

The Facetiae or Jocose Tales of Poggio, Now first translated into English with the Latin Text, in two volumes. Paris: Isidore Liseux, 1879.

The Facetiae of Giovanni Francesco Poggio Bracciolini. Translated by Bernhardt J. Hurwood. New York: Award Books, 1968.

Opera omnia. 4 vols, edited by Riccardo Fubini. Turin: Bottega d'Erasmo, 1964–69.

Further Reading

Barkin, Leonard. *Unearthing the Past.* New Haven, CT: Yale UP, 1999.

Bolgar, R. R. *The Classical Heritage.* New York: Harper & Row, 1964.

Gordon, Phyllis, trans. *Two Renaissance Book Hunters: The Letters of Poggius Bracciolini to Nicolaus de Niccolis.* New York: Columbia UP, 1974.

Grafton, Anthony, ed. *Rome Reborn.* New Haven, CT: Yale UP, 1993.

Legman, G. *The Horn Book.* New York: University Books Inc., 1964.

———. *The Rationale of the Dirty Joke.* New York: Grove Press, 1968.

Martines, Lauro. *The Social World of the Florentine Humanists, 1390–1460.* Princeton, NJ: Princeton UP, 1963.

PORNOGRAPHY

Etymologically, *pornography* is a relatively young term dating from its 1850s medical usage, though deriving from the Greek *pornographos,* writing of or about prostitutes. In modern usage it encompasses any literary or visual materials designed to eroticize its audience, i.e., to stimulate sexual feelings and, presumably, desires in its audience. Pornography has been a troubled concept and, accordingly, a troublesome term especially in the last century. By the late 20th century the term had lost its lexical innocence and did not have a uniform consensus definition. One school of feminists argued that pornography was necessarily an agency of male dominance and that its depictions of women were necessarily degrading and in fact generated male violence toward females. This contention had legal implications by virtue of its designation of pornography as not so much a matter of speech (afforded maximal legal latitude in both British Common and United States Constitutional Law) but rather an *act* of violence against women and therefore prosecutable. In the United States this idea gained momentum especially in the 1980s via the vigorous promotion of an anti-pornography ordinance by certain feminists under the banner of Women Against Pornography, or WAP. But in the court proceedings, another school of feminists, designating themselves the Feminists Against Censorship Taskforce, or FACT, challenged the assumptions informing the ordinance and its definition of pornography as a violent act rather than a legitimate mode of speech. Its primary rebuttal was that pornography was indeed a mode of speech that legally is and culturally ought to be as available to women as it is to men as an agency of self-exploration and knowledge, and its censorship would not only infringe upon free speech but deprive women of a valuable epistemological source. Whatever the merits of these arguments, higher courts in the United States have ruled that the ordinance's language did not meet First Amendment requirements and was therefore unconstitutional.

This decision resolved the legal issue of censorship, but intensive social discourse about the character and effects of pornography continued. To determine whether pornography had discernibly harmful effects, two commissions to study obscenity and its effects were convened in the United States, one in Britain, and one in Canada between 1970 and 1986. The 1970 US, 1979 British, and 1984 Canadian commissions essentially agreed that there was little or no evidence that obscenity caused social harm. The 1986 U.S. commission grudgingly agreed that evidence for harm from obscenity was scarce and problematic, but nonetheless insisted that there was an "association" between the two. Still, the lack of data support and the court decision noted above dispersed activist censorship campaigns. By the last decade of the 20th century the usage of the term *pornography* had ranged widely, from the descriptively passive (pornography as the depiction of sexual acts and situations) to the editorially modest (pornography as such matter "intended to arouse sexual feelings" [*American Heritage Dictionary*]) to the editorially aggressive (pornography as "a demeaning and sometimes violent representation of sexuality and the body, typically the woman's" [*Cambridge Encyclopedia*]). But there was effectually no consensus that pornography constituted a social harm.

Licentious, bawdy, and obscene sexual depictions have been extant and even notorious in both East and West since ancient times, but the concept of pornography as a socially transgressive phenomenon seems to have accompanied its Western development, at least from the advent of the printing press. Pietro Aretino's light pornographic sonnets accompanying Giulio Romano's drawings, called *Posizioni,* were published in 1524, about 50 years after the printing press came to Italy. They circulated throughout Europe and were the first popular "modern" pornography, in that they were broadcast via printing press and were self-consciously a breach of taste and manners. Their printer was jailed at the behest of the Vatican, and Aretino avoided the same by leaving Rome. His offensiveness to the Church, however, was not due solely to pornography. His *Dialogues* incorporated pornography with satirical depictions of priests, nuns, and the Church. Moreover, as David O. Frantz argues, Aretino integrated sexuality into the general humanistic concerns of his time. Further, Aretino's satirical posture anticipated the deconstructivist spirit characteristic of such varied successors in the tradition as John Cleland, the Marquis de Sade, Aubrey Beardsley, Guillaume Apollinaire, D.H. Lawrence, Georges Bataille, and William S. Burroughs.

That there is a legitimate literary tradition of pornography suggests not only the customary distinctions between "soft core" and "hard core" pornography but also its aesthetic function. Hard-core pornography represents explicit sex, usually depicting genitalia in action and usually to the end of eroticizing its audience,

though it may also employ other, subordinate motifs. Soft-core pornography may represent explicit sex but usually within what is perceived to be an acceptable standard of taste and usually subordinate to other motifs, particularly sentimental or parodic ones. While hard-core's principal functions are to evoke sexual obscenity and thereby encourage libido, soft-core tends rather to allude to these things and is consequently more restrained or decorous. These two forms are essentially commercial and are said to constitute an "industry," one that is bigger in the aggregate (magazines, videos, films, photographs, books) than the film or record industries in the United States. A third form, which has been called artistic pornography, may represent explicit genital sex but integrates sexuality as a theme or rhetoric into a context for an aesthetic, usually transgressive, purpose.

All of these forms are sometimes confused with the erotic, but pornography and erotica are distinct. Erotic works evoke sex in the context of physical love, so as to subordinate the former to the latter. For example, Radclyffe Hall's novel *The Well of Loneliness* is about sexual love, but it subordinates sex to love so as to be unequivocally erotic. Pornography of any degree functions in terms of the obscene—the more hard core, the more conspicuous the obscenity. For example, Pauline Réage's novel *The Story of O* is about sexual love, but it so casts love in terms of an obscene sexual imperative that it is unequivocally pornographic. Some readers might well consider it hard-core pornography by virtue of its obscenity, but others have considered it at once hard-core, obscene, *and* artistic. The fluidity of aesthetic dynamics, critical judgment, and public discourse in the face of free-speech traditions and laws has made censorship of pornography via categorization problematic and in general unsuccessful.

In the early years of the 21st century, pornography may be theoretically equivocal but it is pragmatically pervasive as an entertainment industry in movies, television, journalism, pop music, paraphernalia, and books. The postmodern era of the 20th century manifested a radical change in public tolerance of obscenity and pornography, or at least in the ways it defined and/or understood these things to be. This change was very likely facilitated by the integration of mainstream aesthetics into a long-developing literary and artistic underground legacy of naturalism, vulgarity, obscenity, and pornography, as exemplified in works by Jonathan Swift, William Blake, the Marquis de Sade, Walt Whitman, Honore de Balzac, Emile Zola, Guillaume Apollinaire, James Joyce, and D. H. Lawrence. It asserted itself in novels (e.g., Henry Miller's *Tropic of Cancer*), poetry (e.g., Allen Ginsberg's *Howl*), movies (e.g., Bertolucci's *Last Tango in Paris*), theater (e.g., Richard Foreman's *Dionysus in '69*), etc. And in the last quarter or so of the 20th century a substantial body of critical commentary developed a discourse on the subject, along with an increasing body of creative work.

PETER MICHELSON

Further Reading

Bataille, Georges. *Eroticism*. Translated by Mary Dalwood. London: John Calder, 1962.
Dworkin, Andrea. *Pornography: Men Possessing Women*. New York: Putnam, 1981.
Frantz, David O. *Festum Voluptatis: A Study of Renaissance Erotica*. Columbus: Ohio State University Press, 1989.
Friday, Nancy. *My Secret Garden*. New York: Simon & Schuster, 1974.
Griffin, Susan. *Pornography and Silence*. New York: Harper & Row, 1984.
Hite, Shere. *The Hite Report*. New York: Dell, 1977.
Hunter, Nan D., and Sylvia A. Law. *Brief Amici Curiae of Feminist Anti-Censorship Taskforce, et al.* U.S. Court of Appeals, Seventh Circuit, 1985.
Kronhausen, Eberhard and Phyllis. *Pornography and the Law*. New York: Ballantine Books, 1964.
Lawrence, D.H. *Sex, Literature and Censorship*. edited by Harry T. Moore. New York: Twayne, 1953.
Marcus, Steven. *The Other Victorians*. New York: Basic Books, 1966.
Michelson, Peter. *Speaking the Unspeakable: A Poetics of Obscenity*. Albany: State University of New York Press, 1993.
Miller, Henry. *The World of Sex*. New York: Grove Press, 1965.
Ullerstam, Lars. *The Erotic Minorities*. Translated by Anselm Hollo. New York: Grove Press, 1966.
Young, Wayland. *Eros Denied*. New York: Grove Press, 1964.

POSITIONS

All civilizations have produced erotic handbooks. Whereas many cultural or religious traditions demand that the sexual act be conducted in the darkness of the night, *ars erotica* insists upon doing it with the lights on. The erotic handbook overturns the notion of desire as causing the subject to panic and lose his or her composure and to be thrown blindly into the ecstasy of possession (as in the Dionysian mysteries). On the contrary, it is about mastering pleasure, organizing the search for it, and methodically ruling over the torrid relations between the sexes.

A book on sexual positions can take many forms. It can be a compendium of anecdotes, a collection of love stories, a catalog of the world's resources, a gradual arrangement of the figures (from the basic position to the most complex), a book of wisdom, or a medical treatise. Each time, it appears as a reading of how a civilization exposes itself, with its rites, beliefs, history, and imagination. The great *Kâma Sûtra* of Vât-syâyana (who drew inspiration from ancient love codes, or *shastras*) teaches the 64 talents or arts of pleasure, the seven types of union, the three types of kisses a young girl asks for (nominal, shifting, and touching, to which four more are added), the four basic embraces ("ivy," "tree climber," "blend of sesame with rice," "blend of milk with water"), the different "passion marks," done with scratching or biting; and the eight types of screams that correspond to the ways of striking blows during lovemaking. To further the didactic aid in executing the positions, it classifies men and women according to the size of their sexual organs.

The *Tao-te Ching* seeks to promote the harmony between "the rod" and "the jade door." Li Tong-hsuan's *Tong-hsuan tze* differentiates between nine types of penetration (e.g., "like a courageous warrior attempting to disperse the enemy ranks," "like a flock of seagulls playing in the waves") and four basic positions, from which 26 variations can be developed (e.g., "the silkworm spinning its cocoon," "the mandarin ducks," "the white tiger that pounces"). Japan has its "pillow books," which list the many ways to do it, consulted by lovers before making love and given by courtesans to their patrons to read. Al-Jahiz's *Book of the Respective Merits of Maidens and Young Men* is the most ancient treatise of Arab erotology, echoed in the 15th century by Sidi Mohammed el Nefzaoui's *Scented Garden* and, a century later, Ahmed Ibn Souleimân's *Return of the Sheik to His Youth for Vigor and Coitus*.

Ancient Greece has given us Astyanassa, Helen's servant, who was well versed in the art of changing coital positions. It was Astyanassa who popularized the books on sexual positions by the maidens Philaenis and Elephantis; Paxamus's *Dodecatechnon*, which, according to Suidas, lists 12 positions; and Cyrene, the famous hetaira, or sexual entertainer, nicknamed Dodecamechanos because she knew how to practice all 12. To these must be added the didactic, elegiac, or satirical "arts of love" from the Roman poets. Medieval European nouvelles contained many erotic figures, depending on the hero's talents or geographical origins. It was with Aretino (1492–1556), however, that the catalog of sexual positions triumphed in the West. Beyond the *Sonetti lussuriosi* [*Lewd Sonnets*], Aretino's *Ragionamenti* [*Discussions*] introduces a long series of educational talks in which appears "the teaching whore," who transmits her knowledge to a young novice. Through the *Dialogues* that punctuated the history of erotic literature in the 17th and 18th centuries, the number of sexual positions increased from 32 to more than 50, all listed and annotated. In 1790 the French Revolution made best sellers of *Quarante manières de foutre* [*Forty Ways to Fuck*] and *Les travaux d'Hercule ou la rocambole de la fouterie* [*Hercules' Works, or the Attraction of Fucking*], the last edition of which would bring to 15 the feats of the demigod.

Books on sexual positions triumphed in the 18th century because the Enlightenment believed in the sociability of pleasure, linked to the mechanics of the body. The sexual scene was no longer archaic, terrifying, and primitive. It was in harmony with the general sharing of knowledge; it could be controlled and improved upon; there was a positivity of pleasure, to which was added the bliss of numbers (up to Sade's *120 Days of Sodom*) and illustrations—for no book on fuck positions can do without illustrations.

Marcantonio Raimondi engraved *I modi*, a series by Giulio Romano, for which Aretino composed his sonnetti. Titian, Carracci, and many classical painters and engravers illustrated sexual positions. From the Japanese pillow books to the *Quarante manières de foutre*, engravings constituted an essential element. They picked up where religious or scientific iconography left off, to disseminate practical and anatomical knowledge. They were offered as an initiation and also as a stimulant, an incitement to act. Simple form and mental image, dynamic line and universal representation, the drawing of positions make up an alphabet. The representation of the sexes in their union introduced into the world a "schematic" perception, between reality and language, at the point of entry into the world of signs. The picture does not merely replicate the motion of the body, however; it portrays the vitality of the body during the burst of desire. The sexual tableau thus endows the body with the nature of a spectacle. The graffiti of a phallus, a vulva, or two joined bodies might have been the first "image" rendered by humans, to thenceforth be indefinitely conjugated by books of positions.

PATRICK WALD LASOWSKI

Further Reading

Boudhiba, Abdelwahab. *La Sexualité en Islam*. The collection Quadrige-Essais Débats. Paris: PUF [Presses Universitaires de France], 1986.

Cotin, J., ed. *Dictionnaire des postures amoureuse*. Paris: Picquier, 2001.

Etiemble, René. *L'Érotisme et l'amour*. Paris: Arléa, 1987.

Forberg, F.K. *De Figuris Venerisi*, 1824.

Foucault, M. *Histoire de la sexualité*. Vol. 1: *La Volonté de savoir*. Gallimard, 1976.

Lasowski, P. Wald, ed. *La science pratique de l'amour*. Revolutionary erotic texts selected and introduced by the author. Paris: Picquier, 1998.

Van Gulik, Robert. *La Vie sexuelle dans la Chine ancienne*. Gallimard, 1971.

POTTER, WILLIAM SIMPSON

1805–1879
English businessman, bibliophile, and writer

William S. Potter was the founding partner in a coal firm who shared a love of erotic books with Monckton Milnes (Lord Houghton), Sir James Plaisted Wilde (Lord Penzance), James Campbell Reddie, Frederick Popham Pike, Edward Bellamy, and George Augustus Sala. Rumor has it that their novel *The Romance of Lust* was written by these men in a round-robin fashion and then edited by Potter during a journey to the Far East. According to Peter Mendes, William Lazenby (alias Duncan Cameron and possibly Thomas Judd)—one of the main British pornographers during the 1870s and 1880s—published *The Romance of Lust* in four volumes between 1873 and 1876. Shortly after, he fled to Paris to escape a sentence of two years at hard labor for violating obscenity laws. *The Romance of Lust* stands as one of the most expensive pieces of Victorian pornography, costing upward of £10 in 1892, one of the longest at over 600 pages, and one of the best-known pieces of the period (running second place to *My Secret Life* in all categories).

It also has been singled out, quite unfairly, as one of the worst pieces of pornography from the Victorian age. Henry Spencer Ashbee believed that "it contains scenes not surpassed by the most libidinous chapters of *Justine*. The episodes, however, are frequently improbable, sometimes impossible, and are as a rule too filthy and crapulous" (Ashbee: 185). Henry Miles argued that "attempted 'psychological interpretations' may well be stumbling over bad grammar" and that "it takes a special sort of genius to create such a ludicrous situation in such a manner" (Miles: 48–9). Finally, Steven Marcus felt that it "could in fact only have been imagined by persons who have suffered extreme deprivation" (Marcus: 274). *The Romance of Lust* does not deserve the scorn, but neither will it win awards for craftsmanship; instead, as a novel it combines a Victorian attention to detail with an almost Malthusian attention to geometric progressions. Whereas Malthus explained the geometric consequences of procreation, the *Romance of Lust* explores the geometric possibilities for copulation.

The Romance of Lust chronicles an adolescent boy's growth to adulthood almost exclusively through his sexual awakening and activities. The narrator, Charlie, tells of his erotic history that began when he was fifteen years old and his father's death left him to become man of the house. Although he is treated as a child and kept in the nursery, he lusts for his governess and engages in sexual play with his two sisters. He quickly receives a sexual education—oral, genital, and anal—from an older woman who eventually shares him with another female friend. He, in turn, enlightens his sisters. From there, Charlie's sexual exploits begin to ramify, as every conceivable associate in a middle-class life—family friends, family members, servants, teachers, school chums, chance acquaintances—becomes a sexual partner.

In many ways, *The Romance of Lust* uses literary conventions typical of the Victorian novel, like the premise of the orphaned boy, the liminality of the governess, and the endless rounds of country visiting. While more standard Victorian novels use these conventions to explore tensions and ambiguities in a time of social flux, *The Romance of Life* sexualizes them, removing any complications or any need for change. Instead, the novel allows lust to be the only possible motive, a sense of gratified affection between characters to be the only bond or emotion, and sexual activities as the cure-all for all social problems. In doing so, *The Romance of Lust* offers a radically different view of Victorian life from that of mainstream literature but one that lacks any urgency or self-reflection.

Written as a series of vignettes tied together by the continuity in characters and settings, the book examines the sexual combinations available to the boy. The most banal of acts—walking on the beach, going to school, making new friends, talking with family—leads to intercourse, and all intercourse is equally pleasing.

Oral, anal, and genital stimulation give an interchangeable pleasure; pleasure can only be doubled, or tripled, with multiple acts. Incest, menage, anal intercourse, male–male relations, lesbianism, flagellation, wife swapping become commonplace, as the narrator describes them with little tension or reflection. Through sheer repetition, intercourse dominates the sexual, familial, and social world. Each vignette in the novel is composed of the introduction of a new character or scene followed by intercourse and orgasm, and in each case the process builds only to repeat itself. The text gives organs, individuals, social relationships, and locations meaning by their relationship to sexual pleasures. The proliferation of characters and sexual acts gives the novel a circus-like quality in some places, as it tries to detail who does what to whom with multiple partners and overlapping sexual acts. These orgies overwhelm the abilities of the writer(s), and instead of a clear narrative, the reader is left with a sense of disembodied organs tied together through a profusion of orgasms.

Steven Marcus sees the novel as divesting the sexes of difference; both men and women have the same passions and each enjoys the same pleasures. Dildos and enlarged clitorises make women capable of insertion, and anal intercourse allows men to enjoy being penetrated. In some ways, the paring down of gender and sexual differences through an equality of organs and acts makes this work subversive in the rights to pleasure that it authorizes. However, the circus-like quality, the cursory character development in which individuality is developed only through the size of one's bum, and the interchangeability of characters throughout the work ultimately create a sense that women as well as men are mere sexual automatons. This perhaps is the work's most enduring feature and its most telling point about Victorian life. An addenda to the work includes letters from the Cavendish vs. Cavendish and Rochefoucault divorce cases (over which James Plaisted Wilde presided). The descriptive capacities of the letters are superior to that of the novel, but only slightly, hinting that perhaps the literary flaws of the novel are in fact a form of frankness about the lack of emotional attachment in Victorian sexual relations.

LISA Z. SIGEL

Selected Readings

Potter, William Simpson (attributed), with Frederick Pike. *Lascivious Gems.* London: Printed for the booksellers, 1866.
Potter, Simpson (attributed), with James Campbell Reddie and Frederick Popham Pike. *The Power of Mesmerism.* Moscow [London]: Printed for the Nihilists [Lazenby], 1880.

Further Readings

Ashbee, Henry Spencer (Pisanus Fraxi, pseud.). *Catena librorum tacendorum* [1885]. New York: Documentary Books, Inc., 1962.
Kendrick, Walter. *The Secret Museum: Pornography in Modern Culture.* New York: Viking Press, 1987.
Marcus, Steven. *The Other Victorians.* New York: W. W. Norton & Company, 1985.
Mendes, Peter. *Clandestine Erotic Fiction in English, 1800–1930.* London: Scolar Press, 1993.
Miles, Henry. *Forbidden Fruit.* London: Luxor Press, 1973.
Sigel, Lisa Z. *Governing Pleasures: Pornography and Social Change in England, 1815–1914.* New Brunswick, NJ: Rutgers University Press, 2002.

POUGY, LIANE DE

1869–1950
French courtesan and novelist

Anne-Marie Olympe Chassaigne was born in La Flèche, a town some two hundred miles southwest of Paris, into a military family. A few days after her seventeenth birthday, she herself was married off to a naval ensign seven years her senior, giving birth to a son in 1887. The marriage was not a success; within three years, Anne-Marie was installed in Paris, having been ignominiously divorced by her husband, who had caught her *in flagrante delicto* with a fellow officer. In Paris, Anne-Marie would seem to have had the good luck to fall in with Madame Valtesse de La Bigne, a once-fashionable courtesan (the former mistress of Offenbach and Napoleon III and reputed to have been the principal model for Zola's *Nana*) who lived on the other side of the Parc Monceau. This borderland between the 8th and 17th arrondissements was one of the favored residential areas of the demimonde, and there can be no doubt that Anne-Marie, who had by now adopted her famous sobriquet Liane de Pougy, was intent on making her mark.

Among the various men who showered money and jewelry on her were Lord Carnarvon, the celebrated Egyptologist (whose interests were also rumored to include flagellation); Charles de MacMahon (nephew of the field marshal who earned fame in the Crimean War and the battle of Magenta); the Maharajah of Kapurtala (who, according to gossip, proposed marriage to her if she would return with him to India); Henri Meilhac, the wealthy playwright and librettist (about whom a story circulated that he paid her 80,000 francs just to be able to gaze on her naked body); Roman Potocki, a Polish count; Albert Robin, a society doctor (Liane's attempted suicide outside his home earned her further notoriety); Maurice de Rothschild, an eighteen-year-old member of the famous banking clan (who was quickly packed off by the family to England); several English lords (the future Edward VII was said to be not entirely immune to her charm); and, finally, around 1907, Henri Bernstein, a rising, but emotionally overwrought, young playwright. But this list is by no means comprehensive, especially with regard to relationships forged during her travels abroad. Toward the turn of the century, her conduct became even more scandalous as she embarked on a brief but passionate relationship with the American heiress Natalie Clifford Barney (1876–1972).

The fact that so much is known about Liane de Pougy's life explains her very popularity: she was, in essence, the product of her own celebrity. Early in her career, she had learned the value of publicity. Ephemeral periodicals such as *Gil Blas* and *Fantasio* trumpeted her initial conquests and triumphs. After a brief period of mutual misunderstanding, her friendship with Jean Lorrain (1855–1906), one of the main guardians of the Decadent flame, opened his widely read "Pall Mall" column in *Le Journal* to her, even

providing readers with the recipe for a fruit salad soaked in ice-cold champagne and ether that she is supposed to have served her guests (this is almost certainly a fantasy of the author, who was an ether addict). Though an indifferent actress (Sarah Bernhardt is supposed to have advised her to open her mouth only to smile), she appeared in a succession of spectacles, including Lorrain's *L'Araignée d'or* (1896), a short *conte féerique* [fairy tale] at the Folies-Bergère, which kept her in the public eye.

Last but not least, she also celebrated her life as a courtesan in a series of thinly disguised autobiographical novels. The first of these, and by far the most successful, was *L'Insaisissable* (1898), which recounts the amorous adventures of a courtesan named Josiane de Valneige with a sequence of lovers whose real-life counterparts were easily identifiable to a readership that had already followed the author's own exploits in the Parisian press. It was followed the next year by *Myrrhille*, which was serialized in *Gil Blas* prior to publication in book form. *Idylle saphique* (1901) rehearses Liane's affair (and its conclusion) with Natalie Clifford Barney (who become, respectively, Annhine and Flossie). *Ecce homo* (1903), despite its allusion to Nietzsche, contained little fresh material. *Les Sensations de Mademoiselle de La Bringue* (1904), her fifth and most densely populated novel, is also the least coherent. The work bristles with references to a perplexing variety of Parisian social groups, ranging from the demimonde (including real-life rivals such as Cléo de Mérode, who appears as Méo de la Clef) to the Sâr Péladan's twilight world of occultists (including scenes depicting a Roman orgy and a black mass) (see *Péladan, Joséphin*) to literary and theatrical circles. Finally, the series is completed by *Yvée Lester* (1906) and its sequel *Yvée Jourdan* (1908), which treat the subject of lesbianism in a quasi-mystical manner generally lacking in sensational elements.

Though Liane de Pougy obviously did not invent the *roman à clef* (and it is worth remembering in this connection that Valtesse de La Bigne had published an autobiographical novel called *Isola* as early as 1876), her utilization of the form for purposes of self-promotion was perhaps rivaled only by Willy, Colette's first husband. By the time the last of her seven novels appeared, Liane's career as a courtesan was almost over.

In the spring of 1908, she met Georges Ghika, a Romanian prince and a nephew of the queen of Greece. At twenty-four, he was also Liane de Pougy's junior by more than 15 years. Despite the objections of Ghika's family, who were less than delighted at the prospect of welcoming a former courtesan into their aristocratic ranks, the couple wed in 1910. Curiously, this ill-assorted pair managed to weather most of the storms of life together for the next 35 years: through the First World War (Liane's son, Marco, an aviator, died in an accident toward the beginning of the conflict); the financial instability of the interwar years, during which time Liane's savings were constantly eroded; the excesses of travel and increasing ill health; and the search for a safe haven as the clouds of war mounted again in the 1930s. The couple settled in Switzerland; Ghika died suddenly of a cerebral hemorrhage in 1945. As was often the case with the men in her life, Prince Ghika was guilty of a number of sexual peccadilloes, involving voyeurism, exhibitionism, and onanism. Though Liane chided him for these singularities in her private diary, it was only when he began an affair in 1926 with Manon Thiébaut, a young artist whom Liane herself had befriended, that a rupture occurred, and even that was patched up the following year. After Georges Ghika's death, Liane became increasingly drawn to religion, donning the habit of Sister Mary Magdalene of the Penitence and entering a Dominican convent in Lausanne. In 1977, the publication of *Mes cahiers bleus*, Liane's intimate diary, provided considerable insight into her life during the interwar years.

With her marriage, Liane seemed to leave the old life behind; indeed, for some commentators, the event marks the end of *la belle epoque*—with its acquisitive courtesans and excessive displays of wealth and patronage—with as much finality as did the outbreak of the First World War four years later. Liane's reputation, however, outlived her withdrawal from Parisian society. Marcel Proust, who was by no means pleased to learn that Reynaldo Hahn, his lover, had passed a night of passion with her (an experience not renewed), modeled certain characteristics of Odette de Crécy in *A la recherché du temps perdu* on her. But Liane's presence may equally be seen behind several of Jean Lorrain's more bizarre female characters, as well as in works such as Gabriele d'Annunzio's *Il fuoco* (1900) and Colette's *Chéri* (1920).

TERRY HALE

Selected Works

L'Insaisissable, roman vécu. Paris: P. Lamm, 1898.
La mauvaise part. Myrrhille. With a preface by M. William Busnach. Paris: Per Lamm, 1899.
Idylle saphique. Paris: Librairie de la Plume, 1901; reprt. Paris: J.-C. Lattès, 1979.
"Ecce homo"! d'ici de là. Paris: Société parisienne d'édition, 1903.
Les sensations de Mademoiselle de La Bringue. Paris: A. Michel, 1904.
Yvée Lester. Paris: Ambert, 1906.
Yvée Jourdan. Paris: Ambert, 1908.
Mes cahiers bleus. With a preface by R.P. Rzewuski. Paris: Plon, 1977; as *My Blue Notebooks: The Intimate Journal of Paris' Most Beautiful and Notorious Courtesan*, preface by Rzewuski, translated by Diana Athill. New York: Harper & Row, 1979.

Further Reading

Chalon, Jean. *Liane de Pougy. Courtisane, princesse et sainte.* Paris: Flammarion, 1994.

PRITCHARD, MARK

1956–
United States writer, activist, publisher

Mark Pritchard is known as much for his queer activism as for his erotic writing. Having spent his youth in the repression of Midwestern suburbia, followed by two years in Japan, he embraced the sexual freedom of expression offered by San Francisco. Although he'd written for his college newspaper and created theater pieces as a student and young adult in Austin, Texas, his writing became more subversive through the 1980s, culminating in his decision to establish the small-press/underground magazine, or "zine," *Frighten the Horses: A Document of the Sexual Revolution.*

The zine's launch was only one expression of Pritchard's burgeoning activism. Through his volunteer efforts with Queer Nation, Street Patrol, and San Francisco Sex Information (SFSI), he played a significant role in shaping San Francisco's queer climate in the early 1990s.

He had been writing erotica since at least the mid-1980s, but suspected that its content was too transgressive and *outré* for most publishers. Partly for this reason, he founded *Frighten the Horses* in 1990. Pritchard's intention was to publish transgressive sex writing alongside news and features that explored the way women and queer people continued the sexual revolution of the previous decades. "I had a vision of how sex fiction and real events informed each other," Pritchard said.

Pritchard saw what sexual repression did to people and how misinformation about the GLBT (gay-lesbian-bisexual-transsexual/-vestite /-gendered) community often led directly to ignorance as well as hatred. His years of activism and writing reflected his desire to fight these misconceptions and ignorance and to ensure that disenfranchised voices were not only heard but respected.

One of the ways in which he chose to represent those disenfranchised voices was through more "honest" representations of the sexual experience in literature. Although he was heavily influenced by the Anaïs Nin version of erotica that was popular when his erotic consciousness emerged, he gradually became aware of the euphemistic treatment of sexual matters in such work. He sought to "call things by their own names," he said.

In 1999, his first collection of short stories, *Too Beautiful*, was published by Masquerade Books (and later reprinted by Cleis Press). It presents an exploration of bisexuality, the "meaning" of penetration and anal play for heterosexual men, and the possibility of finding love and transcendence through open relationships. His blatant sexual writing was not limited to empty pornographic scenes but, rather, delved into a plethora of sexual orientations and the complicated, powerful emotions behind sexual acts.

Take this excerpt from his short story "How I Adore You," in which one woman struggles with showing her desire for another woman. Notice that the focus is not on the sex act itself but on the emotions and insecurities behind it:

> She doesn't really want you, I told myself, forcing myself not to grind back against her face. I made my hips dance a very light pattern as she put her tongue against my clit. She doesn't want you, I said to myself over and over again, so don't show her you want her.

> "Oh," I let myself say. It meant, Elena, your mouth on me is like the whole fucking ocean. Your mouth is perfect just to look at, and the thought of it, just the thought of your mouth, is enough to make me wet. Just the idea of it being against my pussy is enough to make me come. So what does it mean for you to actually be pressing your lips against me, sucking on my clit, making me do this?

> I let my breaths tell the rest of it. My mind went somewhere where she was sticking long needles into my pussy lips in such a way that the pussy was not shut but pinned open widely, so that to be fucked would simply drive the needles deeper into me.

> That's the kind of thing I don't let myself say or really talk about.

Writer Pat Califia's work also inspired him to write more realistically about sex and about the people engaged in it. As the entire erotica genre entered a new phase of no-holds-barred sexual exploration, Pritchard began to make no distinction between pornography and erotica. In fact, he came to understand that the more honest—even transgressive—erotica became, the hotter it was.

His writing faces themes from incest to drugs to sadomasochism. In *Too Beautiful*, stories run the gamut from dominant/submissive fantasies to one particularly controversial piece called "Lizza," the wild chronicle of incestuous siblings so obsessed with breaking taboos that they careen from downright fierce sex with each other to a violent crime spree. The stories are rarely autobiographical but are influenced heavily by the era in which his activism peaked. "I tried to capture the energy of a time and place, namely early 1990s San Francisco," Pritchard explains. "In the same way that David Wojnaraowicz and Kathy Acker captured the energy of the late '70s and early '80s New York City, I wanted to capture early '90s San Francisco."

Pritchard's latest writing efforts are not erotica based, but he believes that erotica provided a "very useful training ground" for him as a fiction writer. "I tried to use my erotica writing as an apprenticeship to fiction, learning how to construct a story, learn timing and pacing, how to write dialogue, how to write descriptions, and most of all, avoid clichés. Avoiding clichés is particularly important for genre writers because it's all been done before. How many different ways can you write about fucking? How many different ways can you describe cocksucking? The answer is that it's the context that makes it interesting to read about."

Pritchard is currently writing novels, none of which, at this writing, is scheduled for publication.

Biography

Born in St. Louis, April 28. Moved to southern Illinois in 1957, and suburban Houston, Texas, in 1970. Began to experiment with dance and performance art, as well as writing while at the

University of Texas at Austin in 1977. Moved to San Francisco, 1979. Taught high school in San Francisco, 1985–1986. Taught English in Japan, 1987–1988. Queer activism from 1989 to 1993. With Cris Gutierrez, published and coedited the zine *Frighten the Horses*, 1990–1994. Married Cris Gutierrez in 2003.

SAGE VIVANT (JILL TERRY)

Selected Works

Too Beautiful. New York: Masquerade Books, 1999.
How I Adore You. San Francisco, CA: Cleis Press, 2001.
Too Beautiful and Other Stories. San Francisco, CA: Cleis Press, 2001. New edition of *Too Beautiful* with additional stories.
Frighten the Horses. Zine. San Francisco, CA: 1990–94.

Further Reading

Burke, Phyllis. *Family Values: Two Moms and Their Son.* New York: Random House Value Publishing, 1995.
Powers, Ann. *Weird Like Us.* New York: HarperCollins, 2001.

PRIVATE CASE

Segregated cabinet in the British Library

The presence of erotica in great national and academic libraries is not something that is generally advertised but may well be suspected. Often erotic books are merely catalogued in the normal way and lost amidst their more respectable brethren. Sometimes, as with the "Enfer" [Inferno] of the Bibliothèque Nationale or the agreeably punning Φ [fi!] pressmark of the Bodleian Library, Oxford, erotic works are segregated or given special shelf-location codes to distinguish them, but they have always been included in the printed catalogues.

By contrast the British Library took a different course entirely, maintaining for almost 100 years a secret catalogue of its holdings and enforcing special rules on those readers diligent enough to discover what treasures were literally

locked away in the glass-fronted cases of the Arch Room of the old Library at Bloomsbury.

The precise origins of the Private Case are uncertain, and a number of theories on the subject have been proposed. However, the most likely would seem to have been a desire to conceal books that were thought of, in earlier times, as being obscene rather than merely erotic. This would account for the large number of medical or sexological books in the collection until the mid-1960s, as well as the presence of novels like *Naked Lunch* by William Burroughs, which by no stretch of the imagination could be described as erotic.

The earliest entry into the Private Case that I know of is a verse satire called *Paradise Lost; or The Great Dragon Cast Out* (London, 1838) by "Lucian Redivivus." This was acquired by the British Library in 1841 and was probably kept in a cupboard in the keeper's office. Since the collection remained at first relatively small, numeric pressmarks were deemed unnecessary, but eventually the confines of the keeper's cupboard became somewhat restrictive and around 1865 more generous accommodations had to be found, and with them numeric pressmarks. *Paradise Lost* acquired the shelf location P.C. 20. b. 12, but was later "desegregated," as the process is called, to the less restrictive pressmark 1077. d. 70.

The growth of the Private Case was at first slow. Some of the books—for example, Vizetelly's splendid series of unexpurgated translations of Zola—were acquired through the operation of the British copyright laws, which demand that copies of each book published in the United Kingdom be deposited with a number of the nation's major research libraries, including the British Library. Others were purchased with public money, which is perhaps why there are so few mentions of the Private Case and its contents to be found in the minutes of the trustees.

The collection received its first major boost in 1900 with the Ashbee bequest. Henry Spencer Ashbee accumulated one of the best Cervantes collections outside Spain. He also had a substantial erotica collection, which the British Library accepted with rather less enthusiasm, and there is evidence to suggest that many mid- to late-Victorian English erotic books in the collection were destroyed by the Library as being of no value—a pity, since in many cases Ashbee's descriptions of these books in his celebrated three-volume bibliography of erotica are all that we know about them. The books the Library kept can be identified by a small leather label or the accession date stamp of November 10 1900.

Throughout the 20th century, the collection grew thanks to the efforts of Dr. E.J. Dingwall, an honorary assistant keeper in the Department of Printed Books, who apparently purchased for the Library individual books and small collections with his own money. Other bequests, and the transfer of the small Guildhall Library collection to the Private Case in 1950, further enlarged the holdings, until in 1964, the massive Dawes bequest elevated the Private Case to one of the finest collections of its kind in the world.

During the late 1960s, a decision was made to enter the Private Case books into the General Catalogue. By then, the collection amounted to almost 2,800 titles. The process of recataloguing involved checking each volume to see whether, in the light of changing attitudes, they still deserved to be there or could be safely desegregated. A little over 800 titles were weeded out in this way and reshelved in other, less restricted areas of the Library.

As of 1991, the Private Case contained about 1,950 titles. Additions are no doubt made from time to time, but with pornography freely available and a more liberal view of what's acceptable, these are infrequent. Where books are added to the collection today it seems likely that the reason has more to do with their rarity than their indecency.

PATRICK J. KEARNEY

Further Reading

Fryer, Peter. *Private Case, Public Scandal*. London: Secker & Warburg, 1966.

Harris, P.K., ed. *The Library of the British Museum. Retrospective Essays on the Department of Printed Books*. London: The British Library, 1991.

Kearney, Patrick J. *The Private Case. An Annotated Bibliography of the Private Case Erotica Collection of the British (Museum) Library*. Introduction by G. Legman. London: Landesman, 1981.

Mendes, Peter. *Clandestine Erotic Fiction in English, 1800–1930. A Bibliographical Study*. Aldershot: Scolar Press, 1993.

Reade, Rolf S. [Alfred Rose]. *Registrum Librorum Eroticorum vel (sub hac specie) dubiorum: Opus bibliographicum et præcipue bibliothecariis destinatum*. London: Privately printed, 1936. 2 vols. Reprinted in facsimile at New York by Jack Brussel in 1965.

PROSTITUTION

Prostitution covers a wide variety of behaviors and activities; not surprisingly it offers poets, playwrights, and novelists rich subject matter, figuring metonymically for other behaviors, attitudes, and ideals. In erotic literature dating from before the middle of the 20th century, the prostitute is generally viewed as a threat: to masculinity, to the social order, to "good" women. However, the rise of the prostitutes' rights movement and other shifts in representations of female sexuality have offered new versions of the prostitute: her illicit sexuality and erotic explorations suggest economic and personal freedom.

One of the earliest prostitutes in literature, the unnamed "harlot" in the Sumerian *Epic of Gilgamesh* civilized Gilgamesh's companion, Enkidu. She taught him to dress, bathe, and drink wine, but Enkidu cursed her for destroying his power over animals. Obviously, this narrative suggests that the luxury associated with women corrupts masculinity, a familiar theme.

The prostitute character is central to the theatrical canon. Shakespeare's *Othello* has Bianca, Behn's *Rover* includes Angelica, and Brecht's *Mother Courage and her Children* features Yvette. The prostitute in most canonical plays is usually a peripheral figure who displaces tension over correct female behavior in the main plot or serves as a vehicle for the playwright's larger argument. Bianca's promiscuity shadows Desdemona's supposed infidelity, making literal Othello's assumptions about women's "natural" inclinations. In *The Rover*, Angelica is a spectacular figure; Restoration audiences were preoccupied with depictions of sexuality, especially female sexuality, and Angelica provides the body on which some of the play's more obscene jokes and subplots are written. Brecht's whores (Pirate Jenny from *The Three-Penny Opera*, Shen Te from *Good Woman of Setzuan*, and Yvette) stand in for the evils of capitalism. These three examples demonstrate the elasticity of the prostitute metaphor; that these three are exemplars rather than exceptions suggests that the prostitutes' erotic presence thrilled theatre audiences.

Before the 19th-century, few plays featured prostitutes as the central dramatic focus. However, the 19th century fully exploited the dramatic potential of prostitution narratives: "courtesan plays" were immensely popular. Alexandre Dumas *fils' La Dame aux camellias* (*Camille*) is the paradigm here. *Camille*, first produced in Paris in 1849, tells the story of beautiful, desirable Marguerite, a courtesan available to characters in the play and the gaze of the audience. Marguerite dances about her Parisian apartments, bosom heaving; is kissed and fondled by the male characters; and finally dies for the entirety of the final act, falling across couches and beds, onto the floor, and into the arms of her friends and lovers. Marguerite provided erotic spectacle for audience members titillated by the visual representation of a courtesan. Her story of sacrifice and sensuality solidified into a pervasive representation of the theatrical prostitute: she is initially shallow and greedy, but true love brings out her best instincts and she dies rather than continue to pollute her family, friends, and lovers.

These plays and countless imitations present an image of the doomed and morally flawed woman. This theatrical narrative parallels 19th-century novelistic treatments of the fallen woman. The narrative of the fall contained prostitutes in the passive, victim role, and attempted to discursively erase their threat to middle-class ideology. Zola's Nana and Balzac's Esther are both terrifying figures; though ignorant and illiterate, they unleash the depravity suppressed by the bourgeois codes of middle-class society from which they seduce their "victims." Their awesome sexual power is narratively contained, as both women die in diseased corruption. Victorian British novelists also pursued the fallen-woman narrative, albeit with less emphasis on the prostitutes' activities than her moral attitude toward them. For example, Thomas Hardy's *Tess of the d'Urbervilles* is less the story of the initial fall than Tess's struggle to reassert a moral compass. This discursive representation of prostitution had material effects in the nineteenth century. Prostitutes were conceived of as so-called fallen women who necessarily died alone and diseased soon after their initial seduction, and so European and American rescue efforts of prostitutes focused on instilling bourgeois moral values into them rather than offering them specific job skills.

Though high- and middle-brow theatre and literature successfully adapt the prostitute to a variety of rhetorical effects, erotic literature also uses the prostitute. For example, the Roman *Satyricon* contains several stories of sexual excess where the prostitute figures as a central trope, again corrupting masculine power through luxury and weakness. John Cleland's *Fanny Hill, or Memoirs of a Woman of Pleasure* and Daniel Defoe's *Moll Flanders* are two early modern examples of highbrow, literary erotica. In both stories, the innocent girl learns her own sensuality through experimentation before embarking on a career as a prostitute. Shocking when published, and shocking now for its depiction of early modern female sexuality, this erotic literature suggests both corruption and sexual freedom. De Sade also includes prostitutes in his narratives, often using their experience to teach him or the young women under his tutelage new sexual techniques. In important ways, erotica of the 17th to 19th centuries offers prostitutes as representing the limits of all female sexuality; their sexual excess is the extreme with which all female sexual behavior can be compared.

In twentieth-century Western erotic literature, prostitutes are still repositories of sexual knowledge and advanced technique but are rarely depicted as either fallen or depraved. This shift reflects the prostitutes' rights movement, which insists on the agency (sexual and otherwise) of the prostitute. For example, Tracy Quan's *Diary of a Manhattan Call Girl* chronicles the adventures of Nancy Chan, a high-priced, high-class escort. Chan's experiences are clearly modeled on Quan herself, a working prostitute and the activist founder of Prostitutes of New York (PONY). Chan/Quan detailed her sexual encounters with clients in graphic detail but also included her struggle as a woman of color seeking entry into the prostitutes' rights movement. Prostitutes and sex-positive feminists are increasingly writing erotic narratives (Xaviera Hollander's hugely successful *The Happy Hooker* [1972] was an early entry into autobiographical aboveground prostitute erotica), inflecting graphic depictions of sexual adventures with an awareness of the prostitutes' own pleasure and the parallels between sexual and other freedoms.

KIRSTEN PULLEN

Further Reading

Almodovar, Norma Jean. *Cop to Call Girl*. New York: Avon, 1993.

Anderson, Amanda. *Tainted Souls and Painted Faces: The Rhetoric of Fallenness in Victorian Culture*. Ithaca (NY) and London: Cornell University Press, 1993.

Bernheimer, Charles. *Figures of Ill Repute: Representing Prostitution in Nineteenth-Century France*. Cambridge (MA) and London: Harvard, 1989.

Bullough, Vern, and Bonnie Bullough. *Women and Prostitution: A Social History*. Buffalo: Prometheus, 1987.

Carpenter, Belinda J. *Rethinking Prostitution: Feminism, Sex, and the Self*. New York: Peter Lang, 2000.

Hollander, Xaviera. *The Happy Hooker: My Own Story*. With Robin Moore and Yvonne Dunleavy. 30th anniversary ed. New York: ReganBooks, 2002.

Kendrick, Walter. *The Secret Museum: Pornography in Modern Culture*. New York: Viking, 1987.

Kishtainy, Khalid. *The Prostitute in Progressive Literature*. London and New York: Alison and Busby, 1982.

Nead, Linda. *Myths of Sexuality: Representations of Women in Great Britain*. Oxford: Basil Blackwell, 1988.

Parish, James Robert. *Prostitution in Hollywood Films: Plots, Critiques, Casts and Credits for 389 Theatrical and Made-for-Television Releases*. Jefferson (NC) and London: McFarland, 1992.

Pearson, Jacqueline. *The Prostituted Muse: Images of Women and Women Dramatists, 1642–1737*. New York: St. Martin's Press, 1988.

Pepys, Samuel. *The Diary of Samuel Pepys*. Edited by Robert Latham and William Matthews. London, 1970–83.

Pinero, Arthur Wing. *The Second Mrs. Tanqueray*. London: William Heinemann, 1894.

Quan, Tracy. *The Diary of a Manhattan Call Girl: A Nancy Chan Novel*. New York: Crown, 2001.

Queen, Carol. *Real Live Nude Girl: Chronicles of Sex-Positive Culture*. San Francisco: Cleis, 1997.

PULP FICTION

The term *pulp fiction* most often refers to a class of paperback books published in Britain and the United States during the post–World War II period, employing a characteristically colorful style of cover art and exploiting sensational themes of criminality and sexuality. While attempts had been made since at least the 19th century to mass-distribute entire novels in paperback form, certain technological advances made in the late 1930s made this mode of publishing increasingly economical and lucrative following World War II. Among these advances were cheaper and faster paper-making techniques (hence the term *pulp*) and improvements in color reproduction and binding technologies. Added to these was the idea of taking manuscripts directly from the author to paperback, giving unknown authors publishing opportunities and thus saving the cost of paying high manuscript advances and/or paying for expensive reprint rights on hardcover best sellers and classics. An early edition of William Borroughs' novel *Junky*, published in 1953 in paperback by Ace Publications, exemplifies all of the qualities of pulp fiction. Treating what was considered a highly sensational theme and involving much of the kind of material that a congressional committee had termed obscene in the previous year, this novel by an unknown author cost its publisher little and eventually proved a very good investment.

Another innovation, in distribution, was led by the Fawcett publishing house in 1939. Fawcett, which had formerly published only magazines, hit on the idea of distributing books through channels formerly reserved for periodical publications. The lower cost of production made this mass distribution possible. In the postwar United States, pulp paperbacks were available (usually in revolving racks) in virtually every drugstore, bus station, train station, and laundromat. Rachel Bowlby has documented a similar development in Britain, where the W.H. Smith chain of book and stationery stores had placed branches in all major rail stations by the mid-20th century. This led to the rise of the cheap "commuter novel," intended for reading on short train journeys. Alison Hennegan recalls her first sight of one such novel in a London train station in the 1950s. It was a paperback reprint of a classic novel with a lesbian theme—made obvious by lurid cover art which the young writer found immediately desirable and which her mother found objectionable. The incident illustrates the nature of the sexual messages and interactions which occurred around pulp paperbacks throughout the postwar decades.

Along with drugs and violent crime, sexual identity has been a major preoccupation of the pulp paperback genre. Both the cover art and promotional blurbs exploit the position of women as objects of desire in the culture at large, and often add to this the sensational theme of "perversion." Thus lesbians become the perfect marketing tool, and lesbian fiction is perhaps the best-remembered form of the pulp paperbacks of the postwar era. However, pulp houses published many books on the theme of male homosexuality. *Twilight Men: The Story of a Homosexual*, published by Lion Books in 1952, is a good example. It advertised itself on the cover as "the definitive novel on the homosexual male, a frank and honest account of the subject that had always before been spoken of in whispers and medical case histories." It is important to note the mention of medical case histories here. All forms of pulp erotica exploited the association of medical inquiry with so-called sexual perversion. In 1959, Collier published Sigmund Freud's *Fragment of an Analysis of a Case of Hysteria* (often referred to as the "Dora case") inside a sensational cover featuring a woman in a half-laced corset. The cover blurbs make much of Freud's incidental mention of his patient's possible lesbian desires.

In the United States in 1952 a special committee was formed in the House of Representatives for the investigation of then-current pornographic materials. This committee is often referred to as the Gathing's Committee, after the name of the senator who chaired it. In reality, it was an attempt at gaining federal support for censorship moves made by local governments and police forces. Over a month the committee examined pulp paperback fiction alongside periodical and mail order publishing. A senior executive of Fawcett Publishing testified, and among the novels examined were *She Made It Pay* by Les Scott, *Spring Fire* by Vin Packer (see *Meaker, Marijane*), and *Women's Barracks* by Tereska Tores. Though the committee's majority opinion found in favor of censorship, the pulp industry does not seem to have been affected by any real increase in the power of censors.

In the early 1960s, with the erosion of censorship in other popular cultural forms, themes began to broaden. Mass-market paperbacks which dealt with drug addiction increased, and many books which constituted tours of urban bohemia appeared. These combined various taboo sexual subjects such as miscegenation, female promiscuity, lesbianism, and male homosexuality. A good example of these is McFadden Books' *I Love Thee Beast* by H.D. Miller. Its cover announces it as "a scorcher, a white hot shocker about the beatniks of Greenwich Village" and quotes *The Library Journal* as saying that it "touches upon the race problems, Lesbianism, homosexuality, psychoanalysis and sex." Here we see a comprehensive list of the many signifiers of sexual content exploited by postwar pulp advertising.

Though most critics agree on the years between 1950 and 1965 as the golden age of pulp publishing, it is difficult to pinpoint an ending to the genre, if there has been one. Inexpensively produced formulaic paperback fiction continues to constitute the most financially significant sector of the publishing industry. Though it is not often referred to by the term *pulp fiction,* critically we must count mass-market romance novels in the same category. The year 1939, which saw the first innovations in pulp distribution, also saw the publication of Daphne du Maurier's hugely successful romance novel *Rebecca*. Pulp publishers saw something in this particular romance plot that eventually became the formula for the mass-market romance novel. By the 1970s romance publishing houses such as Harlequin in North America and Mills and Boon in Britain commanded a market much larger than anything before seen in the publishing industry. Again, low-cost production techniques and innovative marketing, this time through mailing lists and supermarket distribution, led to enormous financial success. Much feminist criticism has been written on mass-market romance novels. Ann Barr Snitow argues that for women, these novels perform the same function which magazine pornography performs for men. "How different," she writes, "is the pornography for women, in which sex is bathed in romance, diffused, always implied rather than enacted at all. This pornography is the Harlequin (or Mills and Boon) romance" (Snitow, 1983).

Mass-market paperbacks are still a multinational industry, and many are still distributed through newsstand and supermarket venues in the United States and the United Kingdom. Many of these, like the British Black Lace and American Harlequin lines, still function as vehicles for sexual identification and pleasure. Two factors, however, might be seen as contributing to the decline of the "classic" pulp paperback. The increasing use of photography in late-20th-century cover art ended the creation of the colorful and stylized airbrush painting since prized by collectors. Also, after 1970, Western culture began to see itself as increasingly sexually "liberated." Sexual restrictions and taboos were seen in mainstream culture as relics of the past. This narrative of sexual progress detracted from the pose of danger and daring which was the selling point of so many pulp paperbacks.

MEREDITH MILLER

Further Reading

Hennegan, Alison. "On Becoming a Lesbian Reader." In *Sweet Dreams: Sexuality, Gender and Popular Fiction*, edited by Susannah Radstone, 165–90. London: Lawrence and Wishart, 1988.

Longhurst, Derek, ed. *Reading Popular Fiction: Gender, Genre and Narrative Pleasure*. London: Unwin Hyman, 1989.

McCracken, Scott. *Pulp: Reading Popular Fiction*. Manchester: Manchester University Press, 2000.

Miller, Lawrence. "The Golden Age of Gay and Lesbian Literature in Mainstream Mass-Market Paperbacks." *Paperback Parade* 47 (February 1997): 37–66.

Peterson, Clarence. *The Bantam Story: Thirty Years of Paperback Publishing in America*. New York: Bantam, 1975.

Radway, Janice. *Reading the Romance: Women, Patriarchy and Popular Literature*. Chapel Hill, NC: University of North Carolina Press, 1984.

Snitow, Ann Barr. "Mass-Market Romance: Pornography for Women is Different." In *Desire: The Politics of Sexuality*, edited by Ann Snitow and Christine Stansell, 245–63. London: Virago, 1983.

Tebbel, John A. *A History of Book Publishing in the United States, Volume IV: The Great Change, 1940–1980*. New York: R.R. Bowker and Co., 1981.

PUSHKIN, ALEKSANDR

1799–1837
Russian poet and writer

Secret Journal, 1836–1837

In 1986 Mikhail Armalinsky published *Secret Journal, 1836–1837*, an erotic and intimate diary that he attributed to Aleksandr Pushkin. The journal was supposedly written during the final months of the poet's life while he was preparing himself for the duel in which he died.

Armalinsky explains in his "Necessary Preface" that in 1976, before his emigration to the United States, a mysterious stranger, referred to as Nikolai Pavlovich, had given the journal to him to be smuggled out of the Soviet Union for publication in the West. It was supposed to have been originally written in French with only a few words and expressions in Russian, and then translated by Nikolai Pavlovich into Russian. Armalinsky contends that the journal would have been banned had it been discovered by Soviet authorities because of its highly erotic content and explicit language. The cult of Pushkin was strong in the Soviet Union, and any scandal, founded or unfounded, concerning the idol would not have been tolerated.

The authenticity of the *Secret Journal* as Pushkin's work is problematic on several levels. Two major points speak against it: the suspicious circumstances under which it came to be discovered, and the fact that the original manuscript, if one exists, has never surfaced. Since its first publication, the journal has not been conclusively authenticated. Its credibility problems are compounded by the absence of any mention or discussion of this work in the serious Pushkin scholarship of the late 1980s to the early 21st century. The language of the journal as translated—crude, cryptic, and poorly crafted—does not help the cause.

Lending some credence to the work as Pushkin's are the rumors that a secret journal had been written, meant to be published a hundred years after his death. Also there is Pushkin's reputation as both a libertine/freethinker and as the author of two erotic works: the famed "Don Juan list," a notebook that candidly records his sexual exploits, and the scandalous "Graf Nulin," a comic short story with sexual overtones. Both factors could count in favor of the *Secret Journal*'s authenticity. The poor language, so uncharacteristic of Pushkin, may be attributed to its being a private journal, as well as a translation. Perhaps it should be seen as biographical and historical, not to be judged from a literary point of view.

The discussion that follows starts with the assumption that Pushkin is the author of the journal. It is not within the scope of this article to prove or disprove the journal's authenticity.

The journal reads like a fictionalized biographical work with an overtly erotic twist. Intimate details and excesses of the author's sexual life are blended together with a morbid preoccupation with destiny and death, recurring themes in Pushkin's works. A close look at court life, with its hypocrisy, politics, and intrigues adds a new dimension and interest to the plot by bringing to light the suspect court morality. Pushkin was publicly opposed to Tsar Nicholas I, in large part due to the despotic monarch's policy of repression of personal freedom. The journal's obscene language and imagery and repeated use of vulgar words to depict genitalia and the sexual act are almost juvenile in their insistence and can be interpreted as expressions of rebelliousness and defiance; and the sexual excesses and licentiousness can be seen as devices to prove his point.

The journal tells the story of Pushkin's unhappy marriage to Natalia Goncharova, a court beauty and one of the tsar's mistresses; his dissolute and debauched lifestyle with innumerable affairs and liaisons; Natalia's alleged affair with Dantes (D'Anthès), a dashing French officer; Pushkin's decision to challenge his rival to defend his wife's honor; and finally, the duel which resulted in his agonizing death. The journal's ribald tone is diffused in places by the author's musings on the disadvantages and restrictions of matrimony.

The first entry of the journal is dedicated to his wife. The beginning of the journal signals the end with a reference to the duel: "The prediction is coming true—I challenged Dantes to a duel." Alluding to his impending death, he hints that the "notes" are intended for posterity, instructing that they be published in two hundred years or so. The journal, as a "revelation" of his soul, should be made part of his legacy—meant, in his words, "to take my sins, mistakes and torments to the grave with me; they are too substantial not to become part of my monument." The bequeathing of the journal to a future generation is an affirmation of Pushkin's belief that erotica is a legitimate genre.

Graphic descriptions of orgies and trysts abound and are presented in detail; special attention is given to the smell, look, and taste of the sexual partner's genitalia, often accompanied by scatological comments. Scenes of lovemaking even with his wife are presented in a similarly crude manner, with the most intimate details reduced to lasciviousness. Pushkin emerges as a possessive husband, jealous of his wife's success in society as a beauty. He describes his wife as an "ungifted lover," disparagingly comparing her with his other lovers, one of them being Natalia's own sister Katrina, Dantes's wife.

Discussing matrimony, lamenting the loss of the bachelor life and its variety of sexual partners without guilt, he expounds on the benefits of adultery. He admits that his passion for his wife passed a month after their marriage, comparing the married state to a cage and the husband to an animal. The interdictions imposed by matrimony revive lust for other women, turning the "nuptial bed, the cradle of passion, into its grave."

If the *Secret Journal* is proven to be authentic, it would cast a different light on its illustrious author, perhaps unfavorably altering his image. More importantly, Pushkin scholarship would have to be reevaluated and revised by accepting the journal in the literary canon, lending it a postmodern dimension, and thereby keeping his works fresh. Pushkin, long considered an innovator and a visionary, would have again influenced literary discourse.

Biography

Born in Moscow into a noble family. Received the title of National Poet during his lifetime. Poet, playwright, lyricist, and prose writer, he is credited by Russian writers and scholars with having created the modern Russian literary language. His works have been made into operas and ballets by composers like Tchaikovsky, Rimsky-Korsakov, and Mussorgsky. Founder and publisher of *Sovremennik* [*The Contemporary*], a literary and historical review. Considered to be the foremost poet of the so-called golden age (1814–1825) of Russian literature.

TRINA MAMOON

Editions

Tainye zapiski, 1836–1837 godov. Minneapolis, MN: MIP Company, 1986, 1989, 1991; as *Secret Journal, 1836–1837*, translated by Mikhail Armalinsky and Tjody Aan, Minneapolis: MIP Company, 1986, 1990.

Selected Works

Ruslan i Liudmila. 1820
Graf Nulin. 1825
Povesti Belkina. 1830
Boris Godunov. 1825 (publ. 1831)
Malen'kie tragedii. 1830 (publ. 1832–39)
Evgenii Onegin. 1833
Istoriia Pugacheva. 1833
Kapitanskaia dochka. 1836
Mednyi vsadnik. 1833 (publ. posthumously in 1837)
Polnoe sobranie sochinenii. 6 vols. Edited by M.A. Tsyavlovskii. Moscow and Leningrad: Akademia Nauk SSSR, 1936; 16 vols., 1937–59

Further Reading

Arndt, Walter. *Pushkin Threefold: Narrative, Lyric, Polemic, and Ribald Verse*. New York: Dutton, 1972.
Bethea, David. *Pushkin Today*. Bloomington, IN: Indiana University Press, 1993.
Blagoy, Dmitry. *The Sacred Lyre: Essays on the Life and Work of Alexander Pushkin*. Moscow: Raduga Publishers, 1982.
Debreczeny, Paul. *The Other Pushkin: A Study of Alexander Pushkin's Prose Fiction*. Stanford, CA: Stanford University Press, 1983.
———, trans. and ed. *Alexander Pushkin: Complete Prose Fiction*. Stanford, CA: Stanford University Press, 1983.
Nabokov, Vladimir, trans. and ed. *Eugene Onegin*. 4 vols., 2nd ed. Princeton, NJ: Princeton University Press, 1975.
Shaw, Thomas, trans. *The Letters of Alexander Pushkin*. Madison, WI: University of Wisconsin Press, 1967.
Simmons, E.J. *Pushkin*. 2nd ed. Gloucester, UK: Peter Smith, 1971.
Troyat, Henri. *Pushkin*. Garden City, NY: Doubleday, 1970.
Vickery, Walter. *Aleksander Pushkin*. New York: Twayne Publishers, 1970.
Wolff, Tatiana. *Pushkin on Literature*. Evanston, IL: Northwestern University Press, 1999.

Q

QUEER THEORY

Queer theory is a school of literary and cultural criticism that proposes that notions of gender and sexual identities are not fixed entities. It had its beginnings in the development of feminist criticism, postmodern philosophers such as Michel Foucault and Jacques Lacan, and gay/lesbian identity politics of the 1980s. Gay/lesbian studies, in turn, grew out of feminist studies and feminist theory, and gay/lesbian and feminist studies have been interrelated ever since. Foucault's legacy was to inaugurate an understanding of sexuality as socially constructed and as a complex array of social codes and forces, forms of individual activity, and institutional regulatory power. He demonstrates that sex/sexuality has a social history with varying constructions. Foucault resists the naturalizing assumptions of biology and psychoanalytic theory that undergirds normative theories of sexuality. Early constructionist theorists argued with gay/lesbian scholars on the notions of sexuality and gender whether they were socially constructed or do they operate within a transhistorical rubric of what is natural, essential, or biological.

At the end of the 1980s, Queer National activists reclaimed 'queer' as a label for a term of resistance to heterosexuality. It became an inclusive, political term for translesbigays with activists. The popular and political use of 'queer' does not coincide with the academic usage though they all share a common history of resistance to heteronormativity. Queer theory arose in the early 1990s within universities in a number of academic disciplines from literature and the classics to cultural studies. Queer scholars accepted postmodern indeterminacy and diversity as an axiom of critical inquiry. While gay/lesbian studies concentrated mainly on questions of homosexuality, queer theory expanded its realm of investigation to include sexual desire, paying close attention to cultural construction of categories of normative and deviant sexual behaviors. Queer theory expanded the scope of its queries to all kinds of behaviors linked to sexuality, including gender-bending, transvestism, fetishes, and non-conventional sexualities. It analyzed sexual behaviors, all concepts of sexual identity, and categories of normative and deviant. These formed sets of signifiers, which created constructed social and cultural meanings. Queer theory is a set of ideas based around the notion that identities are not fixed and do not determine who we are. As a field of inquiry, queer theory shifts the emphasis away from specific acts and identities to the myriad ways in which gender and sexualities organize and even destabilize society. Queer theory claims that sexual categories shift and change. It differs from earlier gay/lesbian identity politics by arguing that sexual identity templates are not fixed but rather are elastic.

There are several prominent scholars who pioneered queer theory: Eve Kosofsky Sedgwick, Judith Butler, David Halperin, and Michael Warner. This list does not do justice to the proliferation of works on queer theory in the last decade, crossing the fields of literature, history, religion, music, and cultural studies. In *Epistemology of the Closet*, Sedgwick provided deconstructive readings of English canonical literature to unmask the distinctions between homosocial and homosexual relations.

Heterosexuality is privileged in its stigmatization of homosexuality, and the closet is the primary paradigm for structuring knowledge in modern society.

In *Gender Trouble* and *Bodies That Matter*, Judith Butler begins with feminist discussions of gender and advances the argument that gender is not fixed but a cultural fiction. "Gender is the repeated stylization of the body, a set of repeated acts within a highly regulatory frame that congeals over time to produce the appearance of substance, of a natural sort of being." (Butler, 33) Gender is a regulatory construct that privileges heterosexuality as natural and original while homosexuality is understood as its inferior copy. Butler uses the notion of drag as performance that re-inscribes heterosexual norms within a gay context. Drag thus reveals the performative aspects of gender as endless within a regulatory system of sexuality, gender, and desire. Gender becomes something a person performs at particular times rather than a universal characteristic of who you are. Identity categories function as regulatory regimes, whether as normalizing categories or as a counter discourse against normalizing and oppressive regulations.

[]There is no definitional consensus on the limits of queer theory. Jagose proposes that queer theory is a "zone of possibilities...which dramatise the incoherencies in the allegedly stable relations between chromosomal sex, gender, and sexual desire" (Jagose, 2–3). David

Halperin, likewise, takes anti-definitional stance to queer theory: "Queer, then, demarcates not a positivity but a positionality vis-a-vis the normative—a positionality that is not restricted to lesbians and gay men but is in fact available to anyone who is or who feels marginalized because of her or his sexual practices...." (Halperin, 62). For queer theorist Michael Warner queer is a transgressive paradigm, representing "a more thorough resistance to the regimes of the normal" (Warner, xxvi). Queer theory becomes a deconstructive theory, attempting to disrupt cultural normativity by surfacing the heterogeneous and multiple meanings of gender, sexuality, sex acts, and erotic desires. Queer theory has no consistent set of characteristics except denaturalization. It is a mode of critical inquiry that invokes non-normative sexuality and does not refer to anything in particular. It celebrates differences, ruptures, and incoherencies of identities while insisting that all sexual behaviors, either deviant or normative, are social constructs, signifiers of particular social meaning.

Queer theory not only represents a resistance to cultural normativity and to heteronormativity but even a resistance to gay or lesbian normativities. The disassembling of gender and sexual orientation templates has allowed space for the development of bisexuality as a category to undermine the binary categories of heterosexual/homosexual and transgendered/transsexual as categories to subvert gender reification.

Critics such as Max Kirsch and Steve Seidman have also noted that queer theory has subverted the ethnic model of identity politics and that it was difficult to build a political movement on instable identities. For some gay/lesbian critics, the inclusive use of queer and queer theory had the totalizing effect of effacing specific identities and political agendas. Or it disprivileges the positionality of gay and lesbian with emergence of bisexuality, transgendered, and diverse markers of identity. Some have accused queer theory of de-gaying the movement while others claim that it privileges white gay males. The indeterminacy of queer theory has led to such contradictory critiques.

ROBERT E. GOSS

Further Reading

Butler, Judith. *Gender Trouble: Feminism and the Subversion of Identity*. New York: Routledge, 1990.

Dinshaw, Carolyn. *Getting Medieval: Sexualities and Communities, Pre- and Postmodern.* Durham: Duke University Press, 1999.

Foucault, Michel. *The History of Sexuality, Vol. I.* Trans. by Robert Hurley, New York, Vintage Books, 1978.

Halperin, David. *Saint Foucault: Towards a Gay Hagiography.* New York: Oxford Press, 1995.

Jagose, Annamarie. *Queer Theory: An Introduction.* New York: New York University Press, 1996.

Kirsch, Max H. *Queer Theory and Social Change.* New York: Routledge, 2000.

Sedgwick, Eve Kosofsky. *Epistemology of the Closet,* Berkeley, University of California Press, 1990.

Seidman, Steven (ed), *Queer Theory/Sociology,* Cambridge: Blackwell Publications, 1996.

Spargo, Tasmin. *Foucault and Queer Theory.* New York: Totem Books, 1999.

Warner, Michael. *Fear of a Queer Planet.* Minneapolis, MN: University of Minnesota Press, 1993.

QUENEAU, RAYMOND

1903–1976
French novelist

Sally Mara

In 1947, there appeared, in 'French translation from the Gaelic,' a novel by Sally Mara entitled *On est toujours trop bon avec les femmes.* Three years later, the same publishers issued the author's *Journal intime,* a diary of her adolescence written in French, which she had learned from her translator, Michel Presle. In 1962, these two works were reprinted by prestigious publisher Editions Gallimard as *Les Oeuvres complètes de Sally Mara.* This volume included another short text, 'Sally plus intime,' a collection of scurrilous aphorisms. Sally Mara herself introduced the work, although curiously enough she denied the authorship of this new text. Even more curiously, she begins her preface with these words: 'A supposedly imaginary author does not often have the opportunity to preface her complete works, especially when they appear under the name of a so-called real author.' For *Les Oeuvres complètes de Sally Mara* are published here under another's name, one 'Raymond Queneau of the Académie Goncourt.'

This curious trajectory calls for comment: Editions du Scorpion, the publisher of the works of Sally Mara, was set up after World War II to cater to the taste for hard-boiled fiction, and had just published a thriller by Vernon Sullivan, supposedly translated 'from the American' and titled *J'irai cracher sur vos tombes* [*I'll Spit on Your Graves*], which became a cause célèbre for its treatment of sex and violence. Vernon Sullivan, in fact, was a pseudonym for Boris Vian, a young writer influenced and encouraged by the same Raymond Queneau, a highly respected writer, who was later revealed to be the 'author' of the works of Sally Mara.

All this might tend to make one think that Queneau, too, was hiding behind a pseudonym in order to publish a commercial potboiler, especially as *On est toujours trop bon avec les femmes* is, in its outlines, a violent and sexually explicit story, apparently inspired by James Hadley Chase's sensational bestseller, *No Orchids For Miss Blandish.*

Set in 1916 during the Easter uprising in Dublin, it is based on an actual event: the taking of the Central Post Office by Republicans. In the novel, they achieve their aim without much resistance, killing some employees and sending the others home. They think they are masters of the situation, but discover a young English woman, Gertrude Girdle, who was caught in the toilet at the time of the attack. It is too late to send her home, since the British army now surround the building, and they find themselves with an unwanted hostage.

As good revolutionaries, they are determined to act 'properly' and she, a virgin who believes in king and country, has nothing but contempt for these insurgents against the proper order of things. However, when the leader of the rebels, MacCormack, declares the King of England to be 'a stupid cunt,' Gertie is both outraged and liberated. While her fiancé, Commodore Sidney Cartwright, leads the British assault on the Post Office from outside, gallant Gertie systematically sets about seducing the men inside. Discouraged by the success of the British counter-offensive and finding themselves alone in their resistance, they are further demoralized as Gertie undermines their sense of moral purity. On the point of surrendering and with their comrades dead, the two remaining rebels try to persuade Gertie not to reveal what occurred so that their dead comrades will not lose honor. She refuses and one of them, O'Rourke, cursing her as a whore, sodomizes her in order to dishonor her instead. When Commodore Cartwright appears and demands to know whether the rebels had abused Gertie, she replies that they lifted her dress in order to admire her ankles. Cartwright orders that the two rebels be immediately shot.

Although the plot has the ingredients to be a potboiler, Queneau downplays all of these elements. Furthermore, nothing inclines us to believe that writing this novel was an indulgence on his part: it is recognizably a Queneau novel and he makes no concessions to the reader who comes expecting salaciousness. This does not mean that it cannot be considered an 'erotic thriller,' but it is one of a singular kind.

It should be noted that, although based on an actual event, the story is entirely 'literary,' since Queneau has taken the places and characters from James Joyce's *Ulysses*. At one point this fact is even commented upon by one of the characters. Sally Mara, in a footnote, explains Caffrey lets this slip because he, 'being illiterate, could not have known in 1916 that *Ulysses* had not yet appeared.' This brings attention to the complex levels of referentiality at which the novel is working, being about the interplays between appearance and reality and the extent to which fiction assumes its own 'reality.'

Many commentators have seen the novel as an attack on the hard-boiled novel and surrealist black humor, since Queneau had criticized both as being linked into the mentality that had made Nazism possible. This hardly seems satisfactory, especially as the novel contains a scene André Breton would surely have considered as a fine example of pure black humor, indeed it draws directly upon surrealist interests in the predatory aspects of sexuality. In it, Caffrey has his head removed by a shell fired by Commodore Cartwright just as he is being fellated by the latter's fiancée: 'The body continued its rhythmical movement for some seconds, exactly like the praying mantis male when its upper part has been half devoured by the female and which perseveres in the copulation.'

Whatever Queneau's intentions, they are not reducible to facile explanations. *On est toujours trop bon avec les femmes*, taken together with the other works of Sally Mara, reveals a complex web of representation and counter-representation. Characteristic of all of Queneau's work, this theme is given a particular form here by the use of the pseudonym. Sally Mara is less a pseudonym than a female extension of Queneau, bearing much of the same ambivalence as Marcel Duchamp's creation of Rrose Sélavy. The real erotic heart of *Les oeuvres completes de Sally Mara* is to be found in the complex interplays and undercurrents that this relation reveals.

Biography

Born in Le Havre, Raymond Queneau was at first an enthusiastic member of the Surrealist group, from which he split in 1929 'for personal reasons' which he never fully explained. A literary polymath, he was a mathematician, a translator, an editor, a poet, as well as a novelist. A founding member of the College of 'Pataphysics' and the Oulipo, his work is marked by a lightness of touch that does disguise his seriousness of purpose and vast erudition.

MICHAEL RICHARDSON

Editions

"Sally Mara". *On est toujours trop bon avec les femmes*, Paris: Editions du Scorpion, 1947.

"Sally Mara". *Journal intime*, Paris: Editions du Scorpion, 1950.

Les Oeuvres complètes de Sally Mara, Paris: Gallimard, 1962.

We Always Treat Women Too Well, translated by Barbara Wright. London: John Calder, 1981.

Selected Works of Raymond Queneau in English

A Hard Winter. Trans. Betty Askwith. London: John Askwith, 1947.

The Skin of Dreams. Trans. J.J. Kaplan. New York: New Directions, 1948; London: Atlas Press, 1987.

Exercises in Style. Trans. Barbara Wright. London: Gabberbocchus, 1958.

Zazie in the Metro. Trans. Barbara Wright. London: Bodley Head, 1960; London: John Calder, 1982.

The Blue Flowers. Trans. Barbara Wright. New York: Atheneum, 1967.

The Bark Tree. Trans. Barbara Wright. London: Calder & Boyars, 1968.

The Flight of Icarus. Trans. Barbara Wright. London: Calder & Boyars 1973.

The Sunday of Life. Trans. Barbara Wright. London: Calder, 1976.

Pounding the Pavements, Beating the Bushes and other Pataphysical Poems. Trans. Teo Savory. Greensboro, NL: Unicorn Press, 1985.

Odile. Trans. Carol Sanders. Elmwood Park: Dalkey Archive, 1988.

Pierrot Mon Ami. Trans. Barbara Wright. London: Atlas Press, 1988.

The Last Days. Trans. Barbara Wright. Elmwood Park: Dalkey Archive, 1990.

The Children of Clay. Trans. Madeledine Velguth. Los Angeles, CA: Sun & Moon Press, 1998.

R

RABELAIS, FRANÇOIS

c. 1484–1553
French comic writer

Rabelais's humor derives from both a *gaulois* tradition of bawdy parody and an erudite tradition of humanist satire. Erotic themes within the former can be limited to frank obscenity concerning sexual intercourse and a dethroning of the values of chastity and marital fidelity. Yet, as a serious student of Erasmus and St. Paul, Rabelais probably upheld those same values, satirizing unchaste prelates whose celibate life was a fake, just as their obvious wealth defied the vow of poverty. His hero-figures in *Gargantua and Pantagruel* tend to outgrow adolescent sexual dalliances as schoolboys (Gargantua went whoring; Pantagruel had an undisclosed romance) to become responsible adults, and in Gargantua's case a father. However, the licentious themes are maintained via the heroes' exclusively male companions, who, in at least two cases, namely Panurge (anti-hero to Pantagruel) and Frère Jean (anti-hero to Gargantua), claim extravagant sexual appetites and prowess, even though the only one of Panurge's seductions to be described in detail is a failure (see *Pantagruel,* chapters 21–2).

In a fascinating development, Rabelais then makes Panurge, rather than the now chaste and mature Pantagruel, the hero of the *Tiers livre,* which centers on Panurge's terror at being mistreated in marriage now that he feels inclined to woo a bride. Again Rabelais's essentially male perspective conditions the fact that no potential spouse for Panurge is ever selected, named, or introduced, the book instead comprising various unsatisfying predictions concerning his future, and an equivalent series of discussions motivated by his (traditionally Latin) dread of cuckoldry and sexual failure. Meanwhile, the one doctor we meet gives a derogatory, though perhaps only semi-serious, account of female psycho-physiology. Furthermore, Panurge never does marry, and Rabelais, perhaps tiring of his obsessions, turns the *Quart livre* into a sea voyage of exploration rather than that search for the ultimate truth concerning his anti-hero's marital fate, which was its original purpose.

Again, the crew is exclusively male and there are no erotic escapades aboard ship. Nevertheless, the encounters, discussions, and anecdotes comprising their adventures are peppered with the usual lewd details: Frère Jean expresses lust for the maids serving him in chapter 54; a peasant woman uses the "wound" hidden between her legs to scare away a devil; meanwhile, the Queen of the Andouilles, a phallus-shaped race of sausages whom the company defeats in battle, bears a name (Niphleseth) based on the Hebrew for penis. Such incongruity notwithstanding, she is well treated in defeat, while her daughter, also called Niphleseth, ultimately enjoys a happy and fruitful marriage in the French royal court.

The thematic complexity of the Andouilles episode well exemplifies Rabelais's authorial practice whereby an initially simple topic is overloaded with detail to a point where linear interpretations become plainly untenable. As a writer of comic fiction, he thus earns the bonus of allowing many contrasting readings, whilst his erotic themes, applied almost exclusively to comic effect, deliberately stretch his reader's tolerance, yet retain a notable freshness by being so frank and so surprisingly juxtaposed to passages of deep seriousness, mystery, and spirituality.

Biography

Born in or near Chinon, of a middle-class, locally well–established, landowning family. Entered holy orders at some time in his youth, joining the Franciscan house at Fontenay-le-comte, where he pursued humanist scholarship alongside other like-minded intellectuals. Following Church censorship of his Greek studies, left Fontenay for the Benedictine abbey of Maillezais and the tutelage of Bishop Geoffroy d'Estissac, a man of humanist sympathies. At Montpellier by 1530, took various medical degrees, meanwhile gaining employment as town physician in Lyon and encountering his lifelong patrons, the du Bellay family. Early publications were scholarly, but in 1532, following the anonymous *Grandes et inestimables cronicques du grand et énorme géant Gargantua*, which he may also have helped edit, he produced a mock epic, *Les horribles et espovantables faictz et prouesses du tresrenommé Pantagruel*. Encouraged by the success of his book (universally known as *Pantagruel*), he published its prequel, *La vie inestimable du grand Gargantua, pere de Pantagruel* (known simply as *Gargantua*), in 1534/5. With Cardinal Jean du Bellay, Rabelais also made visits to Italy in this period, whereupon, following a lengthy sojourn in Piedmont, then under the French governorship of Guillaume du Bellay (d. 1543), he produced a third volume, now always called *Le tiers livre*, and again featuring the hero Pantagruel. Despite hostility from the Sorbonne, then the center of French Catholic censorship, the du Bellays' patronage also smoothed over various legal matters, including his apostasy and his tenure of religious benefices, a traditional source of revenue for French writers. A partial (possibly pirated) edition of the so-called *Quart livre* appeared in 1548, describing still further adventures of Pantagruel and his followers. A longer *Quart livre*, possibly still incomplete, was published in 1552, only shortly before the author's death. The posthumous publications *L'Isle Sonante* (1562) and *Le cinquième livre* (1564), neither definitively authenticated, are probably adapted from his manuscript notes.

JOHN PARKIN

Selected Works

Oeuvres complètes. Edited by by M. Huchon. Paris: Pléiade, 1994.
The Complete Works of François Rabelais. Translated by D.M. Frame. Berkeley and Los Angeles, CA: University of California Press, 1991.
Gargantua and Pantagruel: The Histories of Gargantua and Pantagruel. Translated by J.M. Cohen. London: Penguin, 1955.

Further Reading

Bakhtin, M.M. *Rabelais and His World.* Translated by H. Iswolsky. Bloomington, IN: Indiana University Press, 1984.
Cave, T. *The Cornucopian Text: Problems of Writing in the French Renaissance.* Oxford: Clarendon Press, 1979.
Etudes rabelaisiennes. Dedicated periodical. Geneva: Droz, 1956–.
Febvre, L. *Le Problème de l'incroyance au XVI siècle.* Paris: Michel, 1942.
Plattard, J. *Vie de François Rabelais.* Paris and Brussels: G. Van Oest, 1928.
Screech, M.A. *Rabelais.* London: Duckworth, 1979.

RACE, RACISM, MISCEGENATION, RACE-BAITING LITERATURE

Histories of the construction of race do not always address the erotic or its role and function in maintaining racism. When the intersections of race and the erotic are explored, however, the arguments are often complicated, powerful, and disturbing. Edward Said's *Orientalism* (1978) offers a compelling account of the eroticized myths of the Orient and how they serve imperialism, and Patricia Hill Collins's *Black Feminist Thought* (2000) powerfully considers the role of self-definition in social knowledge and transformation. The politics of location make any discussion of race and the erotic always partial and definitely problematic. Whose version of race? Whose version of the erotic? Is the erotic always implicated in the politics of race? Can the erotic ever exist outside of or divorced from other systems of power?

In the 1960s, Calvin C. Hernton did much to highlight the way that sex and racism were intertwined, boldly arguing, for example, that "all race relations tend to be, however subtly, sexual relations." Edited volumes, such as *Sex, Love, and Race* (1999) and *Race/Sex: Their Sameness, Difference, and Interplay* (1995), may be said to extend Hernton's argument. In her introduction to *Race/Sex*, for example, Naomi Zack states that "the historical intersection or connection between socially constructed sexuality and socially constructed race has been the sexualization of race in American lived experience." And Martha Hode reminds us: "The history of racial categories is often a history of sexuality as well, for it is partly as a result of the taboos against boundary crossing that such categories are invented." The United States, with its long history of slavery, segregation, and institutional racism, provides a particularly dramatic field for investigating the sexualization of race, though it is important to recognize that other national literatures also tell complex stories about the intersections of race and sex. It is also important to recognize that "race," a metaphor for difference, may refer to various identities, although there are heuristic reasons for focusing on African American identity as it has been represented in the literature of the United States.

Early writings by Africans and slaves in the New World assiduously suppressed the erotic because their primary goal was to argue for the legitimacy, propriety, and humanity of the Negro. Not only was a healthy eroticism missing from African American literature of the nineteenth century but so were negative representations of sex; for example, rape. Despite the very real effects of a slave system that institutionalized the rape of black women and the emasculation of black men, the dominant stereotype of Negroes was that they were primitive and, therefore, more sexually free and even lascivious. Texts such as Harriet Jacob's *Incidents in the Life of a Slave Girl* (1861) risked much by addressing rape and the sexual violence of the slave system, even though the black subject was a victim and not an agent in these accounts. Jacob's account, therefore, was published under the pseudonym Linda Brent. Conversely, the romanticization of whiteness, which found its apotheosis in the purity of the white maiden, promoted an inviolate femininity. These stereotypes were, of course, dependent upon a Manichaean worldview, one that dominated eighteenth- and nineteenth-century literature.

Even the antislavery novel, as Sterling Brown ("Negro Characters") has argued, made use of harmful but sexualized stereotypes, such as the Brute Negro, the Exotic Primitive, and the Tragic Mulatto. In reference to the latter stereotype, Brown states: "If anti-slavery authors, in accordance with Victorian gentility, were wary of illustrating the practice [of concubinage], they made great use nevertheless of the offspring of illicit unions" (158). The Tragic Mulatto may be the most sexualized figure in U.S. literature, often representing the result of illicit unions but also the threat of miscegenation.

Miscegenation laws and mores against the cohabitation or marriage of people of different races betray a complex history of both fear *and* attraction. Novels by African American authors, such as Frances E.W. Harper's *Iola Leroy*, and white authors, such as William Dean Howell's *Imperative Duty*, document this fear and attraction through their use of the "passing" figure: a light-skinned African American who can pass for white. This figure of racial ambiguity, in fact, has been used by many of the most celebrated American authors to explore the interdictions over interracial love, sex, and marriage. Charles Chesnutt's *House Behind the Cedars*, for example, provides an anguished account of the tensions over miscegenation, and William Faulkner's *Light in August* devolves into the horrific and obscene narrative of interracial relations. George Schuyler's *Black No More*, in developing the relationship between a white supremacist and a passing figure, is pure farce. The many narratives of passing, by writers as diverse as Mark Twain and Langston Hughes, are built upon the taboo of interracial love.

The phobia of interracial relationships, however, is most obsessively rendered and disturbingly portrayed in the novels of Thomas Dixon. In *The Clansman* and *The Leopard's Spots*, Dixon portrays the black male body as a hypersexualized threat. Sandra Gunning writes, in *Race, Rape, and Lynching*: "The continual attempt to escape from and return to the black male body is played out whenever Dixon's narratives dramatize the detection, capture, and dismemberment of a black rapist," and: "Dixon is fascinated with the effluvia of black males." In novels such as *The Clansman* and *The Leopard's Spots*, Dixon has presented the most virulent stereotype of a black sexuality that is monstrous. Dixon's work seems inseparable from the phobia and hate that led to so many lynchings in the first half of the twentieth century.

But what use have canonical authors made of—to use Toni Morrison's term—the Africanist presence? In *Playing in the Dark*, Morrison argues that the study of American literature "should be investigations of the ways in which a nonwhite, Africanist presence and personae have been constructed—invented—in the United States, and of the literary uses this fabricated presence has served." In enumerating some of the strategic uses made of race in literature, Morrison describes the fetishization of blackness as "evoking erotic fears or desires and establishing fixed and major difference where difference does not exist or is minimal. Blood, for example, is a pervasive fetish: black blood, white blood, the purity of blood; the purity of white female sexuality, the pollution of African blood and sex. Fetishization is a strategy often used to assert the categorical absolutism of civilization and savagery." The fetishization of race, of course, participates in a broader tradition that romanticizes race.

Few scholars have done more to historicize the romanticization of race than George M. Frederickson, whose *The Black Image in the White Mind* (1971) covers the early 1800s to the beginning of the twentieth century, when there was a "revised form of romantic racialism." Frederickson argues that "[w]hat was new about the image of blacks conveyed in the novels of white writers like DuBose Heyward, Julia Peterkin, and Carl Van Vechten was not the stereotype itself but the lack of moralism in the treatment of what would previously have been defined as black immorality or even animality." This history continues to be written in books such as Robert Entman's *The Black Image in the White Mind: Media and Race in America* (2001) and Marianna Torgovnick's *Gone Primitive* (1990). The greater awareness and critical attention to representations of race have not, of course, eliminated all harmful stereotypes or racist narratives, but there are now more images and more complex renderings of the African American experience.

It was not that long ago that William Styron's *Confessions of Nat Turner* (1967) shocked readers with its transformation of Nat Turner, an historical figure, into a slave who was not only concerned with escaping slavery but also obsessed with raping a white mistress. The formal response to this Pulitzer Prize–winning novel came quickly in the form of *William Styron's Nat Turner: 10 Black Writers Respond*, which challenged Styron's history and politics. Indeed, this rather public debate over the representation of Nat Turner as a sexual threat has been just one in a long series of exchanges concerning the struggle over representative images. The debates, moreover, may be found within the African American community and not solely across racial lines. In the 1920s, for example, W.E.B. Du Bois publicly criticized Claude McKay's *Home to Harlem* (1926), stating that after reading the novel he needed to take a bath. DuBois was concerned with presenting the best qualities of the New Negro, and this did not include his sexuality. Eldridge Cleaver, in *Soul on Ice* (1968), would publicly criticize James Baldwin not so much for addressing sexual themes but for addressing homosexuality, or rather for being a homosexual. Cleaver describes Rufus Scott, the black protagonist of *Another Country*, as "a pathetic wretch who indulged in the white man's pastime of committing suicide, who let a white bisexual homosexual fuck him in the ass, and who took a Southern Jezebel for his woman." Cleaver, moreover, cannot separate his characterization of Rufus Scott as "the epitome of a black eunuch" from his characterization of Baldwin as a "castrated" homosexual.

With these many sordid debates suggesting our profound inability to positively work through the dynamics of race and sex, it is refreshing to consider the example of Audre Lorde, who in essays like "Uses of the Erotic: The Erotic as Power" imagines the erotic as important and powerful. "As a Black lesbian feminist," Lorde writes, "I have a particular feeling, knowledge, and understanding for those sisters with whom I have danced hard, played, or even fought. This deep participation has often been the forerunner for joint concerted actions not possible before." The empowerment Lorde celebrates continues in the voices of Pat Parker and Cheryl Clarke. It can be felt in the growing concert of gay and lesbian writers of color— marginalized no more. Recent anthologies of gay and lesbian literature by African Americans (*Taboo, Go the Way Your Blood Beats,* and *Shade*) document this growing acceptance of taboo themes.

Is there, then, an erotica of race that does not get implicated in racist structures and hierarchies? How should we regard the celebration of race and color in poems like Langston Hughes's "When Sue Wears Red" and Nikki Giovanni's "Beautiful Black Men"? And how should we understand the racially unmarked but deeply erotic poetry of Carl Phillips? And where should we situate the racially and sexually fluid erotics of Samuel Delaney's science fiction? There seems to be, in short, a range of expressions of the erotic in contemporary African American literature that speaks to an evolution toward a greater complexity of self-representations.

JUDA BENNETT

Further Reading

Brown, Sterling. "Negro Characters as Seen by White Authors." In *Dark Symphony: Negro Literature in America*, edited by James A. Emanuel. New York: Free Press, 1968.

Clarke, John Henrik. *William Styron's Nat Turner: 10 Back Writer's Respond.* New York: Greenwood Publishing, 1987.

Cleaver, Eldridge. *Soul on Ice.* New York: Dell Publishing, 1968.

Collins, Patricia Hill. *Black Feminist Thought: Knowledge, Consciousness, and the Politics of Empowerment.* New York: Routledge Press, 2000.

Frederickson, George M. *The Black Image in the White Mind: The Debate on Afro-American Character and Destiny, 1817–1914.* New York: Harper & Row, 1972.

Gunning, Sandra. *Race, Rape, and Lynching: The Red Record of American Literature, 1890–1912.* New York: Oxford University Press, 1996.

Hernton, Calvin. *Sex and Racism in America.* New York: Anchor Books, 1992.

Hodes, Martha. *Sex, Love, Race: Crossing Boundaries in North American Literature.* New York: NYU Press, 1999.

Jacobs, Harriet. *Incidents in the Life of a Slave Girl* [1861]. New York: W.W. Norton & Company, 2001.

Lorde, Audre. "The Uses of the Erotic: The Erotic as Power." In *Sister Outsider: Essays and Speeches.* Ithaca, NY: Crossing Press, 1984.

Morrison, Toni. *Playing in the Dark: Whiteness and the Literary Imagination.* New York: Random House, 1992.

Said, Edward. *Orientalism.* New York: Random House, 1978.

Styron, William. *The Confessions of Nat Turner* [1967]. New York: Modern Library Edition, 1994.

Zack, Naomi. *Race/Sex: Their Sameness, Difference, and Interplay.* New York: Routledge Press, 1997.

RACHILDE

1860–1953
French novelist, dramatist, poet and critic

Rachilde published more than 50 novels, as well as several collections of short stories, poetry, and plays. She wrote extensively in the French press throughout much of her life, and contributed a fortnightly review column to the *Mercure de France*. Diana Holmes (2001) describes her as "a colourful, prolific, combative figure on the French literary scene." Rachilde's scandalous reputation rests to a certain extent on her unconventional behavior. She frequently cross-dressed and referred to herself as "Rachilde, *homme* de lettres," causing Maurice Barrès to christen her "Mademoiselle Baudelaire" in his preface to *Monsieur Vénus*. However, it was the publication, between 1884 and 1900, of her most erotic novels—*Monsieur Vénus, Nono, La Marquise de Sade, L'Animale*, and *La Jongleuse* [*The* (Female) *Juggler*]—which thrust her into the public eye. Rachilde's critics have often commented on the disparity between her relatively innocent, naive existence and the depravity of her novels. This disparity can in part be explained by her literary heritage. She grew up with full and free access to her grandfather's library (a scenario almost unheard of in the moral climate of the 19th century) and had read the works of the Marquis de Sade by the time she was fifteen. Although her novels cannot be described as de Sadean in the proper sense, his influence is clearly discernible, especially in the actions of Mary Barbe in the aptly named *La Marquise de Sade*. In addition, when she moved to Paris, Rachilde became involved in the Decadent literary movement. The Decadents were inspired by the works of Charles Baudelaire as well as de Sade and rejected procreation in favor of the perverse, the artificial, the unnatural. Rachilde's novels share Decadent characteristics with the work of Joris-Karl Huysmans, Jules-Amédée Barbey d'Aurevilly, and Octave Mirbeau.

Rachilde's novels deal explicitly with female sexual desire. Her dominant heroines engage in a range of excessive sexual practices such as sadism (Mary Barbe in *La Marquise de Sade*), necrophilia (Raoule de Vénérande in *Monsieur Vénus*), and bestiality (Laure Lordès in *L'Animale*), as well as erotically motivated murder (Renée Fayor in *Nono*) and suicide (Éliante Donalger in *La Jongleuse*). The powerful sexual desires of Rachilde's heroines are the driving force behind the novels. Her women, who are single-minded, selfish, and emphatically nonmaternal, devote themselves to a quest for female *jouissance* (orgasmic pleasure), which is to be found not in traditional penetrative sex, but in the acts of sexual violence which they inflict on their malleable, helpless, often effeminate male objects of desire. The relentless quest for female sexual pleasure which characterizes the majority of Rachilde's novels means that the desires of submissive male partners are unfulfilled or ignored. However, this quest is rarely successful, and usually results in the death, disappearance, or demise of the central female protagonist, who leaves a trail of bloodshed and heartache behind her. Éliante's orgasm in *La Jongleuse*, which she reaches as she caresses a huge alabaster vase, is one of the rare examples of triumphant female sexual pleasure in Rachilde's work. Although Rachilde's novels were widely considered pornographic at their time of publication, their general lack of scenes of sexual satisfaction means that they are not erotic in the traditional sense. Instead, the scenes of often violent, frequently melodramatic eroticism which they contain are mediated by the novels' sustained interrogation of the tortured existence of their pariah-heroines. The power of Rachilde's narratives comes less from the scenes of sexual activity which they depict than from their engagement with, and perversion of, the accepted gender norms of the 19th century.

When Rachilde writes from the perspective of a male protagonist, as in *Les Hors Nature* [*The Unnatural Ones*] and *La Tour d'amour* [*The Tower of Love*], she demonstrates that male sexual desire is no less problematic than that of her female protagonists. For the most part, her works represent a violent and troubling exploration of the darker side of human sexuality. However, two of Rachilde's novels, *Queue de Poisson* [*Fish-Tail*] and *Le Tiroir de Mimi-Corail* [*Mimi-Corail's Drawers*], represent a more playful, lighthearted, and mainstream kind of *fin-de-siècle* erotica—interestingly, these works have never been republished and are among the least remarkable of her novels.

Monsieur Vénus

Monsieur Vénus is Rachilde's best-known work. Its publication in Belgium in 1884 was a huge *succès de scandale*, earning Rachilde national celebrity and a prosecution for obscenity (the outcome of which cost her two years imprisonment and a fine). Consequently, the courts in Paris ordered immediate seizure of all copies of the book. The novel's celebrity was enhanced by a preface by Maurice Barrès. The heroine of *Monsieur Vénus*, the cruel and youthful aristocrat Raoule de Vénérande, refuses the traditional fate reserved for women—virginity, marriage, childbirth—and elects instead to lead a "masculine" life of sexual freedom. In particular she rejects the kind of male-orientated herterosex in which women's desires remain unfulfilled. In a quest for sexual pleasure, she takes her lover Jacques Silvert from a lower class, sets him up in a sumptuous apartment, and uses him as she wishes. When she discovers that her friend and suitor Raittolbe is also attracted to Jacques, her jealousy leads her to engineer a duel between the two men in which Jacques is killed. The novel ends with an archetypal Decadent scene in which the ghoulish figure of Raoule lavishes her attentions on a wax dummy of Jacques, complete with nails, hair, and teeth which she has taken from his corpse. The scandalized reaction to the novel's publication comes from its clear challenge to the gendered binary oppositions in place in 19th-century France: Raoule's authority, control, and voyeurism are in stark contrast to Jacques's increasingly feminized behavior. Of all Rachilde's work, this novel has best stood the test of time, in part because the "gender trouble" it evokes finds a telling echo in 21st-century identity politics.

Biography

Born Marguerite Eymery in Le Cros, France, February 11, 1868. Received minimal education at home. Began writing in 1870; took the pen name Rachilde in 1876. First published in local newspapers in 1877. Moved to Paris in 1878. Married Alfred Vallette in 1889 (widowed 1935); one daughter. Co-founded the journal *Mercure de France* with Vallette, 1890; contributed a regular review column until 1925. Made officer of the Légion d'Honneur, 1924. Although infamous in the Parisian literary circles of the 1880s and 1890s, Rachilde's fame diminished as she grew older, and she died alone and in poverty on April 4, all but forgotten by the literary establishment.

HANNAH THOMPSON

Selected Works

Monsieur Vénus [1884]. Translated by Madeleine Boyd, in *The Decadent Reader,* edited by Asti Hustvedt. New York: Zone Books, 1998.
Nono, roman de moeurs contemporain, 1885
Queue de poisson, 1885
La Marquise de Sade [1887]. Translated by Liz Heron. Sawtry, UK: Dedalus, 1994.
Le tiroir de Mimi-Corail, 1887
L'Animale, 1893
Les hors nature: Moeurs contemporaines, 1897
La tour d'amour, 1899
La jongleuse [1900]. Translated by Melanie C. Hawthorne. New Brunswick, NJ: Rutgers University Press, 1990.

Further Reading

Dauphiné, Claude. *Rachilde.* Paris: Mercure de France, 1991.
———. "Sade, Rachilde et Freud: Lecture de *La Marquise de Sade.*" *Bulletin de l'association des professeurs de lettres* 17 (1981): 53–59.
Hawthorne, Melanie C. "*Monsieur Vénus*: A Critique of Gender Roles." *Nineteenth-Century French Studies* 16 (1987–88): 162–79.
———. "The Social Construction of Sexuality in Three Novels by Rachilde." *Michigan Romance Studies* 9 (1989): 49–59.
Holmes, Diana. "Monstruous Women: Rachilde's Erotic Fiction." In *French Erotic Fiction: Women's Desiring Writing 1880–1990,* edited by Alex Hughes and Kate Ince. Oxford: Berg, 1996.
———. *Rachilde: Decadence, Gender and the Woman Writer.* Oxford: Berg, 2001.

RADIGUET, RAYMOND

1903–1923
French novelist and poet

Radiguet published two collections of poetry in his short lifetime, *Les Joues en feu* [*Cheeks on Fire*] and *Devoirs de vacances* [*Holiday Works*], while other poems appeared after his death (at twenty). He is best known for his novel *Le diable au corps* [*The Devil in the Flesh*], written between the ages of sixteen and nineteen and published when he was twenty. This novel tells the story of the illicit affair between a schoolboy and a nineteen-year-old married woman whose husband spends most of the novel away fighting in World War I. This first-person narrative created quite a controversy at the time, and a group of American World War I veterans even attempted unsuccessfully to block its translation and subsequent sale in English. *Le bal du comte d'Orgel* [*Count Orgel's ball*], Radiguet's final novel, was published a year after his death, with a preface by Jean Cocteau, his mentor, collaborator, and close friend. Cocteau used this space to establish what has become an abiding legend surrounding the events of Radiguet's "peaceful" death. *Le bal du comte d'Orgel* displays a maturing talent. Written in the third person, this short novel sets in motion a story of passion that is not acted upon, continuing in the psychological tradition most prominently represented by the seventeenth-century novel *La princesse de Clèves* by Madame de Lafayette.

The Devil in the Flesh

Radiguet's career and the impact his figure had upon French society cannot be separated from the way in which he burst upon the literary scene, nor from the brevity with which he shone upon it. The young writer benefited from a savvy promotional campaign. In order to sell *The Devil in the Flesh*, the publisher Bernard Grasset not only placed oversize photographs of the author in bookstores all over Paris, but also had a newsreel made of the signing ceremony in which Radiguet received an unprecedented advance for the novel.

Radiguet's short novel provides a detailed analysis of the mental processes (more than the emotions or physical experience) of love, especially as regards jealousy and egoism. Indeed, it spends very little time describing the act of love itself. The focus is on the extreme youth of the unnamed first-person narrator/protagonist, who claims that although he knows his story will be deemed scandalous, his experiences were normal for someone in his situation: sixteen years old and in no danger of having to serve in the cataclysm of the First World War. His novel is thus not only an examination of a lover's calculations, but also a defense of youth itself: "A quel âge a-t-on le droit de dire 'j'ai vécu'?" [How old must one be before one can say "I have lived"?] ("Diable au corps," *Oeuvres complètes,* 431). The theme of debauching youth is never far, though it is the younger participant, that is, the narrator, who maintains sexual and psychological control over his older lover.

After accompanying nineteen-year-old Marthe on a trip to buy furniture for the house in which she will live with her soon-to-be husband, the narrator begins an affair that is made possible by the atmosphere of permissiveness in which the very young spent the war years. After her marriage to the soon-to-be cuckolded young man, Marthe and the narrator begin to keep regular trysts in her new apartment located above that of an older couple who take to gossiping about the young male caller. The hypocrisy of the adult world's reactions to the affair constitute one of the principal interests of the novel. *The Devil in the Flesh* includes brief references to preliminary sexual encounters, though the focus remains on the narrator's emotional manipulation of Marthe. The narrator's "devilishness" leads him to lure Marthe's Swedish girlfriend to her apartment while she is away in order to force himself upon her.

The Devil in the Flesh contains, alongside its study of the young lover's adventures, an implicit critique of liberal parenting. The narrator gets into trouble, he repeatedly shows, because his father chooses to look the other way once it has become obvious that his son is involved in an illicit affair. Eventually the entire town knows what is happening, and the older couple living below Marthe even invites friends over to come listen to the amorous noises emitted by the scandalous couple upstairs. Later, on a trip to Paris, the young protagonist lacks the courage to take a hotel for Marthe and himself, as he is so young and she is already pregnant with his child. The time spent walking around Paris in the winter trying to find the right hotel aggravates Marthe's incipient illness and, it is implied, seals the narrator's partial responsibility for her subsequent death in childbirth. The highly self-critical narrator views love in terms of obsession and egoism, stating that his love for Marthe has blocked out that for his best friend and family. Yet, the narrator makes clear that above this love for the other remains cold self-love. When he learns that young Marthe's dying words were spent calling the name of her newborn son (the same as his own), he decides that all is for the best.

While in the previous generation, André Gide's *L'Immoraliste* [*The Immoralist*] (1902) had treated homosexuality from the shockingly vivid first-person perspective, Radiguet exploded the myth that the very young do not lead rich sexual lives in just as frank a manner. The book's title comes from the expression "avoir le diable au corps" [to have the Devil in one's body], which was used to describe hyperactive children; since the book's release, however, it has taken on an erotic connotation. The story is best known today through several film adaptations, the most recent of which is Marco Bellocchio's sexually explicit *Diavolo in corpo* (1986).

Biography

Born in Saint-Maur-des-Fossés. Cocteau's heroic preface notwithstanding, Radiguet died alone ravaged with typhoid fever in a hospital in Paris.

MATTHEW ESCOBAR

Works

Poetry, Theatre, Essays

Devoirs de vacances. Poetry. Paris: La Sirène, 1921.
Les joues en feu. Poetry. Paris: Grasset, 1925; as *Cheeks on Fire*, translated by Alan Stone, London: Calder, 1976.
Vers libres et jeux innocents. Poetry. Paris: Ramsay, 1988.
Les pélicans. Play. Paris: Editions de la Galerie Simon, 1921.
Art poétique. Essays. Paris: Émile Paul, 1922.

Novels and Complete Works

Le diable au corps. Paris: Grasset, 1923.
Devil in the Flesh. Translated by Kay Boyle. Paris: Crosby Continental Editions, 1932; translated by Robert Baldick, New York: Penguin, 1971.
Le bal du comte d'Orgel. Paris: Grasset, 1924.
Count d'Orgel. Translated by Violet Schiff. London: Pushkin Press, 1953.
Count d'Orgel's Ball. Translated by Annapaola Cancogni. New York: Eridanos Press, 1989.
Le bal du comte d'Orgel. Critical edition edited by Andrew Oliver and Nadia Odouard. 2 vols. Paris: Lettres Modernes Minard, 1999.
Oeuvres complètes. Paris: Stock, 1993.

Films Based on Radiguet's Books

Le Diable au corps. Dir. Claude Autant-Lara, 1946
Le Bal du conte d'Orgel. Dir. Marc Allégret, 1970
Diavolo in corpo. Dir. Marco Bellocchio, 1986
Devil in the Flesh. Dir. Scott Murray (Australia), 1989
Le Diable au corps. Dir. Gérard Vergez (French television), 1990

Further Reading

Giardina, Calogero. *L'Imaginaire dans les romans de Raymond Radiguet*. Paris: Didier Erudition, 1991.
Goesch, K.J. *Raymond Radiguet, étude biographique, bibliographie, textes inédits*. Paris: La Palatine, 1955.
McNab, James. *Raymond Radiguet*. Boston: Twayne Publishers, 1984.
Odouard, Nadia. *Les Années folles de Raymond Radiguet*. Paris: Seghers, 1973.
Movilliat, Marie-Christine. *Raymond Radiguet ou la jeunesse contredite*. Paris: Bibliophane, 2000.
Noakes, David. *Raymond Radiguet*. Paris: Seghers, 1968.

RAMAYANA

The *Ramayana* of Valmiki is the most renowned and imitated work of South Asian literature. As the primeval exemplar of Sanskrit literary culture, the epic spawned several poetic retellings in Sanskrit, including Buddhist and Jain works, as well as in vernacular languages throughout South and Southeast Asia. The popularity of the broadcast of the *Ramayana* television serial of Ramanand Sagar in 1987–88—the first all-India television hit—is a testament to its continued cultural relevance today.

Scholars agree that a single poet likely authored the core narrative of the *Ramayana,* although there is wide disagreement regarding its date. The traditional dates of the life of Rama occur in the legendary Treta Yuga, one of the epochs of Hindu time, c. 867,102 BCE. Produced from the same bardic tradition as South Asia's other great epic, the *Mahabharata,* in the region of the eastern expansion of the Vedic Aryans, the Ramayana was likely authored either during the late Vedic (c. 750–500 BCE) or early Mauryan (c. 500–300 BCE) period. While the absence of explicit references to the urbanization of the eastern Ganges valley and of Buddhism argue for the former, the developed ideology of divine kingship appears anachronistic before the advent of the Mauryan empire. The epic comprises about 50,000 verses divided into seven books.

The basic plot of the *Ramayana* is as follows. The narrative opens with the birth of the god Vishnu on Earth as Rama, son of Dasharatha, along with his three brothers, Bharata, Lakshmana, and Shatrughna. Later, the sage Vishvamitra calls Rama to the forest to protect his sacrifices from demons. At the conclusion of this sojourn in the forest, Rama wins his bride, Sita, in a test of heroism and returns triumphant to the capital, Ayodhya.

The Book of Ayodhya and the Book of the Forest contain many of the most dramatic events of the epic. Dasharatha desires to install Rama as crown-prince, as do the people of the kingdom. But his youngest wife, Kaikeyi, corrupted by the advice of her servant Manthara, uses two boons granted to her earlier to banish Rama to the forest for fourteen years and demand that Dasharatha install her own son, Bharata, in his place. Rama, far from displeased at this change of fortune, accepts his step-mother's wishes dutifully in a spirit of sacrifice, eager to protect the word of his father, and proceeds to the forest with Sita and his brother Lakshmana at his side. During this time his old father dies of grief. Bharata, who had been away from the kingdom, is aghast when he hears of his mother's actions and beseeches Rama to return, only to be denied. Rama instead gives him the symbol of his own sandals, with which Bharata rules Ayodhya.

Rama, Sita, and Laksmana spend ten years in the forest, culminating in the turning point of the epic—the abduction of Sita by the demon-king Ravana. The trouble begins when the ugly sister of Ravana, Shurpanakha, makes amorous advances to Rama and Lakshmana and abuses Sita, for which Lakshmana mutilates her. Several demons die at the hands of Rama in the ensuing battle, and Shurpanakha, enraged, incites Ravana to intense longing for Sita with her descriptions. Ravana then forces the demon Marica to take the form of a golden deer to lure Sita into sending Rama after it. Disguised as an ascetic, Ravana deceives Sita and takes her off in his aerial vehicle. The brothers return in horror and despair, collecting whatever traces of evidence are available.

The intelligent and heroic monkey Hanuman, one of the most memorable characters of the epic, meets Rama and Lakshmana grieving near Lake Pampa and facilitates an alliance between them and the monkey-king Sugriva, which is cemented by Rama's assassination of Sugriva's brother, Vali, who had usurped the throne. The monkeys set out in troops to seek Sita, but only Hanuman's party succeeds in discovering her presence in the demon capital at the island of Lanka. Hanuman leaps over the ocean, conveys a message to Sita along with Rama's signet ring, and plunders the city, burning it with his tail, which is set aflame by the demons.

The Book of War describes the colossal battle between Rama and Ravana. Vibhisana, Ravana's righteous brother, surrenders to Rama and offers his assistance in the war. Rama, Lakshmana, and the monkeys build a bridge to cross the ocean and then mount their attack on the demons. Rama kills Ravana along with his brothers, sons, and multitudes of the demon army. He is finally reunited with his beloved wife, Sita, but cruelly rejects her; after Sita subjects herself to a trial by fire and the god Brahma himself reminds Rama of his own divinity, he accepts her, claiming that he only intended to demonstrate to the world Sita's unadulterated purity. Rama and Sita return triumphantly to Ayodhya in the aerial vehicle.

The *Ramayana* contains several explicitly anti-erotic elements and yet is at heart one of the great love stories of world literature. While characters displaying deviant or excessive sexuality—Ravana, Shurpanakha, Kaikeyi, and even Dasharatha—eventually meet with death or infamy, Rama's renunciation defines his heroic character, as does Sita's absolute fidelity. Several of the key motifs of the romance genre, including separated lovers, rings and recognition, abduction and rescue, are present. Descriptions of the painful separation between Rama and Sita are passionate and poetic, such as the descriptions in 5.23 of her "brooding," "bathing her full breasts with her flowing tears," and being "afflicted" and "overcome by grief," causing some medieval commentators to classify the aesthetic sentiment of the entire epic as "love in separation" (Goldman and Sutherland 1996). This romantic dimension appealed especially to the poetic imagination of later Sanskrit poets like Kalidasa, whose lyric love poem, the *Meghaduta*, is modeled on Rama's separation from Sita; and Bhavabhuti, who in his poignant *Uttararamacarita* reverses the tragic ending of the subsequently appended last book (where Rama once again abandons Sita) in a long, dramatic meditation on the lovers' mutual, unrequited longing.

AJAY K. RAO

Editions

The Ramayana of Valmiki. 4th rev. ed. Edited by Wasudeva Laxman Sastri Panasikar. Bombay: Nirnayasagar Press, 1930. With the commentary (*Tilaka*) of Rama.

Srimadvalmikiramayana. 3 vols. Edited by Gangavisnu Srikrsnadasa. Bombay: Venkatesvara Steam Press, 1935. With the commentaries of Govindaraja, Ramanuja, and Mahesvaratirtha and the commentary known as *Tanisloki*.

Srimadvalmikiramayana. 7 vols. Edited by T.R. Krishnacharya and T.R. Vyasacharya. Bombay: Nirnayasagar Press, 1911–1913.

The Valmiki Ramayana: Critical Edition. 7 vols. Edited by G.H. Bhatt and U.P. Shah. Baroda: Oriental Institute, 1960–1975.

Translations

Buck, William. *Ramayana: King Rama's Way*. Berkeley and Los Angeles: University of California Press, 1976.

Goldman, Robert, ed. *The Ramayana of Valmiki: An Epic of Ancient India*. 5 vols. Princeton, NJ: Princeton University Press, 1984–1996.

Narayan, R.K. *The Ramayana: A Shortened Modern Prose Version of the Indian Epic*. New York: Penguin Books, 1972.

Further Reading

Brockington, J.L. *Righteous Rama: The Evolution of an Epic*. Delhi: Oxford University Press, 1984.

Jacobi, Hermann. *Das Ramayana: Geschichte und Inhalt, nebst Concordanz der gedruckten Recensionen*. Bonn: Friedrich Cohen, 1893.

Lutgendorf, Philip. *The Life of a Text: Performing the Ramcaritmanas of Tulsidas*. Berkeley and Los Angeles, CA: University of California Press, 1991.

Pollock, Sheldon. "Ramayana and Political Imagination in India." *Journal of Asian Studies* 52 (May 1993): 261–97.

Raghavan, V., ed. *The Ramayana Tradition in Asia*. Delhi: Sahitya Academy, 1980.

Rajagopal, Aravind. *Politics After Television: Religious Nationalism and the Reshaping of the Indian Public*. Cambridge: Cambridge University Press.

Richman, Paula, ed. *Many Ramayanas: The Diversity of a Narrative Tradition in South Asia*. Berkeley and Los Angeles, CA: University of California Press, 1991.

———. *Questioning Ramayanas: A South Asian Tradition*. Berkeley and Los Angeles, CA: University of California Press, 2001.

READER RESPONSE

In erotic fiction, the reader response, generally to other erotic texts, plays such an important part that it has come to represent one of the defining principles of the genre. Of course other characters in non-erotic texts also read (erotic or non-erotic) texts to which they also react (Don Quixote and Emma Bovary to name but two examples of famous avid readers). But in erotic fiction, reader responses are so insistently present that they serve more than the characterization of the novel's hero or heroine. In erotic fiction, the narrative functions of characters' readings are multiple: they contribute to the recognition of the genre and to its characterization as illicit, they help emphasize the narrative and ideological power of the genre as a whole (and thus of each individual text's power), and they also create a supplemental layer of voyeuristic transgression so typical of erotic fiction.

From the very beginning, the erotic novel capitalized on its marginal status. In one of the most prolific periods of erotic fiction production, the Enlightenment, the novel as a whole came under fierce attack. The erotic novel and all obscene productions were condemned by various legal, philosophical, and religious authorities, who had very little in common except their condemnation of erotic fiction. The radical philosopher La Mettrie, who was famous for his iconoclastic views on ethics, fiercely attacked the first famous (and notorious) erotic novel to be written and published during the French Enlightenment, *Histoire de D[om Bougre], Portier des Chartreux* (1740). Such novels, La Mettrie contends, must be avoided at all costs if their dangerous influence is proportionate to the powerful empire of reading on the imagination. Later in the century, a voice from the other side of the ideological spectrum would express a similar concern. In his *Nymphomanie* (1771), Dr. Bienville describes at great length readers' reactions to erotic fiction and other "tender, lascivious, and voluptuous novels" which act on their readers (preferably female) as a "magnifying glass which brings together the sun rays in order to fix them in one small part, and to set it on fire" (110).

From a literary point of view, the tendency of characters in erotic novels to read (and sometimes quote) other erotic novels helps create a strong erotic intertextual presence. Numerous references to preceding texts lead to a historical catalogue of previous productions, contributing to a definition and characterization of the genre itself. At the end of the eighteenth century, de Sade's Juliette comments on erotic books published during the entire century, thus placing her own philosophical ideas and sexual practices (as well as de Sade's novel itself) within the erotic corpus of the eighteenth century. In the absence of an official critical discourse on the genre, the erotic novel itself creates a critical space for discussing (analyzing, criticizing, recommending, or condemning) other erotic novels.

Thematically, the presence of other erotic texts plays a very active role: that of exemplifying the power of the genre and of establishing itself as a transgressive corpus. Capitalizing on the official condemnation of erotic fiction by the church and the medical establishment, erotic texts acknowledge the radical influence of erotic fiction on its readers, but they transform such negative influences into positive ones. The description of the reading character who is systematically, and often delightfully, under (narrative) influence leads to quantitative and qualitative improvements of sexual performances by the reading characters. Some erotic novels aim primarily at improving their characters' sexual performances by providing them with catalogues (sometimes illustrated) of postures to be imitated (see, for example, *Les quarante manières de foutre, dédiées au clergé de France* [*The Forty Manners of Fucking, Dedicated to the French Clergy*], 1790).

In other erotic novels, readers responses are framed to show the power of the erotic novel not only on characters themselves, but also, *en abyme*, on their female and male readers. In the second erotic best seller of the Enlightenment, *Thérèse philosophe* (1748, the same year as *Fanny Hill*), one character who has systematically refused penetration for fear of becoming pregnant has finished reading the first best seller, *Dom Bougre*. As she is "all on fire," she implores the priest who had lent her the lascivious book to penetrate her. At the end of the book, only novels and lascivious prints can convince Thérèse to be penetrated by her lover. Reactions by male readers are similar, as erotic fiction inevitably incites them to imitate described models. One of the protagonists of Restif de la Bretonne (who also wrote pornographic texts) is so inflamed by the reading of *Dom Bougre* that he tumbles the six women who come to visit him within a couple of hours, barely recuperating enough between two orgasms to proceed with the "inflaming readings" (*Monsieur Nicolas*, 1794–1797). A later Victorian novel again self-complacently emphasizes the dangerous power of erotic fiction. In the anonymous *My Secret Life* (1885–1895), the narrator remembers having received a copy of *Fanny Hill*. As had been the case in Restif de la Bretonne's work, an erotic novel causes the reader to lose all restraint. Rather than repeated intercourse, *Fanny Hill* causes the hero to masturbate, and the narrator gives a perfect example of a reader's reaction to erotic fiction: "I devoured the book and its luscious pictures, and although I never contemplated masturbation, lost all command of myself, frigged, and spent over a picture as it lay before me. . . . Fascinated although annoyed with myself, I repeated the act till not a drop of sperm would come" (124). As J.M. Goulemot has put it, and as so many readers (female and male) in erotic texts testify, readers' reactions to erotic novels prove the absolute power of erotic fiction, which breaks all social, moral, and physiological barriers.

When applied to female characters reading, similar scenes can also serve as a physiological incentive to the turgescent male character who observes a hidden female reader. In this instance, the reader's reaction serves as an additional foreplay for the female reader and an additional transgression for the voyeuristic male observer (the targeted audience of many early erotic novels), who finally interrupts the reading for more "solid" pleasures, thus completing physically what had been initiated by the reading.

In general, the effects of all "infernal books" are described at great length, but they are given to the reader less as a warning against spermatic expenditure than as a complicit invitation to similar excesses under their influence. One of the most popular erotic novels from the seventeenth century, *L'École des filles* [*The School of Girls*] (1655), a best seller in France and in England, starts with an "Orthodox Religious Decree" which could exemplify the ideal reader's reaction in, and to, erotic fiction: "Our August father Priapus severely condemns every man and every woman who reads or hears the love precepts, morally explained in the famous *School for Girls*, without spermatizing or being stimulated spiritually or physically in any way" (183).

JEAN MAINIL

Further Reading

Anonymous. *L'École des filles*. In *Oeures érotiques du XVIIe siècle*. Paris: Fayard, 1988.
———. *My Secret Life*. Ware, Hertfordshire: Wordsworth, 1995.
Bienville. *De la nymphomanie ou fureur utérine*. Edited by Jean Marie Goulemot. Paris: Le Sycomore, 1980.
Boyer d'Argens [attributed]. *Thérèse philosophe*. In *Romanciers libertins du XVIIIe siècle*, edited by Patrick Wald Lasowski et al. Paris: Gallimard, 2000.
Cryle, Peter. *Geometry in the Boudoir: Configurations of French Erotic Narrative*. Ithaca, NY: Cornell University Press, 1994.
Darnton, Robert. *The Forbidden Best-Sellers of Pre-Revolutionary France*. New York: Norton, 1995.
Gervaise de Latouche [attributed]. *Histoire de D[om Bougre], portier des Chartreux*. In Lasowski et al., eds., *Romanciers libertins*.
Goulemot, Jean-Marie. *Ces livres qu'on ne lit que d'une main: Lecture et lecteurs de livres pornographiques au XVIIIe siècle*. Aix-en-Provence: Alinéa, 1991; as *Forbidden Texts: Erotic Literature and Its Readers in Eighteenth-Century France*, Cambridge: Polity, 1994; Philadelphia: University of Pennsylvania Press, 1995.
Hunt, Lynn, ed. *The Invention of Pornography*. New York: Zone Books, 1993.
Kearney, Patrick. *A History of Erotic Literature*. London: Macmillan, 1982.
Trousson, Raymond, ed. *Romans libertins du XVIIIe siècle*. Paris: Laffont, 1993.
Wagner, Peter. *Eros Revived: Erotica of the Enlightenment in England and America*. London: Paladin, 1990.

RÉAGE, PAULINE

1907–1998
French novelist and journalist

L'Histoire d'O

In January 1954, Jean Paulhan, chief editor of the *Nouvelle Revue Française*, met Jean-Jacques Pauvert in Paris and gave him the manuscript of *The Story of O*. Pauvert read it overnight and immediately realized that it was "quite obviously one of those books which make an impact on their readers." The author had already signed a contract with another publisher, and the next day Pauvert went to the Editions des Deux Rives, where René Defez sold him the contract, describing as "trivial porn" the book for which Pauvert felt himself to be the ideal publisher.

The Story of O relates the passion of a young woman, formerly carefree and independent, who delights in becoming the "captive" of a man, René. In order to keep his love and give him constant proofs of her abandon, O agrees to become a sexual slave and to undergo initiation in a chateau at Roissy outside Paris. Here, for fifteen days she allows strangers to subject her to tortures, deprivations, and caresses which gradually dispossess her of her sense of being, while creating in her a feeling of deep mystical pleasure. On her return to normal life in Paris she resumes work as a fashion photographer and becomes attracted to a model, Jacqueline, also desired by René. O begins an affair with her and wants to take her to Roissy. When O is given over by René to a more demanding master, Sir Stephen, known as "the Englishman," she is branded with the mark of Sir Stephen and her labia are pierced with rings. But she finds in her absolute submission a sense of extravagant pride. At the end of the story, her tamed body, partly hidden by the mask of a sparrow-owl, is displayed during a party given by a mysterious Commander. The metamorphosis of the heroine into a night bird raises her momentarily above the level of common mortals like a "creature from another world" that the fascinated audience comes to look at and touch, despite its fear and repulsion for the chains and irons which bind and pierce her.

Two short paragraphs conclude the story, offering an alternative between a tragic ending and a degradation of the story. The first one refers to a final chapter in which O will return to Roissy and be abandoned by Sir Stephen. It was written at the same time as *The Story of O* but discarded until its publication in 1969, entitled *Return to the Chateau*, with an introduction, *A Girl in Love*. The second cuts short O's existence like the blade of a guillotine with its account of her voluntary death.

Since June 1954, when the work was first published, a number of ill-founded ideas about *The Story of O* have circulated. The first of these concerns the circumstances of the first publication. *The Story of O* was not published clandestinely but officially, by a man who had begun at the age of 21 a vast, courageous undertaking: to publish the complete works of the Marquis de Sade. Publishing *The Story of O* was a new challenge, as for the first time a woman revealed "the nocturnal and secret part of herself" in language otherwise chaste and mannered. Another ill-founded idea concerns the author. Because of the reputedly masculine dimension of the fantasies referred to, and of his status as preface writer, Paulhan was long considered, mistakenly, to be the author of the novel. He was in fact its privileged addressee. Even if he did not write it, he nevertheless inspired it as a lover and urged its author to publish it. She was deeply in love with Paulhan, a married man and a womanizer. They had been lovers for ten years and she was looking for a way to continue to please him. Paulhan did not believe that a woman could write such a story. The author took up the challenge using the weapons of her intellect. She decided to captivate him by writing down the fantasies which had obsessed her since her youth and which her lover, a well-read man familiar with the works of de Sade, would appreciate. In *A Girl in Love* (1969), written while Paulhan was dying, the author revealed for the first time that the story was a love letter designed to enthrall him.

The fact that the author was a woman gave rise to severe disapproval on the part of the intelligentsia of the time, including Albert Camus, for example, who nevertheless was quite ready to defend the book in court. In *La Coupe est pleine* (1975), Michel Droit still thought that the book had been written by "a well-read, lewd old man." The truth came out in July 1994 when Pauline Réage, in an interview with John de Saint-Jorre in *The New Yorker*, admitted that she was in fact Dominique Aury. At 86 years old she no longer had to fear the disapproval of her deceased family. Yet as early as 1954 some well-known figures close to Gallimard knew her real identity but kept it secret. In *Confessions of O*, her interviews with Régine Deforges, she explains that at the time, even the police knew every detail of her true identity!

Another persistent legend concerns the immediate impact of the book. Its official publication created a scandal only within a limited circle. The press was dumb with stupefaction. Controversy over it did not arise until September 1975, when its screen adaptation by Just Jaeckin, judged "abominable" by the author, popularized the work and was the subject of a dossier in the magazine *L'Express*.

The book came out during a period of austerity marked by censorship, the main weapons of which were the July 29, 1939, statutory order "on the protection of the family and the birth rate" and the more redoubtable July 16, 1949, law prohibiting the publication of any book "constituting an outrage to accepted standards of behavior" by a triple ban on selling to minors, public display, and advertising. The book was subjected to this ban in 1955. Legal proceedings were indeed begun but toward the end of 1955 suddenly abandoned thanks to an "arranged" meeting at a luncheon between Dominique Aury and the justice minister of the time. As for the first edition in English, published by Maurice Girodias at Olympia Press, its sale and circulation were banned in February 1957. The poor translation was quickly replaced by a new one entitled *The Wisdom of the Lash* (May 1957).

The weight of repression partly accounts for the "conspiracy of silence" which greeted *The Story of O* and for its poor sales, hardly 2,000 copies during the first year. The fact that it won the Prix des Deux-Magots in 1955 widened its readership considerably. The first important critical appraisal of the book was undoubtedly Paulhan's preface, "Happiness in Slavery," inseparable from Réage's story. This subtle and provocative text did not quite correspond to the book, according to Aury, but its presence immediately proposed threefold support for it: *aesthetic*, because Paulhan was a highly respected writer and critic (elected to the Académie Française in 1963), whose mere name was enough to recommend the book and guarantee its literary worth; *intellectual*, because the preface provided an initial interpretation of the novel; and *ethical*, because by likening the book to "a fairy tale" and more especially "an impassioned love letter," Paulhan took a clear stand on certain points to forestall the moral objections of censors and reticent readers. The apparently paradoxical title of the preface prefigures Réage's book as the illustration of an idea running counter to common opinion, as it associates love with dependence, not with freedom. Moreover, from the singular case of the heroine, Paulhan posits the existence of a femininity entirely devoted to sexuality—"At last a woman who confesses . . . that they never cease to obey the call of their blood; that everything in them is sex, even their minds"—and needing nothing less than "a good master" to provide an outlet for it! *The Story of O*, far from being an embarrassing story, thus satisfies "a virile ideal."

To preempt a denial of the author's feminine identity, he takes a firm stand in its favor, justifying his position by referring to details in the book. Nevertheless, certain problems are raised—the autobiographical elements, the real name of Pauline Réage, the addressee—but not resolved, and so maintain the aura of mystery surrounding the work.

Paulhan's preface was at times misunderstood and, according to Muriel Walker, would foster "a certain collective psychosis" by insisting on the scandalous content of the book. At any rate it provided a reference point for enlightened criticism of the time. The principal critical reviews recalled by Aury in *Confessions of O* (1975) were "L'Amour fou" by Claude Elsen in *Dimanche-Matin* (August 29, 1954); "Les Fers, le feu, la nuit de l'âme" by André-Pieyre de Mandiargues in *Critique* (May 1955); and

"Le Paradoxe de l'érotisme" by Georges Bataille in *La Nouvelle Nouvelle Revue Française* (June 1955). Yet other articles, of varying interest, appeared in *Combat, Le Courrier des Canettes, Medium,* and again in *Dimanche-Matin.*

These critics all recognize in the subject of the book a woman's painful journey through life, with its tragic outcome, and are all disturbed by O's unusual complacency. Only André Berry in *Combat* (March 14, 1955) lingers over the erotic dimension of the book, considering that *The Story of O* pinpoints lust in its purest state. The others refer to less compromising aspects: the mystic quality of the heroine's quest, the contrast between the audacity of the subject and the discreet style, the risk of legal proceedings, and the repercussions on censorship.

Elsen's review questions the erotic label attributed to the story. He compares *The Story of O* with the *Song of Songs* and *Tristan and Isolde* and proposes that amorous motivation is the informing principle of the novel, at the same time half-denouncing the complacency of the heroine. Mandiargues interprets the story as "a mystic novel" in the tradition of Teresa of Avila, Catherine Emmerich, and *The Portuguese Nun.* For Bataille, the author of *L'Anglais décrit dans le château fermé* (1953), the story is about an ascetism which brings about the degeneration of the flesh while elevating the spirit. Bataille's article is more neutral and conceptual, comparing Réage's novel with *Roberte ce soir* by Klossowski (see *Klossowski, Pierre*). He refers to the gruesome eroticism of *The Story of O* as "the impossibility of eroticism." Recalling the image of Teresa of Avila, who dies "of not being able to die," he sees the object of O's quest as death. These principal commentaries use the term "erotic" with some caution, no doubt for reasons of censorship but also because Réage's book is too complex for facile labels. They free it from a vision reducing it to a sado-masochistic (S&M) story with a single aim, that of arousing the reader by its highly erotic content. Unfortunately, such a positive evaluation of its complexity by the enlightened critics of the time would not prevent the vice squad from unleashing its fury upon Réage's book and from considering it as "violently and deliberately immoral."

It was not until 1969 that the possible alternative expressed in Paulhan's preface between "an experienced lady who has done it all" and "a dreamer" was resolved. *A Girl in Love*, a magnificent text written just before Paulhan's death, provides the key to the reading of the novel. In his review of the *The Story of O*, Francois Mauriac was wrong: the novel is not simply "the confidences of a beautiful woman" but the laying bare of violent fantasies in total contrast with the discreet personality of its author. We also learn from *A Girl in Love* that *The Story of O* was written at night in small notebooks before being read in a car at each secret meeting between the two lovers.

A Girl in Love preceded *Return to the Chateau*, a last chapter formerly discarded. The few reviews it inspired recognized the novel as a work of eroticism. The senselessness of official repressive measures, the fact that eroticism was henceforth a public phenomenon, and the changes in public attitude toward it explain why it was possible in 1969 to discuss the guignolish eroticism of the book without risking the censors' wrath and harming one's literary reputation. For Emmanuelle Arsan, *The Story of O* was the opportunity for "intellectual and moral progress," as it asserted women's long-oppressed freedom of expression. And unlike the "passion for servitude" defended by Paulhan, the novel brought "a stronger taste for freedom." Arsan declared that *The Story of O* had inspired her to dare to write *Emmanuelle,* even if the response of her own radiant heroine to the question of love was more in keeping with modern attitudes. So, between 1954 and 1969 the novel changed status from a *curiosa* to "a great marvel produced by French literature during this period of transition" (Mandiargues), as it influenced the liberation of attitudes toward love, especially for women.

The reaction to *Return to the Chateau* was, on the contrary, one of disappointment. The transformation of the mystic chateau into a vulgar high-class brothel and of the dissolute master into a crook and the degradation of O into a cheap prostitute constituted a desacralization of the mystic aura and was deplored by the critics. The terms of the challenge had changed. Whereas in 1954 the book had breached the then-current fortress of puritanism, in 1969 it appeared as the incarnation of a "real" eroticism, as opposed to a strictly commercial one. The publication of *Return to the Chateau* provided critics with an opportunity to denounce the popularization of eroticism. It was no longer a matter of battling against censorship, now inoperative anyway, but of battling against the foisting of cheap eroticism onto the public at large.

Whereas in France the ban on the advertising of erotica was lifted in 1975 and translations of Apollinaire's *Onze mille verges* became available to the public even in Spain, *The Story of O* was still censored as of 1979, mainly because its author was a woman. In Quebec, while the censorship of *Lady Chatterley's Lover* ended in 1962, *The Story of O* was confiscated by the Montreal vice squad, and in 1967 a new trial opened during which defense witnesses argued that the erotic aspect of the book constituted a positive vector of evolution in public attitudes. The confiscation order was lifted in 1973, but the judges nevertheless ordered the Delorme bookshop, which had put the original edition on sale, to pay a $200 fine.

In September 1974 the author of *The Story of O*, as Dominique Aury, gave her first interview, with Jacqueline Demornex for the magazine *Elle*. That year the movie version of Arsan's *Emmanuelle* broke box-office records, with 700,000 tickets sold in 7 weeks. The sense of public fear and unease sparked by the wave of pornography and sexology then inundating France had inspired the journalist's interest in the author of what was described as "the most widely read contemporary French novel in the world" and of "one of the finest erotic texts ever written." The interview took place shortly before the release of the screen adaptation of the novel by Just Jaeckin—who also made *Emmanuelle*—and of the 12-page dossier in *L'Express* featuring on its cover a topless Corinne Cléry, the actress playing the title role. In Madeleine Chapsal's commentary, the dossier aimed at reviving the topical relevance of the book and presenting it as symptomatic of the present reality, which in 1975 was marked by an upsurge in violence and a lack of communication between the sexes. A year earlier, the American feminist Andrea Dworkin had devoted a chapter in *Woman Hating* to Réage's novel. For Dworkin *The Story of O* is more than simple pornography but a story of demonic possession which posits men and women as being at opposite poles of the universe and which reveals, through O as victim, the true, eternal and sacral destiny of woman: submission to men's power.

The reactions of women who recognized a positive social function in the book were few in number. Fortunately some women critics have thrown new light on the character of O. Jessica Benjamin, for example, maintained that "the desire for submission represents a peculiar transposition of the desire for recognition," and Brigitte Purkhardt considered the depersonalization of O as the precondition for her attaining individuality. Béatrice Didier invited the reader to probe beneath the surface detail, asserting that the essential core of the book lies in "the affirmation of the writing of extreme desire"; Anne-Marie Dardigna examined the subjection of the woman's body as the precondition for erotic narration, at the same time distinguishing O's expressive body from that reduced by de Sade to its anatomic materiality.

The book had already inspired a number of inchoate artistic projects. In the early 1960s, Kenneth Anger had drawn up plans to produce a movie of the book by way of subscription, but his project was never carried out. In 1967 the impresario Norbert Gamsohn had obtained the rights, but apparently without any result. During the same period Maurice Béjart had planned to make a ballet of *The Story of O*, but once again the project had not been realized. The screen version by Just Jaeckin (1975) is the best known adaptation. It took advantage of the success of the book but weakened its significance, diluting its S&M plot and giving it a happy ending in which O, reclining peacefully in Sir Stephen's arms by the fireside, burns the letter "O" onto the back of his hand with the tip of a lit cigar.

The film and the cover of *L'Express* created a huge scandal and resulted in the settling of old scores with the book through broadsides at the film. The novel was the target of a number of attacks by feminists. Janis L. Pallister judged it severely and, despite all the evidence to the contrary, refused to believe that its author was a woman. Susan Griffin, equally fierce in her disapproval, studied the narrative point of view but mistakenly attributed the main narrative instance to just one voice, that of O the slave. When the film was released, militant feminists from the Mouvement de libération des femmes (MLF), outraged over what they perceived as the commercial exploitation of women's bodies in sexually explicit films, stormed the *L'Express* building and daubed vengeful inscriptions in lipstick on its walls. Their action was supported by the archbishop of Paris, Monsignor Marty, by Michel Droit, and by François Chalais, who in an "Open Letter to the Pornographers" called

Réage's book "the Gestapo in the boudoir." The affair was also taken up by politicians and led to a legal decision to give an X rating to pornographic films and to introduce a professional tax on them of 33 percent.

Other screen versions of the book followed Jaeckin's but were unequal in quality and far removed from Réage's text. In 1975 an American film, *The Journey of O*, was made by Chris Latham. In 1979 Lars Von Trier brought out a black-and-white tribute to the book, *Menthe – la bienheureuse*. A Franco-Japanese adaptation based on *Return to the Chateau* was released in 1981. A sequel to *The Story of O* was made in 1984 by Eric Rochat, who in 1995 also created a ten-hour serial for television, with Claudia Cepeda in the title role, which in turn was produced as a shorter, 82-minute film. The Spanish filmmaker Jesus (Jess) Franco released a loosely based *Historia Sexual de O* in 1986, and, more recently, *The Story of O—Untold Pleasures* (2001) was made in the United States by Phil Leirness.

Other graphic artists have sought inspiration in Réage's book, among them illustrators. Léonor Fini, the surrealist painter, illustrated several fine editions; Hans Bellmer designed for the cover of the first edition in 1954 a silver medallion destined for a circle of privileged readers; Guido Crepax made several comic-strip versions of the book as early as 1975; Loic Dubigeon illustrated the 1981 edition with a hundred drawings; Lynn Paula Russell has specialized in erotic illustrations of S&M literature; Stefan Price has created since 1996 over twenty oil paintings and drawings based on the book; and David Wilde illustrated a series of erotic books, including *Story of O*, for a private client.

Interest in the work continued in the 1980s. In 1981 a chapter in Maurice Charney's *Sexual Fiction* dealt with *The Story of O* and with *L'Image* by the so-called Jean de Berg (suspected by some of being Réage herself) (1956). The two books are studied as "erotic/religious fables in the style of Sade." A year later, Susan Sontag in *The Pornographic Imagination,* considered that "the notion implicit in *Story of O* that eros is a sacrament is not the 'truth' behind the literal (erotic) sense of the book . . . but exactly a metaphor for it."

Then, in the 1990s the author's real identity was revealed to the public and critical interest in the book was once again stimulated. John de Saint Jorre, a journalist and writer, first met Dominique Aury while doing research for his book *The Good Ship Venus*. The chapter on *The Story of O* in his book recounts the true story of the novel and its author through the words of the main people involved; Saint Jorre also published a shorter version of this chapter in *The New Yorker* in 1994. Both texts contain a host of details about the genesis of the book and the biography of its author—the circumstances of the publication of what was both a *succès d'estime* and a *succès de scandale*, the liaison between Paulhan and Aury, the origins of the characters, the book's posterity, the origins of *Return to the Chateau* and *A Girl in Love*, the reactions to the book in the United States, the puzzle of the identity of the American translator, "Sabine d'Estrée": all are covered with a maximum of precision and in-depth investigation to reveal the truth about the book.

In 1995 Hector Biancotti interviewed Dominique Aury for *Le Monde* on the subject of "literature as love," a conversation which presented the author's life from the angle of a quest for "pure love." But it was her death in 1998 which gave rise to new articles. In *L'Humanité* Régine Deforges paid tribute to the woman who had enabled her to become a writer herself. In the same newspaper, on May 2, 1998, J.-P.L. (?) announced the death of Dominique Aury and recalled the remarkable feat the sulfurous book represented when it was written. Five days later it was the turn of *The Times* of London to announce the death of the author of "an international bestseller," of "the best-known work of erotic literature this century," which, according to the journalist, showed masculine desire at its extreme. The same year, S&M comic novelist Molly Weatherfield eulogized Dominique Aury as the mother of masochism and mentioned the special place that *The Story of O* held in the context of contemporary pornography. A prefeminist story in which everything revolves around masculine desire, Réage's book is here indeed considered a masterpiece but an outmoded one, due to its 1950s atmosphere of latex and piercings and to its difference from the positive sexual atmosphere of the present day.

In 1999, John Phillips's analytical study of *The Story of O* took up several academic points of view on the novel and clarified some of its aspects with the help of literary theoreticians such as Gérard Genette. Here the worrisome question of the author's identity is put forward as an example of the dangers inherent in any moral or artistic conclusion based on a presumed identity. Phillips also examines the title of the work, the question of the narrative voice, and the powerful suggestiveness of the letter O with its possible symbolic value, already interpreted differently by Andrea Dworkin, Susan Sontag, and Luce Irigaray and here given a fresh appraisal. In order to explain the least evident aspects of this complex, open, and composite work, Phillips draws upon multiple sources of knowledge and theory, notably feminist, and takes a stand in relation to them.

The beginning of the 21st century has seen an ongoing journalistic interest in *The Story of O* and its author. In 2000 the revue *Sigila* published an article by Nicole Grenier revealing the dual personality of the author and studying the resonances between the articles written by Dominique Aury, a privileged witness of the literary scene for 50 years, and Réage's mythical text. In July 2004 Geraldine Bedell, for *The Observer*, disclosed lesser known facts such as the fate in store for the book on feminist campuses during the 1980s (it was burned) and the identity of Aury's son, Philippe d'Argila. Then the audiovisual media took over from the written word. On the literary radio program *Un Eté d'écrivains* on France Inter, Jérome Garcin told the behind-the-scenes story of "the great literary scandal of the 20th century, an erotic masterpiece written by a woman, Dominique Aury, for the love of a man" (also the subject of a long article in *Le Nouvel Observateur*). In December 2004, on the 50th anniversary of the first edition, Paula Rapaport made a documentary film broadcast on the Franco-German TV channel Arte. It not only told the true story of the book, showing Dominique Aury at various moments in her life and interviewing various witnesses, but also reconstructed several scenes from *The Story of O* and the interviews between Aury and Régine Deforges in *Confessions of O*.

Today the book is still in print, translated into 17 languages. It is a classic reference in the literature of eroticism and quoted in most anthologies and essays devoted to this genre, yet hardly is it ever mentioned in textbooks for schools and universities. It is indeed extremely rare for a teacher of literature to recommend reading the book, in spite of its irreproachable literary quality. Controversy over the novel has gradually given way to serious academic interest in internal

analysis of the work, which has made it possible to highlight the complexity of its formal functioning. Among the forerunners in this respect, Gaëtan Brulotte in 1974 proposed a structuralist analysis, considering *The Story of O* as a vast field of opportunity for study. Since then it has inspired a number of dissertations and theses.

Why is it that still today *The Story of O* exerts an irresistible power of seduction over its readers and has lost nothing of its breath of scandal? The classic construction of this book, its discreetly suggestive style and the Sadean imagery haunting it do not make it a "modern" book in the sense that it echoes the aspirations of our time. The idea of love as an absolute gift to the other appeals less and less to our Western conscience. Women are now more attached to their recently won individual liberties. Nevertheless, in choosing to prove her love by the exercise of debauchery, which enables her both to please her lover and to satisfy her own desires at will, the heroine displays a "freedom of mind . . . rarer than a freedom of manners" (Dominique Aury).

The novel's power both to enchant and to disturb lies in a mythic dimension over which mundane reality has no hold, in the seductiveness of a heroine who chooses to assert herself in non-being rather than establish her individuality, in the strange combination of unusual events and the quiet audacity of a narration which assumes responsibility for them without judging them. More than an erotic novel with a strong S&M theme, it is a mystic novel which revitalizes an ancient myth, that of passionate love in which passion is *endura*, that is, suffering which leads inevitably to death.

O resembles neither de Sade's Justine, the prisoner of ancient forms of servitude, nor Juliette, who, according to Apollinaire, the forerunner of 20th-century woman. She is a character unique in literary history, for unlike sentimental or mystic heroines, she uses the sexual mode, as conceived by the man she loves, to give herself and to pursue her own destruction. She plays the man's game not only to go on being loved, even though aware of the precariousness of masculine desire, but also to belong to herself no longer and to disappear, whence the quest of which man is the instrument. She also brings an original slant to the character of a woman in love through her reverse relation with the life of her author: the nocturnal double of Pauline Réage, the incarnation of a secret love affair between a discreet woman and a charismatic man for whom Réage wrote this passionate love letter. We should first read it as such.

Biography

Pauline Réage was the pseudonym of Dominique Aury, who was actually born Anne Desclos on September 23 at Rochefort-sur-Mer. She received a bilingual education and discovered at an early age the works of Kipling, Virginia Woolf, Shakespeare, Laclos, and Fénelon. Her encounter with the works of de Sade came later, when she was 30. After brilliant studies at Condorcet and the Sorbonne, she began working as a journalist. In 1939 she participated in choosing the texts for Thierry Maulnier's *Introduction à la poésie française,* then, during the German occupation, distributed the clandestine *Lettres françaises.* It was when she proposed her *Anthologie de la poésie religieuse* (published 1943) to the *Nouvelle Revue Française* that she met Paulhan, 15 years her senior. After 1944 Aury was subeditor for *Lettres françaises, L'Arche,* and then *Nouvelle Revue Française;* and from 1950, for 25 years she was the only woman on the reading committee at Gallimard. A translator, preface writer, and literary critic, she won the Grand prix de la critique littéraire in 1958 for *Lectures pour tous.* In 1963 she joined the panel of judges for the Prix Femina. She died at the age of 90. *The Story of O* is the only published novel which it can be said with certainty she wrote.

ALEXANDRA DESTAIS

Translated from the French by Valérie Burling

Selected Works by Réage

Histoire d'O [1954]. Preface "Le Bonheur dans l'esclavage" by Jean Paulhan. Paris: Pauvert, 1975.
Retour à Roissy. Une fille amoureuse. Postface by A. Pieyre de Mandiargues. Paris: Pauvert, 1975.
Story of O. Translated by Sabine d'Estrée. London: Corgi, 1985.
Story of O. Translated by John P. Hand. New York: Blue Moon Books, 1993.
Return to the Château (preceded by *A Girl in Love*). Translated by Sabine d'Estrée. New York: Ballantine Books, 1995.

Interviews

St. Jorre, John de. "Une Lettre d'amour: The True Story of *Story of O.*" In *The Good Ship Venus: The Erotic Voyage of the Olympia Press,* 209–40. London: Hutchinson/Random House, 1994.
———. "The Unmaking of O." *The New Yorker* 70, no. 23, August 1994.
Deforges, Régine. *O m'a dit, entretiens avec Pauline Réage.* Paris: Pauvert, 1995.
———. *Confessions of O: Conversation witth Pauline Réage.* Translated by Sabine D'Estrée. New York: Viking Press, 1979.
Grenier, Nicole. *Vocation clandestine.* Paris: Gallimard/ L'Infini, 1999.

Critical Studies

Benjamin, Jessica. *The Bonds of Love: Psychoanalysis, Feminism, and the Problem of Domination.* New York: Pantheon Books, 1988.
Brulotte, Gaëtan. "Oui." *Champs d'application* [Montreal] 2 (Spring 1974): 20–52.
Charney, Maurice. "Erotic Sainthood and the Search for Self-Annihilation: *Story of O* and *L'Image.*" In *Sexual Fiction,* 52–70. London: Methuen, 1981.
Dardigna, Anne-Marie. *Les Châteaux d'Eros ou les infortunes du sexe des femmes.* Paris: Librairie François Maspero, 1980.
Didier, Béatrice. *L'écriture-femme.* Paris: Presses Universitaires de France, 1981.
Dworkin, Andrea. "Woman as Victim: *Story of O.*" In *Woman Hating,* 53–63. New York: Plume, 1974.
Grenier, Nicole. "Anne-Dominique-Pauline-Desclos-Aury-Réage." *Sigila,* no. 6, 2000.
Griffin, Susan. "Sadomasochism and the Erosion of Self: A Critical Reading of *Story of O.*" In *Against Sadomasochism: A Radical Feminist Analysis,* edited by R.R. Linden et al. East Palo Alto, CA: Frog in the Well, 1982.
Pallister, Janis L. "The Anti-Castle in the Works of 'Pauline Réage." *Journal of the Midwest Modern Language Association* 18/2 (1985): 3–13.
Phillips, John. "O, Really! Pauline Réage's *Histoire d'O.*" In *Forbidden Fictions, Pornography and Censorship in Twentieth Century French Literature,* 86–103. London: Pluto Press, 1999.
Salaün, Elise. "Erotisme littéraire et censure: La révolution cachée." *Voix et Images* 23 (Winter 1998).
Sontag, Susan. "The Pornographic Imagination." Appendix in *Story of the Eye,* by Georges Bataille, 85–118. Harmondsworth: Penguin, 1982.
Walker, Muriel. "Pour une lecture narratologique d'Histoire d'O." Section Analyses: Le littéraire et le politique: Points d'ancrage. In *Études Littéraires* 32–33 (Autumn 2000–Winter 2001): 149–69.
Weatherfield, Molly. *The Mother of Masochism* [August 6, 1998]. Retrieved April 1, 2006, from http://www.salon.com/books/feature/1998/08/06feature.html

Web Site

The Corridors of Roissy... The Gardens of Samois..., at: http://www.storyofo.co.uk/Keys.html http://www. storyofo.co.uk/Biblio.html

REBATET, LUCIEN

1903–1972
French novelist, journalist, and critic

There are not many ways of presenting the fascist writer Lucien Rebatet other than in Sartrian terms. Because he was an arch-collaborator under the Nazis, he was very much considered a *salaud* (a very uncomplimentary French epithet) even by René Étiemble, who supported his book against Sartre; an "inexpiable *salaud*" by Marc-Edouard Nabe; and "the very worst of *salauds*" as far as George Steiner was concerned. This judgment of the author contrasts with the high praise earned by his 1,319-page novel *Les deux étendards* [*The Two Battle Flags*]. Although ignored by the critics, it attracted the attention not only (predictably) of young right-wing novelists like Nimier and Blondin, but also of former members of the Resistance and anti-fascists as well known as Jean Paulhan and Etiemble. Failing nonetheless to be discussed widely, it was labeled by Steiner as "the secret masterpiece of modern literature," while Pascal Ifri referred to it as "a damned masterpiece." This seems disputable for a novel whose all-too-classical form is indebted to the nineteenth century and whose very conception is a refusal to engage with the main trauma of the twentieth century. The work which, like much of de Sade's, was written in prison, could be considered as a major piece of erotic literature. One of its most enduring literary achievements consists in its subtle concealing of its erotic dimension. While dealing with questions of theology, as the title (borrowed from Saint Ignatius of Loyola) suggests, as well as of music, painting, theatre, and literature, eroticism appears in fact to be its principal theme. This eroticism is both spiritual and material, marked by ecstatic pleasure and agony, where unveiled desires and the body reveal as much fear as rapture.

Set in Lyon and Paris in the 1920s, it is the story of two highly intellectual twenty-year-old boys: Michel, a former pupil of the Brothers, who has lost his faith and hopes to replace it with a pagan cult of arts and pleasure, and Régis, who wants to become a Jesuit priest but loves a younger girl named Anne-Marie. The two lovers hope that their mystical and pure love will sublimate the flesh; its fulfillment shall come when Régis enters the seminary and when Anne-Marie joins an order of nuns. Michel, who fell in love with Anne-Marie as soon as he met her, sees sharing their spiritual adventure as the only means of being loved by her. The incapacity of Michel to adhere to his new beliefs and his gradual winning over of Anne-Marie from Régis shows what he considers to be the supremacy of eroticism. Yet Anne-Marie's inability to forget her earlier ideals and to find satisfaction, once Michel has successfully convinced her to reject Régis, along with her vow and her faith, shows religion to be a "drug" even more powerful than sex. Rebatet proves his anti-religious point with cruel sarcasm by setting the ultimate failure of eroticism and the final triumph of Régis's God in the holy City of Rome. This frustrating outcome is aimed at showing that the perpetuation of religious prejudice implies the ruin of human happiness. As in de Sade, the novel is ultimately a tale of the destruction of the innocent and trusting Anne-Marie, "the most admirable lover." Yet, it is the Catholic Régis and not the libertine Michel who destroys her.

Whereas in 1942's *Les décombres*, Rebatet's occasional eroticism is descriptive and graphic and serves the metaphorical purpose of highlighting the violation of France by the German armies, in *Les deux étendards*, eroticism thrives in a more subtle atmosphere of a gradually growing desire and a fiery intellectualism. It results from the combination of two opposing erotic strategies. Firstly, the incredibly lengthy pursuit of the desired object, the pious and supremely beautiful Anne-Marie, whose fall is anticipated and awaited with growing excitement for well over 1,000 pages. This fall, preceded and followed by a negation of her purity, gives the narrative its climax and its overriding leitmotif. Secondly, throughout the novel are scattered scenes of intense crudity, told in the language of students from the 1920s and in which portraits of mistresses and emancipated or debauched girls (such as "Gaupette") are contrasted with the physical process of repressed desire by Catholic virgins in the *Années Folles*.

Biography

Lucien Rebatet was born November 15 in Monas-en-Valloire (Drôme) and attended a school in Saint-Chamond led by the Marist order, where he earned a baccalaureate and became an atheist. He studied philosophy and letters first in Lyon (1921) and then at the Sorbonne (1923), without completing his degree. He had several low-paying jobs as a private school teacher and an insurance clerk before and after his military service in Germany (1927), where he became a fascist. He was a journalist for Charles Maurras's monarchist newspaper, *Action Française,* writing celebrated cinema criticism under the pseudonym Francois Vinneuil (1929–1940), and from 1932 for the far-right broadsheet *Je suis partout*, led by Pierre Gaxotte. In 1933, he married Véronique Popovici in Romania. He was overtly pro-Nazi and, together with Drieu La Rochelle and Robert Brasillach, was one of the most prominent figures of French collaboration. His anti-Semitic novel *Les décombres* (1942), describing the French military collapse in the years 1938–40, became the best seller of the occupation years. Like Céline, he followed the officials of the Vichy regime into their German exile in Sigmaringen in September 1944, and was captured on May 8, 1945, in Austria. He was sentenced to death on November 23, 1946, but unlike Brasillach, Hérold-Paquis, or Luchaire, he wasn't executed. He was reprieved on April 12, 1947, and like Maurras and Benoist-Méchin, served a long jail sentence in Clairvaux, where he wrote most of his most important novel, *Les Deux étendards*, published by Gallimard in February 1952, the same year Rebatet was freed. He published another novel, *Les epis murs* (1954) and resumed journalistic activities, with contributions to the journals *Rivarol*, *Les Écrits de Paris,* and *Le Spectacle du Monde*. His book *Une histoire de la musique* was published in 1969. He never expressed regrets or apologized and died embittered and in literary isolation on August 24, 1972.

DOMINIQUE JEANNEROD

Selected Works

Les décombres. Paris: Denoël, 1942.
Les deux étendards. 2 vols. Paris: Gallimard, 1951; new ed., 1 vol., 1971.
Les épis mûrs. Paris: Gallimard, 1954.
Les mémoires d'un fasciste. Vol. 1: Les Décombres, 1938–1940, rev. ed. by author, 1976; Vol. 2: 1941–1947. Paris: Jean-Jacques Pauvert, 1976.
A Jean Paulhan. Liège: Éditeur Dynamo, 1968.
Une histoire de la musique. Paris: R. Laffont, 1969.
Lettres de prison. Paris: Le Dilettante, 1993.

Further Reading

Belot, Robert. *Dialogue de vaincus: Prison de Clairvaux, janvier-décembre 1950* (Lucien Rebatet, Pierre-Antoine Cousteau). Paris: Berg international, 1999.
Etiemble, René. *Hygiène des lettres, II: Littérature dégagée, 1942–1953*, 199–210. Paris: Gallimard, 1955.
Faulkner, Christopher. "Theory and Practice of Film Reviewing in France in the 1930s: Eyes Right (Lucien Rebatet and Action Française, 1936–1939)." *French Cultural Studies* (June 1992): 133–55.
Ifri, Pascal A. *Les Deux Étendards de Lucien Rebatet: Dossier d'un chef-d'œuvre maudit*. Lausanne: L'Âge d'Homme: 2001. See the review by Nicholas Hewitt in *French Studies* 57 (2003): 419.
———. *Rebatet*. Collection "Qui suis-je?" Paris: Editions Pardès, 2004.
———. "Anatomy of an Exclusion: *Les Deux Étendards* by Lucien Rebatet." *Symposium* 45:1 (1991): 343–54.
———. "Le Journal des Deux Étendards ou les coulisses de la création." *Cincinnati Romance Review* (1995): 109–15.
———. "The Epitexts and Allotexts of Lucien Rebatet's Les Deux Étendards." *Romanic Review* (1996): 113–30.
———. "Le Paris des 'Années Folles' dans Les Deux Étendards de Rebatet." *RLA: Romance Languages Annual* (1998): 54–58.
———. "Modern Literature and Christianity: The Religious Issue in Lucien Rebatet's Les Deux Étendards." *Studies in Twentieth Century Literature* (2001): 394–413.
———. "Les Deux Étendards de Lucien Rebatet ou 'Proust refait sur nature.'" *French Review* (March 2004): 705–15.
Reboul, Yves. "Lucien Rebatet: Le Roman inachevé?" *Etudes Littéraires* (Summer 2004): 13–29.
Vandromme, Pol. *Rebatet*. Puiseaux: Pardès, 2002.

REBELL, HUGUES

1867–1905
French poet, translator, and novelist

Among the fiction of Hugues Rebell, some half a dozen or so works have been considered sufficiently interesting to merit being reprinted in recent decades in France in paperback: *Le magasin d'auréoles* (1896), *La Nichina* (1897), *La femme qui a connu l'empereur* (1898), *La Câlineuse* (1899), *La saison à Baïa* (1900), *La Camorra* (1900), and *Les nuits chaudes du Cap Français* (1902). Though none of these works are in themselves pornographic, all include discussions of adult sexual behavior, and several include flagellation scenes. Resolutely pro-aristocratic, much of the prose fiction is best understood as a reaction to the tide of democratic politics which many right-wing commentators feared was engulfing France at the time. Although the Grassal family wealth was considerable (significantly, it derived ultimately from the slave trade), Rebell had been spending money so recklessly that by the beginning of the new century he was in considerable financial difficulty. It was at this moment that he entered into relations with the publisher Charles Carrington (i.e., Paul Fernando), who operated in Paris from about 1890 until his death in the early 1920s. Carrington had been captivated by the flagellation scenes in *La Nichina*, and Rebell produced various works for him in this vein, including: *The Memoirs of Dolly Morton* (1899), *Whipped Women* (1903), and *Cinq histoires vécues* (1904). With regard to *Les Mystères de la maison de la Verveine* (1901), an above-average flagellation novel which some bibliographies attribute to Rebell, it is likely that his involvement was limited to translating and editing the book, since the original work, *The Mysteries of Verbena House* (1882), is usually ascribed to the journalist George Augustus Sala. Various other titles published by Carrington, including *Le Fouet à Londres* (1905), seem unlikely to have been the work of Rebell. Apart from some of the Carrington material, none of his work has been made available in English translation; a certain amount of biographical information has been published in French in recent years, however.

The Memoirs of Dolly Morton

Rebell's authorship of this work has never been comprehensively established, though there is strong evidence in support of the attribution. The fact that the English edition preceded the French only confuses matters, since it is possible that Rebell wrote the novel in his native language and it was then translated into English prior to the French edition, as *En Virginie* (1901). Though Rebell himself was a translator (among his works is the French translation of Oscar Wilde's essays, *Intentions*, in 1905), it is customary for translators to work only into their mother tongue. Perhaps the strongest argument in support of Rebell's authorship, however, is the clearly defined historical context of the novel—the period of the "underground railway" in the antebellum United States (i.e., the network of farms and houses in which escaping slaves were given refuge as they moved north)—and its psychosexual dynamics.

Whether or not Rebell was the author, *The Memoirs of Dolly Morton* has to be considered one of the more able flagellation novels of the period, not only on account of its period style and historical detail but also with regard to the vivacity of the erotic scenes. In essence, the novel is an episodic account of the adventures and progressive humiliation of the eponymous heroine, who, on the death of her father, decides to assist escaped slaves in their bid for freedom. Naturally, in such a work, one moves progressively from one flagellation scene to another. In *Dolly Morton*, the opening chapter describes Dolly's own childhood from the perspective of the domestic discipline she receives. Subsequent chapters detail her plight at the hands of local plantation owners when her political activities regarding slavery become known; the manner by which she is blackmailed into becoming the concubine of another plantation owner (Rebell was particular fascinated by power games of this sort, and practically all his prose fiction involves hierarchies of some sort, whether political or domestic); and the increasingly licentious behavior of her blackmailer. Needless to say, each scenario involves some form of flagellation activity and/or sexual humiliation. Closure of the novel comes in the form of northern military successes, at which time Dolly makes her way to Paris.

Les nuits chaudes du Cap Français (1902)

In 1899, as noted above, Rebell began working for Carrington. In parallel with this, however, he also continued to tout other projects around Parisian publishers. One such project, a two-volume novel with a Caribbean setting (to be entitled *La Caresse des tropiques* and *Noire et créole,* respectively) was offered to a firm called the Maison d'Art in May 1900. Two years later, under the new title *Les nuits chaudes du Cap Français* [*The Hot Nights of Cap-Francais*], and for an entirely different publisher, this would prove to be the author's last work of fiction of any note brought out by a mainstream publishing house. It is also one of the author's most accomplished novels, and certainly one his most dense.

Les nuits chaudes du Cap Français is a complex tale of the web of sexual and emotional blackmail and jealousy which develops on an isolated sugarcane plantation in Saint-Domingo in the aftermath of the outbreak of the French Revolution. Indeed, it might even be claimed that the action of the novel is precipitated by events in France and, more importantly, the subsequent breakdown of law and order, since the starting point of the novel is the murder of the fleeing sister of a plantation owner who is carrying valuable property sewn in the lining of her coat. In the best tradition of the nascent detective story, the sordid details of this crime are not revealed until an advanced stage. The culprits, however, are an apparently honest Creole, Mme Gourgueil, who acts from pecuniary advantage, and her black maid, Zinga, who is motivated by a hatred of whites. Although Mme Gourgueil subsequently adopts the murdered woman's daughter, Antoinette, she will henceforth be always in the power of Zinga.

Although the author had never visited the French West Indies, the claustrophobic nature of colonial life and the petty rivalries and jealousies which develop between neighbors, between masters and servants, and even between stepmother and a pubescent stepdaughter are well defined. Flagellation, for once, is not the central focus of the work, but the relationship, essentially of a sexual nature, which exists between women. This is particularly true of Mme Gourgueil's interest in Antoinette. Naturally, the exoticism of the location lends itself particularly well to this sort of exercise, but Rebell is at pains to locate the story within a clearly defined political and social context. Though far more sophisticated as a novel than *The Memoirs of Dolly Morton*, one sees the same fascination with historical detail, the same power dynamics at work (though here put to the service of a revenge novel something in the tradition of Dumas), and the same manner of closure, as an essentially hierarchical world crumbles in the face of democratic political reform. Indeed, perhaps the most successful single piece of writing that Rebell achieved is the short story *La Vengeance d'un inconnu*, which serves essentially as the introduction to *Les Nuits chaudes du Cap français,* though all the events in it are, in fact, a consequence of the main body of the novel. Here again a complicated revenge intrigue is worked out, this time within the context of Parisian revolutionary politics.

In contrast to the main intellectual preoccupation of nineteenth-century French popular literature, which was to expose aristocratic sexual misconduct, Rebell seeks to celebrate such excesses. It is perhaps for this reason that not only was the author little appreciated in his own time, but remains a largely unknown writer to this day. *Les Nuits chaudes du Cap français* was initially conceived following the success (the only real one of Rebell's literary career) of *La Nichina* (1897), another complicated tale of intrigue and revenge set against the backdrop of Renaissance Venice. Significantly, Pascal Pia lists a 1916 French translation attributed to Rebell of *Queenie*, first published around 1885 (and subsequently issued as *The Adventures of Lady Harpur*), an anonymous flagellation novel with a West Indian setting. Obviously, there must be a lost earlier French edition, but if Rebell really was the translator of this work, it would suggest one not entirely unexpected source for *Les Nuits chaudes du Cap français.*

Whipped Women

Whipped Women, which consists of five short stories, was the last book Rebell prepared for Carrington. Even by Rebell's own standards, this remains a curious and by no means satisfactory work. According to some critics, even Carrington, who brought out an English translation (attributed to the pseudonymous Jean de Villiot) in a limited edition of 300 copies in 1903, would seem to have been aware of the book's limitations, demanding a number of revisions. Stylistically, the book is more simple and straightforward than is usually the case with Rebell, perhaps indicative of the author's declining physical strength and levels of concentration. On the positive side, there is a greater show of humor than elsewhere in Rebell's work, though also an insistence on melodramatic denouement. This is clearly indicated in a story ("Le confesseur") concerning the Princess Elisabeth Bathory, who is subject to an elaborate hoax (which, needless to say, involves the surprisingly naive Elisabeth being flagellated) by a lover who disguises himself as her new confessor; when he reveals the nature of the trick he has played on her, Elisabeth murders him in a fit of passion before killing herself (see *Pizarnik, Alejandra* in this volume for information on the real-life Erzebet Bathory, the "bloody countess." Any relation?). This, and other stories in the collection, contain occasional scatological references (which are not to be found elsewhere in his work). Together with the increasing severity of the flagellation scenes, some commentators see this collection as further tending to indicate the author's mental collapse. The original manuscript, under the title *Femmes Châtiées,* was not published until 1994.

Biography

Georges Joseph Grassal was born in easy circumstances in Nantes and died in abject poverty in Paris. Though by no means academically precocious, as a teenager he became fascinated by such *fin-de-siècle* figures as J.-K. Huysmans (whose 1884 novel *A Rebours* is considered by many to have defined the Decadent movement in France) and the German philosopher Friedrich Nietzsche. Indeed, his identification with the figure of the outsider led him to invent the pseudonym Hugues Rebell by which he subsequently preferred to be known. Between 1886 and 1890 he self-published a handful of works, mainly collections of poetry, initially in Nantes and later in Paris, where he established himself in 1892. Over the course of the following decade, he published some 25 books and contributed to various magazines and journals.

TERRY HALE

Selected Works

Le magasin d'auréoles. Paris: Mercure de France, 1896; reprinted, Paris: Jérôme Martineau, 1970 (one story removed).

La Nichina. 2 vols. Paris: Mercure de France, 1897; reprinted 2 vols. in the collection "Les Classiques interdits," Paris: Editions Jean-Claude Lattès, 1980.

La femme qui a connu l'empereur. Paris: Mercure de France, 1898; reprinted, Paris: Union générale d'éditions, 1979.

La Câlineuse. Paris: Editions de la Revue Blanche, 1899; reprinted, Paris: Union générale d'éditions, 1979.

La saison à Baïa. Paris: Borel, 1900; reprinted, Paris: Union générale d'éditions, 1979 (with *La Camorra*).

La camorra. Paris: Editions de la Revue Blanche, 1900.

The Memoirs of Dolly Morton. Paris: Carrington, 1899; Philadelphia [Paris?]: Society of Private Bibliophiles [Carrington], 1904; ibid., 1910; Los Angeles: Holloway House, 1966; North Hollywood, CA: Brandon House, 1968; introduction by Donald Thomas, London: Odyssey Press, 1970; *En Virginie* (as by Jean de Villiot), Paris: Carrington, 1901.

Les nuits chaudes du Cap Français. Paris: Editions de la Plume, 1902; Paris: Editions Germaine Raoult, 1953 (illustrations by Paul Emil Bécat); Paris: Union générale d'éditions, 1978 (includes *Le Magasin d'auréoles; Femmes Châtiées*).

Whipped Women (as Jean de Villiot). Paris: Carrington, 1903; *Femmes Châtiées,* edited by Thierry Rodange, Paris: Mercure de France, 1994.

Cinq histoires vécues (as by Jean de Villiot). Paris: Carrington, 1904.

Further Reading

Rodange, Thierry. *Le Diable quitte la table ou la vie passionné d'Hugues Rebell.* Paris: Mercure de France, 1994.

REBREANU, LIVIU

1885–1944
Romanian novelist, short story writer, and dramatist

Adam si Eva

Adam si Eva [*Adam and Eve*] was published in 1925. According to the writer's wife, it was inspired by a real incident. While walking on Lapusneanu Street in Iaşi in September 1918, the novelist was suddenly struck by a beautiful green-eyed woman who was looking intently at him. The woman seemed familiar, although the writer was convinced that they had never met. They exchanged a glance, then turned round, walked farther, and after a few steps simultaneously turned their heads to look at each other again. Then they disappeared from each other's lives forever.

Inspired by this event, Rebreanu initially wrote a short story based on metempsychosis. Then he created seven fictional kernels that developed into a novel through repetition and reinforcement of the main theme. Actually, it is difficult to say with certainty whether the composition of *Adam si Eva* is that of a novel or a short story cycle. What is obvious is that *Adam si Eva* is an erotic novel that relies on the idea that the first couple (Adam and Eve) is reiterated in any new couple. The two lovers are elements of the original of the Platonic androgyny. On their quest to restore their initial unity, they must go through the pains of recognition and separation in seven lives. They will be reunited only in the seventh life. Rebreanu's very clear thesis is reinforced by the repetition of the number seven. There are seven chapters (stories), and each of them has seven parts. Everything is sevenfold: the spans of time, space dimensions, and details of significant objects in the story.

In the first chapter, entitled "The Beginning," Toma Novac, a university professor from Bucharest, is on his deathbed, and is suddenly cognizant of all his post lives. In this supreme moment of final comprehension, he will relive, in a flash, all his seven lives. In the first life he is Mahavira, a cowherd, who is the predestined partner of Navamalika, one of the maidens destined to King Arjuna. In a swift moment, Mahavira succeeds in resting his cheeks on Navamalika's maidenly breasts. The punishment is terrible. He will be skinned alive. In the second life he is Unamonu, a high Egyptian government official, and his beloved is Isit, the pharaoh's favorite. Everything is simply longing and desire in this life. In the third life he is Gungunum, a Babylonian scribe, and he loves Umma, a county governor's daughter. The war between Nippur and Babylon will bring him an ironic death among other prisoners of war although his ransom had already been paid. Distant worshipping is all that is allowed to the desperate lover in this life. In the fourth life, the social balance between the two lovers is changed. He is Axius, a Roman cavalier who loves below his rank. His beloved is a slave, Servilia. This is one of the best chapters of the novel. In a sadistic fit Axius asks the flogger to whip Servilia in order to punish her for the desperate passion that she inspires. Trying to get rid of this obsession, Axius travels to the East, but nothing can remove Servilia from his mind. Upon his return, his first question is about Servilia. The jealous Chrysilla, his wife, stabs Servilia to death. Axius will cut his veins open in the bathroom, desperate for having lost the chance of a lifetime. In the fifth life he is Adeodatus, a monk in a German medieval monastery, Hans by his secular name. His desperate love is blasphemous as well. Rebreanu's exploration of obsessive love is both clinical and theological. Adeodatus dies kissing the icon of the Holy Virgin and mumbling "Maria" while Satan grins at him and says that there is nothing more precious in the world than the love of woman. In the sixth life, Rebreanu plays again with social status of his protagonists. He is Gaston Duhem, a revolutionary physician in France during the Reign of Terror. She is Yvonne Collignon de Gargan. They meet in a revolutionary court and are sent, with expediency, to death together. In the seventh life he is Toma Novac, a philosophy professor in Bucharest, Romania, in the thirties of the twentieth century. He is shot to death by the jealous husband of Ileana, his predestined love. Toma's spiritual guide, Tudor Aleman, will set forth the ideological frame of this sevenfold literary structure that is *Adam and Eve*. He appears to verify that Toma does meet the woman that is the embodiment of his other spiritual half and make sure that this life is the seventh, the end of the material journey of the soul.

The fictional discourse of *Adam and Eve* is organized on two levels: a meta-discourse which utters the life of the self in-between the earthly lives in a space and time of pure consciousness and a fictional discourse which is the erotic story. The former always presents the painful separation of the soul from the body, its wandering as pure consciousness, and then its reintegration into another finite body. The latter is a historical and erotic novel. The two partners meet in different historical periods that are described with precision and the pleasure of the picturesque detail. They always belong to different social groups, and this disparity makes their reunification impossible. Sometimes the man has a higher social position, sometimes the woman. The writer varies the circumstances with intelligence and avoids monotonous repetition. Eroticism is mostly distant adoration and desire. Occasionally, hot embraces and even sado-masochistic drives are allowed. Full sexual accomplishment exists only in the seventh life, the last.

Metempsychosis is the vehicle of love, and love is the absolute accomplishment of the human being. *Adam si Eva* is a variation on the same theme of narrative virtue. Rebreanu is able to maintain the delicate balance between the same and the different. The scheme is always the same. The two lovers meet and recognize each other and after a very brief interlude of physical and mostly spiritual reunification they are separated forever. It is only in the Roman and the French story that the woman is killed before the man. Otherwise, she stays in the world after the man's violent death or she remains an idealization, as with Adeodatus. The man always has the initiative of the quest and he is always killed for having transgressed the rules, be they social, moral, or religious. The seven lives are constructed from the man's

perspective, for the woman does not leave the world with her lover even in the seventh life when the cycle is over for the man. Why not for the woman as well? Rebreanu, the male writer, gives no answer. There is usually a third character that fulfills the eternal triangle and thwarts the lovers' reunification. It is the spouse or the partner of one of the lovers. Eroticism permeates the text. Sexuality is explored with delicacy and psychological penetration, especially in the cases when love becomes an obsession bordering on the pathological.

With Rebreanu, Eros is the manifestation of destiny. In his narrative demonstration, Eros and Death meet and complete each other. The tragic dimension of the story is given by the reiteration of the desire. The seven linear plots become a cycle that gets a utopian dimension. Rebreanu's millenarism is individual and erotic. The reader is advised to hope and expect the greatest encounter of any life: one's predestined partner, the other half of one's spiritual self.

Biography

Born in the village of Tirlisua. Died in Valea Mare. He made his debut with a collection of short stories, *Framintari*, in 1912. Rebreanu is considered the creator of the Romanian modern novel. One of his best novels, *Padurea spanzuratilor* (translated as *The Forest of the Hanged*), is set during World War I and expresses the trauma of the Romanian military from the Austro-Hungarian empire obliged to fight against the Romanians from Romania. In 1920 Rebreanu won the Nasturel-Herescu Prize of the Romanian Academy for his novel *Ion*. In 1939 he became a member of the Romanian Academy.

MIHAELA MUDURE

Editions

Adam si Eva. Bucuresti: Cartea romaneasca, 1925; Bucuresti: Eminescu, 1970; Bucuresti: Cugetarea-Georgescu Delafras, 1941; Bucuresti: Minerva, 1974; Bucuresti: Minerva, 1982; Iasi: Junimea, 1985; Bucuresti: Minerva, 1989; Craiova: Valeriu, 1995; as *Adam and Eve*, translated by Mihail Bogdan, Bucharest: Minerva, 1986.

Selected Works

Golanii. 1916
Ion. 1920
Padurea spanzuratilor. 1922
Ciuleandra. 1927

Itic Strul, dezertor. 1932
Rascoala. 1932.
Opere. volumes I–XVIII, 1968–1998

Further Reading

Crohmalniceanu, Ovid S. *Liviu Rebreanu.* Bucuresti: Editura de stat pentru literatura si arta, 1954.

———. *Cinci prozatori în cinci feluri de lectura.* Bucuresti: Cartea romaneasca, 1984.
Dan, Sergiu Pavel. *Proza fantastica romaneasca.* Bucuresti: Minerva, 1975.
Piru, Alexandru. *Liviu Rebreanu.* Bucuresti: Editura Tineretului, 1965.
Rebreanu, Fanny Liviu. *Cu sotul meu.* Bucuresti: Editura pentru literatura, 1963.

RECHY, JOHN

1934–
American novelist

Ben Satterfield once likened John Rechy's writing to "an excerpt from Krafft-Ebing's *Psychopathia Sexualis*" (Satterfield: 81). In fact, Rechy demonstrates an almost Sadean knowledge of sexual variation, gingerly describing the exchange of every conceivable body fluid in scenes of the most abandoned promiscuity. Yet, descriptions of explicit sex actually take up only a part of his writing, and are absent from his most famous book. What makes Rechy an erotic novelist is not his ability to pen a raunchy scenario when he wants to, but his soldierly defense of Eros in its eternal struggle with Thanatos.

After leaving the army, Rechy drifted into the half-world of male prostitution, migrating from city to city until he ended up in New Orleans. A long letter to a friend, eventually published in the *Evergreen Review*, became the nucleus for his brilliant first novel, *City of Night* (1963). Supposedly the semi-autobiographical account of a nameless homosexual street hustler, *City of Night* depicts a hidden world of outlaw sex, peopled by drag queens and bull dykes, hustlers and "scores," chicken hawks and ratty teenagers, all seemingly condemned to pursue a never-ending search for some "substitute for salvation" in a godless universe. Only by refusing to reciprocate, while desperate scores lick his body, can Rechy's hustler feel completely whole. In the process, the distinction between the author and his literary alter ego gradually disappears. As Rechy himself has suggested, autobiography and fiction have become nearly indistinguishable in his life.

While *City of Night* eschewed any graphic description of sex, Rechy's second novel, *Numbers*, was much more explicit. *Numbers* carries the story of the hustler (now named "Johnny Rio") forward, chronicling his return to Los Angeles after an absence of three years. Dropping any pretense of hustling, Johnny resolves to break his old "record" by getting thirty men to get him off, without doing anything in return. Strutting through movie balconies, men's rooms, and parks, he reaches his goal, only to finally recognize that he needs his scores as much as they need him. Since *Numbers*, Rechy has published nine more novels, one "documentary," several plays, and numerous essays. Although much of his early work focused on gay themes, more recent efforts, such as the underrated *Our Lady of Babylon*, have dealt with "straight" sexuality in its various permutations. In fact, he often writes from the perspective of a number of characters in a single book, demonstrating a profound capacity to empathize with a people of either, or every, gender.

Yet, Rechy appears to be deeply conflicted about his own eroticism. Honorah Moore Lynch has thus suggested that he is torn between the need for order and a hunger for rebellion (Lynch: 1). From a sociological perspective, Rechy's work seems to chronicle the decay of bourgeois society and the coming of some new hyper-modern order. On one level, he clearly portrays sexual life as an apparent struggle between opposing forces. On one side are the rich, old, white men who do the looking, and on the other side are the women, young men, and poor who get the looks. While the former have money and power, the latter have only their youth and allure to bargain with. This binary structure not only forces poor males to sell their bodies to the rich, but makes male prostitution the only way that men who want to be looked at can gratify their needs.

On a deeper level, however, Rechy portrays a very different reality that is gradually pushing its way to the surface of social life. Here, men and women, young and old, are all motivated by the same needs, and cursed by the same loneliness. Gender is mere performance, mere artifice dictated by a dying social order. Marriage appears here as an empty convention, and righteous promiscuity as the only kind of sex befitting a democracy. Johnny Rio "c'est nous." While "people wear masks three hundred and sixty-four days a year," an old crone warns, only on Mardi Gras do "they wear their own faces" (*City of Night*). When women gain the right to look at men as men have looked at women, everyone will become equally narcissistic, and the traditional order will pass away. What bourgeois society calls narcissistic is merely the highest form of self-expression. The orgiastic rites of Fat Tuesday reveal not only the real faces of people, but the face of the future itself.

Against this background, Rechy extols street sex as a righteous disruption of the filaments of power, paving the way for a sexual revolution that will make everyone equal (except, perhaps, the old and ugly). Yet, a strange (crypto-Catholic?) guilt haunts this vision. In the fact-based *Sexual Outlaw*, Rechy wonders why after being with "dozens of people, I just want . . . to die." It is perhaps to assuage this guilt that Rechy has felt compelled to distinguish between the life-affirming sex of joyful promiscuity and the deathlike anti-sex of sadomasochism. Rechy's moralistic condemnation of sadomasochism may shed light on why critics have too often ignored his work. Too conservative for the cultural left, but too radical for the right, Rechy has never been "politically correct." The result has been a scandalous silence about his books. Despite the fact that his works have been translated into twenty languages and sold millions of copies, he has never received the critical attention he deserves. As society continues to become increasingly "Rechyan," this may slowly change.

Biography

Born March 10 the child of impoverished but aristocratic refugees from the Mexican Revolution, grew up in El Paso. Studied at Texas Western College (BA degree) and the New School of Social Research in New York. Served a tour of duty in Germany in the U.S. Army. Adjoint professor, Professional Writers Program, University of Southern California; Pen-USA West Lifetime Achievement Award, 1997. William Whitehead Award for Lifetime Achievement, 1999.

LAWRENCE BIRKEN

Selected Works

Novels

City of Night. 1963.
Numbers. 1967.
This Day's Death. 1969.
The Vampires. 1971.
The Fourth Angel. 1972.
Rushes. 1979.
Bodies and Souls. 1983.
Marilyn's Daughter. 1988.
The Miraculous Day of Amalia Gomez. 1991.
Our Lady of Babylon. 1996.
The Coming of the Night. 1999.

Documentaries

The Sexual Outlaw: A Non-Fiction Account, with Commentaries, of Three Days and Nights in the Sexual Underground (1977)

Plays

Tigers Wild (1986)
Momma as She Became—But Not as She Was

Further Reading

Adams, Stephen. *The Homosexual as Hero in Contemporary Fiction*, 83–98. New York: Barnes and Noble, 1980.

Birken, Lawrence. "Desire and Death: The Early Fiction of John Rechy." *Western Humanities Review* 51:2 (Summer 1997).

Bredbeck, Gregory. "John Rechy." In *Contemporary Gay American Novelists: A Bio-Bibliographical Critical Sourcebook*, edited by Emmanuel S. Nelson. New York: Greenwood Press, 1993.

Giles, James R. "Religious Alienation and 'Homosexual Consciousness' in *City of Night* and *Go Tell it on the Mountain*." *College English* 36:3 (November 1974): 369–80.

Hoffman, Stanton. "The Cities of Night: John Rechy's *City of Night* and the American Literature of Homosexuality." *Chicago Review* 17:2–3 (1964): 195–206.

Leyland, Winston, ed. "John Rechy." *Gay Sunshine Interviews I*. San Francisco, CA: Gay Sunshine Press, 1975.

Lynch, Honorah Moore. *Patterns of Anarchy and Order in the Works of John Rechy*. Unpublished Ph.D. dissertation, University of Houston, 1976.

Ortiz, Ricardo. "Sexuality Degree Zero: Pleasure and Power in the Novels of John Rechy, Arturo Islas, and Michael Nava." *Journal of Homosexuality* 26: 2–3 (1993): 111–25.

Satterfield, Ben. "John Rechy's Tormented World." *Southwest Review* 67:1 (Winter 1982): 78–85.

Steuernagel, Trudy. "Contemporary Homosexual Fiction and the Gay Rights Movement." *Journal of Popular Culture* 20:3 (Winter 1986): 125–34.

Website

http://www.johnrechy.com

REICH, WILHELM

1897–1957
Austrian physician, psychotherapist, and scientist

Reich's first published article, under the guise of describing a patient, tells how he had witnessed his mother's sexual relationship with his tutor and then told his father. These events and his mother's subsequent suicide may well have become what his biographer Sharaf called, using Erik Erikson's phrase, "an 'existential debt [remaining] all the rest of a lifetime.'" Certainly the rights of lovers to what Reich called "the genital embrace" remained central to his passionate mission. In a letter to Lou Andreas-Salomé (1928), Freud called Reich "a worthy but impetuous young man, passionately devoted to his hobby-horse, who now salutes in the genital orgasm the antidote to every neurosis."

Reich outlined the phases that are supposed to occur in healthy sexual intercourse and lead up to orgasm. There is pleasurable (not "cold") erection; the man is "spontaneously gentle . . . without having to cover up opposite tendencies"; then, "pleasurable excitation, which during the preliminaries has maintained about the same level, suddenly increases . . . both in the man and in the woman–with the penetration of the penis" (the man feels he is "being sucked in," the woman that she is "sucking the penis in"). The man increasingly feels he wants to penetrate deeper, but not sadistically "pierce" the woman; the "frictions" are "mutual, slow, spontaneous, and effortless," with all consciousness on the pleasurable sensations; finally, there is loss of voluntary control, increased excitation, a "melting" sensation, and clouding of consciousness; ejaculation and orgasm begin in increased frequency of involuntary muscular contractions and with the desire (in the man) to "penetrate completely" or (in the woman) to "receive completely," a release of tension, and the tapering off of excitation in "a pleasant bodily and psychic relaxation."

He considered the moralistic suppression of such experiences, especially in adolescents, the basis for the "mass psychology of fascism" itself, and was drawn to the Communist Party in an effort to oppose sex-denying society, though in time the Communists repudiated him for his sexual beliefs. His break with Freud can be understood not only in terms of his insistence on the genital orgasm, and his subsequent political position, which Freud did not want to be associated with psychoanalysis, but also in terms of his interest in curative technique, for which, as a psychotherapist, he apparently enjoyed remarkable success. In *Character Analysis*, a work still referred to in psychoanalytic literature, Reich developed the theory of "character armor." He noted that patients got better not just because they had insights, but because, along with these insights, they experienced emotional release. For instance, they needed to express their anger, not just know they had it. Reich came to believe that mental repressions are maintained by chronic muscular tensions that inhibit emotional energy. These rigidities reveal the specific "character" and call out for an active therapy rather than the famed analytic neutrality. From here Reich developed his argument against the theory in Freud's later work of a primary masochism and original "death instinct." For Reich, masochism is in no way inborn but the *result* of turning onto the self sadistic impulses that are not primary but caused by suppression of loving, life-affirming impulses. These impulses are the true human biological "core" which patriarchal, sex-denying society has suppressed—the energy that accumulates from the cosmos in the body and is discharged naturally in the uninhibited genital orgasm. Ultimately, then, in a reversal of Freud's views, it is civilization that needs to be cured in order to prevent neurotic unhappiness. In the schizophrenic, the ego itself breaks down because (unlike in "homo normalis," the neurotic who makes up the mass of humanity) the "armor" no longer functions to prevent perception of the free "streaming" of cosmic biological energy in the body. This energy, whether inside the body or responsible for the spiraling of hurricanes or galaxies, is cosmic "orgone" energy.

Thus, Reich came to be less interested in psychological processes than in physical ones, which he believed to be the basis of illnesses like cancer as well as of neurosis, and began to think that because processes such as lightning flashes and orgasms seem analogous, they must in some way be identical. Indeed, the observer's own inner feelings can be a guide to physical research. He called this "functional" thinking. What cosmic and biological processes supposedly share in common is their animation by the orgone energy. Thus orgone is responsible for the blue of the sky, the blue he thought he could see in blood cells at high power, and the blue Reich said he could detect under certain conditions in the dark. He claimed to observe orgone and its effects in experiments using instruments like microscopes, electroscopes, and Geiger counters, and came to believe he could control them through his "orgone energy accumulators" ("orgone boxes"), made of alternating layers of metal and organic material, in which one could sit and be charged with cosmic life-energy. He became notorious for such devices, the use of which led to his federal prosecution and which were treated with some

interest by American literary figures such as Norman Mailer, William Steig, and William S. Burroughs.

In this later phase of his thinking, there is an increasing pessimism about the possibilities of curing "homo normalis," whose unleashed sadism is responsible for all of the horrors of human history, and tampering with the "armor" most likely only causes an outburst of devastating "emotional plague." Reich came to think the only hope for humanity lay in yet unarmored infants. A.S. Neill, founder of the "free school" Summerhill in England, was interested in his ideas and engaged in correspondence with him.

Sometimes those interested in Reich's earlier work try to separate it from his orgone preoccupations of this later phase. But Chasseguet-Smirgel and Grunberger argue that the later work is directly related to the earlier, since Reich's conception of genitality is based on a notion of physical "discharge"; indeed, they stress the resemblance of this discharge—a view of love that leaves out human *relationship*-to excremental functions and conclude that what they see as his later psychosis is related to anal fixations. But perhaps the vision in his later work of a universe animated with life-energy, which can be felt by lovers who experience joyful sexual intercourse with each other, is best understood as a kind of poetry—valid enough as long as one does not try to use an electroscope to assure its "scientific" validity.

Biography

Born March 24, 1897, in Galicia in the Austro-Hungarian empire. Privately educated, entered German high school, 1907. Suicide of mother when he was twelve. Austrian army 1915–1918; medical studies at University of Vienna 1918–1922. In Freud's Psychoanalytic Polyclinic was first clinical assistant, then director of the Seminar for Psychoanalytic Therapy 1924–1930 and vice-director of the Polyclinic 1928–1930. Left Germany in 1933. Research at University of Oslo 1934–1939, then lived in the United States for the remainder of his life. Directed his Orgone Energy Laboratory in Forest Hills, New York, 1939–1941. Founded Orgone Institute, 1942, and set up "Orgonon" in Maine, home of the Wilhelm Reich Foundation, 1949. U.S. Food and Drug Administration complaint in 1954; sentenced to two years imprisonment for criminal contempt, 1956. Died in the federal penitentiary at Lewisburg, Pennsylvania, November 3.

GERALD J. BUTLER

Selected Works

Die Funktion des Orgasmus. 1927; essentially trans. as *Genitality.* 1981.
Der Massenpsychologie der Faschismus. 1933; as *The Mass Psychology of Fascism.* 1969.
Charakteranalyse. 1933. As *Character Analysis.* 1958.
Die Sexualitaet im Kulturkampf. 1936. As *The Sexual Revolution.* 1974.
The Function of the Orgasm. 1942.
Listen, Little Man! 1948.
Ether, God and Devil and *Cosmic Superimposition.* 1951.
Selected Writings: An Introduction to Orgonomy. 1960.
Reich Speaks of Freud. 1972.
The Murder of Christ. 1972.

Further Reading

Boadella, David. *Wilhelm Reich: The Evolution of His Work.* Chicago: Contemporary Books, 1973.
Chasseguet-Smirgel, Janine, and Béla Grunberger. *Freud or Reich? Psychoanalysis and Illusion.* Translated by Claire Pajaczkowska. New Haven, CT and London: Yale University Press, 1986.
Reich, Ilse Ollendorf. *Wilhelm Reich: A Personal Biography.* New York: St. Martin's Press, 1969.
Sharaf, Myron. *Fury on Earth: A Biography of Wilhelm Reich.* New York: St. Martin's Press, 1983.

RELIGIOUS SEXUAL LITERATURE AND ICONOGRAPHY

Although religion is often popularly considered to be an antisexual force, the relations between sexuality and religion are complex and multiple. The production and regulation of desire is a concern of most religions, and religious traditions which severely restrict accepted sexual behaviors may nevertheless generate highly erotic imagery. It is possible that the central concern of the earliest religions was the desire to make sense of the mysterious powers of fertility and sexuality. Ancient religions celebrating female fertility have been posited, and the patriarchal Greek mythology is full of narratives of bizarre sexual encounters and conceptions. Sexual practices may be considered to produce access to the divine in some religious movements, such as the minority Tantric form of Buddhism. Any one religious tradition may fluctuate between considering erotic and religious pleasures as fundamentally similar or fundamentally opposed to each other.

In the West, however, Christianity is the faith which has had the most impact on understandings and discussions of sexuality. The reputation of Christianity for anti-eroticism is, in part, justified. St. Augustine of Hippo (who had prayed, as a youth, "Give me chastity and continence but not yet") identified sexual difference and sexual desire as the product of Adam and Eve's fall and thus as the signs of human imperfection. The ascetic strand of Christianity celebrates virginity as a route to partial restoration of that lost perfection and may include extreme austerities such as Origen's self-castration. But Christianity still allows a regulated marital sexuality, more restrictive but also more egalitarian than most of the various secular codes with which it has coincided and competed, and some contemporary Christians are engaged in the project of resacralizing sexuality.

The dominant Christian attitude to explicit discussions of sexual matters has most often been hostile. St. Augustine was horrified by the lascivious content of pagan worship and theatre; medieval priests were ordered to be circumspect in the investigation of sexual sins for fear of inadvertently informing penitents of the existence of sins they would never otherwise have contemplated. Although many present-day Christians approve a limited celebration of sexuality as part of God's creation, others are vocal opponents of pornography and even of sex education. Material which combines erotic with religious themes is particularly controversial, as demonstrated by the furor over the 1988 film *The Last Temptation of Christ* or the prosecution of *Gay News* in 1977 for blasphemous libel for the publication of James Kirkup's poem "The Love That Dares to Speak its Name," a homoerotic meditation on the crucified Christ. Reproduction of this poem is still illegal in the United Kingdom, though it is easily found on the Internet.

Some Christian practices, however, have enabled the production of erotic speech, literature, and iconography. Michel Foucault's provocative and influential *History of Sexuality* locates the historical roots of sexuality and subjectivity in the Catholic practice of confession, which requires each penitent to construct a narrative of his or her actions. Hagiographic narratives may dwell on the stripping and torture of martyrs with a relish which some modern commentators consider pornographic, or may detail the preconversion activities of penitent prostitutes. Visual representations of saints sometimes emphasize the naked or vulnerable body to potentially erotic effect.

However, it is the mystical tradition which has produced the most characteristically Christian erotic literature. Christian discourse uses metaphors of human relationships to describe those between humans and God: God the Father may be the most familiar of these, but God the Lover has a long-standing presence in Christian thought. Christian celebrations of erotic desire are most likely to be found in the mystic tradition developed from the Song of Songs, also known as the Song of Solomon, or Canticles. Although both Jewish and Christian authorities permitted canonicity to this book only by interpreting its intensely erotic language as metaphorically signifying the contract between God and Israel or God and the Church, it was also used by both male and female mystics to speak of their desire for God. Reinterpreted as a narrative of the soul's longing for God, the Song is in a sense re-literalized and offers a language for speaking of desire, dangerous to unsophisticated readers who might be tempted to read its surface level, but an invaluable sourcebook for the spiritual elite. Its example authorizes Christian mystics, especially in the Catholic tradition, to use erotic language as the most appropriate expression of their apprehension of the divine.

The sixteenth-century Spanish mystic St. John of the Cross adapted the Song into passionate verse: his friend, St. Teresa of Avila, considered herself married to God and famously wrote of an ecstatic experience in which she envisioned an angel piercing her heart with a golden spear. Almost a century later Gianlorenzo Bernini in stone and Richard Crashaw in verse responded independently to the power of her vision with equally sensuous works of their own. Bernini's sculpture of Teresa's ecstasy is so intensely erotic that the psychoanalytic theorist Jacques Lacan cites it as the very image of sexual pleasure: "You only have to go and look at Bernini's statue of her in Rome to understand immediately that she's coming."

Christ is the most common but by no means the only object of mystics' desire: the Virgin Mary may also be addressed in love-lyrics almost indistinguishable from those addressed to women. Scholars of the tradition are divided as to whether such expressions should be understood as reports of sexual fantasies or as metaphorical treatments of mystical ineffability, but it may be that it is impossible, or unnecessary, to distinguish these experiences. In the visions of both male and female mystics, Christ sometimes appears as a feminized figure, suckling his worshippers with his blood, his wound vulval and penetrable. Women who spoke from the position of a bride of Christ might also construct him as a perfectly masculine lover. Such language was also available to male mystics, such as the twelfth-century monk Rupert of Deutz, reporting on his encounter with the figure of Christ on a crucifix:

> I took hold of him whom my soul loves, I held him, I embraced him, I kissed him lingeringly. I sensed how gratefully he accepted this gesture of love when, between kissing, he himself opened his mouth, in order that I kiss more deeply.

Although almost all Christian traditions condemn homosexual acts, God's unique status as object of desire, both the ultimate Same and the ultimate Other, disrupts heterosexual stability. The tradition of erotic mysticism can enable the articulation of desires otherwise rejected by mainstream Christian sexual ethics. Kirkup's poem, though its explicitness gave genuine offense to many Christians, is not without precedent in religious literature.

SARAH SALIH

Further Reading

Astell, Ann W. *The Song of Songs in the Middle Ages.* Ithaca, NY: Cornell University Press, 1990.

Brown, Peter. *The Body and Society: Men, Women and Sexual Renunciation in Early Christianity.* New York: Columbia University Press, 1988.

Bynum, Caroline Walker. *Jesus as Mother: Studies in the Spirituality of the High Middle Ages.* Berkeley and Los Angeles, CA: University of California Press, 1982.

Foucault, Michel. *The History of Sexuality: An Introduction.* Translated by Robert Hurley. Harmondsworth: Penguin, 1978.

Gaunt, Simon. *Gender and Genre in Medieval French Literature.* Cambridge: Cambridge University Press, 1995.

Hollywood, Amy. *Sensible Ecstasy: Mysticism, Sexual Difference, and the Demands of History.* Chicago, IL: University of Chicago Press, 2002.

Kripal, Jeffrey J. *Roads of Excess, Palaces of Wisdom: Eroticism and Reflexivity in the Study of Mysticism.* Chicago, IL: University of Chicago Press, 2001.

Lochrie, Karma, Peggy McCracken, and James A. Schultz, eds. *Constructing Medieval Sexuality.* Minneapolis, MN: University of Minnesota Press, 1997.

Matter, E. Ann. *The Voice of My Beloved: The Song of Songs in Western Medieval Christianity.* Philadelphia: University of Pennsylvania Press, 1990.

Mills, Robert. "Ecce Homo." In *Gender and Holiness: Men, Women and Saints in Late Medieval Europe,* edited by Samantha J.E. Riches and Sarah Salih. London: Routledge, 2002.

Moore, Stephen D. *God's Beauty Parlor: And Other Queer Spaces in and around the Bible.* Stanford, CA: Stanford University Press, 2001.

Murray, Jacqueline, and Konrad Eisenbichler. *Desire and Discipline: Sex and Sexuality in the Premodern West.* Toronto: University of Toronto Press, 1996.

Nelson, James P., and Sandra P. Longfellow. *Sexuality and the Sacred: Sources for Theological Reflection.* London: Mowbray, 1994.

Parrinder, Geoffrey. *Sex in the World's Religions.* London: Sheldon Press, 1980.

Payer, Pierre J. *The Bridling of Desire: Views of Sex in the Later Middle Ages.* Toronto: University of Toronto Press, 1993.

Petersson, Robert T. *The Art of Ecstasy: Teresa, Bernini and Crashaw.* London: Routledge and Kegan Paul, 1970.

Rambuss, Richard. *Closet Devotions.* Durham, NC: Duke University Press, 1998.

Steinberg, Leo. *The Sexuality of Christ in Renaissance Art and in Modern Oblivion.* 2nd ed., revised and expanded. Chicago, IL: University of Chicago Press, 1995.

Turner, Denys. *Eros and Allegory: Medieval Exegesis of the Song of Songs.* Kalamazoo, MI: Cistercian Publications, 1995.

RENAULT, MARY

1905–1983
British novelist

The Charioteer

Self-identified as a bisexual, Renault is best known for her novels about ancient Greece. Their focus on male friendships and ideals of masculinity frequently led readers to assume that she was male. She published her first novel, *Purposes of Love,* in 1939, commencing a number of works focused on nursing (in which she had been trained) and hospital settings. *The Charioteer* (1953) is the last of these and also represents her shift in interest to male relationships.

The novel portrays the essential human drive for the erotic within the context of a bildungsroman which traces the growth of Laurie (Laurence) Odell from naive youth to erotic adulthood. Written within the oppressive context of the 1950s, the novel's eroticism is that of the gesture, the smile, the suggestion, and the implication, much like the later writing of Henry James. *The Charioteer* explores the challenges of integrating the erotic aspects of human nature into an integrated homosexual man. The novel is richly and intensely erotic: every interchange between characters has erotic undertones, as Renault brings to life the experiences of a group of men and women in Britain under the pressure of World War II. The novel's achievement lies in its ability to depict a world in which even innocence has erotic ramifications and in which the ideal of human love emerges in uniting the physical with the spiritual.

Renault develops this unified doubleness through deft use of the myth of the charioteer from Plato's *Phaedrus*. In *Phaedrus* Socrates describes the human soul as a charioteer driving two contrary horses: one noble, self-restraining, and aware of shame, and the other unruly, willful, and desiring. Renault uses the myth on multiple levels in which different characters at once personify the drives of the different horses and wrestle with their own individual ill-matched team. All the major characters are caught in the challenge of managing and reconciling their idealisms and their desires—from Reg, a soldier desperately in love with his unfaithful wife, to Andrew, a tough but naive conscientious objector whose love for Laurie remains on the plane of the ideal.

Synthesis—or mastery of the two horses—is achieved by Laurie, a young man severely wounded at Dunkirk and now enduring a slow recuperation in a military hospital. Aware of his homosexuality, he finds himself lonely and alone because of the tension between his idealized view of human relationships and his own sexual desire, which seems to threaten those ideals. Laurie's personality has been shaped by a pair of crises marked by overtly sexual overtones. The novel opens with Laurie, age five, alone in bed, aware but unclear about the rift in his parents' marriage—specifically his father's infidelities—that leaves him knowing "the burden, prison, and mystery of his own uniqueness" (13). The second, parallel event occurs during Laurie's public school days when the head of the school, Ralph Lanyon, whom Laurie idealizes, is expelled for homosexual behavior with another student. Renault describes Laurie's adolescent idealization of Lanyon as "a kind of exalted dream, part loyalty, part hero-worship, all romance. Half remembered images moved in it, the tents of Troy, the columns of Athens, David waiting in an olive grove for the sound of Jonathan's bow" (31). Laurie's idealism here is doused by the fact that his hero had in fact committed the acts. In parting, Lanyon gives Laurie a copy of *Phaedrus*.

The bulk of the novel explores the adult Laurie's coming to terms with himself. In the hospital, Laurie falls in love with a young Quaker conscientious objector, Andrew Raynes.

Andrew's openness to friendship and affection disarms Laurie by its innocence. Both men are aware of an abiding love for the other, but Andrew's apparent ignorance of his own sexuality keeps this relationship within the Jamesian realm of the wished for rather than the realized. Typical of idealized lovers, they seek out the quiet and comfort of companionship with the beloved without actually moving into the realm of physical touch. Their single kiss is awkward and abortive because a nurse happens to enter the room.

This idealized romance becomes challenged by the reappearance of Ralph Lanyon, now a sailor also wounded during the Dunkirk retreat. Against his own inclinations, Laurie agrees to attend a homosexual party because Lanyon is also expected to attend. Here the men are "specialists," focused only on the physical aspects of their desires. Such behavior appalls Laurie, and Lanyon is critical of it, but has in fact participated widely in that version of his sexuality. However, from the beginning of their reunion, Laurie and Ralph have an intellectual and physical sympathy which much later finds consummation. From that point, Laurie is caught between his Platonic romance with Andrew and the physically rewarding if less ideal involvement with Lanyon.

Eroticism in the novel operates on a number of levels. Men in Laurie's ward make the expected jokes about women; and the erotic life of Laurie's Dunkirk friend, Reg, provides the most overt sexual plot, as the infidelities of his wife, Madge, underscore the challenges of maintaining a faithful relationship, which is precisely what Reg has such a passionate need for. Laurie himself flirts with a heterosexual alliance with the gentle nurse Adrian, which culminates in a kiss and Laurie's confession of another attachment. The blush of Laurie's mother when he suggests she need not remarry provides the most striking image of how heterosexual eroticism is gently but firmly a public fact.

By contrast, homosexual eroticism manifests itself through multiple modes of suggestion, implication, and innuendo. Laurie's idealism had already received a shock from his contact with the homosexual underworld in Oxford before the war. Here, and in the party Laurie attends, the atmosphere of camp banter and presumed promiscuity repels Laurie. The characters in this underworld define themselves exclusively by their homosexuality, and the presumption of ready sexual liaisons among the members of this shadow community underscores a simple physical eroticism devoid of the spiritual affinity that Laurie feels with Andrew.

Laurie's romance with Andrew is very much a spiritual eroticism threatened by the possibilities of physical consummation. By contrast, Ralph Lanyon has lived a life of promiscuity with both men and women even while yearning for the ideals of male friendship, human wholeness, and membership in a broader fellowship. Laurie's challenge is to find this integrity, to cherish the ideal as superhuman, while maintaining its values within the context of a real, physical relationship.

The achievement of the ending is Laurie's integration of his idealistic and desiring selves into a complete eroticism that is both sexual and spiritual and that recognizes the pull of both of the horses in the drive of human nature, allowing Laurie to love both another and himself and to integrate his sexuality into his humanity in a way that most of the other characters of the novel have been unable to accomplish. At the end, Laurie returns to Lanyon, ostensibly to a committed relationship between two strong men. Renault concludes with an image drawn from her governing myth: the horses "are far, both of them, from home, and lonely, and lengthened by their strife the way has been hard. Now their heads droop side by side till their long manes mingle; and when the voice of the charioteer falls silent they are reconciled for a night of sleep" (347).

Biography

Mary Renault is the pen name of Eileen Mary Challans, who was born in London, England, on September 4 and was trained as a nurse in the 1930s. In 1948, with her companion, Julie Mullard, she moved to South Africa (note that in *Phaedrus,* upon which *The Charioteer* is based, Plato designates the two horses as "white," the noble one, and "black," the unruly one). She died of bronchial pneumonia in Cape Town on December 13.

KEITH E. WELSH

Editions

The Charioteer. London: Longmans Green, 1953; New York: Pantheon, 1959; as *El auriga,* Mexico City: Grijalbo, 1986. There is no standard edition for *The Charioteer*; this essay refers to the edition published by Harcourt Brace under their Harvest imprint in 1993.

Selected Works

Purposes of Love. 1939.
Kind Are Her Answers. 1940.
The Friendly Young Ladies. 1944.
Return to Night. 1947.
North Face. 1948.
The Last of the Wine. 1956.
The King Must Die. 1958.
The Bull from the Sea. 1962.
The Mask of Apollo. 1966.
Fire from Heaven. 1969.
The Persian Boy. 1972.
The Praise Singer. 1978.

Further Reading

Burns, Landon C. "'Men Are Only Men': The Novels of Mary Renault." *Critique* 6 (1963): 101–21.
Dick, Bernard F. *The Hellenism of Mary Renault*. Carbondale, IL: Southern Illinois University Press, 1972.
Hoberman, Ruth. "Masquing the Phallus: Genital Ambiguity in Mary Renault's Historical Novels." *Twentieth Century Literature* 42 (1996): 277–93.
Summers, Claude J. *Gay Fictions: Wilde to Stonewall*. New York: Continuum, 1992.
Sweetman, David. *Mary Renault: A Biography*. New York: Harcourt Brace, 1993.
Wolfe, Peter. *Mary Renault*. Boston: Twayne, 1969.
Zillboorg, Caroline. *The Masks of Mary Renault: A Literary Biography*. Columbia, MO: University of Missouri Press, 2001.

RESTIF DE LA BRETONNE, NICOLAS

1734–1806
French novelist, autobiographer, and philosopher

The word *érotisme* did not enter the French language until around 1850. But if 18th-century France did not have the word, it had the thing. Of some 3,500 novels published between 1700 and the French Revolution of 1789, around 200 are classifiable as libertine, and a large quantity of licentious verse also circulated on a permanent basis. While the official culture of church and state frowned at the prevalent level of sexual frankness and pursued authors who overstepped the mark (*Les Bijoux indiscrets* [1748] helped earn Diderot a jail sentence), public attitudes varied considerably. Moralists, critics, censors, and the police drew fine distinctions. Anything classed as "gallant" or "frivolous," though deplorable, could at least be relied upon to be well spoken and was considered socially and aesthetically permissible. Books and pictures described as "lewd," "obscene," and "scabrous" were morally reprehensible, of course, but the label "lascivious" or "lubricious" indicated a far more wicked will to exploit the lusts of the flesh. At the bottom of the heap, unmediated paillardise, or bawdyness—which denoted a vulgar pandering to the beast in man—was beyond the pale. But most libertine fiction had higher ambitions than the mere titillation which is the purpose of pornography, and a measure of licentiousness was tolerated in literature as in public life. For the most part, it operated within the limits of a certain cultural complicity which was part of the mood of contestation that grew as the French Revolution approached. Particularly after 1740, many philosophical (and therefore obliquely political) skirmishes were fought in the erogenous zone.

Restif de la Bretonne was not a libertine in this intellectually combative sense. While he had decided views about how society should be changed for the better, he was more concerned with his own sexuality and how it might be exploited to defeat the real world, which was resistant to his writings, and project him into a region of the imagination which had little to do with reason and promised a haven which legitimized his sexuality and freed him of transgression and guilt. His place in the history of 18th-century eroticism lies somewhere between Casanova's conception of sexual freedom as a means of expressing the total self and Laclos's (and even more so de Sade's) equation of sex with power. Excluded by his social origins and outsiderly life from the traditions of courtly libertinage, he made sexuality an essential ingredient of an inner fantasy which became more lurid, insistent, and hermetic as he grew older. Thus although Restif has a clear place in the history of erotic writing, he may also be considered a case that could have been written about by Krafft-Ebing.

His literary education was undirected and, after he was apprenticed to the printing trade in 1751, largely determined by the books he printed and read in proof. It was thus that at Auxerre he read *Mysis et Glaucé* (1748), Séran de la Tour's mildly erotic neo-Grecian poem. When Restif arrived in Paris, his friends Boudard and Renaud provided him with clandestine scabrous books from the illegal printing shops where they worked. Certainly, Restif's haphazard apprenticeship as a writer gave him more than a nodding acquaintance with erotica, to which he attributed a large capacity to pervert young minds and harm society. Impressionable heroines in his first novels, such as Lucile (1769), are exposed to plays and fiction which glamorize vice but are brought back to the path of virtue by a course of reading which includes Rousseau's *La nouvelle Héloïse* (1762) and the wholesome novels of Marie-Jeanne Riccoboni (1713–92). The corruption of innocence is one of the major themes of the dozen books which preceded *Le paysan perverti* (1775), where Edmond's "perversion" is the loss of his country virtue by exposure to the values of the city. It was a fashionable subject, but Restif approached it from a number of original directions.

First, *Le pornographe* (1769) tackled sexuality as a social problem. The title is a personal noun referring to a "writer on prostitution" (the modern sense of *pornographie* also dates from the mid-19th century), and the book is a "project" which offers a plan for reform of the vice trade and displays no more salacity and no less public spirit than are to be found in the writings of opponents of the so-called white-slave traffic a century later. It is worth noting, to Restif's credit, that while the most famous philosophes tackled the great issues posed by the clash between religious and secular thinking, it was left to minor writers like Restif to identify prostitution as a serious social and medical problem. Poverty, lack of education, the decline of marriage and the family, the bad example set by the rich, and the culpable connivance of the police all figure on his surprisingly modern list of causal factors. He took the view that prostitution is ineradicable, since the demand for it is eternal and the supply endless. It is a necessary evil, and society has a duty to limit the damage done by what it cannot prevent. Whores play a useful role—they are a safety valve for male urges and a protection for decent women—and they deserve better treatment. Restif claimed to have carried out a personal investigation of their attitudes and conditions, though elsewhere his knowledge of the brothels of Paris derived, he said (sometimes self-reproachfully, sometimes with pride), from a more basic imperative. It is clear, however, that his sympathy for the plight of the prostitute is as striking as it was rare in his time. His project was designed to encourage the state to control and regulate the flesh market. He recommends the building of state-run, efficiently policed bawdy houses in quiet suburbs. All social classes would be catered to and medical services would be provided to restrict the spread of venereal disease. Useful employment would be found for superannuated inmates and for the children born in the new, hygienic, socially useful, and classically named "Parthénions." Though quaint in parts and overearnest (Restif's utopianism is never far from the surface), *Le pornographe* is a well-informed and thoughtful inventory of the regulationist case, which has continued to be fiercely advocated and passionately opposed.

Second (and this was the stance which would prevail), Restif approached the corruption of innocence from the personal stance of autobiography. His early novels recall incidents and people from his past. Thinly disguised heroines, some of whom he later identified as girls he had known, and naive, idealistic young men who resemble his younger self, encounter temptation. They may succumb temporarily, but they are guided to safety often by a wiser, older man who is an echo of his father or of respected churchmen he had known as a boy. Until 1775, his novels were far more moral than titillating. But with *Le paysan perverti*, the tone darkens. Edmond, urged on by the cynical Gaudet d'Arras to be "bold" with life and women, rapes Madame Parangon, ushers his sister into prostitution, and is cursed like Cain. Edmond is clearly a transposition of Restif, who identified closely with the character's guilt and failure. In the early 1780s, the heroes of a series of "posthumous" novels which drew heavily on Restif's experience and psyche, labor unavailingly under the weight of a father's curse. Their crimes are never made explicit, but they have been judged by an unforgiving Jansenist God in whom Restif had long since ceased to believe.

This mood had blown itself out by the mid-1780s. But by then Restif had become addicted to using fiction as a way of acting out in his imagination desires which he could not achieve in life. He wrote several versions (notably *Le quadragénaire* [*The Middle-Aged Man*], 1777, and *La dernière avanture d'un homme de 45 ans* [*The Last Adventure of a 45-Year-Old Man*], 1783) of a scenario in which he is deceived by a girl young enough to be his daughter. These novels, though not explicit in any way, carry a strong erotic charge, the reason for which was his attraction to his elder daughter, Agnès. He opposed her marriage in 1781, complaining that Augé was not a suitable husband. When he was proved right and Agnès fled from her brutal, sadistic spouse, Restif wrote his version of her experience in *Ingénue Saxancour* (1786), an early example of a "faction." It contains scenes and reports of sadistic behavior and is one of the rarest of his books, his family later having destroyed all the copies they could find.

Despite these ominous signs, Restif's sexual personality was still capable of objectivity, and in 1783 he began serious work on his autobiography, *Monsieur Nicolas*, which was published in 1796. In it, he traced the development of his "combustible temperament," giving a large place to the precocious fumblings of his early years and not disguising, but often exaggerating, his success with women. A small number, however, were the focus of an idealizing tendency. Jeannette Rousseau, a notary's daughter to whom he was too shy to speak, remained a lifelong icon. Along with Madame Parangon (the wife of his master at Auxerre) and Filette, whom he watched from a distance in the 1790s, she represented an ideal of womanhood which he had failed to find in his wife and which he had expressed rationally in another grandiose project, *Les gynographes* (1777), designed to show how women should be educated and prepared for their role as wives and mothers. He continued to instruct them in their duties of subservience, and *Les contemporaines* (1780–5, 42 vols.), by far his longest collection of tales, showed "a thousand and one" routes to married happiness. But generalities did not electrify his imagination, which required, he said, a basis in fact and a muse to inspire him.

This often meant weaving stories around girls he had known or merely glimpsed. The result was not always a remembered encounter but the imagined tale of what he would like to have happened, with himself as irresistible hero. His heroines acquired graphic reality in the 300 illustrations for *Les contemporaines* which he commissioned mainly from the engraver Louis Binet (1744–c. 1800), with whom he worked closely. He claimed that the women he pictured were distinctive by their bearing, dress, and social class. In fact, they are all versions of a single type which is obsessively re-created: a doll-like head (large eyes, rosebud mouth, oval face) is set above an impossibly narrow thorax; miniaturized shoes peep out under long skirts; legs twice as long as the upper torso eventually turn into exaggeratedly swelling haunches. A small minority are nudes and a few are shown as the victims of sadistic men. Restif took great pains and incurred considerable expense to externalize his inner vision of women who all wear the straitjacket of his obsession.

Most of the stories he published in the 1780s were based on muses he had known, some of whom reappear in a variety of situations. Occasionally he borrowed the experience of third parties. Alexandre Tilly (1764–1816) recalled being approached by Restif, who asked him to provide "erotic episodes" from his life which he could use. Tilly refused and wrote them up himself in his own *Memoirs* (written 1804–5, published 1828) in the sardonic, libertine style

which was a world removed from Restif's compulsive voyeurism. Undeterred, Restif continued to press his lurid imagination into a variety of rational causes. Thus he gave a philosophical twist to his obsession with female dress. He argued that feminine modesty is more stimulating than nudity and insisted that any attempt to dull down female fashions (he instanced the Revolutionary taste for unexciting low heels) undermined the attractiveness of women. The birth rate would fall and the incidence of homosexuality rise. For Restif, the homosexual was an antisocial egotist whose infertility denied man's procreative function and therefore harmed the growth of the population on which the wealth of nations depended. Most unexpected of all these arguments was his account of the creation of the universe.

In the beginning, he argued, all matter was gathered into a small, spinning, fiery sun in empty space. As it whirled, pieces were projected by centripetal force to form secondary suns, which in turn ejected further suns until their energy was exhausted. When they were no longer capable of generating new suns, they still scattered matter, which formed into planets where in time living forms appeared. By analogy with terrestrial creation, Restif argued that the life-giving force was male, that "corporeity" was female, and that male suns impregnated female planets and the "eggs" of plants and breathing creatures by their rays. In time, the cooling of matter reduced the system's procreativity and induced aging and eventually death. Dead planets lost momentum and spiraled back into their local suns, hastening the latter's extinction by choking them with accruing burnt-out matter. Steadily, beginning with the farthest flung, each sun died and returned to its parent until finally all matter congregated in one small mass. Then, like the Phoenix rising, the mass burst into new life, and the cycle, which he called a "revolution," was begun again.

But if the cosmos was a stately sexual ballet, Paris offered Restif, its observer in *Les nuits de Paris* (1788–94, 16 parts), opportunities for chronicling more immediate immoralities— sometimes with graphic vividness, at other times with shameless voyeurism, of which his lurid and purely fictitious account of the activities of the Marquis de Sade may stand as an example. *Le Palais Royal* (1790) was a further, anecdotal incursion into the milieu of prostitution. By then, the ancien regime had fallen, and while Restif joined the pamphlet war with a short series of scurrilous pamphlets directed at the abbé Maury (May 1790), he had no hand in the obscene *Dom Bougre aux États Généraux* (1789), which is still often attributed to him.

But also by then, Restif was losing interest in the real world and retreating into himself and his desires as the source of inspiration. He continued to add to *Monsieur Nicolas* and wrote *Le drame de la vie* (1793), a series of interconnected plays through which he relived old adventures and old loves. But recycling the past ceased to satisfy him, and he grew interested in rewriting his life as it might have been. He likened himself to an artist assigned to sketch an unfinished building and arranged his adventures as he wished they had turned out. In *L'Année des dames nationales* (1791–4, 12 vols.), he made a modest use of his new freedom. Anodyne for the most part, his stories linger over the sexual possibilities of colonial settlers who, far from the world of law, create ideal conditions for sexual domination. A similar power is granted to Multipliandre, magical hero of *Les Posthumes,* which Restif began in 1787, rewrote in 1796, and published in 1802. Multipliandre is a projection of Restif triumphant. He quells all opposition and reorganizes France, the world, and finally the whole universe according to social principles outlined by Restif in the series of reformist, utopian projects he had published between 1769 and 1789. But Restif also exploits Multipliandre's ability to inhabit other bodies to achieve the sexual success denied to him in life.

After 1795, when he was treated for a urinary dysfunction, Restif hints that he was impotent. This may be so, but in any case his libido was unaffected. To *Les Posthumes* he added a handful of "re-vies," or revisionistic essays that revisited familiar characters and situations which he retold according to some new hypothesis. He had shown that the cosmos was a series of so-called revolutions; now he argued that each revolution followed exactly the same pattern and that our lives have been relived many times. This knowledge gave Restif the advantage, because now, on paper, he could correct his mistakes and generate a past not as it *might* have been but as it *should* have been. Hence, with *L'Enclos et les oiseaux* [*The Enclosure and the Quails*] (1796), he returned to a scenario dating back to

a poem which he claimed to have begun in 1749. In it he had imagined transporting twelve girls to a sequestered enclosure of which he was master. In his re-vie, he transforms the situation into a gigantic fantasy engineered by a final autobiographical hero who is omnipotent and made immortal by means of a potion called "spermaton." He fathers immense numbers of daughters, and over many generations, the enclosure spreads until it fills the world with a genetically pure race of Restif clones. *L'Enclos et les oiseaux* was never published, and the manuscript was dispersed. But enough remains to indicate the visionary power of Restif's erotomania.

It does not, however, reach the level of frank obscenity displayed by *L'Anti-Justine* (1798), of which only one volume (of four) was published. It was ostensibly written as an antidote to de Sade, who, he said, made sex a justification for cruelty, pain, rape, and murder and threatened the fabric of society. In the event, Restif's counterblast was another autobiographical exercise which sets no limit on the sexual energies of Cupidonnet/Nicolas. Beneath the squirmings and the ecstasies, Restif is to be observed doing to his enemies—that is, almost everyone he had ever known—what he could not do in life. It is a perverse exercise, an escape, a chronicle of impotence. The rarest of all Restif's books, it is also a compendium of its author's sexual fixations. It is now accepted that he committed incest with Agnès and that his claims to have fathered some 230 daughters (against one son) is part of a wider erotic fantasy. Many stories ring the changes on his carnal feelings for so-called muses who looked like or might have been his daughters. No less insistent was his obsession with women's feet (always daintily visible in his closely supervised illustrations) and with women's shoes, which, as his private journals reveal, he used for onanistic rites. Restif is one of literature's most clearly documented literary cases of foot fetishism.

As a casebook example of an erotomaniac, Restif displays multiple symptoms—incest, daughter fixation, foot fetishism, voyeurism, mild perversion—which intensified as he grew older. In literary terms, however, he was saved from their destructive potential by a creative literary imagination. His reputation may stand on his perverse amours—but there are many other Restifs: the imaginative novelist, the social reformer, the below-stairs observer of Paris life, the explorer of time who has no equal before Proust, the philosophical and political idealist, the anti-intellectual who freed the imagination from the bonds of Enlightenment reason, and not least the autobiographer, who laid his heart bare and still offers us, two centuries on, true reflections of ourselves.

Biography

Born Nicolas-Edmé Restif (or Rétif) de la Bretonne at Sacy (Burgundy), October 23. Took his name from the farm of La Bretonne into which the family moved in 1742. Attended village schools and, for one year (1746–47), the Jansenist college at Bicêtre before being apprenticed to François Fournier, printer at Auxerre (1751–55). Worked as a journeyman typesetter, then as a foreman printer until 1766, when, believing he could write as well as the authors he printed, he became a full-time writer. Between 1767 and 1802, he published some 50 titles in 300 volumes: reforming tracts, novels, over 1,000 short stories, unperformed plays, accounts of Paris seen "from below," and the autobiography for which he is best remembered, *Monsieur Nicolas*. He became famous in 1775 for *Le paysan perverti* but remained, by choice, outside the literary establishment. Married Agnès Lebègue in 1760 (divorced, 1792); two daughters. Died in Paris, February 3.

DAVID COWARD

Selected Works

L'Anti-Justine. Paris: Veuve Girouard, 1798; republished as vol. 11 of the facsimile reprint of Restif's *Oeuvres complètes*, 207 vols., Geneva: Slatkine, 1988.

L'Oeuvre de Restif de la Bretonne. Edited by B. de Villeneuve. Paris: Bibliothèque des Curieux, 1911.
Oeuvres érotiques. Edited by Daniel Baruch et al. Paris: Fayard, 1985.
Monsieur Nicolas. 2 vols. Edited by Pierre Testud. Paris: Gallimard, 1989.
Le Paysan perverti. 2 vols. Edited by François Jost. Paris: L'Âge d'homme, 1977.
Le Pornographe. Preface by Béatrice Didier. Paris: Régine Deforges, 1977.
Ingénue Saxancour. Edited by Daniel Baruch. Paris: Dix dix-huit, 1978.
Les Posthumes. 4 vols. Paris: Duchêne, 1802.

Further Reading

Charpentier, Dr. P.-L.-J. *Restif de la Bretonne. Sa perversion fétichiste*. Medical doctoral thesis, Bordeaux, 1912.
Courbin-Desmoulins, J.-C. "Les Femmes féiques de Binet." *L'Oeil* 81 (September 1961): 22–31.
Coward, David. *The Philosophy of Restif de la Bretonne*. Oxford: The Voltaire Foundation, 1991.
———. "The Sublimations of a Fetishist." In *'Tis Nature's Fault: Unauthorized Sexuality During the Enlightenment*, edited by Robert Purks Maccubbin, 98–108. Cambridge: Cambridge University Press, 1987.
Études rétiviennes. 34 vols. to date. Paris: La Société Rétif de la Bretonne, 1981–.
Heine, Maurice. "L Vieillesse de Rétif de la Bretonne." *Hippocrate* 7 (September 1934): 605–33.
Louys, Pierre. "Un Roman inédit de Restif [*L'Enclos et les oiseaux*]." *Revue des livres anciens* 1 (1913): 87–94.
Rival, Ned. *Rétif de la Bretonne ou les Amours pervertis*. Paris: Librairie académique Perrin, 1982.
Rives Childs, John. *Restif de la Bretonne. Témoignages et Jugements*. Bibliography. Paris: Librairie Briffaut, 1949.
Testud, Pierre. *Rétif de la Bretonne et la création littéraire*. Geneva: Droz, 1977.
Wagstaff, Peter. *Memory and Desire: Rétif de la Bretonne, Autobiography and Utopia*. Amsterdam and Atlanta, GA: Rodopi, 1996.

REVERONI SAINT-CYR, JACQUES ANTONIE

1767–1829
French novelist and librettist

Pauliska ou la perversité moderne

Reveroni Saint-Cyr is currently remembered for only one work, a Gothic novel (though more in the French style than the British tradition) entitled *Pauliska ou la perversité moderne; mémoires récens d'une Polonaise* [*Pauliska, or Modern Perversity: Recent Memoirs of a Polish Woman*] (1798). The novel is imbued with a royalist political agenda far removed from the concerns of any British Gothic novelist of the period. In essence, *Pauliska* recounts the vicissitudes suffered by the eponymous heroine, a beautiful young countess, during her attempted flight from Poland shortly after a Russian invasion. Given the date of the book's publication (1798), commentators have not failed to see parallels between the misadventures of Pauliska and Marie-Antoinette's abortive flight to Varennes in June 1791.

Pauliska is aided and assisted throughout by a young army captain, Ernest Pradislas, who is devoted to her cause. This allows the author, of course, to exploit the sentimental benefits of separating Pauliska from her companion, and, indeed, throughout much of the novel, we follow their separate adventures. At one moment, for example, Pauliska falls into the hands of the sinister Baron d'Olnitz, who has been conducting experiments with love serums. Pradislas, on the other hand, is captures by a gang of female *philosophes* belonging to a clandestine organization whose membership extends from Madrid to Saint Petersburg. During the period of his captivity, Pradislas is subjected to a bizarre sexual experiment. In short, he and a young woman are stripped and placed into a cage in order for the observers to witness whether he becomes sexually aroused. The point of this experiment is to determine whether men's reactions are motivated by the emotion of love or are merely the automatic response to external promptings. In the event, however, the author neatly sidesteps these issues by making Pradislas fall in love with the female member of the sect chosen to participate in the experiment, and the couple manage to contrive an escape.

Interestingly, at the very moment that *Pauliska* was first published in the late 1790s, there was a considerable vogue in Paris for translated English Gothic novels. Indeed, so great was this vogue that a number of French writers produced imitation Gothic novels, sometimes disguised as translations. However, it should not be taken for granted that the French term *roman noir* and the English term "Gothic novel" are entirely identical. English Gothic novels tend to be set not only in the distant past but also in an essentially Catholic and feudal society. French imitation Gothic novels, on the hand, are often focused on more recent French history and may be generally seen as providing a conservative response to the French Revolution. One of the most popular of such works, not only in France but also in countries such as Spain and Italy, was J.-F. Regnault-Warin's *Le cimetière de la Madeleine* (1800), which recounts the final days of Louis XVI's reign and execution in 1793 in the form of eleven "visions."

In Reveroni Saint-Cyr's case, the focus is not only on the tribulations of Marie-Antoinette's alter ego but on Enlightenment science generally (parodied through both the Baron d'Olnitz and the society of *Misanthrophiles* who capture Pradislas) and on the system of Masonic lodges which conservative commentators blamed for the spread of revolutionary ideas. Paradoxically, however, in terms of genre, *Pauliska* seems as indebted to the tradition of the libertine *conte philosophique* as to, say, translations of the novels of Mrs. Radcliffe. In this respect, however, the novel is by no means alone. Indeed, the works of the Marquis de Sade clearly reflect the same binary tradition. More specifically, one can point to a French subgenre of more erotically informed novels employing surface genre markers derived from the English Gothic novel, such as *Rosaide et Valmor, ou les victimes de l'orgueil* (1800), a Gothic flagellation novel deliberately misattributed to Horace Walpole, and *Le Parc aux Cerfs* by de Faverolle (pseudonym of Elisabeth Guénard, Baronne de Méré) (1809), which centers on a clandestine brothel claimed to have been operated for the sexual gratification of Louis XV in the late 1750s.

The brief revival of interest in *Pauliska* in France during the 1970s may perhaps be explained by two factors: the continued interest in cultural manifestations of the French Revolution and the ongoing debate about censorship in contemporary society. Regrettably, little subsequent work has been carried out either into the precise nature of the French *roman noir* or its more philosophical counterpart.

Biography

Jacques Antoine Reveroni Saint-Cyr was born in Lyons. His life would seem to have been spent mainly as an officer in the French artillery and engineer corps, from which he retired in 1814 with the rank of lieutenant-colonel. Among his various military projects, he is known to have prepared a plan for the royalist defense of the Tuileries during the early stages of the French Revolution, worked on strengthening a number of fortifications, and narrowly missed out on participating in Napoleon's Egyptian expedition due to ill health. Like many men in a similar position, he probably took to the pen initially as a means of making a living as a consequence of the financial catastrophe which accompanied the French Revolution; a later flurry of activity suggests a similar pecuniary embarrassment about the time of Waterloo. He published two novels in 1798 and six more later on, wrote more than a dozen plays and operas (some unperformed) during the first two decades of the new century, and acted as occasional librettist for musicians as distinguished as Dalayrac and Cherubini (then at the height of his fame). Reveroni Saint-Cyr's present-day obscurity is probably due more to the immediate topicality of his work than any other fact. The *opéra-comique* was not then the despised form it is today, and audiences were particularly appreciative of parodies (an art form that rarely survives the test of time). *Pauliska*, too, might best be considered to some extent a parody (a French imitation Gothic novel) with considerable topical appeal. None of his work has been translated into English. He died in Paris, possibly in a state of temporary insanity.

TERRY HALE

Editions

Pauliska ou la perversité moderne; mémoires récens d'une Polonaise. 2 vols. Paris: Lemierre, Year 6 [1798].
Reveroni Saint-Cyr: Pauliska ou la perversité moderne; mémoires récens d'une Polonaise. Edited by Béatrice Didier. Paris: Desforges, 1976.

Further Reading

Hale, Terry. "Translation in Distress: The Construction of the Gothic." In *European Gothic: A Spirited Exchange, 1760–1960*, edited by Avril Horner, 17–38. Manchester: Manchester University Press, 2000.

RHETORIC

Rhetoric refers to the theory and practice of persuasive speaking; the word is derived from the Greek verb *rhêtoreúô*, meaning to speak, and more particularly, to speak in public. As a theory, rhetoric has sought since antiquity to understand speech as a force that asserts itself in the energy to act upon others and upon oneself, to affect ideas and actions, will and desire. As the practice of discourse, rhetoric develops through an art of speaking and writing that places the business of seduction at the heart of the exercise of speech.

Rhetoric, at once the well-thought-out experience of discourse and the craft of speech, also claims to teach the art of winning hearts and minds by arousing the desires and passions of the listener or reader. Accordingly, beginning in the Renaissance it was called upon to play a major teaching role in educating Europe's upper classes. Until the nineteenth century at least, this education in eloquent speech encouraged artistic and literary practices which, in keeping with the ideas of Cicero, made every work into a project intended not only to instruct [*docere*], but also to please [*delectare*] and to affect the emotions [*movere*].

In modern Europe, the oratorical training of people of letters was based mainly on the teaching of rhetoric dispensed by the Jesuits. The Jesuit fathers proposed to train young people who, fit for polite society, would be able to win over an audience solely through the art of pleasing by word and gesture. In tune with the spirit of court society and inheritor of the splendors of the Baroque sensibility, this rhetorical tradition is particularly attentive to the theatrical vocation of eloquence, that is, to the emotional aspect of words. By cultivating the seductions of oratorical artifice, it turns language into the instrument of a performance where wit seasons discourse and eroticizes it through the multiplication of sense images or subtle allusions.

It is to this oratorical tradition that erotic literature is most indebted. At least this is what one infers from Boyer's French-English dictionary, whose author, in the 1702 edition, suggests that the French term *libertin* be translated as "wit." That the libertine novelist is often a student of rhetoric as well is likewise affirmed in a novel attributed to the comte de Mirabeau and titled *Hic et Hæc, ou l'élève des Révérends Pères Jésuites d'Avignon* [*Hic and Haec, or the Student of the Jesuit Fathers of Avignon*] (1798). Notice, for example, in what terms the hero of the story, a brilliant student of the Jesuits and a talented prose writer, describes the way in which his first mistress fixes her gaze on his sex: "Et ses yeux, écrit-il, se fixaient sur l'insolent dont l'orgueil augmentait à vue d'œil; il y a peu d'avocats aussi éloquents aux yeux d'une femme : je vis le succès du plaidoyer muet, et reprenant sa main, je la pressai contre l'orateur" [And her eyes, he wrote, rested on the insolent member whose pride swelled visibly; there are few lawyers as eloquent in a woman's eyes: I saw the success of the wordless plea, and taking her hand, pressed it against the orator].

From Pietro Aretino to the marquis de Sade by way of Crébillon *fils*, rhetoric imbues erotic literature with this sense of virtuosity and stylistic ingenuity that is founded upon the art of allusion, wordplay, and double entendre. Over and above this taste for oratorical artifice, rhetoric also questions all forms of private exchange, beginning notably in the Renaissance, a time that differed in this regard from the tradition of classical antiquity, which was concerned primarily with public speaking, whether in the Athenian agora or in the Roman forum. Rhetoric henceforth came to include the art of conversation and repartee, of pleasing one's audience, of seducing it even, within that dialogue par excellence: the exchange between men and women. In moving from the ancient forum to the aristocratic boudoir, the art of speech was now employed in the service of love. This is seen in the novels of Crébillon *fils*, for example, who in *Sopha* (1740) has a lover declare to his lady: "Je vous ai prouvé la nécessité où vous êtes d'aimer encore, et je vais . . . vous prouver actuellement que c'est moi qu'il faut que vous aimiez" [I have proved to you that it is necessary for you to love again, and I will . . . prove to you now that it is I whom you must love].

The importance that rhetoric accorded to the various forms of private exchange influenced erotic literature all the more in that the models par excellence of a speech at once eloquent and intimate were, especially in ancien régime France, considered essentially feminine. In the preface of his *Essai de rhétorique française* (1746), Gabriel Henri Gaillard, for example, specifies that the company of women "est absolument nécessaire pour polir l'esprit . . . [car] leur conversation . . . est une espèce de Rhétorique-Pratique" [The company of women is absolutely necessary for polishing wit . . . [for] their conversation . . . is a kind of practical rhetoric]. Erotic literature constantly echoes this "practical rhetoric" that women are given to, as shown by a text like *Trois voluptés* (1746), a short anonymous play in which the hero describes the love letters he receives from his mistress as follows: "Je sentis dans celles qu'elle m'écrivait ce feu, cette légèreté, . . . enfin cette véritable éloquence qui n'existe que dans le style des femmes" [I felt in the ones she wrote me this fire, this grace, . . .

in short, this genuine eloquence one finds only in the writing style of women].

Finally, rhetoric favors the eroticization of discourse to the extent that since Aristotle, it has been conceived of as "a picture thinking," that is, as the power to represent and to form an image to actualize and to place before the eyes. By magnifying the emotional aspect of speech, rhetoric teaches the art of representing the physiological and sensory intensity of lived life in such a way that discourse, transposed into a visual order, can claim to make what it describes visible. From this point of view, erotic literature can arouse a desire for pleasure in the reader only when it becomes an eloquent picture able to make things seen by creating an illusion of the real that triggers an awakening of desire.

ANDRÉ MARC BERNIER

Further Reading

Bernier, Marc André. *Libertinage et figures du savoir. Rhétorique et roman libertin dans la France des Lumières (1734–1751)*. Québec: Presses de l'Université Laval; Paris: L'Harmattan (République des Lettres), 2001.

Conley, Thomas M. *Rhetoric in the European Tradition*. Chicago and London: University of Chicago Press, 1994.

Dainville, François de, S.J. *L'éducation des Jésuites (XVIe–XVIIIe siècle)*. Paris: Éditions de Minuit, 1978.

France, Peter. *Rhetoric and Truth in France: Descartes to Diderot*. Oxford, 1972.

Fumaroli, Marc. *L'Âge de l'éloquence: Rhétorique et " res literaria" de la Renaissance au seuil de l'époque classique*. Paris: A. Michel, 1994.

Goulemot, Jean-Marie. *Forbidden Texts: Erotic Literature and Its Readers in Eighteenth-Century France*. Translated by James Simpson. Cambridge: Polity Press; Philadelphia, PA: University of Pennsylvania Press, 1994.

Hellegouarc'h, Jacqueline. *L'Art de la conversation. Anthologie*. Paris: Dunod (Classiques Garnier), 1997.

Houle, Martha M. "What the Libertine and Jesuit Have in Common, and the Posing of a Literary Problem." *Continuum: Problems in French Literature from the Late Renaissance to the Early Enlightenment: Libertinage and The Art of Writing*. New York: AMS Press, 1992.

Sermain, Jean-Paul. "Le sens de la repartie." In *Les Agréments du langage réduits à leurs principes. Troisième partie*. Paris: Éditions des Cendres (Archives du commentaire), 1992.

———. *Rhétorique et roman au dix-huitième siècle. L'exemple de Prévost et de Marivaux (1728–1742)*. Oxford: The Voltaire Foundation, 1985.

RICE, ANNE

1941–

American novelist

Best-selling author Anne Rice is one of a select few contemporary American novelists who have successfully published works in both mainstream and erotic literary markets. Most famous for her continuing Chronicles of the Vampire series, which began in 1976 with *Interview with the Vampire*, Rice is most noted in erotic circles for the work published under her two pseudonyms, A.N. Roquelaure and Anne Rampling. However, Rice is an author who infuses sexual and erotic content into all of her works, emphasizing the importance that sexual progression maintains in her writing. The erotic content of all of Rice's novels is fluidly pansexual, a world of sexual opportunity based on the sensuality of new experiences. This is especially true in her vampire novels, in which the transformations of the human characters into vampires allows for nearly overwhelming sensory explorations of the world around them:

> It was as if I had only just been able to see colors and shapes for the first time. I was so enthralled with the buttons on Lestat's black coat that I looked at nothing else for a long time. Then Lestat began to laugh, and I heard his laughter as I had never heard anything before. (*Interview with the Vampire*)

Of course, nothing is as sensuous as the act of drinking blood:

I knelt beside the bent, struggling man and, clamping both my hands on his shoulders, I went into his neck. The sucking mesmerized me; the warm struggling of the man was soothing to the tension of my hands; and there came the beating of the drum again, which was the drumbeat of his heart—only this time it beat in perfect rhythm with the drumbeat of my own heart, the two resounding in every fiber of my being, until the beat began to grow slower and slower, so that each was a soft rumble that threatened to go on without end. (*Interview with the Vampire*)

Rice's focus on the sensory experiences of the narrator—sound, sight, texture, taste—rather than on the corporeal nature of the act itself belies her lush, eros-accentuated style, a hallmark of her later erotic novels. The twin themes of dominance and surrender—the narrator vampire's domination over his victim and his surrender to the transformation that controls his body—reflect Rice's fascination with the gentler side of sado-masochism, creating worlds where the cessation of sexual and physical autonomy need not ally themselves hand in hand with the crueler aspects of dominant sexual play.

This loving representation of sexual slavery often creates a divided self within Rice's protagonists, individuals who both worship and fear punishment, who become valuable animals but still wield extraordinary power because, without their obeisance, their masters signify nothing. This concept of the divided self plays a prominent role in all of her erotic novels. As one character notes, "The best slaves sometimes make the best masters" (*Beauty's Punishment*). The three Roquelaure novels, *The Claiming of Sleeping Beauty* (1983), *Beauty's Punishment* (1984), and *Beauty's Release* (1985), present a sexual satire of the Sleeping Beauty mythos in which Prince Charming wakes Beauty only to claim her for the sado-masochistic theme park governed by his mother, an ill-tempered and leering evil Queen. The three books chart the sado-masochistic adventures of Beauty and the Prince, Tristan, as they are auctioned off to different masters, carried off in village raids, and become the sexual wards of a powerful sultan. In the *Beauty* trilogy, slave psychology becomes an allegory of religious experience, and the need for masochists to seek perfection in both their masters and their selves a divine quest:

There is something undeniable in the true slave who worships those of unquestioned power. He or she longs for perfection even in the slave state, and perfection for a naked slave must be yielding to the most extreme punishments. The slave spiritualizes these ordeals. (*Beauty's Punishment*)

Rice's two Rampling novels, *Exit to Eden* (1985) and *Belinda* (1986), while also largely concerned with the divided self, focus more on the psychological and emotional repercussions of sado-masochistic experiences to the individual. Here, dominance and surrender become a methodology toward the re-essentializing of the actual self—a process of psychological recovery that often ends in, for lack of a better term, social normalcy. *Exit to Eden,* for example, is the story of Elliott, a nihilistic photojournalist who goes to the Club to test his personal mettle. Lisa, the Club manager, chooses Elliott as her own personal slave because she desires a challenge, "the kind of man who submits to no one and nothing in the real world" (*Exit to Eden*). There is a philosophical context to their sado-masochism, and the two become conversational sparring partners as well as master and slave. Ultimately, Lisa abandons the Club to join Elliott in the real world of marriage and social normalcy, giving up their sado-masochistic games in favor of domestic tranquility. Thus in the novel, the master and slave relationship not only gives way to husband and wife, but actually allows for it, securing both Lisa and Elliott into roles they believed, at the novel's commencement, they would never be capable of fulfilling.

Belinda is Rice's version of Nabokov's *Lolita.* In the book, forty-four-year-old children's book artist Jeremy Walker is seduced by sixteen-year-old nymphette Belinda. Quickly abandoned by his adolescent lover, Jeremy obsesses over the conflicting shame and titillation he associates with her. He begins to paint likeness after likeness of her on canvas, as if attempting to both understand and capture the essence of what she signifies to him. Eventually he locates her, and the two begin a wary game of cat-and-mouse, both with each other and with their own inner turmoil. Ultimately, like *Exit to Eden*, this book ends with a happy marriage, conventionality winning out over the perceived indiscretions of the divided self.

Rice's mainstream appeal and lush style have done much for contemporary erotic fiction. Though she no longer writes erotica, her work is continually infused with the themes prevalent in her erotic work. Rice continues to explore and refashion—for better or for worse—the paradigms of surrender and domination and the divided self, thus maintaining a continuing erotic presence on today's best-seller lists.

Biography

Born Howard Allen O'Brien in New Orleans, October 4; changes name to Anne at the age of five. Graduated from Richardson High School, Richardson, Texas, 1959; enters Texas Women's University but leaves for San Francisco after one year. Graduated from San Francisco State University (SFSU) with a BA in political science in 1964; completes MA at SFSU in creative writing in 1972. Married poet Stan Rice 1961; two children, Michele (1966–1972) and Christopher (1978–).

MICHAEL G. CORNELIUS

Selected Works

Cry to Heaven. New York: Alfred A. Knopf, 1982.
Interview with the Vampire. New York: Alfred A. Knopf, 1976.
The Queen of the Damned. New York: Alfred A. Knopf, 1988.
The Vampire Lestat. New York: Alfred A. Knopf, 1985.
The Witching Hour. New York: Alfred A. Knopf, 1990.

As A.N. Roquelaure

Beauty's Punishment. New York: E. P. Dutton, 1984.
Beauty's Release. New York: E. P. Dutton, 1985.
The Claiming of Sleeping Beauty. New York: E. P. Dutton, 1983.

As Anne Rampling

Belinda. New York: Arbor House, 1986.
Exit to Eden. New York: Arbor House, 1985.

Further Reading

Badley, Linda. *Writing Horror and the Body: The Fiction of Stephen King, Clive Barker, and Anne Rice*. Westport, CT: Greenwood Publishing Group, 1996.
Beahm, George, ed. *The Unauthorized Anne Rice Companion*. Kansas City, MO: Andrews and McMeel, 1996.
Haggerty, George. "Anne Rice and the Queering of Culture." *Novel: A Forum on Fiction* 32.1 (1998): 5–18.
Hoppenstand, Gary, and Ray B. Browne, eds. *The Gothic World of Anne Rice*. Bowling Green, OH: Popular Press, 1996.
Keller, James R., and Gwendolyn A. Morgan. *Anne Rice and Sexual Politics: The Early Novels*. Jefferson, NC: McFarland & Company, 2000.
Marigny, Jean. "The Different Faces of Eros in the Vampire Chronicles of Anne Rice." Translated by Victor Reinking. *Para-doxa* 1.3 (1995): 352–62.
Ramsland, Katherine M., ed. *The Anne Rice Reader*. New York: Ballantine Books, 1997.
———. *Prism of the Night: A Biography of Anne Rice*. New York: Plume, 1992.
———. *The Roquelaure Reader: A Companion to Anne Rice's Erotica*. New York: Plume, 1996.
———. *The Vampire Companion: The Official Guide to Anne Rice's "The Vampire Chronicles."* New York: Ballantine Books, 1993.
———. *The Witches' Companion: The Official Guide to Anne Rice's "Lives of the Mayfair Witches."* New York: Ballantine Books, 1994.
Riley, Michael. *Conversations with Anne Rice*. New York: Fawcett Books, 1996.
Roberts, Bette B. *Anne Rice*. Twayne's United States Authors. Detroit: Gale Group, 1994.
Smith, Jennifer, and Jennifer Cruise. *Anne Rice: A Critical Companion*. Westport, CT: Greenwood Publishing Group, 1996.
Ziv, Amalia. "The Pervert's Progress: An Analysis of *Story of O* and the *Beauty* Trilogy." *Feminist Review* 46 (1994): 61–75.

RICHARDSON, SAMUEL

1689–1761
British printer and novelist

Pamela

In 1739, two booksellers suggested that Richardson produce "a little volume of letters, in a common style, on such subjects as might be of use to country readers who are unable to indite for themselves." But while writing this he conceived the epistolary method would serve to tell a story that he had heard fifteen years before—of a young servant girl whose wealthy and powerful master tries to seduce and rape her but cannot succeed in possessing her except by marriage. All Richardson's works have a moral purpose, but in *Pamela*, his most popular, the sexual content is so strong that the novel is often read as if designed to arouse readers sexually. "Good God!" wrote Richardson's contemporary Charles Povey, "what can youths learn from *Pamela*'s letters, more than lessons to tempt their chastity?" The anonymous author of *Pamela Censured* in 1741 pointed out the "images that tend to *inflame*"—and in the process helped sell the book; it was rumored that *Pamela Censured* was a bookseller's trick. Fielding's *Shamela* (1741) gives a parodic version that demonstrates the hypocrisy of Richardson and his pious readers. But Fielding's comic intention distances readers from the heroine, while Richardson, with his minute attention to the sentiments in Pamela's "heart," brings readers into a close—and titillating—identification with her erotic "trials." Although Pamela is always able to fend off her "wicked master," it is evident that she is also responding to him sexually. The sexual content was made necessary by Richardson's desire to make his didactic story effective. "I am endeavoring to write a Story," he told George Cheque, "which shall catch young and airy Minds, and when Passions shall run high in them, to shew how they may be directed to laudable Meanings and Purposes, in order to decry such Novels and Romances, as

have a Tendency to inflame and corrupt: And if I were too spiritual, I doubt I should catch none but Grandmothers." But as the author of *Pamela Censured* pointed out:

> the Modest Young Lady can never read the Description of Naked Breasts being run over with the Hand, and Kisses given with such Eagerness that they cling to the Lips; but her own soft Breasts must heave at the idea and secretly sigh for the same Pressure; what then can she do when she comes to the closer Struggles of the Bed, where the tender Virgin lies panting and exposed, if not to the last Conquest, (which I think the Author hath barely avoided) at least to all the Liberties which ungoverned Hands of a determined Lover must be supposed to take?

The aroused reader then "privately may seek Remedies which may drive her to the most unnatural Excesses"—i.e., of masturbation. D.H. Lawrence called Richardson's work "calico purity and underclothing excitements," and, more recently, Peter Wagner in his *Eros Revived* points out how close *Pamela*'s vocabulary of passion is to eighteenth-century erotic works and how "kinky" (Wagner's word) the novel can be, as in the scene where the master waits in Pamela's bed, disguised in the nightdress of Pamela's bedfellow, to try to rape her with the help of his assistant, the "mannish" Mrs. Jewkes. Richardson made many revisions in subsequent editions to tone down the eroticism. For example, the 1740 version reads: "I found his hand in my bosom; and when my fright let me know it, I was ready to die; and I sighed, and screamed, and fainted away." But in the last edition, published in 1801, this becomes: "The wicked wretch still had me in his arms. I sighed, and screamed, and then fainted way." In innumerable passages she loses her susceptibility, her breasts, even her ears (which previously would "color").

Clarissa and Sir Charles Grandison

Clarissa; or, the History of a Young Lady is the story, told through letters between Clarissa Harlowe and her friend Miss Howe, of an upper-class young woman. She is courted by the rakish

Lovelace, but resists him because of his lack of morals, though she is attracted to him. Her parents seek to force her into a marriage with another she does not want. Lovelace abducts her and drugs and rapes her, and she dies. De Sade thought highly of this novel. But, unlike *Pamela*, this much longer novel does not present us with graphic representations of bodily response. Even Lovelace seems less interested in the woman as a goal of sexual desire than as a prize to conquer sexually—to defeat the idea of chastity by defeating it in this paragon. But it is Clarissa who wins the struggle—by dying. As William Beatty Warner put it, through the very letters she has written, "Clarissa dies so that she may produce the book that will guarantee her triumph. . . . The heroine will be exalted and the witnesses of the tragedy will begin an invidious meditation on the causes of Clarissa's fall. The book ends by pointing an accusing finger towards everyone but Clarissa." Nonetheless, Richardson feels the necessity to editorialize against Lovelace and admonish readers, in the course of the long novel, not to develop a sympathy for Lovelace and his aspirations. He is killed by Clarissa's cousin in a duel.

In *The History of Sir Charles Grandison*—perhaps Richardson's answer to Fielding's *Tom Jones*—the hero rescues the lovely Harriet Byron from a fraudulent marriage ceremony by which the rakish Sir Hargrave Pollexfen would possess her. Harriet and Sir Charles fall in love, but, because of a previous engagement, Sir Charles does not ask to marry her, nor does he try to relieve his desire for her in any other way. At long last the complications are cleared up and they can marry. While Richardson has been credited with a great understanding of the psychology of his female characters, his male characters are generally not regarded as very credible. But Sir Charles is the ideal of the male required by heroines of future fiction. Never attempting to overpower the woman with his sexual desire, the "Grandissonian hero" Lord Orville offers his protective services to Fanny Burney's Evelina and as Darcy or Knightly to the heroines in Jane Austen, but these heroines may often be read as harboring an attraction to the men who do not have high-minded feelings about them. It is not easy to deny that Richardson's works inevitably subvert their puritanical heritage.

Biography

Born in Derbyshire, England, the son of a joiner; after a brief, elementary education apprenticed to a London printer. In 1721 married his master's daughter and set up his own printing business in Fleet Street, then in Salisbury Court, where he lived for the remainder of his life. Wife died in 1731. Remarried in 1733 and had four children who survived, all daughters. Wrote and published *The Apprentice's Vade-Mecum* (1733) and his version of *Aesop's Fables* (1739), *Pamela; or, Virtue Rewarded* (1740), *Letters Written to and for Particular Friends* (1741), *Clarissa; or, the History of a Young Lady* (1747–48), *The History of Sir Charles Grandison* (1753–54). By 1754 had become Master of the Stationers' Company and Printer of the Journals of the House of Commons. Ran his printing house till his death.

GERALD J. BUTLER

Further Reading

Eaves, T.C. Duncan, and Ben D. Kimbel. *Samuel Richardson: A Biography*. Oxford, UK: Clarendon Press, 1971.

Doody, Margaret Anne. *A Natural Passion: A Study of the Novels of Samuel Richardson*. Oxford: Clarendon Press, 1974.

Eagleton, Terry. *The Rape of Clarissa: Writing, Sexuality, and Class Struggle in Samuel Richardson*. London: Blackwell, 1989.

Harris, Jocelyn. *Samuel Richardson*. Cambridge, UK: Cambridge University Press, 1987.

Utter, R.P., and G.R. Needham. *Pamela's Daughters*. New York: Macmillan, 1936.

Warner, William Beatty. *Reading Clarissa: The Struggles of Interpretation*. New Haven, CT: Yale University Press, 1979.

RIMBAUD, ARTHUR

1854–1891
French poet

While Arthur Rimbaud was in Africa, the publication of Verlaine's article "Les poètes maudits" [The Damned Poets] in 1883 did much to promote the myth of the *enfant terrible,* as did the publication in 1886 in *La vogue* of "Marine" (26 May) and "Mouvement" (21 June). These two free-verse poems figure in the collection of otherwise exclusively prose poetry entitled *Illuminations,* which, with *Une saison en enfer* and the verse poems grouped under the heading *Poésies,* traditionally constitute the three major movements of Rimbaud's work (although, with the exception of *Une saison en enfer,* these groupings are not formal poetry collections but rather editorial conventions that have persisted for much of the last century).

Much of the poetry of Rimbaud can be thought of as erotic, albeit in different ways according to the groupings of poems. In the *Poésies,* there is an unmistakable tender sensuality in poems such as "Soleil et chair" [Sun and Flesh], "Sensation," "Roman" [Novel], "Rêvé pour l'hiver" [A Dream for Winter], "La maline" [The Sly Girl], and "Première soirée" [The First Evening], whereas the poetic subject is more impulsive or violent toward women in "Vénus Anadyomène," "Les reparties de Nina" [Nina's Replies], and "À la musique" [To Music]. In "Le cœur du pitre" [The Fool's Heart], the narrator describes a (perhaps fictitious, perhaps real) scene of homosexual rape at the hands of a troop of soldiers. Rimbaud inserted this poem—alternately entitled "Le cœur supplicié" [The Tortured Heart] and "Le cœur volé" [The Stolen Heart]—in his poetic manifesto, his Seer Letter of May 13, 1871. In this letter to his former professor, Rimbaud prefaces the poem with the words, "I beg you, do not underline it with your pencil or too much with your thought" and concludes the poem, and the letter, with the double-negative, "This does not mean nothing."

As the poem "Le cœur du pitre" suggests, much of the eroticism in Rimbaud's poetry has long met with theories that directly equate the poems with specific episodes in the poet's life; "the girl with huge tits and lively eyes" who appears in "Au Cabaret-Vert" is none other than Mia la Flamande, who worked at the real cabaret, La Maison-Verte (Steinmetz: 40), and one of the young girls who would have inspired "À la musique" was either the real-life Blanche Goffinet or Marie(-Henriette) Hubert (Steinmetz: 50–1). This blurring of life and work is most tempting for readers of Rimbaud who find themselves confronted with, on the one hand, a highly suggestive poetry and, on the other, a tantalizing biography, but it is ultimately unsatisfactory and does a disservice to the works.

The temptation is particularly great in *Une saison en enfer* [*A Season in Hell*] (1873), written after Rimbaud's definitive break with Verlaine. In this prose collection, the poet seems to offer a repudiation of his earlier poetic work: "One evening I pulled Beauty down on my knees. I found her embittered and I cursed her." The section entitled "Délires" begins with a rejection of a litany of life experiences in "The Foolish Virgin / The Infernal Bridegroom"—many of which have been attributed to Rimbaud's relationship with Verlaine—and proceeds to retractions of his earlier poetic project in "Alchemy of the Word": "It is my turn. The story of one of my follies. . . . I regulated the form and movement of each consonant, and, with instinctive rhythms, I prided myself on inventing a poetic language accessible someday to all the senses. I reserved translation rights." In "Adieu," the last poem, the poet renews his refusal of his past attempts, personal and poetic: "I have created all celebrations, all triumphs, all dramas. I have tried to invent new flowers, new stars, new flesh, new tongues." He then closes with a look toward the future: "We must be absolutely modern. . . . I shall be free to possess truth body and soul."

The collection of prose and free-verse poems entitled *Illuminations* is certainly replete with erotic tones—particularly in poems such as "Conte" [Story], "Parade" [Circus], "Solde" [Sale], and "Vagabonds"—but the hermetic nature of the poems dominates. While "Parade" marvels in the line "What mature men!", the reader is left with the impossible task of interpreting the procession, especially with the poet taunting, "I alone hold the key to this savage parade."

Also notable is the long prose poem "Un cœur sous une soutane" [A Heart Under a Cassock], in which a young priest falls in love with an ambiguous Thimothina, as well as the collaborative *Album Zutique*, a product of informal dinner meetings attended by Rimbaud, Verlaine, Charles Cros, and a host of other poets, composers, and artists. Best known in this collection is the "Sonnet of an Asshole," written by Rimbaud and Verlaine together and also appearing in Verlaine's erotic collection *Hombres*. The poem's first line, "Dark and wrinkled like a deep pink," begins with the word "Obscur," the oversized capital letter "O" emphasizing the poem's subject matter. Also notable is Rimbaud's contribution, "Remembrances du vieillard idiot" [Memories of the Simple-Minded Old Man], which presents an adolescent's obsessions with his own puberty: "Why puberty so late and the disgrace / Of my tenacious and too often consulted glans?" Finally, there are the poems commonly called *Les stupra* [*Defilements*], most likely contemporary and certainly similar in their explicit nature to the poems in the *Album Zutique,* although not formally included in that collection. In "Les anciens animaux..." [Ancient Animals...], the bestial nature of the human animal is on display ("Moreover, man is equal to the proudest mammal; / The hugeness of their member should not surprise us"), whereas "Nos fesses ne sont pas les leurs" [Our backsides are not theirs] evokes a more intimate account of ecstasy: "Oh! to be naked like that, and look for joy and rest, / My head turned toward my companion's glorious part, / And both of us free murmuring sobs?"

Biography

Born in Charleville, October 20. Educated at the Collège Municipal, where he received numerous awards for his poems. Attempted to leave Charleville several times for Paris, e.g., around the time of the Paris Commune. Met Paul Verlaine in 1871, thus beginning a turbulent homosexual relationship between the two poets that ended July 10, 1873, in Brussels, when Verlaine shot him twice in the wrist. Returned to his family farm to compose *Une saison en enfer,* the only collection he published. After abandoning both Europe and poetry in 1875, enlisted in the Dutch army and traveled to Batavia. Upon deserting, returned to France and subsequently traveled to Austria, Sweden, Denmark, Cyprus, Egypt, and finally Aden. Worked for an export company in Aden, and later in Harar, and explored the Somalia and Galla countries. Lived in Africa until ill health—a tumor on his right knee—forced him to return to Marseille, where he eventually died on November 10.

SETH WHIDDEN

Selected Works

Album Zutique. Facsimile of the original manuscript, edited by Pascal Pia. Geneva: Slatkine, 1981.
Oeuvres complètes. Edited by Antoine Adam. Bibliothèque de la Pléiade. Paris: Gallimard, 1970.
———. Edited by Pierre Brunel, 1999.
———. Edited by Steve Murphy. 4 vols. 1999–.
Complete Works, Selected Letters. Translated by Wallace Fowlie, 1966. Revised and updated by Seth Whidden, 2005.
Rimbaud Complete. Translated by Wyatt Alexander Mason, 2002.

Further Reading

Ahearn, Edward J. *Rimbaud: Visions and Habitations.* Berkeley and Los Angeles, CA: University of California Press, 1983.
Lawler, James R. *Rimbaud's Theatre of the Self.* Cambridge, MA: Harvard University Press, 1992.
Lefrère, Jean-Jacques. *Arthur Rimbaud.* Paris: Fayard, 2001.
Murphy, Steve. *Le Premier Rimbaud ou l'apprentissage de la subversion.* Paris: Editions du CNRS; Lyon: Presses Universitaires de Lyon, 1991.
Murat, Michel. *L'Art de Rimbaud.* Paris: José Corti, 2002.
Robb, Graham. *Rimbaud.* New York: Norton, 2000.
Schmidt, Paul. "Visions of Violence: Rimbaud and Verlaine." In *Homosexualities and French Literature,* edited by George Stambolian and Elaine Marks. Ithaca, NY: Cornell University Press, 1979.
Steinmetz, Jean-Luc. *Les Femmes de Rimbaud.* Paris: Zulma, 2000.

ROBBE-GRILLET, ALAIN

1922–
French novelist, screenwriter, and literary theorist

Alain Robbe-Grillet is the author of novels, *ciné-romans* (screenplays that can be read as novels), short stories, autobiography/fiction, and theoretical essays, is a director of films, and has written texts as part of collaborative works with five different artists or photographers. He is chiefly associated with the *nouveau roman* (new novel) writers, through his publisher, Editions de Minuit, which published works by many other *nouveaux romanciers*. This avant-garde group, although not a literary school, shared some common aims, including literary experimentation and a rejection of literary convention. This perhaps explains why many of Robbe-Grillet's works initially had a mixed reception, in spite of his receiving several literary and cinema prizes. Robbe-Grillet came to be viewed as something of a spokesperson for the *nouveau roman*, partly due to a series of essays he published in the collection *Pour un nouveau roman* [*For a New Novel*]. These explored various topics such as novelistic form, realism and reality, time, and characterization, and expounded an eschewal of previous conventions of literature, particularly those of the nineteenth century realist novel, as exemplified by Balzac. Robbe-Grillet complained that realism constructed its fictional universe from commonly accepted means of representing reality, such as anthropomorphic metaphor—the attribution of human qualities to the world around us—whereas in fact the world is neither significant nor absurd, it simply is. Robbe-Grillet's aim was to remove any apparent psychological depth attached to objects, instead allowing their surfaces to be described, so that objects as they really are may be laid bare. Thus, the object itself, rather than the culturally loaded or metaphoric meaning it has acquired, was foregrounded in the *nouveau roman*. Robbe-Grillet's own theoretical work thus inspired what came to be known as the *chosiste* interpretation of his work, whereby descriptions of things [*choses*] themselves are favored over explanations, and the world is rendered in terms which give it no meaning beyond the bare fact of its existence.

Opposed to this view was the claim that Robbe-Grillet's novels are deeply psychological. A psychological account of his work would assert that in many cases, a disturbed or traumatized mind is at the center of the narrative. The obsessive attention paid to objects, in this interpretation, is indicative of a psychological state wherein the consciousness, disoriented by some shock or trauma, fixes upon certain objects which, for the reader, become associated with that state of mind.

Some scholars of Robbe-Grillet have argued that his interest in the portrayal of objects just as they are perceived is similar in intent to phenomenological philosophy's attempt to describe phenomena as they are given to consciousness in perception, free from the prejudices and preconceptions of science or cultural conditioning. The situated nature of the narrator (or of the narrative perspective) in time and space in Robbe-Grillet's work is also analogous to the phenomenological account of a consciousness with a temporal and spatial bodily situation in the world.

Structuralist studies of Robbe-Grillet's works focus upon an analysis of the formal and structural elements of his texts and films. Patterns are identified across a given work, establishing links between individual words, visual images, or audible elements. These elements are often repeated, recombined, slightly altered each time they appear, or set in opposition to one another, and they give the work its structure and impetus. Structuralism concerns itself with the nonmimetic, purely linguistic interplay of literary and cinematic language. Identifying connections such as these across a work reveals structural devices employed within it and can indicate the way in which formal aspects combine to construct meaning.

As a writer of erotic fiction, the thread of an interest in eroticism runs throughout Robbe-Grillet's career. The erotic content is subtle in his earlier novels and tends to be alluded to rather than explicitly described, but it begins to take the form of very explicit, sado-erotic images and scenes in his later fiction. The reception of his works in terms of their erotic content has been divided. Feminist critics have, for example, indicated the misogynistic nature of the treatment of his female characters, unsurprisingly, since the rape, torture, and murder of young women are themes which pervade many of his works. Robbe-Grillet himself and those who have defended his presentation of eroticism argue that his works aim to exaggerate clichéd sexual stereotypes in order to reveal their banality, to subvert their usually erotic function. This has been questioned by critics, who argue that his exaggeration of sexual stereotypes tends to be repetitive, rather than subversive. Unapologetically, Robbe-Grillet continues to include erotica in his latest works.

Le voyeur

A watch salesman, Mathias, returns to his native island with the intention of spending the day selling watches. His unrealistic projected sales targets prove impossible to achieve; he is forced to abandon them as events on the island take a sinister turn and he develops a feeling of malaise. During his visit, a local girl disappears. It appears that she has been murdered, possibly following a sexual assault, and her body thrown over the cliffs into the sea. Mathias' itinerary, as he realizes in retrospect, had taken him close to where the girl had been minding sheep on a clifftop at the time of her disappearance. He realizes that there is a gap in his memory, a certain length of time he cannot recall or account for, which coincides with the girl's death. Although narrated in the third person, the novel reveals the viewpoint of only Mathias, and thus it is through the filter of his eroticized fantasies that events are described. He frequently notices the postures of girls or young women whose hands are behind their backs, a posture suggesting that they are tied up. This is emphasized further by the mention of the collection of pieces of string he kept as a boy and the length of cord

he keeps in his pocket and touches frequently during his visit to the island. Mathias' guilt, although never conclusively established during the course of the novel, is nevertheless hinted at in his return to the clifftop to recover the cigarette butts and sweet wrappers he had dropped there. Although not a novel that deals with eroticism in an explicit way, the whole work is suffused with erotic tension.

La jalousie

La Jalousie rests upon an ambiguity related to eroticism; the double meaning of *jalousie* in the title is indicative of two possible ways of reading the novel. *Jalousie*, taken to mean "venetian blind," can be understood to indicate the possibility of reading the novel as a camera-like recording of the movements of people through a house, with blinds impeding the view. A psychological understanding of the novel, wherein *jalousie* is understood to mean "jealousy," could indicate the possibility of reading it as the thoughts of a jealous husband witnessing the infidelity of his wife with their neighbor. He spies on them through the venetian blinds, while his jealousy, as well as the blinds, distort his point of view. The husband never mentions himself, although the narrative is always situated from a point in space and time that is suggestive of his presence. The novel has little by way of action, with the gradual rise and ebb of the unmentioned narrator's jealousy of the suspected affair being its main feature. The jealousy at the heart of the novel reaches its zenith in a description of an imagined bedroom scene involving A (the narrator's wife) and Franck, their neighbor. The scene begins to take shape in the narrator's mind when, following A's horror at the sight of a millipede at the dinner table, Franck crushes the insect with his napkin, and A's hand grasps the tablecloth. This gesture could indicate either her fear of the insect or her thrilling at Franck's manliness in dealing with it, and the scene is repeated obsessively throughout the novel, with slight modifications each time. One of its modifications involves the grasped tablecloth transforming into a bed sheet grasped in the throes of sexual pleasure. Thus the scene is transformed from the innocuous crushing of the millipede into an act of adultery between A and Franck, followed by the narrator's imagining one of their visits to a nearby town ending in a car crash.

La maison de rendez-vous

A tale of drug dealing and prostitution in a Hong Kong brothel, *La maison de rendez-vous* [*The House of Assignation*] marks a move to more explicit depictions of eroticism. Lady Ava not only runs the brothel, but appears to control other people and their actions too, including thwarting the attempt of Sir Ralph Johnston to buy Lauren, one of the prostitutes working at the brothel, from her. The prostitutes' duties at the brothel include the performance of an unusual stage act, which involves one of the girls standing in a spotlight and having her dress ripped from her body by a dog, for the delectation of the audience. The novel is complicated not only by the proliferation of narrative voices, between which the narrative jumps unexpectedly, but also by the multiple names given to each character (for example, Lady Ava is also Eva or Eve). Threads of the various characters' stories interweave in a disorienting labyrinth, with the result that it is difficult to establish any definitive account of what occurs in the novel. This is particularly true of the mysterious death of Manneret, which is presented on the stage in the brothel as a performance and is repeatedly recounted and altered later in the narrative as if it were a real event, having consequences in the lives of the other characters. Johnston, for example, is implicated in Manneret's death. Before fleeing in order to avoid being accused, he visits the brothel in a last-ditch attempt to persuade Lauren to accompany him and is finally caught by the police.

Projet pour une révolution à New York

As its name suggests, this novel takes place in New York City, the New York of modern popular culture, a place where modern myths are played out. It abounds with references to, for example, television programs popular at the time it was written (1970), to Robbe-Grillet's own texts, to criminal gangs, and to sexual stereotypes in the form of the delicate flesh of young women subjected to torture. As in *La maison de rendez-vous*, no one narrative voice dominates, characters' names are varied, nothing is certain. The play of exaggerated modern myths is the only content the novel has; there is no underlying reality that these myths refer to. The nature of the revolution itself is somewhat enigmatic—instead of explaining it, only the means of bringing it about are described. The New York portrayed is one where crime has taken over in the name of revolution, although apparently no revolution ever occurs. In terms of its erotic content, a notable feature of this novel is that one of the revolutionary activities involves the graphically described sadistic torture of women, and it is for this reason that it has courted controversy. In spite of the fact that these scenes are described as imaginary, in spite of their theatricality and staged nature, they have nevertheless caused some consternation among critics. The theatricality of these scenes calls into question the extent to which they can be considered real or referential. Those who defend Robbe-Grillet argue that the scenes of violent sexual torture are not to be understood as referring to anything real—they are a metaphor for his destruction of literary norms, they are the revolution he brings about in literature.

Romanesques

The trilogy known as *Romanesques*—comprising *Le miroir qui revient* [*Ghosts in the Mirror*], *Angélique ou l'enchantement* [*Angélique, or the Enchantment*], and *Les derniers jours de Corinthe* [*The Last Days of Corinth*]—consists of part autobiography and part fiction, and Robbe-Grillet deliberately blurs the distinction between the two. As well as recounting the major events of his life and his literary career, the *Romanesques* are an account of the real-life and fantasy events which have inspired his work. Among these are the erotic fantasies which he admits have haunted his dreams since childhood. Whether these fantasies are based upon real people or events is difficult to ascertain, given that Robbe-Grillet does not distinguish clearly between fantasy and reality. Typical of this is the story of Angélique, who is referred to in the title of the second volume of the *Romanesques*. Robbe-Grillet suggests that she really did exist and was the inspiration for the adolescent female character in *Le Voyeur*. He describes a scene during his adolescence or youth in which Angélique undresses and gives him orders (which he dare not disobey) to touch her, introducing him to sexuality and the female body.

The scene bears many of the hallmarks of descriptions of the female body elsewhere in his works, although this early experience engenders fear in the young initiate. When his finger emerges blood stained from her vagina, she claims that he has deflowered her and will forever be cursed by impotence. He fears that he has fatally injured her. In a passage that exemplifies Robbe-Grillet's merging of apparently factual events with fictional ones, the conclusion of his encounter with Angélique is, in effect, a summary of the final part of *Le voyeur*, with the adolescent girl's body found naked in the sea at the bottom of some cliffs, thus suggesting a link between blood, sex, and danger.

La reprise

Eroticism in the form of incest is a major theme in Robbe-Grillet's latest novel, in which there are repeated references to the story of Oedipus. In *La reprise* [*Repetition*] (2001) the ruins of postwar Berlin, a French secret agent named Henri Robin is sent on a mission, the reason for which is unclear. The sense of uncertainty is emphasized by the fact that Henri's identity is constantly changing, he has many names, and the narrative is undermined by a second narrator who contradicts events. Henri suspects that he will be framed for a murder committed by a man who later turns out to be his twin brother, Walther. Walther, who had suffered injuries to his eyes during the war, has murdered their father, suggesting an oedipal parricide. In further family complications, incest is hinted at when it is revealed that Walther may have fathered Gigi, his half-sister, whom he had tortured and interrogated with the aim of ascertaining the whereabouts of their father. Gigi had been made to strip and had her limbs chained down, making it difficult for her to move during the interrogation. Walther admits to having taken pleasure in the sexual torture of Gigi, regardless of any useful information she was able to divulge. Gigi also features in a series of three pornographic drawings signed by Walther, in which she is variously depicted tied down, burned, and crucified, subjected to sexual torture in every case, crying out apparently in pain, although this, according to Henri's narration, could be mistaken for pleasure. Finally, Henri claims to have been raped by Gigi's mother, although he does not find the experience disagreeable.

The sexual encounter between Henri and Gigi's mother (who is described as behaving maternally toward him) thus constitutes a further reference to Oedipus and to the theme of incest which pervades the novel.

Biography

Born in Brest, France, August 18. Early education, Paris, 1929–39; Brest, 1939–40. Entered into the Institut national agronomique (INA), 1942. Requisitioned into the Service du travail obligatoire (compulsory labor organization established under the German occupation) in Nuremberg, 1943–44, then completed studies at INA. In 1945, joined INSEE (French national institute of statistics and economic studies) and worked on the journal *Etudes et conjonctures*. Volunteered in August 1947 for the Brigades internationales de reconstruction, working on the Pernik-Volouïek railway in Bulgaria. Upon leaving INSEE, worked in an animal artificial insemination laboratory in Bois-Boudran, Seine-et-Marne, and, during the long breaks between duties, wrote the manuscript for a novel, *Un Régicide* (turned down by Gallimard; not published by Minuit until 1978). In 1949 became research engineer for the Institut des fruits et agrumes coloniaux, working in Morocco, Guadeloupe, and Martinique. Ill health led to forced resignation from this post and return to France. During boat journey back, began to write *Les Gommes* [*The Erasers*], and resigned from job in order to finish it, marking the beginning of his career as a writer. Became literary adviser at Editions de Minuit in 1955, a post he would hold for thirty years. Married Catherine Rstakian in 1957. In 1960, Robbe-Grillet signed the *Déclaration sur la droit à l'insoumission dans la guerre d'Algérie* (the so-called *Manifeste des 121*) supporting the right to refuse to serve in the Algerian war. In 1961, survived a plane crash with his wife in Hamburg; wrote the screenplay (published as a *ciné-roman*) for *L'Année dernière à Marienbad* [*Last Year at Marienbad*], directed by Alain Resnais. Robbe-Grillet's film and *ciné-roman Glissements progressifs du plaisir* [*Gradual Shifts in Pleasure*] condemned in 1975 by an Italian court as pornographic. Since devoting himself to writing and filmmaking, has been a visiting teacher at several universities around the world, taken part in numerous literary and film conferences, and won several literary and film prizes. He became a member of the Académie Française in 2004.

ELIZABETH NEWTON

Editions

Un régicide [1949]. Paris: Minuit, 1978.
Les gommes. Paris: Minuit, 1953.
Le voyeur. Paris: Minuit, 1955.
La jalousie. Paris: Minuit, 1957.
Dans le labyrinthe [In the Labyrinth]. Paris: Minuit, 1959.
L'Année dernière à Marienbad (ciné-roman). Paris: Minuit, 1961.
Instantanés [Snapshots]. Paris: Minuit, 1962.
L'Immortelle [The Immortal One] (ciné-roman). Paris: Minuit, 1963.
Pour un nouveau roman. Essays on fiction. Paris: Minuit, 1963.
La maison de rendez-vous. Paris: Minuit, 1965.
Projet pour une révolution à New York [Project for a Revolution in New York]. Paris: Minuit, 1970.
Glissements progressifs du plaisir (ciné-roman). Paris: Minuit, 1974.
Topologie d'une cité fantôme [Topology of a Phantom City]. Paris: Minuit, 1976.
Souvenirs du triangle d'or [Recollections of the Golden Triangle]. Paris: Minuit, 1978.
Djinn. Paris: Minuit, 1981.
Le miroir qui reveint. Paris: Minuit, 1984.
Angélique, ou l'enchantement. Paris: Minuit, 1988.
Les derniers jours de Corinthe. Paris: Minuit, 1994.
La reprise. Paris: Minuit, 2001.
Le voyageur. Collection of interviews and short texts, 1947–2001. Paris: Christian Bourgois, 2001.
C'est Gradiva qui vous appelle [Gradiva is calling you] (ciné-roman). Paris: Minuit, 2002.

Collaborative Works with:

Delvaux, Paul. *Construction d'un temple en ruine à la Déesse Vanadé* [Construction of a Ruined Temple to the Goddess Vanadé]. Paris: Le Bateau-Lavoir, 1975.
Hamilton, David. *Rêves de jeunes filles* [Dreams of a Young Girl]. Paris: Laffont, 1971.
———. *Les Demoiselles d'Hamilton* [The Hamilton Daughters]. Paris: Laffont 1972.
Ionesco, Irina. *Temple aux miroirs* [Temple of Mirrors]. Paris: Seghers, 1977.
Magritte, René. *La Belle Captive* [La Belle Captive]. Lausanne and Paris: Bibliothèque des arts, 1975.
Rauschenberg, Robert. *Traces suspectes en surface* [Suspicious Surface Traces]. West Islip, NY: Universal Limited Art Editions, 1978.

Filmography

L'Année dernière à Marienbad. Screenplay. Directed by Alain Resnais. France/Italy, 1961.
L'Immortelle. France/Italy/Turkey, 1963.
Trans-Europ Express. France/Belgium, 1966.
L'Homme qui ment [The Man Who Lies]. France/Czechoslovakia, 1968.
L'Eden et après [Eden and After]. France/Czechoslovakia, 1971.
N a pris les dés [N Took the Dice]. France, 1971.
Glissements progressifs du plaisir. France, 1974.
Le Jeu avec le feu [Playing with Fire]. France/Italy, 1975.
La Belle captive [The Fair Captive], France, 1982.
Un Bruit qui rend fou (as *The Blue Villa*). Written and directed jointly with Dimitri de Clerq. France/Belgium/Switzerland, 1995.

Further Reading

Bernal, Olga. *Alain Robbe-Grillet: Le roman de l'absence.* Paris: NRF Gallimard, 1964.
Brée, Germaine. "What Interests Me Is Eroticism." Interview. In *Homosexualities and French Literature,* edited by George Stambolian and Elaine Marks. London and Ithaca, NY: Cornell University Press, 1979, 1990.
Camber, Melinda. "Robbe-Grillet: The 'Ironic' Treatment of Eroticism." *The Times* (London), October 29, 1974.
Corpet, Olivier, and Emanuelle Lambert. *Alain Robbe-Grillet le voyageur du nouveau roman: Chronologie illustré 1922–2002.* Illustrated biography. Paris: Editions de l'IMEC, 2002.
Critique: Alain Robbe-Grillet 651–652 (August-September 2001).
Dunmars Roland, Lillian. *Women in Robbe-Grillet.* New York: Peter Lang, 1993.
Fragola, Anthony N., & Roch C. Smith. *The Erotic Dream Machine: Interviews with Alain Robbe-Grillet on His Films.* Carbondale and Edwardsville: Southern Illinois University Press, 1992.
Jost, François, ed. *Obliques/Robbe-Grillet* 16–17. Paris, Borderie, 1978.
Magazine Littéraire 402 (October 2001). Contains a collection of features on Robbe-Grillet.
Morrissette, B. *Les Romans de Robbe-Grillet.* Paris: Minuit, 1971.
Ramsey, Raylene L. *Robbe-Grillet and Modernity: Science, Sexuality and Subversion.* Gainesville: University Press of Florida, 1992.
Ricardou, Jean. *Problèmes du Nouveau Roman.* Paris: Seuil, 1967.
Smith, Roch C. *Understanding Alain Robbe-Grillet.* Columbia: University of South Carolina Press, 2000.
Suleiman, Susan. "Reading Robbe-Grillet: Sadism and Text in *Projet pour une révolution à New York. Romanic Review* LXVII (January 1977).

ROCCO, ANTONIO

1586–1653
Italian philosopher and theologian

L'Alcibiade fanciullo a scola

Published anonymously in 1652, *L'Alcibiade fanciullo a scola* [*Alcibiades the Schoolboy*] was first thought to be the work of Pietro Aretino and later of Ferrante Pallavicino. It was only in 1888 that its true author, Antonio Rocco, was established by Achille Neri. It appears to be in connection with Rocco's membership in the Accademia degli Incogniti that he wrote this "carnivalesque."

L'Alcibiade fanciullo a scola, an early classic of homosexual/pederastic literature, became widely known through a new edition in 1862 and a French translation in 1866. (The first English translation of 2000 is based on the 1891 edition of the French translation.) The pioneer homosexual theorist and emancipationist Karl Heinrich Ulrichs knew the book in the French translation and noted in 1868 that it was a "curious book that in addition to deterring frivolities contains much important scientific information." Richard Burton, too, quoted widely from the French translation in his famous "Terminal Essay" to his own translation of *Thousand Nights and a Night* (1888).

The novel is set in Athens and is in the form of a dialogue between the teacher Philotimos ("loving honors") and the boy Alcibiades, presumably the historical general and friend of Socrates. It begins with a glowing description of the boy's physical charms, from head to foot, with broad hints of hidden delights—which his teacher finds irresistible. While ostensibly set in ancient Greece, the dialogue that follows also includes Roman mythology—and the moral arguments almost all relate to Christian teaching. Philotimos makes it clear from the beginning that his goal is penetration. How he proceeds to attain that goal is the subject of the book, for the boy places obstacles in his path. Not that the boy is entirely reluctant, but he has doubts and questions that he wants answered first.

The various questions are answered in different ways. Alcibiades says, "What you wish to practice is a hideous vice which offends Nature, indeed one which is called 'the sin against Nature,' and our law forbids it." That this act was "against Nature" had already been discussed over a century earlier in another carnivalesque, *La Cazzaria* of Antonio Vignali, a book that also came to modern attention about the same time as *L'Alcibiade* (a new edition was published in Brussels in 1863 and a French translation appeared in 1882). But Rocco gives it an original solution with a clever linguistic twist, as Philotimos replies: "First, that this is a vice against nature is a ridiculous allusion spread by the statesmen. Since in women the flower [asshole] is placed against, i.e., on the opposite side to the fig [cunt], which is called nature, they say the use of it is opposed to nature" (my translation here—this argument, although in the French translation, is oddly lacking in the English edition, which is altogether a free adaptation).

One argument that particularly impressed nineteenth-century readers was in answer to Alcibiades' question: "Cannot you, without having dealings with either women or boys, extinguish the flames of love with your own hands—without expense, without trouble, without submitting to anyone?" (75). Philotimos gives a long speech comparing so-called onanism unfavorably with the contact of a beloved person, concluding: "Onanism, by contrast, deprives us of the sight of our lover, of contact with him in the flesh, and leaves us drained and exhausted. We must not then give up our boys for this habit, because our moderate enjoyments with them bring us joy and health; indeed, one of our most famous physicians wrote this sentence: "*Usus et amplexus pueri bene temperatus, salutaris medicina* [The embrace of a boy, when enjoyed in moderation, is a health-giving medicine]" (77 in the English edition, which, however, has "Uses et amplexes," apparently reflecting the misspelling of the Latin in the 1891 French translation). Ulrichs, Burton, and others took this report of "one of our most famous physicians" at face value, but this canard is a sheer invention of Antonio Rocco, as Wolfram Setz pointed out in his excellent commentary to his own German translation (242).

The teacher's arguments become more and more persuasive. The boy admits to some experience with other boys and says, "Without doubt, there is between these childish games and those of which you have spoken the difference between a green fruit and a ripe one. Therefore I am not very far, either, from venturing upon them, and I am listening to you with both my ears" (85). The teacher is eager: "To work then, my son! Experience will teach you more than will lectures and arguments."

But the boy is a bit of a tease after all and replies: "It is certainly my wish, but I fear that when you no longer need to convince me, you will become less explicit in your discourse, and your lessons will become less interesting. Therefore continue with your arguments, and wait patiently for the rest."

The teacher's final argument is that the sperm of a man improves a boy's intellect. "A boy who wishes to be the equal of his master has no other way than this. I admit that to be fucked by any man, given that his fluid is warm and temperate, can make the brain of a boy develop wonderfully, but to bear the true fruits, let him be fucked by a man who is noble and distinguished" (92–3). Now the boy is completely convinced and says, "I give myself to your wishes. It is your desire to instruct me, more than other reason, that decides me. See, I prepare myself for you." With that, he lifts his robe and the master attains his goal.

The book concludes: "How they continued their encounters and their loving caresses is what we will tell you in a second part, even more lascivious." But the second part never appeared.

Biography

Born in Scurzola (Abruzzi, Italy). He studied theology and philosophy in Rome, Perugia, and especially in Padua, where his teacher was Cesare Cremonini, the "Aristotle of his time." Rocco then settled in Venice, where he became a successful teacher and writer. As an Aristotelian, he attacked Galileo's mathematical "Platonism" in 1633—and received a rude reply from Galileo. In 1634, as a member of the Accademia degli Incogniti [Academy of the Unknowns], Rocco gave a lecture on love in all of its manifestations—from love between parents and their children to physical love and love of one's country and God—and brought them all under one formula, "Amore è un puro interesse" [Love is a pure interest]: basically each person loves only himself. In 1636 the city of Venice named Rocco its official teacher of rhetoric and moral philosophy. He died there.

HUBERT KENNEDY

Editions

L'Alcibiade fanciullo a scola. Edited by Laura Coci. Rome: Salerno, 1988.

Alcibiade enfant à l'école. Edited by Louis Godbout. Montréal: Les Editions Balzac, 1995.

Alcibiades the Schoolboy. Translated by J.C. Rawnsley; afterword by D.H. Mader. Amsterdam: Entimos, 2000.

Der Schüler Alkibiades: Ein philosophisch-erotischer Dialog. Original Italian, with German translation and afterword by Wolfram Setz. Hamburg: MännerschwarmSkript, 2002. This volume also contains a valuable dossier of sources, including a section of Antonio Rocco's "Amore è un puro interesse" (1634) in Italian and German translation.

Further Reading

Asoka, Louis. "Alcibiades the Schoolboy." *Paidika: The Journal of Paedophilia*, no. 2 (1987): 49–54.

Dall'Orto, Giovanni. "L'Alcibiade fanciullo a scola." In *Encyclopedia of Homosexuality*, edited by Wayne R. Dynes, 1:34. New York: Garland, 1990.

Maggi, Armando. "The Discourse of Sodom in a Seventeenth-Century Venetian Text." In *Reclaiming the Sacred: The Bible in Gay and Lesbian Culture*, edited by Raymond-Jean Frontain, 25–43. New York: Haworth, 1997.

Neri, Achille. "Il vero autore dell' 'Alcibiade fanciullo a scola.'" *Giornale Storico della Letteratura italiana* 12 (1888): 219–227.

Setz, Wolfram. "Antonio Roccos *Der Schüler Alkibiades*: Ein Buch und seine Leser." *Forum Homosexualität und Literatur* 40 (2002): 99–110.

Vignali, Antonio. *La Cazzaria*, edited by Pasquale Stoppelli. Rome: Edizioni dell'Elefante, 1984.

ROJAS, FERNANDO DE

1465–1541
Spanish novelist

Celestina

This dialogue novel, written in the final years of the fifteenth century by the Salamanca university law graduate Fernando de Rojas and possibly one other hand, is considered to be one of the top half-dozen Spanish masterpieces of world literature. It foreshadows the development of both the theatre and the novel in Spain and Europe and creates one of the archetypal characters of Spanish fiction, the bawd, go-between, and sorceress Celestina.

The genesis of this masterpiece is cloaked in mystery. Rojas claims to have found a one-act play and during his Easter vacation to have added another fifteen shorter acts to it (in 1497 or 1498) and taken it to the publishers where it appeared in 1499 as the *Comedia de Calisto y Melibea*. Its printing success was such that Rojas decided to lengthen it, adding five new acts interpolated into act XIV of the original and renaming it the *Tragicomedia de Calisto y Melibea* (this possibly in 1502, although no editions survive from this date). The nickname *Celestina* was given to the book by the public at a later date.

The story is as follows: Calisto meets Melibea in her garden, which he has entered in search of his falcon. He is smitten but she rebukes him. He returns home and complains bitterly to his man-servant Sempronio, who undertakes to seek out the services of the go-between Celestina on his master's behalf. Sempronio fetches Celestina from her house, where she lives with her companion and sometime prostitute Elicia, also Sempronio's mistress. On their return to Calisto's house they are seen by Parmeno, Calisto's faithful servant, who warns him against the wiles of Celestina, who helped to raise him when he was young. (In fact, Celestina was trained by Parmeno's mother, Claudina, a witch who had

been punished and possibly executed.) Calisto ignores Parmeno's good advice and enlists Celestina's help for a large amount of money, which Sempronio expects to share with her. Celestina has a long conversation with Parmeno and manages to subvert him by promising him the sexual favors of Areusa, Elicia's cousin. The long first act ends here, and according to Rojas, he takes up the dialogue early in act II.

In the second act Calisto's maltreatment of Parmeno seals the lad's defection to Celstina's camp. Act III takes place in Celestina's house, where Sempronio and Elicia go to make love while Celestina prepares the scene for a *philocaptio* spell, viz., to captivate the will of a beloved. She summons up a demon and anoints a skein of thread with snake oil. In act IV she takes the skein to Melibea's house to trade it for a piece of clothing, her girdle or sash. Alisa, Melibea's mother, is called away opportunely to visit a sick relative, a circumstance which Celestina attributes to the Devil's intervention. Melibea is at first angered by Celestina's mention of Calisto but finally lets herself be persuaded to give Celestina her girdle and to see the bawd again after the girls have prepared a prayer for Calisto's alleged toothache. In act V Celestina bears the glad tidings to Calisto, but Sempronio begins to suspect that she will not share the booty with him. Act VI sees Calisto fetishizing the girdle and promising Celestina new clothing. In act VII Celestina makes good her promise to supply Areusa to Parmeno, but she punishes him with a long description of his mother Claudina's witchcraft. Act VIII sees Parmeno and Sempronio sealing their friendship and planning a servants' banquet, which takes place in act IX. Celestina reminisces about the good old days when she ran a large brothel (before these were taken over by the town councils in the mid-1490s after the appearance of syphilis). In act X she returns to Melibea's house and arranges an assignation between the lovers for the next night at the gates of Melibea's garden. Melibea has succumbed to the temptations of lust (or perhaps the magic spell). Act XI finds Calisto rewarding Celestina with a valuable gold chain, much to the envy of Sempronio and Parmeno, as it is not easily divisible. In act XII the lovers' first platonic encounter at the garden gate has a counterpoint in the fears and cowardice of the young men standing guard outside the walls. Afterward they go to Celestina's house and murder her for the gold chain. As we hear in act XIII from one of Calisto's stable boys, they are immediately apprehended and put to death. In the original *Comedia*, the denouement follows. Calisto goes to Melibea's garden and they make love (old act XIV). He hears a noise outside the garden and rushes to help the stable boys, who now accompany him, but slips and falls to his death. Melibea, overcome by grief, bids farewell to her father Pleberio and jumps from the tower of their house to her death. Pleberio is left alone to grieve the death of his only heir (old act XIV).

The five new acts added by Rojas are an excuse to lengthen the lovemaking (act XIX); they also include some comic action between Areusa and her pimp, Centurio, a braggart soldier (act XVIII), whom she tries to cajole into taking action against Calisto and his servants (he instead arranges for a friend to go in his place). Elicia forges a new partnership with Areusa and casts her own curse on Melibea's garden (new acts XV and XVII). The most remarkable of the new acts shows a Melibea who secretly rebels against the wishes of her parents to make a good marriage for her (new act XVI). Also notable is the new ending to act XIV when Calisto exercises his imagination, first, in cowardly mode, upbraiding the judge who condemned his servants to death, then reliving the night of love with Melibea in the garden.

This work was meant to be read aloud by one or more performers over a series of readings, rather than being performed on stage or indeed read silently. The frankness of the sexual scenes in acts XIV and XIX alone would not have allowed for a more graphic and literal setting, nor would the length of the work. With its portrayal of the psychological and persuasive powers of Celestina and her corruption of both Parmeno and Melibea, whose characters change profoundly as a result, *Celestina* is a century ahead of its time in the depiction of psychological realism. It foreshadows the picaresque genre in Spain and *Don Quixote*'s novelistic trajectory.

It also paves the way for shorter theatrical imitations which will help form the early theatrical tradition of sixteenth-century Spain.

The figure of Celestina captured the imagination of the reading public in the same way that the figures of Don Juan and Don Quixote would in the next century. The bawd, sorceress, and sometime witch symbolized the incarnation of evil, but even so was almost attractive in her pride, valor, strength of character, and comic ability to turn a good saying to an evil end. Although Rojas's purpose was essentially didactic and the work was originally aimed at an all-male audience at the University of Salamanca, as an outsider of converted Jewish stock, or a *converso*, Rojas's misogyny was tempered by a sense of identification with the marginalized Celestina and her proto-picaresque cohorts. The women are the strongest characters in the work, and Celestina is a comic figure who subverts the ordered male hierarachy represented by Pleberio and his world. As a genius of misrule, Celestina seduces Melibea on behalf of Calisto and enlists Parmeno to her cause with the promise of sex. Calisto himself is a parodic courtly lover who never lets good sense get in the way of his lust. Although the longer version gives the lovers a month for their love affair, the original shows a Calisto keen to get away from his one-night stand and falling to his death for his pains. Sempronio is an opportunist and Parmeno a weak vessel traumatized by his past. Only Elicia and Areusa emerge as significantly strengthened survivors of the multiple deaths at the end of the work. The most subtle and difficult character is Melibea, who metamorphoses from an inexperienced virgin to a woman resentfully aware of her captivity in her father's home and her powerlessness to escape in the arms of her lover. The ambiguous power of witchcraft in her seduction, her entrapment through an act of Christian charity (the prayer for Calisto), and the failure of her prayer to God for protection make her the best candidate for tragic status in the work. Despite the gory denouement, most of the other deaths are meant to be comic, not tragic. In his closing lament, the pathetic figure of Pleberio faces the failure of the neo-Stoical philosophy which he has followed. He berates fortune, the world, and love, a slight variation on the world, the flesh, and the Devil, and concludes that he stands sad and alone in this vale of tears.

Biography

Fernando de Rojas was born in La Puebla de Montalbán in Castile, Spain, into a family recently forcibly converted from Judaism to Christianity. Around 1488 he went to Salamanca, where he studied Latin, philosophy, and law. He died known better for his success as a lawyer than for the masterpiece that would later be known as *La Celestina.*

DOROTHY SHERMAN SEVERIN

Further Reading

Bataillon, Marcel. *'La Celestina' selon Fernando de Rojas.* Paris: Didier, 1961.

Berndt-Kelley, Erna R. *Amor, muerte y fortuna en 'La Celestina.'* Madrid: Gredos, 1963.

Burke, James. *Vision, the Gaze and the Function of the Senses in 'Celestina.'* University Park: Pennsylvania State UP, 2000.

Castells, Richard. *Fernando de Rojas and the Renaissance Vision: Phantasm, Melancholy, and Didacticism in 'Celestina.'* University Park: Pennsylvania State UP, 2000.

Castro, Américo. *'La Celestina' como contienda literaria (castos y casticismos).* Madrid: Revista de Occidente, 1965.

Deyermond, Alan. *The Petrarchan Sources of 'La Celestina.'* London: Oxford UP, 1961.

Dunn, Peter N. *Fernando de Rojas.* New York and Boston: Twayne, 1975.

Fraker, Charles. *'Celestina': Genre and Rhetoric.* London: Tamesis, 1990.

Fothergill-Payne, Lois. *Seneca in 'Celestina.'* Cambridge: Cambridge UP, 1988.

Gilman, Stephen. *The Art of 'La Celestina.'* Madison, WI: University of Wisconsin Press, 1956.

——. *The Spain of Fernando de Rojas: the Intellectual and Social Landscape of 'La Celestina.'* Princeton, NJ: Princeton UP, 1972.

Lacarra, María Eugenia. *Cómo leer 'La Celestina.'* Madrid: Júcar, 1990.

Lida de Malkiel, María Rosa. *Two Spanish Masterpieces: The 'Book of Good Love' and 'La Celestina.'* Champaign and Urbana: University of Illinois Press, 1961.

——. *La originalidad artística de 'La Celestina.'* Buenos Aires: EUDEBA, 1962.

Márquez Villanueva, Francisco. *Orígenes y sociología del tema celestinesco.* Barcelona: Anthropos, 1993.

Maravall, José Antonio. *El mundo social de La Celestina.* Madrid: Gredos, 1954.

Miguel Martínez, Emilio de. *'La Celestina' de Rojas.* Madrid: Gredos, 1996.

Norton, Frederick John. *Printing in Spain, 1501–1520, with a Note on the Early Editions of 'La Celestina.'* Cambridge: Cambridge UP, 1966.

Penney, Clara Louisa. *The Book Called 'Celestina' in the Library of the Hispanic Society of America.* New York: Hispanic Society of America, 1954.

Russell, Peter E. *Temas de 'La Celestina' y otros estudios.* Barcelona: Ariel, 1978.

Samonà, Carmelo. *Aspetti del retoricismo nella 'Celestina.'* Rome: Università, 1953.

Severin, Dorothy Sherman. *Memory in 'La Celestina.'* London: Támesis, 1970.

——. *Tragicomedy and Novelistic Discourse in 'Celestina.'* Cambridge: Cambridge UP, 1989.

——. *Witchcraft in 'Celestina.'* London: Queen Mary and Westfield College, 1995.

Snow, Joseph T. *'Celestina' by Fernando de Rojas: an Annotated Bibliography of World Interest.* Madison, WI: Hispanic Seminary of Medieval Studies, 1985.

——, ed. *Celestinesca.* 1 to the present (1977–).

ROMANIAN EROTIC LITERATURE

Romania possesses a rich erotic folklore, yet Romanian erotic literature is also bound to popular songs, anecdotes, and especially to epithalamiums, in the form of pornographic songs or verses sung as fertility rituals during the wedding ceremony. Possibly the only writer to use these luscious popular jests as a source of inspiration was Ion Creangă (1837–1889). His short story, *Moş Nichifor, cotcariul [Father Nekifor, the Knave]* (1877) is in fact an anecdote set in a "literary" context about a comic tale of the love between an old carter and a young Jewish woman. The literary history notes that there were two versions of this narrative, the first very explicit, the other simply suggestive, making subtle allusions to the sexual act. Only the second version has reached us, and this is a true masterpiece. Two short pornographic stories have also been preserved: *Povestea lui Ionică cel prost* [*The Tale of Johnny the Silly*] and *Povestea poveştilor* [*The Tale of Tales*], also named *Povestea pulei* [*The Tale of the Dick*]. Similar to Chaucer and the *Canterbury Tales,* Creangă's touch gives a particular charm to the narratives where popular language and humor are mixed with the refined expression of a great stylist, but, nevertheless, one feels that the folk source that is very obvious. The classical critique then came under the influence of French letters, more in the style of Rabelais.

Folklore is the source for two poets who preceded Creangă: Costache Conachi (1779–1849) and Anton Pann (1796–1854). Although Ion Negoiţescu, in History of Romanian Literature, posited that Conachi's poetry borrowed from the ribald character of Alexis Pironăs's *Ode to Priap,* one can say that popular poetry keeps its traces in the poems of Conachi, with echoes of the French rococo. A virile, overflowing eroticism is shown by Conachi in *Amoriul din prieteşug* [*The Love from Friendship*], *Judecata femeilor* [*The Judgment of the Ladies*], and *Scrisoare către Zulnia* [*Letter to Zulnia*].

Anton Pann underwent the influence of suburban folklore. His poems portray elegant love as foreplay to carnal love. The vitality of libidinous longing is impregnated with the sighs and expressions of suffering caused by the kind of love that was highly valued at the time. Among Pann's volumes, perhaps the best known from the point of view of this eroticism is *Spitalul amorului* [*The Hospital of Love*] (1850–52). Pann is a sort of suburban troubadour who doesn't sing the *Amor de lonh,* but sings of love pursued and captured in a time when the wantonness of customs allowed for many carnal possibilities between young men and widows or married women and between the wealthy bourgeoisie and young girls. A traveling artist, Pann set much of his poetry to music, which was sung especially by the fiddlers in the restaurants of Bucharest and other southern Romanian cities.

The development of erotic themes (and sometimes pornography) in modern Romanian literature can be traced in both poetry and prose. Mihai Eminescu (1850–1889), one of the last great Romantics, wrote of erotic frustration in his best-known poem, *Luceafărul* [*The Morning Star*], which speaks of the impossible love between a young princess and a celestial being, and in works on forbidden love: e.g., *Călin, file din poveste* [*Calin, Pages of Fairy Tales*] and *Povestea teiului* [*The Legend of the Lime*]. But he can also be licentious, as in the fable *Antropomorfisme* [*Anthropomorphism*], which, as can be guessed from the title, takes place among poultry and other animals of the barnyard. Many Romanians today still know a few pornographic quatrains assigned to Eminescu.

The poems of Tudor Arghezi (1880–1967) created a stir by their audacity when they first appeared in *Flori de mucigai* [Flowers of Mildew] in 1931. The title recalls Baudelaire's *Fleurs du mal*, but the Romanian is bound rather to naturalism. Arghezi talks about the body in love, as in "Rada": "She unveiled, while jumping, / her black peony, and her sex, / like a box quickly opened and quickly closed, / that hides a jewel of blood." He speaks of the infernal desire of a monk in "Bitterness": "In his cell at the convent, his home, / a lively girl stayed late this night, / with her firm breasts, her fine thigh, / like a Florentine violine"; and speaks of transsexualism in "Hermaphrodite": "You are nearly like a pretty woman, / you, without hair on your face." The poetry of Arghezi is always very naturalistic, but very sensitive also. His language, although metaphorical, has a certain nakedness, audacity, and sincerity, while his eroticism is bound to the sensations and to a sort of aesthetic intelligence of the world. All is picturesque and instinctual, and eroticism can be found everywhere, even in prison, in the dreams of the prisoners. His poetry and, to a lesser extent, his prose are also bound to the aesthetic of the ugly, having its origins in the conceptions of Baudelaire. The sensuality of the texts of Arghezi aren't predicated upon beauty—his characters are sometimes marked by infirmity and an erogenous zone which intermixes normalcy and the pathological.

A true bombshell was Geo Bogza's (1908–1993) *Jurnal de sex şi Poemul invectivă* [*Diary of Sex and the Insult Poem*] (1933). From the beginning, Bogza was linked to the Romanian avant-garde, and this volume constituted a protest against convention, against the bourgeois blandness of society and its hypocritical customs:

> I write this poem on you, to infuriate the bourgeois girls, / To shock their honorable parents, / Although I turned up them several times, this daughter, / I don't want to praise them, / I want to urinate in their face powder, / on their intimate lingerie, / in their piano, /

and in all these artifacts that their beauty make ... / and, like a challenging smile / thrown against the continentes / the abuses perpetrate themselves / under the ice finger / of the future prophets. ("Offending Poem")

Bogza's is poetry of protest and, at the same time, pornographic poetry, of fetishism, rape, and sexual perversion. When he wrote of a woman who used cucumbers to masturbate, a scandal ensued that brought the young poet before the bar of justice. And only after a terrifying press campaign was the case dismissed.

Nichita Stănescu (1933–1983) was one of the most important Romanian poets due to his innovations in the use of language, his particular lyricism, his philosophy, and his poems of love, well in tune with the sensitivity of the young generation of the 1960s. To this slightly pantheistic eroticism, but for a general readership, he added a new volume of poems, *Argotice*. These are the texts of his student youth, full of vivid expressions and an overflowing imagination and sprinkled with visions concocted for their shock value. One senses the development of a great poet, a future candidate for the Nobel Prize. The strength of his poetry recalls that of Arghezi.

Similar to the style of Stănescu, slang is also used by Gheorghe Astaloş (b. 1933) in his remarkable work *Pe muchie de şuriu* [*Over the Edge of the Knife*] (1999). Astaloş was the first to give a programmatic artistic turn to slang in Romanian poetry, while writing twelve long works that combine the rules of classic prosody with the incendiary topic of carnal love. Following Astaloş's traces, Liviu Vişan (b. 1953) created a poetry that employs military slang, e.g., *Licenţioase* [*Libertine Poems*] (2001).

The voluptuous rhymes of Emil Brumaru (b. 1939) make of the erotic game a domestic ritual and a dreamlike escape, on the boundary between the romantic imagination and surrealist paranoia, in such works as *Detectivul Arthur* [*The Detective Arthur*] (1970), *Julien Ospitalierul* [*Julien the Hospitalier*] (1974), *Dulapul îndrăgostit* [*The Wardrobe in Love*] (1980), *Ruina unui samovar* [*The Decrepitude of a Samovar*] (1983), and *Dintr-o scorbură de morcov* [*From a Carrot's Hollow*] (1998). Often his racy dreaming employs characters with names of well-known actresses, but Brumaru's most successful poems are those dedicated to his wife, Tamara, from whence the nickname of these verses, "Tamarettes": "If Apollinaire sang the pussy of Lou, / Tamariushka, what could I sing you? / Your peach wrapped in dew and pepper, / Guarded by an angel with the trembling spear?"

Nina Cassian (b. 1924) is a poet who conveys her erotic impulses with a special talent for resonance. Marian Popa, in *History of Romanian Literature*, defines her as a "Bach of the sensations," cultivating seductive and compelling diabolism. Among her volumes are *Sângele*, [*Blood*] (1966), *Ambitus* (1969), and *Marea Conjugare* [*The Big Conjugation*] (1971).

With Marta Petreu (b. 1955), Romanian erotic poetry in the 1990s became settled under feminine domination. *Poeme neruşinate* [*Shameless Poems*] (1993) seems like the expression of an unlimited fantasy that was the mark of the so-called Generation '90. It also signaled (according to Radu Voinescu in *Today's Feminine Literature*) an intellectual pleasure in eroticism reduced to toying with ideas. *Falanga* [*The Phalanx*] (1998) pushes eroticism to an intense sensuality where carnal love is combined with a sort of mystical devotion.

Thus dominated by female poets, Romanian erotic poetry has become an emancipation of imagination. Much like a new avant-garde, the literary mentality of the 1990s had as its goal indulgence and enjoyment, an exhibitionism certainly driving toward the affirmation of a total freedom. Rodica Draghincescu (b. 1962) tells hitherto inconceivable stories about her experiences, in which a literate woman can valorize and describe her erotic life. She evokes the most intimate places of the body and the most physiological moments of the sexual act and desire, as in her most interesting work, *Obiect de lux ascuţit pe ambele părţi* [*Object of Luxury Sharpened by Its Two Edges*] (1997).

Floarea Ţuţuianu represents a hermetic eroticism, crossed by sexual symbols and impregnated with cultural but very sensual allusions: "I am naked among artists, / I want to be myself, without success, / I speak in the hose of the ear of Mr. Manet, / and together we take lunch on the grass" ("The Lunch on The Grass"). Her creations are very spiritualized, yet keep the essential note of limitless sincerity in a language that is sometimes cruel. In the volumes *Femeia peşte* [*Woman-Fish*] (1996), *Libresse oblige* (1998), *Leul Marcu* [*Mark the Lion*] (2000) her literature makes use of cruel expressions that still remain touching and retain a mysterious charm. It speaks of a femininity lived to its maximal intensity with lucidity and rationality. With *Rochia nesupunerii* [*The Dress of Rebelliousness*] (2001), Paulina Popa shows evidence of a very strong courage to deliver experiences at times abstract, at times concrete, that proclaim their authenticity filtered by poetic culture. Her fashionable style of writing is bound to make proselytes.

As for Romanian erotic prose, the short novel of Bogdan Petriceicu Hasdeu (1836–1907), *Duduca Mamuca* [*Lady Mamuca*] (1863) can be considered its beginning. In it, a young student seduces a girl of sixteen years. The seducer's tricks result in the girls mother falling in love as well. In bed one night, the student looks for his Lolita in the darkness but instead finds the mother and, of course, the delights of love with a well-versed lady. Conceived as a narrative on the erotic tribulations of the characters, the novel also stands against the stereotypes of romanticism of which it represents a true caricature. Hasdeu was indicted for immorality and had to answer to the court. Initially, he lost the case and had to give up his teaching post and pay a large fine; then, he was acquitted and published a new version, *Micuţa* [*The Flapper*] (1864), from which he had eliminated the obscene fragments while keeping the progress of the plot and writing a preface declaiming to the ladies and damsels that his book was meant to alert them to the sly tricks of men. The preface is signed "Doctor Artis Amandi," Doctor in the art of love.

A short story in the style of popular literature, *Păcat* [*The Sin*] (1892) by I.L. Caragiale (1852–1912), questions incestuous love. A village priest has a son with a widow, then gets married (Orthodox law obliges priests to marry) and has a girl. As a widower, many years later, he brings the bastard into his house and observes that there is a sexual attraction between his son and his daughter. The priest explains to his daughter that they are siblings, but she doesn't take this into account. Finally, the father kills the two lovers.

An important symbolist poet, Alexandru Macedonski (1854–1920) was also a prose writer. His short story *Thalassa*, which appeared posthumously in an anthology named *Cartea de aur* [*The Golden Book*] (1975), is a tale of unbridled sensualism and exoticism. On an island, separated from the civilized world, two youngsters grow up together and in adolescence discover physical love. Their innocence makes the narrative and the description of their passion more exciting.

Ion Minulescu (1881–1944) is well known as a symbolistic poet. But he also wrote a very hardcore novel, *Roşu, galben şi albastru* [*Red, Yellow, and Blue*] (the colors of the Romanian flag) (1924). During the First World War, behind the lines of defense in Iassy and far from the tragedy of combat, the hero, a young man who has well-placed connections, is sheltered as an adjutant at army headquarters. He thus has many amorous adventures with the wives of the officers who are fighting in the front lines in combat. Minulescu writes as a great hedonist, and his ironic tone is very caustic.

A poet, fiction writer, and authority on Romanian medicine, Victor Papilian (1888–1956) wrote *Decameronul românesc* [*A Romanian Decameron*] between the two world wars, although it was not published until in 1996. These tales are replete with husbands and wives cheating on each other, in *imbroglios* that may pose many moral problems but which clear the way for the characters to have fun and to find happiness in the moment. The narratives are not told by different characters, as in Boccacio's work, but by the author, who, at the finale of each tale, reestablishes the order that had been briefly disturbed by the piquant misadventures.

With the novels *Maidanul cu dragoste* [*The Waste Ground with Love*] (1933) and *Sfânta mare neruşinare* [*The Big Holy Impurity*] (1935), G.M. Zamfirescu (1898–1939) shows himself to be one of the most important Romanian erotic novelists. The suburbs of Bucharest offer the topics and heroes. Child love, sadomasochism, rape, prostitution hide no secrets from the astonished reader, who is surprised on every page by the novelist's overflowing invention and his taste for the violence of the instincts, for matings sometimes brutal, sometimes sophisticated. The two novels in fact make a single work, the characters of the first being found in the second, with new sexual feats. Zamfirescu is probably the Marquis de Sade of Romanian literature.

Village customs are explored by Zaharia Stancu (1902–1974), such as love among the peasants, their barbaric customs, the dance with the bride's bloody shirt after the wedding night, the sexual initiations of teenagers by aged women, adultery and its punishment, the sexual abuses or seduction that the boyars practice on farmer's daughters, as in *Desculţ* [*Barefoot*] (1948).

One of the most important historians of religion, Mircea Eliade (1907–1986) was at the same time a very important novelist. Concerning love, his writings revive some old myths and use archaic patterns about the mystery of the union between man and woman. In *Isabel şi apele diavolului* [*Isabel and the Waters of the Devil*] (1930), he is an apologist for the orgiastic atmosphere, where the heterosexual couples use the practices of the *Kama Sutra* and have "artificial unions," in which one makes love with someone while thinking about another. *Maitreyi* (1933) purports to tell the real-life experience of the young author as a student in India with a girl of the *kshatryia,* or military, caste, the real-life Maitreyi Devi (who later wrote a book of her own to rebut the fiction of Eliade). This forbidden love is very ardent and is conceived of as a ritual of initiation, with the secret encounters between the two lovers in the night having a mystical quality. *Domnişoara Christina* [*Miss Christine*] (1936) is a fantastic narrative in which the heroine is a girl who dies, becomes a vampire who threatens with her deadly erotic fascination, and makes love with living youngsters. *Pe strada Mântuleasa* [*On Mantuleasa Street*] (1968) is a narrative with some elements of a thriller. One of the two narrative lines looks at the destiny of an uncommon girl, Oana. She is physically very big gigantic and copulates with the shepherds in the Carpathian Mountains each night, but is insatiable and finds a fabulous bull for her sexual pleasure, like a new Pasiphae. Finally, she marries a young professor from Lithuania who is as big as she, and they make a beautiful pair.

Three of the novels of Eugen Barbu (1924–1993) are endowed with an intense eroticism. *Groapa* [*The Hole*] (1957) relates the stories of people who live as outsiders or outcasts from society. Theirs is an amoral world that lives, apparently, for only two goals: to have no attachments and to satisfy its sexual desires. *Princepele* [*The Prince*] (1969) demonstrates a rare sophistication in the scenes of erotica and lovemaking. One of the more accomplished scenes is during an orgy, in which several friends practice sodomy with a fish. *Săptămâna nebunilor* [*The Week of The Incane*] (1981) is a story of

lost love between a young prince from Wallachia and a woman of the Venetian aristocracy. The evocation of the luxury and pleasures of Venice in the middle of nineteenth century is saturated by the memories of adventures of love and of sick, sad, and perverse associations.

Vasile Voiculescu (1884–1963) wrote many short stories about love and magic and about sexual abnormality. *Vaca năzdrăvană* [*The Magic Cow*] tells of the strange behavior of a cow. The narrator discovers that the animal receives daily, far from prying eyes, sex from a gypsy. *Sakuntala* [*Sakuntala*] describes an orgy among gypsies. *Zahei orbul* [*Zakey the Blind*] tells of the customs of homosexuals in jail. Marin Mincu (b. 1944) is a critic who also writes prose. His four-volume novel *Intermezzo* (1984–1997) is a postmodernist text which has elements of experimentalism. The author narrates adventures with many women with frankness and frequently even with great pleasure, as a postmodern Casanova. An essayist interested in erotic themes and armed with a vast libertine culture, Luca Piţu (b. 1947) has written *Eros, Doxa and Logos* (1995).

RADU VOINESCU

Further Reading

Călinescu, G. *Istoria literaturii române de la origini până în prezent* [History of Romanian Literature from the Origins Until Today]. Bucureşti, 1982.

Călinescu, G., E. Petrovici, and A. Rosetti. *Istoria literaturii române* [History of Romanian Literature] 1–2. Bucureşti, 1964–1968.

Cioculescu, Şerban, Ovidiu Papadima, and A. Piru. *Istoria literaturii române* [History of Romanian Literature] 3. Bucureşti, 1973.

Crohmălniceanu, Ovid S. *Istoria literaturii române între cele două războaie mondiale* [History of Romanian Literature Between the Two World Wars]. 3 vols. Bucureşti, 1971, 1974, 1975.

Micu, Dumitru. *Scurtă istorie a literaturii române* [A Short History of Romanian Literature] 1–2. Bucureşti, 1995.

Haneş, Petre V. *Histoire de la littérature roumaine* [History of Romanian Literature]. Paris, 1934.

Popa, Marian. *Istoria literaturii române între 23 august 1944–22 decembrie 1989* [History of Romanian Literature Between 23 August 1944 and 22 December 1989] 1–2. Bucureşti, 2001.

RONSARD, PIERRE DE

1524–1585
French poet

Pierre de Ronsard's love poetry was constantly revised and reclassified throughout his career, and his eventual resolve to place it at the head of his *Oeuvres complètes* signifies an admission that it formed his greatest achievement. It divides into three main sequences, the first being *Premier livre des amours*, now often called the *Amours de Cassandre*. This anthology reflects the classical preoccupations of the Coqueret period, with Petrarch as its clearest influence. Hence the emotions expressed reflect standard patterns of intense admiration and desire of the loved one, contrasting a sadness and frustration at her inaccessibility. Ronsard may well have chosen the name Cassandre for its classical associations rather than because he knew (and might have loved) the real Cassandra Salviati, and the poems often read better as exercises in rhetoric than as investigations of the psychology of love. Conversely he will also apply the Platonist topos whereby love elevates the soul to an experience of ideal rather than mortal beauty, whilst elsewhere describing his persona's erotic fantasies, his straying hands, and a franker admiration of Cassandre's body than one tends to find in Petrarch himself.

These latter themes become more frequent in the *Second livre des amours* [*Amours de Marie*], fewer of which are in sonnet form, and in which the intellectual input is diminished, even if classical influences (including Catullus, Tibullus, and Propertius) remain strong. In partial imitation of their work, the persona and Marie enjoy intimate relations, often in a rural setting. They kiss more often, sleep together, and share playful and bantering exchanges, as a teasing lightheartedness develops at the expense of Petrarchism's more tortured emotions. The *Second livre* concludes with a series of poems on Marie's death, a reversion to Petrarchism which came much later in his career.

The third major sequence, the *Sonnets pour Hélène*, was published at the same time as the verses *Sur la mort de Marie* (i.e., in 1578, in the fifth edition of his complete works), and they certainly constitute his most original, and arguably his richest collection. Petrarchism returns, but with an added psychological realism, for the predominant theme is the love of an older man for a woman much his junior, both represented as members of the royal court. Though one cannot reliably identify the intelligent if not overwhelmingly beautiful Hélène with Hélène de Surgères, a real acquaintance of Ronsard and lady-in-waiting to Catherine de Médicis, this collection explores, not without some irony, the vicissitudes and embarrassments of an incompatible relationship, as the somewhat infirm and certainly aging persona appraises rather than worships his mistress, criticizing her for her Platonist beliefs which deny the physical pleasures of which he fantasizes whilst in reality doing no more than touching or kissing her hand. As Ronsard situates the martial imagery of the love lyric in the genuine context of France's Religious Wars, rounds on Cupid and love as irrelevant to a period of national crisis (Charles IX's death affected him greatly), and finally abandons the relationship with Hélène as unworkable and unworthy, so he achieves something unique in French Renaissance verse.

When responding to Protestant charges of paganism and hedonism, Ronsard frankly admitted (again in a poem), "J'ayme à faire l'amour, j'ayme à parler aux femmes," however a biographical reading of his love poetry remains problematic: the smaller collection of *Sonnets pour Astrée* and the poems on the death of Marie were certainly based on emotions and experiences not his own, and may even have been written on command. What is certain is his intense interest in amorous themes as a wellspring of literary inspiration and creativity. Feeding on a profound and authentic appreciation of classical literature, and ranging from bawdy sonnets on the penis and vagina up to the complex mythography of the *Hymnes*, Ronsard's erotic poetry achieves a matchless variety of form, depth, and expression.

Biography

Born in 1524, the youngest son of a minor nobleman from the province of Vendôme, Pierre de Ronsard became the major poet of the French Renaissance, displaying a talent unequaled at least until the nineteenth century. After periods spent as a page and courtier he gained a classical education in the late 1540s and rallied to the Brigade (later called the Pléiade), a group of scholar-poets led and tutored by Jean Dorat at the Parisian Collège de Coqueret. His early output of neo-classical odes and Petrarchan sonnets betrayed strong humanist influences coupled with an extravagant sense of his own literary importance, but his output spread rapidly beyond Dorat's academic program to finally include, alongside his uncompleted epic (the *Franciade*) and his didactic poetry entitled the *Hymnes*, some polemical verse written during the early Religious Wars, various miscellanies including the lighthearted *Folastries*, whose eroticism is naive and outspoken, plus the sonnet cycles for which he is now most famous. Once he reverted to a more traditional, easier literary style, his standing at court rose rapidly, until by the late 1550s he was acknowledged as its official poet. Greater fame and wealth were to follow in Catherine de Médicis's regency and the reign of Charles IX (1560–1574), during which period, paradoxically, he may have encountered a weakening in his inspiration perhaps not unconnected with the parlous state of his country and its monarchy. The death of Charles IX led to a change of cultural regime as the new king Henri III brought in other favorites, which factor, along with increasing ill health, caused Ronsard to spend much time away from the court. However, notwithstanding these vicissitudes, he continued to produce new material, usually compiled into successive editions of his complete works, and his talent certainly burgeoned again with the later sonnets, including some dictated on his deathbed. A tonsured cleric, Ronsard never married, though his religious benefices guaranteed him considerable wealth. The adult years were afflicted by severe deafness and his old age by gout. He was buried in the small priory of St. Cosme, near Tours, but his memorial service took place in Paris to great pomp and ceremony.

JOHN PARKIN

Editions

Oeuvres complètes. Edited by J. Céard and D. Ménager. Paris; Bibliothèque de la Pléiade, 1994.

Pierre de Ronsard: Selected Poems. Translated by M. Quainton and E. Vinestock. London: Penguin Books, 2002.

Poems of Pierre de Ronsard. Translated and edited by N. Kilmer. Berkeley and Los Angeles: University of California Press, 1979.

Further Reading

Armstrong, E. *Ronsard and the Age of Gold.* Cambridge, UK: Cambridge University Press, 1968.

Bishop, M. *Ronsard, Prince of Poets.* Ann Arbor: University of Michigan Press, 1940.

Cave, T., ed. *Ronsard the Poet.* London: Methuen, 1973.

Cohen, G. *Ronsard: Sa vie et son oeuvre.* Paris: Gallimard, 1956.

Gadoffre, G. *Ronsard.* Paris: Seuil, 1994.

Gendre, A. *L'Esthétique de Ronsard.* Paris: SEDES, 1997.

Quainton, M. *Ronsard's Ordered Chaos.* Manchester, UK: Manchester University Press, 1980.

Simonin, M. *Pierre de Ronsard.* Paris: Fayard, 1990.

ROQUÉ, ANA

1853–1933
Puerto Rican novelist and journalist

Roqué's only novel and most important work of fiction is *Luz y sombra* [*Light and Shadow*] (1903). An epistolary novel, it follows the lives of two young friends: Matilde, who marries for love and settles in the countryside, and Julia, who marries for money and social position and hopes to shine in San Juan's upper-class society. It is an avowedly feminist novel about sexual mores in Puerto Rico's patriarchal planter society at the turn of the twentieth century. Not surprisingly, given its provocative conclusions, it was greeted by Puerto Rican critics with absolute silence, a significant fact on an island where every new publication was widely discussed in the press.

At the center of the plot of *Luz y sombra* is a tale of adultery. While Matilde finds true happiness in her bucolic country retreat despite the death of her child, Julia discovers very quickly that her husband's sexual indifference toward her is at the root of her unhappiness. Having discovered sexual pleasure following her marriage, and finding this pleasure denied to her, she seeks love and admiration from a friend of her husband's with whom she was smitten on the very day of her wedding. The potential lovers' passion is discovered by the husband when it is on the verge of being consummated and prompts from him an acknowledgment of his own guilt in not fulfilling his wife's sexual needs and a promise of greater passion and attention from then on. The eloquent plea for understanding that women's nature is not different than that of men despite society's higher expectations of modesty and purity from women is delivered, surprisingly, by Matilde, Julia's highly conventional friend. The novel ends with the deaths of both Julia and her husband—a death expected given the nature of her transgression and his unprecedented forgiveness—but not before their unconventional tale has given Roqué the opportunity to advance a thesis that was clearly revolutionary at the time.

Roqué's contribution to erotic literature in *Luz y sombra* is rooted in the realistic and detailed portrayal of a young woman's sexual frustration and in Roqué's powerful arguments for societal understanding of women's sexual needs in marriage. The novel's controversial premise led to its being essentially erased from Puerto Rican literary history until the last decade of the twentieth century, when a new edition was published.

Biography

Ana Roqué de Duprey, author, journalist, educator, and suffragist, was born in Puerto Rico. Orphaned at the age of four, she was raised by her father and grandmother, who took charge of her early education. A precocious child, she claimed to have learned to read and write by the age of three and a half and knew the fundamentals of grammar, math, and geography by the time she enrolled in school at the age of seven. She finished her formal education by the age of nine, having exhausted the resources of the local school, and continued to be schooled at home, studying piano, embroidery, and sewing with her grandmother and aunts, and math with her father. She returned to school at age eleven, as assistant to the teacher and, at the age of thirteen had founded her own private school, teaching students often older than herself. She wrote a geography textbook for her school, which was later published, and became known for her accomplishments in literature, foreign languages, astronomy, botany, geography, philosophy, musical composition, and history.

In 1872, Roqué married Luis E. Duprey, a sugar plantation owner, with whom she had five children, three of whom survived. Financial troubles following the emancipation of slaves forced them to move to San Juan, where she continued to develop her scholarly interests and became the first woman to join the Ateneo Puertorriqueño, a cultural and scholarly organization. In addition to her scholarly interests, she was one of the first Puerto Rican adherents to Allan Kardec's theories of Spiritualism and communication with the dead through mediums.

Roqué's marriage did not long survive the couple's financial troubles and she began teaching again as a way to support herself and her children. Her career as educator lasted 30 years, mostly in schools that she founded and directed, among them Colegio Mayagüezano and Liceo Ponceño, which continue as thriving institutions today. She established a normal school in San Juan, considered one of the best centers dedicated to the education of women, and was instrumental in the creation of the University of Puerto Rico.

In 1888, Roque began publishing fiction in magazines and newspapers, which she later collected in *Pasatiempos* [*Entertainments*] (1894) and *Novelas y Cuentos* [*Novellas and Short Stories*] (1895). Around the same period, she also began her work as a suffragist. Her writings and activism were an integral part of the history of feminism in Puerto Rico. In 1917 she established the Liga Feminista Puertorriqueña and in 1924 the Asociación de Mujeres Sufragistas.

She founded several newspapers and magazines devoted to women's issues and used the production of these to train women in the printing trades. Roqué became the honorary president of the Liberal Party of Puerto Rico and received an honorary doctorate from the University of Puerto Rico. In 1929, her efforts were rewarded when the right to vote was granted to women who could read and write. Ironically, Roqué was unable to cast a valid vote in the first elections in which literate women were allowed to vote, as she was found not to be properly registered as a voter. Voting rights for all women did not become law until 1935, two years after Roqué's death.

LIZABETH PARAVISINI-GEBERT

Edition

Roqué, Ana. *Luz y sombra*. Edited by Lizabeth Paravisini-Gebert. Río Piedras: Universidad de Puerto Rico, 1991.

Further Reading

Chen Sham, Jorge. "Sanción moral y castigo: Contradicciones ideológicas en la narrativa de Ana Roqué." In *La voz de la mujer en la literatura hispanoamericana fin-de-siglo*, edited by Luis Jiménez, 167–80. San José: Universidad de Costa Rica, 1999.

Romero-Cesareo, Ivette. "Whose Legacy? Voicing Women's Rights from the 1870s to the 1930s." *Callaloo* 17 (1994): 770–89.

Roy-Fequiere, Magali. "Contested Territory: Puerto Rican Women, Creole Identity, and Intellectual Life in the Early Twentieth Century." *Callaloo* 17 (1994): 916–34.

ROSSETTI, ANA

1950–
Spanish poet, novelist, short story writer, dramatist, and librettist

In the male-oriented and highly literary poetry scene of early 1980s Spain, Ana Rossetti's poems broke new ground with their disruptive eroticism and ironic way with literary conventions. The poems' feminine-gendered voice explores intricate masturbatory fantasies, hints at incest, and revels in ironically lesbianism. Men are framed, manipulated, violated, elevated, and also reduced to icons: saints, sailors, boys in jeans and leather, mere pictures of desire. In the poems "A la puerta del cabaret" [At the Club Door] and "Chico Wrangler" [Wrangler Boy], the male's jeans-clad form is focused on, and, as in the essays in *Prendas íntimas* [Underwear], 1989, Rossetti displays a fascination with the erotic charge of single items of clothing or of accessories on bare flesh. In *Devocionario* [A Devotional] (1986)—a subversively erotic re-creation of the archetext of the fall and an imitation of saintly writings on temptation—this obsession is turned toward the paraphernalia of martyrdom and religious representations of Christ's body, creating a subversive juxtaposition, in the context of the strong Catholic culture of Rossetti's own childhood and of the instincts of spiritual purity and of sadomasochistic desire. Such tactics are further developed in the limited-edition collection of prints by Jorge Artajo and poems by Rossetti, *Virgo potens* [All-Powerful Virgin] (1994). This is a double-edged confession by a virgin who (proudly) accuses herself of causing the downfall of her confessor with her vivid descriptions of the desires and sensations coursing through her (for example, "the tangled swarms of hummingbirds" beneath her starched robes in Poem 4).

In 1991 Tusquets Editores' well-known series of erotic texts "La sonrisa vertical" [The Vertical Smile] published Rossetti's collection of eight stories, *Alevosías* [Betrayals]. The first story, "Del diablo y sus hazañas" [Of the Devil and his Works], is written in the falsely naive voice of a pubescent boy, Buba, whose initiation begins with fantasies constructed around his older female cousin Nela's breasts, in motion like "giant jellyfish" on a train journey, and of her "front bottom," glimpsed during a bedtime cuddle; it moves on to masturbation—taking the "devil" in his hand, and making him "spit" into the holy water by his bed headboard—and finally to "sucking the devil out" of Fred, his older cousin. In the second story, a frigid virgin dreams of watching her sister having prolonged and intricate sex with a stranger, recalls her thrill as a child at helping her sister break her hymen with a stick of candy, and resolves, on waking, to break her own with the heel of her shoe, prior to a casual encounter of her own, thus opening up the connection back to her sister. Childhood as a time of delightful, perverse sexual education had been a constant theme in the poems and, more extensively, in an essay on leather and sex shops in *Prendas íntimas* (113–23). Here, watching DeMille epics during Lent as a schoolgirl is seen as having laid down a rich bed of fantasies about torture, torsos, straps, muscles, and harnesses. All this leaves a mark on the stories of *Alevosías* in particular: in "La cara oculta del amor" [The Hidden Face of Love] a woman confides in a friend that she has been brutally half-raped by her lover, whose violence is fueled by his own fantasies of bondage, whipping, and rape—but the friend turns out to be projecting onto the two of them his own sadomasochistic fantasies; in *Et ne nos inducas* [And Lead Us Not] a novice in the confessional reviews his sin (lusting after choirboys), recalls the in-itself lascivious language of admonition (how "the trunks of ivy which are Babylon's thighs" will strangle the sinner: 117), and submits, naked, to flagellation by his almost equally young confessor.

Rossetti's dominant vocabulary is of moisture, tingling flesh, and tremors of ecstasy and surrender. The scent, texture, and structure of flowers refer to the body in arousal. Bee stings, lava, and fire condensing in the scrotum assault the novice in "*Et ne nos inducas*"; in "La noche de los enamorados" [Lovers' Eve] (2002) a spell cast by a woman on St. John's Eve causes the death of her tiresomely fixated lover but backfires when his spirit—as lustful and thrusting as his body was in life—enters her as "a hurricane of roses" (123). The density of this postmodern baroque language has its own erotic purposes: it stimulates sense and imagination, but it also teases and diverts, delaying narrative closure, dwelling on what would otherwise be passing pleasures, blurring the definitions of gender, preference, and anatomical form. It is also frequently leavened with wit. "La vengadora," in *Alevosías*, adopts the sardonic tone and turns of phrase of the woman some way into her marriage facing the twin facts that "when a man turns off the tap, he turns it off" and that "what seemed to her as inert as . . . a fossil is in fact a snail which is perfectly able to wave its lubricious antennae about elsewhere in search of stimuli" (161). "Dedicado a tus plantas" [Dedicated to Your Feet] is an extended, vicariously homoerotic, pedophiliac fantasy involving a muscular young artist, a gay gallery owner, and a less than bright protagonist smitten by the former and in futile love with the latter. The artist's unlikely participation as a barefoot penitent in a Holy Week procession and Lela's discovery—in a state of quasi-spiritual ecstasy—of his discarded boots on the church altar nicely and mischievously link erotic and religious archetypes in a manner typical of this key literary figure of the late twentieth century in Spain.

Biography

Born in San Fernando (Cadiz Province, southwestern Spain), Rossetti first gained fame as a poet. Her first novel, *Plumas de España* [Flamboyant Spain] was published in 1988 and she has written and performed for various theatre companies, in 1993 writing the libretto for the opera *El secreto enamorado* [The Secret Lover], on Oscar Wilde. She is a regular reader of her work at public events and on air.

CHRIS PERRIAM

Selected Works

"La sortija y el sortilegio." In *Cuentos eróticos*, edited by Paloma Díaz-Mas et al., 1988
Prendas íntimas: El tejido de la seducción, 1989
Indicios vehementes [Signs of Vehemence]. 2nd ed., 1990
Alevosías, 1991
"Dedicado a tus plantas." In *Verte desnudo*, edited by Lourdes Ortiz, 1992
Recuento: Cuentos completos, 2001
"La noche de los enamorados." In *Cuentos eróticos de verano*, edited by Ana Estevan, 2002

Further Reading

Keefe Ugalde, Sharon. "Subversión y revisionismo en la poesía de Ana Rossetti, Concha García, Juana Castro, y Andrea Luca." In *Novísimos, posnovísimos, clásicos: La poesía de los 80 en España*, edited by Biruté Ciplijauskaité. Madrid: Origenes. 1990.
Perriam, Chris. "Jugar, exceder, perder: poemas de Ana Rossetti de los 80 y de los 90." In *Ludismo*

e intertextualidad en la lírica moderna, edited by T.J. Dadson and D. Flitter. Birmingham, UK: University of Birmingham Press, 1997.

Sherno, Sylvia. "Ana Rossetti, o el jardín del deseo erótico." In *Del franquismo a la posmodernidad:* *Cultura española 1975–1990*, edited by José B. Monleón. Madrid: Ediciones Akal, 1995.

Wilcox, John C. *Women Poets of Spain, 1860–1990: Toward a Gynocentric Vision*. Urbana, IL: University of Illinois Press, 1997.

ROTH, PHILIP

1933–

US novelist and short story writer

Philip Roth is the author of more than twenty books as well as essays, reviews, short fiction, and interviews conducted with other writers. His writing has experimented with many forms, from satire and parable to autobiography and memoir, from realism to postmodernism. Roth has challenged not only conventions concerning the representation of erotic life but also customary distinctions between the modes of fiction and nonfiction.

Subjectivity and intimate relations have provided his subject matter. Roth's work examines the intersections between selfhood and history, with special attention to the problems posed to the male subject by cultural constructions of masculinity, embodiment, male sexuality, and Jewish American identity. Roth's characters often displace their desire for autonomous selfhood into the erotic, and his fiction grows sexually explicit when, through illicit behavior, they resist the regulation of their identities. The erotic life Roth represents therefore signifies several conflicts: the male's social and psychoanalytic repression within a culture that at once constrains him to act morally and encourages a transgressive view of manliness; the subject's inevitable objectification by its own erotic desires; and the deceptions and self-deceptions inherent in the pursuit of desire. Roth has viewed eros through the travails of the Rothian body—typically male and Jewish—not in order to question the ethics of the erotic or to subvert cultural prohibitions against erotic performance but to illuminate the ontological implications of eroticism inevitably situated within a time and place.

No stranger to controversy, Roth in his first book, *Goodbye, Columbus*, offered stories that elicited fierce reactions among some postwar Jewish readers who feared that his unflinching comic portraits would expose American Jews to anti-Semitism. Not until the notorious *Portnoy's Complaint* ten years later, however, did Roth find a truly taboo-breaking voice and a liberating mode of representation to express the condition he called in the novel, following Freud, the "degradation in erotic life." *Portnoy's Complaint* broke ground for its unfettered language, slangy and obscene—with chapters titled, for example, "Cunt Crazy" and "Whacking Off"—as well as for its graphic descriptions of phallic sex and its book-length howl of dismay about the bondage of the self. Shaped, like much of Roth's work, by a psychoanalytic view of instinctual repression, *Portnoy's Complaint* makes Freud's influence visible in its narrative frame, within which Alexander Portnoy recounts his busy history of sexual exploits to an analyst. The anguished first-person confession was so convincing that many readers failed to distinguish Roth from his creation.

Portnoy enters therapy complaining of impotence, caught between the urge to be a "Jewboy" and the call to be a "nice Jewish boy" (*Reading Myself:* 35). His appetites run from compulsive masturbation, presented in hilariously humiliating scenes, to disastrous, objectifying sexual relationships with women whom he desires because they are not Jewish, "as though through fucking I will discover America. *Conquer* America." Portnoy feels himself the butt of a "Jewish joke," as he labors under the yoke of a superego displaced from his mother, whose smothering, Oedipal presence causes him at last to cry that he wants to "put the id back in Yid!" Shocking to some readers, the novel became an American cultural event, bringing the title into common parlance as a shorthand reference to sexual liberation from the social repressiveness of the United States in the 1950s.

The range and continuity of Roth's investigations into the degradations of erotic life are suggested by four other representative novels. Three center around the same protagonist and variously prolong the primal scream that closes *Portnoy's Complaint*. In the Kafkaesque parable of *The Breast* (1972), David Kepesh metamorphoses into a six-foot mammary gland. Thrust to the border not only of the "human" but of gender, Kepesh discloses the limitations of the cultural construction of a male/female bipolarity that cannot account for sexual desire. The intense arousal of his nipple, which has replaced his penis, cannot bring him to climax but becomes an obsessive desire as the only "human" pleasure remaining to him. In charting Kepesh's efforts to repress desire in the face of physical abjection, Roth defines "the human" as the confluence of the erotic drive and the will to control it.

Published five years later, *The Professor of Desire* (1977) offers background to *The Breast*, depicting Kepesh's conflict between sexual cravings and impotence imposed by an ethic of restraint. He seeks after objects of desire—including a "good girl"/"bad girl" pairing of women in a youthful ménage à trois—to define his masculinity in terms of erotic power, only to find himself feminized, hysterical, plagued with guilt, and bemoaning the "totalitarianism" of the desiring body. The novel closes with the juxtaposed images of punishment, figured as castration, and succor, in the nostalgic clinging to a lover's breast, ironically foreshadowing Kepesh's fate in *The Breast*. When Roth resurrects Kepesh, no longer a breast, in *The Dying Animal* (2001), the totalitarianism of the body is redefined in relation to aging and mortality. Roth uncovers the naked narcissism in masculine desire that willingly objectifies women and that persists long after the beauty or potency of the flesh. Thrilled by the "radical destabilization" that is the "chaos of eros," Kepesh in his sixties confronts in the fetishized but diseased breast of his youthful conquest a reminder of his own impending abjection.

The prospect of decay likewise motivates the furious exploits of a death-haunted libertine in *Sabbath's Theater* (1995). Framed by Mickey Sabbath's extravagant liaisons with his voracious mistress and his later visits to masturbate and urinate on her grave, the novel traces Sabbath's antic, self-defining acts as a phallic subject whose masculinist ideology is demystified by the treachery of the aging body. The novel punishes Sabbath for displacing Freudian thanatos into pure id and a will to power, but Roth allows him at last, in a Rabelaisian performance of selfhood, to celebrate both the dying body and the erotic life force. The paradoxical view of the erotic in *Sabbath's Theater* as a sign of both human frailty and the power of the human subject stands for Roth's career-long appreciation of the opportunities desire offers for self-invention, his acknowledgment of the wages of desire, and his refusal to censure the desiring subject.

Biography

Born March 19, Newark, New Jersey. Attended Newark College, Rutgers University 1950–51, Bucknell University for BA 1951–54; University of Chicago, MA, 1955 and further study 1956–57. Married Margaret Martinson Williams, 1959 (separated, 1963); married actress Claire Bloom, 1990 (divorced, 1994); no children. Taught at universities from 1956 to 1980, most notably as writer-in-residence at the University of Pennsylvania, 1965–80. Received a National Book Award for his first book, *Goodbye, Columbus* (1959), and subsequently received numerous other literary prizes, including the National Book Critics Circle Award (1986 and 1991), the PEN/Faulkner Award (1993), another National Book Award (1995), and the Pulitzer Prize in Fiction (1997).

DEBRA SHOSTAK

Selected Works

Goodbye, Columbus, and Five Short Stories. 1959
Letting Go. 1962
When She Was Good. 1967
Portnoy's Complaint. 1969
"On the Air." 1970
The Breast. 1972
My Life as a Man. 1974
Reading Myself and Others. 1975
The Professor of Desire. 1977
The Ghost Writer. 1979

Zuckerman Bound. 1981
The Anatomy Lesson. 1983
The Prague Orgy. 1985
The Counterlife. 1986
The Facts: A Novelist's Autobiography. 1988
Deception. 1990
Operation Shylock: A Confession. 1993
Sabbath's Theater. 1995
American Pastoral. 1997
I Married a Communist. 1998
The Human Stain. 2000
The Dying Animal. 2001

Further Reading

Biale, David. *Eros and the Jews: From Biblical Israel to Contemporary America.* Berkeley and Los Angeles, CA: University of California Press, 1997.

Baumgarten, Murray, and Barbara Gottfried. *Understanding Philip Roth.* Columbia, SC: University of South Carolina Press, 1990.

Brooks, Peter. *Body Work: Objects of Desire in Modern Narrative.* Cambridge (MA) and London: Harvard University Press, 1993.

Cooper, Alan. *Philip Roth and the Jews.* Albany, NY: State University of New York Press, 1996.

Gilman, Sander. *The Jew's Body.* New York and London: Routledge, 1991.

Halio, Jay. *Philip Roth Revisited.* New York: Twayne, 1992.

Kelleter, Frank. "Portrait of the Sexist as a Dying Man: Death, Ideology, and the Erotic in Philip Roth's *Sabbath's Theater.*" *Contemporary Literature* 39 (1998): 262–302.

Lee, Hermione. *Philip Roth.* London and New York: Methuen, 1982.

Milbauer, Asher Z., and Donald G. Watson, eds. *Reading Philip Roth.* New York: St. Martin's Press, 1988.

Pinsker, Sanford, ed. *Critical Essays on Philip Roth.* Boston, MA: G.K. Hall, 1982.

Schehr, Lawrence R. "Fragments of a Poetics: Bonnetain and Roth." In *Solitary Pleasures: The Historical, Literary, and Artistic Discourses of Autoeroticism,* edited by Paula Bennett and Vernon A. Rosario II. New York and London: Routledge, 1995.

Searles, George J., ed. *Conversations with Philip Roth,* Jackson and London: University Press of Mississippi, 1992.

Shostak, Debra. "Roth/CounterRoth: Postmodernism, the Masculine Subject, and *Sabbath's Theater.*" *Arizona Quarterly* 54/3 (1998): 119–42.

RUIZ, JUAN

1282?–1349?
Spanish poet

El libro de buen amor

Possibly composed sometime between 1325 and 1345, this narrative poem is a masterpiece of medieval Spanish literature. The title of the work is posthumous, assigned to it in the late nineteenth century. Three manuscripts of the work survive, as well as a few isolated fragments. Numerous annotated editions are available today in several languages. This work is considered one of the most significant literary productions of the Spanish Middle Ages, and has given rise to a rigorous and ongoing critical discussion on questions of meaning, sources, and authorship.

A dynamic and engaging narrative poem written in several different meters and poetic styles of the period, *El libro de buen amor* centers on a number of amorous episodes in the poet's life as well as didactic, allegorical, and satirical pronouncements on other issues. The poem is narrated in the first person, and the poet is identified as the archpriest of Hita, Juan Ruiz. Basically episodic in structure without compromising an ultimate sense of unity, the poem incorporates a wide variety of topics, ranging from the clearly religious (prayers to the Virgin, didactic assertions) to the blatantly erotic (pursuit of women, descriptions of female anatomy). The structure of the poem discourages a coherent plot summary, for the episodes are not tied to one another primarily as functions of a linear plot. This is further emphasized by the continual insertions of fables, tales, and parodies which weave into and out of the first-person narrative at several junctures.

The work has inspired numerous interpretations, many of which have sought to throw light on the seemingly contradictory stances it takes toward physical love from alternating secular and religious standpoints. The very concept of "buen amor" (good love) has generated abundant discussion among scholars. Much debate has occurred on the topic of whether "good love" refers to secular or Christian love.

Coexisting alongside the allegorical and spiritual threads of the poem, one substantial core of the poem is the narrator's account of his amorous pursuits. Aided by three parties—an old go-between, the God of Love [Don Amor], and his companion Doña Venus—the narrator attempts to seduce several women, the most memorable of whom are Doña Endrina [Lady Plum] and Doña Garoça the nun. He also tries his luck with a Moorish woman and is at one point forcibly abducted by parodic inversions of the ideal woman—grotesque anti-portraits of femininity—who take advantage of him on isolated mountain roads. Throughout and in between adventures, the outcome of which is at times left ambiguous, the narrator offers musings on women, seduction, and physical love. The pursuits themselves take the shape of heated dialogues among the narrator, his object of desire, the go-between, the God of Love, and Venus, all of whom attempt to outmaneuver and outwit one another rhetorically as they express their views on physical love.

The poem's achievement as a poetic expression of erotic love is manifold. On the level of plot, it is entertaining and dynamic; the amorous pursuits are presented in lively ways that engage the reader from beginning to end. The frustrations, humorous mishaps, and verbal sparring generated by erotic longing and resistance are chronicled with affection and irony, showcasing the importance of dialogue in seduction. On the level of literary design, Juan Ruiz displays admirable skill in bringing a wide range of sources to his poem and reshaping their function in highly original ways. Present in the poem are references to Ovid, Hebrew and Arabic literature, medieval and ancient fables, medieval Latin comedy, lyric poetry, and the Bible, to mention some of Juan Ruiz's important sources. All are woven into the poem from a fresh and often ironic perspective, creating a deeply reflective ambiguity. On the level of meaning, the poem sustains the paradox of erotic love coexisting with divine love with such humor and complexity that it becomes ultimately trivial to attempt to answer the question, What is good love? With its simultaneous celebration of both tendencies—love of the divine and love of the profane—with no attempt to offer artificial and strained resolutions, *El libro de buen amor* represents a masterpiece of medieval literature, given the rich perspectives on human love it offers the reader.

Biography

Very little is known about Juan Ruiz, the archpriest of Hita. He was born in Alcalá de Henares and held an ecclesiastical post in the village of Hita. The *Libro de buen amor* is his only known work, though he possibly composed other poetry as well.

LEYLA ROUHI

Editions

Libro de buen amor. Edited by Alberto Blecua. Barcelona: Planeta,1999.

The Book of Good Love. Translated by Elizabeth Drayson MacDonald. New York: Everyman's Library, 1999.

Further Reading

Criado de Val, Manuel. *Historia de Hita y su Arcipreste*. Guadalajara: Ediciones AACHE, 1998.

Dagenais, John. *The Ethics of Reading in Manuscript Culture: Glossing the* Libro de buen amor. Princeton, NJ: Princeton University Press, 1994.

Estudios de frontera: Alcalá la Real y el Arcipreste de Hita: Congreso internacional celebrado en Alcalá la Real, del 11 al 25 de noviembre de 1995. Coordinated by Francisco Toro Ceballos and José Rodríguez Molina. Jaén: Diputación Provincial de Jaén, 1996.

Joset, Jacques. *Nuevas investigaciones sobre el* Libro de buen amor. Madrid: Cátedra, 1988.

Libro de buen amor *Studies*. Edited by G.B. Gybbon-Monypenny. London: Grant & Cutler, 1970.

Malkiel, María Rosa. *Dos obras maestras españolas: El libro de buen amor y La Celestina*. Buenos Aires: Editorial Universitaria de Buenos Aires, 1966.

RUSSIAN

The profound sexual phobia of Soviet society was reflected in the almost total suppression of erotic discourse, making "Russian eroticism" something of an oxymoron. The lifting of censorship restrictions in the post-Soviet period, however, has made Western pornography and erotic literature widely available, leading to a rediscovery of Russia's own erotic past, which differs from that of western Europe in a number of significant ways. For example, the split between the idealized, nonsexual concept of love produced within the "high" culture of the church and the literary elites, and the frank, often celebratory representations of sexuality in the "low" culture of the folk, was greater in Russia than in the West. In addition, refined works of erotic art and literature appeared much later in Russia. In fact, Russia produced nothing similar to the chivalric literature of the West that idealized romantic love, and Russian artists were forbidden to paint naked figures until the late eighteenth century. Moreover, the broad censorship of erotic and/or sexually explicit materials meant that many of the greatest works of Russian eroticism were not originally published in Russia, or were circulated there only in manuscript form, often complicating the establishment of publication dates and even authorship.

Censorship in Russia was largely unrestricted by the principle of freedom of the press, and for most of Russian history no distinction was made between erotic art and pornography. The emigré poet and essayist Vladislav Khodasevich was one of the few to address the problem in an article entitled "O pornografii" [On Pornography] (1932), in which he argued that artistic merit (*khudozhestvennost*) distinguished erotic literature from pornography. The legacy of censorship is evident in the continued preference for such terms as *zavetnaia* or *potaennaia* [secret] and *netsenzurnaia* [unprintable] in referring to erotic literature. Furthermore, censorship lent erotic literature a *de facto* political significance, and eroticism and obscenity were often used to parody the church and the state. To the extent that censorship mostly affected printed works, it had little effect on erotic folk culture, which was predominantly oral, thus reinforcing the chasm separating the two erotic traditions.

The love idealized in church teachings was godly and platonic and bore little resemblance to the love celebrated in Russian folk culture, which was never ascetic. Overt expressions of sexual desire can be found in a wide range of folk genres, such as tales, songs, poems (*chastushki*), sayings (*poslivitsy*), incantations (*zagovory*), and plays, but these genres may make different use of erotic elements. A.I. Nikiforov, for example, argues that the use of obscenities and even erotic scenes in folktales had a primarily stylistic function, while Andrei Toporkov maintains that folk incantations have as their primary aim the arousal of sexual desire.

Erotic works of folk culture were collected in earnest throughout the nineteenth century by Aleksandr Afanas'ev and Vladimir Dal', among others, but were not published in Russia until much later. In fact, the first bawdy tales to be published openly in Russia were contained in the collection *Severnie skazki* [*Northern Tales*] (1908) prepared by the folklorist Nikolai Onchukov. Afanas'ev's collection of bawdy folktales, *Russkie zavetnye skazki* [*Russian Secret Tales*], a supplement to his standard collection, *Narodnye russkie skazki* [*Popular Russian Tales*] (1855–64), was first published in Geneva in 1872 and included an apocryphal attribution of the tales to the Russian Orthodox monks of Varaam. The volume's preface was signed "Bibliophile." The tales, which Afanas'ev edited for style, combining some into a single, synthetic text, were soon translated into French and English, but were only published in Russia after the loosening of censorship in 1905 when they were included in the collection *Russkie narodnye skazki*, edited by A.E. Gruzinsky. A collection of erotic writings, *Eros Russe: Russkii erot ne dlia dam* [*Russian Eros: Russian Eros Is Not for Ladies*], was also published in Geneva, a center of Russian emigré publishing, in 1879.

Russian erotic folktales deal with what Mikhail Bakhtin has referred to as the "lower bodily strata" and were clearly produced to entertain, if not explicitly to arouse sexual desire. They exhibit a fairly limited number of motifs and can be easily classified into a typology. Many of the stories involve the comic misrecognition of body parts, physical—often sexual—acts, and bodily functions. Others depict marital infidelity, sexual impropriety on the part of clerics, and the comic humiliation of old men by young women.

A collection of Russian erotic folk poetry, attributed by some scholars to Afanas'ev, was published in the 1870s under the title *Mezhdu druziami: Smeshnya i pikantnya shtuki domashnikh poetov Rossio: Pervoe polnoe izdanie* [*Among Friends: Humorous and Piquant Bits from Russian Folk Poets: First Complete Publication*]. The place of publication was listed as Tsargrad (Constantinople). Dal', most famous as the author of a widely respected dictionary of the Russian language, prepared a collection of erotic folk sayings that was first published in French under the title *Les proverbes erotiques russes: Etudes de proverbes recuillis et non-publies par Dal et Simoni* (1972).

Russia's turn toward the West in the seventeenth and eighteenth centuries made possible the birth of a secular—and erotic—literary tradition. Romantic poetry began to appear in the late seventeenth century and bawdy *lubok* [woodcut] prints, which contained a short narrative text in either poetry or prose beneath an illustration of an erotically suggestive scene, became very popular in the eighteenth century. The translation and adaptation of foreign—especially French—works of erotic literature occurred with particular intensity following the "pornography boom" that took place in France in the mid-eighteenth century. A dependence on foreign models, however, did not consign Russian erotic literature to mere imitation. Russians, for example, exhibited a marked preference for erotic poetry over prose, which was reflected in a tendency to translate foreign works of prose, mainly novels, into Russian verse. The Russian prose tradition would in fact remain remarkably "chaste" throughout the nineteenth century.

One of the most significant moments in the development of Russian erotic literature was the appearance in the mid-eighteenth century of a collection of erotic poems entitled *Devich'ia igrushka* [*A Maiden's Toy*], a reference to the male member, believed to have been authored, at least in part, by Ivan Barkov, a seminarian of plebian origins who worked, among other things, as an editor and translator. This collection was circulated in manuscript form and contained original poems and loose translations that parodied the high genres of eighteenth-century neo-classicism through the use of obscene language and sexually explicit content, as in "Oda Priapu" [Ode to Priapus], "Oda pizde" [Ode to the Cunt], and "Ssora u khuia s pizdoi" [Argument Between a Prick and a Cunt]. So influential was the collection that Nikolai Karamzin would include Barkov in his *Panteon rossiiskikh avtorov* [*Pantheon of Russian Authors*] (1802), and Aleksander Pushkin was purported to have declared him "one of the most eminent figures in Russian literature." Barkov's significance is attested to by the fact that all erotic works that followed, such as the very popular *Luka Mudishchev*, an anonymous narrative tale in verse, would come to be known as *barkoviana*, or, more derisively, as *barkovshchina*. There may even have been a link between Barkov's irreverant parodies and political liberalism in Russia, as suggested by one Russian arrested in the Decembrist uprising of 1825, who, when questioned as to the source of his freethinking ideas, replied: "various compositions (who does not know them?) of Barkov."

Literary parodies played a significant role in the development of Russia's erotic literature. Some notable works of the late eighteenth and early nineteenth centuries include: V.I. Maikov's mock epic set in a bordello, *Elisei, ili razdrazhennyi Vakkh* [*Elisei, or Bacchus Enraged*] (1777); Ippolit Bogdanovich's *Dushenka* (1783), a reworking via La Fontaine of Apuleius's tale of the love of Amor and Psyche; and anonymous parodies of Mikhail Lermontov's poem *Demon* [*The Demon*] and Aleksandr Griboedov's play *Gore ot uma* [*Woe from Wit*].

Many of the greatest Russian poets of the nineteenth century, well acquainted with eighteenth-century French culture, penned erotic verse. Aleksandr Pushkin, for example, wrote a number of erotic and obscene literary works and has long been attributed with the authorship of the erotic tale in verse *Ten' Barkova* [*The Shadow of Barkov*], although his authorship is today in dispute. That work, which takes place in a brothel in St. Petersburg's red-light district, depicts a variety of Russian social types, including a poet and an unfrocked priest, in competition to best "serve Aphrodite." The priest is in the lead until the ghost of Barkov appears to revive the poet's flagging member and help him win the victor's laurels.

Pushkin began writing bawdy epigrams, largely for parodic purposes, while still at the lycée, and his early erotic poems, "Monakh" [The Monk] and "Gorodok" [The Town], reveal the influence of both Russian and French authors—in particular, Barkov and Voltaire. Lengthier works include "Tsar Nikita i ego sorok docherei" [Tsar Nikita and His Forty Daughters] and the blasphemous "Gavriiliada" [The Saga of Gabriel]. "Gavriiliada" is a mock epic in the tradition of Maikov's *Elisei*. Pushkin's "Gavriiliada" parodies church teachings concerning the Annunciation and the virgin birth by portraying a competition between the angel Gabriel and the devil for Mary's sexual favors. God the Father then takes on the form a white dove—a parodic reference to Jupiter as a swan—and makes love to the virgin himself. "Tsar Nikita and His Forty Daughters" tells the story of a tsar's beautiful daughters who lack but one erotic charm: genitalia. Drawing on both French literary works and Russian folktales, the poem recounts how the tsar attempts to solve the problem with the help of a witch who gives the tsar's messanger a box "Full of sinful things / Which we adore." When the box is opened, birds fly out and must be recaptured. Walter Arndt's English translation of the poem was published in the December 1965 edition of *Playboy* magazine, which hailed it as "a ribald classic."

The nineteenth-century poets Nikolai Yaszykov and Mikhail Lermontov also wrote erotic verse. Yazykov penned a cycle of seven erotic elegies between 1823 and 1825 which were very popular and circulated in manuscript. Lermontov, Russia's second great Romantic poet after Pushkin, wrote a number of erotic poems, especially during his years in the cavalry cadet school. Among those works, several depict same-sex desire among the cadets, such as "Oda k puzhniku" [Ode to the John] (1834) and "Tizengauzenu" [To Tiesenhausen] (1834). A.F. Shenin, who worked from 1820 to 1845 as an instructor in the Pavelsky Corps of Cadets, also composed a number of erotic poems dedicated to same-sex love, among them "Svidanie"

[The Rendezvous]; "R——u" [To R——], or "Though feminine charms delight all mortals" ("Khot'zhenskie krasy vsekh smertnykh voskhishchaiut"); and "L——oi" [to L——], or "I swore on glorious Ganymede" ("Klianulsia Ganimedom slavnym").

The tightening of censorship during the reign of Nicholas I, as well as the increasing popularity of the novel in the second half of the nineteenth century, adversely affected the production of erotic literature in Russia. Notable exceptions include selected works of Mikhail Longinov, such as the narrative poems "Bordel'nyi mal'chik" [Bordello Boy] and "Svad'ba poeta" [Marriage of a Poet]; the collection of verse *Dlia chernoknizhnyikh vdokhnovenii* [*For Black Magical Inspiration*], authored jointly by Nikolai Nekrasov, Ivan Turgenev, and Aleksandr Druzhinin, who repeatedly invoke Longinov and his work; the long poem "Pop" [The Priest] by Ivan Turgenev; and the collection *Mezhdu Druz'iami. Smeshnye i pikantnye shutki domashnikh poetov Rossii* [*Between Friends: Amusing and Risque Anecdotes by Homespun Poets of Russia*]. Many of these works are literary parodies or social satires and, as such, add little that is new to the tradition of Russian erotic literature.

In sharp contrast to the tradition of erotic poetry, the classic Russian novel of the second half of the nineteenth century portrayed sexual attraction in tortured and tragic terms. In the works of Fyodor Dostoevsky, for example, there is an almost unbridgeable gap between love and sexual desire. The latter often involves power and is exemplified in its most heinous form by the sexual abuse of children. So central is this motif to Dostoevsky's portayal of sexual desire that Ieronim Iasinkii wrote a short story entitled "Ispoved'" (1888), in which Dostoevsky confesses to his literary nemisis, Ivan Turgenev, that he himself had raped a young girl. The inherent sinfulness of sexual desire was also expressed in works by Lev Tolstoy, such as *Kreitserova sonata* [*The Kreutzer Sonata*] (1889), the unfinished *D'iavol* [*The Devil*] (1890), and *Otets Sergii* [*Father Sergius*] (1898). *The Kreutzer Sonata*, which presents sexual relations as sinful even in marriage, was banned in 1890 from the US mail.

This negative portrayal of erotic desire would be challenged in the last decade of the nineteenth century and the first two decades of the twentieth century, a period referred to as the Silver Age of Russian literature. "In the span of a few decades in Russia," notes Viacheslav Shestakov, "more was written about love than in the span of centuries." This was due to a number of general social factors related to Russia's rapid urbanization and modernization, as well as more specific ones, such as the loosening of censorship restrictions following the revolution of 1905. In the realm of philosophy, Russians under the influence of neo-Platonism saw the sexual union of male and female as symbolizing the resolution of fundamental antinomies. For Vladimir Solov'ev, one experienced in true love the reconciliation of the earthly and the divine, the individual and the eternal, symbolized by Sophia, or the universal feminine principle of love between individuals. The concept of Sophia, which would become a central theme among the Russian Symbolist poets, reflects the traditional gender archetypes and the essential gender differences at the heart of much Silver Age philosophy.

Nikolai Berdiaev further developed the ideas of Solov'ev, arguing that "sexual difference is the basic law of life and perhaps the foundation of the world," that erotic energy was the eternal source of creativity, and that the erotic was linked to the beautiful. Vasilii Rozanov also recognized the central importance of erotic energy and criticized the Christian tradition for denigrating the sexual. In *Liudi lunnogo sveta* [*People of the Moonlight*] (1911), he argued that Christian culture was characterized by latent homosexuality.

In the realm of literature, the Silver Age witnessed a number of important erotic works produced for both elite and mass audiences. Some of the best-selling boulevard literature includes *Sanin* (1907) by Mikhail Artsybashev, *Kliuchi schast'ia* [*The Keys to Happiness*] (6 vols, 1909–13) by Anastasiia Verbitskaia, *Gnev Dionisa* [*The Wrath of Dionysius*] (1910) by Evdokia Nagrodskaia, and selected short stories by Anatolii Kamenskii, such as "Leda" (1906) and "Chetyre" [The Four] (1907). All these works to some degree questioned traditional gender roles and advocated the de-stigmatizing of sexual desire as part of a challenge to middle-class hypocrisy and prudishness, although *Sanin*, with its ambiguous rape scene and the suggestion of incest, represented perhaps the greatest challenge to contemporary morality (see *Artsybashev, Mikhail*).

Erotic works produced by the more elite literary culture of the time include Mikhail Kuzmin's *Kryl'ia* [Wings] (1906), which is considered to be Russia's first "gay" novel, and Lidiia Zinov'eva-Annibal's "Tridtsat' tri urodov" [Thirty-three Abominations] (1907), which treats the subject of lesbian love. Both works were successes by scandal and went through several printings, although in "Thirty-three Abominations" the lesbian affair of the two main characters is overwrought, theatrical, and ultimately tragic, placing it squarely within the Decadent movement, whereas in *Wings* homosexual desire is depicted in positive terms and is associated with both high art and the natural world. In addition to *Wings*, Kuzmin penned a number of highly sensual and homoerotic verse cycles, such as *Aleksandriiskie pesni* [*Alexandrian Songs*]; *Liubo'v etogo leta* [*A Summer Affair*] (1907); *Prervannanaia povest'* [*A Story Interrupted*] (1907); and *Forel' razbivaet led'* [The Trout Breaks the Ice] (1929); as well as the short stories "Kushetka teti Soni" [Aunt Sonia's Sofa] (1907), a reworking of "Le Sofa" by Crébillon *fils;* "Prikliucheniia Eme Lebefa" [The Adventures of Aime Leboeuf] (1907), an adventure tale set in eighteenth-century France that treats the topic of libertinism; "Devstvennyi Viktor" [Virginal Victor] (1914), the story of a young Byzantine nobleman with a strong homoerotic connection to his manservant; and "Pechka v bane" [The Stove in the Bathhouse] (1926), a series of fourteen short sketches on erotic themes. (See *Kuzmin, Mikhail.*)

Another noteworthy contribution to Russian erotic literature of the Silver Age is Aleksei Remizov's *Chto est' tabak?* [*What Is Tobacco?*] (1908), a blasphemous anticlerical tale recounted by a simple monk. Published in a print run of 25 copies, Remizov's tale is accompanied by three illustrations by Konstantin Somov. Somov would also illustrate *Le livre de la Marquise: Recuil de poesie et de prose*, a collection of erotic French epigrams, poetry, and stories, published in St. Petersburg in 1918 and regarded as a classic in the history of Russian erotic book design.

Although the Soviet government would practice a very restrictive censorship, several important works of erotic literature were published in the early post-revolutionary period. Kuzmin put together a collection of homoerotic poems which were published with delicately salacious illustrations by Vladimir Milashevskii, entitled *Zanaveshannye kartinki* [*Draped Pictures*] in 1920. The place of publication was listed fallaciously as Amsterdam. This volume, printed in only 307 copies for private sale, would adversely affect the poet's ability to find work. Also published in 1920 was Remizov's blasphemous *Zavetnye skazy* [*Secret Tales*], but his cycle of stories *Russkii Dekameron. Semidnevets* [*The Russian Decameron: Seven Days*] was published in Revel (Tallinn, Finland) in 1921, and *Skazy obez'ian'ego Tsaria Asyki* [*Tales of Tsar Asuka's Ape*] in Berlin in 1922. The *Eroticheskie sonety* [*Erotic Sonnets*] of Abram Efros, influenced by the Symbolist poets, was published in Russia in 1922 in 260 numbered copies.

By the end of the 1920s, it had become virtually impossible to publish erotic literature in Russia. The poems of Nikolai Agnivtsev, such as "Galantnaia istoriia" [A Courtly Story], with its ironic, playfully erotic depictions of courtly life, and the stories of Aleksei Tolstoi, such as "V bane" [In the Bathhouse] and "Vozmezdie" [Retribution], were circulated in *samizdat*. The avant-garde poet and children's writer Daniil Kharms (pseudonym of Iuvachev) wrote a number of playful and inventive erotic poems which could not be published in his lifetime. Andrei Platonov parodied official Soviet prudery, in particular the war against masturbation, in his short story "Anti-seksus" written in 1925–26 but not published until decades later (see *Platonov, Andrei*). The short story writer Evgenii Kharitonov and the poet Iurii Trifonov, both openly gay, were also prevented from publishing their work.

The loosening of censorship during *perestroika* and in the post-Communist period radically altered the erotic landscape in Russia. It resulted in, among other things, the introduction of hardcore pornography, the publication or republication of suppressed works of Russian erotic literature, and the (re)introduction of eroticism into contemporary Russian literature. Viktor Erofeev's novel *Zhizn' s idiotom* [*Life with an Idiot*] (1991) is a good example of eroticism used as a vehicle for social and political satire. The novelist Vladimir Sorokin has also made use of erotic elements in his often wildly postmodern works. His novel *Tridtsataia liubov' Mariny* [*The Thirtieth Love of Marina*] (1995) features lesbianism, and his novel *Goluboe salo*

[*Blue Lard*] (1998) depicts, among other things, a homosexual relationship between Khrushchev and Stalin. In 2002 Sorokin was charged with publishing pornography by the youth organization *Udushchie vmeste* [*Going Together*].

While it is true that the overwhelming majority of post-Soviet eroticism is directed at the heterosexual male reader, some works, such as *Drugoi Peterburg* [*The Other Petersburg*] (1998), a campy, gay history of St. Petersburg published by the author under the pseudonym K.K. Rotikov, and *Peterburgskaia eroticheskaia prosa: Odna v posteli* [*Petersburg Erotic Prose: Alone in Bed*] (2001), a collection of short works by Russian women writers, offer hope of greater diversity in Russia's erotic literature.

BRIAN JAMES BAER

Further Reading

Afanasyev, Aleksandr. *Russian Secret Tales: Bawdy Folktales of Old Russia*. Annotations by Giuseppe Pitre, introduction by G. Legman, new foreword by Alan Dundes. New York: Genealogical Publishing Company, 1998.

Cross, Anthony. "Pushkin's Bawdy; or, Notes from the Literary Underground." *Russian Literature Triquarterly* 10 (Fall 1974): 203–43.

Goldschmidt, Paul W. *Pornography and Democratization: Legislating Obscenity in Post-Communist Russia*. Boulder, CO: Westview Press, 1999.

Gruzinsky, A.E., ed. *Russkie narodnye skazki*. Moscow: I.D. Sytin, 1913–14.

Heller, Leonid, ed. *Amour et erotisme dans la litterature russe du XXe sielce; actes du colloque de juin 1989/ organize par l'Universite de Lausanne, avec le concours de la Fondation du 450eme anniversaire*. Bern and New York: P. Lang, 1992.

Iliushin, Aleksandr, ed. *Tri veka poezii russkogo Erosa. Publikatsii i issledovaniia*. Moscow: Piat' Vecherov, 1991.

Leavitt, Marcus, and A. Toporkov, eds. *Eros and Pornography in Russian Culture*. Moscow: Ladomir, 1999.

Prokhorova, I.D., S.Iu. Mazur, and G.V. Zykova. *Erotika v russkoi literature: Ot Barkova do nashikh dnei: teksty i kommentarii*. Moscow: Literaturnoe obozrenie, 1992.

Pushkareva, Natalia, ed. *"A se grekhi zlye, smertnye..." Liubov', erotika i seksual'naia etika v doindustrial'noi Rossii (X–pervaia polovina XIX v.)*. Moscow: Ladomir, 1999.

Sazhin, Valerii, ed. *Zanaveshennye kartinki: Antologiia russkoi erotiki*. St. Petersburg: Amfora, 2001.

Shchuplov, Aleksandr, ed. *Eros. Rossiia. Serebrianyi vek*. Moscow: Serebrianyi bor, 1992.

Toporkov, Andrei, ed. *Russkii eroticheskii fol'klor. Pesni. Obriady i obriadovyi fol'klor. Narodnyi teatr. Zagovory. Zagadki. Chastushki*. Moscow: Ladomir, 1995.

S

SACHER-MASOCH, LEOPOLD

1836–1895
Austrian novelist, short story writer, playwright, historian, literary critic and journalist

Despite Sacher-Masoch's enormous output and his widespread recognition during the nineteenth century as a hugely talented writer and the pre-eminent literary defender of the pan-Slavic spirit, he is currently mainly remembered as the author whose name was used by the sexologist Richard von Krafft-Ebing in 1890 to designate a "sexual anomaly". "Masochism", as von Krafft-Ebing called it, has since entered both scientific language and popular parlance as the name for a condition whereby someone derives (sexual) enjoyment from being dominated, humiliated and mistreated. Although Krafft-Ebing indicated that Sacher-Masoch had described this "sexual anomaly" in many of his writings, the text to which most people (including Krafft-Ebing's patients) referred was *Venus im Pelz* (1870). During the twentieth century, *Venus im Pelz* remained the most popular and most widely available of Sacher-Masoch's novellas, to the point where the book acquired cult-status as the original manifesto of masochism. The book inspired films by Massimo Dallamano (1968), Jesus Franco (1970) and, most recently, by Maartje Seyferth and Victor Nieuwenhuijs (1994). It was also immortalised in a song by the Velvet Underground. In recent years, Sacher-Masoch's life and works have enjoyed renewed scholarly attention, and when Graz was named Cultural Capital of Europe in 2003, the city staged a spectacular "Sacher-Masoch Festival", including art exhibitions, concerts, lectures and performances.

Venus im Pelz, 1870

Leopold von Sacher-Masoch's most famous novella appeared as the fifth section of the first volume of a large-scale fictional work entitled *Das Vermächtnis Kains* [*The Testament of Cain,* or *Cain's Legacy*], which he had conceived, rather naïvely, as a grand narrative cycle of philosophical and ideological contemplations on the sources of human conflict. Of the projected six volumes, Sacher-Masoch would publish only the first (on love) and the second (on property), yet he continued to believe in the possibility of finishing his life's work, even during his final days.

The author's overall intention in the first volume was to paint "the battle of the sexes" in its various forms and circumstances. Drawing on Arthur Schopenhauer's bleak picture of human relationships in *Die Welt als Wille und Vorstellung* [*The World as Will and Representation*] (1818), Sacher-Masoch set out to describe, illustrate and demonstrate the fallacies of love, and the impossibility of a sustainable sexuo-erotic desire in the relationship between a man and a woman. In the course of five separate and unrelated novellas, Sacher-Masoch portrayed how each of his (male) protagonists, regardless of the intensity of their feelings and whichever their beliefs about the nature of true love, ends up being disappointed, devastated and often betrayed by the women they are in love with. After so much strife and despair, the book's sixth novella (entitled *Marzella oder das Märchen vom Glück* [*Marcella, or the Fairy-Tale of Happiness*]) was then supposed to show the mechanisms of a steady and happy relationship, which Sacher-Masoch situated in a couple's ability to develop their sex-drive into a higher unity of shared interests. Perhaps expressing his own scepticism concerning the value of his solution, Sacher-Masoch called this story a "fairy-tale," and its philosophical arguments were far less convincing than those he had formulated in the "conflict-section" of the book. In addition, the "fairy-tale" was also generally regarded as the weakest story in the volume from a strictly literary perspective. *Venus im Pelz* thus constitutes the culmination of Sacher-Masoch's narration of the war between the sexes—a struggle which remains all the more pressing and unresolved, here, as its supposedly reformative sequel radically failed to deliver the goods.

Venus im Pelz opens with the account of a dream in which the anonymous narrator, after having fallen asleep whilst reading a book by Hegel, plays host to Venus, the Goddess of Love, who is sitting by the fireplace dressed in a huge fur. The conversation turns to the cruelty of love and the host's preference for "a beautiful, voluptuous, and cruel female despot who capriciously changes her favourites", when he is suddenly stirred by his valet, who reminds him that his friend, Herr Severin, is expecting them for tea. Herr Severin is described as "a Galician nobleman and landowner," who is "barely over thirty" yet whose eccentricities have made him into someone who is regarded as a "dangerous fool", "not just by his neighbors but throughout the district of Kolomea". As the narrator recounts his dream to his friend, he is at one point struck by a painting in Severin's room, which uncannily reproduces part of the scene in his dream: a reclining woman covered in nothing but furs wields a whip in her right hand and has her foot resting on a man who lies on the floor like a slave. When the narrator expresses his surprise at the similarity between his dream (Venus in furs) and the painting (which the narrator presumes must have inspired it), Severin responds that he himself actually dreamt the dream "with open eyes." After alerting his friend to the visual connections between this painting and Titian's *Venus with Mirror,* Severin then presents the narrator with a copy of his journal entitled "Confessions of a Suprasensual Man". Apart from the last paragraphs of Sacher-Masoch's novella, in which the narrator closes the manuscript and asks his friend about the moral of the story, the entire text of the book is then made up of the contents of Severin's recollections, as read by the narrator in Severin's room, whilst the latter "sat down by the fireplace" and "seemed to be dreaming with open eyes."

"Confessions of a Suprasensual Man" tells the story of Severin von Kusiemski, a self-identified "dilettante in life" who summers in the Carpathian mountains contemplating the scenery, endeavouring to read, paint and write poetry, musing about beauty, and worshipping a stone statue of Venus at the back of the garden. His wild infatuation with the statue makes him totally immune to the charms of Ms Wanda von Dunajew, a beautiful widow from Lwów who lives above him. Yet one day Ms Wanda von Dunajew finds the postcard showing Titian's *Venus with Mirror,* carrying a poem and the inscription "Venus in Furs", which her downstairs neighbour had accidentally left in the book that he lent her to read. The lucky find prompts Wanda to introduce herself to Severin and before long they engage in a conversation about Greek sensuality, which encourages Severin to say: "Free, lovely, cheerful, and happy people as the Greeks were can exist only if they have *slaves.*" To his amazement, Wanda replies: "Do you want to be my slave?" Severin admits that he quite likes the idea of being dominated by a beautiful woman, yet Wanda does not seem to take him seriously and simply responds that she likes his depth and enthusiasm, and could potentially start to love him. Severin, however, is completely smitten and asks her to marry him. Instead of accepting his proposal immediately, Wanda explains that she could only imagine "belonging to one man for life" if it were "a total man, a man who commands . . . respect" and who "subjugates . . . with the power of who and what he is". And so she suggests to Severin that they take a year to discover whether they are suitable for one another.

Almost immediately, Severin starts to fear that Wanda will leave him and expresses his unconditional love for her. Wanda warns him that she might take advantage of the situation and become despotic, to which Severin responds: "Then be that! Be arrogant, be despotic," "Make of me what you will, your husband or your slave." Undeterred and seemingly enjoying the power attributed to her, Wanda immediately confronts Severin with her decision: "You were imprudent enough to leave the choice up to me. This is my choice: I want you to be my slave! I am going to turn you into my plaything." Severin readily complies and subsequently engages in elaborate digressions concerning the origin of his suprasensuality. During the following weeks, Wanda more or less succeeds in realizing Severin's sexual fantasy, yet it does not stop Severin from being shattered by the thought that Wanda will leave him. All the while, Wanda is simultaneously warning Severin that she might start to enjoy her despotic act a bit too much, becoming more cruel than he wants her to, and apologizing to him for her inadequacies in meeting his demands, which she nonetheless continues to do out of love for the man she has loved like no other man before. To prove to him that she is serious, she draws up a contract for Severin to sign, in which he agrees that he will be her slave until the moment when she is willing to set him free. Severin is surprised that he has no say in the contract's clauses, and insists that Wanda at least include that she will never leave him and that she will always wear fur when being cruel. Wanda promises that she will revise the contract accordingly and offer it to Severin for signing "in the right place."

Unexpectedly, she instructs Severin to prepare for a trip to Italy, during which he will be known as Gregor and act as her servant. In the province's district seat, Wanda buys a first-class ticket for herself and a third-class one for Gregor. In Vienna, Wanda gives Gregor's clothes to the hotel waiters and equips him with a new set of clothes, appropriate for a servant. In Florence, she allocates him to a hotel room without heating and prohibits him to share a meal with her. Yet when she summons him to her room, she reveals how much she loves him and how much she wants to give him her fur so that he can keep warm during the night. "I'm more in love with you than ever", says Severin, to which Wanda replies: "So you love me when I'm cruel. . . "Go away! You bore me! Don't you hear?" Eventually, Wanda decides to rent a villa on the banks of the Arno. Reserving the entire second floor for herself, she allocates Gregor to one room on the ground floor, nicely equipped with a fireplace. Shortly after settling in, Wanda gives Gregor the contract for signing. Although stipulating that Wanda will always wear fur when being cruel, the contract does not say that she will never leave Gregor and is also accompanied by a second document, in which Severin details his decision to commit suicide, which effectively gives Wanda the opportunity to kill him when she wants to. Wanda and Severin both sign the contract, and as if to celebrate the occasion she calls in three African women, orders them to tie Severin to a column, and proceeds to whip him. During the following month, Gregor is forced to work in the garden, while Wanda is being entertained by a score of admirers. Severin suffers terribly: "Tears came to my eyes; I felt how deeply she had degraded me—so deeply that she didn't even think it worthwhile torturing me, mistreating me." Wanda, for her part, confesses to Severin during a moment of intimacy that she is only doing it to provoke him and to ensure that she does not lose him. And so she explains that she is compelled to take a lover. When a young German painter moves in, she orders him to paint her stretched out on velvet cushions, only dressed in furs, clutching a whip and with one foot resting on the submissive body of Gregor at her feet. The painter decides to call the painting "Venus in Furs."

One day, Wanda apparently falls in love with a handsome Greek. Severin implores Wanda not to give in to her desire, yet she ignores his plea and employs him as a go-between in her seduction ritual of the "arrogant despot." Finally, Severin decides that he has had enough and leaves the villa. Yet he soon discovers that even

1149

if he had the money to go somewhere, he wouldn't know where to go. He tries to commit suicide by jumping into the Arno, yet he fails because the image of Wanda appears above the surface of the water and beckons him back. At the villa, Wanda accepts him with utter disdain, yet Severin notices how Wanda and the Greek seem to be involved in an acrimonious argument. When Severin confronts her, she confesses that they had been arguing about him and that the Greek had been violently jealous. Severin and Wanda in turn start to argue and at one point Severin grabs her by the wrist, throws her to the floor and threatens to kill her if she decides to marry the Greek. Wanda replies: "You appeal to me like this," "Now you're a man, and I know at this moment that I still love you." A moment later, she explains to him "that everything was just a game, just make-believe." Wanda accepts to be Severin's wife and they start preparing their departure from Florence. The next day, Wanda is stretched out on the ottoman in her bedroom, contemplating her love for Severin, when she suddenly offers to tie him up in order to see him "truly in love." Severin is completely entranced and asks her about the whip. "So you absolutely want to get whipped?" asks Wanda. "Yes," says Severin. "Then whip him!" she cries. Enters the Greek, who gives Severin the most violent whipping of his life. As he lies there bleeding in his ropes, Wanda and the Greek take their leave from the villa. More than three years later, long after Severin has been "cured" from his suprasensual desires, Severin receives a letter from Wanda in which she concedes that she had been truly in love with him, but that her love had been "smothered" by his "fantastic surrender." Referring to the disastrous events at the villa, she ends with the words: "I hope that you were healed under my whip; the therapy was cruel but radical. To remind you of that time and the woman who passionately loved you, I am sending you the portrait painted by the poor German."

If *Venus im Pelz* has succeeded in stirring and consolidating the imagination of many a "masochist", as Krafft-Ebing learnt from his patients and as Sacher-Masoch himself was eager to confirm, then the novella is definitely more than a treatise of sexual cruelty and a specialised sample of erotic literature. Both in style and conception, the book stands out amongst the cornucopia of flagellation books that were produced at the end of the nineteenth century, because it delves into the extraordinary complexity of power (im)balances within human sexual relationships and demonstrates the tragic fate of all attempts at bringing these to a satisfactory resolution. *Venus im Pelz* also plays magnificently on the constant blurring of fact and fiction, reality and semblance, in the realm of love and sexuality. Severin is an idealist who derives pleasure from transforming a woman he loves into the desirable figure of a cruel despot who occupies the centre stage of his sexual fantasy. For as long as she resists and he does not succeed in realising his "dream", he suffers unbearably, yet he simultaneously suffers from the possibility that his fantasy is realised into a scene over which he no longer has any control. Severin desires Wanda for as long as she is desirable as a compliant object, yet desire turns into anxiety when she shows no desire at all to satisfy his desire, and equally when she seemingly gives up on responding to his desire by showing a desire of her own.

The multi-layered structures and constantly shifting perspectives of *Venus im Pelz* are further complicated by the peculiar relationship between the contents of the novella and certain events in Sacher-Masoch's own life. It is generally accepted that "Confessions of a Suprasensual Man", the book within the book, was based on Sacher-Masoch's relationship with Fanny Pistor, who called herself Baroness Bogdanoff and who had allegedly contacted the author after reading his novel *Die geschiedene Frau* [*The Divorced Woman*] (1869), which was in itself based on his earlier affair with Anna von Kottowitz-Wasserzieher. In *Die geschiedene Frau*, the unhappy Anna von Kossow tells Sacher-Masoch about her passionate affair with a young writer called Julian von Romaschkan, who had given her a copy of his book *Venus im Pelz*, after which Anna had tried to impersonate its heroine Wanda. Apparently inflamed by this story, Fanny Pistor and Sacher-Masoch started their own relationship in 1869, which was also regulated through the terms of a sexual contract, similar to that which is signed by Wanda and Severin in *Venus im Pelz*. With Fanny Pistor, Sacher-Masoch travelled to Italy as her servant Gregor and during the (contractually determined) time of the relationship he wrote *Venus im Pelz*. Yet when the book was published, he was in turn contacted by Aurora Rümelin, who presented herself to him as Wanda von Dunajew, and who would subsequently engage in a relationship with the author along the lines and conditions set out in the book. With Sacher-Masoch, it is thus very difficult to distinguish between fact and fiction, reality and fantasy, not only within the narrative space of a novella, but also within the wider framework of the author's life and works. Through his fiction, Sacher-Masoch narrated and gave shape to crucial events in his love-life, yet through his love-life he simultaneously validated and elaborated on crucial events in his fictional world.

Biography

Leopold Ritter von Sacher-Masoch was born on 27 January 1836 in the city of Lwów (currently in Ukraine, but then known as Lemberg and part of the Galician province of the Austro-Hungarian Empire) as the eldest son of the city's police commissioner. In 1848, the family moved to Prague, where he studied law, history, philosophy and mathematics, and developed an interest in theatre. The family left Prague for Graz in 1853, where he obtained a degree in law in 1855 and was appointed "Privat-dozent" in German history at the University of Graz one year later. He published his first literary work in 1858, which prompted him to give up his academic career and become a full-time writer. Between 1858 and 1895, Sacher-Masoch published some eighty volumes of fiction, historical studies and criticism, and was widely regarded as one of the most important European writers. In 1873 he married Aurora von Rümelin, who had contacted the author after reading his novella *Venus im Pelz* [*Venus in Furs*], and who adopted the identity and persona of Wanda, after the name of its cruel heroine. In 1881, Sacher-Masoch and his family left Austria for Germany, so that he could escape four days of imprisonment as a penalty received for his slanderous portrayal of a renowned publisher in one of his writings, and they settled in Leipzig. Two years later he received the "légion d'honneur" from the French government for his contributions to literature. At the end of January 1883, Sacher-Masoch separated from Aurora Rümelin and went to live with his secretary and mistress Hulda Meister, whom he subsequently also married, in the German town of Lindheim,

near Frankfurt am Main. During these years, Sacher-Masoch's reputation as a literary genius gradually dwindled into that of an inferior pulp-author and pornographer. He died on 9 March 1895.

DANY NOBUS

Editions

Venus im Pelz. Frankfurt: Insel, 1980.
Venus in Furs. Trans. Joachim Neugroschel, with an introduction by Larry Wolff. Harmondsworth: Penguin Books, 2000.

Selected Works

Der Aufstand in Gent unter Kaiser Carl. 1857.
Don Juan von Kolomea. 1864.
Die geschiedene Frau: Passionsgeschichte eines Idealisten. 1869.
Das Vermächtnis Kains: Novellen I: Die Liebe. 1870.
Über den Wert der Kritik: Erfahrungen und Bemerkungen. 1873.
Das Vermächtnis Kains: Novellen II: Das Eigentum. 1877.
Die Gottesmutter. 1883.
Jüdisches Leben in Wort und Bild. 1892.

Further Reading

Amiaux, Mark. *Un grand anormal. Le Chevalier de Sacher-Masoch*. Paris: Les éditions de France, 1938.
Bang, Karin. *Aimez-moi! Eine Studie über Leopold von Sacher-Masochs Masochismus*. Frankfurt am Main: Peter Lang, 2003.
Bransiet, Maurice. *La vie et les amours tourmentées de Sacher-Masoch, le père du masochisme*. Paris: Quignon, 1910.
Cleugh, James. *The First Masochist: A Biography of Leopold von Sacher-Masoch, 1836–1895*. London: Anthony Blond, 1967.
Deleuze, Gilles. "Coldness and Cruelty." (1967). Translated by Jean McNeil, in *Masochism*. New York: Zone Books, 1991.
Exner, Lisbeth. *Leopold von Sacher-Masoch*. Reinbek bei Hamburg: Rowohlt, 2003.
Farin, Michael (ed.). *Leopold von Sacher-Masoch: Materialien zu Leben und Werk*. Bonn: Bouvier, 1987.
Gratzke, Michael. *Liebesschmerz und Textlust. Figuren der Liebe und des Masochismus in der Literatur*. Wurzburg: Königshausen und Neumann.
Hasper, Eberhard. *Leopold von Sacher-Masoch. Sein Lebenswerk, mit vorzüglicher Berücksichtigung der Prosadichtungen*. Greifswald: H. Adler, 1932.
Koschorke, Albrecht. *Leopold von Sacher-Masoch. Die Inszenierung einer Perversion*. München: Piper, 1988.
Kossmann, Alfred. "Over leven en werk van Leopold von Sacher-Masoch." (1959). In *Leopold von Sacher-Masoch: Martelaar voor een dagdroom – Een studie en twee verhalen*. 'S-Gravenhage: BZZTÔH, 1985, pp. 7–91

Michel, Bernard. *Sacher–Masoch (1836–1895)*. Paris: Robert Laffont, 1989.

Milojevic, Svetlana. *Die Poesie des Dilettantismus. Zur Rezeption und Wirkung Leopold von Sacher-Masochs*. Edited by Manfred Kuxdorf. Frankfurt am Main: Peter Lang, 1998.

Noyes, John K. *The Mastery of Submission: Inventions of Masochism*. Ithaca NY-London: Cornell University Press, 1997.

Quignard, Pascal. *L'être du balbutiement. Essai sur Sacher-Masoch*. Paris: Mercure de France, 1969.

Rudloff, Holger. *Pelzdamen. Weiblichkeitsbilder bei Thomas Mann und Leopold von Sacher-Masoch*. Frankfurt am Main: Fischer, 1994.

Sacher-Masoch, Wanda von. *The Confessions of Wanda von Sacher-Masoch.*, Translated by Marian Phillips, Caroline Hébert and V. Vale. San Francisco, CA: Re/Search Publications, 1990.

Schlichtegroll, Carl Felix von. *Sacher-Masoch und der Masochismus. Literarhistorische und kulturhistorische Studien*. Dresden: H.R. Dohrn, 1901 (reprinted as *Sacher-Masoch*, München, Belleville, 2003).

Spörk, Ingrid and Alexandra Strohmaier, eds., *Leopold von Sacher-Masoch*. Graz: Literaturverlag Droschl, 2002.

Stern, Léopold. *Sacher-Masoch, ou l'amour de la souffrance*. Paris, Bernard Grasset, 1933.

SADE, MARQUIS DE

1740–1814
French novelist, dramatist and philosopher

Donatien-Alphonse-François de Sade (1740–1814) was the author of a large number of novels (many of which are perfectly respectable), of plays (all conventional in style and content), journals, letters, and a few essays, but those writings on which the Marquis's sulphurous reputation rests, and which have been of particular interest to critics as much as to the general reader are the four "libertine" novels composed over a 12-year period from 1785 to 1797. The essential interest of Sade's writing lies less in its literary qualities (although these are certainly not lacking), than in its transgressive power generating the relentless movement of the narrative towards excess that underpins all Sadean eroticism. The so-called "libertine" or "obscene" novels – *The 120 Days of Sodom, Justine, Philosophy in the Boudoir* and *Juliette* – are among the most excessive works of erotic fiction ever composed. The novels explore the murkier depths of human sexuality, shunned by earlier writers of erotica: coprophilia, and of course, the practice of sexual sadism that bears his name, are probably the most extreme.

Sade's libertine fiction is on one important level the expression of his philosophy, a combination of atheistic materialism and the utopian vision of total sexual freedom. His atheism was heavily influenced by the work of two materialist philosophers of the Enlightenment: La Mettrie's *L'Homme Machine*, published in 1748, and d'Holbach's *Système de la nature*, which appeared in 1770. Materialism rejected belief in a soul or afterlife, reducing everything in the universe to the physical organization of matter. According to La Mettrie, scientific observation and experiment are the only means by which human beings can be defined, and this method tells us that Man is quite simply a machine, subject to the laws of motion like any mechanism of eighteenth century science. The sole purpose of existence, in this scheme of things, is pleasure – a doctrine espoused with relish by so many of Sade's libertine characters. Baron d'Holbach views the human being as a collection of atoms, so that even the conscience has a material origin, acquired from our education and experience. d'Holbach's system does not, therefore, allow for free will, since all our decisions are determined by our personal interest. For d'Holbach, then, all morality is a matter of social utility or pragmatism. Sade described *Système de la nature* as the true basis of his philosophy and a book he would be prepared to die for, and indeed, lifted whole passages from it practically verbatim to place in the mouths of his protagonists, as they railed against the various dogmas of religion.

Although these writers furnished Sade with the essentials of his thinking, and he certainly plagiarised from them liberally, it is also possible to identify features of his philosophy that are peculiarly his own. The most important of these is his conviction that every human being is utterly alone. This "isolisme" helps to explain the lack of expression in his work of any fraternal feeling: if we are fundamentally cut off from all others, then our only motivation can be self-interest. Sade wants to abolish the social, not merely in the form of the *ancien régime* society that he constantly attacks, but in the guise of any society worthy of that name, that is, one based on a code of ethics which protects the individual while observing what Rousseau called "the general will".

The self-interest at the heart of Sade's thinking, which makes possible the unfeeling exploitation of others, is justified because it is "natural". Since nature treats us all equally, and so does not allow for any special cases, we are free to dominate others; indeed, in doing so, we are conforming to nature's wishes, expressed in the universal "law of the jungle", according to which the strong survive at the expense of the weak. All laws are therefore inimical to nature's plan, since they are designed to protect the weak, and neither God nor morality has any meaning in a universe governed entirely by natural forces. Nature in fact needs crime in order to preserve a necessary balance (for instance, for the purposes of population control). Any absolute distinction between good and evil breaks down because the preservation of this natural equilibrium will have different requirements in different societies and at different times. There are thus no moral absolutes, only culturally and temporally relative values. On the shifting sands of Sade's moral universe, reason alone is Man's guide. As the seat of prejudice, emotion can never be trusted. On the other hand, reason can only operate on the basis of physical sensations. Taking materialism to its logical extreme, Sade locates reason in the body, and the Sadean body being entirely subordinated to sexual desires, only these desires make any sense.

The laws of Nature are the only laws to which we are subject, and these do not obey any ordering intelligence – Nature is blind. It is this dependency on forces that are arbitrary but also unpredictable that elicits an ambivalent response from the Sadean hero. While, on the one hand,

Nature justifies all his crimes (which in fact cease to be crimes because they are simply necessary to the natural order), Nature completely lacks either rationale or compassion, either reason or emotion. In the psychoanalytic perspective of Melanie Klein, Nature is an absent mother, a "bad breast", stirring up feelings of longing but also of resentment and hatred, and prompting a power-struggle by the child against its parent. Like the Kleinian infant, Sadean Man thus experiences an intense desire to destroy the absent and yet all powerful and all nurturing maternal breast that Nature represents to him. But Nature is infinite, and if Man is to best Nature, then he too must achieve the power and status of infinity. This quest for infinity, for a transcendence that will challenge mother nature's monopoly on power is a dominant and recurring theme in the Sadean text, especially in the four libertine novels for which Sade is best known and which now deserve our close attention.

The 120 Days of Sodom

The 120 Days is often considered as Sade's final work, as the peak of a steep curve of ever more pornographic writing. This impression is apparently confirmed by the Introduction to the work, in which the narrator proudly describes his narrative as "the most impure tale that has ever been told since our world began". It was in fact Sade's first long work of fiction. Its unfinished nature perhaps fuels this particular misapprehension, and the dramatic circumstances surrounding its composition and eventual loss have also contributed to the creation of the work's mythical status. Sade began it in prison on 22 October 1785, writing in microscopic handwriting on long narrow roles of paper that he glued together into a roll that was eventually 14.7 metres (49 feet) long, kept hidden in a hole in the wall of his cell in the Bastille. He wrote every evening after dinner for three hours or more in the paradoxically named Tower of Liberty where his cell was located, taking only 37 days to produce a novel-length draft of the first of four sections and detailed notes for the remaining three. When Sade was suddenly moved from the Bastille ten days before it was stormed during the Revolution of 1789, he became separated from this rudimentary manuscript and never saw it again. When the Bastille was taken, the work was discovered and found its way into the hands of the

Villeneuve-Trans family, remaining in their possession until its sale in around 1900 to a German collector. In 1904, the German psychiatrist, Dr Iwan Bloch, published a limited edition of 180 copies under the pseudonym of Eugen Dühren. Maurice Heine, the father of modern Sade studies, acquired the manuscript in 1929 on behalf of Viscount Charles de Noailles, and provided a much revised version in the early 1930s – also in a limited print-run of fewer than 400 copies, reserved for the members of the *Société du Roman Philosophique*. Both of these early editions were aimed at those doctors and scientists working in the new field of sexology who saw the novel as providing the first-known encyclopedia of sexual aberrations, predating the work of Freud and Krafft-Ebing by more than a century.

Sade's own admission that he wept tears of blood at the loss of the work has also probably helped to give the impression that this was his most important and therefore most mature undertaking. Although his first and not his last work, however, the *120 Days* is for many, quite simply the foundation-stone of the Sadean edifice, containing many of the features that would become characteristic of his novel-writing: a passionate concern with order and categorization, a preoccupation with numbers, the uniquely Sadean rhythm of orgy following dissertation or narrative, of practice following theory, and above all, the encyclopedic mission to "say all" in the area of human sexuality. The work represents an audacious attempt to catalogue all known sexual perversions (or "passions", as Sade called them), and in both conception and form clearly seems inspired by Boccaccio's *Decameron*.

Four libertines have planned an orgy that is scheduled to last 120 days or four months, during which they will hear about and themselves enact 600 "passions" or perversions at the rate of 150 per month or five per day. These passions will be narrated by four story-tellers, one for each month and for a different class of perversion, which are to be illustrated by "case-histories" of an increasingly violent nature, from the "simple passions" of November via the "passions de seconde classe ou double" of December, and the "passions de troisième classe ou criminelles" of January, to the "passions meurtrières ou de quatrième classe" of February. Sade in fact only completed Part 1, but wrote detailed notes for the remaining three parts.

Sade's aim was to cover all conceivable sexual manias, in other words, to produce a veritable encyclopedia of sex, in which incest, coprophilia, torture, and murder are given pride of place.

The work is set in the first decade of the 18th century during the last years of the reign of Louis XIV. The novel's four libertines are wealthy enough to embark on a murderous three-month orgy thanks to the huge profits they have made from Louis XIV's expansionist wars. As in all of Sade's narratives, the violence is framed by a violent historical context, one sufficiently long ago to be "just outside the collective memory of the writer's contemporaries", as Joan De Jean puts it, but nevertheless a past not too distant to suggest an underlying critique of the entire contemporary period, that is, of a century whose rulers all share some responsibility for the impoverishment and ruin of both the Sade family and the French nation. In a negative image of Rousseau's fraternal utopia, the libertines form a pact cemented by their wealth and influence. Right from the start, Sade distances himself from his characters, holding up a mirror to a corrupt society in which money is power. The four main characters and orchestrators of the four-month orgy, which forms the main subject-matter of the novel, represent the four sources of authority and power in 18th-century France (the nobility, the Church, the courts and high finance), and their largely negative portrayal reinforces the impression gained by the reader in the opening lines that one of Sade's aims is political satire. The book presents the reader with a gallery of social types as physically and morally unattractive as the four libertines: bankers, lawyers, magistrates, priests, courtiers, landowners, military officers, all old, rich and powerful, they represent a wide cross-section of the ruling classes, whom Sade had every reason to hate. In this work, if not in Sade's later novels, libertinage is certainly not painted in seductive colours.

The orgy takes place in a remote castle, the château of Silling, located on a high peak in the depths of the Black Forest. Sade emphasises Silling's total inaccessibility, "a remote and isolated retreat, as if silence, distance, and stillness were libertinage's potent vehicles". Silling offers no hope of rescue or survival to those unfortunates captive within its impenetrable walls, and womb-like security to their nefarious captors. Completely cut off from the outside world for the four winter months of their protracted orgy, the main characters realise a universal unconscious fantasy of unlimited power over others. In this more than any other of his works, Sade was creating the fantasy of total licence as an antidote to the restraint of his own circumstances. Writing in his cell in the Bastille each evening, Sade created an exaggerated libertine utopia in his unfettered imagination to make up for the physical freedom he had lost. This utopia of total sexual and ethical licence is indeed only possible in the imaginary world conceived in and framed by prison walls. In this sense, the *120 Days* may be, in De Jean's words, "the ultimate work of prison literature".

Philosophy in the Boudoir

Unlike the *120 Days*, *La Philosophie dans le boudoir* (*Philosophy in the Boudoir*) was composed during Sade's extended period of freedom during the 1790s, and its upbeat tone reflects this. Published in 1795, the work fizzes with self-confidence, and is by far the most light-hearted (some have called it the least cruel) of his libertine works. The language is certainly obscene and there are moments of sadism, but these features are counterbalanced by a tongue-in-cheek and often self-reflexive humour that is both verbal and physical. The work also operates on a number of complex levels – dramatic dialogue, philosophical and political polemic, literary parody, Chaucerian farce – which make it Sade's most innovative and, at the same time, most accessible piece of writing.

At one important level, the work reads as a savagely ironic denunciation of Robespierre's "virtuous republic", founded on repression and the guillotine. *Philosophy in the Boudoir* was begun in 1794 during Sade's confinement in the Picpus sanitorium, in a room from which he could see the guillotine and its operations. (It had by now been moved from the Place de la Concorde because of complaints about the smell of blood). Its victims were even buried in the grounds of the sanatorium, "1,800 in thirty-five days", and Sade's letters leave little doubt that the horror of this spectacle marked him profoundly.

Not surprisingly, then, *Philosophy in the Boudoir* is strongly satirical in character and conception, in appearing to justify vice and, above all, murder, on the grounds that such things are good for a republic. Set sometime between 1789 and 1793, the work positions itself unambiguously in the middle of the French Revolution, and can be read as a powerful critique of its aims and methods. *Français, encore un effort, si vous voulez être Républicains* [*Frenchmen, One More Effort if You Wish to Become Republicans*], a polemical pamphlet intercalated in the middle of the work, is itself, on one level, a pastiche of the many political and philosophical "libelles" or underground pamphlets that circulated during the revolutionary period. But the work's main impact has always been as sexual pedagogy. Here, Sade was almost certainly influenced by two earlier models. The first of these was *L'École des Filles*, produced by Michel Millot and Jean l'Ange in 1665. Published in England in 1688 as *The School of Venus*, this relatively innocent tale concerns the sexual education of a young girl by her older female cousin. The second, Nicolas Chorier's more sexually explicit *L'Académie des dames* of about 1660, consists of a number of dialogues in which one young woman instructs another in the art of love-making. The similarly dialogic form of *Philosophy in the Boudoir* is obviously a development of Chorier's technique.

The title itself seems to sum up the whole Sadean project, which is to bring the body, and in particular the female body, back into philosophy. The work's subtitle, "or the immoral teachers", reflects the author's growing boldness at this time, explicitly acknowledging its immoral content. Suggesting its status as possibly the first modern work of sex-education for young girls, the subtitle also implies the legitimization of bodily desires within an accepted framework of instruction – the school classroom – while the adjective "immoral" undermines this legitimacy, announcing with titular pride the illicit pleasures associated with the sexual corruption of innocence. The binarism of both title and subtitle, then, encapsulate the two dominant impulses in Sade: the intellectual and the erotic, the mind and the body, the proselytising and the transgressive.

The actors of this obscene tragicomedy are all fit, healthy and, above all, young – Dolmancé at 36 is the eldest of the whole group. Eugénie, whose sexual initiation is the pretext for the party, is a delicious young virgin of 15 (her father, himself a well-known libertine and one of the richest merchants of Paris, has given permission for all that both daughter and mother are to undergo). The bisexual Madame de Saint-Ange, who will play a leading role in Eugénie's debauchery, is 26. Her brother, the Chevalier de Mirval, is at 20 the youngest of the libertines, and his youthful vigour seems emblematic of a sexual athleticism, which is also enhanced by the extraordinary size of his penis: "Oh, dearest friend, what a monstrous member!... I can scarcely get my hand around it!" cries Eugénie on seeing it for the first time. He prefers women, but can be persuaded to engage in sodomy with "an agreeable man" like Dolmancé. In addition to these five principals, there are two minor characters: Augustin, a young gardener of "about eighteen or twenty", who is even more impressively endowed than the Chevalier, his member measuring 14 inches in length and having a circumference of eight and an half, and Lapierre, Dolmancé's similarly well equipped but syphilitic valet.

Seven actors who, in the course of seven "dialogues" or scenes, will reenact Christianity's founding myth, inverting its central message, as the Eve-like Eugénie's rejection of God and her passage from sexual innocence to sexual knowledge are celebrated rather than lamented. It is Eugénie's pious mother, Madame de Mistival, not the sacrilegious and debauched daughter, who is finally expelled from this perverse paradise of the body. Madame de Mistival's expulsion follows a gruesome scene of black comedy in which Eugénie is instrumental in punishing her mother for her prudishness by infecting her with venereal disease and sewing up her vagina.

A paradisiacal space of sexual freedom for women (if not for mothers) as well as for men, the boudoir becomes a kind of model state, and like all states, it has to have a constitution, embedded in philosophical thought: hence the pamphlet, *Frenchmen, One More Effort if You Wish to Become Republicans*, whose hundred or so pages form the centrepiece of the work. Dolmancé, who just happens to have bought this pamphlet, hot off the press, at the Palais de l'Égalité, reads it out in response to a question from Eugénie about whether morals are necessary to government.

The pamphlet temporarily suspends the fiction of the dramatic dialogues and takes us outside the text, so to speak, and into the politics of the French Revolution. This part of Sade's text, at least, is firmly rooted in its historical context. In a sense, the insertion of the pamphlet into an anonymously published work of fiction provides a further protective barrier against discovery. Sade is thus able to express his views on topical ideas and events from a position of relative safety.

In spite of its final scene, *Philosophy* is probably the most optimistic of Sade's libertine works. Like its mythical model, the libertines' own Eden is a "delightful boudoir", a privileged and almost timeless space isolated from the outside world, but unlike the Christian version, the joys associated with it are physical, not spiritual. The only serpent is Augustin's delightfully monstrous penis and Eugénie and her mentors display an awareness of their nudity that is completely without shame.

Justine

There are no fewer than three separate versions of *Justine*, which grew from a mere infant text of 138 pages, to mature some ten years later as a triple-X rated adult entertainment of more than a thousand. The original version, *Les Infortunes de la vertu* [*The Misfortunes of Virtue*], not so much a novel as a short story with satirical aims (critics describe it as a "conte philosophique" or "philosophical tale"), was composed in 15 days in the Bastille in 1787. Largely conventional in style, and lacking any characteristics that might now be termed obscene, this short, snappy novella could safely be recommended nowadays to most maiden aunts. Some critics have found this first draft of Sade's tale of virtue despoiled to contain an intensity and clarity of vision absent from the two subsequent versions, but it was destined never to reach the reading public in the author's lifetime. The unpublished *conte* was, nevertheless, to grow into the novel-length, *Justine; ou, Les Malheurs de la vertu* [*Justine; or, Good Conduct Well Chastised*] which appeared in 1791, a year after the author's release from Charenton. Sade claimed that money problems and editorial pressure had forced him to write a "spicy" bestseller. The editor must have been delighted with the result. *Les Malheurs* was considerably more violent and sexually explicit than *Les Infortunes*, and sold so well that five further editions had to be printed in the space of ten years. While the public's appetite for Sade's first published work was evidently insatiable, critical responses of the time were mixed. An article of 27 September 1792 praises the author's "rich and brilliant" imagination, while exhorting young people to "avoid this dangerous book" and advising even "more mature" men to read it "in order to see to what insanities human imagination can lead", but then to "throw it in the fire".

In spite of the popular success of *Les Malheurs*, Sade's financial affairs remained in the doldrums. Maurice Lever tells us that *Justine* did not make its author any money, nor did any of his other books. It did however achieve a *succès de scandale*. This apparent success and the writer's continued impecuniousness doubtless provided sufficient incentive for the composition of the much extended and more openly obscene final version of Justine's adventures, entitled *La nouvelle Justine; ou, Les Malheurs de la vertu* [*The New Justine*], which appeared six years later in 1797 in a ten-volume edition that also included *L'Histoire de Juliette*. *La nouvelle Justine* is, in a number of important respects, significantly different from the two earlier versions. According to Rétif de la Bretonne and Sébastien Mercier, writing at the time, sales were brisk among the booksellers of the Palais Royal, and it was more than a year before the authorities began to seize copies. Gradually, however, the work and its author were systematically hunted down. Sade was accused of having written "l'infâme *Justine*" in a press article that appeared in 1800, and despite his vigorous denials, he was eventually arrested the following year, together with his publisher, Nicolas Massé, for the authorship of these "dangerous" and "detestable" works, and detained without trial at the "maison de santé de Charenton" until his death in 1814.

In a sense, then, Sade fell victim to his own creation. Perhaps all along, as his narrative became increasingly bolder, more challenging to the censor, the Marquis was unconsciously driven to a point of coincidence with his fictional heroine, for both author and character are acutely aware of their own status as victim. After all, it was not Juliette, but Justine that preoccupied him for more than ten years of his own less than happy existence to the point of composing three separate versions of her woeful tale. Such, in fact, was the association of Sade with his less fortunate heroine that he would be known throughout the 19th century as the author, not of *Juliette* but of *Justine*. This identification of the writer with his ingenuous creation

outside of the text can perhaps be explained by what some have seen as an unconscious authorial identification on psychological and emotional levels with the character herself. How justified are we in positing such an identification between author and character? In the first-person narratives of *Les Infortunes* and *Les Malheurs*, the young woman often appears to speak with her creator's voice. Sade's appreciation of feminine beauty, for example, certainly shows itself in Justine's all too enthusiastic evocation of the beauty of other young women. There is, moreover, a marked discrepancy in the first two versions between the stereotypes of Justine's initial portrait and the more positive ways in which, through her own words and actions, she is subsequently portrayed.

From the outset, Justine appears to us as a passive creature, destined for martyrdom. A devout young girl of 12 at the beginning of her remarkable odyssey, her religious faith remains implausibly unshaken by the unending catalogue of disasters that befall her throughout her relatively short and miserable existence.

In a few lines at the start of the narrative, Sade deftly sketches the charm of this "delicious" young creature in terms of what we would now consider to be a stereotype of feminine beauty (big blue eyes, teeth of ivory, lovely blond hair). For the modern reader, the same physical features make up another stereotype – the dumb blonde – which is reinforced here by character traits connoting "girlishness" and vulnerability (ingenuousness, sensitivity, naivety). Like her beauty, these traits can be also read on her physiognomy, at the very surface of her body: modesty, delicacy, shyness, and above all, the "look of a virgin". In fact, in line with her creator's materialist thinking, physique and temperament become one in Justine, naivety is graceful, vulnerability attractive, sexual innocence seductive. Justine is the first "girly girl", the young ingénue so beloved of 19th- and 20th-century theatre and film, a blonde whose dumbness here means ignorance of sexuality, an essential prerequisite of the female victim. Justine's physical appearance immediately suggests that this is the part she will play: in Sade's terms, she is primed to be a victim of her own virtue (which will prevent her from enjoying the sexual attentions forced upon her, but which more importantly will determine the very nature of her attraction for the men and women who abuse her). She will also be the victim of the religious and social prejudices of a society that places a high value on the status of virginity, and in so doing, creates a taboo that cries out to be transgressed. Innocence, virtue, beauty are all synonymous in Justine, who initially at least is nothing more than a cluster of nouns and adjectives. She is simply, we are told, the embodiment of virginal innocence and sensibility, having a potentially erotic vulnerability, "an ingenuousness, a candor that were to cause her to tumble into not a few pitfalls" (*Good Conduct*, p. 459). A construct of Platonic ideals expressed nonplatonically in physical terms, Justine exists in abstraction only, as an object promised to the reader's sexual curiosity – until the narrative brings her to life, that is.

When both parents die, Justine and her 15-year-old sister, Juliette are left penniless orphans. Juliette's only response is the pleasure of being free. Even if we had not already been told at the beginning of the narrative of the fortune her beauty will help her to amass, we would know from this display of lack of feeling that, far from being a victim, the insensitive and self-serving Juliette will be one of life's winners. Not so the "sad and miserable Justine".

Justine's narrative follows more or less the same pattern in all three versions, although in the second and especially the third versions events are narrated in considerably more detail and there are some new episodes and characters. For a thumb-nail sketch of Justine's tale up until her reunion with her sister, Juliette (or Madame de Lorsange, as she is known by then), the reader is referred to the young woman's own summary of her wretched life, told to her sister, Juliette and her lover, as she waits to be hanged for a crime she did not commit.

In the first two versions, when she finishes her sad tale, Justine is recognized by her sister Juliette, whose rich and powerful lover succeeds in rescuing her from the gallows, and she goes to live with them in their château. Fate, however, cruelly cuts short Justine's life and her new-found happiness. In a savage metaphor for the sheer perversity of providence, she is finally split asunder by a thunderbolt during a violent storm. The evolution of this scene and its repercussions in the narrative reflects both the increasingly transgressive sexualization of *Justine* from one version to the next and, perhaps also, the author's changing attitude to his heroine. In

Les Infortunes, the bolt enters her right breast and comes out through her mouth, whereas in *Les Malheurs* the bolt exits through her abdomen and in *La nouvelle Justine* through her vagina. Furthermore, in the final version, in which there is no happy reunion, Justine's horrific death is not so much an accident, as an event engineered by Juliette and her libertine friends, who sadistically drive her outside as the storm reaches its peak.

The common theme of all three narratives is that the heroine's unreasonable attachment to virtue (and in particular, to her virginity) attract nothing but misfortune, as she is exploited and abused physically and sexually by almost everyone she encounters, and is even framed for crimes of theft and murder. Like Voltaire's *Candide*, which Sade had almost certainly read, *Justine* was originally conceived as a satire, attacking the corruption of contemporary institutions, including the judiciary, banking, the bourgeois-dominated world of finances in general, and above all the Catholic Church, with divine providence the principal religious target. In these respects, Sade's *conte* is decidedly Voltairean, but where Voltaire never quite found a satisfactory solution to the problem of physical and moral evil, other than to posit the totally implausible concept of an indifferent God, Sade's libertines dismiss belief in a deity altogether, and draw somewhat different conclusions from the observation, familiar to Candide, that the virtuous perish while the wicked survive. Candide and his fellow truth-seekers do eventually find a kind of contentment in the simple virtue of hard work. In contrast, Justine is repeatedly reminded of what the author-narrator had told the reader on the very first page: that "in an entirely corrupted age, the safest course is to follow along after the others" (*Good Conduct*). Rousseau's idealistic faith in Man's natural goodness is directly challenged in a dissertation delivered to Justine by Roland the counterfeiter: the only truth is the law of the jungle according to which the strong not only survive but flourish at the expense of the weak. In the original version, even Justine herself comes to the conclusion on encountering the monstrous counterfeiter that "Man is naturally wicked". The note of optimism on which *Candide* ends is completely absent from the far bleaker vision of life and death that closes *Justine*.

The Story of Juliette

Sade's most violent and most shocking complete work, the marathon picaresque novel, *The Story of Juliette* was published between 1798 and 1801, following the appearance in 1797 of its companion, *The New Justine*.

Juliette and *The New Justine* provide the reader with an unadulterated account of Man's inhumanity to Man, and in this sense are the cynical product of their author's personal and painful experience of the Terror and its evil. Geoffrey Gorer called *Juliette* "the final vomiting of de Sade's disgust and disappointment". As Gorer's observation implies, the novel represents a savage attack on the corruption of 18th-century French society, in which money is power, and power facilitates the unrestrained pursuit of pleasure. *Juliette* can also be read, of course, as the barely unconscious expression of a desire for such unfettered freedom – a utopian vision of power that is almost divine in its totality: "Oh, my love" cries the libertine, Saint-Fond to Juliette, "how delicious are our crimes when impunity veils them, when duty itself prescribes them. How divine it is to swim in gold and, as one reckons up one's wealth, to be able to say, here are the means to every black deed, to every pleasure; with this, all my wishes can be made to come true, all my fancies can be satisfied; no woman will resist me, none of my desires will fail of realization, my wealth will procure amendments in the law itself, and I'll be despot without let or hindrance."

Only the leisured upper classes could afford to use sex recreationally as well as procreationally, and only the political masters of a land could indulge with impunity in a perverse sexuality that favoured rape and murder, manipulating the justice system for their own ends. More generally, *Juliette* has been read as an implicit indictment of male sexuality as utterly selfish, intrinsically violent and fundamentally tyrannical, and yet, paradoxically (or so it seems), Sade chooses a female rather than a male character as the central focus of this sexual tyranny. Indeed, the novel is dominated by the activities of a number of violent and depraved *femmes fatales*.

Sade's longest novel is scandalously provocative with regard to the role and status of women, as well as to a whole range of moral and philosophical issues, and there is no doubt that many will continue to find both the ideas contained within its pages and its outright obscenity unpalatable.

On the other hand, it is a work of breath-taking geographical and historical scope and of remarkable scholarship, replete with learned allusions and references and detailed philosophical arguments. But at the simple story level, too, the novel's sheer nervous energy carries the reader along with its heroine as she races through a Europe ruled by sexual deviants and ruthless megalomaniacs. Among its hundreds of characters, we encounter lascivious monarchs and psychotic politicians, atheistic clerics and man-hating lesbians, giants and sorcerers, vamps and virgins. The entirely fictional rub shoulders with the verifiably historical; the real blends with the surreal (a black mass at the Vatican, the giant Minski's "human" furniture) to produce a work of layered complexity. Sade's *Juliette* can be read on many levels: as an adult fairy-tale and a manual of sexology, as a political and philosophical satire and a Gothic horror, as an Italian travelogue and an 18th-century road movie, above all, perhaps, as a terrifying journey into the murkier depths of human eroticism. On all of these levels, *Juliette* goes much further than *Justine*. The narrative moves faster, the crimes are greater, and the reader feels swept along from one location to another to encounter ever more extreme situations and behaviour.

Juliette, Justine's beautiful but wicked elder sister, is her opposite in every way. Like her sister Justine, her character and temperament are initially expressed in physical terms: not blond, but brunette, with eyes not credulously blue but dark and "prodigiously expressive"; not timid but spirited, not naive but incredulous, not innocent, but wordly wise thanks to the best possible education that a father's untimely ruin will deny her younger sister:

> (...) she was brought up (...) in one of the best convents in Paris where, until the age of 15, she was never denied good counsel or teachers nor good books or talents. (*The Misfortunes of Virtue*)

She has, in fact, much in common with Eugénie, the mother-hating apprentice libertine of *Philosophy in the Boudoir*. Fifteen years old when she and Justine are orphaned, she is Eugénie let out of the boudoir into the great, mad, bad world. Already awakened to the pleasures of the body as well as to its power by the mother superior of the convent where the two sisters had resided before their father's financial ruin, she immediately sets out to make her living as a prostitute, becoming the mistress of two extremely dangerous libertines, Noirceuil and Saint-Fond. The latter is a government minister who abuses his position to line his pockets and to evade the consequences of the rapes and lust-murders that he and his associates regularly commit. Under the protection of these two monsters, she embarks with her lesbian lover, the equally bloodthirsty Clairwil, on an epic tour of Europe, in particular Italy, encountering en route a series of libertines, each more depraved than the last, and leaving a trail of pillage, death and destruction in her wake. These libertines include a number of historical figures, such as Catherine the Great, the atheistic Pope Pius VI, and two of Marie-Antoinette's homicidal siblings, Grand Duke Leopold of Tuscany and the wife of the King of Naples. Unsurprisingly given the revolutionary period in which the novel was written, kings and pontiffs are seen as surpassing all others in their debauchery and corruption. Eventually, following many gruesome and often gratuitous crimes, which include the murder of her friend, Clairwil, Juliette returns to France considerably enriched. There she is reunited with Noirceuil, whose iniquities are seen to be rewarded when the King makes him prime minister, assuring him and his fellow criminals of a glorious future. With a note of self-referential irony, Noirceuil draws the obvious moral from their story:

> Come, good friends, let us all rejoice together, from all this I see nothing but happiness accruing to all save only virtue – but we would perhaps not dare say so were it a novel we were writing.

In continuing ironic vein, Juliette adopts and defends the real author's point of view:

> Why dread publishing it, said Juliette, when the truth itself, and the truth alone, lays bare the secrets of Nature, however mankind may tremble before those revelations. Philosophy must never shrink from speaking out.

So the novel ends with Juliette stepping out of the pages of her own story to take a cheeky swipe at the censor, who is implicitly positioned as the enemy of truth.

Sade's world is an interior world, a world of castles and dungeons and boudoirs and monasteries in which the reader can feel as trapped as Justine. The claustrophobic sexual arena of the Sadean imagination reflects the loss of physical and sexual freedom the author was forced to endure. Though stages for the *mise-en-scène* of the body, the interior spaces of the fiction are, at the same time, therefore, both representations and projections of the internal world of the mind. In the dissertations and footnotes and philosophical dialogues that alternate with and seek to justify the acts of extreme violence and sexual abuse conducted by his libertine anti-heroes, Sade invites us to rethink received wisdoms, and reinterpret long-standing values, challenging essentialist conceptions of morality and truth.

If Sade is now worthy of a place in the local bookstore and public library, as well as on university syllabi, it is not only because of the enormous and undisputed influence of his writing and thought over the last two centuries, but also because, in so many regards, his work once again finds resonance with the current artistic climate: our suspicion of modern political credos, the fragmentation of our value-systems and the ubiquitous pursuit of sexual ecstasy and physical immortality. Although, like all writers and thinkers, undeniably a product of his own times, Sade raises moral, social and even political questions that are as relevant now and everywhere as they were in 18th-century France: the threat of religious fundamentalism, the repression and persecution of non-normative forms of sexuality, the obsession with physical perfection, the sexual motives underlying our fascination with violence, and the emergence of greater pluralism in the way we organize our societies, for example, are all important Sadean themes.

Sade deserves to be called a great erotic writer because of the extraordinary modernity of his thinking, because of the breadth of his vision and the novelty of his perspectives, because he alone dares say what others before him considered unmentionable, because he says it in a form of some artistic depth and complexity, and perhaps most of all, for the unambiguous warnings he so fearlessly and stubbornly sounds against the ever-present dangers of self-deception and ignorance:

> I authorize the publication and sale of all libertine books and immoral works; for I esteem them most essential to human felicity and welfare, instrumental to the progress of philosophy, indispensable to the eradication of prejudices, and in every sense conducive to the increase of human knowledge and understanding. (*Juliette*)

JOHN PHILLIPS

Biography

Born in Paris, 2 June 1740. Educated at Collège Louis-le-Grand, Paris, 1750–54; then attended a military school in 1754, becoming 2nd lieutenant in 1755. Served in the French army during the Seven Years War: Captain, 1759; resigned commission, 1763. Married Renée Pélagie Cordier de Launay de Montreuil in 1763 (separated 1790); two sons and one daughter. Succeeded to the title Comte, 1767; arrested and imprisoned briefly for sexual offences, but pardoned by the king, 1768; condemned to death for sex offences, 1772, but sentence commuted to imprisonment; held in Miolans, 1772–73 (escaped); convicted again and imprisoned in Vincennes, 1778–84, Bastille, Paris, 1784–89, and Charenton, 1789–90; liberated and joined Section des Picques, 1790: organized cavalry and served as hospital inspector; made a judge, 1793, but condemned for moderation and imprisoned, 1793–94; arrested for obscene work (*Justine*) and imprisoned in Sainte-Pélagie, 1801, and confined again in Charenton, from 1803 until his death on 2 December 1814.

Selected Works

Justine; ou, Les Malheurs de la vertu (published anonymously). 2 vols, 1791; as *Justine; or, Good Conduct Well Chastised*, translated by Pierralessandro Cassavini, 1953; and in *Justine, Philosophy in the Bedroom, and Other Writings*, edited and translated by Richard Seaver and Austryn Wainhouse, 1990.

La Philosophie dans le boudoir. 2 vols, 1795; as *Philosophy in the Boudoir*, translated by Austryn Wainhouse and Richard Seaver in *The Complete Justine*, 1965.

La Nouvelle Justine; ou, Les Malheurs de la vertu, suivie de l'histoire de Juliette, sa soeur. 10 vols, 1797; second part as *Juliette*, translated by Austryn Wainhouse. 1968.

Les 120 Journées de Sodome; ou, L'École du libertinage. Edited by Eugen Dühren, 1904; edited by Maurice Heine, 3 vols, 1931–35; as *The 120 Days of Sodom*, translated by Austryn Wainhouse and Richard Seaver, in *The 120 Days of Sodom, and Other Writings*. 1966.

Dialogue entre un prêtre et un moribund. Edited by Maurice Heine, 1926; as *Dialogue between a Priest and a Dying Man*, translated by Samuel Putnam, 1927; translated by Richard Seaver and Austryn Wainhouse in *The Complete Justine*. 1965.

Les Infortunes de la vertu. Introduction by Jean Paulhan, 1946; as *The Misfortunes of Virtue and Other Early Tales*, edited and translated by David Coward, 1992*Letters from Prison*, translated by Richard Seaver. 1991.

References and Further Reading

Airaksinen, Timo. *The Philosophy of the Marquis de Sade.* London and New York: Routledge. 1995

Allison, David B., Mark S. Roberts and Allen S. Weiss (editors). *Sade and the Narrative of Transgression.* Cambridge: Cambridge University Press. 1995

Barthes, Roland. *Sade, Fourier, Loyola.* Paris: Seuil, 1971; as *Sade, Fourier, Loyola*, translated by Richard Miller. New York: Hill and Wang. 1976.

Beauvoir, Simone de. "Must We Burn Sade?" Translated by Annette Michelson,, London and New York: Nevill, 1953; also in *The 120 Days of Sodom and Other Writings*, edited and translated by Austryn Wainhouse and Richard Seaver, New York: Grove Press; London: Arrow. 1990.

Bongie, Laurence L. *Sade: A Biographical Essay.* Chicago: University of Chicago Press. 1998.

Carter, Angela. *The Sadeian Woman: An Exercise in Culture History.* London: Virago Press. 1979.

Cryle, Peter. *Geometry in the Boudoir: Configurations of French Erotic Narrative.* Ithaca, New York: Cornell University Press. 1994.

De Jean, Joan. *Literary Fortifications: Rousseau, Laclos, Sade.* Princeton, New Jersey: Princeton University Press. 1984.

Frappier-Mazur, Lucienne. *Writing the Orgy: Power and Parody in Sade.* Translated by Gillian C. Gill. Philadelphia: University of Pennsylvania Press. 1996.

Gallop, Jane. *Intersections. A Reading of Sade with Bataille, Blanchot, and Klossowski.* Lincoln: University of Nebraska Press. 1981.

Gorer, Geoffrey. *The Life and Ideas of the Marquis de Sade.* London, 1934; revised edition, London: Peter Owen. 1953; New York: Norton. 1963.

Goulemot, Jean Marie. *Forbidden Texts: Erotic Literature and its Readers in Eighteenth Century France.* Translated by James Simpson. Philadelphia: University of Pennsylvania Press. 1994

Hénaff, Marcel. *Sade: The Invention of the Libertine Bod.*, Translated by Xavier Callahan. University of Minnesota Press. 1999.

Klossowski, Pierre. *Sade My Neighbour.* Translated by Alphonso Lingis. London: Quartet. 1992.

Lever, Maurice. *Marquis de Sade: A Biography.* Translated by Arthur Goldhammer, London: HarperCollins and New York: Farrar Straus. 1993.

Paglia, Camille. *Sexual Personae: Art and Decadence from Nefertiti to Emily Dickinson.* New Haven, CT: Yale University Press. 1991.

Paulhan, Jean. "The Marquis de Sade and His Accomplice." In *Justine, Philosophy in the Bedroom, and Other Writings.* Edited and translated by Richard Seaver and Austryn Wainhouse. New York: Grove Weidenfeld, 1990; London: Arrow, 1919.

Plessix Gray, Francine du. *At Home with the Marquis de Sade.* London: Chatto and Windus and New York: Simon and Schuster. 1999.

Phillips, John. *Sade: The Libertine Novels.* London: Pluto Press. 2001.

Thomas, Donald. *The Marquis de Sade.* London: Weidenfeld and Nicolson and Boston: New York Graphic Society, 1976; London: Allison and Busby, 1992.

SADO-MASOCHISM

Sado-masochism, a term derived from sadism and masochism, is the name given to the group of sexual behaviours and attitudes that combine sex with pain, or which use pain symbolically for erotic pleasure. The word sadism derives from the Marquis de Sade (1740–1814), whose writings can be characterised as extreme sexual violence towards, and humiliation of, the 'victim', and masochism from Baron Leopold von Sacher-Masoch (1836–95), who eroticised the subaltern's treatment. These terms, however, are far from able to capture the complexity of the theoretical manifestations of sado-masochism in sexological discourses, and the other literary writing, throughout history, let alone more recent writings by aficionados of such practices. For this reason, alternative names, such as BDSM (bondage and discipline (BD), dominance and submission (DS), and sadism and masochism (SM)), algolagnia, and algophily have been proposed by some authors. Furthermore, there are significant epistemological problems with assuming that sado-masochistic behaviour is able to be addressed as trans-historical. As such, this entry follows many of the sexological discourses in their location of prior sado-masochistic acts, even though many of these acts were recorded before the concept of sado-masochism was first formulated, and would not be counted as such today by practitioners of sado-masochism.

One of the key organising points of sado-masochism throughout all of the writings addressed is the passive and active aspects of sexual expression which are manifest in extreme form in sadism and masochism. In these discourses, sadism is active, while masochism is passive. There are highly gendered connotations for these two phases that are formalised within the sexological discourses and in some of the other sources: the feminine sexual impulse being masochistic and a masculine one being sadistic. Nevertheless, these gendered notions are a part of a long history of writing about sexuality which has been used by both sexologists and readers who were aroused by descriptions of flogging and sexual domination.

The early writing about sado-masochstic acts can be traced to the ancient world. In these discourses we see the first formulations of a masochistic feminine sexual impulse, and a sadistic masculine one. For example, the eighth Dialogue of Lucian's *Dialogues of Courtesans* (Lucian 299; Lucian, vol 7, trans. M.D. MacLeod, Loeb Classics, Harvard UP, p.403), asks "If a man isn't jealous or angry, Chrysis, and never hits you, cuts your hair off, or tears your clothes, is he still in love with you?", although this text can be read as an enquiry about the role of jealousy in love. Ovid's *Ars amatoria* explains less equivocally that:

> Though you call it force: it's force that pleases girls: what delights
> is often to have given what they wanted, against their will.
> She who is taken in love's sudden onslaught
> is pleased, and finds wickedness is a tribute.
> And she who might have been forced, and escapes unscathed,
> will be saddened, though her face pretends delight.
> Phoebe was taken by force: force was offered her sister:
> and both, when raped, were pleased with those who raped them.

Plutarch's *Life of Pompey* described the relationship of the courtesan Flora with Pompey, noting that "she could never part after being with him without a bite." The historian Livy retells the legend of how the Sabine women were snatched from their families at a religious festival to populate Rome and how their hearts and minds were won over by violence followed by sweet words and childbearing. In all of these instances, it is the domination of women by men that captures the later sexological basis of female masochism–that women truly love when they are dominated–and male sadism, that they prefer to dominate women against their wills.

Although these examples play up female passivity and modesty as the basis for true sexual desire, there are some examples of men being sexually excited when punished; for example, in Petronius' *Satyricon*, Œnothea whips Encolpius with nettles, a practice which sexually excites him.

These Western examples are not the only ones that underlie the 'naturalised' basis of sado-masochism as a gendered manifestation of the sexual impulse. The classic Indian text, the *Kama sutra* of Vatsayayana, specifies the place in which a woman should be struck (the shoulders, the head, the space between the breasts, the back, the middle part of the body, and the sides). This striking is of four kinds: with the back of the hand, with the fingers a little contracted, with the fist, and with the open palm of the hand (*Kama sutra*, part two, chapter 7, trans. Richard Burton, 1883). There are also remarks made about biting and scratching during sexual congress that are worth further considering.

Having established that it was sometimes considered normal and natural in the Ancient world for men to behave aggressively during sex towards women, and that women responded positively, it is worthwhile considering how this tradition was maintained. There are a number of examples from the early modern period, up until the Enlightenment, which are worthy of mention, such as Johann Heinrich Meibom's (1590–1655) medical text, *Tractus de usu flagrorum in re Medica & Veneria* (1639; English trans. Edmund Curll, 1718): "there are Persons who are stimulated to *Venery by Strokes of Rods, and worked up into a Flame of Lust by Blows*, and that the Part, which distinguishes us to be Men, should be raised by the Charm of invigorating Lashes" (pp. 34–35). Other texts that followed a more traditional line concerning the sexual domination of women included Pierre de Brantôme, whose 1587 *Recueil des Dames* [*Les Dames Galantes*], noted that a woman who is "a little difficult and resists gives more pleasure to her lover." (cited in Ellis *Love and Pain*, 1903, p. 79). If we are to believe Enlightenment author, Restif de la Bretonne, writing in his 1798 *Anti-Justine*, "All women of strong temperament like a sort of brutality in sexual intimacy and its accessories" (cited in Ellis, *Love and Pain*, 1903 , p. 79), these ideas persisted from the Ancient world.

One of the most famous Enlightenment descriptions of masochism was recorded by Jean-Jacques Rousseau, in book one of his *Confessions*, where he annotated his erotic awakenings, aged eight, when he was whipped by Mlle Lambercier. Rousseau noted that "this punishment increased my affection for the person who had inflicted it. All this affection, aided by my natural mildness, was scarcely sufficient to prevent my seeking, by fresh offences, a return of the same chastisement; for a degree of sensuality had mingled with the smart and shame, which left more desire than fear of a repetition. . . . Who would believe this childish discipline, received at eight years old, from the hand of a woman of thirty, should influence my propensities, my desires, my passions, for the rest of my life, and that in quite a contrary sense from what might naturally have been expected? . . . Even after having attained the marriageable age this odd taste still continued and drove me nearly to depravity and madness."

These rather coy descriptions of sadistic and masochistic desire were seriously overshadowed by the first of the eponymous authors with which this entry is concerned: Donatien Alphonse Francois, Marquis de Sade. Sade's novels, which were written while he was imprisoned, graphically describe a 'philosophy of evil', derived from La Mettrie and Holbach's Enlightenment philosophies which conceived of nature as a system that exists without God. A logical extension of these atheistic philosophies is a world that is not governed by morality, in which pleasure is sought and an egocentric domination of the world is permissible, because any appeal to a higher morality is precluded by the denial of the existence of God. This is the world that Sade created. In his works, the most famous ones including *One hundred and twenty days of Sodom, Justine, Juliette, and Philosophy in the Bedroom*, the reader is exposed to tales of rape, sodomy, torture, coprophilia, etc. These are organised under the rubric of imposing one's will on one's lover. Sade is not interested in the moral aspects of these acts–for he does not believe in conventional Christian morality. Rather, he is pushing the boundaries of philosophical convention by celebrating the individual ego, and by exerting his desires onto the world. It is the association of cruelty with sexuality that gave us the name sadism, although it is a rather superficial linkage that denies Sade's philosophical system, and focuses only on the erotic aspects in a way similar to that in which many people seem to have since read him.

There are other ways of imposing one's will than humiliating and torturing one's paramour. Baron Leopold von Sacher-Masoch (1836–95) is famous nowadays for having his name given to the forms of erotic submission known as masochism, although he was not pleased with this appropriation by Austrian sexologist, Richard von Krafft-Ebing (1840–1902), who in turn borrowed it after one of his patients referred to themselves as a masochist. Masoch was an historian and novelist who emphasised contractual domination by women. An important novel that encapsulates this is *Venus im Pelz* [*Venus in Furs*, 1870], in which the heroine, Wanda, is made to treat the protagonist like a slave, and to socially and sexually humiliate him. As with sadism, there are strong power relations at play in this scheme, but it is the masochist who is in power, controlling the ways his mistress maltreats him through carefully devised contracts. The sexological use of this word has denied these power relations, and focuses on arousal by submission.

Before finishing with pre-sexological writing about sadism and masochism, it is important to note other relevant forms of erotica which are not considered classical, high literature, or Enlightenment philosophy, such as the erotic writing produced in England in the eighteenth and nineteenth centuries. It is noteworthy that flagellation was considered the 'English vice'. Throughout Victorian erotica, there are numerous descriptions of flagellation and birching, more often than not of young women with big bottoms, either by strict mistresses or old *roués*. Often after such a scene, the young girl is deflowered, having been aroused by the domination with the rod. Occasionally, it is the man who is dominated, a point which is also cast in 'high literature' by Algernon Swinburne in some of his poems, such as "Authur's flogging," written under the name 'Etonensis.' This poem details the whipping of a young boy on many occasions in a manner that is difficult to remove from any homoerotic associations, describing in graphic lines the state of Arthur's bottom as it is flogged by his school-master.

As the discipline of sexology emerged, it soon began to focus on sado-masochistic issues, and it reformulated the relationship between sex, pain, and power accordingly. There had always been some form of medical interest in these issues, from the forensic work on rape, although rarely did these texts attempt to understand these forms of behaviour. Some of the early work of Chicagoan biologist and psychiatrist, S.V. Clevenger, addressed the gendering of active and passive sexuality. This work was based on the notion that in the early history of life, there were two ways for bacteria to combine heritable material: either by eating or being eaten. Bacteriophages were considered active; those that 'submitted' to being eaten in order to pass on their genetic material were considered passive. The "hunger impulse" developed from this primordial desire, and later so did the sexual impulse, according to Clevenger. Another Chicagoan psychiatrist, James Kiernan, began to apply Clevenger's ideas to the sexual impulse more directly, arguing that the active phases of sexual desire were masculine, and the passive feminine. He also formulated the doctrine that these impulses were normal in their more restrained manifestations, which allowed copulation, but that they could become exaggerated and thus pathological. This idea was picked up by Krafft-Ebing, who denoted the two behaviours as sadism and masochism in the third edition of his *Psychopathia Sexualis* (1890). After Krafft-Ebing, there was a general sexological consensus about sado-masochism, although some dissenters emphasised other aspects. For example, Munich hypnotherapist, Albert von Schrenck-Notzing, developed the concept of algolagnia to emphasise the relationship of pain and lust, derived from Kiernan. Kiernan himself later preferred the term 'algophily', as neither Schrenck-Notzing nor Kiernan believed that either Masoch or Sade were the ideal masochist or sadist, and both Schrenk-Notzing and Kiernan thought that the two mechamisms were linked. English sexologist Havelock Ellis agreed, and preferred to think about the pain as a form of erotic symbolism that stimulated the otherwise evident sexual deficiency of the patient. Ellis also emphasised that there were perfectly normal phases of erotic play that had the same roots as sado-masochism, including kisses, love bites, spanking, etc. He further agreed with the ancient writers that there was a gendered differentiation of the sexual impulse, with women being naturally passive and deriving pleasure from being dominated, and men being naturally inclined to dominate during sexual play. He considered it difficult for a woman to be a pathological masochist, as they were predisposed to this behaviour, and thus it was basically normal except in the most extreme manifestations. He also thought that instances of male masochism and female sadism were similar in aetiology to homosexuality, which he considered a form of gender inversion with a congenital basis. Male sadism, he believed, was the extreme signification of male domination that had to be controlled, as it vitiated his otherwise feminist beliefs in the importance of consensual, non-harmful sex.

This sexological trajectory did much to formalise the approach to sado-masochism prior to activists within the community gaining a voice for themselves on the fringes of popular culture and on the internet. Other contemporary evidence for the existence of sado-masochistic behaviour was being sought by ethnologists and anthropologists, who found such behaviours in practices of marriage capture, as described in the works of John MacLennen and E. B. Tylor, and more subtly described by Edward Westermarck and other later anthropologists. Many of these ethnological texts were enrolled by sexologists as supporting evidence, as were historical descriptions of sadistic practices, such as marriage by capture, which was graphically portrayed in Fustel de Coulanges *Cité d'Antique* (1864). In all cases, there was a maintaining of the gendered distinction between sadistic and masochistic behaviour, and this historical and cultural evidence did much to support this theory.

Significant sexological developments were made when the distinction was forged between perversions of aim and perversions of object. Perversions of aim included sadistic and masochistic practices, because it was not penetrative sex that was desired, but practices of sexual domination. Berlin sexologist, Magnus Hirschfeld, stressed this distinction, which had an important impact on the sexual psychology of Sigmund Freud. After Freud, within sexology as well as psychoanalysis, sado-masochism began to be treated not only as a simple paraphilia involving pain, but became emphasised as a personality trait (especially in psychoanalysis) and as a basic phenomenon that was manifest in many other sexual activities. In this vein, another Chicagoan psychiatrist, Harold Moyer, described both lesbianism and bestiality as forms of sadistic behaviour, the former being a masculine desire to dominate other women as sexual partners, the latter as the desire to actively seek non-compliant sexual partners and to dominate them. Some of Moyer's more extreme examples come from sadistic lesbians who forced their (masochistic) partners to fellate dogs before having sex with the same dogs. In all of these instances, Moyer employed a significantly modified interpretation of sadistic and masochistic behaviour that was much more in line with current psychiatric conceptions of the issue. Within psychoanalysis, there was a tendency to utilise the existing sexological categories in a similar way. Further theoretical developments were contributed by Clara Thompson and Karen Horney in particular, as they strove to overcome many of the overtly gendered assumptions of psychoanalytic theory, and began treating their female patients as individual women rather than embodied theory.

Some resistance, or at least alternatives, to these emerging scientific conceptions of sado-masochism came from contemporary literature. For instance, Freud's early critic, Viennese author Robert Musil, in *Confusions of Young Törless* (1906), described the homoerotic humiliation and beating of one boy in a military academy. Musil rejected many of Freud's ideas about the upbringing of a child impacting on the later sexual development, preferring a volition-based scheme derived from Friedrich Nietzsche which superficially shared much with Sade. Other texts which explicitly made use of social and sexual conceptions of sadism and masochism include the character Baron de Charlus, in Marcel Proust's *A la recherche du temps perdu* (1913–25). Charlus is both sadistic in his sexual and social behaviour, but also masochistic in his old age, needing to be beaten violently in order to be sexually satisfied (as shown in the scene in the Hotel during the war). Neither Proust nor Musil maintained the Freudian ideas about sado-masochism that would become important later in the century, in works such as Georges Bataille's *The Story of the Eye* (1928), which employed sadism to symbolic ends, including descriptions of defiling a priest, and other eroticised violence.

Philsophically, there was a growth in interest in Sade's work after the Second World War, partially as it was perceived as a precursor to some of Nietzsche's ideas which had become popular in the early 1900s, but also because it was published in better editions in the early part of the century when works previously considered missing came to light. Important philosophical engagements came from assorted French philosophers, including Pierre Klossowski, whose *Sade mon prochain* (1947) put the Enlightenment philosopher back on the agenda (although he had written an important psychoanalytic treatment of Sade in *Le revue français de psychanalyse* in 1933). Others who engaged with Sade in this early period included Simone de Beauvoir ("Faut-il bruler Sade?" *Les temps modernes*, 1951–52), Georges Bataille (who wrote two essays in 1947 and 1953, and who also translated the 1440 trials of the serial killer, Gilles de Rais), and Maurice Blanchot (who wrote series of essays on Sade in 1946–48). This work was later followed by Roland Barthes' *Sade, Fourier, Loyola* (1971). In all of these instances, there was no interest in criticising Sade, but rather employing him as a test for further sexual and social possibilities. In this, Sade was hailed as a champion, although the readings became more and more sophisticated, with Barthes declaring that Sade had created an erotic utopia.

Significant literary examples of masochism were produced after the Second World War, including Dominique Aury's (under the pen name of Pauline Réage) *The Story of O* (1954), an instant erotic classic which was lauded for its literary ability and awarded the *Prix Deux-Magots* in 1955. In many ways, the publication of this work, when considered concurrently with the growing philosophical engagement with Sade, was a significant step towards the acceptance of sado-masochism as a part of the mainstream sexual and social world, a position that it had not enjoyed since before the Enlightenment, and which had never been as explicit in earlier times. Other evidence for this acceptance might include the demise of Widmerpool into a subservient character in Anthony Powell's epic *Dance to the Music of Time* (1954–75), or some of the masochistic fantasies in Nancy Friday's *My Secret Garden* (1973), which contributed to the de-pathologization of sado-masochism as it showed the extent to which 'normal' female fantasies could operate. Although one could maintain that these gendered ideas about dominating that are so central to most thought about sado-masochism are not abandoned in Friday's work, a more general idea about the restrictive earlier ideas being gendered is exploded by demonstrating the breadth of female desire, for there are more dominating fantasies as well.

The explosion of contemporary erotica, greatly facilitated by the internet, has allowed for the growth of writing about BDSM, a term used to capture some of the variation of sado-masochism. In this respect, it would seem that sado-masochsim is a widely accepted and practiced sexual manifestation, if amplified in some circumstances, although it should be remembered that different fields define sado-masochism in different ways, and thus is it problematic to speak as if it was one trans-historical phenomenon. There are numerous erotic websites and stories devoted to it, and there are nightclubs which laud its practices in public. It should, however, be noted that contemporary psychiatry fits sexual masochism and sadism under the general heading of paraphilias in the latest edition of the American Psychiatric Association's *Diagnostic and Statistical Manual–Text Revised, 2000*. Both behaviours are recognised as extreme manifestations of normal sexual desires, but of course, they are heavily gendered as well, which provides for a certain 'scripted' performativity which has been adopted and exploited by readers and writers in many fields, as well as by practitioners of these desires.

IVAN CROZIER

Further Reading

Barthes, Roland. *Sade, Fournier, Loyola*. 1971. Translated by Richard Miler. Baltimore: Johns Hopkins University Press. 1997.

Bataille, Georges. "Sade (1740–1814)." *Critique*, 9, 1953.

———. "Le secret de Sade." *Critique*, 3, 1947.

———. *The Story of the Eye*. Translated by Joachim Neugroschel. San Francisco: City Lights Books 1987. Orig., 1928, as *Histoire de l'oeil*.

Beauvoir, Simone de. "Faut-il bruler Sade?" *Les temps modernes*, 7, 1951–52, trans. Autryn Wainhouse and Richad Seaver, repr. in Sade, *Justine, Philosophy in the Bedroom and Other Writings*. New York: Grove Press. 1990.

Blanchot, Maurice. "Quelques remarques sur Sade." *Critique*, 2, 1946.

———. "À la rencontre de Sade." *Les temps modernes*, 3, 1947–48.

Bloch, Iwan. *Marquis de Sade: His Life and Works*. New York: Castle Books. 1931.

Clevenger, S.V. "Comparative Physiology and Psychology," New Englander and Yale review, 49, Issue 222, September 1888, pp. 221–222.

Clevernger, S.V. *Comparative Physiology and Psychology*. Chicago: Jansen, McClurg & Co. 1885.

Diagnostic and Statistical Manual–Text Revised, 2000. American Psychiatric Association, Washington DC. 2000.

Deleuze, Gilles. "Coldness and Cruelty" in *Masochism.* New York: Zone Books. 1991.

Ellis, Havelock. *Love and Pain: Studies in the Psychology of Sex.* Vol. III. Philadelphia: F. A. Davis and Co. 1903.

Freud, Sigmund. *Three Essays on the Theory of Sexuality.* Trans James Strachey. *Standard Edition.* 1905.

Gebhard, Paul. "Fetishism and Sadomasochism.," In Jules E. Masserman, (ed.): *Dynamics of Deviant Sexuality.* New York-London: Grune & Stratton. 1969.

Hekma, Gert. "Sade, Masculinity and Sexual Humiliation," http://www.pscw.uva.nl/gl/

Hirschfeld, Magnus. *Sexual Anomalies and Perversion: A Summary of the Works of the Late Magnus Hirschfeld.* Edited by Norman Haire. London: Encyclopaedic Press. 1938.

Horney, Karen. "The problem of feminine masochism." *Psychoanalytic Review,* 22, 1935.

Kiernan, James. "Psychological Aspects of the Sexual Appetite." *Alienist and Neurologist.* 1891.

———. "Responsibility in sexual perversion." *Chicago Medical Recorder,* March, 1892.

———. "Responsibility in Active Algophily." *Medicine,* April, 1903.

Klossowski, Pierre. *Sade my neighbour.* Translated by Alphonso Lingis. London: Quartet Books. 1992.

Niekirk, Carl and Michael C. Finke, eds. *One Hundred Years of Masochism: Literary Texas, Social and Cultural Contexts.* Amsterdam-Atlanta: Rodopi. 2000.

Moyer, Harold. "Is Sexual Perversion Insanity?" In *Alienist and Neurologist,* May, 1907.

Ovid. *Ars amatoria.* Book I Part XVII. Translated by A. S. Kline 2001 http://www.tkline.freeserve.co.uk/Webworks/Website/ArtofLoveBkI.htm (accessed 7/5/02)

Thompson, Clara. *On Women.* New York: New American Library. 1964.

SADOVEANU, MIHAIL

1880–1961.
Romanian novelist and short story writer

Creanga de aur [*The Golden Bough*]

The novel was published in 1933. Upon its appearance, critics and ordinary readers were shocked by the exquisite style and by the esoteric significance of the book. In *Creanga de aur,* Eros becomes a fundamental epistemological experience surpassing the limitations of time, space and senses.

The novel purports to be a posthumously-discovered manuscript written by the author's alter ego, a researcher named Stamatin, a narrative device that lends verisimilitude to the story. The author presents his lyrical fiction as nonfiction. In the tradition of moralizing or "improving" literature, the novel offers the reader a moral lesson. At the same time it is a very moving love story. The story begins in 1926, when Stamatin returns from an expedition to the Eastern Carpathian mountains, claiming to have discovered a manuscript from the eighth century. In 780 CE, the venerable master of the old law—the ancient traditions of the Dacian (Romanian) priests, who lived somewhere in the Eastern Carpathians—sends Kesarion Breb, the best of his apprentices, to Egypt to become an initiate. He is to study asceticism for seven years, and to learn to transcend matter and open his spirit to the divine. This foreshadows the love story, for Kesarion will close off not only his senses, but any bodily feeling from now on. After he completes his studies and initiation—which leaves a physical trace on his body in the form of three wrinkles forming a triangle on his forehead between his eyebrows—he is to go to Byzantium and rejoin human society by immersing himself among ordinary people.

The human world that he rejoins in Byzantium is tormented and polluted, especially as he has arrived during a time of great upheaval. The conflict between the Iconoclasts (the destroyers of icons) and the Iconodules (those who venerate them) has recently ended, leaving the Iconodules with a shaky victory. The conflict is not only religious, but political. Empress Irina, an Iconodule who above all loves power, does not want to give executive powers to her son, Emperor Constantine. Therefore, she breaks her son's engagement with Rotruda, the daughter of Charlemagne, and decrees that Constantine will marry a Byzantine girl. The decision has serious political implications. Had Constantine married Rotruda, it would have cemented an alliance between Byzantium and the Frankish empire, but Irina and her faction can control a Byzantine maiden much easier. Kesarion Breb befriends Bishop Plato of Sakkoudion, the eminence grise of the Iconodoule party and one of Irina's advisors. He is responsible for vetting bridal candidates. While the advice that Kesarion gets at the beginning of his journey is reminiscent of Polonius' famous speech to his son, his quest most resembles that of the prince from *Cinderella*. The girl's foot must fit the glass slipper. But literary references do not stop here. Like Tristan, Kesarion is looking for a bride for a royal master, but he will fall in love with his her himself. He becomes completely besotted with the winning candidate, the maiden Maria of Amnia, the poorest but most virtuous of the candidates. There is only a single, immortal instant that connects Kesarion and Maria forever. The power of this encounter is stronger than any physical desire, and merely seeing each other is more satisfying than sex. Sadoveanu implies that Bishop Plato also has a role in introducing them, but leaves open the possibility of supernatural action as well.

The emperor and Maria do not live happily ever after. Maria is only a toy for the tempestuous Constantine, who is soon at open war with his mother, the dowager empress Irina. A coup d'etat meant to restore Constantine to power is thwarted with Maria's inadvertent help—she reports the Emperor's bedroom talk to his mother. A second coup is successful, although it is too late for any reconciliation in the imperial marriage. Maria is exiled to Halki, and Teodota, an aristocratic courtesan, replaces her. Kesarion also suffers: his ability to transcend the material world has been compromised, even though the only interaction he has with Maria is completely chaste. Eros is an intoxicating illusion, which Kesarion knows full well, but he cannot resist falling in love. Eros will be for these two a lost moment that will haunt them both forever. Maria is for Kesarion a vision of Beauty incarnate, and it is not accidental that their affair, a purely spiritual one, is conducted under the shadow of the Cathedral of St. Sophia. Beauty is wisdom and wisdom is Beauty. Finally, the Emperor is deposed and mutilated—blinded—by order of his mother. Maria takes holy orders at Halki and Kesarion, now known as the

Egyptian, returns north of the Danube to assume the duties that had been those of his mentor, the old priest of the Dacians, in the Eastern Carpathians. It is only at their final separation that Maria and Kesarion the Egyptian discuss their feelings openly and give some physicality to their erotic impulses. They touch hands and the Empress rests her head on his shoulder. For them, Eros is the knowledge and the awareness of the transience of the material world. Expressed in terms that echo the Gnosticism predating Byzantine Christianity, long after the destruction of "this delusion"—the material world—their love will continue to glow beyond the confines of space and time like a golden bough.

Stylistically brilliant and beautiful, *Creanga de aur* is a unique novel of delicate, discreet but pervasive eroticism that escapes the possibility to be ever satiated by physical acts.

Biography

Born in 1880 in Pascani, Romania. Died in Bucharest in 1961. Debuted in 1904 with four books: *Povestiri, Soimii, Dureri inabusite, Crasma lui mos Precup*. The last book is dated 1905, although it was already being sold in bookshops in 1904.

Sadoveanu wrote several novels, short story collections, and travelogues. Some of his books are masterpieces of the twentieth century Romanian literature. He contributed to practically all the Romanian literary magazines of his time and his style is unique. After 1945 he made several compromises with the Communist regime, which ensured him a privileged political and social status.

MIHAELA MUDURE

Editions

Creanga de aur, Revised edition, Bucuresti: Cartea romaneasca, 1943; *Opere, vol. XII*, Bucuresti: Editura de stat pentru literatura si arta, 1958; Bucuresti: Minerva, 1976; Iasi: Junimea, 1986; Bucuresti: Minerva, 1981; Bucuresti: Minerva, 1986; Bucuresti: Allfa, Paideia, 1996; as *The Golden Bough*, translated by Eugenia Farca, Bucuresti: Minerva, 1981.

Selected Works

Povestiri. 1904.
Bordeeni. 1912.
Neamul Soimarestilor. 1915.

Strada Lapusnean., 1921.
Venea o moara pe Siret. 1925.
Hanu Ancutei. 1928.
Zodia Cancerului sau Vremea Ducai-Voda. 1929.
Nunta Domnitei Ruxandra. 1932.
Locul unde nu s-a intamplat nimic sau Targ moldovenesc din 1890. 1933.
Viata lui Stefan cel Mare. 1934.
Cazul Eugenitei Costea. 1936.
Divanul Persian. 1940.
Oamenii mariei-sale. 1942.
Anii de ucenici., 1944.
Nicoara Potcoava. 1952.
Opere, volumes I-XXII. 1954–1974.

Further Reading

Manolescu, Nicolae. *Sadoveanu sau utopia cărţii.* Bucuresti: Minerva. 1976.

Paleologu, Alexandru. *Treptele lumii sau calea către sine a lui Mihail Sadoveanu.* Bucuresti: Cartea Romaneasca. 1978.

Spiridon, Monica. *Sadoveanu. Divanul înţeleptului cu lumea.* Bucuresti: Albatros, 1982.

Vlad, Ion. *Cărtile lui Mihail Sadoveanu.* Cluj-Napoca: Dacia, 1981.

SALE, ANTOINE DE LA

c. 1386–c.1461
French writer

As is frequently the case with medieval writers, modern scholarship has argued the authorship of texts ascribed to Antoine de la Sale. This is especially true for *Les Cent Nouvelles Nouvelles*, *Les Quinze Joyes de Mariage* and the *Livre des faits de Jacques Lalaing*. It is possible, however, that he is the author of tale 50 ["Like Father, Like Son"] and tale 98 ["The Star-crossed Lovers"] in *Les Cent Nouvelles Nouvelles* (most likely between 1456 and 1461). The former tells the story of a prodigal son who returns home after a 16-year absence. His grandmother is much more joyful that his parents about his return and kisses him profusely. As there are only two beds in his parents' cottage, he reluctantly shares his grandmother's bed while his parents share the other one. Not knowing why, the young man starts to make advances to his grandmother. Her crying wakes up her own son who, once he discovers the incestuous intent of his son, swears that he will kill him. The son runs out of the house and escapes. After having promised his mother that he would avenge her, the father finds the lad a few days later. He tries to stab him but is retrained by a throng. The son explains that his father is mad at him for once wanting to lie with his mother while he has never said a word to his father for doing the same thing over five hundred times with his own mother. Everyone laughs at this answer and eventually the father and the son are able to forgive each other. In another fugitive tale, "The Star-crossed Lovers,"a young couple flees the girl's father's court to avoid an unwanted marriage. While they spend the night at an inn, four ruffians who want to rape her kill the young knight she is in love with. Rather than submit to their assault, and realizing that her love has been killed, she cuts her own throat.

The author of *Les Quinze Joyes de Mariage* uses satire to relate the difficulties of married life. After a prologue that begins by stating that "(...) man hath greater felicity in this world when he liveth frank and free (...)", there follows a description of each *joie* told from the point of view of the husband and designed to correspond to the various episodes of married life, such as monetary and material concerns, changes that occur with the birth of children, and the couple's changing interests. The first ten *joies* as presented in a quasi-chronological order while the last five discuss less frequent occurrences such as remarriage or extra marital affairs.

Le Petit Jehan de Saintré

Antoine de la Sale's most important text is *Le Petit Jehan de Saintré*. This prose romance is composed of 86 chapters of varying length. It tells the adventures of a young page who finds that a cousin of the queen reciprocates the love he feels for her. With her support and his own prowess, he becomes a great knight who overwhelms many knights during tournaments. My Lady, as she is commonly referred to, has made some very specific stipulations as to the comportment of her young lover, in a manner that will remind of the tenets of a relationship – such as maintaining secrecy, accepting blame in public without flinching, and obeying the every command of the lady – as it progresses, step by step, within the realm of courtly love.

One day, the young knight decides of his own initiative to perform knightly deeds, she lets him go reluctantly. Concerned over her physical and mental state, the queen suggests that she go home to rest. Soon after she reaches her ancestral home, she responds favorably to the advances of a young abbot. When the knight comes looking for her, there ensues a fight between the abbot and the knight in which the latter is ridiculed by his adversary and his former love. The knight finds his revenge in an inn where both combatants put on a coat of armor. This time, the knight is victorious and enjoys his revenge. At the same, the knight removes My Lady's blue girdle tipped with gold. At the end of the romance, back at the king's court, Saintré retells all that has happened in his relationship with the unnamed lady up to the moment when he removed the girdle. The lady's identity is soon revealed when Saintré returns her girdle.

Much discussion has been generated as to whether Antoine de la Sale favors or condemns chivalry in Le Petit Jehan de Saintré. The author's interest in chivalry is amply demonstrated by the many chapters that deal with this subject matter that is also demonstrated by his work on tournaments mentioned above. Saintré offers also interesting glimpses into court life in the fifteenth century.

Biography

Antoine de la Sale was born in southern France (either in Agenais or near Arles-en-Provence) the illegitimate son of Bernard de la Sale and Périnète Damendel. After his father's death in 1391, Antoine was taken into the service of Louis II of Anjou and continued to serve this house for most of the next fifty years. In the early 1400s, he resides in Italy, as the Princes of Anjou were also Kings of Sicily, and in Flanders, where he is known to have attended two tournaments. In Italy, it is possible that Antoine de la Sale met a Marshal of France, Jean le Meingre, called Boucicault, introduced in the 47th chapter of La Sale's Little John of Saintré. In 1420, Antoine de la Sale fights for Louis III in his war against Alphonse of Aragon. His early writings, such as his Excursions aux Iles Lipari are of limited literary value especially when compared to his latter works. What little is known of his life at that time does not seem to indicate any interest on his part for the budding humanist spirit to which his repeated stays in Italy should have exposed him. In the 1430s, he is also known to have held a magistrate position in Arles.

Once Louis III selects him to become the tutor to his son John, Duke of Calabria, Antoine de la Sale begins to work on a text entitled La Salade for his student that is of very limited literary worth except for some personal reminiscences. After he leaves the service of king Rene of Anjou, he becomes tutor to the sons of the Comte de St Pol in 1448, for whom he writes La Sale (1451), another pedagogical treatise that relies on classical writings to bring forth lessons in morals. In 1459, Antoine de la Sale wrote Des anciens tournois et faictz d'armes, a subject matter with which he had already dealt in some details in Le Petit Jehan de Saintré (1456). Antoine de la Sale most probably died in 1461 in Châtelet-sur-Oise where he had spent most of his time and written some of his better known works after leaving the service of the house of Anjou.

Selected Works

Jehan de Saintré, édition et présentation de Joël Blanchard; traduction de Michel Quéreuil. Paris : Livre de poche. 1995.
Oeuvres Complètes, Paris : E. Droz, 1935–41.

SALTEN, FELIX

1869–1945
Austrian novelist, dramatist and journalist

The position in German-language Literature of the novel *Josefine Mutzenbacher* (1906), "the story of a Viennese prostitute, told by herself," can be compared to that of John Cleland's novel *Memoirs of a Woman of Pleasure (Fanny Hill)*. It is likely the best-known example of German erotic literature and, like its English eighteenth-century predecessor, has frequently been the subject of court cases seeking to prevent its widespread distribution. The ban of one edition (Rowohlt, 1978) caused a long-term court battle in Germany, which ended in a ruling by the Federal Constitutional Court in 1990. It revisited the delicate relationship between the freedom of artistic expression and the protection of minors from writings considered harmful to them by stating that "a pornographic novel can be art" and should therefore be constitutionally protected, thereby forming the legal basis for decisions on similar cases.

While other names such as Arthur Schnitzler have been mentioned in connection with the anonymously published novel, it is nowadays usually attributed to his friend Felix Salten, who is best-known for his novel *Bambi, Eine Lebensgeschichte aus dem Walde* (1923), the literary basis of Walt Disney's classic film *Bambi* (1942). In 1931, a first English translation of the book under the title *Memoirs of Josefine Mutzenbacher. The Story of a Viennese Prostitute* came out in Paris. A sequel under the title *Meine 365 Liebhaber* was, again anonymously, but probably not by the same author, published sometime between 1917 and 1925, and 1970 saw the release of the first of a number of films (*Josefine Mutzenbacher*, Germany) based on or loosely connected to the novel.

Even though the fictitious narrator claims ignorance concerning previous "biographies" by prostitutes, *Josefine Mutzenbacher* continues a long tradition of such works in German-language literature, one of its better-known predecessors being *Aus den Memoiren einer Sängerin* (1862[–]75). Josefine begins the narrative of her life with a short look back and a reflection on the reason for writing down her story: she wants to show her clients how she and other prostitutes became what they are. Josefine grows up as the youngest of three children in a poor family in mid-nineteenth century Vienna. At the age of five, she has her first sexual contact with a boarder in her family's apartment and, two years later, her brother Franz becomes one of her lovers. Soon, neighbors, friends, and strangers, both male and female, are added to her array of sexual partners. When she is thirteen years old, her mother dies, and, after a sexual relationship with a teacher is exposed, her father begins having intercourse with his daughter on a regular basis. After another boarder finds out about the incestuous affair, he persuades Josefine to become a prostitute, with her father as her pimp. The long remaining portion of the novel then describes her experiences during her first day in the sex trade. As if to mirror the introduction, Josefine finishes her narrative by looking back on her life, the disintegration of her family, and the estimated 33,000 men with whom she had sexual intercourse over her thirty years as prostitute.

Josefine Mutzenbacher has been called a "grotesque mechanical ballet" (Hellmuth Karasek, Die Zeit 47, November 21, 1969), which at first seems an accurate assessment. Except for the introduction and the conclusion, the book appears to contain nothing but blatantly explicit descriptions of the encounters between a sexually curious Josefine longing for her defloration, and her always willing partners. In line with existing prejudices, the novel names the sexual insatiability of women, not social circumstances, as the major reason for prostitution. The characters, except perhaps for Josefine in her reflective passages and her oldest brother, are mostly reduced to their sexual drive, "Körper sind hier funktionale Maschinen des Geschlechtsverkehrs" (bodies are here functional machines of sexual intercourse) (Ruthner, *Gegen-Pornographie*).

Also, the fact that the novel describes the sexual education of a girl between the ages of five and thirteen, an education that consists "im Wesentlichen aus einer Serie von Akten sexuellen Missbrauchs" (essentially of a series of acts of sexual abuse) (Ruthner, *Gegen-Pornographie*), may leave readers with mixed feelings towards the book.

Besides this criticism, however, critics have also pointed out the artistic merits of *Josefine Mutzenbacher* and called it the "einzigen deutschsprachigen Klassiker des Erotik-Genres" (the only classic of the erotic genre in the German language) (Ruthner, *Gegen-Pornographie*, 166). One of the factors meriting a positive evaluation is the language that is used, especially in the dialogue passages. By having the characters speak a version of the local Viennese dialect that is frequently interspersed with sexual expressions, the author adds a naturalistic touch to the description of the heroine's environment. Another point concerns the conclusion, which disrupts the otherwise unreflective character of the narrative. After the uncritical casting of women in the role of sexual objects, with men ever willing to accept their offerings, the last paragraph suddenly questions, from the point of view of an aging prostitute, the whole concept of (physical) love. She considers it to be absurd and states that the only difference between the genders is that men lie on top, while women lie on the bottom.

Critics have also seen a connection between *Josefine Mutzenbacher* and Sigmund Freud's theory of infantile sexuality, which was published just one year earlier (1905) in *Drei Abhandlungen zur Sexualtheorie* (Three Essays on the Theory of Sexuality). According to Freud, infantile sexuality has previously been generally ignored; yet it is of central importance in *Josefine Mutzenbacher*. Freud claims that in early childhood the foundation for a person's later sexual development is laid, a fact that Josefine's creator corroborates in the novel. Freud further states that seduction can lead to a child's proneness to sexual excesses, since its mental defenses against such excesses do not yet exist, which again is reflected in Josefine's narrative. The author of *Josefine Mutzenbacher* might well have used the story of the fictitious character both to profit from the uproar following Freud's publication and to comment upon his theories.

Biography

Born 6 September 1869 in Budapest (modern-day Hungary) as Siegmund Salzmann. Married to actress Ottilie Metzl on 13 April 1902 (two children: Paul, Anna-Katherina). Traveled to the USA at the invitation of the Carnegie Foundation in 1930, returned to Austria in 1931. Fled to Switzerland after the German annexation of Austria to avoid persecution as a Jew in 1938. Died October 8, 1945 in Zürich, Switzerland. 1927–1933 President of the Austrian P.E.N.-Club. Wrote for *Berliner Morgenpost*, *Wiener Allgemeine Zeitung*, *Neue Freie Presse*

MARKUS WUST

Editions

Josefine Mutzenbacher oder die Geschichte einer wienerischen Dirne: von ihr selbst erzählt, n.p.: Privatdruck, 1906; Vienna: Kunz, 1929; Reinbek: Rowohlt, 1978; Stuttgart: Parkland, 1992 (ed. Michael Farin); Vienna: Tosa, 1999; as *Memoirs of Josefine Mutzenbacher. The Story of a Viennese Prostitute*, Paris: Privately Printed, 1931; as *The Memoirs of Josephine Mutzenbacher*, translated by Rudolph Schleifer, North Hollywood: Brandon House, 1967; as *Oh! Oh! Josephine*, London: Luxor Press, 1973.

Selected Works

Der Hinterbliebene. 1899.
Der Gemeine. 1901.
Die Gedenktafel der Prinzessin Anna. 1902.
Die kleine Veronika. 1903.
Gustav Klimt. Gelegentlichen Anmerkungen. 1903.
Der Schrei der Liebe. 1904.
Das Buch der Könige (Karikaturen). 1905.
Wiener Adel. 1905.
Herr Wenzel auf Rehberg und sein Knecht Kaspar Dinckel. 1907.
Künstlerfrauen. 1908.
Die Geliebte Friedrichs des Schönen. 1908.
Vom anderen Ufer. 1908.
Das österreichische Antlitz. 1909.
Olga Frohgemuth. 1910.
Die Wege des Herrn. 1911.
Das Schicksal der Agathe. 1911.
Wurstlprater. Huldigung an den Wiener Prater. 1911.
Das stärkereBand. 1912.
Kaiser Max, der letzte Ritter. 1913.
Gestalten und Erscheinungen. 1913.
Die klingende Schelle. 1914.
Prinz Eugen, der edle Ritter. 1915.
Abschied im Sturm. 1915.
Kinder der Freude. 1917.
Der alte Narr. 1918.
Im Namen des Kaisers. 1919.
Die Dame im Spiegel. 1920.

Der Hund von Florenz 1921; as The Hound of Florence, translated by Huntley Paterson, 1930.

Schauen und Spielen. Studien zur Kritik des modernen Theaters, 2 vol. 1921.

Das Burgtheater. 1922.

Bambi. Eine Lebensgeschichte aus dem Walde. 1923; as Bambi. A Life in the Woods, translated by Whittaker Chambers, 1928.

Geister der Zeit. 1924.

Bob und Baby. 1925.

Schöne Seelen. 1925.

Neue Menschen auf alter Erde: eine Palästinafahrt. 1925.

Martin Overbeck. 1927.

Simson, das Schicksal eines Erwählten. 1928.

Gesammelte Werke 6 vols. 1928–1932.

Fünfzehn Hasen 1929; as Fifteen Rabbits: A Celebration of Life, translated by Whittaker Chambers, 1976.

Fünf Minuten Amerika. 1931.

Freunde aus aller Welt 1931; as The City Jungle, translated by Whittaker Chambers, 1947.

Samson und Delilah 1931; as Samson and Delilah, translated by Whittaker Chambers, 1931.

Lousie von Koburg. 1932.

Mizzi. 1932.

Auf Leben und Tod. 1932.

Florian. Das Pferd des Kaisers 1933; as Florian, the Emperor's Stallion, translated by Erich Posselt and Michel Kraike, 1934.

Kleine Brüder 1935; as Good Comrades, translated by Paul R. Milton, 1942.

Die Jugend des Eichhörnchens Perri 1938; as Perri, translated by Barrows Mussey, 1938.

Bambis Kinder 1940; as Bambi's Children: The Story of a Forest Family, translated by Barthold Fles, 1939.

Renni der Retter 1941; as Renni the Rescuer: A Dog of the Battlefield, translated by Kenneth C. Kaufman, 1940.

Kleine Welt für sich 1944; as A Forest World, translated by Paul R. Milton and Sanford Jerome Greenburger, 1942.

Djibi, das Kätzchen 1945; as Jibby the Cat, 1948.

Further reading

Doppler, Bernhard, ed. Erotische Literatur 1787–1958. Vienna: Böhlau. 1990.

Ehneß, Jürgen. Felix Saltens erzählerisches Werk: Beschreibung und Deutung. Frankfurt/Main: Lang. 2002.

Farin, Michael, ed. Josefine Mutzenbacher. Stuttgart: Parkland, 1992 (Includes an extensive collection of background material).

McCombs, Nancy. Earth Spirit, Victim, or Whore? The Prostitute in German Literature, 1880[–]1925. New York and Frankfurt: Lang. 1986.

Riess, Curt, Erotica! Erotica! Das Buch der verbotenen Bücher, Hamburg: Hoffmann und Campe, 1968.

Ruthner, Clemens, "Gegen-Pornographie? Albert Drachs intertextuelle Antwort auf 'Josefine Mutzenbacher'". Österreich in Geschichte und Literatur (mit Geographie), 3 (2000): 159–172.

Schönfeld, Christiane, ed. Commodities of Desire. The Prostitute in Modern German Literature. Rochester, NY: Camden House, 2000.

SAMANIEGO, FÉLIX MARÍA DE

1745–1801
Spanish poet and man of letters

Jardín de Venus

Jardín de Venus is the name given by the twentieth-century publisher Joaquín López Barbadillo to a collection of erotic poems by Samaniego, which he claimed to have edited from an eighteenth-century manuscript. Samaniego's poems had circulated in this format among his contemporaries, and the celebrated writer and statesman Gaspar de Jovellanos recounted his amusement at hearing some of the texts read by the author. A few poems were apparently included in the currently unlocatable Álbum de Príapo (ca. 1860), but sixty-three compositions were attributed to Samaniego in the collection entitled Cuentos y poesías más que picantes, believed to be compiled by the French scholar Raymond Foulché-Delbosc and printed in Barcelona in 1899. However, it was the 1921 edition in the series "Obras festivas" by Joaquín López Barbadillo, which put the poems on the map under the title Jardín de Venus. Renewed interest only resumed after the end of the repressive Franco regime when Emilio Palacios Fernández followed up his thesis on the author with the first scholarly edition of the Jardín de Venus. Palacios has continued his researches and in his Biblioteca Nueva edition of 2004 (used in the references below) includes a total of 77 erotic compositions, having added some newly-discovered texts.

While some of the poems in *Jardín de Venus* reveal a clear debt to Jean de la Fontaine's *Contes et nouvelles en vers* of 1665[–], others draw on the French and Italian fable traditions, though the author's domestication of the stories gives no hint of their origins. All share the characteristic of popular or folk literature of revealing few concrete aspects of historical timing or geographical location, though one has a Turkish context (5), another the Holy Land (44), and two are set in Ancient Greece (23, 49). Six are clearly situated in Spain and feature Galicians (19, 65) in addition to inhabitants of Madrid (29, 37, 40) and Extremadura (33). Whereas most participants are nameless, being referred to by their roles or professions (farmer, monk, nun, soldier, muleteer, student, Inquisitor, widow, young man, married woman), religious figures feature prominently (Augustinians, Benedictines, Capuchins, Carmelites, Franciscans, Jeronimites, Trinitarians), to the extent of their alleged sexual powers being compared (25). Cardinals, Bishops, Priests, friars, monks and nuns are usually presented as more subject to uncontrollable sexual desire than lay figures and the author skilfully manipulates the reader's expectations in this respect (16, 31, 39, 56, 59).

As is usual in the popular style the poems exhibit great narrative economy, focusing quickly on sexual matters, though nevertheless revealing a masterful handling of elements of suspense and closure. The shortest of the compositions has a mere eight lines, three are sonnets, while others range from 20 to 212 lines, though the norm is around 80. Two poems have sequels (25, 42), and another is presented in alternative versions (46, 47). The author mixes seven- and eleven-syllable lines in accordance with the reasonably free Spanish 'Silva' form; rhyme alternates between full consonantal rhyme, frequently in couplets, and the characteristically Spanish, assonantal rhyme.

The erotic practices portrayed are mostly heterosexual, though a few poems feature homoerotic behaviour (1, 5). Enthusiasm for sexual pleasure is equally matched in male and female participants and can be made the subject of comedy when mis-matches occur (37, 44, 65). Humour often derives from behaviour featuring the polarities of experience and inexperience (16, 19, 32), knowledge and innocence (9, 13, 15, 17, 27, 30, 41, 61), sometimes with evident folk origins. The Spanish world of Catholic Christianity is evident in the prominence given to Catholic practices, especially confession and its opportunities for sexual abuse of penitents by confessors (33, 48). The supposedly enclosed world of convents of nuns and monks is portrayed in which the inhabitants give full rein to their bodily desires (4, 8, 16), while priests and friars are the most frequent protagonists in the narratives, almost without exception shown as oblivious of their vows of chastity, and with voracious sexual appetites.

The poems present the exaggerations to be expected of poems whose intention is humour derived from human sexuality. So if in one poem all the nuns in a convent enjoy the sexual services of a willing young man (4), a Jeronimite Friar is similarly capable of servicing his partner 11 times in a single session (25). And the hyperbole extends, as is common in such literature, to the size of male sexual organs (18, 42, 6). The economy of style focuses on the centrally featured activities in these tales to sharpen the humorous effect and expose human hypocrisy in not accepting as natural the reality of sexual passion. Samaniego's linguistic skill is evident in the choice of language, which exhibits the clarity of expression to be expected from a neoclassical poet who rejects complex metaphor but can also make wit derive from word play involving figurative language when the opportunity for humour allows (20). Sexual organs, often subjects of humour in themselves, are most frequently described in euphemistic terms; occasionally more earthy language appears, though minimally (35). The overall thrust of the poems is the celebration of sexuality and an implicit accusation of hypocrisy against clerical guardians of morality who belittle its importance.

Biography

Born into a wealthy Basque family, and great-nephew of the progressive cultural and political figure, the Count of Peñaflorida, Samaniego is best known for his moralizing *Fábulas* (1781–4), which enjoyed immense success in Spain and its overseas possessions. He was educated in Bayonne and on returning to Spain devoted himself to culture and public works. Literary friends were aware that, like his model La Fontaine, Samaniego also wrote erotic poetry, often versions in Spanish of the French author's originals. Such poems could not be published in Spain in the author's lifetime but evidently circulated in manuscript copies. One of these must have come to the notice of the Inquisition, but the author was tipped off and, through the offices of the Basque politician Eugenio de Llaguno, was seen privately by the Inquisitor General. No trial ensued and the matter was buried without the poems or their author being officially named in an Edict of condemnation.

PHILIP DEACON

Editions

Cuentos y poesías más que picantes (Samaniego, Yriarte, anónimos). Edited by "Un rebuscador de papeles viejos." Barcelona: L'Avenç. 1899.
Jardín de Venus. Madrid: Joaquín López Barbadillo. 1921.
El Jardín de Venus. Cuentos eróticos y burlescos con una coda de poesías verde. Edited by Emilio Palacios Fernández. Madrid: Biblioteca Nueva. 2004.

Further Reading

Cerezo, José Antonio. "Samaniego, Felix Maria" in *Literatura erótica en España: Repertorio de obras 1519–1936.* Madrid: Ollero y Ramos. 2001.
Gies, David T. "El XVIII porno." In *Signoria di parole. Studi offerti a Mario Di Pinto.* Edited by Giovanna Calabrò. Naples: Liguori. 1999.
Haidt, Rebecca. *Embodying Enlightenment. Knowing the Body in Eighteenth-Century Spanish Literature and Culture.* New York: St Martin's Press, 1998.
Niess, R.J. "La Fontaine and the 'cuentos' of Samaniego." *Revue de Littérature Comparée.* 18 (1938): 695[–]701.
Palacios Fernández, Emilio. "Introducción." In Félix María de Samaniego, *El Jardín de Venus. Cuentos eróticos y burlescos con una coda de poesías verdes.* Madrid: Biblioteca Nueva. 2004.
Palacios Fernández, Emilio. *Vida y obra de Samaniego.* Vitoria: Caja de Ahorros Municipal. 1975.
Palacios Fernández, Emilio. "Félix María de Samaniego, adaptador de cuentos eróticos de La Fontaine." In *La traducción en España (1750–1830). Lengua, literatura, cultura.* Edited by Francisco Lafarga, Lleida: Universitat de Lleida, 1999.
Ribao Pereira, Montserrat. "Del humor y los humores en *El jardín de Venus.* Las otras fábulas de Samaniego." *Dieciocho* 24 (2001): 203[–]216

SÁNCHEZ, LUIS RAFAEL

1936–
Puerto Rican prose writer and dramatist

In Luis Rafael Sánchez's work, the idealised collectivity of traditional Latin American nationalism is humorously replaced by a Puerto Rican communality rooted in everyday popular culture, eroticised, and set in the context of Puerto Rico's rapid modernisation under U.S. colonisation since 1898.

The internationally acclaimed novel of 1976, *La guaracha del Macho Camacho,* [*Macho Camacho's Beat*], explores Puerto Rico's stagnation under American capitalism. In this situation, the incapacity of official politics to conceive a postcolonial project that might fulfil national aspirations is countered by a type of carnivalisation of capitalism and its commodities. Carnivalisation takes place according to the physical terms of the human body as the centre of popular communal life exemplified by the importance of music in the lives of all the characters. The novel traces how the mass media commodification of music parallels that of personal relationships under capitalism. At one point, the sexual act takes place as a sequence from a pornographic film, while amorous assignations are set in supermarkets, featuring characters who model their identities on media stars with the intention of attracting rich sexual partners who can feed their overwhelming consumerism. However, modernisation is represented as a two-way process that, though commodifying physical pleasure, only partially does so with regard to popular culture. The latter still allows physical freedom and pleasurable fellowship. Meanwhile, in his 1985 play *Quíntuples*

[*Quintuplets*] commodified versions of gender identity are fetishistically erotised by the six characters, all played by two actors, in a compelling masquerade that pushes Puerto Rican stereotypes of masculinity, femininity, and nationality over the edge of credibility, thus clearing a space for the reinvention of Puerto Rican identity.

The concern with reinventing Puerto Rican identity was initiated by Sánchez in his 1966 collection of short stories, *En cuerpo de camisa* [*Shirt Sleeves Unbuttoned*], particularly in the short story, 'Aleluya negra' [Black Halleluyah], where essentialist associations of black Caribbeanness with a lyrically fervent sexuality are coarsely parodied in favour of contextualising Afro Puerto Rican eroticism in the island's colonial history and its ensuing racial tensions. The process of reinvention continues in the novel-length text of 1988, *La importancia de llamarse Daniel Santos* [The Importance of Being Daniel Santos], a book which, by ironically representing the mythical extremes of masculine sexuality in the Caribbean and Latin America offended many readers, who criticised it of exalting machismo and sexual aggression. The explicit homoeroticism of several lengthy passages was also daring in the context of the Caribbean's traditional homophobia, so savagely satirised earlier in the short story '¡Jum!' This book constitutes perhaps Sánchez's most explicit and sustained exploration of eroticism. In it, the idealised collectivity of nationalism is replaced by a Puerto Rican communality that is both part of a greater Latin Americanism and a dynamic agent of the inevitable divisions of national identity. Travelling to several Latin American towns and cities, a narrator carries out research and interviews fans of the bolero singer Daniel Santos, as part of an investigation into the legend of the historical Puerto Rican artist. By using a series of popular vernaculars in his chronicle of first-hand reports, the narrator gives free rein to a barrage of enjoyably coarse language, sexual imagery, and an admiring portrayal of Daniel's monumental machismo. Through these, the author perhaps ironically expresses his sympathies with what, through a low-life brazenness opposes social inequality and the entrenched official culture that upholds it. As a popular hero, Daniel offends by not lending himself to assimilation into the easy categories of conventional virtue misrepresented by corrupt politicians and the exploitative classes to which they belong. Moreover, as a mulatto, Daniel offends the bourgeois myth of Hispanic values traditionally promoted by elite powers in Puerto Rico. Though the book has been accused of deploying a distorting Caribbean masculinity, it is more likely that his recourse to stereotypes with powerful resonances constitute a strategically offensive position from which to attack the supposedly virtuous machismo traditionally promoted by Puerto Rican writers and politicians. Sánchez's Daniel represents a humorous vulgarisation of the supposedly noble virility they believed was necessary in the emasculating context of modernising American colonialism. Meanwhile, the author's concern with bad language, gross sexuality and machismo is far from gratuitous. Instead, in ironic dialogue with literary and political tradition, the book portrays a type of popular self-assertion taking the form of histrionic sexual aggression. Such machismo attempts to compensate for the degrading status of Latin American men who, as third-world, colonised, or tentatively democratised subjects of, in all cases, economically dependent nations, are incapable of measuring up to the nostalgic masculine ideal of nationalism. Furthermore, it is clear that an exclusively heterosexual reading is untenable. Certainly the book's exhaustive assertion of male physicality may also be read as a homoerotic discourse, where masculinity is staged, takes place and is imitated in all-male environments as a baroque display of machismo. With regard to this, the singer's *machista* prowess is commemorated by the narrator as a series of tales recounted to him in accompaniment of Daniel songs, which are heard in countless Latin American bars and billiard halls. The extended eroticisation of identity in this novel-length text is the culmination of Sánchez's challenge to traditional nationalism in favour of an informal Caribbean nationhood and Pan-American affiliations that emerge surreptitiously as popular rituals of belonging in the absence meaningful nation-statehood in the Caribbean and Latin America.

Biography

Born in Humacao, Puerto Rico, 17 November 1936, into a working-class family. Family moved to San Juan, 1948. Actor for Puerto Rican radio in his late teens; also acted in the theatre.

Studied at Humanities Faculty of the University of Puerto Rico, 1956. Scholarship to Columbia University, New York, 1959. Master's degree from New York University, 1963. PhD from University of Madrid, 1967. Lecturer in Hispanic Literature, University of Puerto Rico, 1969. Awarded Guggenheim Fellowship in 1985, which allowed him to start writing *La importancia de llamarse Daniel Santos* [The Importance of Being Daniel Santos]. From the 1990s spends half the year teaching at the City University of New York (CUNY) and the rest of the time travelling and writing.

JOHN D. PERIVOLARIS

Selected Works

Novel-length texts and short fiction

En cuerpo de camisa. 4th ed., San Juan, Puerto Rico: Cultural, 1984.
La guaracha del Macho Camacho. Madrid: Cátedra, 2000; as *Macho Camacho's Beat*, translated by Gregory Rabassa. New York: Pantheon, 1980.
La importancia de llamarse Daniel Santos. Hanover, NH:, Ediciones del Norte. 1988.

Play

Quíntuples. Hanover, NH: Ediciones del Norte. 1985.

Further Reading

Barradas, Efraín. *Para leer en puertorriqueño: acercamiento a la obra de Luis Rafael Sánchez*. Río Piedras, Puerto Rico, Cultural, 1981.
Birmingham-Pokorny, Elba D. (editor). *The Demythologization of Language, Gender and Culture and the Remapping of Latin American Identity in Luis Rafael Sánchez's Works*. Miami: Universal. 1999.
Fernández Olmos, Margarite. 'Luis Rafael Sánchez and Rosario Ferré: Sexual Politics and Contemporary Puerto Rican Narrative.' *Hispania* 70 (1987).
Gelpí, Juan. *Literatura y paternalismo en Puerto Rico*. Río Piedras: Universidad de Puerto Rico. 1993.
Perivolaris, John Dimitri. *Puerto Rican Cultural Identity and the Work of Luis Rafael Sánchez*. Chapel Hill, NC: University of North Carolina Press. 2000.
Vázquez Arce, Carmen. *Por la vereda tropical: notas sobre la cuentística de Luis Rafael Sánchez*. Buenos Aires: La Flor. 1994.

Bibliography

Hernández Vargas, Nélida and Daisy Caraballo Abréu (editors). *Luis Rafael Sánchez: crítica y bibliografía.*, Río Piedras: Universidad de Puerto Rico. 1985.

SARDUY, SEVERO

1937–1993
Cuban prose writer and poet

In Sarduy's texts eroticism is a mercurial element that serves as the vehicle for a deconstructive drive. Revisiting Latin American writers' traditional search for their origins, Sarduy's texts reveal the fissures, fluidity, and plurality behind the myths of nationality and identity underpinning Cuban and Latin American literary tradition. Influenced by the ideas of Jacques Lacan, structuralism, and, eventually, post-structuralism, with which Sarduy had come into contact in Paris, novels such as *Gestos* [*Gestures*] (1963) and *De donde son los cantantes* [*From Cuba with a Song*] (1967) subvert those myths.

The realization of such myths is constantly deferred and diverted by the inability of culture and language to fulfil the desire for stability, essence, unity, and origins. For example, in *De donde son los cantantes* gender roles are confused by the switching of Spanish grammatical genders when referring to the two protagonists, a pair of transvestites. As a result, the impossibility of ascertaining their true sex is associated with their freewheeling, polymorphous sexuality. Desire becomes perversion through a sexual role-playing which, in turns, parodies the heterosexual, political, religious, and scientific desire for power, unity, and fulfilment which is explored in this and subsequent novels, such as *Cobra* (1972), *Maitreya* (1978), *Colibrí* [*Hummingbird*]

(1984), *Cocuyo* [*The Glowworm*] (1990), and *Los pájaros en la playa* [*The Birds on the Beach*] (1993).

Traditionally, sexual, nationalist, and cultural politics in the Caribbean and Latin America have been publicly transacted through patriarchal discourses. Therefore, the absence of conventionally nuclear family groups, the parody of patriarchal and matriarchal authority, and the haphazard, nonreproductive sexual relations that take place in Sarduy's novels highlight eroticism as a subversive but also liberatingly dynamic force that allows change to take place. In this context, the characters' desire often enables them not only to cross genders but also to metamorphose into other biological species. In Sarduy's world, freedom involves breaking free from the gravity of historical, ideological, cultural, and even biological, origins, to achieve a free-floating, promiscuous indeterminacy that is by definition erotic. This is increasingly matched by the transnational or indeterminate geographical settings of the novels. *De donde son los cantantes* involves a journey across Cuba from east to west; *Cobra* a journey through India, Cuba, and China; and *Maitreya* a pilgrimage from Tibet to Cuba, Miami, New York, and Iran on the eve of the Islamic Revolution.

Colibrí, Cocuyo, El Cristo de la rue Jacob [*Christ on the Rue Jacob*] (1987), and the essay *La simulación* [*Simulation*] (1982), mark a shift towards autobiographical representations of the *bildungsroman* and a greater concern with the individual's survival of his fragmentation in the face of culture, language, and repression by historical authority. Sarduy's reflections on the individual's endurance, albeit as a fractured self, is lent poignancy by Sarduy's rise to fame as a writer associated with the cultural upheaval of the Cuban Revolution and his subsequent self-exile in France during the persecution of homosexuals in Cuba. The autobiographical vein intensifies in the posthumously published novel, *Los pájaros en la playa* and the miscellaneous collection, *Epitafios, Imitación, Aforismos* [*Epitaphs, Imitation, Aphorisms*] (1994), written after the author had been diagnosed with AIDS and dealing respectively with life in an island AIDS sanatorium and his own personal reflections while experiencing the illness. In Sarduy's last novel eroticism constitutes a release from the abjection of identity, with *pájaro* being a derogatory term for identifying homosexuals. Homosexuality is cast out to the margins of society in the novel's very title, and in the situation of the sanatorium on the beach, a liminal space between land and sea. However, Cosmógrafo, a central, autobiographical, character with AIDS, escapes the confines of identity through cosmological meditations that he vainly hopes will lead him to the origins and cure of the illness. These reflections resemble Sarduy's own in his 1987 essay *Nueva inestabilidad* [*New Instability*].

Part of the complexity of Sarduy's skepticism towards language and culture, as an eternally receding series of repressive structures, is his eternal, inescapable return to their promise of freedom. In this sense, they are structures synonymous with an eroticism that is both transcendental and hopelessly text-bound. Hence, at the end of Cosmógrafo's diary, with which Sarduy's novel also ends, a poem by the Soviet lesbian poet Marina Tsvetayeva is reproduced, in a gesture of citation and literary collage that characterizes Sarduy's work in general. This is textually promiscuous, built out of layers of intricate reference to mass culture, painting, literature, and other cultural texts, and tenuously holding together as a body of literature whose linguistic extravagance is both pleasurable and fatally infectious.

Biography

Born in Camagüey, Cuba, 25 February 1937. Attended the Instituto de Segunda Enseñanza de Camagüey; Faculty of Medicine, University of Havana, 1956–60; École Pratique des Hautes Études at the Sorbonne. Contributed to the journal *Lunes de Revolución*, 1959, and in the same year left Cuba to study in Paris. Lived in Paris for the rest of his life; became a French citizen in 1967. Director of the Latin American collection at the publishing house Editions du Seuil, 1969–1990, and of the Latin American division at the publishing company Gallimard, 1990–1993. Received the Medicis International Award, 1972 for *Cobra*; Paul Gibson and Italia Awards for radio and television, 1983. Died of AIDS in Paris, 1993.

JOHN D. PERIVOLARIS

Selected Works

Novels

Gestos. Barcelona: Seix Barral, 1963.
De donde son los cantantes. Madrid: Cátedra, 1993; as *From Cuba with a Song*, translated by Suzanne Jill Levine, in *Triple Cross: Three Short Novels*, New York: Dutton, 1972; reprinted as a separate volume, Los Angeles: Sun and Moon Press, 1994.
Cobra. Buenos Aires: Sudamericana, 1972; as *Cobra*, translated by Suzanne Jill Levine, New York: Dutton, 1975.
Maitreya. Barcelona: Seix Barral, 1978; as *Maitreya*, translated by Suzanne Jill Levine, Hanover, New Hampshire: Ediciones del Norte, 1986.
Colibrí. Barcelona: Argos Vergara, 1984.
El Cristo de la rue Jacob. Barcelona: Mall, 1987; as *Christ on the Rue Jacob*, translated by Suzanne Jill Levine and Carol Maier, San Francisco: Mercury House, 1995.
Cocuyo. Barcelona: Tusquets, 1993.

Essays

La simulación. Caracas: Monte Avila, 1982.
Nueva inestabilidad. Mexico City: Vuelta, 1987.
Epitafios, Imitación, Aforismos. Miami: Universal, 1994.

Further Reading

González Echevarría, Roberto. *La ruta de Severo Sarduy*. Hanover, New Hampshire: Ediciones del Norte, 1987.
Hayman, David. "Excesos de la escritura: violaciones verbales." *Quimera* (Madrid), 12 (1981): 28–31.
Henric, Jacques. "Severo Sarduy dans le temple et le bordel." *Art Press* (Paris), 42 (1980): 30–31.
———. "Severo Sarduy, la lumière et l'excrément," *Art Press* (Paris), 166 (1992): 55–57.
Pérez Firmat, Gustavo. "Riddles of the Sphincter," in his *Literature and Liminality: Festive Readings in the Hispanic Tradition*. Durham, NC: Duke University, 1986: 53–74.
Prieto, René. "The Ambivalent Fiction of Severo Sarduy." *Symposium* (Washington, DC), 1 (1985): 49–60.
Rivero-Potter, Alicia. "Algunas metáforas somáticas-erótico-escripturales en *De donde son los cantantes y Cobra*." *Revista Iberoamericana*, 123–24: 497–507.
———. (editor). *Between the Self and the Void: Essays in Honor of Severo Sarduy*. Boulder, CO: Society of Spanish and Spanish-American Studies, 1998.

SARTRE, JEAN-PAUL

1905–1980
French philosopher, novelist, dramatist, essayist, and critic

Jean-Paul Sartre is not primarily regarded as an author of erotic literature, yet characters of dubious or deviant sexuality, enmeshed in bizarre or dysfunctional relationships, abound in his major works of fiction and theater. The three *dramatis personae* of his best-known play *In Camera*, for example, are a lesbian, an infanticidal nymphomaniac, and a macho philanderer who torments his wife by entertaining his mistresses in the marital bed. The hero of his famous political drama, *Dirty Hands*, is an impotent young intellectual who has a pseudo-incestuous, yet seemingly asexual, relationship with his girlish and apparently frigid wife, who finally falls into the arms of the mature 'Proletarian Party' boss, provoking his overdue assassination by her husband's hand. The central character of Sartre's last original play, *The Condemned of Altona*, sustains a fully incestuous relationship with his sister, and attempts for good measure to seduce his sister-in-law, while the entire family is under the same roof!

In his first novel, *Nausea*, Sartre's *alter ego*, Antoine Roquentin, exacerbates his debilitating apprehension of the viscous plenitude and disconcerting flux of contingent physical existence, by indulging in perfunctory sexual intercourse with the landlady of a local bar. Additionally, three episodes of child molestation in the book (recounted by Roquentin, rather than involving him) caused his publisher's lawyers to advise a toning-down of the more vulgar and explicit vocabulary. In Sartre's later trilogy of novels, *The Roads to Freedom*, the protagonist Mathieu divides his energies in the first volume, *The Age of Reason*, between trying to procure an abortion for his mistress, Marcelle, and trying to seduce his androgynous and probably lesbian pupil, Ivich. He fails on both counts, and Marcelle finally marries their mutual friend Daniel, a repressed and self-loathing homosexual, who views marriage as an exquisite punishment for his guilt-ridden deviancy.

However, it is Sartre's second work of fiction—a collection of short stories entitled *The Wall*—which reveals his potential as an erotic writer. These five novellas brought him, simultaneously, commercial and critical success (the *Prix du roman populiste* of 1940) and widespread notoriety. Critics in the press made comparisons with Céline's *Voyage au bout de la nuit*, and accused Sartre of, *inter alia*, "sexual obsession," "crudity," and "visceral realism." Even Albert Camus, although laudatory in the main, queried the "use the author makes of obscenity." In fact, three of these stories contain little reference to sex. The first, "The Wall," includes some scatological details, but these are not gratuitous in the context of a prison cell holding Spanish Republican partisans faced with torture and execution. The fifth story, "Childhood of a Leader," is the length of a short novel, and contains episodes in which the hero, Lucien Fleurier, indulges adolescent homosexual tendencies before confirming his conventional heterosexuality with a young woman whom he regards as his social inferior, yet a necessary stage on his way to male, bourgeois respectability. The second story, however, introduces a sexual theme which builds throughout the third into a kind of "dry orgasm" in the fourth, where the focus is emphatically, perversely, and paradoxically upon impotence, frigidity, masturbation, abstention, and frustration.

"The Room" recounts the visit of Monsieur Darbédat to his daughter Ève, whose husband—a psychotic invalid called Pierre (meaning "stone")—refuses to leave his darkened room where he is tormented by flying statues, terrifying hallucinations in which he implicates and humiliates his submissive wife by calling her "Agathe," a name in French which sounds like that of the mineral "agate." The nub of the narrative is Monsieur Darbédat's realization that his wife's intuition is right: Ève stays with Pierre

only because "they still do *that*." The mesmeric fascination of exclusively sexual—and subliminally sadomasochistic—relations is implicitly privileged, and ironically reflected by the evidently continent relationship existing between Monsieur and Madame Darbédat, who are exemplars of middle-class propriety, and transparent parodies of Sartre's grandparents, who slept separately from the early days of their marriage, according to his account in *Words*.

"Erostratus" concerns the ambition of Paul Hilbert, a petty employee in Paris, to make himself immortal—like the eponymous arsonist of the Temple at Ephesus—by means of a gratuitous act of violent destruction, namely the random shooting of people in the street, followed by suicide: both projects fail abjectly. His sexual quirk is a voyeuristic auto-eroticism, evoked explicitly, yet subtly, in a scene where he employs a prostitute to parade naked in front of him, and then to masturbate with his walking-stick, until he ejaculates spontaneously while himself remaining fully-clothed, "right down to his gloves." So audacious or titillating was this passage for the British publishers of Lloyd Alexander's 1949 translation of the book—as *Intimacy*—that it is crucially censored by a combination of judicious excision and deliberate, or possibly inept, misconstruction.

"Intimacy" is the story that attracted most vehement censure in France, and most extensive censorship in the English translation, no doubt because—as Geneviève Idt has observed—its theme is *female* sexuality. Lulu is married to the impotent Henri, but having an affair with the sexually accomplished Pierre. Through a promiscuous combination of stream-of-consciousness monologues, dramatic dialogues and orthodox third-person narration, the story explores Lulu's dilemma: should she abandon Henri for a new life in Nice with Pierre? She is actively encouraged in this by her girlfriend, Rirette, who appears to be sexually voracious, yet is actually lonely, celibate, jealous of Lulu, and apt to flirt pathetically with café waiters, whilst secretly fantasizing about eloping with Pierre herself. The obvious attraction of life in the sun with an attentive lover is, however, vitiated for Lulu by the revulsion she feels for the sexual act, her accounts of which place vivid stress on the repellent hardness of taut male muscle—particularly of the erect penis—and on her object-status as a "musical instrument being played upon by a maestro," whose legacy is nevertheless a cold, damp, soiled bed. By contrast, the sweet softness of Henri's impotent "thing" is a reassurance of purity and a justification for her habit of masturbation: "Only I can give myself pleasure," Lulu tells herself, "the doctor said so, it's a medical fact." Constructing a socially respectable and morally plausible pretext, Lulu eventually rejects Pierre because she is "indispensable" to Henri, who would "kill himself" without her. Rirette is disappointed that Pierre does not consequently turn his attention to her, and both women revert to the *status quo ante* in an atmosphere of muted desperation.

These overt references to female auto-eroticism were evidently taboo at the time and were completely excised in the first English translation. However, it is clear from the body of his work as a whole that Sartre is not especially interested in the erotic as such. Rather, in *The Wall*, he exploits the erotic as a vernacular idiom in which to transpose metaphorically one of the central preoccupations of his philosophy, namely the characteristically human paradox of simultaneous aspirations towards thing-like stability (the "in-itself"), and self-conscious subjectivity (the "for-itself"), and the tension between freedom and responsibility that flows from this contradiction.

Biography

Born Paris 21 June 1905. Lives with widowed mother (Anne-Marie Schweitzer) and her parents in Meudon, 1906–1911, then in Paris, attending Lycée Henri IV, until mother's remarriage, 1917. After "three unhappiest years of [his] life" in La Rochelle, returns to Paris, Lycée Louis-le-Grand, then École Normale Supérieure. Fails Agrégation de philosophie 1928, but graduates first 1929 (with Simone de Beauvoir second). Military service 1929–1931, teaching in Le Havre 1931–1936, except for scholarship in Berlin to study under Husserl, 1933–1934. Appointed to Lycée Pasteur, Paris, publishes *La Nausée* and *Le Mur*, 1937–1939. Mobilized, captured, released, 1939–1941, assumes post at Lycée Condorcet, Paris. Makes mark in philosophy and theater with *L'Être et le néant*, *Les Mouches* and *Huis clos*, 1943–1944. "Existentialism" enjoys postwar vogue with publication of novels, plays, essays, and periodical *Les Temps modernes*, 1945–1950.

Increasingly active politically, as critical fellow-traveler of French Communist Party and opponent of government policies in Indochina and Algeria, 1950s. Refuses Nobel Prize for literature, 1964, chairs Russell Tribunal on American war-crimes in Vietnam, 1966–1967. Supports "Prague Spring" and student-led "events" of May 1968, condemns Soviet invasion of Czechoslovakia. Remains close to extreme-left movements, notably Maoists, post-68, becomes nominal editor of banned newspapers, La Cause du Peuple and Libération. Deserts Marxism, espouses "libertarian socialism," 1970s. Sight failing, devotes last years to interviews and vocal support of dispossessed until death, 15 April 1980.

BENEDICT O'DONOHOE

Selected Works

La Nausée. Paris: Gallimard, 1938. (*Nausea*, trans. Robert Baldick, Harmondsworth: Penguin, 1965.)

Le Mur. Paris: Gallimard, 1939. (*Intimacy*, trans. Lloyd Alexander, London: Panther Books, 1960.)

L'Être et le néant. Paris: Gallimard, 1943. (*Being and Nothingness*, trans. Hazel Barnes, London: London University Press, 1976.)

Les Mouches. Paris: Gallimard, 1943. (*The Flies*, trans. Stuart Gilbert, London: Hamish Hamilton, 1946.)

Huis clos. Paris: Gallimard, 1945. (*In Camera*, trans. Stuart Gilbert, London: Hamish Hamilton, 1946.)

Critique de la raison dialectique I. Paris: Gallimard, 1960. (*Critique of Dialectical Reason*, trans. Alan Sheridan-Smith, London: Verso, 1976.)

Les Séquestrés d'Altona. Paris: Gallimard, 1960. (*Loser Wins*, trans. Sylvia and George Leeson, London: Hamish Hamilton, 1961.)

Les Mots. Paris: Gallimard, 1964. (*Words*, trans. I. Clephane, Harmondsworth: Penguin, 1964.)

L'Idiot de la famille: Gustave Flaubert de 1821 à 1857, tomes I, II, III. Paris: Gallimard, 1971–1972. (*The Family Idiot: Gustave Flaubert, 1821–1857, vols. 1–5*, trans. Carol Cosman, Chicago: Chicago University Press, 1981–1993.)

Further Reading

Boulé, Jean-Pierre. *Sartre: Self-Formation and Masculinities*. New York and Oxford: Berghahn, 2004.

Clack, Beverley. *Sex and Death: An Appraisal of Human Mortality*. Cambridge, UK: Polity Press, 2002.

Davison, Ray. "Sartre and the Ithyphallic: An Interpretation of 'Ersotrate.'" In *The Short Story: Structure and Statement*. Edited by William F. Hunter, Exeter: Elmbank Publications, 1996.

Ghamari-Tabrizi, Sharon. "Feminine Substance in *Being and Nothingness*." *American Imago* 56:2 (Summer 1999): 133–144.

Giles, James. "Sartre, Sexual Desire, and Relation with Others." In *French Existentialism*, edited by James Giles, Amsterdam: Rodopi, 1999.

Leak, Andrew N. *The Perverted Consciousness: Sexuality and Sartre*. Basingstoke: Macmillan, 1989.

Martin, Thomas. "Sartre, Sadism, and Female Beauty Ideals." In *Feminist Interpretations of Jean-Paul Sartre*, edited by Julien S. Murphy, University Park, PA: University of Pennsylvania Press, 1999.

O'Donohoe, Benedict. "Fraternity: Liberty or Inequality? Incest in Sartre's Drama." *French Studies* 50:1 (January 1996): 54–65.

O'Donohoe, Benedict. "Sartre's Heroine Addiction: Leading Women in his Theatre and the *comédie familiale*." *French Studies* 55:1 (January 2001): 47–58.

Slaymaker, Doug. "When Sartre was an Erotic Writer: Body, Nation and Existentialism in Japan after the Asia-Pacific War." *Japan Forum* 14:1 (2002): 77–103.

SCANDINAVIAN LANGUAGES

In the three Scandinavian countries censorship is as old as printing itself. It was directed against papal heretics, people with dangerous political messages, and obscene writers. But since history differs, we will deal with them separately.

In Denmark, censorship was formalized in 1537. Except for a short period from 1770–1773 censorship was exercised until the first democratic constitution of 1849. With the Act of Liberty of the Press in 1799, a direct prohibition on offences against public decency was for the first time installed. But at that time the first ban on an erotic book had already taken place. In 1783, Thomas Christopher Bruun's *Mine Frie-Timer* [*My Free Hours*], a series of versifications of Boccaccio and Fontaine, was seized by the police by order of the government. Actually, Bruun was sentenced not only to a fine but also to a reconfirmation since his knowledge of Christian values "seemed to be too weak."

There were attempts to translate European erotic classics such as de Laclos' *Les Liaisons dangereuses* or Crébillon's *Le sopha*, but both were banned. Modern realism was introduced with Georg Brandes' path-breaking lectures at the University in 1872 in which he defined living literature as 'literature putting things under debate.' With his radicalism a new naturalist literature grew dealing with, for instance, marriage and sexual relations. An uproar was caused by the novel *Haabløse Slægter* [*Hopeless Kindred*] (1880) by Herman Bang. The book tried to give passion a new and more realistic voice. This was too much for the court and the book was banned

and Bang fined. He rewrote the book without the passages criminalized by the court in order to have the book published.

In the same decade the first publications commercially exploiting the borders created by police and court were printed. A collection of short stories with erotic themes were published with the title *Forbudne Frugter* [*Forbidden Fruits*] (1886). These stories were deliberately written within the legal border of decency, and they paved the way for an erotic, underground a specific spicy genre, which published work; secretly until abolition of the anti-porn regulations in the penal code.

From the 1880s, how to integrate the sexual world into text became a problem for literature. To make representations of erotic scenes directly was out of the question. But it was possible to let these scenes begin, for instance, with a kiss and then continue with ellipses (...). Or the result could be indirectly referred to by a pregnancy or a birth. The possibilities for authors were thus to use their imaginations to create lust-provoking settings. One bestseller was, for instance, written as a book about atrocities committed by the Germans in World War One and called *Barbarkvinder* [*Barbarian Women*] (1917). It came out in seven printings before the police discovered the fraud and confiscated it.

A new phase began around 1920 when modernism hit Danish culture in many aspects. The introduction of psychoanalysis as well as literary modernism prepared the way for making the fight for sexual reform an issue for the progressive culture. All the modernist themes were introduced and articulated by a group of intellectuals later known as *cultural radicals*.

The new phase was marked by the trial against an expressionist collection of poems by Rudolf Broby called *Blod* [*Blood*] (1922). The book introduced a series of sexual motives which the court didn't like. For instance, a poem describing a prostitute provoking an abortion on herself with a knitting pin. The poems were not in any sense arousing, but still they were considered pornographic, banned, and were fined.

When Josephine Baker visited Copenhagen in 1928, one of the leading cultural radicals, the architect Poul Henningsen, wrote an article in a journal on 'The Pedagogic Value of Pornography.' He defended the rights of artists, but also the rights of adults to be aroused. He thought of it as a democratic issue. The police took the opposite position: they didn't care to ban *Lady Chatterley's Lover* in English, since it was expensive and in a foreign language. Only men of the elite would be customers and therefore of no harm. But a Danish translation saw daylight only in a censored version.

During the 1930s, the fight for sexual reform was integrated in the anti-fascist struggle. In this the cultural radicals associated themselves with the freedom-discourse going back to the Enlightenment. But the decade was also the first period for home-grown Danish pornography. In the police archives we find what the police termed 'typewritten books': the producers of porn simply wrote the novels on a type-writer and bound them. Then they were hired out (often with photos glued to the blank pages) from second-hand bookshops in Copenhagen. Printed pornography was still imported from the mass-producing countries: Britain, France, and Germany.

In the last years of the 1930s and during World War II, the police were busiest. Pictures were banned, and even paintings with erotic motifs were prohibited. The Obscenity Act was made more severe, and there was a series of cases against a sexual reform journal, *Sex og Samfund* [*Sex and Society*]. Also translated American crime fiction with erotic elements was prosecuted.

Although the police suggested many possible cases to the Public Prosecutor, none came to trial after the war. When Henry Miller's *Tropic of Cancer* was translated into Danish in 1954, no trial followed. The following year, *Tropic of Capricon* was translated without repercussion. The Public Prosecutor had reflected the public mood by renouncing a trial against Miller's publisher. This was really the beginning of the abolition of the Obscenity Act. To understand this change, we must call attention to at least two important changes in Danish culture: first, the opening of Danish culture to modern life had happened through the cultural radicalists and their emancipatory program; second, the democratic culture in Denmark had favored a relativistic view on class cultures and as a famous Danish female politician, Else Merete Ross, formulated the problem: "Why should one class dictate to other classes their view on sex, when sex is a private affair?"

A new wave of translated erotic books created a new open market and even new Danish books were published. The translation of John Cleland's classic *Fanny Hill* was the last battle. In 1965, the Supreme Court acquitted the Danish publisher and numerous Danish and translated books were published before the Obscenity Act was abolished for texts in 1967 and for pictures in 1969.

The period 1961 to 1969 was the golden period of Danish erotic literature. Both commercial and artistic books sold very well and stimulated the market. A milestone was publication of the author Sven Holm's anthology *Sengeheste* [literally: *Bedstaves*, but in Danish: *Bed-Horses*] in three volumes (1965–1967) in which well-known Danish authors published short stories with erotic themes. But the flourishing market began to dry up when picture-porn was legalized in 1969.

Although the market for erotic fiction as such dried up, it never completely disappeared but lived more or less through translations. Most important was, however, that a new fictional language had grown from this experience and erotic scenes were more or less easily integrated into artistic fiction. The porn language could be used in connection with the opening of all spheres of human activity for fiction works. The sexual revolution was thus also a textual revolution.

Norway was constitutionally and legally a part of Denmark until 1814 and in a union with Sweden until 1905. The breaking up of the old society caused a new public discourse on the modern society. Henrik Ibsen's plays *Et Dukkehjem* [*A Doll's House*] (1879) and *Gengangere* [*Ghosts*] (1881) displayed an emancipatory outlook towards marriage and womens' role and spoke of venereal diseases. They were accused of indecency.

Ibsen and the modernists in Kristiania (now Oslo) were adherents of Brandes' radicalism. In the 1880s, this trend clashed with the legal system. In 1884, Hans Jæger published the two-volume novel *Fra Kristiania-Bohêmen* [*From the Kristiania Bohemian*]. It is a naturalistic book about two young men and the pressure they experience from their sexuality. Jæger was probably the first one to go as far in describing intercourse, and the book was seized only an hour after its release. He was imprisoned and fined. He later issued the book under the title *Julefortællinger* [*Christmas Tales*] and the printer sold them in Sweden. But the Swedish legal system put Jæger on trial again in Norway, and he was sent to jail again, he lost his job as a stenographer in Parliament and was kicked out of university.

In 1886, Jæger's friend, the painter Christian Krohg, published the novel *Albertine* about a poor and beautiful girl who becomes a prostitute. Not only a graphic rape scene, but also the outspoken way in which he addressed prostitution and social conditions, caused confiscation—but it was said in a contemporary newspaper that it was because of the author's critical attitudes towards the police.

At the same time, Arne Garborg published his book *Mannfolk* [*Men*] which was much more outspokenly erotic than Krohgs novel, and actually Garborg demanded his novel be seized also. But it wasn't. Perhaps the reason was that Garborg's novel was written in 'landsmål,' the Norwegian language spoken in the countryside in opposition to the official Danish-like 'bokmål.'

Both Jæger and Garborg saw sexuality as determined by societal (dis)order and wrote their novels in the wake of naturalism. And they both pursued this tendency in the following books, especially Jægers trilogy *Syk kjærlihet* [*Sick Love*], which he published privately in France, where he lived in exile, which is a very radical book also in its erotic passages. The love is considered sick not only because it has certain sadomasochistic traits, but most of all because it tends to rule Hans Jæger's (the main character) life. The book was reviewed by a Danish journalist, Jean-Jacques Ipsen, and he was then sentenced to one month in jail due to this review.

Cultural radicalism also had a strong impact in Norway in the inter-war period and brought erotic fiction back on the agenda. In 1931 one of the leading Norwegian cultural radicalists, the author Sigurd Hoel, published the novel *Syndere i sommersol* [*Sinners in Summer-sun*] about four young men and four young women living together one summer while on vacation. The novel is based on psychoanalysis as well as on a kind of sensual rite. Sex, the body, moving, and eating is a pleasure which is humanly divine. The book caused a lot of religious indignation most of all because the women were described as sexually hungry and self-confident—they were more emancipated than contemporary men thought feminine. Later, in the 1930s, Hoel became a pupil of Wilhelm Reich who lived in Norway before emigrating to the United States.

We have to go to the 1950s to find the next wave of erotic literature. One of its peaks were the case against Agnar Mykle's *Sangen om den røde rubin* [*The Song of the Red Ruby*] in 1956. Also his novel *Lasso rundt fru Luna* [*Lasso Around Mrs. Luna*] in 1954 should be mentioned with the *Ruby* as some of the finest erotic books in Norwegian literature. Both books are about a young man, Ask Burlefot, from a puritanical background, who becomes an adult and seeks his own way. The first book ends in a kind of failure of his, but the second one shows that passionate love can also be part of a solution.

Mykle's description of intercourse search caused a scandal. And the details were too much for the public prosecutor and so were his attacks on puritanical Protestantism. After some months of public witchhunting, the prosecutor, in February 1957, accused Mykle of offending public decency. In October, he was acquitted, but the remaining books were still confiscated. In May 1958, they were also acquitted by the supreme court. The book was a tremendous success (17 printings the first year), but for Mykle, the outcome of the witchhunt was disastrous. He withdrew from public life and stopped writing.

In the wake of Mykle's book, an order of confiscation was made against the Norwegian importers of the Danish translation of Henry Miller's *Sexus*. In 1959, the supreme court found the book obscene and the confiscation was sustained.

The most significant legal process was the one against Jens Bjørneboe's *Uten en tråd* [*Without a Stitch*] in 1966. The book came out anonymously and was written as many pornographic books are: with only erotic scenes, and little else.

Bjørneboe became known as the author and turned the process into a farce. He accepted that the book wasn't of very high artistic value, but it had been nescessary for him to write in order to arrive at his next novel. The book was confiscated and in 1967 the supreme court sentenced Bjørneboe to a fine of 1000 Nkr. and a fine of 10,000 Nrk. to his publisher.

Although both Denmark and Sweden lifted the ban on pornography, Norway didn't and Section 211 of their penal code is still in force. The actual enforcement of it has changed, however. Pornography is in fact sold in Norway without police action.

In Sweden, censorship has been the rule. From 1684 a royal ordinance was issued with the result that everything to be printed was pre-censored. With the exception of a short period of freedom under Gustav III this system functioned until the military coup in 1809 and the Freedom of the Press Act of 1810. The new legal system required all press cases to be tried by a jury, which might be the reason that many press cases ended in acquittal.

The first legal case against literature was the famous case against Agust Strindbergs *Giftas*, part 1 [*Getting Married*], a collection of short stories from 1884. They were about marital relations and quite open and realistic. But one story, 'Dygdens lön' [The Reward of Virtue], was read as blasphemic, and he was prosecuted, but later, acquitted. It labelled him as obscene for many years, and he had difficulties in getting the play *Fröken Julie* [*Miss Julie*] published in 1888.

In 1896, Gustaf Fröding published *Stänk och flikar* [*Splashes and Flaps*]. In one of the poems, 'En morgondröm' [A Morning Dream] there was a description of intercourse, which both in words and in rhyme was considered highly obscene. There was an uproar in the press and a demand for confiscation. Fröding was actually prosecuted and the book confiscated. As in the case of Strindberg it was tried by a jury, the jury voted not guilty, and Fröding was acquitted. But as the collection was re-edited, the lovemaking passage was omitted. As a result of the Fröding-case, the press law was changed. The old wording about texts that "furthered a demoralizing manner of life" was changed so that these texts would be criminalized if they offended "decency and morality."

In the inter-war period, Nazism and extreme-Rightist tendencies were rather strong in Sweden, and surfaced during the so-called Krusenstjerna-fight in 1934–1935. In 1930–1935, Agnes von Krusentsjerna published the seven-volume novel-cycle called *Fröknarna von Pahlen* [*The Misses von Pahlen*] about some Swedish noble-women. In these novels she describes sexuality rather openly and especially a lesbian scene and one scandalous lovemaking scene between a brother and a sister. She was heavily attacked from the Right. Her novels became a theme in the fight between democracy and womens' rights on one hand and Right-wing morality and the church on the other. But it never went as far as a legal prosecution.

In Sweden in the inter-war period there was a radical movement for sexual enlightenment (RFSU). The movement represented some of the same points of view as cultural radicalism in Denmark and Norway. In the post-war period these enlightened views became the leading trend. One of the first instance came with Ivar Lo-Johansson's novel *Geniet* [*The Genius*] (1947) in which he wrote about the sexual misery of youth, and especially about masturbation and the propaganda against it. Also Bengt Anderberg's novel *Kain* of 1948 with some descriptions of intercourse and his *Svensk Decamerone* [*Swedish Decameron*] from 1949 were also in this first round.

Influences by the openness of Swedish film-making, literature also moved towards more openness. Even though the film *491* by Vilgot Sjöman was banned in 1963, other films by him and by Ingmar Bergmann in the 1960s broke through the walls of censorship.

In 1965, Bengt Anderberg started the series *Kärlek* [*Love*] published in 14 volumes until 1970. The books contained short stories by Swedish authors produced for the eotic market. Anderberg wanted to produce 'good pornography for everybody,' and the series was a tremendous success. Pornography was a "legitimate need," wrote a Swedish intellectual. The acknowledged Swedish literary journal *Ord och Bild* [*Word and Picture*] even published an issue with pictures from porn magazines.

As a result of the ban of the film *491*, a parliamentary commission was set up, and in 1969 it recommended the abolition of censorship for adults. The parliament didn't agree, and even today, films are precensored in Sweden. But in 1970 the regulations in the penal code on obscenity were abolished, and even in the area of film the trend became rather liberal. In the 1970s, it even became possible to see *491*.

MORTEN THING

Further Reading

Brusendorff, Ove and Poul Henningsen. *Love's Picture Book: The History of Pleasure and Moral Indignation, Polybooks*. London 1973.

Gentikow, Barabara. *En skitten strøm: samfunnskritikken i den "umoralske" litteraturen i Norge 1880–1960*. Gyldendal, Oslo 1974.

Kutchinsky, Berl. *Studies on Pornography and Sex Crimes in Denmark: A Report to the US Presidential Commission on Obscenity and Pornography*. Nyt fra-samfundsvidenskaberne, Copenhagen 1970.

——. *Law, Pornography and Crime: The Danish Experience*. Pax, Oslo: The Scandinavian Research Council for Criminology, 1999.

Thing, Morten. *Pornografiens historie i Danmark*. Aschehoug, Copenhagen 1999.

Fröding, Gustav. *Splashes and Patches: Poems*. Oak Tree Press, Wintringham 1998.

Hoel, Sigurd. *Sinners in Summertime*. Iq Pub., New York, 2002.

Ibsen, Henrik. *The Doll's House*, Nick Hern Books, London, 1994.

——. *The Oxford Ibsen*. Vol 1–8, University Press, Oxford, 1960–1977.

Krusenstjerna, Agnes von. *The Misses von Pahlen*. Vol. 1–7, Women's Street, Melbourne [198?].

Mykle, Agnar. *Lasso 'Round the Moon*. Dell, New York, 1961.

——. *The Song of the Red Ruby*, Dell, New York, 1962.

Strindberg August. *Getting Married I–II*. Quartet Books, London, 1977.

——. *Plays: The Father, Countess Julie, The Outlaw, The Stronger*. IndyPublish, Boston, 2003.

SCHNITZLER, ARTHUR

1862–1931
Austrian dramatist and narrator

Through his composition of early poetry and aphorisms, scandalous plays, innovative short stories and novellas, and select novels Arthur Schnitzler is known today as one of the most important Austrian authors of the turn of the century. The entirety of his œuvre reflects both inner and outer mechanisms of late-Imperial Austria and its subjects, often leaving his readers with the task of coming to terms with the conundrum of what is truth/being or just appearance/semblance, the German *Sein* und *Schein*. His works, including Schnitzler's 8,000-pages-long diary manuscript, offer a detailed chronicle of the Viennese fin-de-siècle period (1890–1925) and thematize among many issues the dilemma of assimilation for Austrian Jews (*Der Weg ins Freie*, 1908; *The Road into the Open*), the Catholic Church's promoting of anti-Semitic prejudice against established professionals (*Professor Bernhardi*, 1912), and, in general, his times' attitudes, beliefs, prejudices, and political and social practices. In this vein, his play *Fink und Fliederbusch*

(1917), which depicts a duel between two rivaling journalists, is equally about the enduring fascination with the militaristic honor code and the influential as well as calculating power of contemporary media outlets.

Despite this broad range of themes, Schnitzler is perhaps best known for exploring in his narratives and plays the erotic and decadent stimuli that linked the entirety of society, regardless of noted social differences. His introduction into literature of the *süßes Mädel* type, the sweet girl, exemplifies such constant exploration of sexuality that transcends all class barriers. The *süßes Mädel* is described aptly as a young girl from the *Vorstadt*, the Viennese outskirts, who both lovingly and frivolously pursues sexual adventures with young men of better social standing, only to reach in later years perfect petit bourgeois haven by marrying the solid, ordinary workman type. Her sexual openness and availability together with the understanding that the sweet girl will not pursue her relationship beyond a certain point cultivate her intense attraction. The frailty of bourgeois respectability and of society's demands of moral decency thus take center stage in Schnitzler's quest to unveil sexual libido as the defining element that links all social classes. Sigmund Freud, whose *Traumdeutung* [*Interpretations of Dreams*] (1900) mirrors Schnitzler's understanding of sexuality as the key mover of mankind's behavior, expressed in a letter to Schnitzler in 1922 to what degree he viewed the writer as an intimidating double of himself. Schnitzler's talent for portraying his characters' inner processes, albeit primarily through what is unspoken, shows how close his literature of the subconscious is to Freudian concepts.

Easily the most controversial Schnitzler play, *Reigen* [*Hands Around: A Cycle of Ten Dialogues*] (1903) unmasks its characters' moral façade as each experiences the full circle of a sexual merry-go-round in which society's entirety is linked in both directions from the prostitute up to the aristocrat by ten implied sexual acts. Illustrating these acts only by means of dashes in the written play, Schnitzler's concern is to highlight the duplicity of verbal exchanges before and after each encounter. The play's scenes, which have been compared to a medieval *Totentanz* (a traditional Austrian ritual of the dance of death), exemplify a simultaneous presence of anticipation and dissatisfaction, subordination and brazenness, the desire for adventure and marital duty, frivolity and naiveté, all bundled in the constant expectation of achieving pure sexual pleasure. After the 1920 premiere of the play in Berlin and its 1921 performance in Vienna, a wave of disapproval spread across the German-speaking lands and denunciations of Schnitzler as pornographer were ubiquitous. Organized public disturbances in Vienna and Berlin, initiated by nationalistic and anti-Semitic organizations, culminated in a trial involving the entire Berlin ensemble and ultimately in Schnitzler's withdrawal of his permission to have his play performed. Only after his son, Heinrich, lifted the sanction in 1981, could it be seen once again in European theaters. Max Ophuls' celebrated French film adaptation, *La Ronde* (1950), was banned as well until the United States Supreme Court overruled a ban in the state of New York in 1954.

Defying the literary convention and what is familiar to readers, in the three-act play *Liebelei* [*Light-O'-Love*] (1895) the sweet girl disobeys the stereotypical relationship. Christine reveals unexpected emotions that go beyond the comprehension of her surroundings as she falls in love with her cheating lover Fritz, and this despite her awareness of the evanescence of their relationship:

> CHRISTINE: Love!—He?—I was nothing else to him but a way of passing the time—and he died for another woman!—And I—adored him!—Did he not know?...

Light-O'-Love, Act 3

Fritz's affair with a married woman betrays his initial affair with Christine, only to die in the end during a duel with the married woman's husband. Yet again, the vision of sexual desires and engagements becomes the primary determinant in unveiling tensions and emotions, underneath the veil of a deceptively ordered life, in what appears to be a stable society. In this example, sexuality takes shape in what many view as the typically Austrian duality of politeness and malice.

Schnitzler's plays rarely reach the level of erotic explicitness as in the interior monologue of the novella *Fräulein Else* (1924). It exposes a young woman's psychological state that is torn between respectful love for her father and the powerful sexual desire to reveal her virginal body to unknown onlookers. She finds a seeming exhibitionist solution to this dilemma in the covering of her naked body with only a coat, which she drops in front of everyone in a hotel, only to lose consciousness and eventually commit suicide. Once again, hints of frivolity that were so provocative to the superficial prudery of Schnitzler's contemporaries are engulfed by more complex arrangements. Else is trapped in a psychological and in a social conflict, since her wish to expose herself originates in a need to sell her body in order to guarantee the financial survival of her family. Without a doubt, it is because of such sexual thematics and because of these hermeneutic possibilities that many of Schnitzler's plays are still frequently performed today. And for similar reasons, many of his texts have been reinterpreted by film makers, such as the well-publicized adaptation of *Traumnovelle* [*Rhapsody: A Dream Novel*] (1926) in Stanley Kubrick's *Eyes Wide Shut* (1999).

Biography

Born in Vienna, Austria, May 15, 1862. Youngest of four children of the well-known laryngologist

Johann Schnitzler. Educated at the Akademisches Gymnasium (1871–1879); attended the University of Vienna medical school (1879–1885; MD 1885). Served as assistant and intern to Theodor Meynert, one of Sigmund Freud's teachers, in the Wiener Allgemeines Krankenhaus (1885–1888); assistant to his father in the Polyklinik (1888–1893). After his father's death (1893), Schnitzler ran a private practice and specialized in nervous disorders. His increasing literary productivity reduced the focus on medical practice. In the 1890s, Schnitzler had close contact with the Zionist Theodor Herzl, but he did not support his ideals. Schnitzler's literary assessment of the dubious qualities of the Austrian military honor code in the novella *Leutnant Gustl* [*Lieutenant Gustl*] (1901) culminated in a court's revoking of his reserve officer title. Recipient of numerous literary awards: Bauernfeld Prize, 1899, 1903; Franz Grillparzer Prize, 1908; Ferdinand Raimund Prize, 1914; Vienna Volkstheater Prize, 1920. He died in Vienna on 21 October 1931.

ARNE KOCH

Selected Works

Anatol (produced 1910). 1893; translated by Frank Marcus, 1982.

Sterben. 1894; as "Dying," translated by Harry Zohn in *The Little Comedy and Other Stories*, 1977.

Liebelei (produced 1895). 1896; as *Light-O'-Love*, translated by Bayard Quincy Morgan in *The Drama*, August 1912; as *The Game of Love*, translated by Carl Mueller in *Masterpieces of the Modern Central European Theatre*, 1967; as *Love Games*, translated by Charles Osborne in *The Round Dance and Other Plays*, 1982; as *Flirtations*, translated by Arthur S. Wensinger and Clinton J. Atkinson in *Plays and Stories*, 1982; as *Dalliance*, translated and adapted by Tom Stoppard, 1986.

Die überspannte Person. 1896; as *The High-Strung Woman*, translated by Paul F. Dvorak in *Illusion and Reality*, 1986.

Halbzwei. 1897; as *One-Thirty*, translated by Paul F. Dvorak in *Illusion and Reality*, 1986.

Der Grüne Kakadu. 1899; as *The Green Cockatoo*, translated by G.J. Weinberger in *Paracelsus and Other One-Act Plays*, 1995.

Reigen. Zehn Dialoge (written 1897; scenes 4–6 produced 1903; complete production in Hungarian, 1912; in German, 1920; private print, 1900). 1903; as *Hands Around: A Cycle of Ten Dialogues*, 1920; as *La Ronde*, translated by Eric Bentley in *From the Modern Repertoire*, 1955; translated by Hans Weigert and Patricia Newhall in *Masters of the Modern Drama*, 1962; translated by Carl Mueller in *Masterpieces of the Modern Central European Theatre*, 1967; translated

by Sue Davies and adapted by John Barton, 1982; as *Dance of Love*, 1965; as *The Round Dance*, translated by Carles Osborne in *The Round Dance and Other Plays*, 1982.

Komtesse Mizzi oder Der Familientag (produced 1909). 1908; as *Countess Mizzie; or, the Family Reunion*, translated by Edwin Björkman in *Plays and Stories*, 1982.

Das weite Land. 1911; as *Undiscovered Country*, translated by Tom Stoppard, 1980.

Casanovas Heimfahrt. 1918; as *Casanova's Homecoming*, translated by Edan and Cedar Paul, 1921.

Die Schwestern oder Casanova in Spa (produced 1920). 1919; as *The sisters, or Casanova in Spa*, translated by G.J. Weinberger in *Three Late Plays*, 1992.

Komödie der Verführung, 1924; as *Seduction Comedy*, translated by G.J. Weinberger in *Three Late Plays*, 1992.

Fräulein Else. 1924; translated by Robert A. Simon, 1925; by F.H. Lyon, 1925.

Traumnovelle. 1926; as "Fridolin and Albertine," translated by Erich Posselt in *Vanity Fair*, October 1926; as *Rhapsody: A Dream Novel*, translated by Otto P. Schinnerer, 1927.

Spiel im Morgengrauen. 1926; as *Daybreak*, translated by William A. Drake, 1927.

Im Spiel der Sommerlüfte (produced 1929). 1930; as *In the Play of Summer Breezes*, translated by G.J. Weinberger in *The Final Plays*, 1996.

Further Reading

Arnold, Heinz L. (editor). *Arthur Schnitzler*. Munich: Edition Text und Kritik, 1998.

Daviau, Donal G. (editor). *Major Figures of the Turn-of-the-Century Austrian Literature*. Riverside: Ariadne Press, 1991.

Lindken, Hans-Ulrich. *Arthur Schnitzler: Aspekte und Akzente. Materialien zu Leben und Werk*. New York [and Frankfurt]: Lang, 1984; revised edition, 1987.

Liptzin, Solomon. *Arthur Schnitzler*. Riverside: Ariadne Press, 1932; revised edition, 1995.

Perlmann, Michaela L. *Arthur Schnitzler*. Stuttgart: Metzler, 1987.

Scheible, Hartmut (editor). *Arthur Schnitzler in Selbstzeugnissen und Bilddokumenten*. Reinbek: Rowohlt, 1976; revised edition, 1994.

Schneider, Gerd K. *Die Rezeption von Arthur Schnitzlers "Reigen," 1897–1994*. Riverside: Ariadne Press, 1995.

Swales, Martin. *Arthur Schnitzler: A Critical Study*, Oxford: Clarendon, 1971.

Thompson, Bruce. *Schnitzler's Vienna: Image of a Society*. London: Routledge, 1990.

Wagner, Renate. *Arthur Schnitzler: Eine Biographie*. Vienna [and New York]: Molden, 1981.

Weinberg, G.J. *Arthur Schnitzler's late plays: a critical study*. New York [and Frankfurt]: Lang, 1997.

Weinzierl, Ulrich. *Arthur Schnitzler: Lieben, Träumen, Sterben*. Frankfurt: Fischer, 1994.

Yates, W.E. *Schnitzler, Hofmannsthal, and the Austrian Theatre*. New Haven, CT [and London]: Yale University Press, 1992.

SCIENCE FICTION AND FANTASY

Science Fiction and Fantasy (SF/F), at least in theory, allows writers considerable leeway in the presentation of explicit or alternative material. It is possible to explore themes under the cloak of the alien or the fantastic that would be too risqué in a mainstream format. SF/F publishing has always been culturally marginalized and while this fact is often lamented by practitioners, publishers, and readers, it does allow for a modicum of invisibility. SF/F publishing, broadly defined, includes a wide spectrum of publishing practices, from large commercial publishers to fan-produced items with limited circulation. Since much of this latter material exists "under the radar" it pays little regard to commercial considerations, "community standards," or copyright. Then there is the nature of the genre itself: as Stanislaw Lem writes, "only in science fiction does a writer have room to vary biological and cultural phenomena so that they extend beyond the reader's experience" (2).

Bram Stoker's *Dracula* (1897) and J. Sheridan Le Fanu's earlier lesbian vampire tale, *Carmilla* (1872), are foundational narratives in which fear of the alien is conflated with fear of a more powerful sexuality. Fear of women is evident in many early texts, exemplified by *She* (1887) by H. Rider Haggard, a fantastic voyage narrative in which two explorers encounter an ancient and powerful seductress. There are similar scenarios in Edgar Rice Burroughs's novels and Robert E. Howard's *Conan* series of the 1930s. But in all these texts sexuality, though powerful, is only implied. John Clute writes that "traditionally sf has been a puritanical and male-oriented literature" (1088). From early in the twentieth century until the "new wave" of the 1960s, publishers assumed a readership of male adolescents, which meant that the titillation promised by lurid covers featuring semi-clad women menaced by multi-tentacled aliens (see Harrison) was rarely mirrored in the texts. Throughout its early history, then, SF/F placed considerable emphasis on fear of women and sexuality, and on violence, but while it engaged with sexual themes and images, it was usually in a cautionary way.

By the 1980s there was a "radical exploration of alternative sexual possibilities" (Clute 1089), in part due to ground-breaking work by writers and publishers in the preceding two decades. Robert A. Heinlein's *Stranger in a Strange Land* (1961), though dated today, was a landmark in its exploration of free love. Ursula K. LeGuin's classic *The Left Hand of Darkness* (1969) describes a society of androgynous humans who can take on the characteristics of either sex during their period of "kemmar." John Varley created a culture of polymorphous sexuality in his Gaen trilogy (*Titan* [1979], *Wizard* [1980], and *Demon* [1984]), and gender-as-costume has become a convention in various high-tech futures, as in Iain M. Banks's *Culture* novels (*Consider Phelbus* [1987] and *Passim*) in which characters regularly change sex.

Samuel R. Delany's *Aye and Gomorrah* was "the first major work about gender (and sex!) to win an award [a Nebula award in 1967] in the field" (Notkin, x). Sex is a literal metaphor for the interface between humans and technology in J. G. Ballard's taboo-breaking *Crash* (1973) and in the intervening decades, cybersex, defined by Richard Glyn Jones as "sex that depends to a greater or lesser extent on technology" (xv), has become a given of the genre.

The increased visibility of women writers had an incalculable impact on the field. A number of women-only utopias were published in the 1970s, radically different from the sexless utopias of earlier periods such as Charlotte Perkins Gilman's *Herland* (1914). Joanna Russ has been credited for introducing lesbian feminism to SF/F with *When It Changed* (1972) (Garber and Paleo, xi). Suzy McKee *Charnas's Motherlines* (1978) and Sally M. Gearhart's *The Wanderground* (1979) are also central texts.

In 1999, Wendy Pearson wrote that "lesbians and gay men have become less alien in the world of sf in the last little while; we have, indeed, experienced a minor boom in the publishing of stories of 'alternative sexuality'" (53). Theodore Sturgeon is often considered to have pioneered the use of gay themes in SF/F with his story "The World Well Lost" (1953) about two aliens exiled from their culture for homosexuality (Garber and Paleo). Marion Zimmer Bradley incorporated gay themes into her *Darkover* series in the same period. Samuel Delaney's *Stars in My Pockets Like Grains of Sand* (1984) is a densely beautiful proclamation of same-sex desire. Melissa Scott and Nicola Griffiths are both award-winning authors who feature lesbian characters. Some other contemporary writers who treat gay and lesbian themes are Clive Barker, Perry Brass, Pat Califa, Jewelle Gomez, Keith Hartman, Jeffrey N. McMahan, Mercedes Lackey, Maureen F. McHugh, Severna Park, Anne Rice, Lawrence Schimel, and Jean Stewart.

In a relationship parallel to that between mainstream literature and erotica, there is also a subgenre of erotic science fiction. Universal's Beacon Books claims to have published the first true "science fiction pornography" in its "Galaxy Prize Selections" series between 1959–1961 with titles like *Sin in Space* by Cyril Judd (pseud. of C.M. Kornbluth and Judith Merril, 1961). Greenleaf was an important publisher of SF erotica in the mid-1960s with over fifty titles. After the US Supreme Court ruling on pornography in 1967 there was an outpouring of SF/F erotica. Essex House, an imprint of American Art Enterprises with "unusual aspirations" (Clute, 392), published forty-two titles in less than two years, half of which have SF/F themes. David Meltzer, Michael Perkins, and Philip José Farmer were all important writers for Essex House (Jakubowski, 55–61) whose works have become collectors' items. Farmer's three Essex House novels have been described as "probably the best known examples of SF pornography" (Johnson, 5) and his novel *The Lovers* (1961) is credited by several critics as having played a significant role in opening up sexuality as an acceptable SF theme (Lem, 5–7; Stevens, 30). Other notable presses were Olympia (*Satyr Trek* by Ray Kainen, 1970), Ophelia (*A Flutter of Lashes* by Morgan Drake, 1970) and Travellers' Companion (*Frankenstein 69* by Ed Martin, 1969), all imprints of Maurice Girodias's Olympia. Bee-line Books (*Pleasure Planet* by Edward George, 1974) was also a prolific publisher of SF/F-themed erotica. By the end of the 1970s,

the flurry subsided, though in recent years there has been a resurgence, notably with the various collections edited by the prolific Cecilia Tan, author of *Telepaths Don't Need Safewords* (1992) and founder of Circlet Press, publishers of "the cutting edge" of erotic SF/F. Other presses include Alyson (gay and lesbian themes), Cleis, and Leyland (gay male press with some SF erotica).

SF/F art is itself a genre with calendars and coffee-table books by artists such as Frank Frazetta and "adult" graphic novels such as Morbus Gravis, a series which features the gravity-defying Druuna, by Paolo Eleuteri Serpieri. Originally published in France by Dargaud Editeur, translated episodes appeared in *Heavy Metal: The Illustrated Fantasy Magazine* and in book form (*Heavy Metal/Kitchen Sink in the International Album Line*). Eurotica and Catalan are also prolific publishers of adult graphic narratives.

Fan-produced texts are an important lode of eroticism in SF/F. According to Eric Garber and Lynn Paleo, some of the first gay and lesbian publications in North America were fannish publications in the 1950s. Considerable academic attention has been paid to "slash," named for the Kirk/Spock narratives and artwork that predominated the field for so long. Print is still strong but the mimeographed zines of the past, sold from boxes under the tables at conventions and through the mail, have given way to Web sites.

MIRIAM JONES

Further Reading

Clute, John, and Peter Nicholls (editors). *The Encyclopedia of Science Fiction*. 1993; rpt. New York: St Martin's Press, 1995.

Farmer, Philip José. *Blown*. Los Angeles: Essex House, 1969.

———. *A Feast Unknown*. Los Angeles: Essex House, 1969.

———. *Image of the Beast*. Los Angeles: Essex House, 1968.

Garber, Eric, and Lynn Paleo. *Uranian Worlds: A Reader's Guide to Alternative Science Fiction and Fantasy*. 1983, 2nd ed. Boston: G.K. Hall, 1990.

Harrison, Harry. *Great Balls of Fire: An Illustrated History of Sex in Science Fiction*. New York: Grosset and Dunlap, 1977.

Jakubowski, Maxim. "Essex House: The Rise and Fall of Speculative Erotica." *Foundation: Review of Science Fiction, 14* (1978): 50–64.

Johnson, Kenneth R. "Science Fiction Pornography," *The Science-Fiction Collector 4* (July 1977): 4–18; 42–44.

Jones, Richard Glyn. *Introduction, Cybersex: Aliens, Neurosex and Cyborgasms*. New York: Carroll and Graf, 1996.

Lem, Stanislaw. "Sex in Science Fiction," translated by Franz Rottensteiner. *SF Commentary, 22* (July 1971): 2–10, 40–49.

Notkin, Debbie. "Why Have A Tiptree Award?" in *Flying Cups and Saucers: Gender Explorations in Science Fiction and Fantasy*, Debbie Notkin and the Secret Feminist Cabal (editors), Cambridge, Mass.: Edgewood Press, 1998.

Pearson, Wendy. "Identifying the Alien: Science Fiction Meets Its Other." *Science Fiction Studies, 26.1* (March 1999): 59–53.

Stevens, Paul. "Sex in Science Fiction." *SF Commentary, 6* (Sept. 1969): 27–33.

Selected Anthologies and Collections

Brite, Poppy Z. (editor). *Love in Vein: Twenty Original Tales of Vampire Erotica*, New York: Harper Prism, 1994.

Datlow, Ellen (editor). *Alien Sex: Nineteen Tales By the Masters of Science Fiction and Dark Fantasy*. New York: Dutton, 1990.

Datlow, Ellen (editor). *Off Limits: Tales of Alien Sex*. New York: St Martin's Press, 1996.

Datlow, Ellen, et al. (editors). *Sirens and Other Daemon Lovers*. New York: HarperPrism, 1998.

Dozois, Gardner (editor). *Killing Me Softly: Erotic Tales of Unearthly Love*. New York: Harper, 1996.

Dozois, Gardner (editor). *Dying for It: More Erotic Tales of Unearthly Love*. New York: HarperPrism, 1997.

Elder, Joseph (editor). *Eros in Orbit: A Collection of All New Science Fiction Stories About Sex*. New York: Trident Press, 1973.

Eliot, Jeffrey M. (editor). *Kindred Spirits: An Anthology of Gay and Lesbian Science Fiction Stories*. Boston, MA: Alyson Publications, 1984.

Griffith, Nicola, and Stephen Pagel (editors), *Bending the Landscape: Original Gay and Lesbian Writing, Vol. 1: Fantasy*. Clarkson, GA: White Wolf Publishing, 1996, *Vol. 2: Science Fiction*, Woodstock, NY: Overlook Press, 1998, *Vol. 3: Horror*, Woodstock, NY: Overlook Press, 2001.

Hill, Douglas (editor). *The Shape of Sex to Come*, London: Pan Books, 1978.

Hollander, Evan. *Virtual Girls: The Erotic Gems of Evan Hollander*. Cambridge, MA: Circlet Press, 1996.

Jones, Richard Glyn (editor). *Cybersex: Aliens, Neurosex and Cyborgasms*. New York: Carroll and Graf, 1996.

Keesey, Pam (editor). *Dark Angels: Lesbian Vampire Stories*. San Francisco: Cleis, 1995.

Keesey, Pam (editor). *Daughters of Darkness: Lesbian Vampire Stories*. 2nd ed. San Francisco: Cleis, 1998.

Kessler, Joan C. (editor). *Demons of the Night: Tales of the Fantastic, Madness, and the Supernatural from Nineteenth-Century France*. Chicago and London: University of Chicago Press, 1995.

Manning, Reed. *Earthly Pleasures: The Erotic Science Fiction*. Cambridge, MA: Circlet Press, 1996.

Parry, Michel, and Milton Subotsky (editors). *Sex in the 21st Century: A Collection of SF Erotica*. London: Granada, 1979.

Rowe, Michael, and Thomas Roche (editors). *Sons of Darkness: Tales of Men, Blood and Immortality*. San Francisco, CA: Cleis, 1996.

Scortia, Thomas N. (editor). *Strange Bedfellows: Sex and Science Fiction*. New York: Random House, 1972.

Slung, Michele (editor). *I Shudder at Your Touch: Twenty Two Tales of Sex and Horror*. New York: New American Library, 1991.

Slung, Michele (editor). *Shudder Again: Twenty Two Tales of Sex and Horror*. New York: New American Library, 1995.

Stewart, Alex (editor). *Arrows of Eros*. West Warwick, RI: Necronomicon Press, 1989.

Szereto, Mitzi. *Erotic Fairy Tales: A Romp Through the Classics*. San Francisco: Cleis, 2001.

Tan, Cecilia. *Telepaths Don't Need Safewords: And Other Stories from the Erotic Edge of SF/Fantasy*, Cambridge, MA: Circlet Press, 1992.

Tiptree, James, Jr. [Alice Sheldon]. *Warm Worlds and Otherwise*. New York: Ballantine, 1975.

Selected Critical Texts

Bacon-Smith, Camille. *Enterprising Women: Television Fandom and the Creation of Popular Myth*. Philadelphia, PA: University of Pennsylvania Press, 1992.

Bozetto, Roger, Max Duperray, and Alain Chareyre-Mejan (editors). *Eros, sciencefiction, fantastique*. Aix-en-Provence: University de Provence, 1991.

Delany, Samuel R. *The Motion of Light in Water: Sex and Science Fiction in the East Village. 1957–1965*, New York: Arbor House, c1988.

Delany, Samuel R. *Silent Interviews on Language, Race, Sex, Science Fiction, and Some Comics*. Hanover, NH: Wesleyan University Press; University Press of New England, 1994.

Duffy, Maureen. *The Erotic World of Faery, 1972*. London: Cardinal, 1989.

Hollinger, Veronica, and Joan Gordon (editors). *Blood Read: The Vampire As Metaphor In Contemporary Culture*. Philadelphia, PA: University of Pennsylvania Press, 1997.

Jenkins, Henry. *Textual Poachers: Television Fans and Participatory Culture*. New York: Routledge, 1992.

Palumbo, Donald (editor). *Eros in the Mind's Eye: Sexuality and the Fantastic in Art and Film*. New York and London: Greenwood Press, 1986.

Palumbo, Donald (editor). *Erotic Universe: Sexuality and Fantastic Literature*. New York and London: Greenwood Press, 1986.

Penley, Constance. "Brownian Motion: Women, Tactics, and Technology." In *Technoculture*, edited by Constance Penley and Andrew Ross, Minneapolis, MN: University of Minnesota Press, 1991.

Penley, Constance, Elisabeth Lyon, Lynn Spiegel, and Janet Bergstrom (editors). *Close Encounters: Film, Feminism, and Science Fiction*. Minneapolis, MN: University of Minnesota Press, 1991.

SEDUCTION

The concept of seduction implies notions of persuasion and power. In order for techniques of seduction to be necessary, there must exist some obstacle to the sexual encounter: one party's unwillingness to comply, whether it be for reasons of morality or more pragmatic fear of the potential consequences of the act. As such, the structure of seduction has historically been associated with the masculine conquest of female resistance. However, modern representations of seduction often diverge from this model and in the process highlight the neglected history of seduction by the female. Equally, acts of seduction are not limited to the characters depicted in an erotic narrative, but form a vital part of a text's strategy with regard to the reader. Modern critics have begun to theorize this relationship in terms of seductive behavior, the story acting as a 'flirt' in order to attract readers.

The word 'seduction' finds its roots in the Latin *seducere*, to lead astray or apart (se—apart, ducere—to lead). This meaning is explicitly figured in perhaps the earliest literary instance of seduction, that of Odysseus by the Sirens. Aware that many a sailor has altered his course to seek out the source of the Sirens' enchanting song only to find death on the treacherous rocks of their island, Odysseus plugs the ears of his crew with wax and ties himself to the mast. Already in this ancient representation of seduction, sexual pleasure is offered only in association with compulsion and danger. The Siren is also the first of many mythical creatures (vampire, succubus, sylph ...) endowed with supernatural powers to overcome the will of mere mortals.

The word's etymological meaning persisted into eighteenth-century libertinism which many have seen as the ultimate expression of seduction. Titles such as *Les Égarements du cœur et de l'esprit* by Crébillon *fils* [*The Wayward Head and Heart*] (1738) preserved connotations of corruption and diversion from the proper moral course. But by this time the gender structure of seduction had been inverted. A long tradition of courtly romance dating from the Middle Ages

had fixed the positions of male and female as ardent suitor and reluctant maiden respectively, as can be seen in the many Troubadour love ballads of the time, or even in Shakespeare's sonnets.

It was at about this time that the legend of the (male) serial seducer gained widespread popularity. From Molière (1665) through Mozart (1787) to Byron (1819–1823), the character of Don Juan gave rise to the enduring figure of the 'love-'em-and-leave-'em' cad, whose sexual stamina and number of conquests are virtually unlimited. Such fictional achievements were paralleled by the real-life antics of Casanova recounted in his *Mémoires* [*History of My Life*] (1821), whose journeys to the cultural capitals of Europe were always accompanied by a generous sampling of the local female talent.

This focus on quantity was not, however, at the expense of quality. Many of the eighteenth-century libertine novels describe in detail the minute manipulation of language and situation required to effectuate a successful seduction. Seducers like Valmont in Laclos' *Les Liaisons dangereuses* [*Dangerous Liaisons*] (1782) seem to view the challenge of persuading one virtuous woman to give herself up as emblematic of their triumph over the entire female sex. But the novel ends unhappily for this character as Valmont is himself overcome by the persuasive power of his own language—falling in love with his victim, he spends his last days tormented by regret.

The advent of Sade's fiction marked the end of a libertine tradition that pinned its reputation to obtaining the female's consent despite herself. Violence and compulsion outweigh persuasion and rhetoric in his texts, destroying the delicate balance of active and passive participation required by the act of seduction. Sigmund Freud's development of a 'Seduction Theory' around the turn of the twentieth century did little to enhance the bad reputation the act had acquired. Freud's theories of hysteria posited a real or imagined event of sexual trauma in the patient's past, which, when repressed, would emerge in the symptoms of the illness. This event, first described as 'attack' or 'abuse' came later to be known as 'seduction.'

One of the main reasons why Freud's seduction theory caused controversy was its application to describe the 'seduction of the daughter' by her father. The idea that a potential victim of child abuse could somehow be complicit in an act of seduction shocked many. Once more, this reaction highlights the delicate balance of persuasion and consent at work in strategies of seduction, by assuming the female participant's essential collusion in the act. Scenes depicting the seduction of men by women have existed throughout history, but twentieth-century representations were to magnify and popularize this theme, increasingly placing women in a position of power over men. The character of Mrs. Robinson in *The Graduate* (1967, Mike Nichols) employs the persuasive techniques of an experienced older woman against the resistance of a younger man in a gender reversal of the traditional initiation scene. Nevertheless, for women, power still stems from physical allure and it is only when combined with beauty that female seductive discourse may be assured of success.

This structure remains even when the act of reading is itself transformed into one of seduction in Barthes' *Le Plaisir du texte* (1973, *The Pleasure of the Text*). Here, the narrative acts as a female seducer, attempting to persuade the reader of its meaning through striptease, revealing just enough to whet his appetite and offering pleasure "où le vêtement baille" ("where the garment yawns"). More recent theoretical endeavors have tried to break down this male–female opposition, viewing the seductive encounter as a potential space for the exposure and reconfiguration of desire through language, with the potential for transgender and anti-patriarchal effects (Baudrillard, Clément). Seduction has always been premised on the existence of an unequal relation of desire, and on a struggle for power. But recent critics have shown that it is a struggle not always won by the dominant party.

SUSAN GRIFFITHS

Further Reading

Ballaster, Ros. *Seductive Forms: Women's amatory fiction from 1684–1740*. Oxford: Clarendon, 1992.

Barthes, Roland. *The Pleasure of the Text*, Oxford: Blackwell, 1990.

Baudrillard, Jean. *Seduction*. London: Macmillan, 1990.

Becker-Theye, Betty. *The Seducer as Mythic Figure in Richardson, Laclos and Kierkegaard*. New York: Garland, 1988.

Beebee, Thomas O. *Clarissa on the Continent: Translation and seduction*. London: Pennsylvania State University Press, 1990.

Chebel, Malek. *Le Livre des séductions*. Paris: Payot, 1996.

Clément, Catherine and Hélène, Cixous. *The Newly Born Woman*. Minneapolis, MN: University of Minnesota Press, 1986.

Cummings, Katherine. *Telling Tales: The Hysteric's seduction in fiction and theory*. Stanford, CA: Stanford University Press, 1991.

Felman, Shoshana. *Le Scandale du corps parlant: Don Juan avec Austin, ou, La Séduction en deux langues*. Paris: Seuil, 1990.

Gallop, Jane. *Feminism and Psychoanalysis: The Daughter's Seduction*. London: Macmillan, 1982.

Gross, Nicholas P. *Amatory Persuasion in Antiquity: Studies in theory and practice*. London: Associated University Presses, 1985.

Hartmann, Pierre. *Le Contrat et la séduction: essai sur la subjectivité amoureuse dans le roman des Lumières*. Paris: Champion, 1998.

Haslett, Moyra. *Byron's Don Juan and the Don Juan Legend*. Oxford: Clarendon, 1997.

Hunter, Dianne (editor). *Seduction and Theory: Readings of gender, representation and rhetoric*. Urbana and Chicago, IL: University of Illinois Press, 1989.

Kierkegaard, Søren. *Either/Or: Part One*, Princeton, NJ: Princeton University Press. 1987.

Marchal, Roger, Moreau, François and Crogiez, Michèle (editors). *Littérature et séduction: mélanges en l'honneur de Laurent Versini*. Paris: Klincksieck, 1997.

Monneyron, Frédéric. *Séduire: l'imaginaire de la séduction de don Giovanni à Mick Jagger*. Paris: Presses universitaires de France, 1997.

Reed, Toni. *Demon Lovers and Their Victims in British Fiction*. Lexington, KY: University Press of Kentucky, 1988.

Rouhi, Leyla. *Mediation and Love: A Study of the medieval go-between in key Romance and Near-Eastern texts*. Leiden: E.J. Brill, 1999.

Saint-Armand, Pierre. *The Libertine's Progress: Seduction in the eighteenth-century French novel*. Hanover, NH: University Press of New England, 1994.

SEI SHÔNAGON

c. 965–c. 1013
Japanese diarist

Makura no Sôshi [*The Pillow Book*]

Makura no Sôshi is the unique example of "zuihitsu," or essay for the Heian period. It is a rare testimony on a woman's life and her surroundings. The conditions in which Sei Shônagon wrote this essay are still unknown, and different versions exist. Some parts of it are similar to the "nikki" (diaries). It forms a chronicle of court life, especially of gallant intrigues. The author gives a personal glimpse of Heian's life and sensibility, with a special sense of irony and humor. *The Pillow book* is part of the "kanabungaku," written in a phonetic writing (the kana), without any Chinese elements; "onnade," writings of women, were written in hiragana. In fact, "kambun" (literature in Chinese) is reserved for erotic terms, imported from China. Licentious literature was only written in "kambun."

The title refers to the pillow, though the first title was only *Shônagon no Ki* [*The Book of Shônagon*], as Sei used to write her intimate thoughts on a pile of white paper just as if the pillow became her confident, each evening, in the secret of her room. This book, often associated with the *Genji Monogatari*, is considered as a masterpiece for its realistic quality and insight into universal feelings. At the beginning of the eleventh century, the aristocratic life seemed quite free, and related to the aesthetic rather than to morality, to the beautiful rather than to the good, and the search of voluptuous sensations was characteristic of that period.

Sei is particularly sensitive to visual, auditory and olfactory pleasure, and is successful in transmitting the precious sensations she received as if it were yesterday, and not a thousand years ago. Within these notes, many characters are brought to life, among which, numerous lovers. She doesn't refer in any way to her own sentimental life, and it appears that her notes were read and stolen. It is hardly possible to find any reference to sexuality or nudity in the modern sense, though the main problems of men and women of the court concerned love affairs.

The lover had to follow special codes of behavior: the very important moment was at dawn, at the moment of departure. He should not be concerned about tidying up his clothes or look for his belongings. On the contrary, he should forget his things for example, and express regret at leaving his mistress in despair.

He should be especially gallant at dawn, because it is the moment of departure that remains in the memory of the woman. Summer is considered as the best period for secret dates, and dawn is specially favored in this season.

Very often, the author spies on the lovers, and can therefore describe the quality of their clothes. She watches the comings and goings of men, looking carefully at their hair, or clothes dampened with fog. On the other hand, men often peep at women sleeping, because it is said that the face of an awakening woman is particularly beautiful. A beautiful woman awakening from her siesta and even a sick woman, are valuable sights. Sei alludes to her own situation when she writes that she lives in a place where it is hardly possible to be visited, and where everybody is trying to avoid being watched. Aristocrats used to live in semi-darkness, which adds to the mystery of women, and creates some misunderstanding about the identity of the partner, and the houses of Heian-kyô, the capital, were ideal for peeping through the hedges [*kaimamiru*]. Women used to live in the shadow of screens and curtains, and the aim of the lover was to pass on the other side of the screen, and reach the body of the woman with whom he chatted for a long time. Sei manages to listen to noise through the partition, and she can guess that it is a man who has come secretly to visit one of the ladies. She likes to watch and to listen to other people's love affairs.

As for seductive physical aspects, the body is never described naked. Despite this, the color of the flesh of a young lord, slightly pink, is admired; young men and women, and children, should be plump to be beautiful. As for women, their teeth should be blackened in a perfect way, and very often, Sei describes the beauty of their hair. At that time, women's hair was the most important asset for seduction, and should be naturally black. It had to be straight, glittering, and as long as possible, reaching to the feet if possible. This is the only part of a woman's body that is described. The skin had to be white, a sign of aristocracy, the mouth small and painted like a rosebud, with white powder around it; the eyebrows were often shaved or plucked, and replaced by painted ones higher up on the forehead.

The beauty of costumes for aristocrats of high rank is an essential asset for seduction, and Sei notes many details about men's and women's beautiful clothes. Women used to wear several layers of clothes, and the matching of colors was considered especially elegant, especially for sleeves. Sei loved the chamberlain's brilliant silk clothes.

No court event was complete without poetry, and no lord or lady was considered as such without poetical skills. A woman would forget chastity and shyness in front of a beautiful poem; along with poetry, calligraphy was considered a skill of the highest rank, and venerated nearly like a religion, said Arthur Waley. Therefore, the way to use a brush was considered the best way to know one's sensibility and personality. Penmanship was as important as beautiful eyes. A woman or a man could easily fall in love while reading a poem or a letter. Sei considers a letter a beautiful thing. She loves looking at the charming face of a lady who has just received a letter at twilight.

Biography

Sei Shônagon is supposed to have been born in 965 (or 968), and her father was probably Kyohara no Motosuke, the grandson of prince Toneri, who mainly compiled the *Nihongi* (annals of Japan). She belonged to the Kyohara family, and was then introduced to the imperial palace around 993. She became the maid of princess Sadako, aged fifteen. After 1000, after the death of Sadako, the life of Sei remains unknown. She may have remained at court until 1013.

MARK KOBER

Further Reading

Beaujard, André. *Sei Shônagon, son temps et son oeuvre:: une femme de lettres de l'ancien Japon.* G.P. Maisonneuve, 1934.

Morris, Ivan. *La vie de cour dans l'ancien Japon au temps du prince Genji,* (first edition, 1964). Transl. M. Charvet, Gallimard, Paris, 1969.

Pigeot, Jacqueline and Jean-Jacques, Tschudin. *La Littérature japonaise.* P.U.F, "Que Sais-je ?," N°710, 1983 (reed. 1995)

Revon, Michel. *Anthologie de la littérature japonaise des origines au vingtième siècle.* Vertiges, Paris, 1986.

Editions

Notes de chevet. Translated by André Beaujard, Gallimard/Unesco. Paris, 1966.

The Pillow book. Partly translated by Arthur Waley. 1972. Complete translation in 1984.

The Pillow Book. Editions Dis Voir, Paris, 1996.

The Pillow Book, Dir. Peter Greenaway, 1996.

SELBY, HUBERT, JR.

1928–
American novelist and short story writer

Last Exit to Brooklyn

The 1964 publication of Hubert Selby's *Last Exit to Brooklyn* aroused considerable controversy because of its often profane language and its graphic descriptions of sexual violence. It occasioned a widely publicized obscenity trial in England and extensive debate in the British House of Commons. In Italy, the novel was banned. In fact, the pre-novel magazine publication of one section of *Last Exit* resulted in the editor of the *Provincetown Review* being arrested and charged with distributing pornography to a minor. In retrospect, this controversy involves no little irony since the prevailing tone of Selby's novel, which focuses upon the interrelationship of sexuality and power, is determinedly anti-erotic. *Last Exit* is a grim exploration of the wages of the sins of lust and human exploitation. The penalties that its central characters pay for their sins are so grotesquely excessive that the novel has been discussed as a modern experiment in Swiftian satire.

Last Exit to Brooklyn is episodic in structure, consisting of five sections each with its own artistic integrity and a coda that, at first glance, seems the least integrated part of the novel. In fact though, the coda entitled "Landsend" dramatically underscores the fate that awaits the inhabitants of Selby's fictional world and the harsh vision that underscores the five central sections of the text: "Another Day Another Dollar," "And Baby Makes Three," "The Queen Is Dead," "Tralala," and "Strike." Selby's cumulative characterization of a Brooklyn street gang that functions as a kind of avenging force and reappears throughout these five sections is an important unifying device in the novel. Therefore, the five sections stand out as especially memorable.

"The Queen Is Dead" recounts the psychological destruction of Georgette, a young and sensitive drag queen. Georgette makes the mistake of falling in love with Vinnie, an especially brutal member of the street gang who proceeds to debase and humiliate Georgette in a number of ways. First, the street gang isolates her as the center of a grotesque game in which its individual members take turns throwing a knife at her feet forcing her to leap out of the way. Inevitably she is injured by the knife whereupon Vinnie procures some iodine and, along with the rest of the gang, laughs sadistically as he applies it to her wound. This assault on Georgette symbolically foreshadows Vinnie's forcing her to perform fellatio on him during an orgiastic party. Selby has said that Georgette, easily the most sympathic character in the novel, was based upon a real-life counterpart who inspired his novel. The obvious narrative compassion for Georgette led to the mistaken impression that the novelist was himself gay.

"Tralala" describes the harrowing destruction of the title character, a cold and calculating prostitute. Initially, Tralala is content to work with the street gang in systematically assaulting and robbing her clients. Along with "Another Day Another Dollar," "Tralala" gives the clearest indication that the novel is set in war time, and Tralala especially targets young enlisted men who wander into her section of Brooklyn. She is baffled and enraged when an army officer, after having sex with her, offers her love instead of money before he is shipped overseas. Seemingly disoriented by this unexpected occurrence, Tralala initiates a prolonged self-abasement which culminates in her becoming the victim of a gang rape. The gang rape scene is described in graphic and extensive detail and constitutes the most horrific moment in Selby's grim naturalistic text.

"Strike," the longest section of the novel, is also a detailed account of self-destruction. It is especially important in the Selby canon for thematic reasons and because it focuses upon one incarnation of a recurring character type. "Strike" is an investigation of the deadly nature of obsession, a major emphasis in Selby's subsequent fiction; and its main character is the first of several Selby protagonists named Harry. Selby has confirmed that he envisions the various Harrys as constituting one evolving character type, the obsessive and addictive male who hates women and can respond to them only by objectifying them. A lathe operator in a Brooklyn factory, the Harry of "Strike" is provocatively incompetent on the job. Married and the father of an infant son, he hates his wife and child, perceiving them as traps from which he can never escape. Two unrelated experiences offer Harry temporary release from his professional and personal entrapment. First, after the workers in his factory strike, Harry is given the job of running the strike headquarters because no one else wants it. In addition, Harry, who has always been militantly homophobic, begins to find himself attracted to drag queens. He starts frequenting a gay bar where he feels truly empowered for the first time, not realizing that his obsessive personality frightens the young homosexuals whom he tries to pick up in the bar. Eventually Harry becomes involved with a cynical drag queen who, after taking most of Harry's money, dumps him. The strike is ultimately settled, and the union consents to Harry's firing as a concession to management. In such profound despair that he is hardly aware of what he is doing, Harry sexually propositions a young boy and suffers a horrifying retribution for his sin. A street gang appears and beats him so severely that he is left barely conscious and hanging from a chain-length fence in a grotesque parody of Christ's crucifixion.

Last Exit to Brooklyn is a harrowing exploration of an urban subculture, a waste land in which all potentially redemptive emotions are distorted by a vengeful power that resides externally in the external slum landscape, but more importantly inside the psyches of its lost and desperate characters. The residents of Selby's wasteland are specifically victimized by debased and dehumanizing forms of eroticism.

Biography

Born in 1928 in Brooklyn, New York. *Last Exit to Brooklyn*, his first novel, was published by Grove Press in 1964. Selby has published four subsequent novels and one short story collection, as well as short fiction in *New Directions 17* and the journals *Enclitic, Evergreen Review, Black Mountain Review,* and *Provincetown Review.*

JAMES R. GILES

Editions

Last Exit to Brooklyn. New York: Grove Press, 1964; London: Calder & Boyars, 1966.

Selected Works

Last Exit to Brooklyn. 1964.
The Room. 1971.
The Demon. 1976.
Requiem for a Dream. 1978.
Song of the Silent Snow and Other Stories. 1986.
The Willow Tree: A Novel. 1998.

Further Reading

Giles, James R. *The Naturalistic Inner-City Novel in America.* Columbia, SC: University of South Carolina Press, 1995.
———. *Understanding Hubert Selby, Jr.* Columbia, SC: University of South Carolina Press, 1998.
Hendin. *Vulnerable People: A View of American Fiction Since 1945.* New York: Oxford University Press, 1978.
Howard, June. *Form and History in American Literary Naturalism.* Chapel Hill, NC: University of North Carolina Press, 1985.
Hurm, Gerd. *Fragmented Urban Images; The American City in Modern Fiction from Stephen Crane to Thomas Pynchon.* Frankford am Main & New York: Peter Lang, 1991.
Oates, Joyce Carol. *New Heaven, New Earth.* New York: Vanguard, 1974.
Volume 1, 1981 issue of *Review of Contemporary Fiction* was devoted to Selby's fiction.

SELLON, EDWARD

1818–1866
English writer, translator, and illustrator

Annotations on the Sacred Writings of the Hindüs

Printed for private circulation, the *Sacred Writings* is an anthropological exploration of Indian sexual beliefs and practices. Among other rituals, Sellon describes that of the Kauchilüas, a branch of the Sactas sect. He describes their practice which throws into confusion all the ties of female relationships, and disregards natural restraints. "On the occasions of the performance of divine worship the women and girls deposit their Julies or bodices in a box in the charge of the Gurü or priest. At the close of the rites, the male worshippers take a Julie from the box, and the female to whom it belongs, even were she his sister, becomes his partner for the evening in these lascivious orgies."

The New Epicurean; or The Delights of Sex

Five hundred copies were run off initially selling for £1.113.6d. According to *MS Arcana* most of the first edition stock was seized and destroyed by the Society for the Suppression of Vice after a raid on Dugdale's publishing house in Holywell Street in the summer of 1868 (see Mendes, p. 346). Under the character of Sir Charles, Sellon depicts a life entirely to his tastes, "I am a man who, having passed the Rubicon of youth, has arrived at that age when the passions require a more stimulating diet than is to be found in the arms of every painted courtesan." This was essentially a reworking of his sexual adventures.

Phoebe Kissagen; or the Remarkable Adventures, Schemes, Wiles, and Devilries of Une Maquerelle, being a sequel to the "New Epicurean." Sir Charles leaves £3000 to Phoebe and Chloe which allows them to buy a bagnio in Leicester fields. The book contains "the Bagnio Correspondence", letters from prostitutes' clients describing their various sexual experiences.

The Ups and Downs of Life

Sellon's life has best been told by himself in his "erotic autobiography" (as he called it), *The Ups and Downs of Life*. First published by Dugdale in 1867, it was later reprinted by Auguste Brancart in Brussels in 1892, as *The Amorous Prowess of a Jolly Good Fellow or His Adventures with Lovely Girls as Related by Himself*. The book is a first-hand account of his sexual experiences in both India and England and a demonstration of his uninhibited libertinism. *The Ups and Downs* is a lucid account, wittily describing his foolhardy adventures. Sellon refuses to use euphemisms to describe his sexual activities but leaps into explicit account of his escapades, including a comic transvestite episode. The manuscript was left unfinished mid-sentence just before his death.

Cytheral's Hymnal

Sellon is attributed to having contributed to *Cytheral's Hymnal*, a collection of bawdy and sacrilegious verse, with the mock imprint "Oxford. Printed at the University Press, for the Society for the Promoting of Useful Knowledge," 1870. Containing fifty-one erotic limericks, it is believed to be a joint production between Sellon, George Augustus Sala, Swinburne and several other Oxford men.

Unpublished Tales

Sellon also wrote a handful of tales which remained unpublished. "Scenes in the Life of a Young Man" was intended as an erotic tale as a prelude to *Phoebe Kissagen* but was never printed. He also wrote two other short erotic tales, "The Confessions of a Single Gentleman exemplified in the Erotic Adventures of a Gentleman," originally intended to be printed at the end of *New Epicurean*, and "The Delights of Imagination."

Illustrations

Ashbee believes Sellon illustrated many of his own books including *The Ups and Downs of Life, the New Epicurean, Phoebe Kissagen,* and *Adventures of a Gentleman.* He did six obscene watercolors to illustrate *Memoirs of Rosa Belle-fille* published by Dugdale in 1865. He wrote *Adventures of a Gentleman* (c. 1865) which remained unpublished, plus four watercolor drawings to accompany the tale. He also produced a drawing intended for a new edition of *The Amorous Quaker* which was never published. He designed the illustrations to *The Adventures of a Schoolboy* and *The New Lady's Tickler*, London: Dugdale, 1866.

Biography

As well as a writer and a translator of erotica, Sellon was, at various times in his life, a soldier, a stagecoach driver, and a fencing master. He was born in England in 1818 to a family of moderate fortune, his father dying when he was a child. He received a good education in languages and the classics. He joined the army as a cadet at the age of sixteen where he rose to captain by the time he was twenty-six. While serving in India, he engaged in foolhardy escapades and amorous intrigues with both European and native females. In his words, "I now commenced a regular course of fucking with native women. The usual change for the general run of them is two rupees." After remaining in India for 10 years, in 1844 he arrived back in England where his mother had arranged a marriage for him with a reputed heiress, "a young lady of considerable personal attractions." On discovering she was not as rich as he had been led to believe, he left his wife and moved out for two years, keeping a mistress in "a little suburban villa." He was temporarily reconciled with his wife but among his numerous affairs was a young servant girl of fourteen which dalliance his wife soon discovered. He continued with his sexual adventures, intermittently living with his wife, who along the way bore him a son whom he did not like. His mother lost her fortune, and he was obliged to become a stage driver to keep himself, driving the Cambridge mail for two

years, and then started teaching fencing in London. He finally shot himself in April 1866 at Webb's hotel, 219 and 220 Piccadilly at the age of forty-eight years.

JULIE PEAKMAN

Selected Works

Herbert Breakspear, A Legend of the Mahratta War. London: Whittaker, 1848.

Edited the English translation of the *Gita-Radhica-Krishna, a Sanskrit Poem.* London, William Roch, 1850: London: 1865.

Annotations on the Sacred Writings of the Hindüs. London: H. Weede, 1865: London, Privately printed, 1902.

The Monolithic Temples of India. c. 1865.

The New Epicurean; or The Delights of Sex. London: Dugdale, "1740"; actual date of original publication 1865. Reprinted with identical title in 1875 by "D. Cameron" [Lazenby]: New York: Olympia Press, c. 1968.

Sellon gave a paper *On the Linga puja, or Phallic worship of India* to the Anthropological Society on January 17, which was printed in *The Reader*, 21 January 1865. Another manuscript paper was written on *Some remarks on the Same Sancti Puja or The Worship of the Female Powers* and *A Reply to the Attack in the Ethnographical Review*, December 1865.

Translated *Selections from the Decameron of Giovanni Boccacio. Including all the Passages hitherto Suppressed.* London: 1865.

The Ups and Downs of Life. London: Dugdale, 1867. Reprinted 1987.

Phoebe Kissagen; or the Remarkable Adventures, Schemes, Wiles, and Devilries of Une Maquerelle, being a sequel to the "New Epicurean." London: Dugdale, "1743," actual date of original publication 1866. Reprinted 1876.

The Index Expurgatorious of Martial. London: 1868. Translation from the Latin of more explicit epigrams of the classic Roman author. Undertaken along with George Augusta Sala and F.P. Pike.

Further Reading

See indexes "Sellon" and his works as cited above in the following books:

Fraxi, Pisanus [Henry Spencer Ashbee]. *Index Librorum Prohibitorum, Centuria Librorum Absconditorum* and *Catena Librorum Tacendorum.* London: privately printed, 1877. Reprinted as *Bibliography of Forbidden Books.* New York: Jack Brussel, 1962.

Kearney, Patrick. *The History of Erotica*, London: Macmillan, 1982.

Legman, G. *The Horn Book. Studies in Erotic Folklore and Bibliography.* London: Cape, 1970.

Mendes, Peter. *Clandestine Erotic Literature in English 1800–1930.* London: Scholar Press, 1993.

McCalman, Iain. *Radical Underworlds. Prophets, Revolutionaries and Pornographers in London 1795–1840.* Oxford: Oxford University Press, 1988.

SEWALL, ROBERT

c. 1915–
American novelist

The Devil's Advocate

Often called the greatest of American underground erotic novels, *The Devil's Advocate* has a confusing history. Legman implies that Sewall originally wrote the novel for the Oklahoma millionaire Roy Johnson, to whom Sewall had sold several Henry Miller parodies (*Horn Book*, p. 36). The erotic book dealer C.J. Scheiner spoke to Sewall during the 1980s to confirm that the novelist had actually written the work in 1942 for the "RCA Collection," a group of manuscripts commissioned by yet another wealthy collector, this one from Albany, New York; Scheiner owns the original manuscript. Disturbed by the novel's graphic sadomasochism, Legman, working from the carbon copy, expurgated, expanded, and retyped the manuscript for a red-covered mimeographed edition bound by the bookman Herman Miller in New York. On the title page, Legman falsely ascribed authorship of the revised manuscript to "Wood C. Lamont" as a way of twitting the American poet Clement Wood, who had also written erotic stories for Roy Johnson (Legman, *Horn Book*, p. 36). Appalled at Legman's censorship, Sewall two years later retyped the manuscript from memory, having already delivered the original to "RCA." This 1944 retelling, *The Sign of the Scorpion*, shorter than Legman's version and stylistically inferior to Sewall's own original, bore the pseudonym "Bruce Abbott"; this edition was also run off in bound mimeographed form by Herman Miller. Most subsequent editions, variously called *The Devil's Advocate*, *The Sign of the Scorpion*, and *The Devil's Brand*, have reproduced this 1944 manuscript, but the original 1942 version was issued under the name "Robert Sewell" in 1998.

The Devil's Advocate eroticizes a tale that blends "hard-boiled detective" with "country youth corrupted by city" genres. Though told mostly in third person, the novel is framed by the musings of Conrad S. Garnett, an attorney known as the "devil's advocate" after his practice of defending celebrated criminals. The frame makes clear that Garnett is ruthless and opportunistic as an attorney and as a sexual predator. When a woman offers sex in exchange for his defending her boyfriend, he takes advantage of her with no intention of accepting the case. As the novel opens, he has just cast off a pleading lover. His justification is "Garnett's Law: 'Never do anything for anybody unless you're sure that the profit derived from your generosity will far exceed the expenditure'". When Clara Reeves, a "hick" from upstate, talks her way into his office, her desirability and his own arrogance make Garnett forget that law. Clara claims that she has sought out Garnett because of his reputation. She is searching for her sister Rita, who has disappeared but left in her New York apartment whips, dildos, and other appliances, a diary detailing her seduction by an unnamed but clearly powerful man, and a ring in the shape of a scorpion. He will help her, Garnett says, if Clara will obey his instructions. Making use of a cherished erotic plot device, Garnett says that she must go undercover, which also means she must shed her inhibitions. To prepare her, he has her read aloud graphic passages from Rita's diary, strip naked, and learn to masturbate him. Garnett tells her to put an ad in the paper offering to return the curious scorpion ring to its owner. A woman responds, and introduces Clara to friends who gradually seduce her into sexual acts, all of which Clara reports to Garnett, who makes her perform the same acts on him; she reluctantly confesses to enjoying them. The Scorpion's trail leads to a secluded Long Island estate.

According to Scheiner, the novel fictionalizes real sex parties held at Bozenkill, Clement Wood's Long Island home; to make this connection clear, Legman dedicated his expurgated version to "Gloria," the name of Wood's wife. Roman-à-clef or not, the novel depicts decadent upper-class swingers. At the estate, Clara participates in orgies, even allowing herself to be flogged, in order to find the Scorpion, convinced that she is on the right track when during lesbian encounters she discovers two women who carry scorpion brands above their vaginas. The force of fetishes on those she meets both bewilders and arouses Clara. Although she engages in oral and anal intercourse with various partners, Clara remains technically a virgin, a circumstance that becomes sinister when she hears that there is to be a Black Mass, a ceremony in which a virgin, functioning as an "altar," is ritually deflowered. The Scorpion, Garnett claims to have learned, will personally sacrifice her maidenhead. After a mysterious masked woman prepares Clara for the Mass, Garnett reveals himself as the Scorpion and his masked assistant as Clara's sister Rita, still in thrall to her seducer. As the ceremony begins, however, police disguised as apostate priests arrest Garnett on accusations by Clara, who has been secretly working for the authorities all along. The plausible plot foregrounds the power of sexuality even as it undercuts suspense: readers anticipate rather than fear what will happen to the seemingly compliant Clara. Sewall's skilled use of language, his credible characters, and his psychologically-rendered sex scenes permit the reader to savor the "immoral" pleasures for which the unrepentant villain is brought to justice.

Biography

The mysterious Robert Sewall was probably born in Scranton, Pennsylvania, around 1915. Patrick Kearney has surmised that "Sewall" was merely a pseudonym of Gershon Legman, the erotic bibliographer, but according to Legman's widow, Sewall in fact attended elementary school with Legman, and possibly married a Scranton sweetheart. Certainly Legman and Sewall met again in New York, where they might have worked together for a Planned Parenthood organization there. Sewall was later a postmaster in Vermont, and still later yet, postmaster in a small town on Long Island. During the late 1930s and early 1940s, Sewall wrote erotic stories on commission from collectors. In addition to *The Devil's Advocate*, these included imitations of Henry Miller, and, under the pseudonym "L. Erectus Mentulus" (see entries on Mentulus and Legman), *The Oxford Professor*.

JOSEPH SLADE III

Selected Works

The Devil's Advocate. By "Wood C. Lamont" [Robert Sewall, as typed and enlarged by Gershon Legman], Chicago [New York]: mimeographed, 1942; rewritten and retyped by Sewall as *The Sign of the Scorpion*, by "Bruce Abbott," New York: Private edition [of mimeographed copies], 1944; *The Devil's Advocate* [excerpts], Nice: M. Seuferin, c. 1948; *The Devil's Lawyer* [excerpts], [Tijuana]: Esoterica Press, c. 1955; *The Devil's Brand. First Complete and Unexpurgated Edition of The Devil's Advocate, An Erotic Classic*, Los Angeles: Holloway House, 1969; *The Sign of the Scorpion*, by Bruce Abbott, New York: Grove Press, 1970; *The Devil's Advocate*, by "Robert Sewell," New York: Quality Paperback Book Club, 1998 (rpt. from the original manuscript). Also mistakenly attributed to "Bob De Mexico" [Robert Bragg], *The Devil's Advocate*, Mexico City [New York: mimeo, c. 1942]; to "M. D. R.," *The Devil's Advocate*, Industry, CA: Collectors Publications, 1968; and to "Marcus Van Heller" [John Stevenson], in *Seduced: Two Celebrated Erotic Novels by Marcus Van Heller*, New York: Carroll & Graf, 1995.

The Oxford Professor, In which L. Erectus Mentulus, Ph. D., late of Oxford College, is taken further in the narration of his adventures and misadventures, erotic, alcoholic, and otherwise; not to mention a choice accompaniment of drolleries, notes and excursi of one sort or another, metaphysical & also miscellaneously edifying and entertaining. Done by the Hand of the Author Into a Manuscript at Natchitoches, Louisiana [New York, Shomer, c. 1948], by Sewall and Gershon Legman—see entry for Mentulus, L. Erectus.

Attributed

Manuscript stories modeled on Henry Miller's *Tropic of Cancer*, 1930s.

Further Reading

Franklin, Benjamin, IV. "Adventures in the Skin Trade; Or, the Enigma of White Stains," In Search of a Continent: A North American Studies Odyssey, ed. Mikko Saikku, Maarika Toivonen, and Mikko Toivonen. Helsinki, Finland: University of Helsinki Renvall Institute for Area and Cultural Studies, 1999, pp. 262–274.

Legman, Gershon. *The Horn Book: Studies in Erotic Folklore and Bibliography*. New York: University Books, 1964.

Luboviski, Milton. "Epilogue: Affadavit," *Opus Pistorum*, by Henry Miller. New York: Grove Press, 1983, pp. 287–288.

Nin, Anaïs. *The Diary of Anaïs Nin: 1939–1944*, ed. Gunther Stuhlmann. New York: Harcourt, Brace and World, 1969.

Scheiner, Clifford J. *Encyclopedia of Erotic Literature*. 2 vols. New York: Barricade Publishing, 1996.

Wolfe, Bernard. *Memoirs of a Not Altogether Shy Pornographer*. Garden City, NY: Doubleday, 1972.

SEX MANUALS

Over the centuries, sex manuals have offered a wide range of advice not just on sex, but on hygiene, the workings of the body, masturbation, and procreation. They have discussed the broader issues of childbirth, birth control, and afflictions such as impotency and venereal diseases. Content has ranged from serious polemics to sensational, titillating material promoting quackish sexual potions.

The earliest notions about sex and the body came from Hippocrates (c. 460–377 BE) and were incorporated into Galenic physiology during the second century CE with advice based around humoral medicine. By the seventeenth century, material incorporating their advice was being published in sex manuals which carried humoral notions about bodily fluids. For example, Joannes Benedictus Sinibaldus''s *Geneanthropeiae* (1642) admits to being a collection of ancient Greek and Roman physicians' and philosophers' sexual texts. Parts of *Geneanthropeiae* were translated into English and incorporated into *Rare Verities, The Cabinet of Venus Unlocked and her Secrets Laid Open* (1657). In turn, *Rare Verities* was popularized by Nicolas Venette in *Tableau de L'Amour Conjugal* (1686) which first appeared in English as *Mysteries of Conjugal Love Revealed* (1703) and again in 1740 as *The Pleasures of Conjugal Love Explain'd*. It advised on the age at which to marry since "Every age is not capable of tasting the Sweets of Matrimony: the first and last Years have their obstacles; Children being too feeble and old Men too languishing. The Middle Part of out Life is the most proper Age for Venus who, like Mars, requires only Young People full of Fire, health and courageous." Furthermore when it comes to making love, it warns against certain times as unsuitable for kissing, "There is nothing ruins our Stomach, and weakens Digestion more than Love: it exhausts us to that degree, by dissipating our Natural Heat, and wasting out Spirits, that we feel great Inconveniences in the principal Parts. Physicians agree that one ought not to kiss fasting, but nor straight after eating."

Throughout the eighteenth century, sex manuals continued to be mixtures of earlier works; books frequently borrowed texts from each other or amalgamated parts of older printed material. The intention of the books was frequently ambiguous. Although allegedly written with the purpose of sexual instruction, publishers recognized a market for reprinting old medical texts for the purpose of titillation. Readers were intentionally alerted to the sexual nature of the book through disingenuous "warnings" about its content inserted in the prefaces.

Many of the eighteenth-century sex manuals were taken up with the problems of identifying a virgin, a task thought worth investigating at some length. In *Aristotle's Masterpiece* (1690), a whole chapter is devoted to all aspects of virginity—what it is, and how it is violated, suggesting that doctors were generally in agreement that the hymen is broken after intercourse; "most are of the opinion that the Virginity is altogether annihilated when this Duplication is fractured and dissipated by violence, and that when it is found perfect and intire, no penetration had been made. Also some learned Physicians are of opinion that there is no Hymen or Skin expanded containing blood in it, which divers imagine in the first Copulation, flows from the fractured expanse." *Aristotle's Masterpiece* was published in various formats and editions with slightly differing titles throughout the eighteenth century, and became a bestseller. The book was popular not only for its interest in medical facts but for its erotic appeal.

Sex manuals were keen to offer help to couples encountering problems. G. Archibald Douglas in his *The Nature and Causes of Impotence in Men, and Barrenness in Women, Explained* (1758) addressed those incapable of intercourse and those having difficulty bearing children. Some books were specifically aimed at women for instruction purposes such as *The Ladies Dispensary, or Every Woman her Own Physician* (1770), thus enabling women to detect and cure their own ailments. Others were aimed at married couples as indicated by the titles such as one nineteenth-century book *Marriage Ring: A Gift-Book for the Newly Married, and those Contemplating Marriage* (undated, late-nineteenth century).

Few new hegemonic texts appeared in the nineteenth century, the bestseller still being *Aristotle's Masterpiece*, albeit in a more prudish style. Gone were the explicit references to sex included in the more frank eighteenth-century versions. The later publication removed any anatomy of genitalia, erased bawdy language and explicit references, threw out the advice on how to create the right atmosphere or lovemaking, and mentioned nothing about how to conceive a boy or a girl. In its place came new material in the form of moralizing tracts, "You find some men indulging their vicious inclination by following the 'strange woman,' the street harlot, to her den of guilt and shame, or by alluring some simple girl by promises false and heartless to sin in that transgression which society forgives in a man, but never forgives in a woman." It warns men to be on guard against weakness or recklessness but should regulate themselves through prudence and benevolence to be sure of a virtuous life.

Whether these books were written for doctors or the general public is often difficult to discern. Some writers pitched their books directly at the intended audience such as Sylvanus Stall (1847–1915) who targeted bachelors in *What a Young Man Ought to Know* (1847). Other, such as Robert J. Brodie's *The Secret Companion* (1845) was a medical work on onanism, yet he lets his readers know that he could be consulted in Queen Anne Street for all cases of nervous and physical debility, including 'premature decay.' Other books with formally sounding scientific title such as Dr. George Drysdale's *Elements of Social Science: or Physical, Sexual and Natural Religion* (1854) enjoyed a wide circulation and appears to be produced primarily for a lay audience. Drysdale advocated the use of contraceptive methods in marriage castigating the popular advocacy of sexual restraint. Havelock Ellis believed the book was read by many people who had never previously read anything before on sexual topics.

Isaac Baker Brown's *On the Curability of Certain Forms of Insanity, Epilepsy and Hysteria in Females* (1866) was criticized by his colleagues for attracting the attention of his readers, particularly women, to the subject of self-abuse. Some books which proposed contraception were subjected to prosecution including Henry Arthur Allbutt's *Wife's Handbook* (1886), which went through at least 56 editions up to 1922; and Knowlton's *Fruits of Philosophy* (1845).

Discussion about sperm evacuation and its weakening effect on the male continued unabated in nineteenth-century sex manuals. The first female doctor, Elizabeth Blackwell, wrote *The Human Element in Sex* (1884). She warns "The amount of nervous energy expended by the male in the temporary act of sexual congress is very great; out of all apparent proportion to its physical results, and is an act not to be too often repeated." She believed instruction was necessary in order to elevate oneself from the "grossly unchaste" found in behavior of "savages." Samuel Hough Terry offered advice specifically on obtaining the required sex of a child. In *Controlling Sex in Generation; The Physical Law Influencing Sex in the Embryo of Man and Brute* (1885). He wrote, "When the husband possesses an ardour in the sexual embrace so much greater than the wife that female conceptions ordinarily ensue, it is, of course, not desirable that he should be shorn somewhat of this ardour by fasting or otherwise, as this would tend to the general weakening of the offspring, but rather measures should be taken to increase the general health and strength, and incidentally thereby her sexual vigour." He goes on to explain that "most of the wives whose sexual ardour is feeble, have some inherent taint of disease inherited of personal which, if cured, would greatly restore to them the vigour they lack."

Sexologists came on the scene towards the end of the nineteenth century. By this time, sexual science was tabulating a variety of sexual dispositions delineating the normal sexualities from those of the abnormal or deviant (see *Sexology*]. Patrick Geddes and J. Arthur Thomson, *The Evolution of Sex* (1889) was the first book to be published in Havelock Ellis's Contemporary Science series and found favor with the intelligent reading public. These works advocated temperance and unlike the other sexologists, emphasized the biological norm. Havelock Ellis (1859–1939) wrote on human sexuality in *Man and Woman* (1894) but his seven volume studies in the *Studies in the Psychology of Sex* (1897–1928) was the one for which he is most famous. Ellis made sex into a science extending the terminology of psychosexual types into homosexuals, paedophiles, nymphomaniacs, fetishists, transvestites, zoo-philes and so forth, creating a labeling system rare before the twentieth century. Ellis made inroads into the taboo status held by sexuality and morality and was to make the discussion of sex more acceptable for scientific inquiry.

In 1894, Edward Carpenter (1844–1929) wrote a series of small pamphlets on sex reform: *Woman and her ..., Sex and its..., Marriage and its..., Homogenic Love and its /...Place in Society* culminating in a book *Love's Coming-of-Age* (1896), the topic on "The Intermediate Sex" being omitted by publishers following the Oscar Wilde scandal. Carpenter argued for sex as a proper union and that the sexes should not be "two groups hopelessly isolated in habit and feeling from each other."

Dr. Lyman Beecher Sperry in his *Confidential Talks with Husband and Wife: A Book of Information and Advice for the Married and Marriageable* (1900) explored the difficulties of the introduction of sexual intercourse. Sperry offers his opinion on the unsuitability of some people for marriage declaring, "It is almost equally evident that persons who are decidedly scrofulous, consumptive or cancerous should not intermarry; and it is questionable whether persons of such morbid tendency ought ever to marry at all." He advised that prior to taking a honeymoon, a newly married couple should first spend a few months at home so the husband could show himself to be a man, "instead of a selfish sensualist or a careless and ungovernable brute."

The issue of retention of sperm was still being considered in the twentieth century. Sperry declared, "When the intense energies of men which seem to be exclusively of sexual origin—and which, to many, seem to be intensified for sexual expression—are then expended along those lines of activity directly intended for reproduction, they naturally find expression in deeds of gallantry, courage, heroism, philanthropy and other benevolent efforts contributive to the general good of humanity." Dr. Emma Drake reiterates Blackwell's views on over-evacuation of sperm in *What a Young Wife Ought to Know* (1901) attributing to it a man's moral weakness. "Vast amount of vital force used in the production and expenditure of seminal fluid," if wasted, could lead to feebleness and depravity; alternatively, if conserved, it could enhance a man's "mental and moral force" lifting him to a higher plane. She warns that masturbation causes dreadful side effects "some of the terrible results are epilepsy, idiocy, catalepsy and insanity."

Marie Stopes (1880–1958) was one of the most popular sex advisers in the early twentieth century, most famous for her advocating of birth control. She claimed that its practice would allow families to space their children and ensure an optimal family size. Her book *Married Love* (1918) was "a new contribution to the solution of sex difficulties," with *Wise Parenthood* (1918), a treatise on birth control for married people. Stopes cautioned her readers against thinking that regular ejaculations were good for a man and that it is a great mistake "to imagine that semen is something to be got rid of frequently."

By 1930, in her *The Sex Factor in Marriage*, Helena Rosa Wright was proposing that "A woman's body can be regarded as a musical instrument awaiting the hand of an artist." Her book *Sex, an Outline for Young People* (1932) was republished in 1963, and was still on sale in the 1970s. Gladys Cox followed these up with *The Woman's Book of Health: A Complete Guide to Physical Well-Being* (1933) also issued under the title *The Lady's Companion*. Many advice books were directed at married people. In his book, *Love Without Fear: A Plain Guide to Sex Technique for Every Married Adult* (1940), Dr. Eustace Chesser went so far as to carry a disclaimer, declaring "The author has written this book for those who are married or about to be married, and in this connection the bookseller's co-operation is requested." From his study, he found that out of 925 women he interviewed, 237 felt repelled by their husband during their initial sexual transaction in marriage. He believed that any virgin would find the size of a man's penis huge and it was therefore up to the man to take the initiative with his wife since "The normal women likes to feel herself conquered."

William S. Sadler in *Courtship and Love* (1952) echoed views about the submissive female expressed in many sexual guides through the first half of the twentieth century. He reminds the husband "his wife had been bought up to resist the sexual advances of all men and to defend her chastity with her life." Hence Isabel Emslie Hutton's advice to wives in *The Hygiene of Marriage* (1953) that sexual intercourse is "something rather unpleasant which they will have to put up with." Women should not therefore expect orgasm at their first time of sex, but this was not something to worry about; as she reminds wives, they "have several decades of married life ahead...."

Dr. Gilbert Oakley in his *Sane and Sensual Sex* (1963) warned his reader that a new bride should be recognized "as a highly sensitised human being." She would be modest and needed to be treated "with delicacy." The bridegroom was given advice on how to proceed, "He should not seem to be too gloating, but should reduce her with his eyes, his touch and with the things he may say to her, to the imagined status of a small girl who is helpless and resigned at husbands." Oakley expounding on the efficacy of masturbation for teenage boys, declares that it "helps him clear his face of adolescent spots and blemishes [and] purifies his blood stream. Yet continuation of this habit has dire effects on the adult male such as "shaking limbs...poisoning of the blood stream...impotence... priapism...," the list goes on. Sex during menstruation was however "most unsafe for the husband, for he may well contract an unpleasant condition on his member through having contact with the menstrual flow which is, after all, poison leaving a woman's body."

During the 1960s and 1970s, various new contributions came from T. A. A. Hunter edition, *Newnes' Manual of Sex and Marriage* (1964), Benjamin Spock's *A Young Person's Guide to Life and Love* (1971), Jane Mills' *Make It Happy* (1978) and David Heyman's *Help with Sex Problems* (1979). New suggestions could be found in The *Sensuous Woman* (1970) which detailed the latest techniques in lovemaking, the writer the anonymous "J" (Joan Terry Garrity) suggesting "you must train like an athlete for the act of love." Allying fears about venereal disease, the author adds, "the risks aren't adequate reasons for you to deprive yourself of a wonderful sex life."

In her book *The Total Woman* (1973), Marabel Morgan warns women to keep an eye out for competition "... would your husband pick you for his mistress..." she inquires to the "girls" insisting that, "One of your husband's most basic need is for you to be physically attractive to him...." Mabel Fonseca in her *All About Your Intimate Sex and Married Life* (1976) also blames women for not stirring themselves enough. "The working wife mixes with attractive men all day and comes back home to tell her husband the passes he made at her. Whether these are teasing reports or false, they are meant to make the husband jealous and shake him out of the take-me-for-granted-attitude wives find so frustrating and infuriating." She suggests men are driven to adultery by nagging frigid wives or women who are full of ridicule or let their appearance go. If an old love affair comes between marital happiness, it should be best overcome but she warns, "taking to alcohol can be hazardous." In such a situation the best thing to do "is to take up some good hobbies, do social work, and generally keep busy." Meanwhile, Tim LaHaye's popular Christian guide, *The Act of Marriage* (1976) advises on having sex during the week that "twice will probably be sufficient at this stage of the marriage."

By the 1980s, men were being offered the chance to learn about achieving multiple orgasm just like women. By now, it is woman's assertiveness, not men's, which is perceived as a barrier to good sex. *The Complete Book of Love* (1983) remarks on the women's movement over the last twenty years having caused increasing anxiety for men about their sexual performance "the assertiveness of women outside the bedroom had also adversely affected many men, and this is reflected in their reduced practical interest in sex." England's Dr. Miriam Stoppard provided sexual instruction for all the family from *Talking Sex* (1982) "a book about growing up" to advice for women in *Everywoman's Lifeguard* (1982). Her American counterpart, Dr. Ruth, proved a stalwart through the 1980s and 1990s with *Dr. Ruth's Guide to Good Sex* (1983) and *Dr. Ruth's Guide to Safer Sex* (1992). From the 1980s onwards, with the onslaught of AIDS, advice on safe sex became prevalent in many manuals from Michael Callen and Richard Berkowits's *How to have Sex in an Epidemic* (1983) through to Peter Tatchell's *Safer Sexy; the Guide to Gay Sex Safely* (1994). Alex Comfort's *Joy of Sex* (1972) has proven remarkably durable, a newly edited version reprinted in 2002.

JULIE PEAKMAN

Further Reading

Beall, Otho T. Jr. "Aristotle's Master-Piece in America: A Landmark in the Folklore of Medicine.' *William and Mary Quarterly*, 3rd series. xx, 1963, pp. 207–222.

Bush, Michael. "The Rise of the Sex Manual" in *History Today*. Vol 49, No. 2 Feb 1999.

Erickson, Robert E. "The Books of Generation': Some Observations on the Style of the British Midwife Books, 1671–1764." In Boucé, Paul-Gabriel (ed.), *Sexuality in Eighteenth-Century Britain* (Manchester: Manchester University Press, 1982), pp. 74–94.

Melody, M.E. and Linda M. Peterson. *Teaching America About Sex. Marriage Guides and Sex Manuals from the Late Victorians to Dr. Ruth.* New York/London: New York University Press, 1999.

Porter, Roy, and Lesley Hall. *Facts of Life: The Creation of Sexual Knowledge in Britain, 1650–1950.* New Haven, CT: Yale University Press, 1995.

Rusbridger, Alan. *Concise History of the Sex Manual.* London: Faber, 1986.

SEXOLOGY

Sexology is the group of disciplines that concern themselves with the study of human sexual behavior: physiology, psychology, psychiatry, and sociology. It has always been a difficult disciplinary area to define since its emergence in the late-nineteenth century, for many of the practitioners see themselves as operating within their broader disciplines (such as psychiatry), rather than being 'sexologists' from the start.

In order to appreciate this multifarious area of writing, a few words about its history are necessary. Prior to the sexological studies of William Masters, Virginia Johnson, or Alfred Kinsey, it was doctors who were interested in sex. The main areas of medicine that addressed sex were venereology (which also addressed prostitution), the study of systemic diseases such as spermatorrhoea (the excessive leaking of semen which caused all manner of debilitating problems, usually deriving from the patient's over-indulgence in masturbation), forensic medicine (insofar as there were sexual crimes such as rape and sodomy that needed discussing), and those few doctors interested in birth control. There was no psychiatric theory of the sexual impulse for the bulk of the nineteenth century; rather, sex was considered to be either normal, or to be criminal or morally wrong, depending on whether it had been sanctioned by the Church, general public, or legal institution.

Sexology as a medical specialty emerged in order to understand the so-called perversions, the main ones being homosexuality, sadism and masochism, and fetishism, which were catalogued in detail, most notably by Richard von Krafft-Ebing in his *Psychopathia Sexualis* (1st edition, 1886). Theories of the sexual impulse were formulated in order to deal with the complexities of these three main groupings, as it was deemed necessary by the early sexologists to understand why people persisted in crimes such as rape, sexual mutilation, and sodomy when there was sufficient judicial deterrence and social opprobrium when they were committed. Initially, the two main strands of thought were based on either a principle of congenital predisposition towards certain perversions (this owed a fair amount to degenerationalist theories, as being promulgated in Italy and elsewhere), and upon an acquired model for perversity. These differences reflected a significant political aspect as well, for many of those who argued that perversions such as homosexuality were congenital were likely to argue that it should be decriminalized as it was 'natural,' such as English sex psychologist, Havelock Ellis, whereas those who held that homosexuality was acquired usually had an agenda that included a cure, such as Munich-based hypnotherapist, Albert von Schreck-Notzing, and later psychoanalysts.

After the initial scuffles around whether sexual 'types' were congenital or acquired, with many sexologists arguing that there was a significant congenital predisposition that needed to be 'triggered' in some personal, psychological—and thus acquired—way (a position held by French psychologist, Charles Féré, in his later writings), more sophisticated mechanisms of the sexual impulse were formulated. These were aimed specifically at describing all sexual desires, and thus were relatively non-prescriptive. The most important of these was put forward by Berlin psychiatrist, Albert Moll, who noted that there were two phases of the sexual act: the *detumescence-impulse*, from *detumescere*, to decrease in size, and the *contrectation-impulse*, from *contrectare*, to touch (Moll, *Libido Sexualis,* 1897). It could be used to describe almost any sexual activity as normal: for instance, a shoe fetishist is aroused by the sight and touch of a partner's shoes; they are able to consummate the relationship involving the specific use of the shoe, and the fetishist achieves orgasm. Only in cases where there is no arousal, or where there is no orgasm, could the sexual impulse be called physiologically abnormal. There were, of course, social barriers to the free expression of the impulse, such as not involving children or hurting people, and non-procreative forms of sexual expression were by and large disparaged. While sexological theories allowed for more sexual possibilities, the social responses were much more constraining.

Havelock Ellis expanded Moll's theory by emphasizing the psychological aspects of the arousal stage, which he called *tumescence*. Ellis also emphasized individual desires and gender sexual equality in his writing, and rather than merely producing a cornucopia of sexual perversions, was politically motivated to explain all sexual activities as outside the ambit of moral and legal control, unless they injured people or involved the under-aged. Not all sexologists were predominantly interested in the paraphilias, however. Indeed, even those like Ellis, who wrote about perversions in so much detail, were merely trying to understand the full scope of sexual behaviors.

After this initial excessive attention to the 'perversions,' there was an increased attention to heterosexuality. This came about firstly through the detailed attentions of gynecologists such as Robert Latou Dickinson, who kept meticulous case notes from fifty years of practice from which he could generalize on the sex lives of women. The same kind of trajectory informed Alfred Kinsey, whose 1948 *Sexual Behaviour of the Human Male* and 1953 *Sexual Behaviour of the Human Female* employed large-scaled and detailed sexual surveys in order to locate exactly what people did in bed. This attention to 'normal' sexuality was taken further with Masters and Johnson, who paid specific attention to the physiology of sex as well as the psychological aspects, and found that the classical Freudian distinction between the vaginal and clitoral orgasm was false.

More recently, sexology has turned its attention much more towards the control of infectious diseases, most notably HIV, but also to other venereal infections. Important knowledge about sexual practices and their relations to risk activities has emerged which has been deployed in the fight against AIDS. Another topic with which sexology is currently concerned is sexual dysfunction, including gender dysmorphia and intersexuality. Certain contemporary sexologists have also taken a leading role in sexual and marriage counseling.

Sexological texts have been utilized for erotic purposes, as well as by students of medicine and law. Not only do many early sexological texts have detailed case histories from people who identified with the previously published cases, and wrote to doctors to tell them their own experiences and theories of perversion, thus using sexological texts as locations of erotic self-expression, but the erotic use of these texts should also be considered as important. In previous ages where there was a certain prohibition on sexually explicit material, sexology was one place to which those interested in sex, but not willing to pay vast sums for banned 'pornography,' could turn.

IVAN CROZIER

Further Reading

Bland, Lucy and Laura Doan (eds.). *Sexology in Culture*. Chicago, IL: University of Chicago Press, 1998.

Oosterhuis, Harry. *Stepchildren of Nature: Krafft-Ebing, Psychiatry and the Making of Sexual Identity*. Chicago, IL: University of Chicago Press, 2000.

SEXUAL ALCHEMY LITERATURE, CHINESE

The three central problems of Chinese religious thinking are family solidarity, microcosm–macrocosm harmony, and immortality. The three paths to immortality are alchemy, inner alchemy, and sexual alchemy. Medicine's mastery of acupuncture and herbs gave hope of defeating disease; alchemy's mastery of chemical transformations gave hope of defeating death. Inner alchemy absorbed the theory and terminology of medicine and alchemy and combined it with meditation; sexual alchemy absorbed the theory and terminology of medicine and alchemy and combined it with the techniques of meditation and the bedroom arts. Medicine highlighted the importance of sexual essence in the body's energy economy, the bedroom arts sought control of it, and inner alchemy and sexual alchemy undertook to transmute it into elixir.

Although the received sexual alchemy literature dates from the Ming dynasty (1368–1644), the origins and theoretical foundations of the sexual school can be traced back to at least the fourth century, when its existence is attested in alchemy apologist Ge Hong's (283–363) *The Master Who Embraces Purity* (Bao Pu zi): "There are more than ten masters of the sexual arts....The essential teaching is to 'return the sexual essence to nourish the brain....' One branch of Daoists seek solely by means of the art of intercourse to achieve immortality without preparing the medicine of the golden elixir. This is sheer folly."

Although the householder sex craft literature is chiefly concerned with health, harmony, pleasure, and eugenics, the note of more ambitious possibilities is sounded in the Sui dynasty (581–618) *Classic of Su Nü* [*Su Nü jing*], when the legendary immortal Peng Zu declares: "Because heaven and earth have attained the dao of union, they are eternal.... If we could but avoid those things that gradually injure our bodies and learn the art of yin and yang, this would truly be the dao of immortality." Tang dynasty (618–907) physician Sun Simiao's "Health Benefits of the Bedchamber" (Fangzhong buyi) is the first medical sexology text to combine *coitus reservatus* with specific meditation technique: "When both man and woman are aroused, he should grasp [the penis] in his left hand and imagine that there is red qi in the dantian, which is yellow within and white without. This then becomes transformed into the sun and moon, which move about in the dantian in the lower abdomen and enter the niyuan point in the center of the brain, where the two halves reunite as one."

Transitional texts from the Ming that retain the health and gender harmony emphasis of the early householder tradition, while prefiguring the marriage of essence absorption and the immortality project, include the *Wondrous Discourse of Su Nü* [*Su Nü miaolun*], the *True Classic of Perfect Union* [*Jiji Zhenjing*], and the *Exposition of Cultivating the True Essence* [*Xiuzhen yanyi*], which reveals:

> The secret transmissions state that by using one human being to supplement another, one naturally obtains the true essence....When this art is thoroughly mastered, and when the true essence released by the partner is obtained and one's own unshed essence 'returned,' then this is of little harm to the woman and of great benefit to oneself....Refine and receive it, circulating it upward from the weilü (coccyx), ascending the two 'white channels,' passing through the jiaji (midback), penetrating the kunlun (head), entering the niwan (midbrain), and flowing into the mouth. Here it is transformed into 'jade juice,' (saliva) which should be swallowed down the 'storied pavilion' (throat) until it reaches all the way to the dantian (lower abdomen). This is called "the reverse flow of the Yellow River," and has the ability to augment the sexual essence and supplement the marrow, increase longevity and lengthen the years.

The first distinguishing characteristic of the sexual alchemy literature proper is the assertion of its superiority over other techniques of immortality. Sun Ruzhong's *Introduction to Cultivating the True Essence* [*Xiuzhen rumen*] lays out the argument for sexual practices:

> When it comes to strengthening the qi, there are two theories: some advocate strengthening it through "pure practices" and others by yin and yang (sexual cultivation)....
>
> However, for those who have already experienced seminal leakage, rapid strengthening is difficult, and it is not easy to rein in the scattered mind. This is not as effective as the mutual strengthening of yin and yang, for here there is something concrete to work with.

The Preface to *Seeking Instruction on the Golden Elixir* [*Jindan jiuzheng pian*] states: "I have perused countless works on the elixir of immortality, and all insist that the great medicine of longevity requires the primordial undifferentiated true qi. If one asks from whence comes this qi, the answer is that it can be found in the 'other.'" The "other," of course, refers to young women, and the theoretical defense continues, "At the onset of puberty, yin and yang begin to interact, and the prenatal qi flees to the middle of Kun (trigram representing earth). As a result, the three unbroken lines of the pure Qian (heaven) are ruptured, and it becomes Li (fire)....Therefore, the elixir method borrows from Kan (water) to repair the broken Qian, supplement its empty line, and restore its pure yang body. This is the theory of the returning elixir of immortality." The next level of theory explains the necessity for reversing nature, as the *True Transmission of the Golden Elixir* [*Jindan zhenzhuan*] states: "If I fail to obtain the true lead from a partner, absorbing it upstream to join the mercury, how can I form the holy fetus and become a Buddha or an immortal? The opposite sex is by nature yin on the outside and yang on the inside, represented by the trigram Kan, or lead. If she fails to obtain my true mercury, and going downstream combine it with lead, how could she form the worldly fetus and give birth to sons and daughters? Therefore, following what is natural results in a human being, while going contrary to it results in the elixir." *The Rootless Tree* expresses the need for dual cultivation in a homely metaphor: "An unfertilized egg produces no chicks, for this violates the creative process of yin and yang....Practicing only solitary meditation, the qi dries up."

Each of the sexual alchemy texts is structured as a kind of syllabus for the stages of cultivation. Although not identical in content and sequence, they share a stock of common elements. The *Summary of the Golden Elixir* [*Jindan jieyao*] explains the first stage of practice, often called "establishing the foundation," which consists of locking the gate against ejaculation, "Immortals and Daoist priests do not have the aid of the gods. They achieve the True by saving jing and accumulating qi."

The next stage involves "refining the self," as the *True Transmission of the Golden Elixir* [*Jindan zhenzhuan*] says, "When the mind is without random thoughts and foolish notions have been banished, only then does one receive the proper results from 'crucible' (cultivator's body) and 'stove' (woman's body)."

In the third stage of practice, it is necessary to secure a supply of essence donors, as the *Summary of the Golden Elixir* says, "There are three grades of 'crucibles.' The first is metal, the second fire, and the third is water. What is meant by the 'metal crucible?' It refers to the metal of a fourteen-year-old girl, represented by Dui (trigram representing the youngest daughter)....At this time, her menses is about to commence, and her 'yellow path' regularly opens. A woman's first menses is the 'true metal' and is a priceless treasure."

In the next phase of practice, it is essential to excite the donor without becoming carried away oneself, as the *Secret Principles of Gathering the True Essence* [*Caizhen jiyao*] says in verse: "When dragon occupies the tiger's lair, intrinsic nature and emotion are one. At this moment one must play dead....Although my partner's passion has become intense, I am oblivious. With trusting sincerity, she reveals her secret, as I wait for the right moment."

In the fifth stage, the adept, with the help of the "yellow dame" (female coach) and "companions" (male assistants), must calculate the precise moment to harvest the partner's ripe essence. The bedroom arts manuals focused on female orgasm as the object of absorption, but sexual alchemy seeks a more rarified prenatal prize. Although there is no concept of ovulation, as such, in Chinese medicine, the *Secret Principles* speaks of gathering a kind of premenstrual essence described as the "golden flower before the petals have fallen" and the "jade bud newly opened." *Seeking Instruction* advises the adept to approach his partner at the very beginning of her period, "before it becomes visible," a stage which the *Summary* calls, "the approaching tide." The *True Transmission*, using the terrestrial branches system, distinguishes between the ren (premenstrual) stage of the cycle and the gui (menstrual), but also tries to synchronize the individual biological cycle with the cosmic cycle of moon and sun, recommending the fifteenth day (full moon), of the eighth month (late summer), during the zi hour (midnight) to maximize the potency of the cosmic yang energy.

The sixth stage involves allowing the "enemy" to seize the high ground and the initiative, as the *Summary of the Golden Elixir* says, "Have your partner sit on the 'three-legged crescent moon chair' and assume the position 'earth over heaven' as in the hexagram Tai (peace)."

In the seventh stage, the adept harvests the woman's "lead" and combines it with his own "mercury," as the *Secret Principles* says, "The 'true lead' (female sexual essence) is the prenatal monadal true qi....It is especially important that one mobilize a bit of 'true mercury' (male sexual essence) in the region of one's own anus to welcome it." This enables the volatile mercury to revert to the stable state of cinnabar.

The elixir formed from the marriage of yin and yang essences must now undergo a process variously called "refining," "watering and cultivating," or "incubation." In the words of the *True Transmission*, "The elixir forms, and in ten months the holy fetus is complete. Now naturally the immortal appears."

After gestation, and in keeping with the principle of reversing nature, the holy fetus is born at the fontanel, as the *True Transmission* says, "When the 'gate of the crown' bursts open, this then is the time of the dragon's offspring emerging from the womb. The yang spirit now appears, and one has earned the title of Immortal."

In the final stage, the dematerialized immortal, formed of pure prenatal yang energy and unbounded by space and time, is presented with the "mysterious pearl" of enlightenment and welcomed at the "Jade Pool of the Immortals" in paradise. The last verse in *The Rootless Tree* [*Wugen shu*] puts the capstone on the process, "Strive for the true emptiness and return to the great void. Received in the paradise of the immortals, accept the heavenly tally."

Chinese sexual alchemy harnesses the scientific spirit of medicine, alchemy, meditation, and the bedroom arts in the service of salvation through self-deification. The richly allusive language and exalted vision give it a unique place in the history of sexology and religious literature.

DOUGLAS WILE

Bibliography

Gulik, Robert van. *Sexual Life in Ancient China.* Leiden: E.J. Brill. 1961.

Maspero, Henri. "Les Procédés de 'Nourir le Principe Vital' dans la Religion Taoist Ancienne." *Journal Asiatique* 229. 1937.

Needham, Joseph. 1962, 1986. *Science and Civilization in China.* Vol. 2, pp. 146–152; Vol. 5, pp. 184–218. Cambridge: Cambridge University Press.

Schipper, Kristofer. Karen Duval, trans. *The Taoist Body.* Berkeley, CA: University of California Press. 1993.

Wile, Douglas. *The Chinese Sexual Yoga Classics, Including Women's Solo Meditation Texts.* Albany, NY: SUNY Press. 1992.

SHAKESPEARE, WILLIAM

1564–1616
English Playwright and Poet

Although generally acknowledged as the celebrator of romantic marriage, in his many plays and poems, Shakespeare employs his remarkable insight to probe the enigma of human sexuality in all of its multiple manifestations. Moreover, while many of his plays dramatize such socially sanctioned rituals as courtship and marriage, his works also explore illicit sexual relations such as extra-marital sex, adultery, prostitution, rape, incest, and homosexuality.

Heterosexual Courtship

Most people in Western society accept without question the linking of love and marriage; however, this conception is actually a relatively recent innovation, emerging approximately 400 years ago in Western Europe and Britain and much later in Eastern societies. The genesis in England of the ideal of the consensual, companionate marriage—a union whose primary goal is not economic, dynastic, or procreative, but rather affectionate companionship—remains one of the most vigorously debated topics in early modern scholarship. However, whether scholars credit the Renaissance with transforming the romance of adultery into the romance of marriage, or locate amorous matrimony within the Puritan art of love, or praise consensual conjugality as the signal achievement of the high Middle Ages, most agree that this conjugal pattern, which unites respect and desire in amorous mutuality, had become the dominant social ideal, if not always the reality, by the late-sixteenth century when Shakespeare began writing his plays and poems.

However, although Shakespeare has traditionally been praised as the great poet of married love, close scrutiny indicates that his plays celebrate not so much the romance of marriage as the romance of courtship. Following the traditions of Latin New Comedy, introduced and popularized by Plautus (254–184 BCE) and Terence (195–159 BCE), one of Shakespeare's tragedies (Romeo and Juliet) and numerous comedies and romances dramatize the erotically-charged courtships of young men and young women, usually concluding in multiple marriages (often three, but sometimes as many as four). During these passionate courtships, the lovers surmount numerous obstacles—disapproving parents, romantic rivals, scandalous rumors, misunderstandings, even their own homosocial or homosexual bondings—to couple with the mates of their choice; and in the rare dramas, such as Pericles and The Tempest, in which the course of true love does run smoothly, the wise fathers, Simonides and Prospero, invent impediments to matrimony. Despite the libidinal urges motivating these courtships, in all but one of these wooings, Measure for Measure (in which

the transgressive couple is betrothed but not yet married), the chastity of the beloved lady is preserved until the wedding day and the fetishizing of virginity in these plays mirrors the high estimation awarded chastity in the society of the time. Although sexuality is zestfully extolled in all of these dramas of courtship, this sexuality must await the conjugal bed.

Married Love

Yet despite the many plays in which multiple couples march joyfully to the altar, presumably to live happily ever after, Shakespeare's canon offers few positive portraits of the erotically, emotionally, and intellectually fulfilling union envisioned as the consensual, companionate marriage. Indeed, there are few merry wives and devoted, trusting husbands in Shakespeare's plays. Many of the plays present no mature married couples at all, and scholars have commented on the absence of mature wives and mothers in Shakespeare's dramas. Moreover, even initially blissful unions—such as those of Desdemona and Othello in Othello, Hermione and Leontes in The Winter's Tale, and Imogen and Posthumus in Cymbeline—are soon clouded by the paranoid fear of female unfaithfulness that casts dark shadows over so many of Shakespeare's dramas. Shakespeare's plays do frequently portray devoted wives—Kate in Henry IV, Part I, Portia in Julius Caesar, Richard II's adoring Queen in Richard II —but these wives are marginalized by their spouses, relegated to the private sphere, almost always with unfortunate consequences. Kate in Henry IV, I offers a particularly apt exemplum of this marginalization. Although the spirited Kate seems a perfect mate for the fiery Hotspur, at a time of crucial decision-making, her husband unwisely banishes her from his bed and from his confidence primarily because she is a woman. Paradoxically, the happiest, most fulfilling marriages in Shakespeare are often the most destructive. Hamlet's Claudius undoubtedly loves Gertrude; he insists that "She is so conjunctive to my life and soul / That, as a star moves not but in his sphere, / I could not but by her," and the play verifies this devotion. Nevertheless, at the play's dénouement, Claudius allows his beloved wife of only a few months to die from poison rather than reveal his own treachery. Moreover, the marriage, constructed on murder and perhaps adultery, acts as catalyst to tragedy. Similarly, at the beginning of a later tragedy, the eponymous hero Macbeth and his Lady—his "dearest partner of greatness"—appear to exemplify the reciprocity and companionship idealized in the Puritan dream of romantic marriage. However, this dream soon becomes a nightmare as this very reciprocity—what some commentators cite as Macbeth's uxorious love for his wife—leads to his destruction and that of his beloved partner. Of course, contented conjugal partners are hardly the stuff of effervescent comedy or rousing drama, but even this does not explain the almost total absence of mutually fulfilling marriages in Shakespeare. Indeed, many commentators would agree that, paradoxically, Shakespeare's most incandescent study of mature love—a marriage of both true minds and physical bodies—is the adulterous romance of Antony and Cleopatra.

Illicit Heterosexuality

Many of Shakespeare's male characters are obsessed with dark fears of dangerous female sexuality and paranoid fantasies of female unfaithfulness. In four of his plays—one comedy (*Much Ado About Nothing*), one tragedy (*Othello*), and two late romances (*Cymbeline* and *The Winter's Tale*)—Shakespeare replays the familiar topos of the chaste woman slandered, and cuckold jokes run like a refrain throughout Shakespeare's comedies. Yet despite this male fixation with female betrayal, actual adultery (at least by wives) occurs relatively rarely in the plays. There is, of course, the problematic adultery of Gertrude with Claudius in *Hamlet*, implied but never explicitly verified in the text, and Goneril's attempted but never consummated adultery with Edmund in *King Lear*. Moreover, illicit sexual relationships, of various kinds—some historical, some fictitious—crop up occasionally in the history plays: these include Joan la Pucelle's carnal encounters with both men and demons in *Henry VI, Part I*; Hastings's fatal affair with Jane Shore in *Richard III*; Lady Faulconbridge's adultery in *King John;* Falstaff's trysts with Doll Tearsheet in *Henry IV, Part II*; and Henry VIII's infidelities in the play by that name. However, only in the Greek and Roman plays do extra-marital relationships assume center stage.

Shakespeare's first tragedy, *Titus Andronicus*, depicts the adultery of Tamora, Queen of the Goths and Empress of Rome, with the vice-like Moor Aaron, an instance of miscegenation that culminates in revenge, rape, and many grisly deaths. Moreover, multiple illicit sexualities fill the dramatic canvass of *Troilus and Cressida*, Shakespeare's cynical satire on chivalric honor and courtly love: Helen's famous adulterous affair with Paris launches a thousand ships and burns the topless towers of Ilium; Cressida's courtly love romance with Troilus (by definition an erotic union outside of marriage) dwindles into unfaithfulness and disillusionment when the Trojans unceremoniously barter Cressida to the Greeks and the deserted lady switches her affections from Troilus to Diomedes; finally, Achilles's liaison with Patroclus (perhaps homosocial but more probably homosexual) motivates the fabled hero's craven ambush of Hector and complete loss of honor. The dramatic action thus deflates the glorious rhetoric of chivalric honor and courtly love into brutal war and sexual betrayal.

Although the majority of interpreters would agree that *Antony and Cleopatra* presents Shakespeare's most complex and sympathetic treatment of illicit passion, nevertheless, this quintessential exploration of adultery has also aroused fervent and antithetical responses from commentators. These range from moralistic critics, who view the tragedy as a condemnation of irresponsible lust, to romantic critics, who laud the play as a celebration of a magnificent passion transcending conventional morality. However, most contemporary interpreters, avoiding these polarities, adopt an ambivalent reading of the play, arguing that the tragedy dramatizes an oxymoronic passion, at once sensually intoxicating and intellectually stimulating, yet, at the same time, vitiated by the jealously and suspicion that plague so many of Shakespeare's amorous partners, an instability perhaps accentuated, in this case, by the absence of marital commitment. Cleopatra frequently harps on marriage and when she discovers that Antony has married Octavia after the death of his wife Fulvia, she flies into a tempestuous rage. Thus, insecure in Antony's love, Cleopatra plays elaborate games to hold his interest and seeks to dominate him lest she lose him. Similarly, unsure of Cleopatra's commitment, Antony invariably mistrusts his lover and in every problematic circumstance believes the worst of her. Only in death do the mercurial lovers become "marble constant" and totally accepting of each other, and, in her triumphant suicide, with the asp at her breast, Cleopatra finally claims the title so long denied her, proclaiming, "Husband, I come! / Now to that name my courage prove my title!" In her mystic deathbed union with Antony, Cleopatra may fleetingly experience the felicitous merging of desire and esteem associated with the consensual, companionate marriage.

Prostitution

Since, according to Hamlet, drama should hold a mirror up to nature, prostitutes and bawds people Shakespeare's dramatic universe even as they did the society that these dramas reflect. Shakespeare sometimes depicts these transgressive figures with good-natured, jovial wit, sometimes with scorn, often with pity. However, in only two of his plays—*Measure for Measure* and *Pericles*—does prostitution assume central importance, and in both of these dramas the bawdy house functions as a symbol for the dissolute societies that must be redeemed, the former by a *deus ex machina* Duke, the latter by a chaste virgin.

Rape

Although characters from Proteus in *The Two Gentlemen of Verona* (an early romantic comedy) to Caliban in *The Tempest* (probably Shakespeare's last play) either attempt or fantasize about rape, in only two of his works does Shakespeare treat this brutal sexual crime as a *fait accompli*: In his first tragedy, *Titus Andronicus*, and in a long poem, *The Rape of Lucrece*, both written in the early 1590s and both set in a Roman milieu.

At the beginning of the tragedy that bears his name, Titus Andronicus, the victor over the Gauls, makes several tragic errors in judgment, among them the ritual sacrifice of Alarbus, son of Tamora, captured Queen of the Goths. In retaliation for the slaying of her son, Tamora, guided by her paramour Aaron, incites her other two sons to rape and mutilate Titus's daughter Lavinia, whose tongue is torn out and hands

hacked off to prevent the identification of her assailants. The rape of Lavinia is motivated both by the sons' lechery and by Tamora's thirst for revenge. Ironically, because Tamora's voice was silenced at the beginning of the play when she pleaded for her son's life, Lavinia will be stripped of both her chastity and her voice. Lavinia, sexually violated, mutilated, and muted, has often been interpreted as a symbol not only for the sexual vulnerability but also for the legal and educational silencing of women at this period. Ultimately, although Lavinia, with the help of Ovid's *Metamorphosis*, does succeed in disclosing both the nature of her violation and the names of her attackers, she lacks agency. Significantly, she does not kill herself, but is executed by her father to remove the stigma of rape polluting her honor and that of his house.

The Rape of Lucrece opens with a boasting match in which a group of military men vaunt the chastity of their wives (adumbrating a similar bragging contest and wager in one of Shakespeare's late romances, *Cymbeline*, a dramatic descendent of *Lucrece*). Significantly, the warrior Collatine extols his wife Lucrece only for her chastity, but when another of the warriors, Sextus Tarquinius, curious to meet this paragon of virtue, views the lady, her beauty inflames him with lust. The rape of Lucrece by Tarquin is thus motivated partially by male competition and desire for dominance, and partially by the reduction of women to objects of sexual desire, all salient aspects of a patriarchal society. The first half of the poem focuses on Tarquin, narrating the circumstances leading up to the rape. Tarquin stays as a guest in Lucrece's home while his military ally Collatine remains at camp. During the night, the licentious Tarquin penetrates Lucrece's bedchamber to view the sleeping lady, torn between guilt and desire even as he ravishes her with his gaze (much as the leering Iachimo will visually violate the slumbering Imogen in *Cymbeline*). Visual violation progresses into actual rape, and the latter half of the poem recounts Lucrece's anguish following her ravishment. Unlike the muted, victimized Lavinia, Lucrece is granted both voice and subjectivity; however, as Coppélia Kahn observes in "*Lucrece*: The Sexual Politics of Subjectivity," the loquacious Lucrece speaks with the tongue of the patriarchy.

Moreover, although Lucrece achieves agency as well as subjectivity—unlike Lavinia, she plans her own suicide, affirming that she is "mistress of her Fate"—her decision to kill herself to remove the stain besmirching her honor and that of her husband operates within a patriarchal paradigm. Thus, both *Titus Andronicus* and *The Rape of Lucrece* pose vexing problems for scholars of Shakespeare. Both clearly examine the role of the violated woman in the patriarchal family, which accepts the female as the property of the father or the husband, but whether these works interrogate this structure or merely reinscribe it has been much debated.

Incest

Only once in his entire canon does Shakespeare explicitly dramatize society's most taboo sexual transgression, incest. *Pericles*, one of Shakespeare's late romances, exposes the liaison between Antiochus, King of Antioch, and a character designated only as Daughter of Antiochus. Surprisingly, although most people today place exclusive blame for father–daughter incest on the violating parent, Gower, the Chorus of *Pericles,* judges the nameless daughter complicit, branding both the victim and the victimizer as "Bad child, worse father." Moreover, the play sentences both offenders to incineration by "a fire from heaven," which Gower proclaims the just reward of sin. Although the blatant sexual violation of Antiochus and his daughter offers the only explicit example of incest in the play, father–daughter relationships dominate *Pericles,* and commentators have interpreted Simonides—the king who readily bestows his daughter Thaisa on the man of her choice—and Pericles—who leaves his infant daughter Marina with a king and queen unrelated to him, only returning to reclaim her many years later—as inverted mirrors reflecting the father's flight from incest.

Critics focusing on father–daughter relationships in Shakespeare, such as Lynda E. Boose, Betty Flowers, and Lagretta Tallent Lenker, posit this "flight from incest" as a dominating motif of all of Shakespeare's late romances, including *Cymbeline, The Winter's Tale,* and *The Tempest.* Moreover, plumbing the sub-text of Shakespeare's plays, interpreters have discovered other innuendoes of incest—in the outrageous "love contest" in *King Lear,* and in the

fathers' possessive love for their daughters in *The Two Gentlemen of Verona* and *Othello.*

However, the most famous "incest" interpretation in all of Shakespeare is the Oedipal reading of *Hamlet.* Applying a Freudian paradigm to decipher the many ambiguities of Shakespeare's most debated play, Ernest Jones in *Hamlet and Oedipus* theorizes that Hamlet's hesitancy in fulfilling his dead father's command to slay Claudius results from his unresolved Oedipus complex, the infantile desire to kill his father and marry his mother. This Oedipus fixation paralyzes Hamlet, who cannot avenge his father's murder because he unconsciously identifies with the murderer Claudius. Although advocates of this reading can adduce no explicit testimony from the text, they often cite as support for this interpretation Hamlet's obsession with his mother's sexuality, particularly as revealed in the "closet scene" between mother and son. Moreover, even through this once popular theory lacks currency with contemporary critics, it has influenced a number of popular films, particularly those by Laurence Olivier and Franco Zeffirelli.

With the exception of Antiochus and his daughter in *Pericles,* all of the suggested instances of incest discussed above must rely for their validation on sub-textual innuendoes and subjective interpretations. However, this does not mean that they have no credibility. Indeed, Shakespeare's characteristically "open-ended" texts invite subjective interpretations, and his famed ambiguity may be a strategy for treating tabooed subjects without fear of censorship or reprisal.

Homosexuality

In his influential book, *The History of Sexuality,* Michel Foucault reminds the reader that the modern concept of an exclusively homosexual orientation, a construct of medical discourses of the nineteenth century, was unknown in the early modern period. Foucault does not deny the occurrence of homosexual acts during Shakespeare's time—indeed, he would probably agree with most contemporary scholars that this activity was widespread, even institutionalized, in early modern England. Rather, Foucault insists that during this period orthodox morality regarded this particular infraction—like other violations of official sexual edicts—as a temporary aberration, not a congenital abnormality or a distinctive mode of identity. Moreover, scholars have marshalled a plethora of evidence to show that at this period, the widely accepted, "orderly" homosexual relationships between masters and servants, princes and their minions, or consenting adults of the same class were generally tolerated or ignored unless perceived as disruptive of the social order, particularly the culturally sanctioned institution of marriage. Furthermore, these acts were rarely associated with the monstrous capital crime of "sodomy," which at this time became a synecdoche for a number of heinous actions; these might include anal penetration, along with sexual violations such as rape and incest, but only when these transgressions were associated with more socially threatening offenses such as treason, sorcery, and witchcraft.

According to many contemporary critics, just as homosexual practices flourished in early modern England, homoerotic nuances also saturate Shakespeare's plays, particularly his comedies. The theatrical convention of the period, whereby boys played all the female roles, further complicates the issue and scholars have actively speculated on the probable response of early modern audiences to the spectacle of cross-dressed boys being wooed and embraced by adult male actors. The transvestite heroines of Shakespeare's comedies and romances (Julia in *The Two Gentlemen of Verona*, Portia and Jessica in *The Merchant of Venice*, Rosalind in *As You Like It*, Viola in *Twelfth Night*, and Imogen in *Cymbeline*), in which the boy actor plays a girl disguised as a boy (and, in *As You Like It*, the boy actor plays a girl disguised as a boy pretending to be a girl), have excited particular debate. Reactions to these sexually ambiguous figures include the following: The affirmation of these doubly cross-dressed characters as exemplars of androgynous wholeness dissolving rigid gender categories; the insistence that the so-called "androgyny" of these cross-dressed actors serves to stress their maleness rather than their femaleness and thus to titillate homoerotic fantasies in the audience; the argument that these transvestite disguises accentuate the characters' femaleness rather than their androgyny. These diverse reactions to Shakespeare's clever gender bending demonstrate the difficulty of decoding erotic responses in an historical period far removed from our own.

Accentuating these erotic valences is the conflict between male/female friendships and heterosexual love dominating many of Shakespeare's comedies. Numerous comedies dramatize close, loving friendships between men and women. In *The Two Gentlemen of Verona*, the self-sacrificing Valentine incredibly offers his beloved Silvia to his inconstant friend Proteus, thus elevating male friendship above heterosexual passion. However, in all of Shakespeare's other comedies, the devoted friends—the melancholy Antonio and the enterprising Bassanio (*The Merchant of Venice*), the mournful Helena and the feisty Hermia (*A Midsummer Night's Dream*), the jesting Benedict and the caddish Claudio (*Much Ado About Nothing*), and the charismatic Rosalind and the loyal Celia (*As You Like It*)—must all ultimately subordinate their affectionate homosocial bondings to heterosexual love. Most commentators would agree with David Bevington in *Shakespeare* that these plays (with the exception of *The Merchant of Venice*, which treats more mature relationships) dramatize the normal process of maturation in which the young boy or girl must eventually relinquish his or her original, semi-narcissistic, same-sex love object and graduate into mature heterosexual attachments leading to marriage.

However, some contemporary critics demur that often the relationships traditionally identified as friendship include homoerotic desire as well as homosocial affection. Focusing particularly on *As You Like It*, both Valerie Traub in *Desire and Anxiety* and Mario DiGangi in *The Homoerotics of Early Modern Drama* comment on what they interpret as the multiple sexualities dramatized in the play, not only the heterosexual attachments—the romantic love of Rosalind and Orlando, the courtly love vagaries of Phoebe and Silvius, and the earthy lust of Touchstone for Audrey—but also the homoerotic attractions–Celia's passionate devotion to Rosalind, Orlando's marked interest in Ganymede, and Phoebe's infatuation with Rosalind disguised as the boy Ganymede. According to Traub, Rosalind enjoys evoking both homosexual and heterosexual desires, and Shakespeare punctuates the homoerotic nuances of Rosalind's performance through her adoption of the name of Ganymede, an allusion to the young Trojan youth loved by Zeus and a slang term at this time for the passive member of a male homosexual liaison. For Traub, Phoebe's crush on

Ganymede also suggests sexual ambiguity. Consciously, of course, Phoebe believes Ganymede to be a man and when she discovers otherwise, she loses interest. Unconsciously, however, Phoebe is clearly enamored of Ganymede's femininity, and her blazon to the girl disguised as a boy, in which she praises his/her shapely leg, ripe red lips, and damask cheek, parodies the traditional blazon of the courtly lover to his lady.

Both Traub and DiGangi also discover multiple sexualities in the Illyria of *Twelfth Night*, which include Olivia's infatuation for Viola, disguised as the effeminate page Cesario (paralleling Phoebe's crush on Ganymede); Orsino's sexual attraction to the same Cesario, whom he believes to be a youth (recalling the youth Ganymede's similar appeal to Orlando); and, most significantly, Antonio's homoerotic love for Viola's twin brother Sebastian. However, with typically ambiguity, Shakespeare never clarifies the exact nature of these attachments. Of all of these relationships, the strongest case can be made for Antonio's single-minded dedication to Sebastian, expressed throughout the play in the soaring language of courtly love, as transcending the early modern code of passionate male/female friendship.

Nevertheless, even if we grant that in the Saturnalian worlds of Arden and Illyria homoerotic fantasies may be briefly indulged, these fancies must ultimately surrender to the demands of heterosexual marriage and procreation. Olivia must wed Sebastian, not Viola, even as Phoebe must accept Silvius, not Ganymede, and Celia must live with Olivier, not Rosalind. Moreover, Rosalind and Viola will win Orlando and Orsino, and the wedded pairs will be rounded out with Touchstone and Audrey in *As You Like It* and Sir Toby and Maria in *Twelfth Night*. Only Antonio, the putative homosexual lover of Sebastian, remains alone.

Another Antonio—the Merchant of Venice, in the play by that name—also remains odd-man-out at the dénouement, this time amid three jubilant sets of newly-weds. A popular reading of this play asserts that the plucky heroine Portia must overcome two challenges in order to possess the man she loves, Bassanio. First, she must circumvent the restrictions of her father's will; secondly, she must win Bassanio from his friend or lover (depending on one's interpretation). The shrewd and determined lady

accomplishes both of these feats, and, at the end of the play, as with almost all of Shakespeare's comedies, homosocial (or homosexual) bonding must surrender to heterosexual love.

However, all of the relationships cited above, and even the most overt example of homoerotic pairing—the attachment in *Troilus and Cressida* of Achilles and Patroclus, legendary homosexual lovers dating back to Homer—are shrouded in characteristic Shakespearean ambiguity. Thersites slurs Patroclus as Achilles's "male varlet" or "masculine whore," epithets that Patroclus does not deny, but then this scurrilous malcontent reduces everything to lechery. Moreover, the affiliation between the two warriors provides no impediment to Achilles's love for Priam's daughter Polyxena, at least not until the death of Patroclus in battle drives Achilles to madness and dishonor.

Other posited homosexual attachments are even more problematic. Interpreters frequently adduce repressed homosexuality as an explanation for the hidden motivations of both Shakespeare's villains and heroes, such as the motiveless malignity of Don John (*Much Ado About Nothing*) and Iago (*Othello*), and Leontes's irrational jealousy of Hermione (*The Winter's Tale*). Still other commentators discover homoerotic innuendoes in the friendships of Bertram and Parolles (*All's Well That Ends Well*) and Richard II and his minions (*Richard II*), as well as in the intense masculine rivalry of Coriolanus and Aufidius (*Coriolanus*). However, as Stanley Wells remarks in his reasonable and open-minded appraisal (*Looking for Sex in Shakespeare*), all of these interpretations must rely on the possible psychological sub-texts of the plays rather than on explicit statement.

The same conflict between male friendship and heterosexual desire and the same ambiguity between passionate same-sex friendship and homosexual love animates Shakespeare's great sonnet cycle. The sonnet cycle, initiated by Dante and Petrarch, popularized in England by Wyatt and Surrey, and perfected in the sixteenth century by Sidney, Spenser, and Shakespeare, traditionally recounts the emotional tribulations of a lover enamored of an unattainable, idealized lady, who must remain on an unreachable pedestal, either because she is pledged to chastity or because she is someone else's wife and too virtuous to break her marriage vows. In either case, these sonnet cycles typically depict an oxymoronic love, simultaneously a source of pleasure and pain, elevation and degradation.

Always the innovator, Shakespeare adapts the sonnet cycle in numerous ways, rejecting the unobtainable Petrarchan mistress and substituting instead two highly unconventional objects of poetic desire—the Fair Young Man and the Dark Lady. Most critics concur that the first 126 verses of the Sonnets are dedicated to the Fair Young Man (although a few dissenters argue for two or more addressees) and agree that these poems contain some of the most rapturous love lines that Shakespeare ever wrote. Yet Sonnet 20 strongly implies that the poet's homoerotic passion for the Fair Young Man must remain unconsummated, at least if we accept Helen Vendler's highly influential reading in *The Art of Shakespeare's Sonnets*. In this sonnet, the poet examines the remarkable confluence in the beloved youth of a beautiful woman's face and a man's anatomy, explaining that Nature originally created the beloved as the ideal woman, but soon "fell a-doting" on her own creation and, being female herself, "pricked out" this paragon for women's pleasure, adding genital equipment that renders the Fair Young Man unavailable to the poet, at least for heterosexual intercourse. According to Vendler, the poet never considers homosexual intercourse with his love object, and thus the passion of the poet for the Fair Young Man, although both erotic and romantic, must remain a "marriage of true minds" only (Sonnet 116), not a union of physical bodies. However, other interpreters argue against such a literal exegesis of this sonnet, while still others insist that this two-line statement provides insufficient evidence on which to reject a homosexual union between the poet and the beloved youth. As so often in Shakespeare, the explicit nature of the relationship between the poet and the "Master/Mistress" of his passion remains obscured, although few commentators today would deny the eroticism permeating the sonnets to the Fair Young Man.

Sonnets 127–154, dedicated to the Dark Lady, narrate a very different kind of ardor. Even though, unlike the traditional unattainable Petrarchan mistress, the sexually available Dark Lady treads on the ground rather than balancing on a pedestal (Sonnet 130), she is both promiscuous and probably married to another (Sonnet 152 accuses her of breaking her "bed [marriage] vow") and thus cannot be permanently possessed

by the poet. The Dark Lady sonnets recount a tumultuous, love/hate liaison, which moves from joyous sexual fulfillment through the torments of betrayal, jealousy, humiliation, rage, and disillusionment, finally concluding with the disenchanted poet still in thrall to his sexual obsession for his unfaithful mistress. Thus, Shakespeare's much-praised Sonnets, containing the most passionate love poems the poet ever wrote, both celebrate and deplore two ultimately unfulfilling relationships, juxtaposing the poet's elevated yet erotic love for the Fair Young Man (his good angel), whom the poet idealizes but cannot possess sexually, with his obsessive lust for the Dark Lady (his bad angel), whom he can possess sexually but cannot idealize.

Harold Boom, in *Shakespeare: The Invention of the Human*, identifies Shakespeare as the inventor of the modern concept of "the self." Whether or not we accept this rather grandiose claim, Shakespeare certainly ranks as one of literature's most intrepid explorers of the human psyche, navigating a path into the tangled human id that would later be followed by Freud and other psychologists. Since sexuality is inextricable from human psychology, Shakespeare investigated the various manifestations of sexual relations as boldly as was allowed within a culture that practiced censorship and punished violators of socially acceptable behavior. Thus, Shakespeare left the literary world a rich legacy of insights into the sexual attitudes of his era, granting us glimpses of the early modern fascination with love, lust, and the unruly libido.

Biography

William Shakespeare was born in Stratford-upon-Avon, April 23, 1564. Although little is known of his education, he presumably attended the King's New School at Stratford. At the age of eighteen he married Anne Hathaway, with whom he had three children, his eldest daughter Susanna, and a pair of twins, Hamnet and Judith. Nothing is known of Shakespeare's activities during the seven years from 1585, when the twins were baptized, until 1592, when Shakespeare first appeared as an actor and playwright of significance for the Lord Chamberlain's men. Shakespeare later became chief playwright of this company and a shareholder in the Globe Theatre. During an extraordinarily productive career, spanning nearly twenty years,

Shakespeare wrote thirty-seven plays (although he may have collaborated on others), four poems, and a celebrated sonnet sequence. Sometime in 1611 or 1612, he retired to Stratford, where he died on his birthday in 1616 at the age of fifty-three.

SARA MUNSON DEATS

Editions

Shakespeare, William. *The Complete Works of Shakespeare* ed. David Bevington, New York: HarperCollins Publishers, 4th Edition, 1992.

References and Further Reading

Bevington, David. *Shakespeare*. Malden, MA: Blackwell Publishing, 2002.

Bloom, Harold. *Shakespeare: The Invention of the Human*. New York: Riverhead Books, 1998.

Boose, Lynda E. and Betty Flowers, eds. *Daughters and Father*. Baltimore: John Hopkins University Press, 1989.

Bredbeck, Geogory W. *Sodomy and Interpretation: Marlowe to Milton*. Ithaca, NY: Cornell University Press, 1991.

Charney, Maurice. *Shakespeare on Love and Lust*. New York: Columbia University Press, 2000.

Deats, Sara Munson. "Shakespeare's Anamorphic Drama: A Survey of *Antony and Cleopatra* in Criticism, on Stage, and on Screen." In *Antony and Cleopatra: New Critical Essays*, edited by Sara Munson Deats. New York and London: Routledge, 2005.

DiGangi, Mario. *The Homoerotics of Early Modern Drama*. Cambridge: Cambridge University Press, 1997.

Foucault, Michel. *The History of Sexuality*, Vol. 1. New York: Pantheon Books, 1978.

Greenblatt, Stephen. *Will in the World*. New York and London: W.W. Norton & Company, 2004.

Hagstrum, Jean H. *Esteem Enlivened by Desire: The Couple from Homer to Shakespeare*. Chicago, IL: University of Chicago Press, 1992.

Jones, Ernest. *Hamlet and Oedipus*. New York: Doubleday, 1954.

Kahn, Coppélia. "*Lucrece*: The Sexual Politics of Subjectivity." In *Rape and Representation*. Edited by Lynn A. Higgins and Brenda R. Silver. New York: Columbia University Press, 1991.

Lenker, Lagretta Tallent. *Fathers and Daughters in Shakespeare and Shaw*. Westport, CT: Greenwood Press, 2001.

Sale, Carolyn. "Representing Lavinia: The (In)significance of Women's Consent in Legal Discourses of Rape and Ravishment." In *Women, Violence, and English Renaissance Drama*, edited by Linda Woodbridge and Sharon Beehler, Tempe, Arizona: AZ: Center for Medieval and Renaissance Studies, 2004.

Smith, Bruce R. *Homosexual Desire in Shakespeare's England: A Cultural Poetics*. Chicago, IL: University of Chicago Press, 1991.

Traub, Valerie. *Desire and Anxiety: Circulations of Sexuality in Shakespearean Drama*. New York and London: Routledge, 1992.

Vendler, Helen. *The Art of Shakespeare's Sonnets*. Cambridge, MA: Harvard University Press, 1997.

Wells, Stanley. *Looking for Sex in Shakespeare*. Cambridge: Cambridge University Press, 2004.

SHANQING HUANGSHU GUUODUYI [YELLOW BOOK SALVATION RITUAL OF HIGHEST PURITY]

The *Yellow Book Salvation Ritual, a Shangqing Scripture* is a complete liturgy for conducting the rite of salvation through sexual intercourse in the Daoist religion. The text is absolutely unique in Chinese literature for its fusion of Daoist ritual with sexual yoga, meditation, medicine, and shamanism. Hidden in plain view for centuries in the *Daoist Canon*, the text was rediscovered by Kristofer Schipper in the 1970s. Although, the date and provenance of the work has yet to be determined from internal evidence, it is clearly a direct descendent of the rite of "harmonizing the qi" from the late Han dynasty (206 BCE–220 CE) and cannot be later than 1445, the date of its publication in the Ming *Daoist Canon*.

The earliest antecedents of sexual rituals in China may be seen in Neolithic cave paintings depicting naked dancers engaged in what appears to be fertility rites. There is also folkloric evidence of the survival of sexual rituals among the peasants and non-Han peoples in China up until the modern period. The *Yellow Book*, however, represents the absorption and refinement of sexual ritual within the Daoist religious movement of the second century CE, a movement which arose to fill the political and spiritual vacuum left by the disintegration of the Han dynasty by ministering directly to the people and maintaining the cosmic covenant until a legitimate new dynasty could be founded with the mandate of Heaven.

In 142 CE, Zhang Daoling claimed to have received revelations from the deified Laozi to bring about the restoration of the Era of Great Peace and took for himself the title Celestial Master. Popular movements seeking to actualize this ideal, the Yellow Turban rebellion and the Five Pecks of Rice community, ended with the defeat of the Yellow Turbans and the capitulation of Daoling's grandson to General Cao Cao in 215 on the condition that Celestial Master Daoism become the state cult of Cao's Wei dynasty (220–265). Since neither the *Scripture of Great Peace* [*Taiping jing*] nor the *Xiang'er Commentary to the* Laozi [*Laozi xiang'er zhu*], the two texts most closely associated with early Celestial Master Daoism, contain direct references to sexual rituals, our only contemporaneous accounts of the marriage and initiation rite of "harmonizing the qi" is from its Buddhist, Daoist, and Confucian rivals.

Buddhist monks Dao An, Xuan Guang, and Fa Lin attack the "harmonizing the qi" ceremony as "demonic methods" and "false doctrines." Chen Luan, in his 570 CE *Ridiculing the Daoists* [*Xiao dao lun*], recounts his early participation in such rites before being converted to Buddhism: "We were first instructed in the practice of 'harmonizing the qi' after the teachings of the *Yellow Book* and the three-five-seven-nine method of sexual intercourse." Daoist alchemist Ge Hong's (283–343) biography of Zhang Daoling mentions his use of sexual practices, and Tao Hongjing's (456–536) *True Decrees* (*Zhen gao*) also refers to revelations warning Highest Purity Sect medium Yang Xi against Zhang Daoling's sexual rites. The *History of the Wei Dynasty*'s (Weishu) "Account of Buddhists and Daoists"

[*Shi lao zhi*] speaks of "The three Masters Zhang's teachings on the harmonization of qi between men and women" and the efforts of Kou Qianzhi (d. 448) to adapt Daoism to the taste of literati elites and deflect Buddhist criticism by abolishing the old Celestial Master's sexual ceremonies.

As described in the *Yellow Book* text, the rite is limited to couples twenty or younger, and by way of prologue, the celebrants bathe, observe abstentions, perfume themselves with incense, and pay respects to the altar of the priestly lineage. The twenty stages of the ritual engage every aspect of the participant's psyche and sensorium. In spatial terms, the ceremony is choreographed on an imaginary grid laid out according to the cardinal and ordinal compass points and their corresponding sexegenary cycle binomials, *Book of Changes*' trigrams, five phases, and yin and yang. Left–right directionality defines the orientation of the partners to each other, to hand selection in gesture and touching, foot placement, clockwise and counter-clockwise massage, and qi circulation. Time is evoked in summoning the qi of the four seasons and the five gods of the year, month, one's birth year, one's age, and the present day. Color is represented in the chromatic correspondences of qi visualized in meditation, in the divinities conjured, and their vestments. The celebrants occupy space in prescribed postures—standing, sitting, kneeling, reclining—and move through space—bowing, saluting, perambulating—on their own power, and also manipulating each other's limbs.

Verbally, the couple engages in call and response prayers with the officiating priest and with each other, often invoking long lists of deities of the civil and martial god/officials of the three realms of the Daoist universe (heaven, earth, and water), the gods of the four directions, gods of the sexegenary cycle, and gods of the body—organs and psychic centers. In their prayers, they identify themselves by name and residence and appeal for health, immortality, unity with the dao, to be inscribed in the book of life and expunged from the register of death, and to become the "seed people" for the regeneration of the world; they plead to be delivered from sickness, demons, and calamity and to avoid transgressing taboos and escape the disapproval and plots of their fellow men. Parallel prayers for male and female use their respective gender associations: heaven for male, earth for female; yang for male, yin for female; odd numbers for male, even for female, and so forth. Often prayers are punctuated with breathing exercises involving inhalation of the qi of life and exhalation of the qi of death, and movement, too, is synchronized with breath work. Numerology permeates every aspect of the ritual, from numbers of fingers joined, to repetitions of breathing, prostrations, and massage, from rounds of perambulations to the dimensions in inches of visualized qi. Qigong practices include teeth gnashing, cranial finger tapping, massage, and auto-massage.

On the purely interior level, there are visualizations and meditation. The devotees visualize spheres of colored qi, which circulate throughout and suffuse the body, and protective deities standing guard around them. The supplicants practice many rounds of microcosmic orbit meditation, moving qi up the posterior midline of the body and down the anterior to gather in the dantian (elixir field) below the navel, or laterally, up the left side of the body and down the right, with variations of each.

Physical contact between the partners includes hand clasping and hand covering, cradling of each other's heads, and massage, particularly of the heart, dantian, and pubic area. In section fourteen, the priest assists the couple in removing their clothes and unbinding their hair, and finally, in section sixteen, the ritual coitus is described in this passage:

> With his right hand he massages her lower dantian three times. Approaching the "gate of birth," he opens the "golden gate" with his right hand, while lifting the "jade key" with his left hand and casting it upon the "gate of birth." Now supporting her head with his left hand, he massages the "gate of life" up and down and from side to side, while reciting the following three times: "Water flows to the east and clouds drift to the west. Yin nourishes yang with a qi so subtle. The mysterious essence and nourishing liquid rise to the 'tutorial gate.'" The first partner (man) recites: "The 'divine gentleman' holds the gate, and the 'jade lady' opens the door. As our qi is united, may yin bestow her qi upon me." The second partner (woman) recites: "Yin and yang bestow and transform, and the ten thousand creatures are nourished and born. Heaven covers and earth supports. May qi be bestowed upon the bodies of these humble supplicants...." Raising his head and inhaling living qi through his nose, he swallows yang according to the numbers three, five, seven, and nine and recites:

"May the dao of Heaven be set in motion." The second partner now recites: "May the dao of earth be set in motion." Following this, he enters the "gate of birth" to a depth of half the head, while reciting: "Oh, celestial deities and immortals, I would shake Heaven and move earth that the 'five lords' might hear my plea." Now the second partner recites: "Oh, celestial deities and 'dantian palace,' I would move earth and shake heaven that the five gods of the body might each be strong." He then penetrates to the greatest depth, closes his mouth, and inhales living qi through the nose and exhales through the mouth three times. Gnashing his teeth, he recites: "May nine and one be born in the midst." Now he withdraws and returns to a depth of half the head.

The literary value of the *Yellow Book* cannot be judged by the standards of poetry or fiction, for as ritual, performer, and audience are one and the same. The practice differs from the bedroom arts or sexual alchemy, however, in that it is ritualized, communal, monogamous, egalitarian, and devoid of arousal, orgasm, and sexual vampirism. From the point of view of religious literature, the *Yellow Book* stands for transformation through somatic performance and the sacralization of sex. The sexual element here is not ecstatic but estheticized and embedded in a dense structure of cosmological and polytheistic symbolism deployed for its power of renewal in a religious movement that hoped to heal the individual, restore the community, and knit back together the broken pieces of civilization.

DOUGLAS WILE

Further Reading

Andersen, Poul. 1989–1990. "The Practice of Bugang." *Cahiers d'Extreme-Asie* 5: 15–54.

Bokenkamp, Stephen. 1999. "Tianshidao hunyin yishi 'heqi' zai Shangqing, Lingbao xuepai de yanbian" (Transformations of the Celestial Master marriage ritual 'joining pneumas' in the Shangqing and Lingbao scriptures). *Daojia wenhua yanjiu*, 16: 241–245.

———. 1997. *Early Daoist Scriptures*. Berkeley: University of California Press.

Despeux, Catherine and Livia Kohn. 2003. *Women in Daoism*. Cambridge, MA: Three Pines Press.

Kohn, Livia, ed. 2000. *Daoism Handbook*. Leiden: E.J. Brill.

Lagerway, John. 1986. *Daoist Ritual in Chinese Society and History*. New York: Macmillan Publishing Co.

Liu Dalin. 1993. *Zhongguo gudai xing wenhua* (Sex culture in ancient China): Yinchun: Ningxia renmin chubanshe.

Ruan Fangfu. 1991. *Sex in China: Studies in Sexology in Chinese Culture*. New York: Plennum Press.

Schipper, Kristofer. *Le Corps Taoiste*. Paris: Fayard. 1982.

Shangqing huangshu guodu yi [Yellow Book Salvation ritual, a Shangqing Scripture]. Li Yimang, ed. *Daozang*. Beijing: Wenwu Press.

Wile, Douglas. *The Chinese Sexual Yoga Classics, Including Women's Solo Meditation*. Albany, NY: SUNY Press. 1992.

SHIBUSAWA, TATSUHIKO

1928–1987

Japanese scholar of French literature, critic, and novelist

On the basis of eroticism as a new thought, he was a pioneer like Gaius Plinius Secondus. He was the first researcher about Sade in Japan, as many as three times published "The selection of Marquis de Sade" (3 vol, 1956–1967; 5 vol, 1962–1964; 8 vol, 1965–1966). In addition, he has translated Huysmans, Bataille, Pieyre de Mandiargues, Cocteau, and Desnos. He quickly estimated the value of Sade in Japan, though his translation of *Akutoku No Sakae: Zoku* [*L' Histoire de Juliette; ou, Les Prosperites du vice*] was censored in 1960. Shusaku Endo, Kenzaburou Ôe, etc., defended him. Finally, he was fined 70,000 yen. He always arrived to the tribunal too late, and escaped the final judgement. According to him, he was not escaping, but he considered the debates were of no interest. He said there was no obscenity, and that obscenity existed only in the reader's mind. Finally, according to him, there was no obscenity in the world.

Mishima said that, "if Shibusawa didn't exist, Japan would die from boredom." He was a very close friend, but they had opposite views on Sade. Mishima liked Sade "Raw" and "Bloody," while Shibusawa liked the literature of Sade as a dramatic tale with his historical implications pronounced by a taler. Mishima always waited for the translations. The only biography of Sade in Japan was *Sado Kôshaku No Shôgai* [*Life of Marquis de Sade*] (1964) was the basis for Sado Kôshaku Fujin [Madame de Sade] (1965), of Mishima.

From 1968 to 1969, Shibusawa was chief editor of *Chi To Bara*. The subtitle of the review was "Synthetical review for researches on eroticism and cruelty." In this journal, he translated Morion's "L'anglais Decrit Dans Le Chateu Ferme." These researches leaded to a publication of great value. Many photographs were included, and Shibusawa was the model for "La Mort de Sardanapale," and Mishima for "Le Martyre de Saint Sebastien." They presented several paintings and objects, such as Paul Delvaux, Pierre Molinier and Clovis Trouille. This review was of real value, also because such writers as Nosaka and Yoshiyuki participated in it.

After his travel in Europe, he extracted the quintessence of all literatures of any times and places, like a narrator. His style is luxuriant, as if you were invited to labyrinthe ou museum:

His father was third of the Shibusawa family who became wealthy during Edo period. Shibusawa wrote about this childhood in the essay *Kitsune No Danbukuro* [*The Trousers of Fox*]. When he was a pupil, he read a lot of adventure novels and his health was poor. He was a brilliant student. During World War II, he had to work as a laborer. He then passed the high school entrance exam, but was delayed admission due to the war until July. He attended a boarding school. At that time, he admired Akutagawa and Dazai. At first, he was a scientist, but changed to study literature. He studied French at the "Athénée Français." After he discovered Cocteau and Gide, his great passion became surrealism, and the works of Sade. He studied theses two fields while attending university courses and then wrote his thesis: "The Presence of Sade."

He considered eros to be a sensual experience which is peculiar to sex, and at the same time, he was like a "spotless child," driven by intellectual curiosity. He always considered objects as seen from an apper point of view, like a bird. As if children were collecting their treasure in a coffer, Shibusawa named his inner world "Draconia," and he built his "Micro Cosmos" with a pen. It is not an exaggeration to say that eroticism for him was always like an object hidden in a coffer.

Biography

Born in Tokyo, 8 may 1928, he studied French literature at Tokyo University, especially surrealism and its surroundings between 1950 and 1953. He moved from Tokyo to Komachi, in Kamakura in 1946. He translated from Jean Cocteau, "le Grand Ecart," 1954. About the Marquis de Sade, he published an anthology in three volumes (1956), and translated *L'Histoire de Juliette; ou, Les Prosperites du vice*. This book was submitted to censorship, and the publisher and translator were prosecuted for obscenity. He married Sumiko Yagawa (writer, poet, translator), in 1959 (then divorced in 1968). With the *Yume No Uchû-Shi* in 1964, he dignified the essay gender to an original way of thinking, and introduced in Japan the heretical art and literature, magic art, occultism, and the western utopical and epicurian ideal. He fled to Yamanouchi, Kamakura, in 1966. In 1968–1968, he was redactor in chief for the review *Chi To Bara*, together with Mishima and others. The final judgement in the Sade trial condemned him to a fine of 70,000 yen (the average monthly wage was then 50,000–60,000 yen). He married Tatsuko Maekawa (editor of an art review) in

1969. He began to publish the "Compilation Shibusawa Tatsuhiko," and made his first trip to Europe in 1970. Since the essay *Kurumi No Naka No Sekai* [*World in a Walnut*] unto 1974, and the essay *Shikou No Monshô-Gaku* [*Heraldry of Thought*] in 1977, he wrote on various kinds of subjects. He received the Izumi Kyouka award in 1981 for the tale Karakusa Monogatari wrote the tale Utsuro Bune in 1986, received the Yomiuri award for "Takaoka shin'nou Koukai-Ki" in 1987. His style is beautiful and erotic and is linked to oriental mythology. He lost his voice because of cancer of the hypopharynx since September 1986. He died in 5 August 1987.

SACHIE SHIOYA

Selected Works

Kenrou toshi [*Cynopolis*]. A collection of short stories, Tougen sha, 1962.
Karakusa monogatari (Karakusa story), a collection of short stories, Kawade shobô shinsha, 1981.
Utsuro bune (Hollow ship), a collection of short stories, Fukutake shoten, 1986.
Takaoka shin'nou koukai-ki [Prince Takaoka's sailing records]. Nobel: Bungei shunjû, 1987.

Critique and Essay

Eros no kaibou (Anatomy of eros). Essay, Tougen sha, 1965.
Homo eroticus. critique, Gendai shichou sha, 1967.
Tougen sha. 1967.
Kikaijikake no eros [*A clockwork eros*]. critique, Seido sha, 1978.
Eros teki ningen, (Erotic human), critique, library, Chûou kouron sha, 1984.

SHORT STORY, FRENCH

From the history of the French short story with its origins in the fifteenth century, there are many examples of short texts, in which sex has a significant role. Some examples of French writers include Guy de Maupassant, Jean Lorrain, Daniel Walther, and Vincent Ravalec at the end

of the twentieth century. It is rather exceptional to find a text, erotic from beginning to end, with everything this involves in the choice of subjects, situations, descriptions, and vocabulary. Since the nineteenth century, there has been a tradition of the fantastic short story, since the twentieth century, science fiction and crime have developed; but there is no trace of the erotic short story. This essay will try to provide an explanation for this.

The short stories of the fifteenth and sixteenth century, which are in a similar vein to Boccaccio's *Decameron* and the Italian licentious story-writers, are gathered in *The One Hundred New Short Stories – Les Cent nouvelles Nouvelles* the first French collection of short stories. It uncovers with delightful coarseness the sexual adventures of libertine monks, the dalliances of discontented married women who are henceforth satisfied: "So he led her into a very beautifully apparelled wardrobe, locked the door and lay on the bed. Master Monk took her sheets away, and instead of his finger, he drove his hard and stiff stake into her."

After these, eroticism disappears from the short story is shelved for three centuries. We come across *Nouvelles galantes* in the seventeenth and eighteenth centuries, where the adjective merely calls up sentimentalism (the precious character of classicism is expressed in the *One Hundred Short Stories—Les Cent Nouvelles*, (1732–1739) by Mme de Gomez). Moralizing short stories appear in the wake of Marmontel at the end of the eighteenth century and dramatic short stories become available thereafter in the first half of the nineteenth century. These are characterized by bloodshed and violence. In *One Hundred and Short Stories of the One Hundred and One—Les Cent-et-Une Nouvelles des Cent-et-Un* (1833) like Madame de Gomez's collection is not a patch on the spirit of the fifteenth century's eponymous collection. Realistic short stories at the end of the nineteenth century are centered on social drama and some other novellas are dominated by conservative middle-class conformism with a *New Decameron—Le Nouveau Décaméron*, (1884–1887) which is a poor imitation of Boccaccio's work). At the very least, we can list a few of these examples:

- *Tales and Short Stories—Contes et Nouvelles* (1665–1668—forbidden by the police!) by Jean de la Fontaine, yet these are only successful adaptations in verse of earlier texts.
- The *Love Short stories or The Abused Fair Sex—Nouvelles amoureuses ou le beau sexe abusé* (1760—"à l'isle de Cythère"), including 'Swindled Virginity'—'Le Pucelage

excroqué' and 'Well-Hung Brother Abélard'—'Frère Abelard bien monté.'
- *The Monastic Adventures or the Scandalous Life of Brother Maurice Among Nuns - Les Aventures monacales ou la vie scandaleuse du frère Maurice parmi les eligieuses* (1763–1777) including 'Mornings of the Nuns'—'Les Matins des nonnes'—and 'The Mule in the Dormitory'—'Le Mulet dans le dortoir.'

If *The Crimes of Love. Heroic and Tragic Short Stories* [*Les Crimes de l'amour, nouvelles héroïques et tragiques*] (1799) by Sade and the collections by Restif de la Bretonne (*Contemporary Women* series—la série des *Contemporaines*, 1780–1783) are not named in this list, because these works have only few similarities with the other novels by these authors. Editors may claim that they are sexually explicit, but they are not.

One still has to recall the nineteenth century's fiery works of Balzac and his *A Passion in the Desert* [*Une passion dans le désert*] (1830) and *The Girl with (the) Golden Eyes* [*La Fille aux yeux d'or*] (1834), Theophile Gautier's *The Loving Death* [*La Morte amoureuse*] *Nouvelles* (1845) and lastly Barbey d'Aurevilly with his *The Demonic* [*Les Diaboliques*] in 1874. The appearance of coarse novellas is noted with Maupassant and Montifaud, for example *The Innocent Suzanne, Comical Short Stories* [*La Chaste Suzanne, nouvelles drôlatiques*] in 1895. The licentious tale by Catulle Mendès appears in 1884 entitled *To Read in the Bath* [*Pour lire au bain*]. The list is endless. The analysis of these works is outside the realm of this article in much the same way as the history of the erotic short story in the nineteenth century, which remains untouched.

In the twentieth century, the situation does not change much at first. Here are a couple of works written before 1940 (to which we could add *The Story of the Eye* by Georges Bataille):

- *The Secret Week of Venus—La Semaine secrète de Vénus* (1926, 1985 - a first edition of only 275 copies) by Pierre Mac Orlan.
- *The Singapore's Dancer—La Danseuse de Singapour* (1936) and *Beauties for Rent—Belles à louer* (1939) by Louis-Charles Royer, a specialist of the time in soft eroticism (with curious fetish for breasts), who wrote five other collections of short stories.

The further we move into the twentieth century, the more interest we find in erotic short stories, so much so that it almost became a fashionable genre in the 1990s. From 1940 to 2000, I counted 136 works (collections, special issues of magazines or newspapers, independently published texts). Yet this is just an estimate. Frenchmen wrote 103 of these, Quebecians wrote 22, Belgians 10, and Swiss 2. This is puzzling because the voice of the novelist is not absent: *Ten Swiss Erotic Short Stories* [*Dix nouvelles érotiques helvétiques*] (1989) by Salio de Vries, *Eleven Unpublished Erotic Tales* [*Onze contes érotiques inédits choisis*] (1995).

From the beginning, some titles set the tone insofar as they do not allow for any ambiguity: *Torrid Geometry* [*La Géométrie dans les spasmes*] (1959), "*... Help Us Against Evil Men*" ["*...Et délivrez-nous du mâle*"] (1960) by Belen (Nelly Kaplan), *Emmanuelle III*, [*Short Stories From Erosphere—Emmanuelle III, nouvelles de l'érosphère*] (1969) by Emmanuelle Arsan (Maryat et Louis Rollet Andrianne). Some others include *Eros Exists, I Met Him* [*Eros existe, je l'ai rencontré*] (1970) by Philippe de Jonas, *The Traveller From Antibes and Other Improper Stories* [*Le Voyageur d'Antibes et autres récits inconvenants*] (1978) by Jude du Lacques, *Oedipus at the Brothel and Other Immoral Tales* [*Oedipe au bordel suivi d'autres contes inconvenants*] (1993) by André Thirion, *Tales That Make Little Riding Hoods Blush* [*Contes à faire rougir les petits chaperons*] (1987) by Jean-Pierre Enard, *Perverse Tales* [*Contes pervers*] (1980) by Régine Deforges (1980), *Laura Colombe, Tales for Perverse Little Girls* [*Laura Colombe, contes pour petites filles perverses*] (1981) and *Tales for Perverse Little Girls* [*Contes pour petites filles perverses*] (1995) by the Belgian Nadine Monfils, *Perverse Chronicles* [*Chroniques perverses*] (1986) by Olivier Dazat, and *Mechanical Eros [Eros mécanique]* (1995) by Pierre Bourgeade. If the words "eroticism," "Eros" and "erotic" are not rare in the titles ('Erotic Bullfights'—'Corridas erotiques' in *Tales and Legends of the One-Eyed W...* 1970, by Eric Gordès; *Eros in a Chinese Train, Short Stories* [*Eros dans un train chinois, nouvelles*], 1990, by Haitian René Depestre), the term "erotic tale" is to be found only in five titles and quite late: *The Lips' Edge* [*Le Tranchant des lèvres*] (1990) by Geneviève Hélène, *Tales to Make You Blush. Erotic Short Stories* [*Histoires à faire rougir, nouvelles érotiques*] (1994) by the Quebecian

Marie Gray, *Three Erotic-Fantastic, Short Stories* [*Trois nouvelles érotico-fantastiques*] (1998) by Mauricette Lecomte, *Erotic Short Stories* [*Nouvelles érotiques*] (1999, a collection), *Torrid Embraces, Erotic Short Stories* [*Etreintes torrides, nouvelles érotiques*] (2000) by Sam Titus, *As Black As Eros, 33 Erotic Black Short Stories* [*Noir comme Eros, 33 nouvelles noires érotiques*] (2000).

Pervading all kinds of short stories—whether serious or amusing, using the conventions of Science fiction, fantasy or crime, eroticism has many aspects:

- **Soft Eroticism:** more allusive than daring as shown in the following examples, considered now as curiosities of the middle-class ideology between the early 1930s to the late 1950s: Louis-Charles Royer, Clarmide (*Simulacras of Love, Novels and Short Stories* [*Les Simulacres de l'amour, romans et nouvelles*], 1949). The impact of other texts depends on an insidious way of representing or suggesting the unusual perversity of the subject. For example in a park, a man is observing a woman being raped by two strangers, which turns out to be a set-up, but the woman was not compliant. (Raymond Jean, 'Mira' in *A Bella B's Fantasy and Other Stories* [*Un fantasme de Bella B. et autres récits*], 1983). This type of eroticism does not exclude violence: a man stabs his lover's sex—"I lock you up inside of me. I seal you there and tomorrow you will have a special place among those I have honoured." (Jude du Lacques, *The Traveller From Antibes and Other Improper Stories* [*Le Voyageur d'Antibes et autres récits inconvenants*], 1978). This eroticism is the prerogative of authors who are more willing to write about eroticism rather than be frank about it. Here are some other examples: Gilles Plazy (*The Bitches Academy* [*L'Académie des chiennes*], 1993), Claude Louis-Combet (*Augias and Other Infamies* [*Augias et autres infamies*], 1993), Richard Millet (*White Heart, Short Stories* [*Coeur blanc, nouvelles*], 1994).

- **Open Eroticism:** Here the eroticism is explicit: "At the fourth drink, David plunged his fist softly but without hesitation between Sylvia's thighs and he got an electric shock right in the spinal cord when he reached the humid mass of her bushy tuft, which proved that she wore no knickers." (Belgian writer Jacques Sternberg, *Cuckold and Bull Stories* [*Histoires à dormir sans vous*], 1990). Those short stories are comprised of erotomaniacs, nymphomaniacs, masturbation scenes, straightforward or extravagant copulations. This kind of eroticism, which rests on complete shamelessness, has unfortunately given birth to an impressive number of insipid works, which under the pretence of provocation, are but an accumulation of clichés, as is the case with Régine Deforges and Françoise Rey (*Black Nights* [*Nuits d'encre*], 1994).

- **Neurotic Eroticism:** a man achieves satisfaction with a dog (by Quebec writer Marie-José Thériault, 'Cyclops in the Park'—'Les Cyclops du jardin public' in *The Ceremony, tales,* 1978), a little girl spends her time caressing old men (by Quebec writer Jean-Yves Soucy, 'The Buzzard'—'La Buse' in *The Buzzard and The Spider, Stories* [*La Buse et l'araignée, récits*], 1988). These are some strong, almost unbearable examples of an eroticism, which is dominated by perversion, neurosis, cruelty, and morbidity. Here are some examples: a man is making love to a woman, who had the inside of a body tattooed on the outside of her body (Philippe Djian, 'Life Size'—'Grandeur nature' in *50 To 1, Stories* [*50 contre 1, histoires*], 1981), a man makes love to a dead woman (Claude Louis-Combet, 'Yeside' - in *Augias and Other Infamies* [*Augias et autres infamies*], 1993). This type of eroticism is not geared towards the general audience and is becoming altogether unwholesome and sordid. The reader is also confronted with shady ceremonies or other secret societies characterized by perversion, and to sadomasochistic scenes: a masked woman is submitting to the fancies of a man (Robert Margerit, *Ambiguous* [*Ambigu*], 1946, 1956, Janine Aeply, 'Love Shutters', 'Les Volets d'amour' in *Eros zéro*, 1972, 1997). This intellectual eroticism becomes quite sulphurous with Pierre Bourgeade (a nun longs to make love to God: 'Mystics' in *Immortals* 1968), and especially in these two collections, bordering on obscenity, full of a distressing sexual madness: "The matron, always more perplex, looked

like an ecstatic beast. A thousand cocks, flags at half-mast, charged to order. The bearded man, boosted by drugs, was masturbating with a syringe. Mr. Cooper orchestrated the orgasms of the patients, carefully watching out for the matron to prevent her from having an orgasm." (Joyce Mansour, *Noxious Stories* [*Histoires nocives*], 1973): "Mark's penis, constantly stiff, and Rosa's cunt, always wet and open, were the sacred instruments of an eternal mass." (Nicolas Meilcour, *Rose and Carma*, 1969—or the love life of a man and a young mental defective).

- **Homosexual Eroticism:** Men are normally attracted to women and vice versa hence the presence of homosexual writers is rather rare. However, in France we have Olivier Delau (*Clear as Night* [*Clair comme la nuit*, 1986]), Hugo Marsan ("He must be so beautiful stark naked," *Your Lordship's desires* [*Monsieur desire*], 1992). The female writers from Quebec are the only ones to assert their differences and they do so in a much more forthright way than their masculine counterparts. This is to be found in their collections and in a review called *La Vie en rose* (in the 1980's).

- **Surrealist Eroticism:** mainly represented by one author. A prime example is André Pieyre de Mandiargues. From his fifties collection *Sun of the wolves* [*Soleil des loups*] (1951) a man is reduced to the size of a greenfly, living in a loaf of bread that is covered with bees, he experiences extreme delight ('The Red loaf of Bread'—Le Pain rouge) This illustrates a personal universe, insofar as it remains unique, fantastic, bizarre, and obsessional: the naked or stripped body of a woman ("Is she, under her dress, as naked as her feet, as he felt her tits were?" *Under the Wave, Stories*), sex drives ("...a tremendous desire for black skin seized all the women," *Black Museum* [*Le Musée noir*], 1946), its favorite places (brothels), its key scenes (rapes, sexual murders), in which the boundary between dream and reality is hardly perceptible. The following is a list of some of the authors associated with Surrealist Eroticism: Quebecians Daniel Gagnon (*Love Peril, Short Stories* [*Le Péril amoureux, nouvelles*] 1986), Marie José Thériault, *The*

Ceremony, Tales [*La Cérémonie, contes*] (1978), the twins Claire Dé et Anne Dandurand (*The She-Werewolf* [*La Louvegarou*], 1982) and Belgian Nadine Monfils (*Tales for Perverse Little Girls* [*Contes pour petites filles perverses*], 1995).

- **Humorous Eroticism:** Some authors follow a deliberately different path from these stories, probably considered as too unsubtle, too clumsy, or ... too obvious, and write surprising and humorous stories, characterized by weirdness and by a delightful humor: "Your weddings to fifteen do not seem to be getting better" (Philippe de Jonas, *Eros exists, I Met Him* [*Eros existe, je l'ai rencontré*], 1970), *Small Horizontal Stories* [*Petites histoires horizontales*] (1985) by Cécile Philippe, "I have been finding myself in an uncomfortable situation for some time; every morning, in the bus—between Glacière and Opera—a homosexual wearing an undershirt scrutinizes me crudely and scot free. Most unpleasant" (Olivier Dazat, *Perverse Chronicles* [*Chroniques perverses*], 1986), the Quebecian Yves Thériault (*Work of Flesh—Oeuvre de chair*, 1976, an association between the pleasures of the clash and good meals. The Haitian René Depestre championed this "happy" eroticism: a doctor, a sex maniac, spreads scandal with "his gyratory syringe with intravaginal injection" (*Alleluia For a Woman-Garden, Stories* [*Alléluia pour une femme-jardin, récits*], 1973, 1981) not forgetting the "Glossary of Terms That Design the Masculine and Feminine Sexual Organs in Fictions" and the "Catalogue of Some Generally Accepted Ideas About the Extraordinary Adventures of Sexual Organs" that conclude *Eros in a Chinese Train, Short Stories* [*Eros dans un train chinois, nouvelles*] (1990). Humorous eroticism is also represented by Belen and her fantastic tales characterized by a devastating sense of humor that is most delightful: 'Solidarity Pleasure' ['Le Plaisir solidaire,'] 'The function creates the Orgasm' ['La Fonction crée l'orgasme'] (*Torrid Geometry* [*La Géométrie dans les spasmes*], 1959), 'Circe's Glottis' ['La Glotte de Circé,'] 'The Erection of Mister Universe'—L'Erection de M. Univerge,' 'The Extreme Function'—'L'Extrême ponction,' 'Love each upon the other'—La Reine de Sabbat'—*La Reine de Sabbat*, 1960—the collections have been published together in one book: *The Reservoir of the Senses—Le Réservoir des sens*, 1966, 1988). Sex can be funny, as in the works of Jean-Pierre Enard, who reinterpret childhood tales: "Snow White could not satisfy anymore the seven dwarves as they wished." (*Tales That Make Little Riding Hoods Blush—Contes pour faire rougir les petits chaperons*, 1987, p. 31) and with Frank Spengler: "Did fairies make love?" (preface to *The Love Life of the Fairies—La Vie amoureuse des fées*, 1997, 2000).

Two other curiosities are to be mentioned: *The Sexameron* (1990) by Jean Ikaris (in which a few people gathered in a tavern tell about their erotic exploits on holidays) and *It Looks Like Some Pushkin, Short Stories—Tiens, on dirait du Pouchkine, nouvelles* (1999) by Pierre Rival (in which the heroes of erotic adventures are called Marguerite Duras, André Gide, Françoise Sagan, and Patrick Modiano with two pastiches of Sade and Georges Bataille).

It may first appear that erotic tales are for men alone. The fact is only 41 works were written by women (20 of these storeis is the same five writers: were written by Belen (4), Régine Deforges (2), Nadine Monfils (5), Claire Dé (4), Anne Dandurand (5)). However, except for Louis-Charles Royer, who was completely forgotten, André Pieyre de Mandiargues and Pierre Bourgeade, the writers who devote themselves to the erotic tale today are women. In comparison to the situation one or two decades earlier, when the domination was clearly masculine in collections (for example, 3 women out of 15 in the science fiction collection *Venus' Boobies* [*Les Lolos de Vénus*], 1978), the tendency has reversed, the masculine presence having completely disappeared: 14 out of 14 (*Women's Disorders* [*Troubles de femmes*], 1994).

The erotic tale is part of a provocative literature: "The purpose of these adventures or tales is to shock the spectator or listener. In his convictions, in his most honourable feelings, in his beloved culture, in his modesty..." as is written on the back cover of *The Extravagant Door, Stories* [*Porte dévergondée, récits*] (1965) by André Pieyre de Mandriargues.

Even though eroticism has become fashionable, it remains scandalous. Just like this collection by Claire Dé, *Desire as Natural Catastrophe* [*Le Désir comme catastrophe naturelle*] (1989), which has raised a controversy after having won the Prix Stendhal of the short story. This recalls the sharp response of some subscribers of *L'Encrier Renversé* when the First Prize of the Short Story Competition organized by the review was awarded to an erotic tale.

RENÉ GODENNE

Further Reading

Aeply Jeanne. *Eros Zero - Eros zéro*. Paris: Mercure de France, 1972.

Belen (Nelly Kaplan). *Torrid Geometry - La Géométrie dans les spasmes*. Paris: Le Terrain Vague, 1959.

Bourgeade Pierre. *Mechanical Eros—Eros mécanique*. Paris: Gallimard, 1995.

Depestre René. *Alleluia For a Woman-Garden, Stories— Alléluia pour une femme-jardin, récits*. Paris: Gallimard, 1989.

Enard Jean-Pierre. *Tales That Make Little Riding Hoods Blush—Contes à faire rougir les petits chaperons*. Paris: Ramsay, 1987.

Jean Raymond. *A Bella B's Fantasy and Other Stories - Un fantasme de Belle B. et autres récits*. Actes-Sud, 1983.

MacOrlan Pierre. *The Secret Week of Venus—La Semaine secrète de V énus*. Paris: Minerve, 1985 (rééd.).

Margerit Robert. *Ambiguous, Short Stories - Ambigu, nouvelles*. Paris: Gallimard, 1956 (réed.).

Meilcour Nicolas. *Rose and Carma—Rose et Carma*. Paris: Bourgois, 1969.

Monfils Nadine. *Tales for Perverse Little Girls - Contes pour petites filles perverses*. Ed. du Rocher, 1995.

Pieyre de Mandiargues André. *The Extravagant Door, Stories—Porte dévergondée, récits*. Paris: Gallimard 1965.

The One Hundred Tales. Translated by Judith Bruskin Diner. New York: Garland, 1990.

Tales and novels in verse by J. de La Fontaine, with eighty-five engravings by Eisen and thirty-eight after Lancret, Boucher, Pater, etc. London: Privately printed for the Society of English Bibliophile, 1896.

Sade Marquis de. *The Crimes of Love: Heroic and Tragic Tales*. Preceded by an Essay on Novels: A Selection Translated with an Introduction and Notes by David Coward. New York University Press, 2005.

Thériault, Marie José. *The Ceremony*. Translated by David Lobdell. Ottawa: Oberon Press, 1980.

SHORT STORY, SPANISH-AMERICAN

Colonial Times

Being a fundamental part of life, sexuality and eroticism have been present in Spanish-American society and literature since its beginnings. The clash between pre-Hispanic cosmogonies and the medieval-renaissance minds of European conquerors and priests results in a steady flow of short anecdotes transmitted both orally and through the written word. Often, those with an erotic element speak about unfulfilled loves and transgressions, going against social institutions and Catholic dogma. *El Carnero* (1636–1638), by a Creole son of a conquistador, Juan Rodríguez Freyle (1566–1640), illustrates the presence of the erotic during these times. Several pieces in the book, extracted from a wastebasket found at Bogotá's court of appeals, relate marriage infidelities and offer a critique of the corruption in colonial society. This work has been

called a "kind of Spanish colonial *Decameron*" (see González Echevarría 1997, p. 50). It must be noted, however, that what critics describe as the literary short story had not been born yet. Both the royal decree in 1577 forbidding the publication of fictional works in Spanish America, and the pre-eminence of other genres (epic and lyric poetry), account for the lack of a literary vehicle for tales during the sixteenth, seventeenth, and eighteenth centuries.

The Nineteenth Century

The independence of Spanish America from colonial rule brings forth the process of nation building. The novel and the essay are the preferred genres for literary expression. During these times, as Enrique Pupo-Walker explains, the short story is not yet fully defined and moves "slowly amid the many hybrid forms employed by nineteenth-century writers of fiction" (1996, p. 514). Between 1830 and 1880, stories bare the imprint of the romantic aesthetic, based on a sentimental sensibility, idealized characters, and local customs and traditions. Erotic content is sprinkled minimally in the *Tradiciones*, by Peruvian Ricardo Palma (1833–1919), the most important short story writer of this period. "Secret Love," by Mexican Manuel Payno (1810–1894), however, is a good example of the representation of eroticism in the short story in this time frame. The protagonist describes his passion for Carolina as "ardent, pure, and holy" (Menton 1991, p. 38), in a tale about undeclared love, implicit promiscuity, and love to the grave (literally).

Between 1880 and 1910, Realism, Naturalism, and *Modernismo*—the first literary movement to have arisen from Spanish America—coexist with different agendas: the observation of both urban and rural reality (realism), with a clinical eye on the predicament of marginalized populations (naturalism) versus the aesthetics of "art for art's sake" of *Modernismo* that renovated literary language and form. Given the social criticism of most realist and naturalist fiction, the erotic is frequently found in short stories dealing with violent emotions. In *The Well*, by Chilean Baldomero Lillo (1867–1923), a romantic triangle infused with sexual desire advances to the sheer physicality of fighting among the characters. This is not romantic passion; Lillo's reformist prose chastises both the animal instincts in human beings and the degrading condition of the society they live in. On the other hand, the *Modernistas* seem detached from the Spanish-American social milieu. A closer look at their literary output, though, unveils a reaction against the values upheld by a *bourgeoisie* class that embraced the positivist thinking linked to Realism and Naturalism. In this context, sexual desire was to be regulated and made to conform to society's needs. Nicaraguan Rubén Darío (1867–1916) wrote poetic short stories that often projected a literary aesthetic. In "The Death of the Empress of China," under the guise of a flourishing style, a Parisian setting and Oriental allusions, lays an erotic tale of a wife's jealousy that ends with the destruction of the Chinese statue that had alienated her from her husband. The positioning of desire within the realm of artistic creation—the sculptor's obsession with the object—is meant, according to Naomi Lindstrom, "to serve as a counterforce to the repressive influence of conservative Catholic-Hispanic culture" (1985, p. 62).

Twentieth and Twenty-First Centuries

It could be argued that in the twentieth century Spanish-American literature shines the brightest in the short story. Nevertheless, it is difficult to identify an erotic short story writer, because the erotic short story is a thematic modulation on a genre. Not a history, but an erotics of the short story is best suited to examine the representations and functions of sexualities during this period. This erotics can, in turn, be divided into the laconic, the symbolic, and the explicit.

"Cristián threw down the cigar he had just lit and said evenly, 'Let's get busy, brother. In a while the buzzards will take over. This afternoon I killed her. Let her stay here with all her trinkets, she won't cause us any more harm'" (Borges 1970, p. 166). The end of "The Intruder," by Argentine writer Jorge Luis Borges (1899–1986), offers the reader a point of departure for the laconic erotic. In these types of stories, explicit sexual imagery is mainly absent; what is found instead are allusions, repressed desires, violence, and death.

The tale of two brothers, the Nielsens, and Juliana Burgos, the woman that Cristián brings to live with them in the Argentine *pampas*, is a love story: Juliana is for Cristián, but Eduardo, the younger brother, falls for her. Once they start sharing her sexually, they start arguing. They sell her to a whorehouse and soon thereafter they are both paying visits to the place; they bring her back home. Because "a man never admits to anyone—not even to himself—that a woman matters beyond lust and possession," the killing seems unavoidable. One man's love for a woman, two men's love for a woman, a woman's love (or desire) for two men? Critics have even suggested homoerotic desire between Cristián and Eduardo, a reading that Borges, always prudish about these matters, vehemently denied. All of this happens without a single overt sexual scene. Nonetheless, desire is undeniably the protagonist in "The Intruder," and the attempt to eliminate it only strengthens its hold on the narrative.

Before and after Borges parted the waters of the Spanish-American short story, two masters of the genre also infused some of their stories with an erotic element that was never totally disclosed. The father of the modern Spanish-American short story, Uruguayan Horacio Quiroga (1878–1937), was interested in the role sexuality plays in relationships. In "The Feather Pillow," the reason given for the death of the young bride—a spider-like animal that, hidden in her pillow, sucked her blood, leaves the reader wandering about the vampire-like qualities of her strange husband. And even if Argentine Julio Cortázar (1914–1984) was more sexually explicit in his novels, "Blow Up," widely viewed as an experiment with metafiction, is also an erotic story: the central scene of seduction ends up with the protagonist, a translator–photographer, trying to "save" a boy from homosexual initiation. Although this category cuts across the twentieth century, most examples fall between 1910 and 1960, a period wherein the sexual revolution and the rise of feminist consciousness had not yet taken place. The laconic erotic does not, however, shy away from issues of sexual objectifying, dysfunction, or homosexuality.

The translation to Spanish of Georges Bataille's seminal work on eroticism in 1960 was key for the gradual freeing of literary language from social constraints in Spanish America. During the 1960s there is also an interest in the dialogue between psychoanalysis and sexuality, and the women's liberation movement begins to have an impact on cultural production. The effect is felt on many fronts: the emphasis on *jouissance* (enjoyment, bliss) and the fragmentation of identity opposes the notion of sexuality linked to procreation, social stability, or instinctual urges; the body is increasingly seen as a political space; "alternative" sexualities surface to the forefront of the social fabric and there is a corresponding rise of homosexual and transsexual issues; and women start their transition from desired objects to desiring subjects.

For the symbolic erotic, stories can be more or less explicit in their depiction of sexuality; however, their erotic content is representative of something beyond. "Lyrics for Salsa and Three Made-to-Order Soneos," by Puerto Rican Ana Lydia Vega (1946–) is a case in point. In a story rich with the language of the streets, the stereotypical chase between man and woman gets turned upside down. She takes charge, drives to the motel, pays, and gets undressed first. The result: The man excuses his impotence by saying,

"I have a stomach-ache" (Menton 1991, p. 700). Vega experiments with three *soneos* (in salsa music, a *soneo* is the improvisational part where the singer goes off the lyrics and sings whatever comes to mind) which function as alternative endings: In the first and the second, the sexual act is consummated; its description mimics both Marxist and feminist discourse. The third one closes with frustration for both lovers and a circular return to the neverending flirting language from the street man. Sexuality is mixed with humor, but the symbolic erotic in this story speaks about the pitfalls of women's liberation, about Puerto Rico's status as a colony of the United States, and about the power of language to demystify issues of economics, politics, and gender.

For Argentine Luisa Valenzuela (1938–) private sexuality is inextricably linked to the political. In "At Night I Am Your Horse," there is only one sexual scene; the woman narrator says: "I fell asleep with him still on top of me" (Giardinelli 153). The individuals that are looking for the fugitive torture her, and finally she is thrown into jail. Here, the erotic symbolic links sexuality with power and refers to the repressive military regimes prevalent in South America in the 1970s. In a story like "The Orgasmographon," Mexican Enrique Serna (1959–) presents a delirious take on science fiction through a case of inverted morality: a totalitarian society where sexual pleasure is the norm and the people must fulfil a quota of orgasms. Accordingly, the Spiritualist Front members will take up the resistance. In these stories, eroticism provides a matrix for social commentary.

The favorite space for the explicit erotic is interpersonal relationships. In "The Cat," Mexican Juan García Ponce (1932–2003), strongly influenced by Bataille, presents many obsessions within the context of intimacy that constitutes his trademark: the role of desire in daily life, the gaze at the feminine body, the voyeuristic discourse, and a mysterious sexual connection (in this case, between the woman and the cat). García Ponce tries to establish a path of communion outside established social conventions and closely linked to the language of the body. Two women, Argentine Tununa Mercado (1939–) and Uruguayan Cristina Peri Rossi (1941–) are among the most representative erotic short story writers, largely due to Mercado's *Canon de alcoba* (1988) and Peri-Rossi's *Desastres íntimos*

(1997). In Mercado's "To See," the *motif* of the voyeur in the window gets an objectivist treatment. The ending is surprising: while the woman and the man both reach sexual climax (her by listening on the phone and him by watching her on the phone), the reader realizes the observed was listening precisely to the observer, which begs the question of who is watching whom. In Peri Rossi's "To Love or To Ingest," sexual acts such as the narrator introducing a cigarette in his lover's vagina and then smoking it are intertwined with reflections on the relationship between sex and eating and on his future destiny: "We all become the orphans of pregnant women" (Hughes 2004, p. 6).

The explicit erotic in the Spanish-American short story renews old themes and brings forth new ones, but the depiction of sexual content is what changes: more matter-of-fact and more daring, pushing the limits of what is considered acceptable. This is one of the directions eroticism follows in the Spanish-American short story; other writers choose to be laconic or symbolic. Although many taboos still remain well within the twenty-first century, a historic look at the erotic content of many Spanish-American short stories reveal that pushing the limits has been, is, and perhaps will be, what defines them.

PABLO BRESCIA

See also **Bataille, Georges; Caribbean; Cortázar, Julio; Cyber sexualities; Darío, Rubén; Exhibitionism and Voyeurism; Latin America; Mercado, Tununa; Modernismo; Peri Rossi, Cristina; Psychoanalysis; Science Fiction; Short stories; Valenzuela, Luisa; Vega, Ana Lydia; Women's Writing: Spanish Language Twentieth Century**

References and Further Reading

Short Story Authors, Short Story Anthologies, Erotic Short Story Anthologies

Borges, Jorge Luis. *The Aleph and Other Stories 1933–1969.* Translated by Jorge Luis Borges and Norman Thomas di Giovanni. New York: E.P. Dutton, 1970.

Cortázar, Julio. *End of the Game and Other Stories.* Translated by Paul Blackburn. New York: Pantheon Books, 1967.

García Ponce, Juan. *Encounters.* Hygiene: Eridanos Press, 1989.

Giardinelli, Mempo and Graciela Gliemmo, eds. *La Venus de papel.* Buenos Aires: Beas, 1993.

González Echevarría, Roberto, ed. *The Oxford Book of Latin American Short Stories.* Oxford: Oxford University Press, 1997.

Iturri Salmón, Jaime, ed. *Antología del cuento erótico boliviano.* La Paz: Alfaguara, 2001.

Hughes, Psiche, ed. *Violations: Stories of Love by Latin American Women.* Lincoln and London: University of Nebraska Press, 2004.

Jaramillo Levi, Enrique. *El cuento erótico en México.* Mexico City: Diana, 1975.

Menton, Seymour, ed. *El cuento hispanoamericano. Antología crítico-histórica.* 4th ed, Mexico City: Fondo de Cultura Económica, 1991.

Mercado, Tununa. *Canon de alcoba.* Buenos Aires: Ada Korn, 1988.

Peri Rossi, Cristina. *Desastres íntimos.* Barcelona: Lumen 1997.

Quiroga, Horacio. *The Decapitated Chicken and Other Stories.* Austin, TX: University of Texas Press, 1976.

Salinas Paguada, Manuel and Galel Cárdenas Amador, eds., *En el círculo del cobre. Antología del cuento erótico Centroamericano.* Tegucigalpa: Argos, 1993.

Serna, Enrique. *El orgasmógrafo.* Mexico City: Plaza y Janés, 2001.

Criticism

Balderston, Daniel. "The Twentieth-century Short Story in Spanish America." In *The Cambridge History of Latin American Literature*, Vol. 2: *The Twentieth Century*, Cambridge: Cambridge University Press, 1996. 465–496.

Brushwood, John S. "The Spanish American Short Story from Quiroga to Borges." In *The Latin American Short Story. A Critical History*, Ed. Margaret Sayers Peden, Boston: Twayne, 1985. 71–96.

Foster, David William. *Gay and Lesbian Themes in Latin American Writing.* Austin, TX: University of Texas Press, 1991.

Leal, Luis. *Historia del cuento hispanoamericano.* Mexico City: Ediciones de Andrea, 1966.

Lindstrom, Naomi. "The Spanish American Short Story From Echeverría to Quiroga." In *The Latin American Short Story. A Critical History*, Ed. Margaret Sayers Peden. Boston, MA: Twayne, 1985. 35–70.

McMurray, George R. "The Spanish American Short Story From Borges to the Present" in *The Latin American Short Story. A Critical History.* Ed. Margaret Sayers Peden. Boston, MA: Twayne, 1985. 97–137.

Pupo-Walker, Enrique. "The Brief Narrative in Spanish America: 1835–1915." In *The Cambridge History of Latin American Literature*, Vol. 1: *From Discovery to Modernismo.* Cambridge: Cambridge University Press, 1996. 490–535.

SHULMAN, ALIX KATES

1932–
United States novelist and memoirist

Alix Kates Shulman, whose career as a writer has spanned more than thirty years, has produced an impressive range of texts from novels to memoirs to nonfiction studies of Emma Goldman to children's books. In all of these, she has kept at the center an attention to one of the central messages of the women's movement of the sixties and seventies, in which she was an early and active participant: the dictum that the personal is the political, that no writing ever emerges without a connection between the writer's lived experiences and her imagination. In so doing, Shulman gives literary life to themes of critical importance to young women maturing in the fifties, sixties, and seventies, especially sexuality, dating, marriage, divorce, motherhood, sexual harassment, abortion, parenting, and the political struggle for women's liberation.

Shulman writes with an airy wit and an eye for details of daily life that exposes the subtle conventions and ridicules the blatant practices by which gender has been constructed and deconstructed in post-World War II United States. In particular, her humorous take on growing up as a teenager in the fifties and breaking free as a young woman in the sixties allowed her to confront some of the most tabooed of topics in middle-class American culture, including the loss of virginity, the female body and its emerging sexuality, and the female desire to experience and to give pleasure. Her treatment of female sexuality is both forthright and evocative, clinical and sensual, and in all cases presented as both a natural mystery about which one must be daring enough to seek the truth and a literary trope to critique American Puritanism.

Memoirs of an Ex-Prom Queen, which Shulman began in 1969 and published in 1972, is a female *bildungsroman* and semi-autobiographical. It is the story of Sasha, a young midwestern, middle class girl struggling to escape identity as a girlfriend, wife, and mother and to find own her identity as beautiful, intelligent, and sexual. The book, frequently referred to as the first novel to have emerged from the women's movement, developed an underground reputation when it was still in galley form, circulating amongst the secretaries in the reprint houses. Written as a conventional first-person narrative, the novel describes young Sasha's sexual explorations, which range from petting with her high school boyfriend, to "going all the way" with him the night she's crowned prom queen, to having an affair with her college philosophy professor, to engaging in quasi-nymphomanical behavior with a Spanish boyfriend. Shulman presents Sasha's sexuality as initially a paradoxical mark of teenage popularity and embarrassment that is then characterized as an invasion of the female body and eventually develops into intense pleasure functioning as an act of political liberation.

Shulman's descriptions of sex emphasize the act as lyrical expression undercut with metaphoric humor. Fellatio, for example, is presented as the art of kissing her "very center," which brings "little shock waves" and a "whimper of joy." The tenderness of the moment culminates in penetration, the transcendental interpretation of which Shulman negates by having Sasha describe actual coitus as the undulation of "a quarter's worth of nightcrawlers." The effect is to highlight both the beauty of sex when allowed full expression and the ordinariness of sex when understood as a natural act.

Burning Questions, published in 1978, is also autobiographical fiction, telling a story similar to that of *Memoirs*, although *Burning Questions* recounts more specifically the heroine's coming of age in the women's movement. Zane IndiAnna, fueled by stories of revolutionary women from the turn of the century, leaves her comfortable midwestern home for life as a beatnik in Greenwich Village, where she finds free-love, opts out for a conventional marriage, and becomes radicalized by the heady polemics of grassroots feminism. *Questions* critiques many middle-class practices that constrain the development of female consciousness, but in contrast to *Memoirs* its attention to sex is subordinated to the narrative of the feminist movement. Zane does share Sasha's whimsical perceptions of sex, describing her first night of love with a beatnik poet as "a pair of koalas—I am the little one clinging to him with my legs, he feeding my mouth with wet kisses like eucalyptus leaves." But subsequent evocations of heterosexual and lesbian sex avoid literary or clinical language, more often taking a more distanced, reportorial stance, avoiding the erotic altogether.

Such is not the case in Shulman's short story "A Story of a Girl and Her Dog," written in 1975. This daring narrative presents in a tone of playful innocence a snapshot of a teenage girl named Lucky, who discovers the pleasure of orgasm by allowing her pet dog to sniff and lick her clitoris. Shulman manages in this short fiction to not only explore the most hidden of sexual secrets but also to portray it as natural, harmless, and sensual. Lucky's private moment with her dog is compared to that of Adam and Eve—only their tasting of the fruit of the tree of knowledge brings not sin but rather the expanse of the world in all its virginal glory.

In her most recent works, Shulman has turned to memoir and the exploration of what it means to be a daughter and to care for aging parents, but her earlier fictional studies of female sexuality continue to find an audience with which they resonate, one seeking liberation through realism and the erotic.

Biography

Born in Cleveland Heights, Ohio, a suburb of Cleveland, on August 17, 1932; graduated at the age of twenty in 1953 from Case Western Reserve University with a bachelor's degree in English and history; moved to New York City, where she briefly studied philosophy at Columbia University and mathematics at New York University; earned on MA in humanities from NYU; married and divorced twice; has two children, a son Teddy, born in 1961, and a daughter, Polly, born in 1963; has taught at the University of Arizona, The Ohio State University, New York University, and the New School for Social Research; received a National Endowment for the Arts fiction grant in 1983; has been a visiting writer at the MacDowell Colony for the Arts Fellow (1975–1977, 1970, 1981); was a final

selection for a National Book Award in 1972; lives in New York City and Maine.

NANCY M. GRACE

Selected Works

Novels

Memoirs of an Ex-Prom Queen. Alfred A. Knopf: New York, 1972; reissued, Penguin Putnam, 1997.
Burning Questions, A Novel. Alfred A Knopf: New York, 1978.
On the Stroll. Alfred A. Knopf: New York, 1981; reissued, Academy Chicago: Chicago, Il., 1987.
In Every Woman's Life. Alfred A. Knopf: New York, 1987.

Nonfiction

"A Failed Divorce." In *Women on Divorce: A Bedside Companion.* Eds. Penny Kaganoff and Susan Spano. New York: Harcourt, Brace & Co., 1995, 153–165.
To the Barricades: The Anarchist Life of Emma Goldman. Crowell: New York, 1971.
Drinking the Rain. Farrar, Straus and Giroux: New York, 1995.
Red Emma Speaks: An Emma Goldman Reader. Humanities Press: Atlantic Highlands, New Jersey, 1996.
"A Marriage Disagreement, or Marriage by Other Means." In *The Feminist Memoir Project*, eds. Rachel Blau du Plessis and Ann Snitow. Three Rivers Press, 1998.
"A Story of a Girl and Her Dog." *Too Darn Hot: Writing About Sex Since Kinsey.* Eds. Judy Bloomfield, mary McGrail, and Lauren Sanders. Persea Books: New York, 1998, 30–35.
A Good Enough Daughter. Schocken Books, Inc.: New York, 1999.

Children's Books

Bosley on the Number Line. McKay: New York, 1970.
Awake of Asleep. Young Scott: Reading, MA, 1971.
Finders Keepers. Bradbury Press: Scarsdale, New York, 1971.

Further Reading

Bell, Pear. Review of *Burning Questions. New York Times Book Review.* March 26, 1978, 12.
Bender, Marilyn. Review of *Memoirs of an Ex-Prom Queen. New York Times Book Review.* April 23, 1972, 36.
Breines, Wini. *Young, White, and Miserable: Growing Up Female in the Fifties.* Boston: Beacon Press, 1992.
Hendin, Josephine. *Vulnerable People: A Review of American Fiction since 1945.* New York: Oxford University Press, 1978.
Michelson, Peter. *Speaking the Unspeakable: A Poetics of Obscenity.* Albany, NY: State University of New York Press, 1993.
Muchnik, Laurie. Review of *Memoirs of an Ex-Prom Queen. Voice Literary Supplement*, October 1993, 21.

SLASH FICTION

Slash is homoerotic writing featuring characters borrowed from popular media. It is written almost exclusively by women, cannot be commercially published due to copyright restrictions, and has flourished as an amateur art form since the 1970s. Most slash depicts two male media characters, though a small percentage is written about female couples.

Fans assert that as early as 1966 or 1967 private stories paired Napoleon Solo and Illya Kuryakin of the popular TV series "The Man from U.N.C.L.E.," but the first documented slash stories were privately circulated in Great Britain based on "Star Trek's Captain Kirk and his Vulcan First Officer, Spock. An example is "The Ring of Shoshern," written in 1968 but not published until 1987.

Heterosexual "adult" fan fiction based on "Star Trek" was already available to science fiction fans in a few fanzines, a format used primarily for nonfiction since the 1930s. The first published same-sex story was the two-page "A Fragment Out of Time" by Diane Marchant, in *Grup*, Number III, September 1974. The first line of the story is, "Shut up... we're by no means setting a precedent." But they were. 1976 saw the publication of Gerry Downes's all-Kirk/Spock zine *Alternative: Epilog to Orion* and the historically recognized first fully-developed published Kirk/Spock story, "Shelter," by Leslie Fish. Multi-issue zines devoted solely to Kirk/Spock stories then appeared thick and fast, including, by 1978, *Obsc'zine, K/S Relay, Thrust, Companion, Naked Times*, and *The Sensuous Vulcan*, followed by a flood of hundreds of zines and the birth of a genre.

These Kirk/Spock stories came to be known as "K/S." At the advent of other early couples, like Starsky and Hutch (S/H) and Bodie/Doyle (B/D) (from the British show "The Professionals"), an inclusive term for this type of story was needed. The slash mark used to join the two characters' names or initials, the emblem of the union at the heart of the genre, was adopted as its name.

The number of stories published is staggering to the uninitiated: there were thousands upon thousands of them, documented in bibliographies and lists of zines available for sale—at cost: all slash publishing is and must be not-for-profit. They were nevertheless expensive, often spiral bound with glossy color covers and explicit black and white interior artwork. Zines might contain a single long novel, or an anthology of many authors' short stories. They were reproduced by traditional science fiction fanzine mimeography (often this material was too controversial for commercial printers of the day), and later by photocopying. Slash was considered by many to be a secret art, best kept hidden due to its homoerotic content and issues of copyright. In the early days, and even into the 1990s, some copyright owners reacted with legal threats when startled into awareness of the frolickings of their hero-characters in bed with one another. Over the years, as both homophobia and fear of loss of revenue dissipated, and as the courts consistently recognized a sort of usufruct in nonharmful and nonprofit use of copyrighted material, studios and other copyright holders have tended to pursue a "don't ask/don't tell" policy toward slash, recognizing also the folly of attacking their own fan base. In the 1970s and 1980s, however, mutual fears were rampant, and much slash fiction (as well as some heterosexual erotic fan fiction) was circulated only clandestinely, mailed on private "circuits," each recipient making her own copies before mailing on the original. Thus, much slash was never published, and is now lost; however, at least one such circuit, for "The Professionals" slash, was still in existence in 2002, and had its own central library. Some Web sites are attempting to locate and archive old fanzine stories.

By the mid-1990s, slash started aggressively moving onto the Web. In 2005, a Google search using the search terms "slash" and "fiction" returned 1,180,000 results; the phrase "fan fiction," 1,260,000. Thousands of archives and individual Web sites feature slash fiction and art based on every conceivable television show, many movies, and even some book series.

Sex in slash is rarely described euphemistically, but is shown with at least Tab-A-in-Slot-B detail, and in the most sophisticated works with original, telling, and highly literate extravagance. With some authors, a single sex act may run to many pages. Praise from readers often centers around how "hot" they found the story.

Though some slash writing only implies or refers to a sexual relationship, traditionally at least one explicit sex scene is expected in each story. Canon—the "facts" established by the original TV show, movie, comic book, etc.—must be adhered to, unless the story is an "AU" (alternate universe) tale, and clever twisting of canon to achieve one's erotic purpose is much admired.

Slash has recognized subgenres, often defined by the way eroticism is used. "First time" stories are the most popular, as they lay out ingenious rationales for two canonically heterosexual males to discover mutual attraction and act on it. PWPs (Plot? What Plot?) focus on the sex act itself, with setting or rationale barely sketched in. "Established relationship" stories depict a more intimate couple, with the sex scene, again, requiring little 'set-up.' "Hurt/comfort" stories are traditionally defined as nonsexual, using injury, torture, rape, or illness of one partner to elicit comfort (often of a cuddling nature) from the other, but hurt/comfort-type scenarios are also freely used in stories that do lead to open passion. Subgenre names also serve as "warnings" in the header material of stories, so that readers likely to be upset by them can avoid them; for example, rapefic, BDSM, death of a major character. "Angst," meaning trauma, conflict, sturm und drang, is another love-it-or-hate-it category, the drama frequently rooted in the nature of the eroticism itself, as in prostitution, homophobic rejection, or abuse, creating much highly eroticized tension (usually resolved in sex and confessions of love). A few categories are almost universally looked down upon, yet continue to be written: "curtain fic" (frilly domesticity), "mpreg" (male pregnancy), and Mary Sue stories (a wildly idealized OFC—original female character—inserted into the normal cast).

Intriguingly, an entirely independent homoerotic phenomenon called 'yaoi' arose in Japan based on Japanese comic books and anime, and also created entirely by women. No early connection between the two genres has ever been shown, though with the advent of the Web, the two traditions became peripherally aware of one another by the turn of the millennium.

CAMILLA DECARNIN

See also **Fan fiction; Manga; Yaoi**

Further Reading

Aestheticism Articles: Why the Guys? or, Navel-Gazing on a Sunny Afternoon http://www.aestheticism.com/visitors/editor/jeanne/whytheguys.htm

Aestheticism Articles: The Self-Lubricating Penis and Other Yaoi Anomalies http://www.aestheticism.com/visitors/editor/jeanne/self_lube/

Amy-Chinn, Dee. "Queering the Bitch: Spike, Transgression and Erotic Empowerment," presentation, *Blood, Text and Fears: Reading Around Buffy the Vampire Slayer.* University of East Anglia, U.K., 19–20 October 2002.

Bacon-Smith, Camille. "Spock Among the Women." New York Times Book Review, 1 (November 16, 1986): 28–29.

Barker, Meg. "Slashing the Slayer: A Thematic Analysis of Homo-Erotic Buffy Fan Fiction." Presentation, *Blood, Text and Fears: Reading Around Buffy the Vampire Slayer.* University of East Anglia, U.K., 19–20 October 2002.

Clute, John and Nicholls, Peter (editors). *The Encyclopedia of Science Fiction.* London: Orbit (Little, Brown), 1993.

Curtin, Mary Ellen. *The Foresmutters Project for the History of Slash,* undated. http://www.foresmutters.org/

Dery, Mark. "Slashing the Borg: Resistance is Fertile" http://www.levity.com/markdery/borg.html

Jenkins, Henry. *Textual Poachers: Television Fans and Participatory Culture.* New York: Routledge, Chapman and Hall, 1992, 1994.

Jenkins, Henry. "Star Trek Rerun, Reread, Rewritten: Fan Writing as Textual Poaching." *Critical Studies in Mass Communications,* 5, 2 (June 1988): 85–107. Reprinted with revisions in *Close Encounters: Film, Feminism and Science Fiction,* edited by Constance Penley, Elizabeth Lyons, Lynn Spigel and Janet Bergstrom, Minneapolis: University of Minnesota Press, 1991. Reprinted in *Television: The Critical View,* 5th Edition, edited by Horace Newcomb, New York: Oxford University Press, 1994.

Jenkins, Henry, and Tulloch, John. *Science Fiction Audiences: Doctor Who, Star Trek and Their Followers.* London: Routledge, Chapman and Hall, 1995.

Jenkins, Henry. "A Conversation with Henry Jenkins: Interview on the Intersections of Fan and Academic Criticism," in *Enterprise Zones: Critical Positions on Star Trek,* edited by Taylor Harrison and Sara Projansky, Boulder: Westview Press, 1997. http://web.mit.edu/21fms/www/faculty/henry3/harrison.html

Jenkins, Henry. "Television Fans, Poachers, and Nomads," in *The Subcultures Reader,* edited by

Susan Thornton. New York: Routledge, Chapman and Hall, 1997. Reprinted from Textual Poachers: Television Fans and Participatory Culture.

Jenkins, Henry. "The Poachers and the Stormtroopers: Cultural Convergence in the Digital Age." Presentation, University of Michigan, *Red Rock Eater Digest*, Spring 1998. http://www.strangelove.com/slideshows/articles/The_Poachers_and_the_Stormtroopers.htm

Jenkins, Henry, Green, Shoshanna and Jenkins, Cynthia. "'The Normal Female Interest in Men Bonking': Selections from The Terra Nostra Underground and Strange Bedfellows." In *Theorizing Fandom: Fans, Subculture, and Identity*, edited by Cheryl Harris and Alison Alexander, Cresskill, NJ: Hampton Press, 1998. http://web.mit.edu/21fms/www/faculty/henry3/bonking.html

Jenkins, Henry. "'Out of the Closet and into the Universe': Queers and Star Trek." In *American Cultural Studies*, edited by John Hartley and Roberta Pearson, Oxford: Oxford University Press, 2000.

Jenkins, Henry. "Intensities interviews Henry Jenkins @Console-ing Passions," *Intensities: The Journal of Cult Media*. Issue 2, Autumn/Winter 2001. http://www.cult-media.com/issue2/CMRjenk.htm

Jenkins, Henry. "Interactive Audiences? The 'Collective Intelligence' of Media Fans." In *The New Media Book*, edited by Dan Harries, London: British Film Institute, forthcoming. http://web.mit.edu/21fms/www/faculty/henry3/collective%20intelligence.html

Jenkins, Henry, III and Jenkins, Henry, IV. "'The Monsters Next Door': A Father-Son Conversation about Buffy, Moral Panic, and Generational Differences." In *Red Noise: Buffy the Vampire Slayer and Critical Television Studies*, edited by Elaine Levine and Lisa Parks, Durham: Duke University Press, forthcoming. http://web.mit.edu/21fms/www/faculty/henry3/buffy.html

Lamb, Patricia Frazer and Veith, Diana L. "Romantic Myth, Transcendence, and Star Trek Zines." In *Erotic Universe: Sexuality and Fantastic Literature*, edited by Donald Palumbo, New York: Greenwood Press, 1986.

National Public Radio, *All Things Considered*, "Harry Potter Fan Fiction," http://www.npr.org/ramfiles/atc/20021229.atc.08.ram http://www.npr.org/ramfiles/atc/20021229.atc.08.ram http://www.npr.org/ramfiles/atc/20021229.atc.09.ram The Ethicist <http://www.npr.org/ramfiles/atc/20021229.atc.09.ram>, 29 December 2002.

Penley, Constance. "Brownian Motion: Women, Tactics, and Technology." *Technoculture*, Minneapolis, MN: University of Minnesota Press, 1991. 135–161.

Penley, Constance. "Feminism, Psychoanalysis and the Study of Popular Culture." In *Cultural Studies*, edited by Lawrence Grossberg, Cary Nelson, and Paula A. Treichler, New York: Routledge, 1992. 479–450.

Russ, Joanna. "Pornography By Women For Women, With Love." In *Magic Mommas, Trembling Sisters, Puritans and Perverts: Feminist Essays*, Trumansburg, New York: The Crossing Press, 1985.

Russ, Joanna. "Another Addict Raves About K/S." Nome #8 or 9, 1986.

Saxey, Esther. "Why is BtVS so Slashable?" presentation, *Blood, Text and Fears: Reading Around Buffy the Vampire Slayer*. University of East Anglia, U.K., 19–20 October 2002.

Sinclair, Jenna. *A Short History of Early K/S, or How the First Slash Fandom Came to Be*. Undated. http://beyonddreamspress.com/history.htm

Stein, Atara. "Minding One's P's and Q's: Homoeroticism in *Star Trek: The Next Generation*." *Genders*, 27, 1998.

Slayage: The Online International Journal of Buffy Studies http://www.slayage.tv/ [peer-reviewed scholarly articles about "Buffy the Vampire Slayer"]

A few slash and fan fiction archives

Fanfiction.net http://www.fanfiction.net/
The Gossamer Project http://fluky.gossamer.org/
Slash Fan Fiction on the Net http://members.aol.com/KSNicholas/fanfic/slash.html

SODOMY

During the classical era, sodomy was first and foremost linked with male homosexuality and pederasty. Religious writings, philosophical essays, historical dissertations, libertine novels, and satirical poems show how much in favor the "masculine wedding" was in Ancient Greece, in Rome, and with the Oriental princes.

Voltaire used the word "sodomy" to evoke the Jesuits, helping to spread their bad reputation. However, as early as Nicolas Chorier's *L'Académie des dames* [*The Ladies' Academy*] - *Aloisiae Sigeae Toletanae Satyra sotadica de Arcanis Amoris et Venris. Aloysia Hispanice scripsit Latinitate donavit Johannes Meursius*

1235

(1659 or 1960), translated into French for the first time in 1680, heterosexual sodomy was being debated (using the same argument between the two Aphrodites that was already found in antiquity as a topic for discussion in the philosophical *banquets* inspired by Plato).

The homage rendered to the Aphrodite with "beautiful buttocks" was violently condemned by Tullie and Octavie, the two characters from *L'Académie des dames*. They exposed this "dirty sensual pleasure," this "ridiculous and vile" posture, this "extravagant rage" that "violates the laws of nature." Against all logic, since the girls were only seeking pleasure, the aim was to preserve the generation principle. The discourse on pleasure showed a limitation by suddenly becoming moralizing: the truth of nature, the demands of the natural order, the need for procreation acted as censorship within the praise of pleasure.

Commonly attributed to the Italians and the Spaniards (it was the "Florentine vice," a "Roman pleasure"), sodomy was only tolerated as a preliminary, provided one returned to the "ordinary place" when reaching the moment of pleasure. That was what *Les Quarante manières de foutre* [*Forty ways to fuck*] (1790) also suggested with the "Milanese attraction." The fortieth posture to be itemized, sodomy added spice; it was an additional "stew," but it could not be a substitute for the customary way.

It was found in Indian and Oriental literature. It was also found in the famous Arab treatise written during the first half of the sixteenth century, *Le Retour du cheikh à sa jeunesse pour la vigueur et le coït* [*The Return of the Sheik to his Youth for Vigor and Coitus*], by Ahmed Ibn Souleimân, in which the author offered up to sixteen positions for the sodomy of women. Still, Sinistrati, in his *De Sodomia tractatus* (part of the book *De delectis et voenis*, Rome 1754), reminded that sodomy was a vice against nature, that it was the silent sin par excellence (*peccatum mutum*) because it scandalized the ears and was related to heresy. Thus it was condemned by all, be it from the Church or from those who eulogized pleasure. Often painful, humiliating for women (since it negated the difference between the sexes), sodomy was sign of heresy, a unnatural position, an "odd" or "disguting" form. The same discourse ridiculing or protesting sodomy could be found in *Thérèse philosophe* (1748) or in the *Catéchisme libertin à l'usage des filles de joie* [*Libertine Catechism for Ladies of the Night*] (1791).

Such was the paradox of sodomy: although present in all the libertine or erotic texts, it was always the subject of a debate, the opportunity for an objection. Enlightened minds saw in its denunciation a prejudice to be rid of: "proof of love," said one; "proof of madness," answered the other. The "anti-physical" pleasure presented a problem. As if sodomy was to the erotic narrative what the scene of sexuality was to the novel, a subject of resistance, the place of suggestion or silence, a realm of worry, scandal, and secret. Until it became common through the diffusion of pornographic movies, it would retain this sulfurous dimension—last interdict, eliciting an ultimate transgression—throughout the erotic literature of the nineteenth and twentieth centuries, imposing itself as the position reached by those who got liberated at the end of their journey.

The violence of Sade's text, which turned sodomy into the libertine gesture par excellence, is then easier to grasp. Such was the defiance of the *Cent Vingt Journées de Sodome* [*One Hundred and Twenty Days of Sodom*]. Sade thus went to the ultimate consequences of the liberating discourse on pleasure. There was no divine law, no natural law to uphold. In Sade's work, sodomy was an insult to the Church, a parody and reversal of sexuality, which remained subjected to the "natural order." There were no limits to the transgression. And sodomy asserted itself not as the ultimate conquest, but as the starting point from which Sade led his libertines on the path of crime, in the reversal of values, discourses, and representations.

PATRICK WALD LASOWSKI

Further Readings

Kearney, Patrick. *A History of Erotic Literature.* London: Macmillan, 1982.

Klossowski, Pierre. *Sade, mon prochain.*

Mainil, Jean. *Dans les règles du plaisir.* Kimé, 1996.

SOLLERS, PHILIPPE

1936–
French writer, critic, and theorist

Portrait du Joueur has a self-conscious, playfully autobiographical dimension: the first-person narrator (a Philippe Diamant who chose the pseudonym of Philippe Sollers) shares numerous biographical elements with Philippe Sollers the writer (whose real name is *Joyaux*, that is, Jewels), both being Bordeaux-born successful writers of controversial books and married to foreign academics. The *Player* whose *Portrait* is skillfully painted as a sophisticated combination of Sollers-Diamant and Sollers-Joyaux keeps playing this game of hide-and-seek, with constant allusions to genuine events, people, and places, a trap for the reader which Sollers himself has acknowledged in terms of narrative reflexivity: 'My novels are a mythobiography, meant to confuse by giving too many tracks. A writer is someone who makes a biography impossible' ("Une biographie officielle," *Le Figaro Littéraire*, 19 mars 1990, p. 8).

Portrait du Joueur has a rather loose narrative: its major thread is provided by the narrator's reminiscences, reflections, and digressions on a variety of themes including catholic theology, world literature, languages, surveillance, Bordeaux, French history, libertinism, non-monogamous relationships, sex, artificial insemination, metaphysics, and so forth. Those streams of consciousness (occasionally peppered with dialogues between the narrator and a hypothetical reader) take place against various backgrounds and settings, from Bordeaux to Venice. At the beginning of the book, Dowland (the family château near Bordeaux) represents nostalgia, half-forgotten bourgeois traditions, consumerism, capitalism, and betrayal as the old vineyard property has been sold, demolished, and replaced by a typical modern superstore. At the end of the book, after sojourns in Paris and New York, the narrator settles down in Venice, the heavily connoted city of Casanova, love and eroticism, games of masks and carnivals,

where he seemingly plans to die and be buried, having already written his epitaph mentioned in capital letters at the end of the book: 'DIAMANT DIT SOLLERS, VENITIEN DE BORDEAUX.'

Those rich albeit disorganized reflections (reminiscent of Montaigne's *Essays*, another Bordeaux-born writer and a recurrent reference in the book) could rapidly become vain if it were not for the humanizing presence of numerous women. His mother Lena, his sister Laure, his nieces Lise and Blandine, his masseuse Sumiko, his daugher Julie, his half-estranged American wife Norma, and his three mistresses Sophie, Ingrid, and Joan surround the narrator and ceaselessly bring him back to reality, to the world of bodies and feelings. Men only appear as disruptions or ludicrous figures (such as the Spanish chambermaid's overjealous boyfriend and the ignorant supermarket assistant): *Portrait du Joueur* is a novel about women, about the narrator's women, which creates a direct link to Sollers' previous novel precisely entitled *Femmes* (and in fact *Femmes*, *Portrait du Joueur* and Sollers' following novel *Le Coeur Absolu* form a trilogy of some sort). That exclusive heterosexuality stance, repeated several times, is barely balanced by the mention of two gay secondary characters and the extract from a wan gay novel the narrator starts to read then rapidly discards. At an erotic level, the four key women for the narrator are Ingrid, Norma, Joan, and Sophie, giving him 'four rather interesting lives where most people have only one, one and a half, or one and three quarters.' Ingrid is a Dutchwoman sixteen years older than him, a living connection to the past and to their love story when he was faking schizophrenia to be released from military service. Norma, despite being the narrator's wife, is very absent from the book: we only learn that she gets a regular alimony and raises their daughter. Joan is a much more erotic character: a *femme fatale* journalist, she becomes a good friend of the narrator after having sex with him. She often tells him about all her sexual partners, explaining that she has sex with them out of charity, to be nice to them: her best orgasms are always when she masturbates on her own, lying on the carpet, listening to Bach or Handel and telephoning the narrator whose fake insults ('you little bitch!') help her come. Yet the erotic interest and originality of *Portrait du Joueur* really resides in the character of Sophie and her complex relationship to the narrator, who qualifies this relationship both as 'physical communication' and 'religious experience.' Sophie is a 28-year-old, sexy, timid-looking bourgeois brunette, married to a catholic German diplomat. She lives in Geneva where she works as a doctor, yet she comes to Paris on a weekly basis for business, seizing those opportunities to meet Philip for sex, always following specific scenes she describes in short letters she sends him beforehand. This rather unexpected intrusion of the epistolary genre in the very center of the novel is more than a direct allusion to *Les Liaisons Dangereuses*, to which several references are made elsewhere in the book; those 15 letters, brief and straightforward (half a page on average), constitute the erotic nexus of the book by presenting and combining two types of eroticism: eroticism of situation and eroticism of language.

Firstly, the narrator's regular meetings with Sophie all comply to precise and prearranged scenarios of her own making: she is the one who decides every single time what will happen sexually between them. With minimal spontaneity and leeway, they follow strict role-plays where she is always in control. At times she is a doctor who slowly examines a patient's genitalia and scrupulously extracts his sperm for research purposes; at times she is a provincial butcheress perverting her young and shy apprentice; other times she is a modern Lady Chatterley contemptuously using her valet, footman, or gardener. The narrator equally refers to those scenes as 'contracts,' 'rituals,' 'games' and 'erotic sessions,' which stresses the complex nature of their sexual relationship, both ludic and solemn, both serious and frivolous. Sophie's punctual arrivals, her business-like attitude, his obedience to follow her instructions as well as her coldness and apparent detachment could lead one to believe that their relationship is only physical, yet it gradually transpires that she is deeply in love with him, which gives an emotional layer to

their complex erotic relationship on the verge of sadomasochism.

Secondly, Sophie's sexual language also contributes to the eroticism of the book. Whereas she is presented as socially most respectable and conventional, if not a prude, her sexual language with the narrator is a subtle mix of obscene words and poetic phrases: 'How I felt your cock fucking me yesterday! My voice is still colored by your sperm: smooth and deliciously languorous,' 'I feel a constant happiness: I want to suck you, always. I long for you. I love you getting hard for me. Just like I love getting wet for you, always.' This dual tonality is reflected in the way she keeps shifting between an intimate *tu* and a formal *vous* both in her letters and in the few words she utters when having sex with him. Her choice of intentionally blunt and crude words (such as 'fuck me and come, bastard!') feels so much out of context and out of character that those very phrases get an erotic connotation, that language being the marker of their sexuality — then after sex, she turns back into a most respectable bourgeoise, creating a clear and rigid distinction between her sexual interactions with the narrator (when she uses words such as 'cunt, fuck, and cock') and social interactions with him (when after sex she lights a cigarette and politely asks him about his work, his travels, his life).

Those two dimensions (eroticism of situation and eroticism of language) are eventually subsumed in what Sollers named 'the unrelated sentence: the message from the woman that must trigger ejaculation.' A key aspect of their sexual relationship (integrating both her control in their role-plays and the power of her language) is the fact that a specific and also pre-decided sentence, unrelated to the context, must trigger his orgasm at once whenever she decides, whenever she utters the sentence, which can be 'Remind me to buy roses on the way back,' 'It's been really hot today' or 'You shall accompany me to mass tomorrow.' Several pages intellectually analyze this technique which totally negates the natural aspect and timing of male ejaculation and male pleasure, and is supposed to enter the annals of human sexuality, presumably because of the underpinning erotic creativity. This form of orgasm control, unexpected in the book as a whole where the narrator is always the one who plays, the *joueur*, and not someone being played with, gives a certain erotic edge both to the central character Philippe and to *Portrait du Joueur*.

The character of Sophie only appears in one tenth of the book, yet its importance in the history of erotic literature cannot be underrated. Not only does Sophie enable Sollers to show his erotic creativity in terms of scenarios, language, and relationships, not to mention the original 'unrelated sentence,' but she also provides him with the opportunity to illustrate the ideas on erotic literature outlined elsewhere in the book. The narrator, working on a complex novel whose key themes and dynamics are that of *Portrait du Joueur*, explains and justifies his own principles on erotic writing throughout the book. His premise is that the first thing (if not the only one) readers are interested in is the sexual aspect of any book, which they then endeavour to relate to, with reference to their own sexual experience, and possibly to integrate into their own erotic repertoire. No matter what some conservative, hypocritical critiques may say, such is the critical importance of sex in a book. Pornographic language is one aspect thereof, yet a limited one: the narrator, reflecting on the choice of explicit words which some readers may (or ideally will) find shocking, analyzes how most readers never go beyond the signifier/signified association: 'Cock, fuck, suck, cum... You tell them words, they see things.' The objective is less to arouse the reader than to develop an aesthetics of eroticism, yet few people seem to understand that, or so explains the narrator with regret when his niece asks him why he writes porn. Besides the fact that all comments on eroticism are irregularly scattered throughout the book, the main difficulty to make sense of the interesting aesthetics of eroticism presented in *Portrait du Joueur* is the fact that it relies heavily on aphorisms: 'eroticism is a cardinal virtue,' 'to write, to sleep, to shag: that's the same wheel,' 'eroticism has its own algebra' are powerful ideas and good quotations, yet their possible meanings are not necessarily convincing.

In *Portrait du Joueur*, Sollers explores a bourgeois fear of language, as sexual language is understood as taboo and undisclosed except in very particular sexual circumstances. As a postmodern novel *Portrait du Joueur* is a landmark in the history of erotic literature because it is both a theory of erotic writing and an applied example thereof — which is actually typical of Sollers, as it is often said that it is difficult, if not impossible, to separate his critical/theoretical texts from his fictional ones.

Biography

Born in 1936 in Bordeaux, a city often mentioned in his books. A media-savvy novelist and editor, critic and theorist, he got his first Literary Award (*Prix Médicis*) at the age of 25 for his second book *Le Parc*. In 1960, he founded the leftist *avant-garde* literary review *Tel Quel* and the intellectual group of the same name, which had a huge impact on the political and cultural debates of France in the 1960s and 1970s (most of the major French post-structuralist thinkers have indeed been associated with *Tel Quel*, notably Roland Barthes, Michel Foucault, Jacques Derrida, Marcelin Pleynet as well as Julia Kristeva to whom Sollers has been married since 1967). *Tel Quel* was dissolved in 1983 when Sollers left the publishing company *Le Seuil* to found a new journal called *L'Infini* with competitor *Gallimard*.

LOYKIE LOÏC LOMINÉ

Editions

Une Curieuse Solitude. Paris: Seuil, 1957.
Le Parc. Paris: Seuil, 1961.
Sur le Matérialisme. Paris: Seuil, 1974.
Femmes. Paris: Gallimard, 1983.
Portrait du Joueur. Paris: Gallimard, 1984.
Le Coeur Absolu. Paris: Gallimard, 1987.
Les Folies Françaises. Paris: Gallimard, 1988.
Le Lys d'Or. Paris: Gallimard, 1989.
La Fête à Venise. Paris: Gallimard, 1991.
Le Secret. Paris: Gallimard, 1992.

Further Reading

Clement, C. *Philippe Sollers*. Paris: Julliard. 1995.
Forest, P. *Philippe Sollers*. Paris: Seuil. 1992.
———. *Histoire de Tel Quel 1960-1982*. Paris: Seuil. 1995.
Pollard, M.C. *The Novels of Philippe Sollers: Narrative and the Visual*. Amsterdam: Rodopi. 1994.

SOLOGUB, FEDOR

1863–1927
Russian prose writer, poet, and dramatist

Fedor Sologub was the author of a large number of poems, five novels, over a dozen plays, and numerous theoretical articles. His early works were influenced by authors such as Charles Baudelaire, Auguste Villiers de L'Isle-Adam, and Joris-Karl Huysmans. Shocked Russian critics labeled Sologub and others "decadent" because they continued the erotic, demonic, pessimistic, and solipsistic themes of their French counterparts. In his later works Sologub turned away from portrayals of the depravity of Russian provincial life toward using the author's powers to produce a "legend in creation," an artistic recreation of this world. The use of erotic themes and images remained a constant throughout his works.

Bad Dreams

Considered by many to be Russia's first modernist novel, *Bad Dreams* (1895) describes the efforts of the schoolteacher Vasilii Login to rise above the stifling philistinism of his provincial surroundings. Sologub vividly compares the base sensuality of the masses to Login's denial of the erotic impulses within him in an attempt to overcome ordinary mores. For example, Login sees the beautiful Nyuta Ermolina (his eventual savior) nude, but rejoices at her beauty (i.e., truth) and feels no ordinary sexual desire. Similarly, he has suggestive daydreams about a young boy but only contemplates his innocent beauty. *Bad Dreams* was the first of several Sologub works to feature young boys as potential objects of sexual desire. In a minor plot line, Login's erotic experimentation is paralleled by Paltusov's incestual relationship with his stepdaughter Klavdiia; they escape from the repressive atmosphere of the novel by fleeing abroad, where they can love each other openly. Critics decried Sologub's "sick fantasy" and "base sensual perversion" and equated the author with

Login. Out of fear of censorship, Sologub omitted several erotic scenes that were published only in the third edition (1909), which he considered the true text.

The Petty Demon

As in *Bad Dreams*, in *The Petty Demon* depraved eroticism is the defining characteristic of Sologub's provincial hell, whereas erotic experimentation is practiced by those looking to escape from mundane reality. The gloomy, increasingly-insane school teacher Ardalion Peredonov is the personification of the former; several scenes in the novel portray the animalistic intercourse between him and his partner Varvara. Peredonov's imagination is aroused by rumors that a new student, Sasha (the name in Russian can be applied to males or females), is in fact a girl in disguise. He dreams of whipping and humiliating Sasha the same way he does other boys in the school. Liudmila Rutilova hears the same rumors and befriends Sasha. Locked away in her room, she draws him into innocent sexual games, which include cross-dressing, dousing him with perfume, and exploring the sweet side of pain through light flagellation. Liudmila enjoys the beauty of young boys' bodies, whereas Peredonov takes great delight in seeing this beauty perverted. Unfortunately Liudmila's vision of beauty is fleeting; as Sasha reaches puberty, he increasingly exhibits the same feelings of lust and animal instincts seen in the other inhabitants of Sologub's provincial world.

The Created Legend

Sologub's reputation as an "incomparable Russian pornographer" was confirmed in 1909 when, based on the first volume of *The Created Legend*, a mock student trial at St. Petersburg University convicted him of describing "unnatural tendencies known as sadism" (the notorious writers Mikhail Kuzmin and Mikhail

Artsybashev were found innocent by the same group!) (see Baran). In this novel Sologub presents one controversial scene after another: after making love with the hero Grigorii Trirodov, his mistress Alkina discusses sadomasochism and describes her desire to be humiliated; in the local police station arrested girls are stripped and beaten; Elizaveta Rameeva is raped and seems to enjoy the experience. Far from provincial Russia on the United Islands lives Queen Ortruda, for whom "free feelings are never depraved, only constrained ones are." She fights against constraint by engaging in a series of affairs with lovers of both genders and indulging in sexual games in the underground passages of her castle. With Elizaveta Trirodov represses average sexuality and strives for a platonic relationship free of erotic or degrading impulses. Like Login he is connected with young boys, especially the "quiet boys" who live on his estate and who are the subject of many rumors. After Ortruda dies in a volcano eruption, Trirodov is elected king of the United Islands and flies there to start putting his utopian plans into action.

Other Works

Sologub's reputation as an erotic writer is due mostly to his novels, but similar themes echo throughout all of his works, for example in his short stories. In "The Queen of Kisses" the young wife of an impotent old merchant wishes to become "the queen of kisses," and her dream is realized; the next day she undresses and rushes out to the street and calls upon all of the youths of the town to enjoy her caresses. This orgy lasts all day, until she is killed by a soldier, who visits her that evening and has intercourse with her cold body. In "The Red-Lipped Guest" Lydia Rothstein, who prefers to be called Lilith, promises Nikolai Vargolsky that kisses from her vampire lips, which result in death, are sweeter than this life. Initially he yields to her, but before her last visit (on Christmas Eve), he resists and is saved by a radiant Youth. Other important erotic stories include "The Beloved Page" and "Lady in Bonds."

The erotic plays a similarly important role in Sologub's drama. The two-act *Loves* is Sologub's most intensive exploration of a Nietzschean morality in which everything is allowed. Apollon

Reatov returns from years of traveling to discover that his daughter has grown into a beautiful young woman. He declares his love for her; she replies that she loves him as well, and the play ends with them affirming their support for a new morality in which desire alone determines behavior. They thus fit in with Sologub's other positive characters, all of whom distinguish themselves by daring to approach the erotic differently from the masses.

Biography

Born Fedor Kuz'mich Teternikov in St Petersburg, March 1 1863. In 1882, he graduated from the Petersburg Teachers' Institute and spent the next eleven years teaching mathematics in provincial cities. While still in the provinces, he began publishing poetry in the journal *Severnyi vestnik* [*Northern Herald*], where his novel *Tiazhelye sny* [*Bad Dreams*] also appeared after his return to Petersburg in 1893. In 1894, his mother, Tat'iana Semenovna Teternikova, passed away; Sologub recalled that she frequently whipped him right up to her death. The publication of *Melkii bes* [*The Petty Demon*] in 1907 brought Sologub national fame and allowed him to retire from teaching. This same year his beloved sister Ol'ga died. In 1908, he married Anastasiia Chebotarevskaia; they had no children. For the next ten years he was a major figure in the Russian Symbolist movement and one of Russia's bestselling authors. After the revolution Sologub and Chebotarevskaia unsuccessfully attempted to emigrate to Europe; she committed suicide in 1921. In the 1920s he published little, mostly translations from French (Rimbaud, Verlaine). From 1923 on he occupied important posts in the Leningrad Writers' Union. He died in Leningrad, 5 December 1927 from myocarditis.

JASON MERRILL

Selected Works

Tiazhelye sny. In *Severnyi vestnik* (1895); as *Bad Dreams* translated by Vassar W. Smith, 1978.
Melkii bes. In *Voprosy zhizni* (1905); as *The Little Demon* translated by John Cournos and Richard Aldington, 1916; as *The Petty Demon* translated by Andrew Field, 1962 and Samuel Cioran, 1983.
"Milyi pazh." In *Vesy* (1906); as "The Beloved Page" translated by Murl Barker, 1977.

Liubvi. In *Pereval* (1907); as *Loves* translated by Jason Merrill, 2002.

"Tsaritsa potseluev." In *Pereval* (1907); as "The Queen of Kisses" translated by Murl G. Barker, 1977.

Tvorimaia legenda. In the almanacs *Shipovnik* 1907–1909; and *Zemlia* 1912–1913; as *The Created Legend* translated by John Cournos, 1916 and Samuel Cioran, 1979.

"Krasnogubaia gost'ia." In *Utro rossii* (1909); as "The Red-Lipped Guest" translated by Murl G. Barker, 1977.

"Dama v uzakh." In *Ogonek* (1912); as "The Lady in Bonds" translated by Murl G. Barker, 1977.

Further Reading

Baran, Henryk. "Fedor Sologub and the Critics: The Case of *Nav'i čary*" in *Studies in Twentieth-Century Russian Prose* (Stockholm Studies in Russian Literature 14). Edited by Nils Åke Nillson, Stockholm: Almquist and Wiksell, 1982.

Barker, Murl G. "Erotic Themes in Sologub's Prose." *Modern Fiction Studies*, 26/2 (1980): 241–248.

Christensen, Peter G. "Politics, Fantasy, and Sex in Fedor Sologub's *The Created Legend*." *New Zealand Slavonic Journal*, (1995): 77–91.

Ehre, Milton. "Fedor Sologub's *The Petty Demon*: Eroticism, Decadence and Time" in *The Silver Age in Russian Literature* (Selected papers from the Fourth World Congress for Soviet and East European Studies, Harrogate, 1990). Edited by John Elsworth, New York: St Martin's, 1992.

Greene, Diana. "Images of Women in Fedor Sologub." *Proceedings of the Kentucky Foreign Language Conference (Slavic Section)*, 4/1 (1986): 90–103.

Masing-Delic, Irene. *Abolishing Death: A Salvation Myth of Russian Twentieth-Century Literature.* Stanford, CA: Stanford University Press, 1992.

Merrill, Jason. "The Many 'Loves' of Fedor Sologub: The Textual History of Incest in His Drama." *Slavic and East European Journal*, 44/3 (2000): 429–447.

Pavlova, Margarita. "Iz tvorcheskoi predystorii 'Melkogo besa.' (Algolagnicheskii roman Fedora Sologuba) in *Anti-mir russkoi kul'tury*. Edited by N. Bogomolov, Moscow: Ladomir, 1996.

Peters-Carlson, Stephanie. "The Dichotomy of Lilith and Eve in Fedor Sologub's Mythopoetics." *Russian Literature* 18 (2000): 1–14.

Rabinowitz, Stanley J. "From the Early History of Russian Symbolism: Unpublished Materials on Fedor Sologub, Akim Volynsky, and Lyubov' Gurevich." *Oxford Slavonic Papers* 27 (1994): 121–143.

SOMATOPIA

By the Renaissance, metaphor was so common a strategy for dealing with sexual subjects that Pietro Aretino demanded that authors "speak plainly" and eschew "thy rope in the ring, thy obelisk in the Coliseum, thy leek in the garden, thy key in the lock, thy pestle in the mortar, thy nightingale in the nest, thy dibble in the drill, thy syringe in the valve," and "thy stock in the scabbard," for "otherwise thou wilt be understood by nobody."

British authors, however, largely ignored Aretino's advice, and took sexual innuendo to new heights, developing a very specific type of extended metaphor that would persist well into the nineteenth century. They created an entire erotic genre that presents women's bodies (or more accurately, a generalized female body) as a pseudo-geographic site of male pleasure: a utopian sexual landscape. These carefully constructed and, for the most part, fairly well developed conceits are somatopias, derived from the Greek soma (body) and topos (place). The term is innately ambiguous: a "body-place" could be either a place composed of a body, or designed for a body (as in providing bodily pleasure). Yet the term works both ways, since the places are simultaneously composed of female bodies and designed for male bodily satisfaction.

Examples of the genre include Thomas Stretser's 1741 *A New Description of Merryland*, in which "Captain Roger Pheuquewell" expounds at length on the relatively uncomplicated geography of Merryland, consisting of "a pleasant Mount called MNSVNRS" which "overlooks the whole country; and... round the Borders of Merryland is a spacious Forest which... seems to have been preserved for the Pleasure of Variety, and Diversion of Hunting." The only other features worth noting are two mountains, known as BBY, "which tho' at some Distance from

Merryland, have great Affinity with that Country, and are properly reckoned as at an appendage to it." Charles Cotton's 1648 *Erotopolis: The Present State of Bettyland* presents women as agricultural landscapes, demanding constant plowing and seeding; as game preserves ripe for hunting (although the animals here are a devious sort, and frequently ensnare the hunters); and as fortresses yearning to be conquered.

When males appear in somatopias, they usually take the form of a wandering penis in search of a warm refuge. In "The Geranium" (1789) for example, woman is the earth in which the "Tree of Life" must be planted. The poet shows young Susan his "Tree" and explains that it is like a geranium: blooming, falling, only to bloom again at a later date. Susan is of course enthusiastic, noting her own "tumultuous throbs of bliss?" and remarking that "Sure 'tis this tree that tempted Eve! / The crimson apples hang so fair, /Alas! what woman could forbear?" Similarly, *Mimosa: or, The Sensitive Plant* (1779) notes that although the penis/Mimosa has been planted in "many different soils....England, if not peculiarly, is at least happily adapted to the culture and use of it." Perhaps the most unusual (and mobile) phallus is that found in "The High-Mettled Peho": depicted as a thoroughbred horse, which runs "Full stretched, crossing, justling" over the female racetrack. Three times around is about all he can manage, however; then "weary'd, worn out, we behold Peho tame/ As he crawls of the course lifeless, jaded and lame."

The earliest British somatopias are relatively egalitarian and agricultural, employing the simplest of nature metaphors: women as fields to be plowed. Males, on the other hand, function as emblems of western culture, whose project is to tame nature. As men assumed more and more technological control, women were denatured, transformed into artifacts celebrating the glory of such cultural forces as domesticity, technology, law, and commerce: from metaphors for wild Nature, women become houses, factories, dungeons and banks. In "Banking," for example,

(1798) "Pudenda" is a "receiver, cashier," who "Always acts upon credit and honor," who, "When her customer's credits run low... takes their affairs in her hand." The poet marvels that the bank has not been crushed, given "the numberless drafts it doth take in," but "Mother Bank" has "bullion enough for them all." And in Robert Burns' 1793 "A Scots Ballad," the vagina becomes a dungeon. In Edinburgh, a new law has supposedly been enacted: "standing pr-cks are fauteurs [offenders] a,'" and must be imprisoned in the "dungeons deep" which "Ilk [every] lass has ane in her possession." The felonious phalluses must remain there until they "wail and weep... for their transgression."

DERBY LEWES

Selected Works

"Banking." *Hilaria, the Festive Board*. Ed. Charles Morris. London: n.p., 1798. 139–142.

Cotton, Charles. *Erotopolis: The Present State of Bettyland*. London: Thomas Fox, 1648.

"The Geranium." *The Pleasures, That Please on Reflection*. Selected from the Album of Venus. London: W. Holland, 1789. 35–38.

"The High-Mettled P—o." *Hilaria, the Festive Board*. Ed. Charles Morris. London: n.p., 1798. 14. L

Mimosa: or, The Sensitive Plant; A Poem. London: W. Sandwich, 1779.

"A Scots Ballad." 1793. *The Merry Muses of Caledonia*. Ed. James Barke and Sydney Goodsir Smith. Edinburgh: Macdonald, 1982. 52.

[Stretser, Thomas]. *A New Description of Merryland. Containing a Topographical, Geographical, and Natural History of That Country*. By Roger Pheuquewell [pseud.]. Bath: J. Leak and E. Curll, 1741. [London: Edmund Curll.]

Further Reading

Kolodny, Annette. *The Lay of the Land: Metaphor as Experience and History in American Life and Letters*. Chapel Hill, NC: University of North Carolina Press. 1975.

Lewes, Derby. *Nudes from Nowhere*. Rowman and Littlefield, 2000.

Parker, Patricia. *Literary Fat Ladies*. London: Methuen. 1987.

SONG OF SONGS, THE

The Song of Songs (also known as the *Song of Solomon* or *Canticles*) is a sequence of ancient Hebrew erotic poems that have been preserved in the canons of Jewish and Christian scripture. It is impossible to date the poetry with any precision, owing to its lack of specific historical references. Although the superscription to the book, "The Song of Songs which is Solomon's," associates it with King Solomon (who lived in the tenth century BCE), it is clear that the language of the poetry represents a much later form of Hebrew and that Solomon is not the author. A rough consensus among biblical scholars dates the book to the fourth or third centuries BCE. Its author or authors are anonymous.

Like nearly all ancient Hebrew poetry, the *Song of Songs* makes primary use of short parallel lines, which mostly occur in a sort of couplet form with the second line heightening, concretizing, or otherwise modifying the first; occasionally a third line is added to complement or extend the image or metaphor. Thus, to the two classically parallel lines in 6:4, "You are beautiful as Tirzah, my love, / comely as Jerusalem," is added a third line, "terrible as an army with banners" (citations are from the New Revised Standard Version, cited here and below by chapter and verse). Elsewhere the poetry of the Song of Songs exhibits a greater freedom than most ancient Hebrew poetry in relating the parallel lines. In 2:2 for example, as a male voice describes his female lover, the poet pairs a simile in the first line with its referent in the second: "As a lily among brambles, / so is my love among maidens."

The book alternates between a male and a female voice, with occasional interruptions by a female group voice (e.g., 5:9; 6:1) and a male group voice (e.g., 8:8–9). The main male and female voices represent two young, obviously unmarried lovers, who spend most of the poem expressing their erotic yearnings and describing each other's physical attractions in lush, sometimes hyperbolic imagery. Thus, a quote from the male voice: "Your breasts are like two fawns, / twins of a gazelle, / that feed among the lilies. // Until the day breathes / and the shadows flee, // I will hasten to the mountain of myrrh / and the hill of frankincense" (4:5–6). And from the female voice in 2:3: "As an apple tree among the trees of the wood, / so is my beloved among young men. // With great delight I sit in his shadow, / and his fruit was sweet to my taste." Despite the alternating voices of the lovers the poetry is not fundamentally dramatic—there is no overarching plot, and little narrative development—but rather remains squarely within the realm of lyric. As in the quotes above, much of the imagery is drawn from the natural world, and it often contains double entendres (e.g., "his fruit was sweet to my taste"; or "Let my beloved come to his garden, / and eat its choicest fruits" [4:16]).

One striking consequence of the alternation of female and male voices in the *Song of Songs* is an underscoring of the egalitarian nature of erotic love with regard to gender roles (see Trible, 144–165). The intermingling of voices disallows the gender stereotypes that would assign the active role of "lover" to the man and the passive role of "beloved" to the woman. The two voices are given roughly equal amounts of space in the book, each describes the body of the other, and each expresses the desire they feel for the other. This mutuality is exhibited also in the range of imagery with which the lovers are imagined: both lovers (not just the woman) are associated with the beauty and grace of doves, lilies, and fawns or gazelles; and both lovers (not just the man) are described in terms of power and strength, the man being associated with marble columns and cedar trees (5:15) and the woman with ramparts and towers (8:10).

The poetry of the *Song of Songs* is, for the most part, a wholly positive celebration of the pleasures of erotic love. Yet it does acknowledge, if only briefly, the dangers of Eros—dangers that arise from outside the erotic relationship and threaten the young lovers, as well as dangers inherent to the nature of eros itself.

With regard to the former, see especially 5:2–8, where the young woman imagines herself wandering the streets at night searching for her lover, only to be met and beaten by the "sentinels of the walls." With regard to the latter, see 8:6: "Set me as a seal upon your heart, / as a seal upon your arm; // for love is strong as death, / passion fierce as the grave. // Its flashes are flashes of fire, / a raging flame." Though thoroughly rooted in the body, Eros here takes on near-cosmic dimensions. The language of the body, elsewhere in the *Song of Songs* so positive, teeters in this instance on the brink of obsession. The passage represents a sort of crescendo to the book, offering for the first time a second order reflection on the nature of erotic love, even the metaphysics of Eros, rather than the first person declarations and descriptions that one encounters to this point.

Given that the Song of Songs is preserved as a part of Jewish and Christian scripture, the question is often asked, where is God in all this? In fact, God is never mentioned in the book. Nevertheless, for centuries complex allegorical interpretations, by both Jewish and Christian religious authorities, have prevailed in interpretations of the book. The alleged allegory takes the two young lovers as ciphers for God and humanity. In traditional Jewish interpretation, Israel is cast as the female lover and God as the male lover. For Christian interpreters the lovers of the biblical book are taken to refer variously to God and the church, or Christ and the individual soul, or even to Jesus and the Virgin Mary. Modern scholars have tended to dismiss these allegorical interpretations, since they so obviously do violence to the text's metaphorical meanings. But while it is true that such a mode of interpretation *spiritualizes* the *Song of Songs*, and thus tames its potentially subversive role in a Bible that has so often been taken as shoring up borders and fencing in sexuality, it is no less true, as Howard Eilberg-Schwartz has pointed out, that such interpretation *eroticizes* theological discourse, with potentially very radical results for doing theology.

A critical edition of the Hebrew text of the Song of Songs may be found in *Biblia Hebraica Stuttgartensia*. Standard biblical translations into English include the King James Version, the New Revised Standard Version, the Jewish Publication Society Version, and the New American Bible. Other notable translations that are freestanding—that is, not included in an edition of the Bible—include those of Marcia Falk (1993; *The Song of Songs: A New Translation*) and Ariel Bloch and Chana Bloch (1998; *The Song of Songs: A New Translation with an Introduction and Commentary*).

TOD LINAFELT

Further Reading

Alter, Robert. *The Art of Biblical Poetry*. New York: Basic Books. 1985.

Cohen, Gerson. "The Song of Songs and the Jewish Religious Mentality." In *Studies in the Variety of Rabbinic Cultures*. Philadelphia, PA: Jewish Publication Society, 1991.

Eilberg-Schwartz, Howard. *God's Phallus, and other Problems for Men and Monotheism*. Boston, MA: Beacon, 1994.

Fox, Michael. *The Song of Songs and the Ancient Egyptian Love Songs*. Madison, WI: University of Wisconsin Press, 1985.

Landy, Francis. *Paradoxes of Paradise: Identity and Difference in the Song of Songs*. Sheffield: Almond Press, 1983.

Linafelt, Tod. "Biblical Love Poetry (... and God)," *Journal of the American Academy of Religion* 70:2 (2002): 323–345.

Trible, Phyllis. *God and the Rhetoric of Sexuality*. Philadelphia, PA: Fortress, 1978.

Turner, Denys. *Eros and Allegory: Medieval Exegesis of the Song of Songs*. Kalamazoo, MI: Cistercian, 1995.

SOREL, CHARLES

1602–1674
French eclectic writer

Histoire comique de Francion

Frank Sutcliffe argues that on one level *Francion* is an expression of the problems of the old provincial nobility as it confronts the new nobility of the court. Sorel's Francion is a young, sometimes poor provincial nobleman, a little like D'Artagnan. Francion goes to Paris for his education, but suffers at the hands of the foppish court nobles. Significantly, though, he is still honored by the king.

Francion also suffers from the antequated teachings of his Sorbonne professors, and this expresses the sentiments of the seventeenth-century libertines (the likes of Theophile de Viau and Saint-Amant), who favored the new science of Galileo and the like against the old, Aristotelian knowledge of the schools.

Francion would not be at home in this volume, however, if his libertinage were purely scientific or philosophical. In the opening section he seeks to seduce the beautiful Laurette, a castle steward's wife, while for her part she is content to take instead the robber who happens to be the first man up the ladder.

In his noble quality, Francion judges an *épreuve du congrès*, in which a peasant proves his ability to have intercourse with his wife, and does so before a large crowd.

Later in a country inn, Francion hears the stories of the Elderly Agathe, an enlightened libertine prostitute and procuress in early Paris. Unlike some fictional prostitutes, she enjoys her work. Her companions urge her to play hard to get with the customers. However when she meets a young Englishman, he is so "handsome and blond" that "I would have had to be prouder than a tigress to withold anything."

Francion, in turn, recounts a really remarkable dream, full of pre-Freudian sexual symbolism. Unlike the typical dream of early modern literature, coherently foretelling events to come

in the rest of the story, Francion's dream is "without reason and without order." Sorel adds that "you know that all dreams are thus, just made up of "this and that."

Francion's dream places him in a boat with a leak that he stuffs with his penis—not without a feeling of superiority toward other men whose penises are too small to stop the leaks in *their* boats. He visits the sky, where he finds the gods dragging stars across the heavens with ropes and pullies. He visits a kind of temple of lost hymens, including Laurette's, and he sees and tries to touch Laurette, who turns out to be encased in a form-fitting glass sheath. And much more like that.

Francion is befriended by Raymond, a nobleman he has known in the past but does not recognize. Raymond frightens Francion: Francion did something bad in the past and will be judged severely. But then Raymond leads him to meet four noblemen and five charming girls. They decide he shall be judged by Laurette, who enters from another room. Raymond explains: "I sent for your Laurette, so that if you still love her, her presence will bring you joy, and not only that, I brought these five girls, one of whom is my own Helene, so that you can choose; these four noblemen are among the finest of the country, and the most worthy of your company...."

There follows a sort of good-natured orgy. In the midst of the celebrations, Francion proposes to invent new and more genteel language to talk about sexual intercourse. When Raymond objects that noble people make love just like peasants and might as well use the same language they do, Francion replies that "we do it in a different way; we use many more caresses than they do... they do it just with the body, and we do it (Descartes?) with body and soul together...."

Everyone begs Francion to invent this new language. Sorel adds that "women principally approved of his reasoning, since they would be happy to have new words to express the things they liked the best...."

Francion—whose approach to sex is original—promises to oblige, and "Moreover, he swore that as soon as he had time, he would compose a book of the practice of the most exquisite games of love"—a project at that time without precedent in the Occident, but which was to be realized in France in succeeding decades by Michel Millot (*L'Ecole des filles,* 1655; q.v.) and Nicolas Chorier (*L'Académie des dames,* 1660?; q.v.)

Biography

Born in Paris, perhaps towards 1600, Charles Sorel published his masterpiece, the *Histoire comique de Francion.,* in 1623. Before and after he wrote in many genres—poems, other novels (notably *Le Berger extravagant,* which seeks to do for the pastoral novel what *Don Quixote* did for the novels of chivalry, essays on *La Science universelle,* speaking machines, surveys of the books available in his time (*Bibliothèque française, De la connaissance des bons livres*),

games—and seemingly every other imaginable subject.

HERBERT DE LEY

Editions

Sorel, Charles. *Histoire comique de Francion,* in *Romanciers du XVIIe siecle,* Pléiade. Paris: Gallimard, 1958 and ss. See the preface and bibliography of Sorel's works by Antoine Adam (pp. 16–34; 1343–1347).

Further Reading

De Vos, Wim. *Le Singe au miroir... romans comiques de Charles Sorel.* Tübingen: G. Narr, 1994.

Howells, Robin. *Carnival to Classicism. The Comic Novels of Charles Sorel.* Tübingen: Biblio 17, 1989.

Leiner, Wolfgang. "Le Rêve de Francion...," *La Cohérence intérieure. Studies... Judd D. Hubert,* ed. J. Van Baelen and David L. Rubin. Paris: J.-M. Place, 1977.

Sorel, Charles. *L'Anti-roman ou l'Histoire du berger Lysis.* Paris, 1633–1634 [revised version of Sorel's *Le Berger extravagant;* the other most erotic work of Charles Sorel is *L'Orphise de Chrysante,* 1626].

Sutcliffe, Frank. *Le Réalisme de Charles Sorel.* Paris: Nizet, 1965.

SOUTHERN, TERRY AND MASON HOFFENBERG

Southern, Terry

1924–1995
American novelist and screenwriter

Mason Hoffenberg

1922–1986
American writer and editor

Candy (Terry Southern and Mason Hoffenberg, writing as Maxwell Kenton)

After the Paris publisher Maurice Girodias approved an outline of the adventures of "a sensitive, progressive" girl from Racine, Wisconsin,

Southern asked the help of Hoffenberg, but seems to have written most of *Candy* himself. Though published in 1958, *Candy* anticipates and mocks the American aesthetic and social idealism that would flower in the 1960s. Targets include sexual freedom, academia, psychoanalysis, medicine, television, bohemianism, spiritualism, and Zen Buddhism, all of which are subjected to raucous but rarely mean-spirited humor. Modeled on Voltaire's Candide, the naive protagonist, Candy Christian, misconstrues the lecherous overtures of a succession of comic characters in her search for meaning. Persuaded that her widowed father does not "need" her, and yearning to help humanity, Candy writes a paper extolling "selflessness" as a precept. Her professor, Mephesto, promptly urges his "needs" on the girl, who recoils. When she discovers Mephesto cavorting nude with a male student, she blames her own reluctance to "share her beauty," and resolves to make amends by giving herself to her father's poor Mexican gardener, who "needs" her more. Discovered in bed with the naked Candy, Emmanuel the gardener in panic cleaves with his shovel the skull of Candy's father, effectively lobotomizing the hapless Mr. Christian. Candy is comforted by her father's twin brother, Jack Christian, and his randy wife Livia, whose fascination with Candy's voluptuousness vies with the narrator's own fixation on "the darling girl's" genitals. Livia reads aloud a television script about an encounter between a battle-shocked soldier and a repressed female patient that prefigures events in *Candy*, but the scene is almost swamped by the madcap pacing that animates the narrative. Chaos erupts when Jack attempts to seduce his niece in her father's hospital room: Candy's catatonic father disappears, while a nurse mistakenly puts an unconscious Jack in his brother's bed. Candy's nubile innocence destabilizes a hospital teetering on the verge of sexual lunacy. Dr. Krankheit, who prescribes masturbation as therapy, treats another doctor in a rocket-countdown sequence climaxed by ejaculation, then masturbates himself while inserting acupuncture needles into the naked Livia. The distraught Candy herself flees Racine for New York.

The novel's language veers between Candy's predictable liberal homilies on the downtrodden and the epithets she screams during intercourse ("Fuck! Shit! Piss! Cunt! Cock! Crap! Prick! Kike! Nigger! Wop!"); the latter scandalized liberal and conservative audiences alike. When a retarded hunchback from the Greenwich Village streets attracts the girl, her sympathy leads inevitably to intercourse. Her orgiastic cries—"Give Me Your Hump!"—passed for a time into American idiom. Searching for the wandering hunchback, Candy allows Dr. Howard Johns, a demented gynecologist, to give her a pelvic examination in the bathroom of a Greenwich Village bar to test her "clitoral reflexes." Their exertions destroy a toilet, whose overflow creates pandemonium in the bar. Police arrest Johns and Candy, but when one of the officers attempts to molest the naked girl, their car crashes into a gay bar, whose patrons riot. Candy is rescued from this melee by Pete Uspy,

from the Cracker Foundation, a spiritualist cult. Uspy sends her to a Foundation commune in Mohawk, Minnesota; on the way, she dreams that her father needs her. Candy succumbs to the commune's leader, Grindle, who takes charge of her "spiritual advancement," a series of naked, comically-rendered erotic exercises that leave Candy convinced she is pregnant. Grindle hastily sends her off to Tibet. At a stop-over in Calcutta, Candy receives a letter from Aunt Livia telling her that her father is still missing. Feeling superior to materialistic American tourists, Candy is moved by the sight of a nearly naked "holy man" encrusted with filth. Days later, in Lhasa, relieved by the onset of her period, she resumes her own spiritual quest. As she seeks shelter from rain in a Buddhist temple, she finds there the same holy man she saw in India. Lightning strikes the temple. A statue of Buddha, falling against her, its giant nose pressing into her anus, leaves her vagina impaled on the holy man's penis. Motifs—incest, religion, delusion, obsession—rush together. As rain pouring through the ruined temple washes the dung from the holy man's face, Candy, wide-eyed as always, cries, "Good Grief—It's Daddy!"

More parable than parody, *Candy* is both an erotic novel and a send-up of the genre. More whimsical than satirical, it is as much about the resilience of innocence as it is about the persistence of sexual hypocrisy. Candy, though constantly beset, is never victimized; she enjoys her own sexual reactions, though she mistrusts them. The novel's disdain for realism permits narrator and reader alike to be amused by Candy's rationalizations of the pleasure she takes in being ravished.

Biographies

Southern was born May 1, 1924 in Alvarado, Texas. He left Southern Methodist University (1942–1943) to enlist in the Army. Discharged, he attended the University of Chicago and Northwestern University, graduating from the latter in 1948. The GI bill enabled him to study at the Sorbonne in Paris, where he met expatriates who wrote erotica for Maurice Girodias's Olympia Press. Later celebrated for novels such as *The Magic Christian* and *Blue Movie*, Southern achieved greater fame for screenwriting *Dr. Strangelove*, *The Loved One*, *Barbarella*, and *Easy Rider*. Southern married Pud Gadiot

(1953–1954) and Carol Kauffman (1956–1972) before living with Gail Gerber (1964–1995). He had one son, Nile (b. 1960). He died October 29, 1995 of cancer in New York. Mason Hoffenberg was born in 1922 in New York. He also used the GI Bill to live in Paris, where excellent French earned him a job as an editor for Agence France-Presse. Hoffenberg wrote two other "dirty books" for Olympia Press, *Sin for Breakfast* (as Hamilton Drake) and *Until She Screams* (as Faustino Perez). He was married to Couquitte Faure, with whom he had two children, adopting her first by another marriage. He died June 1, 1986 of lung cancer in New York.

JOSEPH SLADE III

Selected Works

Candy. With Southern and Hoffenberg writing under the pseudonym Maxwell Kenton, Traveller's Companion # 64, Paris: Olympia Press, 1958; retitled to counter a police ban two months after publication as *Lollipop*; again as *Candy*, Paris: Olympia Press, 1958; New York: Putnam, 1964; New York: Dell, 1964; New York: Lancer, 1964; North Hollywood, CA: San Diego, CA: Brandon House, 1964; Greenleaf Classics, 1964; New York: Grove Press, 1996; London: Bloomsbury, 1997; screen version 1968

Southern

Flash and Filigree. London: Andre Deutsch, 1958; New York: Grove Press, 1996; London: Bloomsbury, 1997.
The Magic Christian. London: Andre Deutsch, 1959; New York: Grove Press, 1996; London: Bloomsbury, 1997.
Writers in Revolt. Edited with Richard Seaver and Aexander Trocchi, New York: Frederick Fell, 1962.
Red Dirt Marijuana and Other Tastes. New York: New World, 1967; New York: Grove Press, 1996; London: Bloomsbury, 1997.

Blue Movie. New York: New World, 1970; New York: Grove Press, 1996; London: Bloomsbury, 1997.
Texas Summer. New York: Little Brown, 1992.
Virgin. With Perry Richardson. London: A Publishing Company, 1995.
Now Dig This: The Unspeakable Writings of Terry Southern, 1950–1995. Ed. Nile Southern and Josh Alan Friedman, New York: Grove Press, 2001.

Selected Screenwriting Credits

Dr. Strangelove. 1964.
The Cincinnati Kid. 1965.
The Loved One. 1965.
Casino Royalle. 1967.
Barbarella. 1968.
Candy. 1968.
Easy Rider. 1969.
The Magic Christian. 1970.

Hoffenberg

Sin for Breakfast (as Hamilton Drake). Paris: Olympia Press, 1957.
Until She Screams (as Faustino Perez). Paris: Olympia Press, 1956; New York: Olympia Press, 1969.

Further Reading

St. Jorre, John de. *Venus Bound: The Erotic Voyage of the Olympia Press and Its Writers*. New York: Random House, 1996; (aka *The Good Ship Venus*, London: Hutchinson, 1994.
Hill, Lee. *A Grand Guy: The Art and Life of Terry Southern*. New York: Harper Collins, 2001.
Plimpton, George. "The Quality Lit Game: Remembering Terry Southern." *Harper's Magazine*, 303: 1815 (2001): 71–76.
Sawyer-Laucanno, Christopher. *The Continual Pilgrimage: American Writers in Paris. 1944–1960*, New York: Grove Press, 1992.

SPENSER, EDMUND

c. 1552–1599
English poet

Edmund Spenser was the greatest non-dramatic poet of the Elizabethan age. His style is richly descriptive and intensely allusive, with images often carrying multivalent meanings. Of special relevance here are certain key passages of his epic *The Faerie Queene*. Some of these relate also to parts of *Colin Clouts Come Home Againe* and *The*

Fowre Hymnes, and to his personal celebration of love and desire in the *Amoretti* and *Epithalamion,* written for his second marriage.

The Faerie Queene

Spenser's epic is a formal allegory of great complexity, set in a Faerie Land which partly mirrors and is adjacent to his and our own historical continuum. Only six of the twelve books originally planned were completed. Each presents the knightly quest of a specific virtue. These cross with the journey of the future King Arthur, who has come into Faerie Land to find his love, the Faerie Queene herself, Gloriana, Elizabeth's royal analogue. In his introductory *Letter to Sir Walter Raleigh,* Spenser states that, 'The general end therefore of all the booke is to fashion a gentle man or noble person in virtuous and gentle discipline': his subject is the whole fallen human condition and the delighted fulfillment of each aspect of its moral and spiritual potential. The energies of love and lust are polarized as vital elements of this schema, appropriately to the register of each Book. In Book I, *Of Holinesse,* they center especially on the juxtaposition of Duessa, spiritual corruption espressed in sexual terms, with Una, truth, the 'blisful ioy' (I xii 41) of whose eventual marriage to her champion Redcrosse, Saint George, the English Church, Everyman reveals its divine opposite. A number of patterns are established in Book I that will recur throughout the poem, and these apply to the handling of erotic imagery and reference among other foci. First, that the negative should appear before the positive and so arouse the reader's desire for the latter; the disturbing and chaotic sensuality of the House of Pride (I iv) is counteracted by the House of Holiness and its gracious inhabitants (I x). Again vice, here specifically the negative aspects of eroticism, may appear either deceptively attractive, like the evil Duessa, or immediately repulsive, like Lust in the procession of the Sins (I iv). Virtue is never disguised, though like Una's loveliness, veiled in mourning black, its full revelation may be gradual.

In I. i.-ii the crucial separation of Redcrosse and Una, traveling to deliver her parents' kingdom from the Dragon, is effected by sexual deceit: the sleights of the wicked magician Archimago. The reader sees the whole action, and so cannot be deceived, unlike Redcrosse,

who is first tempted with erotic dreams of sickly sweetness:

> And made him dream of loues and lustfull play. That nigh his manly hart did melt away, Bathed in wanton blis and wicked ioy. (I i 47)

There follow graphic visions of Una as seductress and harlot. Leaving her in a jealous fury, Recrosse meets Duessa, whose over-rich adornments of scarlet and gold at once suggest her archetypal identity of the Whore of Babylon (Rev 17), and are characteristic of the false glamour of evil elsewhere in the poem. He becomes her sexual prey, in the House of Pride and later, until she betrays him to her lover the Giant Orgoglio. Una meanwhile is saved from the lust of the Saracen Sansloy by the 'wyld woodgods' (I vi 9 ff), whose innocent worship of her establishes an important and recurring motif of the whole poem: the progression from instinctive to fully rational virtue. Later Una meets Prince Arthur, Redcrosse is rescued, and at Una's bidding Duessa is revealed in her true monstrous shape, to which sexual revulsion gives special force:

> That her misshaped parts did them appall, A loathly wrinckled hag, ill- fauoured, old, Whose secret filth good manners biddeth not be told (I viii 46).

This horror, like Redcrosse's faults and weaknesses, is corrected in the House of Holiness. Here Charissa, Charity with her many children, appears as love gloriously and physically fulfilled:

> Full of great loue, but *Cupids* wanton snare As hell she hated, chaste in worke and will; Her necke and breasts were euer open bare, That ay thereof her babes might sucke their fill. (I x 30)

Book II is *Of Temperaunce,* and the schemata introduced in Book I are redeployed accordingly to express degrees and nuances of excess and deficiency on the one hand and on the other the poise of the titular virtue itself, the golden mean. Erotic imagery and association play an important, often very subtle part. Early in his quest to destroy the wicked enchantress Acrasia Sir Guyon encounters two of her victims. Mordant was one of her lovers, rescued by his wife Amavia from 'drugs of foule intemperance' only to die when Acrasia's parting spell cast on him takes effect. Amavia stabs herself before Guyon can prevent her. The erotically romantic description is ironic—tragedy is displaced by self-indulgence:

> In whose white alabaster brest did sticke A cruel knife, that made a grisly wound. From which forth gusht a streme of gorebloud thicke...(11 i 39)

Guyon has no Lady, his companion and counselor is an aged Palmer, but in the course of his journey he encounters two feminine representatives of his own virtue, and the reader a third. In Canto ii Medina's 'gracious womanhood' is thrown into relief by the undisciplined lewdness of her sisters, and in Canto ix the beauty of Alma, the chaste soul governing her castle, the temperate body, is expressed in terms of sexual desirabilty; 'woo'd of many a gentle knight.' In Canto iii the reader first encounters Belphoebe: a virgin huntress whose exquisitely detailed beauty startles the reader into perceptive admiration, and the base Bragadoccio into attempted rape, decisively foiled: contrasting reactions that are perfectly calculated.

These passages are set against specific negatives. In Canto vi Guyon is distracted from his quest by the 'light behauior and loose dalliance' of Phaedria, whose pretty silliness will later be recognized as offering a dangerous stage on the way to Acrasia's Bower of Blisse itself. In Canto vii Guyon is offered the hand of Philotime (ambition), whose 'glistering glory,' like that of Duessa, is merely 'counterfetted shew.' The central theme is developed through recurrent glimpses of Acrasia's Bower: Amavia's agonized account in Canto i of her husband 'In chaines of lust and lewd desires ybound' is expanded in Canto v, when Atin goes to fetch Acrasia's latest lover, Cymocles, to the help of his brother, who has been wounded by Guyon. Here we learn that Acrasia, like Circe before her, transforms her discarded lovers 'to monstrous hewes,' appropriate to their loss of human rationality.

As the loveliness of the Bower is described it becomes clear that lust is merely one, almost metaphorical, aspect of its destructive power. Cymocles in a flowery arbour whose art, significantly is 'striving to compare' with nature, is surrounded by 'loose Ladies and lascivious boyes,' with naked and half-naked 'Damzels fresh and gay' striving in every way for his attention. It is his 'idle mind,' not his body that responds:

> He, like an Adder, lurking in the weeds, His wandering thought in deepe desire does steepe, And his fraile eye with spoyle of beautie feedes...
>
> Whereby close fire into his heart does creepe: So them deceiues, deceiu'd in his deceipt, Made drunke with drugs of deare voluptuous receipt (II v 34)

The emphatic reiteration of Amavia's reference to 'drugs' is revealing. Acrasia's enchantments affect the mind, the rational faculty, of any given victim according to their specific sensual weaknesses, that of Cymocles being sloth.

This is made explicit in Canto xii, describing the voyage of Guyon and the Palmer to the Bower of Blisse. They pass many perils, including the Gulf of Greediness and the Quicksand of Unthriftyhed as well as Phaedria, in her 'little skippet' 'faining dalliance and wanton sport,' and the mermaids singing so sweetly that Guyon is almost beguiled. They are attacked also, by sea-monsters, and foul birds and, as they land by wild beasts: all former lovers of Acrasia. The Porter of the Bower is the false Genius of the place, who charms those who enter with 'semblaunts sly,' drawn from their own minds. He has no power over Guyon, who passes on with the Palmer in to the Bower itself. The almost stifling beauty of the place is exemplified by the vine-grown arbour of Excesse, where golden fruit is hung among those from which she squeezes the wine that Guyon refuses, and by the fountain, wreathed in 'lascivious armes' of gold enamelled ivy. Here 'Two naked Darnzelles' play seductively. Guyon pauses,

> Them to behold, and in his sparkling face
> The secret signes of kindled lust appeare,

but he is recalled to himself by the Palmer. They come at last to the 'secret shade' where Acrasia lies with her new lover, Verdant:

> And all that while, right ouer him she hong,
> With her false eyes fast fixed in his sight,
> As seeking medicine, whence she was stong,
> Or greedily depasturing delight...
> And through his humid eyes did sucke his spright,
> Quite molten into lust and pleasure lewd...

This vampiric image makes the same point as Marlowe's Faustus when the succubus in Helen's shape kisses him:

> Her lips suck forth my soul: see where it flies! (1. 1330, 1604 ed.)

1251

Even Acrasia's 'vele of silk' is a spiderish entrapment:

> More subtile web *Arachne* cannot spin.

Guyon captures Acrasia and razes her Bower: her beasts are restored to human shape by the Palmer. The regret felt for the utter destruction of all that has been so tempting described is calculated to arouse longing for such loveliness uncorrupted: this will be satisfied in Canto vi of the following Book.

Books III and IV, of Chastity and of Friendship, have a continuous though complicated narrative line. Their joint subject is love: universal and human. The divine impulse to create is presented in terms of erotic delight in the Garden of Adonis (III vi) as is the continuum of that creation in the Temple of Venus (IV x) and its fulfillment in elemental concord in the Marriage of the Thames and the Medway (IV xi–xii). The narrative lines explore human love in its different aspects, positive and negative, and its part in the individual's growth to maturity and self-awareness as their adventures are involved in the universal allegories. The Knight of Chastity is the British Princess Britomart, who has fallen in love with a vision of her destined husband, Artegall, in Merlin's mirror, and who has come into Faerie Land to find him: they meet in iv–vi, and their narrative runs on through much of Book V. Her own virtue dictates that Britomart should encounter and defeat its enemies. Florimel, whose transcendent beauty acts on every male who sees her according to his nature, good or ill, first appears in Canto i. Only Marinell, whom she loves, is indifferent to her, until his awakening into adulthood at the end of Book IV. The stories of Belphoebe and her twin Amoret present compementary aspects of femininity, properly fulfilled in comradeship and marriage respectively.

Britomart's first adventure occurs in Canto i, when she comes to the Castle Ioyeous; a place of purely sensual delight, rich in deliciously erotic tapestries and 'superfluous riotize.' Its inhabitants, like Britomart herself are young: 'Damsels' and 'Squires';

> And *Cupid* still emongst them kindled lusfull fires.

Their Lady, Malecasta, deceived by Britomart's knightly armour, goes to her by night, and the resulting tumult brings her attendant knights, to find,

> ...the warlike Mayd All in her snow-white smock, with locks vnbound, Threatening the point of her auenging blade...

The whole episode accesses a register close to that of Chaucerian comedy. Ma1casta's temptations are primarily to folly and self-indulgence. Their fashionable manifestations in the outer circles of Elizabeth's own court are satirised in *Colin Clouts Come Home Againe:* 11 762–792. They are dangerous nonetheless: Britomart is slightly wounded by Gardante's arrow in the ensuing fracas before she arms herself and goes on her way.

Early in Canto i, Prince Arthur and his squire Timias saved Florimel from a forester intent on rape: Arthur follows her, and Timias remains behind, to vanquish the forester and his companions in Canto v. He is gravely wounded, but rescued by Belphoebe. In the Prologue to this Book we are told that Belphoebe is a mirror of the Queen's 'rare chasti tee' in his own world: her appearance here gives the opening for Spenser's account of her birth and upbringing in Faerie Land in Canto vi. She and Amoret are twin daughters of the virgin nymph Crysogone, begotten by the sun's rays. They are found by Venus, searching for her son Cupid with Diana's reluctant help. The goddesses agree each to foster one of the babes: Diana takes Belphoebe and Venus' Amoret.

The Garden of Adonis, to which Venus takes her charge, is in every way the counter to Acrasia's corrupted Bower. Its Porter is the true Genius:

> He letteth in, her letteth out to wend,
> All that to come into the world desire.

The Garden itself is that aspect of the Creator's mind in which substance is drawn from Chaos and given forms, passing each into time in due succession. The central image is that of joyous love. Here,

> Frankly each paramour his leman knows. In 'the middest of that Paradise' is Venus' Mount, where the Goddess, as substance, delights in her Adonis, .'..the Father of all forms,' and: Possesseth him and of his sweetnesse takes her fill.

After many adventures, in Canto ix Britomart comes with the false knight Paridell to Malbecco's house for a night's shelter. Paridell seduces Malbecco's young wife Hellenore, using all the arts of the Ovidian sophisticate, as spilling his wine, and,

...therein write to let his loue be showne,
Which well she red out of the learned line.

They elope, and Pari dell deserts her. She wanders through the forest, and is rescued by a group of Satyres (x 36ff). Malbecco follows after, and finds her with them, entirely happy in her new life. The episode is almost an inverted mirror to that of Una's sojourn with the wood-gods in I vi. Hellenore's Satyres entertain her with garlands, and music and dancing and tireless sex. She refuses to return with her husband, and that she is content to abandon full humanity for unthinking sensuality is Spenser's sole condemnation of her. Malbecco, jealous, mean, possessive, fares far worse, pining in 'selfe-murdring thought' until he becomes *Gealousie* itself.

Britomart has no contact with this intrigue. She leaves at dawn, before the elopement takes place. Presently, in Canto xi, as she is riding through the forest, she comes upon a knight 'all wallowed Vpon the grassy ground,' his shield, with Cupid's picture as its device, and his armour all cast from him as he lies there weeping. This is Sir Scudamour, who tells Britomart that his Lady, Amoret, has fallen into the power of Busirane, an evil enchanter:

Whilest deadly torments do her chast brest rend,
And the sharpe steele doth riue her hart in twain,
All for she *Scudamour* will not denay.

Britomart's response Scudamour's rather theatrical dispair is briskly practical: she catches his horse, helps him on with his discarded armour, and acompanies him to Busirane's House. Its doors are blocked by flames and sulphurous smoke. Scudamour cannot pass through, but Britomart does.

The House is mysterious, threatening as an evil dream which resonates on many levels of consciousness differently shared between at least the three main characters. Certain clues as to what may Busirane's real nature are given in retrospect in the following Book. Here Britomart passes into the first chamber. No-one is there: only heavy tapestries, where the interwoven gold shows, 'Like a discolord Snake.' (Canto xi 28 ff). These depict the metamorphoses of the Gods into swan and bull, Centaur, and grapevine and many other shapes in pursuit of their loves. As with Acrasia's victims, such change is itself a degredation, as is made explicit by the inscription beneath the statue of Cupid at the far end of the room: *Vnto the Victor of the Gods this bee.*

Britomart goes on into the second chamber, richly adorned with 'warlike spoiles,' like Scudamour's cast-off armour, of kings and heroes in whom love 'wrought their owne decayes.' Again, all is silence and 'wastefull emptinesse.' Then Britomart sees written round the room, 'Be Bold,' and over an iron door at the end, 'Be not too bold.' She is puzzled, but the reader should not be: these are the inscriptions found in *Mr. Fox's* frightful Castle in the savage English analogue to Bluebeard. Night falls at the opening of Canto xii, and presently a trumpet sounds, heralding a frightful storm. At last there enters from the last door the Masque of Cupid himself: a procession of all the trials and cruelties he can inflict. He is mounted on a lion, and wears no blindfold, the better to see and delight in the agonies of Amoret, who is led before him by Despight and Cruelty:

Her brest all naked, as net iuoryoo.
And a wide wound therein (O ruefull sight)
Entrenched deepe with knife accursed keene...
At that wide orifice her trembling hart
Was drawn forth, and in siluer basin layd,
Quite through transfixed with a deadly dart,
And in her bloud yet steeming fresh embayd.

The procession circles the room three times, and returns as it came, leaving the question of how, since he could not enter the House, Scudamour had such specific knowledge of Amoret's sufferings. Their description also recalls the death of Amavia, (II i), though Amoret is not dead but entrapped in nightmare. The details of her apparent torment however reveals the procession as a horrible parody of the Grail procession of the Arthurian romances: a spiritual sickness perceived through phantasmagoric sado-masochism.

The day passes, and when at night the door opens again, Britomart enters the last room (xii 29 ft). There is no sign of Cupid or his Masque, only Amoret, bound to a 'bras en pillour.' Before her sits Busirane himself: 'Figuring straunge characters of his art' in the blood that drips,

...from her dying hart,
Seeming transfixed with a cruell dart,
And all perforce to make her him to loue.
Ah who can loue the worker of her smart?

The question is not merely rhetorical, as appears later. Britomart springs forward and smites Busirane to the ground, but Amoret prevents her from killing him, since only he can cure her pain. Britomart forces him, '...his charmes backe to reuerse,' and as he does so Amoret's chains fall away, and her wound is healed. As they leave the House with the captive Busirane it falls into empty desolation.

The Book has two endings. In the 1590 edition of Books I–III they rejoin Scudamore; he and Amoret embrace as though, '...they had beene that faire Hermaphrodite,' and Britomart, seeing them, '...wisht like happinesse.' In the 1596 edition of Books I–VI Scudamour has left, dispairing of their return, and Busirane disappears from the story.

In Book IV Canto i Britomart escorts Amoret as they go in search of Scudamour, but first we are told the circumstances of Amoret's abduction.

Amoret 'neuer ioyed day' since Scudamour first won her, in circumstances to be detailed in Canto x, for at her wedding feast, '...before the bride was bedded,' Busirane,

> Brought in that mask of loue which late was showen:
> And there the Ladie ill of friends bestedded,
> By way of sport, as oft in maskes is knowen,
> Conveyed quite away to liuing wight unknowen.

Amoret's agony in the House can be seen as virginal fear exacerbated to near insanity, with Busirane as the embodiment of her terror: her vision or sexual perception of Scudamour himself. Although his Masque is a phantom, a projection of perverse imaginings, the enchanter is something more. Britomart defeats her own enemy as well as Amoret's tormentor, and reaches her own maturity as she does so.

Most of the manifold adventures recounted in Book IV deal in different ways with strife or misunderstanding and their reconciliation. In Canto x Scudamour has occasion to describe his wooing of Amoret in' the place of peril': the Temple of Venus. The account is his own, not the narrator's. He passes its guardians and comes to a marvellous garden where fond lovers and true friends consort in bliss. In the temple itself is Venus' androgynous statue, veiled and with the tail-biting serpent of eternity about her feet, and about her, 'A flocke of litle loues.' Here are,

> Great sorts of louers, piteously complaining...
> As euery one had cause of good or ill.

One sings a hymn, closely derived from the opening of Lucretius' *De Natura Rerum*, praising the Goddess as,.'.the root of all that ioyeous is' throughout the natural order, and above all for her gift of sexual desire to birds and beasts and men, by which the cycle of creation begun in the Garden of Adonis is sustained in time. This theme recurs and is elaborated in *Colin Clouts Come Home Againe,* 11.793–893 and in the *Hymne of Loue.* At the feet of the statue is Amoret, surrounded by all the meeker feminine virtues. Scudamour siezes her hand, 'Like warie Hynd within the weedie soyle,' and leads her away dispite her tears and protests. What follows from this brash wooing the reader already knows. The contrast with the warmth, wit, and delicacy of *Amoretti,* written for Spenser's future wife, is marked.

Cantos xi and xii describe the Marriage of the rivers Thames and Medway: a marvelously sustained metaphor for that concord of the physical elements which is yet another aspect of the power of divine love. Here gather all the world's rivers, praised for their fish, and for their fertile land and the cities that link them with human history. This celebration becomes the context for the new-found love of Florimell and Marinell, so that elemental concord is expressed also on the human scale.In his *Epthalamion,* 11 37–72, Spenser makes a very similar point, invoking the nymphs of river and mountain to deck and attend his Lady for their wedding.

In Book V Artegall is the Knight of Justice. Unlike Holiness, Temperance and Love itself, Justice, necessary only in a fallen world, cannot easily appear delightful, least of all through erotic attraction, and the ills Artegall faces are too obvious to need hightening by more than occasional faint of sexual repulsion.

Book VI was the last to be completed. Its subject, Courtesie, will be defined by the poet himself in his pastoral persona of Colin Clout as the .'..skill men call Ciuility' (x 23): the art of living in human society. As such it impinges naturally on sexual mores and their violation: the brutal pride of Crudor and Briana in Canto i, for example, and the sexual arrogance for which Mirabella does penance in Cantos vii-viii. The quest of its Knight, Calidore, is to render harmless the Blatant Beast: that is malicious slander, and his narrative is interwoven with a number of others.

There are two episodes in which the diversified themes of the book are ritualistically concentrated through erotic imagery and association. The first is negative. In Canto viii Serena, separated from her Lord, Calepine, falls asleep in the forest and is captured by cannibals. Then,

> Vnto their God they would her sacrifize,
> Whose share, her guiltlesse bloud they would present,
> But of her dainty flesh they did deuize
> To make a common feast, and feed with gourmandize.

They watch her sleeping, and, .'..with their eyes the daintiest morsels chose,' while their priest prepares fire, vessels, and garlands. The cannibals strip Serena naked, and it becomes clear that not only hunger excites them:

> Those daintie parts, the dearlings of delight,
> Which mote not be prophan'd of common eyes,
> Those villains vew'd with loose lasciuious sight...

This base confusion of appetites expresses the nadir of social order. It is only their priest who restrains them from rape. They build an altar of turf and deck it with flowers, and at nightfall, as the priest raising his sacrificial knife, 'Gan mutter close a certaine secret charme' they shout to the barbaric sounds of bag-pipe and horn. The noise brings Calepine upon them. He rescues Serena with great slaughter of her tormentors. The rituals of cannibalism are an inversion of human decency at all levels: here specifically those of hospitality, sexuality and religious order, but they indicate it as being still human, not merely bestial. Neither is the behavior of the cannibals obsessive, like that shown in Busirane's house. Anyone might be their victim.

Recollection of the prurient emphasis given to Serena's helpless nakedness sharpens the positive shift of focus in the second episode: the Vision of the Graces. In Canto ix Calidore has come to the Valley of the Shepherds, where he falls in love with Pastorella. There he lingers, and in Canto x comes one day upon Venus' lovely mountain, Acidale. There in her sacred glade he sees,

> And hundred naked maidens, lilly white,
> All raunged in a ring, and dauncing in delight.

Their music is the piping of Colin Clout: Spenser's own persona. In their midst dance the Graces themselves, showering their gifts upon Colin's own beloved, as they do in *Epithalamion,* 11. 103–109. Sacramental love in that other very personal context is a part of their dance, as the mysteries of the marriage bed belong to Venus herself, whose sons, .'..little winged loues' (1 357) flutter round it as they do about her Temple's statue. The vision beheld on Acidale is expounded in universal terms of 'Ciuilitie.' The Graces are naked, being,.'.. without guile, Or false dissemblaunce.' They are desireable, not as an erotic end in itself, but as their 'gracious gifts' are to be desired, 'Which decke the body or ad orne the mynde.' They move so that,

> ...two of them still froward seem'd to bee,
> But one still towards shew'd herself afore:
> That good should from vs goe, then come in greater store.

Their dance replays the cycles of creation, generation and love at the highest level of human order. For these expanding perceptions erotic delight has been a triumphant metaphor throughout the epic, resonant above a full awareness of its perversions.

Biography

Born in London in or around 1552: educated at the Merchant Taylors' School from 1561 and Pembroke Hall, Cambridge from 1569: BA 1573, MA 1577. Secretary to John Young, Bishop of Rochester in 1578. He began *The Shepheardes Calender,* his first original published work, while still at Cambridge: it appeared in 1579. In the same year he married his first wife, Macabyas Childe, the date of whose death is unknown. He was by then in the service of the Earl of Leicester, but left to take up the post of private secretary to Lord Grey, the newly appointed Lord Deputy of Ireland. He remained in Ireland for the greater part of his life. There he held a number of posts, civil and military. In 1589, he was granted the manor of Kilcolman, in Cork, where much of his greatest poetry was written, including most of his epic *The Faerie Queene,* dedicated to Elizabeth I, to whom he presented Books I–III before their publication in 1590. He was rewarded with a pension of £50 a year, at that time a respectable income. He married his second wife, Elizabeth Boyle, for whom he wrote the sonnet sequence *Amoretti* and the *Epithalamion,* in 1594. In October 1598, Kilcolman was burned in the Tyrone rebellion. Spenser escaped with his family to Cork, and was subsequently sent to London with dispatches, where he fell ill and died, January 16, 1599.

ELIZABETH PORGES WATSON

Editions

The Poetical Works of Edmund Spenser, ed. J.C. Smith and E. de Selincourt. Oxford University Press, 1912.

Works...A Variorum Edition. Ed. E. Greenlaw, C.G. Osgood and F.M. Padelford, Baltimore, 1932–1957.
The Faerie Queene. Ed. Thomas P. Roche, Jr. Penguin Books, 1978.

Further Reading

Cavanagh, S.T. *Wanton Eyes and Chaste Desires, Female Sexuality in The Faerie Queene.* Bloomington and Indianapolis, 1994.
Paglia, C. *Sexual Personae.* London, 1992.
Reale, E. *The Faerie Queene: A Reader's Guide*, Cambridge University Press, 1987.
Roche, Thomas P. Jr. *The Kindly Flame: a Study of the Third and Fourth Books of Spenser's 'Faerie Queene.'* Princeton, NJ, 1964.

STENDHAL

1783–1842
French novelist

Stendhal was the author of several novels, numerous short stories, various autobiographical writings, a large amount of non-fictional philosophical and historical writings, and many essays, articles, and letters. However, in terms of erotic writing, and literary critical success, his most interesting works are his novels, both finished and unfinished. Love was the predominant concern of Stendhal's life, thoughts, and writing. In his early years he was a dedicated pupil of the Ideologue Destutt de Tracy, and was greatly influenced by his ideas about the relationship between man and society. Following his example, he attempted to analyze the emotion of love scientifically in the non-fictional essay *De l'Amour* [*Love*], published in 1822. In this work, he separates love into four distinct categories: *amour passion* [*passionate love*], *amour-goût* [*mannered love*], *amour physique* [*physical love*], and *amour de vanité* [*vanity-love*]. Dismissing physical, or sexual, love as a purely sensual experience, he focused mainly upon the other three types of love, matters for the mind and soul. *Amour passion* is true love, an ideal that Stendhal presents as

man's ultimate aim, although only attainable in reality by a privileged few. It is natural and spontaneous, transcending social constraints and allowing lovers to experience a superior state of being. In contrast, the remaining two forms of love, *amour-goût* and *amour de vanité*, are presented as artificial, imitated emotions, the product of human vanity. A crucial element of Stendhal's philosophy was the conflict between nature and society; socialization is presented as restrictive and harmful to man's natural instincts, in particular destroying spontaneity, or what Stendhal termed 'énergie.' Throughout his work, he is highly critical of nineteenth-century French society, claiming that it has created a country of false, dull, artificial people, governed by vanity rather than passion; this he contrasts to Italy, a country he fell in love with, he claims, due to its 'natural' passion and spontaneity.

The opposition of the different types of love can be seen to guide and influence Stendhal's fictional writing. This is particularly evident in one of his most successful novels, *Le Rouge et le noir* [*Scarlet and Black*]. In this novel the protagonist, Julien Sorel, is presented with a choice between two very different women. For the motherly figure, Mme de Rênal, he experiences *amour passion*, although initially his social ambition prevents him from appreciating the true value of this passion. He moves to Paris, where he comes to experience *amour de vanité* for the aristocratic, masculine, Mathilde de la Mole. Julien's seduction of Mathilde enables him to achieve his dreams of social success; their relationship is flawed, however, in that they cannot relate to each other openly on an emotional level. Mathilde's love for Julien is essentially based on his feigned emotional immunity; if at any point Julien reveals the true nature of his love to Mathilde, she loses interest in him. At the height of Julien's success, a defamatory letter from Mme de Rênal provokes him into the rash act of attempting to shoot her. In prison, separated from the social pressures of the outside world, Julien comes to experience the full joy of his *amour passion* for Mme de Rênal, with whom he is reunited, and rejects Mathilde's attempts to save him. The novel ends with his execution, which is presented less as a tragedy than as a welcome escape from the mundane world which, through *amour passion*, Julien has already transcended.

This narrative structure, focused around two types of love and two types of women, is repeated in Stendhal's other major successful novel, *La Chartreuse de Parme* [*The Charterhouse of Parma*]. This novel is set in Italy, the land of spontaneous passions. The hero, Fabrice, is loved passionately by his aunt, the celebrated Gina Sanseverina, whose existence revolves around the social realities of life at court: the focus of her passion for Fabrice is thus to promote his social and material success. Fabrice, however, being one of Stendhal's emotional elite, prioritizes spiritual matters over worldly concerns. He rejects his aunt's love in favor of a deep *amour passion* for Clélia Conti, a passion that is almost religious in its strength and devotion. As with Julien, this passion develops while Fabrice is in prison in the Farnese tower, high above the world and cut off from the social maneuvering and politics taking place below. Another of Stendhal's protagonists, Lucien Leuwen, also experiences this divide of passions, his *amour passion* for Mme de Chasteller being contrasted with the passion he feigns for Mme Grandet. The crucial element of *amour passion*, in all of Stendhal's novels, is its complete independence from social considerations. Social obstacles prevent the fulfilment of the lovers' passion: only once they have overcome these obstacles can they achieve the state of total bliss associated with Stendhalian true love.

As Stendhal specifies in *De l'Amour*, this blissful *amour passion* is a spiritual and mental attraction: sexual attraction is not only unimportant but irrelevant. This is made explicit in Stendhal's final novel, *Lamiel*. Dispassionately, in a purely scientific quest for knowledge, the heroine pays her father's servant to relieve her of her virginity. Unlike typical romantic descriptions of such episodes, Stendhal is cold, clinical, and brutally factual. Lamiel herself expresses complete disillusionment, unable to understand why society assigns such a basic animal act so much importance. This disillusionment has been considered to mirror that of Stendhal himself, who, in the autobiographical *La Vie de Henry Brulard* [*The Life of Henry Brulard*], dismisses the long-awaited loss of his virginity in a couple of lines, a meaningless event which he claims to have forgotten. Love, for Stendhal, is a purely spiritual affair. It has been suggested by many critics that the dissociation of physical and emotional love in Stendhal's works is the result of his own obsession with his mother, the barrier of incest preventing further development of this emotional attachment in his mind.

An interesting aspect of Stendhal's writings is that not one of his heroines retains her virginity, although, with the exception of Lamiel, the actual episodes of defloration are implied rather than described in detail. Refreshingly, for Stendhal the loss of the heroine's virginity is neither over-romanticized nor the first step on the path to her doom: it is presented simply as a natural progression of her love for the hero. Indeed, in a reversal of traditional sexual power relations, it is often the Stendhalian heroine who offers herself to her lover: Mathilde declares herself to Julien and invites him to her room, Clélia comes to Fabrice's cell, Lamiel controls and directs all of her sexual relations with men and the heroine of one of his shorter stories, Vanina Vanini, not only offers herself to her lover, but socially disgraces herself of her own accord. The creation of these 'masculine' heroines has often been praised by feminists, and is complemented by the feminization of many of the male protagonists, whose actions are driven by their emotions rather than their ambition or intellect. This traditionally 'feminine' quality is praised by Stendhal, and marks his protagonists out as superior in their fictional world, capable of reaching the heights of *amour passion*. Definitions of masculinity and femininity thus play an important role in his fiction, particularly in his first novel, *Armance*, where the hero, Octave, feels inadequate for the male role assigned him by society, resulting in his psychological impotence.

Stendhal's fiction can thus be seen as an exploration of, and a challenge to, conceptions of love, sex, and sexuality in nineteenth-century French society. Stendhal accurately predicted that his ideas would not be appreciated by his contemporaries, and the fact that most of his success was indeed posthumous demonstrates the radical nature of some of his views.

Biography

Born Marie-Henri Beyle, in Grenoble, January 23, 1783. Educated at the École Centrale de Grenoble, 1796–1799; then moved to Paris to take the entrance exam for the École polytechnique, but renounced this idea in favor of writing. In 1800, Beyle began working for the Ministry of War; in October of that year he was called up to the 6th regiment of the dragoons. However, he hated military life and in 1802 he returned to Paris, where he dedicated himself to reading and attending the theater. In 1806, he accompanied Martial Daru to Germany, entering Berlin behind Napoleon. He participated in the campaign in Vienna in 1809, and in 1810 returned to Paris, where he was given an administrative role. In 1814, Paris was taken by the Allies, and, unable to find employment after the fall of the Empire, Beyle left France to settle in Italy where he wrote his first works, *l'Histoire de la peinture en Italie* and *Rome, Naples et Florence*, which were published in 1817, the latter being the first work to be published under the pen name Stendhal. In 1821, he returned to Paris and made a name for himself in the salons. Following the 1830 revolution he was appointed consul at Trieste and in the small port of Civitavecchia. From then until his death on 23 March 1842, he spent large periods of time living in various Italian cities and returning to Paris as often as his duties allowed.

SARAH F. DONACHIE

Selected Works

De l'Amour. 1822; edited by Victor Del Litto, Paris: Éditions Gallimard, 1980; as *Love*, translated by Gilbert and Suzanne Sale, Harmondsworth: Penguin, 1975.

Armance: ou quelques scènes d'un salon de Paris en 1827. 1827; edited by Jean-Jacques Labia, Paris: GF Flammarion, 1994; as *Armance: a novel*, translated by C.K. Scott Moncrieff, London: Soho Book Co., 1986.

Le Rouge et le noir: Chronique du XIXe siècle. 1830; edited by Pierre-Georges Castex, Paris: Garnier, 1973; as *Scarlet and Black: a chronicle of the nineteenth century, translated by Margaret R. B. Shaw, Harmondsworth: Penguin, 1953*.

La Chartreuse de Parme. 1839; edited by Ernest Abravanel, Levallois-Perret: Cercle du Bibliophile, [1969]; as *The Charterhouse of Parma*, translated by Margaret R.B. Shaw, Harmondsworth: Penguin, 1958.

Lucien Leuwen. 1855; edited by Anne-Marie Meininger, 2 vols, Paris: Imprimerie Nationale, 1982; as Lucien Leuwen, translated by H. L. R. Edwards and edited by Robin Buss, Harmondsworth: Penguin, 1991.

Lamiel. 1889; edited by Victor del Litto, Évreux: Cercle du Bibliophile, [c.1971]; as *Lamiel*, translated by T. W. Earp, Norfolk, Conn.: J. Laughlin, [c.1952].

La Vie de Henry Brulard. 2 vols, 1890; edited by Victor del Litto, 2 vols, Levallois-Perret: Cercle du Bibliophile, 1968; as *The Life of Henry Brulard*, translated by John Sturrock, London: Penguin, 1995.

Chroniques italiennes. 1960; edited by Béatrice Didier, Paris: GF Flammarion, 1977.

Further Reading

Berthier, Philippe. *Stendhal et la Sainte Famille*. Genève: Droz, 1983.

Blin, Georges. *Stendhal et les problèmes du roman*. Paris: J. Corti, 1983.

Bolster, Richard. *Stendhal, Balzac, et le féminisme romantique*. Paris: Lettres modernes, 1970.

Brombert, Victor. *Stendhal: fiction and the themes of freedom*. New York: Random House, [c.1968].

Crouzet, Michel. *Nature et société chez Stendhal: La révolte romantique*. Lille: Presses Universitaires de Lille, 1985.

Pearson, Roger. *Stendhal's Violin: A Novelist and His Reader*. Oxford: Oxford University Press, 1988.

Pearson, Roger (editor). *The Red and the Black* and *The Charterhouse of Parma*, London: Longman, 1994.

Sangsue, Daniel (editor). *Persuasions d'amour: Nouvelles lectures de 'De l'Amour' de Stendhal*. Geneva: Droz, 1999.

Waller, Margaret. *The Male Malady: Fictions of Impotence in the French Romantic Novel*. New Brunswick, NJ: Rutgers University Press, 1993.

STRETZER, THOMAS

d. 1738
English poet and novelist

The Natural History of the Frutex Vulvaria, or Flowering Shrub and Arbor Vitae; or, The Natural History of the Tree of Life

In 1732, two humorous pieces of erotica, *Arbor Vitae* and *The Natural History of the Frutex Vulvaria* were published, which contained detailed descriptions of the nature and functions of the male and female sexual organs. Published under the pseudonym "Philogynes Clitorides," *The Natural History of the Frutex Vulvaria, or Flowering Shrub* has been ascribed to Stretser. The vagina is described as a shrub:

> The *Frutex Vulvaria* is a flat low Shrub, which always grows in a moist warm Valley, at the Foot of a little Hill, which is constantly water'd by a Spring, whose Water is impregnated with very saline Particles, which nevertheless agree wonderfully well with this *Shrub*.

Arbor Vitae was originally published as a poem and frequently emulated. It was regularly reprinted along with prose, or with *Natural History of the Frutex Vulvaria.* The prose version of *Arbor Vitae* was written under the pseudonym of "Roger Pheuquewell," and has been ascribed to Stretser. The work was a skit on the *Catalogus Plantarum* complied by Philip Miller, known and respected gardener of the day. The penis is described as the tree of life:

> *Arbor Vitae, or the Tree of Life,* is a succulent Plant; consisting of one straight Stem, on the Top of which is a *Pistillum,* or *Apex....*Its *Fruits,* contrary to most others, grow near the Root; they are usually no more than two in Number.

In this material, botanical metaphors for genitalia were used to question scientific ideas circulating during the early eighteenth century. Although presented as titillating bawdy facetiae, these texts conveyed a certain set of attitudes towards the body and expose underlying assumptions about male and female sexual behavior. Written as ribald humor, it satirised questions on generation, degeneration, and venereal disease which were current amongst the medical elite. Scathing attacks were made on the *virtuosi* and their new botanical notion of attaching gender to plants. As such, this erotica was a weapon parodying debates already taking place on scientific and medical issues.

A New Description of Merryland

Written under the pseudonym of "Roger Pheuquewell," in *A New Description of Merryland,* the country was depicted as a woman's body:

> Near the Fort is the Metropolis, called CLTRS [clitoris]; it is a pleasant Place, much delighted in by the Queens of MERRYLAND, and is their chief Palace, or rather *Pleasure Seat*; it was at first but small, but the Pleasure some of the Queens have found in it, has occasion'd their extending its Bounds considerably.

A New Description of Merryland (1741) and *Merryland Displayed* (1741) provided erotica in the form of analogies between the body, nature, and landscape. An earlier example can be seen in Charles Cotton's Ετόπλι, *The Present State of Betty-land,* (1684) which undoubtedly influenced Stretser's work. This erotica created "other worlds" in which the terrain is defined as the female body, a mini-cosmos.

Both the Renaissance cosmic view of man and medical analogies of women/nature depicted the body as a metaphor for the cosmos. Stretzer's erotica used the same ploy to describe the sexualized body constructing sexual parables wholly in terms of metaphorical ribaldry. These scenes were loaded with agricultural metaphors, pelagic allegories, and classical allusions producing the image of the landscaped body as a minicosmos. This use of the human body to describe the workings of the world was an ancient trope, the classical tradition of the erotic landscape and garden continued to resurface. Women's bodies become a euphemistic landscape; hills become breasts, caves become vaginas, and shrubs become pubic hair.

A *New Description of Merryland* (1741) (an updated and modernized version of Ἐρoτóπoλiς, *The Present State of Betty-land*) and *Merryland Displayed* were reprinted in a collection of erotic works entitled *Potent Ally*. This new description of Merryland parallels the themes and style of seventeenth-century Bettyland but it has moved on from agricultural descriptions of the farmer and his land. The analogies more reflective of the wider world setting of coasts and topography with explicit anatomical terminology defining the female body. This time the analogy was extended to depict a woman's body as a whole continent, with its own government, religion, canals, tenures and coastal surveys. Merryland sits in "a *low* Part of the Continent, bounded on the upper Side, or the Northward, by the little Mountain called MNSVNRS [Mons Venerus], on the East and West by COXASIN [left hip] and COXADEXT [right hip], and on the South or lower Part it lies open to the TERRA FIRMA."

In the stance of a gynecological exploration, Merryland and "its Divisions and principal Places of Note" is investigated, with specific explorations of the clitoris and the hymen. Doubts surface around the detectability of the hymen. In *Merryland*,

> Another part of the Country, often mentioned by Authors, is HYM [hymen], about which there has been great Controversies and Disputes among the Learned, some denying there was ever such a Place, others positively affirming to have seen it.

Seduction is described as a battle:

> At the End of the great Canal toward the *Terra Firma*, are two Forts called LBA [labia], between which every one must necessarily pass, that goes up the Country, there being no other Road. The Fortifications are not very strong, tho' they have *Curtains, Hornworks,* and *Ramparts;* they have indeed sometimes defended the Pass a pretty while, but were seldom or never known to hold out long against a close and vigorous Attack.

A *New Description of Merryland* mentions sodomy only to dismiss the subject as disagreeable; "I shall leave the Affair of the *Antipodes* to those who have a *Taste* that Way; only shall observe, there are some People who very

preposterously (as I think) give the Preference to the PDX [podex]." The text addresses problems of both venereal disease and the production of too many children. Condoms are advocated as protection against disease rather than as a contraceptive measure. The narrator advises "always to wear *proper cloathing,* of which they have a Sort that is very commodious, and peculiarly adapted to this Country; it is made of extraordinary fine thin Substance, and contrived so as to be all of one Piece, and without a Seam, only about the Bottom it is generally bound round with a scarlet Ribbon for Ornament."

Merryland Displayed

Written in the style of a mock critique of *A New Description of Merryland,* Stretser probably wrote *Merryland Displayed* spurred on by Curll in an attempt to cash in on further sales and publicity. Curll published at least two editions of *Merryland Displayed* in 1741. *Merryland Displayed* states that *New Description of Merryland* went through seven editions in three months it was so popular "besides some Thousands of pirated Copies that were sold in the Town and Country."

Biography

Little is known about the life of Stretser (sometime known as Stretzer) apart from that he was a hack employed by the notorious pornographer, Edmund Curll, to write some of his publications. As with many writers of pornography in the eighteenth century, there is a question about whether he wrote everything ascribed to him.

In a literary context, Stretser was among those who developed a form of erotica containing botanical and agricultural analogies in which landscapes were depicted as a woman's body. These "other worlds" displayed anatomical details while depicting both classical and contemporary images of landscapes and gardens. Within these erotic settings, genitalia are described in botanical euphemisms; the penis described as "the tree of life," the vagina as the "flowering shrub," the woman's body as a geographical terrain, a country called *Merryland*.

JULIE PEAKMAN

Editions

It should be noted that Curll was well-known for using false imprints, including false dates and "borrowing" the names of respectable publishers.

The Natural History of the Frutex Vulvaria, or Flowering Shrub. London: W. James, 1732; London: E. Hill 1741.

Arbor Vitae Or, The Natural History of the Tree of Life. London: W. James, 1732: London: E. Hill 1741: London, E. Curll, 1741.

A New Description of Merryland. London: Curll, 1741: 4th edition, Bath: W. Jones, 1741: 5th edition, Bath: W. Jones, 1741: Bath: J. Leake, 1741; 6th edition, Bath: J. Leake, 1741; London: E. Curll, 1741: 8th edition Bath: J. Leake, 1741.

Merryland Displayed, Or Plagiarism, ignorance and impudence detected.

Being observations upon a pamphlet intitled [sic] *A New Description of Merryland*. A satirical pseudo-criticism of the work written previously by himself. London, E. Curll, 1741: Bath: J. Leake, 1741.

Potent Ally, or The Succours from Merryland. London, Curll, 1741.

Further Reading

Boucé, Paul Gabriel. "Chronic and Pelagic Metaphorization in Eighteenth Century English Erotica." *Eighteenth Century Life*, No. 9, 1984—1985.

Boucé, Paul-Gabriel. "The Secret Sex Nexus: Sex and Literature in Eighteenth Century Britain." In Alan Bold (ed.) *The Sexual Dimension in Literature*, London: Vision Press Ltd, 1983.

Kearny, Patrick, J. *A History of Erotic Literature*. London: Macmillan, 1982.

Peakman, Julie. "Medicine, the Body and the Botanical Metaphor in Erotica." In Kurt Bayertz & Roy Porter (eds.), *From Physico-Theology to Bio-Technology*, Rodopi B.V., Amsterdam—Atlanta, 1998.

Straus, Ralph. *The Unspeakable Curll*. London: Chapman and Hall, 1927.

Thompson, Roger. *Unfit for Modest Ears: A Study of Pornographic, Obscene and Bawdy Works Written or Published in England in the Second Half of the Seventeenth Century*. London: Macmillan, 1979.

SUN WEI

C. tenth century
Chinese author

Biographies of Goddesses

Most, if not all, of the six stories about divine women that make up the collection entitled *Shennü zhuan*, and ascribed to the rather obscure author, Sun Wei, are to be found nearly verbatim in the great compendium of stories completed during the Taiping era (976–983), the *Taiping guangji* [*Extensive gleanings of the Reign of Great Tranquility*], which devotes twenty-five chapters out of five hundred to stories related to gods or goddesses. The first biography has but its title changed, the second one, quoted by Robert van Gulik not even that: *Wanruo* is the name of an elder sister-in-law on the husbands side; she acts as a medium for the goddess. The *Taiping guangji*, chapter 491, gives its sources: the *Han Wu gushi* (ancient stories about Emperor Wu of the Han dynasty, reigned 140–187 BCE), a sort of fictional romance of Taoist inspiration, popular in the period when Zhang Zu's novelette, *Visiting the Fairy Cave*, was written. The text of the *Han Wu gushi* which came to us is likely to be a garbled version.

The other story, partially translated by van Gulik, is the third one in the collection; it too has been copied from the above-mentioned compendium, at the end of chapter 295, under the title *Liu Ziqing*; the source is given as the *Bachao qiongguai lu* [*Records of Fathomless Strangeness From Eight Dynasties*], a lost work by an unknown author living at the beginning of the seventh century. Some ten pieces of it survive, copied or quoted in various compendia, half being rather elaborate stories about encounters with goddesses. The original text is slightly shortened and the title changed into *Kang wang miao nü* [*The Girls From the Temple of King Kang*]. Liu Ziqing is the name of a poor scholar who received the visit of two girls in their teens. They come every ten days to make love with him, both of them, for years, till he discovers their figures among the nearby temple statues.

The idea that a divine woman, a goddess, could have cured General Huo Quping by having sex with him, instead of depleting him as a demonic woman would have (fairy-fox with or without nine tails, etc.) may testify to a common belief rather than clearly reflect the influence of the handbooks of sex and their theories about Yin supplementing Yang during sexual intercourse properly mastered. Is not the reversal of what is commonly believed extraordinary enough to make a good story?

Biographies of Goddesses is included in several collections of Tang fiction published in the eighteenth and early nineteenth centuries. The work was taken as genuine until recently and more research would be needed to ascertain the time of the forgery.

Several of its pieces do belong to a period close to the time of composition of Zhang Zu's *Visiting the Fairy Cave,* vindicating van Gulik's point about this closeness. We may as well quote his excellent summary of *Wanruo:*

> The second story relates that the Han Emperor Wu used to make sacrifices to a female deity on the Po-liang Terrace. When his famous general Huo Quping fell ill, the Emperor advised him to go and pray to this deity for recovery. She appeared before the general in the shape of a beautiful girl and invited him to have intercourse with her. He refused indignantly. Then his illness grew worse, and shortly afterwards he died. Thereupon the goddess revealed to the Emperor that the general had been failing in Yang essence. She intended to supplement this with her Yin essence and his refusal brought about his death.

Biography

Sun Wei probably lived in the early tenth century. While *Biographies of Goddesses,* compiled from ancient pieces no later than the eighteenth century, has long been attributed to him, none of it is likely to be of his composition.

ANDRÉ LÉVY

Editions

Tangdai congshu. 1806, Taipei 1968 (reproduction), p. 620–624.

References and Further Reading

Gulik, Robert van. *Sexual Life in Ancient China, A preliminary survey of Chinese sex and society from ca. 1500 B.C. till 1644 A.D.* Leiden, E.J. Brill 1961, p. 208–210.

SURREALISM

From the time of its foundation in 1919 in France, the Surrealist movement responded to the trauma of the First World War through an active endeavour to bind desire with human creativity. It did so through poetry (Paul Eluard, André Breton), the pictorial arts (Salvador Dali), and cinema (Louis Buñuel) amongst other art-forms. While Surrealism must be seen in the context of the politics of the avant-garde movements of the time, in particular the Dadaist movement as founded by Tristan Tzara in 1916 in Zürich, it can also be read partly as a response to the rationalist philosophical tradition in France with its insistence on will as a primary ordering factor in human life. Contrary to this philosophy, Surrealism took as one of its main objects the promotion of eroticism, in all of its forms, and the reinvention of the arts through an immense confidence in desire and the breaking of taboos—both in literary and philosophical terms.

The word "surrealism" in all probability stems from Guillaume Apollinaire's 1918 theatrical farce les *Mamelles des Tirésias* [*Breasts of Tiresias*] (1964), which was subtitled "une drame surréaliste." The word itself was then adopted by the self-proclaimed official leader of the Surrealist movement: the writer and poet André Breton.

In 1924, Breton pushed the movement into the public domain with the publication of the Manifeste du surréalisme, in which the main tenets of surrealism were outlined. The 'manifeste' presented the idea that the subconscious mind could be accessed through a form of automatic writing, a procedure of non-revisionist writing enacted under a semi-hypnotic state, in which language would simulate as well as regenerate the use of dreams as a valid springboard for artistic revolt and subsequent liberation.

In spite of the inner contradiction inherent in ruling out the poet's reasoning faculties during moments of creativity—the so-called automatic process—the Surrealists saw their practice in the light of an imaginative role-play rather than an attempt to mimic earlier symbolist practices and discourses. According to them, it was within the nature of believing in simulation as a creative process in its own right that the erotic could be privileged as the most effective way to temporarily move out of a restrictive and bourgeois way of life. Despite differences amongst the Surrealists in terms of how they wrote on the erotic, most efforts shared a fascination with the prohibition of desire in bourgeois society, the random divisions between reason and madness, and an affirmative faith in the poetic qualities of the unconscious.

More than any other Surrealist of the 1920s and 1930s, André Breton's literary output extended the main tenants of surrealism, whilst at the same time focusing on the erotic and romantic aspects of the urban environment that formed the backdrop for most Surrealist fiction.

In *Nadja* (1928), Breton's chance encounters with a woman of the same name constitute the acknowledged meeting of the fantastical and the irrational with the erotic attributes of the female, usually through a series of meetings mysteriously connected to Breton's own independent wanderings through Paris. As such the erotic for Breton, and for other members of the surrealist group—in particular Louis Aragon and the poet Paul Eluard—was fundamentally linked to a belief in the supernatural and fantastical properties of the signs and portents that guide the "urban flaneur" (see *Baudelaire*) through the urban landscape. While these signs and portents may be of an overtly fetishistic nature, Nadja's gloves for example, they are also often the very

locations in which sexual behavior is unleashed from its bourgeois trappings. Hence the arcades and parks of nineteenth Century Paris become erotically charged due to their convenience as places for prostitution and secret rendevous.

The linking of the erotic aspects of the Surrealist romance with a nostalgia for a form of life prior to the twentieth century, not only feeds into the unattainable quality of the female figure but becomes one of the prerequisites for Breton's desired "amour fou" (lending its name a later Breton romance: *L'Amour fou* (1936) as well). In one of Breton's earlier artistic collaborations, with the surrealist Philippe Soupault: *Les Champs magnétiques* (1921) the feminine is equated with the hysterical and the irrational in ways influenced by Freudian principles of sexuality by way of a deeply romanticized vision of insanity as a viable revolt against the bourgeois code of rationalism. According to Breton and Soupault the actual sources of *Les Champs magnétiques* were accounts given by mental patients at the Saint-Dizier hospital in 1916 combined with extensive readings of Freud's theories on sexuality. Thus while madness is celebrated in both eroticized and poetic terms it also, in line with Surrealist politics, refers to the anguish of survivors of World War I.

In this respect, Surrealism's attitude to the erotic and to women in particular may appear intrinsically flawed by its paradoxical relationship to reason, but the Surrealists nevertheless unashamedly promulgated the disavowal of rationality and saw love as demarcated precisely in these terms. Partly due to its uncompromising stance on the issue of rationalism vis-à-vis contemporary politics (disagreements regarding their various Communist affiliations also caused problems) the Second World War saw a lessening of the surrealist impact on literary and intellectual life as Existentialist thought entered the arena in France and elsewhere. During the 1970s, 1980s, and 1990s interest on Surrealism resurfaced; for example on the impact of female Surrealists in what was traditionally considered a predominantly male field.

CAROLINE BLINDER

Selected Works

Les Champs Magnétiques. 1921.
Le Libertinage. 1924.
Les Pas perdu. 1924.

Aragon, Louis. *Le Paysan de Paris*. 1926 (*Paris Peasant* translated by Simon Watson Taylor, Boston: Exact Change, 1994).

Soupault, Philippe. *Les Derniérs Nuits de Paris*. 1928 (*Last Nights of Paris* translated by William Carlos Williams, Cambridge: Exact Change, 1992).

Breton, André. *L'Amour fou*. 1936 (*Mad Love* translated by Mary Ann Caws, Lincoln: University of Nebraska Press, 1988).

Breton, André. Nadja, 1928 (*Nadja* translated by Richard Howard, New York: Grove Press, 1960).

L'immaculee conception. 1930.

Les Vases communicants. 1932.

La vie immediate. 1932.

Les Marteau sans maître. 1934.

Une semaine de bonté. 1934.

Further Reading

Bate, David. *Photography and Surrealism: Sexuality, Colonialism and Social Dissent*. London: Tauris, 2004.

Breton, André. *Manifestoes of Surrealism*. Translated by Richard Seaver and Helen R.Lane. Ann Arbor: University of Michigan Press, 1972.

Caws, Mary Ann. *Surrealist Painters and Poets—An Anthology*. Edited by Mary Ann Caws, Cambridge: M.I.T. Press, 2001.

Chénieux-Gendron, Jacqueline. *Surrealism*. Translated by Vivian Folkenflik, New York: Columbia University Press, 1990.

Eluard Paul, André Breton and Philippe Soupault. *The Automatic Message, The Magnetic Fields, and The Immaculate Conception*. Translated by David Gascoyne, New York: Grove Press, 1997.

Matthews, J.H. *Surrealism, Insanity and Poetry*. New York: Syracuse University Press, 1982.

Pierre, José. *Investigating Sex, Surrealist Research 1928—1932*. Edited by José Pierre and translated by Malcolm Imrie with an afterword by Dawn Ades, London: Verso, 1992.

Rosemont, Franklin. *What is Surrealism? Selected Writings*. Edited and with an introduction by Franklin Rosemont, London: Pathfinder, 2001.

SUSANN, JACQUELINE

1918–1974
American author and actress

Jacqueline Susann was widely derided in her lifetime as a hack writer of trash, and her best-selling work has only recently been acknowledged as a major influence on popular erotic literature. An actress turned writer, Susann never had pretentions to literary refinement; but her novels combined sincerity, compelling narratives, and an almost anthropological eye for detail in order to explore the varieties of human sexuality. The extraordinary success of her books brought to a mass audience subjects found (and perhaps better handled) in more recondite erotica, thus allowing greater visibility to erotic literature as a whole in American and Anglophone culture. In fact, it is hard to overestimate Susann's importance in mainstreaming erotic themes for popular literature.

Valley of the Dolls

Jacqueline Susann's first published novel, *Valley of the Dolls* (1966), was a *roman à clef* that followed the lives of three successful career women working in the entertainment business that Susann knew so well, concentrating on their experiences of love, sex, and drugs. Its core theme is innocence corrupted. The protagonist is Anne Welles, an innocent whose progress through romance, sexual knowledge, and ultimately to drug abuse forms the central plot of the book. Her story is intertwined with those of her friends Neely O'Hara, a worldly entertainer who ultimately betrays her, and Jennifer North, a blonde bombshell with a lesbian past. Their adventures permit Susann to present a conspectus of sexual attitudes and mores from 1944 to 1966 with the starkness of a medieval morality play. In successive scenes, *Valley of the Dolls* addresses a series of sexual "issues" (e.g., abortion, divorce, homosexuality, pornography, etc.) within a compulsively readable narrative that makes the reader suspend disbelief. One of the remarkable features of *Valley of the Dolls* is its relatively sympathetic treatment of women in lesbian relationships—these romantic and idealized figures are in sharp contrast to the haunted, guilt-ridden lesbians found in the work of Susann's contemporaries. In general, *Valley of the Dolls* treated sexual relations with a frankness and matter-of-factness that provided much of the book's appeal. Although it is certainly not as sexually explicit as other writings available at the time, its then-unusual combination of sex and drugs, the voyeuristic thrill of its *roman à clef* aspects and a shrewdly orchestrated marketing campaign made *Valley of the Dolls* one of the bestselling and most widely distributed novels of all time.

The Love Machine

Susann followed the success of *Valley of the Dolls* with *The Love Machine* in 1969. With its male protagonist, absence of lesbian subplot, and "happy ending," it is somewhat anomalous in Susann's output, but this difference gave her the opportunity to examine more threatening manifestations of sexuality. Sexual violence and the degradation of prostitution are juxtaposed with stunning images of sexually motivated body transformations. Again Susann used the format of a *roman à clef* to explore her themes, this time basing her characters on personalities from the television industry. Robin Stone, a newscaster turned television executive, acts out a series of sexual relations while attempting to come to terms with his complex and abused past. His insatiable sexual appetite and mechanical attitude towards its satisfaction make him the "love machine" of the title. Drug use is still a minor theme, but this time around Susann was more interested in exploring the possibilities of surgical body modification to enhance sexual attraction and change sexual identity. She develops this most fully in the episode where Robin Stone visits the prostitutes on Hamburg's Reeperbahn, culminating in an encounter with a transsexual dancer. Later, Stone's violent assault on another prostitute enables him to understand why he equates sex and violence, and so comes to a greater self-knowledge. The novel adopted the ancient Egyptian *ankh* sign as a symbol of

sexual power and vitality, so providing a uniquely recognizable cover image that greatly aided promotion of the book. *The Love Machine* is also notable for its positive treatment of male homosexuality through a sympathetic portrayal of a minor character. Although not as well received as *Valley of the Dolls, The Love Machine* did much to establish Susann's reputation in Europe.

Once Is Not Enough

In her final major novel, *Once Is Not Enough* (1973), Susann returned to an initially innocent female protagonist while casting a (perhaps surprisingly) jaundiced eye on the world of sexual permissiveness and licence that she herself had earlier helped to promote, if not create. The novel is, in essence, a tale of a sexual utopia gone haywire through excess—seen through a daughter's incestuous longing for her father in world of people too rich, too beautiful, and too powerful for their own good. In some ways, the heroine of the novel, January Wayne, is a fantasy portrait of Susann herself in her earlier years as an aspiring actress. January's childhood is characterized by her worship of her movie-producer father Mike Wayne, her innocence kept secure in a girls' school and a Swiss clinic. Her defloration and initiation into the "swinging" sexuality of 1970s New York is guided by Linda Riggs, a hip women's magazine journalist based on *Cosmopolitan* editor Helen Gurley Brown. Linda introduces the reader to an unsentimental world of sex and drugs that is continually contrasted with January's idealized childhood. January reluctantly accepts Linda's guidance while continuing to worship her father, but later transfers this attraction to a married novelist with sexual dysfunction. January's adventures are paralleled by Susann's caustic running commentary on contemporary mores. She satirizes the dangerous advice of women's magazines and then-popular trends such as "nude theater" as well as several literary figures who had ridiculed her earlier work, including Norman Mailer and Truman Capote, who appear as grotesque caricatures. A major subplot revolves around the lesbian relationship of January's step-mother, socialite Dee Milford Granger, with reclusive Garbo-based actress Karla. An extensive digression covers Karla's past: her early lesbian desires and war years in Poland, culminating in a startling account of mass rape in a convent. The deaths of January's father and step-mother make January unimaginably wealthy, but also cut her adrift in a world she is unequipped to handle. Her wanderings take her from a sexually explicit play to a drug-fueled orgy that is one of the most astonishing scenes in the book. Susann uses a stream-of-consciousness narrative style to convey January's dislocated experience of a variety of group sex situations while under the influence of LSD. The final resolution of the book reworks Susann's then-unpublished scifi fantasy *Yargo*. January hallucinates a handsome alien that looks like her father and, her dreams fulfilled, disappears and is presumed dead. Her sense of erotic dislocation is taken to its logical conclusion as she flees this world altogether.

Other works

Susann's short roman à clef *Dolores* (1976), based on Jacqueline Kennedy Onassis and her sister Lee Radziwill, explored the themes of love, sex, and drugs among the very rich. Initially commissioned as a story for *Ladies' Home Journal*, it was published as a book only after Susann's death; perhaps out of fear of libel or deference to her magazine audience, this novella is relatively unexplicit, but intriguingly develops themes of sex and class. A number of unfinished projects never saw the light of day, but Susann's early attempt at a science fiction romance, *Yargo*, was published in 1979 to disappointing sales. The afterlife of Susann's work has been considerable: each of the major novels has been filmed, some more than once, and have appeared in various forms on stage and television. An estate-sanctioned sequel to *Valley of the Dolls, Jacqueline Susann's Shadow of the Dolls* by Rae Lawrence, was said to be based on a detailed outline by Susann herself, but failed to capture either the tone or the spirit of the original, and was poorly received. Various unauthorized sequels and parodies of Susann's work have had greater success. Of especial interest in the reception of Susann's work has been its enthusiastic adoption by young authors of lesbian erotica: the stories published in the irreverent tribute zine *Dead Jackie Susann Quarterly*, for example, show the unmistakable influence of Susann on a wide range of authors.

Biography

Born in Philadelphia, 20 August 1918, also educated there. Worked in theater and television in New York from 1936; married publicist Irving Mansfield in 1939, one son. Began writing plays in collaboration with Beatrice Cole, of which "The Temporary Mrs. Smith" and "Lovely Me" were produced on Broadway; began work on prose fiction in the 1950s. Diagnosed with breast cancer in 1962, first book (*Every Night Josephine*) appeared in 1963. First published novel, *Valley of the Dolls* (1966) was enormously successful, as were two others, *The Love Machine* (1969) and *Once Is Not Enough* (1973), in part because of innovative promotion techniques. Appeared in the films of all three novels. Died of cancer, 21 September 1974; posthumously published works include a novella, *Jacqueline Susann's Dolores* (1976), and a romantic science fiction fantasy, *Yargo* (1979, written 1953–1956).

T.G. WILFONG and DOMINIC MONTSERRAT

Selected Works

Every Night, Josephine. New York: Bernard Geis Associates, 1963.
Valley of the Dolls. New York: Bernard Geis Associates, 1966.
The Love Machine. New York, Simon and Schuster, 1969.
Once is Not Enough. New York: William Morrow Company, 1973.
Jacqueline Susann's Dolores. New York: William Morrow Company, 1976.
Yargo. New York, Bantam, 1979.

Further Reading

Ehrenreich, Barbara. *Remaking Love: The Feminization of Sex.* New York: Doubleday, 1986.
Lawrence, Rae. *Jacqueline Susann's Shadow of the Dolls*, New York. Crown, 2001.
Mansfield, Irving, and Jean Libman Block. *Life With Jackie: The Personal Story of Jacqueline Susann.* New York: Bantam, 1983.
Seaman, Barbara. *Lovely Me: The Life of Jacqueline Susann.* Rev. ed., New York, Seven Stories, 1996.
Ventura, Jeffrey. *The Jacqueline Susann Story.* New York, Award Books, 1975.

SUYŪTĪ, JALĀL AL-DĪN AL-

1445–1505
Pre-modern Egyptian polymath

Al-Suyūtī is, by all accounts, the most prolific author in Arabo-Islamic history. It is estimated that he authored 900 works in various genres and fields. His most famous and important contributions are in Qurānic commentary, theology, exegesis, and history. At least eleven of his works, most of them extant, but not all edited or published, are solely concerned with sexology (al-bāh)- an established genre in pre-modern Arabo-Islamic culture. The most important and famous of these are the following:

Rashf al-zulāl min al-sihr al-halāl [*Drinking the Sweet Water of Licit Magic*]. Also known as *Maqāmat al-nisā* [*The Harangue on Women*]. This work is a collection of twenty *maqāmas* (harangues; a pre-modern Arabic narrative genre written in rhyming prose). The overarching frame narrative of the work centers around a group of scholars who went to the mosque on the feast and listened to a sermon in which the imam encouraged them to abandon adultery and homosexuality and to marry. Having heeded his advice, they meet afterwards and each narrates, in painstaking detail, his sexual intercourse with his bride. The work is chock-full of punning as each narrator employs terminology, concepts, and titles from his own field of knowledge to describe intercourse. Among the twenty narrators are a Qurān teacher, exegete, *hadīth* scholar, jurist, linguist, grammarian, prosodist, mathematician, physician, logician, and mystic. This approach undoubtedly allowed al-Suyūtī to display his erudition, wit, and mastery of the various fields and their respective terminology.

Shaqā al-utrunj fī rāqā īq al-ghunj [*The Citron Slices of Delicate Coquetry*] is an epistle centering around the theme of ghunj [coquetry, both verbal and physical]. However, in delineating the wide semantic field of the word, al-Suyūtī, as in many of his works and the genre in general, tackles many other related themes and terms such as *rafath* [obscene, lewd, or immodest language, especially during intercourse]. The epistle expounds on the theme following the typical structure of the *bāh* [sexology] genre in Arabic. The general division starts out with related and relevant quotations from the Qurān and the *hadīth* [prophetic tradition] on the term or theme under question. This is usually followed by anecdotes, excerpts, and sayings from various sources of belles-lettres and, finally, excerpts of poetry. This is one of his most popular erotic works in the Arab world and is available in a few popular editions.

Mabāsim al-milāh wa-manāsim al-sabāh fī mawāsim al-nikāh [*The Mouths of the Beautiful and the Morning Breeze of the Seasons of Intercourse*] is a lengthy encyclopedia divided into seven parts. The first part includes excerpts from the prophetic tradition on sex, the second focuses on sex in lexicography, the third prose anecdotes, the fourth poetry, the fifth is devoted to the anatomy of male and female sex organs, the sixth: medicine, and the seventh focuses on sexology. The work was so large that al-Suyūtī abridged it himself and entitled the smaller selection *al-wishāh fī fawā id al-nikāh* [*The Sash on the Advantages of Intercourse*]. The section on lexicography, for example, is subdivided into four parts covering the various terms used to describe intercourse (a mini dictionary of sorts), a section on the various names for the penis and its parts, a similar section for the vagina, and finally a section on the various expressions and terms for sexual acts, positions, and related themes.

Nawādir al-ayk fī ma rifat al-nayk [*The Fresh Branches in the Knowledge of Intercourse*]. Al-Suyūtī, in the introduction to this work, writes that it is an addendum to the aforementioned *The Sash*. This, too, is a smaller compilation of quotes, anecdotes, and verses spread out in chapters on sexual intercourse and its pleasures, the various types of penetration, various sexual positions, a taxonomy of sizes and shapes of sexual organs, advice on achieving the greatest sexual pleasure. *Nuzhat al-muta ammil wa murshid al-muta ahhil* [*The Sojourn of the Reflective* and the Guide for the Married] is a manual for newlyweds. It is divided into nine parts dealing with intercourse and its advantages and disadvantages (maladies and sicknesses), foreplay, preferred and religiously sanctioned positions and conditions, a taxonomy of preferred types of women and erotic physiognomy, a similar section on men, the rights of the wife and husband, and the protocols and rituals of copulation. *Al-Īdāh fī ilm al-nikāh* [*The Book of Exposition in the Science of Intercourse*] is attributed to al-Suyūtī, but probably originally composed by al-Shīrāzī. Aside from the general scheme and obvious subject, what distinguishes this work is the relatively extensive use of Egyptian colloquial language in its various anecdotes.

A significant number of al-Suyūtī's works, including erotic ones, have yet to be edited and published. Many others are forever lost. Of these it is worth mentioning al-*Yawāqīt al-thamīna fī sifāt al-samīna* [*The Precious Stones in Praising Plump Women*].

Biography

Born in Cairo in October 1445. His father was a teacher and judge. He was precocious (started writing at the age of seventeen) and possessed a prodigious memory. Al-Suyūtī was trained in the Islamic sciences by the prominent teachers of the day, including some women who

taught him the science of *hadīth*. In 1463, he inherited his father's position as a jurist and law teacher and his fame quickly spread outside Egypt. He retired from public life in 1486 due to tensions with the rulers and his disdain of widespread corruption. In 1501, he shunned public life and retreated to his house where he dedicated his time to editing his own works until his death on October 17, 1505.

SINAN ANTOON

Selected Works

Khawam, Rene R., tr. *Nuits de Noces (Ou Comment Humer le Doux Breuvage de la Magie Licite)*, Paris: Editions Albin Michel, 1972.
——, tr. *Les Branches Robustes de la Foret Dans les Cas Extraordinaires de Conjonction*, Paris: Editions Albin Michel, 1972.
al-Suyūtī. *The Book of Exposition: Literally Translated from the Arabic by an English Bohemian*, London: Darf Publishers, 1987.

Further Reading

Bouhdiba, Abdelwahab. *Sexuality in Islam*. London: Routledge & Kegan Paul, 1985.
Jaghām, Ahmad Husayn. *Al-Jins fī amāl al-imām Jalāl al-Dīn al-Suyūtī (Sex in the Works of the Imām Jalāl al-Dīn al-Suyūtī)*. Sūsa (Tunisia):Dār al-Maārif, 2001.
Sartain, E.M. *Jalāl al-Dīn al-Suyūtī*. London: Cambridge University Press, 1975.

SWINBURNE, ALGERNON C.

1837–1909
English poet, dramatist, and critic

Lesbia Brandon

Swinburne's incomplete novel survives in fragmented form. It is impossible to reconstruct the exact details of the plot from the various chapters and detached passages that remain. The poet, having begun it in the mid-1860s, had intended to finish and publish it at various stages

in the 1870s. But it seems that his friend Theodore Watts, later Watts-Dunton, did what he could to prevent this, including losing parts of it and muddling the script. The volume was first made available only in 1952 in an edition by Randolph Hughes (who gave it its title). *Lesbia Brandon* explores some of Swinburne's consistent preoccupations including the sea and sea swimming, and the death of the desired and beautiful. It also touches on radical Italian politics. But central to *Lesbia Brandon*'s energies is sadomasochism, in particular the relations between sexual desire and flogging. In this it testifies to Swinburne's relatively new enthusiasm for the works of the Marquis de Sade to whom Swinburne pays the tribute of imitation not least by titling chapter XIV "Les Malheurs de la Vertu," the subtitle of the version of de Sade's *Justine* published in 1791.

Lesbia Brandon begins with the childhood story of Herbert Seyton who, perhaps, articulates some of Swinburne's own feelings as a young boy at Eton. Seyton, after his father's death, is taken to live with his sister, Margaret, and Lord Wariston, her husband, at a house named Ensdon, a place of "stately recluse beauty" (195). There, he takes pleasure in sea swimming, and his enchantment with the sea's dangers marks the beginning of the sadomasochistic discourse of the novel. For him, the sea is both beautiful woman and vicious animal, and Seyton's passionate engagement with it prompts the most memorable sexualized lyricism of the novel. The knowledge [of] how many lives went yearly to feed with blood the lovely lips of the sea-furies who had such songs and smiles for summer, and for winter the teeth and throats of ravening wolves or snakes untameable, the hard heavy hands that beat out their bruised life from sinking bodies of men, gave point to his pleasure and a sheathed edge of cruel sympathy to his love (198).

Seyton's private delights, the religious intensity of which make him a "small satisfied pagan" (199), are soon disturbed by the arrival of a new tutor, Mr. Denham. Denham is appointed to improve Bertie's chances of succeeding at school. But training the "crude mind" necessitates, his new instructor believes, the disciplining of the "vile body" (200).

Swinburne's own interest in the sexual pleasures of flogging began at Eton. In *Lesbia Brandon*, the flogging scenes—both regular and motivated by the least transgression—include a particularly brutal occasion when Denham beats his pupil while still dripping wet from the sea. The motivation for "swishing" Bertie increases as Denham vents his frustration for his growing, unrequited passion for Margaret by viciously beating her brother, and this enables new combinations of the language of pain, hatred, and sexual yearning. Throughout, Bertie's sense of what is admirable masculinity becomes associated with the acceptance of being beaten,

though he admonishes himself for his failure to be indifferent to it. Swinburne adds what appears to be a brief incest theme to the novel's presentation of dissenting sexuality as, in chapter III, Bertie and Margaret kiss ardently, leaving Bertie to dream "passionately of his passion till he woke" (265). Jean Fuller suggested that one of Swinburne's original intentions for the novel was to sustain the incest plot, having Bertie, in the end, kill himself for love.

The character of Lesbia Brandon, "poetess and pagan" (350), is introduced late in the surviving novel. The beautiful daughter of Sir Charles Brandon, she falls in love with Margaret while Bertie falls in love with her (she turns out to be Denham's half-sister). Her self-inflicted death from poison precipitates a new configuration of contrary feelings that look forward to the violently oscillating emotional world of D.H. Lawrence. Bertie, seeing her on her deathbed, "felt a cruel impersonal displeasure, compound of fear and pain, in the study of her last symptoms. Then by way of reaction came a warm sudden reflux of tenderness" (347). Rooksby (1997) proposed that the death of Lesbia reflected Swinburne's memories of the final illness of his favorite sister, Edith. The generically and stylistically composite nature of *Lesbia Brandon* means that it includes various songs and ballads. Rooksby (1997) referred to it as "like a mad tea-party story told in turn by Jane Austen, Emily Brontë, an Eton schoolboy and an anthologist of Northumberland border ballads" (101).

Biography

Algernon Charles Swinburne was born in London into a distinguished family. Taught first by his mother, he entered Eton and Balliol College Oxford, though was sent down from the former and briefly rusticated from the latter. He left Oxford without a degree. His first published work was dramatic (1860) but he attained prominence with the controversial *Poems and Ballads* (1866), reflecting his interest in the Marquis de Sade, to whose work he had been introduced in 1862, and in paganism. *A Song of Italy* (1867) and *Songs before Sunrise* (1871) arose from his life long commitment to radical politics that led to an enthusiasm for Blake. Swinburne was a prolific writer, and in his later years he continued to publish extensively, though critical preference remains in favor of the earlier work. His *oeuvre* includes many volumes of poetry, essays, translations, criticism, and two novels: *A Year's Letters* (1877) and the unfinished *Lesbia Brandon* begun in the early 1860s. Swinburne died in Putney and was buried at Bonchurch on the Isle of Wight.

FRANCIS O'GORMAN

Edition

The Novels of A.C. Swinburne: Love's Cross-Currents, Lesbia Brandon. With an introduction by Edmund Wilson, New York: Farrar, Straus and Cudahy, 1962.

Selected Works

The Queen-mother. Rosamond. 2 plays. 1860.
Atalanta in Calydon, a Tragedy. 1865.
Poems and Ballads. 1866.
A Song of Italy. 1867.
Songs before Sunrise. 1871.
Bothwell. 1874.
Poems and Ballads, 2nd series. 1878.

Tristram of Lyonesse and other poems. 1882.
Poems and Ballads, 3rd series. 1889.

Further Reading

Alexander, Jonathan. "Sex, Violence and Identity: A.C. Swinburne's Uses of Sadomasochism." *Victorian Newsletter* 90 (1996): 33–36.
Fuller, Jean Overton. *Swinburne: A Critical Biography*. London: Chatto and Windus, 1968.
Rooksby, Rikky. "Swinburne's Reginald." *Notes and Queries*. 38 (1991): 322–23.
Rooksby, Rikky. "A.C. Swinburne's *Lesbia Brandon* and the Death of Edith Swinburne." *Notes and Queries*, 40 (1993): 487–490.
Rooksby, Rikky, *A.C. Swinburne: A Poet's Life*. Aldershot: Scolar, 1997.
Rooksby, Rikky and Nicholas Shrimpton (editors). *The Whole Music of Passion: New Essays on Swinburne*. Aldershot: Scolar, 1993.
Vincent, John. "Flogging is Fundamental: Applications of Birch in Swinburne's *Lesbia Brandon*." In *Novel Gazing: Queer Readings in Fiction*, edited by Eve Kosofsky Sedgwick. Durham, NC: Duke University Press, 1997.

SZÛ-MA HSIANG-JU

d. 117 BCE
Chinese poet

Szû-ma Hsiang-ju has traditionally been regarded as the greatest exponent of the *fu* or rhapsody. The rhapsody, an essay marked by the use of rhyme and meter, is an intermediate literary form between poetry and prose. During the Han dynasty (206 BCE–220 CE) this was an extremely popular court literary form, and many rhapsodies were commissioned by royal or imperial patrons. Rhapsodies were intended to entertain the reader with the rich and beautiful language used, and often described scenes of great luxury and exoticism. Szû-ma Hsiang-ju's work was noted for the elements of fantasy that he liked to incorporate. His rhapsodies were marked by the use of lists, cumulatively conjuring up impressions of sensual pleasure and

physical beauty. Rhapsodies were traditionally supposed to contain a critical element, for they were thought to be a good means of advising rulers and directing them away from dangerous pleasures. This was a comparatively minor part of Szû-ma Hsiang-ju's work, perhaps because so many of his rhapsodies were commissioned by members of the imperial family.

According to the catalogue of the Han Imperial library, Szû-ma Hsiang-ju wrote twenty-nine rhapsodies. Six of these survive as more or less complete works. Three more survive in a handful of quotations. Of these surviving pieces, four are of unquestioned authenticity, since they were included in Szû-ma Hsiang-ju's official biography in the Han dynastic history. These are the *Tz'u-hsü fu* [*Rhapsody of Master Empty*], and its companion piece *Shanglin fu* (*Rhapsody of Shanglin Imperial Park*), which was presented to the emperor in 138 BCE. Also of unquestioned authenticity are the *Ai Ch'in Erh-shih fu* [*Rhapsody in Mourning for the Second Emperor of Ch'in*] and the *Da-jen fu* [*Rhapsody of the Great Man*]. Of more dubious authenticity are Ssu-ma Hsiang-ju's two erotic works: the *Mei-jen fu* [*Rhapsody of Beautiful Women*] and the *Ch'ang-men fu* [*Rhapsody of the Tall Gates*]. Both were to prove highly influential in traditional Chinese erotic literature. The three fragmentary surviving rhapsodies are the *Li fu* [*Rhapsody of the Pear Tree*], *Yu-tsu fu* [*Rhapsody of Salt Fish*] and *Hsin-tong shan fu* [*Rhapsody of Camphor Mountain*]. Too little survives of these works to be able to guess the subject. Szû-ma Hsiang-ju was also credited with the composition of a short love-song, describing the mating of phoenixes, with which he was said to have wooed Cho Wen-chü;n. This musical seduction inspired a key scene in the famous erotic play, the *Hsi-hsiang-chi* [*Romance of the West Wing*].

Traditional scholarship on Szû-ma Hsiang-ju's rhapsodies focused on trying to relate these works with events in his life, or with specific historical individuals. The *Mei-jen fu* described in lyrical terms how an attractive and handsome young man resisted all attempts by a series of beautiful women to seduce him. This rhapsody was frequently said to be autobiographical, although some scholars have suggested that this rhapsody should be understood as about Szû-ma Hsiang-ju (a famously good-looking man) rather than by him. According to tradition, when Szû-ma Hsiang-ju arrived at the court of the king of Liang, one of the other court poets accused him of licentiousness. Szû-ma Hsiang-ju was said to have written this poem to exculpate himself. At the culmination of the rhapsody, one woman approached the poet naked, and her beauty was lyrically described. Although some translations suggest that the couple end up making love, this rhapsody was in fact about sexual continence. The *Mei-jen fu* has other counterparts in traditional Chinese literature, and a number of Han dynasty poets wrote verse on the theme of sexual continence, most famously the *Teng t'u-tz'u hao-se fu* [*Rhapsody of Master Teng-t'u, the Lecher*] by Song Yü; (fl. 3rd century BCE). In this witty rhapsody a handsome young man accused of licentious behavior points out that he has resisted all attempts by his neighbor's beautiful daughter to seduce him,

while his accusor has a disgustingly unattractive wife with whom he has had many children.

The *Ch'ang-men fu* was supposedly commissioned by Empress Ch'en, the neglected wife of the Han emperor Wu-ti. Some scholars have doubted the story of the commission, which is given in a separate introductory paragraph, but regard the rhapsody itself as genuine. This rhapsody described in great detail the emotions of the neglected wife, and her sexual frustration. This rhapsody was highly unusual, if not unique in Han dynasty literature, in its portrayal of female sexuality. Subsequently the *Ch'ang-men fu* was to prove enormously influential, as many later poets were drawn to the theme of the loyal and loving abandoned wife, pondering her bleak life as her husband enjoys himself with a new favorite. Although only two of Szû-ma Hsiang-ju's works contained a significant exploration of erotic themes, but both were important and influential literary works, which inspired numerous later Chinese poets.

Biography

Szû-ma Hsiang-ju was born in Ch'eng-tu, the capital of Shu (Szechuan province) in western China in approximately 179 BCE. During the reign of the Han emperor Ching-ti (r. 157–141 BCE), Szû-ma Hsiang-ju held a minor court appointment but did not find favor with the emperor, therefore he accepted an appointment with Liu Wu, King of Liang (r. 168–143 BCE). The king of Liang was a great patron of the arts, particularly poetry. During his stay in Liang, Szû-ma Hsiang-ju wrote the earliest of his surviving works. When the king died, Szû-ma Hsiang-ju returned to Szechuan, where he met and eloped with a young widow, Cho Wen-chü;n, the daughter of one of China's wealthiest men. They lived in great poverty until Cho Wen-chü;n was reconciled with her father. Szû-ma Hsiang-ju was employed as an official by the Han emperor Wu-ti (r. 141–187 BCE), and played a crucial role in promoting the acceptance of Chinese rule in Szechuan. The emperor also periodically commissioned poetic works from him. Thanks to his wife's wealth, from 130–120 Szû-ma Hsiang-ju was able to concentrate on his poetry. Szû-ma Hsiang-ju retired in 119, and went to live in Mao-ling outside the Han capital Ch'ang-an, where he died in 117 BCE.

OLIVIA MILBURN

pan-she, 1993. This contains complete texts for all rhapsodies attributed to Szû-ma Hsiang-ju, including those that only survive in fragmentary quotations.

Selected Works

Ssu-ma Ch'ien. *Shih chi*. Peking, Chung-hua shu-chü;, 1959. The biography of Szû-ma Hsiang-ju containing four of his rhapsodies was translated in Burton Watson: *Records of the Grand Historian of China, vol. II, The age of Emperor Wu 140 to circa 100 BC*, New York: Columbia University Press, 1961.

Li Shan. *Wen-hsüan Li chu-yi-shu*. Peking: Chung-hua shu-chü;, 1985. Four of Szû-ma Hsiang-ju's rhapsodies were included in this important ancient anthology, translated by David R. Knechtges, *Wen Xuan or Selections of Refined Literature*, Princeton: Princeton University Press, 1982–. To date three volumes have been published, Vol. One: *Rhapsodies on Metropolises and Capitals*; Vol. Two: *Rhapsodies on Sacrifices, Hunting, Travel, Sightseeing, Palaces and Halls, Rivers and Seas*; Vol. Three: *Rhapsodies on Natural Phenomena, Birds and Animals, Aspirations and Feelings, Sorrowful Laments, Literature, Music, and Passions*.

Fu Chen-kang, Hu Shuang-pao, Ts'ung Ming-hua. *Ch'üan Han fu*. Peking: Pei-ching ta-hsü;eh ch'u-

Further Reading

Gong Kechang. *Studies in the Han Fu*. New Haven, CT: American Oriental Society, 1997.

Hervouet, Yves. *Un poète de cour sous les Han: Sseu-ma Siang-jou*. Paris: Presses Universitaires de France, 1964.

Kern, Martin. "The "Biography of Sima Xiangru" and the Question of the *Fu* in Sima Qian's *Shiji*." *Journal of the American Oriental Society* 123.2 (2003), pp. 303–316.

Knechtges, David R. *Court Culture and Literature in Early China*. Aldershot: Ashgate Publishing, 2002.

Nienhauser, William J. *The Indiana Companion to Traditional Chinese Literature*. Bloomington, IN: Indiana University Press, 1986.

Shih, Vincent. *The Literary Mind and the Carving of Dragons*. New York: Columbia University Press, 1959.

Van Gulik, Robert. *Sexual Life in Ancient China: A Preliminary Survey of Chinese Sex and Society From Ca. 1500 B.C. Till 1644 A.D*. Leiden: Brill, 2003.

T

TABOOS

The term "taboo" entered Western culture in 1777 when the English explorer Captain James Cook encountered and appropriated the Tongan word *tabu*. *Tabu* is one variation of a word found throughout Oceanic languages; another form, occurring in Maori and Polynesian, is *tapu*. Deriving from *ta*, "to mark," and *pu*, an adverb of intensity, *tabu* literally means "very marked" as in "very marked off" or set apart. In its original context *tabu* and its equivalents describe a complex system of ritual, superstition, and social restriction.

In the West "taboo" has come to signify those things or acts which are forbidden through social or religious prohibition and the threat of punishment. During the 20th century, "taboo" was extended to often offensive or obscene words, expressions, or topics. A "taboo word" or "taboo topic" is one which should not be used or spoken of in social intercourse.

By separating that which is allowed from that which is not, taboos mark a boundary between the socially allowed and the socially prohibited. Taboos are the strongest inhibitions which a culture imposes on itself in order to guarantee its own survival; they protect and maintain the complex framework of regulation and division upon which civilization depends. Although most taboos are culturally or historically specific (and constructed), many regard the two oldest and most universal taboos: incest and murder. The fact that these acts are universally prohibited illustrates that taboos refer to the basic codes of civilization and to what humanity most fears and abhors. As such, "taboo" carries a more powerful sense of the forbidden than, for example, "unlawful." However, if taboos represent prohibition and fear, then it is also important to note that these feared acts are often accompanied by desire for that which is forbidden—after all, there is no need to forbid acts which no one wishes to perform, only those which are somehow desired. As domains where the feared and/or socially unacceptable often meet desire and fascination, sexual behavior and eroticism are principal sites where the interplay between taboo and transgression occurs.

Taboo's powerful associations derive from its original location at the boundary between human culture and more potent, universal forces. Oceanic religion regarded both the sacred, pure world of Gods, idols, tribal chiefs, and priests, as well as the unclean or impure (e.g., menses and decaying bodies) as powerful and potentially dangerous to society. Based on the belief that such danger was contagious and could be transferred to others, taboos served to segregate these sources of "contagion" from the profane realm of human society. Thus taboos surrounded the clothing and sleeping places of menstruating women as much as tribal chiefs, sacred icons, and priests. In this way it is important to note that taboos existed to protect the inviolability of the sacred as much as to protect ordinary people *from* the power of the sacred.

Despite their power, at specific times (such as during festivals) taboos could be freely broken. As a general rule, however, to break a taboo meant (and indeed means) punishment. The punishment depended on the taboo which had been violated: sometimes ritual atonement was possible. If atonement was not possible, the risk to society posed by the defiled and now "contagious" transgressor could be nullified only by his or her execution.

The study of taboos in "primitive" societies formed a major part of 19th-century, Western discussions concerning the origin of religion and civilization. European anthropologists collected and listed thousands of "primitive" taboos as examples of how early spirituality affected early social existence. These studies often used taboos to discuss primitive concepts of the sacred. Because taboos protected against both the pure and the impure, primitive religions were seen as lacking any distinction between the holy and the dangerous. Influenced by contemporary evolutionary theory, such discussions usually posed Christianity—in which the sacred refers only to purity—as a more "evolved" form of religion.

Influenced by these earlier discussions, Sir James Frazer's *The Golden Bough, Part 2: Taboo and the Perils of the Soul* (1911) provides a seminal study of the topic. Frazer shows how all "primitive" societies throughout history have relied on temporary or permanent taboos. Comparing and contrasting different taboos from various societies, he illustrated how taboos regulated all aspects of traditional culture and life events, including birth, sexual behavior, and death—and (among other things) eating, clothing, worship, property, hunting, warfare, knotting, and naming.

The 20th century saw a change in the perception of taboos and their transgression. It became clear that as much as taboos regulated "primitive" societies, taboos remained central to modern culture. Just as "primitive" civilizations depended on them, so taboos maintained a framework of restriction within and around modern civilization. Discussions of taboo shifted to illustrate the similarities, rather than the differences, between the "primitive" and the modern. The most influential 20th-century analyses of taboos presented them as social creations (no longer as religious prohibitions) vital to the functioning of civilization.

Sigmund Freud's influential *Totem and Tabu* (1913) suggests that taboos prohibit acts which are unconsciously desired. Freud identified the desire to perform murder and incest as intrinsic to human nature and traces these desires back to his theory of the Oedipus complex.

In 1957, the French erotic writer Georges Bataille, whose fiction describes murder, incest, necrophilia, and other taboo acts, published *L'Érotisme* [*Eroticism*]. *L'Érotisme* is an exploration of human history in which equal importance is ascribed to both taboos and their transgression. According to Bataille, civilization depends upon taboos because they protect society from mankind's primal, violent urges. However, just as civilization depends on taboos, so taboos cannot exist without their transgression. Thus, for Bataille, taboos, civilization, and transgression are mutually dependent forces.

Another influential text, Mary Douglas's *Purity and Danger: An Analysis of the Concepts of Pollution and Taboo* (1966), aligns human civilization with order; an order rigidly enforced and emphasized by social divisions such as within and without, male and female, right and wrong. Opposed to this order, dirt, decay, and unregulated sexual activity represent disorder. As much as "primitive" man, modern man perceives disorder—that which is outside the socially ordained, allowed, and "civilized," and therefore taboo—as dangerous, contagious, and threatening.

Emerging from all previous writing on taboo, however, is the recurrent motif of realization that throughout history, as much as humanity has erected taboos, so too has it been, and continues to be, drawn by desire and fascination toward that which taboos prohibit.

BEN JACOB

Further Reading

Bataille, Georges. *L'Érotisme*. Paris: Editions de Minuit, 1957.

Cook, Capt. James. *A Voyage to the Pacific Ocean*. London: W. and A. Strahan, 1784.

Douglas, Mary. *Purity and Danger: An Analysis of the Concepts of Pollution and Taboo*. London: Routledge and Kegan Paul, 1966.

Durkheim, Émile. *Les Formes élémentaires de la vie religeuse*. Paris: Félix Alcon, 1925.

Frazer, Sir James George. *The Golden Bough, Part 2: Taboo and the Perils of the Soul*. London: Macmillan, 1911.

Freud, Sigmund. "Totem and Taboo." Translated by James Strachey. In *The Origins of Religion*. Penguin Freud Library, Vol. 13. Harmondsworth: Penguin, 1990. Originally published as *Totem und Tabu*, Leipzig and Vienna: Heller, 1913.

Lévy-Bruhl, Lucien. *La Mentalité primitive*. Paris: Félix Alcon, 1922.

Smith, William Robertson. *Lectures on the Religion of the Semites*. Edinburgh: Adam and Charles Black, 1889.

Steiner, Franz. *Taboo*. London: Cohen and West, 1956.

Van Gennep, Arnold. *Les Rites de passage*. Paris: Nourry, 1909.

Wundt, Wilhelm. *The Elements of Folk Psychology*. Translated by Edward Leroy Schaub. London: Allen and Unwin, 1916.

TANG YIN

1424–1524
Chinese scholar and poet

The Ocean of Inequities of Monks and Nuns

The book called in Chinese *Sengni niehai* is a compilation of stories about the sexual misdemeanor of Buddhist monks and nuns—most in classical Chinese language, some in colloquial, and others in a mixed style. Sources have been identified for almost half of them, and the tales are sometimes copied verbatim. The anthology must have been published between 1618 and 1631, the earlier date found in one of the stories and the later one in another work mentioning this title. It survived in two incomplete manuscripts and one print in Japan's library entitled *Saeki bunko*. These slightly different copies amount to 36 monks' stories, besides the appendix, with 11 for the nuns.

Some stories end with more humorous than moral comments. Though there is no homogeneous style to speak of, the work seems to be of erotic import and often jocular, rather than a castigation of Buddhist clerics. For example, the very first story, about the Tanxian affair of mid-sixteenth century, in which Queen Hu was "compelled by her licentiousness and lust to do things repellent to even the most lewd women and prostitutes," concludes: "According to the karmic retribution, if a person thinks of the Buddha at the time of death, he can cross over to the other bank to Nirvana's shores. But if his mind is on animal lust, then he sinks to the rebirth wheel. Since Queen Hu had sown many good seeds of enlightenment, both in life and after death, she must have been thinking about Buddha all the time. So she must have been reborn as a happy and carefree monk."

Whether practiced by widows, nuns, or monks, celibacy is portrayed as pretense, for sexual urge cannot be contained: such is the axiomatic truth to be found in every tale. And the longer the urge is restricted, the wilder it eventually bursts out. Women, religious or not, even procuresses, are usually indulged more than monks, who are often condemned to death when hidden affairs, discovered, turn into judicial cases. The second tale about monks, the longest one, offers, besides many others explicit sights, an uncommon one in Chinese erotica: "With two young monks sitting [on] either side, she looked to her right and left and could hardly control herself. She let the two monks make love to her, her one vagina accommodating two penises" (Levy and Yang: 27). Deflowered by a monk, the girl is later married to an unknowing husband.

The fifth tale is a brief account of the strange case of a bisexual nun who is condemned to death. The sixth nuns' tale consists of a few lines introducing three satirical poems about girls leaving their religious state in order to get married. In fact, the first two stories are the only ones with sophisticated plots.

Such a collection of tales hardly amounts to an anticlerical tract. It should be noted that the anthology called *Jingu qiguan*, published less than a decade later, did not retain any of the monks' few judicial cases of its sources. One of the earlier stories, "The Stolen Slippers," has been translated several times. Tales based on judicial cases of the judge Bao Zheng (999–1062) or other clever judges, quite popular in the sixteenth century, would yield many more topics on brutal monks or lewd nuns.

Biography

Tang Yin cannot be the author of this work, as it contains several pieces dated or referring to events more than half a century following his death. His erratic career as a scholar, painter, and poet created a legendary aura of a figure overindulging in wine and women. A favorite in popular literature, he became the main character of the *Romance of Three Smiles* [*Sanxiao yinyuan*], which copies the plot of a play written several centuries earlier.

ANDRÉ LÉVY

Editions

Chan Hing-ho and Wang Qiugui. *Siwuxie huibao.* Taipei: Encyclopedia Britannica Book Co., 1995.

Translations

"The Stolen Slippers." Translated by Leo Comber, in *The Strange Cases of Magistrate Pao*, Tokyo: Tuttle 1964; as "The Monk's Billet-doux," translated by Gladys & Hsien-yi Yang, in *Courtesan's Jewel Box,* Peking, 1957; as "The Monk with a Note Cleverly Tricks Huangfu's Wife," translated by Shunhui and Yunqin Yang, in *Stories Old and New* by Feng Menglong (1574–1646), Seattle: University of Washington Press, 2000.

Levy, Howard, and Richard Yang. *Monks and Nuns in a Sea of Sins.* Sino-Japanese Sexology Classic Seies, Vol. II, 1971 (31 items).

Huang San, Jean Blassé, and Oreste Rosenthal. *Moines et nonnes dans l'océan des péchés.* 42 items, 2,453 pp. Arles: Philippe Picquier, 1992.

Rummel, Stefan M. *Zhang und die Nonne vom Qiyun-Kloster.* 36 items, 235 pp. Munich: Wilhelm Heyne. Postface (pp. 206–29) by Helmut Martin (1940–1999) on Chinese erotic literature.

Further Reading

Gulik Robert van. *Sexual Life in Ancient China: A Preliminary Survey of Chinese Sex and Society from ca. 1500 B.C. till 1644 A.D,* 320. Leiden: E. J. Brill, 1961.

Rummel, Stefan. *Der Mönche und Nonnen Sündenmeer. Der buddhistische Klerus in chinesischen Roman- und Erzählliteratur des 16 und 17 Jahrhunderts.* Series "Chinathemen," Band 68. Bochum: Universitätverlag Brockmeyer, 1992.

TAXIL, LÉO

1854–1907
French polemicist and hoaxer

Although Taxil has often been described as a pornographer, he preferred salacious innuendo and imputation to graphic description and always claimed to be serving the interests of morality. His innumerable anticlerical works draw on the shocking juxtaposition of religion and sex, in the tradition of Gothic fiction and sensational melodrama. His absurd *Amours de Pie XI* [*Love Life of Pius XI*] (serialized 1881) portrayed the recently deceased pontiff as an indefatigable womanizer who would stop at nothing, including abduction and torture, to procure a tasty virgin. The book version (1884) was attributed to an ex–papal chamberlain and provoked a lawsuit instituted by the pope's heir. Taxil was hit with a fine of 60,000 francs and a beating by a *Le Figaro* reporter on whom he had tried to pin the real authorship.

The unending proliferation of Taxil's libels was enabled by recycling his own and others' work, at the risk of being labeled a plagiarist. *Les Livres secrets des confesseurs* (1883) is simply a reprint of a number of manuals for parish priests and seminarians, excerpting those chapters on questions of sex, chastity, and conjugal relations. Defending his infringement of copyright in the interests of the public welfare, Taxil declared that state-subsidized seminaries are breeding grounds for lust and that these manuals, put into the hands of susceptible young celibates, lead them in turn to seduce the working-class women who flock to their confessionals. *Lettres d'un Ignoratin à son élève* is a somewhat expurgated reissue of the much-circulated pornographic *Lettres amoureuses d'un frère à son élève* (1878), in which an ecclesiastic tries to win over his pupil to sodomy.

One of Taxil's non-anticlerical treatises on sex was *La Prostitution contemporaine. Étude d'une question sociale* (1883–84). This massive work conflated earlier publications of physicians and police inspectors, mingling statistics and muncipal ordinances with lurid anecdotes. It introduced a mass public to such recondite topics as "labial and anal masturbation" and the eccentric brothel patron who wanted a burning omelette dropped onto his belly. The next year Taxil was sentenced to a 2,000-franc fine and a fortnight in prison for the alleged obscenity of three of the work's engraved illustrations of perversions (necrophilia, pederastic foot fetishism, and brothel lesbianism). As usual, to raise money to pay his fines, Taxil brazenly published the trial proceedings. In 1891, he updated the work as *La Corruption fin-de-siècle,* with even greater emphasis on homosexuality.

Biography

Born Gabriel-Antoine Jogand-Pagès in Marseilles, March 21, son of a devout Catholic businessman. Molested by a priest at a Jesuit academy; ran away; was apprehended and placed in a rural borstal. At 16, working on a newspaper, changed his name to Léo Taxil. Run out of Geneva, 1875, for peddling aphrodisiac bonbons. Moved to Paris, where in 1879 he founded *L'Anti-clérical,*

a weekly whose popularity prompted him to publish a spate of vitriolic screeds against the Catholic Church, the clergy, and the pope, bringing him excommunication and several lawsuits for outrage to religion and defamation of character. Legal costs and growing competition forced his publishing house into bankruptcy. To recoup his losses, he returned to the Church, overwhelming his confessor with trumped-up "facts" about his part in a murder. Delighted to have such a notorious convert, the Church paid his debts and set him up as a dealer in pious, anti-republican, and, especially, anti-Masonic works. From 1885, Taxil's ferocious "exposés" of Freemasonry earned him a small fortune and celebrity in religious circles. Under the name Dr. Bataille, 1892–95, Taxil issued a series of attacks on spiritism, *Le Diable au XIXème siècle,* which purported to reveal a secret, devil-worshipping Masonic order called the Palladium. At a public meeting in Paris on April 17, 1897, Taxil confessed that his anti-Masonic polemics of the past twelve years had been a tissue of fabrications, invented to embarrass the Catholic Church. Thereafter, served as copy editor in the government printing office, republished some of his anticlerical works, and churned out racy novelettes; his exposés were now directed at adulterated groceries. Died Paris.

LAURENCE SENELICK

Selected Works

A bas la calotte. 1879
Calottes et calotins, histoire illustrée du clergé et des congrégations. 1880
Les amours sécretes de Pie IX, par un ancient camérier du pape. 1881
Les pornographes sacrés: La Confession et les confesseurs..., 1882
Un pape femelle: Roman historique. 1882
L'Affaire Léo Taxil-Pie IX. with E. Delattre and G. Mastai, 1882
Pie XI devant l'histoire, sa vie politique et pontificale, ses débauches, ses folies, ses crimes. 1883
Les livres secrets des confesseurs dévoilés aux pères de famille. 1883
Le célibat ecclésiastique et l'enseignement réligieux: Plaidoyer pour Léo Taxil..., with E. Delattre. 1883.
Les maîtresses du Pape. roman. 1884
Les trois cocus, roman. 1884
La prostitution contemporaine: Étude d'une question sociale. 1884
Les mémoires d'un ex-libre-penseur. Paris, 1887

La France maçonnique. 1888
Supplément à la France maçonnique, nouvelle divulgations. 1889
Y-a-t-il des femmes dans la Franc-Maçonnerie? 1891
La Corruption fin-de-siécle. 1891
(as Dr. Bataille) *Le Diable au XIXe siècle; ou, les Mystères du spiritisme, la Franc-Maçonnerie luciférienne... Révélation complètes sur la Palladisme...,* 1892
Mémoires d'une ex-Palladiste, parfaite initée, indépendante, 1895; translation as *Miss Diana Vaughan: Priestess of Lucifer by Herself, Now a Nun,* 1904
(as l'Abbé de la Tour de Noë) *La Vérité sur Miss Diana Vaughan, la Sainte et Taxil, le Tartuffe,* 1897
(as Prosper Manin) *Le Journal d'un valet de chambre,* 1899
(as Prosper Manin) *L'Amant des veuves,* 1900

Further Reading

Gruber, Hermann. *Leo Taxils Palladismus-Roman, oder, Die Enthüllugen, Dr Batailles Margiottas und Miss Vaughans über Freimaurerei und Satanismus.* Berlin: Verlag der Germania, 1897.
Laurant, Jean-Pierre. "Le Dossier Taxil." *Politica Hermetica* 8 (1996).
Muracciole, Bernard. *Léo Taxil: Vrai fumiste et faux frère.* Paris: Éditions Maçonniques de France, 1998.
Élisabeth Ripoll. "Taxil ou Le Feuilleton de l'anticléricalisme." In *Le Populaire à l'ombre des clochers,* edited by Antoine Court. Saint-Étienne: Université de Saint-Étienne, 1987.
Weber, Eugène. *Satan Franc-Maçon, la mystification de Léo Taxil.* Paris: R. Julliard, 1964.

TEMPLE D'APOLLON, LE

Seventeenth-century French collection

Le temple d'Apollon occupies a minor place among the libertine collections that flourished in France during the first quarter of the 17th century. In fact, the collection does not properly belong to this genre, for it contains numerous non-erotic poems, including conventional amorous sonnets, occasional verses addressed to the king, and funereal consolations. Nevertheless, the collection also contains a certain proportion of bawdy poems. This means that although it is not part of the libertine collections, the work partakes of the general permissive spirit that allows for their publication. In fact, during the reign of Henri IV, then in the regency of Marie de Médicis, and in the first years of the reign of Louis XIII, censorship displayed a relative tolerance. It was a time during which the young nobility was able to brandish its atheism, to frequent cabarets, and to celebrate carnal bliss. In such a context of loose morals, important sensual literature made its appearance, including *Le temple d'Apollon.*

The foreword to the book purports, as is often the case with this type of preamble, that it presents only new material. This is only a half-truth: *Le temple d'Apollon* comprises two volumes, but the second is a collection of four compilations previously published (from 1597 to 1600) by the same printer, Raphaël du Petit Val, of Rouen. One supposes that with this work of 1611 he was intent, in part, to profit handsomely from a commercial affair, for half of the collection is only a disguised reissue. However, the first volume does contain a certain number of previously unpublished poems, or at least poems that have never appeared in earlier collections published by Raphaël du Petit Val.

Among the new authors, one finds in particular François de Malherbe (1555–1628), the Court's official poet, the initiator of French classicism, and writer of religious poetry, but also known in private for his libertinage (his friends called him "Father Lewdness") and his erotic writings. Jean Bertaut (1552–1611), the king's secretary, first almoner of the queen, Marie de Médicis, also distinguishes himself by his 27 poems. Jean Bertaut was appreciated in his time for his love verse, and *Le Temple d'Apollon* contains, among others, a poem narrating the origin of Hermaphrodite, emblem of perfect love. It is also important to note that about a quarter of the poems published in this first volume are anonymous. Anonymity was a common practice in the collections of the time, especially in the satirical collections, and points to the growing importance the author's figure took with regard to the judicial institutions and moral norms. The disappearance of the author's name testifies to the increased risk linked with the production of erotic writings.

Eroticism as presented in *Le temple d'Apollon* is opposed to the rules acknowledged and imposed by society. Above all, eroticism seeks to manifest blasphemy with a maximum of presence, by shocking our proprieties. For example, one poem opposes honor, which is considered a simple, inconsequent word in comparison with the reality of the flesh. Honor is but an arbitrary convention whose effects are terrible: shame creeps in, consumes woman, and wastes her youth. The different ages of woman constitute an object of preoccupation for the poets of this compilation, asking which woman is most suited for love: the virgin, the mature woman, or the widow, thus echoing Brantôme's fourth discourse in *Les dames galantes* [*Lives of Fair and Gallant Ladies*]. Generally, they incline toward the virgin, whose fire still burns and who is therefore the most fitted to awaken desire. To initiate the young girl to sensual pleasures is held by man to be an incomparable privilege. Thus defloration constitutes a recurrent fantasy. However, contrary to modern eroticism, which usually shows hatred of childbirth and babies, some poems of *Le temple d'Apollon* describe pregnancy as a natural and estimable result of the sexual act. The pleasure to reach maturity follows the pleasure of knowing a man for the first time: "Non, vous nous direz la belle, / Le bon soir d'une pucelle, / Et demain au point du jour / D'une femme le bon jour" [Nay, you will bid us, fair one / The goodnight of a maiden / And tomorrow at dawn / You will greet us as a woman] (vol. 1: 246).

Men-women relations presented in this work are fairly balanced between the sexes: most of the time, man displays roughly his desire, but the sexual act itself reveals mutual respect. In this sense, a long comparison between love and music is the occasion to show one lover resting while the other continues to play the piece. Like music, sexuality is based upon a perfect harmony, of which each note is made of a "blow": "Je sçay qu'à divers coups se forme l'harmonie, / Et naist de la parole un doux contentement, / Et sçay qu'encore il faut pour l'accomplissement, / Qu'on employe deux corps à la rendre fournie"

[I know that many blows shape harmony / And that from speech arises sweet comfort / And I know that for its completion it takes / Two bodies to make it plentiful]. Here, two characteristics of the libertine *ars erotica* are worthy of notice. First, the inexhaustible energy. In the same poem, the lover declares: "Souvent passe le jour sans que j'aye cessé, / De pousser, d'entonner, de monter, et de descendre. / Je suis d'un naturel qui travaille et endure" [Often the day goes by without seeing me cease / From pushing, striking up, going up and down. / I have a patient and industrious disposition]. The stamina of the libertine lover is in proportion to the intensity of his desire. The other noticeable element is the fundamental value attributed to dynamism in the course of sexual coupling. For this reason, French erotic poetry from the beginning of the 17th century, following that of the 16th century, distinguished itself from that of Pietro Aretino (*I Sonetti lussuriosi* [*Lascivious Sonnets*]) by the fact that it does not have recourse to the figure of the positions (*posizioni*). The tradition founded by Aretino shapes the carnal act according to predetermined postures, or at least it gives preference to the bodies' precise disposition in space in order to describe the lovers. On the contrary, in the libertine *ars erotica* of the beginning of the 17th century, the body's gestures and spatialization is subordinate to the synthetic power of movement. It seems that agitation abstracts and incorporates the entire body. Thus the sexual act is described using verbs that, above all, denote animation: "Et qu'au retour de l'Aurore / Soyez fretillans encore / Que les premiers esveillez / Vous trouvent enfretillez" [And upon Aurora's return may you / Be still quivering / So that those first awake / May find you quivery] (vol. 1: 248).

DAVID DORAIS

Editions

Le Temple d'Apollon ou nouveau recueil des plus excellens vers de ce temps. Rouen: L'Imprimerie de Raphaël du Petit Val, Libraire et Imprimeur du Roy, 1611.

Further Reading

Few serious works have been written about French erotic poetry of the 17th century. The best reference is still the voluminous work of Frédéric Lachèvre, *Le Libertinage au XVIIe siècle*, 15 vols., 1909–1928, Geneva: Slatkine Reprints, 1968.

The following two works deal directly with the subject but are of little interest:

Bougard, Roger G. *Érotisme et amour physique dans la littérature française du XVIIe siècle*. Paris: Gaston Lachurié, 1986.

Loude, Michel. *La Littérature érotique et libertine au XVIIe siècle*. Lyon: Aléas, 1994.

These two articles are valuable for the background information they provide:

Houdard, Sophie. "Vie de scandale et écriture de l'obscène: Hypothèses sur le libertinage de mœurs au XVIIe siècle." *Tangence* 66 (2001): 48–66.

Simonin, Michel. "Éros aux XVIe et XVIIe siècles." In *Eros in Francia nel Seicento*, 11–29. Bari: Adriatica; Paris: Nizet, 1987.

TENCIN, CLAUDINE

1682–1749
French novelist and *salonnière*

Inevitably associated with the excesses of the Regency, Claudine Tencin was known for her audacious affairs with the elite of Paris, her central role in literary salons of the early eighteenth century, and, finally, her novels.

At the age of eight, Claudine Tencin was sent to a convent, where, by all accounts, she was miserable. Even before being compelled by her father to take her vows, she made it clear that she wished only to be relieved of them. After her father's death, she left the convent, had her vows annulled, and made her way to Paris, where she entered public life as Madame de Tencin. She immediately earned renown as the mistress to a long succession of some of the most powerful men in Paris, including Philippe d'Orléans, Richelieu, Cardinal Dubois, and Lord Bolingbroke, to name only a few. Her liaison with the Duc d'Orléans was short lived: it was widely reported that he disliked her habit of talking politics in bed. She mingled with the literati at Mme de Lambert's salon and after Lambert's death, hosted one of the most important salons of the day, with regulars including Montesquieu, Fontenelle, Helvétius, Madame du Châtelet, and Marivaux.

The most scandalous of the many episodes of her Paris life occurred in 1726 when one of her estranged lovers shot himself in Tencin's house. The day before, he had given his solicitor a letter to be read in the event of his untimely death, accusing Tencin of wishing to assassinate him.

She was arrested, then transferred to the Bastille, where she remained for several months, until she was finally acquitted. She emerged from prison the notorious subject of gossip and calumnious songs and verse.

After her acquittal, she focused her attention on salon life and, at the same time, quietly began writing novels. She published her first and best-known novel anonymously in 1735, *Les mémoires du comte de Comminge*. After the relative success of her first novel, she wrote and published two more. Surprisingly, perhaps, her novels offer little of the worldliness, vulgar language, and sexual improprieties for which she was notorious. On the contrary, the tales were praised for their unflinchingly virtuous women and duty-bound men. Her novels all treat similar themes: mistaken identity, paternal authority, forced vows, the conflict between love and duty, and the improbability of consummating true love.

Written in the popular tradition of the first-person memoir novel, *Les mémoires du comte de Comminge* was a literary success, reprinted in nearly twenty editions throughout the eighteenth and nineteenth centuries. It is the story of the young comte de Comminge, who, traveling under a false name to recuperate documents that will restore his father's fortune, falls instantly in love with Adélaïde, the daughter of his father's rival. This *coup de foudre* [love at first sight] sets in motion a chain of events that perpetually keep the two apart. Adélaïde marries a cruel man she doesn't love; Comminge stabs him and flees to a monastery, where, several years later, the deathbed confession of a monk reveals that a fellow monk at the monastery is, in reality, Adélaïde, who never stopped loving Comminge and had disguised herself as a man in order to be close to him. Adélaïde dies immediately after her unveiling, and Comminge retreats to a hermitage to mourn his twice lost love.

Set at the time of the Hundred Years' War, *Le siège de Calais* is a novel that opens with a seduction scene based on mistaken identity: the charming comte de Canaple, aided by a groggy valet, ends up in the wrong bed. He finds himself in the company of his friend's wife. The sleepy Mme de Granson does not realize until the next morning that the man in her bed was not her husband. Canaple has already retreated in haste, wracked with guilt at his act of betrayal. In spite of the passion Mme de Granson feels for Canaple, she acts with uncompromising virtue, offering him only a cold shoulder. In the end, many years, intrigues, and battles later, virtue is rewarded. The husband dies and Mme de Granson, disguised as a man, tries to be executed in the place of Canaple. Touched by the display, the queen intervenes and in the end Granson and Canaple marry.

Published two years before Tencin's death, *Les malheurs de l'amour* is the story of the thwarted love between Pauline and M. de Barbasan. Barbasan is sent to prison for his part in a duel and escapes by seducing the jailer's daughter. Meanwhile, out of duty, Pauline marries the upstanding Hacqueville; distressed at not being truly loved, he dies of grief. Barbasan then returns only to be mortally wounded while saving Pauline from an attacker.

Beginning with the Goncourt brothers in the nineteenth century, literary historians have been more concerned with Tencin's life than her works, recounting her biography as a libertine tale: multiple lovers, escape from a convent, murder, and prison. This emphasis on her sensational biography however, led to the invention of Tencin as a paradox: her legacy is one of a conniving, immoral woman who nevertheless created virtuous, dutiful characters. While ignoring Tencin's own novels, literary historians have compared her to two fictional characters: Suzanne Simonin, the recalcitrant nun in Diderot's *La Religieuse,* and Madame de Merteuil, the calculating libertine from Laclos's *Les liaisons dangereuses.* The very inclusion of Tencin in an encyclopedia of erotic literature is symptomatic of a persisting conflation of her life and texts.

The seduction scenes in her novels serve to promote fidelity and warn of the consequences of unchecked passion; the eroticism that fueled her public and private life is inevitably sublimated in her own literary creations. Perhaps the task still at hand today is the same task feminist critic Naomi Schor outlined for another woman writer, George Sand, whose scandalous life has often overshadowed her texts. For Schor, it is imperative "to devise a reading strategy" that will allow readers to "make sense of the fused texts of her fiction and her life" (183).

Biography

Born in Grenoble, April 27. Sent to a convent at Montfleury, 1690; took vows in spite of her written, notarized protest, 1698; death of her father, Antoine de Tencin, in 1705, which allowed her to leave the convent, 1708; arrived in Paris and began a series of liaisons with some of the most powerful men in Paris, including the Duc d'Orléans, around 1710; official annulment of her vows, 1712; gave birth to and abandoned a son (Jean le Rond d'Alembert, the future editor of the *Encyclopédie*), 1717; imprisoned for the alleged murder of a lover, Charles de La Fresnaye, April 1726; acquitted, July; initiated her own salon, 1733; published her first novel, 1735; died at her home in Paris.

DIANE BERRETT BROWN

Selected Works

Les mémoires du comte de Comminge [1735]. Paris: Mercure de France, 1996.
Le siège de Calais [1739]. Paris: Desjonquères, 1983.
Les malheurs de l'amour [1747]. Paris: Desjonquères, 2001.
Anecdotes de la cour et du règne d'Edouard II, roi d'Angleterre [1766]. Posthumous.
Histoire d'une religieuse, écrite par elle-même [1786]. Posthumous, not confirmed.

Further Reading

Descottignies, Jean. Introduction to *Les Mémoires du comte de Comminge*. Lille: René Giard, 1969.
Duc de Castries, René de La Croix. *La Scandaleuse Madame de Tencin*. Paris: Librairie Académique Perrin, 1987.
Jensen, Katharine Ann. "The Inheritance of Masculinity and the Limits of Heterosexual Revision: Tencin's *Les Mémoires du comte de Comminge*." *Eighteenth-Century Life* 16 (May 1992): 44–58.

Jones, Shirley. "Madame de Tencin: An Eighteenth-Century Woman Novelist." In *Woman and Society in Eighteenth-Century France*, edited by Eva Jacobs et al. London: Athlone Press, 1979.

Masson, Pierre-Maurice. *Une Vie de femme au XVIIIe siècle: Madame de Tencin (1682–1749)*. Originally published in Paris by Hachette, 1909. Geneva: Slatkine, 1970.

Miller, Nancy K. "1735: The Gender of the Memoir-Novel." In *A New History of French Literature*, edited by Denis Hollier. Cambridge, MA: Harvard University Press, 1989.

Schor, Naomi. *George Sand and Idealism*. New York: Columbia University Press, 1993.

THAI EROTIC LITERATURE

An overview of Thai literature available in English translation reveals a frank acknowledgment of the erotic throughout a variety of texts, ranging from the *Ramakien*, the ancient Thai epic based upon the *Ramayana*, to courtly poetry of the Ayutthaya period, to novels and short stories exploring the mores and ramifications of contemporary Thai life in both country and city. The rich heritage of the Hindu-based epics—such as the *Ramakien*—in conjunction with open acknowledgment by Theravadin Buddhism of desire (ideally to be mastered in order to avert suffering), provides a foundation for a literary use of the erotic remarkable for its integration into portrayals of complete lives. While works that present themselves as specifically erotic exist (*The Story of Jan Darra*, 1966, for example), they seem less remarkable given the way that many more mainstream novels and stories incorporate the erotic as a matter of course of everyday life.

Klaus Wenk traces the origins of Thai literature into the 13th century, though the Hindu epics and stories of Buddha's life predate the writings of the Sukhothai court. These provide the founding models for literary structures which inhere to this day. For most of its history, "literature" was the province of the court—kings often being noted and celebrated for their ability to compose elegant poetry. At the same time, there was a strong tradition of oral literature and visual art that frankly represented human—and divine—sexual desire. These gradually came to influence one another, first in the form of drama, and then, with the rise of literacy in the twentieth century, in fiction.

The *Ramakien*, an epic of kingship that involves petty jealousies, drives for revenge, fantastic battles, attempted rapes, presumed infidelities, and divine interventions, is richly erotic, though its eroticism is often more apparent in visual, theater, or dance representations than in the literal translations. The idyllic love of Rama and his consort Sita is disrupted when Ravana, a giant, kidnaps Sita because he desires her beauty. There follows a number of struggles and schemes to rescue Sita from Ravana's realm. Upon rescue, Sita insists on proving her fidelity to Rama through a test of fire, but even that is ultimately not enough to quell the jealousy in Rama's heart, and ultimately Shiva must intervene to reconcile the couple. The short story "Sita Extinguishes the Flames" by Sidaoru'ang (collected in *The Sergeant's Garland*) provides an excellent illustration of a reworking of a *Ramakien* episode into a tale of contemporary marital infidelity.

The themes of female chastity and male promiscuity (because of the woman's ravishing beauty) persist throughout the courtly poetry of the 15th–18th centuries. Unlike courtly love poetry of the West, Thai poetry of this period is marked by far more overt willingness to discuss sexual desire without coding it in complex symbolic systems, as suggested by, for example, "The Boat Song in Praise of Copulation" cited by Wenk.

Much of the literature of the Ayutthaya kingdom was lost when the Burmese sacked the capital in 1767. With the relocation of the capital to Bangkok and the foundation of the Chakri dynasty in the 1780s, Thai literature revived. Rama I, the first Chakri king, wrote (or had written) a new text of the *Ramakien*. Under the Westernizing influences of King Mongkut (Rama IV) and King Chulalongkorn (Rama V), public literacy became a high priority. At the turn of the 20th century, Western novels became available to Thai intellectuals, and these in turn served as models for the generations of writers that followed.

A relatively early Thai novel, *The Prostitute* (1937) by Kanha Surangkhanang, surprised many at its publication in the late 1930s. Attacked as pornographic, the novel in fact sympathetically explores the fate of a beautiful young girl, Reun, from rural Thailand who is seduced to Bangkok and then abandoned in a brothel. There she falls in love with Khun Wit, a young man of good family who, despite his feelings for her, abandons her, unaware that she is carrying his child. She and her fellow prostitute, Samorn, set up housekeeping, with Samorn continuing to work in the sex industry while Reun keeps house and raises the child. This portrait of female friendship and support is rich in love, if not sexualized, and adds an erotic dimension to what would otherwise be a novel of despair. Predictably, their fortunes sour. Samorn dies and Reun is forced back into prostitution, where she reconnects with Wit shortly before she herself dies. Khun Wit, a typical—if generally more decent—young man exploring his sexuality before marriage, is nonetheless also an ethical character and accepts responsibility for his daughter.

Surangkhanang frames the novel with two men who meet on a train and speak slightingly of Wit's early attachment to Reun, thus counterpointing the difference between male and female attitudes toward erotic relationships. Men, in general, are simply more casual about such relationships, and women are left to pay a high price for male promiscuity. This theme can be observed in many works, including *Snakes* (1984) by Wimon Sainimnuan and the story of the prostitute in M.R. Kukrit Pramoj's *Many Lives* (1954). Novels that deal with the historical periods of the late 19th and early 20th centuries, including *Four Reigns* (1953) by Kukrit Pramoj, candidly deal with the practices of multiple wives and husbandly infidelity. Pramoj's heroine, Phloi, is adjured by her mother not to accept the role of a minor wife, and early on has her

heart broken by an attractive young man who pledges himself to her but then marries someone else.

Utsana Phleugntham's *The Story of Jan Darra* treats male sexuality and the desirability of women with almost salacious candor. The novel details the diverse sexual exploits of its hero, Jan, including most notoriously his liaisons with the mistresses and lovers of his own (presumed) father. The author himself advises in an introductory note: "This is the writer's first novel, and he must insist that his work of fiction is unsuitable for kids and most offensive to sanctimonious pricks." Told in the first person, the novel uses its overt eroticism to explore the development of character and to expose the complexity of power relationships within an aristocratic Thai household.

As almost a polar opposite, Chart Korbjitti's *The Judgment* (1981) pursues the fate of a young man, Fak, whom everyone in the village assumes is sleeping with his stepmother. Again, the people of the village, and the men in particular, make broad assumptions about male sexual behavior and the "easiness" of women which, in Fak's case, prove to be untrue. They make vulgar jokes, attempt to spy on Fak, and torment his stepmother. The villagers' hatred drives Fak to drink—and ultimately to his death.

Heterosexuality and the tensions between carnal desire and spiritual love provide the center of most eroticism in Thai literature. But that is not to say that homosexuality, passionate friendships, unrequited love, and idealized romance do not also appear. While much remains inaccessible to those who do not read Thai, there are a number of works in translation which give fine representations of the variety and power of the erotic in Thai literature and culture.

KEITH E. WELSH

Selected Readings

Choophinit, Marlai. *The Field of the Great.* Translated by Marcel Barang. Bangkok: Thai Modern Classics, 1996.

Korbjitti, Chart. *The Judgment.* Translated by Phongdeit Jiangphattana-Kit and Marcel Barang. Nakhon Rachasima, Thailand: Howling Books, 2001.

Phleungtham, Utsana. *The Story of Jan Darra.* Translated by Phongdeit Jiangphatthanarkit. Bangkok: Thai Modern Classics, 1995.

Pramoj, Kukrit. *Four Reigns.* Translated by Chancham Bunnag (1981). Chiang Mai, Thailand: Silkworm Books, 1998.

———. *Many Lives*. Translated by Meredith Borthwick. Chiang Mai, Thailand: Silkworm Books, 1996.

Sainimnuan, Wimon. *Snakes*. Translated by Phongdeit Jiangphatthanarkit. Bangkok: Thai Modern Classics, 1996.

The Sergeant's Garland and Other Stories. Translated by David Smyth and Manas Chitkasem. Oxford, UK: Oxford UP, 1998.

Siburapha. *Behind the Painting and Other Stories* [1936–7]. Translated by David Smyth. Chiang Mai, Thailand: Silkworm Books, 1995.

Surangkhanang, K. *The Prostitute*. Translated by David Smyth. Oxford, UK: Oxford UP, 1994.

Thai Ramayana (Abridged) Retold from the Original Version Written by King Rama I of Siam. Bangkok: Chalermnit, 2000.

Further Reading

Bumroongsook, Sumalee. *Love and Marriage: Mate Selection in Twentieth-Century Central Thailand*. Bangkok: Chulalongkorn UP, 1995.

Nagavajara, Chetana. *Comparative Literature from a Thai Perspective*. Bangkok: Chulalongkorn UP, 1996.

Phillips, Herbert P. *Modern Thai Literature with an Ethnographic Interpretation*. Honolulu: U of Hawai'i Press, 1987.

Rutnin, Mattana Morjdara. *Dance, Drama, and Theatre in Thailand: The Process of Development and Modernization*. Chiang Mai, Thailand: Silkworm Books, 1993.

Wenk, Klaus. *Thai Literature: An Introduction*. Translated by Erich W. Reinhold. Bangkok: White Lotus, 1995.

THANATOS

In Greek mythology, Thanatos is the personification of death, who bears away men's spirits when the threads of their lives have been cut by the Fates. He was portrayed in classical art not as the wizened or skeletal figure one might expect, but as a beautiful winged youth, bearing a sword and an extinguished torch. In the context of modern philosophy, *Thanatos* is a conceptual term, coined by Sigmund Freud in 1920 and used to describe the principle of death as a driving force of psychical and cultural life.

Thinking about Thanatos in relation to erotic literature raises an apparent paradox. Sexuality appears at first sight and in a "commonsense" understanding to be wholly in the service of the creation and preservation of life. However, as suggested by the unlikely image of death embodied in a virile Greek youth, the idea that mortality is inexorably linked to eroticism is deeply rooted and widely represented in our culture. Various causal relations have been posited to account for this link. Firstly, there is the fact that nonprocreative sexual intercourse, masturbation, and homosexuality are condemned as sins in Judeo-Christian discourses, creating a climate of guilt and mortal danger around the idea of pleasurable sex. Even those who have consciously rejected religious faith cannot easily escape these deep-rooted cultural associations.

Pursuing different lines of inquiry, philosophers of transgression have drawn on the very dynamics of sexual excitement to account for its fatal overtones. Georges Bataille has posited that sexual rapture shares qualities with death, as both are states in which the integral boundaries of the self are transgressed and put into danger. In *The Accursed Share* he writes: "Anguish, which lays us open to annihilation and death, is always linked to eroticism; our sexual activity finally rivets us to the distressing image of death, and the knowledge of death deepens the abyss of eroticism."

More prosaically, it has been pointed out that the sexual act entails the exercising and exorcising of the initial motivating desire, the temporary exhaustion of the impulse which led to the act. The economy of sexual pleasure (at least of male sexual pleasure), with its energetic rhythms of buildup and discharge accounts, perhaps, for the equation of sexual release with the point of no return of mortality. The universality of this idea is encapsulated in such linguistic phenomena as the French euphemism for orgasm: "la petite mort" [the little death], a phrase which has been incorporated into most European languages.

The linking of sexuality and death is found in literature from the earliest times and persists as a motif in modern and postmodern writing. Many examples can be found in classical myth. Aphrodite, the goddess of love, is said to have sprung into being from the semen of a murdered man. Similarly, in Egyptian mythology, Isis, wife of the god of death, Osiris, gives birth to her son Horus after impregnating herself with the seed from her husband's corpse. While such myths can be read as being about the triumph of life *over* death, it is also possible to read them as foregrounding the very centrality of the ideational qualities of death in the erotic imagination.

It is possible to identify (though not always to dissociate completely) two ways of thinking about the fusion of desire and death. The first strand of thought posits that death is structurally intrinsic to sexuality or, to quote Shakespeare, that "Desire is Death" (Sonnet 147). The philosophical concept of the deathly insatiability of desire can be traced through the works of prominent thinkers such as Plato, Hegel, Schopenhauer, and Lacan. A comprehensive account of this idea and the texts it produces is found in Jonathan Dollimore's *Death, Desire and Loss in Western Culture* (1998). One literary trope which expresses the lack-driven quality of desire is that of idealized and impossible Romantic love, ending in death. The popular medieval myth of Tristan and Iseult provides a particularly apt illustration of the seamless collapse of the erotic and the thanatic in the love relationship. Unable to sate their desire for each other in life, the lovers must die in a consummatory *Liebestod* (love-death). The concept of the love-death, which continues to resonate in literature and art, suggests that death is the true *aim* of desire, as well as an escape from its sovereignty.

The second way in which the link between death and sexuality is commonly articulated is by means of fantasies, images, and practices in which death itself becomes a conscious object and/or necessary condition of sexual excitement. The aphrodisiac properties of death are testified to by Thom Gunn in his poem "In Time of Plague" (1992):

My thoughts are crowded with death
and it draws so oddly on the sexual
that I am confused
confused to be attracted
by, in effect, my own annihilation.

While considered rare and pathological in the medical sphere, extreme fantasies regarding death are relatively often represented in literature and, moreover, occur frequently in otherwise mainstream erotic and pornographic writing. A good example is found in Anaïs Nin's short story "The Woman on the Dunes," commissioned and written in the 1940s and published in the collection *Little Birds* (1979). The story contains an anecdote recounting a woman's encounter with a stranger, which takes place while she is standing in a crowded town square watching a public execution. As the condemned man's death grows nearer and tension mounts in the crowd, the woman feels herself being held and penetrated from behind by an unknown man she cannot even see. Nin exploits the juxtaposition of the two actions (the hanging/the sexual encounter), suggesting that what is particularly exciting about the proximity to death is precisely that it makes the living subject feel more alive. She writes: "[T]he pain of watching him was so great that it made this touch of flesh a relief, a human, warm, consoling thing," and, "As the condemned man was flung into space and death, the penis gave a great leap inside of her, gushing out its warm life." What is unspoken, however, in this description is the similarity of the two experiences, given that a hanged man's final sensation will be ejaculation in his moment of death (see *Erotic Asphyxation*). Identification with the dying man, then, is implicit in this apparent celebration of life and pleasure.

Another literary figure which links death and sexuality is the "murder as sex" conceit. In Robert Browning's poem "Porphyria's Lover" (1836/1842), for example, the lover cannot bear to be separated from his adulterous mistress. He dreams of a lasting and deep consummation with the object of his desire. Finally, he settles upon a resolution:

That moment she was mine, mine fair
Perfectly pure and good: I found
A thing to do, and all her hair
In one long yellow string I wound
Three times her little throat around
And strangled her.

The eroticism implicit in this poetic murder is neutralized by the Romantic conventions Browning deploys. His possessive killing of the lover is re-encoded as an act of love.

Some poets have been less squeamish regarding their mapping of murder onto sex. Charles Baudelaire's *Les Fleurs du mal* [*The Flowers of Evil*] (1855) contains many explorations of this idea. One of the most striking, "A celle qui est trop gaie" [Against Her Levity], describes a fantasy of murderous wounding. The poet recounts his desire to create a new hole in his mistress's abdomen, more beautiful than her original sexual opening, into which he can inject his "venin" [venom]. This poetic fantasy of wounding suggests a metaphorical means of transforming sex into murder. This is particularly visible in the climactic image of ejaculation, in which the substance ejected is not life-giving sperm, but fatal poison.

A few texts exist in which the erotic frenzy of sexual murder is explicitly described. The final section of the Marquis de Sade's *Les 120 Journées de Sodome* [*The Hundred and Twenty Days of Sodom*] (1784–5), entitled "Les Passions meurtrières" [Murderous Passions], is devoted to the many varieties and configurations of eroticized killing. Typically, these killings are designed to juxtapose Eros and Thanatos for aesthetic effect, as in the following example, which conjoins maternity and murder, life-giving and death:

> Un grand partisan de culs étrangle une mère en l'enculant; quand elle est morte, il la retourne et la fout en con. En déchargeant, il tue la fille sur le sein de la mère à coup de couteau dans le sein, puis il fout la fille en cul quoique morte [An *amateur* of arses strangles a mother while buggering her. When she is dead, he turns her over and fucks her in the cunt. While ejaculating, he kills the daughter on the mother's breast with a knife blow to the heart; then he buggers the daughter, even though she is dead].

For de Sade, destruction epitomizes the most erotic experience, as it confirms man's agency and power in the world. Moreover, for de Sade, murder is "natural," since, he argues, Nature herself carries out random creation and destruction of all of her creatures, with no guiding principle of morality.

As has been demonstrated above, expressions of the link between death and eroticism are not limited to one historical period or culture. However, an important moment in the conceptualization of this link, and one which demands specific attention, is the late nineteenth century, which marked the dawning of modernity in Europe. The rise in clinic-based psychology at this time, coupled with the birth of the modern science of sexology, saw an increased interest in understanding and naming the varieties of sexual expression and dysfunction. The Enlightenment principles underpinning this project meant that sexuality was seen as a knowable and analyzable concept for the first time. However, significantly, this ambitious scientific project was also contemporaneous with pessimistic currents of thought such as degeneration theory and literary decadence, prevalent in England, Germany, France, and Italy at the end of the nineteenth century. In his philosophical work on *fin-de-siècle* European subjectivity, *The Decline of the West* (1950), Oswald Spengler describes a phenomenon that "suddenly emerges into the bright light of history," which he goes on to describe as "a *metaphysical* turn towards death."

The historical co-incidence of the Scientific Revolution and Decadent philosophy produced a certain strand of European writing about sexuality and death that blended both cultural influences. One of the most interesting example [s] of this kind of literature is Emile Zola's *La Bête humaine* (1889), which tells the story of Jacques Lantier, a young man who is troubled by an obsessive desire to kill any woman he finds sexually attractive. As a writer influenced by the scientific theories of heredity popular at the time, Zola presents this desire as a flaw inherited from a tainted bloodline. The story of Jacques Lantier approximates a case history of a lust murderer such as would be found in the works of Krafft-Ebing and other sexologists. However, as well as incorporating features of fashionable scientific discourse, Zola proposes in *La Bête humaine* an ambitious philosophy of masculine sexuality based on the proximity between sexual feeling and murderous aggressiveness.

Following Jacques's first sexual experience with the heroine, Séverine, he is amazed by the fact that he feels satisfied and does not experience the urge to kill her. Framing the question from Jacques's narrative point of view, Zola asks whether sex and death are psychically the same thing: "Depuis qu'il la possédait, la pensée du meurtre ne l'avait plus troublé. Était-ce donc que la possession physique contentait ce besoin de mort? Posséder, tuer, cela s'équivalait-il dans le fond sombre de la bête humaine?" [The thought of murder had not troubled him since he had possessed her. Could physical possession satisfy that need for death? Possessing, killing: did they mean the same thing in the dark heart of the beast in man?] The novel pursues the theory that owing to deep-rooted, atavistic impulses, the male of the species is inclined to equate the aggression of sexual conquest with the absolute possession of destruction.

However, of the two terms—murder and sex—Zola's protagonist ultimately prefers the former. The novel's climax takes the form of Jacques's murder of Séverine. In a gesture of passion, Séverine offers her bare throat to Jacques to be caressed. Unable to resist this incredible provocation, Jacques plunges his knife into her neck. The fact that Séverine hastens her own death in this way stands as Zola's bitterly ironic comment on the fatal impossibility of passion between the sexes.

The flavor of these turn-of-the-century European writings, both theoretical and literary, would influence one of the most important and ambitious theories of death and sexuality to emerge in the twentieth century. In *Beyond the Pleasure Principle* (1920), Freud postulated controversially that alongside the drive to survive, procreate, and flourish (Eros, or the life drive), there exists an apparently opposing principle, the death drive, or Thanatos. While the life drive seeks to decrease tension and to maintain the organism in a state of equilibrium (the pleasure principle), the death drive works in excess of this, seeking to return the subject to an originary state of nothingness, of radical absence. Drawing on Empedocles's opposition between φιλία (love) and νῖκος (discord), Freud thus portrays psychical life as characterized by a constant struggle between two forces which battle for supremacy. When internalized, the death drive leads to a masochistic repetition of unpleasurable experiences and fantasies. When externalized, it manifests as aggression.

It has been suggested that literary creation is one of the spaces in which we have privileged access to the workings of Eros and Thanatos. In his classic text of narrative theory, *Reading for the Plot*, Peter Brooks argues that the processes of literary storytelling reveal, by their very construction, the impetus toward ending. He writes: "Desire is the wish for the end, for fulfilment, but fulfilment must be delayed so that we can understand it in relation to its origin and to desire itself." Brooks reads Freud's *Beyond the Pleasure Principle* as a work of literature as well

as a theoretical text. For him, it is the exemplary tale of the relation between beginnings and endings. The desire to achieve a state of stasis is seen as the driving force that motivates the forward-flung desire of any text, as well as of any individual life. In suggesting that the death drive operates an intrinsically destructive creation, Brooks offers up literature as a privileged space for examination of the workings of Thanatos, directing the course of sexuality into dying *only in its own way*. For Brooks, the novel's form may be said to demonstrate mimetically the *structural* properties of Thanatos.

In *The Ego and the Id* (1923), Freud discussed those cases in which the death drive and the life drive merge and are made manifest in the world. Freud proposes that the fusion of the drives (*Triebmischung*) is visible in sadistic and masochistic performances of human sexuality. Freud's notion of the death drive as a repetition beyond what is pleasurable provides an elucidatory tool for reading certain texts which do not at first appear to be about an erotic relation to death. Annie Ernaux's *Passion simple* (1991) is a semi-autobiographical, first-person erotic narrative which recounts an obsessive love affair. The narrative describes the repetitive rituals undergone by the female narrator, who has spent a year of her life doing "rien d'autre qu'attendre un homme" [nothing other than waiting for a man]. Her sexual thrall is described as an addiction, something consummately pleasurable while at the same time destructive of the other aspects of her life. Ernaux, read through the lens of Freud, exposes the death-driven impulses at the heart of the apparently most erotic relationships and the most life-driven sexual practices.

Several feminist critics in the twentieth century have critiqued the linking of death and sexuality, claiming that it reveals a pervasive masculine fantasy of power and dominance. They posit, variously, that the male fear of femininity and of death leads to the sexualization of dead women in culture (Bronfen); that the figure of the male killer is eroticized and glamourized in popular culture (Caputi); and, most radically, in an argument that echoes the logic of Zola's *La Bête humaine*, that penetration is innately aggressive and always already accompanied by a fantasy of destruction (Dworkin).

Some twentieth-century literary texts play with and mobilize the dominant paradigm of male aggression and female victimization that these accounts identify. Muriel Spark's *The Driver's Seat* (1970) offers a particularly inventive example of this strategy. The novel opens with the heroine, Lise, about to go on holiday to Italy in search of a particular—and unnamed—type of erotic encounter. On the plane, she spots a man whom she recognizes instantly as "the one" with whom she wishes to have her adventure. However, he appears afraid and resistant to her approaches and, on arrival at their destination, he manages to give her the slip. Evading her pursuit of him throughout the course of the holiday, he is finally cornered in the closing pages of the book, whereupon she leads him to a park and tells him what it is that she wants: "'Kill me', she says, and repeats it in four languages." When Lise's chosen killer/victim (for the roles have become radically confused at this point) indicates he would much rather have sex instead, her response is uncompromising: "'You can have it afterwards.'"

Certain commentators, who take the novel at face value, have criticized it heavily for its apparent endorsement of female masochism to the point of self-destruction. Passages of dialogue such as the following appear to universalize the desire for victimization:

> "A lot of women get killed in the park." . . .
> "Yes, of course. It's because they want to be."

However politically incorrect it may be, Spark's novel is extremely self-conscious in its intention to amuse and to shock. It disconcerts our perceptions of aggression and passivity by focusing throughout on the driving subjectivity of the "victim" who seeks out, predatorily, her (reluctant) killer. By naming death as the aim of the sexual encounter, this self-aware novel makes radically transparent the commonplace representations of discourses of sexuality, in which death is the omnipresent but unspoken underside of eroticism.

Thanatos occupies a paradoxical position in erotic representation. Death, as we have seen, is central to discourses of eroticism, yet its presence is either undertheorized or dismissed as politically problematic by critics. This co-presence of obsession and silence is characteristic of the human relationship to death in general. In Freud's 1915 essay "Our Attitude Towards Death," he describes the cultural tendency, in peacetime, to disavow death, to eliminate it from life. Several commentators on Western culture, most notably Phillippe Ariès, have written about this tendency in the context of a particularly modern consciousness. In Ariès's historical account of attitudes toward death (1974), he asserts that while medieval culture understood mortality with reference to discourses of mysticism, in the atheistic modern period, death has become shameful and taboo. Ariès goes on to claim that the rich history of eroticizing death finds its pathological apotheosis in the modern fascination with erotic violence: he contends that death has become "admirable in its beauty." Given the thanatic qualities of much erotic writing, literature may present the most privileged site available to us for exploration of the problematic relationship between desire and destruction that has informed thought since the earliest time.

LISA DOWNING

Further Reading

Ariès, Phillippe. *Western Attitudes Towards Death: From the Middle Ages to the Present.* Translated by Patricia M. Ranum. Baltimore and London: Johns Hopkins University Press, 1974.

Bataille, Georges. *The Accursed Share.* Translated by Robert Hurley. 3 vols. New York: Zone Books, 1988, 1991.

Boothby, Richard. *Death and Desire: Psychoanalytic Theory in Lacan's Return to Freud.* New York and London: Routledge, 1991.

Bronfen, Elisabeth. *Over Her Dead Body.* Manchester: Manchester University Press, 1992.

Brooks, Peter. "Freud's Masterplot." In *Reading for the Plot*, 90–112. Oxford: Clarendon Press, 1984.

Caputi, Jane. *The Age of Sex Crimes.* London: Women's Press, 1987.

Dollimore, Jonathan. *Death, Desire and Loss in Western Culture.* Harmondsworth: Penguin, 1998.

Downing, Lisa. *Desiring the Dead: Necrophilia and Nineteenth-Century French Literature.* Oxford: Legenda, 2003.

———. "On the Limits of Sexual Ethics: The Phenomenology of Autassassinophilia." *Sexuality and Culture* 8 (2004): 3–17.

Dufresne, Todd. *Tales from the Freudian Crypt: The Death Drive in Text and Context.* Stanford, CA: Stanford University Press, 2000.

Dworkin, Andrea. *Intercourse.* London: Secker & Warburg, 1987.

Freud, Sigmund. "Our Attitude Towards Death" [1915], "Beyond the Pleasure Principle" [1920], and "The Ego and the Id" [1923]. All in *The Standard Edition of the Complete Psychological Works*, translated from the German under the general editorship of James

Strachey. 24 vols. London: Hogarth Press and the Institute of Psycho-Analysis, 1953–74.

Laplanche, Jean. *Life and Death in Psychoanalysis.* Translated by Jeffrey Mehlman. Baltimore and London: Johns Hopkins University Press, 1976.

Rougemont, Denis de. *Love in the Western World* [1940]. Translated by Montgomery Belgion. New York: Fawcett, 1966.

THÉÂTRE ÉROTIQUE DE LA RUE DE LA SANTÉ, LE

French pornographic puppet shows

In the early 1860s, a small group of writers and actors would gather on Sundays at the home of the man of letters Amédée Rolland (1819–1868), at 54 rue de la Santé, in the Parisian suburb of Batignolles. Along with Georges Bizet, Alphonse Daudet, and Théodore de Banville, the regulars numbered the journalist Jean Duboys (1836–1873), humorist and caricaturist Henri Monnier (1799–1877), itinerant actor-poet Albert Glatigny (1839–1873), and Louis Lemercier de Neuville, nicknamed Lemerdier (1830–1918), littérateur and budding puppeteer. To enhance their amusement, they created a little marionette theatre in a glassed-in antechamber. The spatial limitations meant that only two operators—Lemercier and Duboys—could work the dolls, and no more than four puppets could be on stage at one time. The author of a play would stand beside the stage and read out his work, while the wooden actors mimed it. There were eight puppets in all, their heads carved by the actor Demarsy.

The first performance of what Rolland called the *Erôtikon théatron*, May 27, 1862, was attended by fifteen persons, including two actresses. Irreverence, derisive irony, and bawdiness were the hallmarks of these entertainments. For the second performance, a burlesque poster announced that the play *Le dernier jour d'un condamné* was not Victor Hugo's, that *les misérables* would be anyone who didn't applaud, and that the performance would conclude with *La puce enceinte ou l'innocence reconnu.*

The three-scene play performed at the opening, and revived five times thereafter, was *Signe d'argent* by Rolland and Duboys. A nobleman who has managed to get his wife with child (actually the servant's) is eager to indulge all her cravings, including sticking a peacock's feather in his arse (a joke as old as pre-Revolutionary obscene libels of Marie Antoinette). In the next scene, a soldier and a peddler defecate in a country landscape, a parody of the realist school of painting and literature. The pregnant Marquise develops a craving for the smell of a turd, a situation developed to the point where her husband is made to eat it.

Le dernier jour d'un condamné, played only once, at the second performance, was written by the actor-playwright Jean-Hippolyte Tisserant (1809–1877), author of a dramatization of *The Vicar of Wakefield.* A sardonic attack on French law, the scenes unfolded in three acts against a traveling panorama three meters long, starting at the Palace of Justice and ending at the guillotine. The play's interest lies in its blasphemy, cynicism, and use of underworld argot. Its protagonist, the murderer Jean Coutaudier, recurs in Monnier's dialogues as Jean Hiroux, and there was an debate over which character came first.

Scapin maquereau (originally *Scapin ruffian,* January 1863), written by Glatigny in alexandrines, centers on a girl who doesn't know the use of a bidet. Scapin the brothelkeeper promises the girl's father to teach her cleanliness at his place. It's just before her wedding, and when her bridegroom comes to the brothel to try his luck, he runs into his bride. Scapin brings him the basin of water and all ends happily with the purification of the bride's bottom and the crowning of a bust of de Sade.

The most famous of these plays is *La grisette et l'étudiant* by Monnier, although he repudiated authorship even while reciting all three roles. A period piece, set between 1830 and 1840, it offers a steamy episode from the Romantic *vie de bohème*: a student and a working-class girl making strenuous love in a garret are interrupted by the indignant voice of the next-door neighbor, M. Prud'homme, Monnier's hybrid of Pecksniff and Mrs Grundy. As the girl gasps in ecstasy, Prud'homme is heard to bellow through the wall: "Here, that'll do! If you don't stop I shall be forced to lay violent hands on myself!"

Les jeux de l'amour et du bazar by Lemercier de Neuville, whose characters' names come from Marivaux's neoclassic comedy *Le jeu de l'amour et du hasard* but whose dialogue is in slang, introduces us to Sylvie, a whore who wants to taste true love. While on the game, she is met by the pimp Dorante, who decides to play at being a john. Charmed by his considerable virility, Sylvie lets him have her without payment. When he reveals his identity and says he wouldn't keep such a stupid cow on his team, she agrees to let him be her manager. The finale included a chorus of policemen painted on a single piece of cardboard manipulated by one puppeteer. This innovation was then adapted to other plays.

The title of *Un caprice*, also by Lemercier (October 1863), alludes to Alfred de Musset's comedy. In this two-hander, a husband, who likes to visit whores, can't get an erection and goes back to his wife. At the moment when the tart Urinette peed in a pot, the German scholar Louis Wihl, who was under the misapprehension that he was attending a serious literary puppet show, insulted his hosts and erupted from the room. *Un caprice* was later revived at Emile Renié's marionette theatre.

Indeed, the fame of the *Erôtikon théatron* was such that newspapers carried glowing though veiled reviews, and the puppets were invited to other venues. The first external exhibition of the *pupazzi* was in *Le bout de l'an de la noce* (1863), a parody of a sketch by Théodore Barrière, played at the home of the fashionable photographer Carjat. The psychologically subtlest of the plays of Lemercier and Duboys, it depicts two newly married society ladies waiting for their former lovers in a private room in a restaurant. As they while away the time recounting their various disappointments with men, they begin to develop a romantic interest in one another and, when the waiter announces the gentlemen's arrival, escape through a side door to taste the joys of Lesbos.

Finally, *La Grande Symphonie des Punaises*, an operetta about an epic battle between military men and bedbugs, penned by the journalist, caricaturist, and photographer Nadar (Félix Tournachon, 1820–1910) and the writer Charles Bataille (1831–1868), was performed at the home of Jacques Offenbach. He composed the score for it, recycling some of the music into *La Belle Hélène*.

This Rabelaisian theatre lasted only a year and a half (1862–3) but was perpetuated in print. A guest at the premiere was Auguste Poulet-Malassis (1825–1878), the publisher of Baudelaire's *Les Fleurs de mal* (1857), for which he had been prosecuted and fined, along with the author. In 1864 he issued from Brussels the five plays of the *Erôtikon théatron* plus the bedbug operetta, with his own prefaces and a frontispiece by Félicien Rops, as *Le Théâtre érotique de la rue de la Santé*. An expanded octavo edition of 1866 added another Rops plate and a facsimile of the original invitation. Later editions include *Les deux gougnottes*, Monnier's licentious playlet in which two persuasive lesbians recruit a third woman to their pleasures. (It may have been inspired by an incident when Glatigny surprised Rolland's cook and servingmaid in their sapphic lovemaking.)

LAURENCE SENELICK

Editions

Le Théâtre érotique de la rue de la Santé, suivi de La grande symphonie des punaises. With a priapic frontispiece by SPQR [Félicien Rops]. Everywhere and nowhere [Brussels: Poulet-Malassis], 1864; expanded edition, Batignolles, 1866; as *Le Théâtre érotique de la rue de la Santé: Précédé de son histoire et suivi de Les Deux gougnottes*, Paris: Cercle du Livre Précieux, 1963; Paris: L'Or du temps, 1969; as *Le Théâtre érotique du XIXe siècle*, Paris: Lattès, 1979.

L'Enfer de Joseph Prud'homme, c'est à savoir: La Grisette et l'étudiant et les deux Gougnottes dialogues agrémentés d'une figure infâme et d'un autographe accablant, Paris [Brussels]: to the sixth chamber, 1877; as "The Tart and the Student," translated by Daniel Gerould, *The Drama Review* (March 1981).

Further Reading

Delvau, Alfred. *Le Théâtre érotique sous le bas-Empire.* Paris: Pincebourse [1871].
Lemercier de Neuville, Louis. *Histoire anecdotique des marionettes modernes.* Paris: Calmann Lévy, 1892.

————. *Souvenirs d'un montreur des marionettes.* Paris: M. Bauche, 1911.
Place, Georges G., and Jean-Pierre Seguin. *Henry Monnier.* Paris: Éditions de la Chronique des lettres françaises, 1970.

THEOCRITUS

c. 285–246 BCE
Greek poet

Theocritus is credited with 24 surviving epigrams and a body of 30 or so poems, some of which are of doubtful authenticity. The poems bear the general title "Idylls," meaning "pictures" or short descriptive pieces on rustic, bucolic, or pastoral subjects, but also on town life, legends of the gods, or passages of personal experience. Theocritus has a sharp eye for realistic detail, and his poetry is elegant, witty, and charming. Love plays an important part in his subject matter, but Theocritus is more interested in portraying the emotional states of the victims of love than depicting sensual details.

Unrequited passion is described in a number of poems. In Idyll 2 (one of his finest), the enchantress Simaetha has been jilted by her handsome lover Delphis. Fired by erotic jealousy and torn between hope and despair, she casts a spell to bring him back to her ("I want to chain to me my dearest love who causes me such pain"). In her loneliness, she tells the story of her love to Selene, goddess of the Moon. In Idyll 3, a lovesick goatherd approaches his beloved Amaryllis and pleads with her, but she remains cold and indifferent. The ugly Cyclops Polyphemus in Idyll 11 shows his infatuation and naive vanity in trying to woo the nymph Galatea: he recalls the beginning of his love and dreams of a future life with the object of his desire. The poem, which may be satirizing some Alexandrian romantic clichés, declares: "There is no remedy for love, except the Muses's song" and closes with the advice that the Cyclops should find another girl (compare Idyll 29). Idyll 14 is the story of a jealous lover and a faithless girl. In Idyll 20, an oxherd complains that Eunica, a town girl, has unreasonably rejected him. Idyll 23 is on a pederastic subject: a young man, scorned by the boy he adores, comes to the latter's house, predicting that the boy's beauty will eventually fade and that he in turn will experience the pangs of unrequited love. The man hangs himself, and the boy, unmoved, goes off to the gymnasium where a statue of Eros falls and kills him. Other poems also have homosexual themes. Idyll 12 is a monologue addressed to a boy whose brief absence the poet regrets; on their coming together again, he expresses the wish that posterity will remember their perfect union. This poem contains references to the youths who competed in the "Contest of Kisses," held at the town of Megara. Idyll 13, a conversation on love and the sufferings which it causes ("No one is proof against love, not even the mightiest of men"), tells the story of Hercules's strong but tragic passion for Hylas, the youth who was treacherously seduced and drowned by some nymphs. Idylls 29 and 30 are both titled "Paedica" [Lads' Loves]. The former is addressed to a fickle boy ("I'm only half alive because of your beauty: when you agree, I'm in Heaven, when you don't, I'm in Hell"). Together with advice to remember that youth is fleeting (a characteristic observation on pederastic love), the poet hopes that when the boy has grown a beard, they will both be the firmest and noblest of friends. There is, however, a sting in the tail: "I'll go through fire and water for you, but if you say 'Why do you keep on bothering me,' you'll call for me in vain—for I'll be cured." Idyll 30 is a dialogue between the poet and his soul on the theme that now that he is growing old, he should behave correctly and not let himself be seduced by a boy's smile.

A large number of the idylls are constructed in dialogue form, usually as a song contest or conversation between two pastoral characters. This allows more than one view of a subject to be expressed. Thus in Idyll 1, Thyrsis, a shepherd, sings the celebrated story about Daphnis, who angers the goddess Aphrodite by being indifferent to love. In consequence she makes him fall victim to a violent passion from which he dies. In Idyll 5, Lacon, a shepherd, and Comatas, a goatherd, have an angry exchange of words and then engage in a singing contest, part of which deals with their amorous adventures. In the course of their argument, Comatas, the elder, forcefully reminds Lacon how he had once sodomized him. Idyll 6 provides a variant on Polyphemus's story: here Damoetas, taking on the role of the Cyclops, sings how his feigned indifference to Galatea is a trick to bring her down a peg and make her surrender. In Idyll 7, Lycidas sings how he wishes Ageanax a prosperous sea voyage on condition he grants him his favors, for he is in love with him. This is answered by Simichidas's song describing Aratus's love for Philinus, who, it seems, is past his prime. The charms and snares of love are wittily and delicately evoked. Idyll 10 is a song contest at harvest time. Boucaios is so deeply in love he cannot sleep. He sings in praise of his girl, Bombyca, but in reality she is skinny and sunburned. Milon, who hears all this, is unimpressed. Of the remaining idylls where love is the subject, Idyll 27 ("Sweet Talk") is charming, but unfortunately incomplete at the beginning: Daphnis, a cowherd, persuades a shepherdess to go with him to the nearby woods, where he does not have to try too hard to get her to yield. Idyll 18 is a marriage hymn sung to Helen by her maiden companions before her wedding. Helen, its hearers would have known, was the epitome of beauty and was destined to commit adultery and cause the

Trojan War. Theocritus's *Idylls* have been widely appreciated since they first appeared in print in about 1480, but before the twentieth century most translations were simply censored by omitting alleged indelicacies, or bowdlerized by the substitution of female for male pronouns.

Biography

A Greek poet of the Hellenistic period, Theocritus was probably born at Syracuse (Sicily) and left there at a relatively early age to go to the royal court of the Ptolemies at Alexandria in Egypt. Details of his life are simply inferences, drawn from his poetry, and no reliable biographical information has come down to us.

PATRICK POLLARD

Selected Works

Theocritus. Edited with a translation and commentary by A.S.F. Gow. 2nd ed. Cambridge: Cambridge University Press, 1952.
Bucoliques grecs: Théocrite. Translated and edited by P.E. Legrand. 5th ed. Paris: Les Belles Lettres, 1972.
Greek Pastoral Poetry: Theocritus, Bion, Moschus, the Pattern Poems. Translated with an introduction and notes by A. Holden. Harmondsworth: Penguin Books, 1974.

Further Reading

Gutzwiller, K.J. *Theocritus' Pastoral Analogies.* Madison: University of Wisconsin Press, 1991.
Hunter, R. *Theocritus and the Archaeology of Greek Poetry.* Cambridge: Cambridge University Press, 1996.
Lawal, G. *Theocritus' Coan Pastorals.* Washington, DC: Center for Hellenic Studies, 1967.
Rosenmeyer, T.G. *The Green Cabinet: Theocritus and the European Pastoral Lyric.* Berkeley and Los Angeles: University of California Press, 1969.
Segal, C. *Poetry and Myth in Ancient Pastoral: Essays on Theocritus and Virgil.* Princeton, NJ: Princeton University Press, 1981.
Walker, S.F. *Theocritus.* Boston: Twayne Publishers, 1980.

THEOTOKIS, CONSTANTINOS

1872–1923
Greek novelist

Constantinos Theotokis is a Greek naturalist writer who figures at the origin of the Greek social novel. His works bear the brand of a hard and crude naturalism inspired by Zola.

Theotokis's works arouse a feeling of horror. His characters live in a rural world marked by rapes, murders, suicides, blackmail, and death threats. The human body is depicted in its least noble functions. Dishonor, when it is abused, is obscene and ugly, and hurts decency and intimacy. Theotokis is very far from the beauty Plato celebrated in *Hippias majeur*. Indeed, he conveys only violated and violating pleasure—the sensual appeal of Cicero's taste and distaste finds a wonderful illustration in Theotokis.

Honor and love often trigger murder or suicide. As in the case of Petros Peponas in *O Κατάδικος* [*The Convicted*] (1919), the individual cannot escape from the tyranny of the code of honor: the deceived husband is forced to kill his wife to win his honor back. Violence is always directed toward women: they find themselves abandoned, like Rini in *Η Τιμή και το χρήμα* [*Honor and Money*] (1912), or they are left to die after being repeatedly raped, like Chrysavgi in *Αγάπη παράνομη* [*Forbidden Love*] (1906). Murder adds to this gloomy picture of a society in which love is missing: In *Πίστομα* [*On the Stomach*], the amnestied bandit Coucouliotis, on his return home, kills his wife's lover out of revenge and forces his wife to bury alive the child they had together. Similarly, in *Ακόμα* [*Not Yet?*] (1904), Kourkoupos, another deceived husband, takes his revenge by stabbing his wife to death in their own house.

Theotokis's entire work stages ugly, disgusting, and loathsome situations, which shock the inner self and the very harmony of the mind and offend moral standards. There is no love in his works. This lack of love is conveyed in its most sublimated form—evoking the birds' nuptial songs and dances become extreme and pathological, turning man into an animal. There is neither magic nor rapture in these lives, only acts of violence which degrade man; neither duality nor complicity (except perhaps Rini in *Honor and Money*), only carnal and violent instincts. Under the yoke of sexual desire, Theotokis's male characters obey a primitive, violent force which thwarts chastity and honesty. It is precisely this primitive force, this appetite, this voracity, this ravenous force that Theotokis tried to highlight in those of his novels considered most outrageous—at the dawn of the twentieth century, he dared to put brain, mind, and sex together.

More than the theme of dishonor in *Honor and Money* (which highlights the bargaining of marriage), and much more than *Η παντρειά της Σταλαχτής* [*Stalachti's Marriage*] (1905), in which the dishonored and desperate heroine throws herself into a well to put an end to her sufferings, *Forbidden Love* stages the incestuous love of Stathis Therianos with Chrysavgi, his daughter-in-law. A calculating criminal, Stathis hatches a monstrous scheme to get Chrysavgi: he has his son marry the young woman in order to have her at hand under his roof. A ravenous power seems to be at the origin of all these depraved behaviors, the metaphysical root of obscenity. The satisfied but not totally assuaged desire of Stathis, a modern Oedipus without the shame and heartbreaks of Sophocles's character, turns into an incestuous urge to possess his daughter-in-law. The forced sex act takes place in his house with the concupiscent complicity of his wife Diamanto, in the shameful alcove where the young woman will leave her weary flesh. The affair she is forced to have with her father-in-law is doubly perverse.

More than any of his other works, *Η ζωή και ο θάνατος του Καραβέλα* [*The Life and Death of Karavelas*] (1920) is a book of crime and perversity. With fierce Naturalism, it portrays a sexually obsessed old man, manipulated by a couple in the grip of cupidity. In this work where obscenity reigns supreme, Eros is no longer the chubby and winged boy poised in an ethereal sky, the very emblem of human lightness and amorous exhilaration, luxury, calm, and delight. Theotokis's Eros is taken from the Platonic figure of the Banquet: he inherited from Shortage, his mother, the lack of beautiful and good qualities and from Makeshift, his father, the means to achieve them, thanks to procreation: "He is filthy and brutal and has absolutely no delicacy or pleasantness" (Lacarrière: 272–3). Persevering and stubborn, he is always up to no good, plotting some mischief. Thomas Kranias, the protagonist, is no sympathetic character: he is perverted, lustful, cruel, violent, and short-tempered. Possessed by a demonic lechery, he lusts after his young neighbor Maria. He even makes a deal with her brother-in-law: the house in exchange for Maria's body. He first has to get rid of his old, sterile wife as quickly as possible to be able to taste of this longed-for happiness. So he murders his wife, abandoning her in her bed, where she suffers horrible death pangs and is to be found there in a putrefying state. Suffering from unassuaged desire, driven to despair because he cannot possess Maria, Kranias is slowly led to suicide. In an attempt to debase mankind, Theotokis gives his characters the frenzy of filth.

In this novel, Eros generates Thanatos. The theme of Eros-*nosos* [*illness*], which leads to madness, was elaborated by Sophocles and taken up again by Euripides, who distinguishes two Eroses: the one which leads to virtue and the one which leads to indignity (Lévy-Bertherat: 564–73). It is precisely this pleasure which can be seen in Theotokis's works. Indeed, the novel includes many allusions to the psychological appetites of a pervert, but Maria shows herself as she really is, namely, a whore. Impervious to shame, she displays her private parts in front of the old man with a daring quietness, convinced as she is of the all-powerfulness of her flesh. She is a maneater. She both delights in arousing the old man's real and concrete desire and frustrates it, out of perversity. Karavelas's desire is below human love. It is pure concupiscence. Maria represents two things: a womb likely to bear children and a free servant.

Theotokis's moral nakedness imparts to all his characters, above all to Maria and Thomas Kranias, the frenzy of garbage. *The Life and Death of Karavelas, The Convicted,* and *Forbidden Love* are novels of the flesh, studies of social customs of a rural society considered at their most erotic or most amoral. Perverted men and women, the preys to victims of the unleashed frenzy of their desires, indulge in incredible adventures of shame and madness. Such is the prevalence of the relationship between Eros and Thanatos in our modern literature.

Biography

Constantinos Theotokis was born into the Corfú aristocracy. He studied in Graz, Austria, where he was influenced by the Russian novel and became a committed socialist.

EFSTRATIA OKTAPODA-LU

Selected Works

Η ζωή και ο θάνατος του Καραβέλα [The Life and Death of Karavelas]. Athens: Hestia, 1977.

Η Τιμή και το χρήμα [Honor and Money]. Athens: Printing Keimena, 1984; as the film *Η Τιμή της αγάπης* [The Price of Love], directed by Tonia Marketaki, 1984.

Ο Κατάδικος [The Convicted]. Athens: Nefeli, 1990.

Διηγήματα. Κορφιότικες ιστορίες [Novels. Corfu's Stories] [1898–1912]. Athens: Printing Keimena, 1981. Includes "Πίστομα" [On the Stomach], "Ακόμα" [Not Yet?], "Τίμιος Κόσμος" [Fair World] [1905], "Η παντρειά της Σταλαχτής" [Stalachti's Marriage], and "Αγάπη παράνομη" [Forbidden Love].

Further Reading

Lacarrière, Jacques. "Éros." In *Dictionnaire amoureux de la Grèce* [The Love Dictionary of Greece], 271–74. Paris: Plon, 2001.

Lévy-Bertherat, Ann-Déborah. "Éros." In *Dictionnaire des mythes littéraires* [Dictionary of Literary Myths], edited by Pierre Brunel, 564–73. Paris: Éditions du Rocher, 1988.

Platon. *Le Banquet, Oeuvres complètes.* Vol. 1. Paris: Gallimard/La Pléiade, 1989.

Thibaudet, Albert. " Langage, littérature et sensualité." In *Réflexions sur la littérature.* Vol. 2, 205–13. Paris: Gallimard, 1940.

———. "Le roman du plaisir." In *Réflexions sur le roman*, 161–68. Paris: Gallimard, 1938.

THÉRIAULT, YVES

1916–1983
Canadian novelist and short story writer

Oeuvres de chair

The title of Yves Thériault's erotic short story collection, *Oeuvres de chair* [*Ways of the Flesh*], brings to mind the common religious exhortation: "The ways of the Flesh shall be had in wedlock only." The religious connotation is linked to sexual activities and brings to mind the notion of sin, or even transgression, since in many of Thériault's short stories, the protagonists are priests, nuns or monks who do not abide at all by their vows of chastity. The title also evokes the pleasures of the table—*flesh* can refer both to sensual pleasures and to meat served as food—and the short stories play on this ambivalence to offer detailed recipes as well as fine meals as preludes to sexual intercourse. *Ways of the Flesh,* then, combines the pleasures of the table and those of the bed.

The period used as a setting for the three short stories "Sister Jeanne's Coq en pâte," "The Monastic Stew," and "Quill and Quail" is the Middle Ages and consequently the characters are a nun, a countess, a monk, and a peasant, who indulge without any restraint or remorse in sexual transgression. Thus, Sister Jeanne flees her convent, intent on losing her virginity. She meets Flavian and arouses and seduces him: "In the twinkling of an eye, Sister Jeanne bared her breasts, then pulled her long skirt up over her head. To Flavian's surprise, she was naked underneath, and suddenly all his fears gave way before the onrush of desire" (14). Later on, Sister Jeanne invites Flavian to the convent so that he can reveal the ways of the flesh to her virgin companions. Flavian and the nuns first share an abundant meal of hams, roasts, and ribs whose *piece de resistance* is, of course, Sister Jeanne's *coq en pâte*, a delicious capon in a crust, prepared with her own hands. Once he has been well fed, Flavian must tackle the delicious task of initiating the nuns to sexual pleasures: "The several deflowerings were performed quickly, methodically, and without embarrassment. Flavian, who was fairly bursting with desire, applied himself vigorously to his task" (22–3). Suddenly, the mother superior enters the room where the collective sexual initiation is taking place and discovers her nuns in flagrante delicto. Thinking they will be seriously upbraided, the nuns hang their heads, but to the surprise of all, the mother superior gives Flavian fellatio as a preliminary to wild sex. Thus, religious authority becomes completely subverted in "Sister Jeanne's Coq en pâte," since the mother superior becomes a sort of procuress.

"The Monastic Stew" bears analogy to "Sister Jeanne's Coq en pâte" in that the main character is a mendicant friar, Sebastian, who goes from village to village collecting alms. He arrives in a big farmhouse where he finds three idle sisters, Gervaise, Marie, and Dominique Péclet. The teenagers, gripped by intense sexual desire, cook a monastic stew, a kind of beef stew they offer to the mendicant. Once the monk's hunger has been satisfied, the three sisters get to the business of seducing him: "It therefore wasn't long before the saintly man showed hard, tangible evidence of his reaction to this abundance of temptations. Dominique was the first of the girls to discover the holy staff and enjoy its initial discharges" (177). Here again, the characters indulge in collective lovemaking in which neither family ties nor vows of chastity hinder their climax.

The third and last short story set in medieval times, "Quill and Quail," describes the heterosexual love affair of a countess and Joachim, a peasant. This story, drawn from *Lady Chatterley's Lover*, tells of the countess's love story. Like Constance Chatterley, she is married to an old, impotent aristocrat. In order to fulfill her cravings, she follows the peasant to his hut in the woods. There they partake of a preliminary feast: a pair of truffle-stuffed quails. Sexual intercourse occurs as soon as the meal is over, when the noble countess abandons herself in the peasant's arms. Here as in Lawrence's novel, the transgression takes place at the social level where an upper-class woman gets involved with a commoner who is much more adept at satisfying her sexual appetites than his betters in rank.

Ways of the Flesh includes several short stories with a contemporary setting, such as "Two Chicks Are Better Than One," in which Myrielle meets Hans Bjering on an Air Canada jetliner and invites him to comply to her whims and eat chicks before he is to provide the dessert: "You're going to have me first, then I'll share Amelia with you, and to finish off, Amelia will have me. I can't think of a more irresistible and sophisticated conclusion to our dinner" (45). Whereas the short stories set in the Middle Ages describe transgression emanating from the looseness and insouciance of the characters, in the more recent ones transgression is justified by modernity, by the evolution and opening of mindsets in opposition to traditional religious interdicts. The story "Ecclesiastical Meatballs" is, without any doubt, the most exemplary of "erotic modernity." The main character is Gertrude, a former nun who has only recently left her order and who has known only masturbation as sexual activity. She is still a virgin, but a haunting question is gnawing at her: where then is her man? (102). She gets to meet him on a Saturday in a bookstore in the shape of Germain Constant, who claims to be a social worker but does not get into any detail. Gertrude falls under his spell and he invites her home to dinner, where he prepares his own dish of meatballs. The recipe offered in the text describes an extremely refined variation on a traditional beef stew. Afterward, in keeping with the structure of the short stories in the book, they end up in bed for Gertrude's initiation: "Once she felt the unaccustomed member inside her, this sudden revelation of virility, Gertrude began to thrash about in the throes of an incredible orgasm and let loose a long throaty cry" (105). The end of the short story reveals a characteristic of the modern period, which is even more permissive in terms of sexuality and the decline of religious institutions, when Germain tells Gertrude: "I'm afraid you'll have to be off soon, my dear. I'm the priest of the neighboring parish and tomorrow is Sunday" (105).

The short stories in *Ways of the Flesh* explore all avenues of sexual variants—homosexuality, lesbianism, sex across age differences, etc. Each short story, without exception, presents a very detailed cooking recipe. On reading Yves Thériault's book, the reader can but acknowledge the fact that, after all, the recipes are presented in greater and much more precise detail than the sexual acts. It is important to note here that this collection of short stories is the first of its kind in Quebec; its merit lies in the fact that it combines various sensual pleasures and overcomes taboos that had so long silenced any erotic expression.

Biography

Thériault was born in Quebec City on November 28. He dropped out of school when he was 15 and started writing for the National Film Board and Radio Canada, 1945. His best-known work is *Agaguk* (1958), a tale of cultural conflict between Eskimos and white men. Thériault died October 20.

Élise Salaün
Translated by Henry C. Mera, Ph.D.

Selected Works

Oeuvres de chair. Montréal: Stanké, 1975; VLB Éditeur, 1982; as *Ways of the Flesh*, translated by Jean David. Agingourt, ON: Gage Publishing, 1977.

Further Reading

Beauregard, Micheline, and Andrée Mercier. "Une lecture d'*Oeuvres de chair*, récits érotiques d'Yves Thériault." *Études littéraires*, Spring 1988.
Godenne, René. "Yves Thériault, nouvelliste." *Études littéraires*. Spring 1988.
LaRoque, Gilbert. "Les Plaisirs solitaires d'Yves Thériault." *Le livre d'ici*, 1976.

THOMAS, D.M.

1935–
British novelist, poet, translator, editor

The White Hotel

Donald Michael Thomas's *The White Hotel* continues to shock readers with its mixture of eroticism and suffering, of Eros and Thanatos. This binarism of what Sigmund Freud conceived of as love and death is particularly apparent in the first two sections and in the Holocaust scenes.

Section One immerses readers in "Don Giovanni," a poem Thomas had written earlier, offering a dozen pages of obsessive sexual activity in a context of death and destruction. The poem's persona addresses a "Professor" (Freud) whose son seduces her on a train and takes her to an Alpine hotel where the two engage in a nonstop orgy. The poem details his titillating her anus and sucking her nipples so long and so hard that they begin to produce milk, as well as her masturbating him and performing fellatio. Their sexuality includes other guests, especially a middle-aged corset maker who joins the couple in bed. The persona shares the milk from her breasts in the dining room, particularly with the "kind old priest," later identified as "Freud." While this "polymorphous perverse" sexual activity goes on tirelessly, there are reports of drownings and avalanche fatalities and of a fire in the hotel itself, which claims more lives.

Section Two, "The Gastein Journal," offers a prose narrative rendition of the events in Section One. This section is a bridge between the rhapsodically erotic fantasy of the first section and the "scientific" rendition of the persona's experience in Section Three, "Frau Anna G.," a fictional "case study" written by the novel's "Freud," a character almost as important as Anna G./Lisa Erdman. Section Two thus modulates the extreme eroticism of the earlier section, which many readers would judge pornographic. It ends with the woman being "mounted from behind" by Freud's son, or the hotel's chef—she cannot be certain which. This image of a sexual threesome will prove central to Anna/Lisa's analysis. Sexuality becomes more "human" and personal here, evident in the episode of Freud's son and the persona's al fresco lovemaking, interrupted by a kindly nun who apologizes for her intrusion and bids them return to their intercourse.

These two sections provide an apt contrast between the "pornographic" and the "erotic," as clarified by D. H. Lawrence in his essay "Pornography and Obscenity." Lawrence states: "No matter how hard we may pretend otherwise, most of us rather like a moderate rousing of our sex. It warms us, stimulates us like sunshine on a grey day" (Lawrence: 173). "Pornography [in contrast] is the attempt to insult sex, to do dirt on it" (175). Lawrence might worry, as some readers have, that the mechanical or compulsive nature of the sexual act diminishes the erotic. In Section One, for example, the persona notes the "man's unresting stroke . . . driving like a piston in / and out, hour after hour."

Section Three of *The White Hotel,* "Anna G.," describes the period of Lisa Erdman's analysis by "Freud" in 1919. The date is important because Freud was working on *Beyond the Pleasure Principle*, a major turning point in his theorizing. Freud could not explain why shell-shocked World War I veterans were compulsively drawn to painful battlefield nightmares. Observing his grandson casting away and retrieving a spool on a string, Freud theorized that compulsive repetitions of painful experience are motivated by a death wish, the desire to recover of an Edenic, prenatal quiescence, before the fall into sentience with the infant's explosion into a world of sensory stimuli at birth.

The remaining sections of *The White Hotel* continue the erotic tendencies within a Freudian context of faith in reason to explain sexual dysfunction. "Freud" narrates the life of "Anna G.," or Lisa Erdman, whom he treated for "hysteria," evidenced by pains in her left breast and pelvic area, with no apparent physical cause.

Anna/Lisa also experienced "breathlessness" in anticipation of full sexual intercourse with her husband who was returning from World War I. (She had been insisting on coitus interruptus to forestall an early pregnancy.) "Freud" focuses on breasts and ovaries as maternal images, leading back to Anna's early loss of her mother in a hotel fire and the subsequent rejection by her father.

Anna/Lisa leads "Freud" to believe that she sought a "white" relationship with A., as later with her husband, because she feared pregnancy and motherhood. She narrates an episode on a yacht in which A. torments her by having intercourse in her presence with another woman in *more ferarum*, or entering the woman from behind. She tells "Freud" of witnessing a "primal scene" of her "aunt" and uncle in an erotic embrace in a summer house. Lisa's "uncle" and her mother were having an affair, and their bodies may have been in a sexual embrace when the two were consumed by the hotel fire.

Section Four moves forward a decade from 1919 to the correspondence between the middle-aged Lisa Erdman, who has achieved modest success as an opera singer, and the aging Freud, recovering from mouth and throat surgery for cancer. The "corrections" Lisa offers to the manuscript of Section Three's "case study" take readers further into the erotic details of her past. Her letter begins with acknowledgment of the "painful pleasure" his case study caused her. Lisa reveals how the misrepresented yacht scene with A. and the summer-house scene were "screens" for an earlier "primal scene" when as a child she saw her "uncle" having sex with her mother and aunt, identical twins, aboard her father's yacht. It is also "intercourse a tergo," a threesome in which the man is entering the kneeling woman from behind. Lisa's parents had had an essentially "white marriage" following her older brother's birth, suggesting the distinct possibility that her father was actually her uncle, making her Christian, like her mother, aunt, and uncle, rather than Jewish like her father. Lisa offers another correction to her earlier rendition of the episode on a ship which was more "vile and frightening" than she had told her analyst. In her "baptism," the sailors berated her as a Jewess and forced her to perform fellatio. Later, it is revealed that even her corrective letter was incomplete because she had not included the loss of her virginity to a stranger on the train from Odessa to Petersburg. The letter was already too long, she adds.

Section Five, "The Sleeping Carriage," brings the narrative to its powerful climax at Babi Yar, the Nazi concentration camp in Russia where thousands of Jews were machine-gunned and buried in a ravine. Lisa has married and become the adoptive mother of Kolya, the son of an opera star whose wife, the singer whom Lisa replaced at La Scala Opera House, died giving birth to Kolya. At Babi Yar, Lisa and Kolya are beaten and forced to strip before being marched to their gravesite, the victims attempting unsuccessfully to cover their genitals. In a moment of anagnorisis, or tragic recognition, Lisa discovers why she feared pregnancy. It was not Freud's "hysteria" which haunted her during sexual intercourse, but foreseeing her present dilemma: if she proclaims she is not a Jew she lives, but with "survivor guilt," for as a Jew Kolya will die. Now, as in Sophocles's *Oedipus*, she and the readers know fully the implications of her early statements that she could never feel pleasure while others were suffering on the "other side of the hill" and the worst horror was knowing that a child was suffering. Accordingly, Lisa *chooses* to be a Jew to ease the pain of Kolya's dying. Still alive in the sea of corpses, she is almost raped by a Nazi soldier, who covers his impotence by kicking her breast and pelvis before mock-raping her with his bayonet. This tragically revealing conglomeration of rape and sexual love, Eros and Thanatos, points up Freud's painfully inadequate attempt to explain Lisa's pains and sexual dysfunction scientifically as "hysteria."

Section Six, "The Camp," offers an afterlife, a purgatory, set in "Palestine." The Camp is clearly a return to the "white hotel" of the mother's body, the mother being both Lisa's biological mother she lost as a child and Lisa herself as mother now. The daughter suckles at the mother's breast and then suckles her mother in a closing of the circle.

Thomas has continued to explore the relationship of Eros and Thanatos. His 1993 novel *Pictures at an Exhibition* focuses on Nazi experimentations with sexuality at the Auschwitz death camp.

Biography

Born Redruth, Cornwall, January 27. He published poetry for over a decade before his first novel, *The Flute Player*, appeared in 1979, receiving the Gollancz Fantasy Novel Prize. His *Selected Poems* appeared in 1983. He has published almost a dozen novels, including the five-novel sequence *Russian Nights*, on the theme of improvisation. He has also published translations of Russian poets, preeminently Anna Akhmatova. None of his other work has achieved the fame of his best seller, *The White Hotel*, short-listed for the Booker Prize in 1981.

EARL G. INGERSOLL

Editions

The White Hotel. London: Gollancz, 1981; New York: Viking, 1981.

Selected Works

The Flute Player. 1979
Birthstone. 1980
Selected Poems. 1983
Ararat. 1983
Swallow. 1984
Sphinx. 1986
Summit. 1987
Memories and Hallucinations. 1988
Lying Together. 1990

Flying in to Love. 1992
Pictures at an Exhibition. 1993
Eating Pavlova. 1994
Alexander Solzhenitsyn: A Century in His Life. 1998

Further Reading

Bartkowski, Frances, and Catherine Stearns. "The Lost Icon in *The White Hotel*." *Journal of the History of Sexuality* 1.2 (1990): 283–95.

Coward, David. "Being and Seeming: *The White Hotel*." *Novel: A Forum on Fiction* 19.3 (1986): 216–31.

Cross, Richard K. "The Soul Is a Far Country: D.M. Thomas and *The White Hotel*." *Journal of Modern Literature* 18.1 (1992): 19–47.

Hutcheon, Linda. "Subject in/of/to History and His Story." *Diacritics* 16.1 (1986): 78–91.

Lawrence, David Herbert. *Phoenix: The Posthumous Papers of D.H. Lawrence*. Edited by Edward D. McDonald. New York: Viking, 1936, 1972.

Michael, Magali Cornier. "Materiality versus Abstraction in D.M. Thomas's *The White Hotel*." *Critique: Studies in Contemporary Fiction* 43.1 (2001): 63–83.

Siegelman, Ellen Y. "*The White Hotel*: Visions and Revisions of the Psyche." *Literature and Psychology* 33.1 (1987): 69–76.

Wirth-Nesher, Hana. "The Ethics of Narration in D.M. Thomas's *The White Hotel*." *Journal of Narrative Technique* 15.1 (1985): 15–28.

THOUSAND AND ONE NIGHTS, THE

In medieval Arabic literature there was no taboo on erotic or sexual explicitness. Apart from treatises on sexuality and love, which were used as medical handbooks and to enhance marital pleasures, erotic motifs and themes occurred in various genres, ranging from humorous anecdotes to entertainment literature, folktales, and farcical shadow plays. Poetry was concentrated on love themes from its beginnings, but it became increasingly sensual in Baghdad and Andalusia from the 9th century onward. Scabrous poetry appeared in the form of light verse seemingly without objection and it was sometimes composed by quite respectable scholars. Comical tales often played upon erotic motifs, and epic cycles usually contained several obscene passages.

Examples of most of the genres in which eroticism was explored can be found in the famous collection *Thousand and One Nights* [*Alf layla wa-layla*], which was probably based on Sanskrit or Persian models and which entered Arabic literature in approximately the 9th century, in an embryonic form. About the textual history of the *Thousand and One Nights* there is still much uncertainty. It seems that between the 10th and 15th centuries the original collection was reworked and supplemented to become a refined collection of entertaining tales, which was especially appreciated by the urban elite. The earliest extant version of the *Thousand and One Nights* is a Syrian manuscript dating from the 15th century, which probably contains a reworking of the oldest core of the work, consisting of 282 nights. This manuscript was brought to light by the French Orientalist Francois Galland (1646–1715), who used it for his translation, which appeared from 1704 to 1715. After the "discovery" of the work by Galland, several "complete" Arabic versions of the work were produced, some of which were based on obvious mystifications composed to satisfy European demand, while others may have been serious efforts to reconstruct what may have been the original *Thousand and One Nights*. As we will see below, some of these reconstructions show a remarkable preference for scabrous tales.

During the course of time, the *Thousand and One Nights* acquired the reputation of being an erotic masterpiece of world literature. This perception was inspired first of all by the frame story of "Shahriyar and his brother," in which it is explained how the cycle came into existence: After having discovered the adultery of his wife with a black slave, Sultan Shahriyar, disillusioned by the perfidity of women, decides to marry a new virgin every evening and have her executed in the morning. After a while, Shahrazad, the vizier's daughter, decides to put an end to this vicious cycle. She marries the Sultan and starts telling tales after their love-making until daybreak, inducing the Sultan to keep her alive in the morning to hear the continuation of the tale the following night. The story-telling continues for a thousand and one nights and Shahrazad and the virgins of the empire are saved. Apart from several references to sexual acts, the frame story explores the overlapping fields of storytelling and eroticism, and since it serves as an explanatory introduction to the collected tales, it puts the work as a whole in a specifically erotic perspective. Even if stories hardly refer to sexual activity, the reader is induced to believe that the stories somehow have an erotic dimension. This erotic subtext is preserved especially in the oldest core of stories, which contains, for example, "The Porter and the Three Ladies of Baghdad," with its playful and explicit erotic references, and the tales collected in the cycle of the "Hunchback," which contain many ironic erotic motifs. As in the frame story itself, these stories can be read as a comment on traditional gender roles and perceptions of female sexuality.

There is no evidence that in medieval times the *Thousand and One Nights* was condemned for its frivolity or obscenity, but in more recent times Muslim scholars have sometimes expressed their disapproval of the collection, which, in their view, presents an incorrect image of the Arabo-Islamic tradition. It is true that the work, due mainly to its stylistic properties and fantastic elements, does not belong to the classical canon, with its strict stylistic and generic conventions, but was rather part of the corpus of entertainment literature. It enjoys a wide popularity among Arab literati and intellectuals, but many new reprints which appear in Arabic countries are severely bowdlerized.

Part of the objections of the religious scholars no doubt derives from the way in which the *Thousand and One Nights* has been incorporated into European culture, which especially relished its more scabrous aspects. The first translation which appeared in Europe—the French version compiled by Antoine Galland—was adapted to what was called the *bienséance*, or "good taste," of the audience. Certain passages were skipped with the excuse that they were too obscene or too rude for the readers' taste. Similarly, the first English translation, by Edward Lane (1801–1876), which appeared in 1838–1840, was censored to accommodate the prudish taste of the Victorian public, explicitly stating that the omitted parts and stories were too obscene. Of course, the lacunae in the translations of Galland and Lane aroused the curiosity of the public, and in the course of the 18th and 19th centuries the narrative material provided by the *Thousand and One Nights* was widely used for erotic and pornographic publications. Stereotypical images of cruel sultans, passionate odalisques, fierce eunuchs, and jealous lovers were utlized to evoke the image of a sensual Orient which indulged in wealth and physical pleasures. Examples of "decent" literary works with erotic motifs inspired by the *Thousand and One Nights* are *Les Bijoux indiscrets* by Dénis Diderot (1713–1784; published in 1748) and *Le Sopha* by Crébillon *fils* (1707–1777; publ. 1740). It should be noted that at the same time, the *Thousand and One Nights* also served as a source for didactic tales and children's books.

In 1885–88 the Orientalist, traveler, soldier, explorer, polyglot, and ethnographer Richard Burton (1821–1890) published his famous, or notorious, English translation of the *Thousand and One Nights*. Burton stated that the translations made by Galland and Lane gave a wrong, anemic image of the Oriental temperament, and especially its erotic component. As an expert on Oriental sexuality, he proposed a new, unexpurgated, translation which would set this straight. Burton's translation is marked by the erotic interests of its translator. Not only is the text itself adapted at some occasions to accentuate erotic details, but the work is supplemented with numerous footnotes, many of which provide information of a sexual nature, and a "Terminal Essay," which includes chapters on pornography and pederasty. Evidently, the fixation on sexuality in Burton's translation reflects the "other side" of Victorian prudishness, which hid an increased interest in sexual matters, prostitution, and pornography. It is obvious that Burton used the *Thousand and One Nights* to confront what he saw as the narrow-minded morality of his contemporaries and that he hoped to contribute to a form of sexual liberation. Burton's translation was banned on several occasions, both in Britain and in the United States, and in 1886–87 an expurgated version was published under the auspices of his wife, Isabel.

In France, the scabrous reputation of the *Thousand and One Nights* was confirmed by the translation of Joseph Mardrus (1868–1949), which appeared in 1899–1904. The translation should perhaps rather be called a reworking, since it was not based on an Arabic manuscript or printed text but consisted of tales taken from a variety of sources, revised to emphasize their sensual and erotic aspects. Mardrus succeeded in evoking a romantic vision of the Orient, which, together with Edmund Dulac's *art nouveau* illustrations, generated a wave of Oriental fashions and tastes. Léon Bakst (1866–1924) was inspired by it while designing the costumes and backdrops for the Ballets Russes (*Shéherazade, Alladin*), and Paul Poiret created harem costumes, made of silk and transparent tissues, and Oriental perfumes and gave a notorious "Thousand and Second Night" dress party. Again, the *Thousand and One Nights* was used to create the image of a sensual and passionate Orient, exploiting age-old fantasies of palace harems and lascivious odalisques.

The erotic image of the *Thousand and One Nights* found expression, too, in the visual tradition which was inspired by the work, starting especially in the 19th century. From time to time "adult" editions' appeared, which were often accompanied by erotic illustrations. Although in Burton's translation some evocative, but unprovoking, nude pictures occur, it is only with Mardrus's text that the erotic potential of the work is exploited in illustrations, some with the aim of arousing the reader, some only exploring the visual possibilities of frivolous Oriental themes. It should be noted that the illustrations to the *Thousand and One Nights* were only remotely linked to the tradition of Orientalist painting which emerged throughout Europe in the second half of the 19th century. Special mention should be made of the lithographs of Kees van Dongen for the 1955 edition of the Mardrus translation, which combine Oriental exoticism with modern imagery inspired by the Folies Bergères. Other visual media which made use of the erotic aspects of the *Thousand and One Nights*, in the course of the 20th century, were comic books, advertisements, and cinema, focusing on figures such as Aladdin and Sinbad, belly dancers, kohl-eyed princesses, and mean and lustful viziers.

Due to the various imaginative translations of the *Thousand and One Nights* and the visual imagery which accompanied them, Shahrazad became the prototype of Eastern sensuality and a paragon of beauty. This image is only partly corroborated by the Arabic versions, in which not her beauty, but rather her intelligence and knowledge are accentuated. According to modern Western standards, the scabrous passages which occur in the Arabic texts are not very shocking, and when erotic intrigues are woven into the story, they are usually meant to enliven the narrative, add an element of playfulness, or give the story a touch of humor. There are only a few examples of stories or passages which are intended to arouse or to shock the readers, although there is no aversion to bizarre sexual habits or violent passions. There are differences between the various texts, of course. It seems justified to say that the Wortley-Montague manuscript, which dates back to the 18th century, contains the most obscene anecdotes, some of which were incorporated by Burton into his translation.

In his survey of erotic motifs in the *Thousand and One Nights*, or, more precisely, in the version of Mardrus, Dehoï contrasts European visions of sexuality—subject to taboos and moral reprehension—with Oriental perceptions, in which love is seen as a natural part of life, as a form of art, conceptually linked to a mystical worldview. Although this idea may have been inspired by a romantic vision of the Orient, it is true that in the *Thousand and One Nights* eroticism is linked to idealized concepts of love and that the narrator shows little inhibition in relating physical details. The story of "The Porter and the Three Ladies of Baghdad" has already been mentioned above. In this story a humble porter is teased by three beautiful nude ladies in a swimming pool in a quite explicit play of words. It also contains the tales of the three qalanders, or dervishes, which include motifs of love, incest, adultery, and homoeroticism. In these stories eroticism is embedded in a world governed by magic and the inescapable interaction between love and fate. A similar fateful view of sexuality can be observed in the story of "Aziz and Aziza," in which a young man is initiated into the world of love and sexuality by his cousin—to whom he is intended to be married—and two demanding lovers, one who keeps testing his refinement and dedication in matters of love and another who commands him to do with her "what the cock does to the hen" and locks him up for a whole year. Eroticism is described here as a world full of confusion, dominated by the unfathomable desires of women, who communicate through secret signs and messages. In this domain dominated by women, the hero finally loses his manhood.

Dominating women are a recurrent theme, too, in several anecdotes—for instance, the tales collected in the story of the "Hunchback." In one of these tales, the hero has his thumbs and toes cut off because he ate a spicy dish just before approaching his beloved, a slave girl in the harem of the caliph (the "Reeve's Tale"). In other stories, men are humiliated for their lascivious fantasies by women who are in control of the situation. According to some observers, these stories characterize the *Thousand and One Nights* as a work of proto-feminism, in accordance with the purport of the frame story, but according to others the stories were conceived by men and meant to be related to a male audience. The occurrence of dominating women should be seen as conforming to a male fantasy.

In love stories, too, men are often portrayed as anti-heroes, as compared with the vigilant and courageous heroines. In these stories, some of which probably date back to pre-Islamic times, social conventions and the prohibitions of strict

fathers have to be overcome before the loving couple can be united. In general these stories are rather prudish and conform to social conventions, but there are some exceptions—for example, the story of "Qamar al-Zaman and Budur," which begins with an erotic encounter and ends with a *démasqué* during an erotic game. It is suggested that the hero is averse to women but is subsequently "cured" by Princess Budur, who was from the beginning destined to marry him. In the story of "Ali Nur al-Din and Maryam the Girdle-Girl," the hero is ruined by an amorous escapade, but he is later saved—after numerous adventures—by a willful girl who defeats the forces of evil in the name of love. This story contains some explicit erotic poetry, which can also be found in the story of "Harun al-Rashid and Hasan the Merchant of Oman." In the latter story the hero visits a brothel and falls desperately in love with the daughter of the owner.

A separate cluster of stories comprise the anecdotes situated at the court of Harun al-Rashid. Some of these tales refer to the famous love between the caliph and his spouse, Queen Zubayda, others to the figure of Abu Nuwas, here presented as a court poet, a composer of scabrous verse, and an unscrupulous lover of young boys. It is these stories that have the libertine atmosphere usually associated with palace harems ("Harun al-Rashid and Queen Zubayda in the Bath," "Harun al-Rashid and the Two Slave Girls," "Abu Nuwas with the Three Boys"). A taste for the bizarre can be found in anecdotes such as "The King's Daughter and the Ape," about a princess who keeps an ape hidden in her closet, and "Wardan the Butcher," about a lady who has a bear as her secret lover. Typically obscene anecdotes from the Wortley-Montague manuscript include "The Lady with the Two Coyntes," "The Youth Who Would Futter His Father's Wives," and "The Goodwife of Cairo and Her Young Gallants." There are a number of stories, finally, that describe the love between humans and jinn, but these do not explore the erotic possibilities of encounters of this kind.

The survey given above shows that a great variety of erotic themes and motifs occur in the *Thousand and One Nights* comprising various genres and types of tales. Erotic intrigues are often cleverly woven into the narrative fabric in the form of plots and subplots, humorous and scabrous intermezzos, and characterizations of love and human passions, of the struggle between the sexes, and of sophisticated urban life. Eroticism allows the narrator to show his skill in ingenious descriptions, forms of elegant rhymed prose and verse, plot deferment, the creation of suspense, and other narrative techniques which, if Shahrazad is to be believed, are all part of the art of love.

RICHARD VAN LEEUWEN

Editions

Burton, R. *Plain and literal translation of the Arabian nights entertainments. Now entituled the book of the Thousand nights and a night.* 17 vols., edited by Burton Club.

Galland, A. *Les Mille et une nuits.* 2 vols. Paris: Éditions Garnier Frères, 1960.

Lane, E. *The Thousand and One Nights.* 3 vols. London: Charles Knight & Co., 1839–1841.

Mardrus, J. C. *Le Livre des Mille et une nuits.* 16 vols. Paris: Éditions de la Revue Blanche, 1899–1904.

Further Reading

Bürgel, J.C. "Love, Lust and Longing: Eroticism in Early Islam as Reflected in Literary Sources." In *Society and the Sexes in Medieval Islam*, edited by A Lutfi al-Sayyid Marsot, 81–117. Malibu, CA: Undena 1977.

Christman, H.M., ed. *Gay Tales and Verses from the Arabian Nights.* Austin, TX: Banned Books 1989.

Dehoï, E.F. *L'Érotisme des Mille et une nuits.* Paris: Pauvert 1960.

Ghazoul, F.J. *The Arabian Nights: A Structural Analysis.* Cairo: UNESCO 1980.

Hamori, A. "Notes on Two Love Stories from the Thousand and One Nights." *Studia Islamica* 43 (1976): 65–80.

Irwin, R. *The Arabian Nights: A Companion.* London: Allan Lane/Penguin Press, 1994.

Leeuwen, R. van. *Space, Travel and Transformation in the Thousand and One Nights*, to be published in London by Routledge, 2006.

Marzolph, U., and R. van Leeuwen. *The Arabian Nights Encyclopedia.* 2 vols. Santa Barbara, CA: ABC-Clio, 2004.

Naddaf, S. *Arabesque: Narrative Structure and the Aesthetics of Repetition in 1001 Nights.* Evanston, IL: Northwestern University Press, 1991.

TĪFĀSHĪ, AL-

1184?–1253
Arab poet and story writer

A compilation of amusing and indecent tales of mixed verse and prose, *The Delight of Hearts: or, What you Will not Find in Any Book* [*Nuzhat al-Albāb fīmā Lā Yujadu fi Kitāb*] is ascribed to al-Tīfāshī. It belongs to the traditional genre of *munjun*, a style of composition which was particularly popular in Baghdad in the 9th and 10th centuries CE and was characterized by "verbal liberation from the shackles of decency" (M. Schild). There are similarities with the scabrous stories in the *Arabian Nights* and, in the West, with the tales of Boccaccio in the *Decameron*. In his preface the author is careful to claim that a knowledge of indecent matters teaches us to avoid them. He claims that he is writing his book for a sophisticated audience who will appreciate his wit and intellect, for such people, unlike common humanity, will be motivated more by their minds than by their sensual appetites. Allah is to be praised for giving us the Word and for providing witty literary anecdotes, since mankind is so vulnerable to boredom. The salt of such pleasant tales is not for the uneducated, for where cultivated men see delicacy, ordinary folk can see only signs of weakness and immorality. The book is divided into twelve sections, the majority of which deal with sexual encounters between men:

1. "On the Twenty-two Types of Pimps and Go-Betweens" describes with illustrations and anecdotes the tricks, excuses, and subterfuges which women use to evade the vigilance of husbands, servants, and the like.
2. "On Adultery" advises how men between the ages of 16 and 30 can seduce both willing and not-so-willing wives.
3. and 4. "On Libertine Women and Men" includes stories of old men who, feeling

the urge to have sex, can be satisfied in various ways thanks to their own ingenuity and the compliance of the women they seduce.

5. "On Lovers of Males" gives advice in story and verse on the seducer's need to be well set up with convenient rooms, soft cushions, sweetmeats, and money.

6. "On Youths Who Play the Field" includes stories of a boy who increases his price for every extra sexual refinement his client requests and of a richly dressed servant who replies to indiscrete questions that the Royal Mint is in his pants. A variety of tricks are described and commented on with witty aphorisms and verse.

7. "On Corporal Blows," which are described as elegant and health giving when delivered in the full flood of joy (examples are provided). They are often without corrective effect when administered as a punishment.

8. "On Pederasty," specifically the love of boys and youths, praises their beauty with tales that often have a reversal as conclusion. One story tells of the honorable judge who thinks his privacy is assured behind a curtain in the Baths, but who, slipping on a piece of soap, careers across the public space while still joined to his beloved. Another describes a gang of old men who seduce youths by appealing to their greed but withhold payment. Others illustrate a variety of dirty tricks, some of which are practiced by men who at first pretend to be passive.

9. "Advice on Sodomizing Youths in the Dark," for which, in one story, the would-be perpetrator needs a variety of objects, such as a needle and thread, three small stones, some powder, a pair of scissors, other bits and pieces, and one raw egg. The need for these is explained as the predator progresses. Several tales and poems in this section describe how the desired outcome is not always achieved, and several old men become the unwitting objects of nocturnal attentions.

10. "On Sodomizing Women." Several stories in this section illustrate the joys of this activity, and the women are often only too happy to comply. In one tale a presiding judge does not see it as a fault.

11. "On Love Between Women." This section gives the medical reasons for such behavior (eating too much celery and rocket, for example) and a descriptive list of different types of lesbians. Several stories illustrate the theme, among them one of a judge who catches two women in the act of love. He arrests one but is hoodwinked into putting her onto his mule, whereupon the beast gallops off in the wrong direction.

12. "On Passive and Effeminate Men," which ends with the medical opinions of Rhazes (c. 860–924) on the causes and treatment of effeminacy. The characters who feature in these stories are grown men with tastes for passive sexual activity. Here are witty anecdotes of shameless "inverts" and incorrigible old men who enjoy the charms of generously endowed youths, an analysis of the various desires of such men and how they can be satisfied, a debate on the relative attractiveness of penises when they are short, long, fat, or thin, and an allegedly moral tale on how a promisingly beautiful exterior can hide a disappointingly minute sexual instrument. Celebratory and condemnatory stories and verses illustrate a variety of situations among which feature the rags-to-riches tale of a well-hung stable boy and an educational manual detailing the joys of sodomy.

In this collection we generally find that conventional gender roles are adhered to: adult males (except the old) are active; youths, effeminate men, and eunuchs (there are not many of these latter) are passive; women are sexually demanding, and their modesty is often a pretense. The exceptions, often resulting from mistaken purpose or error of circumstance, give a witty twist to many of the stories. Although there are explicit descriptions of sexual acts, the narrative style, even in translation, enables us to appreciate the tongue-in-cheek lewdness of the author, who, when asked his opinion on a passive tomcat (section 12) replies that when witnessing these practices we should pray to Allah, the dispenser of all good things, to free us from them.

Biography

Al-Tīfāshī (Abu 'l-Abbās Ahmad bin Yūsuf al-Tīfāshī) was probably born in Qafsa, in present-day Tunisia, and traveled widely in North Africa. He studied law, natural sciences, medicine, and astrology and wrote a treatise on precious stones. He earned the nickname Shihāb al-Dīn [Meteor of Religion], or Sharaf al-Dīn [Honor of Religion]. He died in Cairo.

PATRICK POLLARD

Selected Works

The Delight of Hearts: or, What You Will Not Find in Any Book. San Francisco: Gay Sunshine Press, 1988.

(A translation of the French version: *Les Délices des cœurs, ou ce que l'on ne trouve en aucun livre.* Translated and edited by R. R. Khawam. Paris: Phébus, 1981.)

Further Reading

Murray, S.O., and W. Roscoe, eds. *Islamic Homosexualities: Culture, History and Literature.* New York: New York University Press, 1997.
Wright, J.W., and E.K. Rowson, eds. *Homoeroticism in Classical Arabic Literature.* New York: Columbia University Press, 1997.

TRANSGRESSION

The English language acquired the word "transgression" via the French *transgression,* from the Latin *transgredi*—which means "to step across" (from *trans* meaning "across" and *gradi* "to step").

Simply speaking, to "transgress" is to overstep a boundary. Although "transgression" can be used in a spatial sense—akin to trespassing—the boundaries it commonly refers to are more abstract and ideological: religious, legal, moral, or sexual. When it first appeared, "transgression" was used solely in a religious sense to refer to blasphemy or sin. Since then, "transgression" has acquired a host of secular definitions. Thus, transgression may be a violation of rights or duty, a breaking of the law, or a deviation from the socially acceptable. These are simple definitions. Rather like many aspects of sexuality (and for many of the same reasons), during the latter half of the twentieth century, transgression became linked to the theoretically loaded issues of cultural politics such as subversion, deviance, dissidence, and resistance. It has become a byword for any political or expressive act perceived as challenging the structures, limits, or framework inherent to society—this includes, in the field of textual theory, challenging the regulations and representative ability of culture's symbolic system, language.

Even such a brief summary reveals that to talk about transgression is to address, alongside a complex, shifting concept, many intricate cultural issues. It is also true to say that transgression has a history as long as civilization and an intimate—some would say integral—relationship to humankind. This is so because civilization depends upon a framework of boundaries. These boundaries are policed by prohibitions or taboos, and wherever taboos exist, so too does man's temptation to transgress them. As the body and sexual practice are the most tabooladen sites in human culture, it is possible to see how an understanding of transgression relates to the wider cultural implications of sexual behavior—especially "transgressive" sexual desires or conduct, that is, any practice which deviates from the socially accepted norm.

Within, but certainly not limited to, the linked sites of the body, sexuality, and the taboos which control them, it is possible to see how powerful the temptation to transgress may be. It is also a temptation toward which culture exhibits a contradictory attitude. On the one hand, acts which violate socially acceptable behavior, taste, or ideology induce reactions of disgust and shock; they are perceived as offensive, perhaps immoral, and often threatening to "civilized" values and civilization. Often artists intend certain artistic, literary, or cinematic works to induce shock. Their purpose is to force the audience to react and question accepted social values. Such intentions also play into people's eagerness to be shocked and their fascination with the transgressive, for, on the other hand, transgression has a long association with knowledge, pleasure (there is, after all, a great thrill in doing wrong, and part of the excitement associated with erotic material is that it violates laws and the socially acceptable) and liberation, as if a more authentic existence or identity exists outside of civilization's restrictive taboos. Transgressive figures—such as the rebel, the mass murderer, and the sexual "pervert," or, as with the notorious Marquis de Sade, figures who embody all three—are thus subject to both cultural repulsion and fascination. It is as if, by breaking culture's limits, these figures are privy to forbidden knowledge and/or forbidden pleasure.

One need only think of an ancient Judeo-Christian story—that of Adam and Eve (Genesis 3)—to see how the themes of forbidden knowledge, pleasure, sexuality, sin, liberation, morality, and mortality (which represents the violation of the boundaries of life itself) have haunted humankind and the notion of taboos and their transgression for millennia.

The influential 4th-century writings of Saint Augustine, *Confessions,* explored the same themes in terms of theological belief, temptation, sin, and divine forgiveness. More recently, transgression and taboo were theorized by the French writer of eroticism, Georges Bataille. Bataille's study *L'Érotisme* (1957) presents an exploration of human history and the importance of transgression within it. Although Bataille does not cite Freud, rather as Freud does in his essay *Totem and Taboo* (1913), Bataille shows how ritualized celebrations which allow individuals and entire communities to transgress acceptable behavior have existed throughout history. Bataille points out that although transgression is the violation of a taboo, transgression never actually destroys the taboo: for there to be transgression, the norm or acceptable must remain apparent. By suggesting that no taboos can exist without their transgression, Bataille extends the notion that without taboo there is no transgression and without transgression there is no pleasure, into a reading which challenges the division of transgression and taboo into mutually exclusive opposites. The two—transgression and taboo—depend on each other and, in Bataille's study, are indissolubly entwined with that search for boundary experience, the erotic.

Since the 1960s, the implications of Bataille's study have been appropriated and extended by a number of influential critics. In *Préface à la transgression* [*A Preface to Transgression*] (1963), an essay written shortly after Bataille's death, the French philosopher Michel Foucault introduced and developed many of Bataille's theories alongside his own interpretation of transgression. This intepretation emphasizes transgression's link to sexuality and a secular world in which God is dead. Another seminal study is Peter Stallybrass and Allon White's *The Politics and Poetics of Transgression* (1986). In this work, transgression is explored in terms of the emergence and construction of the European bourgeoisie. Other cultural critics have argued that if transgression and taboo are mutually interdependent, then the same can be said of many cultural values; for example, sexual "perversion" and the socially accepted sexual "norm." As in the earliest myths, however, integral to all these theories is that taboo-laden center of culture, the body, and the forbidden pleasure it promises.

BEN JACOB

Further Reading

Augustine. *Confessions*. Translated by C. Bigg. London: Methuen, 1897.

Bataille, Georges. *Eroticism*. Translated by Mary Dalwood. London and New York: Marion Boyars, 1987. Originally published as *L'Érotisme,* Paris: Editions de Minuit, 1957.

Dollimore, Jonathan. *Sexual Dissidence: Augustine to Wilde, Freud to Foucault.* Oxford: Clarendon Press, 1991.

Foucault, Michel. "A Preface to Transgression." In *Language, Counter-Memory, Practice: Selected Interviews and Essays*, edited by Donald Bouchard, translated by Donald Bouchard and Sherry Simon. Ithaca, NY: Cornell University Press, 1977. Originally published as "Préface à la transgression" in *Critique* 195–6 (1963): 751–770.

Shattuck, Roger. *Forbidden Knowledge: From Prometheus to Pornography.* New York: St. Martin's Press, 1996.

Stallybrass, Peter, and Allon White. *The Politics and Poetics of Transgression.* London: Methuen, 1986.

Wilson, Elizabeth. "Is Transgression Transgressive?" In *Activating Theory: Lesbian, Gay, Bisexual Politics,* edited by Joseph Bristow and Angela Wilson. London: Lawrence and Wishart, 1993.

TRANSLATION

In his pioneering study *Libertine Literature in England, 1660–1745*, David Foxon noted that "every time a major pornographic book appeared on the continent, it was known in England within a year, and in many cases appeared in translation right away." The same remark would generally hold true, despite the various efforts of the authorities to regulate the trade in pornography, throughout the second half of the eighteenth century and for much of the nineteenth century.

In many respects, the market for translated erotica mirrors the market for other forms of literature over the course of the last three hundred years. Although commentators in Britain have been keen to promote the idea that English fiction represents an independent cultural tradition, there is little evidence for such a view. Indeed, as far as subgenres such as science fiction, the Gothic novel, or erotic writing are concerned, there is overwhelming evidence for the view that the continental contribution to their development was very considerable, paramount even. The origins of science fiction, for example, may be clearly be seen in the *conte philosophique* of the 1750s; early British Gothic novelists such as Charlotte Smith or Sophia Lee began their careers as translators of French sentimental fiction; finally, with regard to erotic writing, the sophistication and extent of the French tradition tended to set the agenda for what was written and published elsewhere.

France was, of course, the dominant cultural force in Europe generally for much of the period in question. Even as late as 1900, let alone 1700 or 1800, there would have been few commentators who would have predicted that the English language would ever achieve sufficient prominence to replace French as the language of international diplomacy and commerce, as well as social and intellectual interaction. When Voltaire, one of the first great continental Anglophiles, sought refuge in England in the 1720s, being unable to speak English did not present a serious drawback: the language of the English court was French and most of his aristocratic friends were fluent in his native language. In the second half of the century, British authors as diverse as Horace Walpole, William Beckford, and Edward Gibbon were sufficiently fluent in French as to be able to write complex works of fiction or scholarship directly in that language. Thus, it should come as no surprise that when, in early 1668 Samuel Pepys purchased a copy of Michel Millot's *L'École des filles*, he bought a French edition rather than a translation.

The implication of this, however, is that translated erotic works in Britain (and, indeed, even in America) were aimed at a different class of readers to those whose education and taste allowed them to dispense with translations. Moreover, given the extremely fluid notion of translation that existed until quite recently, it cannot be taken for granted that any English edition represents a version of the original that might be described as faithful. Broadly speaking, translation is a word that has been used at various times to include activities as diverse as adaptation, rewriting, translocation, and, on occasion, even entirely original writing disguised as translation. Thus, the "translation" of Restif de la Bretonne's *L'Anti-Justine; ou, Les Délices de l'amour* (1798), published by Charles Carrington in 1895 as *The Double Life of Cuthbert Cockerton,* not only anglicizes all the names of the characters but, surprisingly, relocates the setting of the action to Sheffield. Similarly, the first translation of J.-K. Huysmans's *A Rebours* (1884), brought out by the American firm Lieber and Lewis in 1922 as *Against the Grain,* was considerably censored. Among many changes, the whole of chapter 6 (concerning a homosexual brothel) was omitted. Historically, such derivative or expurgated works have tended to be ignored or dismissed by scholarship; however, the modern view is increasingly that such cultural artifacts are far from valueless but should be studied and assessed on their own terms.

The history of translation in relation to erotic writing, however, must also include an account of the massive decline in the market for translated erotic works in English. Again, this reflects a decline in translation generally in Britain and America, where translated fiction nowadays (in 2003) accounts for no more than 2% or so of new titles published (this should be compared with other major European countries, where translation still accounts for as many as 25% of new titles published). This is clearly a reflection of the dominance of American (and, though to a much less extent, British) book and magazine publishers in international markets, such that the flow of works is now generally from English into other languages. Moreover, since the liberalization of censorship regimes in Britain and America in the 1960s, many of the niche markets developed by small publishers such as Olympia Press are now occupied by corporate magazine publishers. By and large, the strategic importance of Paris as a center of the erotic book trade from the late nineteenth century through to the mid-1960s was, in any event, a historical anomaly caused by the fact that the rate at which leisure time has become eroticized has varied from culture to culture.

The shifting relationship between French and English as the language of power and prestige is an important one with regard to the development of erotic literature. Indeed, translation could and often did determine the dominant style of erotic writing at particular historical junctures. Little work has been undertaken, however, with regard to the various strategies adopted by translators at different times, the extent to which translated works were forced to conform to the cultural norms of the host community, or the relationship between translation and creative writing with respect to erotic writing. Many translators have been authors, or, indeed, publishers in their own right, and perhaps in no other literary field has the distinction between the profession of author and that of translator been so continually and systematically blurred. Generally speaking, translations commissioned since the early 1960s have tended to be much more scholarly and reliable than earlier translations, though this in itself perhaps indicates that the market for translated works of an erotic nature is motivated by different interests than those prevailing in, say, 1800 or 1900.

TERRY HALE

Further Reading

Foxon, David. *Libertine Literature in England, 1660–1745.* New Hyde Park, NY: University Books, 1965.

TRANSVESTISM

All through history when it has been possible to relax societal barriers between the sexes, as during special festivals, gender blending has taken place, temporarily at least equalizing or destroying the inequality of gender and the rigid barriers which existed. Cross-dressing also often was part of the initiation ceremony into various cults or groupings. Both mythology and history are full of examples of individuals who broke gender barriers by living in sex roles different than their biological sex (Bullough and Bullough). The erotic implications of such activities, however, while undoubtedly a part of such behavior, are not always easy to document.

It was not until the sixteenth and seventeenth centuries that what might be called "playing with gender" became an erotic and titillating pursuit and that erotic connotations could be documented. While males playing women's roles had been a standard of much of medieval and early modern drama, it was the increasing appearance of women on stage in England following the Restoration in 1660 which seemed to have imparted more erotic implications to crossing the gender barriers. Both sexes engaged in playing the roles of the opposite sex, and cross-dressing festivals or holidays associated with Mardi Gras or Halloween increased. In literature, playing with gender became a major theme. from Ariosto's (1474–1533) poetic masterpiece, *Orlando Furioso*, to the *Arcadia* of Sir Philip Sidney (1554–86), to many of the plays of Shakespeare.

Women who actually managed to change roles and status in society through cross-dressing seemed to have been much admired by other women when knowledge of what they had done was reported, provided of course that the exposed woman finally settled down and married. Women readers seemed to enjoy the fact that the cross-dressing woman could successfully challenge male dominance, and undoubtedly fantasized that they too might be able to do so if they had had the opportunity. We know of hundreds if not thousands of ordinary women who temporarily or more or less permanently crossed over the gender divide. Public fascination is illustrated by over a hundred ballads that dealt with women cross-dressers between 1650 and 1850, all with more or less the same theme of a girl in love, who leaves her father's house, is forced to disguise herself as a man, has a stormy love relationship in which she shows unusual courage, and generally ends up married.

The men who donned feminine garb (except on comedic or carnivalesque occasions) seem to have belonged to the princely or upper classes. Some aristocratic boys were actually brought up as girls, like the most famous of the seventeenth-century female impersonators, François de Choisy, who has recorded his erotic escapades for us. The effect of cross-dressing, on both the individual and those who observed it, is illustrated quite effectively in Théophile Gautier's 1835 novel *Mademoiselle de Maupin*.

The more rigid separation of the roles of males and females which seemed to dominate much of the nineteenth and early twentieth centuries simply increased, at least for males, the eroticization of all aspects of the female, particularly in terms of clothing and cross-dressing. In the words of a nineteenth-century observer, women's underclothes were comparable to a "tinted flower, whose innumerable petals become more and more beautiful and delicate as you reach the sweet depths of the innermost petals." Describing lingerie on display, Émile Zola (1840–1902), in one of his novels, said that it looked "as if a group of pretty girls had undressed, piece by piece, down to the satin nudity of their skin" (Steele: 201). In short,

women's underclothes for some men seemed to replace women, and wearing them, or holding them, seemed particularly erotic.

Even viewing postcards of photos of women in underwear seemed to be arousing to some men. The novelist Colette (1873–1954), in *My Apprenticeship*, describes Willy's apartment as "strewn" with postcards "celebrating" the attractions of underclothes. The eroticism of female "unmentionables" to men inevitably led to fictional and "true" reports of men wearing women's underclothes or even dressing as women in such magazines as the *Englishwoman's Domestic Science*, *English Mechanic*, and *Knowledge*, the last two magazines edited by Richard Proctor. Both of these latter often ran special articles on women's underclothes and received much correspondence, either real or made up, from men who delighted in the erotic joy of wearing women's clothes (Farrer: 4; Kunzle: 225).

As gender divisions became more formalized in the course of the nineteenth century, impersonation by both sexes became a staple of the stage. During the first part of the nineteenth century, more women than men played cross-dressing roles, but increasingly toward the end of the century, female impersonation dominated the game. One woman observer of the male impersonators stated that the impersonation illustrated the obsessive concern women had with sexual imagination. The heroes kill dragons and monsters, brave demons, outwit enemies, and rescue maidens, enabling women vicariously to have the mythic adventures they desired, to explore sexual boundaries, and to be excited or aroused by this, without threatening the males in the audience. Male impersonation was not confined to pantomimes or burlesque, but went on the serious stage with women playing Hamlet, Romeo, and such obvious roles as Peter Pan. Opera also included erotic scenes of women playing the male role, from Mozart's *The Marriage of Figaro* to Richard Strauss's *Der Rosenkavalier*, although here they often portrayed either effeminate men or youths whose voices had not yet changed. Women writers such as Virginia Woolf, in her novel *Orlando* (1928), had fun in illustrating gender change. The feminism of the 1960s led to a new wave of plays featuring women playing men's roles, seemingly satisfying erotic dreams of both men and women, as women not only achieved fictional equality but approached it in real life as well.

Female impersonation remained more or less at the same level of popularity throughout much of the twentieth century, not only in vaudeville, but in the mainstream theater as well. Perhaps the dominant person in the first part of the century was Julian Eltinge (born William Dalton, 1882–1941), who was particularly liked by the women in the audience perhaps because he was so realistic that his "obvious femininity" threatened many males' own concept of masculinity. Increasingly in the last part of the twentieth century, however, female impersonation came to be associated with the gay community. Esther Newton (1972) distinguished two different patterns for professional female impersonators, one of which she called the street impersonator, and other, the stage impersonator. Street impersonators tended to conform to the homosexual stereotype of the feminine male, and their lives were strongly oriented toward survival in the present. They were closely associated with prostitution, acting as B-girls pushing drinks to customers, arousing them enough to eventually have sex with them. The stage impersonators generally were more skillful and talented and played to both the gay and straight communities. Many men and women who see impersonators, such as Julie Andrews in *Victor Victoria* and Jack Lemmon and Tony Curtis in *Some Like It Hot,* find them erotically stimulating. Perhaps the greatest line in *Some Like It Hot* is its last, when Jack Lemmon snatches off his wig and tells his ardent pursuer Joe E. Brown that he is not a woman, to which Brown replies, without batting an eyelash, "Well, nobody's perfect."

As male transvestism began to come out of the closet in the 1950s, there was a growing erotic literature designed especially to appeal to transvestites. Virginia Prince, the founder of the modern transvestite movement, began publishing erotic short stories in her magazine *Transvestia* in the 1960s. They never mentioned sex or used the word *penis,* and when the person cross-dressed, he wore special items of clothing to keep "his manliness" under control. Her readership was so stimulated by such stories that her efforts were soon supplemented by a number of publishers issuing 100- to 200-page novelettes which increasingly became more graphic. Robert Stoller, who has studied transvestite fiction, called it simply pornography, since its purpose was to "excite lust." In a study of a random sample of materials available since 1950, Vern and Bonnie Bullough analyzed 96 works of fiction. The fantasy stories written under Prince's influence in the first two decades of the study period featured more of a Barbie-doll type of cross-dresser, were aimed clearly at a heterosexual audience, and often involved the wife of the cross-dresser lovingly embracing her husband, while others simply leave the main character happy and contented simply to belong to the world of women when he/she has a desire to do so. In the 1970s, as the known population of cross-dressers expanded and more publishers entered the market for transvestite fiction, special audiences seemed to develop, some emphasizing sadomasochistic and others homosexual themes. These novels were far more sexually explicit. Surgical sex change began to enter into some of the stories. Still there remained a substantial base of transvestite fiction aimed at a heterosexual audience, although all the cross-dressing men in the stories seemed to be able to pass in public as a women when they wanted to. A lot of attention was paid to wardrobe. Increasingly the fictional accounts were written in a variety of languages and settings, emphasizing that there was a large audience of men interested in partaking in what they fantasized was the feminine world.

There has been little comparable fantasy fiction dealing with female cross-dressers, although role change and the wearing of male clothing has been a subject of popular lesbian fiction since Radclyffe Hall's *Well of Loneliness* (1928), if not before. The works that are extant seem to emphasize the ability of women to perform tasks traditionally regarded as men's work. It seems clear, as Stoller emphasized, that wearing or seeing females wearing items such as denim jeans, engineer boots, and false mustaches can produce orgasmic sensations in women (Stoller: 135–36). As in the cross-gender fiction aimed at the male transvestite, some erotic changes have begun to appear in fiction aimed at the gender-bending woman. Nancy Friday, for example, in *My Secret Garden*, a collection of sexual fantasies, tells of a woman admiring herself in the mirror wearing male jockey shorts with a tampon penis protruding from them. The sale of devices to create a male-looking crotch has been increasing each year, as has that of two-pronged dildoes, which two women are able to use together.

Cross-dressing, transgenderism, or playing at gender bending is a significant erotic fantasy.

Vᴇʀɴ L. Bᴜʟʟᴏᴜɢʜ

Further Reading

Bullough, Vern, and Bonnie Bullough. *Cross Dressing, Sex, and Gender*. Philadelphia, PA: University of Pennsylvania Press, 1993.

Farrer, Peter, ed. *Men in Petticoats*. Liverpool: Karn Publications, 1987.

Garber, Marjorie. *Vested Interests*. New York: Routledge, 1992.

Kunzle, David. *Fashion and Fetishism*. Totowa, NJ: Rowman and Littlefield, 1982.

Newton, Esther. *Mother Camp: Female Impersonators in America*. Englewood Cliffs, NJ: Prentice-Hall, 1972.

Steele, Valerie. *Fashion and Eroticism*. New York: Oxford University Press, 1985.

Stoller, Robert J. *The Erotic Imagination*. New Haven, CT: Yale University Press, 1985.

TRIGO, FELIPE

1864–1916
Spanish novelist

Felipe Trigo is, perhaps along with Eduardo Zamacois, the first systematic cultivator of the erotic novel as a subgenre in modern Spanish literature. He wrote almost twenty full-length novels and more than twenty novellas, in addition to a collection of short stories, *Cuentos ingenuos*. Most of these works display an explicit element of eroticism, and many of them explicate his personal conception of Eros as one of their fundamental components. Trigo also wrote several books of essays, two of which, *Socialismo individualista* and *El amor en la Vida y en los libros*, closely reflect his ideas about sexuality and society as developed in his novels.

Trigo defends the establishment of a new moral order based on what he terms "total love." This new order reached beyond the conventional rules of erotic conduct prevalent in the society of his time. Influenced by the ideas of socialist utopians such as Charles Fourier and Robert Owen, Trigo envisioned a harmonious society in which the achievement of personal happiness resided in creating a collective environment of justice and of freedom that allowed for the expression of sensual and erotic impulses. This social and erotic ideal is, however, quite far from being fulfilled in his own fictional worlds. If it is fulfilled at all, satisfaction is attained only within a limited personal sphere, as in *Alma en los labios* or as part of a scenario set remotely apart from Western civilization, as in *Las Evas del Paraíso*.

The clash between the real and the ideal provides the basic framework for the twofold depiction of eroticism present in many of his novels. The idealistic impulse allows for the recurrent creation of young and pure female characters endowed with delicacy, refined spirituality, and a beauty that approximates physical perfection. Not infrequently, these characters have been subjected to pernicious environments which have rendered them "fallen angels." The possibility of redemption usually presents itself through the woman's encounters with a male protagonist. Yet the protagonist himself has to overcome problems arising from the inadequate education offered by his social milieu, especially when he belongs to an upper class that for the most part is selfish and corrupt.

Trigo's conception of such female characters is strongly influenced by the aesthetic premises of Decadent, *fin-de-siècle* literature and Hispanic modernism. In his hands, the balanced proportions, smooth surface, and quasi-pictorial perfection of the body seem to coincide with a liberation from the cultural conditions that unnaturally limit erotic exploration. The more these women are able to satisfy their natural desires, the more beautiful they become. Trigo's texts advocate a "religion of life" alien to the constraints and frequent hypocrisies of conventional religion. The narrators of these novels (usually the male protagonists) repeatedly present themselves as proponents of women's development and autonomy. Certainly, these novels attempt a progressive defense of women's intellectual expression, and they proclaim the legitimacy of women's search for pleasure and for mastery over their own bodies as a mode of contributing to an enlightened society. There remains, however, a paternalistic attitude on the part of the narrators which, as some critics have noted, precludes a truly emancipatory perspective on the ideological subjugation of Spanish women at the beginning of the 20th century.

In contrast to the development of these stylized figures, the expression of eroticism in Felipe Trigo's novels also accounts for what is perhaps the most common characterization of his work, which views him as a Naturalistic writer. Trigo repeatedly voiced his admiration for Emile Zola and, in spite of his frequent statements highlighting his unequivocal differences with the French novelist, he can be considered one of the most enthusiastic practitioners of Zolesque literary doctrine in Spanish literature. Although he eventually gave up his medical practice to devote all his efforts to literary creation, he was himself a doctor and thus enjoyed a profound familiarity with scientific methods and principles. In accordance with Zola's proposals, he viewed the novel as a space for the acquisition of knowledge through experimentation with the human personality, in an attempt to evaluate scientifically all the environmental forces that condition the development of the self. In this sense, what he termed his "clinical notes" provided a vast source of primary materials for the construction of his fictional worlds.

The contemplation of sexual reality through the Naturalistic/materialistic lens results in a presentation of eroticism that is quite different from the one already discussed. This perspective tends to underscore the degraded character of a purely material carnal interaction. Prostitutes, *cocottes*, and aged bourgeois gentlemen become the protagonists of these sexual encounters; the repellent carnality of their worn-out bodies is barely hidden behind the falsehood of their makeup. Often, these two viewpoints of sexual relations (one with a materialistic, one with an idealistic emphasis) coexist in the same work, depending on which characters engage in them.

The relatively explicit character of the sexual encounters described in Trigo's books earned him a reputation as a pornographic writer, and not surprisingly, also a wide audience almost unsurpassed by any other Spanish author of his time. It must be noted, however, that such labeling frequently came from persons who had not even read his works, as he himself complained on several occasions. Although unquestionably advanced as compared with the general tone of romantic literature of the time, Trigo's works would hardly be considered pornographic by even the most prudish reader today. Generally, his love scenes limit their adventurousness to descriptions of nude female bodies and to mild accounts of explicit sexual interaction that are either very stylized, "spiritualized," or brief.

Affected by neurasthenia, a disorder that he would repeatedly re-create in the fictional realm, Trigo became progressively obsessed with the concept of a pagan religion of love that would advance the notions of inner purity and naturalness achieved through sensual satisfaction. Even while enjoying a stable family environment and a prosperous economic situation, Trigo's emotional and mental states continued to deteriorate during his final years, when he was a victim of acute depressive crises. According to his biographers, during this period he may have engaged in turbulent extramarital affairs. The gap between his inner aspirations and the surrounding reality would only be exacerbated by the onset of the First World War, a conflict which prompted in him deeply disillusioned reflections regarding the present and future state of European civilization. All these circumstances intertwine in what has been considered his literary testament, the novel *Sí sé por qué* (1916), published a few months before his death as a final expression and reformulation of his long-established views regarding eroticism, society, and individual achievement.

Biography

Born in Villanueva de la Serena (Badajoz, Spain), February 13. Studied medicine at the University of Madrid. At age 21 married 18-year-old Consuelo Seco de Luna. Worked as a military doctor at a penitentiary in the Philippines, a Spanish colony. Wounded during a prison uprising, he received military honors and public acclaim on his return to Madrid. His first novel, *Las ingenuas*, was published in 1901, and his first erotic novel, *La sed de amar*, appeared in 1903. He committed suicide, shooting himself in the head, September 2.

RICARDO KRAUEL

Selected Works

Las ingenuas. Madrid: Fernando Fe, 1901; Madrid: Otero Ediciones, 1996.

La sed de amar (Educación social). Madrid: Fernando Fe, 1903; Madrid: Renacimiento, 1920.

Socialismo individualista (Indice para su estudio antropológico). Madrid: Fernando Fe, 1904; Madrid: Renacimiento, 1920.

Alma en los labios. Madrid: Pueyo, 1905; Montevideo: Clio, 1945.

"La Altísima," "El moralista," "Los abismos," "El domador de demonios" [c. 1907]. In *4 Novelas eróticas*. Badajoz: Diputación Provincial, 1986.

El amor en la Vida y en los libros: Mi ética y mi estética. Madrid: Pueyo, 1907; Madrid: Renacimiento, 1920.

En la carrera (Un chico buen estudiante en Madrid). Madrid: Renacimiento, 1909; Madrid: Turner, 1988.

Cuentos ingenuos. Madrid: Pueyo, 1909; Madrid: Clan, 1998.

La clave. Madrid: Renacimiento, 1910.

Las Evas del Paraíso. Madrid: Renacimiento, 1910.

El médico rural. Madrid: Renacimiento, 1912; Madrid: Ediciones Turner, 1974.

Jarrapellejos (Vida arcaica, feliz e independiente de un español representativo). Madrid: Renacimiento, 1914; Madrid: Espasa Calpe, 1988.

Crisis de la civilización (La guerra europea). Madrid: Renacimiento, 1915.

Sí sé por qué. Madrid: Renacimiento, 1916.

Further Reading

Abril, Manuel. *Felipe Trigo: Exposición y glosa de su vida, su filosofía, su moral, su arte, su estilo*. Madrid: Renacimiento, 1917.

Dendle, Brian John. *The Spanish Novel of Religious Thesis (1876–1936)*. Madrid: Castalia, 1968.

Fernández Cifuentes, Luis. *Teoría y mercado de la novela en España: Del 98 a la República*. Madrid: Gredos, 1982.

Fernández Gutiérrez, José Maria. *La novela corta galante: Felipe Trigo (1865–1916)*. Barcelona: Promociones y Publicaciones Universitarias, 1989.

García Lara, Fernando. *El lugar de la novela erótica española*. Granada: Diputación Provincial, 1986.

González Blanco, Andrés. *Felipe Trigo: Antología crítica de sus obras*. Madrid: La novela corta, 11 June 1921.

Litvak, Lily. *Erotismo fin de siglo*. Barcelona: Antoni Bosch, 1979.

Longares, Manuel. *La novela del corsé*. Barcelona: Seix Barral, 1979.

Manera, Danilo. *Letteratura e società in Felipe Trigo*. Roma: Bulzoni, 1994.

Martínez San Martín, Ángel. *La narrativa de Felipe Trigo*. Madrid: Consejo Superior de Investigaciones Científicas, 1983.

Sainz de Robles, Federico Carlos. *La promoción de "El cuento semanal" (1907–1925) (Un interesante e imprescindible capítulo de la novela española)*. Madrid: Espasa-Calpe, 1975.

Ton, Jan Pieter. *Felipe Trigo: Estudio crítico de sus obras novelescas*. Amsterdam: Academisch Proefschrift, 1952.

Watkins, Alma Taylor. *Eroticism in the Novels of Felipe Trigo*. New York: Bookman Associates, 1954.

TROCCHI, ALEXANDER

1925–1984
Scottish novelist and poet

Alexander Whitelaw Robertson Trocchi wrote erotic fiction out of financial necessity rather than a desire to contribute to the genre. He was the founder and editor of the Paris-based literary journal *Merlin*. The magazine was an artistic success—publishing Samuel Beckett, Eugene Ionesco, and many others—but a financial failure. In order to raise funds for the project, Trocchi and other Merlin contributors entered into a deal with Maurice Girodias of Olympia Press to translate French erotic classics into English. Thus, Trocchi's translation of Apollinaire's *Les Onze mille verges* was published in 1953. Shortly afterward, Girodias encouraged the Merlin group to write their own "dirty books." In 1954, Olympia published Trocchi's *Helen and Desire, Young Adam, The Carnal Days of Helen Seferis, School for Sin,* and *Frank Harris—My Life and Loves: Volume 5.* In 1955 followed *Thongs* and *White Thighs.* He left *Merlin* and Olympia Press in 1956 to move to the United States. There he published his final erotic works, *Sappho of Lesbos* and *Angela* (a rewrite of *Helen and Desire*).

Trocchi did not consider the aforementioned erotic works as important as his serious novels—the original version of *Young Adam* and *Cain's Book*—and it is on those two books that his literary reputation rests. Trocchi's sense of himself as an author is seen in the way he differentiated his work. Olympia Press published his books under the pseudonym of Frances Lengel. Trocchi completed *Young Adam,* his first novel, in 1952 but was unable to find a publisher. He inserted several gratuitous erotic scenes in order to render it salacious enough for Girodias and it was published as a Frances Lengel book in 1954. However, as soon as he found a mainstream publisher for the work, he removed the extraneous passages and released it under his own name. Another measure of his attitude is that while he labored for months over his serious work, he spent only one week writing *Helen and Desire* and ten days on *Frank Harris—My Life and Loves: Volume 5.* This last work was published as if the real-life Harris, author of *My Life and Loves,* had written it. In fact, Trocchi created it from a handful of Harris' notes, which Girodias had acquired. Many years later, when it was reprinted under Trocchi's name, he claimed to have undertaken the project in order to "take the piss out of [Harris] using his own execrable style." Likewise, he originally claimed *Sappho of Lesbos* was his translation of her long-lost autobiography, when it was actually his own work merely incorporating poetic fragments of Sappho.

Trocchi's erotic work is often lightweight, escapist, and derivative. *Helen and Desire,* for example, is indebted to John Clelland's *Fanny Hill;* and its sequel, *The Carnal Days of Helen Seferis,* reads like a hard-boiled detective novel. The sex itself is mostly conventional (though the novels with female protagonists inevitably contain some lesbian scenes) and described with florid prose. Trocchi's style, though, is to interject moments of brutality and violence into what are otherwise adventurous erotic romps. Helen, for example,

ends up a slave in an Algerian brothel. His male characters fare no better, and the private detective who narrates *The Carnal Days of Helen Seferis* is whipped and humiliated by a group of women. The theme of torture emerges in several other novels. In *Thongs,* the female protagonist runs afoul of a secret society of sadomasochists, and in *White Thighs* the narrator's father marks each sexual conquest with a carving in her inner thigh. Despite the violence, there is something lighthearted about Trocchi's erotic work. The portrayals of sexuality in his serious novels reflect the existential gloom that permeates these semi-autobiographical works, as exemplified by the scene in *Young Adam* where the protagonist rapes his girlfriend. In contrast, writing erotic fiction seems to have offered him the freedom of detachment. He often wrote from the female perspective, described cities and countries he had never been to, and incorporated fantastic (perhaps unbelievable) plot developments. This almost carefree approach was perhaps necessitated by the lack of time he spent on the manuscripts, but it also serves to undercut some of the violent tension present in the books and more often than not works to their strength.

Trocchi was an anti-authoritarian rebel his entire life and clearly saw his erotic books as a way to challenge and offend conservative sensibilities. However, it is clear in his letters and essays that he thought that drugs, rather than sexuality, were the key to true cultural subversion. He described himself as a "cosmonaut of inner space" and sometimes signed his correspondence "Alexander Trocchi—Junkie to the Queen." Indeed, when magistrates, in a ruling that expanded the scope of the Obscene Publications Act, declared *Cain's Book* obscene in 1964, it was due to the graphic depiction of drug use in the novel. Ironically, his heroin addiction cut his literary career short, leaving *Young Adam* and *Cain's Book* as his only "serious" works. Because of this limited output, Trocchi's erotic novels, however flawed, remain an important, if not central, part of his body of work.

Biography

Born in Glasgow, July 30. Enrolled at Glasgow University for a BA in English, political economy, and logic in 1942. Conscripted February 1943 and served in the Royal Navy. Released from service in November 1946. Married Betty White, January 1947 (divorced 1954); two daughters. Returned to Glasgow University in 1947 with an ex-serviceman's grant as a student of English and philosophy. Awarded a Second Class Honours degree in English and philosophy in 1950; settled in Paris. Wrote a monthly "Paris Letter" for the *Scots Review,* November 1950–April 1951. Sold his first work (a poem) to the editor of the literary magazine *Botteghe Oscure* in the summer of 1951. Founded the literary magazine *Merlin* in 1952. Published erotic novels under a pseudonym for Olympia Press, 1954–55. Moved to New York City, 1956. Married Lyn Hicks, 1957; two sons. Published *Cain's Book,* 1960. Arrested for supplying drugs to a minor, April 1961, and fled to England to avoid prosecution. *Cain's Book* declared obscene by Sheffield magistrates and the ruling upheld by the High Court in the Strand, 1964. Lecturer in the sculpture department of St. Martin's School of Art, 1964–1966. Became an antiquarian book dealer, 1972. Died of pneumonia following lung cancer surgery, in London, April 15.

CHAD MARTIN

Selected Works

"Frances Lengel." *Helen and Desire.* Paris: Olympia Press, 1954.
———. *Young Adam.* Paris: Olympia Press, 1954.
———. *The Carnal Days of Helen Seferis.* Paris: Olympia Press, 1954.
———. *School for Sin.* Paris: Olympia Press, 1954.
———. *Thongs.* Paris: Olympia Press, 1955.
———. *White Thighs.* Paris: Olympia Press, 1954
"Frank Harris." *Frank Harris—My Life and Loves: Volume 5.* Paris: Olympia Press, 1954.
"Jean Blanche." *Angela.* New York: Castle Books, 1959.
Trocchi, Alexander. *Sappho of Lesbos.* New York: Castle Books, 1960.

Further Reading

Campbell, Allan, and Tim Niel. *A Life in Pieces: Reflections on Alexander Trocchi.* Edinburgh: Rebel Inc., 1997.
Scott, Andrew Murray. *Alexander Trocchi: The Making of a Monster.* Edinburgh: Polygon, 1991.
———, ed. *Invisible Insurrection of a Million Minds: A Trocchi Reader.* Edinburgh: Polygon, 1991.

TURGENEV, IVAN

1818–1883
Russian novelist, short story writer, and playwright

Turgenev favored social reform as the means for Russia's advancement and called for a Western-style democracy. Unlike those of his two great contemporaries Tolstoy and Dostoevsky, Turgenev's works reflect little mysticism or religious zeal. He maintained a moderate political view, alienating both reactionaries and radicals and facing bitter criticism from both sides. His works can be divided into two broad categories: the short fiction focused on courtship, marriage, unrequited love, and extramarital affairs, and the controversial social novels dealing with more abstract issues of societal justice and freedom. The so-called social novels, the most famous of which is *Fathers and Sons* (1862), often have an erotic subplot or revolve around a love story, as in *Rudin* (1856) and *On the Eve* (1860).

Asya

Narrated in the first person, *Asya* (1858) is highly autobiographical. It is a story of an illegitimate child and her frustrated love affair with the narrator. Both the heroine Asya and the "cruel widow" of the story are characters drawn from real life. Turgenev's uncle had a daughter Asya with a peasant woman, who, because of social taboo, was never acknowledged to be his.

The widow is modeled after Turgenev's lover Pauline Viardot, a French opera singer with whom the author had a love affair which lasted many years and who was then having a passionate affair with another man, becoming pregnant by him.

The illegitimate Asya, like her real-life counterpart, was doomed to a life of ambiguous identity and status, neither a servant nor ever quite a "lady," inhabiting an uncomfortable social space. Turgenev weaves a tale of incest (the relationship between Asya and her half-brother), deceit (the attempt to cover up the facts of Asya's birth), and adultery (her father's numerous affairs with peasant women), but veiled in insinuation, suggestion, and implication.

Despite the strong attraction between Asya and the narrator, their relationship is never consummated and they part in the end. The narrator, though inwardly critical of the social stigma attached to illegitimacy, proves incapable of opposing it. Similar to many of the weak Turgenevian heroes, he resigns himself to his fate and does not commit to Asya for fear of societal disapproval.

First Love

This 1860 novella recounts the story of Turgenev's sexual awakening at sixteen: his infatuation with the seductive nineteen-year-old Zinaida. Another autobiographical story informed by Freudian pre-Oedipal impulses, it reveals intimate details of Turgenev's own dysfunctional family: the sadistic and overbearing mother and the distant and philandering father. His lifelong pathological relationships with domineering women—his mother and then his mistress Viardot—left him irresolute and passive, often regretting his romantic decisions. Feminist readings of this work have interpreted it as misogynistic, challenging traditional views of Turgenev as a "lyrical" and "gentle" portraitist of the human heart.

It is a story within a story, as an old man, Valdemar, relives the pain and disillusionment of his first love. Zinaida, initially cast as a kind of high priestess with a strong sexual hold over men, finally emerges as a tragic seductress who dies young in childbirth. The obsessed and frustrated Valdemar, too young to be of any interest to her, can only fantasize about Zinaida as he watches her from afar. With voyeuristic precision he records every movement, every gesture of Zinaida and her various suitors, deriving what vicarious fulfillment he can. His constant shadowing of Zinaida ends in a devastating discovery which will scar him for life. Realizing she has been secretly meeting a lover, Valdemar is determined to discover the man's identity and to kill him. Following her into a forest, Valdemar witnesses a sadomasochistic encounter between Zinaida and her mysterious lover, who whips her with a riding crop, drawing her blood; she responds by kissing him passionately. After this ritualism of dominance and submission, Valdemar recognizes the secret lover: it is his father.

Torrents of Spring

This story, from 1872, like so much of Turgenev's short fiction, juxtaposes sexual love (or *eros*) with the spiritual love of *agape*: the hero Sanin, modeled after the author himself, is torn between the two. Like his prototype, Sanin chooses the erotic excitement of the *femme fatale* over the quiet, wifely love, so highly prized in the sentimental novel of the nineteenth century, of an ordinary woman.

Following his engagement to a naive young girl, Jemma, Sanin finds himself under the spell of a dominatrix, whose strong sexual appeal (like that of Viardot) draws him into a relationship of bondage and enslavement, a lifelong *ménage à trois*. Her impotent and ridiculous husband acts as her procurer, recruiting new lovers and buying provocative lingerie, his only reward being the erotic gratification of watching her with her partners. At the end of the story Sanin laments having lost Jemma, whom he now sees as the "true love" of his life. This story may have been something of a catharsis for the author. In 1854 Turgenev was engaged to a much younger woman, Olga, but unable to break free from Viardot (whom he called a "Circe"), he called off the engagement, a decision he was later to regret.

At the core of Turgenev's erotic works lies his preoccupation with the destructive power of sexual desire and its unshakable hold over people. Though not a moralist in outlook, Turgenev often portrays *eros* as a dark, irrational drive, in opposition to *agape*, which is portrayed as "pure" but elusive and unattainable. Turgenev's women tend to come in two types: some, like his domineering mother, are depicted as sexual predators who ruin their inexperienced lovers, while others are portrayed as noble and self-sacrificing heroines, paragons of virtue, and models of Russian womanhood. His male characters are sensitive but weak, faltering under the spell of strong women caused by deep-rooted neurosis. Their inability to act leaves them disssatisfied and regretful in the end.

Biography

Ivan Sergeevich Turgenev was born in the province of Oriol, Ukraine, into a serf-owning aristocratic family. His collection of short stories depicting the injustice of serfdom, *A Hunter's Sketches* (1852), influenced Tsar Aleksandr II's decision to emancipate the serfs in 1861. Called "the novelist's novelist" by Henry James, and befriended by Gustave Flaubert and Emile Zola, in the West Turgenev was considered to be the foremost Russian novelist of his time.

TRINA R. MAMOON

Editions

Asia [Asya]. In *Sovremennik* [Contemporary Review], January 1858; in *Polnoe sobranie sochinenii* [Complete Collection of Works], vol. 3, Moscow: Izdanie N.A. Osmovskogo, 1860; as *Acia*, in *A Lear of the Steppes and Other Stories*, translated by Constance Garnett, London: Heinemann, 1899; in *First Love and Other Tales*, translated by David Magarshack, New York: Norton, 1960.

Pervaia liubov' [First Love]. In *Sovremennik*, April 1860; in *Polnoe sobranie sochinenii*, vol. 3, Moscow: Izdanie N. A. Osmovskogo, 1860; in *Torrents of Spring, First Love, and Mumu*, translated by Constance Garnett, London: Heinemann, 1897; in *First Love and Other Tales*, translated by David Magarshack, New York: Norton, 1960.

Veshnye vody [Torrents of Spring]. In *Vestnik Evropy* [The European Herald], January 1871; in *Polnoe sobranie sochinenii*, vol. 6, Moscow: Izdanie Brat'ev Salaevykh, 1874; in *Torrents of Spring, First Love, and Mumu*, translated by Constance Garnett, London: Heinemann, 1897; in *The Torrents of Spring*, translated by David Magarshack, New York: Farrar Straus, 1959.

Selected Works

Zapiski okhotnika [A Hunter's Sketches]. 1852
Mesiats v derevne [A Month in the Country]. 1855
Rudin. 1856
Dvorianskoe gnezdo [Nest of the Gentry]. 1859
Nakanune [On the Eve]. 1860
Otsy i deti [Fathers and Sons]. 1862
Dym [Smoke]. 1867
Nov' [Virgin Soil]. 1877
Polnoe sobranie sochinenii i pisem [Collected Complete Works and Letters]. Edited by M.P. Alekseev. Moscow: Akademiia Nauk SSSR, 1960–68, 28 vols.

Further Reading

Allen, Elizabeth Cheresh. *Beyond Realism: Turgenev's Poetics of Secular Salvation*. La Jolla, CA: Stanford University Press, 1992.

Costlow, Jane T. *Worlds Within Worlds: The Novels of Ivan Turgenev*. Princeton, NJ: Princeton University Press, 1990.

Costlow, Jane, and Stephanie Sandler, eds. *Sexuality and the Body in Russian Culture*. Stanford, CA: Stanford University Press, 1993.

Freeborn, Richard. *Turgenev: The Novelist's Novelist*. Greenwood Publishing Group, 1960.

Magarshack, David. *Turgenev: A Life*. London: Faber, 1954.

Moser, Charles. *Ivan Turgenev*. New York: Columbia University Press, 1972.

Nabokov, Vladimir, V. *Lektsii po russkoi literature: Chekhov, Dostoevskii, Gogol', Gor'kii, Tolstoi, Turgenev*. "Literaturovedenie" series of the journal *Nezavisimaia*, 1998.

Pritchett, V.S. *The Gentle Barbarian: The Life and Work of Turgenev*. New York: Random House, 1977.

Yarmolinsky, Avram. *Turgenev: The Man, His Art, and His Age*. New York: Century Company, 1926.

TUSQUETS, ESTHER

1936–
Spanish novelist

Trilogy (*El mismo mar de todos los veranos, El amor es un juego solitario, Varada tras el último naufragio*)

A stylistic tour de force in the "new novel" mode (Servodidio: 160), Tusquets's trilogy (1978–80) made literary headlines no less for the powerful erotic charge that drives it. The subject matter—the first substantial account of lesbianism in Spanish narrative (Smith: 91)—explores a range of crisscrossing heterosexual and lesbian relationships among the upper middle class of Barcelona who traditionally decamp to their residences on the Costa Brava for the summer. Its publication coincided with and spearheaded a boom in erotic literature in Spain following the abolition of censorship at the end of the Franco regime. This cleared the way in Spanish literature for the particular prominence of writing by and for women.

Although the majority of critical writing on Tusquets has focused on this trilogy, she has produced other fiction of an equally high standard, in which she has maintained the importance of the erotic element but developed new contexts, angles, and characters to rearticulate her recurrent preoccupations with the search for sexual satisfaction and true love, as well as the obsessive concern with the impact of her characters' past on their present selves (Molinaro: 15), always in the world of the Catalan elite, which she knows well, as she herself belongs to it. *Para no volver* [*Never to Return*] (1985) is about Elena, who in late middle age is struggling to come to terms with the disappointments of her marriage, her husband's philandering with younger women, and the end of her own youthfulness, by recourse to a psychoanalyst and an extramarital heterosexual affair of her own; *Con la miel en los labios* [*With Honey on Her Lips*] (1997) deals with a passionate lesbian love affair between two students at Barcelona University that ends with both partners capitulating to societal expectations and getting married. Two collections of short fiction, *Siete miradas en un mismo paisaje* [*Seven Looks at the Same Landscape*] (1981) and *La nina lunática y otros cuentos* [*The Odd Girl and Other Stories*] (1996), allow Tusquets to sketch out and experiment with different amorous conflicts and combinations, but all the stories bear her hallmark of an atmosphere imbued with eroticism, woven into the searching psychological exploration of her female protagonists. In a different vein altogether, Tusquets has also published some children's fiction.

One of the distinctive features of Tusquets's literature for adults is her habit of reusing certain first names for characters in different stories. In this way is created a certain continuity, as the people bearing the same name often have much in common with one another, yet are not reappearances of a single character in the realist mode. Tusquets's world is therefore not like that of Balzac in *La Comédie humaine,* for example, where one meets the same characters in successive novels at different stages in their lives; rather, the impression is analogous to musical variations on a theme, and this writer's theme is undoubtedly the quest for love expressed as physical passion and how relationships wax and wane, the euphoria followed by the misery of the end of an affair that seemed perfect and eternal, and the intense pathos generated when there is a lack of total reciprocity: when one partner's trajectory of falling in or out of love fails to synchronize with the other's. Coupled with the stream-of-consciousness style, in which characters' abiding preoccupations and experiences that have marked them keep coming back in their thoughts, an air of circularity—of endlessly repeated mirrorings and echoes—pervades Tusquets's oeuvre as a whole and ironically undercuts her internal characters' impressions that they are living through a unique and life-changing experience.

One element typical of Tusquets's fiction, which enhances and intensifies the reading experience, is linked to her richly metaphorical use of other narratives: *Peter Pan* is utilized to develop ideas around the meaning of growing up, for example; classical mythology provides a rich source of topoi too, as do the Hollywood films watched by her characters. But the key aspect of her consummate technique in creating the erotic charge that marks out her distinctive style is probably her integration of these intertextual references into the stream-of-consciousness discourse, which delves into her narrators' deepest consciousness and keeps the reader's eye running on for page after page, with few paragraph divisions or full stops to offer the usual breaks. Amongst the effects this creates is an urgency, a breathlessness in the reading experience which echoes well the characters' own yearnings. Some critics (e.g., Servodidio) find that the tortured syntax and uninterrupted flow slow down the reading process, but there does seem to be agreement that this style "fortifies" the thematic concerns of the author. The two examples which follow contrast two sex scenes. The first, a short extract from a much longer account in *El mismo mar de todos los veranos*, is an emotionally powerful one between the protagonist and her young lover, Clara, which takes place in a box at the Barcelona opera house during a performance; the second is an excerpt from a portrayal of a meaningless and mechanical experience for Elena with a man she hardly knows in *Para no volver*; in both cases the stream-of-consciousness discourse evokes with almost painful accuracy the precise feelings of the narrator during the lovemaking.

> Siento que la herida que el gemido [de Clara] ha abierto en mí se hace honda y lacerante, la punzada feroz de un hierro al rojo vivo, . . . y cojo a la ninfa entre mis brazos, y la oprimo, la mezo, le acaricio una y mil veces el pelo largo, sedoso, lacio, las mejillas mojadas, los hombros estremecidos, y entre beso y beso, en los breves momentos en que mis labios se separan un poco de sus labios, la arrullo con palabras increíbles, tan extrañas, palabras que no he dicho nunca a ningún hombre, . . . palabras que ignoraba yo misma que estuvieran en mí, en algún oscuro rincón de mi conciencia, agazapadas, quietas y a la espera de ser un día pronunciadas, ni siquiera pronunciadas, sino salmodiadas, cantadas, vertidas espesas y dulcísimas en una voz que tampoco reconozco aunque debe forzosamente ser la mía, tantos años oculta esta voz y estas palabras. (137–38)

> [I feel that the wound which [Clara's] moan opened up in me is growing deep and lacerating, the ferocious jab of a red-hot iron, . . . and I take the nymph into my arms, and I press her to me, I rock her, one and a thousand times I stroke her long, silky, smooth hair, her wet cheeks, her trembling shoulders, and between one kiss and the next, in the brief moments when my lips are slightly parted from her lips, I soothe her with incredible words, so strange, words I have never said to any man, . . . words I myself didn't know were inside me, in some dark corner of my consciousness, crouching quietly and waiting to be one day uttered, not even uttered but chanted, sung, poured thickly and oh so sweetly in a voice which I don't recognize either, although it must necessarily be mine, this voice and these words for so many years concealed.]

> Había permitido . . . que . . . la empezara a besar en el sofá, y luego la llevara al dormitorio y la desnudara y la acostara — . . . ¿habría dejado de ser una mujer que se acuesta, para pasar a convertirse en una muñeca grande, de goma o de porcelana, a la que se quita la ropita y se mete en la cama? — y comenzara a acariciarla, sin dejar ni por un instante — mientras le daba la vuelta, la manipulaba, le separaba las piernas de trapo, las flexionaba, le colocaba en una posición o en otra los brazos perfectamente articulados, la tocaba por todas partes, la lamía, la chupaba, le conducía con su mano de ella, la incitaba la golpeaba, la penetraba — ni por un solo instante de hablar. . . . De modo que no le parecía a Elena-robot, Elena-muñeca-de-porcelana que estuvieran haciendo de veras el amor, no se asemejaba aquello casi en nada a una escena vivida y real, parecía, por el contrario, la escena retransmitida de una serial radiofónica. (114–15)

> [She had allowed him . . . to start kissing her on the sofa, and then to take her to the bedroom and undress her and put her to bed—had she stopped being a woman who goes to bed, to become a large doll, made of rubber or china, whose little clothes you take off and you put to bed?—and to start caressing her, without for a single moment—while he turned her over, manipulated her, opened her cloth legs, flexed them, positioned one way or another her perfectly jointed arms, touched her everywhere, licked her, sucked her, guided her hand, incited her, hit her, penetrated her—not for a single moment stopping talking. . . . So that robot-Elena, china-doll-Elena did not feel as though she was making love for real, that bore virtually no resemblance to a real, lived scene, it seemed, on the contrary, like a broadcast scene from a radio serial.]

Biography

Esther Tusquets was born in Barcelona, placing her in the same age-group as the so-called

Midcentury Group, who launched themselves on the Spanish literary scene in the 1950s, when they were in their twenties. However, unlike these contemporaries, Tusquets did not embark on her career as an author until after Franco's death; she was forty-two and running a successful publishing business when her debut novel was published in 1978. The first of her trilogy, *El mismo mar de todos los veranos* [*The Same Sea as Every Summer*], created a critical sensation, which Tusquets sustained with its sequels, *El amor es un juego solitario* [*Love Is a Solitary Game*] and *Varada tras el último naufragio* [*Stranded After the Last Shipwreck*].

ABIGAIL LEE SIX

Selected Works

El mismo mar de todos los veranos. Barcelona: Lumen, 1978.
El amor es un juego solitario. Barcelona: Lumen, 1979.
Varada tras el último naufragio. Barcelona: Lumen, 1980.
Siete miradas en un mismo paisaje. Barcelona: Lumen, 1981.
Para no volver. Barcelona: Lumen, 1985.
La nina lunática y otros cuentos. Barcelona: Lumen, 1996.
Con la miel en los labios. Barcelona: Anagrama, 1997.

Further Reading

Davies, Catherine. *Spanish Women's Writing, 1849–1996*. London: Athlone Press, 1998.
Gil Casado, Pablo. *La novela deshumanizada española (1958–1988)*. Barcelona: Anthropos, 1990.
Ichiishi, Barbara F. *The Apple of Earthly Love: Female Development in Esther Tusquets' Fiction*. New York: Peter Lang, 1994.
Lee Six, Abigail. "Protean Prose: Fluidity of Character and Genre in Esther Tusquets's *Siete miradas en un mismo paisaje*." In *Changing Times in Hispanic Culture*, edited by Derek Harris, 177–86. Aberdeen: Centre for the Study of the Hispanic Avant-Garde, 1996
———. "Home and Away: *Con la miel en los labios* in the Light of 'En la ciudad sin mar.'" *Hispanic Research Journal* 3 (2002): 31–42.
———. "Why *Giselle*? Tusquets's Use of Ballet in *Siete miradas en un mismo paisaje*." In *Crossing Fields in Modern Spanish Culture*, edited by Federico Bonaddio and Xon de Ros, 155–64. Oxford: Legenda, 2003.
Molinaro, Nina L. *Foucault, Feminism, and Power: Reading Esther Tusquets*. Lewisburg, PA: Bucknell University Press, 1991.
Perez, Janet. *Contemporary Women Writers of Spain*. Boston, MA: Twayne, 1988.
Perriam, Chris, Michael Thompson, Susan Frenk, and Vanessa Knights. *A New History of Spanish Writing: 1939 to the 1990s*. Oxford: Oxford University Press, 2000.
Servodidio, Mirella. "Esther Tusquets's Fiction: The Spinning of a Narrative Web." In *Women Writers of Contemporary Spain: Exiles in the Homeland*, edited by Joan L. Brown, 159–78. Newark, NJ: University of Delaware Press, 1991.
Smith, Paul Julian. *Laws of Desire: Questions of Homosexuality in Spanish Writing and Film, 1960–1990*, especially 91–128. Oxford: Clarendon, 1992.
Soliño, María Elena. *Women and Children First: Spanish Women Writers and the Fairy Tale Tradition*, especially 221–64. Potomac, MD: Scripta Humanistica, 2002.

TWAIN, MARK

1835–1910
American novelist, journalist, and lecturer

[Date, 1601.] Conversation, as it was by the Social Fireside in the Time of the Tudors

Mark Twain's *1601* embeds scatalogical banter and sexual anecdotes in a comic contrast between the elevated reputation of Queen Elizabeth's court and its vulgar behavior. Written in 1876 between revisions of *Tom Sawyer* and plans for *Huckleberry Finn*, *1601* circulated only in manuscript and private editions until published in the *Oxford Mark Twain* (1996). Twain first sent the manuscript in a letter to his friend the Reverend Joseph Twichell, but it found its way into print through unwitting support from the US government. John Hay wrote to Alexander Gunn of Cleveland on U.S. Department of State stationery in June 1880 offering to share a "masterpiece"; veiled requests thereafter led to 4 printed copies (Meine: 12–16). In 1882 Lieutenant Charles Erskine Scott Wood printed 50 copies—the first authorized edition—at the U.S. Military Academy (West Point) to spare Twain hand-copying. Apparently with Twain's permission, Wood used archaic fonts and coffee-stained paper to represent *1601* as "a species of forgery." Franklin J. Meine identified 42 other editions by 1938, when he collected the first two printings (the 1882 edition in facsimile) into an elaborately annotated volume.

Twain's 2,400-word narrative in Elizabethan eye-dialect (mock-Shakespearean spellings that may not correspond to variant pronunciations) strings together witticisms on flatulence and sexual availabililty purportedly witnessed by "the Pepys of that day," a cupbearer to Queen Elizabeth who witnessed her conversations with [William] Shaxpur, Lord [Francis] Bacon, Ben Jonson, Francis Beaumont, Sir Walter Rale[i]gh, the Duchess of Bilgewater, the Countess of Granby, and the Ladies Alice Dilberry, Helen of Granby, and Margery Boothy. As snobbish as Pepys, *1601*'s narrator objects to the "righte straunge mixing truly of mighty blode with mean" (33) and resents having to remain on duty until dismissed. The tale begins when a member of the party "did breake wind, yielding an exceding mightie and distressful stink." When the Queen tries to identify "ye author," her visitors' elegant and eupemistic disclaimers turn the conversation from flatulence to genitalia, sexual maturity, and potency. Characters' comments reveal individual traits as well as collective vulgarity—to the dismay of the cupbearer over "the foul and deadly stink" (34) and the Queen's company, which becomes a comic sufferer's chorus. When Bacon ends his denial with flattery ("haply shall ye finde yt 'tis not from mediocrity this miracle hath issued"), the cupbearer rails against "this tedious sink of learning" (34). When Ralegh admits to the fart, but dismisses it as "so poor and frail a note, compared with such as I am wont to furnish," and then delivers another, the narrator bemoans "this swaggering braggart" [35]. The cupbearer judges Shaxpur's *Henry IV* "not of ye value of an arsefull of ashes" (38). The narrator is haughty, not prudish. He condemns those who feign offense at "a little harmless debauching,

when pricks were stiff and cunts not loathe to take ye stiffness out of them," asking, "who of this company was sinless?" (certainly not the Duchess Bilgewater, "roger'd by four lords before she had a husband," nor Lady Alice or Lady Margery, both "whores from ye cradle" [38]). And he enjoys Elizabeth's end to Lady Alice's "grandiose speeche": *"O shit!"* (39). The themes of *1601* culminate in a narrative and sexual anticlimax—a joke equating sexual failure, bodily waste, debunked status, and verbal success—as Ralegh tells how a witty maiden escaped an archbishop's rape: *"First, my lord, I prithee, take out thy holy tool and piss before me; which doing, lo his member felle, and would not rise again"* (39).

1601 draws on Twain's stock comic contrasts between characters' high status and low manners, between Elizabethan culture's elevated reputation and this tale's topics, between British and American literary traditions. A key joke—a pun conflating intestinal gas and speech—debunks great literature: eloquent Elizabethans are full of hot air. (Hence Ralegh, the "windy ruffian" (38), authors the initial fart and the last joke.) Reversing the literary principle of decorum, the noblest figures speak most vulgarly. Elizabeth jokes, "widows in England doe weare prickes . . . betwixt the thighs, and not wilted neither, till coition hath done that office for them" (36). Like the teller of an American tall tale, Lady Margery elevates life experience over book learning to end Bacon and Jonson's dispute over the spelling of *bollocks* (testicles): *"Before . . . my fourteenth year I had learnt that them that would explore a cunt stop'd not to consider the spelling o't"* (37, italics in original).

Unlike some other instances of eroticism and scatology, *1601* occupies an honored place in Twain's career as an experiment in language, setting, and point of view, well timed to assist his creativity as a writer and cultural critic. *1601* is the first of Twain's works, including *The Prince and the Pauper* and *A Connecticut Yankee*, to draw on European literary and historical sources (such as Rabelais and Pepys) that fired his imagination long after. The model of Pepys's *Diary* attracted Twain as late as 1905, when his *Eve's Diary* followed *Adam's Diary*. *1601*'s critique of British laureates and royalty recurs in *Huckleberry Finn*, with the sunken *Walter Scott* and the con man Duke. Twain considered the cupbearer's point of view the most important element of *1601*'s humor, Walter Blair has pointed out, putting this narrator—like Huck—in the "long procession of figures . . . in American humor . . . who were lacking in humor and some sorts of perception but who nevertheless communicated important insights of their creators" (Blair: 97). Equally important, Twain's ridicule of Elizabethan English in *1601* not only exploited American fondness for eye-dialect and comic misspellings, but also built upon his recent forays into black dialect in "Sociable Jimmy" and "A True Story"—key elements in his decision to turn away from conventional literary diction in favor of the vernacular voice that made *Huckleberry Finn* a masterpiece and landmark of American fiction.

Biography

Born Samuel Langhorne Clemens, November 30 in Florida, Missouri, though primarily associated with nearby Hannibal, to which his family moved in 1839. Following stints in Missouri, Nevada, and California as a typesetter, riverboat pilot, and journalist, Clemens came to national attention as Mark Twain, author of "Jim Smiley and His Jumping Frog" (1865) and *The Innocents Abroad* (1869), the latter based on his humorous newpaper reports of a cruise to the Holy Land and nearby countries. Married Olivia Langdon, 1870; lived in Hartford, Connecticut, 1871–1891, when Clemens supplemented his writing career with several others, most notably publisher (Buffalo *Express*, American Publishing Company), inventor (scrapbook), and comic lecturer. His lecturing career, which began in 1867 at Cooper Union in New York City, eventually took him across the nation and around the world. He read from *Life on the Mississippi* (1883), *Adventures of Huckleberry Finn* (1884), and other writings on an American tour with G. W. Cable in 1884–85. Spent long periods in Europe in 1873, 1878, 1891–95; charted his 1895–96 tour of Australia, New Zealand, India, and southern Africa in in *Following the Equator* (1897). But even in tales set abroad, his great theme was the promise of American culture, and his great technique the language spoken by Americans of different regions, races, and classes. His complete works fill 29 volumes and have been translated into dozens of languages. At age eighty-four, having outlived his wife Olivia

(1845–1904) and three of their four children, Clemens died of angina pectoris at his Redding, Connecticut, home, "Stormfield," on April 21.

JUDITH YAROSS LEE

Editions

Conversation, as it was by the Social Fireside, in the Time of the Tudors, Cleveland: n.p., 1880; *Date 1601, Conversation, as it was by the Social Fireside, in the time of the Tudors*, West Point, NY: Academie Presse, 1882; *Mark Twain's [Date, 1601.] Conversation, as It Was by the Social Fireside in the Time of the Tudors*, edited by Franklin J. Meine, [Chicago:] Mark Twain Society of Chicago, 1939; *1601, and Is Shakespeare Dead?* New York: Oxford University Press, 1996.

Selected Works

"A True Story, Repeated Word for Word as I Heard It." *Atlantic Monthly* 34.205 (Nov. 1874): 591–94. Rpt. *Sketches New and Old*, 1875.
"Sociable Jimmy." *New York Times*. November 29, 1874, 7.
"Some Thoughts on the Science of Onanism" (speech). 1979
The Prince and the Pauper. 1882
The Adventures of Huckleberry Finn (English ed.). 1884
Adventures of Huckleberry Finn (American ed.). 1885
A Connecticut Yankee in King Arthur's Court. 1889
Adam's Diary. 1893
"The Mammoth Cod." Comp. 1902
Eve's Diary. 1905
"Wapping Alice." Comp. 1877–1907, pub. 1981. A tale of a cross-dresser.

Further Reading

Baetzhold, Howard G. *Mark Twain and John Bull: The British Connection*. Bloomington, IN: Indiana University Press, 1970.
Blair, Walter. *Mark Twain and Huck Finn*. Berkeley and Los Angeles, CA: University of California Press, 1960.
Kronhausen, Eberhard, and Phyllis Krohnausen. *Pornography and the Law: The Psychology of Erotic Realism and Pornography*. New York: Bell Publishing Company, 1959.
Meine, Franklin J., ed. "Introduction." *Mark Twain's [Date, 1601] Conversation, as It Was by the Social Fireside in the Time of the Tudors*. New York: Lyle Stuart [privately printed], 1939.
Twain, Mark. *1601, and Is Shakespeare Dead?* Foreword by Shelley Fisher Fishkin, introduction by Erica Jong, afterword by Leslie A. Fiedler. The Oxford Mark Twain. New York: Oxford University Press, 1996.

TYNAN, KENNETH

1927–1980
British drama critic and theatrical producer

Oh! Calcutta

During his tenure as literary manager of the British National Theater, Kenneth Peacock Tynan also struck out on his own as a theatrical producer in the United States, staging a series of sex farces he solicited from such well-known writers as Jules Feiffer, John Lennon, Edna O'Brien, Sam Shepard, and most notoriously Samuel Beckett. Called *Oh! Calcutta* and subtitled "An Entertainment with Music," it was "devised" by Tynan and directed by Jacques Levy, and was less a species of Marxist political commitment than a good-natured sexual romp. As he said to the *Village Voice*, "[T]here was no place for a civilized man to take a civilized woman to spend an evening of civilized erotic entertainment. . . . We're trying to fill that gap" (so to speak). After an unprecedented 39 cautious previews off-Broadway (to which New York City officials were repeatedly invited to ensure that no civil action be taken against the production), it finally opened on June 17, 1969, at the Eden Theater in New York City, moved to Broadway on February 26, 1971, and ran until August 6, 1989, that is, for a full nine years after Tynan's death. An astonishing 85 million people saw 1,314 performances over a twenty-year period. The play took its title from a surrealist painting by Clovis Trouille called "Oh! Calcutta! Calcutta!" which suggested the French surrealist pun, "Oh quel cul t'as" [Oh what a lovely ass you have!]. The image of a posterior odalisque whose *fesse* was framed by a drape, each cheek decorated by a variety of *fleur-de-lys*, was simultaneously innocent and erotic, as was the show itself. The Trouille painting was exploited in publicity posters for the show and for the cover of the subsequent book (Grove Press, 1969), which made the wildly exaggerated boast that the sketches dealt "with every conceivable erotic fantasy and sexual reality that Western man has dreamt up or experienced."

The most unlikely of the "sex farces" was Samuel Beckett's unwitting contribution called *Breath,* but renamed "Prologue" by Tynan. Although the text had nothing to do with his theme, Tynan made it fit, and in the process infuriated Beckett. To Beckett's "Miscellaneous rubbish," for example, Tynan added, "including naked people." And Beckett's two cries, one of birth and one of death (the entire text of the play), were turned into erotic groans in production. To add to the folly, the altered text of *Breath* was published by Beckett's American publisher, Grove Press, under Tynan's title (although still attributed to Beckett), "Prologue," the text facing a production photo of naked bodies protruding from a heap of rubbish. A furious and surprisingly prudish Beckett scurried to stop the performance but found that his American contract forbade his intervention. He did succeed in forbidding use of the "Prologue" in all subsequent countries where the play was produced, including the United Kingdom. The final irony may have been, however, that the "Prologue" became Samuel Beckett's most viewed play—ever.

Much of Tynan's decline as a theater critic and his failing health are detailed in a series of journals covering the years 1971–1980. They were kept from publication by Tynan's second wife, Kathleen, a novelist, Tynan's biographer, and the editor of his letters. The journals were finally released by his daughter Tracy, edited by John Lahr, in 2001. Writing in *The Observer* (October 7, 2001), playwright David Hare concludes his review of the journals, which he called "All Passion Spent," with Tynan's own measure of his decline: "One reason I cannot write nowadays is because I no longer have a stance, an attitude, what [T.S.] Eliot called 'the core of it, the tone.'"

Biography

Born in Birmingham, England, April 2 to an unwed, middle-class couple. Tynan was something of a "terrible child prodigy," according to Harold Clurman. At the age of 16, two years before he entered Oxford University on scholarship, he wrote his first theater review and grew to become what some have called "the greatest theater critic since Shaw." At Oxford he was drama critic for *Isis*, the university literary magazine, secretary of the debating society, and president of the Experimental Theatre Club. After an aborted attempt at acting (in Alec Guinness's *Hamlet*) in 1951, he was hired first by the *London Evening Standard*, then three years later as the theater critic of *The Observer*, where he had made his reputation as a pugnacious, stylistically elegant drama critic from 1954 to 1963. Beginning in 1956, he championed the new British theater, that realistically gritty art that focused on the underclasses and was dubbed "Kitchen Sink" drama, since it broke with the tradition of setting British drama in Mayfair drawing rooms or in elegant country houses. He became spokesman for a new generation of upstart, left-wing dramatists, particularly John Osborne, Arnold Wesker, and Shelagh Delaney. In 1958 he went to the United States to be drama critic for the *New Yorker* magazine, and those early reviews were collected under the title *Curtains: Selections from the Drama Criticism and Related Writings*. By 1963 he had been lured away from drama criticism by Laurence Olivier to become literary manager of the nascent British National Theater, at the time little more than an idea, a position that he held until his forced withdrawal in 1973. A champion of the "Angry Young Men" movement in the United Kingdom (a fine essay on which appears in *Curtains*), he also championed Arthur Miller and Lorraine Hansberry in the United States and Bertolt Brecht and Samuel Beckett from abroad, although he tended to lose patience with the latter's aesthetic preoccupations. Of Beckett's *Endgame*, Tynan wrote in 1957: "Last weekend's production, portentously stylized, piled on the agony until I thought my skull would split. . . For a short time, I am prepared to listen in any theatre to any message, however antipathetic. But when it is not only disagreeable but forced down my throat, I demur." Tynan would grow from an advocate of "the theatre of fantasy and shock" to a more Marxist-oriented perspective where "art, ethics, politics, and economics were inseparable from each other." Among experimental theater artists he preferred the ideology of Bertolt Brecht to Beckett's modernist formalism and would also have his revenge on the Irish dramatist in 1969 with *Oh! Calcutta*. He died in Santa Monica, California, from pulmonary emphysema.

S.E. GONTARSKI

Editions

Oh! Calcutta! An Entertainment with Music. Devised by Kenneth Tynan, directed by Jacques Levy. New York: Grove Press, 1969. (Video version by VidAmerica, directed by Guillaume Martin Aucain, 1980.)

Selected Works

He That Plays the King: A View of Theater. 1950.
Bull Fever. 1956.
Tynan Right and Left: Plays, Films, People, Places, and Events. 1967.
The Sound of Two Hands Clapping. 1975.

Further Reading

Lahr, John. *The Diaries of Kenneth Tynan*. 2001.
Tynan, Kathleen. *The Life of Kenneth Tynan*. 1987.
Tynan, Kathleen, ed. *Profiles*. 1990.
———. *Kenneth Tynan: Letters*. 1994.

U

UEDA AKINARI

1734–1809
Japanese poet, scholar, and writer of fiction

Ueda Akinari was the most important Japanese writer of fiction in the eighteenth century, a formidable scholar of ancient Japanese literature, and perhaps the finest *waka* poet of his generation. A sober, reclusive man who strove in his best work to approach the refinement of court literature, he thought of himself primarily as a scholar and poet, and certainly not as a writer of erotica in a society that was unabashed in its eroticism. Akinari's elegant masterpiece, *Ugetsu monogatari* [*Tales of Moonlight and Rain*], is one of the classics of Japanese fiction and the work for which he is remembered today. It has had a strong influence on subsequent Japanese writers, including Tanizaki and Mishima, and inspired Mizoguchi's 1953 film classic, *Ugetsu*.

Akinari's first ventures into fiction are now considered to have been the last significant *ukiyo zōshi* [floating-world books], a genre pioneered by Ihara Saikaku. Often lighthearted, they typically satirize the foibles of townspeople. His first collection, *Shodō kikimimi sekenzaru* [*A Worldly Monkey Who Hears About Everything*],

purports to repeat gossip from the streets. Examples will suggest the flavor. In the seventh story (the titles are too long to include), a samurai tries to seduce a beautiful Buddhist nun, only to be challenged to a contest in martial arts; he flees when she proves to be the more accomplished. In the ninth, the promising, handsome son of a retired dancing girl ends up as a male prostitute who caters to men. Akinari's next collection, *Seken tekake katagi* [*Characters of Worldly Mistresses*], focuses on relations between men and women, but with more emphasis on wives than on mistresses. In the second story, an eternally youthful woman outlives three husbands and a male concubine until finally, when age catches up with her, her fourth husband abandons her for a mistress. Buddhism is satirized in the fifth, when six monks lust after a beautiful woman who leads them on, pretending to be a widow; after accepting their gifts, she and her husband drive the monks away. In the story some critics consider the best (the seventh), Fujino, a former prostitute, returns to the brothel when her lover falls on hard times. He uses her advance to start a new enterprise, but it fails and he commits suicide. Fujino then honors not only her contract with the brothel-keeper but also her vows to her lover and remains single after her indenture is complete. The seriousness of this story anticipates the solemn beauty of Akinari's masterpiece.

Ugetsu monogatari consists of nine tales about revenants and other anomalies. Gone are the playfulness and satire of Akinari's earlier work; the *Ugetsu* tales are neoclassical gems of high artistry, reflecting the author's studies in Japanese and Chinese literature. Four of the stories contain erotic elements. The title of "Kikka no chigiri" [The Chrysanthemum Vow], hints at its subject, because the supposed resemblance of the chrysanthemum flower (*kikka*) to an anus made the blossom a common symbol of male homosexual intercourse. In this story, the bond between a scholar and a samurai is tested when the latter finds himself unable to meet his younger friend on the date he has promised to return. He fulfills his vow by committing suicide, knowing that his spirit will be able to traverse the distance in time. The scholar, overjoyed by his friend's loyalty until he learns the truth, faithfully avenges the suicide by killing the man who had unjustly detained his friend. The commitment demonstrated by these men contrasts with the fecklessness of a farmer in "Asaji ga yado" [The Reed-Choked House]. Leaving his wife behind, he goes to the capital to make his fortune, but procrastinates six years before returning home. He finds his wife waiting there for him faithfully and they go to bed; in the morning, he realizes that he has slept with her ghost, which had come back to welcome him home. In "Jasei no in" [A Serpent's Lust], a naïve young scholar is seduced by a murderous serpent that has assumed the form of a woman in order to satisfy her lust for him. Though he soon becomes aware of the deceit, the youth cannot resist her charms. Both of these stories—the two on which Mizoguchi based his film—subtly demonstrate the affinities among danger, death, and sexual attraction. These themes achieve their most passionate statement in "Aozukin" [The Blue Hood], in which an esteemed Buddhist abbot falls in love with a servant boy, then goes mad with grief when the boy dies. His despair, longing, and loneliness, which culminate in his playing with the boy's corpse, then eating it, are presented in such powerful language that the reader is moved to sympathy for the abbot, even when the priest-turned-demon begins to devour bodies

from the cemetery. Few stories of necrophilia and cannibalism have been more compelling. The abbot's homosexual behavior is not stigmatized; the problem is that his attachment to something ephemeral deters him from progress toward enlightenment. The story's ideology is summarized by another priest, who says that one who loses control of his mind turns into a demon, while one who governs his mind achieves enlightenment.

Akinari's other major work of fiction, *Harusame monogatari* [*Tales of the Spring Rain*], avoids the erotic altogether, even when it tells the life story of a courtesan in "Miyagi ga tsuka" ["The Grave of Miyagi"].

Biography

Born in Osaka, 1734, to a prostitute; his father's identity is unknown. Adopted in 1737 by Ueda Mosuke, a prosperous merchant. Received a good Confucian education, possibly at the Kaitokudō Academy; later studied ancient Japanese literature, especially *waka*. Married Ueyama Tama in 1760; they had a happy marriage but no children. Mosuke died in 1761, leaving the family business to Akinari, who ran it until it burned in 1771. Practiced medicine until 1787; retired and devoted himself to scholarship, teaching, and writing. Moved to Kyoto in 1793, lived in poverty; his wife died in 1797. Akinari died August 8, 1809, in Kyoto.

ANTHONY H. CHAMBERS

Selected Works

Shodō kikimimi sekenzaru, 1766, and *Seken tekake katagi*, 1767, are not available in English translation.
Ugetsu monogatari, 1776; as *Ugetsu Monogatari: Tales of Moonlight and Rain*, translated by Leon M. Zolbrod, 1974; and as *Tales of Moonlight and Rain* by Anthony H. Chambers, forthcoming. Chambers's translations of "The Chrysanthemum Vow," "The Reed-Choked House," and "A Serpent's Lust" appear in Shirane, ed., *Early Modern Japanese Literature*, 2002.
Harusame monogatari. 1808–1809; as *Tales of the Spring Rain*, translated by Barry Jackman, 1975.

Further Reading

Keene, Donald. *World Within Walls: Japanese Literature of the Pre-Modern Era, 1600–1867*. Chapter 16, "Fiction: Ueda Akinari." New York: Henry Holt & Co., 1976.

Leupp, Gary. *Male Colors: The Construction of Homo-sexuality in Tokugawa Japan*. Berkeley, Los Angeles, London: University of California Press, 1996.

Richie, Donald. "The Ghoul-Priest: A Commentary," in *Zen Inklings: Some Stories, Fables, Parables, and Sermons*. New York: Weatherhill, 1982, pp. 79–90. (On "Aozukin.")

Screech, Timon. *Sex and the Floating World: Erotic Images in Japan, 1700–1820*. Honolulu: University of Hawaii Press, 1999.

Shirane, Haruo, ed. *Early Modern Japanese Literature: An Anthology, 1600–1900*. New York: Columbia University Press, 2002.

Young, Blake Morgan. *Ueda Akinari*. Vancouver: University of British Columbia Press, 1982.

See also **Japanese: Medieval to Nineteenth Century; waka; Ihara Saikaku; Tanizaki Jun'ichirō; Mishima Yukio**

V

VAILLAND, ROGER FRANÇOIS

1907–1965

French journalist, novelist, dramatist, and film scriptwriter

Vailland was the author of nine novels, two of which earned him major literary awards. He also wrote travel books, plays, and film scripts, most notably the adaptation with Roger Vadim of Laclos's *Dangerous Liaisons* (1959). Except for a few "notes for an erotic narrative" published posthumously, Vailland did not write erotic or "libertine" fiction: In his novels, sexuality and the relationships between men and women serve essentially as means of characterization and illustrate his emotional and intellectual development. It is in his essays, his book on Laclos (*Laclos par lui-même*), and his notebooks, diaries, and correspondence published posthumously (*Écrits intimes*) that his interest in and practice of libertinism are at their most explicit.

Some critics have emphasized the tension, or even contradiction, between Vailland's intense individualism, manifest in his fascination for eroticism and the aristocratic figure of the eighteenth-century libertine, and his left-wing convictions, his desire to participate in collective action in order to fight against oppression. Others have attempted to show that the two are not as irreconcilable as may first appear: Both stem from an atheistic, materialistic stance, and sex and political activism are both areas in which the individual can strive for and exercise freedom. Vailland defines libertinism as the "art of pleasure practiced by a free mind." There is something fundamentally austere in the uncompromising rationality of Vailland's "true libertine." Far from being a self-indulgent figure without morals, his libertine bravely rejects reactionary morals and emotional dependency. Hence, the rejection of passionate love in favor of pleasurable love, an opposition likened to that between servitude and liberty, passivity and action.

Esquisses pour un portrait du vrai libertin

Sketches for a Portrait of the True Libertine was first published in 1946 together with *Les Entretiens de Madame Merveille avec Lucrèce, Octave et Zéphyr* [*Dialogues Between Mrs. Marvel, Lucrecia, Octavio, and Zephyr*]. Vailland begins by stressing that libertine thinking differs from both romantic notions of love and the Schopenhauerian view of sexual attraction as serving the reproductive interests of the species. He then praises the sacrilegious audacity of the early libertines who dared equate love with pleasure alone, before discussing de Sade as a precursor to Freud and the true founder of erotology. In these *Esquisses*, which essentially rehearse the points made in *Les Entretiens avec Madame Merveille*, Vailland insists on the key role of prostitutes, the "professionals," in the systematic pursuance of pleasure, and most notably that of the madam. For Vailland, the brothel is essentially a theatre, and the madam the stage director who selects the members of the cast, creates the appropriate setting, and defines the rules. Combining the tact of the confessor with the imagination of the poet, she is the one who makes up for the shortcomings of her clients's fantasies. To the sentimental souls who cry: "But what about tenderness?" Vailland replies that it is reserved for the woman who has proved herself to be a worthy adversary, thus becoming his equal, his accomplice. This is exemplified in the relationship between Valmont and Mme de Merteuil (in *Dangerous Liaisons*), who, having loved and hurt one another, eventually support one another in their quest for pleasure. This feeling of tenderness, born out of mutual respect and akin to the pity one feels for those who have devoted the whole of their existence to a purely gratuitous pursuit, might eventually become, Vailland concludes, the purest form of love.

Les Entretiens de Madame Merveille avec Lucrèce, Octave et Zéphyr. Notes à l'usage d'un essai sur le plaisir

Meeting by chance at Mme Merveille's brothel, three libertines (a woman and two men, one of whom is a homosexual) agree to devote the following twelve evenings to a systematic exploration of the nature of sexual pleasure: Each evening will start with a discussion on a particular theme, supported by the recounting of personal stories and followed by sexual activities related to the given theme. Having drawn a parallel between his chosen structure and that of de Sade's *120 Days of Sodom*, Vailland points out that the dialogic form was used long before by Plato in *The Banquet* and Lucian in *Dialogues of*

the Dead and that the madam as a Socratic figure in matters sexual was not invented by de Sade. The first evening begins with the assertion that pleasure and the satisfaction of the reproductive instinct are unrelated and that so-called vice cannot therefore be a perversion of the latter; this is evidenced by the fact that the erotic experiences of children are not linked to the representation or enactment of reproductive acts. The second evening is a further theoretical and practical investigation of the initial topic: Erogenous zones coincide only occasionally with reproductive organs. The following evening is spent recapitulating on previous discussions and deploring the social consequences of a "finalist" conception of sexuality with references to Gide's *Corydon*. Having refuted the notion of perversion, the libertines come to the conclusion that de Sade's classification of pleasures from the "natural" to the increasingly "perverted" is inappropriate and that there is a need for a new type of classification, which is simultaneously "genetic, evolutional, and dialectic." The first two phases outlined on the fourth evening are pre-puberty chaos (which foreshadows all future developments) and solitary onanism (when primarily the self appears as a source of pleasure). Then comes the time when the individuals become beings of pleasure, subjects able to satisfy their desire through conquest. In the course of the fifth evening, the libertines profess the utmost scorn for those individuals (the woman chaser or the man hunter) who do not develop beyond the conquest stage and remain, as far as pleasure is concerned, eternal adolescents. The sixth evening focuses on infatuation: By making the fulfillment of desire dependent on one person, and one person only (a choice often based on diverse or contradictory factors, if not mere chance), the lover becomes the victim of passion, and thus condemned to a life of suffering. True, passion may give way to love, but then physical pleasure is merely a by-product and, as such, devoid of value; hence the need to call on the services of professionals once the mature, austere, and truly libertine phase is reached. The eighth discussion stresses that the sexual makeup of the individuals (their degree of femininity, masculinity, or homosexuality) has no bearing on their development: All go through the five successive phases. The following evening, Octave talks about his need for particular rituals, and Mme Merveille explains that virtue does not consist in combating one's tendencies but in containing them within a wider erotic framework. In the course of the tenth and eleventh evenings, Lucrèce and Zéphyr confirm that for them too, pleasure has become increasingly ritualized: While Octave can be described as a masochist, Lucrèce is a sadist and Zéphyr a fetishist. They do not elaborate on the matter by documenting their practices, however, their ambition being merely to provide a definition of pleasure and examine the laws governing it. And this is where *Les Entretiens* departs from its de Sadean model: Although the meetings are meant to combine theory and practice, the practical activities are never described in any great detail, not even those staged on the last evening to show that "the tragic grandeur of eroticism lies in the conflict between the infinity of possible variations and the formal narrowness of its themes."

Les Quatre figures du libertinage

In this short essay, *The Four Figures of Libertinage,* published in 1950, Vailland sets out to define what he sees as the four basic "patterns" of eighteenth-century *libertinage*: the choice of an appropriate victim, the ensuing seduction, the fall, and the breaking off. As there is no merit in choosing an easy prey, the person to be seduced must be virtuous and of a blameless character. The seduction process itself is likened to hunting, but it is not enough to possess the hitherto virtuous; there must be a willing surrender. This surrender, or fall, is the equivalent of the clean kill in bullfighting: It allows neither lingering nor ambiguity. The same applies to breaking off the relationship, which constitutes the "moral" of the libertine story: It must follow the fall as quickly as possible so that the seducer cannot be suspected of having in turn been seduced, and moreover must be executed with a flourish of impudence. In all this, Vailland's point of reference is obviously Laclos's *Dangerous Liaisons*, whose heroes, Vailland explains, have little in common with Casanova, Don Juan, or de Sade's characters. Unlike Casanova, who was motivated by love and the appreciation of female beauty, and for whom seduction was a last resort, Valmont's interest lay not in the object of his attentions but first and foremost in the chase: He was emotionally detached. Unlike Molière's Don Juan, whose behavior was a negation of the existence of God, a metaphysical gamble, Valmont belonged to the age of Enlightenment, and played an essentially social game. Finally, in terms of the risks incurred, Valmont's highly codified and flamboyant love games had little in common with de Sade's extreme variations on the theme of freedom.

Laclos par lui-même

Dangerous Liaisons is again at the core of the book on Laclos—*Laclos by Himself*—that Vailland published in 1953. It focuses on the social and economic conditions that prevailed in eighteenth-century France, just before the Revolution, and proposes a detailed analysis of the internal workings of Laclos's novel. Vailland begins by dispelling the idea that Laclos was an aristocrat like the vicomte de Valmont: Laclos, he explains, was a bourgeois whose military career as an artillery officer suffered from the fact that he had neither title nor money; hence his idea of making his mark on the world by writing a novel. By doing so, he not only made a name for himself but provided the middle classes who aspired to power with useful ammunition against the ruling aristocracy. If Valmont is the epitome of the aristocracy, the Présidente de Tourvel, the wife of a magistrate and the only sincere character in the book, represents the bourgeoisie; she is the "ideal" woman described by Laclos in his treaty *De l'éducation des femmes* [On Women's Education]. This treaty is presented as key to a proper understanding of *Dangerous Liaisons*: Although socially and economically oppressed, woman is, by nature, equal to man, and it is up to her to bring about the revolution that will secure her freedom, Laclos said, thus anticipating Marxist analyses of female oppression quoted at length by Vailland. His close analysis of the epistolary novel develops the points made in *Les Quatre figures du libertinage*. Although he gives a detailed account of Laclos's commitment to and active participation in the French Revolution, responsible for the downfall of the likes of Valmont and Mme de Merteuil, Vailland does not comment on the tragic fate of the libertines at the end of the novel. In fact, he concludes his book with quotations from twentieth-century French writers praising the "eroticization of will" in the character of Mme de Merteuil (André Malraux), and the beauty and sophistication of the evil, shocking, yet "perfect" libertine couple (Jean Giraudoux).

Esquisses pour un portrait du vrai libertin, Les Entretiens de Madame Merveille, and *Les Quatre figures du libertinage* were reprinted in 1963 in *Le Regard froid* [*The Cold Look*], a collection of essays which also includes *Eloge du cardinal de Bernis* [*Eulogy of Cardinal De Bernis*], another libertine greatly admired by Vailland and presented here through the eyes of Casanova, who shared a mistress with De Bernis. Vailland describes the Cardinal as a man whose words, however cruel, and whose affability, however perfidious, are "the most exquisite signs of the distance that someone endowed with reason can put between himself and the rest of humanity in order to have a clear vision of the world and of his own position within it." This eulogy was written in 1956, only months after Stalin's crimes were made public. Vailland did not leave the Communist Party immediately but withdrew from political activism, opting for the detached stance epitomized in the *regard froid* that de Sade attributed to the libertine.

Biography

Born in Acy-en-Multien (Oise), October 16. Secondary education in Paris, 1918–19, and Rheims, 1919–25. Higher education in Paris at Lycée Louis-Legrand and then at the Sorbonne, 1925–28. In 1928, fell out with his Catholic family, graduated in philosophy, and became a reporter at *Paris-Midi*. Having cofounded a literary journal (*Le Grand Jeu*) inspired by the Surrealists in 1927, was accused of political complacency in his reporting and excluded from the group, 1929. Traveled extensively for *Paris-Midi* and *Paris-Soir*, and frequented the hottest Paris night spots, 1930–39. Underwent treatment for drug addiction in 1938 (again in 1942 and finally in 1947). During the German occupation of northern France in World War II, moved to Lyon with his paper, 1940, and joined the Resistance movement, late 1942. War correspondent, 1944–45; freelance journalist, 1945–65. Joined the Communist Party in 1952 but failed to renew his membership after 1958. Married Andrée Blavette in 1936 (separated, 1946); met Elisabeth Naldi in 1949 (married 1954). Left Paris in 1951 and lived near Bourg-en-Bresse (Ain) until his death on May 12.

MIREILLE RIBIÈRE

Selected Works

"Esquisses pour un portrait du vrai libertin" and "Les Entretiens de Madame Merveille avec Lucrèce, Octave et Zéphyr" [1946], "Les Quatre figures du libertinage" [1950], and "Eloge du cardinal de Bernis" [1956]. In *Le Regard froid: réflexions, esquisses, libelles, 1945–1962.* Paris: B. Grasset, 1963.

Laclos par lui-même. Paris: Seuil, 1953.

Ecrits intimes. Edited by Jean Recanati. Paris: Gallimard, 1968.

"La Jeune fille couverte de bittes." In *N'aimer que ce qui n'a pas de prix,* edited by René Ballet and Christian Petr. Monaco: Editions du Rochet, 1995.

Further Reading

Courrière, Yves. *Roger Vailland ou un libertin au regard froid.* Paris: Plon, 1991.

Flower, J.E. *Roger Vailland: The Man and His Masks.* London: Hodder and Stoughton, 1975.

Picard, Michel. *Libertinage et tragique dans l'œuvre de Roger Vailland.* Paris: Hachette, 1972.

Recanati, Jean. *Vailland: esquisse pour la psychanalyse d'un libertin.* Paris: Éditions Buchet/Chastel, 1971.

"Le Libertinage, une passion de liberté." *Cahiers Roger Vailland* 9. Le temps des Cerises Éditeurs, 1998.

Ballet, René. "Jeu de la passion et passion du jeu. Roger Vailland et les femmes." *Europe* 712–713 (Aug.–Sep. 1988): 38–51.

Senegas, Jean. "De la souveraineté selon Vailland." *Europe* 712–713 (Aug.–Sep. 1988): 52–61.

Information and documents by and on Roger Vailland can be obtained from "Les Amis de Roger Vailland," Médiathèque Elisabeth et Roger Vailland, 1 rue du Moulin-de-Brou, 01000 Bourg-en-Bresse.

VALDÉS, ZOÉ

1959–
Cuban novelist

Valdés began her writing career as a poet, and her first collection, *Respuestas para vivir* (1986), won the Roque Dalton prize in 1982. Her volumes of poetry include *Todo para una sombra* (1986), *Vagón para fumadores* (1996), *Cuerdas para el lince* (1999), and *Breve beso de espera* (2002).

Her international fame, however, rests with her novels, which draw sometimes polarized responses from critics and readers. Admirers praise the unabashed eroticism, sardonic humor, and candor of her prose. Detractors find her work repetitive, crude, and bordering on the pornographic, and charge that her productivity has a negative impact on the quality of her writing.

Valdés's first novel, *Sangre azul*, was published in Cuba in 1993. Its protagonist, Attys, a beautiful adolescent girl, moves from Cuba to Paris in pursuit of Gnossis, a painter who had offered his love only to withdraw it later, initiating her in the search for an impossibility, that of an absolute blue which can be gleaned only from the most intimate connection to the senses but is invisible on the surface. A finalist for the Sonrisa Vertical prize for erotic fiction, it already gave evidence of Valdés' daring imagery and the vitality of her expression of the erotic.

Valdés first came to international notice as a writer in 1995 with the publication of *La nada cotidiana*, translated immediately into a dozen languages. "She was born on an island that sought to build paradise"—the opening and closing line of the novel—frames the story of Patria, born in 1959 with the Cuban revolution, and like the revolution, mired in the frustration of the collapse of what began as endless promise. Patria, street-smart and irreverent, narrates a tale that seeks to capture the urgency and despondency of life in Cuba after the collapse of the Soviet Union, the "período especial" that has reduced everyday life in Cuba to a new level of despair. Patria's openness to sexual experimentation—depicted graphically in the novel—opens a possibility of asserting an identity through her body. It in turn allows her to escape from the sordidness of her surroundings and counteract the politicized identity imposed on her by her father's choice of name, Patria. Patria's frank appropriation of erotic discourse accounted in great part for the novel's critical and popular success. *La nada cotidiana* was praised by critics for its humor and biting critique of Cuban reality. Many critics found it style—built on an inventive use of language that is both highly poetic and deeply earthy—dazzling and bold.

Valdés followed this success with a third novel, *La hija del embajador* (1995), for which she won the Premio Novela Breve Juan March Cencillo. In this novel Valdés draws upon her experiences in the Cuban embassy in France to tell the tale of Daniela, the daughter of the Cuban ambassador to Paris, as she struggles between her identity as a Cuban, marked by its exuberant sensuality, and the studied eroticism and inner coldness she finds in Europe. The furious eroticism of the tale becomes an act of defiance against the stifling oppression of diplomatic mores.

In *Te di la vida entera* (1996), a finalist for the Planeta Literary Prize, Valdés returns to the topic of desire, hope, and disillusionment, this time through sixty years in the life of her heroine, Cuva, who comes to prerevolutionary Havana shortly after her sixteenth birthday. Exploring the flavor and rhythms of Havana night life in the 1950s with two voluptuous older prostitutes who befriend her, she encounters a mysterious man who after a frenzied dance and a passionate kiss disappears without a trace, leaving her hopelessly in love and holding on to a one-dollar bill he has entrusted to her care. When they reunite eight years later, they embark on a fiery love story. Left alone again, Cuva's life mirrors the story of the revolution, moving from elation and passion through degradation, want, misery, and absurdity. The novel takes the reader along this path to the rhythm of Cuban music, chiefly *boleros*, that seem to control Cuva's life.

In *Café Nostalgia* (1999), Valdés returns to the *bolero* as the evocative backdrop to her tale of a Cuban woman living in Paris who seeks to hold on to her memories of Havana through her readings. As she reads, she writes letter to the people who have been important to her in her life; the letters, which remain unsent, become her text. Here, the elements familiar to readers of Valdés's work—eroticism, the plight of women in unrequited love, separation from the home-land—lack the freshness and vitality of earlier work. But the musical evocation, as an element that Valdés incorporates fully and organically into the text, offers enough of the new to ac-count for the interest of this recent work.

Valdés's *Querido primer novio*, published in 2000, also explores the problems of memory and of living in the past. Dánae, living in frus-trated claustrophobia in the city, pursuing her domestic chores as if they were battles against fierce foes, finds refuge in the memories of child-hood, in particular those of a first boyfriend through whom she had discovered the vital power of eroticism to fulfill a woman's life.

Valdés's other novels include *El pie de mi padre* (2000), *Milagro de Miami* (2001), *Lobas de mar* (2003), and *La eternidad del instante* (2005), all of which continue to explore the erot-ic as a path to self-fulfillment for her female characters.

Biography

Zoé Valdés, a Cuban writer of Chinese descent, was born in Havana in 1959. She worked toward a degree in Spanish philology before leaving Cuba in 1984 to work at the Cuban delegation to UNESCO. She also worked as a scriptwriter at the Cuban embassy in Paris before returning to Havana in 1988 to become the assistant direc-tor of the *Revista de Cine Cubano*. Disenchanted with Castro's regime, she returned to France in 1995. Valdés has been a Spanish citizen since 1997 and lives in Paris with her daughter and second husband, filmmaker Ricardo Vega.

LIZABETH PARAVISINI-GEBERT

Works

Los aretes de la luna. Leon, Spain: Everest, 1999.
Breve beso de espera. Barcelona: Lumen, 2002.
Café Nostalgia. Barcelona: Planeta, 1997.
Cólera de ángeles. Barcelona: Lumen, 1996.
Cuerdas para el lince. Barcelona: Lumen, 1999.
El pie de mi padre. Barcelona: Planeta, 2000.
La eternidad del instante. Barcelona: Plaza y Janés, 2005.
La hija del embajador. Barcelona: Emecé, 1996.
Lobas de mar. Barcelona: Planeta, 2003.
Milagro en Miami. Barcelona: Planeta, 2002.
La nada cotidiana. Barcelona: Emecé, 1995.
Querido primer novio. Barcelona: Planeta, 1999.
Respuestas para vivir. Havana: Letras Cubanas, 1986.
Sangre azul. Havana: Letras Cubanas, 1994.
Te di la vida entera. Buenos Aires: Seix Barral, 1997.
Todo para una sombra. Barcelona: Taifa, 1986.
Traficantes de belleza. Barcelona: Planeta, 1998.
Vagón para fumadores. Barcelona: Lumen, 1996.

Further Reading

González-Abellás, Miguel Angel. "'Aquella isla': Intro-ducción al universo narrativo de Zoé Valdés." *Hispa-nia* 83.1 (2000): 42–50.
———. "Sexo trasnacional: La cubana como mercancía en la obra de Zoé Valdés." *Alba de América: Revista Literaria* 22 (2003): 277–85.
Ortiz Cerebro, Cristina. "La narrativa de Zoé Valdés: Hacia una reconfiguración de la na(rra-)ción cubana." *Chasqui* 27.2 (1998): 116–28.
Seung Hee, Jung. "*Te di la vida entera*, una versión en bolero de la Revolución cubana." *Espéculo: Revista de Estudios Literarios* 25 (2003–2004).
Zamora, Hilma Nelly. "La memoria del exilio y el abismo de la destrucción en *Café Nostalgia* de Zoé Valdés." *Explicación de Textos Literarios* 28: (1999–2000): 125–32.

VALENZUELA, LUISA

1938–

Argentine novelist and short story writer

Luisa Valenzuela is the author of many novels and short story collections. As a part of the "post-boom" generation of women writers in Latin America, she has consistently used her writing as a locus for searching out a female voice, which for her is inextricably linked with the body. The erotic infuses much of Valenzuela's work. Sometimes it serves as a glance into the personal, which reveals links to both the public and the political. At other times, female eroticism is expressed overtly through a subversive use of the word, challenging patriarchal authority and language. Finally, in many of Valenzuela's later works, the erotic link between the personal and the political evolves into an exposure of the link between sexual perversion and the perversion of power, particularly in the form of torture and oppression in the writer's native Argentina during the "Dirty War."

Valenzuela's first short novel, *Hay que sonreír* [*Clara*], details the story of a young prostitute who, despite abuse by men, continues to search for a "true love," a man who will treat her lovingly. A link between the personal and the public is clear through sex in the novel—Clara is a prostitute, selling the private act of lovemaking to the public. In addition, despite her personal experience of sex as an act of exploitation and abuse (men continually mold her to their desires, ignoring her own needs), she still believes the popular societal rhetoric of romantic love. In the end, however, this conflict is resolved not through Clara finding this love. Instead, she marries a man who continually dominates her mentally and physically, telling her, "Hay que sonreír" [one must keep smiling], despite the acts of degradation performed on her. Finally, this husband kills Clara in a last act of domination, slitting her throat in order to silence her and assure her complete submission.

Valenzuela's next novel, *El gato eficaz*, expresses its theme of eroticism through a much more experimental language than any of her previous work. Written shortly after her involvement with the *Tel Quel* group in Paris, this text bears the imprint of its positions and ideologies. Language is central to the anti-realist *El gato eficaz*, a novel without a plot, which contains characters only as rudimentary figures. In addition, language is employed for its own destruction, as Valenzuela uses such devices as wordplay and free association to undermine any notion of a fixed referent. Eroticism is intimately linked with language in the novel, and it too is under erasure. Valenzuela attempts to express a new form of female sexuality which undermines traditional sex/gender dichotomies. Thus, the main narrator, although primarily female, is constantly in flux, sometimes becoming male (or even an animal or plant). Sex is also portrayed with the same playful enthusiasm with which Valenzuela approaches language in the novel. In one chapter, entitled "El juego de fornicon" [The Fornication Game], Valenzuela writes of the sexual act in the language of game rules, stating, "Es este un juego inventado por mí para pasar bien el rato en compañía. Cualquiera puede aprenderlo; es sencillo, no se desordena demasiado la casa, y distrae de las cotidianas preocupaciones" [This is a game I invented to pass the time with company. Anyone can learn it: it is simple, does not mess up the house, and distracts one from daily preoccupations] (*El gato*, 70). In *El gato eficaz*, Valenzuela expresses a sexuality from the unconscious, an eroticism that falls outside the rigidity of traditional linguistic rules and patterns.

Luisa Valenzuela's later novels and short stories depart from the linguistic experimentalism of *El gato eficaz* while nevertheless retaining eroticism as a central theme. These works, rather than presenting female desire, instead focus on the links between sex and power, often looking at the links between sexual perversion and the abuse of power. In her 1983 novel *La cola de lagartija* [*The Lizard's Tail*], she comments on the political situation in Argentina in the 1970s and early 1980s, once more using the personal as a gateway to the political. The novel focuses on the character of "El Brujo" [The Sorcerer], a fictionalized version of Isabel Peron's Minister of Social Welfare (an infamous torturer). In this novel, El Brujo is a megalomaniacal, fantastic creature with three testicles, bent on world domination. His unwavering quest for power is mixed with his sexual perversion, as he believes that he will procreate with himself (since his third testicle is female) and is obsessed with his own bodily fluids.

Valenzuela's short stories from this time period onward are not quite as fantastically lyrical as *La cola de lagartija* but they do reflect the same preoccupation with the relationship between sex and power. *Cambio de Armas* [*Other Weapons*] deals with this relationship from the female perspective (all of the narrators are women) as it criticizes women's plight by evoking the tension between political and erotic relations. In the title story, the female protagonist is heavily drugged and locked in her house. She suffers from severe amnesia and at first cannot even remember her husband's name. As the story progresses, however, she slowly regains her memory, and the reader begins to realize that her husband (a high military official) had killed her leftist lover and tortured her brutally before marrying her. Their intense and often violent sexual encounters become an extension of the torture that was committed on her in the political context. In addition, her story becomes a metaphor for masculine control over and cruelty toward women. The protagonist cannot remember her husband's name and thus calls him all sorts of different men's names, making him into an Everyman. The story directly intermingles the personal and political, the private and public, in such a way that issues of eroticism cannot be separated from issues of power and politics.

Although Luisa Valenzuela's works span different styles and genres, all are concerned with eroticism, specifically as it relates to female subjectivity. Her works explore the relationship between language, eroticism, and politics/power through various lenses, commenting on both specific political realities and universal issues. For Valenzuela, eroticism and the realm of the personal are not only keys to the "outer" public world, they are inseparable themes. By juxtaposing these themes, she questions and problematizes both the dichotomy of the public/private and the relationship between eroticism and power.

Biography

Born in Buenos Aires, Argentina. She began work in Argentina as a journalist, writing for the newspaper *La nación* and the magazine *Crisis*. She moved to France, where she wrote her first novel *Hay que sonreir* in 1966. In 1979, she moved to the United States, where she lived for ten years, leading writing workshops at Columbia and New York Universities. She has written 12 books, and received a Guggenheim fellowship, as well as being a fellow at the Institute for the Humanities in New York.

TRACY FERRELL

Selected Works

Hay que sonreír. 1966; as *Clara (Discoveries)*, translated by Andrea G. Labinger, 2000
Los heréticos. 1967
El gato eficaz. 1972
Aquí pasan cosas raras, 1975; as *Strange Things Happen Here*. Translated by Helen Lane, 1979
Cambio de armas. 1982; as *Other Weapons*, translated by Deborah Bonner, 1985
Cola de lagartija. 1983; as *The Lizard's Tail*, translated by Gregory Rabassa, 1992
Realidad nacional desde la cama. 1990; as *Bedside Manners*, translated by Margaret Jull Costa, 1995
Simetrías. 1993; as *Symmetries*, translated by Margaret Jull Costas, 1998

Further Reading

Cordones-Cook, Juanamaria, ed. *Poética de transgresión en la novelística de Luisa Valenzuela*. New York: Peter Lang, 1991.
Díaz, Gwendolyn, and María Ines Lagos, eds. *La palabra en vilo: Narrativa de Luisa Valenzuela*. Santiago: Editorial Cuarto Propio, 1996.
Magnarelli, Sharon. *Reflections/Refractions: Reading Luisa Valenzuela*. New York: Peter Lang, 1988.
Martinez, Nellie. *El silencio que habla: Aproximación a la obra de Luisa Valenzuela*. Montreal: Corregidor, 1994.
Marting, Diane. "Female Sexuality in Selected Short Stories by Luisa Valenzuela: Toward an Anthology of Her Work." *Review of Contemporary Fiction* 6.3 (1986): 48–54.

VALLEJO, FERNANDO

1942–
Colombian novelist

Fernando Vallejo's purpose is to unmask human misde eds. His novellas expose them in humorous, beautiful, and sometimes cruel prose. Colombia dominates his work, as does his birthplace, Medellín. Historical memory is central to his task. In his fiction he uses imaginative memory to blur distinctions between the real and the fantastic. By depicting reality on a continuum Vallejo invites readers to reflect on its veracity, a technique which encourages them to consider their own role in humanity's failings.

The narrator describes his erotic desires at greatest length in *La Virgen de los Sicarios*, *El fuego secreto* [*The Secret Fire*] and *Mi hermano el alcalde* [*My Brother the Mayor*]. He portrays his attraction to adolescent males economically but powerfully, as in this passage from *La Virgen* about his lover Alexis, a *sicario* (teenage contract killer):

Si por lo menos Alexis leyera. … Pero esta criatura en eso era tan drástico como el gran presidente Reagan, que en su larga vida un solo libro no leyó. Esta pureza incontaminada de letra impresa, además, era de lo que más me gustaba de mi niño. ¡Para libros los que yo he leído! y mírenme, véanme. ¿Pero sabía acaso firmar el niño? Claro que sí sabía. Tenía la letra más excitante y arrevesada que he conocido: alucinante que es como en última

instancia escriben los ángeles que son demonios. Aquí guardo una foto suya dedicada a mí por el reverso. Me dice simplemente así: "Tuyo, para toda la vida", y basta. ¿Para qué quería más? Mi vida entera se agota en eso. (64)

[If at least Alexis read. … But in that this child was as extreme as the great President Reagan who, in his long life, read not a single book. This purity uncontaminated by print, moreover, was that which I most liked about my lad. As for the books I have read! and look, look at me. But did, perhaps, the boy know how to write? Yes of course he knew. He had the most exciting, ornate writing I've known: mind-blowing like that of the demon angels in the end times. Here I keep his photo, dedicated to me on the back. It says simply: "Yours, for life," and that's it. Why would I want more? My entire life ends there.]

El fuego secreto depicts the narrator's coming of age in Medellín's homosexual netherworld and recounts, from the tragic to the comic, his attempted sexual relationships, all of which founder. At one point, after the narrator stands up a potential boyfriend, he describes his inability to love:

Y acúsome padre de haberle dado la espalda al amor. Tras de buscarlo tanto, cuando lo encontré di media vuelta y me fui corriendo. Y ni supe cómo se llamaba. Le decían por apodo, por cariño, Joselito. … Vive Dios y es testigo, no había otro como él. Dueño de lo que buscaba en todos y no encontraba en ninguno: la inocencia esencial. (293–4)

[Father, I accuse myself of having turned my back on love. After looking so hard for it, when I found it, I did an about-face and went running away. And I never knew his name. They called him, affectionately, by the nickname Joselito. … As God lives and is witness, there was no other like him. Owner of that sought in all and found in none: essential innocence.]

In *Los caminos a Roma* [*The Roads to Rome*], the narrator, now in his early 20s, recounts trysts in hidden public places, such as on the Aventino and under the Seine's bridges in Paris. The novella depicts two longed-for romantic relationships that fail, one with an Italian boy, the other, in an exquisitely written dreamlike sequence, with a Sephardic girl. *Años de indulgencia* [*Years of Indulgence*] shows him as a man cruising the docks and trucks of Manhattan's lower west side seeking anonymous sex; relationships are no longer mention ed.

Death eclipses sex in the three following novellas. His one successful bond, that with Alexis, is truncat ed. Sex is only a memory in *El desbarrancadero*, about the narrator's return to Medellín to help his terminally ill father and brother die, and *La Rambla paralela* [*The Parallel Rambla*], where he is an old man facing his death.

Mi hermano el alcalde breaks with this arc and its presentation of male–male sexuality. The narrator's brother Carlos wins the mayoralty of the Colombian mountain town Támesis. Homoeroticism is as public as the administration's accomplishments: Carlos and his two male lovers adopt a child, preside over civic events, and pursue their erotic desires across the story's landscape, usually to humorous effect. During the campaign, Carlos sends his friends Ritiña and Lucho to survey the municipality's *veredas* (districts):

> Con el pretexto del informe iban el par de maricas de vereda en vereda a conseguir muchachos y a pelearse entre sí por ellos delante de niños, mujeres y viejos, dando un espectáculo bochornoso con el consiguiente desprestigio de mi hermano y caída en la intención de voto. Para Ritiña y Lucho la política era el homoarte de pichar. (40)

> [From *vereda* to *vereda* went the pair of fairies, using the pretext of the survey to find boys and to fight among themselves over them in front of children, women, and the old, presenting a degrading spectacle with the consequent discrediting of my brother and drop in his poll numbers. For Ritiña and Lucho, politics was the homo art of screwing.]

The narrator's signification *homoarte* reveals a concept heretofore unnamed in Vallejo's fiction: an ethos of male–male love. To signify a thing implies its apprehension, and hence a degree of ownership. *Mi hermano*'s narrator elaborates on *homoarte*, as in this summation of his brother's most notable contribution as mayor:

> Que piche cada quien con quien quiera y que el niño aprenda. … Támesis hoy en día gracias a él es un pueblo alegre y pichanguero, sin remordimientos sexuales que le corroan la conciencia y que son tan inútiles y feos y que tanto mal les hacen a los niños. (23–4)

> [May each do it with whomever may want to and let the child learn. … Thanks to him, today Támesis is a festive and doing-it kind of town, without the sexual guilt which corrodes the conscience, and which is so unproductive and nasty and which harms children so much.]

Vallejo's biographies and accompanying volumes of poems and letters illuminate unrecorded facets of Latin American history. He brings a novelist's voice to his meticulously researched accounts of the Colombian poets José Asunción Silva (1865–1896) and Porfirio Barba Jacob (1883–1942). Each gained a reputation in Latin America as much for the erotic ambiguities of his life as for his work. Silva was a modernist whose poems pointed the way to the twentieth century. Barba Jacob was a brilliant newspaper editorialist and bohemian who expressed his homoerotic desires openly in poetry and prose; his verses remain at the summit of Colombian letters.

Biography

Born in Medellín, Colombia, October 24. Studied philosophy and arts in Medellín and Bogotá and film at Rome's Cinecittà. Lived in New York City before moving to Mexico City in 1971. Vallejo is best known for the novella *La Virgen de los Sicarios* [*Our Lady of the Assassins*], translated into six languages and made into a movie for which he wrote the script. The novella followed a five-volume autobiographical cycle compiled in *El río del tiempo* [*The River of Time*]. Since then he has published four novellas. All nine are told by a first-person narrator, unnamed except in *La Virgen*, where he is called Fernando. Vallejo has also written a pair of biographies, a book on grammar, and a book on biology. Early in his career, he directed two short movies in Colombia and three feature-length movies in Mexico. In 2003 he won one of the most prestigious prizes in Spanish literature, the Premio Rómulo Gallegos, for *El desbarrancadero* [*The Precipice*].

MARK MCHARRY

Selected Works

Books

Logoi: Una gramática del lenguaje literario [Logoi: A Grammar of Literary Language]. México, DF: Fondo de Cultura Económica, 1983, 1997.
Barba Jacob, el mensajero [Barba Jacob: The Messenger]. México, DF: Séptimo Círculo, 1984; Bogotá: Planeta, 1997.
Barba Jacob: Poemas recopilados y anotados por Fernando Vallejo [Barba Jacob's Poems Compiled and Annotated by Fernando Vallejo]. Bogotá: Procultura, 1985.
Los días azules [Clear Days]. Bogotá: Planeta, 1985.
El fuego secreto. Bogotá: Planeta, 1986.
Los caminos a Roma. Bogotá: Planeta, 1988.
Años de indulgencia. Bogotá: Planeta, 1989.
El mensajero [The Messenger]. Bogotá: Planeta, 1991.
Cartas de Barba Jacob [Barba Jacob's Letters]. Bogotá: Revista Literaria Gradiva, 1992.
Entre fantasmas [Among Ghosts]. Bogotá: Planeta, 1993.
La Virgen de los sicarios. Madrid: Alfaguara, 1994, 1998; Suma de Letras 2002; as *Our Lady of the Assassins*, translated by Paul Hammond, London: Serpent's Tail, 2001.
Almas en pena [Souls in Torment]. Bogotá: Alfaguara, 1995; republished as *Almas en pena, chapolas negras* [Black Butterflies: Souls in Torment], Barcelona: Suma de Letras, 2002.
Cartas de Silva: 1881–1896 [Silva's Letters]. Bogotá: Casa Silva, 1996.
El río del tiempo (comprises: *Los días azules*; *El fuego secreto*; *Los caminos a Roma*; *Años de indulgencia*; *Entre fantasmas*). Bogotá: Alfaguara, 1999, 2002.

La tautología darwinista y otros ensayos de biología [The Darwinist Tautology and Other Essays About Biology]. México, DF: Universidad Nacional Autónoma de México, 1998; Bogotá: Ediciones de la Revista Número, 1999; Madrid: Taurus, 2002.

El desbarrancadero. Madrid: Alfaguara, 2001, 2002.

La Rambla paralela. Bogotá, Madrid, and México, DF: Alfaguara, 2002.

Mi hermano el alcalde. Bogotá: Alfaguara, 2004.

Movies, Feature Length

Crónica roja [Crime Pages], 1979, Conacite 2 (México).

En la tormenta [In the Storm], 1980, Conacite 2 (México).

Barrio de campeones [Neighborhood of Champions], 1981, Conacite 2 (México).

Movies, Short Documentaries

Un hombre y un pueblo [A Man and a People], 1968, Bogotá, about Jorge Eliécer Gaitán.

Una vía hacia el desarrollo [A Road to Development], 1969, Bogotá.

Movie Scripts

Nueva York, Nueva York, 1971, México.

La Virgen de los Sicarios [Our Lady of the Assassins], 2000, Medellín, Les Movies du Losange / Le Studio Canal Plus / Vertigo Film / Tucan Producciones, dir. Barbet Schroeder.

Plays

El médico de las locas [Doctor of the Lunatics], 1971, México, DF.

El reino misterioso o Tomás y las abejas [The Mysterious Kingdom, or, Thomas and the Bees], published in *México, sus raíces y su folklore* (*2o concurso nacional de obras de teatro: hombres de México y el mundo*), México, DF: IMSS, Subdirección General Administrativa, Jefatura de Servicios de Prestaciones Sociales, Departamento de Prensa y Difusión, 1975.

Further Reading

Cabañas, Miguel A. "El sicario en su alegoría: la ficcionalización de la violencia en la novela colombiana de finales del siglo XX." *Taller de Letras* 14 (November 2002): 7.

DuPouy, Steven M. "Vallejo, Fernando." In *Latin American Writers on Gay and Lesbian Themes: A Bio-Critical Sourcebook*, edited by David William Foster and Emmanuel S. Nelson. Westport, CT: Greenwood Press, 1994.

Fernández, Javier. "Fernando Vallejo: La voz del muerto." *Literate World*. Retrieved May 31, 2004, from http://www.literateworld.com.

Foster, David William. "Utopian Designs." In *Gay and Lesbian Themes in Latin American Writing*. Austin, TX: University of Texas Press, 1991.

———. "Political Intersections." In *Queer Issues in Contemporary Latin American Cinema*. Austin: University of Texas Press, 2004.

González, Pablo. "Visión y evocación de Medellín en *La Virgen de los Sicarios* y *El Fuego Secreto* de Fernando Vallejo." *Con-Textos* 7 (April 2000).

Martínez, Fabio. "Fernando Vallejo: El ángel del apocalipsis." *Boletín Cultural y Bibliográfico* 25 (1988). Bogotá: Biblioteca Luis Ángel Arango; retrieved May 31, 2004, from www.lablaa.org/blaavirtual/boleti5/bol14/angel1.htm

McHarry, Mark. "Killers in Love." *The Guide* [Boston], November 2001.

———. "Fernando Vallejo." In Thomson Gale's *Literature Resource Center*.

Ospina, Luis (director). *La desazón suprema.* Documentary about Vallejo, 90 minutes, Colombia 2003.

Zeiger, Claudio. "En la ciudad de la furia." *Página/12* [Buenos Aires], August 5, 2001; retrieved May 31, 2004, from www.pagina12.com.ar/2001/suple/radar/01-08/01-08-05/nota1.htm

———. "La belleza y la furia." *Página/12* [Buenos Aires], September 23, 2001; retrieved May 31, 2004, from www.pagina12.com.ar/2001/suple/libros/01-09/01-09-23/nota1.htm

VARGAS VILA, JOSÉ MARÍA

1860–1933
Colombian novelist

Vargas Vila was the first Latin American author to make eroticism a centerpiece of his work, and his erotic imagination took many forms. He was the first to feature prostitutes as heroines, excelling in the description of the seduction of female innocence leading to prostitution, as in *Flor de fango* (1895). He was also very adept at the depiction of how corrupted female innocence can turn very quickly into unprincipled depravity. In many of his fictional works, women, as repositories of animalistic instinct, represent sexuality in its most elemental essence, becoming in turn vehicles for the devil. In *Ibis* (1900), an avowedly erotic novel that he considered his first fully realized literary text, he portrays a heroine—a novice at a convent who is the victim of a sexual attack—whose voracious sexual appetite and depravity acknowledge no religious or ethical concerns. In some of his later work he would turn to irreverent portraits of biblical female characters as hedonistic destroyers of men, as temptresses leading them to their destruction, which added to his already established reputation as a misogynist who actually saw women that way.

In *Magdalena* (1916) and *Salomé* (1920), for example, the protagonists' demand for an independent sexual life leads directly to men's corruption. *María Magdalena* caused a scandal due to the author's portrayal of Jesus as a man who has lost his physical and intellectual powers after allowing himself to be seduced by a prostitute. In *El huerto del silencio* (1921), the protagonist is an apostate priest whose desire for his young cousin leads to murder at his hands when he learns of her pregnancy.

Vargas Vila's eroticism, as these examples illustrate, is closely linked to death and damnation, often embodied in incestuous relationships that break religious and societal taboos. His approach to sexuality owed much to contemporary social and psychological theories about illness (particularly venereal) and sexuality, and his sensibilities were those of the Naturalistic movement so much in vogue during a seminal period in his literary career. Although his work continues to receive scant critical attention, it remains popular with readers, many of whom know his work through illustrated novels and film melodramas.

Biography

José María Vargas Vila was born in Bogotá, Colombia, the son of a general who died when he was four, leaving the family penniless. A self-taught young man, Vargas Vila tried his hand at teaching in the provinces before returning to Bogotá to work at a prestigious school, from which he would be dismissed following accusations of pedophilia. When his accuser was later found to have embezzled funds from his army battalion and to have prowled the streets of Bogotá dressed as a woman, Vargas Vila turned the incident into a novel, *Alba roja* (1901).

After his failure at teaching, Vargas Vila became involved in political life as a newspaper reporter, political activist, and orator. His participation in an uprising against the government led to his fleeing to Venezuela. His first of more than a hundred books, *Pinceladas sobre la última revolución de Colombia*, was so scathing in its grotesque caricatures of Colombia's political leaders that it led to a price being put on his head.

Vargas Vila established himself in Venezuela, where he turned his attention to the writing of novels, sold as pamphlets in installments. In New York City, where he settled in 1891, he developed close friendships with many exiled Latin American intellectuals and politicians, among them Cuban patriot José Martí. He also published *Los Providenciales*, a furious diatribe against the arrogance of Latin American dictators. In the late 1890s Vargas Vila joined the Latin American exiles in Paris, where he continued to publish articles, essays, novels, and political pamphlets at a feverish pace. In 1902, he wrote *Ante los bárbaros*, a passionate denunciation of the United States' incipient expansionism.

Following this publication, he became prey to neuroses caused by intense loneliness, a feeling of persecution, and the rejection of his work in intellectual circles. Having grown aggressive and intolerant with friends, he left for a restorative sojourn in Venice, returning to Paris in 1904 not fully recovered. The breakdown intensified the black legend growing around Vargas Vila. Gossip had it that he was immensely rich and lived like a prince in luxurious decadence. He was reputed to hate women, clerics, and nuns, a hatred stemming from being the child of a priest and a depraved nun. It was said that he was an anarchist who supported Errico Malatesta's assassinations and bombings against Italian aristocrats. It was generally reported that he was a homosexual who presided over Satan-worship ceremonies and that he was an impotent hermaphrodite who hated everything living.

In 1905 Vargas Vila settled in Madrid and in 1912 moved to Barcelona. The period of his greatest productivity and widespread fame followed, and he became the best known and most widely read writer in Spanish. His 1923 tour of Latin America, when he lectured to huge crowds in Buenos Aires, Montevideo, Rio de Janeiro, Mexico City, and Havana, among other cities, was the event of the year in the continent. Loudly vilified by priests everywhere, his books were banned by the Church. During this tour he contracted a rare disease that would ultimately leave him blind.

Vargas Vila's prolific work was invariably greeted with scandal, controversy, and critical repudiation, but these seemed to have only encouraged his readers. His work appealed to the masses, among whom he found an enthusiastic following. His rejection of literary canons, his virulent anticlericalism, and his eroticism, coupled with the melodrama and rhetorical excesses of his prose, brought to his writing and public persona much notoriety. He was in turn persecuted, barred from returning to Colombia, and excommunicated by the Catholic Church. Nevertheless, he was a master at producing works for popular consumption; and as such, a precursor or twentieth-century mass culture. His winning formula was a controversial mixture of anti-imperialistic, leftist, pro-worker political diatribe, sentimental melodrama, and eroticism. He died in Barcelona.

LIZABETH PARAVISINI-GEBERT

Works

Alba roja. Madrid: R. Fé, 1902.
Aura o las violetas; *Emma*; *Lo irreparable*. Paris: Bouret, 1901.
Flor de fango. París: Bouret, 1902 [1895].
El huerto del silencio. Barcelona: Maucci, 1917.
Ibis. Paris: Librería Americana, 1917 [1900].
María Magdalena. Barcelona: R. Sopena, 1916.
Salomé. Barcelona: R. Sopena, 1918.

Further Reading

Castillo, Jorge Luis. "The Gospel According to Vargas Vila: Religious and Erotic Discourses within *María Magdalena*." *Romanische Forschungen* 111 (1999): 600–21.
Domínguez Michael, Christopher. "El increíble caso Vargas Vila." *Letras Libres* 2 (2000): 92–93.
Gomez, Rafael. "José María Vargas Vila." *Boletín Cultural y Bibliográfico* 16 (1979): 203–09.
Gómez Ocampo, Gilberto. "El discurso ensayístico en *De sobremesa* e *Ibis*." In *Leyendo a Silva*, edited by Juan Gustavo Cobo Borda, 97–107. Bogotá: Instituto Caro y Cuervo, 1990.
———. "Secularización, liturgia y oralidad en José María Vargas Vila." In *Actas Irvine-92, Asociación Internacional de Hispanistas*, edited by Juan Villegas, Vol. 4, 259–67. Irving, CA: University of California at Irvine, 1994.
Osorio, Betty. "Erotismo y poder en la narrativa de José María Vargas Vila." In *Literatura y cultura: Narrativa colombiana del siglo XX*, 112–30. Bogotá: Ministerio de Cultura, 2000.

VASSI, MARCO

1937–1989
American novelist and essayist

An intellectual adventurer in the real and fictional realms of Eros, Marco Vassi brought a keen and wry intelligence to bear on the turbulent times of the 1960s and 1970s in America. He was on the barricades of the sexual revolution, personally involved and yet viewing it with Jesuitical acuity and detachment. His first novel, *Mind Blower* (1970), was published by the legendary Maurice Girodias, who proclaimed him the new Henry Miller.

Mind Blower is an awkward novel, suffering from woodenness of plot, characterization, and dialogue, more interesting for its ideas and erotic scenes than for the story it tells. A young man named Michael, desiring to "get in touch with people who were playing serious sexual games," answers an ad in the *New York Times* for an assistant to a master of arcane studies. When he interviews for the position, he meets an extraordinary fat man named Dr. Tocco, who heads the Institute for Sexual Metatheater. Tocco shocks him by insisting that he make love to a young girl even before they talk.

Michael is a familiar figure in erotic fiction: the seeker of erotic knowledge. What follows in *Mind Blower* is the narrative of Michael's progress to sexual enlightenment. Tocco calls Michael's various sexual experiments "role actualization." By acting out every fantasy, subtle or monstrous, Michael is able to shed his individuality like old skin. For Vassi, ego transcendence is achieved only by people strong enough to discard conventional sexual morality, who recognize that "in our society, everything is a lie."

In *Mind Blower* the protagonist learns the necessity of denying love itself, of seeing that tenderness is an emotion no better or worse than others; emotional attachments inhibit his progress to erotic enlightenment. *Mind Blower* introduces Vassi's idea of metasexuality—a concept central to his thought—which he elaborates on in his essay "The Metasexual Manifesto," included in the book *Metasex, Mirth and Madness* (1975). Metasexuality requires that its adepts give no more weight to one emotion than to another. This Zen-like attitude is adopted by the protagonists in Vassi's second and third erotic novels, *The Gentle Degenerates* (1970) and *Saline Solution* (1971). Metasexuality is a concept that does away with categories like homosexuality, heterosexuality, bisexuality, and perversions, replacing them with sexual modes: theatrical, masturbatory, romantic, therapeutic, and procreative. Vassi is one of the few writers since Georges Bataille to express his perceptions about eros along philosophical lines.

Vassi bothers very little with plot or characterization in his fiction. He is a didactic artist, an explorer with findings to present. Like such writers from de Sade onward, his narratives are vehicles for the exposition of his ideas. In *The Gentle Degenerates*, the breakup of a marriage is his subject; in *The Saline Solution*, it is abortion. Vassi once said that the conflict in all his novels is that of approach/avoidance, between the desire to live in a relationship and an even stronger desire to be free of it. Vassi's intimate knowledge of the subtle interplay of power between men and women and his honesty with himself (for all his work is autobiographical) help to ameliorate an unattractive narcissism that manifests itself in the attitude that others exist only insofar as they help him learn how to live.

His fourth novel, *Contours of Darkness* (1972), is his longest and most ambitious. It has more than one major protagonist, is told in the third person, and possesses a skeletal plot. In it he attempts a broader scope than in previous novels. Its theme is once again relationship, but without the sharp, ruthless focus of the more openly autobiographical novels. In *Contours of Darkness* Aaron is a school teacher in Berkeley, California, involved in a threesome with his wife, Cynthia, and a younger student, Conrad. They explore homosexuality and lesbianism in the context of radical politics of the late sixties.

Metasex, Mirth and Madness is Vassi's most important book because it is a good introduction to his thought. In it he presents in essays and fables the thinking of a unique, courageous intelligence about a sexual philosophy derived from personal experience. The seven essays in the book are pungent with the smell of erotic experience.

Just as Vassi's concept of metasexuality encompasses all the forms of eroticism, so his books exhibit the range possible within erotic literature, from genre entertainment to philosophy.

Biography

Born Ferdinand William Vasquez-D'Acugno in New York City, 1937. He took his BA at Brooklyn College, with further studies at The New School For Social Research and Yale University's Institute of Far Eastern Languages. His first novel, *Mind Blower*, was published by Olympia Press in 1970. Simon & Schuster published his autobiography, *The Stoned Apocalypse*, in 1972. Many novels and essays followed. He died of AIDS-related complications.

MICHAEL PERKINS

VEGA, ANA LYDIA

1946–
Puerto Rican short story writer

Vega emerged as a writer with the publication of her first collection of short stories, *Vírgenes y mártires* [*Virgins and Martyrs*] (written with Carmen Lugo Filippi, 1982). This collection, and the two books of short fiction that followed—*Encancaranublado y otros cuentos de naufragio* (1983) and *Pasión de historia y otras historias de pasión* (1987)—set the tone for Puerto Rican feminist literature in the 1980s and early 1990s. Her books were greeted with critical acclaim. *Encancaranublado y otros cuentos de naufragio* won the Casa de las Américas short story prize in 1982. Her story "Pasión de historia," in which she parodies detective fiction, won the 1984 Juan Rulfo International Short Story Contest. In 1989 she received a Guggenheim Fellowship for the completion of *Falsas crónicas del Sur* (1991). Vega co-wrote the script for the Puerto Rican feature film *La gran fiesta*, with director Marcos Zurinaga, which was nominated for an Academy Award for Best Foreign Film.

From the beginning, Vega's style was characterized by her command of colloquial Puerto Rican Spanish and street jargon, her parodic approach to sexuality, and her subversion of linguistic and literary structures. As an avowedly feminist author, one of Vega's principal parodic targets was the Puerto Rican version of machismo, which she ridiculed in stories such as "Letra para salsa y tres soneos por encargo" [Lyrics for a Salsa] and "Pollito Chicken." In these and other stories, Vega subverted male sexual aggressiveness through humor, depicting it as turning impotent the moment it is matched by outspoken female desire. In "Letra para salsa," her best-known short story, she tells of a young woman determined to lose her virginity who carries off the first man who yells a compliment to her on the street to a motel room, with hilarious consequences. Their attempt at a sexual encounter is given three possible endings, each tied to a particular ideological position. The bold and irreverent depictions of sexual encounters in this and other stories, coupled with the irrepressible humor with which she addresses sexuality made Vega an icon of comic erotic literature internationally. Her short stories have appeared in magazines and anthologies internationally and have been translated into many languages. Part of the appeal of her comic-erotic fiction comes from Vega's ability to use the sexual conflicts between men and women to voice larger political and social concerns. Her erotic clashes are always rooted in the class and gender struggles, racial oppression, and political strife of her native Puerto Rico and the broader Caribbean region. This erotic component of her fiction, which was usually drawn from situations familiar to readers from sensationalist newspapers and publicity campaigns, when coupled with her command of street jargon and popular culture, has gained Vega a broad readership and critical acceptance.

In 1991, with the publication of *Falsas crónicas del sur*, which gathers eight tales inspired by Puerto Rican history, Vega broke with the comic eroticism of her earlier collection. As she did with detective fiction in *Pasión de historia*, where she parodied that popular genre as the basis for her exploration of a wife's puzzling disappearance (à la *Rear Window*), here Vega calls upon a number of genres—the Romantic novel, the tale of adventure, social satire, the political chronicle—to turn history inside out, helping us to look at familiar incidents from the individual's perspective, bringing history (and the folkloric interpretation of history in the process) into the realm of everyday occurrence and personal drama. In her preface to the book, Vega speaks of her commitment to extensive research for this project, which involved visits to libraries and archives as well as countless interviews with Puerto Ricans of the southern coastal towns, as a tribute to the world of her mother. The resulting stories are testimonies to the Puerto Rican collective imagination and its distinctive take on history, and although critics considered them to represent her best and more mature work, they did not have the success with the general public of her earlier comic-erotic work.

Vega has not published any additional books of fiction since *Falsas crónicas del sur*, although she has completed a book of essays: *El tramo ancla: ensayos puertorriqueños de hoy* (1988), which Vega edited with fellow columnist Kalman Barsy, gathering the essays published in "Relevo," the column appearing throughout 1985 in the leftist weekly *Claridad*, by Vega, Barsy, Mayra Montero, and Carmen Lugo Filippi. A second collection, *Esperando a Loló y otros delirios generacionales*, published in 1996, gathers an assortment of Vega's satiric essays on Puerto Rican society, politics, and mores. The texts, autobiographical and feminist as we have come to expect from Vega, expand on the critique of Puerto Rico's abortive bilingualism and ambivalent nationalism that has been deemed responsible for the island's continued identity crisis. They also expose, as did Vega's fiction throughout the 1980s, the problematic role of women writers in a society such as that of Puerto Rico, where patriarchal role models and rampant machismo continue to relegate them to the periphery of the literary tradition. In 1998 Vega published two books for children, *Celita y el mangle zapatero* [*Celita and the Shoemaker Mangrove*] and *En la bahía de Jobos* [*In the Bay of Jobos*], with illustrations by Yolanda Pastrana Fuentes, about the preservation of Puerto Rico's rich mangrove environments.

Biography

Ana Lydia Vega was born in Santurce, Puerto Rico, the vibrant working-class sector of San Juan, whose characters she brings to life in her fiction. She studied French at the University of Puerto Rico and received a master's degree in French literature from the Université Paul Valéry in Montpellier and a doctorate in comparative literature from the Université de Provence. She joined the faculty of the University of Puerto Rico in 1971 and retired after a thirty-year teaching career. As a scholar, Vega was a pioneering figure in pan-Caribbean cultural studies, helping train several generations of students in the comparative study of Caribbean societies across languages and cultures.

LIZABETH PARAVISINI-GEBERT

Editions

Encancaranublado y otros cuentos de naufragio. Río Piedras: Antillana, 1983.

Esperando a Loló y otros delirios generacionales. Río Piedras: Universidad de Puerto Rico, 1994.

Falsas crónicas del sur. Río Piedras: Universidad de Puerto Rico, 1991.

Pasión de historia y otras historias de pasión. Buenos Aires: Ediciones de la Flor, 1987.

El tramo ancla: ensayos puertorriqueños de hoy. Río Piedras: Universidad de Puerto Rico, 1988.

Vírgenes y mártires. Río Piedras: Antillana, 1982.

Further Reading

Aparicio, Frances R. "'Así son': Salsa Music, Female Narratives, and Gender (De)Construction in Puerto Rico." *Poetics Today* 15:4 (1994): 659–84.

Craig, Linda. "Intersections in Ana Lydia Vega's 'Pasión de historia.'" *MaComère* 4 (2001): 71–83.

Feracho, Lesley. "Ana Lydia Vega, True and False Romances." In *Reading U. S. Latina Writers: Remapping American Literature*, edited by Alvina Quintana, 181–96. New York: Palgrave/ Macmillan, 2003.

Hernández, Carmen Dolores. "A Sense of Space, a Sense of Speech: A Conversation with Ana Lydia Vega." *Hopscotch* 2:2 (2000): 52–59.

Labiosa, David J. "Ana Lydia Vega: Linguistic Women and Another Counter-Assault or Can the Master(s) Hear?" In *Sharpened Edge: Women of Color, Resistance, and Writing*, edited by Stephanie Athey, 187–201. Westport, CT: Praeger, 2003.

Velez, Diana. "Ana Lydia Vega's 'Pasión de historia': A Text Within Two Genres." *Torre de Papel* 14 (2004): 44–51.

VENEREAL DISEASE

The emergence of syphilis in Europe struck like a thunderbolt, dating from Charles VIII's campaign in Italy in 1495 and the return to the Continent of the sailors and soldiers who had accompanied Columbus to America. It was a *coup de foudre* because of its surprise and the extent of its violent harm to the body, and also because of its resonance within the bosom of the *social* body—its inscription in collective fantasies and the intensity of its bond, over the next several centuries, with literature.

It spread like an epidemic, borne across Europe by mercenaries and prostitutes, and characterized as a leper's leprosy, the plague of God, and divine punishment upon sexual intercourse. Those who were contaminated were rejected from social circles and marked as accursed. The writers of the Renaissance presented this *grosse vérole* as a major face of the carnival of exorbitance and disorder constituting the world. Rabelais dedicates his oeuvre to the "most precious poxed." The disease makes one of its first appearances in a novel in 1528, in the picaresque *La Gentille Andalouse* by Francisco Delicado. Two years later, Fracastor coined its name in his poem *Syphilis sive morbus gallicus* (1530). One finds it throughout all the tales of Boccaccio. In Elizabethan theater, it is omnipresent in the characters of the prostitute and the libertine seducer, in Shakespeare, Ben Jonson, and John Ford. The anonymous author in 1539 thus celebrated *Le triomphe de haute et puissante dame vérole, reine du puys d'amour* [*The Triumph of the High and Mighty Poxed Woman, Queen of the Country of Love*]. In the next century, it inspired comic tales and satirical poems, which sarcastically justaposed mutilated genitalia and ruined bodies to the gallantry and dreamy love of preciosity.

The 17th century conceived of syphilis as a test of or challenge to civilization. Newspapers and other forms of public correspondence had never before given so much advertising to physicians—or to charlatans—who claimed to have an anti-syphilitic remedy. In "girl stories" and libertine novels are painted the experience of going to "the pool" at a general hospital, where, in scenes from the banks of the Ganges, mercury baths were taken. These libertine texts (e.g., Diderot and Rousseau) were frank about the circumstances under which they had contracted the disease.

Voltaire above all took the measure of the threat of syphilis in his fight to defend European civilization. To those, like Diderot in his *Supplément au voyage de Bougainville* (1777), who denounced the colonizers who were purportedly carrying syphilis to the New World and corrupting the innocence of noble primitive societies, Voltaire responded with the reminder that the disease had first seen the light of day in America, that nature alone was guilty, and that the intelligent person had to resist the temptation to conceive of either natural utopias or divine reigns of terror condemning sexuality. On the contrary, society should be about reviving the precautions against the disease, in terms of themes of pleasure and of the exchange and circulation of commodities, ideas, and men.

However, it was in the 19th century that writers had their most significant encounters with the subject syphilis—mainly because most of them (Stendhal, Flaubert, Heine, Baudelaire, Jules de Goncourt, Daudet, Maupassant, Lorrain) had contracted it. Although syphilis was a collective disease, bourgeois society made those infected face up to it in shame and secret. Writers were thus brought face to face with painful questions of identity. Rejected by society, whose values he was no longer able to share, the artist (e.g., Baudelaire) tended to find in prostitution a condition analogous to his own. Syphilis may even have attested to a certain "malediction" of genius. It is the melancholy "venom" of the *Fleurs du mal*. It is the muse of literature. It was synonymous with modernity for the Decadent writers, who, from Jules de Goncourt to Joris-Karl Huysmans, claimed—again, in juxtaposition to the beautiful form—an aesthetics of rags, of pargeting, of poxed decomposition. Modernity thus found its favored expression in the image of the prostitute excessively made up—to hide venereal sores. The exorbitance of this makeup designates an extravagance where life and death, desire and morbidity (eros and thantos?) meet and exchange their essences, in a sort of desperate baroque (e.g., Barbey d'Aurevilly).

Bubu de Montparnasse by Charles-Louis Philippe (1901) was no doubt one of the last chants to syphilis. The identification of the bacterium *treponema pallidum* in 1905 demystified it, the discovery of penicillin effectively cured it, literature went in a new direction (e.g., Gide, Claudel, Valéry), viz., back to classicism, and the disaster of the First World War finally put an end to the fantastic influences of the disease.

It popped up again, here and there, in literature, as in Thomas Mann's *Doctor Faustus* (1947), which echoes the ethos of the tormented relationship of disease (cholera, tuberculosis, syphilis) with the artist and the genius, negotiated once again by the figure of the prostitute. The outbreak of AIDS, toward the end of the 20th century, tended to have the same effect, but now with the potency of years of sexual liberation and the recognition of diversity and homosexuality as acceptable alternatives in society. Initially identified with the gay scene, then with the contaminated syringes of drug addicts, AIDS revives some of the archaisms of the collective syphilitic fantasy. Again emerge a "terror" mindset and an ethos of divine punishment, the labeling of minority groups as vectors, and phobias of spatial contamination and infection by mere proximity. And literature, again, looked to reconcile the terrifying, impossible relation of a subject with a virulent disease, that a subject maintains with the disease (e.g., *As is* by W. H. Hoffmann [1984], *A l'ami qui ne m'a pas sauvé la vie* [1990] and *Le Protocole compassionnel* [1991] by Hervé Guibert, *Les Quartiers d'Olliver* by Jean Noel Pancrazi [1990]). All the more urgent, all the more intense is the impetus of the writer who faces the imminence of physical disease.

PATRICK WALD LASOWSKI

Bibliography

Corbin, A. *Les Filles de Noce. Misere sexuelle et prostitution.* Paris: Flammarion, 1982.

Nelson, E.S. *AIDS: The Literary Response.* New York, 1992.

Quetel, C. *Le Mal de Naples. Histoire de la syphilis.* Paris: Seghers, 1986.

Sontag, S. *Illness as metaphor.* New York: Farrar, Straus and Giroux, 1978.

Wald Lasowski, P., *Syphilis. Essai sur la litterature française du XIXème siècle.* Gallimard, Paris, 1982.

———. *L'Ardeur et la galanterie.* Paris: Gallimard, 1986.

VÉNUS DANS LE CLOÎTRE [*VENUS IN THE CLOISTER*]

Whereas most so-called pornographic novels of the seventeenth and eighteenth centuries were unsigned and published anonymously, *Vénus dans le cloître* [*Venus in the Cloister*] begins with an introductory letter, addressed to "Madame D.L.R., très digne abbesse de Beaulieu" and signed by one abbé Duprat, in which he proclaims, in the opening sentence: "As I would find it difficult not to execute what you acknowledge to desire, I have not deliberated a single moment about the request which you have addressed to me to reduce in writing at the earliest possible time the gentle interviews in which your Community has taken such a creditable part" (313). He never explains precisely how he has been informed of those interviews nor what amount of "reduction," or editing, he has been forced to do. At the same time, he wishes his text to be read by this abbess only and fears what would happen to their likes if "such secret conferences were to become public" (314); in other words, he does not wish the interviews to be published. This is the typical kind of double-talk to be found in editor's notes of typical eighteenth-century novels, the editor himself being a hybrid subject halfway between the publisher or the real author and the fictional characters present in the text. The real author who signed this dedication "abbé Duprat" to protect his anonymity and his good name was probably, as most specialists seem now to agree, l'abbé Barrin (1640–1718), the translator of Ovid's *Oeuvres galantes et amoureuses.*

The date of first publication of this novel has not been established with certainty. Many bibliographers still consider it to be an eighteenth-century novel if only because the only extant copies date from that period; but Alexandre Cioranescu claims that the first edition came out in 1672, and Jules Gay mentions many seventeenth-century editions, the first one having apparently been published around 1682 (*L'Enfer,* vol. 7: 291). How many interviews did the first edition contain—three, five, or six? Nobody knows for sure, but the editor of *L'Enfer de la Bibliothèque Nationale* thinks that there were only three (the ones that will be analyzed below) and that the fourth and fifth, though they may have been written by the same author as the first three, came out later; as to the sixth, which involves new characters, Séraphique et Virginie, it was probably written much later by a different author, as its style seems to suggest. Paradoxically, such uncertainties about the name of the author, the date of first publication, and the number of interviews are largely due to the fact that this novel, contrary to *L'Ecole des filles,* was not censured at the time; it would have received a great deal more publicity otherwise.

These three dialogues between two young nuns, sixteen-year-old Agnès and twenty-year-old Angélique, do not contain a single obscene word, the only coarse one being *pisser* [to piss]. Whereas, in *L'Ecole des filles,* the author clearly sought to excite "l'homme moyen sensuel" [the man of sensual ways], to borrow Judge Woolsey's expression in his decision concerning *Ulysses,* and used every trick possible to achieve this goal, the author of *Vénus dans le cloître* soon became as preoccupied with moral and political issues as with creating an erotic text. The novel contains comparatively few erotic scenes like the opening one, in which Angélique comes upon half-naked Agnès, who is masturbating, and starts kissing her and caressing her inflamed bottom and later her genitals, modestly called her "Nature." This scene is described with decorous metaphors; here is, for instance, Agnès's reaction to Angélique's most intimate caresses:

> I beseech you, take off your hand from that spot if you don't want to kindle a conflagration there which it might be difficult to extinguish. I must confess my weakness to you: I am the most sensitive girl that can be found, and what would not cause the least emotion in others is often the source of confusion for me. (329)

When Agnès starts flogging Angélique's buttocks (*maison de derrière*), there is hardly any suggestion that she does it for sadistic purposes: "Do you realize that this spot only becomes more beautiful as a result? The very special fire which animates it lends it a vermilion which is more pure and brilliant than any coming from Spain" (331). She does not so much take pleasure in hurting her companion as in enhancing the voluptuousness of her sexual parts.

Gradually, there develops something akin to a love relationship between the two girls, Angélique acting the part of the monitor of pleasure as well as confessor and teacher because of her higher rank in the community's hierarchy, and Agnès that of the compliant and highly voluptuous pupil. Angélique opens her moral argument with the following introduction:

> For me, I must say that I have been instructed by a learned man as to how I was supposed to behave myself in order to live happily all my life without doing anything, however, which might offend the eyes of a regular Community or could be unequivocally opposed to God's commandments. (320)

She then goes on to quote the learned man, a Jesuit and therefore a casuist, who held that religion was composed of two bodies, one political, liable to change from country to country and from century to century, and the other mystical, which, coming directly from God, is universal and eternal. The religious orders were not founded basically for mystical reasons but for political ones, to dispose of the younger children of the aristocratic families. Whatever the nuns do within their community cannot affect public tranquillity, since they do not belong to society anymore, as Agnès is prompt to understand. The first interview ends with a long evocation of the said Jesuit's affair with one of the nuns, Virginie. The learned man, whose name, Father Raucourt, Angélique finally discloses to Agnès, who knows him, has the ability "to convince you of what he desires" (335). When he had fallen in love with Virginie, he had cast aside another nun who had so far been his favorite and who, out of jealousy, now vows to bring about his downfall: she spies on the lovers with another nun as a witness, sees how the Jesuit "manipulates the spots consecrated to chastity and continence" (339) through a small opening in the grille, and then tells Virginie that she has seen everything and wants her to terminate her affair with the Jesuit. Virginie feigns to comply but, a few weeks later, sends her lover a letter in a cap she has made for him; he uses the same trick to communicate with her, claiming that the cap does not fit. The trick is finally exposed and the Jesuit is expelled to another province. This cap, which goes back and forth between the lovers, gradually becomes the potent signifier of their passion.

The second interview takes place immediately after Angélique's retreat. In the meantime, Agnès has been instructed by the priests recommended by Angélique, especially by the community's abbot, who told her that "there was nobody more dissolute than all the recluses and bigots when they find occasion to enjoy themselves" (347) and showed her an opening in the grille through which they could get together and to make love. Here again, the language is never crude but highly metaphorical:

> Then after many protests from both of us, the abbot easily got through the straits and reached port, where he was ushered in; but it was a little painful and was effected only after he had assured me that his entrance would have no bad consequences. (348)

Then she proceeds to tell about her sexual games with the Capuchin and with the Cistercian who had a reliquary full of pubic hairs lifted from his many mistresses. Angélique, pleased with what she has heard, quotes a Benedictine who told her about the various orders' sexual habits, especially masturbation. She also narrates the amorous adventure of sister Cécile, an Augustinian, and Father Raymond, the provincial of the Jacobins, and shows how the nun's superiors punished her when they discovered her attachment to a member of another order. After Agnès, who takes great pleasure in such narra-

tives, has provided a list of the pornographic books that she has received from her lovers, Angélique embarks upon another indecent story, that of sister Scolastique, who every evening availed herself of the perfumed bath prepared for the abbess's morning ablutions and, through a clever stratagem devised by the abbess, was exposed and severely flogged. At the end of the second interview, after a reading of some of the letters exchanged between Virginie and Father Raucourt, some comments on their respective styles and the evocation of the Jesuit's eventual escape to England, Angélique discourses on the vanity of the religious vows and the difference between freedom and licentiousness, pursuing her pliant pupil's instruction.

At the beginning of the third interview, Angélique explains why their abbess, who has had many lovers, is presently indisposed and won't disturb them: she likes to feed many different kinds of animals, among them a crawfish, which, because its water had not been changed, got out of its tank and took refuse in the abbess's chamber pot, and when "it felt sprayed by a rain a little too hot, jumped towards the spot whence it seemed to flow" (373); as it refused to relax its grip, one had to cut its paw. The two friends having retired into an alley in the garden, Angélique undertakes to discuss the subject of confession and instructs Agnès on how to deal with their present confessor, who is a particularly austere man, giving her a sample of a confession in which she withheld two thirds of what she should have said regarding her sexual transgressions. Intent as she is to show her pupil how aggravating it can be to repress one's sexual instincts, she narrates the story of sister Dosithée, a young nun endowed with a particularly amorous nature, who fell under the authority of an old and vicious confessor and, following his exhortations, fought too hard to repress her natural inclinations and succeeded only in getting more sexually aroused; finally, experiencing an orgasm after a flogging session, she decided henceforth to follow her nature. Through this example, Angélique wishes to show Agnès the vanity of many values and the necessity "always to preserve one's mind free and unobstructed by silly thoughts and stupid maxims" (385). She illustrates this principle during a kissing session with Agnès and begins to discuss the comparative merits of various pornographic books, especially *L'Ecole des filles,* which is too insipid and silly to her taste, and *L'Académie des Dames,* which is as dangerous, though "the purity of its style and its placid eloquence have something pleasant about them" (389). Free-spirited as she is, Angélique refuses to condone debauchery and libertinage, for, as she says, "the pleasures we propose must be curbed by the laws, as well as by nature and prudence" (390). Like Horace, who promoted "proper measure in all things," she favors a refined economy of pleasure, concluding:

> Let us live for ourselves only and without making ourselves ill with alien infirmities; let us establish within ourselves such spiritual peace and tranquillity as are the very principle of joy and the beginning of such happiness as we can reasonably desire. (392)

Vénus dans le cloître is neither a sexual manual nor a crude pornographic novel. The erotic scenes, as in de Sade's works, are always a pretext for promoting moral, political, and philosophical principles. The author clearly inveighs against church and nobility, which together conspire to imprison helpless girls for political and economic reasons and hinder them from enjoying a normal sexual life. As the refined style of the novel and Angélique's measured principles testify, the author does not plead in favor of a slackening of morals. The authors of *L'Ecole des filles* and *Thérèse philosophe* can be accused of bad faith, holding as they do two contradictory discourses; here, the text has a great discursive coherence and consistently pleads in favor of those poor creatures who, behind their grilles, are deprived of their natural right to know sexual desire and to indulge it, and who develop harmful frustrations as a result.

Vénus dans le cloître was translated into English and published in 1724 by Edmund Curll, and, along with *A Treatise of the Use of Flogging in Venereal Affairs* (1718), caused his arrest. It is this edition, obviously, that Fielding's heroine must be reading in *Shamela*. The case was difficult to try because there existed no previous case of the kind in English jurisprudence, only strict moral principles laid out by religion, as a judge had to admit: "Whatever tends to corrupt the morals of the people ought to be censured in the Spiritual Court, to which properly all such cases belong" (proceedings of the trial quoted in Hunter et al.: 50) The court had to devise a way to convert religious principles, which had little or no legal force in public life, into a legal jurisprudence, which was done by the judge, who considered that the government was responsible for public order when the latter was threatened by immorality. The court took into consideration the fact that since *Venus dans le cloître* was published in an English translation, it was now accessible to a much larger public and therefore deserved to be banned. Eventually, Curll was convicted, sentenced to pay a fine of 25 marks for each of the books, and pilloried, a comparatively light sentence.

MAURICE COUTURIER

Edition

"Vénus dans le cloître." In *L'Enfer de la Bibliothèque Nationale.* Vol. 7, ed. by Michel Camus. Paris: Librairie Arthème Fayard, 1988. The quotations were translated by the author of this article.

Further Reading

Couturier, Maurice. *Roman et censure ou la mauvaise foi d'Eros.* Seyssel: Champ Vallon, 1996.

Delarun, Jacques. *L'Impossible sainteté: La vie retrouvée de Robert d'Arbrissel.* Paris: Le Cerf, 1986.

Hunter, Ian, David Sauders, and Dugald Williamson. *On Pornography: Literature, Sexuality and Obscenity Law.* London: Macmillan, 1993.

Rustin, Jacques. *Le Vice à la mode, Etude sur le roman français de la 1ère partie du XVIIIe siècle.* Paris: Ophrys, 1973.

VERLAINE, PAUL

1844–1896
French poet

If critics often speak of the real life of Paul-Marie Verlaine in discussing his poetry, it is because of the inextricable link between the two. Generally speaking, the poems of Verlaine's that have received the greatest critical reception are those that were clearly inspired by strong emotional influences: his adolescent yearnings in *Poèmes saturniens*; his courtship of Mathilde in *La Bonne chanson* [*The Good Song*] (1870); his tumultuous affair with Rimbaud in *Romances sans paroles* [*Songs Without Words*] (1873); and his imprisonment in the poems intended for a collection originally entitled *Cellulairement* [*In Confinement*] and later included in *Sagesse* [*Wisdom*] (1881) and *Amour* (1888). While Verlaine's indecision—notably his inability to choose between the respectable heterosexual existence of his marriage to Mathilde and the drunken, tormented savagery of his homosexual relationship with Rimbaud—is the juicy recurrent theme that has proven most fertile for critics, the poet's other collections have been largely ignored. In addition to the poems inspired by Verlaine's religious conversion in his jail cell, he contributed to the collaborative *Album Zutique*, a product of informal dinner meetings attended by Verlaine, Rimbaud, and a host of other poets, composers, and artists. Best known in this collection is the "Sonnet of an Asshole" (reproduced in *Hombres*), written by Verlaine and Rimbaud together. The poem's first line ("Dark and wrinkled like a deep pink") begins with the word *Obscur,* the capital letter *O* emphasizing the poem's subject matter.

The first collection of Verlaine's that is filled with erotic themes is *Parallèlement* (1890), which, as its title indicates, was written alongside Verlaine's other collections, *Sagesse* and *Amour* (the latter indicating a sacred, rather than erotic, love). In a letter in August 1887 to Charles Morice, Verlaine said that "*Parallèlement* is the overflow, the dumping ground of all the 'bad' feelings that I am susceptible to express." Its first section, "Les Amies," first stood alone when it was published clandestinely in 1867 under the pseudonym Pablo de Herlagnez. "Les Amies" is composed of six poems that evoke a lesbian love. In part, Verlaine reproduces themes found in the lesbian poems of Baudelaire's *Les Fleurs du mal* [*Flowers of Evil*] (1857). The language ranges from the delicate, in "Per amica silentia" or in "Spring": "Swelling sap and growing flour, / Your childhood is an arbour: / Let my fingers wander in the moss / Where the rosebud glistens," to the more crude, as in "Pensionnaires." *Parallèlement*'s next section, "Filles," takes its themes from love scenes in bordellos. Later in the collection, Verlaine praises homosexual love in the poem "These passions that only they still call loves …" and recalls his relationship with Rimbaud in the aptly titled "Læti et Errabundi" [Joyful Vagabonds].

Most recently, more attention has been paid to two companion volumes of erotic poetry: *Femmes* and *Hombres*. The two collections were finally recognized as part of Verlaine's poetic work when they were included in the "Oeuvres libres" [Free Works] supplement to the highly respected Pléiade edition in 1989, and the first critical edition of *Femmes* and *Hombres* was published the following year. *Femmes* was first published in Brussels in 1890, again under the pseudonym Pablo de Herlagnez, and this time with the description: "printed clandestinely and not for sale anywhere"; and *Hombres* first appeared posthumously in 1903. While they appeared separately at first, they are—and should be—treated as two parts of a larger, erotic work. In fact, there is a marked intertextuality between the two collections: for example, between "Childishness" from *Femmes*:

Since it suits me better
To fuck you from below, I love
This position …

and the seventh poem from *Hombres:*

Climb up on me like a woman
So that I can fuck you from below
There. That's it. Are you well in hand?
While my cock enters you, a blade
In butter …

Whether in the heterosexuality of *Femmes* or the homosexuality of *Hombres*, debauchery is one of the poet's attempts at redemption. Unlike the undercurrent of prostitution in parts of *Parallèlement*, there is a sheer and free pleasure taken in both *Femmes* and *Hombres*.

Biography

Born in Metz, March 30, raised in Paris, where, after brief university studies amid periods of heavy drinking, worked at the Hôtel de Ville. After *Poèmes saturniens* [*Poems Under Saturn*], (1866), married Mathilde Mauté, nine years his junior. Having taken the side of the rebel Communards after the end of the Franco-Prussian War in 1871, he fled Paris until August, when he returned to the capital to live with Mathilde's parents. Received Arthur Rimbaud in 1871 and restarted his drinking, creating arguments with then-pregnant Mathilde. Left Paris with Rimbaud in 1872 for Belgium, and then London. Ever conflicted, Verlaine missed Mathilde, and ultimately left Rimbaud and London to be reunited with her in Brussels, only to rejoin Rimbaud and, in the same hotel in which Mathilde and Verlaine's mother were staying, to shoot him twice in the wrist in July 1873. While Rimbaud tried to have the charges dropped, Verlaine was condemned to two years in prison. After his return to Catholicism, Verlaine lived in England and France, teaching; relationship with his pupil Lucien Létinois (to whom was dedicated a section of *Amour*) lasted until 1883. Published the series "Les Poètes maudits" [The Damned Poets] in revues *Lutèce* and *La Vogue*, 1883–1886, and the last ten years of his life were divided between Parisian hospitals and drinking binges in cafés. Died in Paris, January 8.

SETH WHIDDEN

Editions

Oeuvres complètes. Edited by Antoine Adam. Paris: Gallimard/Bibliothèque de la Pléiade, 1972; as *Complete Works, Selected Letters*, translated by Wallace Fowlie, Chicago: University of Chicago Press, 1966.
Oeuvres poétiques. Edited by Jacques Robichez. Paris: Garnier, 1986.
Femmes/Hombres. Edited by Jean-Paul Corsetti and Jean-Pierre Giusto, 1990; translated by William Packard and John D. Mitchell, 1977; translated by Alistair Elliot, 1979; translated by Alan Stone 1980.

Selected Works

Album Zutique: Fac-similé du manuscrit original. Edited by Pascal Pia. Geneva: Slatkine, 1981
Parallèlement. 1889
Femmes. 1890
Chansons pour elle. 1891
Odes en son honneur. 1893
Elegies. 1893
Dans les limbes. 1894
Chair. 1896
Hombres. 1903

Further Reading

Buisine, Alain. *Verlaine: Histoire d'un corps.* Paris: Tallandier, 1995.
Cornea, Doina, and Livia Titieni. "Symboles de la féminité dans l'œuvre de Verlaine." *Studia Universitatis Babes-Bolyai, Philologia* 25.1 (1980): 41–47.
Milech, Barbara. "'This Kind': Pornographic Discourses, Lesbian Bodies and Paul Verlaine's *Les Amies.*" In *Men Writing the Feminine: Literature, Theory, and the Question of Genders*, edited by Thaïs E. Morgan. Albany: State University of New York Press, 1994.
Minahen, Charles D. "Homosexual Erotic Scriptings in Verlaine's *Hombres.*" In *Articulations of Difference: Gender Studies and Writing in French*, edited by Dominique D. Fisher and Lawrence R. Schehr. Stanford, CA: Stanford University Press, 1997.
Richard, Jean-Pierre. "Fadeur de Verlaine." In *Poésie et profondeur.* Paris: Seuil, 1955.
Richardson, Joanna. *Verlaine.* New York: Viking Press, 1971.
Schmidt, Paul. "Visions of Violence: Rimbaud and Verlaine." In *Homosexualities and French Literature*, edited by George Stambolian and Elaine Marks. Ithaca, NY: Cornell University Press, 1979.
Schultz, Gretchen. "Verlaine's Sexualities." In *The Gendered Lyric: Subjectivity and Difference in Nineteenth-Century French Poetry.* West Lafayette, IN: Purdue University Press, 1999.
Whidden, Seth. "'A la Marie-Antoinette': L'érotisme bisexuel dans 'Reddition.'" *Revue Verlaine* 7 (2002): 115–25.
Zimmermann, Eléonore. *Magies de Verlaine.* Geneva: Slatkine, 1981.

VERVILLE, BÉROALDE DE

1556–c. 1629
French novelist

Primary Work: *Le Moyen de parvenir*

In spite of the various works he published during his lifetime, Béroalde is perhaps most recognized for his novel *Le Moyen de parvenir* [*The Way to Success*]. Arguably, it is one of the greatest and most influential works of seventeenth-century French literature. Appearing after the French Renaissance and predating the literature of the Enlightenment, the novel was possibly written around the year 1558 and published between 1610 and 1620. Much controversy surrounds the work. In addition to the confusion regarding its year of publication, the authenticity of the novel as an original work has been long contested. It has been suggested that de Verville may not have been its true author, while some academics and critics have even proposed that the novel is either a reworking or an exact copy of an earlier text. However, the style of *Le Moyen de parvenir* suggests otherwise. Like many of de Verville's works, it is rich in imagery and contains countless examples of French dialect, jargon, and argot.

Le Moyen de parvenir is a substantial piece of writing. As a work professing to explain "all that was, is, and shall be," it sets out to debate countless philosophical and moral subjects. Béroalde described it thus: "[J]'ai fait un oeuvre, lequel est une satire universelle, où je reprends les vices de chascun" [I have created a work that is a world satire, where I capture the vices of each and everyone] (quoted by Monnoye: viii). Situated in a limbo-like setting, the focus of the novel is a grand banquet, attended by an assembled crowd of the most revered historical figures, presided over by Socrates as the master of ceremonies. The worthies (*gens d'honneur*) in attendance include philosophers, religious figures, royalty, and writers, all of different nationalities.

In short, *Le Moyen de parvenir* is a collection of thoughts and observations of life, told as anecdotes by the novel's various personages. Among the many themes discussed, religion is one subject that occurs at regular intervals throughout the course of the novel. De Verville's own experiences of Protestantism and Catholicism may have influenced his views of the clergy (all quotations are from the 1900 edition):

> Vous estes bien trompé d'autant qu'il n'y a gens qui soient plus sur le cul que moines et gens benis, ministres et sçavans qui estudient assi, et qui au lieu de conserver les saincts ordres qui leur ont esté conferez, les quittent et, abandonnant l'ordre de Dieu, se rangent aux ordres du diable, qui leur confere grace d'estre plus ribauds que jamais, et plus putains que les autres gens. (192)

> [You are all the more mistaken that there are no people more obsessed by sex than monks and clergymen, ministers and scholars who study diligently, and who, instead of keeping the holy orders, which have been conferred upon them, part from them, and abandoning God's holy orders, place themselves at the Devil's command, who awards them the honor to act more like a strumpet than ever, and more like a whore than other people.]

Similarly, de Verville writes at great length about women. He examines the emotional and sexual relationship between men and women, while analyzing the differences between the female and male character. A conversation between "the King of Egypt" and a Mme "le seigner de Danois" elicits perhaps his true view:

> Nous estions sur le subjet des dames. —Vroiment, madame, le subjet est unique en perfection. —Mais qu'en dites-vous? —Tout bien, madame. —Et encore? Dites-nous-en, à bon escient, vostre opinion. —Puis qu'il vous plaist, madame, par la mordong, toutes les femmes sont putains. (47)

> [We were discussing the subject of ladies. —Really, Madame, there is no other subject like it. —But what do you have to say about it? —Very well, Madame. —Well? Give us your wisdom. —If it should please you, Madame. God's death, all women are whores].

There are several examples of violence toward women in the text:

Cest officer avoit une femme assez fascheuse, et qui tourmentoit. Il la battit plusieurs fois, et à dur, don't elle se contrista, et menaça son mary du consistoire, qui est le purgatoire des Huguenots. Remis qu'il fut au consistoire, il y alla; et on luy remonstra que cela n'estoit pas beau de batter sa femme. "Elle estoit battable," dit-il. —Allez, allez, luy dit le diseur, sça-chant la pensée de nostre seigneur le consistoire, retirez-vous; et qu'il y ait de la mesure en vos actions, et qu'on n'oye plus parler de vous. (372).

[This officer had a wife, who was quite irritating and who tormented him. He beat her several times, and hard; she was grieved and threatened her husband with the consistory, which is the purgatory for Huguenots. Sent to the consistory, he went there and was taught that it wasn't nice to beat his wife. "It was so easy to beat her," he said. —Go now, said a voice, knowing the thought of our lord the consistory, leave us; Be sure to behave with more moderation in future, and don't let us hear about you again.]

Béroalde intended *Le Moyen de parvenir* to be a satire, a criticism of human weakness and vice. In numerous ways, it is reminiscent of Rabelais, with moments of cruelty and sadism given a comedic treatment. Kritzman notes: "The rabe-liaisian text ... transcribes a sadistic tendency to destroy an aggressor through the enactment of a comic allegory in which latent hostility is sublimated and yet unconsciously adheres to the ideological imperatives that dictate the power of repression" (201). Many passages in *Le Moyen de parvenir* are obscene, and some contain examples of scatological violence. Béroalde's decisions regarding use of language and certain words has also contributed to its notoriety; for example: "[J]e vous demande, Lipsius, pourquoy les femmes qui ayment le desduit hantent les gens de cloister? ... C'est pource qu'elles ont le feu d'enfer au cul; il faut des c....... benites pour l'esteindre" (103) [I ask you, Lipsius, why women who love pleasure regularly visit men of the cloister? It's because they're in heat and only blessed balls can put out the fire].

Subsequently, *Le Moyen de parvenir* was long classed as pornographic, relegated to the "l'enfer" [inferno] of libraries (i.e., access was closed to the general public).

Biography

Born François Brouard in Paris. His father was the renowned Protestant minister and humanitarian Mathieu Béroald, who had been closely involved with Agrippa d'Aubigné and Pierre de l'Estoile. In 1562, his mother died of the plague in Orléans, when de Verville was very young. After the death of his father, he converted to Catholicism, although he converted back again to Protestantism during the later years of his life. His education and subsequent career were a conflict of science, medicine, and religion. He was not only a preacher, but also was characterized as "a poet, chemist, physician, philosopher, grammarian, [and] mathematician" (Monnoye: xiii). His writings, consequently, were varied with regard to style and genre. As a poet, he composed several works, including romantic poetry (*Soupirs Amoureux*), philosoph-ical poetry (*Connaissances Nécessaires*), and religious poetry (*Muse Céleste*). In addition to his works of fiction and prose, Béroalde wrote the political work *L'Idée de la République* and produced various scientific pieces of research, primarily on alchemy. The date of de Verville's death is uncertain, and to this day he remains an author about whom little is actually known.

SARAH BERRY

Editions

Le Moyen de parvenir. 2 vols. Edited by Hélène Moreau and André Tournon. Paris: Champion, 2004.

Le Moyen de parvenir: Oeuvre contenant la raison de tout ce qui a este, est et sera. (Nouv. ed.) Paris: Garnier, 1900.

Anthologie Poétique de Béroalde de Verville. Introduc-tion by V.L. Saulnier. Paris: Haumont, 1945.

Translation

Machen, Arthur. *Fantastic Tales, or The Way to Attain: A Book Full of Pantagruelism.* Privately printed by Carbonnek, 1890.

Further Reading

Bancquart, Sophie, ed. *Dictionnaire des Littératures de Langue Française (Vol. A–F)*. Paris: Bordas, 1984.

Kritzman, Lawrence D. *The Rhetoric of Sexuality and the Literature of the French Renaissance.* Cambridge: Cambridge University Press, 1991.

Monnoye, Bernard de la. "Dissertation sur *Le moyen de parvenir.*" In *Le Moyen de parvenir.* Paris: Garnier, 1900 [Nouv. ed.].

Zinguer, Ilana. *Les Structures narratives du Moyen de Parvenir de Béroalde de Verville.* Paris: Nizet, 1979.

VIAN, BORIS

1920–1959
French writer

Eroticism figures quite naturally in the bizarre and hyperbolic universe of Vian's texts, as an integral part of the human condition. As such, it is at odds with society's hypocritical anti-erotic stance, in particular that of the clergy, which Vian denounces and mocks vigorously. Yet love is always twofold. Physical attraction to beauty and youth is presented as life affirming and playful (oftentimes in a tongue-in-cheek manner), and sensual details such as colors, dress, songs, and scents are the joyful anticipation of lovemaking. However, once consummated, the sexual relationship, and those living it, begin to wear and decay, all too often resulting in the death of the initial object of desire. The women portrayed are clichés. Sexually assertive women (and/or lesbians) are frowned on or ridiculed. Despite Vian's notoriety, his few downright erotic texts (*Écrits pornographiques*) were not published until 1980, featuring among other things the conference *Utility of Erotic Literature* from 1948, and a Dracula parody of deadly sex. In the works he penned under the pseudonym of Vernon Sullivan, sex is both a sales strategy and a way to expose the voyeuristic desires of the general public.

Boris Vian was many things: novelist, poet, playwright, screenwriter, actor, translator, singer/songwriter, jazz trumpeter, critic, essayist, and member of the Collège de Pataphysique, and "prince" of the St. Germain-de-Prés district of Paris. His first novel, *L'Ecume des jours* [*Foam of the Days*], was nominated for the 1946 Prix de la Pléiade. In that same year, the noir racial thriller *J'Irai cracher sur vos tombes* [*I'll Spit on Your Graves*] became the first of four novels written by Vian under the pseudonym "Vernon Sullivan." The *succès de scandale* of 1947, the book earned Vian a reputation as a "master pornographer," thwarting his aspirations to join the literary establishment and denying his subsequent works the critical attention they deserved. These included the novels *L'Automne à Pékin* (1947), *L'Herbe Rouge* (1950), and *L'Arrache-coeur* (1953), along with novellas (e.g., *Les fourmis*), plays (*L'Équarissage pour tous, Les Bâtisseurs d'empire*), and poetry (*Cantilènes en gelée*). His anti-war song *Le Déserteur* (1955) and the iconoclastic character of his versatile work has assured him postmortem cult status.

J'Irai cracher sur vos tombes

Vian is said to have written *J'Irai cracher sur vos tombes* in ten days in August 1946 on a wager with publisher Jean d'Halluin. Vian posed as the supposed French translator of an African American writer who was unable to find a publisher in the United States, a ploy that both excused and allowed for the over-the-top eroticism and violence of the novel. When in real life in 1947 the body of a young woman strangled by her lover was found in a Montparnasse hotel with the novel next to her opened to the page where the protagonist kills his mistress in a similar fashion, a scandal erupted and Vian was labeled an "assassin by proxy." Charges and lawsuits led to the book's being banned in France from 1949 to 1953; Vian was convicted of affronting public morals and was sentenced to pay a 100,000-franc fine.

In the novel, Lee Anderson, a black man passing for white, seeks revenge for the death of his younger brother, who was lynched for having dated a white girl. Befriending a gang of adolescents, Lee acts as the indefatigable, ever-ready "sex machine" and supplier of alcohol. He pursues and promises marriage to two daughters of a plantation owner. As he attempts to implicate the younger one in the murder of her pregnant sister, she attacks him to prevent the crime. He massacres her and proceeds to rape and kill the other sister. The police apprehend and kill him, leaving the body for the townspeople to hang.

In this violent plot Lee's numerous sexual encounters serve to confirm that he is white (as when he has sex with a 13-year-old black girl) and to prove his overall prowess, or as "foreplay" to the eventual killings. Sex is a way of dominating and humiliating women, of manipulating them and their sexual pleasure, which is ultimately used against them. Hence the "colonized becomes the colonizer," but at the same time this white impostor sexually behaves like the racial stereotype of a "black man," lusting for and seeking to violate white women. Some few episodes are truly erotic, as when Lee tries to seduce the contrary younger sister, who employs the classic apparatus of female seduction and demands that he act out the respective male part. The restless pace of sexual acts rouses and strings along the reader, but seduction always and inevitably ends in violence. If there is *jouissance* in this novel, it comes with a bitter aftertaste, with the reader feeling as manipulated and abased as the female characters. A pastiche of hard-boiled as well as black American protest literature, which makes for some well-meaning racism, this hoax of a novel is also an allegory of the workings of literature and of the French literary establishment. It also satirizes male–female relations, and with Vian's ideas on erotic literature in mind, it might be read as a deliberate challenge to female writers to voice their own erotic or violent fantasies involving men.

Utilité de la littérature érotique

In the form of a talk or seminar, *The Utility of Erotic Literature* explains some of the principles according to which the Vernon Sullivan novels (in particular *J'Irai cracher sur vos tombes*) were composed and advertised. The erotic content of these novels, announced and implicit in the supposed censorship (and partly the cause of the actual censorship following its publication) was meant to be a "weapon of subversion." Yet, it was probably less the "revolutionary quality" of his erotic writing than the forbidden touch and the potential for transgression that enticed people to buy the book. As it engages the reader by provoking a visceral response, erotic literature is one way to "sell" such an urgent message.

Rather than propounding a coherent argument, the author concludes in his own implicit defense by proposing that literature does not create eroticism or violence but evokes something already existing in the reader's mind. But while eroticism rouses the reader as much as do matters of death, the two are diametrically opposed, violence is the worst enemy of sexual pleasure, and Vian underhandedly admits that his Sullivan novels are not erotic but pseudo-erotic at best.

Biography

Born in Ville d'Avray near Paris, March 10. Civil engineering degree from the École Central Paris in 1942; worked with AFNOR (L'Association française de Normalisation) and the Office du Papier until 1946. Having suffered from heart and lung conditions since adolescence, Boris Vian died June 23 at the age of 39.

INA PFITZNER

Editions

J'Irai cracher sur vos tombes. Paris: Scorpion, 1946; as *I Shall Spit on Your Graves*, translated by Boris Vian. Paris: Vendome Press, 1948; *I Spit on Your Graves*, translated by Boris Vian and Milton Rosenthal, Tam-Tam Books, 1998.

L'Écume des jours. Paris: Gallimard, 1947; as *Froth on a Daydream*, translated by Stanley Chapman, London: Rapp and Carroll, 1967; as *Foam of the Daze* [sic]. translated by Brian Harper, TamTam Books, 2003; as a motion picture, *Spray of the Days*, directed by Charles Belmont, 1968.

Mood Indigo. translated by John Sturrock. New York: Grove Press, 1968.

L'Automne à Pékin, Paris: Scorpion, 1947; as *Autumn in Peking*, translated by Paul Knobloch, with an introduction by Marc Lapprand, TamTam Books, 2005.

Écrits pornographiques, comprising "Utilité de la littérature érotique." Paris: Bourgois, 1980.

Selected Works

Vercoquin et le plancton. 1947
(Vernon Sullivan) *Les Morts ont tous la même peau*. 1947
(Vernon Sullivan) *Et On tuera tous les affreux*. 1948
Barnum's Digest. 1948
Les fourmis. 1949
Cantilènes en gelée. 1949
L'Herbe Rouge. 1950
(Vernon Sullivan) *Elles Se rendent pas compte*. 1950
L'Équarissages pour tous, follow-up to *Le Dernier des métiers*. 1950
L'Arrache-coeur. 1953
En avant la zizique... et par ici les gros sous. 1958
Les Bâtisseurs d'empire ou Le Schmürz. 1959
Je voudrais pas crever. 1962
Trouble dans les Andains. 1966
Le Chevalier de neige. 1974
Manuel de Saint-Germain-des-Prés. 1974
Le Ratichon baigneur. 1981

Further Reading

Arnaud, Noël, *Les Vies parallèles de Boris Vian*. Paris : Bourgois, 1981.

Arnaud, Noël, and Henri Baudin, eds. *Colloque de Cerisy: Boris Vian*. 2 vols. Paris: U.G.E., 1977.

Baudin, Henri. *Boris Vian: La Poursuite de la vie totale*. Paris: Centurion, 1966.

Héchiche, Anaïk. *La Violence dans les romans de Boris Vian*. Paris: Publisud, 1986.

Lapprand, Marc. *Boris Vian: La vie contre. Biographie critique*. Ottawa: Les Presses de l'Université d'Ottawa, 1993.

Noakes, David. *Boris Vian*. Paris: Éditions universitaires, 1964.

Pestureau, Gilbert. *Boris Vian, les Amarlauds et les Godons*. Paris: U.G.E., 1978.

Rybalka, Michel. *Boris Vian: essai d'interprétation et de documenation*. Paris: Minard, 1984.

Scott, J.K.L. *From Dreams to Despair. An Integrated Reading of the Novels of Boris Vian*. Amsterdam and Atlanta: Rodopi, 1998.

VIAU, THÉOPHILE DE

1590–1626
French libertine writer

Théophile de Viau was the author of a large body of poetry and a play and was known in his lifetime as the "prince of libertines." The fact that posterity has come to refer to him simply as "Théophile" is a legacy of a contemporary strategy of depriving libertine authors of their surnames in order to undermine the identity of and infantilize individuals who found themselves outside of the literary establishment. He undoubtedly owed some of his later heterodox opinions to the influence of Marc Duncan, a liberal Scottish professor at Samur who became his mentor in 1611. Duncan rejected mysticism and superstition, and for Viau this deconstructed a Counter-Reformation theology firmly rooted in expressions of mystical spirituality. As early as 1612, Viau's verse questions the concept of a personal, provident God. After his return from Spain in 1612, the young writer became a wandering troubadour around several chateaux throughout France and acquired a certain celebrity. The writer was among the best-known and most successful members of those associated with the libertine group of authors: his collected poetry (*Les Oeuvres poetiques*) of 166 poems went through 93 editions during the seventeenth century alone. His poetry is characterized by an undercurrent of sensuality that can best be described as bawdy; moreover, it was as much for his heterodox opinions as for the content of his works that Viau attracted censure.

Viau was nonconformist not only in matters of religion, but also in his choice of sexual partners, and several poems contain overt homoerotic elements, a feature of some other libertine writers such as Des Barreaux and Boisrobert. When he was imprisoned on suspicion of sodomy and freethinking, he penned the poem "A un sien ami" [To His Own Friend], probably addressed to his former lover, Des Barreaux, who renounced him at the time of his imprisonment. The poem is notable for its unambiguous treatment of same-sex love, as well as for its stark representation of betrayal. The theme of homosexuality is a leitmotif in Viau's work, though the positive image it is given, unlike its portrayal in Petronius or Martial, marks a radical departure from the Christian tradition. It was this factor, together with the increasing boldness with which libertines were attacking sections of the clergy, that guaranteed natural enemies. A Jesuit preacher, François Garasse, was determined to ensure Viau's downfall and published his *Doctrine curieuse des beaux esprits de ce temps ou prétendus tels* [*Curious Beliefs of the So-Called Freethinkers of This Age*] (1623) as a riposte to Viau and his immediate circle, and criticizes their blasphemy and obscenity. When the cleric examined the *Parnasse satyrique* and saw the name Théophile on the first page, he immediately assumed that this denoted Viau (although this attribution has never been proved one way or another), and the author was duly arrested in September 1622. Another Jesuit, André Voisin, was obsessed with seeing Viau perish at the stake "to defend Our Lady and the saints." While the Jesuits at this time enjoyed the favor of the queen mother, Louis XIII was more sympathetic to the libertines' cause, and on the very day that Viau was banished (a sentence that was never enforced thanks to royal protection and the assistance of the duke of Montmorency), the monarch sent Voisin into exile. Viau had become acquainted with the Duke of Buckingham during his early exile in England, and the duke's arrival in Paris on May 14, 1625, to collect the king's sister, Henriette-Marie, to marry Charles I, strengthed the writer's position with the French court and helped him gain a relatively light sentence.

Viau's most influential work is the tragedy *Pyrame et Thisbé* (performed c. 1617; printed 1623), based on a story appearing in Ovid's *Metamorphoses*. This deals with two young lovers whose neighboring families are at war and forbid the couple from courting. The pair continue seeing each other by the means of a gap in the wall separating their estates, and they make plans to elope. They fix a date for their escape and arrange to meet at the tomb of Ninus, located by a fruit tree and a fountain. Thisbé arrives first but is chased by a wild lion. Pyrame arrives a little later and discovers her blood-splattered veil lying on the ground. He commits suicide and his blood mingles with Thisbé's blood on the garment. She initially believes him to be asleep, then commits suicide on realizing the truth. In Viau's hands, this tale becomes an erotically charged love story, but a passion proscribed by society. In act II, scene 2, Pyrame invokes immortality of the soul and the prospect of an afterlife as merely one hypothesis amongst others. This play inspired Pierre Corneille's *Clitandre* (1632)—a drama with an obvious homoerotic subtext—and Viau's work is recognized as influencing Jean de La Fontaine, and, much later, the nineteenth-century poets Théophile Gautier and Stéphane Mallarmé. In his lifetime and the subsequent decades, Viau was the visible figurehead of the libertine movement and would be remembered as its honorary founder. His condemnation was a landmark in the history of French literature, for it effectively meant that from that point, erotic works could be printed only clandestinely.

Biography

Born near Agen in Clairac to a noble Protestant family. Educated at Samur (1610–11); completed his studies at Leiden, 1613. Obliged to leave France for suspect poetry, 1619; returned from Spain and England, 1621. Converted to Catholicism, 1621. Arrested for suspected debauched writing, September 1622; condemned and burned in effigy, August 1623. Capital sentence commuted to banishment by Parlement of Paris, July 1625. After a period of imprisonment in the Conciergerie, he spent the rest of his life in four French residences thanks to Louis XIII's protection. Died aged 36 years, September 25.

PAUL SCOTT

Selected Works

Les Advantures de Théophile, au Roy, par lui faites pendant son exil en un vieux désert où estoit sa retraicte, [Paris?]:1624
Les Amours tragiques de Pyrame et Thisbé. Paris: J. Martin, 1626.
Les Oeuvres du Sieur Théophile. 2nd ed., 2 vols. Paris: Pierre Bilaine, 1622.
Oeuvres complètes. Edited by Guido Saba. Paris: Champion, 1999.

Further Reading

Adam, Antoine. *Théophile de Viau et la libre pensée française en 1620.* Paris: Droz, 1935.
DeJean, Joan. *Libertine Strategies: Freedom and the Novel in Seventeenth-Century France.* Columbus: Ohio State University Press, 1981.
———. *The Reinvention of Obscenity: Sex, Lies, and Tabloids in Early Modern France.* Chicago: University of Chicago Press, 2002.
Duchêne, Roger, ed. *Théophile de Viau: Actes du colloque du CMR 17.* Biblio 17, 65, Tubingen: Narr, 1991.
Gaudiani, Claire Lynn. *The Cabaret Poetry of Théophile de Viau: Texts and Traditions.* Études Littéraires Françaises 13. Tubingen: Narr, 1981.
Rizza, Cecilia. *Libertinage et littérature.* Paris: Nizet, 1996.
Saba, Guido. *Théophile de Viau: Un poète rebelle.* Paris: Presses Universitaires Françaises, 1999.
Schoeller, Guy, ed. *Dictionnaire des œuvres érotiques.* Paris: Laffont, 2001.

VIGNALI, ANTONIO

1501–1559
Italian satirist

Primary Work: *La Cazzaria*

This 16th-century dialogue (written c. 1525, published clandestinely c. 1530) is one of the earliest European texts to explore the "infinite ways of fucking" (*infiniti modi di fottere*) (Stoppelli: 134; all citations from Stoppelli's edition). Whereas his contemporary Pietro Aretino wrote for mass publication, demonic and literally pornographic, Vignali wrote for manuscript circulation among the members of his private academy, and his dialogue promotes elite homosexuality in a mock-erudite tone, alternating between crude vocabulary and lofty philosophical discourse.

The word *cazzaria* seems to mean a shop that manufactures and sells *cazzi*, or penises, hence a penis, or phallus, factory (153). Like *coglioneria,* it could mean no more than "a load of cock" or rubbish, but in Vignali's dialogue it suggests the visual motif of the *testa de' cazzi*, the human head made up of writhing penises. Vignali's preface invents a scene in which another member of the intellectual elite, waiting for an assignation in a state of phallic arousal ("a cazzo dritto" [with a stiff prick]), discovers a manuscript of this work and declares it "il maggiore viluppo di cazzi che vi fusse" [the greatest tangle of pricks there ever was]. The reader then loses interest in his date, much preferring "the excessively great pleasure of finding all the reasons and circumstances of fucking" in this book (38). Nicolò Franco claimed, in a sonnet supposedly spoken by Vignali himself, that "to stock the Cazzaria properly, here are millions of pricks, the number that Pietro Aretino has tried in his lifetime" (153).

La Cazzaria itself takes the form of a Socratic dialogue between two members of the elite Academy of the Intronati, Arsiccio (Vignali) and Sodo, the youthful Marcantonio Piccolomini. In contrast to Aretino's *Ragionamenti*, the speakers are privileged males rather than plebeian courtesans, and it emerges that the whole dialogue takes place in bed: "Sodo, see that you don't interrupt when I have my prick inside your arse" (94). The discourse proceeds through a series of pseudo-Aristotelian scientific questions about the shape, origin, and function of the genitalia, as discussed in the Academy; Arsiccio is collecting material for his scholarly *Lumen Pudendorum,* or *The Light of the Pudenda*, in three volumes corresponding to the three erogenous zones (82). Vignali's purpose is as much political as sexological, since his main narrative—the war between Cunts, Pricks, Arses, and Balls that resulted in their current disastrous state—allegorizes the factions and conflicts that led to the collapse of Sienese autonomy. But half the dialogue pursues sexo-philosophical questions for their own sake: "why humans are unwilling to be seen while fucking" (134); why nature placed pubic hair in certain places and not others (58); why lovers' tongues interlace when they kiss (134); "why pricks are depicted with wings and feet" on university walls (125–6); why sodomy is said to be "against nature" (67); whether the phallus was originally made by women (70); what the true meanings of paradise, nectar, and ambrosia are (61).

Arsiccio's ostensible goal is to train Sodo in libertine heterosexuality: only by becoming a "scholar," able to "find out the modes and secret ways," will he appeal to the discriminating lady, who values "intellectual sublimity" [*sublimità d'ingegno*] and "acute and subtle inventions," not to mention contraceptive advice (44–6). As the question-and-answer dialogue develops, however, its "inventions" become increasingly misogynist, dwelling on the grotesque anatomy of the vagina. Vignali frequently laments the fall from happier "ancient" days, when *potta* and *culo* [cunt and arse] coexisted in a "pact" of amity, when the genitalia could speak properly and "do their deeds" openly and honorably in public view. Now, in the fallen world, we are cursed with shame, repulsion, secrecy, and an "insatiable appetite" for "forced and disastrous" new postures (134–5). Homoeroticism is conceived of not as a rehearsal for "sublime" heterosexuality but as a preferable alternative: "Paradise" means the *dolcezza* [sweetness] experienced "with your prick up a soft, white, boyish arse"; nectar and ambrosia refer to the "exclusive pleasure" [*chiuso piacere*] of sodomizing a handsome youth (60–1).

Two later works should be considered here. An unknown author ("C.M.") borrowed the *Cazzaria* title to celebrate in verse "the trophies of prick in arse," and Vignali's original prose dialogue prompted an apocryphal "Second Part" that brings "academic" homosexuality back to the street. In this continuation Sodo abandons his legal and philosophical studies to become a common prostitute, while the mentor-figure Arsiccio becomes a crude feeder of questions. Except in its final pages, this second *Cazzaria* emphasizes the similarities between homo- and heterosexuality and the interchangability of the male and the female whore. Sodo sets up business with his pimp, or *ruffiano,* just like his female counterpart and performs all the same postures: "grazing sheep," "legs-around-the-neck," etc. (Vatican MS Capponiano 140, ff. 78–9, 81, 92v, 101v; all citations from this manuscript). While he proceeds from keeper to keeper, he also sleeps with a "puttana" [whore], and often "I, he, and my whore made three happy at once" (f. 92v).

Notable episodes, related in the matter-of-fact tone of the case-hardened professional, include being "well fucked" in rapid succession by 19 monks (ff. 82–v) and being invited by the sacristan to see his etchings, a prelude to rapturous fellatio (ff. 85v–86). In contrast to the expressionless Sodo, these ecclesiastical clients pour out their adoration and frustration in poetic language, adorned with echoes of classical mythology and religious worship, as in the friar's litany for the youth's "culo di zuccaro" [sugar arse] (f. 101v). As in the original *Cazzaria,* however, pleasure comes before a fall. Sodo suddenly realizes that he has outgrown the "Land of Cockaigne" or "Golden Age." His youthful beauty vanishes: "I found myself 20 years old, I was getting completely covered in hair, ... and a Coach with 6 Horses could drive through my Arse-hole" (ff. 84, 93–v).

Though Sodo's survival narrative dwells more and more on his criminality, the author does make a final effort to simulate Vignali's lofty academic dialogue. The rent-boy turns philosopher, giving a lecture on the history and etymology of buggery and citing a string of homosexual lovers that includes Cain and Abel, Plato and Alcibiades, Jupiter and Argus, and Apollo and Hyacinth (ff. 106v–109). These arguments—from geometry, anatomy, mythology, and history—circulated widely in the academies and show up in the most sophisticated homoerotic text of the 17th century, Antonio Rocco's *L'Alcibiade fanciullo a scola* [*Alcibiades the Schoolboy*]. After establishing this prestigious genealogy, Sodo concludes by equating his kind of transgression with courtly privilege: "[J]ust as only the Eagle, Queen of Birds, is permitted to fix her gaze on the Sun, so the Arse, the similitude of that Planet, is permitted to fix its gaze on Princes" (f. 109v, numbered "110").

La Cazzaria del C.M. is a virtuoso poem in which every line ends with *cazzo* or *culo.* With its companion poem, an "Effective Persuasion" to sodomy, it launches ingenious arguments similar to those of Vignali and Rocco: the *cazzo* desires the *culo* because nature has made them both round; heterosexual vaginal intercourse is fit only for animals (and Germans), but "I want to do it as *persons* do it"; nature has created us to "fuck and refuck," which makes it quite natural to seek new ways and abandon the old ones forever (ff. A2v, A4v). Man-and-boy coupling is described in some detail, and this union is given an aesthetic and symbolic property: "Il cul possi chiamar, specchio del cazzo, / Può dirsi il cazzo l'anima del culo" [The arse can be called the mirror of the prick, and the prick the soul of the arse] (f. A2). In fact, the ultimate happiness would be a state of blissful self-fusion. "If only Man could bugger himself in his own arse," how peaceful the world would become; no "clamors on earth and sea" would disturb this new Golden Age, no frenzy, no weapons of hunting or warfare, no yearning for the other (f. A4v).

Vignali's *Cazzaria* was never well known, but it influenced several later writings as well as the homoerotic texts mentioned above. Its question-and-answer format reappears in the French *L'Escole des filles* [*The Girl's School*] (1655), the English *Practical Part of Love* (1660), and most directly in the 18th-century Italian poem *Il Libro del perché* [*The Book of Why*]. A copy of this work, combined into an anthology with other libertine classics, graced the library of King George III of England. Vignali's original has been translated into English at least twice, and the recent version by Ian Moulton is widely available.

Biography

Born in Siena, Antonio Vignali (or Vignale) di Buonagiunta came from the most powerful oligarchy in that city. He attended classes in law at the University of Pisa, though under suspicion for murdering a cousin, and went on to found the Sienese Accademia degli Intronati [Academy of the Thunderstruck], a circle of educated humanists and aristocrats devoted to cultural patronage and playful intellectual inquiry. Vignali was involved in the Sienese coup d'etat (1524) and the subsequent fall of the republic to imperial encroachment. He fled his native city in 1530 and exiled himself in various courts in Seville, Madrid, and Milan. As well as the comic-erotic dialogue *La Cazzaria*, he wrote a variety of letters, translations, poetry, and drama, much of it never published. Vignali died in Milan.

JAMES GRANTHAM TURNER

Editions

Dialogo intitolato la Cazzaria [Dialogue Entitled The Prick Factory]. Biblioteca Apostolica Vaticana (Vatican City), MS Capponiano 140; ff. 78–110 contain the unique "Second Part." In his edition of Vignali's original, Stoppelli notes that the author of this spurious continuation is "not Sienese" but apparently still 16th-century (156).

La Cazzaria del C. M. [The Prick Factory, by Sir M.] N. p., n.d. Bibliothèque nationale de France shelfmark Enfer 562; ff. A4–v are a separate poem entitled "Persuasiva efficace, per coloro, che schifano la delicatezza del tondo" [Effective Persuasion for Those Who Despise the Deliciousness of the Round Part]. This printed poem, with a woodcut portrait of a cleric, is evidently too early to be by "il Cavaliere Marino [C.M.]," as Pascal Pia claimed in *Les Livres de l'Enfer*, 116.

Il Libro del perché. Place and date of publication: "Nullibi et Ubique, nel XVIII secolo" [Nowhere and everywhere, in the 18th century]. British Library shelfmark P.C. 22.c.1; as *The Why and the Wherefore, or The Lady's Two Questions Resolved*. London: J. Lamb, 1765, shelfmark P.C. 27.b.10 [see *Private Case*].

La Cazzaria del Arsiccio Intronato [The Prick Factory by "Burnt Thunderstruck"]. Edited by Pasquale Stoppelli, introduction by Nino Borsellino. Rome: L'Elefante, 1984. Based on several early printed editions and MSS (see 31[-]2 for several other works in MS identified); Paris: Isidore Liseux, 1882, and Cercle du Livre Précieux, 1960; German translations, 1924, 1963, 1988.

La Cazzaria, Dialogue on Diddling, by Sir Hotspur Dunderpate of the Maidenhead Academy. translated by Samuel Putnam, in typescript at the Kinsey Institute Library, Indiana University. City of Industry, CA: Collectors Publications, 1968.

La Cazzaria (La Carajeria). Edited by Guido M. Cappelli from another early MS, en-face Spanish translation by Elisa Ruiz García, introduction by Francisco Rico. Mérida: Regional de Extremadura, 1999.

La Cazzaria: The Book of the Prick. Edited and translated by Ian Frederick Moulton. New York: Routledge, 2003. Not "the first English translation," as the cover claims, but accurate and with a long, informative introduction.

Selected Works

La Floria, commedia. Florence: Giunti, 1560; reprinted 1567, 1965.

Alcune lettere piacevoli, una dell'Arsiccio Intronato. Siena: Luca Bonetti, 1571; reprinted 1610, 1618, 1864, 1975.

Further Reading

Findlen, Paula. "Humanism, Politics and Pornography in Renaissance Italy." In *The Invention of Pornography: Obscenity and the Origins of Modernity, 1500–1800*, edited by Lynn Hunt. New York: Zone Books, 1993.

Lawner, Lynne. *I Modi. The Sixteen Pleasures: An Erotic Album of the Italian Renaissance*. Evanston, IL: Northwestern University Press, 1988.

Leibacher-Ouvrard, Lise, "Transtextualité et construction de la sexualité: la *Satyra sotadica* de Chorier." *L'Esprit créateur* 35/2 (Summer 1995): 51–66.

Pia, Pascal. *Les Livres de l'Enfer* [1978]. Rev. ed. Paris: Fayard, 1998.

Thurman, Judith. "The Anatomy Lesson." *The New Yorker*, December 8, 2003. Review of Moulton's translation.

VILLENA, LUIS ANTONIO DE

1951–
Spanish poet, novelist, and journalist

A prolific writer, Villena has published poetry, prose fiction, essays, and anthologies of poetry. Two of his main characteristics are dissidence and a search for pleasure. Life cannot be understood as a mere acceptance of reality, with its moral and cultural codes. Literature becomes then the appropriate field for an exploration of the meaning of life and its diverse aspects.

Symbolism, aestheticism, and a passion for beauty are the basic features of his early work. Life may not be perfect, but literary and cultural masks can hide its dark side. Dissidence is another feature. Villena does not accept either a poetics of realism or a poetics of the majority. As a consequence, he claims to be a literary inheritor of unknown, extravagant, or marginal authors such as Strato of Sardes, Bertran de Born, Luis de Góngora, Don Juan de Tassis, Bocángel Unzueta, Quasimodo, Sandro Penna, Porfirio Barba-Jacob, August von Platen, César Moro, Lord Dunsanny, and Oscar Wilde. For Villena, literature is pleasure and artifice. It is a representation that mixes life and fiction, experience and desire, memory and reality. Villena experiences reality as a brief moment of intense pleasure that is followed by a long period of dullness. Consquently, he is a skeptic who feels the impossibility of sustaining beauty, pleasure, or love for long periods of time. What is more, he knows that the fusion of life and literature does not lead him to a sort of paradise on Earth. This is the reason why literature is identified with masks; as a writer he can create a literary reality in which a different and better life is fulfilled; a life in which the moral codes of contemporary puritan society are not present.

For Villena, love means homoerotic love. This adds another important feature to his poetry and his life, since he grew up during the last phase of the Francoist dictatorship and the beginnings of the Spanish democratic system. Homosexuality was then a taboo that took time to be socially accepted. An early literary vocation and late adolescent maturity have to be added to his literary characteristics. The nostalgia in his works cannot be properly understood if the reader does not know these two simple facts. He was a precocious reader but did not have a firsthand experience of those readings and of his innermost desires till an advanced stage in his life.

His first book of poems, *Sublime Solarium*, is set in exotic places and past times and shows a variety of prestigious characters surrounded by luxury, decadence, and death. It is the poetry of an unexperienced young boy. This was one of the works that signaled the departure from the previous dominant poetics of social realism in literature. Language was regarded as autonomous and nonutilitarian or committed to society and politics. Impersonality was predominant in the poems, in the sense that there was not a direct reference to his experience and his self. *El viaje a Bizancio* is the next step. Experience makes its presence, although shyly, in his poetry. Young boys and nature are the prevalent characteristics of the book. The work is an apology for desire through either imagination or contemplation. In the first case, the result is painful awareness and melancholy; in the latter, an access to desire via the pleasant contemplation of a male body. Nature is thus depicted in its lushness and corresponds to the mapping of the male body. Love and desire act as a cosmic force of union. The experience of bodily pleasure is also paralleled by the experience of the pleasure of language. The reader perceives the same intensity in the erotic relationship as in the use of language. *Hymnica* and *Huir del invierno* represent the summit of his early phase. *Hymnica* is a passionate chant to youthful beauty. The poet feels and writes on those young bodies with whom he can experience sexuality. It goes beyond mere contemplation, to an immediate living experience. Pagan themes are present throughout *Hymnica*, since Villena views homoerotic love under the species of ancient Greek homoeroticism. Thus Villena creates a world in which the concepts of sin, guilt, and condemnation are compeltely absent. His is not a mere hedonistic eroticism; it contains an ethics and a metaphysics, both of them directly taken from ancient Greek philosophy, i.e., from a civilization in which the destructive concepts of Christianity were not present.

La muerte únicamente represents a shift in his poetry. Villena moves from Decadence toward a more pessimistic and realistic account of life. *La muerte únicamente* thematizes the symbols, myths, and reality of death. Villena moves away from his paradise to enter a more somber terrain. From then onward, and leaving aside the Decadent and aesthetic features I have mentioned, which means that to a certain extent he has moved aways from Luis Cernuda—his former model—he writes a more socially commited poetry.

This does not mean that he avoids or dismisses sexuality as a suitable topic for his writings, since he has written several novels in which this can be found playing a central role, as for example, *Chicos* [Boys] or *El burdel de Lord Byron* [Lord Byron's brothel]. However, his passionate account and contemplation of beautiful young male bodies is not so present and has been replaced by a more pessimistic view of life.

As a journalist Villena has defended gay and lesbian rights in his articles. He has also reviewed gay and lesbian literature for daily journals and has always maintained an active stance in favor of equality.

Biography

Luis Antonio Villena was born in 1951 in Madrid; BA, 1974; worked as a journalist for *El Mundo*, *El País*, *ABC*, and for the Spanish radio networks SER and RNE.

DR. HONORIS CAUSA

Selected Works

Sublime Solarium. 1971
Ante el espejo [Before the Mirror]. 1972
Introducción al Dandysmo [Introduction to Dandyism]. 1974
El Viaje a Bizancio [Voyage to Byzantium]. 1976
Catulo. 1978
Oscar Wilde. 1979
Hymnica. 1979
Para los dioses turcos [For Turkish Gods]. 1980
Huir del invierno [Escape from Winter]. 1981
La muerte únicamente [Only Death]. 1984
En el invierno romano [In the Roman Winter]. 1986
La tentación de Ícaro [Icarus's Temptation]. 1986
Amor-pasión [Love-Passion]. 1986
Como en lugar extraño [As in a Strange Place]. 1990
Chicos. 1998
Poesía 1970–1984. Madrid: Visor, 1988.

Further Reading

Debicki, Andrew P., ed. *Studies in 20th Century Literature. Contemporary Spanish Poetry: 1939–1990* 16 (1992) [Manhattan, KS]. Special issue.
Jiménez, José Olivio. "La poesía de Luis Antonio de Villena." In Villena, *Poesía 1970–1984*, 9–64.
Moral, Concepción G., and R.M. Pereda, eds. *Joven poesía española.* Madrid: Cátedra, 1987.
Provencio, Pedro. *Poéticas españolas contemporáneas. La generación del 70.* Madrid: Hiperión, 1988.

VILLON, FRANÇOIS

1431–c. 1463
French poet, criminal

Written within the context of his imprisonment, Villon's semi-autobiographical and mostly first-person poem *Le Grand Testament* is presented as a last will and testament. Characterized by social satire, this lyric text of just over 2,000 Middle French verses is often colored by cynicism, bitterness, and irony. Villon calls into question religious and social conventions through the humorous advice he gives to those he leaves behind. In his mock bequests to friends and foes, he expresses many regrets and is nostalgic for his youth, health, virility, bitter love affairs, and lack of sexual satisfaction. Much Villon criticism has been biographical.

Stylistically, Villon's *Poésies diverses*—comprising lais, ballads, rondeaux, and virelais—have been considered a formidable antithesis to France's *Grands Rhétoriqueurs,* with his playful and subversive language. Villon is no stranger to scatological scenes, sexual humor, and obscenity. From flatulence to erections, from growling bellies to drunken lovemaking, Villon uses corporeal language and images of bodily functions to parody literary conventions. One well-known example is his use of the Latin prayer *Ave salus tibi decus,* in which the French *d'escus* [coins] is interchangeable with *des culs* [anuses]. Villon makes similar veiled references to male and female genitalia, sodomy, flatulence, intercourse, and prostitution throughout.

The human body and its hungers, suffering, and sexual appetites are frequent themes, as are poverty and material goods. The conception of love is associated with the passionate and often destructive desires of *fol amour,* as exemplified in the sarcastic *Double Ballade,* in which "passion turns people into animals." Love and sexual desire are one and the same for Villon, both associated with death and decay as well as madness. He "swears on his testicle" that he "dies a martyr to love." In *Le Testament,* it is love that "pricks him" and "spurs" him on and love that has "abused" him.

Not wholly misogynistic, Villon's treatment of women may be characterized by desire and fear, disdain and disappointment, but can be ambiguous at times. Villon writes of his mistresses and prostitutes, of his own mother and the Virgin Mary. Women are most often sexual objects, portrayed as sanctuary for his body and soul; Villon seeks sexual release but is often left frustrated by his intimate relationships with women. He considers women "danger" and writes of his own failed relationships with such women as Marthe or Katherine de Vausselles, whom he blames for his own downfall; Jehanneton is an everywoman figure: a beautiful, tempting, and dangerous sexual partner; in contrast, Ambroise de Loré becomes his ideal woman. *La Ballade des dames du temps jadis* treats legendary women (Heloise, courtesans of antiquity) and their reputations as intelligent women, good companions and lovers, or unfaithful temptresses.

The negative image of women and the female body is evident in ballads such as *Les Regrets de la belle Heaulmière,* an unfavorable graphic portrait of aging, female sexuality, and desire. Her once attractive body is reduced to deflated sexual organs; her breasts, thighs, and vagina are "shriveled up" and she laments that her thighs are nothing but sticks, "spotted like sausages." Elsewhere, Villon evaluates the female body and its appearance in positive sexual terms, as "so tender, smooth, gentle, and precious," but conversely as dangerous in youth and hideous in old age. Other acquaintances are evaluated according to sexual abilities, such as the "le bon fouterre."

Prostitution is a central image in Villon and was widespread on the streets of Paris during his lifetime; he even suggests comically that a school for prostitutes be established in Meung Prison. *La Ballade de la Grosse Margot* mocks the highly idealized contemporary medieval motifs of the devoted knight and his ladylove and the enamored troubadour and his unattainable *domna* as Villon describes the affectionate, erotic, abusive, and financial relationship between pimp (the narrator Villon) and prostitute (Margot). Parodying a knight of courtly romance defending his lady, he vows to "love and serve" his lady and her refined desires, pledging that he would gladly arm himself with shield and dagger for her. But their love is equated with lust, violence, and commerce, far from the idealized or Platonic *fin' amour* of the troubadours. Moreover, their home is not the court but rather a bordello. He becomes irritated if she comes to their bed with no profits, making her pay with her body. Sexual intercourse and monetary exchange are often related in Villon. He expresses his love for Margot, seeing her as an equal and a good match because they both "enjoy filth." Together they are "bad rat, bad cat." Comically, Margot shows her affection through flatulence, laughter, manual stimulation, and drunken intercourse. Her large, pregnant body crushes him beneath her and their union "wipes out all lust" in him. The lustful pair are equally immoral and lecherous [*paillart*], and Villon's affection for her grows from this shared depravity.

Le jargon, printed posthumously in 1489, is a short work composed of lyric ballads. *Le jargon,* like *Le Testament,* is rich in witty wordplay, acrostics, puns, slang, sarcasm, and sexual double entendres. *Le jargon* and *Le Testament* also center on images of excessive sexual activity, the immoderate consumption of wine and food, and anti-matrimonial themes. Villon was published in the mid-sixteenth century by poet Clément Marot.

Biography

Born in Paris into a family of modest means, orphaned, and educated at the University of Paris. Arrested following a fatal street fight in 1455 and pardoned in 1456, François Villon left Paris accused of robbing a religious institution in 1457. It has been suggested that Villon became an outlaw for several years. At the age of thirty, he was imprisoned in 1461 in Meung. He was imprisoned again in 1462 for theft and found guilty of assault in 1463. His death sentence was repealed and he was banished, disappearing from record in 1463. The self-described miserable, impoverished *"povre* Villon" suffered from hunger and illness, from the poverty of student life, from the torments of passionate love affairs and cruel rejections, and from the tortures of prison.

SARAH GORDON

Editions

Dufournet, Jean, ed. and trans. *François Villon, poésies.* Paris: Imprimerie Nationale, 1984.

Rychner, Jean, and Albert Henry, eds. *Le Testament Villon.* 2 vols. Geneva: Droz, 1974.

Thiry, Claude, ed. *François Villon, poésies complètes.* Paris: Librairie Générale Française, 1991.

Further Reading

Dufournet, Jean. *Recherches sur "Le testament" de François Villon.* Paris: SEES, 1973.

Fein, David A. *François Villon Revisited.* New York: Twayne, 1997.

Freeman, Michael. *François Villon in His Works: The Villain's Tale.* Amsterdam and Atlanta: Rodopi, 2000.

Freeman, Michael, and Jane H.M. Taylor, eds. *Villon at Oxford: The Drama of the Text.* Amsterdam and Atlanta: Rodopi, 1999.

Pinkernell, Gert. *François Villon: biographie critique et autres études.* Heidelberg: C. Winter, 2002.

VIRGINITY

Virginity has been a major theme in erotica throughout history. The reason for the prominence of virginity as subject matter lies, to a large extent, in its importance within society. As far back as ancient Greece, respectable women were expected to be virgins until they married, and therefore within texts, the loss of virginity was given high prominence. Portrayals of loss of virginity, or the deflowering of innocent young girls, were depicted in a wide variety of scenes: husbands' first marriage nights with their wives, priests molesting naive nuns, masters corrupting their female servants, guardians depraving their innocent charges, and bosses seducing their young workers. Examples of these scenes appear in all sorts of erotica from ancient Greece to the wall paintings of Pompeii to modern-day features in *Playboy*.

Virginity and its loss in erotica pinpoints the time when a girl becomes a woman, opening the door on the heroine's sexual awareness. The reluctant virgins invariably turn into nymphomaniacs in their desire for sex once they have been initiated. In the seventeenth and eighteenth centuries, French erotica concentrated on lost virginity tales in *L'Escole des filles* (1655), *Académie des dames* (1680), *Venus dans la cloître* (1683), *Histoire de Dom B* (1741–2), *Thérèse Philosophe* (1748), and the works of the Marquis de Sade. Extant signs of virginity were considered important, as reflected in the proliferation of scenes which describe the loss of virginity in detail and at some length. Examination of a woman for an intact hymen, bleeding on intercourse, and depictions of pain are all motifs within the virginity scenarios. In *Dialogue Between a Married Lady and a Maid* (1740), Tullia relates the tale of her wedding night, when her husband checked for an intact hymen by inserting his fingers inside her. He "thrust it a little way up, till he met with a stop, and I complained he hurt me: This he did on Purpose, to be satisfied whether I was a Maid or not as afterwards he himself confessed." For Tullia, intercourse is described as a painful experience. She cries out to her husband, "I never can endure it, it will split me in two, you'll kill me, if all this must go into my Body."

In England, John Cleland's *Memoirs of a Woman of Pleasure* (1749) introduced a series of tales narrated by prostitutes on how they lost their virginity. Gentlemen's magazines took up the theme—the *Bon Ton* for March 1793 showed manliness as gained through "breaking in" virgins. The qualifications of becoming a member of the Adam and Eve Club was "that every member must produce a similar certificate of having deflowered his virgin, or debauched his married woman, and the more of those feats he has achieved, the greater is his station in the assembly."

Nineteenth-century narratives followed much the same pattern, with beys initiating harem members in *The Lustful Turk* (1828); the eager, young, virginal Bella being introduced to sex in *Autobiography of a Flea* (1885); nuns being corrupted in convents in *Nunnery Tales* (c. 1888); virginal Indian girls being bought in *The Ups and Down of Life* (1867); and young servant girls being seduced in *My Secret Life* (1890). Since the late twentieth century, porno videos, magazines, and websites devoted to young girls being introduced into sex have created virtually their own genre of "nude teen virgins," "free tight virgin pussies," and the like.

Male virginity was also explored in erotic texts. In *My Secret Life*, Walter not only relates his taking of virgins but recalls how he lost his own virginity at sixteen years old, and describes the pleasure he felt: "The next instant a delirium of my senses came, my prick throbbing and as if hot lead was jetting from it, at each throb; pleasure mingled with light pain in it, and my whole frame quivering with emotion." *The Romance of Lust* (1870) explores the sexual education of Charles Roberts, including his sexual initiation by one of his mother's friends.

Throughout the nineteenth century, female initiation scenes became increasingly more stylized and formulaic. By the end of the century, homosexual initiations were being included in erotica such as *Teleny, or The Reverse of the Medal* (1893). The tried and trusted flagellation of virgins included pederasty in *Frank and I* (1902); incest was added in *Sweet Seventeen: The True Story of a Daughter's Awful Whipping and Its Delightful Consequences* (1910), when Mr. Sanderson delights in his daughter's budding sexuality.

In erotica overall, there is less interest in the loss of male virginity, and a double standard of sexual mores has existed for men and women. Narratives generally attach a greater importance to female virginity. Although some erotica explores tales of young men's initiation into sex, these adventures do not affix the same qualities to the loss of male virginity.

JULIE PEAKMAN

Selected Works

Anonymous. *Dialogue Between a Married Lady and a Maid*. London, 1740.
Bon Ton 3, March 1793, 21–22.
Cleland, John. *Memoirs of a Woman of Pleasure*. London: George Fenton, 1749.
"Walter." *My Secret Life*. Amsterdam: August Brancart, 1890.

Further Reading

Bloch, Iwan. *Sex Life in England, Past and Present*. New York: Panurge Press, 1934.
Foyster, Elizabeth A. *Manhood in Early Modern England. Honour, Sex and Marriage*. London: Longman, 1999.
Merians, Linda E., ed. *The Secret Malady. Venereal Disease in Eighteenth-Century Britain and France*. Lexington: University Press of Kentucky, 1996.
Peakman, Julie. "Initiation, Defloration and Flagellation: Sexual Propensities in Memoirs of a Woman of Pleasure." In *This Launch into the Wide World: Essays on Fanny Hill*, edited by Patsy Fowler and Alan Jackson. New York: AMS Press, 2002.
———. *Mighty Lewd Books: The Development of Pornography in Eighteenth-Century England*. London: Palgrave, 2003.
———. *Lascivious Bodies. A History of the Eighteenth Century*. London: Atlantic, 2004.

Simpson, Anthony, E. "Vulnerability and the Age of Female Consent." In *Sexual Underworlds of the Enlightenment*, edited by G.S. Rousseau and Roy Porter. Manchester: Manchester University Press, 1987.

Thomas, Keith. "The Double Standard." *Journal of History of Ideas*, no. 20, 1959.

Trumbach, Randolph. *Sex and the Gender Revolution: Heterosexuality and the Third Gender in Enlightenment London.* Chicago and London: University of Chicago Press, 1998.

Wagner, Peter. *Eros Revived: Erotica of the Enlightenment in England and America.* London: Secker & Warburg, 1988.

VIVIEN, RENÉE

1877–1909

French Symbolist poet, novelist, and short story writer

Renée Vivien was a prolific writer who published over a dozen volumes of verse, two short novels, two collections of short stories, and the first major translation of the works of Sappho in French—all in less than eight years, from 1901 to 1909. Her early works appeared under a male nom de plume, Renée or R. Vivien, but with the 1903 publication of *Evocations*, she revealed that a woman was the author of passionate poems to women. She may also have written or collaborated on other novels under the name of Paule Riversdale.

Today, Vivien's literary achievements have been eclipsed by her torrid affair with Natalie Clifford Barney—American salon hostess, writer, and seductress of women—and by her romantic longing for death, which she finally embraced at the age of thirty-two. Most of her books are out of print, though a few poems have been anthologized in collections of women writers.

Yet, despite the possible ebbing of her literary fame, Vivien remains a pivotal figure in the history of erotic literature. Her work is not sexual in and of itself, but her sonnets were addressed to other women in a way that boldly and unapologetically announced Vivien's lesboerotic predilections. Her lesbian sexuality was complex and often tortured; orgasm connoted both rapture and death; pure happiness was compromised by guilt and sorrow over the death of her first romantic attachment, Violet Shiletto, in 1901. In *Etudes et préludes* (1901) and much of her subsequent poetry, Vivien created a cult of death—her ultimate lover:

> She exults, strange lover of death. …
> Her desire, fainting over some pale mouth
> From which she knows how to tear an unrequited kiss,
> Fervently turns her attention to the supreme spasm,
> More terrible and more beautiful than love's spasm.

Vivien's most important contribution to the history of erotic literature was her reconstruction of the life and legacy of Sappho, the ancient Greek poet. Though most today associate Sappho with lesbianism, prior to the discovery of additional Sapphic fragments in Egypt in 1897, the poet was generally lauded as a wife and mother who eventually leapt to her death over the Leucadian cliffs after Phaon, a ferryman, rejected her. For poets such as Swinburne and Baudelaire, Sappho was "lesbian," but this designation connoted someone who was both decadent and perverse. For Vivien, Sappho was a goddess.

Vivien studied classical Greek from circa 1900 to 1902, after which she obsessively returned to Sappho's fragments. She wrote four plays about the life of Sappho, including two which appear in *Evocations* (1903); in addition, *La Vénus des aveugles* appeared in 1903 and "Dans un verger" appeared in *Sillages* (1908). In *Les Kitharédes* (1904), Vivien focused on several minor Greek poets, who were possibly disciples of Sappho. Finally, in 1909, she produced the first major translation of the more complete, post-1897 fragments into modern French.

Her mission was to reconstruct Sappho's life and fragments in order to create a new lesbian whole. In doing so, she established a literary ancestor, to whom all lesbian poets could trace their work, and at the same time, placed her own work in this Sapphic canon. One of the most interesting aspects of her work was that Vivien used Sappho and her school of poetry on Lesbos to demarcate lesbianism as markedly different from the Socratic model of male homosexuality. This model was very much on the minds of Vivien and her contemporaries in the wake of the trials, imprisonment, and exile of Oscar Wilde, whose sexual tastes ran to those who were younger and lower class. In the minds of the public, homosexuality was often equated with pederasty.

Since the figurative Sappho's life is, as Monique Wittig and Sande Zeig skillfully put it in their *Lesbian Peoples: Material for a Dictionary*, a blank page onto which anyone might inscribe her idea of the poet's life, Vivien re-created her idol against the Socratic mold. Vivien reconfigures the traditional teacher/student relationship to give the power to the disciples instead of the master. Vivien's Sappho finds herself in thrall to this idea. "And I cry for Atthis whom I once loved" becomes Sappho's refrain in several of Vivien's poems and plays. Thus, in Sappho's school, the power, if there is any, has shifted to the disciples. As the older woman, Sappho offers her followers wisdom and friendship, admiration and encouragement. The concept of erotic initiation by the leader is downplayed, yet the Edenesque circle of attractive and seductive women is sexually charged. In an unpublished journal, Natalie Barney called it "a divinely honest era when modesty was immodesty, when perverse things, far from being calumnious, were joyous and simple."

Vivien and Barney attempted to re-create the Sapphic circle they so much admired. After they were reunited in 1904, they traveled to Lesbos, where they purchased some houses in the hopes of creating a colony for lesbian writers. But they were unable to emulate the calm and collaborative atmosphere of their idol, and Vivien quickly abandoned Barney to return to the Baroness de Zuylen de Nyevelt.

Though Vivien continued to write after her return from Lesbos, her poetry began to spin inward, the themes and tropes slightly diminishing with each repetition. She spent much time traveling to Asia and the Middle East, but when she was in Paris, she tended to enclose herself in her apartment and consume too much alcohol. Finally, in 1909, she attained the early death she had so longed for, one that would join her forever with her idol, Sappho.

Vivien's readers admired the Symbolist purity of her poetry and ignored its lesboerotic implications. As a foreigner and a Protestant woman of means, she, like others in her expatriate circle, were immune to the scorn heaped on "aberrant" French women like Colette, Vivien's neighbor and friend.

Vivien is remembered more for her sexual liaisons and untimely death than for her writing, yet she created a very modern Sappho and erotic lesbian poetry. By doing so, she created a canon for aspiring lesbian writers and a permanent place for herself within it.

Biography

Born Pauline Mary Tarn in London, June 11. Moved to France as an infant; received little formal education from governesses and Parisian schools. Returned to London in 1886 after father's death. Became a ward of the court in London after her mother tried unsuccessfully to commit Vivien to an asylum. Upon reaching her majority, she returned to Paris in 1898 . Became companion of Natalie Clifford Barney 1899–1901 and 1904 and companion of the Baroness Hélène de Zuylen de Nyevelt from 1901 on. Studied ancient Greek 1900–2. Traveled to Lesbos with Barney, 1904; traveled widely but was also reclusive in Paris, 1905–9. Possible conversion to Catholicism, 1909. Death from alcoholism and anorexia, November 18.

KARLA JAY

Selected Works

Etudes et préludes. 1901
Evocations. 1903
Sapho. 1903
La Vénus des aveugles. 1903
Une Femme m'apparut..., 1904; as *A Woman Appeared to Me*. Translated by Jeannette F. Foster, 1976
La Dame à la louve. 1904; as *The Woman of the Wolf*, translated by Karla Jay, 1983
Sappho. 1909.
Les Kitharédes. 1904
Sillages. 1908

Further Reading

Colette. *The Pure and the Impure*. New York: Farrar Straus, 1967.

DeJean, Joan. *Fictions of Sappho, 1546–1937*. Chicago and London: University of Chicago Press, 1989.

Germain, André. *Renée Vivien*. Paris: Crès, 1917.

Goujon, Jean-Paul. *Tes blessures sont plus douces que leurs careses: Vie de Renée Vivien*. Paris: Desforges, 1986.

Gubar, Susan. "Sapphistries." *Signs* (Autumn 1984): 43–62.

Jay, Karla. *The Amazon and the Page: Natalie Clifford Barney and Renée Vivien*. Bloomington and Indianapolis, IN: Indiana University Press, 1988.

Le Dantec, Yves-Gérard. *Renée Vivien: femme damnée, femme sauvée*. Aix-en-Provence: Editions du Feu, 1930.

VOISENON, L'ABBÉ DE

1708–1775
French novelist, poet, and playwright

"Always dying, always charming," with an asthma attack continually looming, Voisenon began by writing fashionable comedies. A penpal of Voltaire, intimate with Mme de Pompadour, the Duchess of Maine, and the Duke of Orléans (the Regent's grandson), Voisenon is the perfect incarnation of the society abbot, who shoots out witticisms and circumstantial verses. He was one of the most active members of the society of the Bout-du-Banc, collaborating on its collective compendia made up of licentious tales, burlesque farces, and parodies which did not allow the possibility of determining each author's contribution (see *Caylus*). Voisenon thus contributes his libertine tales within this context of effervescent sociability, where one has to trick and outwit the other. His most famous tale is *Le Sultan Misapouf et la princesse Grisemine, ou les Métamorphoses* [The Sultan Misapouf and the Princess Grisemine, or the Metamorphoses], published in 1746.

Misapouf, the Sultan, tells his wife, the Sultana, how, while under the curse of the Fée Ténébreuse [Dark Fairy], he was turned into a tub (and had to endure the sight of the "fat and oily dark ass" of the mean fairy and her black eunuch), then had to break the spell cast upon a princess, strangle his parents, friends, and mistresses, and devour an entire family in one single day. The Sultan's "little finger" fits the "ring" of the princess Trop-est-trop [Too-much-is-too-much], whom he frees from a spell with the help of Cerasin, a Buddhist priest, while the ring of her sister, the princess Ne-vous-y-fiez-pas [Do-not-trust-it] swallows Misapouf's two cousins and closes shut on the nose of a knight "caught as in a trap." Turned successively into a hare, a hound, and a fox, he eats his former acquaintances and Grisemine's six young rabbits (she had been metamorphosed into a rabbit). The prediction is fulfilled. It is then the turn of the Sultana to tell of her travels, during which she was metamorphosed into a brill, a rabbit, and a chamber pot.

The entire appeal of the text rests on this unbridled imagination, this ease that Voisenon drives all the way to obscenity. Of course, the "licentious" tale opposes to the usage of the term itself the metaphors of the veiled language. Yet, never has the veil been so sheer. Sexual intercourse besets the tale so much that the "decency" of the veil is canceled by the "filth" of the scenes and situations.

Indeed, it is only a question of "rings" and "little fingers," of all sizes and for every taste. The giantess is endowed with too small vagina, while the midget lady reveals an immense one. Mouths turn into rings. A real mouth can be found where the vagina should be, showing all its teeth. A temple is entirely decorated with rings that knights try to catch at the end of their lances. Voisenon develops the theme to saturation. Disproportionate or tiny, the female vagina is a trap for simpletons into which the heroes of the tale rush at full speed. The male sex is constantly threatened: nothing could be easier to cut off.

Voisenon is having fun. His stories parody folktales, greatly popular since the end of the 17th century, as well as the oriental tale, popularized by the *Thousand and One Nights* (1704). Fairies, genies, and oracles are made fun of. The heroic quest is that of a hero who seeks a vagina measuring up to him. Blasé and skeptical, but playful, Voisenon unleashes a profusion of wit at the expense of his too naive readers, who marvel at the tales. Such is the lesson from the *Sultan Misapouf*: sexual cues are everywhere.

However, be it with the oralization of the vagina (and the vaginization of the mouth), the teethed vagina and the cut penis, the forms of personification of both genitalia, the magic tooth turned into a phallus, or the devouring mother, Voisenon re-creates a mythological scene (such as the adventures of Uranos, Gaia, or Cronos) through which archaic anxieties and desires are expressed. This is the secret strength and power of the story, beyond the obscene and flighty parody.

Voisenon's other important erotic work is *Tant mieux pour elle, conte plaisant* [*Good for Her: A Pleasant Tale*]. According to Grimm (from his *Correspondance littéraire* of February 1763), this work is "filled with obscenities and filth." Published in 1760, it contains the satirical spirit and the obsessions that so characterize Voisenon's tales. The ugly and deformed prince Potiron ("Pumpkin"), son of the fairy Rancune ("Grudge"), wants to marry the fairy Tricolore ("Tricolor"), daughter of the Queen of the Patagons. The young princess, however, is in love with Prince Discret ("Discreet"), son of the fairy Rusée ("Wily"). Numerous misadventures ensue that, once again, must fulfill an absurd and incomprehensible prediction. The two fairies compete with each other, each favoring her own child. Discret is turned into a partridge and a firefly with "a spark of fire on its tail." Tricolore, who owes her name to her mother's three lovers at the time of her conception (one was a blond, another brunette, and the third auburn haired), puts up a peculiar resistance to Prince Potiron once he becomes her husband. When he comes to claim his due, the Princess's bewitched vagina shows a rose bordered with thorns and two big fingers making the sign of the cuckold's horns. The Grand-Instituteur (a character similar to Cesarin in *Sultan Misapouf*) must intervene to lift Tricolore's curse before Discret can become her lover.

Tant mieux pour elle shows the same obsession for the obstacles to sexual intercourse. They are not only due to the acts of malfeasant fairies and genies, but, so to speak, to the female sex itself that renders possession impossible. Burlesque, scatological, and obscene, *Tant mieux pour elle* also harks back to ancient myths, through one of the most accomplished sections of the tale. To recover her virginity (as did Hera), the Patagons fairy dives into an enchanted spring. The result is not what she expected: as she steps out of her bath, the queen finds the portraits of all her lovers, pages, servants, and members of her entourage drawn on her body. The pictures are true to life, with the lovers shown in pose. The king, with bonhomie, cannot but admire the finesse of the drawings. Once again, the sexual secret is revealed to all, indelible, engraved on the skin itself.

Biography

Born in Paris, Claude-Henri de Fusée de Voisenon was the vicar-general of the cathedral of Boulogne before becoming the abbot of Jard. His abundant and light work consists of comedies for the theater, libertine novels and tales, songs and epigrams, and sacred poems. In the theater, he was known as the "archbishop of Italian comedy," while at the Academy his nickname was "the Harlequin of the French Academy."

PATRICK WALD LASOWSKI

Selected Works

Zulmis et Zelmaïde. 1745
Le Sultan Misapouf, et la Princesse Grisemine. "London" [Paris]. 1746
Histoire de la Félicité, conte moral. 1751
Tant mieux pour elle, conte plaisant, il y a un commencement à tout. N.p., n.d. [1760]
Romans et contes de M. l'abbé de Voisenon. 1798, with illustrations
Contes légers. Followed by *Anecdotes littéraires*, 1885

Further Readings

Comoy, Jean. *Un abbé de cour sous Louis XV. M. de Voisenon. 1708–1775.* Paris: La Science Historique, 1959.
Robert, Raimonde. *Le Conte de fées littéraire en France de la fin du XVIIe siècle à la fin du XVIIIe siècle.* Presses universitaires de Nancy, 1981.
Wald Lasowski, Patrick. *L'Ardeur et la galanterie.* Paris: Gallimard, 1986.

VOLTAIRE

1694–1778
French satirist, historian, and dramatist

La Pucelle

Voltaire's *La Pucelle* (1762) is a mock-heroic narrative poem in 21 cantos. It recounts in rhyming decasyllables an irreverent account of the story of Joan of Arc, and, along the lines of Pope's *Rape of the Lock*, makes use of the techniques familiar from the burlesque genre. Besides its use of "mock-solemnity"—underscored by Voltaire's tongue-in-check allusions to the Bible, Homer, Virgil, and Arioste—the poem juxtaposes the sublime and the trivial. *La Pucelle* revolves around the notion that Joan of Arc's virginity was essential to her role as the savior of France—an idea which Voltaire thought a huge joke and presented with great ribaldry. (In a letter, Voltaire suggested, as a piece of hilarity, that Joan of Arc might one day be canonized!) Beginning in the 1730s, Voltaire worked on this poem on and off for over 30 years, and from 1736 onward manuscript copies of *La Pucelle* (or parts thereof) were in circulation. Numerous pirated editions were published until Voltaire's first authorized edition finally appeared in 1762.

The themes of *La Pucelle* are familiar from his other writings: denunciation of superstition, ignorance, and the intervention of providence in human affairs. The poem also inveighs against the perils of religious sectarianism. Its chief protagonists are, on the French side, Joan of Arc; King Charles VII and his mistress, Agnès Sorel; La Trimouille and his lover Dorothy; the monk Grisbourdon; the King's confessor, Père Bonifoux; and, finally, Joan's admirer, Count Dunois. Voltaire's portrait of the English noblemen and soldiery (Chandos, Bedford, Tirconel, Arondel) is one-dimensional, and only the characters of Talbot and Monrose come to life. There are no women on the English side, and so, for the sake of love interest, Voltaire confers the role of amorous cavalier to the King's mistress, Agnès Sorel, on the young and charming Monrose. The English do, however, act as an essential foil to the French, for they serve to represent the rationality and pragmatism the poet clearly favors. Another character in the poem is the fantastic Hermaphrodix, a necromancer who, as his name suggests, is male in the day and female at night, ("Je veux aimer comme homme et comme femme, / Être la nuit de sexe féminin, et tout le jour du sexe masculin," 4: 277–79).

Written along the lines of classical epic poetry, the story of *La Pucelle* is fairly convoluted. A summary of its action can, nevertheless, be attempted. Canto 1—in which the King is described as a "hero in bed"—recounts the love affair of Charles VII with the beautiful Agnès Sorel. So obsessed is Charles with Agnès that, under his rule, the authority of the French crown has been undermined and the kingdom completely overrun by the English. To remedy this state of affairs, Saint Denis, patron saint of France, appears before Joan of Arc, arms her, and, having verified her status as a "virgin," accompanies her to Tours (Joan flying on her trusty mule Pegasus). Once at Tours, Joan inspires the King to take up arms against the English: in Canto 3, the "Palace of Silliness." Meantime, Agnès dresses up in Joan's armor (including codpiece) and is captured by the English. Now without armor, Joan and Dunois are captured by the magician Hermaphrodix and are about to be impaled when, tied up and completely naked, the couple fall in love. Rescued by the monk Grisbourdon, Joan begins to fear for her virginity, but not because she loves Dunois. Rather, the lecherous Grisbourdon tries to take advantage of her vulnerability: a crime for which he is sent to hell (Canto 5). Canto 6, the Temple of Fame sequence, is devoted to the love affair of the English page "the fair" Monrose and the King's mistress, Agnès Sorel. We also learn that the beautiful Dorothy, hitherto unmentioned, is about to be burned at the stake in Milan for her amorous peccadilloes. Flying on his mule, the gallant Dunois learns of Dorothy's plight and saves her from the Inquisition. The two fall in love, but in the interim Dorothy's lover, La Trimouille, sets off for Milan to recover his mistress. Needless to say, he finds her with Dunois, who suddenly vows to return to France, to Joan, and to the wars. Inspired by Dunois's patriotism, La Trimouille vows to return to France as well. At the same time, Dorothy resolves to wait for her lover in a convent at Lorette. Thus the two lovers undertake a journey, during the course of which they meet the Englishman Arondel and his mistress Judith. The two ladies are kidnapped (Canto 8) and then found (Canto 9). Meanwhile, in another part of the kingdom, the King bewails the loss of his beloved Agnès. In love with the King, yet infatuated with the youthful Monrose, Agnès takes refuge in a convent, where, once in bed with the mother superior, she discovers that "mother Besogne" is in fact "a young bachelor" (Canto 10). Still, rather than cause a fuss, she allows nature to take its course. The young bachelor's plans fall apart, however, when, in Canto 11, the English attack the convent and rape all the nuns. Agnès happily escapes this ordeal. In the same canto, Saint Denis and Saint George engage in one-on-one combat. Agnès then finds Monrose, and the two take refuge in the Castle of Cutendre [Tender Bottom], where Charles finally recovers his mistress (Canto 12).

Leaving the chateau, Joan is challenged by the Englishman Chandos, who, discovering that she is a virgin, tries to deflower her. As is always the case, Joan is saved by Saint Denis, who casts a spell on Chandos and renders him unable to "enjoy the laws of conquest." Enraged, Chandos turns his libidinous attention to Dorothy (Canto 14) and is immediately struck down by Dunois. Following this symbolic victory, the King is feted at the town hall of Orléans. Canto 17 sees Charles, Agnès, Joan, Dunois, La Trimouille, and Dorothy imprisoned in Hermaphrodix's palace. Under their host's malevolent spell, the protagonists take leave of their senses. Agnès falls in love with Père Bonifoux, Dorothy thinks that La Trimouille is the Englishman Tirconel, King Charles mistakes the monk Boneau for his belle Agnès, and so on. Finally Bonifoux recognizes the work of the Devil and exorcises his malevolent influence. Free from Hermaphrodix, Charles and his suite head for Rheims.

As the poem concludes, Triconel kills Dorothy and La Trimouille in Canto 19 and, overcome with guilt, becomes a hermit. Dunois longs for Joan, who, protected by Saint Denis, still clings to her virginity. At this point the Devil takes on the form of Joan's flying mule and tries to seduce the heroine, who, in spite of that animal's singular attraction, remembers her divine mission and saves her virginity. Finally, in Canto 21 Pegasus repents his "sin" and together he and Joan, flying through the night, destroy the English armies. Charles is victorious; Joan and Dunois consummate their love when it is revealed to the entire world that indeed Joan was a virgin.

Voltaire clearly thought highly of *La Pucelle*, and it was immensely popular in its day. And yet, like much of Voltaire's poetic output, it is largely ignored today. *La Pucelle* is nevertheless a stunning example of Voltaire's wit. Never vulgar, Voltaire was unrivaled in the use of periphrasis, allowing obscene allusions with a lightness of touch rarely equaled. In short, *La Pucelle* is a genuine example of the "lurid refinement" that was such an important part of eighteenth-century civilization.

Biography

François-Marie Arouet was born on November 21 in Paris into a middle-class family. His godfather was Abbé de Châteauneuf, who was the first to recognize the boy's talent and oversaw his education at the Jesuit Collège Louis-le-Grand (1704–11). In due course, Châteauneuf presented François-Marie to the famous and dissipated coterie of the Temple. Alarmed by the company his son was keeping, Arouet *père* pressed François-Marie to study the law, and then, in order to remove him from Paris, arranged that he serve as a secretary to the French ambassador to Holland. Here François-Marie fell in love with a penniless girl and, because of the resulting scandal, was sent home. His father promptly put him to work in a lawyer's office, but François-Marie's talent for getting into trouble, this time by writing libelous poems, convinced the elder Arouet that his turbulent son should go the country (1714–15). A year later François-Marie was back in Paris and back in trouble with the authorities. Accused of lampooning the Regent, Philippe d'Orléans, he was imprisoned in the Bastille for eleven months, from May 1717 to April 1718.

It was there that he recast the tragedy *Oedipe*, on which he had been working for some time. Performed to great acclaim in November 1718 under the author's name of Voltaire—an anagram of Arouet l(e) j(eune)—*Oedipe* established the young man's reputation as a playwright and poet. Other tragedies followed, but during the 1720s Voltaire enjoyed the admiration of Parisian society and the court. A humiliating altercation with the Chevalier de Rohan in 1726, however, exposed Voltaire's vulnerability. Abandoned by his titled friends, he was imprisoned after unsuccessfully challenging Rohan to a duel. Hurt and out of favor, Voltaire left for England, where he spent the years 1726–29.

Once there, he wasted little time establishing his reputation as one of the foremost literary men in Europe. The Walpoles, Doddington, Bolingbroke, Congreve, Sarah, Duchess of Marlborough, and Pope became his English friends, and within a year he published—in English—his first critical and historical works. The *Essay upon Epic Poetry* and *The Essay upon the Civil Wars in France* both appeared in 1727. He also brought out his first extensive narrative poem, the long-awaited *Henriade* (1728), dedicated to Queen Caroline.

Celebrated in England, Voltaire was granted license to return to Paris in 1729, and there he continued to write plays, poetry, and historical and scientific treatises. He also began about this time his mock-epic poem *La Pucelle*, though it was published only in 1762. During the 1730s, Voltaire wrote the *Histoire de Charles XII* (1731), followed by his *Philosophical Letters*, which were published in 1733. The second of these books was banned, and Voltaire was forced to flee Paris, but the English edition became a bestseller. Living in fear of imprisonment, Voltaire took up residence with Madame du Châtelet, outside French jurisdiction at Cirey in the Duchy of Lorraine (1734–49). The couple traveled annually to Brussels, Paris, and Versailles, where Voltaire—thanks to Mme de Pompadour—was by the mid-1740s in favor once again at court; in 1745 he was appointed historiographer to Louis XV, and a few months later, he was elected to the French Academy. During his long sojourn at Cirey, and later Lunéville, Voltaire enlarged and altered *La Pucelle*. He also gathered material for the *Essai sur les mœurs,* which was published over two years (1761–63) and the *Siècle de Louis XIV* (1751). It was during these years that he began writing the short prose works for which he is best remembered. *Zadig* (1747) was Voltaire's first philosophical novel, and others followed right to the end of his life (*Micromegas*, 1752; *Candide,* 1759; *L'Ingénu* 1767; *La Princesse de Babylone*, 1768; *Le Taureau blanc*, 1774).

Following Madame du Châtelet's sudden death in 1749, Voltaire moved to Berlin at the invitation of Frederick the Great, who had, as Crown Prince of Prussia, first paid homage to the philosopher in 1736. "Master and pupil," as Bloggs said, finally met in 1740 and quickly established a complex friendship. Frederick wanted to attract the most celebrated man in Europe to his court. Voltaire being Voltaire, however, no sooner arrived at Potsdam than the two fell out. He nevertheless remained in Berlin for almost three years, and it was there that he published *Le Siècle de Louis XIV* and began the *Dictionnaire Philosophique*. Finally, in 1753, Voltaire left Berlin, settling briefly in Lausanne and then Geneva before crossing the French border at Ferney. Here, in relative peace, he spent the rest of his life, working, entertaining visitors, and taking up the cause of the oppressed. As an essayist, the elderly Voltaire defended freedom of thought and religious tolerance. His *Dictionnaire Philosophique* (1764) was condemned in Paris, Geneva, and Amsterdam. Finally granted permission to return to Paris, Voltaire died there on May 30, at the age of eighty-four, the undisputed leader of the age of Enlightenment. More than 14,000 of his letters have survived, and his oeuvre encompasses many hundreds of published works, including books, verse, and pamphlets.

E.M. LANGILLE

Editions

La Pucelle d'Orléans. Critical edition by Jeroom Vercruysse. *The Complete Works of Voltaire*, Geneva, 1971. This edition gives a full account of the eighteenth-century editions of *La Pucelle*.

Further Reading

Voltaire en son temps. Edited by René Pomeau. Paris and Oxford: Fayard and The Voltaire Foundation, 1995.

W

WALTER, ANNE

1950–
French writer

Les relations d'incertitude

Les relations d'incertitude is set in contemporary Paris. The narrator is a single, well-read, middle-aged woman who co-owns and co-manages a small shop of antiques and rare books with her like-minded cousin Theo. At his suggestion and recommendation, she starts posing for a renowned painter he has known for some years. The ageing painter is called Volodia, though by and large he is only referred to as 'V*,' the way he signs his paintings. From the very first sessions, he appears aloof and laconic, if not cutting. One day, as she poses nude for him, he brutally yet detachedly shoves the ivory handle of a shaving brush between her thighs. Coldly ordering her not to lose the pose, he then twirls and further pushes the thick shaft into her—this materializes the beginning of his physical domination over her, which she accepts as 'a cruel and refined game' (p. 30).

From them on, V* becomes more productive and the quality of his paintings does improve, whilst the narrator goes through what she calls her 'summer of submission' (p. 32). She becomes his prostitute: evenings, he makes her wear 1900s style old-fashioned undergarments (tight corsets and Victorian waist petticoats) and he sells her to other men, sometimes in his workshop on Quai Bourbon, sometimes at other locations in Paris, including the Bois de Boulogne. He usually watches while they abuse her, which occasionally involves violence and bondage. Sometimes it is not one man but two men who use her at the same time, including two brothers. V* himself rarely touches her, which she construes as a form of proxy: she is emotionally his through his portraits, and physically his through all those other men. Besides describing what he does to her, she also reflects on her condition: she feels 'enslaved, humiliated, ill-treated... most certainly, yet infatuated too!' (p. 33), she is 'humble, fearful, yet bewitched by that man' (p. 35). Their relationship, somehow comparable to that of O and René in *Histoire d'O*, is based on his domination and her love for him—though in *Les relations d'incertitude* there is limited evidence that the authoritarian man really cares for the subservient woman: for V*, obsessed with the quality of his painting, she is but a model and an object, rather than a lover; he treats her rather like an inept maid and shows little care. In the logic of emotional sado-masochism, this only makes her love him even more: 'My pleasure is to give up. Because it's him. Because he decides, contemplates and enjoys himself' (p. 38). Then one day Theo tells her that V* is leaving Paris and does not wish to see her any more—this would naturally dispirit her heavily, yet that aspect is not developed. Theo himself gets ill and is hospitalised for a couple of months—with his cousin he only talks about his hepatitis in inverted commas, which clearly indicates that it was something else, possibly a more serious AIDS-related disease ('une maladie d'amour, ou de l'amour?' p. 71). A few months later, at the end of winter, V* is back in Paris and organizes one more meeting with the narrator, showing her some paintings he had mysteriously made of her as a child, implying that he had known her then, yet this is not clear at all. On the night of V*'s death shortly afterwards, the narrator gives herself one more time to a foreign man, as a sort of ultimate homage to V*.

As implied by the title, the relationships between the characters in the book are very complex, if not too uncertain to analyze. Besides the triad narrator/Theo/V*, two other strange characters keep being mentioned: a woman named Olga, with whom the narrator shares on uncanny resemblance (Olga, who was also Theo's girlfriend, posed for V* too and was his prostitute until her death) and a man wearing loden green who regularly and inexplicably turns up, watching her through shop windows and car windows as if stalking her, eventually buying her for sex from his friend V*. What is the relationship between Theo, V*, and the man in loden green?

Why did V*'s health so suddenly deteriorate? Did Olga too die of AIDS because of V*'s prostituting her to numerous men without any sexual protection? Did she in turn contaminate Theo? *Les relations d'incertitude* shows how erotic literature can discreetly tackle sensitive contemporary issues, whilst respecting the complexity of real-life relationships as opposed to perfect, novel-like structures and situations.

Eventually, a strong originality of *Les relations d'incertitude* is the way the author makes use of the French theologian and writer Fénelon (1651–1715). The narrator, Theo, and V* all have one of his books in hand at some stage, and Fénelon is also quoted directly several times, with reference to his theory of Pure Love. As a key exponent of Quietism, a form of religious mysticism developed in the seventeenth century and rapidly condemned by Rome, Fénelon indeed wrote about Pure Love (for God) as involving submission, self-annihilation, and self-abnegation—and the relationship between the painter and his model in *Les relations d'incertitude* is presented as a secular application of that mystical conceptualisation of Pure Love.

Biography

Anne Walter worked in the cinema industry before becoming a writer and settling in Britanny.

LOYKIE LOÏC LOMINÉ

Selected Works

Les relations d'incertitude. Actes Sud, 1987.
Troisième dimanche du temps ordinaire. (1988).
Monsieur R. 1989.
Rumeurs du soir. 1990.
La nuit coutumière. 1990.

WARD, EDWARD

1660/7—1731
English pamphleteer and journalist

Edward 'Ned' Ward once viewed writing as a form of prostitution: 'the condition of an Author,' he wrote in his preface to *A Trip to Jamaica* (1698), 'is much like that of a strumpet.' Both shared, he believed, a talent for pleasing and a willingness to perform acts 'which we are very much asham'd of' in order to subsist. Ward's shame is ironic for his writing is a deliberate celebration of popular culture with its vibrant scatological turns of phrase, vulgar colloquialisms, and coarse humor. His style of pleasing is to 'tantalize and divert his readers' in a language of 'exaggerated characterization embellished with abundant metaphor and bawdy comment' (Howard Troyer, *Ned Ward of Grubstreet*, p. 29). In addition, Ward intends to please by making his readers participants in, rather than voyeurs of, the low-life scenes he describes. He achieves this by recreating scenes and sensations for his readers' enjoyment that he himself had experienced (Steven Earnshaw, *The Pub in Literature*, p. 112). The eroticism in Ward's work, therefore, resides in his graphic portrayal of the language, pleasures and vices of his contemporary society and especially of London's low-life.

The low-brow literature resulting from Ward's encounters with the lives, aspirations, and activities of the Capital's underclass stood in sharp contrast to prevailing literary tastes for Augustan ideals of propriety, refinement, and decorum. In 1728, Pope attacked Grub Street's hack-writers, including Ward, in *The Dunciad* for appealing to low culture and for their destruction of literary, cultural, and moral standards. With specific reference to Ward, Pope suggested that his 'viler rhymes' would find their main appeal in America where they could be exchanged for cheap tobacco (Bk1: 233). Ward responded in *Durgen, Or a Plain Satyr Upon a Pompous Satyrist* (1728) and *Apollo's Maggot in his Cups* (1729) where he heaped personal abuse on Pope for his hump-backed deformity and his poetic pretensions.

A Trip to Jamaica (1698) was one of Ward's first successes and is an early indication of his characteristically coarse and ribald style. Written during Ward's visit to the island in 1697 where he hoped to escape the debts he had accumulated over the previous six years as a sometime hack-writer, the pamphlet ruthlessly parodied publications used to recruit settlers. It also exposed the island's corruptions by suggesting its male inhabitants had 'just knock'd off their fetters' and its females had been transported there for prostitution.

In November 1698, Ward published the first edition of his periodical *The London Spy* which ran in eighteen monthly editions until May 1700 and which met with such overwhelming success that it was subsequently reprinted in book form. The *Spy* followed the predictable format of aiming to expose 'the vanities and vices of the town' through the eyes of an artless country visitor who passed ingenuous commentary on his city ramblings in the company of a more guileful former school-friend whom he met on his second day in the City. Written in an informal style that marries prose and poetry, *The Spy* is innovative in that it makes ordinary Londoners and their milieu the subject of its study of the city, bringing 'the supposedly marginal or insignificant work and recreations of common people to the fore.' (Paul Hyland, *The London Spy*, xv). The *Spy* teems with erotic reference as it recreates the sensory atmosphere of eighteenth-century London with its coffee-houses, taverns, fairs, and brothels and introduces London's inhabitants including prostitutes, criminals, rogues, tavern-keepers, astrologers, and soldiers whom Ward met and observed at work and play. By the end of the first issue, the reader is invited to pry 'into the dark intrigues of the Town... the whims and frolics of staggering bravadoes and strolling strumpets' and in the ensuing months meets with many a Covent Garden Lady and 'weather-beaten strumpet' (Paul Hyland, *The London Spy*, 194). At every turn on the Spy's perambulations, the reader is ambushed by some form of lewdness, but the eroticism is peculiarly English, in that it combines titillation with bawdy humor. Thus, when an elderly man ogles dirty prints of gentlemen and milkmaids in print-shop windows in St Paul's, the reader is told that 'as many smutty prints were staring the church in the face as a learned debauchee ever found in Aretino's *Postures'* and an over-weight fair-ground entertainer had buttocks that 'trembled when she stirred, like a quaking pudding' (Paul Hyland, *The London Spy*, p. 196). Although Ward's coarse form of eroticism aimed at pleasing his readers, *The Spy* did not shirk its moral responsibility for Ward also used his character sketches of the poor to expose the 'self seeking and dishonest behavior of the governing orders' who regulated their lives (Paul Hyland, *The London Spy* p. xvii).

Ward was prolific and by 1715, had produced over seventy publications, twenty of which had been written during the time of *The London Spy*. He wrote on a wide range of subjects including some lengthy works such as *The Secret History of Clubs* (1709), a two-volumed edition in hudibrastic verse of *The Life and Notable Adventures of Don Quixote (1711–1712),* and a three-volumed *History of the Grand Rebellion (1713)* in verse form. It is in his ephemeral writings, however, where Ward introduces a variety of Londoners, that the reader encounters his particular blend of eroticism which collapses at times into humor, bawdiness, and obscenity. For example, in *The Rise and Fall of Madame Coming-Sir* (1703) the heroine is an innocent country girl, abandoned by her officer lover and forced into prostitution with men of ever-descending status until she catches venereal disease and is cast out. In *A Frolick to Horn Fair,* (1700) it is the hostess of a tavern who relates a risqué story of the origins of the fair and the cuckolding of a miller by King John. In *The London Terrae Filius* (1707–1708), the reader meets the mistress of a flogging school in Moorfields and in *The Reformer, Exposing the Vices of the Age (1700),* an 'Insatiate Wife.' Neglected by her husband, the wife finds pleasure with a gallant on the pretext of going to church but always returns home in time to give her husband a goodnight kiss. The titles of other works suggest their prurient nature: *The City Madame and the Country Maid* (1702), *The Forgiving Husband and Adulterous Wife* (1708), *The Northern Cuckold* (1721). This ephemeral material should not be regarded as mere prurience for, as Hyland has argued, Ward took his work seriously enough to begin, from about 1700, to collect his writings, in varying forms of completeness, into a six-volumed *Miscellaneous Writings in Verse and Prose.* By so doing, Ward demonstrated that he aimed at more than pure erotic pleasure for his readers, rather he intended to provide 'an epic panorama of popular society and culture' (Paul Hyland, *The London Spy*, p. xx).

Biography

Born in Oxfordshire in either 1660 or 1667 and poorly educated, Edward Ward moved to London about 1689 where he became a prolific Grub Street journalist and a publican, keeping taverns in Clerkenwell, Moorfields, and Fulwood Rents successively. As a hack-writer, Ward produced over ninety publications including periodicals, plays, character sketches, travel pieces, and pamphlets which ranged over topics from tiger-baiting to political commentary against the whigs and low-church party. He is best remembered for *The London Spy* (1698–1700) and hudibrastic sketches of London life. In 1706, he was pilloried and fined for seditious libel against Queen Anne's administration in *Hudibras Redivivus* (1705–1707). Ward died at Fulwood Rents near Gray's Inn on 20th June 1731, leaving a wife and children.

BARBARA WHITE

Selected Works

The Poet's Ramble After Riches. 1691.
A Trip to Jamaica. 1698.
The London Spy. 1698–1700.
The World Bewitched: a Dialogue between Two Astrologers and the Author. 1699.
The Cock-Pit Combat; or the Baiting of the Tiger. 1699.
A Trip to New England. 1699.
The City Madame and the Country Maid. 1702.
Secret History of the Calves-head Club; or the Republican Unmasked. 1703.
The Rise and Fall of Madame Coming-Sir. 1703.
The Dissenting Hypocrite; or Occasional Conformist. 1704.
Hudibras Redivivus; or a Burlesque Poem on the Times. 1705–1707.
The London Terrae Filius; or the Satirical Reformer. 1707–1708.
Adam and Eve stripped of their Furbelows; or the Fashionable Virtues and Vices of both Sexes exposed to Publick View. 1710.
Nuptial Dialogues and Debates. 1710.

The History of the London Clubs, or the Citizens' Pastime. 1710.
Vulgus Britannicus; or the British Hudibras. 1710.
The Life and Notable Adventures of Don Quixote de la Mancha. 2 vols, 1711—1712.
The History of the Grand Rebellion, Digested into Verse. 3 vols, 1713.
The Morning Prophet; or Faction revived by the Death of Queen Anne: a Poem. 1714.
St Paul's Church; or the Protestant Ambulators: a Burlesque Poem. 1716.
British Wonders. 1717.
The Delights of the Bottle; or the Compleat Vintner: a Merry Poem. 1720.
The Wandering Spy; or the Merry Travellers. 1722.
News from Madrid. 1726.
Durgen; or a Plain Satire upon a Pompous Satirist. 1729.

Apollo's Maggot in his Cups; or the Whimsical Creation of a little Satirical Poet. 1729.
The Fiddler's Fling at Roguery. 1734.

Further Reading

Earnshaw, Steven. *The Pub in Literature: England's Altered State*. Manchester: Manchester University Press, 2000.
Hyland, Paul, (ed). *The London Spy: From the Fourth Edition of 1709*, East Lansing: Colleagues Press, 1993.
'London in 1699: Scenes from Ned Ward' in *The Gentleman's Magazine and Historical Review*. October 1857, pp. 355–365.
Troyer, Howard W. *Ned Ward of Grubstreet: A Study of Sub-Literary London in The Eighteenth Century*. Cambridge Mass: Harvard University Press, 1946.

WEDEKIND, FRANK

1864–1918
German dramatist and poet

Lulu (Erdgeist [Earth Spirit]; Die Büchse der Pandora [Pandora's Box])

Although Wedekind experimented from an early age with erotic sexuality in his plays, for instance his adolescent *Das Gastmahl bei Sokrates* [*Supper at Socrates*] (1882) with Socrates' directive to his wife to undress, or his celebrated early masterpiece *Frühlings Erwachen* [*Spring's Awakening*] (1891) with its principal elements of masturbation and homoeroticism, it is his two closely linked *Lulu* plays with their explicit focus on the adult world that helped establish Wedekind next to Bertolt Brecht as one of the most influential German dramatist of the twentieth century. The editorial history of the drama is rather complex and often directly impacted by official and unofficial censorship. Initially conceptualized as a five-act play, the earliest version is the manuscript *Die Büchse der Pandora. Eine Monstretragödie* [*Monster Tragedy*] (1894) and premiered almost a century later under the auspices of Peter Zadek (1988). It did not appear in print until 1990. The original drama was divided

into two parts, an additional act was inserted and *Erdgeist* premiered in 1898 in Leipzig, while *Die Büchse der Pandora* (published 1902) did not premiere until 1904 in Nuremberg. Various external pressures, including repeated censoring and the need to adjust the plays to different theatrical stages, led Wedekind to rework the plays repeatedly until 1913. From this point on, it appeared under the unifying title *Lulu*. Wedekind's cleaned-up version of 1906 first included the *Prolog in der Buchhandlung* [*Prologue in the Bookstore*], which polemically refers to the measures of censorship and formally parodies Johann Wolfgang von Goethe's *Vorspiel auf dem Theater* [*Prologue in the Theatre*].

The play's title figure, Lulu, in her function as the "Urgestalt des Weibes" (the prototype of woman), the true, wild, and beautiful beast, as which she is introduced by an animal trainer in the prologue, represents a combination of sexual desires and primitivity, absoluteness and simultaneous naiveté as well as sweet innocence. Throughout the acts, all of these sometimes conflicting traits and her involvement with numerous characters from both sexes directly relate to bourgeois society and its high moral grounds, which are revealed to be grounded in lies and deceit. The central conflicts are but the product of the clash between the contradiction between sexuality and society.

As a young girl, Lulu was rescued from the harsh life on the streets by the newspaper publisher Dr. Schön, who marks her his mistress. To rid himself of Lulu, in order to marry a high-ranking woman, Schön arranges for Lulu to get married: first, to the medical doctor Goll; after that, to the portraitist Schwarz; and, in due course, to Schön himself. In the four acts of *Erdgeist*, each relationship culminates in the eventual destruction of Lulu's men. While the demises appear to be alike, there is a notable intensification of the dramatic development. In each instance, Lulu betrays her current partner with her future partner. However, Goll simply dies from a stroke when witnessing Lulu's rendezvous with Schwarz; Schwarz slits his own throat after Schön informs him of the ongoing affair with Lulu; and, finally, Lulu guns down Schön after he surprises her with a group of devotees and after he desperately attempts to free himself from her, leading her to commit suicide.

Erdgeist is about Lulu's rise and increasing control in life; *Die Büchse der Pandora* follows Lulu's demise and tragic end. Assisted by the infatuated Countess Geschwitz and some of her lovers, Lulu manages to flee from prison and escape to Paris. Together with her new husband, Schön's son Alwa, she leads a luxurious, yet fraudulent existence. Faced by the threat of being sold to the Middle East as a slave by one of her dubious guests, Lulu flees to London together with her entourage (Alwa, Countess Geschwitz, the criminal and Lulu's supposed father Schigolch) after repeated denunciations to the police. Now a prostitute, Lulu brings her customers to their shared attic and her second customer strikes Alwa dead; after unsuccessfully trying to hang herself, the Countess Geschwitz and Lulu are killed by Lulu's fourth customer, Jack the Ripper.

Lulu's path of destruction is not that of a black widow that willingly and deliberately consumes and kills her suitors. Lulu is at once animalistic and infantile. In the end, all interpretations Lulu leave her to be the victim in her passive and innocent, yet destructive life. It is through her mythical status as paradise's serpent, as the animal trainer introduces her, and, simultaneously, as Pandora, as the fantasies Helena (Nelly), Eva or Mignon that her various

men employ to project their desires onto her and shape her. Wedekind's treatment of the rise and fall of this beautiful woman in a male-dominated society, in a society where men's violence against women is exposed, reveals mankind as the victim of its own natural desires. Everyone is a puppet of his or her own instinct, and by showing Lulu literally strolling across the corpses who fell victim to her natural impulses, the play manages to hold a mirror to the souls of the members of the audience. The play evokes the spectators' desperate attempt to hold on to their intricately fabricated structure of bourgeois morality.

The play, which is really more of a grotesque than a tragic drama, is in essence a set of different situations that are all self-contained and geared at baffling and awaking its audience with its constant bombardment of sexual topics. Therefore, as surprising as Klaus Völker's observation may sound, it is perhaps correct to view Lulu as a practical model of Friedrich Schiller's theoretical conjecture, namely the "ästhetische Erziehung des Menschen" [the aesthetic education of man]. Lulu is not a sexual deviant. And she is not the vamp as film and later stage adaptations portrayed her to be. Instead, her natural sexuality provides the essential element of her emancipating powers; some might say of her feminism, which only culminates in destruction because of the overall failure of society to emancipate itself.

Wedekind saw eroticism as a tool with a far-reaching impact, and although his subversive intent in his *Lulu* plays cannot necessarily be traced to social changes, one is correct to view audiences' outrage and ensuing restrictions as confirmation of his effort to convey to the public, how deeply their society was (and given today's occasional uproar following performances: still is) caught within the appearance of morality and rejection of sexuality.

Biography

Born Benjamin Franklin Wedekind in Hanover, Germany, 24 July 1864. Second of five children. Family moved to Switzerland in 1872 for political refuge. Educated at Gymnasium Aarau, 1879–84; studied at universities of Lausanne, Munich, and Münster, 1884–86, and Zurich, 1888. Employed at advertisement section of Maggi in Zurich, 1886–88. Writer for the satirical magazine *Simplicissimus* in Munich, 1896.

Affair with Frieda Strindberg and birth of their son Friedrich Strindberg in Munich, 1897. Incarceration for satirical verses about the emperor, 1899–1900. Married actress Tilly Newes, birth of daughter Pamela and beginning of commercial success of his plays despite repeated altercations with censors, 1906. Birth of daughter Kadidja, 1911. Following a failed appendectomy (1918) and a period of complications related illnesses, Wedekind died in Munich on March 9 1918.

ARNE KOCH

Editions

Lulu, in Gesammelte Werke. Munich and Leipzig: Georg Müller, 1913; Stuttgart: RUB, 1989; as *The Lulu Plays*, translated by Carl Richard Mueller, Greenwich, Connecticut: Fawcett, 1967; as *Lulu: a sex tragedy*, translated by Charlotte Barnes, London: Heineman Educational, 1971; London: Methuen Drama, 1989.

Die Büchse der Pandora: Eine Monstretragödie. Darmstadt: Jürgen Häusser, 1990; as *Lulu: a Monster Tragedy*, translated by Edward Bond and Elisabeth Bond-Pablé, London: Methuen, 1993.

Der Erdgeist. tragödie in vier aufzügen. Munich: A. Langen, 1895; Munich: Georg Müller, 1911; Munich: Goldmann, 1980; as *Erdgeist*, translated by Samuel A. Eliot, New York: A. and C. Boni, 1914; as *Earth-Spirit*, translated by Samuel A. Eliot in *Tragedies of Sex*, New York: Boni and Liveright, 1923; translated by Frances Fawcett and Stephen Spender in *Five Tragedies of Sex*, New York: Theatre Art Books, 1952.

Die Büchse der Pandora. Tragödie in 3 Aufzügen. In *Die Insel*, 10 (1902); Berlin: B. Cassirer, 1903; Munich: Goldmann, 1980; as *Pandora's Box*, translated by Samuel A. Eliot, New York: Boni & Liveright, 1918; translated by Frances Fawcett and Stephen Spender in *Five Tragedies of Sex*, New York: Theatre Art Books, 1952.

Selected Works

Frühlings Erwachen. Eine Kindertragödie (produced 1906), 1891; as *The Awakening of Spring*, translated by Francis J. Ziegler, 1909; as *Spring's Awakening*, translated by Samuel A. Eliot in *Tragedies of Sex*, 1923; translated by Frances Fawcett and Stephen Spender in *Five Tragedies of Sex*, 1952; as *Spring Awakening*, translated by Tom Osborn, 1969; translated by Edward Bond, 1980.

Der Liebestrank [The love potion]. 1899.

Mine-Haha oder Über die körperliche Erziehung der jungen Mädchen [Mine-Haha or About the corporal education of young girls]. 1901.

Der Marquis von Keith. 1901; as *The Marquis of Keith*, translated by Beatrice Gottlieb in *From the Modern Repertoire*, 1957; translated by Carl Richard Mueller in *The Modern Theatre*, 1964.

Hidalla oder Sein und Haben [Hidalla or Being and Having] (produced 1905). 1904; as *Karl Hetmann, der Zwergriese* [Karl Hetmann, the dwarf-giant], 1911.

Totentanz. 1906; as *Tod und Teufel*, 1909; as *Dead and Devil*, translated by Frances Fawcett and Stephen Spender in *Five Tragedies of Sex*. 1952.

Franziska. 1912.

Schloss Wetterstein (produced 1917), 1912; as *Castle Wetterstein*, translated by Frances Fawcett and Stephen Spender in *Five Tragedies of Sex*, 1952.

Die Tagebücher: Ein erotisches Leben. Gerhard Hay (editor), 1986; as *Diary of an Erotic Life*, translated by W.E. Yuill, 1987.

Further Reading

Boa, Elizabeth. *The Sexual Circus: Wedekind's Theatre of Subversion*. New York and Oxford: Blackwell, 1987.

Hibberd, J.L. "The Spririt of the Flesh: Wedekind's Lulu." *The Modern Language Review* 79/2 (1984): 336–355.

Jones, Robert A., and Leroy R. Shaw. *Frank Wedekind: A Bibliographical Handbook*. 2 vols. Munich: Saur, 1996.

Lewis, Ward B. *The Ironic Dissident: Frank Wedekind in the View of His Critics*. Columbia, SC: Camden House, 1997.

Libbon, Stephanie E. "Frank Wedekind's Prostitutes: A Liberating Re-Creation or Male Recreation?" In *Commodities of Desire: The Prostitute in Modern German Literature*, edited by Christine Schönfeld, Rochester: Camden House, 2000.

Völker, Klaus. *Frank Wedekind*. Hanover: Friedrich Verlag Velber, 1965.

Wilke, Sabine. "Die peruanische Perlenfischerin und der jugendliche Buddha: Über stumme und verschwindende Frauenkörper bei Wedekind." *Michigan Germanic Studies* 23/2 (1997): 126–145.

WELSH EROTIC LITERATURE

The richest erotic literature in Welsh is to be found in the strict-meter poetry of the later Middle Ages, from the fourteenth to the sixteenth centuries, before the onset of the Puritanism which suppressed erotic elements in Welsh literature until the late twentieth century. This poetry was the work of trained bards, and exhibits a high degree of technical sophistication in language and meter, particularly in the elaborate consonances of *cynghanedd*, which are inevitably lost in translation. The poems would have been performed to musical accompaniment before audiences in the halls of the nobility, originally by the poets themselves, and subsequently transmitted mainly by oral tradition. The bulk of the poetry was preserved by collectors from the sixteenth century onwards. None was published until the eighteenth century, and very little of the erotic material until the publication of Dafydd Johnston's *Medieval Welsh Erotic Poetry* (1991).

The mainstay of the Welsh bardic tradition was eulogy of noble patrons, but as Wales became more open to external influences in the wake of the Edwardian Conquest of the late thirteenth century, love poetry as entertainment formed an increasingly significant part of the poets' repertoire, using the new *cywydd* meter. This love poetry was mostly perfectly respectable, dwelling extensively on the beloved's beauty and the lover's sufferings, and dealing with the physical fulfilment of his desire only by implication and innuendo. But a small minority of poems are much more explicit in their depiction of the body and the sexual act.

The outstanding love poet of medieval Wales was Dafydd ap Gwilym (c. 1320–1360), a nobleman from north Ceredigion by whom some 150 poems of extraordinary complexity and imaginative power have survived. Although these express an ardent physical desire for two women in particular, the virginal, aloof Dyddgu and the accessible but fickle Morfudd (a merchant's wife with whom Dafydd seems to have had a prolonged affair), the sexuality is usually only implied, as when he makes use of the traditional metaphor of ploughing for sexual intercourse, describing Dyddgu as unploughed land and himself as a young ox, only too ready to draw the plough. Similarly, there is undeniable eroticism in his image of Morfudd's nipples glowing beneath her smock like pennies in heat. But Dafydd ap Gwilym also composed the earliest and most remarkable of all Welsh erotic poems, an address to his own penis, *Cywydd y Gal* [*The Penis*]. In the form of a complaint at the penis's unruly behavior which is constantly getting the poet into trouble, it is in fact a boast of his own sexual prowess, magnified by the bardic technique known as *dyfalu*, a kaleidoscopic series of visual metaphors describing the penis, which is among other things a rolling-pin, a chisel, a bolt, a pestle, and a gun. That is by far the earliest use of the English loan-word 'gun' in Welsh; it referred to the recently-invented cannon. The personification of the penis is achieved by the image of its one eye which finds all girls attractive, and thus the poet manages to detach himself from any moral responsibility for his sexual behavior. This poem is a good instance of the censorship which has suppressed Welsh erotic writing, for it was excluded from Thomas Parry's standard edition of 1952 for no stated reason, and remained infamous but little-known until a reliable text was published in 1985.

A number of other sexually explicit poems are attributed to Dafydd ap Gwilym in the manuscripts, but most are clearly apocryphal. Among these is an ingenious poem which may indeed date from the fourteenth century, although it exists in a single seventeenth-century copy. It draws on and subverts the convention of the *llatai*, or love-messenger, the poet sending his own genitals which, he claims, are sure to win over his beloved. This might be seen as a literary conceit which parallels depictions in medieval iconography of genitals as creatures with feet and wings; on the other hand, it could be interpreted as an elaborate metaphor for rape.

Rape is a topic which occurs in a couple of poems giving sexual advice to young men. One uses the voice of an old woman to give authenticity to the claims about female nature (perhaps influenced by a similar passage in the French *Roman de la Rose*). The advice is to use force to take a girl despite her protests, since her deceitful nature leads her to conceal her need for sexual satisfaction. This advice is seen to be acted upon in another poem from the Dafydd ap Gwilym apocrypha in the *pastourelle* genre in which the narrator meets a peasant girl in a woodland setting and takes her by force. She soon responds enthusiastically, and the poet's smug certainty that having had her once he can have her a hundred times is accompanied by the telling image of an eel caught on a fishing line (the point being that an eel when hooked will draw the line deeper into its body). The same assumption about the voracity of female desire once aroused lies behind a poem by the sixteenth-century cleric 'Sir' Dafydd Llwyd the Scholar about the seduction of a young virgin, a piece chiefly memorable for its inventive series of different expressions for intercourse as she insists on making love again and again.

Dafydd ap Gwilym's address to his penis is often accompanied in the manuscripts by a poem which is in a sense its natural companion piece, although in fact there is no direct connection between the two. The *cywydd* in praise of the vagina by the late fifteenth-century poetess Gwerful Mechain is no personal boast, but rather a celebration of the female body as a poetic topic, complaining that the detailed rhetorical descriptions by male poets ignore the finest part of a girl's body. The series of metaphors which follow serve to demonstrate the poetic potential of this silky, sour grove. Gwerful Mechain also asserted female sexuality in another challenge to the male-dominated poetic tradition by complaining about jealous wives who refuse to share their husbands' fine members with other women—an ironic counterpart to countless poems attacking the jealous husband. And Gwerful Mechain showed herself capable of answering obscenity in kind when challenged by a male poet, Dafydd Llwyd of Mathafarn, who addressed her with a verse purporting to be spoken with penis in hand asking her if she had a dish big enough to contain it. She replied with four verses in similar vein, offering to take him on and culminating with the image of the firing of a cannon. Gwerful Mechain produced a quite substantial body of verse on a variety of topics,

but because of these three erotic poems no full edition of her work was published until 2001.

Medieval Welsh literature is on the whole not tolerant of sexual deviation. A sixteenth-century poem about a boy dressed as a girl (presumably a boy-actor) concentrates on the paradoxical contrast between appearance and reality, with riddling references to two feet and three thighs. A profounder sense of unease with deviance from the norm is to be felt in a poem by the late fifteenth-century poet Llywelyn ap Gutun depicting a couple making love in an unusual posture, with the girl's legs raised up over the man's shoulders. The effect of the series of metaphors here is one of alienation, turning a sexual act into an anti-erotic spectacle, the girl like a hedgehog on a spike, like a horse on its back holding a bear, like a sheep being sheared by a wild dog.

Venereal disease was a recurrent cause of concern, as seen in a rueful comic poem by the fifteenth-century nobleman Ieuan Gethin of Glamorgan, which perhaps reveals profounder fears in its warning against trusting in such a long and crooked thing as a vagina. And in the eighteenth century there is dark humor in Iolo Morganwg's poem about a maid who countered sexual abuse from her master by putting a sickle between her legs to cut his hand when he groped beneath her clothes.

Obscenity features prominently as a weapon in bardic satires, abuse poems with either serious or humorous intent. One of the most vicious of these is by the fourteenth-century poet Prydydd Breuan attacking a woman by the name of Siwan Morgan of Cardigan, a repugnant piece of misogyny focusing on the fluids which flow from her vagina. Dafydd ap Gwilym is reputed to have sung a satire which caused the death of a poet called Rhys Meigen who had composed a verse claiming to have shafted Dafydd's mother. On the other hand, obscenity could be a means of amusement. Two of the most highly respected poets of the fifteenth century, Dafydd ab Edmwnd and Guto'r Glyn, exchanged poems in which Dafydd mocked Guto's swollen testicles (apparently the result of a hernia), and Guto replied by mocking Dafydd's long floppy penis with surreal imagery, likening it to Offa's Dyke!

The complex linguistic situation of medieval Wales could be the source of some erotic frisson in the literature. There are at least two macaronic poems in which a Welshman makes indecent proposals to an uncomprehending Englishwoman. The best-known is by Tudur Penllyn in the mid-fifteenth century, and from the Englishwoman's responses in that poem it can be deduced that the Welshman's actions speak louder than his words, although he is left wondering whether or not she is willing. Of course, such poems presuppose a bilingual audience able to appreciate the whole dialogue and laugh at both the monoglot speakers.

Erotic poetry in the strict meters more or less came to an end with the demise of the old bardic order in the seventeenth century. But from that period onwards there is a wealth of free-meter verse deriving from folk tradition, sometimes known as *penillion telyn* [harp stanzas]. These were almost all anonymous, and they seem to have been the vehicle for women to express their feelings on a variety of subjects, including sexuality. The harp itself becomes a sexual symbol in a group of verses in which a girl longs for a harpist as lover, likening his fingering of the harp to the caressing of a girl's body. Lewis Morris (1701–1765) of Anglesey imitated that tradition in his long poem about an old miller who married a lusty lass, which gives sexual significance to milling and its paraphernalia, the grinding, filling of the hopper, and so on. Such folk traditions were suppressed as a result of the dominance of nonconformist religion from the late eighteenth century onwards, although ribald verse-making did not die out altogether, but took on a purely oral existence amongst agricultural workers.

Since the Welsh novel had its roots in the nonconformist culture of the nineteenth century, it tended to take a puritanical view of sexual relationships, and eroticism had no place in it until well into the second half of the twentieth century. Indeed, neurosis about sexuality can be seen to underlie much of the fiction of Kate Roberts (1891–1985), the foremost practitioner of the short story in Welsh. A crucial turning point was the publication of *Un Nos Ola Leuad* [*One Moonlit Night*] by Caradog Prichard in 1961. Based on reminiscences of his childhood in Bethesda, this novel was written when Pritchard was a journalist in London, and its catalogue of sexual deviance, including incest, child-abuse, transvestitism, and a sex-murder, can be seen as a reaction against the stifling respectability which had so long blighted Welsh literature. It was some time before other writers followed Prichard's lead, but by the 1980s eroticism was as prominent in Welsh fiction as in that of any other language, although there remains a sense of rebellion against the Puritanism of the chapel. The old tradition of strict-meter erotic poetry also resurfaced at this time with the publication in 1973 of *Englynion Coch* [*Red* (i.e., blue) *Englynion*] by the radical Lolfa press, a collection of obscene verses some of which are attributed to major twentieth-century poets.

DAFYDD JOHNSTON

Primary Sources

Johnston, Dafydd. *Canu Maswedd yr Oesoedd Canol / Medieval Welsh Erotic Poetry*. Cardiff: Tafol, 1991; second edition, Bridgend: Seren, 1998.

Howells, Nerys Ann. *Gwaith Gwerful Mechain ac Eraill*. Aberystwyth: Canolfan Uwchefrydiau Cymreig a Cheltaidd, 2001.

Donovan, P.J. *Cerddi Rhydd Iolo Morganwg*. Cardiff: University of Wales Press, 1980.

Jones, Glyn. *A People's Poetry: Hen Benillion*. Bridgend: Seren, 1997

Prichard, Caradog (trans. Philip Mitchell). *Un Nos Ola Leuad / One Moonlit Night*. London: Penguin, 1995.

Further Reading

Johnston, Dafydd. 'Cywydd y Gal' by Dafydd ap Gwilym.' *Cambridge Medieval Celtic Studies*, 9 (Summer 1985), 71–89.

Johnston, Dafydd. 'The Erotic Poetry of the *Cywyddwyr*.' *Cambridge Medieval Celtic Studies*, 22 (Winter 1991), 63–94.

Johnston, Dafydd. *A Pocket Guide: The Literature of Wales*. Cardiff: University of Wales Press, 1994.

Johnston, Dafydd. 'Erotica and Satire in Medieval Welsh Poetry.' in Jan M. Ziolkowski (editor), *Obscenity: Social Control and Artistic Creation in the European Middle Ages* (Leiden: Brill, 1998), 60–72.

WHARTON, EDITH

1862–1937
American novelist, short story writer, and poet

Beatrice Palmato

Beatrice Palmato is a manuscript which includes a plot of a projected short story and a fictional fragment described by Wharton as an "unpublishable fragment of Beatrice Palmato." The manuscript is located at the Wharton Archive, Beinecke Library, Yale University. It was probably written around 1919, and was first published by Cynthia Griffin Wolff in her 1977 study of Wharton, *A Feast of Words; The Triumph of Edith Wharton.*

The plot summary of the projected short story is about as long as the unpublishable fragment. It describes the tragic short life of Beatrice Palmato, the daughter of a rich and cultured half-Levantine and half-Portuguese banker living in London. The Palmatos lead a life of cultivated pleasure. Beatrice's older sister, who looks like their English mother, unexplainably commits suicide at the age of seventeen. Their mother has a nervous breakdown, after which she is sent away to recuperate. Beatrice remains with her father, who takes charge of her education. The mother comes home after a year, and all is well for a while. However, Mrs. Palmato has another breakdown, grows mad, tries to kill her husband, and dies in an insane asylum a few months later. Mr. Palmato takes Beatrice to Paris with him, and engages a young governess, whom he marries a few years later. Beatrice is very close to her father and to her step mother, but at eighteen marries a young Englishman of good family and no artistic or intellectual tastes, who falls madly in love with her. They settle in the English countryside.

Beatrice doesn't see her father for some time, and then starts visiting Mr. Palmato. Early in her marriage her friends notice deep changes in her, "Her animation and brilliancy have vanished, and she gives up all her artistic interests...."

She goes with her father on a short trip to Paris, and "comes back brilliant, febrile and restless...." After several years of married life Beatrice has two children, a boy and a girl, at which point her attachment to her husband increases. Mr. Palmato dies around the time of the birth of Beatrice's daughter. Beatrice's husband loves both children, but exhibits a particular attachment to their little daughter. As the little girl grows to be five or six years old Beatrice becomes morbidly jealous of the affection between her husband and daughter. It seems that Beatrice is growing "queer" like her mother. One day the husband goes away for a week. He returns unexpectedly, and finds his daughter alone in the drawing room. As father and the child hug and kiss each other, Beatrice comes in and screams "Don't kiss my child. Put her down! How dare you kiss her?" She snatches the little girl from his arms. As husband and wife stare at each other, he begins to comprehend the horrifying secret which has come between them. Beatrice, realizing what she has unwittingly betrayed, runs to her bedroom and shoots herself dead. While most people assume that Beatrice succumbed to the madness running through her mother's side of the family, her brother comes to visit her husband and they have a long talk about Mr. Palmato.

The "unpublishable fragment" describes in great detail a love-making encounter between Mr. Palmato and his daughter Beatrice, which sequentially takes place after she is married. While Beatrice marries a virgin, it is obvious from the fragment that she and Mr. Palmato have had erotic encounters before. While the plot summary describes a tragic story of a family rent apart by madness and sexual perversity, the fragment describes the love-making, consisting mostly of oral sex, as an exuberant encounter, much different from the painful and rough advances of Beatrice's husband.

While the fragment is extraordinary in its explicitness, it and the plot summary may be seen as an integral part of Wharton's work.

Critics have assumed that *Beatrice Palmato* was to be a ghost story, one of two types which Wharton wrote. Short stories such as *Mary Pask* and *All Souls'* included a spectral double, an alter-ego, a reflection of an evil and foreboding impulse shared by a character within the story. Other short stories, including *Kerfol* and *The Pomegranate Seed*, centered around a jealous love triangle which included a ghost as a romantic interloper. The plot summary for *Beatrice Palmato* reached into both types of stories.

Parental power is another theme evident in Wharton's writings. For example, the character of the mother is an important element in the horror of *Ethan Frome*, and in *Summer*, the major novel published before *Beatrice Palmato* was written, the heroine marries her foster father. In a later novel, *The Mother's Recompense*, for which Wharton sketched the characters as early as 1919, the portrait of Beatrice Cenci, a sixteenth-century Italian woman who was supposedly raped by her father, confronted the heroine in her husband's bedroom. Wharton's interest in barbarism, taboos, and ritual sacrifices, exhibited in her travel notes on Morocco (first published in 1919), also came through in such novels as *The Age of Innocence*, the first novel written after *Summer*, and published after *Beatrice Palmato* was conceived. The precocious sexuality Wharton observed while traveling in Morocco was reflected in the exoticism and sexuality of Mr. Palmato's Mediterranean character.

The name Beatrice, as well as the incestuous nature of the fragment, resonated personally with Wharton. Beatrice was the nickname given by Wharton's lover, Morton Fullerton, to his cousin, Katherine Fullerton, who grew up in the same household with him, believing at first she was his sister. Morton Fullerton almost married her around the time he began his long love affair with Edith Wharton.

Edith Wharton was a prolific writer, and there has been considerable interest in her work since the 1960s. Despite the unusually explicit pornographic nature of the *Beatrice Palmato* fragment, it has been published only once, in 1977, shortly after its discovery in the Wharton Archive, and very little has been written about it since.

Biography

Born in New York City in 1862, Edith Newbold Jones Wharton was the most famous American female novelist of her time. Her novels and short stories were informed by her experiences growing up in the Dutch Protestant and nouveaux riches milieu of New York. From 1902 until her death she published on average one book a year. From 1913 she lived in Europe, and died of a heart attack in Brice-sous-Forêt, France in 1937.

RUTH WALLACH

Editions

Wolff, Cynthia Griffin. *A Feast of Words: The Triumph of Edith Wharton.* New York: Oxford University Press, 1977.

Selected Works

Fast and Loose. 1877.
Verses. 1878.
The Decoration of Houses. 1897.
The Greater Inclination. 1899.
The Touchstone. 1900.
Crucial Instances. 1901.
The Valley of Decision. 1902.
Sanctuary. 1903.
The Descent of Man and Other Stories. 1904.
Italian Villas and Their Gardens. 1904.
Italian Backgrounds. 1905.
The House of Mirth. 1905.
Madame de Treymes. 1907.
The Fruit of the Tree. 1907.
A Motor-Flight Through France. 1908.
The Hermit and the Wild Woman & Other Stories. 1908.
Tales of Men and Ghosts. 1910.
Ethan Frome. 1911.
The Reef. 1912.
The Custom of the Country. 1913.
Fighting France, From Dunkerque to Belfort. 1915.
Xingu and Other Stories. 1916.
Summer. 1917.
The Marne. 1918.
French Ways and Their Meaning. 1919.
The Age of Innocence. 1920.
In Morocco. 1920.
The Glimpses of the Moon. 1922.
A Son at the Front. 1923.
Old New York. 1924.
The Mother's Recompense. 1925.
The Writing of Fiction. 1925.
Here and Beyond. 1926.
Twelve Poems. 1926.
Twilight Sleep. 1927.
The Children. 1928.
Hudson River Bracketed. 1929.

Further Reading

Lauer, Kristin O. "Is This Indeed 'Attractive'? Another Look at the 'Beatrice Palmato' Fragment." *Journal of Evolutionary Psychology* 11, no. 1–2 (March 1990): 1–8; reprinted in *Edith Wharton Review* 11, no. 1 (Spring 1994): 26–29.

WHITMAN, WALT

1819–1892
American poet

Walt Whitman's writing career began in the early 1840s, when he began writing both prose and verse for journals. Of these, the *Democratic Review* was most important in that it vociferously espoused the "Young America" program of demotic literature, culture, and social structures that also informed even Whitman's early work. But to the social platform Whitman added an amalgam of transcendentalism and materialism that has, often simultaneously, attracted and dismayed subsequent generations. The terms of Whitman's dialectic were manifest throughout the first edition of *Leaves of Grass* but especially in "Song of Myself." In part 5, for example, there is his credo of the soul ("I believe in you my soul"); however, the soul is not the transcendental oversoul but rather one in dialectical tension with the body ("the other I am," and that there be no doubt, in part 24 he compounds the credo, "I believe in the flesh and the appetites"), and neither is to "be abased to the other." Four verses later he evokes a distinctly erotic image, notwithstanding that it is a metaphor of the soul, recalling a summer morning on, appropriately, the grass, where "you settled your head athwart my hips and gently turn'd over upon me, / And parted the shirt from my bosom-bone, and plunged your tongue to my bare-stript heart." This is promptly elevated by infusing the atmosphere with "the peace and knowledge that pass all the argument of the earth." But if

transcendence is a continuous imperative for Whitman, it ever abides in the good earth, as he insists in part 3: "Always the procreant urge of the world. / Out of the dimness opposite equals advance, always substance and increase, always sex...." Whitman's position in this respect is essentially Blakean; contraries—as in male/female, body/spirit, passion/reason, "good"/"evil"—generate creative energy.

The question of how much correspondence there was between the exuberant sensuality in Whitman's verse and the manifestation of it in his personal life is necessarily a matter of speculation. Testimony from friends quotes Whitman as saying that "the ardent expression in words of affection often tended to destroy affection," as in the myth of Cupid and Psyche, also citing personal experience of just such an occurrence. But testimony from other friends indicates that Whitman could be demonstrative: "And so kind, sympathetic, charitable, humane, tolerant a man I did not suppose was possible. He loves everything and everybody. I saw a soldier the other day stop on the street and kiss him [in Washington, DC, where Whitman tended to Civil War soldiers in military hospitals]. He kisses me as if I were a girl." An article by Whitman about his hospital work in the *New York Times* notes, "To many of the wounded and sick, especially the youngsters, there is something in personal love, caresses, and the magnetic flood of sympathy and friendship, that does more good than all the medicines in the world." In his letters to one young soldier Whitman walks a thin line between lover and comrade. One letter addresses "my dear darling comrade," another "my dearest comrade," and at points he seems the awkward suitor, hoping "God will put it in your heart to bear toward me a little at least of the feeling I have for you." Whatever these anecdotes and letters may suggest about Whitman's sexual disposition, they do indicate a correspondence in the frequent effusiveness of amorous vocabulary in both Whitman's private and his public styles.

For the third edition of *Leaves of Grass* (1860) Whitman consciously adopted a challenging, not to say abrasive, erotic stance with the inclusion of the "The Children of Adam" and "Calamus" sequences. He included them over Emerson's objections because, as he had already insisted in "Song of Myself," the dialectic of nature demanded the body and the soul on equal terms. His poetic mission required that he articulate, indeed declaim, not only a democratic ethos of freedom but also the ethos of nature, "Creeds and schools in abeyance, / ...I harbor for good or bad, I permit to speak at every hazard, / Nature without check with original energy." If America was to grow beyond cultural mimicry of the old world, Whitman's essential agenda, it required the full focus of America's native genius, its harmony with natural energy, its fecund ground for, as he had said in "Starting from Paumanok," "A world primal again, vistas of glory incessant and branching, / A new race dominating previous ones and grander far, with new contests, / New politics, new literatures and religions, new inventions and arts." Accordingly, the erotic and its generative "body electric" were imperative.

Whitman's original conception for the two sections was that "Children of Adam" should represent "the amative love of woman" just as "Calamus" reflected "adhesiveness, manly love." The terms amative and adhesive he appropriated from phrenology. In the first sequence Whitman evokes the primary theme of sexual energy, sometimes as the procreative force we have noted and sometimes as exuberant excess and transgression. The Adamic motif opens the sequence, invoking the Garden and its loss as if the poet wanted to exorcise the accompanying shame and its fig leaf. The poet is "determin'd... my own voice resonant, singing the phallus / Singing the song of procreation, / Singing the need of superb children...." But his song is

"Renascent of grossest Nature" and soon swells to ecstatic extremity, "The female form approaching, I pensive, love-flesh tremulous aching / ... The mystic deliria, the madness amorous, the utter abandonment." If generation is natural, a corollary theme, so is it, here, transgressive, "Two hawks in the air, two fishes swimming in the sea not more lawless than we." Erotic images abound, some certainly obscene by the standards of the time: "love-flesh swelling and deliciously aching, / Limitless limpid jets of love hot and enormous, quivering jelly of love, white-blow and delirious juice," or "Love-thoughts, love-juice, love-odor, ... / lips of love, phallic thumb of love, breasts of love, bellies press'd and glued together with love." But Whitman vigorously insists on the "divinity" of the erotic, and the physique of sex is rendered transcendental, "O I say these are not the parts and poems of the body only, but of the soul." But then that dialectic, mediated by a passionate love that is sometimes platonic and sometimes palpable, is characteristic of Whitman's erotic rhapsody.

While Whitman compromised his initial candor a bit in "Children of Adam," deleting his embrace of prostitutes for example, with "Calamus" he seems to have felt the need for still greater masking of intent. The 1953 discovery of the original manuscripts revealed the narrative of a homoerotic relationship reaching heights of happiness and then, to the poet's despair, devolving. This was clearly delineated in a sequence of twelve poems that were distinctly informed by erotic impulses but did not evoke the pulsing erotic imagery of the Adamic sequence. The images of the former poems, however, hover over the even more transgressive narrative of "manly love" in the latter. But in the publication Whitman disguised the story, first, by inserting several unrelated poems between the two complementary sets, and secondly by interspersing revised versions of the twelve poems among thirty-three others so as to dilute the narrative implications of the sequence.

Nonetheless, such images as the male speaker—throughout *Leaves of Grass* identified with the poet himself—sleeping in the arms of a male lover carried considerable impact. Still, the exact nature of Whitman's erotic life remains a matter of speculation. What continues to be true is that the poet's embrace of human being—from its grossest character to its most transcendent aspirations—was of such magnitude, candor, and eloquence as to earn him the admiration of both his elder and junior contemporaries—for example, Thoreau, Emerson, Longfellow, Whittier, Twain, Holmes, and Tennyson. And likewise these qualities make him one of, if not the most distinctive erotic poet in the history of the art.

Biography

Walt Whitman was born May 31, 1819 to Walter and Louisa Van Velsor Whitman, the second of nine siblings. His mother was a follower of Elias Hicks' Quaker mysticism, and his father subscribed to the politics of Tom Paine and the anti-capitalist stance of early nineteenth-century radicalism. After five years of public school in Brooklyn, he became a printer's apprentice, and printing and journalism were to be staple employments throughout his life. Between 1836 and 1850 Whitman worked as a school teacher, a newspaper editor, and contributed to substantial dailies and journals, where he engaged political issues such as slavery, free soil, territorial expansion, and the Mexican war, among others.

Whitman's political sympathies were to find their eloquence in his 1855 Preface to *Leaves of Grass*, where he located the "genius" of the United States in the "common people," and announced his poetic credo of "perfect personal candor" that would assert itself so conspicuously in the third, 1860, edition of *Leaves*. Meanwhile his work attracted the attention and praise of the great transcendentalists Ralph Waldo Emerson and Henry David Thoreau. Whitman's earliest poems of 1850 reflect his hostility to slavery, but the 1860 edition of *Leaves* expand his level of candor with the inclusion of two distinctly erotic poetry sequences considered by the proprieties of the time to be obscene, "The Children of Adam" and "Calamus."

Following discovery of Whitman's original "Calamus" manuscript in 1953, homoerotic interpretations of his life and work proliferated. During the Civil War, Whitman worked as a volunteer in army hospitals, and some of his extensive correspondence with former patients has also been construed to confirm his homoeroticism. Be that as it may, by the 1870s Whitman's work was being sold in Europe, providing welcome finances and recognition, as well as lecture and reading opportunities. In the early '80s he was able to buy a house in Camden, New Jersey, but subsequently both his finances and his health deteriorated until his death on March 26, 1892.

PETER MICHELSON

Editions

Complete Poetry and Selected Prose and Letters. Emory Holloway, ed., London, 1938.
The Complete Writings of Walt Whitman. Richard Maurice Buck, et al., eds., New York and London, 1902.
Leaves of Grass and Selected Prose. John A. Kouwenhoven, ed., New York, 1950.

Selected Works

Leaves of Grass. First edition. 1855.
Leaves of Grass. Third edition. 1860 [including "Children of Adam" and "Calamus" sequences].
Drum Taps. First edition. 1865.
Sequel to Drum Taps. 1866 [including "When Lilacs Last in the Dooryard Bloomed"].
Democratic Vistas. First edition. 1870.
Specimen Days. First edition. 1882.
Leaves of Grass. Tenth and final authorized edition. 1892.
Complete Prose Works. First edition. 1892.
Complete Poetry and Selected Prose and Letters. Emory Holloway, ed., London, 1938.
The Complete Writings of Walt Whitman. Richard Maurice Buck et al., eds., New York and London, 1902.

Further Reading

Allen, G.W. *The Solitary Singer: A Critical Biography of Walt Whitman*. New York, 1955
———. *Walt Whitman Handbook*. Chicago, 1946.
Bowers, Fredson, ed. *Whitman's Manuscripts: "Leaves of Grass" (1860): A Parallel Text*. Chicago, 1955.
Cavitch, David. *My Soul and I: The Inner Life of Walt Whitman*. Boston, 1985.
Faner, Robert D. *Walt Whitman and Opera*. Philadelphia, 1951.
Folsom, Ed, ed. *Walt Whitman: The Centennial Essays*. Iowa City, 1994.
Martin, Robert K. *The Continuing Presence of Walt Whitman: The Life After the Life*. Iowa City, 1992.
Schmidgall, Gary. *Walt Whitman: A Gay Life*. New York, 1997.

WILDE, OSCAR

1854–1900
Irish playwright, novelist, and aesthete

Oscar Wilde was a leading representative of the late nineteenth-century movement in art and literature known as "Decadence." The decadent artist, or "aesthete," was known for his cultivated manners and dandyish appearance. Decadents rejected the conventional canons of morality and professed a contempt for the ordinary. As in Wilde's case, the decadent often spent more time perfecting his pose of "exquisiteness" and contemplating beauty, than he did in creating his own works of art. Indeed, Wilde claimed that his life was his art, and he became known for his quotable one-liners, or "the quip" and for his flamboyant style of dress and living. A proponent of the platonic philosophy of homophile friendship, Wilde revealed the fine line many men had to walk between fin-de-siecle decadence and "homosexuality"—a new legal and medical identity that had emerged by the 1870's and was declared illegal in England in 1885 under the Criminal Amendment Act. His 1895 trial for homosexuality erased the public's doubts about Wilde's sexuality and also created a larger moral panic and justification for censorship of art and literature. While Wilde has become one of the most celebrated "queer" playwrights, homosexuality as a theme is not always obvious in his works.

Wilde achieved popularity and fame for his comedies of Society, such as "Lady Windemere's Fan," (performed 1892), "A Woman of No Importance," (Performed 1893), and "An Ideal Husband" (performed 1895). All three plays contain formidable dowagers, dandified aristocrats, and female innocents forced to confront the sordidness of social and political life. Wilde's most famous and posthumously most successful play, "The Importance of Being Earnest" (performed 1895) does seem to have a homosexual subtext. A farce about guilt, secrecy and the double life, the play deals with two friends, Algernon and Jack, who use alternative identities (Jack's Ernest and Algernon's Bunbury) and the women who love them. The false identity allows the men to escape debt and enjoy a life of pleasure in London and conceal their vices from those in the country. Queer theorists read the play as homoerotic, as the friends, portrayed as effete, leisured, and amoral, discuss their fondness for "bunburying" in London, perhaps a code word for homosexual jaunts, cruising for "rough trade" which Wilde secretly practiced outside of his marriage. Critic Alan Sinfield says of the play, "the whole ambience reeks...of queerness." However, the conversations of the two men tend to dwell on women and property and the play ends with the upcoming marriages of both.

Wilde's most famous novel, *The Picture of Dorian Gray* veered away from his usual attempt at wit and parody. Borrowing the premise of Stevenson's *Dr. Jekyll and Mr. Hyde* Wilde introduces the character of Dorian Gray, the eternal youth who seeks to escape moral punishment. At Oxford, Wilde had belonged to a circle of students whose poetry worshipped male beauty and youth and the writings of Plato. Dorian's very name evokes the Ancient Greeks. In this novel, the homoerotic bond between Dorian Gray and the artist who paints him, Basil Hallward, are evident. Wilde champions the superiority of the leisured gentleman who "has discovered how to live." Dorian's "new Hedonism" and lack of self-control lead to debaucheries that include adultery, murder, opium addiction, and the moral corruption of others, but only his painting registers his guilt; Dorian remains ageless, beautiful, and innocent on the exterior. Having driven the woman he loves to suicide and murdered to keep the secret of his portrait, Dorian at last rediscovers the power to feel; he slashes the painting and thereby kills himself. In 1890 the *Daily Chronicle* called the novel "a poisonous book, the atmosphere of which is heavy with the mephitic odours of moral and spiritual putrefaction" and filled with "effeminate frivolity." Five years later the novel was used as evidence at Wilde's trial of "relations, intimacies, and passions of certain persons of sodomitical and unnatural habits, tastes, and practices."

Another of Wilde's controversial works was his play "Salome" written in 1891 and published in 1893 along with Aubrey Beardsley's erotic illustrations. Wilde never saw the play performed in his lifetime as the London Lord Chamberlain's Office banned the work which represented a Biblical subject. Wilde threatened to leave England and move to Paris, "I will not consent to call myself a citizen of a country that shows such narrowness in artistic judgement." The character of Salome was an icon of female sexuality for *fin de siecle* writers and artists, the ultimate *femme fatale* whose unquenchable desire challenges the conventions of patriarchal culture. In the play Wilde transforms the political execution of John the Baptist into a sexually perverse lust murder. As the prophet denounces female sexuality, Salome tries to seduce him, and agrees to perform for Herod her Dance of the Seven Veils in exchange for the prophet's head on a platter. After the prophet's death, she then horrifies Herod as she lovingly speaks to and even kisses the decapitated head, and Herod orders his guards to kill her. Critics at the time described Wilde's play as bizarre, ferocious, and repulsive, and some compared Salome to the feminist New Woman of the late nineteenth century. Wilde, hinting at the homosexual subtext of the play, posed for a photograph dressed as Salome and declared "Salome, c'est moi."

During and after his imprisonment, Wilde used his writing to contemplate his own life and express his sexuality in a more open manner than his previous works allowed. "I don't regret for a single moment having lived for pleasure.... There was no pleasure I did not experience ... Tired of being on the heights I deliberately went to the depths for new sensations." The trial altered the public's perception of Wilde from the witty dandy to that of a criminal, and his writing changed in response to his public's hostility. In "The Ballad of Reading Gaol" (1898) Wilde used the story of Trooper Charles Thomas Woolridge, a fellow convict sentenced to death for the murder of his wife, as an analogy for his own fate as a condemned man. He also used the poem to link sexuality and death, as he did in "Salome," and laments "each man kills the thing he loves." In his long prison letter to Lord

Alfred Douglas, "De Profundis," (published after Wilde's death), Wilde notes the lack of a distinct boundary between his public figure and artistic persona: "I was a man who stood in symbolic relations to the art and culture of my age." In the work, he meditates on the nature of Christ as well as his own self-destructive behavior that led to his downfall. The letter opens with a section on Wilde's and Douglas's three-year love affair, Wilde's generosity, and Douglas's selfishness. He acknowledged his attraction to young males, calling it "feasting with panthers...the danger was half the excitement." Although he tried to celebrate his sexuality which he had been forced for so long to conceal, Wilde notes in his letter that his sexuality was also the source of his personal and professional suffering: "Of all possible objects I was the most grotesque. When people saw me they laughed."

Biography

Born in Ireland, 1854 to a poet mother and eminent Dublin physician. Educated at Trinity College, Dublin, and then Magdalen College, Oxford where as a disciple of Walter Pater he founded the Aesthetic Movement, which advocated "art for art's sake." From 1878—1881, Wilde became a well-known dandy and party guest in London, known not for his writings but for his wit and flamboyant attire of velvet coat, knee breeches, silk stockings, pale green tie, cane, and shoulder-length hair. In 1882, he toured North America for a year. When a customs officer asked if he had anything to declare, Wilde replied, "nothing but my genius." At 28 he lectured in 70 American and Canadian cities on the arts and literature, attracting crowds as varied as West Coast intellectuals and Kansas farmers. Upon his return to London he worked as a literary critic, journalist, and author of several children's books; he married Constance Lloyd in 1884, and fathered two sons. He reached the peak of his career from 1890–1895 as a playwright and novelist, and his works, with their critique of Victorian mores and hypocrisy, helped usher in the modern era. In 1895, Wilde sued the eighth Marquess of Queensberry (the father of Wilde's young lover, Lord Alfred Douglas) for libel. The suit backfired and Queensberry's accusations of Wilde's homosexuality led to the writer's arrest and trial for "acts of gross indecency." The trial, which resulted in two years' imprisonment with hard labor in Reading Gaol, destroyed Wilde's career, reputation, and alienated him from his family and friends. Upon his release from prison in 1897 he wandered around Europe, in poor health and financially ruined. He died in 1900 in Hotel d'Alsace in Paris, of cerebral meningitis, under the pseudonym "Sebastian Melmoth."

JULIE ANNE TADDEO

Selected Works

Collected Edition of the Works of Oscar Wilde. Ed. Robert Ross, 15 vols., London: Methuen, 1908; reprinted 1969.
The Importance of Being Earnest and Other Plays. Ed. Peter Raby, Oxford: Oxford University Press, 1995.
The Picture of Dorian Gray. Ed. Isobel Murray, Oxford: Oxford University Press, 1974.
Salome: A Tragedy in One Act: Translated from the French of Oscar Wilde: Pictured by Aubrey Beardsley. London: Elkin Mathews and John Lane, 1894.

Further Reading

Behrendt, Patricia Flangan. *Oscar Wilde: Eros and Aesthetics.* London: Macmillan, 1991.
Cohen, Ed. *Talk on the Wilde Side: Toward a Genealogy of a Discourse on Male Sexualities.* New York: Routledge, 1993.
Dellamora, Richard. *Masculine Desire: The Sexual Politics of Victorian Aestheticism.* Chapel Hill, NL: University of North Carolina Press, 1990.
Dollimore, Jonathan. *Sexual Dissidence: Augustine to Wilde, Freud to Foucault.* Oxford: Clarendon Press, 1991.
Ellmann, Richard. *Oscar Wilde.* London: Hamish Hamilton, 1987.
Eltis, Sos. *Revising Wilde: Society and Subversion in the Plays of Oscar Wilde.* Oxford: Clarendon Press, 1996.
Gagnier, Regenia, ed. *Critical Essays on Oscar Wilde.* New York: G.K. Hall, 1991.
Hyde, H. Montgomery, ed. *The Trials of Oscar Wilde.* London: Hodge, 1948.
Knox, Melissa. *Oscar Wilde in the 1990s: The Critic as Creator.* Rochester, NY: Camden House, 2001.
Nassaar, Christopher. *Into the Demon Universe: A Literary Exploration of Oscar Wilde.* New Haven, CT: Yale University Press, 1974.
Powell, Kerry. *Oscar Wilde and the Theatre of the 1890s.* Cambridge: Cambridge University Press, 1990.
Raby, Peter, ed. *The Cambridge Companion to Oscar Wilde.* Cambridge: Cambridge University Press, 1997.
Sandulescu, C. George, ed. *Rediscovering Oscar Wilde.* Princess Grace Irish Library: 8. Gerrards Cross: Colin Smythe, 1994.
Showalter, Elaine. *Sexual Anarchy: Gender and Culture at the Fin de Siecle.* London: Bloomsbury, 1991.
Thornton, R.K.R. *The Decadent Dilemma.* London: Edward Arnold, 1983.
Sinfield, Alan. *The Wilde Century: Effeminacy, Oscar Wilde and the Queer Movement.* New York: Columbia University Press, 1994.
Woodcock, George. *The Paradox of Oscar Wilde.* London: T.V. Boardman, 1949.

WILLY (HENRY GAUTHIER-VILLARS)

1859–1931
French writer and critic

By his early thirties, Henry Gauthier-Villars was not only a successful journalist, he was also the father of an illegitimate son whose mother had died before her divorce could be finalized. Colette's family, with whom he was on familiar terms, looked after this child at their home in the countryside for a time before other arrangements could be made. Presumably it was at this moment that Colette, who harbored ambitions of her own, first came into contact with him. Given the disparity in fortune (while Gauthier-Villars came from a wealthy family, Colette was little more than a poor girl without a dowry or any visible marks of intellectual distinction), the marriage between this ill-assorted couple, which occurred in 1893, was viewed by contemporaries as an unusual arrangement. Within a short while, Colette, like many others, was producing work which her husband edited and signed with his own name.

The two most entertaining works produced by Willy's "fiction factory" were probably dashed off in haste by Jean de Tinan (1875–1899), one of the more able minor decadent writers of the period. The first of these, *Maîtresse d'Esthètes* (1897), manages to combine a racy narrative about the tangled love life of an artist's model, Ysolde Vouillard, with an entertaining satire at the expense of the advanced artistic and literary fashions of the day. The novel begins with Ysolde's seduction of the fashionable sculptor Franz Brotteaux (she performs a striptease in his studio). When Brotteaux, emotionally and physically exhausted by her demands (it is hinted that they make love five times a day), decamps to the coast, she forces herself on his best friend, the writer Jim Smiley (Willy's own alter-ego), who has already adopted another former girl friend of Brotteaux's, Clarisse, as his own. On one hand, the novel seems to be a study of male empowerment with the two men casually trading women between themselves. However, though both men find Ysolde fascinating, especially because of her active solicitation of sex, both are also ultimately glad to escape her importunities. Smiley even claims to prefer the almost asexual domestic satisfactions offered by Clarisse, an uncomplicated *grisette*, more to his taste.

Indeed, the general tone of the novel is misogynistic rather than erotic. Predictably, Ysolde is repeatedly defined in terms of the hysterical woman. More unusually, her behavior is also explained in terms of an artificial voluptuousness which is a literary construct of the period. In fact, Ysolde is the illegitimate daughter of a street prostitute whose knowledge of art and literature derives almost exclusively from her contact with writers and musicians. Indeed, her first lover, a failed Wagnerian composer, is responsible for introducing her to the work of Sotaukrack (with whom she also conducts an affair), the leader of an avant-garde esoteric coterie. Self-educated, Ysolde's understanding of these new ideas is at best unreliable and a source of ribaldry for her male companions. *Un vilain Monsieur!* (1898), also largely written by Jean de Tinan, contains a similar satirical note.

Most of the works published under the "Willy" soubriquet contain transparent references to real people. Ysolde in *Maîtresse d'Esthètes* is probably based on Henriette Maillat, a former mistress of the prolific Joseph Péladan,

the leading esoteric novelist of the day. The latter is clearly the model for Sotaukrack. Brotteaux, with his Christ-like face and numerous sexual conquests, resembles a youthful Catulle Mendès. The various references in the novel to Jean de Tinan's writing perhaps confirm his hand in the authorship as does the theme of impotence, a subject about which we wrote elsewhere. Overall, *Maîtresse d'Esthètes* is an extremely sophisticated novel in terms of the hints and asides it makes (both cultural and sexual), though Ysolde's highly fetishistic striptease (she retains her hat, gloves, and stockings) and subsequent semi-rape of Smiley constitute the main erotic episodes. Despite its quirkiness, the novel may still be read with some pleasure.

Willy and his team of ghost-writers, despite such salacious tendencies, generally managed to avoid legal complications. In 1903, however, *La Maîtresse de Prince Jean* was prosecuted for obscenity. The novel itself concerns an affair between Maurice Lauban, a young poet, and Gaëtane Girard, a middle-aged actress rumored to be the mistress of the elusive (and probably non-existent) Prince Jean of the title. Lauban, who is mean, vulgar, and provincial, is mainly motivated by snobbery, the notion of cuckolding a minor aristocrat appealing to his self-conceit. Although this allows for some low comedy in the opening chapters (Lauban has to defer his first tryst with his new mistress because of the lamentable state of his underwear), the novel is otherwise unremarkable. The most entertaining passages concern an account of a fictitious duel that Lauban persuades Maugis to write for *Gil-Blas*. This simple hoax not only provides Lauban with an excuse for his earlier non-consummation of the affair with Gaëtane but also adds to his own prestige in her eyes. Despite the casual portrayal of sexuality through the work (calling on Maugis, Lauban finds him in bed with a *grisette*; later he becomes obsessed with the idea that Gaëtane has lesbian proclivities, referring in passing to the relationship of the ostensible author's former wife with Polaire), *La Maîtresse de Prince Jean* has little to recommend it as a work of fiction. Willy managed to generate a considerable amount of publicity from the trial (even calling Huysmans as a witness), recouping the cost of the fine that was handed out to him (1,000 francs) many times over in increased sales.

Biography

Henry Gauthier-Villars was born on August 10, 1859, at Villiers-sur-Orge in the Seine-et-Oise. After completing his studies at the Lycée Fontanes and the prestigious Collège Stanislas, he turned down a position with the family publishing and printing firm founded by his father (a staunchly conservative concern) in favor of pursuing a literary career on his own hedonistic terms. His first work, a collection of sonnets, was published in 1878. By the early 1880s, even while completing his military service in Le Mans and Besançon, he was contributing articles and stories to various Parisian and provincial newspapers and journals. By the mid-1880s, he was also publishing material under the pseudonym Henry Maugis; later he would also write criticism under the name Jim Smiley. In 1887, having decided to ingratiate himself with his father, he finally joined the family firm, which was located on the Quai des Grands-Augustins. From his ground-floor office, he held open house for such *fin-de-siècle* literary celebrities as Catulle Mendès, Mallarmé, Paul Verlaine, Marcel Schwob, Pierre Louÿs, Jean de Tinan, and Rémy de Gourmont. Most of the numerous works signed "Willy" demonstrate a similar interest in the erotic, including several works published in the 1920s which deal with the fashionable theme of homosexuality. Such works continued to appear until the eve of his death in 1931.

TERRY HALE

Selected Works

Works signed "Willy" [i.e., Henry Gauthier-Villars]
La Maîtresse du Prince Jean. Paris: A. Michel, 1903.
Maîtresse d'Esthètes. Paris: H. Simonis Empis, 1897.
Le troisième sexe. Paris: Paris-Édition, 1927.
Un Vilain Monsieur! Paris : H. Simonis Empis, 1898.

Further Reading

François Caradec. *Willy—Le père des Claudine*. Paris: Fayard, 2004.
Willy. *Souvenirs littéraires... et autres*. Paris, Editions Montaigne, 1925.

WILMOT, JOHN, SECOND EARL OF ROCHESTER

1647–1680
English poet and satirist

Rochester's writings were intended for manuscript circulation among a coterie of courtiers who valued wit and extremity, violent debauchery, and polished epigrams. He added a sexual twist to almost everything he wrote. When he revised John Fletcher's tragedy *Valentinian*, a drama already steeped in decadent lust, he added extra details about the emperor's love for eunuchs and boys (p. 161; all citations from *Works*, edited by Harold Love). His letters, like his poems, often express the absurdity of sex, the incongruous mismatch of "head" and "tail." Scholars still cannot decide whether Rochester is a libertine poet (the most striking example in English literature) or an anti-libertine, who exposes the emptiness of desire by acting out its contradiction in extreme personas—the woman wit tempted to become a whore, the "disabled debauchee" frenetically encouraging others to sin because he himself is diseased and impotent. His famous *Satyr against Mankind* shocked contemporaries by defining "right reason" as a device to keep up the pleasures of sensuality, and yet suggests the idiocy and filthiness of human passions.

Rochester's poetry is often erotic and obscene, though not always both at once. Lyrics like "An Age in her Embraces Passed," "Love and Life," "Absent from thee I languish still,"

"A Young Lady to her Antient Lover," or "The Fall" show a profound understanding of the erotic bond, its cruelty and fragility. Rochester laments (or perhaps celebrates) the separation of volition, desire, and performance, the fleeting nature of feeling, the compulsion to betray, and the philosophical doubts that force lovers to torture one another: "Love raised to an extream" through anguish and jealousy gives them a sense of reality, since "pain can ne'er deceive" (p. 28). In equally elegant drinking songs, Rochester's various personae strive to "Raise pleasure to the topp" (p. 23) by alternating bouts of wine, boys, and "Cunt."

The verbally obscene poems themselves range from surprising tenderness to hysterical aggression. "Faire Cloris in a Pigsty lay" makes a pastoral out of the pig-girl's masturbatory dream, and even the violent *Ramble in St James's Parke* has a moment of pathos, when the jealous lover recalls the former "tender hours" that Corinna has now "betrayed,"

When leaning on your Faithless Breast
Wrapt in security, and rest,
Soft kindness all my powers did move,
And Reason lay dissolved in Love.

(p. 79)

In other poems (and in other parts of the long *Ramble*) obscene words and images are thrown in the reader's face. A female character wants her "eyes fucked out." A courtesan is savagely attacked for her power to enslave men—or more accurately, to arouse men so that their own "Bollox" make them "slaves" to her. To begin his curse Rochester invokes the mock-epic "Bawdy Powers," dipping his pen in menstrual rather than poetic "Flowers." He ends with a perfectly-manicured explosion of disgust and degradation: "Her Belly is a Bagg of Turds, / And her Cunt a Common sewer" ("On Mrs Willis," p. 37).

Many of Rochester's more outrageous poems interconnect sex and politics. The ingenious ode "Upon Nothing" brackets together kings' promises and whores' vows. One notorious lampoon, slipped "by mistake" into Charles II's pocket, asserts that the monarch's "sceptre and his prick" are not only the same length but equally manipulable by whomever lays her hand on them. Britain may be famous "For breeding the best Cunts in Christendome," but its ruler is completely dominated by his phallus, a single-minded, "peremptory" creature who will

"break through" all religion and law "to make its way to Cunt." Illogically, this all-governing organ is also so "disobedient" that Nell Gwyn has to use "Fingers, Mouth and Thighes" to raise it, while even in its regnant state the "graceless Ballocks" weigh it down and render it ridiculous (pp. 85–89).

Rochester turned every syllable and every gesture into Wit, which meant not just humor but literary sophistication and creativity. Rather than simply *producing* erotic literature, he explores the similarities between literature and the kind of sex he knows best, scandalous and illicit. Whores and men of wit are alike because their patrons first "enjoy" them and then "kick them out of doors," but "a threatening doubt remains" in both cases, since the satirist's sting lingers on like the burning of syphilis (p. 58). One of his aristocratic speakers claims to have "never Rhymed but for my Pintles sake," that is, on behalf of his penis (p. 259). A female character with literary ambitions at first hesitates because "Whore is scarce a more reproachfull name / Than Poetesse," but this recognition then makes her all the more eager to write, like her author "Pleased with the Contradiction and the Sin" (p. 64). Transgression itself is the chief spur to writing.

The contradictions central to Rochester's life and work include the violent contrast between the "lacy precision" of the verse and the obscenity of its content, and the comical disjunction between the sublime grandeur of eros and the gross anatomy of sex. Writing to an obese male friend, he describes the ludicrous spectacle they made when running naked in the park (revealing "the strange decay of manly parts"); writing to his wife, he laments the "disproportion 'twixt our desires and what [Fate] has ordained to content them." (See *Letters*, edited by Treglown, pp. 159, 241–242.) Even writing to his actress mistress, he seems taken with the irony of it all; with a typical logical twist, he assures her that his passion must be sincere because it sounds so false.

The unpredictable autonomy of the genitals haunts Rochester's longer poems of debauchery. *A Ramble in St James's Parke* proclaims that "There's something generous in mere Lust," and yet reduces the faithless mistress to a "Cunt" that speaks in her mouth and "came spewing home, / Drencht with the Seed of half the Town" (pp. 78–79). "The Disabled Debauchee" celebrates drunken brothel riots and bisexual orgies, but in the voice of a syphilitic, impotent man. Impotence is the classic theme of *The Imperfect Enjoyment*, where the penis becomes in rapid succession an "all-dissolving Thunderbolt," a spear which "Where e're it pierced, a Cunt it found or made," a withered flower, a "wishing, weak, unmoving lump," a cowardly street hooligan, and "a Common Fucking Post." The phallus is at once the *raison d'être* of Rochester's poem and the "worst part of me" (pp. 14–15).

Rochester was luridly imitated during his lifetime and extravagantly praised after his early death. Religious leaders paid tribute to the "subtilty and sublimity" of his wit, the "heightening and amazing circumstances of his sins" (repented at the last minute). Women poets like Aphra Behn and Anne Wharton (his niece, adopted sister, and reputed lover) celebrate Rochester for embodying "all the charms of Poetry and Love." He became the prototype for every brilliantly wicked rake in English literature.

Publishers rushed to cash in on Rochester's notoriety. Any obscene or erotic poem they could find was posthumously printed as his, and for this reason it is still difficult to know precisely what he wrote. Most of the poems in underground editions can be attributed to other writers, as David Vieth proved long ago. In his great edition of 1999, Harold Love has shown convincingly that Rochester had no connection with the bawdy classics "Signior Dildo" and *Sodom* (treated as his in popular works like Stephen Jeffreys's drama *The Libertine*, 1994). The mock-heroic drama *Sodom*, evidently written by an individual or group of would-be wits outside the Court circle, imitates Rochester at certain points (for example when King Bolloxinian declares "with my Prick I'le governe all the land"). But it rarely rises above what film critics call the teenage gross-out mode: in one scene, for example, the courtiers make up culinary dishes of "Cunts" garnished with crablice or infected vaginal discharges, and discuss the pleasures of "Turkey's arse." The version entitled *Sodom and Gomorah*—published only in Love's appendix of spurious works—is more extreme and more coherent.

Biography

Born April Fool's Day 1647, at Ditchley in Oxfordshire, to a pious mother and an absentee father exiled (and given the title Earl of Rochester) for his personal commitment to the defeated King Charles II. After his father died in 1658, Rochester was in effect adopted by the King (restored to power in 1660), who generally acted as a rakish companion rather than as a patriarchal authority figure. Entered Wadham College, Oxford, at the age of twelve, and took the Grand Tour of France and Italy in 1661–1664. Fought valiantly (and lost his religious faith) in a naval campaign against the Dutch; later gained a reputation for cowardice by fighting the police and running away, leaving a friend dead. With no profession and little inherited estate, Rochester lived partly off his heiress–wife Elizabeth Malet (abducted 1665, married 1667, four children by her and one by the actress Elizabeth Barry). Court pensions and synecures, such as Keeper of Woodstock Park and Gentleman of the Bedchamber, allowed him to live and frolic in the inner circles of Whitehall.

Drunk for five years continuously—as he candidly admitted in conversations recorded by the Scots clergyman Gilbert Burnet—Rochester still took his hereditary seat in the House of Lords. Several times imprisoned, banished the Court, or sent abroad for his impulsive behavior, he always managed to regain the King's personal favor. Burnet records many of Rochester's beliefs, presumably sincere even if stated for effect: Christianity is a fraud necessary to keep the lower classes in order; a benevolent God would never prohibit the promiscuous "use of women"; all pleasure is legitimate provided it does no harm. His two ruling passions, Burnet observed, were "a violent love of Pleasure, and a disposition to extravagant Mirth"; he particularly "took pleasure to disguise himself as a Porter, or as a Beggar, ... to follow some mean Amours, which, for the variety of them, he affected." (Burnet's memoir is reprinted in *Rochester: The Critical Heritage*, edited by David Farley-Hills.) Rochester died of syphilis and alcoholism at the Christ-like age of thirty-three (26 July 1680), after a much-publicized conversion from his earlier flamboyant atheism.

JAMES GRANTHAM TURNER

Selected Works

The Gyldenstolpe Manuscript Miscellany. Edited by Bror Danielsson and David M. Vieth, Stockholm: Almqvist and Wiksell, 1967; shows how erotic and obscene poetry circulated in hand-written books.

Poems on Several Occasions, by the Right Honourable, the E. of R——. "Antwerp" [London], 1680; contains many lewd verses by other authors, as Vieth has shown.

Poems, Etc., on Several Occasions, with Valentinian, a Tragedy. London: Jacob Tonson, 1691; reliable edition, often reprinted, but excludes all the obscene poems.

The Works of the Earls of Rochester, Roscomon, Dorset, Etc. "4th" edition, London: Edmund Curll, 1714; numerous editions, each one with more smutty "Rochester" poems.

The Letters of John Wilmot, Earl of Rochester. Edited by Jeremy Treglown, Oxford: Blackwell, 1980.

Rochester, Complete Poems and Plays. Edited by Paddy Lyons, London: Everyman, 1993; convenient paperback, but unreliable attributions (accepts Rochester's authorship of *Sodom*, for which there is no evidence).

The Works of John Wilmot Earl of Rochester. Edited by Harold Love, Oxford: Oxford University Press, 1999; includes works unreliably attributed to Rochester ("Appendix Roffensis"), with full scholarly evidence for authorship and distribution.

Further Reading

Burns, Edward (editor). *Reading Rochester*. Liverpool: Liverpool University Press and New York: St. Martin's Press, 1995.

Chernaik, Warren. *Sexual Freedom in Restoration Literature*. Cambridge: Cambridge University Press, 1995.

Coltharp, Duane. "Rivall Fopps, Rambling Rakes, Wild Women: Homosocial Desire and Courtly Crisis in Rochester's Poetry." *The Eighteenth Century: Theory and Interpretation*, 38 (1997): 23–42.

Combe, Kirk. *A Martyr for Sin: Rochester's Critique of Polity, Sexuality, and Society*. Newark, NJ: University of Delaware Press and London: Associated University Presses, 1998.

Farley-Hills, David (editor). *Rochester: The Critical Heritage*. London: Routledge, 1972; essential documents on his contemporary reception and influence, including funeral tributes, Gilbert Burnet's *Some Passages of the Life and Death of John Earl of Rochester*, and literary criticism defending the aesthetic validity of his obscenity.

Fisher, Nicholas (editor). *That Second Bottle: Essays on John Wilmot, Earl of Rochester*. Manchester: University of Manchester Press and New York: St. Martin's Press, 2000.

Greene, Graham. *Lord Rochester's Monkey, Being the Life of John Wilmot, Second Earl of Rochester*. New York: Penguin, 1974; brilliant insights, but uses works almost certainly not by Rochester.

Griffin, Dustin H. *Satires Against Man: The Poems of Rochester*. Berkeley and Los Angeles: University of California Press, 1973.

Lamb, Jeremy. *So Idle a Rogue: The Life and Death of Lord Rochester*. London: Allison and Busby, 1993; popular biography, emphasizing alcoholism, but accepts apocryphal works like *Sodom* without scholarly evidence.

Thormählen, Marianne. *Rochester: The Poems in Context*. Cambridge: Cambridge University Press, 1993.

Treglown, Jeremy (editor). *Spirit of Wit: Reconsiderations of Rochester*. Oxford: Blackwell, 1982.

Turner, James Grantham. *Libertines and Radicals in Early Modern London: Sexuality, Politics and Literary Culture, 1630–1685*. Cambridge: Cambridge University Press, 2001, Chapter 6.

———. *Schooling Sex: Libertine Literature and Erotic Education in Italy, France, and England, 1534–1685*. Oxford: Oxford University Press, 2003, Chapters 6 and 8.

Vieth, David [later Diana] M. *Attribution in Restoration Poetry: A Study of Rochester's "Poems" of 1680*. New Haven and London: Yale University Press, 1963; essential information on authorship, also included in Vieth's modern-spelling edition of *The Complete Poems*, New Haven and London: Yale University Press, 1968 (the first edition to combine the canonical and obscene poems).

WITTIG, MONIQUE

1935–
French novelist

Monique Wittig received the 1964 Prix Medicis for *L'Opoponax* [*The Opoponax*], the first major novel of education from a non-male point of view and the first book of her trilogy which systematically experiments with gender in pronouns and narrative subjectivity. Following the "events" of May '68, an epic from a revolutionary feminist point of view, *Les guérillères*, was published in 1969. In 1974, her most deconstructive work appeared: *Le corps lesbien* [*The Lesbian Body*], where the female body is figuratively taken apart and reconceptualized from a lesbian point of view.

The trilogy was followed by three significant rewritings: a rewriting of the dictionary, *Lesbian Peoples: Material for a Dictionary* which Wittig coauthored with Sande Zeig in 1976; a play rewriting Cervantes's *Quixote, le voyage sans fin* [*The Constant Journey*], first performed in 1985, starring Sande Zeig; and a rewriting of Dante, *Virgile, non* [*Across the Acheron*], published in 1985.

In 1992, Beacon Press published *The Straight Mind and Other Essays*, Wittig's collected theoretical essays previously published in *Feminist Issues* and other journals over a period of a dozen years. Wittig developed an argument that foregrounds the centrality of obligatory heterosexuality as a political régime. Women, for Wittig, belong to a class constituted by the hierarchical social relation of sexual difference that gives men ideological, political, and economic power over women. What makes a woman is a specific relation of appropriation by a man. A feminist is one who fights for women as a class and for the disappearance of that class. "Sex" is the naturalized political category that founds society as heterosexual. All the social sciences based on the category of "sex" must be overthrown. Because lesbians are outside the political economy of heterosexuality, "lesbians are not women."

In 1999, *Paris-la-politique et autres histoires* was published. A parable about power struggles in political groups, it is a collection of hard-to-find short texts that Wittig had previously published. She described them as "parasite texts that fall whole out of the main body on which they had grafted themselves."

In June 2001, Marie-Hélène Bourcier's translation of *The Straight Mind and Other Essays* was published in Paris as *La Pensée straight*. To celebrate this event, the publisher, Editions Balland, cosponsors with the University of Paris, Nanterre, a colloquium on the work of Monique Wittig. Scholars from Canada, Italy, and the United States as well as France presented papers to an overflow crowd in Reid Hall of Columbia University in France. Monique Wittig read excepts from her work in progress, "Un Chantier littéraire" (A Workshop Space). She also discussed, with her partner, Sande Zeig, their new film, "The Girl," based on an unpublished Wittig short story and directed by Zeig. The film premiered in Paris June 17, 2001.

Biography

Monique Wittig was born in Dannemarie (Alsace) France July 13, 1935. She was an experimental writer, lesbian feminist theorist, and activist. As author of experimental fiction she translated from French into a dozen languages. She was the best-known lesbian materialist theorist of the twentieth century becoming a founding member of MLF (French), Gouines Rouges (Red Dykes), and Lesbiennes Radicales (Radical Lesbians). Wittig died in Tucson, Arizona (US) January 3, 2003.

NAMASCAR SHAKTINI

Selected Works

L'Opoponax. Paris: Minuit, 1964.

The Opoponax. tr. Helen Weaver. Plainfield, VT: Daughters Press, 1966.

"Bouvard et Pécuchet." *Les Cahiers Madeleine Renaud-Barrault* 59 (1967): 113–122.

"Voyage: Yallankoro." *Nouveau Commerce* 177 (1967): 558–563.

[Trans.] *L'Homme unidimensional*. Paris: Minuit, 1968. (Trans. of *One Dimensional Man*, by Herbert Marcuse.) Les Guérillères. Paris: Minuit, 1969.

[With Gilles Wittig, Marcia Rothenburg, and Margaret Stephenson (aka Namascar Shaktini)] "Combat pour la libération de la femme." *L'Idiot international* 6 (1970): 13–16.

Les guérillères. tr. David Le Vay. London: Peter Owen, 1971. rpt. Boston, MA: Beacon, 1985.

"Le Grand-Cric-Jules," "Récréation," "Dialogue pour les deux frères et la soeur." Radio plays. Radio Stuttgart, 1972.

"Un moie est apparue...." [*Le Torchon Brûle* n⁰ 5, juillet 1972, Paris, p. 3], revue *Minuit*, 1972, p. 43–46.

Le corps lesbien. Paris: Minuit, 1973.

"Une Partie de campagne." *Le Nouveau Commerce* 26 (1973): 13–31.

[Trans., with Evelyne Le Garrec and Vera Prado] *Nouvelles lettres portugaises*. Paris: Seuil, 1974. (Trans. of *Novas Cartos Portuguesas*, by the Three Marias [Isabel Barreno, Teresa Horta, and Fatima Velho Da Costa].)

[With Sande Zeig] *Lesbian peoples: material for a dictionary*. New York: Avon, 1975.

The Lesbian Body. tr. David Le Vay. London: Peter Owen, 1975. rpt. Boston, MA: Beacon, 1986.

[With Sande Zeig] *Brouillon pour un dictionnaire des amantes*. Paris: Grasset, 1976.

"Un Jour mon prince viendra." *Questions féministes* 2 (1978): 31–39.

[With Sande Zeig] *Lesbian Peoples: Material for a Dictionary*. New York: Avon, 1979.

"Paradigm." In *Homosexualities and French Literature*. Ed. Elaine Marks and George Stambolian. Ithaca, NY: Cornell University Press, 1979. 114–121.

"La pensée straight." *Questions féministes* 7 (1980). Rpt. in Amazones d'hier, lesbiennes d'aujourd'hui 3, no. 4 (1985): 5–18.

"The Straight Mind." *Feminist Issues* 1, no. I (1980): 103–111.

"On ne naît pas femme." *Questions féministes* 8 (1980): 75–84. Rpt. in Amazones d'hier, lesbiennes d'aujourd'hui 4, no. 1 (1985): 103–118.

"One is not born a woman." *Feminist Issues* 1 no. 2 (1981): 47–54.

[Trans., with "Avant-Note"] *La Passion*. Paris: Flammarion, 1982. (Trans. of *Spillway*, by Djuna Barnes.)

"Les Questions féministes ne sont pas des questions lesbiennes." *Amazones d'hier, lesbiennes d'aujourd'hui* 2, no. I (1983): 10–14.

"Les Tchiches et les Tchouches." *Le Genre humain* 6 (1983): 136–147.

"Le lieu de l'action." *Digraphe* 32 (1984): 69–75.

"The Trojan Horse." *Feminist Issues* 4, no. 2 (1984): 45–49.

"Le cheval de Troie." *Vlasta* 4 (1985): 36–41.

"The Mark of Gender." *Feminist Issues* 5, no. 2 (1985): 3–12. Rpt. in The Poetics of Gender. Ed. Nancy Miller. New York: Columbia University Press, 1986. 63–73.

"Paris-la-Politique." *Vlasta* 4 (1985): 8–35.

Virgile, non. Paris: Minuit, 1985.

Le voyage sans fin. Vlasta 4 supplement, 1985.

Across the Acheron. London: Peter Owens, 1987.

"On the Social Contract." *Feminist Issues* 9, no. I (1989): 3–12.

The Straight Mind and Other Essays. Boston: Beacon, 1992.

Paris-la-Politique. Paris: P. O.L., 1999.

La pensée straight. trans. Marie-Hélène Bourcier. Paris: Balland, 2001.

"The Girl," film of Sande Zeig, scenario by Wittig and Zeig. 2001.

WOMEN'S MAGAZINES

In the broadest sense of the term women's magazines might refer to any serial publication consciously marketed at women. However, there are, and have been, a number of such publications which are not included in the category which cultural critics and common usage refer to as women's magazines. The term is generally taken to refer to a set of mass-marketed, serial publications aimed at middle- and upper-class women and containing domestic advice, romantic fiction, and in the later twentieth century sexual advice and discussion. From about 1970 a sub-genre of these has taken an overtly political stance in labeling themselves as feminist and arranging content accordingly. In a discussion of women's magazines in relation to erotic writing it is important to note that magazines are distributed through entirely different channels than literary books. Newsstands, supermarkets, and other neighborhood venues display women's magazines. Thus women interact with this form of writing in the course of everyday lives and do not have to seek it out in venues reserved for "high art" literature associated with middle- and upper-class culture.

Most scholars agree that publications identifiable as women's magazines first began to appear in Europe in the late seventeenth century. First aimed at upper-class women, these publications contained little domestic advice and a good proportion of romantic fiction which detailed the sexual exploits of women both married and unmarried. By the mid-nineteenth century, mass-market publications which addressed the concerns of what was now culturally identifiable as the middle-class housewife began to appear in Europe and the United States. A formula of domestic, romantic and sexual advice, (often with erotic fiction added) emerged and lasted for at least the next century and a half.

A number of "women's" magazines are also read by teenage girls and many women have echoed Janice Winship's description of her first search for erotic knowledge in their pages:

Women's magazines became more intriguing as I tried to glean hints of the mysteries of sex and, perhaps more importantly, seek reassurance that my sprouting and increasingly alien body was not in the first stages of some dreadful illness. It was dissapointing that my mother only had *Women's Weekly*. Mrs. Marryat gave little away on her problem page. But I used to love the romance and adventure of the serials...like Neville Shute's *A Town Like Alice*...mainly because of one (or so I remember it) highly erotic scene in which the heroine lets down her sari robe to reveal and offer up her nakedness to the man she loves. (Winship, 2–3)

This passage highlights several important attributes of the erotic function of the women's magazine in the late twentieth century. Firstly, there are both fiction and non-fiction sources of sexual pleasure within the conventional layout of the women's magazine. The non-fiction elements include problem pages, advice, and information articles and quizzes which test a woman's romantic and sexual knowledge and predilections. These often allow women readers of all ages a vehicle for the discussion of sex and the exploration of their sexuality. They function as a way to communicate the sexual imaginary. (Until the 1990s this imaginary confined itself, in mass-market publications, largely to conventional, heterosexual sex). Fiction pieces contained within these magazines, at first often serialised but increasingly in short story form, often explore the ground between sexual desire and the myth of romance in creating erotic fantasies for women and girls.

In her landmark article, "Pornography for Women is Different," Ann Barr Snitow discusses the tension between romance (the emotional excitement involved in "catching a man") and sexual fullfillment in regards to mass-market paperbacks aimed at heterosexual women. More accurately, she argues that romance and sexual excitement are one and the same thing for women, that the negotiation of social structures of gender and the social function of womanhood must be addressed in order for women to find sexual pleasure within fiction. Therefore the heroines of heterosexual, mass-market fiction (in magazines as well as paperback books) are often caught up in the desire for an inaccessible man, between the needs of their self-respect and good social standing as women and their desire for sex. Sex is thus often delayed and the majority of the story involves the anticipation and negotiation through which the heroine is able to engage in the final sex act without guilt and achieve satisfactory orgasm. This anticipation and negoatiation are part of the sexual pleasure of these texts. Snitow argues that romance is foreplay for the women who read this fiction. The crux of Snitow's argument is that

in a sexist society we have two pornographies, one for men, one for women. They both have, hiding within them, those basic human expressions of abandon.... The pornography for men enacts this abandon on women as objects. How different is the pornography for women, in which sex is bathed in romance, diffused, always implied rather than enacted at all. (Snitow, 269)

Ann Snitow's use of the term pornography represented a radical step for a feminist scholar when the article was first published in 1979. A strong (though not universal) voice within the second wave feminist movement condemned pornography as inherently degrading to women. In particular, the involvement of violent fantasies in the pursuit of sexual pleasure was viewed with alarm and distrust. An issue of the American feminist women's magazine *MS.* (November 1978) attempted to discuss the representation of sex in women's erotic fiction and to articulate what would be acceptable within feminist politics. Gloria Steinem, founding editor of *MS.*, wrote an article for this issue which sought to delineate the difference between erotica and pornography and to articulate a framework for representations of sex which could give women readers and viewers pleasure without exposing them to images which would damage their newfound sense of empowerment.

Snitow's argument is open to attack on the grounds of its neat categorization of erotic literature according to the presumed gender and sexual orientation of readers, and its assumption that it can predict the uses to which readers will put a text. At the same time, it also ignores a range of publications which may be marketed at women, and/or have significant female readership, but are not commonly included in the category of women's fiction, or—for the purposes of this entry—women's magazines.

Since at least the ninenteenth century a number a mass-market, serial publications which do not fit into the commonly accepted defnition of women's magazines have offered erotic pleasure to women. These include so called pulp magazines like the American *True Confessions*, which in the guise of non-fiction offer any number of transgressive sexual fantasies for the pleasure of women readers. The advent of women's magazines like *MS.* in the United States and *Spare Rib* in the United Kingdom in the 1970s began to open up new ground in the sexual content of women's magazines. This in turn influenced more widely circulated publications.

Throughout the twentieth century the involvement of lesbians in the production of women's magazines has offered direction to women's magazines as they seek to expand the possibilities of erotic expression for women readers. The U.S. lesbian publication *On Our Backs,* which began publishing in the 1980s, offers an example of the kind of lesbian feminist sex magazine which arose in the late twentieth century throughout the United States and western and eastern Europe. These publications consciously defy second wave feminist distinctions between erotica and pornography and seek to encroach upon what has been seen as the male domain of transgressive pornography. Through fiction and visual spreads they offer sexual fantasy clearly aimed at women which seeks power through the breaking rather than the creating of taboo.

MEREDITH MILLER

Further Reading

Dancyger, Irene. A *World* of *Women: An Illustrated History of Women's Magazines.* Dublin: Gill and Macmillan, 1978.

McCracken, Ellen, *Decoding Women's Magazines: From Mademoiselle to MS.* Basingstoke: Macmillan, 1993.

Snitow, Ann Barr. 'Pornography for Women is Different.' *Powers of Desire: The Politics* of *Sexuality.* London: Virago, 1983, pp 258–275.

White, Cynthia. *Women's Magazines 1693–1968.* London: Joseph, 1970.

Winship, Janice. *Inside Women's Magazines.* London and New York: Pandora, 1987.

WOMEN'S WRITING: ANGLOPHONE, TWENTIETH CENTURY

Women's erotic writing in the twentieth century is a rich and varied literary phenomenon which is fundamentally engaged with the active challenging of women's social and political positions throughout the century. Erotic writing appears early in the century and much of its themes, forms, readership, and the debate surrounding its production and consumption parallel various historical developments. Historically, during the twentieth century there was consistent engagement with questions to do with women's rights as individuals, both legal political rights and their rights as sexual and reproductive beings. From the turn of the century, the idea and reality of the New Woman, a liberated, freethinking, intellectual version of women established in the late-nineteenth century, continued into the development of the suffragette movement and Marie Stopes' fight for women's rights to choose on issues of childbearing. Early erotic writing accompanied these developments so that the poetry of HD (Hilda Doolittle), some elements of Virginia Woolf's writing, erotic writing by lesbian and other literary modernists such as Djuna Barnes, established both topics and modes of expression on which those who followed them built. The historical changes of the twentieth century in the United Kingdom, the United States, and Australia/New Zealand, and that changing geographical construct the British Commonwealth, saw women gaining the vote, debates about the right to control their own sexual activity and reproduction, and a more general liberation of women's opportunities to write about their sexual desires, needs, and activities using the language and forms of erotic writing whether in explicit and focused work, or as part of acceptable expression in the full variety of poetry and prose.

The Politics of Erotica

For lesbians, the opportunity to write about the erotic was problematized for many years since love between women was unnamed or considered Sapphic (after Sappho the Latin poet) and perverse. If it was difficult for E.M. Forster to write of "the love that dare not speak its name" and homoeroticism during his own lifetime, (while some short stories were published, *Maurice*, his novel of homosexual love and the difficulties of conformity was published posthumously in 1970), it was so much more difficult for women whose sexual feelings and expressions were frequently misunderstood, denied, and overlooked in heterosexual contexts, let alone same-sex contexts. One result of silencing and distrust of expressions of sexuality, sexual desire, and the erotic was its codifying into other images, myths, motifs, symbols, so for some erotic writing, particularly in oppressive circumstances (whatever country and period) the reader must search in the discourse and narrative to discover the eroticism since it is suggested, hinted at, expressed covertly. The trial over the publication and distribution of D.H. Lawrence's *Lady Chatterley's Lover* in 1960 was then a significant moment for those writing of sexuality, sex, and the erotic. Censorship and the division between pornography and the erotic, notions of harm and freedom of speech and behavior all underlay this trial, and those who spoke up for the novel (such as E.M. Forster, Helen Gardner, and Raymond Williams) as often great literary figures were part of a changing moment in history. Another change in the opportunity to write, publish, and express the erotic came with the trial of Allen Ginsberg's long political and sexually charged Beat poem "Howl," which was banned in 1956, published abroad by fellow Beat Lawrence Ferlinghetti, so beginning his City Lights publishing venture. Legal moments such as these freed up writers of both genders to explore sexuality and sex in their works and to write erotic fiction. They contributed also to the recognition of the status of erotic writing as frequently more than sleazy pornography, but instead often the sexual political language which expressed an awareness of identity, as a sexual being, and as an individual and member of society. In this context and this respect, and using the theories of Foucault (1978) which link power and control to discourse and the expression of sexuality and identity, much erotic writing can be seen as an expression of individual liberty and identity. This is certainly one of the ways the Beat poets, particularly Diane di Prima used it, though it would be stretching the case to suggest all the authors and readers of, for example, the romances in the Black Lace series were making a decided blow for freedom throughout their pages. Erotic writing also sells well, and part of the enjoyment of it might be that it is still often rather frowned on—as sleazy porn.

Feminism and the Erotic

Major changes and liberating moments mid-century, the sexual revolution accompanying the contraceptive pill in the 1960s and second wave feminism, underpin a new explicitness in erotic writing and fuel women's claims to the right to explore and write about varieties of sexual choice, taste, experiences, and also fantasies. Debates and legislation of the century began to establish equal rights not only in terms of jobs (Equal Pay Act 1970), property ownership (Married Women's Property Act 1964), and marriage/divorce (Divorce Act 1969), but more broadly in terms of equal citizenship, which includes the recognition and expression of sexuality and the erotic.

Freedom to express a sense of liberated sexuality in erotic writing and reading might seem to be a logical creative step from the social, political, psychological, and biological liberation which women sought and to some extent achieved during the twentieth century. However, the situation of erotic literature is not so clear cut. It has been fundamentally intertwined with feminism's most outspoken and vitriolic debates concerning what could be seen as a sexual and erotic continuum but which has more often been argued as a polar opposition. The continuum commences at one end with freedom of expression, assertion of individual liberty to write and read according to taste and choice, celebration of the body, writing the body, and the recognition of the importance of expressing sensuality and acknowledging and expressing sexual desire. With this writing, these beliefs, there is a refusal of censorship as an outmoded insistence on restraining women's self awareness and expression, a dangerous limitation. At the other end of the continuum lies the recognition that pornography debases women and men (see Dworkin, 1981), and relates in many cases to a legitimization of violence against women, removing women's rights and individual expression. Some writers align the erotic with the pornographic, although others distinguish between the two largely in terms of issues of freedom of choice, that is, pornography degrades women and can be seen to turn women into objects for someone else's voyeuristic pleasure. In some cases, pornography is accompanied by violence against women. In other instances however, pornography can perhaps be seen as a shared construction, representation, and experience for men and women or women and women, and so there are no victims, only explicit sex and in many cases erotic expression. At the other end of the continuum, erotic expression in itself does not necessarily involve pornography but instead is a liberated exploration of sensuality, fantasy, experience, and pleasure. Anglophone women's writing is produced from any number of these positions and often the stages between them are blurred.

Angela Carter's much critiqued mid-century text *The Sadeian Woman* (1979), captures the flavor of this debate when she celebrates de Sade's creative, imaginative liberation of men and women's sexuality and their erotic selves while she also explores the fate of the two sisters, Justine and Juliette, indicating that one person's liberty could be another's suffering and oppression, and that status, money, language, power, and the relationships of these to gender are crucial in such a delicate balance. Michèle Roberts' *Flesh and Blood* (1995) explores similar territory considering erotic encounters between a range of characters notably a young girl "sold" by her father in marriage to an older wealthy rake, who, on meeting his decadent older mistress in the carriage on the way to their mansion, is expected to engage in a perverse threesome.

A key question of the century is how to engage creatively on a path which empowers and enables women's erotic expression in literature but which avoids falling into the trap of merely reproducing discourses and texts which fix women as someone else's sex object. A feminist argument here is that of subjectivity, and sexuality; the importance of the recognition, expression, and power of the individual subject, the recognition of individual and different subjectivities alongside actions which recognize individual and different sexualities. Much erotic writing by women in the century explores these debates, some has focused on developing what could be described as a feminist erotic, some a lesbian erotic, and some forms of erotic writing which appeal more to the general reader.

The issue of readership raises another debate within the production and consumption of erotic writing; its literary status as high and or popular art. In the latter part of the twentieth century, Black Lace books began to appear on the top shelf of the most popular magazine and bookshop chains, ironically perhaps, giving erotic tales by women for women the same position and status as "girlie" magazines for men, also on the top shelves. Meanwhile, other readers were beginning to reread the difficult, high art, and modernist or post-modernist writers, Virginia Woolf for example, and discovering what was overlooked in literary critical comment on her and other great writers' erotic vein.

Virginia Woolf (1882–1941)

> She was letting her imagination sweep unchecked around every rock and cranny of the world that lies submerged in the depths of our unconscious being... And then there was a smash. There was an explosion...The imagination had dashed itself against something hard. The girl was aroused from her dream. She was indeed in a state of the most acute and difficult distress. To speak without figure she had thought of something, something about the body, about the passions which it was unfitting for her as a woman to say. Men, her reason told her, would be shocked. The consciousness of what men will say of a woman who speaks the truth about her passions had roused her from her artist's state of unconsciousness. She could write no more. (Woolf, 1931)

Woolf here confronts and explores, enacts the erotic. She expresses erotic, possibly lesbian desire and the censoring reactions against its expression, poetically and rather straightforwardly indicating as she does, that which must not be recognized or spoken of, passion voiced, powerful, politicized. This is erotic writing and the immediate censorship is fundamentally linked to her right of expression as an artist and a woman. So in this light the piece is an articulation of the hidden sexual expression, the erotic, in social contexts, using and exposing the language which would suppress it, so highlighting how its expression is both highly personal and highly political, both in the arena of sexual and of wider social politics. Erotic writing of the kind produced by Woolf, in particular, is fundamentally linked to free expression and the freedom to develop one's sexuality, and of a piece with her other polemical but not erotic work, *A Room of One's Own, Three Guineas.*

Debates

Perhaps one of the problems ranged around the erotic and its recognition, acceptance, and variety, lies fundamentally with some of the issues upon which feminist theories and practices have been based, and on that very difficult (it sometimes seems) distinction between the erotic and the pornographic. The problem also lies with definitions, recognitions, and appreciations of the erotic, which will differ in relation to cultural context, visibility or invisibility, and reception and taste.

Pornography and the erotic have been linked culturally and historically, largely because the erotic is most frequently seen perhaps as a male preserve, and linked in its representation and construction with issues to do with power, and with pain. The difficulty of differentiating between pornography and the erotic and the moral lobby which surrounds any discussion of pornography threatens to hamper recognition, representation, and reading or appreciation of the erotic. In *Sex Exposed: Sexuality and the Pornography Debate* (Segal and Macintosh, 1992) there are several enlightening debates about these issues:

> Over and over again, what we read as women's testimony against pornography are stories of women coercively pressured into sex they do not want. But surely the harm we are hearing about cannot reside in the pornographic image, nor even the possibility for men enacting the practice they depict – ....The harm is contained in the social context which deprives the woman of her ability to reject any sexual activity she does not want. (Segal in Segal and Macintosh, 1992, p. 86)

Some of the questions we might have in discussing erotic writing by women and that are for or about women are:

> Would an erotica for women merely replicate that for men, with power over men as a key point? (if that is what is one key point in the erotics for men?)
>
> How far does the erotic/do erotics relate to relationships of power, whether partners are male or female? Does this matter?
>
> What kinds of beliefs, actions, and fantasies are involved in different versions of what is perceived to be erotic?

It is hardly surprising that "a women's erotica" is a challenging concept since it is difficult to be exact about what the genre encompasses.

In addition to aspects of feminism and postfeminism, the question of whether lesbian, bi-sexual, and heterosexual texts should be viewed under one heading of "women's erotica" is equally questioned. Contemporary erotica can be seen to be in the process of *becoming*, rather than in a fixed state of *being* (Bakhtin 1981, p. 7, Guattari, 1996).

Post-World War II Erotica

Kate Millett's polemical *Sexual Politics* (1977) commended the work of Jean Genet (1910–1986), for suggesting that sexuality is the "very prototype of institutionalized inequality" (Millet 1977, p. 20), which must alter in order to elude its quotidian or everyday existence. Utilizing theories of sexuality and power, in his play *The Balcony* (1957), Genet explores a pathology of virility,

> sexual congress as a *paradigm of power* over other human beings . . . His critique of the heterosexual politic points the way toward a true sexual revolution, a path which must be explored if any radical social change is to come about. In Genet's analysis, it is fundamentally impossible to change society without changing personality, and *sexual personality* as it has generally existed must undergo the most drastic overhaul. (Millet, 1977, p. 22)

Foucault helps us to read Genet here, recognizing a similarity in the argument about power controlling or enabling the expression of sexuality and the self.

Sexuality as a "paradigm of power" emerges as one of the most important factors in considering the postwar "sexual personality" which has undergone multiple psychological transformations. The current proliferation of women's erotic literature is evidence of a struggle to explore and express female sensuality. We might ask here whether and how "myths" of gender and sexuality have insinuated themselves into contemporary women's erotic texts.

In one respect we seem to have been enabled to recognize and reclaim the erotic for women, bringing into the light that which was taboo, and this is partly a cultural change. However, some of the aspects of that change might just be in different power relations and force different versions of desire on others and on us. The sixties and seventies peddled a liberation for women which confusingly coupled not only the demand for equality of pay and opportunity, but for sexual activity—and we don't need Germaine Greer to point out to us that this was a con which left many flower-power ladies of the canyon washing the nappies out while their men not only celebrated love and peace but some wilderness porn games as well. Margaret Atwood's *Surfacing* (1972), the books Maria Lauret considers in *It's My Party* (1994)—all show that this particular sexual revolution sold an ultimately painful and conformist lie (you had to have a man, several, then what?) to women of that generation and beyond. Was this erotics for women? For feminists? If it was, what would possibly be in it for us now that we have seen through it?

Lesbian or heterosexual, women have difficulties with the ways in which the erotic interfaces with structures and relationships of power. We also have difficulties sometimes in recognizing the erotic itself, as Bronwen Levy points out, because it is veiled, or does not appeal to our tastes.

As Bronwen Levy puts it:

Even recognising erotics when they are depicted may be a problem, let alone developing ways of adequately analysing the historical and cultural context of textual representations. ...Just what is erotic for women is a further important question. ...cultural questions, especially to do with sexual preference, but also to do with class, race, age, and so on, will need to be considered, so that the critic, rather than seeking erotica by a process of relatively straightforward identification or categorisation, as if to say, "now that's erotic," as if this is the last word, will need to rephrase her question: what, for different groups, might be erotic, "Now what is erotic? (Levy, 1992, p. 228)

Susannah Radstone comments in *Sweet Dreams:*

It has also been repeatedly and insistently argued of late, that in order to gain even a limited insight into the ways in which popular texts appeal to us, then the pleasures of those texts must be interrogated to reveal the ways in which they intertwine with the real concerns, needs, and desires of readers. Once however, it soon became apparent that an analysis which revealed only the conscious desires awoken, spoken to or fulfilled by particular genres would be limited by its inability to address the ways in which those genres speak to our unconscious as well as our conscious reading selves. (Radstone, 1988)

Radstone is suggesting here that we moved onto psychoanalytically informed readings. It is not always necessary to do this if we want to look at varieties of writing which deal with and relate to or represent feminist erotic(s) since some feminist writing is more overt:

In fiction the debate over what constitutes the erotic for women is to a large degree constructed by the capacities of various genres for various kinds of representation, as well as by the reading practices thereby encouraged. (Levy, 1992, p. 227)

A broader reading of what the erotic might mean comes from the essayist and poet Audre Lorde who traces the word back to its Greek roots *eros* born of Chaos, and celebratory of all things creative and harmonious. She says:

when I speak of the erotic, then, I speak of it as an assertion of the lifeforce of women, of that creative energy empowered, the knowledge and use of which we are now reclaiming in our language, our history, our dancing, our loving, our work, our lives. (Lorde, 1992, p. 80)

Celebration of the body and writing from the body relate to much of the erotic writing by and for feminists.

Jeanette Winterson, in her introduction to *Erotica: An Anthology of Women's Writing* (Reynolds, 1990), talks of pornography as men's control and ownership of women's bodies, whether women are earning or not through this. The book, she says:

seeks to return women to their bodies by offering a looking glass and not a distorting mirror. Here women can speak for themselves and by doing so deliver a valuable counter-argument to the lies, secrets, and silences that typically pass for a woman's sex-life. Redefining the erotic in terms of female rather than male experience is crucial to the pornography debate, not only to introduce some truth telling but also to remind those who want to protect and sanctify that censorship may replace one kind of gag with another. We don't want men to package us but we must have the freedom to describe ourselves. (Winterson, in Reynolds, 1990, p. xx)

It recognizes that nuance, suggestion, myth, and allegory are often the forms which women adopt in order to write of and in the erotic, and also that reception is a key factor. One person reads or receives as erotic what does not seem so to another. While the introduction tends to veer towards essentialism, stating that women are in tune with their bodies (all women?) and have different notions of the erotic, it does vindicate itself by recognizing taste and differences.

Women, unlike men, do not agree on the broadstream of what is sexy. I do not know whether it is a fact about women per se or whether it is a result of our fragmented inheritance. I do know that such a lively dispute takes us away from the monolithic tedium of male pornography. (Winterson, in Reynolds, 1990, p. xxii)

She argues that sex and titillation are not disturbing, and asks "can women arouse and engage without exploitation?" (Winterson, in Reynolds, 1990, p. xxii) Her views on the erotic are closely related to those of:

Erotica consists of those portraits which are used honestly and with love. This explains why one woman's pornography is another woman's erotics. (Reynolds, 1990, p xxix)

In considering the erotic, there are other issues beyond those of censorship and pornography. One very clear problem is taste. Trying to discover and define what is erotic and then discuss it with others and expect some kind of a consensus is fraught with difficulties. As a topic among friends and colleagues it is more likely to cause disruption and disagreement than politics and religion ever will. It is just this kind of response which I have found in the various collections of self acclaimed erotic writing by and for feminists, (*Moments of Desire*, Hawthorne and Pausacker, 1989; *Erotica*, Reynolds, 1990) and critical discussion of what the erotic and a more traditional, conventional, or feminist erotic might be, what it is for, and what kinds of sexual politics they engage with.

Sappho, George Sand, Colette, and Aphra Benn are seen by Winterson as the "good time" grandmothers of a feminist erotica. An exploration of a range of individual women writers and some themes within women's erotic writing follows.

Anais Nin (1903–1977)

Nin was born of artist parents in Paris and at age 11 started her lifelong diary. She spent her teenage years in New York with her mother, married artist and banker Hugh Guiler in 1923 and had a number of affairs, living a largely bohemian lifestyle. Her earliest published works were the surrealist *House of Incest* (1936) and the novelette *Winter of Artifice* (1939). In 1944, she wrote the infamous sexual fantasies which were in 1977 collected into *Delta of Venus: Erotica* and *Little Birds* (1979). Her novel sequence *Cities of the Interior* came out in 1959. Feminists took up her cause in the 1970s

when her unexpurgated seven volume diary was published posthumously as *The Journal of Love* (first volume in 1986). Her life was one of sexual experiment, performance, and record.

Anais Nin discovered the taboo on women's sexual feelings and more particularly on their expression of these feelings when her erotic writing from the 1940s was published in 1976. Noting differences between her own and male sexual expressions, she attributed the male with explicitness and gusto, the female with ambiguity and poetry arguing:

The true liberation of eroticism lies in accepting the fact that there are a million facets to it, a million forms of eroticism, a million objects of it, situations, atmospheres, and variations. We have, first of all, to dispense with guilt concerning its expansion, then remain open to its surprises, [and] varied expressions . . . (Nin, 1992, p. 9).

An avant-garde writer, Nin studied psychology and famously wrote erotica for a dollar a page. In her article entitled "Eroticism in Women" (1974), she noted "the erotic writings of men do not satisfy women" (Nin, 1992, p. 6), and as men and women have different erotic fantasies it is "time we wrote our own" (ibid.). Her comment on the difference between pornography and erotica is that "[p]ornography treats sexuality grotesquely to bring it back to the animal level/Eroticism arouses sensuality without this need to animalize it." (ibid. p. 7).

Djuna Barnes (1892–1982)

Djuna Barnes, 1892–1982, born in America, Barnes lived and wrote largely in Paris and the United Kingdom. A modernist in style and a Bohemian in lifestyle, she mixed with journalists and expatriates, with Natalie Barney's lesbian group, whom she satirises in *Ladies Almanac*, 1928. Her greatest work is based on the doomed and bizarre relationships she had with actor Thelma Wood, whose dark wanderings and promiscuity form the basis of characterization and action in *Nightwood* (1936), published by TS Eliot. The novel's spokesperson, Matthew O'Connor, is based on a real life doctor, an underworld character. The novel refuses the continuities of character and narrative, scene and reality, and is located in the imagination as much as the streets. It evokes an eroticized nightmarish world of transvestism, lesbian and multiple affairs, identity blurring, and dangerous desires.

Pauline Réage (1907–1998)

Réage's *The Story of O* (1954), has caused great controversy, sitting as it does on the borderline between being erotic or pornographic. In its portrayal of a traditional male fantasy of a totally submissive woman/slave who becomes a commodified object of value between men (in particular, René and Sir Stephen) it offers no erotic liberty for women but confirms the unpleasantness of some male-authored pornography. Angela Carter argues in *The New Statesman* (1975):

> A piece of comment I once read about that monstrous book, *The Story of O*, suggested that only a woman could have written it because of some curious metaphor about, I think, curlers, somewhere in the book . . . but it seemed to me that *The Story of O*, bore all the stigmata of male consciousness, not least in that details about clothes are just the sort of thing a man would put into a book if he wanted the book to read as though it had been written by a woman. (Carter 1982b, pp. 207–208).

However, James Marriott (editor, Nexus Publishing—owned by Virgin Publishing) confirms that Pauline Réage is now an elderly woman living in an old people's home in France. Since *The Story of O: Part Two* (1969), shorter, more prosaic, less elaborately stylized and more aware of the realities of pain and venereal disease is so different from its predecessor, it is possible they have two different authors. "O" is left to choose between remaining at the Roissy château/brothel and returning to the outside world, leaving us to consider whether she now seems free, or still imprisoned in her role.

Erica Jong (1942–)

Erica Jong is the author of eight novels including *Fear of Flying* (1973); *Fanny, Being the True History of the Adventures of Fanny Hackabout-Jones* (1980); *Shylock's Daughter (* formerly titled *Serenissima)* (1987); *Inventing Memory: A Story of Mothers and Daughters* (1997), and *Sappho's Leap* (2003). Several of her novels have been worldwide bestsellers. Her other books include the non-fiction works *Fear of Fifty: A Midlife Memoir* (1995); *The Devil at Large: Erica Jong on Henry Miller* (1994); *Witches* (1981); *What Do Women Want* (1998), and six

volumes of poetry. (*About Erica Jong*, www.ericajong.com/abouterica.htm) *Fear of Flying* (1973), *Parachutes & Kisses* (1984), and *Sappho's Leap* (2003) are erotic novels. She won the United Nations Award for Excellence in Literature (1998) and the Sigmund Freud Award for Literature (1975).

In 1973, *Fear of Flying* explicitly explored women's sexuality. On publication it was praised by such prominent writers as John Updike and Henry Miller. In *The New Yorker* Updike wrote of the novel's "class, sass, brightness, and bite," noting that "[Chaucer's] Wife of Bath, were she young and gorgeous, neurotic and Jewish, urban and contemporary, might have written like this," while Henry Miller in the *New York Times*, predicted "this book will make literary history, that because of it women are going to find their own voice and give us great sagas of sex, life, joy, and adventure." *The Wall Street Journal* argued it "transcends being a woman's book and becomes a latter-day Ulysses, with a female Bloom stumbling and groping, but surviving." (*More About Erica Jong*, www.ericajong.com/abouterica2.htm)

Jong's work both entertains and illuminates the needs, desires, and rights of women (*More About Erica Jong*, www.ericajong.com/abouterica2.htm)

Anne Rice (1941–)

Anne Rice is best known for her *Interview with the Vampire* (1976) filmed with Tom Cruise and Brad Pitt in 1994, but she has also published works of erotica. As Anne Rampling she has published two erotic books *Exit to Eden* and *Belinda*, though *Belinda* has less of a raw erotic tone than does *Exit*, and is more of a romance involving an older man and a teenage girl. Under the pen name A.N. Roquelaure, she wrote the Beauty series, *The Claiming of Sleeping Beauty* (1983), *Beauty's Punishment* (1984), *Beauty's Release* (1985), a trilogy of erotic novels with the same vividness and level of intensity as her other works.

Rouquelaure was a cloak designed by Count Rouqelaure in the eighteenth century, and Anne used it because of its meaning—"Anne under a cloak"—as well as for its erotic sound.

> "I love being a controversial writer. It's only in a free, open marketplace where people can develop," – Anne Rice

The Beauty trilogy sparked controversy when the Columbus Metropolitan Library (Ohio) removed the books from the shelves and banned them following a complaint. The library then defined them as hard core S&M pornography, but when asked to produce their written definition of "pornography," the library's director, Larry Black, admitted that he did not have one. (*Erotic Writings of Anne Rice*, http://www.empirezine.com/spotlight/rice/rice-erotica-of.htm)

Anne Rice's *Interview with the Vampire* (1976) rejects the images and language of disgust, repulsion, and loathing to be found in Bram Stoker, and uses instead the language of the erotic to describe the vampire Lestat's draining of Louis, and Louis of Claudia and others, the strongest and chosen of whom are then turned by this draining and re-filling with the vampire's own blood into a vampire themselves. While Louis hates Lestat for this act which condemns him to be a child of the night himself, destined to feed on small animals, and people, nevertheless the first person description of this and other acts of vampirism is languorous, intense, hypnotic, ecstatic. Louis, turning Claudia's woman friend Madeleine (a favorite vampiric name) into a vampire, by their mutual request, enables both of them to soar (literally in the film) to amazing heights of passion and new life. It is a compellingly eroticized description:

> She gasped as I broke the flesh, the warm current coming into me, her breasts crushed against me, her body arching up, helpless, from the couch. And I could see her eyes, even as I shut my own, see that taunting, provocative mouth. I was drawing on her, hard, lifting her, and I could feel her weakening, her hands dropping limp at her sides, 'Tight, tight' I whispered, 'look at it! 'Her heart was slowing, stopping and her head dropped back from me on the velvet, her eyes dull to the point of death........I felt the gentle pressure of her mouth, and then her hands closing tight on the arm as she began to suck. I was rocking her, whispering to her trying desperately to break my swoon; then I felt her powerful pull. Every blood vessel felt it, I was threaded through and through with her pulling, my hand holding fast to the couch now, her heart beating fierce against my heart, her fingers digging deep into my arm, my outstretched palm. (Rice, 1976, p. 292)

It is a mutual exchange of near death swooning, and life-giving passions, traditional erotic ingredients. The rhythm of the language involves the reader in this powerful exchange, all encompassing and life dominating as Madeleine takes blood from Louis in return.

Anna Couani (1948–)

Australian author Anna Couani's erotic monologue in *Moments of Desire* (Hawthorne and Pausacker, 1989) depends on writing and revelling in the body. Her work consistently uses a flow of writing, monologues of trapped housewives afraid to leave the house unless they check and counter-check all the windows, and here a celebration of self/orgasm:

> The map of the world if felt from the inside. Rough around the coastlines and smooth over the hills and sand dunes. Warm and moist through the rivers which lead outside to the forests like long hair then sparser like shorter more bristly hair.

> Flying low but fast across the land masses. Make yourself feel like the world. As old but not as troubled. (Couani in Hawthorne and Pausacker, 1989)

The rhythms of this piece are fluid, repetitive, and the imagery concentrates on equating the woman/self, each part of the body part of a living whole, with the world, its oceans and its curves. This woman is returning descriptions of herself as a natural force, a natural being, to their rightful owner, herself, rather than the traditional male poet/lover who would see her from the outside, not the inside. She refuses to be the object of male gaze. "The map of the world if felt from the inside" gives back women's bodies as organic and natural, to themselves/ourselves for our own subjective experience, and it is a positive experience. You end up as a world/like the world and yet not as troubled and suffering. The piece explores and enacts self recognition and celebration.

Kathy Acker (1947–1997)

Beat-influenced Kathy Acker is a radical writer who exposes social and romantic lies about women's roles and lack of power. Stream of consciousness reproduces the inner thoughts and feelings most of which would be far too sanitized by the formality of conventional fiction, even more conventional prose poetry. Kathy Acker in *The Adult Life of Toulouse Lautrec by Henry Toulouse Lautrec* (1975) manages to mix her modes of writing and response. She gets inside the graffiti culture and critiques it, while celebrating the erotic and its freedoms. She is radical and critical in her awareness of the dangers inherent in forgetting self, others, poverty, the sickness of the street and living rough in a capitalist society of which street-based teenage lovers are an indictment, on which they are like a running sore. But she also envelopes the reader, draws you in with the second person invocation "you" and involves you in the rhythms and the overwhelming nature of the sexual embrace of the lovers, Marcia and Scott, who forget their poverty, and so ultimately are both escapees from it and its victims:

> being wet and dark with women.
> Being touched and being able to know the person will touch you again. (Acker, 1975)

Kathy Acker's work is always confrontational. While she explores the fantasies of the erotic and its other overwhelming powers of sexual desire, lust, love, showing them to be an explosive force upsetting all the old-world lies and values, she still shows how such desires and dreams can be a very insidious part of a sick society in which the individual has no place, and where money and power politics rule, all sexual relationships are destructive, and the only real response left is graffiti—a radical written refusal and taunt.

Foucault is clear about the policing of desire through discourse and the socially conformist, repressive ends this serves. Kathy Acker, developing the energies of the Beat generation into post-punk feminism, exposes the lies fed through politics and conventionality, aligning cultural insight and critique with the explosiveness of desire, the transgressive power of the erotic.

> Every position of desire, no matter how small, is capable of putting to question the established order of a society; not that desire is asocial; on the contrary, but it is explosive; there is no desiring-machine capable of being assembled without demolishing entire social sections. (Acker, 1984, p. 125)

One of the most destructive forces in the world is love: "Love can tear anything to shreds" (Acker, 1984, p. 125). This writing overtly politicizes the erotic, uses the same kinds of rhythms as the more personal, celebratory writing, but determinedly makes a claim for the erotic as an arena of power politics and sexual controls. Denials, suppression, repression, and lies are exposed and indicted, and

both erotic writing and graffiti are the vehicle for this.

Audre Lorde (1934–1992)

African American lesbian writer Audre Lorde widens the definition of the erotic as a celebration of woman's life-force, an empowerment: "the erotic is the nurturer or nursemaid of all our deepest knowledge." (Lorde, 1992) For her the interpretation is essential and broad, the erotic is directly related to a sense of joyousness, celebration, self recognition, and enjoyment of many different activities, not just the sexual.

> Another important way in which the erotic connection functions is the open and fearless underlining of my capacity for joy. In the way my body stretches to music and opens into response, hearkening to its deepest rhythms, so every level upon which I sense also opens to the erotically satisfying experience, whether it is dancing, building a bookcase, writing a poem, examining an idea........That self connection shared is a measure of the joy which I know myself to be capable of feeling. (Lorde, 1992, p. 81)

Erotic knowledge is empowerment. It stops us from being docile and suppressing truths, and for Audre Lorde it is also a matter of recognizing self in woman-identified relationships. But this is not the only way to reach the erotic. Audre Lorde's celebration of the erotic then is a broad one which recognizes self and others, joy, and power. It is in relation to this kind of version of the erotic that Alice Walker's politicized *Possessing the Secret of Joy* (1992) can be read. Audre Lorde's statement about the power of the erotic is central to Walker's novel:

> in touch with the erotic, I become less willing to accept powerlessness, or those other supplied states of being which are not native to me, such as recognition, despair, self-effacement, depression, self-denial. (Lorde, 1992, p. 82)

Lorde asks how Black women can seize and recognize an erotica which enables them to be anything other than wild objects? She asks:

> So how do we speak of our desires for each other to each other in a language where our relationships to our bodies and desires lack dignity as well as nuance? (Lorde, 1992, p. xx)

> What are our names and the touch taste of our bodies? Where do our tongues linger on each other and

what is the nature of the language we speak? (Lorde, 1992. p. xx)

What she claims are present in the collection are owned by the producers, there is no recognition of the difficulties of reception really here, but the celebration is lively and rich.

Here in these stories we are not myths and stereotypes, art forms or sex objects. We are simply folks at intimate play; our fierce rhythms of desire, the exotic unencumbered by the ' other ' close and hot. (Lorde, 1992, p. xx)

Any investigation of a Black erotics by White writers and readers steers close to the imperialistic appropriation of later nineteenth-century travel and exploration narratives as well as those fictions of colonial power which consistently represented Black women in particular as equitable with a nature which needed taming, redefining, but whose lush tropical pleasures could be revelled in in the meantime, prior to that necessary civilizing taming. This notion builds on Freud's use of the term "dark continent" (1953) to signify female sexuality. Audre Lorde enters the debate and differentiates between pornography and the erotic:

Pornography is a direct denial of the power of the erotic, for it represents the suppression of true feeling. (Lorde, 1992)

The difference between eroticism and pornography is the difference between celebratory and masturbatory sex. (Marcuse, 1955)

Alice Walker (1944–)

Alice Walker's *Possessing the Secret of Joy* (1992) is overtly political. It focuses directly on the suppression and oppression of women's sexuality and their erotic lives and in so doing raises key issues of cultural context, difference, and the censorship/pornography/erotica debate.

However, Alice Walker treads on dangerous ground as a westernized Afro-American intellectual investigating the cultural practices of Africa (Wisker, 1994), clitoridectomy, surely a practice which ensures the denial of an erotic life for women. Her recognition of her roots as well as the comparability if not actual identicality of oppressive practices in the United States, Europe can nonetheless be labeled a kind of post-colonial imperialist appropriation: her superiority of developed culture, especially in the accompanying book (Walker and Parma, 1993) and "Arena"

program "Warrior Marks," casting the critique of this traditional, horrific practice in the light of the culturally "primitive." Celebration of a denied and hidden erotic is powerful, however, if we look at the seizing of individuality, sexual empowerment by women in the stories of African American women writers including Walker.

Women's rights to an erotic element in their lives is politicized in *Possessing the Secret of Joy* (1992) where Tashi's discovery of the politicized nature of genital mutilation and denial of women's power and erotic lives, comes when she recalls that as a child she heard the (male) elders under a tree recounting a myth intended to explain how to deter women's active sexuality. Tashi's metaphorical liberation takes place sadly only at her death when she, having recalled, challenged, and undercut the myth of repression of women's sexuality, the queen ant myth, destroys the national heroine M'Lissa who performs the genital mutilation (clitoridectomy) underlying the myth, the outward show of the repression. Tashi understands her own sexuality and that of other repressed, mutilated women, not merely of the Olinka, her own village, but of westernized societies adopting both genital mutilation in the name of purity and order, and oppression of women in a more general fashion.

Ntozake Shange (1948–)

Poet, prose, and drama writer Ntozake Shange frequently explores the erotic lives of her characters such as the protagonist in *Liliane* (1995) who grows away from the middle class expectations of her parents, and the increasing stifling of her boyfriend to find a newly liberated erotic self. An erotic self is linked with achievement of freedom and identity as Liliane realizes, "The freedom you wage your most serious battle for is your very own mind." (1995, p. 44) Using an alternation between first and third person narrative, Shange has artist Liliane learning to speak out, against racism and the denigration of her boyfriend. When he criticizes her "labia boxes" art she retaliates and finds her own identity, developing eroticized language, recalling sensual affairs.

African American Erotica

There are considerably more complex problems around the definitions of a Black feminist erotics which are not engaged with fully in the introduction to *Erotique Noire* by Ntozake Shange (1992). This might well be because the book is centrally about Black erotica rather than Black female/feminist erotica or because there is no sense of a problematizing of female erotica in relation to male, just the celebration of a black erotics. While she certainly acknowledges the difficulties of Afro-American women, and Latin American women consistently appropriated by a White male gaze throughout time, their bodies used as commodities, exploited, degraded, and devalued, she also recognizes that the myths surrounding Black men and women are jungle myths—a version of the Black as perpetually hot and lustful which itself denigrates Black men and women.

More African American writers, male and female, are devoting books to eroticism in the African American context. Reginald Martin's new book, *Dark Eros: Black Erotic Writings: An Anthology*, (1997) is part of a Black erotica movement developing round Martin, a professor of English at the University of Memphis who argues that while Black erotica resides mainly in pop and hip-hop lyrics concerning sexuality, its expression is growing in literature and art. Gail E. Wyatt, sex therapist and author of *Stolen Women: Reclaiming Our Sexuality, Taking Back Our Lives* (1998), says that talk about erotica is premature: "We need to understand our own sexuality before we can understand erotica." Wyatt suggests the African-American community ask itself one important question: What is erotic to us? The poetry, fiction, and essays contained in this urban anthology follow *Erotique Noir/Black Erotica* (1992), by Martin, Miriam DeCosta-Willis, and Roseann P. Bell, which sold 150,000 copies and is cited in the publishing world as a pioneer in Black erotica. While *Erotique Noir* features the writings of African-American, Latin-American, and Caribbean-American men and women, *Dark Eros* is a collection of erotic writings by African Americans only.

Martin enabled young writers to write from their own experiences and imagination, so cultivating erotica with fresh angles. "Black sexuality has never been properly written about," he says. "Instead, what you had was a white view of sexuality." A stereotype which figured African Americans as sex obsessed. (James L. Dunn Jr., 1997).

Female novelists Zane, Shonda Cheekes, JD Mason, and Eileen M. Johnson have each written erotic novellas for *Blackgentlemen.com* (2002) a Web site for African-American bachelors who hope to find love. The novellas, about women who meet men from the site are *Duplicity* and *Delusions* by Zane; *Lessons Learned* by Shonda Cheekes; *Your Message Has Been Sent*, JD Mason; and *The Adventures of the Bold and Bourgeois* Eileen M. Johnson (*Blackgentlemen.com*, Maryland: Strebor Books).

Zane

"Porn is just straight sex. My books have a story. If I took the sex out of it, you'd still have the story," says Zane ('Little black books,' *The Guardian*, Saturday September 18, 2004. www.guardian.co.uk/week endstory/0,3605,1305854,00.html)

Author of erotic novels including *Breaking the Cycle* (2005), *Afterburn* (2005), and *Addicted* (2001), Zane is a bestselling popular fiction author specializing in Black erotic fiction. Zane retains her anonymity.

'Zane is to urban erotica what J.K Rowling is to children's fiction' (Kalyn Johnson, 'Zane, Inc.'). She has much more on her mind than black erotica. Behind the best-selling author's pseudonym is a shrewd businesswoman, astute publishing entrepreneur and – oh, yes – a wife and mother of four.' (*Black Issues Book Review*, September–October 2004, v6, i5, p. 17, (3))

Widely translated into Japanese, Danish, and Greek ('Little Black Books,' *The Guardian*, Saturday September 18, 2004. www.guardian.co.uk/weekendstory/0,3605,1305854,00.html) and having sold more than two and a half million books, Zane, who began writing out of boredom, producing an erotic legal-based short story thriller, "First Night," which first gained acclaim as it traveled round her friends, has entered a hugely lucrative world in which the central theme—sex—is universal. Her characters, plotlines, and language belong to black America. She says:

Pity the Japanese translator who had to offer a faithful rendition of: "No matter how hoochie I tried to be, she out-hoochied me every single time. She had on a skin-can't-get-no-tighter-unless-you-embed-the-clothes-in-your-ass-tight black sundress and some black leather pumps." ('Little black books,' *The Guardian*, Saturday September 18, 2004. www.guardian.co.uk/weekendstory/0,3605,1305854,00.html)

Zane's books and those of her contemporaries are part of a newly resurgent genre in which middle-class African-American women work and play hard, asserting both financial and sexual independence, hectic jobs, and frantic love lives.

> In February came *Cosmopolitan Girls*, by Charlotte Burley and Lyah Beth LeFlore, currently in its second printing, in which the two main characters bond over cocktails and the woes of work and family in New York. *Sexual Healing*, by Jill Nelson, is about two women in San Francisco who set up a sex spa in Nevada offering male prostitutes. And there is *Bling*, by Erica Kennedy, about a young woman from Ohio who nets a recording contract in New York and mixes it with hip-hop's elite. ('Little black books,' *The Guardian*, Saturday September 18, 2004. www. guardian.co.uk/weekendstory/0,3605,1305854,00. html)

Themes developed here can be described as ''chicklit,'' also seen in the work of Helen Fielding, (*Bridget Jones' Diary*, 1996), Terry McMillan's *Waiting To Exhale* (1992), and *How Stella Got Her Groove Back* (1996), Bebe Moore Campbell's work, and that of rapper and broadcaster Sister Souljah with her novel *The Coldest Winter Ever* (1999).

These works range from the highly raunchy to the everyday, blending concerns with race, sex, and class in a world where Black lives and ways are central, in Black neighborhoods, where folk listen to Black music.

In 1999, Zane set up an e-zine with dirty jokes, stories, and sex advice: www.eroticanoir. com. She sent people extracts for which they paid, published her first collection of short stories called *The Sex Chronicles: Shattering the Myth* (1991) herself, then used Black distributors to get her books out to street stalls and Black bookstores, where they were noticed.

Poppy Z Brite (1967–)

Poppy Z Brite, who has variously been an exotic dancer and Goth, has a number of gay-themed erotic horror stories (collected in *Swamp Foetus*, 1993, *Lost Souls*, 1992, *Drawing Blood*, 1993, and *Exquisite Corpse*, 1996) which show a fascination with vampirism, necrophilia, and the lost lower-middle class post-Vietnam war youth generation of rock bands, deserted children, and drug addicts. Their often bizarre, fetishized relationships combine the sexually rapacious and the

deadly. Her eroticism is dark, appearing in the vampire exchange or devouring which usually leads to death. She identifies our fascination with vampires as a metaphor for transgression.

The vampire is everything we love about sex and the night and the dark dream-side of ourselves: adventure on the edge of pain, the thrill to be had from breaking taboos (Brite, 1994) and in her tales homoerotic exchanges (for the most part) frequently presage unpleasant deaths. Her exquisite, visceral language is at its best in "His Mouth will taste of wormwood" which traces the decadent adventures of Howard and Louis in New Orleans. They drink the outlawed absinthe for "the treasures and the pleasures of the grave," moving beyond sex, drugs, fetid skulls, and all manner of erotic involvements, to a fatal, erotic fascination with death:

> Louis and I, you see, were dreamers of a dark and restless sort...both of us were dissatisfied with everything. We drank straight whiskey and declared it too weak. We took strange drugs, but the visions they brought us were of emptiness, mindlessness, slow decay. The books we read were dull....For a time we distracted ourselves with carnality...When we had exhausted the possibilities of women we sought those of our own sex, craving the androgynous curve of a boy's cheekbone, the molten flood of ejaculation invading our mouths. Eventually we turned to one another, seeking the thresholds of pain and ecstasy no one else had been able to help us attain. (Brite, "His mouth will taste of wormwood," 1993, p. 55)

Eroticism here is mixed with perversity and death.

Black Lace Books

Black Lace books are erotic novels for women about women by women (on the whole) and could be perceived as either the prey of myth or as attempts towards creating artificial myths.

Launched in 1993, as an experiment to a blaze of media attention. (About Black Lace, www. virginbooks.com/go/sp/InfoPageErotic_46.html) the explicit Black Lace books explore female sexuality, sexual fantasy, and erotica in a contemporary setting. Over 300 Black Lace books have been published in several different languages including Japanese and Czech. Recent books include *Bedding the Burglar* (2004) by Gabrielle Marcola and *Wild in the Country* (2003) by Monica Belle.

Black Lace books are unashamedly explicit and have explored areas of sexual fantasy where other women's erotica has feared to tread. With many of the books exploring the experimental side of sex, they've attracted considerable attention (*About Black Lace*, www.virginbooks.com/go/sp/InfoPageErotic_46.html).

They have now published over 250 titles, sold over three million books, and been translated into languages as diverse as Japanese and Czech. "These days, as many women as men are reading and writing porn fiction and feeling very comfortable with what has traditionally been seen as a male-only preserve." Notes the site, define the books as "Upbeat contemporary stories with loads of outrageous sex" (*About Black Lace*, www.virginbooks.com/go/sp/InfoPageErotic_46.html).

They are "escapist fiction, not instruction manuals. Every novel starts with the statement: Black Lace novels are sexual fantasies. In real life always practise safe sex" (*About Black Lace*, www.virginbooks.com/go/sp/InfoPageErotic_46.html).

The logo which is displayed on all "Black Lace" books declares them to be "erotic fiction written by women for women" (although anecdotal evidence suggests that men read them too). Lengthy guidelines to prospective authors are creatively proscriptive, and many of their plots are based on traditional male pornographic writing. So in de Sade the despicable Dubourg refers to masculine power in explaining to the young Justine, "here on earth, my child, nothing but what brings in gain or insures power is accounted" (Sade, 1991, p. 470). Paradoxically, sadomasochism is a common theme in Black Lace novels and the influence of the writings of the Marquis de Sade are firmly embedded in them. Roland Barthes argues that Sadeian writing is not in itself erotic:

> But what is eroticism? It is never more than a word, since practices cannot be so coded unless they are known, i.e., spoken; now our society never utters any erotic practice, only desires, preliminaries, contexts, suggestions, ambiguous sublimations, so that, for us eroticism cannot be defined save by a perpetually elusive word. On this basis, Sade is not erotic. . . (Barthes, 1977, p. 26).

The books contain varying degrees of pornography, and belong to the "popular fiction"/"low art" end of the erotic fiction spectrum. In her paper, "From Ann Radcliffe to Black Lace: Female Gothic for the 1990s," Laura Kranzler explores the influences of de Sade.

> . . . I would suggest that many Black Lace books derive their plots [from the Marquis de Sade], but they do so with an emphasis on a woman's experience of sexuality within a libertine narrative. (Kranzler 1997, p. 1).

While typically patriarchal literary devices are appropriated in these texts, they are often used to empower women. In *Silken Chains*, Abbie notes

> . . . possession wasn't love. It was domination. And while domination in his [Leon Villiers'] fantasy world was something she found acceptable to the point of delirious excitement, in real life there should be equal respect on both sides. (Nicol, 1997, p. 216).

Erotica for women is now seen as a valid genre as Kerri Sharp, Black Lace editor notes In her introduction to *Pandora's Box*, a Black Lace anthology:

> . . . [Women's] fantasies haven't always met the approval of the media . . . Articles began to appear with shock headlines like *Women Writers betray their own sex* and *Is this really the fantasy of British women?* . . . Things have improved over the past couple of years but it seems that we've still got a long way to go before we get to a sex-tolerant society which isn't riddled with double standards. (Sharp, 1996: vii–viii).

Owned by Virgin Publishing (owned by Richard Branson) popular Black Lace plots and topics include necromancy, vampirism, fairytales, mythology, and witchcraft, from heterosexuality, lesbianism, homosexuality, bi-sexuality, fetishism, and sadomasochism. Reviews problematize some of these sexual preferences where otherwise socially liberated women seem to want to be dominated. However the series and collection are popular and provide a glimpse into a new culture of erotic tales written by women for women.

Susie Bright (1958–)

Born in March, 1958, Susie Bright is an author, editor, performer, and educator who has written and directed several erotic stories including *How to Write a Dirty Story*, 2002, *SexWise*, 1995, and the journal *Herotica*, 10th Anniversary Edition, with an afterword by the editor, 1998.

JD Mason

JD Mason was born in Paris, Texas and lives in Denver. She is author of *Don't Want No Sugar* (2004) and *One Day I Saw a Black King* (2003).

Susannah Indigo

Susannah Indigo is a writer and editor of erotic fiction. Her novels include *Oysters Among Us* (2001), and *Going Mad from Roses* (2000). Susannah Indigo is the editor-in-chief of *Clean Sheets Magazine*—an online weekly erotic zine.

Mary Anne Mohanraj (1971–)

Mary Anne Mohanraj was born in Sri Lanka in 1971. She moved with her family when she was two years old to Connecticut and attended the University of Chicago. Her erotic novels include *Aqua Erotica: 18 Stories for a Steamy Bath* (2000) *Bodies in Motion* (2005), *Wet: More Aqua Erotica* (2002).

Portia Da Costa

In *Gothic Blue,* Portia Da Costa's plot is Gothic, set in an isolated priory, with freak weather conditions, and a (230-year-old) hero who should long since be dead, a heroine whose life is endangered, magic, sexuality, and humor. But it is clichéd: when Belinda describes 'her sex felt empty and in need of male possession' (Da Costa, 1996, p. 23), and 'his cock was a rod of iron now' (ibid., p. 42).

Laura Kranzler

Dr. Laura Kranzler is an academic whose *The Name of an Angel* is very different from the usual Black Lace style. While she works within the publishing guidelines, she has written an erotic novel considering complicated gender issues and using many literary allusions. The central character, Clarissa Cornwall, an English Literature lecturer regularly attends the gym and conducts an affair with one of her students. She has a "strong, curvy and voluptuous" body, (Thornton [Kranzler], 1997, p. 3). Her course is "Representations of the Erotic."

Clarissa's affair with one of her young students, Nicholas St Clair, is set off by her reading John Donne's "The Flea" in class.

The relationship is taboo, experimental, and Clarissa has more emotional responses than many Black Lace heroines. She is herself actually writing a book on erotic literature—very self reflexive and intertextual, but subject to some of the same defences that Kranzler herself has had to construct with her university colleagues:

> "It is *not* a dirty book,' Clarissa snorted defensively, then added somewhat pretentiously, 'It's a post-modernist, post-structuralist, post-foundationalist analysis of the representation of the erotic, and it's on its way to my editor even as we speak. Don't mock this weighty tome . . . I need this book to be really great or I may not have a job here next term'' (Thornton, 1997, p. 103).

She visits a Gothic, sadomasochistic cellar club called 'Glory Box,' derived from descriptions in the Marquis de Sade where normally restrained colleagues enact sadomasochistic fantasies.

One dowdy Monica Talbot is dressed in:

> . . . a black mask across the top half of her face, conical breasts atop a black leather-and-metal corset, fishnet stockings gartered up over her plump white thighs, and fetishistic black patent leather boots with cruelly pointed toes and impossibly high heels (Thornton, 1997, p. 3).

Candace Bushnell (1959–)

The highly popular TV series based on the novels by Bushnell, *Sex and the City*, both reinforces the sense that women are unable to sustain an intelligent conversation, and depict them searching for and bedding a variety of men in ways more common among groups of male friends. Sexual olympics and a challenging attitude make the series entertaining, liberating in some respects, erotic and sexually lively, but also reinforce some rather more conservative relationships in the end.

Writing the Body

Writing the body has given feminists an opportunity for erotic writing which fulfils Audre Lorde's desires that the erotic be celebratory of all living. It has also enabled women to express and feel themselves in the world as subjects, rather than objects, because they are speaking from the inside, from the interface between body and world, rather than perceiving ways in which they are represented in writing and art aimed more obviously at a male readership and gaze. Adrienne Rich says of writing from the body:

> I am really asking whether woman cannot begin, at last to *think through the body,* to connect what has been so cruelly disorganized—our great mental capacities, hardly used; our highly developed tactile sense; our genius for close observation; our complicated, pain-enduring, multi-pleasure physicality (Rich in Reynolds, 1990).

She goes on to eroticize women's ability to experience pleasure:

> We are neither "inner" nor "outer," constructed; our skin is alive with signals; our lives and our deaths are inseparable from the release or blockage of our thinking bodies.

> The repossession by women of our bodies will bring far more essential change to human society than the seizing of the means of production by workers. The female body has been both territory and machine, virgin wilderness to be exploited and assembly-line turning out life. We need to imagine a world in which every woman is the presiding genius of her own body (Rich, 1976).

Others who have written about women's celebration of and awareness of the body include Helene Cixous whose "The Laugh of the Medusa" (*Signs,* 1976) in celebrating women's right to write also uses eroticized language, comparing orgasm to the free expression of writing, flying to breaking free and speaking out. So too Jeanette Winterson writes in a fashion which uses the erotic in her *Written on the Body* (1992).

Jeanette Winterson (1959–)

Much of Winterson's work deals with sexuality and relationships of gender and power. While *Oranges Are Not the Only Fruit,* (1985) which brought her to fame, deals with adolescent lesbian relations, later books explore the erotic, reverse gender role expectations and stereotypes. *Written On The Body* (1992) enacts writing the body, and is erotic and sensual in places.

Of Louise it is said:

> Louise's tastes had no place in the late twentieth century where sex is about revealing not concealing. She enjoyed the titillation of suggestion. Her pleasure was in slow certain arousal, a game between equals who might not always choose to be equals. She was not a D.H. Lawrence type; no-one could take Louise with animal inevitability. It was necessary to engage her whole person. Her mind, her heart, her soul and

her body could only be present as two sets of twins. She would not be divided from herself (*Written on the Body,* pp. 67–8).

Love, loss, and emotional pain are detailed rather than the sadomasochism which briefly appears in the later *Sexing the Cherry* (1989). It is difficult to determine the gender of the narrator who wishes to rescue Louise for the tangle of gender stereotyping and labeling of the past. Critics have suggested that undoing the patriarchal past requires more than representing a bisexual or sexually unlabeled narrator.

> Lesbian or not, the story re-enacts a patriarchal control over women. In order to abolish gender distinctions and rewrite the laws of sexual desire, a novelist needs to do more than linguistically castrate her narrator (Barr, 1993).

However, Cath Stowers in "The Erupting Lesbian Body: Reading *Written on the Body* as a Lesbian Text," suggests that Winterson is fantasizing, experimenting with how to write female pleasure through "redefining the erotic in terms of female rather than male experience." (p 90). Later love for Louise is explored through the naming of her body parts in which she is compared to various smells, beings, and objects from the mythical past. Questions are asked about the texture of love, and the erotic is recreated in such lines as:

> Can love have texture? It is palpable to me . . . I weigh it in my hand the way I weigh your head in my hands . . . Your hand prints are all over my body. Your flesh is my flesh. You deciphered me and now I am plain to read. The message is a simple one; my love for you (ibid. pp. 105–106).

Winterson's first novel of adolescent lesbian passion and religious challenge *Oranges Are Not The Only Fruit,* winner of the *Whitbread First Novel Award* in 1985, enabled expression of eroticized relations between women both in text and in the televised version. Jeanette's love for Melanie, although short lived, redressed the lies of romantic fictions, helped her establish her own sexuality as an individual despite her repressive household, and set her on the path for future interactions.

Vampire Erotic

Vampirism is, in Rosemary Jackson's words "perhaps the highest symbolic representation of eroticism" (Jackson, 1981). Richard Dyer in

"Children of the Night" (1988) locates the attraction of the vampire as erotic metaphor in the private setting, both our beds and our innermost thoughts. The equation of blood draining with sexual ecstasy, the domination and swooning, the sensuality, the promise of eternal love and life make the vampire motif central to that of romantic love and central to erotic depiction and imaginings.

It is not merely a feminist erotic that vampiric narrative celebrate and embody of course, and the immensely popular *Interview with a Vampire* as text can be interestingly explored as a fine version (?) of the feminist erotic at times and the homoerotic at other times. Richard Dyer's essay (1988) concentrates on the latter. Vampirism is a metaphor both for social controls and fears of sexuality walking the night streets, and an expression of the taboo of eroticism.

Dyer comments:

> The ideas in vampire fiction of what sexuality is like—privacy, secrecy, uncontrollability, active/passive—have a complex relationship to the place of sexuality within the social order. Until the 1960's—and, really still today—sexuality was approved within marriage. Vampirism takes place outside of marriage. Marriage is the social institution of the private of sexuality—the vampire violates it, tapping at new windows to get in, providing sexual scenes for the narrator to witness. Marriage contains female sexuality—hence the horror of the female vampire walking the streets at night in search of sex. Men are allowed to walk those streets for that purpose, hence the ambivalence of the male vampire, the fulfilment of the importunate nature of male sexuality, dangerous, horrible, but also taken to be what men, alas, are. Finally marriage restricts sexuality to heterosexuality—vampirism is the alternative, dreaded and desired in equal measure (1988).

Dyer concentrates on also equating vampirism as metaphor for homosexuality/lesbianism but in point of fact it is the rather catholic sexual tastes (except that the victim must be attractive! they can be of either gender) of vampires which provides part of the frisson. The male vampire seeks female victims/partners, and often also males, while female vampires, the paradigmatic oversexed demonic women also traditionally seek both sexes. "Carmella" (Le Fanu, 1992) the Romantic's female vampire is the first in the tradition of lesbian vampires. Perhaps the lesbian/gay reading is but one of the most contemporary readings of how vampirism is used to depict the thrill and the fear, repulsion and attraction, temptation, fulfilment, and threat of potential danger inherent in eroticized sexual encounters. With the curse of the AIDS crisis founded upon the exchange of bodily fluids, vampirism emerges as ironically both a metaphor for bad blood, the dangers of the sexual exchange, and an alternative to it—vampires are not often seen kissing or making love; they get their kicks by drinking blood and while this can in most cases kill the prey, it soars above the threat of AIDS in ensuring the predatory vampire further eternal life-giving draughts.

Angela Carter (1940–1992)

Carter frequently used imagery and settings from de Sade to explore the constraints, inequalities, and eventual liberation of female sexuality and uses language which is replete with oxymorons, and are often erotic. Carter's "Lady of the House of Love" (1979) and "The Loves of Lady Purple" (1986) turn romantic love on its head, the one depicting a cursed countess who dies upon a kiss, in a reversal of fairytales, the other a man made vampiric predatory creature, the fruit of a male compulsion to depict woman as sex object and automaton, who comes to life and acts out the scripted life as femme fatale prostitute. Carter's tales and versions of the vampiric are less obviously celebratory, more problematic, but still highly eroticized in their language.

In *The Bloody Chamber* collection (1979), she deconstructs the patriarchal structures and reverses the sexual politics of short stories based on Perrault and other fairytale sources. In the title tale a Bluebeard Marquis recognizes in his young, lower-middle-class bride, the potential for the enjoyment of sadomasochistic relations—assessing her "like a housewife inspecting cuts on the slab"—the erotically charged tale gets to the heart of the contradictions in de Sade. The young woman's sexuality is awakened but on his power terms: "of her apparel she retains only her sonorous jewellery." Both she and the reader are troubled by suggestions of cannibalism, impalement, and then the revelations of previous dead wives soon to be joined by the new wife seeking after knowledge on his deadly trail. But the erotic awakening of women's sexuality goes unpunished in Carter's reversals of patriarchal fairytales. In *The Bloody*

Chamber the girl is rescued by her warrior mother on horseback, in "The Company of Wolves" (1979) Little Red Riding Hood laughs in the face of the deadly courtship rituals of the predatory carnivorous wolf, burning both their clothes and leaping into bed with him, satisfying her own erotic nature.

In "Love in a Cold Climate"—a paper given at a Conference on the Language of Passion, University of Pisa, Italy, 1990—Carter writes that:

> Repression, not ecstasy, is the goal towards which British lovers strive and which they applaud themselves upon achieving. The language of passion is extruded with extraordinary difficulty through the stiff upper lip. Georges Bataille opines that 'the essence of mankind lies in sexuality.' That may be true on the continent, perhaps. In Britain, no.

In *The Passion of New Eve* (1977) the exchange between Evelyn and Leilah is more one based on sadism leading to Leilah's abortion, and Carter explores both the ways in which society constructs and represents a perfect woman, (a transvestite, Tristessa de St Ange, given the same name as Madame de Saint-Ange in the Marquis de Sade's *Philosophy In The Bedroom*, Sade 1991, pp. 179–367) on the screen and how conventional representations of sex and gender roles might be troubled by gender reversals. Evelyn, captured by a matriarchal cult beneath the sands, is castrated and turned into a woman (a *Playboy* centerfold, p. 75), only to recognize how women suffer at the hands of men like himself. Less erotic writing per se and more an expose of the inequalities which produce conventional pornography and some eroticism, this powerful fantasy novel explores the male gaze, defamiliarizing the reader and inverting classical erotic themes.

In "The Company of Wolves" Carter's rewrite of "Little Red Riding Hood," Rosaleen spots traces of her missing, devoured granny, like a trained sleuth and although she fears the blood "she must spill" (Carter 1979, p. 117, his or hers?), she answers him back, forgets her fear, and throws both their clothes in the fire, having undressed him. His practiced moves and lines are absurd!: he is in control: "'All the better to eat you with.' The girl burst out laughing. She knew she was nobody's meat" (p. 118). Sleeping between the paws of the tender wolf, Rosaleen has her sexual partner tamed her own way.

The horror/fairytale has a resolution returning sexual power to women.

Angela Carter's young Rosaleen reveals herself as an equal partner in the sexual games the werewolf initiates. If werewolfishness connotes unleashed sexuality, Rosaleen's answering of his standard questions and her burning all their clothes, trapping them in their werewolf condition, connotes her desire to embrace and take control of her own sexual fate. In a closure in which women's sexuality is allowed energetic free rein despite male attempts at control (rape and devouring, or rescue) the result is a new celebratory howling. The trajectory of the cautionary horror tale is evident until the end of the tale. A restoration of normality and order at the story's end *doesn't* return Rosaleen as the daughter of patriarchy, but rewards her sexual energies. There is harmony without everyday restoration of status quo.

Carter's tale serves as a paradigm for much radical women's horror. It utilizes the tropes and trajectory of a conventional horror tale: threats amid the familiar; the deceptiveness of what seems attractive and safe; the instability of ordered lives and norms (granny's precautions, warnings to Rosaleen) to protect from real danger, but it then disturbs them, with Rosaleen's embracing of werewolfishness, and so of her own sexuality. Recognizing her own sexuality, Rosaleen chooses embrace over devouring. Conventional closure is refused, sexual energies triumph. There are several other eroticized werewolf encounters in Pam Keesey's collection *Women Who Run with the Werewolves* (1996).

Sarah Gamble describes Carter as being influenced by the "graphic extremism of pornographic forms" (Gamble 1997, p. 8), discovered in Japan. Her short story, "Flesh and the Mirror," is set in Tokyo with a heroine suffering from "the Bovary syndrome" (Jones & Williams 1996, p. 223). The city is bizarre, and she moves like a sleepwalker into a relationship with a stranger in an "unambiguous" (ibid. p. 224) hotel, shocked to find the experience somewhat pleasurable, despite the potential danger.

> None of the lyrical eroticism of this sweet, sad, moon night of summer rain had been within my expectations; I had half expected he would strangle me . . . The mirror annihilated time, place and person; at the consecration of this house, the mirror had been dedicated to the reflection of chance embraces. Therefore

it treated flesh in an exemplary fashion, with charity and indifference (ibid.)

Despite some feminist criticism, it can be argued that Carter's play with pornography demythologizes traditional views of women's sexuality as passive.

Lesbian Erotic Writing and Debates

Lesbian erotics have, since those days, been brought out into the open, celebrated, more clearly defined as a way of seizing identity and the creative power of love, beauty, relationships with others, for women recognizing their sexuality as woman-identified there is a political freedom which like Rich's lesbian continuum (1980) enables a celebration of sexuality and eroticism which is able to avoid the debasing power relations seen in this equation as concomitant with women's role in heterosexual relations. Heterosexual gender relations, whether they include an erotic element or not, carry with them an enormous social baggage of power politics, ideologically dubious discourse, and enculturated roles:

> Perhaps the problem of (heterosexual) sex is substantially a problem of what often goes along with it—the demands of marriage and motherhood (although motherhood and the social demands of sexual relationships will also create problems for lesbians).... That women, as opposed to men, may enjoy sex outside marriage or a committed relationship is still not culturally acceptable has witnessed much discussion, including among feminists, upon the topics of women, casual sex, and prostitution. But sexual politics will still cause difficulties with sex itself for relatively 'liberated'' women. The still largely masculine construction of women's sexuality, of women's bodies being prostituted as much by the "male gaze," results in obstacles which women must negotiate if they wish to develop alternative accounts, and practices, of sexuality (Levy, 1992, p. 226).

Debating popularized accessible and acceptable versions of erotica for lesbians is seen by Jenny Kitzinger and Celia Kitzinger (in Griffin, 1993) as fraught with problems. Some male and female producers of pornography and/or erotica assume that lesbians take pleasure from the same representations of women's bodies as do heterosexual consumers. Kitzinger and Kitzinger are explicit about the dangers of re-reading male porn or of celebrating sadomasochism, which they see as a range for practices lesbians

should come to terms with and recognize as likely to be dangerous rather than liberating. In this they agree with Audre Lorde: "Even in play, to affirm that the exertion of power over the powerless is erotic, is empowering, is to set the emotional on stage for the continuation of that relationships, politically, socially, and economically" (Lorde 1982, p. 68) They comment "We believe that critical representations of such activities are fine: uncritical celebrations of them are not" (in Griffin 1993, p. 24). Sadomasochism and aping male pornography are not the only versions of lesbian erotics imagined. Theirs assume representations of lesbian sex or erotica must be "coy and acceptable" featuring "cats and pot plants" or sweet. Kitzinger and Kitzinger argue:

> Lesbian sex is not always pretty, or sweet. Nor do we wish to deny the passion of lesbian desire. But we do think that the current emphasis on the active lesbian audience re-reading male porn for their own 'revolutionary' purposes, and the celebration of sadomasochistic lesbian porn is misguided and dangerous' (p. 24). The images are merely by lesbians and for lesbians (Barbara Smith, 1988, p. 180) is not enough.

> Moving beyond clichéd symbols and both the traditional male sexual codes and their inversion is necessary if new representations are to be possible. We would like to see the invention of new ways of exploring sexuality, which challenge and deconstruct (instead of simply affirming) desire as it currently exists (p. 24).

The Australian anthology of erotic writing, *Moments of Vision* (Hawthorne and Pausacker, 1989)—an explicit and available anthology of such writing is criticized by Levy (1992, p. 233) for its limiting stance anti-pornography and violence, which the editors set out deliberately to ensure: "We know we were looking for writing what did not use the structural power differences between women and men as the basis for eroticisation" (Hawthorne and Pausacker 1989). An argument put forward by Stevenson and Levy is that what results is "rather bland and not particularly erotic" (Hawthorne and Pausacker 1989, p. 233). This opens up the whole debate about the place of violence and sadomasochism in "acceptable" (politically/sexually/morally acceptable?) feminist relationships, whatever they might be. For lesbians in particular, the issue of sadomasochism is raised in Pamela May's recent "Easy come, Easy Go" (1990) about the acceptability of lesbian sadomasochism as a version and image of the erotic.

Contemporary Women's Erotic Horror Writing

Particularly Vampire erotica transgresses the boundaries of both the horror genre and the kinds of finally conformist, comfortingly "normal" social behavior which conventional horror initially destabilizes and ultimately restores, offering instead radical, creative, and liberating alternatives.

Not only does it critique and disturb social conventions, it also refuses to conform to the formulae of conventional horror. Its celebration of the erotic, the Other, the dark exciting side of life/death, dream/nightmare is essentially creative and liberating. Like the erotic in its many selves, contemporary women's radical horror writing challenges conventional norms, translates and rescripts the discourses of oppressive ideologies and their popular manifestation in fictional and filmic formulae, refusing the value systems which underlie them. Desire, it seems to argue, does not have to be linked to sin and duty. Much contemporary women's horror denies the destructive polarities of male/female, good/bad, passive/active, and life/death. The formulae of horror, rescripted, revalued, can be used to critique rather than reinstate forms of power. Examples are Angela Carter's "Company of Wolves" (1979), Pat Califia's "Vampire" (1993), Katherine Forrest's "O Captain, My Captain" (1993), and Cheri Scotch's *The Werewolf's Kiss* (1992) each of which rescripts to celebrate the erotic, with a certain forbidden *jouissance*.

The "point at which the lines between sexuality and violence become blurred" (Keesey 1993, p. 16) is pivotal for Pat Califia's groundbreaking lesbian S&M "The Vampire" (1993). Waspwaisted, blonde Iduna, whose "complexion was so pale it was luminous. In the dark she almost seemed to glow" (p. 170) actively seeks out the leather-clad dominatrix, Kerry, who takes her male victims literally, beating them past endurance, but refusing the blood she needs. Iduna represents an alternative partner, no victim, freely offering her blood and enjoying the exchange, conditioned and "well schooled" (p. 183), which she has actively hunted out, as needy as Kerry,

adapted to this new kind of vampire relationship of mutual exchange. At the height of vampire passion: The venom that had prevented her blood from clotting and closing the wound sang now in her veins, making her see colors behind her closed eyelids, making her warm inside, simultaneously relaxed, alert. No other drug could ever duplicate this ecstasy, this calm. She should know, she had had long enough to search for a substitute (Califia 1993).

Sex, then, is "not out of the question."

Not all women's horror radically rescripts the convention to promote active, equal erotic exchange, however. Some contemporary women's erotic horror concentrates on the kinds of scenarios and relationships which could horrify or disgust women in particular. Highly eroticized, dark, bestial rape fantasies seem to be popular choices for the intermixing of both horror and the erotic personae which, to many feminists, is problematic to say the least.

A case in point is the Australian Darryle Caine who tends to play with highly eroticized, deadly scenarios. In "Predators" (in Kinhill, 1996) the predatory couple, the female narrator and Tiger, her boyfriend, indulge in sexual safaris along Surfer's Paradise, picking up and sharing women whose own isolation and slightly underachieved attractiveness made them succumb easily to flattery and friendship.

The language of seduction and destruction—"devour" (p. 16), "target" (p. 18)—and the erotic foreplay hinting at danger, pales into insignificance once their most recent prey, Elvi (anagram for evil) plays them at their own game, seducing Tiger. The seduction is based on the kind of danger they are used to inventing and controlling for themselves. Caine's erotic writing is more like conventional (male produced) pornography. In this story as in several others in *Screams* (1996) and *Scream Again* (1997), there are any number of descriptions of such as the "angry red rod he packed, its purple tip bursting with the intensity of his arousal" (*Screams* 1996, p. 19) and "roughly his knees parted her thighs and he sank that angry, purple tip into her sopping, swollen sex lips. Up, deep and smooth he plunged, to the hilt with a deep-felt groan" (1996, p. 19). Elvi's inhuman gaze and growing fangs terrify the narrator who cannot extricate her impaling lover. This is a hermaphroditic monster, for when it has finished with the dying Tiger, it turns on the narrator:

I could not guess what sort of gruesome weapon she packed between her legs. For the tatters that remained of his sex looked like he had been having it off with a giant pencil sharpener... And then the demon-creature turned on me. It had transformed further, and now a ferocious looking device was protruding from its groin, like some giant, deformed penis weapon. And it was meant for me! (1996, p. 21)

Imagery of violence, invasion, and destruction characterize sex acts in Caine's work. Her erotic horror fantasies replicate many of the stereotypical abject scenes involving women — Medusa, the Iron Maiden, the *vagina dentata*— and combine these with horrors specifically designed for women—invading, throbbing, barbed monster penises, inhuman power, bestiality, the helplessness of the female victim whose life, partner, unborn children, everything are threatened or destroyed.

Some contemporary women writers in the vampire genre deliberately reverse and trouble the forms and figures of the genre, and refuse the narrative trajectory which would condemn female and lesbian vampires in particular to a permanent death as a punishment for their transgression.

The use of the erotic in women's horror is not only transgressive, however, it is also transgressive in order to suggest new ways of behaving and relating in both heterosexual and homosexual love/sex/erotic unions. A mutual recognition of the other as a subject, however similar or different, is the basis of positive human relations. Erotic horror works in several ways. Some of it exploits the sadomasochistic tendencies which fuel many relationships, and perhaps replicates the Otherising and the power imbalances on which such relationships are predicated and which they uphold and reinforce. Other erotic horror explores the creative and celebratory potential of relationships of mutuality, where difference is a reason for celebration not destruction.

In *Bonds of Love: Psychoanalysis, Feminism and the Problem of Domination* (1988), Jessica Benjamin, a psychoanalyst, suggests that healthy relationships and development demand "mutual recognition, the necessity of recognizing as well as being recognised by the other" (1988, p. 23), "the reciprocity of self and other, the balance of assertion and recognition (p. 25).

In this definition, erotic expression is seen as an element of health. Vampire erotic horror combines the *frissons* of horror with the charged, eternal promise of fulfilled and constantly refulfilling desire. What could be more transgressive in a censorious society, and what more celebratory and liberating?! There are similar needs for mutual self recognition in romance fictions, and in women's erotic horror fictions.

Melding the genres of science fiction, romance, and horror, and blending the Gothic motif of the vampire with the science fiction motif of the alien Other, Katherine Forrest's short story "O Captain, my Captain" (1993) utilizes the tropes of all three genres to create an erotic horror in which the space captain vampire Drake (Dracula, but the adventurer Sir Francis also), captain of the ship Scorpio IV, does not prey upon her traveling companion but instead awakens her to the pleasure of her body in a highly erotic union graphically, but never tackily described. The lesbian relationship is initiated by Drake with the military lieutenant, Harper (after Jonathan Harker). It is then entered into mutually with full awareness of what each "is," what they can offer, and the limitations of this relationship. Vampires in contemporary women's erotic horror do not need to drain their victims unto death; they embrace in a mutually aware exchange which refuses to turn the temporary or long-term mate into a member of the undead. Forrest and others can use the transgressive power and the liberating eroticism of the vampire relationship to suggest and describe new heights of a passion which is mutually sought and exchanged.

Jewelle Gomez (1948–)

As Paulina Palmer has explored at length in her *Lesbian Gothic* (1999), Gomez's chief radical act in writing *The Gilda Stories*, in terms of the treatment of the eroticism of the relationships of the vampire, is to reappropriate and positively revalue that psychoanalytically conventional abjection of the mother and the mother's body which we find in so much male-produced horror. In so doing, she dramatizes a lesbian erotic which valorizes a sensual, sexual, maternal, erotic exchange between (mostly, here) female vampires. Blood exchange is a moment of high sensuality and the act of suckling equates the maternal with eroticized relationships. Blood is a life-giving, not an abject defiling, fluid.

A vampirish encounter which takes place between Bird and Gilda illustrates these contrary associations. Here Gomez brings together the displaced image of the child suckling the mother's breasts, the act of birthing, and the mother's abject bleeding body. She describes how Bird, making an insertion in the skin beneath her own breast:

> pressed Gilda's mouth to the red slash, letting the blood wash across Gilda's face. Soon Gilda drank eagerly, filling herself, and as she did her hand massaged Bird's breast, first touching the nipple gently with curiosity, then roughly. She wanted to know this body that gave her life. Her heart swelled with their blood, a tide between two shores. To an outsider the sight might have been one of horror: their faces red and shining, their eyes unfocused and black, the sound of their bodies slick with wetness, tight with life. Yet it was a birth. The mother finally able to bring her child into the world, to look at her. It was not death that claimed Gilda. It was Bird. (Gomez, 1992, p. 40)

In *The Gilda Stories* the real horror is the racial and sexual violence from which Gilda, originally called "the Girl" initially fled when escaping the plantation, before being rescued by Bird and the original Gilda, who ran a rather friendly brothel. Gilda witnesses lynchings.

Conclusion

Eroticism *is* mystique; that is, the aura of emotion and imagination around sex. It cannot be 'fixed' by codes of social or moral convenience, whether from the political left or right . . . There is a daemonic instability in sexual relations that we may have to accept. (Paglia, 1992, p. 13)

Despite disputes and differing interpretations, women's erotic writing is growing. Some use the erotic to entertain, others to explore the potential for intellectual and individual liberation and demythologizing of constraining myths.

GINA WISKER

References

Acker, Kathy. *The Adult Life of Toulouse Lautrec: By Henry Toulouse Lautrec*. New York: TVRT Press, 1975.

———. *Blood and Guts in High School*. London: Picador, 1984, p. 125.

Atwood, Margaret. *Surfacing*. London: Virago, 1972.

Bakhtin, M. *The Dialogic Imagination*. Emerson, C. & M. Holquist, trans., University of Texas Press, Texas, 1981, p. 7.

Barnes, Djuna. *The Ladies Almanac*. New York: New York University Press, [1928], 1992.

———. *Nightwood*. New York: The New Directions, 1936.

Barr, H. Review of *Written On The Body* by Jeanette Winterson. *The English Review*, Volume 3, Issue 4, April 1993, pp. 22–23).

Barthes, Roland. *Sade, Fourier, Loyola*. Trans. R. Miller, London: Jonathan Cape, [1971] 1977, p. 26.

———. *Mythologies*. Trans. A. Lavers, London: Vintage, [1957] 1993, p. 135.

Belle, Monica. *Wild in the Country*. London: Virgin Publishing, 2003.

Benjamin, Jessica. *Bonds of Love: Psychoanalysis, Feminism and the Problem of Domination*. New York: Pantheon, 1988, pp. 23, 25.

Black Issues Book Review. September–October 2004, vol. 6, i. 5, p. 17, (3).

Bright, Susie. *SexWise*. San Francisco, Cleis Press, 1995.

———. *Herotica*. 10th Anniversary Edition, with Afterword by the editor, San Francisco: Down There Press, 1998.

———. *How to Write a Dirty Story*. New York: Simon and Schuster, 2002.

Brite, Poppy Z. *Lost Souls*. Harmondsworth: Penguin, 1992.

———. *Drawing Blood* (originally called *Birdland*). New York: Delacorte Press, 1993.

———. *Love in Vein 1*. New York: Harper Prism, 1994, p. vii.

———. "His Mouth Will taste of Wormwood" in *Swamp Foetus*. Harmondsworth: Penguin, 1993, p 55.

———. *Exquisite Corpse*. London: Orion, 1996.

Bushnell, Candace. *Sex and the City*. New York: Warner Books, 1997.

Caine, Darryle. "The Predators." In Madeleine Kinhill ed. *Screams*, Queensland: AMS Ironbark publication, for Wild Child, 1996, pp. 16, 18, 19, 20, 21.

Califia, Pat. "The Vampire." In Pam Keesey ed. *Daughters of Darkness*, San Francisco: Cleis Press, 1993, pp. 170, 182, 183.

Carter, Angela. In *The New Statesman*. 1975, pp. 207–208.

———. *The Passion of New Eve*. New York: Harcourt Brace Jovanovich, 1977.

———. "The Company of Wolves" in *The Bloody Chamber*. London: King Penguin, 1979, pp. 117, 118.

———. "Lady in the House of Love." In *The Bloody Chamber*. London: King Penguin, 1979.

———. *The Sadeian Woman*. Virago Press, London, 1979.

———. "The Loves of Lady Purple." In *Wayward Girls and Wicked Women*. London: Virago, 1986.

———. "Love in a Cold Climate." Conference on the Language of Passion, University of Pisa, Italy, 1990.

Cheekes, Shonda. *Lessons Learned*. Blackgentlemen. com, Maryland: Strebor Books, 2002.

Cixous, Hélène. "The Laugh of the Medusa" [1975], in *The Signs Reader: Women, Gender, and Scholarship*. Elizabeth Abel and Emily K. Abel, eds., Chicago, IL: University of Chicago Press, 1976.

Costa, Portia, da. *Gothic Blue*. London: Black Lace, 1996, pp. 23, 42.

Couani, Anna. "The Map of the World." In Susan Hawthorne, Jenny Pausacker, eds. *Moments of Desire: Sex and Sensuality by Australian Feminist Writers*. Victoria, Australia: Penguin, 1989, p. 1.

Dworkin, Andrea. *Pornography: Men Possessing Women*. New York: Perigee Books, 1981.

Dunn Jr., James L. *American Visions*. Vol 12, no. 5, (Oct–Nov 1997): 31, (3).

Dyer, Richard. "Children of the Night: Vampirism as Homosexuality/Homosexuality as Vampirism." In Susannah Radstone ed. *Sweet Dreams: Sexuality Gender and Popular Fiction*, London: Lawrence and Wishart, 1988, pp. 54.

Forrest, Katherine. "O Captain, my Captain." In Pam Keesey ed. *Daughters of Darkness, Lesbian Vampire Fictions*, San Francisco, CA: Cleis Press, 1993, p. 225.

Forster, E.M. *Maurice*. London: Arnold, 1970.

Foucault, Michel. *The History of Sexuality, Volume 1, An Introduction*. London: Penguin Books, 1978.

Freud, Sigmund. "The Question of a Lay Analysis: Conversation with an Impartial Person." In S. Freud, ed. and trans. James Strachey. *Standard Edition Vol 20*, London: Hogarth, 1953, p. 212.

Gamble, Sarah. *Angela Carter: Writing from the Front Line*. Edinburgh University Press: Edinburgh, 1997, p. 8.

Genet, Jean. *The Balcony*. New York: Grove Press, 1958.

Ginsberg, Allen. "Howl." San Francisco: City Lights Books, 1956.

Gomez, Jewelle. *The Gilda Stories*. London: Sheba, 1992, p. 40.

Guattari, Felix. *Soft Subversions*. New York: Semiotext (e), 1996.

Hawthorne, Susan and Jenny Pausacker, eds. *Moments of Desire: Sex and Sensuality by Australian Feminist Writers*. Victoria, Australia: Penguin, 1989, p. 233.

Indigo, Susannah. *Going Mad from Roses*. West Emerald Press, 2000.

———. *Oysters Among Us*. Denver, CO: Samba Mountain Press, 2001.

Jackson, Rosemary. *Fantasy*. London: Methuen, 1981.

Johnson, Eileen, M. *The Adventures of the Bold and Bourgeois*. Blackgentlemen.com, Maryland: Strebor Books, 2002.

Jones, R.G. & S. Williams, S. eds. (1996) *Erotic Stories By Women*. London: Penguin Books, 1995, pp. 223, 224.

Jong, Erica. *Fear of Flying*. New York: Henry Holt. 1973.

———. *Parachutes & Kisses*. New York: Granada Publishing, 1984.

———. *Sappho's Leap*. New York: W.W. Norton, 2003.

———. *Fanny: Being the True History of the Adventures of Fanny Hackabout-Jones*. New York: Granada Publishing, 1980.

———. *Shylock's Daughter* (formerly titled *Serenissima*), Boston, MA: Houghton Mifflin, 1987.

———. *Inventing Memory: A Story of Mothers and Daughters*. New York: HarperCollins, 1997.

———. *Fear of Fifty: A Midlife Memoir*. London: Chatto and Windus, 1995.

———. *The Devil at Large: Erica Jong on Henry Miller*. New York: Random House, 1994.

———. *Witches*. New York: Harry N. Abrams, 1981.

———. *What Do Women Want*. New York: HarperCollins, 1998.

Keesey, Pam. *Women Who Run with the Werewolves*. San Francisco: Cleis Press, 1996, p. 16.

Kitzinger, Jenny and Celia Kizinger. "'Doing It': Representations of Lesbian Sex" in Gabriele Griffin ed. *Outwrite: Lesbianism and Popular Culture*. London: Pluto, 1993, p. 24M.

Kranzler, Laura. *The Name of an Angel*. London: Virgin Publishing, 2003.

———. "From Ann Radcliffe to Black Lace: Female Gothic For the 1990s." P. 1, presented at the conference, "The Legacies of Walpole: The Gothic After Otranto," St. Mary's College, London 15–18 July, 1997, pp. 1, 3, 103.

Kristeva, Julia. *The Powers of Horror: An Essay on Abjection*. Trans. S. Roudiez, New York: Columbia University Press, 1982.

Lauret, Maria. "It's My Party: American Bestsellers of the 1970s." In Gina Wisker, ed. *It's My Party: Reading Twentieth Century Women's Writing*, London: Pluto, 1994.

Lawrence, D.H. *Lady Chatterley's Lover*. London: Heinemann, 1963.

Le Fanu, Sheridan. "Carmella." In *Blood and Roses: The Vampire in 19th Century Literature*, London: Creation Press, 1992.

Levy, Bronwen. "Now What's Erotic? Sexuality, Desire and Australian Women's Writing." In Carole Ferrier ed. *Gender, Politics and Fiction*, Brisbane: University of Queensland Press, [1985] 1992, pp. 226, 227, 228, 233.

Lorde, Audre. "When the Spring Came." In Martin, DeCosta-Willis and Bell, *Erotique Noire* New York: Anchor Books, 1992, p. 80.

———. "Uses of the Erotic: The Erotic as Power." In Martin, DeCosta-Willis and Bell, *Erotique Noire*. New York: Anchor Books, 1992, pp. xx, 81, 82.

Marcola, Gabrielle *Bedding the Burglar*. London: Virgin Publishing, 2004.

Marcuse, Herbert. *Eros and Civilisation*. Boston, MA: Beacon Press, [1955] 1966.

Martin, Reginald, Miriam DeCosta-Willis, and Roseann P. Bell. *Erotique Noir/Black Erotica*. New York: Anchor Books, 1992.

Mason, J.D. *Your Message Has Been Sent*. Blackgentlemen.com, Maryland: Strebor Books, 2002.

———. *Don't Want No Sugar*. New York: St Martin's Press, 2004.

———. *One Day I Saw a Black King*. New York: St Martin's Press, 2003.

Martin, Reginald. *Dark Eros: Black Erotic Writings: An Anthology*. New York: St Martin's Griffin. 1997.

May, Pamela. "Easy Come Easy Go." Broadway: Women's Redress, 1990.

Millett, K. *Sexual Politics*. London: Virago Press Limited, [1969] 1977, pp. 20, 22.

Mohanraj, Maryanne. *Aqua Erotica: 18 Stories for a Steamy Bath*. Three Rivers Press, 2000.

———. *Wet: More Aqua Erotica*. Three Rivers Press, 2002.

———. *Bodies in Motion*. New York: HarperCollins, 2005.

Nicol, Jodi. *Silken Chains*. London: Black Lace, 1997, p. 216.

Nin, Anais. *House of Incest*. Athens, OH: Ohio University Press, [1936] 1992.

———. *Winter of Artifice*. Athens, OH: Ohio University Press, [1939] 1961.

———. *Delta of Venus: Erotica*. New York: Harcourt Brace Jovanovitch, [1944] 1977.

———. *Cities of the Interior*. Athens, OH: Ohio University Press, [1959] 1975.

———. *The Journal of Love*. Denver, CO: Swallow Press, 1986.

———. *Little Birds*. Penguin Books: London, 1979.

———. *In Favour of the Sensitive Man*, London: Penguin Books, [1966] 1992, p. 9.

———. (1992) "Eroticism in Women" [1974], in *In Favour of the Sensitive Man*. London: Penguin Books, pp. 6, 7.

Paglia, Camille. *Sexual Personae: Art and Decadence from Nefertiti to Emily Dickinson*. London: Penguin Books, 1992.

Palmer, Paulina. *Lesbian Gothic*. London: Cassell, 1999.

Radstone, Susannah ed. *Sweet Dreams: Sexuality, Gender and Popular Fiction*. London: Lawrence and Wishart, 1988.

Rampling, Anne. *Exit to Eden*. London: Time Warner, 1985.

———. *Belinda*. London: Time Warner, 1986.

Réage, Pauline. *The Story of O*. Paris: Jean-Jacques Pauvert, 1954.

———. *The Story of O: Part Two*. Paris: Jean-Jacques Pauvert, 1969.

Reynolds, Margaret, ed. *Erotica: an Anthology of Women's Writing*. London: Pandora, 1990, p. xxix.

Rice, Anne. *Interview with the Vampire*. London: Futura, 1976, p. 292.

———. Afterword to *Of Woman Born: Motherhood as Experience and Institution*. New York: W.W. Norton, [1976] 1995.

———. "Compulsory Heterosexuality and Lesbian Existence." In *Signs* 5 no. 4, 1980, pp. 631–660.

Rich, Adrienne. In Margaret Reynolds ed. *Erotica: an Anthology of Women's Writing*, London: Pandora, 1990.

Roberts, Michèle. *Flesh and Blood*. London: Virago, 1995.

Roquelaure, A.N. *The Claiming of Sleeping Beauty*. London: Time Warner, 1983.

———. *Beauty's Punishment*, London: Time Warner, 1984.

———. *Beauty's Release*. London: Time Warner, 1985.

Sade, Marquis de. *Three Complete Novels: Justine; Philosophy in the Bedroom; Eugénie de Franval and Other Writings (1782–1791)*. London: Arrow Books Ltd, 1991, p. 470.

Scotch, Cheri. *The Werewolf's Kiss*. New York: Diamond Books, 1992.

Segal, Lynne and Mary Macintosh, eds. *Sex Exposed: Sex and the Postmodern Debate*. London: Virago, 1992.

———. "Sweet Sorrows, Powerful Pleasures" in Lynne Segal and Mary Macintosh, eds. *Sex Exposed: Sex and the Postmodern Debate*, London: Virago, 1992, p. 86.

Shange, Ntzoke. Introduction in Martin, DeCosta-Willis and Bell, *Erotique Noire*. New York: Anchor Books, 1992.

———. *Liliane*. London: Methuen, 1995, p. 44.

Sharp, Kerri. Introduction to *Pandora's Box*. London: Black Lace, 1996, pp. vii–viii.

Stoker, Bram. *Dracula*. Harmondsworth: Penguin, [1897] 1979.

Stowers, Cath. "The Erupting Lesbian Body: Reading *Written on the Body* as a Lesbian Text." Pp. 90, 105–106.

Walker, Alice. *Possessing the Secret of Joy*. London: Jonathan Cape, 1992.

———, and Parma, Pratibha. *Warrior Marks*. London: Jonathan Cape, 1993.

Winterson, Jeanette. Introduction, in Margaret Reynolds ed. *Erotica: An Anthology of Women's Writing*. London: Pandora, 1990, pp. xx, xxii.

———. *Oranges Are Not the Only Fruit*. London: Pandora, 1985.

———. *Sexing the Cherry*. London: Jonathan Cape, 1989.

———. *Written on the Body*. London: Jonathan Cape, 1992, pp. 67–68.

Wisker, Gina. Review essay on *Possessing the Secret of Joy* in *Over Here* Summer, 1994.

Woolf, Virginia. "Professions for Women." New York: Harcourt, [1931] 1978.

Wyatt, Gail E. *Stolen Women: Reclaiming Our Sexuality, Taking Back Our Lives*. New York: Wiley, 1998.

Zane. *The Sex Chronicles*. Maryland: Strebor Books, 2001.

———. *Addicted*. New York: Pocket Books, 2001.

———. *Duplicity*. Blackgentlemen.com, Maryland: Strebor Books, 2002.

———. *Delusions*. Blackgentlemen.com, Maryland: Strebor Books, 2002.

———. *Breaking the Cycle*. Maryland: Strebor Books, 2005.

———. *Afterburn*. New York: Simon & Schuster, 2005.

TV

"Arena." TV production of "Warrior Marks," dir. Pratibha Parma, producer Alice Walker, Channel 4, 1993.

"Sex and the City." Darren Star, creator. 1998.

Web Sites Accessed

Blackgentlemen.com, Maryland: Strebor Books, 2002.

About Black Lace, www.virginbooks.com/go/sp/Info PageErotic_46.html

Indigo, Susannah. *Clean Sheets Magazine*, www.cleansheets.com. 'Little black books,' *The Guardian*, Satur

day, September 18, 2004, www.guardian.co.uk/week
endstory/0,3605,1305854,00.html

Jong, Erica. *About Erica Jong*, www.ericajong.com/
abouterica.htm

Jong, Erica. *More About Erica Jong*, www.ericajong.
com/abouterica2.htm

Rice, Anne. *Erotic Writings of Anne Rice*, http://www.
empirezine.com/spotlight/rice/rice-erotica-of.htm)

WOMEN'S WRITING: FRENCH, TWENTIETH CENTURY

Women writers who have included eroticism as a primary theme in their work have had to submit to or find ways around the diktats of censorship more than their male counterparts.

So one cannot deal with the question of erotic writing by women without first studying the rules that govern publishing and the evolution of women's rights throughout the twentieth century in France: the literary prize "Vie Heureuse" (1904), which became the "Prix Fémina" in 1922, was founded by Anna de Noailles and other women who were concerned about providing a space for women, a space refused them in the very officious and very masculine world of letters. It was only in the 1960s that women were granted the right to publish without the authorization of a male sponsor or, for that matter, the right to have a sexual life with a non-procreative purpose (the Neuwirth law of 1967 on oral contraception).

This said, since the end of the 19th Century and the beginning of Rachilde's literary career, "feminine" writing has been popular, even if some women were obliged to publish anonymously. In fact, male authors sometimes used female pseudonyms to publish erotic stories, proving that the sexual prohibitions governing women were also a powerful force of titilation and transgression: the naughty Adrienne Saint-Agen was probably a man, Raymond Queneau published under the name Sally Mara, and perhaps Eric Losfeld under the name of Loulou Morin. And of course many women, constrained by social pressures, published erotic stories either in collaboration with a man who was in some sense their protector (the famous couple of Willy/Colette or the less well-known duo of Jean de Létraz/ Suzette Desty), or under a pseudonym. Marguerite Eymery gave birth to Rachilde; Renée Dunant was also Louise Dormienne, who secretly published *Les Caprices du sexe, ou les audaces érotiques de Mademoiselle Louise de B.* (1929) and perhaps also Spaddy, who, in her 1938 novel *Colette, ou les amusements de bon ton* joyously and obscenely plagiarized the famous kiss that the narrator of *A la recherche du temps perdu* (Proust) gave to Albertine; Pauline Tarn takes the name Renée Vivien, marvelously described by Colette in *Le Pur et l'impur*; Anne Desclos, better known under the respectable name of Dominique Aury, was the famous Pauline Réage, a secret that she would keep until the end of her life. Women authors of erotic texts are doubly handicapped: they are women, a difficult position to begin with in the male-dominated publishing industry, and they are immoral in a century that has long made sexuality something forbidden. And this also accounts for the impact of translations of such works as those by Radcliffe Hall (1938), and later those of Dorothy Bussy (1950), Virginia Woolf (1951), Claire Morgan (alias Patricia Highsmith, 1952), Anais Nin (1978), or Eve Ensler (1999).

From the Belle Epoque to the 1940s: Eroticism and Psycho-Social Deviance

It is no accident then that the French pioneers of feminine erotic literature are already, by their life style and their attitudes, considered to be fugitives from the established social order, and often they come from a different world: theater, music hall, literary circles, Natalie Barney's salon, and even some courtesans. Especially during the time of Victor Marguerite's *La Garçonne* (1922), these women are living what is generally considered to be a reprehensible lifestyle: multiple sexual partners, and often homosexual or bisexual. This free life style translates into a freedom and frankness in their writing as well, and will lead Colette to separate from Willy and to produce the rest of the Claudine series by herself. There are also a few of these women who may have regrets later on in life, like the fashionable Liane de Pougy or the lesbian Pauline Tarn, both of whom will finish their lives in the arms... of religion.

One can understand that the themes evoked by these singular writers might have shocked readers. *M. Vénus* (1884) by Rachilde, considered by Maurice Barrès to be the product of a feminine "nervous exhaustion," tells the story of a young man of modest means under the thumb of a woman who supports him and gradually leads him to madness and death. *Cendres et Poussières* (1902) and the poems of the American Renée Vivien, *Idylle saphique* (1901) and *Les Sensations de Mlle de la Bringue* (1904) by Liane de Pougy are so many hymns to Sappho. *Le Poème de l'amour* by Anna de Noailles describes feminine versions of sexual pleasure. Transgression becomes the rule and it goes all the way to a very explicit threesome in one of Spaddy's works, and even to zoophilism from the pen of the sixty year old Rachilde in *Refaire l'amour* (1928) who doesn't hesitate to mention, without describing it of course, a scene between a dog and a woman... The 1920s witness successes that demonstrate the hypocritical expectations of French society in those days; Colette has become an established author, *Un Mois chez les filles* by Maryse Choisy reveals the world of prostitution to its numerous readers in the most explicit terms. Raymonde Machard with *Tu enfanteras?* (1919) and *L'Œuvre de chair* (1925) as well as Renée Dunan with *Une Heure de désir* (1929) describe the convulsions of sexual pleasure.

But on the whole the style remains very much that of the period and even classical despite some very lively dialogue. The exception is Colette whose sensual prose deals with socially incorrect erotic situations: her Claudine books describe the joys of feminine homosexuality and of sexuality in general, her *L'Ingénue libertine* (1909) describes the heroine's desperate quest for sexual pleasure (who, in a rather conformist twist, will find it in the arms of her husband), her *Le Blé en herbe* (1923) recounts adolescent yearnings, and the *Chéri* series (1920 to 1936) describes the agony of a mature woman who is overly sensitive to the attractions of a young Ephebe. Nothing particular to report under Vichy France and its moral order except perhaps for Colette's ongoing work and a few underground works such as the anticlerical *Histoire d'une petite fille* (1943) by Laure, Georges Bataille's partner.

Renewal in the Fifties: Censorship versus Public Acceptance of Erotic Writing

There is a definite break at the beginning of the 1950s—censorship becomes more strict for one thing (post-war concern for birth rate politics perhaps), and a book may be struck by three different prohibitions: sales prohibited to minors under age 18, prohibition on posters and display, and prohibition of advertising. The only public notice of a censored book would be in the *Journal Officiel*, publishing graveyard. The only remaining recourse then becomes anonymous or clandestine publication, and especially the energy of editors like Jean-Jacques Pauvert, Eric Losfeld, Régine Deforges, to mention only a few.

In 1949, Simone de Beauvoir published *Le Deuxième Sexe* which would encourage an ever growing awareness of a woman's right to write about gender and sexuality. Her work didn't have the impact yet that it would have at the end of the 1960s and two symptoms show that nothing had really been won yet in the struggle to publish erotic works by women. Even with the support of Beauvoir, Violette Leduc's novel *Ravages* (1955) has its most explicit and poetic lesbian scenes cut by Gallimard, who has no qualms about publishing *in extenso* male writers who are much more explicit. "Thérèse et Isabelle," an excised chapter, was later published separately as a special edition by Leduc's friend Jacques Guérin. Leduc referred to this censorship of her novel as an "assassination" and she would die in 1972 without ever seeing her novel officially published in an uncensored version. Similarly, the publisher of *Angélique, marquise des Anges* (1956), a text that would become, along with the volumes that followed it, an international best seller, at first refused to publish the novel under the name of Anne Golon (pseudonym for Simone Changeux), preferring to use her husband's name instead. The husband refused since he had only helped his wife with some of the historical research, and the book was finally published with the names Anne and Serge Golon. Even if Angélique remains emotionally and erotically dependant on the man whom she loves, she nevertheless represents a rebellious heroine for the time. The various attempts to guess the author of *Histoire d'O* are clearly symptomatic of a total resistance to the possibility of a feminine eroticism that would participate in male fantasies: Camus could not accept the idea that a novel about the love of submission could possibly be written by a woman, and the anagram Egérie Paulan encouraged people to think that Jean Paulhan was the author. It would be another forty years before anyone knew that the novel was in fact addressed to him as a testimony to unconditional love by a woman, Dominique Aury, alias Pauline Réage. The gradual success of this novel, classically drawn with a spare, almost precious style, recounting the adventures of a slave–heroine ended up becoming a classic—it received the Prix des Deux Magots in 1955, but not without a struggle, to which we will return.

Feminine erotic writing developed in several different directions during the 1950s: the existentialist style, in crude documentary form, in *Vie d'une prostituée* (1946, published in *Les temps modernes*) by an unknown author named Marie-Thérèse; the sober style, quite different from Violette Leduc, but so important for the impact that they had on the public, of Françoise Mallet-Joris (*Le rempart des béguines*, 1951) or Christiane Rochefort (*Le repos du guerrier*, 1958); deviant themes such as incest with a father, experienced as shame in Suzanne Allen (*La mauvaise conscience*, 1955); the violent, sensual, and poetic style in the "histoires nocives" by the Egyptian surrealist, Joyce Mansour (*Cris*, 1954; *Jules César*, 1956) If one considers that with the *Angélique* series a popular and long lasting form of feminine eroticism has finally appeared, the real revolution came in 1959 with the clandestine publication of *Emmanuelle* by an anonymous author (Emmanuelle Arsan, wife of a French diplomat). Thwarting the censors, her editor, Eric Losfeld, managed to publish the text which became an immediate hit.

Emmanuelle's quest (not a completely autonomous one since she is guided by a man, Mario) is not simply one of sexual initiation, but a quest for happiness: the novel describes a world before sin, a world indifferent to Good and Evil, free and utopian. Sexual pleasure is presented as natural, children are able to witness it without taboo, and we are given, perhaps for the first time and from the very beginning of the novel, a precise organic description of feminine sexual response. The freshness of the novel and its feeling of eternal renewal seems to prefigure the great upheavals in French society after May, 1968, and it is no accident that the novel was reissued in a new and this time official version in 1967. Eroticism then begins to move from the individual towards the political and it begins to assume philosophical positions as well: on the Surrealist side, Valentin Penrose, with her *Erzsébet Bathory, la comtesse sanglante* (1962) comes out with a novel of incredible violence, and it shows that a woman can be just as perverse a torturer as a man; the torture and mutilation scenes couple Eros to Thanatos, in the tradition of Bataille, and suggest a retooled gothic redolent of twentieth-century concentration camps.

The 1970s: Politics and Eroticism

The May 1968 movement; the demands for a sexuality liberated from its age-old restrictions; the public affirmation of feminism (for instance with the founding of the publishing company, Editions des Femmes, by Antoinette Fouque in 1973); and theoretical writings on the social implications of sex by authors as different from one another as Monique Wittig and Luce Irigaray, will all contribute to a real evolution in erotic expression. The reissue of *Emmanuelle* in 1967 was an enormous success and it coincided with an explosion in female production as demonstrated by the public reissue of Laure's writings in 1971. Jérôme Martineau created his own publishing house and, after a stint as editor of the collection "L'Or du temps," Régine Deforges created her own publishing house called "Régine Deforges." It is important to note that Deforges would be one of the first "pornographers" who refused to defend erotic literature by arguing for its literary merit, a standard defense in French jurisprudence since the trial of Flaubert's *Madame Bovary* in 1857. In 1969, Pauline Réage published *Une fille amoureuse*, a book that gives special emphasis to the link between eroticism and the spoken word. Monique Wittig, one of the co-founders of Women's Liberation Movement in France, after *Opoponax* (Prix Médecis, 1964), published *Les guérillères* (1969) in an innovative and polyphonic prose, incorporating collage techniques, and then brings *Le corps lesbien* (1973) into the broad daylight of legitimacy, demonstrating that eroticism can be integrated into the new stylistic experiments of the day. This link between literary freedom and sexual liberation is also evident, on a different plane, in the sexual onirism of Janine Aeply or Annie Lebrun, in the alternating coarseness and poetry of Françoise Lefèvre, and especially in the subtle undercurrents of eroticism in Marguerite Duras's work, to which we will return below. Even the themes became more radical, usually provoking the wrath of the censors, and they were reinforced by the use of the narrative conceit of real life stories (fictional or not) like the text by the prostitute Grisélidis Réal, *Le noir est une couleur* (1974). Xavière, with the publication of *La punition* in 1971, wrote a hyper-realistic version of *Histoire d'O*, focusing on the sadistic motivations and the concrete effects of masculine torture, and she even offers, in *F.B.* (1970), an explicit canine zoophilic scene in which the sexual act finishes with nausea, in stark contrast to the more indirect style of Rachilde. Belen (Nelly Kaplan) who had already published many texts in the 1950s, took the guilt out of incest with *Mémoires d'une liseuse de draps* (1974), contrary to the previously mentioned stance of Suzanne Allen. Gabrielle Wittkop, with *Le nécrophile* (1972), describes quite obviously a man's sexual relations with dead bodies, among them that of a young girl. Of course many texts cling to a more classical style of writing like those of the baroness Maud de Belleroche, Céline Rolin, Léone Guerre, or Régine Deforges. But political consciousness remains the hallmark of the literature and of the public stances of the period: *Le Cahier volé* by Deforges in 1978 serves as a reminder of the narrowminded views of the 1950s, and Just Jaeckin's 1975 film adaptation of *Histoire d'O* (he had just brought *Emmanuelle* to the screen in 1974) incurred the wrath of numerous feminists at the time who found both the novel and the film to be reactionary.

From the 1980s to Today: A Return to Moral Order versus Feminine Kamasutras

The 1980s would witness the institutionalization of a certain type of feminism and along with it a backlash (Susan Faludi). But feminine eroticism had earned a clear legitimacy and was now more or less available to the general public through the sale of many different works in airports, train stations, and supermarkets or through the creation of a series like the Harlequin "Désirs," using feminine pseudonyms. One might accept as testimony to this broad acceptance the clear success of the volumes that would follow *La bicyclette bleue* (Régine Deforges, 1981), whose heroine, Léa, is a contemporary French version of Margaret Mitchell's marvelous Scarlett. And further testimony to this legitimacy would be the enthusiasm that greeted Marguerite Duras's narratologically complex novel *L'Amant* (Prix Goncourt, 1984), in which sensual scenes between a man and an adolescent girl are woven into the background of a conflictual and disturbing mother/daughter relationship. The victory in the publishing world for these women who have spoken out is accompanied by a desire, dating from the 1970s, to write about the body and about sexuality without recourse to coded allusions or to secret publication (bookstores specializing in erotic literature are firmly established businesses). At least that is what these commercially appealing titles would seem to suggest: *Jouir* (Catherine Cusset, 1997), *Viande* (Claire Legendre, 1999), *Putain* (Nelly Arcan, 2001), *Des désirs et des hommes* (Françoise Simpère, 2004), *Le divan* (Sophie Cadalen, 1999), *Sept petites histoires de cul* (Anne Cécile, 2001), the collective series such as *Fantasmes/Caprices/Désirs/Passions/Troubles de femmes*, or the somewhat more restrained *Vendredi soir* (Emmanuèle Bernheim, 1997) or *Corps de jeune fille* (Elisabeth Barillé, 1986)... More than ever, women novelists were looking for new avenues of expression or they were taking up pornographic themes that had previously seemed reserved only for men, at least in their public versions. And the men in fact are more often than not transformed into mere puppets, represented only by initials, or even, in the case of Virginie Despentes, Clothilde Escalle, or Chloé Delaume, then objects of violence that is presented as legitimate revenge. On the thematic level adultery, sodomy, fellatio, imaginative masturbation, bi- or homosexuality, multiple partners, or even orgies have become common fare in women's literature, to an extent that one might speak of veritable literary kamasutras (Détrez, Simon, 2006). Some have even tried to stretch the rules of the genre playing with codes and expectations. Catherine Millet or Alice Massat (*Le ministère de l'intérieur*, 1999) write anatomical descriptions of scenes but using a very cerebral style, *Pas un jour* (Prix Médecis, 2002) by Anne Garetta can legitimately be read through the prism of queer theory, Alina Reyes in *Derrière la porte* (1994), alludes to the notorious pornographic film *Behind the Green Door*, but playing with the narrative structures in such a way as to remind us of both Sade and of *A Thousand and One Nights*. The point of all this, mixed with a bit of humor and irony, would seem to be the creation of a "Nouvelle Pornograhie" (Marie Nimier, 2003) that is conjugated in the feminine. This literature, often written in the first person, may be integrated into the domain of autofiction, but also that of autobiography. Grisélidis Réal, active in the struggle for prostitutes rights, has published both documents (*Carnet de bal d'une courtisane*, 2005) and real life stories (*Le noir est une couleur*, 1974, reissued in 2005). Use of the first person allows specific erotic identification for both male and female readers, but and without even mentioning its clear commercial impact, it also raises issues concerning literary history. It is clear that women, who have been linked since time immemorial to the sphere of the intimate and the uterine, are at risk of conforming to a vision of the feminine that will of necessity be defined by the body and sexuality. This is especially true of certain women writers who may not be as subversive as they would have us believe. Catherine Millet may have posed nude for the cover *La vie sexuelle de Catherine M.* (2001), but the very commercial writer, Bénédicte Martin, ups the ante with her own attention grabbing pin-up shot on the cover of *Warm Up*. Alice Ferney, for her part, still exploits femininity, fragility, and emotional instability in *La conversation amoureuse* (2000). The return to a moral order and to age-old clichés hidden behind the scandalous prose and the obvious provocation end up being that much more effective because they remain implicit. There are many women authors of erotic texts who still promote the Pygmalion myth of the man who opens the woman up to a

previously unknown world of sexual pleasure, even through rape and this from writers who consider themselves to be feminists. The "obligatory" link between love and sexuality is a constant, and one even finds advice in women's magazines recommending "polyfidelity" (multiple faithfulness) as a means to keep one's couple together, supreme value of a sexualized contemporary world that is also concerned with social stability. Françoise Rey is thus presented by one of her publishers as a very proper wife, mother, and school teacher, and books appear with explicit titles such as *Le bonheur de faire l'amour dans sa cuisine et vice-versa* (Irène Frain, 2004) or, with an allusion to Mara, *Carnets d'une soumise de province* (Caroline Lamarche, 2004). Finally, censorship laws, updated in 1994, are still there and despite the development of Internet creations: an 'X' rating, meaning it is not allowed to be shown in regular theaters, was given to the film *Baise-moi* by Virginie Despentes and Coralie Trinh Thi in 2000 (that 'X' rating was revised the following year under pressure from the media which wasn't fooled by the political fear-mongering that wanted to silence hard core, anarchical feminism); a court case by parents against a high school teacher who had his 9th-grade students study Agotha Kristof's *Le Grand Cahier* (Prix Inter, 1992); feminine eroticism evicted from all high school textbooks; the creation of special sections dedicated to gay and lesbian literature or erotic women writers in bookstores like FNAC, sections that one might consider less as a form of recognition than as a new means of ghettoizing eroticism. It is nevertheless true that erotic literature written by women, from the time of its early and illustrious representatives at the beginning of the century, has finally found a legitimate place in the contemporary world of publishing.

ANNE SIMON

References and Further Reading

Bennett, Paula, and Vernon Rosario, eds. *Solitary Pleasures: The Historical, Literary and Artistic Discourses of Autoeroticism*. New York: Routledge, 1995.

Benstock, Shari. *Femmes de la rive gauche, Paris 1900–1940*. Paris: Editions des Femmes, 1987; as *Women of the Left Bank*. Austin, University of Texas Press: 1986; London, Virago: 1994.

Bessard-Banquy, Olivier, "L'écriture du sexe aujourd'hui." *Revue d'Etudes Culturelles*, n°1, "Erotisme et ordre moral," Dijon: Abell, mai 2005, p. 47–58.

Brewer, Daniel, Miniche Brewer, and Maria Schehr Lawrence, eds. "Writing After the Erotic." *L'Esprit créateur*, number 3, vol. XLIV, Minneapolis: University of Minnesota, Fall 2004.

Brulotte, Gaëtan. *Œuvres de chair. Figures du discours érotique*. Québec: Presses de l'université de Laval/L'Harmattan, 1998.

Cairns, Lucille. *Lesbian Desire in Post-1968 French Literature*. New York/Ontario/Lampeter: Edwin Mellen Press, 2002.

Célestin Roger, DalMolin Eliane, Prince Gerald, eds. "Eroticisms/Erotismes." *Contemporary French and Francophone Studies: Sites*, vol. 6, issue 1, New York & London: Spring 2002.

Cusset, Catherine. "The Nieces of Marguerite. Novels by Women at the Turn of the Twenty-First Century." *Beyond French Feminisms*, Célestin, Roger, DalMolin, Eliane, De Courtivron, Isabelle, eds., Palgrave Macmillan: New York, 2003.

DeJean, Joan, Miller, Nancy K., eds. "Placing Women in French Literature." *Yale French Studies*, number 75, New Haven: 1988.

Détrez, Christine, Simon, Anne. *A leur corps défendant*, Paris: Seuil, 2006.

Détrez, Christine, Simon, Anne. "Erotisme et familialisme: la nouvelle morale?" *Revue d'Etudes Culturelles*, n°1, "Erotisme et ordre moral," Dijon: Abell, mai 2005, p. 75–85.

Huston, Nancy. *Mosaïque de la pornographie* (1982). Paris: Payot, 2004.

Heathcote, Owen, Hughes, Alex, Williams James S., eds. *Gay Signatures: Gay and Lesbian Theory, Fiction and Film in France, 1945–1995*. New York: Berg, 1998.

Mahuzier, Mc Pherson, Porter, Sarkonak, eds. "'Same Sex/Different Text?' Gay and Lesbian Writing in French." *Yale French Studies*, 90: Yale University Press, 1996.

Phillips, John. *Forbidden Fictions: Pornography and Censorship in 20th Century French Literature*. London: Pluto Press, 1999.

Robinson, Christopher. *Scandal in the Ink. Homosexuality in Twentieth Century French Literature*. London: Cassel, 1995.

WOMEN'S WRITING: LATIN AMERICAN, TWENTIETH CENTURY

An Uncomfortable Script

Hispanic-American Women: the mere formulation of this adjective implies having to present a script that substantiates the main difficulty arising from the elaboration of this presumably evaluative compilation of women writers from Latin America and Spain. Joined by a common language, these two worlds are made up of very distinct cultures and societies. Each has an obvious impact on what their women write, even as they continue to occupy the role of anonymous protagonists of History on both sides of the Atlantic. Then, let us begin by commenting briefly on two problematic themes that are derived from these different origins: the construction of a literary tradition and within it the weight of multiculturalism.

Dating back to the tenth century, erotic literature in Spain is linked to a genre that is as ancient as the *jarchas* of Arabic descent, later rescued and recognized as a formative stream in Spanish culture. What are believed to be the first manifestations of erotica in Latin America, however, were either obliterated by the violence of the conquest or simply ignored during the process of colonization, whereby a foreign language was imposed. The preservation of an important text written in Náhuatl, a poem called "Canto de las mujeres de Chalco"/ "Song of the Women of Chalco" is indeed a rare feat.

Another thorny issue: Even though the Spanish language, within the realm of what is published/publishable, acts as a binding force, cultural heterogeneity in Latin America has been considered and studied as having a thematically timely imprint on women's literature. In Spain, on the other hand, that which has not been acknowledged sufficiently within a recognized framework has yet to be debated in literary terms: the peninsula's cultural diversity is even reflected in its different literary languages. This fact alone, for example, prevents us from including Spanish authors as important as Mercé Redoreda, (1908–1983) who wrote in Catalan.

A third aspect is worth mentioning, though it certainly merits more attention: the representation of social struggles in Spanish and Latin-American women's literary production. If we follow Fourier's line of thought in that the level of development of a society can be measured by the degree of emancipation that women are able to achieve, then Spain and Latin America would not be as distant from each other as their respective historical roles of metrópolis (Spain) and colony (Latin America) would seem to dictate. Common characteristics of both include being made up of underdeveloped societies whereby the State is a tool used by the Catholic church in setting standards for certain behavioral patterns that are reinforced through education and legislative measures. These two characteristics, economically and morally speaking, have acted as obstacles for the development of women's rights. In the realm of politics, traces of masculine superiority have been found in the remotest forms of indigenous government, call it what you will, the Spanish code or American *caciquismo*.

While it's true that in Spain women won their right to vote in 1931, it wasn't until after the end of the Franco regime that society began to include women in the process of modernization that continues to sweep the country today. The suffrage movement in Cuba is successful during comparatively early years, 1934, while in other countries of the continent, such as Mexico and Colombia, to cite two examples, this occurs twenty years later. For the most part, Latin-American societies subjected to armed struggles and dictatorships have not enjoyed the kind of profound democratizing transformation that would insert women in truly egalitarian spaces.

Paradoxically, the struggle undertaken by women writers in Latin America, rooted in an awakening of Creole consciousness, has been the most authentic and stable base from which the Continent enjoys the splendor of feminine literature. With the passing of time, this battle has taken on different nuances. In some places it remains closely tied to the political sphere. Central American literature comes to mind, the testimony of Rigoberta Menchu (1959–), or Claribel Alegría's (1924–) poetry of social protest. But it also manifests itself in the construction of a new language to express the wars of liberation from a feminine perspective. This characteristic stands out in the lyrical-realist narration of the *Sandinista* episode related in Nicaraguen writer Gioconda Belli's (1948–) novel *El país bajo mi piel* [*The Country Under My Skin*] and in Luisa Valenzuela's (1938–) absurd and imaginative works such as *Cambio de armas* [*Change of Arms*] and *Cola de lagartija* [*Tail of a Lizard*] which criticize misogamy and the alliances among dictatorships. Creating new deterritorializing metaphors that reflect the phenomenon of Latin-American cultures in diaspora has also been an aesthetic preoccupation for women writers, be it a product of exile, as in the case *Memoria del silencio*, by Miami-based Cuban writer Uva de Aragon (1944–), or in dealing with the theme of emigration in texts such as *Santitos* by Mexican writer Amparo Rendón, Esmeralda Santiago's (1940–) *Cuando era Puertorriqueña*, or *Yo* by Julia Alvarez (1950–).

At the end of the century, a Spanish woman was referred to as "el ángel del hogar"/ "the angel of the home." Before the twentieth century, Spanish feminism was able to advance only within the scope of education thanks to initiatives set forth by Krausism and the Institute of Free Education. The vindications demanded by women were tied to the struggles for obtaining suffrage rights, income equality, access to education, rights within the institution of marriage, maternity protection, etc. All of these issues are reflected in literature. The style of naturalism in vogue was used by Emilia Pardo Bazan (1851–1921) to denounce the sordid lives of women in the Spanish countryside in novels such as *Los pazos de Ulloa* (1986) and *La Madre Naturaleza* (1887). Due to her work experience and studies on the penal system, Concepción Arenal (1820–1893) was able to publish courageous works, truly ahead of her time, about the correctional institutions for women. In Spain, like Celia Amoros has theorized, feminism has always been closely tied to the conquests of the Enlightenment, and faithful to the demands of Modernity. Nevertheless, in the last decade novels such *Beatriz y los cuerpos celestes* [*Beatriz and the Celestial Bodies*] and *Amor, curiosidad, prozac y dudas* [*Love, Curiosity, Prozac and Doubts*] by Lucía Extebarría (1966) are a reminder that narrative fiction moves complaisantly toward a postmodern cosmology, without renouncing to social critic.

Essential Genealogies

Long before the twentieth century, women in Spain and Latin America, many of them anonymous, took it upon themselves to forge an alternative space within masculine literary canons, an enduring and creative space, though peripheral and almost invisible. As feminist critic Elaine Showalter (*A Literature of Their Own*) has asserted: it's almost always the case that a woman writer shines in the wake of a wave-like movement; while it's true that the crest, with its white foam, is the only thing we can perceive on the surface, underneath there are other profound forces at work, giving rise to a subterranean seismic rumble that makes her visible. Sor Juana Inés de la Cruz (1648–1695), Rosalía de Castro (1837–1885), Clorinda Matto de Turner (1852–1909), Concepción Arenal (1820–1893), Gertrudis Gómez de Avellaneda (1814–1873) and Emilia Pardo Bazán have stayed behind, to mention several literary icons that remain alive despite the lives of their contemporaries who were blinded by incomprehension. Although their works were published posthumously, it is important to remember that such pioneering efforts began to awaken in readers and critics alike the sensibility required to understand the peculiarities of feminine writing today, its texture, tones, and themes.

However, perhaps for the common reader the Chilean writer Isabel Allende (1942) with her *House of the Spirits* (1982) was the one who led the avalanche of editorial and public interest for feminine writing in Latin America that has taken place in the last decades of the twentieth century. This is not entirely untrue given that the novel was translated into various languages, among them Danish, was re-edited innumerable times, and even portrayed on the giant Hollywood screen in the spectacular though inaccurate cinematic rendition of the same title. Works on Allende popped up in every literary magazine; she was interviewed, analyzed during congresses, and invited to give conferences around the world. From academia to the mass media, everyone paid tribute to who was nonetheless referred to as "Garcia Marquez's imitator." Although this isn't the time to discuss this assertion, it's worth remembering that Gabriel Garica Marquez recognizes having been deeply influenced by Elena Garro's (1920–1998) style with her *Recuerdos del porvenir*, and is grateful to Virginia Woolf for having inspired him to experiment with the flow of narrators. Paying debts, recognizing loans, in the same way, Jorge Luis Borges and Bioy Casares would have to be studied in relation to the influence they received from the group of narrators that coalesced around Sur, the leading magazine founded by an Argentine woman named Victoria Ocampo (1891–1979) that became the platform for post avant garde reactions. Works by María Luisa Bombal (1910–1980) and Silvina Ocampo (1903–1993), published before those by such acclaimed masculine names reached the pinnacle of fame, introduced to Hispanic-American literature atmospheres and word games like the ones later recognized as the sole patrimony of the binomial: Borges-Bioy.

In post-Civil War Spain, (1936–1939) a polyphony of women's voices erupt in literature with the strength derived from its ties with Social Realism, a current of wide-ranging traditions in Spanish prose once under the dominion of such great male authors as Pío Baroja, Ramon del Valle Inclán, Miguel de Unamuno, and Blasco Ibañez, among others. Among the traits of these works there is a desire to change a society that deeply wounded the lives of women caused by the war's heartrending impact on the family. They are stories about the inability to adapt, death, and frustrating loneliness. However, soon these women writers begin to be recognized by important awards. Carmen Laforet (1921–2004) is the first woman to win the Nadal prize for her novel *Nada,* in 1944. Another new voice is that of Ana María Matute (1926–); her writing also reflects the desolate aftermath of the war from a pessimistic and existential perspective. In 1957, Carmen Martín Gaite (1925–2000) is awarded with a Nadal for her *Entre visillos*. Although it may seem heretical I feel it's fair, from an anti-canonical standpoint, to include in this list of women authors who wrote from the entrails of the dark world of franquismo, the voice of a woman who achieved the then incredible sum of 400 million books sold. I'm referring to Corín Tellado (1926–), better known as the author of a genre called *novelas rosas* that captivated the feminine public for whom they were conceived. Undoubtedly full of stereotypes, for which her work was condemned to the realm of subliterature, Tellado's work however broke the regimented silence surrounding the world of women.

Support Networks

The sedimentation of a literary feminine anti-canon would be unthinkable without the connections that women writers, critics, journalists, editors, professors, and cultural promoters have created throughout the years. They are at the helm of anthologies dedicated to women, monographical courses, radio and television programs, interviews, academic and editorial publications. Two examples that stand out are *El cuarto propio* [*A Room of One's Own*], in Chile, and *Torremozas* in Spain, dedicated exclusively to feminine productions and used strategically to bear witness to the existing gap so that indifference yields to curiosity from which we finally arrive at recognition. However, literary contests, perhaps the most prestigious avenue in establishing a reputation and reaching effective dissemination, continue to be dominated by men.

Undoubtedly, Spain has been prodigal in creating awards for the divulgation of narrative works. Poetry, on the other hand, cannot rely on equally renowned contests. It may be that in this area Latin America is ahead of the rest in sponsoring the Casa de las Americas awarded in Havana, Cuba.

Spain's Planeta Prize, created in 1952, would acknowledge new feminine voices echoing a new era, although always at a numerical disadvantage in relation to that of their male colleagues. Ana María Matute receives it in 1954 for *Pequeño Teatro*, Lucía Extebarría (1966) was recently bestowed with this award in 2004 for *Un milagro en equilibrio*. In the interim, Planeta Prize has been awarded 52 times and only twelve women, including the two already mentioned, have been honored—Rosa Montero (1951–), Maruja Torres (1943), Carmen Posadas (1953–), and Soledad Puértolas (1947–) are among the women writers who have been awarded between 1989 and 2000, an evident sign of recognition that was long overdue and one which has remained consistent since the fall of Franco.

"Sonrisa Vertical" (Vertical Smile) was also created in Spain. It is the only prize in Iberian American literature that is awarded to narrative works of explicitly erotic themes. Surprisingly, once more in 2004 it went without a recipient, (this had happened three other times since the award's inauguration in 1979). Of 26 awards that have been bestowed a ratio of fifteen men to eight women have walked away the winners. The lower number of female winners can be analyzed symbolically in light of the taboo that has been lifted only recently in relation to this theme. I don't think it's a topic reserved exclusively to women but surely we have much to say on the subject since only a century ago we were completely repressed.

Still Some Treats

However, despite the good news circulating the world regarding the sales of *El albergue de las mujeres tristes*, by Chilean writer Marcela Serrano or *Malena es un nombre de tango* by Spanish writer Almudena Grandés, we should challenge two tendencies that threaten feminine Hispanic American literature, especially that which is produced in Latin America: the reception of its local aspects as exotic and picturesque; and the homogenization of feminine writings within a pattern that conjugates certain stylistic traits, such as poetic language and the use of humor, as an established collection of themes. Let us think of the words used in the compositions of *boleros* and in the culinary recipes that we were bombarded with after the success of *Like Water for Chocolate* by Laura Esquivel (1954–). Parody and the freedom of poetic language have been used as tools in the deconstruction of a masculine vision that they inherit from the strong literary models dictated by men. But once this stage, known by the critiques of Gilber y Gubar as the "anxiety of authorship" (*The Madwoman in the Attic*), is overcome, certain literary models that are too predictable should be dismantled. In literature, formulas are as useful as they are dangerous. A woman writer's worst advisors are hurried editors and shallow criticism in the media.

The Erotic in Feminine Textuality. Problematic Definitions, Expressions, and Risks

Faced with the polemic over the existence of a kind of literature that can be referred to as feminine, we instead adopt Nelly Richard's term "feminine textuality." The stamp of her socio-cultural life experience as a woman and the socio-biological elements that define her are considered here literary traces that conform the text through textual, not only thematic expression.

For this very reason we prefer to use the phrase "literature written by women" in place of "feminine literature." However, we find that much of what has been postulated by Helene Cixous in creating the concept of "feminine writing" is suggestive and useful. In the pages that follow we refer to the eroticism in the writings of Hispanic-American women authors only within narratives and poetry leaving for a brief, final coda theatrical expressions.

Literature that, while being cautious with labels, could be classified as erotic, is also polemic, sometimes bordering on the categorization of pornography and threatened with being excluded from the realm "beaux lettres." The fact that much of the literature written by women enunciates its discourse from the body—the subject's last space of resistance— according to Foucault, could be explained as the search for a place that attempts to decontaminate itself from canonical–patriarchal formulations of feminine sexuality. This simple fact serves to explain that erotic literature can be found broadly represented among works of feminine authorship.

However, the editorial market, with is powerful classifying function, has judged that this literature, precisely because of its iconoclastic nature, "sells." Binary judgments have a tendency to try to impose themselves and the feminine textualization of the erotic is judged from extreme, irreconcilable opposites: that which is vulgar/cultured; that which is popular/elitist. Hence, a female author of such incisive humor and raw eroticism as Cuban writer Zoé Valdés (1959–) can be read, due to the massive circulation of her work as a result of Planeta's promotion, from a pre-judgmental trivializing perspective. Or even worse, devalued by the label of "pornographic writer." Meanwhile, others such as Uruguayan writer Cristina Peri-Rossi (1941–), who works with the theme of alternative sexualities or whose characters and conflicts within the erotic realm can be considered disfunctional, doesn't gain much success from her published works and is read primarily in academic circles. An interesting case that ruptures this trend is reflected in the work of Spanish writer Espido Freire (1974–), who has been awarded Premio Planeta, enjoys surprising popularity, and at the same time is recognized by critics for her unique aesthetics, not only in her treatment of the erotic but in her overall

vision of Spanish society and the challenges that modernization implies.

I turn then to the Argentine Silvia Molloy (1938), one of most renowned scholars of literature written by women in Latin America. One of her opinions may shed light on the interpretation of literature written by women from both sides of the ocean. Presumably rereading Roman Jakobson and his seminal differentiation in the uses of metaphors and metonymy, Molloy has signaled out that: "Turn-of-the century representation of women, in Latin America and else-where, is haunted by dismemberment. In a frenzy of synecdoche, (male) poets will exalt woman's hair, her eyes, her feet, one foot, a glove, a stocking, as *loci* of desire. Only through that mediation, plenitude-woman in her totality, woman complete-proves intolerable..." On the contrary, when Molloy examines the symbols of fragmentation in the feminine body in a text that is written by a woman, she finds that: "the erotic component, and by extension, the fetishization impulse, becomes much more extense in nature." (117)

Molloy looks to the poetry of Alfonsina Storni (1892–1938); I add another example: the work of Cuban writer María Elena Cruz Varela (1953–), whose erotic images also have politically subversive codes. Her poem "El circo" [The Circus] with its strong graphic element, imposes a woman's act of exhibitionism:

> "..I will be the dancer who gallops in the nuderevealing the sparkling arch of her pubes.The round hip. The erect breastsare also for all of you. All of it is a great fanfare..." (*)

As I've demonstrated more extensively in my book about this author, the body, exposed and violated by a gaze, can simultaneously represent the writer or the communal body, that in a country like Cuba is exposed to the controlling vigilance of the State.

On the contrary, to the metonymy that objectifies and ties the image to its physical referent, we find in "ecriture feminine" the feminine metaphor that openly shifts, and situates the process of eroticization of the text (and of reading) into the creation of an image in movement, that can only be captured as a process, an ebb and flow that beckons participation. Let us see it in the lyrical and dynamic way in which Costa Rica native Ana Istarú (1960–) proposes her description of the act of copulation between a man and a woman from a feminine perspective that is fairly recurrent in other female voices. Expressed as a symbiosis with nature, the traditional passivity of the body as an object of desire by the Other is excluded.

"The center of my body
Of my body is the center.
A piece of ebony in two branches,
A tangled dye.
A crescent moon
Rides between my legs.
In my golden thighs,
Steed, the nascent sun

A similar approach to both bodies, that of the female and male loved one, where there are no hierarchies imposed by an objectifying gaze, is the splendid love poem of Spanish poet Ana Rosseti (1950–), who has been able to create a unique style by combining the art of eroticism and liturgical rituals. See such titles as "Exaltación del dulcísimo nombre"/ "The Exaltation of a Very Sweet Name," "Misterios de pasión"/ "Mysteries of Passion," "Porque mi carne no te quiere verbo"/"Because My Flesh Doesn't Want You As A Verb," and a brief demonstration of her graphic and sensual "El jardín de tus delicias"/ "The Garden of Your Delicacy:

Flowers, pieces of your body;
His sap reclaimed me.
I squeeze between my lips
The lacerating bow of the gladiolus.
I could sew lemons to your torso
Their hard tips on my fingers
Like the erect nipples of a young woman..."

"There is no great erotic literature, only eroticism in great works of literature." In that, I agree with Mario Vargas Llosa. This is palpable when we inquire into the production of women whose works can be classified as "historic novels." Many of them distinguish themselves for having female protagonists who experiment with historic changes as part of the very development of their lives. Generally they are bildungsromans such as *Arráncame la vida* [*Take My Life Away*] by Mexican writer Angeles Mastreta (1949–). In this text the progressive disassociation of women from their subordinated conjugal roles and from their acceptance of the political context that dissolves revolutionary ideals run parallel. The nexus Eros-Politics is even more clear in *La otra conquista* [*The Other Conquest*] by another Mexican writer, Marisol

del Campo, where the colonization and destruction of the Aztec empire is reread from the point of view of Malinche, giving her the status of protagonist, portraying her as a character of strong sentiments, not simply as Cortez's concubine as she is cast in traditional History books.

The very relationship between that which is personal and that which is public, psychological, and sociological is more indirect and complex in *La canción de Dorotea* [*Dorothy's Song*], a novel by Spanish writer Rosa Regas (1933–) that merited the Planeta Prize in year 2001. The Civil War is like lime for today's Spain, likewise the repressed desires of middle-class women burn between a traditionally feudal society and modernity. The novel's protagonist, a professional women named Aurelia Fontana, will one day discover the intimate bonds between fear and desire, violence and corruption, in a work of literature where dramatic codes dissolve on the surface in the creation of atmospheres.

We could continue to inquire about the creative uses that women have applied to literary models sanctioned for their effectiveness in an editorial world dominated by men. The case of the so-called *bildungsroman* is also interesting when exploring the feminine vision of one of the principal component episodes of said novelistic style: sexual initiation. Gaetan Brulotte, arguing with Foucault, has observed with certainty that in the erotic arts of the west "sexual truth is essentially not contained in the discourse of confession, but in that of apprenticeship."

By becoming a mentor in bed the female subverts her position as the dominated other and takes on the role of the dominating one by mastering knowledge about sex that is secret and joyful. This inversion of roles gives her back the power and agency that are restricted by moral norms. It is also an ironic paradox that teaching as a profession has traditionally been an occupation that's allowed Hispanic-American women certain influence in the public arena, though only as a service to society.

La nada cotidiana [*The Daily Nothing*] by Zoé Valdés is already a classic reference on erotic language in episodes dealing with sexual initiation. In her style the illustrious Cuban writer uses oral expressions as a renovating source of artistic language and corruptor of stereotypes. By drawing upon humorous, local jargon, very typical of Havana youth, the writer narrates as the protagonist, Yocandra, decides to rid herself of her virginity, which she considers a bothersome obstacle to achieving pleasure. She then searches for a man, who by her own initiative she will turn into a *devirginator* [desvirgador]. Her strong orality gives rise to neologisms, barbarisms, regionalisms, and the eruption of obscene words that typify Valdes's work, leaving an imprint of excess and a fusion between high and pop culture compared with the neobaroque impulse, as Severo Sarduy defines it.

While these explorations in orality can always be studied as signals of the desire to reach the implicit Other in feminine writing, they can also be read as stylistic features of postmodernism in Spain and Latin America, equally reflected in the works of Angela Vallvey (1964–) or Amparo Rendón. Their female protagonists are on the prowl, living itinerant lives in every sense, and open to having contact with the marginal, popular, and extravagant worlds... The works of these writers, one of which was conceived in Mexico's border lands, *Santitos* by Rendón, the other in today's Madrid, *A la caza del último hombre salvaje* [*To the House of the Last Savage Man*], by Vallvey, irradiate the destructive magma of the postmodern where high and pop culture fuse and sexual transgression is only one among a panoply of possibilities. Although the female emerges triumphant this cannot be read as an ideologically explicit feminist vindication. The problematic of gender is also blurred. In works like these, erotica is redefined by trivializing itself, incarnating in the most basic carnal instincts that remain as the only basis of identity for these characters struggling with their circumstances and with themselves.

The charged discussion on pornography as erotica's degenerative limit, the transgression that art cannot afford to commit if it is to be considered art, collects such indispensable voices as Susan Sontag's and George Bataille's. Hence, it must also have a space in this brief summary of what has been done in the area of erotica by women writers. Precisely because they are interested in probing all of its limits, it is very possible that we may frequently find texts written by women who are not frightened of being classified as pornographic as it occurred with Rosario Ferré's (1938–) "Cuando las mujeres quieren a los hombres" [When Women Love Men]. However, the Puerto Rican writer affirms that the very language used for controlling feminine sexuality can also be utilized to redeem it.

Others are less ambitious and use language as a playful, openly defiant instrument. Marcia Morgado (1951–), a Cuban-American author who writes in Spanish is worthy of attention. Her novel's title *69: memorias eróticas de una cubana norteamericana* [*69: Erotic Memories of a North American Cuban*] is a revelation of its context. Morgado pokes fun at the old approach of the turn-of-the-century Latin American *criollista* novel that set out to establish a glossary of names of the continent's flora and fauna that was believed should form part of collective knowledge if we were to interpret our identity. Morgado's glossaries teach us the thousands of ways in which Cuban slang identifies sexual organs, both female and masculine. Finally, I should mention the huge success obtained by Spanish writer Almudena Grandés (1960–) with her novel *Las edades de Lulú* [*Lulu's Ages*]. It won the Sonrisa Vertical Prize in 1989 and made it to the big screen in a cinematographic version in 1990 that exploits through images the pornographic element latent in the novel.

Brief Coda for Theater Written by Spanish-American Women

In the previous pages we've touched on the narrative and poetic genres. Theatre deserves a separate space in its treatment of erotica, be it conceived by a female or male writer. The performance nature of this literary genre bestows it with a fresh singularity. Theater is word in action that cannot exist without voice or body. A character takes on life through the live actor and the presence of a peripheral element: the spectator. It is indeed the most dynamic, participatory, and to a certain degree the most unpredictable of the genres due to the fact that the nature of the text is subject to changes in each enactment.

In following Judith Butler's line of thought when she denies the existence of a "pre-discursive sex" (*Bodies that Matter*: 6) the theatrical arena could be an ideal stage for applying her theories about the importance of performance in defining the sexualized subject, according to which the process of enunciation of the self is inseparable from its generic constitution. The current production by women writers from both sides of the Atlantic apparently takes an interest in experimenting with the materiality of the body that leads to the theatrical scene.

One clear example of this subversive use of the body's materiality in theatrical scenes among Latin-American women writers is the work of Argentine writer Griselda Gambaro (1928–). Recognized by an atmosphere reminiscent of Kafka in her work and for her use of techniques that deal with the ironic and absurd, Gambaro creates characters that interchange their roles of victim and victimized. In this way she makes it clear to what degree we are accomplices of the mechanisms of control. The problem of genre in her work materialize in her feminine and masculine characters. The latter, characterized as caricatures, represent the best criticism of the patriarchal power that they claim for themselves and are therefore reduced to.

In the Spanish dramaturgy written by women Paloma Pedrero (1957–) and Lidia Falcon (1935–) stand out. In both writers, an interest in the world of women seems obvious. At least in Falcon the reiterated presence of female characters immersed in circumstances typical of the roles that real women perform in contemporary Spanish society has served to label her work as propagandist literature. For her part, Pedrero seems to be more interested in the psychoanalytic problematic, as she demonstrates in her most recent work "La Estrella" [The Star], a sort of inner voyage that attempts to salvage her dead father's past that permits the daughter to explore the generational tensions that arise among the two. Realist and contemporary, the theater created by these female authors does not resist being defined as feminist.

Eroticism and Lesbianism: Dangerous Relationships?

Because lesbianism is a particular kind of love shared by two women, this cultural practice can be thought of as having a corresponding rich written expression. However, this apparently doesn't seem to be the case. A recent article that summarizes bibliographical findings from the last decade addresses "the almost inexistence of a 'lesbian literature' written by Spanish or Latin-American authors in their own language" and place even more emphasis on "the scarce translations of the works produced in this area by the anglosaxon culture," (relatoslesbicos. homestead.com) as if it was even known that the audience of our Hispanic countries is not prepared to absorb this theme without prejudice.

The possible reasons for these two absences can be searched for in the deep roots Catholic precepts have in our culture, sanctioning the union between homosexual couples as a sin. On the other hand, the cult of motherhood, a figure venerated in these lands, could imply a total disdain for those women, who by making love to people of the same sex, do not observe the copulative principles of procreation, thus threatening the sacred duty of women as reproducers of the species. However, from the open niche of North American Academia the studies dedicated to Latin-American writers who live and work in the United States (mainly Chicanos, Cubans, and Puerto Ricans) have created a space for research and divulgation of lesbian literature also written in Latin America and Spain. See for example the work of geneological construction presented by the anthology *Hispanism and Homosexualities* where we find a bold rescue of the novelistic creation of a precursor of this type of writing: Venezuelen Teresa de la Parra (1889–1936), in perhaps an even more daring attempt, demonstrating that some of the poems of "The Teacher of America" Gabriela Mistral (1889–1957), also reveal her lesbian sexuality. Fortunately, the contemporary writers no longer have to hide their sexual orientation or its effects on their writing. Uruguayan Cristina Peri-Rossi, Chicana Gloria Anzaldúa (1942–2004), Cuban-American Achy Obejas (1956–), Ena Lucía Portela (1972–) from Cuba, Puerto Rican Magali García Ramis (1946–), and Argentine Silvia Molloy (1938–), write, are recognized and divulged as lesbian writers. Another consequence of the intolerance imposed by the Franco regime was the fact that lesbian characters were scarce in Spanish literature during the first half of the century. Exceptional cases were the rare characters included in works such as *Los soldados lloran de noche* [*Soldiers Cry At Night*] (1964) by Ana María Matute and *El último verano en el espejo* [*The Last Summer in the Mirror*] (1967) by Teresa Barbero. Not until the appearance of *Julia* (1970) by the Catalán writer Ana María Moix (1947–) is this theme treated openly. Then, in 1979, Esther Tusquets continues along this line with her novel *El mismo mar de todos los veranos* [*The Same Sea of All Summers*] where the context of a lesbian relationship also represents the intellectual atmosphere of a university. These two authors are the most outstanding within this genre in Spanish literature.

A point of contact between Latin-American and Spanish writers is an interest to delve in the very process of construction of the relationship, in its internal complexities as well as in confrontations with public moral. Of course this doesn't exclude the recreation of atmospheres and scenes of sexual contact among the characters, but it could be said that lesbian erotica is not essentially constructed upon sexuality but instead on intimacy, the new forms of communication, be it verbal or physical, that two women create in their relationship as lovers.

In Their Own Words

Meanwhile, for female writers, as Rosario Ferré affirms, writing is above all "corporal knowledge" since "it is only through pleasure that we can successfully code... the testimony of our history and our time." Erotic literature, then, can be defined as something much more simple and human, as Argentine Alicia Steimberg does in an exemplary way: "The difficulty in reproducing sexual history rests on the fact that it is an unbinding mix of things and life circumstances; if one attempts to extract those elements the result is strange and frequently pathetic."

MADELINE CÁMARA and LISSETTE CORSA

Further Reading

Araujo, Helena. *La sherezada criolla. Ensayos sobre escritura femenina latinoamericana*. Bogota: Universidad Nacional de Colombia, 1989.

Brulotte, Gaetan. *Oeuvres de chair. Figures du discourse erotique*. Quebec, Presses de l'Universite Laval; Paris: L'Harmattan, 1998.

Butler, Judith. *Bodies that Matter: On the Discursive Limits of Sex*. New York & London: Routledge, 1993.

Charnon-Deutsch, Lou. (ed and comp). *An Annotated Bibliography of Hispanic Feminist Criticism*. Stony Brook, NY: Feministas Unidas, 1994.

Cixous, Helene. "The Laugh of the Medusa." Trans. Keith and Paula Cohen. *Signs*.1 (1976): 875–893.

Davies, Catherine. *Spanish Women's Writing 1849–1996*. London: Athlone, 1998

———. *A Place in the Sun? Women Writers in Twentieth-Century Cuba*. London & New Jersey, 1997.

Foucault, Michel. *Histoire de la sexualite I*. Paris: Gallimard, 1976.

Franco, Jean. *Plotting Woman*. New York: Columbia University Press, 1989.

Gubar, Susan and Sandra Gilbert. *The Madwoman in the Attic. The Woman Writer and the Nineteen Century Literary Imagination*. Second Edition. London: Yale University Press, 2000.

Guerra, Lucia. *La mujer fragmentada: historias de un signo*. La Habana: Casa de las Americas, 1994.

Kaminsky, Amy. *Reading the Body Politic: Feminist Criticism and Latin American Women Writers*. Minneapolis, MN: Minnesota University Press, 1993.

Molloy, Silvia, Sara Castro-Klaren and Beatriz Sarlo. *Womens Writing in Latin America.An Anthology*. Boulder, CO: Westview Press, 1991.

———. and Robert McKee Irwin, eds. *Hispanism and Homosexualities*. Durham and London: Duke University Press, 1998.

Ortega, Eliana and Elena Gonzalez, ed. *La sarten por el mango. Encuentro de Escritoras Latinoamericanas*. Puerto Rico: Huracan, 1985.

Perez, Janet, ed. *Contemporary Women Writers of Spain*. Boston: Twayne, 1988.

Richard, Nelly. "De la literatura de mujeres a la textualidad femenina." *Escribir en los bordes*. Comp. Carmen Berenguer at al. Santiago de Chile: Editorial Cuarto Propio, 1990. 39–52.

Rivero, Eliana. *Discursos sobre la diaspora*. Madrid: Ediciones Aduana Vieja, 2004.

Sarduy, Severo. *Escrito sobre un cuerpo.: ensayos de critica*. Buenos Aires: Editorial Sudamericana, 1969.

Showalter, Elaine. *A Literature of Their Own*. New Jersey: Princeton University Press, 1977.

XAVIÈRE

1941–
French novelist

F.B. and La Punition

F.B. and *La Punition* constitute a striking denunciation of women's self-destructiveness and men's exploitation of their masochism. In both novels the erotic genre's habitual dreamy, seductive staging gives way to a realistic environment and, despite the presence of familiar motifs, Xavière's personal voice, her literary talent—although a minor one—and the questions she addresses bring these novels close to what might be termed high erotic literature.

F.B., like its prototype *The Story of O*, is written in the third person and resorts to the same elegant euphemisms. It takes the reader into a shady network of drifting young women trapped in prostitution, wealthy pimps, and upper-class patrons, without clearly distinguishing between the latter two categories. Cora, the protagonist, is taken by her lover Michel to a luxurious apartment, whose door is opened by a splendid woman in the nude, F.B., with whom

she passionately falls in love. Symmetrically, Michel turns out to be in love with the master of ceremonies, a motif that brings out into the open the homoerotic relationship between René and Sir Stephen in *The Story of O*. While Cora's love for F.B. leads her to accept bondage—figuratively and literally—the novel foregrounds the morbid pride and satisfaction she derives from her growing degradation. The story of F.B., presented as a model of Cora's impending fate, is seen through Cora's own eyes. It is a story of passion and betrayal between women who can love each other in no other way than by allying themselves with the men who torment them and participating in each other's destruction. The women's tortures and humiliations at the hands of their masters culminate in hunting parties in which they are made to act as game. Just as the offenders remind them at regular intervals that they have chosen this way of life—although there would be a severe penalty for trying to refuse it—they also tell them that they are entirely free to run into hiding and escape their pursuers during the hunt. Sometimes there is an "accident" and a woman dies. In the end, F.B. is wounded, and invoking

Rimbaud in a rather failed attempt at sounding literary, Cora is confirmed in her intimate conviction that she has "belonged to an inferior race from all eternity."

In *La Punition*, a loose sequel published shortly after *F.B.*, the first-person narrator writes: "My Lyons punishment, I had somehow wanted it even before knowing of its existence. This is why I could not accuse anybody without first accusing this stranger within myself whom I discovered in Lyons and with whom, from then on, I had to live." This statement summarizes what may be considered the dominant message of both novels: the masochistic wish to be physically and morally "punished" (a recurring word) and the loss of self that ensues from its fulfillment. Whereas the masters find a reason for inflicting punishment in any minor act of disobedience toward them, the women's motivation is not clearly defined, but seems to arise from a despair that leads to self-abasement. Thus, *F.B.* forcefully conveys the obscure pleasure of masochism and its sadistic underpinning, and *La Punition*, a more original attempt, even more realistically details a living through of the willed sentence. The narrator has chosen Lyons after hearing from F.B. that it offered the most severe punishment. The sordid hotel where she is taken by M. and Raymond turns out to be a low-class brothel. Confined to a dirty room, she has to service men on a box spring (without a mattress) all day long, to the accompaniment of a woman's incessant screaming in the next room. This other victim, Gloria, considered insane by the masters, mirrors the narrator's own abjection and will become the instrument of her salvation. Taken back to Paris after an indeterminate number of months, the narrator "forgets" Lyons within a week and resumes her life as a prostitute-hostess. Once, incomprehensibly, she refuses herself to a patron and receives a stern warning from Raymond, who threatens to take her back to Lyons. She consequently resolves to commit suicide. To celebrate this decision, she meets in her usual bar with a male friend. Gloria is there, back from Lyons, and so are M. and Raymond. Gloria then does what the narrator "would never have dared": amid mounting silence, she starts insulting the two men and describing what they did to her in Lyons, "less to take her money than to demolish her." The men beat her and leave her bleeding on the floor. Later, when the paramedics arrive, one of them starts laughing and tells

the others: "It's that madwoman again. Let's hope this time she won't get away with it and they will put her away. Unless she croaks before." Experiencing a new consciousness, the narrator then decides she owes it to Gloria, and to the woman she herself used to be before her subjection, not to die, but to live and remember Lyons. Thus, as opposed to *F.B.*, *La Punition* ends on a note of revolt and hope.

Indeed, the whole narrative of *La Punition*, written in retrospect, conveys this sense of revolt, not so much because it is consistently told from the point of view of the victim, but because the latter's beatings and humiliations, her solitude (she prefers her weekday travails to the loneliness of Sundays, when she does not see any patrons) and, throughout, her depersonalization take place amid everyday, minute happenings that ring only too real and run counter to the erotic effect.

In addition, common themes of erotic fiction are subtly diverted and demystified in both *F.B.* and *La Punition*. Thus, lesbianism is not given the usual stereotypical treatment. In both novels, love for a female prostitute motivates the protagonist's consent to her own prostitution. Lesbianism, however, far from appearing inferior to heterosexual relations—a mere occasion for male voyeurism—also constitutes an emotional refuge and crystallizes the women's strongest love feelings, for which reason it is frowned upon by the masters. Similarly, the women's mutual betrayals and their complicity with their tormenters are not viewed by the narrative voice as originating in nature, but rather as evidence of their inevitable disintegration after repeated sexual humiliations. There is nothing sugar-coated about their debasement. Trained into passivity, they take pleasure in their sense of shame, learn not to stand up for one another, and defy the masters only in order to be punished. Cora in particular feels joy under the whip, euphoria after torture, and an intense sensation of life after watching F.B.'s rape by a dog. Despite her lover's obvious contempt, the narrator of *La Punition* is turned into a groveling supplicant in her terror of being left alone. Most noteworthy perhaps is the pervasive irony in the depiction of the masters' power trips, callousness, and hypocrisy. As in *The Story of O*, they protest their love to the women, especially before torturing them, remind them that they are free, and solemnly orchestrate a ludicrous initiation ceremony, which they crown by forcing Cora to masturbate with a rope "without cheating." The men see themselves as trainers performing their experiments on female animals. Their victims' frigidity does not bother, but suits, them. Alleging their will to know, they observe their victims with dispassionate interest ("It is not funny, but it is interesting") and tend their wounds with expert gentleness. One of them asks for F.B.'s forgiveness when torturing her, while solidly maintaining her "riveted" on a table.

It is not inconceivable that some readers might experience erotic excitement when reading *F.B.* and *La Punition.* No doubt, the choice of scenes and their crudeness place these works squarely in the category of erotic fiction. At the same time, their raw cruelty and analytic tone consistently maintain a distance, and their satiric intent is unmistakable. They were written in the 1970s, at a time of feminist protest, and it is significant that Xavière's production does not seem to extend much beyond that period. *La Punition* was a best seller in its time and in 1973 was the object of a film adaptation by director Pierre-Alain Jolivet, starring Karin Schubert.

Biography

Born in 1941, Xavière Lafont is reported to have worked in Parisian nightclubs in the early 1960s. Her novels were published between 1970 and 1982.

LUCIENNE FRAPPIER-MAZUR

Editions

F.B. Paris: C. Bourgois, 1970; (with *La Punition*), France Loisirs, 1980; Editions J'ai Lu, 1984.
La Punition. Paris: C. Bourgois, 1971; La Table Ronde, 1973; Editions J'ai Lu, 1974, 1998.

Selected Works

Ô gué vive la rose. 1974
Thank you, monsieur. 1975
Quand le vent sèchera tes larmes. 1978
Une chaîne au pied droit. 1982

Y

YAMADA, AMY

1959–
Japanese novelist

Amy Yamada first gained notice with her rambunctious, sexually charged story *Bedtime Eyes*, which was peppered with graphic depictions of sexual encounters between the protagonist, a Japanese club singer named Kim, and a black American soldier named Spoon. First published in the middlebrow literary journal *Bungei*, it was awarded the journal's *Bungei Award* for that year. The story garnered attention for its bold depiction of sexuality from a female's point of view but also because of sensational reports in the media about the author's own experiences (with black American soldiers). Amy Yamada has since become one of the best-known contemporary women writers. Her real-life experiences and their subsequent fictionalizations fanned an underground fascination with black hip-hop culture among her younger readers.

Yamada seems to have made a conscious decision to use the potent image of a black soldier as a central trope for many of her narratives. She purposely blurs the line between her own life and that of her female protagonists, living a glamorous, at times unconventional, life in the full view of the reading public. Yamada's early works are demarcated by two major tropes: sex and race. Her female personae are bold and aggressive in their pursuit of sexual pleasure, transcending the traditional, male-dominated gender relationships that characterize Japanese society. Most of her female characters work in the sex industry and are not bashful. The empowered sexual subjectivity represents a type of liberated contemporary young woman who is not bound by personal inhibitions or traditional roles.

The openness of Yamada's female character toward sex and sensual pleasure is unusual, as is the persistent focus of her gaze on black bodies. In *Bedtime Eyes*, culinary and animalistic metaphors are used to encode Spoon, focusing on color, smell, and texture. Kim compares Spoon's shiny, black body to sweet chocolate, with a "sweet juice that bursts out when one bites into it." She also describes Spoon's body as emitting "the sweet rotting fragrance of cocoa butter" that "smells fetid but not unpleasant. No, not unpleasant, but rather like as if I am aware of myself becoming cleansed while placed in the filth, a smell like that. His smell makes me feel superior." This last comment reveals the complex associations of black ethnicity in Japanese culture. Yamada emphasizes the erotic nature of her protagonists' black partners, and they certainly represent an exotic Other within Japanese society, but she cannot wholly escape the discriminatory attitudes prevalent in Japan, which equate lightness of skin color with high status and social superiority. Moreover, she elides the political questions raised by the presence of foreign troops on Japanese soil, a remnant of the postwar occupation era that reflects a continuing asymmetrical power relationship between Japan and America, with colonialist overtones.

In *Finger Play* (1986), the protagonist Ruiko reunites with a former boyfriend, a black GI named Leroy. Having been expelled from the army, Leroy now works as a pianist. Ruiko suffers frequent physical abuse in this sadistic relation, until one day, as he is about to leave her, Ruiko accidentally kills him. Leroy's nimble fingers, which play the piano and her body with equal dexterity, also deal out violence, and the line between violence and masochistic pleasure is often blurred. The sadomasochistic (S/M) theme continues in *Kneel Down and Kiss My Feet* (1988), where Shinobu, the queen of an S/M club, delineates the ethics of prostitution.

In *Jesse's Backbone* (1986), the themes of drugs, sex, jazz, and S/M are toned down in a touching portrayal of an unexpected relationship between Coco, a Japanese woman, and her black lover Rick's young son, Jesse. This sets the stage for the novel *Trash*, in which the relationship with Rick comes to an end, while her love for Jesse survives.

Other than the black–yellow love relationships that pervade in Yamada's earlier works, her works with teenagers as protagonists are also worth noticing. *The Bound Feet of the Butterflies*, *Wind Burial Classroom*, *Keynote after School*, and *A Child of Old Age* sensitively capture the perils and ambivalence of growing up. Yamada avoids heavy-handed sermons and opts for an airy, lighthearted, colloquial style that makes her characters sound natural and approachable. Her sense of dry humor is best captured in her short story collection, *Verbs for Happiness*.

Lately, Yamada has turned to portraying more mature relationships between men and women. *A 2 Z* (2000), a novel consisting of 26 vignettes based on the letters of the alphabet, depicts a couple, Natsumi and Kazuhiro, who are both having extramarital affairs. The marriage is saved and they are able to reaffirm their love for each other when Kazuhiro punches Natsumi at the end. Domestic violence does not exist in Yamada's lexicon.

Amy Yamada's writing highlights the sexual subjectivity of contemporary Japanese women who deem the pursuit of sexual pleasure their birthright. This assertion, however, is not without its problems. Though Yamada addresses issues of race and discrimination in works such as *Animal Logic* (1996), they tend to remain at the level of superficial observation. The sensual language and the accessibility of the subject matter have made Yamada a favorite of young readers, but the combination of a racialized gaze and the desire to be sexually dominated (although Shinobu in *Kneel Down and Kiss My Feet* is a dominatrix, she does it as a profession) have stimulated criticism among some Japanese critics but especially among Western academics. The complex interweaving of sexuality and race in her writings raises many questions, but it is also what elevates her writing above soft-core sexual fantasy.

Biography

Born as the eldest daughter of a middle-class Tokyo family in 1959, Yamada began her career as an author of *manga* (Japanese visual narrative comics) in the early 1980s. After working at jobs such as club hostess, nude model, and adult video actress, Yamada turned her own experience of living with a black American soldier on a U.S. Army base outside of Tokyo into her first novel, *Bedtime Eyes* (1985). Her subsequent works, *Jesse's Backbone* (1986) and *The Bound Feet of the Butterflies* (1987), were both nominated for the prestigious Akutagawa Literary Award.

FAYE YUAN KLEEMAN

Editions

Bedtime Eyes. Tokyo: Kawade shobo. 1985.
Finger Plays. Tokyo: Kawade shobo. 1986.
Jesse's Backbone. Tokyo: Kawade shobo. 1986.
Kneel Down and Kiss My Feet. Tokyo: Shinchosha. 1988.
Trash. Tokyo: Bungei shuju. 1991.
Verbs for Happiness. Tokyo: Benesse Corporation. 1993.

Animal Logic. Tokyo: Shinchōsha. 1996.
A 2 Z. Tokyo: Kodansha. 2000.

Selected Works

The Bound Feet of the Butterflies [*Chōchō no tensoku*]. 1987
Harlem World [*Haaremuwaarudo*]. 1987
Soul Music Lovers Only [*Souru myūjikku rabāzu onrī*]. 1987
Tropical Rocking Chair [*Nettai anraku isu*]. 1987
The Coffin of the Canvas [*Kanbasu no hitsuki*]. 1987
Wind Burial Classroom [*Fūsō no kyōshitsu*]. 1988
I Am Beat [*Boku wa biito*]. 1988
Freak Show [*Furīku shō*]. 1989
Keynote After School [*Hōkago no kīnōto*]. 1989
Chewing Gums [*Chūinguganu*]. 1990
Son of Colors [*Shikisai no musuko*]. 1991

A Child of Old Age [*Bannen no kodomo*]. 1991
Rabbit Disease [*Rabittobyō*]. 1991
24·7 [*Towentifō sebun*]. 1992
I Can't Study [*Boku wa benkyō ga dekinai*]. 1993
4 U. 1997
Magnet [*Magunetto*]. 1997
The Royal Princess [*Himekimi*]. 2001

Further Reading

Cornyetz, Nina. "Power and Gender in the Narratives of Yamada Eimi." In *The Woman's Hand*, edited by Paul Shallow and Janet Walker, 425–60. Stanford, CA: Stanford University Press, 1996.
Yasue Kuwahara. "Make Me Sick: Perceptions of Traditional Sex Roles in Japanese Society in Novels by Yamada Amy." *Journal of Popular Culture* 27:4 (Spring 1994): 107–16.

YAOHU YANSHI [*THE VOLUPTUOUS HISTORY OF FOX DEMONS*]

Seventeenth-century Chinese novel

This novel in twelve chapters, intended for a readership fond of eroticism and craving for cheap entertainment, is not easier to identify than most novels of the same kind. It most likely dates back to the first half of the Qing dynasty (1644–1911). Its author is assuredly not Xu Lin (1462–1538), the poet to whom it was attributed, even though the set of pseudonyms displayed may suggest so. Incidentally, this is also the case for the *Taohua yanshi* [*The Peach Blossom Fantasy*], another short novel of similar construction which may well have been put together in the same publishing studio.

The *Yaohu yanshi* is known to us only through the single surviving copy of a version that could actually be a shortened one; at least, the roughness of the narrative leads one to imagine that such is the case. Only the first part of the novel is clearly erotic; as for the second, it's entirely devoted to some edifying entertainment blending various aspects of Chinese literature in vernacular language, as if it were intended to make amends for the aberrations of the first one. The

narrator, it is true, doesn't skimp on his effects: he unceremoniously throws the hero, Mingmei, a deceptively naive and inexperienced young man, into the lustful hands of two she-fox demons, who, for quite some time—five centuries, in fact—have been regenerating their power by pumping sexual energy out of their lovers. After both vixens have taken the appearance of irresistible beauties, the first one gives in to Mingmei's every playful whim, while the other sets to watch two young he-foxes cavort about and enjoy sodomite pleasures. A while later, the four demons gather around Mingmei, who soon becomes aware of his decrepitude and, as terrified as he is incredulous about the whole thing, has to witness their trial's proceedings led by the deity in charge of the creatures of the great Beyond: while the male demons are straightaway slain, the female ones are sentenced to two centuries of inactivity. Once relieved of such baleful company, Mingmei stumbles across yet another she-fox spirit, who, fortunately for him, turns out to be closer to immortality than his earlier acquaintances. With the help of her mentor, Hu the Immortal, she sends him back to the human

1443

world and will from then on protect him and his folks under all circumstances.

For, while Mingmei was away his father fell into the clutches of two villains, whose nasty plans do not work out because both human justice and divine wisdom are on lookout. One of Mingmei's neighbors, a former serf who intended to take advantage of the situation, is punished as well. Still under the secret support and protection of the Immortals, Mingmei brilliantly passes the mandarin examinations, an achievment that brings him to the attention of an influential minister. The latter, confident in his might and disregarding a previously sealed union, compels Mingmei to marry his daughter. But, once again, this hideous crime is soon punished. Unfailing support from the spirits eventually eases a happy conclusion for the hero, who will end up marrying two brides, while it precipitates the tragic fate of the disloyal minister whose concupiscence finally leads him to his death. In short, it is success and happiness for the deserving ones, who managed to right the helm in time, and expiation and violent death for those who let themselves get carried away by vile thoughts.

Beyond the moralizing speech that the novel conspicuously develops and its resort to countless overused set phrases which are typical of literature in vernacular Chinese, the true originality of the *Yaohu yanshi* lies in the importance taken on by fox spirit characters. While the male spirits appear particularly dubious and malicious, as they seem solely concerned with the satisfaction of their own needs, the vixens present two diametrically opposed facets of this eerie creature, which has been haunting Chinese fiction ever since the early days. On one hand, we thus have a succubus who tries to take advantage of the vital energy of her victim, and on the other we have a grateful and protective she-fox spirit who even shows the ability to give way to a mere mortal woman. These vulpine characters also refer to other readings, such as the *Zhaoyang qushi* [*The Lascivious History of Zhaoyang*], to name but one.

As regards the sex scenes, they diffusely echo other works too. Some are duly quoted, such as the *Ruyi jun zhuan* [*The Lord of Perfect Satisfaction*] and the *Nongqing kuaishi* [*A Joyful History of Passion*], about the mischiefs of Emperess Wu Zetian (624–705) with her sensual entourage. As for the scenes involving the two sodomite foxes,

they implicitly refer to collections of tales which used to flourish in Hangzhou during the late Ming (1368–1644). But whereas those would promote such practices, our novel here firmly condemns them while simultaneously taking pains to depict them in great detail. The bantering tone that punctuates the protagonists' successive exchanges thus gives way to a warning against what is here presented as a deviance, a base instinct one should be wary of and try to guard one's children against.

Nevertheless, this novel above all remains a farce. The endpaper of the sole surviving old edition mentions "laughter guaranteed as soon as the book is opened" ("Kaijuan yixiao"). Except for the spirits, deities and demons, all the characters in this novel come from a low- or middle-class background in Confucian society; and to the reader, they appear as puppets at the mercy of the author's fancy, the latter obviously taking great pleasure in showing us their flaws and foibles.

Another outstanding and unusual feature is the depiction, in the first chapter, of an erotic theatre which appears quite unlikely insofar as, contrary to the rules of Chinese dramatic art, it shows rather than suggests love relationships and the complementarity of the sexes: "On the first stage 'Ximen Qing Wreaks Havoc Under the Vine Arbor' was being performed, and on the second one they were playing 'Wen Leiming Meets up with Miss Luan.' On both sides, the actors in the title roles were wearing skin-tight outfits: both male and female leads sported trousers made of some see-through gauze which would cling to their legs so well that one could have thought they were naked, incidentally displaying the boys' stiff penises on either stage. The girls' little golden lotuses could also clearly be seen, as they were resting on their partner's shoulders. Tenderly entwined, sex organs against each other, the bodies were banging away as vigorously as a hen pecks about or a pestle hits the bottom of a mortar. Their stage business left none cold."

PIERRE KASER

Editions

Galantes chroniques de renardes enjôleuses. Translated by Aloïs Tatu. Follow-up to *Les renardes par l'une d'elles* by Solange Cruveille. From the collection "Le pavillon des corps curieux." Arles: Picquier, 2005.

YAOI

"Yaoi" is an acronym for ya*ma nashi, ochi nashi,* i*mi nashi:* "no climax, no point, no meaning." It is amateur homoerotic literature based on the young male characters in Japanese manga (comics) and anime (cartoon animations). In Japan, Yaoi comprises mostly *dōjinshi* [fan-produced manga], while in the West it is usually found as stories and artwork on the Internet. The majority of Yaoi creators are young women. The creation of Yaoi is a popular activity in many world regions.

Yaoi stories portray characters overcoming obstacles, often internal, to be together. Many Yaoi works are sexually explicit. Many are not, but as sex underlies romantic love, it is present as a means of giving urgency to desire. In Japan and the West, Yaoi transgresses societal boundaries. Besides same-sex eroticism, these can include relationships between a minor and an older partner, between siblings, among multiple partners, and with authority figures, such as teachers. Sexual acts may be nonconsensual, violent, or carried out in public spaces.

The end of many Yaoi works is idealistic, belying the acronym. Yaoi authors use the tension of crossing boundaries to explore issues central to sex and love. The genre allows young people to redefine the adult-created media characters of their childhood and to express erotic desire publicly, free of editorial constraint and parental control.

Yaoi is a visible activity in Japan. In 2002 almost 400,000 people, most of them young women and teenage girls, attended Tokyo's Comiket, a twice-yearly fan-organized event, to buy or sell *dōjinshi*, much of it Yaoi-themed, created by small circles of friends. Comiket grew rapidly from its 1976 start; since the mid-1980s it has occupied Japan's largest exhibition center. There are smaller similar exhibitions in cities such as Osaka, which attract tens of thousands, and there are stores which sell *dōjinshi* commercially and informal fan networks to exchange *dōjinshi* via mail.

In the West, Yaoi is an activity mostly on the Internet and at events such as Yaoi-Con, a convention held yearly in the United States since 2001. Authors post stories to thousands of websites and online journals, as well as to fan-fiction archives, at least one of which, http://www.fanfiction.net, had close to a million works of all types archived in February 2005, many of them Yaoi stories.

Those unaware of Yaoi may encounter it when searching the Web for anime or manga. One example is a North American boy's e-mail to a Yaoi site in 2000 asking if it was true that his favorite character, the 15-year-old Duo (one of a quintet of space pilots in the popular commercial anime *Gundam Wing*), is gay, as his schoolmates had claimed upon coming across Yaoi illustrations on the Web. The site owner's response marks a discourse between the young and adults around same-sex erotics among the young. In the West this tends to be via LiveJournals, blogs, comments to website guest books, posts to discussion groups, and comments on Yaoi works stored on archive sites; in Japan it is also via letters to printed magazines, especially the popular commercial genre of homoerotic "boy love" [*shōnen-ai*] manga, which arose a few years before Yaoi.

The *dōjinshi* authors of *Rappori Yaoi Tokushū Gou* [*Rappori: Special Yaoi Issue*] (1979) coined the acronym because their work was a collection of episodes with no overarching structure. The story features two youths in a suggestive but not sexually explicit relationship. There were Yaoi parodies of Gundam in the early 1980s, but it was the popularity of a *dōjinshi* in 1985 based on *Captain Tsubasa*, a manga about boys' soccer, and another in 1987 based on the manga *Saint Seiya* which put "Yaoi" into the Japanese vernacular. The early Yaoi works reflect three attributes which have come to distinguish the genre: (1) amateur products outside of commercial editorial controls (2) based on known characters and settings (so far, not so much unlike the

"Tijuana Bibles" well known to connoisseurs in the West) and (3) whose characters are depicted as ordinary teenage boys or young men in their twenties, the same age group as many Yaoi fans.

Yaoi has encountered controversy in Japan. A moral panic occurred in 1989 after a manga fan (not a Yaoi aficionado) murdered four children. Police arrested about 80 amateur manga artists, almost all teenagers or in their twenties, and confiscated thousands of *dōjinshi* from Tokyo stores. In 1992, a debate took place in the feminist magazine *Choisir* after a gay-identified man complained that Yaoi characters had nothing to do with "real gay men." Readers responded that Yaoi was a way to critique and overcome heterosexist gender norms. One said there was no reason why one's sex should determine the gendering of the subject or object of one's desire—a position which agrees with the critique of identity offered by queer theory, which emphasizes the processes of identification through which identities are formed, rather than identity as an ontological given. Neither incident seems to have diminished Yaoi's popularity.

Yaoi's popularity in the West is due in part to the increasing amount of anime shown on commercial television for children as well as the Web as an easy-to-use and pervasive dissemination medium for fan-written stories and artwork. A notable factor in Yaoi's cross-cultural popularity is the dissimilarity of Western and Japanese cultural contexts. The representation of male adult/ adolescent eroticism [*nanshoku*] has been prevalent in Japanese cultural products since about 800–850 CE, ending only with Japan's adoption of Western psychosexual theories in the late 19th and early 20th centuries. Gender ambiguity has been a topos in Japanese culture since the publication of works such as the widely read 12th-century story *Torikaebaya* [*Changelings*]. Sexually explicit depictions have been common since the advent of inexpensive prints produced by woodblock printing in the Edo period (c. 1600–1868) and continue today in manga.

Many Yaoi works resemble fairy tales, in that they show the protagonist(s) triumphing against the odds. Unlike Western literary fairy tales, which started as didactic stories designed to uphold the status quo, Yaoi stories are about desire. As such, they usually explore, not circumscribe, possibilities.

As yet there are no formal published surveys of Western Yaoi creators. Some resist labels,

including "queer," even in its sense of being unable to signify gender monolithically. They report different reasons for why they like Yaoi. Key seems to be erotic attraction to the characters coupled with freedom: Yaoi transcends gender roles and finds young male bodies attractive. Another common reason is that Yaoi provides a relatively safe place from which to explore sex and desire.

Thematically, Yaoi is similar to the works Western women and some men have created about male characters from TV programs, movies, and books (see *Slash Fiction*). The U.S. generation of the 1930s and 40s had Tijuana Bibles: cheap, vest-pocket fuck comics featuring the cherished, cherubic characters of the mainstream funny papers. A difference in Yaoi is the younger age of the media characters and the fans. Yaoi shares with commercial romance fiction and fan-written *gen* (nonsexual) fiction the idea of imagining a different social state; unlike them, Yaoi's discourse appears to be less accepting of gender roles as scripted in the cultures in which it is produced. A smaller genre derived from Japanese anime and manga, *yuri*, denotes fan works about relationships, often represented explicitly, between girls or women.

MARK MCHARRY

See also **Manga; Slash Fiction**

Further Reading

Aestheticism.com. Retrieved April 11, 2006, from http://www.aestheticism.com/visitors/index.htm

Avila, Kat Kaneko. "Yaoi Comics: Two Guys in Love and the Female Voyeur." *JADE Magazine* January-February, 2002.

Barral, Etienne. "Le Comiket, royaume des fanzines." Centre d'Études et de Recherches Internationales (CERI), 2000. http://www.ceri-sciences-po.org

Berry, Chris, Fran Martin, and Audrey Yue, eds. *Mobile Cultures: New Media in Queer Asia*. Durham, NC: Duke University Press, 2003.

Jenkins, Henry. *Textual Poachers: Television Fans and Participatory Culture*. New York: Routledge, 1992.

Kinsella, Sharon. "Amateur Manga Subculture and the Manga *Otaku* Panic." *Journal of Japanese Studies*. Washington University Press, Summer 1998.

———. *Adult Manga: Culture and Power in Contemporary Japanese Society*. Honolulu, HI: Curzon Press and University of Hawai'i Press.

McHarry, Mark. "Yaoi: Redrawing Male Love." *The Guide* 23 (2003): 29–34.

McLelland, Mark. 2000. "No Climax, No Point, No Meaning? Japanese Women's Boy-Love Sites on the Internet." *Journal of Communication Inquiry* 24 (3): 274–91.

————. "Why Are Japanese Girls' Comics Full of Boys Bonking?" *Intensities* 1 (2001).

————. "Japanese Queerscapes: Global/Local Intersections on the Internet." In Berry et al., *Mobile Cultures*, 52–69.

Pflugfelder, Gregory. *Cartographies of Desire: Male–Male Sexuality in Japanese Discourse, 1600–1950.* Berkeley and Los Angeles, CA: University of California Press, 1999.

Radway, Janice. *Reading the Romance: Women, Patriarchy, and Popular Literature.* Chapel Hill, NL: University of North Carolina Press, 1984.

Sabucco, Veruska. "Guided Fan Fiction: Western 'Readings' of Japanese Homosexual-Themed Texts." In Berry et al., *Mobile Cultures*, 70–86.

Suzuki, Kazuko. "Pornography or Therapy? Japanese Girls Creating the Yaoi Phenomenon." In *Millennium Girls: Today's Girls Around the World*, edited by Sherrie Inness, 243–67. London: Rowman & Littlefield, 1998.

Thorn, Matt. "Girls and Women Getting Out of Hand: The Pleasure and Politics of Japan's Amateur Comics Community." In *Fanning the Flames: Fans and Consumer Culture in Contemporary Japan*, edited by William W. Kelly. Albany, NY: State University of New York Press, 2004.

Vincent, Keith J. "Envisioning the Homosexual in Yaoi." Presentation at the conference *Conceptualising Gender in Different Cultural Contexts*, School of Oriental and African Studies, University of London, May 2-3, 2002.

Welker, James. "From The Cherry Orchard to Sakura no Sono: Translating Sexualities." Presentation at the AsiaPacifiQueer3 conference *The Uses of Queer Asia: Research, Methods and Diasporic Intellectuals*, University of Melbourne, Australia, December 8, 2002.

Zipes, Jack. *When Dreams Came True: Classical Fairy Tales and Their Tradition.* New York: Routledge, 1999.

YASUNARI KAWABATA

1899–1972
Japanese novelist

The House of the Sleeping Beauties

Yasunari Kawabata's *The House of the Sleeping Beauties* is a unique 20th-century Japanese erotic novel. Like many of Kawabata's novels, it was initially serialized in literary journals and then published in book form. *The House of the Sleeping Beauties* was serialized intermittently in the literary journal *Shinchō* from January to June of 1960, and from January to November of 1961, the publication being interrupted by two trips abroad to the United States and Brazil. It was later published as a single book in 1961 by the publisher Shinchōsha and has since appeared in numerous reprints and various editions. It has been translated into many languages, including English, French, Italian, Chinese and Korean. E. Seidensticker's English translation is used as the base text for quotes in this essay.

Reading Yasunari Kawabata's *The House of the Sleeping Beauties* is an intense, hypnotic, and yet somewhat disturbing experience. Readers familiar with Kawabata's spirited earlier short story *The Izu Dancer* or the more ethereal novels *Snow Country*, *A Thousand Cranes*, and *The Sound of the Mountain*—which reflect upon nature and the fragility of human nature—will no doubt be taken aback by this airless and constricted narrative world that is cloistered in a secret chamber. To appreciate this chillingly beautiful poetic meditation on the twin themes of sexuality and death, the reader must surrender his daily reality to a world of imagination and fantasy. The work also demands that we investigate our understanding of eroticism in general and erotic literature in particular. What charges eroticism? Is there a fundamental structure of eroticism that is viable and effectual cross-culturally? Is the eroticism of this novel derived from the naked bodies of beautiful young virgins; or is it the highly sexualized memory of the old man Eguchi unleashed in the artificial, cloistered realm that ignites both his and our erotic fantasy? What are the relations between sexual eroticism and violence, death and old age? Where is the thin line between eroticism and perversity? The novel seems to beget more questions as one reads on.

Structure

The House of the Sleeping Beauties begins with the old man Eguchi, who is persuaded by a friend to visit a mysterious house of sleeping beauties. In this secret club, economically and socially successful older men who are sexually impotent come to spend a night sleeping next to a beautiful naked virgin who has been drugged into a deep slumber and is completely unaware of the encounter. The novella documents five such visits by the protagonist Eguchi, from his totally unanticipated first trip to an abrupt and shocking ending involving the death of one of the young girls. There are only two active characters in the narrative: the old man Eguchi and the proprietor of the secret club, a middle-aged woman who speaks with polite but distant deference. The narrative thus consists of the sparse dialogues between the two characters that serve as a frame narrative, while the greater part of the novel transpires in the old man's head, focusing on his observations of the six young virgins, his recollections of the past, and the dreams and nightmares triggered by the young girls lying naked beside him.

Eguchi's fantasies of the six sleeping virgins and his drug-induced, dreamlike meditations on the pivotal females he encountered in his life composes the core of this internalized narrative. Many readers are struck by the lack of action in the narrative and the absence of interaction between characters other than the laconic, businesslike dialogues between the old man and the proprietor. Kawabata uses a complex layering of textual space and time to tell a story essentially occurring within the physical space of a small secret chamber. There are five interactions between the old man and the proprietor woman and five silent interior monologues of the old man, each set in motion by the contours, colors, and smells of the different naked bodies while Eguchi is in a semiconscious, dreamlike, drugged state. The most revealing images, however, are Eguchi's reminiscences of his own past (sexual) encounters with women who left a mark on his life. In these hallucinatory states, the past is invoked and past losses are reexamined. Thus this is not only a novel about an uncanny encounter between the old and the young, the

waking and the sleeping; it is also a pathology of Eguchi's sexual autobiography.

Motif of the Virgin Maiden

Kawabata's obsession with young maidens started with his first work *The Izu Dancer* (1927) and lasted all through his long and prolific career. Rumor has it that his suicide may have been related to his infatuation with a young maid working at his house at the time of his death. That aside, the eternally youthful, preadolescent girl has become one of the most important tropes in Kawabata's literature. In *The Izu Dancer*, a young college student on a sentimental journey to a hot spring area encounters a troupe of itinerant performers, who in those days were looked down upon as outcasts. The buoyancy and liveliness of one precocious 14-year-old dancer in particular, Kaoru, catches his fancy and they strike up a quick friendship as he travels with the group. Though he enjoys the homey comfort he has with the troupe, there is an unspoken sexual tension, as the protagonist wonders whether the dancer will be forced to service the hot springs clientele sexually, as female itinerant performers often did in those days. The protagonist's anxious suspicions are relieved the next morning, when he sees the young dancer waving innocently from afar, naked, beckoning the protagonist to join her in the hot spring. The young man is elated to see her child-like body, not yet a woman, and realizes that his sexual fantasy and tension was misplaced and all is well.

These images of virginal females, kept safe by their inaccessibility to male desire, form a recurring motif in Kawabata's later writings. The young dancer of Izu transformed into the two opposite feminine ideals in his most celebrated work, *Yukiguni* [*Snow Country*] (1937), as the fiery, passionate geisha Komako and the serenely ethereal Yōko. The trope of female purity continues to resurface in his postwar masterpieces: in the mysteriously refined yet distant Yukiko in *Senbazuru* [*Thousand Cranes*] (1952), the forever youthful Kikuko who rejuvenates and comforts her father-in-law Shingo's dreary existence in *Yama no oto* [*The Sound of the Mountain*] (1954), and later in a darker variant in *The House of the Sleeping Beauties*.

In all the novels mentioned above, while the male protagonists progress and mature in conjunction with the author's own life experience, the idealized female is forever frozen at that initial virginal stage of purity, ethereal and untainted by the outside world and thus remaining youthful forever. In contrast to this untainted feminine innocence, what is perceived as ugly, repulsive, and undesirable in femininity is always related to maturity and aging. Madame Ōta in *The Sound of the Mountain*, a worldly, middle-aged seductress who was the mistress of the protagonist Kikuji's father and now resurfaces to meddle in his life, is depicted as dangerous and threatening. In *Birds and Beasts*, a misanthropic man who lives a lonely and isolated life with his many birds and dogs visits his old lover, who is a dancer of Japanese traditional *buyō* dance, at her recital. Ten years ago, the woman dancer, against the protagonist's advice, gave birth to a child, thus shattering the virginal quality of the protagonist's ideal woman. This time, the male protagonist notices the aging of the dancer and her dance which he describes as "degenerated. . . . Form had gone to pieces with the decay of her body" (146). Beauty for Kawabata exists only in an elusive and precarious liminal moment between girlhood and womanhood, and his literature is forever trying to capture that glint of innocence verging on sensuality. Thus, in Kawabata's narrative, the eroticism lies not in direct sexual contact and physical intimacy but rather in the emotions aroused by the distant and inaccessible object of desire. In fact, a rather counterintuitive drive away from actual physical consummation becomes the force that propels Kawabata's narrative movement. It is the sensuality, not the sexuality, informing the male gaze and imagination that interests Kawabata the writer.

In *The House of the Sleeping Beauties*, the precise description and almost clinical details of the six virginal bodies, all different yet equally alluring, form the main trope of the narrative. Describing the first girl he encounters, Eguchi focuses on her upper limbs: "Her right thumb was half hidden under her cheek. The fingers on the pillow beside her face were slightly curved in the softness of sleep, though not enough to erase the delicate hollows where they join the hand. The warm redness was gradually richer from the palm to the fingertips. It was a smooth, glowing white hand. . . . He caught the scent of maidenly hair. After a time the sound of the waves was higher, for his heart had been taken captive"

(18–19). Here, Kawabata uses a technique that is seen, for example, in Ozu Yasujirō's films, in which Ozu alternates close shots and long shots in a seemingly random manner, juxtaposing unrelated images in order to highlight and accentuate the object that he is presenting. After Eguchi is aroused by the smell of the girl's hair, the intensity of the sexual desire is deflated somewhat by the insertion of the natural sound of the waves. The technique of intercutting intense erotic descriptions with nature (be it landscape, seasons, or audio effects) keeps the carnality in the narrative under the author's tight reign. Kawabata's writing, like his beloved young virginal figures, is always demurely seductive and suggestive.

The virginal quality is pushed to its limit in *The House of the Sleeping Beauties* when Eguchi seeks solace from sleeping virgins who are not able to respond to his aesthetic yearning. The virgins here become mere objects of desire and admiration, but not real living human beings who could provide an old man with emotions ranging from sexual gratification, joy, or comfort to disappointment and rejection. The safe haven of the house of the sleeping beauties, a secret chamber shielded from the outside world, provides Eguchi with unbounded access to these young girl's bodies but never their minds. After the first visit, Eguchi had thought that he would not visit the place again, but an irresistable impulse drives him to the house again and again. The inanimate naked female bodies that satisfy the old man's insatiable gaze become fetish objects for the spectator—he refers to them as "living dolls." This voyeuristic micro-description repeats itself five times, each time focusing its attention on different aspects of the bodies, from meticulous descriptions of their physicality to the milky scent and "music of love" exuded by their young bodies (21). Through contact with these bodies, the old man revives memories of his past sexual encounters with various women in his life. In short, these beautiful, sensual, youthful bodies became the medium, or portal, to the sexualized memories embedded in the precarious realm of the old man's subconscious that are about to fade away due to old age and impending death.

Kawabata pushes this fetish theme even further in the short story *Kataude* [*One Arm*] (1964), written several years after *House of the Sleeping Beauties*. This surrealistic story depicts a man spending a night with a woman's arm that he borrowed from her. The erotically and symbolically charged story, with the man caressing and frolicking with the arm, suddenly turns ominous when he wakes up from his dream and realizes, to his horror, that the girl's arm is attached to his body. In *One Arm,* the fetishism of the *object petit* (the part of the body ambivalently related to the person's somatic totality because it appears detachable) turns into revulsion when he realizes that he cannot remain a detached spectator. A similar realization also underlies the *House of the Sleeping Beauties* when the romanticized bliss Eguchi enjoys is abruptly disrupted by the sudden death of the fifth young girl.

Homosocial Bonding, Aging, and Death

The secretive nature of eroticism in *The House of the Sleeping Beauties*, a private club for successful (but sexually impotent) older men, reveals a social dimension of eroticism that is distinct from the aesthetic dimension discussed so far. The clandestine sexual activity permits these men to indulge their sexual fantasies in a secure environment secluded from the prying eyes and questions of normative society. In a society where virility and masculinity are intimately linked to one's sense of self, aging and impotence are taboo subjects. However, Eguchi hides a more perilous secret: he is in fact still virile and capable of breaking the house taboo on sexual intercourse with the sleeping girls. Though warned repeatedly by the proprietor "not to do anything in bad taste," Eguchi is tempted on several occasions to act out his fantasies of sexual transgression. His thoughts of violent, even sadistic, aggression against the girls as a way to avenge all the humiliation he and his male comrades have endured due to their old age in a sense consolidates a satiated and privileged masculine position. The ending is ambiguous, and the reader is left to wonder whether Eguchi did in fact unconsciously strangle the dark-skinned girl.

Though eroticism is the central focus of the narrative, *The House of the Sleeping Beauties* is often mentioned with another contemporary masterpiece, *Fuden rōjin nikki* [*The Diary of an Mad Old Man*] (1965) by Tanizaki Junichirō, as the two apexes of "old-aged literature" [*rōjin bungaku*], a distinctive subgenre in Japanese literature that depicts the travails of aging. Just like Tanizaki's 77-year-old Utsugi, whose spirits are buoyed by a growing erotic obsession with his daughter-in-law, Eguchi's residual libidinal drive is similarly aroused by youthful femininity. Though Eguchi's fear of death and aging is diminished by the comfort he receives from spending time with these young girls, the "ugliness" of age is not wholly elided. He notes his "lonely emptiness" and "cold despondency" and contemplates that the chamber of his fantasies would also be "the most desirable place to die" (93). Eguchi finally confronts death on his last night spent at the inn, when he encounters two girls, one with white skin, and the other dark. The night brings back primordial memories of his mother as the first woman in his life and the miserable way she had died when he was only 17 years old. The young girls' breasts merge with an image of his mother's faltering chest, and when he wakes up to reality, the dark-skinned girl is dead.

The House of the Sleeping Beauties, unlike Kawabata's more traditional works, is a difficult text and has aroused controversy. The reception of the text has shifted recently. Early admiration for Kawabata's visual precision, the subtle eroticism created by his pure and refined language, and the extraordinary detail in his depictions of male lust and female sensuality has given way to a more pathological exploration of the text employing feminist and gender-critical theories. The critics point to the inhuman objectification of the girls as "living dolls," the unrelenting intensity of the male gaze, and the precarious boundaries separating his aestheticism from pedophilia or even necrophilia. No matter how one reads it, *The House of the Sleeping Beauties* is sure to invoke in its readers complex and contradictory senses of awe and bewilderment.

Biography

Born in Osaka. One of the founding members of the avant-garde literary movement known as the Neo-Sensualist school [*shin-kankakuha*]. In the 1920s Kawabata dabbled in experimentalism as a pioneer modernist writer of fiction and the newly nascent art form of cinema. Despite his early incarnation as a modernist, Kawabata later turned to a more realistic and lyrical style, gradually moving toward subject matter concerning traditional culture and aestheticism.

Combining a laconic lyricism, a heightened sensitivity to nature, and Zen-like plot structures, his short stories, most notably the hundreds included in the collection *Palm-of-the-hand Stories,* read more like poetry than narrative. Kawabata also created a rich body of novels, including *Snow Country, The Sound of the Mountain, Old Capital,* and *A Thousand Cranes,* masterpieces that epitomize traditional Japanese pathos and aestheticism. Together with Tanizaki Jun'ichirō and Mishima Yukio, he is regarded in the West as the quintessential Japanese writer, who captures the illusory essence of a feminized Japanese sensibility for beauty. Kawabata received the Nobel Prize for Literature in 1968, the first in Japan to have received the honor and only the second Asian writer after India's Tagore to have been awarded the coveted prize. He committed suicide in his studio in Kamakura.

FAYE KLEEMAN

Editions

House of the Sleeping Beauties and Other Stories. Translated by Edward Seidensticker. New York: Kōdansha International, 1969, 1980. With an Introduction by Yukio Mishima, 1994.

Selected Works

The Izu Dancer. 1968
Japan the Beautiful and Myself. 1969
Snow Country. 1969

The Sound of the Mountain. 1970
The Master of Go. 1972
The Lake. 1974
Beauty and Sadness. 1975
Collected Works of Kawabata Yasunari. 37 vols., 1980
Thousand Cranes. 1981
The Old Capital. 1987
Palm-of-the-Hand Stories. 1988
The Dancing Girl of Izu and Other Stories. 1997
First Snow on Fuji. 1999
El Maestro de Go. 2004
The Scarlet Gang of Asakusa. 2005

Further Reading

Brunet, Yuko. *Naissance d'un etude sue Kawabata Yasunari.* L'Asiathèque, 1982.
Kawabata Yasunari zensakuhin kenkyu jiten. Bensei Shuppan, 1998.
Peterson, Gwenn Boardman. *The Moon in the Water: Understanding Tanizaki, Kawabata, and Mishima.* Honolulu, HI: University of Hawai'i Press, 1979.
Pollack, David. "The Ideology of Aesthetics: Yasunari Kawabata's *Thousand Cranes* and *Snow Country.*" In *Reading Against Culture,* 100–20. Ithaca, NY: Cornell University Press, 1992.
Silberman, Elizabeth Ann. *"A Waste of Effort": Psychological Projection as a Primary Mode of Alienation in Selected Novels by Kawabata Yasunari.* Silberman, 1977.
Starrs, Roy. *Soundings in Time: The Fictive Art of Kawabata Yasunari* (Japan Library). Routledge/Curzon Press, 1999.
Sakai, Cécile. *Kawabata, le clair-obscure: Essai sue une écriture de l'ambiguité.* Paris: Presses Universitaires de France, 2002.

YEATS, WILLIAM BUTLER

1865–1939
Irish poet and playwright

To an extraordinary degree the work of William Butler Yeats reflects the dual influence of his parents. His mother seems to have induced a strong inclination in Yeats for the sensuality of the Irish countryside and the mysterious, not to say mystical, beliefs of Irish country folk. This was kept at bay until Yeats's young manhood, however, by his father's vigorously assertive rationalism. Yeats came of age in an era as much marked by the contention between scientific materialism and religious authority as it was by the tensions of Irish nationalism, and these dynamics were quintessential to the development of Yeats's work. He notes in his autobiography that at about the same time that his father was immersing him in poetry, reading aloud from Shakespeare, Scott, Shelley, Blake, Byron, and others, he was having adolescent erotic dreams that took the form of romantic narratives. In these dreams he first encountered the urges of sexuality confronting the spiritual desire to transcend physicality, describing a binary paradigm that would take various forms persistently through his life and mark the pattern of erotic preoccupations that informed both his life and his work.

This counterpoint induced his concept of a divided consciousness that is especially elaborated in *A Vision* by the symbol of the gyres. These interpenetrating spirals or cones form a vortex where subjectivity and objectivity are "intersecting states struggling one against the other." Such antitheses are generative and imply an existential dialectic between beauty and truth, value and fact, particular and universal, abstract and concrete, life and death, etc. They seem to derive from William Blake's theory of contraries in *The Marriage of Heaven and Hell*. And they also have an obvious sexual symbolism, which Yeats construed as a sign of the grounding of his theory. In the early work *The Wanderings of Oisin* (1889) he is not so at ease with the sexual extension and seems somewhat bemused by the prospect that Oisin might have sexual as well as psychic intercourse with his beloved. A few years later, however, in an 1895 essay titled "The Moods" he declares of the artist that "the only restraint he can obey is the mysterious instinct that has made him an artist, and that teaches him to discover immortal moods in mortal desires, . . . a divine love in sexual passion." He confirmed this synthesis the following year when he took rooms of his own for the first time in order to consummate an affair with Olivia Shakespeare. Still, in 1898 he thought of himself as a symbolist romantic and identified with writers "all over Europe" who are "struggling . . . against that 'externality' which a time of scientific and political thought has brought into literature," and joins Arthur Symons' call for "a poetry of essences . . . because of an ever more arduous search for an almost disembodied ecstasy."

But as he continued the ruminations of his erotic dialectic, attempting to synthesize the competing claims of sexuality and spirituality, disembodied ecstasy became problematic. In "No Second Troy" (1910) he's once again distraught about Maud Gonne, but in comparing her to a composite Agamemnon/Helen figure he

hit upon a mythological key to his aesthetic, if not his personal problem. Much of his work, motivated by Irish nationalism, revived or reinvented Irish folktales and mythology, such as the Cuchulain legends. In *The Green Helmet*, for example, Yeats gestures toward an integration of sexual and spiritual love when Cuchulain, supposing that he is about to sacrifice his life, tells his wife that she is beautiful and smart and that she will be better off without him, as in his travels he has been unfaithful. "Live, and be faithless still," she replies. While this evokes a love that transcends the carnal, it rather leaps over the conflict than resolves it. "No Second Troy" did not solve the problem, but it did expand Yeats's frame of reference to the conspicuous promiscuity of the Graeco-Roman heroes, gods, and goddesses. He had, of course, always had the Bible at his disposal, and in 1916, possibly just before Maud Gonne rejected his last proposal of marriage, he evoked Solomon and Sheba in "On Woman." Contemplating Sheba's interrogation of Solomon's proverbial wisdom and imagining a tryst, a "shudder that made them one," Yeats prays that God grant him to "live like Solomon / That Sheba led a dance." It is perhaps the only poem in which Yeats plays humorously, if only slightly, with his erotic sensibility.

In *The Tower*, published when Yeats was 63 and, as he said, in a rage at his advancing age, "Sailing to Byzantium" seems to mark Yeats's withdrawal from the sensual aspect of the erotic dialogue. Byzantium is the symbolic repository of the soul, and that is where the old man is going, "Into the artifice of eternity." That would seem to be the myth of the spirit, a closeted refuge from the relentlessly "sensual music" of life. Still, in the title poem, Yeats identifies with his character Hanrahan, "Old lecher with a love on every wind," even as he himself faces decrepitude fondling "memories of love . . . of the words of women." As always, however, his erotic imagination not only revealed his psychic landscape but scanned mythologies for cosmic revelation. "Leda and the Swan," in that same volume, almost lubriciously evokes the lust of gods engendering Western culture and racial memory, apparently synthesizing his old antitheses of body and spirit. But the "Crazy Jane" sequence of the early 1930s subtly gives priority to the body, though the dialectic continues as such, summed up when "Crazy Jane Talks with the Bishop," a virulently holy man: "Love has pitched his mansion in / The place of excrement; / For nothing can be sole or whole / That has not been rent." Crazy Jane's disposition had been anticipated in the *A Woman Young and Old* sequence of 1929, where sex and its pleasures are also made the existential requisite for love and its transcendance.

Yeats was particularly, and idiosyncratically, concerned in his later years to explore the communion of the spiritual and material worlds in general as well as his own distinctive erotic dialectic. Dorothy Wellesley, his close friend and voluminous correspondent, observed in her memoir of Yeats's final year: "Sex, Philosophy, and the Occult preoccupy him. He strangely intermingles the three." This is confirmed in *Last Poems*, which were written in his last three years. The sexual motif is especially prominent in "The Three Bushes" and a sequence of "songs" that accompany it. The incident of the poem derives from the Abbe Michel de Bourdeille's "Historia mei Temporis" and concerns a lady who sends her chambermaid to lie disguised by dark with her lover in order to preserve her own chastity and yet satisfy him. The lover is thus deceived for a year, at which point he dies in an accident, whereupon the lady, whose love was unconsummated, dropped dead as well, "for she loved him with her soul." The chambermaid tends their adjoining graves and eventually confesses to her priest, who, when she dies, buries her also "beside her lady's man" where the three are blessed and commune via a common rose bush. The lady's songs, like the longer poem, reflect a conventional eroticism, where she dubiously forfeits the pleasures of the body to enhance those of the soul. The chambermaid's songs are earthy but, were it not for the context of the poem's spiritual sanction, would leave the dialectic up in the air, where the lover's "bird . . . for the womb seed sighs." It is as if eroticism and its dynamics vexed him to the end. As he said in "The Spur," also in 1938, "You think it horrible that lust and rage / Should dance attention upon my old age; / They were not such a plague when I was young; / What else have I to spur me into song?"

Biography

William Butler Yeats was born in Dublin in 1865 to Susan Pollexfen Yeats and John Butler Yeats.

His mother was a Protestant country woman, and his father was an assertively skeptical intellectual who declined the religion and Church of Ireland ministry of his father as well as a career in law to become an artist of some reputation but with little business acumen. Consequently the family income was irregular. William absorbed a lifetime love of nature, the countryside, and the supernatural from his mother, but it was the intellectual vigor and poetic appreciation of his father that constituted W.B. Yeats's most sustained influence.

The introspective isolation and awkwardness of his childhood plagued him throughout life, but at 15 his erotic dreams swept him into a sexual awakening, and it was in this passionate intensity that he began experimenting with verse and romantic aesthetic theories. Even as Yeats entered the literary and political life of Ireland, he carried with him the teenage residue of sexual anxiety manifest in a tension between sexual and spiritual desire that he feared was unnatural. Still wrestling with this moral dichotomy, in 1889 Yeats met and promptly fell in love with Maud Gonne, who became the symbolic icon of his life, though she did not reciprocate his passion.

Now living in London, Yeats was immersed for the next several years in the esoterica of Theosophy and Rosicrucianism and at the same time intensified his involvement with Irish nationalistic literary and political movements. He had written *The Countess Cathleen* (1892) for Maud Gonne, and its production in Dublin in 1899 effectively inaugurated the Irish National Theater, which he founded with Lady Gregory, George Moore, and Edward Martyn. The *fin de siècle* decade produced his first significant works, including *The Land of Heart's Desire* (1894), *Poems* (1895), and *Wind Among the Reeds* (1899), as well as several prose and editorial works.

In 1908 he first met Ezra Pound, the American expatriot poet who was to influence Yeats's poetry in more modernist directions. This was especially manifest in *The Wild Swans at Coole* (1917) and such subsequent books as *Michael Robartes and the Dancer* (1921) and *The Tower* (1928); in such later works as *The Winding Stair and Other Poems* (1933) and *Last Poems* (1939) he recuperated traditional styles. In 1917 he married Georgie Hyde-Lees, a longtime friend and colleague in mystical and literary endeavors whose adeptness at automatic writing helped Yeats articulate the long-elusive mystical system of *A Vision* (1926). In 1922 he became a senator of the Irish Free State. And in 1923 he was awarded the Nobel Prize for Poetry in Stockholm.

A Woman Young and Old (1929), *Words for Music Perhaps* (1932), *A Full Moon in March* (1935), and *Last Poems* (1936–1939) all featured poems evoking distinctly erotic themes and images, a substantive motif especially in Yeats's later work. He declined denouncing fascist and Nazi regimes on the ground that governments were uniformly despotic. Meanwhile his friends and allies were dying—Lady Gregory in 1932, George Russell in 1935—and his own health was in steady decline. Shortly after his last visit from Maud Gonne in September 1938, he was reconciled with his wife. He died on January 28.

PETER MICHELSON

Selected Works

The Autobiography of. New York: Collier Books, 1965.
Essays and Introductions. New York: Collier Books, 1968.
The Collected Plays of. New York: Macmillan, 1953.
The Collected Poems of. New York: Macmillan, 1956.
A Vision. New York: Collier Books, 1968.

Further Reading

Bloom, Harold. *Yeats.* New York: Oxford University Press, 1970.

Ellmann, Richard. *Yeats—The Man and The Masks.* New York: E.P. Dutton & Co., 1958.

Jeffaries, A. Norman. *W. B. Yeats, Man and Poet.* 2nd ed. New York: Barnes and Noble, 1966.

Keane, Patrick J., ed. *William Butler Yeats.* New York: McGraw-Hill, 1973.

Moore, Virginia. *The Unicorn: William Butler Yeats' Search for Reality.* New York: Macmillan, 1954.

Stallworthy, Jon. *Between the Lines: Yeats' Poems in the Making.* Oxford: Clarendon Press, 1963.

Wellesley, Dorothy, ed. *Letters on Poetry from W.B. Yeats to Dorothy Wellesley.* London: Oxford University Press, 1964.

Z

ZAYAS, MARÍA DE

Spanish novelist
1590–c. 1661

The Spanish Baroque author María de Zayas's erotic imagination is a troubled and troubling one. In the nineteenth and early twentieth century she was reviled by scholars for her "shameless indecency" and her "libertine histories." However, from the late 1930s onward, she has been more celebrated for her woman-oriented, realistic tales of amorous (mis)fortune and her "fine sensuality." Although she wrote sonnets and a verse play (*La tracion en la amistad* [*Friendship Betrayed*]), she is best known for her two volumes of short stories (containing ten stories each). The sensational *Novelas amorosas y ejemplares* [*Amorous and Exemplary Novels*, also called in English *The Enchantments of Love*] was so popular that Zayas published a darker sequel: *Parte segunda del sarao y entretenimientos honestos* [*Second part of the entertaining and honest soiree*]; in modern editions it is often titled *Desengaños amorosos* [*Love Undeceived, or The Disenchantments of Love*]. These stories are all either positive or negative "exemplars" about sexual desire, but the majority end ambiguously or negatively. That Zayas was suspicious of men (and conventional 'happy endings' resulting in marriage) is definite; that she was an unequivocal proto-feminist (as some modern scholars have suggested) is more open to question. Clearly she found female erotic desire natural, empowering, and ubiquitous—but also fraught with negative and sometimes gruesomely tragic consequences.

Biographically, we do not even know if Zayas was married or single. We believe her to have been born in 1590 into Madrid aristocracy, but we have no evidence even of her date of death, and allegations that she may have lived much of her life in various other cities of Spain and Europe rely solely on textual descriptions. Her sexual orientation is also in question; Lope de Vega compared her talents to those of Sappho, and other contemporary commentators spoke (perhaps jokingly) of her manly, or even whiskered, appearance and her apparent inability to secure a husband. That she was a passionate advocate for women's intellectual and literary ability, and that she was indeed taken seriously as a writer even in her own repressive era is not in doubt. After the exemplary novels of Miguel de Cervantes, those of Zayas were the best known in Western Europe in her day, and paradoxically Cervantes himself was erroneously given credit for writing three of them.

As in Cervantes, there are numerous examples of cross-dressing female characters in Zayas's work. On the stage, of course, this device was used (as Samuel Pepys notes in his Diary) so male audiences could be titillated by the forbidden sight of female legs in tight male breeches. Normally any hint of "butch" lesbianism is dispensed with because the female character often resorts to masculine garb solely in order to pursue a male love object, or to protect herself in a male-dominated society. For example, in "The Judge in Her Own Case" and "Aminta Deceived," Claudia and Aminta dress as men in order to have the freedom to pursue their male lovers, for reunion or for revenge. In "Venturing and Losing," Jacinta dresses as a shepherd in order to protect herself from robbers. In her *Disenchantments of Love* volume, Zayas presents us with two transvestite males (which was *not* a common literary convention). In "The Most Infamous Revenge," don Juan avenges his sister Octavia's seduction by dressing as a woman to gain entry into the house of the seducer's wife Camila. Upon doing so he proceeds to rape Camila before announcing his true (male) identity to one and all. In "Love for the Sake of Conquest," a young man disguises himself as a woman in order to befriend a woman he intends to seduce—to the point that he truly seems to transform himself from Esteban into "Estefanía" (and is comically but earnestly pursued by Laurela's father). These tales seem bizarre and emasculating until the reader remembers that in Golden-Age Spain, a woman of good breeding would never have been allowed to be left unchaperoned with a male who was not an immediate family member; thus, cross-dressing as an "unthreatening" female often led to successful heterosexual seduction. However, the best life for a woman, according to Zayas, may have been to evade permanent sexual possession by a man; she comments of her heroine Lisis's resorting to convent life that "Hers is not a tragic ending, but rather the happiest that could be given her, because while being both desiring and desired by many [males], she became subjected to none of them."

In "Love for the Sake of Conquest," Zayas discusses the possibility of love between women.

Although eventually she rejects the possibility in that story (after having one of the characters, a transvestite man, claim "The power of love also extends between women, as between a lover and his lady"), she raises it again in "Marrying Afar: Portent of Doom" in which two women, each badly treated or neglected by their men, find solace in their (platonic?) love for each other. (In this story Blanca's husband is eventually caught by his wife *in flagrante delicto* with his beloved sixteen-year-old pageboy.)

Zayas is also known for her "phallic women" and her creation of castration anxiety in men (as Margaret Greer reminds us). In her daring stories we also find instability of gender definition ("Judge Thyself"), female characters' dreams of erotic desires ("Venturing and Losing"), and unflinching depictions of sexual violence against women ("Everything Ventured"). She also writes (sometimes in veiled terms) of incest ("Too Late Undeceived"), interracial passion ("Forewarned but Not Forearmed"), narcissism ("Everything Ventured"), sex magic ("Innocence Punished"), male sexual miserliness ("A Miser's Reward"), and even hermaphroditism ("Love for the Sake of Conquest" and "Disillusionment in Love and Virtue Rewarded"). However, even as Zayas probes the mysterious origins of sexual desire (from her very first story, "Everything Ventured"), she cautions that women who are the active, desirous pursuers of men are usually destined to become victims of their own lust. Despite many feminist suggestions and stances, sexual aggression, which is rampant among Zayas's female characters, nevertheless seems to be the proper province of "lion-like" men in these tales (see Jacinta's dream in "Everything Ventured"), notwithstanding Zayas's sly gender-role subversion and episodes of female autonomy in "Slave to Her Own Lover" and "Judge Thyself."

It can be argued that for Zayas, sexuality is a cruel, multilayered masquerade in which the verbally-expressed erotic interests of both genders inexorably lead to the ruin of women, regardless of their courage, ingenuity, or intellectual capacity. Or that she presages Lacanian theory in her endless repetition of insatiable Need, Desire, and Demand. Or that she hints at a Utopian vision wherein women withdrawn into a convent-like realm become thus blessedly free of the dangers, desires, and depredations of men. Yet some of her stories (in her first collection) have conventionally "happy endings," replete with wedding bells and beautiful progeny. Given how little we know about the historical María de Zayas Sotomayor, her own true sexual desires, intents, preferences, and ideals need remain a matter of speculation.

Biography

María de Zayas Sotomayor was born into the Spanish aristocracy the 12th of September in 1590 in Madrid. She probably spent most of her life in this city, which was the epicenter of her literary activity, but she may have lived with her father in Naples for a period of time, and she may have had sojourns in Zaragoza, Seville, Granada, or Barcelona. Her parents were María de Barasa and Fernando de Zayas y Sotomayor. Her father was allegedly a military officer and/or knight in the service of the count of Lemos. She wrote ("flourished") in the 1620s and 1630s (her *Novelas ejemplares y amorosas* was published in 1637 and her *Desengaños* was published a decade later). It is not known for certain if she were married or single. It is possible that she ended her life in a convent, but nothing is known of her for sure after 1647. Scholars posit that she died between 1647 and 1661.

C.A. PRETTIMAN

Selected Works

La traición en la amistad (Friendship Betrayed); edition and notes by Valerie Hegstrom; translation by Catherine Larson. Lewisburg: Bucknell University Press; London: Associated University Presses, 1999.

The Disenchantments of Love. Translated by Harriet Patsy Boyer. Albany NY: SUNY Press, 1997.
The Enchantments of Love. Translated by Harriet Patsy Boyer. Berkeley: University of California Press, 1990.

References and Further Reading

Brownlee, Marina S. *The Cultural Labyrinth of María de Zayas*. Philadelphia, PA: University of Pennsylvania Press, 2000.
Greer, Margaret Rich. *María de Zayas Tells Baroque Tales of Love and the Cruelty of Men*. University Park, PA: The Pennsylvania State University Press, 2000.
Levine, Linda Gould, Ellen Engelson Marson, and Gloria Feiman Waldman, eds. *Spanish Women Writers: a Bio-bibliographical Source Book*. Westport, Conn.: Greenwood Press, 1993.
Soufas, Teresa Scott. *Dramas of Distinction: a Study of Plays by Golden Age Women*. Studies in Romance Languages 42. Lexington: University Press of Kentucky, 1997.
Vollendorf, Lisa. *Reclaiming the Body: María de Zayas's Early Feminism*. Chapel Hill: University of North Carolina Press, 2001.
Williamsen, Amy R. and Judith A. Whitnack, eds. *María de Zayas: the Dynamics of Discourse*. Madison: Fairleigh Dickinson University Press; London; Cranbury, NJ: Associated University Presses, 1995.
Wilson, Katharina M. and Frank J. Warnke, eds. *Women Writers of the Seventeenth Century*. Athens: University of Georgia Press, 1989.
Zayas Sotomayor, Maria de. *La traición en la amistad (Friendship Betrayed)*; edition and notes by Valerie Hegstrom; translation by Catherine Larson. Lewisburg: Bucknell University Press; London: Associated University Presses, 1999.
———. *The Disenchantments of Love*. Translated by Harriet Patsy Boyer. Albany NY: SUNY Press, 1997.
———. *The Enchantments of Love*. Translated by Harriet Patsy Boyer. Berkeley, CA: University of California Press, 1990.

ZHANG ZU

657–730
Chinese scholar, novelist, and poet

Visiting the Fairy Cave

Such is the title translated by Robert van Gulik from the Chinese *Yu xianku*, but the English translation by Howard Levy uses a different grouping of the three characters, *Yuxian ku*, or *The Dwelling of Playful Goddesses*, based on the traditional Japanese interpretation. In fact, the author does claim to make an unexpected visit to some quite hospitable creatures: rather than fairies or goddesses, the two girls are human beings of prestigious lineage turned into immortals, but of a "real" sort as they do not simply vanish instantaneously but dwindle slowly out of sight at the end of the encounter. It is the first Chinese "novelette" and the only surviving example of this subgenre of Chinese fiction which was soon supplanted by a new genre of longer short stories in a freer style. It was probably composed at the beginning of Cheng Tsu's career, around 680, when the movement for a return to antique prose came into full swing. The *Yu xianku* is written in a mixture of poetry and prose in parallel style, which quickly fell out of fashion. It is unusually lengthy and told in the first person, a rare case in traditional Chinese fiction. The narrator tells how on an official mission he came to a dwelling somewhere in the Northern province of Gansu where he was greeted by two witty and attractive girls, Lady n°10 and Sister-in-law n°5, both widows. After tirelessly exchanging jokes, puns, and poems with both of them, and being entertained with singing and dancing, he is most willingly left to spend a torrid night with Lady n°10, rather cursorially described in no more than hundred and fifty characters out of nine thousand devoted to the whole tale, still enough for a translator in modern Chinese to have skipped them. It may explain why the text disappeared from China and would have remained unknown there, had it not been discovered in Japan by Chinese envoys around 1880. We may well imagine how such a style would have taken the fancy of the Japanese court in its infancy as well as later, when both sexes mingled in aristocratic society. We know for sure that manuscripts of the tale reached Japan shortly after or even before Zhang Zu's death. Later, a great number of printings testify to the high level of appreciation of this text in written Chinese.

The core of the story, visiting a fairy cave, is hardly a new theme. Liu I-ch'ing (403–444) in his *Youming lu* [*Records of the Otherworld*] noted the still famous story of two fellows, Liu Zhen and Juan Zhao, who spent a month with two attractive immortals, and, returning home, learned that seven generations had since succeeded. But here nothing of the sort is mentioned. It is a tale celebrating the pleasures of courtship and making love out of marriage, of the sort reproved by the Confucian orthodoxy

of late imperial China. Equally censurable was the sprinkling of colloquialisms. In Japan, on the contrary, it added to the attractiveness of the text in a readable classical Chinese for cultured people.

The author's reputation for frivolity is probably as unreliable as the idea, circulated in Japan, that he wrote the story to court the favors of the Empress Wu Zetian, who reigned as Emperor of China from 690 to 705. But it is not unlikely that the text is full of contemporary allusions we have no way to decipher.

The authorship of *Yu hsien-k'u* has been contested and unconvincingly assigned to an obscure contemporary of Zhang Zu.

Biography

Born in 657 in Shenzhou (southern Hunan), Zhang Zu graduated and entered the civil service in 679. His career was marred by the personal enmity of the Great Councillor Yao Chong (651–721). He enjoyed a high literary reputation in his time. Korean and Japanese envoys carried back several of his works. However, in China his fame soon declined. Historians still value his *Records of Affairs Within and Outside the Court*. He died in 730 after having attained a prominent position in the central imperial bureaucracy at the capital.

ANDRÉ LÉVY

Editions

Wang Pi-chiang. *T'ang-ren Hsiao-shuo*. Guji, Shanghai 1978, p. 19–36.

Translations

Levy, Howard S. *The Dwelling of Playful Goddesses*. Dai Nippon insatsu, Tokyo 1965, including a bibliography of ninety items, mostly Japanese.

References and Further Reading

Gulik, Robert van. *Sexual Life in Ancient China: A Preliminary Survey of Chinese Sex and Society from ca. 1500 B.C. till 1644 A.D.* Leiden: E.J. Brill, 1961, p. 208.

Wang Chung-han. "The Authorship of the Yu-hien K'u." *Harvard Journal of Asiatic Studies* 11, 1948, p. 153–162.

ZHAOYANG QU SHI

The earliest extant edition of *Zhaoyang qu shi* bears the date 1621. Adopting the plot of *Zhao Feiyan wai zhuan* [*Unofficial Biography of Flying Swallow*], which is attributed to Ling Xuan (first century BCE), the novel depicts the sexual adventures of Flying Swallow (Zhao Feiyan, ?–1 BCE) and her sister Combined Virtue (Zhao Hede, ?–?), two women of humble upbringing who became queen and imperial concubine, respectively, during the reign of the Cheng Emperor (32–7 BCE) of the Han dynasty.

The story begins in a mountain of the Taoist mythic realm, where a fox spirit has been cultivating herself for several thousand years to attain divinity. One day, as she instructs her followers in the technique of collecting yin and yang, she recognizes that the lack of Pure Yang has formed an obstacle to her goal. Thereupon, she leaves her mountain and transforms herself into a beautiful woman, intending to lure a man for his Pure Yang. Meanwhile, a lustful swallow spirit also leaves his mountain and transforms himself into a man, aiming to acquire Pure Yin. He encounters the fox spirit and takes her home, but it results in his loss of Pure Yang during their mating. The swallow spirit leads his clan to attack the foxes, but a Taoist deity passing through the region captures both of them and sends them to the Jade Emperor. The Jade Emperor punishes each of them with a life in the human realm, where the spirits shall be reborn as sisters and become members of the imperial family.

In the mundane world, a handsome musician, Feng Wanjin, is kept by his master Zhao Man as a catamite. Feng, however, conducts an illicit affair with Zhao's wife, the Princess of Gusu, who has been neglected by her husband. As a consequence, the princess becomes pregnant and secretly gives birth to twin daughters in her maternal home. The girls are sent to Feng, who raises them outside the Zhao household.

The two sisters grow into unparalleled beauties. The elder one is nicknamed Flying Swallow and the younger one is named Combined Virtue. When both Feng and the princess die, the girls become homeless and wander to the capital, Chang'an, struggling for a living by making straw sandals. In the capital, a young man nicknamed Bird Shooter often helps them with daily supplies and becomes the lover they share. Zhao Lin, an attendant gentleman, adopts both of them and trains them in singing and dancing. One day, he presents Flying Swallow to the Cheng Emperor, who is immediately captivated and soon dethrones the queen and designates Flying Swallow as the new queen.

Fan Yi, a lady-in-waiting, mentions the beauty of Combined Virtue to the emperor. The emperor summons her to an imperial audience, but she replies she will enter the palace only under her sister's command. Fan Yi, therefore, tricks both sisters in order to bring Combined Virtue to the emperor, who is enticed by the new girl at once and gradually alienates Flying Swallow. To relieve her distress, Fan Yi arranges for Bird Shooter to enter the palace to satisfy Flying Swallow's sexual desires.

Flying Swallow fascinates the emperor once more when she sings and dances for him on a jade serving plate during a voyage on a lake. It becomes a problem, however, that she has not conceived. Trying to become pregnant, she seeks foreign remedies and further engages in sexual activities with Bird Shooter, a court musician, and sixteen youths Fan Yi secretly brings into the palace. The emperor senses her pursuit and intends to execute her, but Combined Virtue calms his anger. She visits her sister and advises her to stop. Flying Swallow, in great fear, sends the youths away. But soon she obtains a substitute, a new attendant, with whom Combined Virtue also has sex.

One day, the emperor spies on Combined Virtue bathing and becomes greatly aroused. Learning about the incident, Flying Swallow also bathes in front of the emperor. However, remembering his queen's lustful affairs, the emperor leaves in silence. Flying Swallow, in distress, continues to satisfy herself with Bird Shooter, and soon she reintroduces him to Combined Virtue to rekindle their old affair. Yet, the sisters still don't conceive. Flying Swallow decides to pretend she is pregnant. At the end of the tenth month, she accepts a suggestion to bring an infant into the palace, pretending it is hers, but the scheme fails and she announces she has lost the child. Combined Virtue, on the other hand, puts a baby of a lady-in-waiting to death to prevent the possibility of the emperor designating an heir that is not her son. The childless emperor finally installs the King of Dingtao as the crown prince. In the meantime, Bird Shooter's health declines, and he begs Flying Swallow to let him go. He finally leaves the palace and becomes a monk. The emperor, who is becoming impotent, takes an aphrodisiac from an alchemist, but Combined Virtue overdoses him for her pleasure and the emperor finally dies of over ejaculation. In fear of the punishment she has to face, Combined Virtue dies by coughing blood. Flying Swallow commits suicide a few years later, when the new emperor also dies. The spirits of Flying Swallow and Combined Virtue return to the court of the Jade Emperor. Having being punished for their sinful previous lives, they are allowed to continue their spiritual cultivation in the mythic realm.

Zhaoyan qu shi is a good example of seventeenth- to nineteenth-century Chinese erotic fiction: it presents a popular mythic framework and a standard combination of fabricated stories and official history. The use of aphrodisiacs is a stock feature of this genre, and death caused by over ejaculation is also common in erotic fiction after *Zhaoyan qu shi*, most notably in *Jin ping mei*. Like all other works in this genre, *Zhaoyan qu shi* was repeatedly banned in imperial China. Modern editions are not widely available, and in-depth study is certainly underdeveloped.

Biography

Gu Hang Yan Yan Sheng [Gorgeous Student of Ancient Hangzhou] is the pseudonym of an anonymous Chinese writer of the sixteenth or seventeenth century. In addition to *Zhaoyang qu shi* (*Pleasure History of Zhaoyang Palace*), he edited *Yufei mei shi* (*Seduction History of the Jade Consort*).

I-HSIEN WU

Editions

Cheng Qinghao and Wang Qiugui, eds. *Zhaoyang qu shi*. Vol. 3 of *Si wu xie huibao*. Taipei: Taiwan Daying baike, 1994.

Zhaoyang qu shi. Vol. 4 of *Zhongguo gu yan xipin congkan*. Unknown publisher.

Further Reading

Chen Qinghao. "Chuban shuoming." In Cheng Qinghao and Wang Qiugui, eds., *Zhaoyang qu shi*. Vol. 3 of *Si wu xie huibao*. Taipei: Taiwan Daying baike, 1994.

Li Mengsheng. "*Zhaoyang qu shi*." In *Zhongguo jinhui xiaoshuo baihua*. Shanghai: Shanghai guji, 1994.

Van Gulik, R.H. "Ming Dynasty, 1368–1644 A.D." Chap. 10 in *Sexual Life in Ancient China: A Preliminary Survey of Chinese Sex and Society from ca. 1500 B.C. till 1644 A.D.* Leiden: E.J. Brill 1961.

ZHULIN YESHI [*UNOFFICIAL HISTORY OF THE BAMBOO GROVE*]

Zhulin Yeshi, a novel in sixteen chapters, takes place in the distant past, about 600 BCE, during the "Spring and Autumn" period. It is about the daughter of the Duke of Cheng, Su E. When she reaches puberty, she meets a Daoist adept in a dream who initiates her into the secrets of sexual intercourse, particularly the way to absorb the male vital essence and nourish her own, known as "the Plain Girl's Method of Reaping the Results of Battle." He explains to her that through this method she will be able to stave off old age and continually rejuvenate herself. The *sunü* "plain girl" is the Yellow Emperor's interlocutor in the foundational medical text, *Huangdi Neijing,* [*The Yellow Emperor's Classic*]. Su E's name, also meaning "plain girl," evokes the discourses of the "plain girl," both canonical and "secret," and frequently on the topic of sex and medicine.

Su E teaches her maid, Hehua, this method of sexual combat, and the two women set out on a sexual odyssey to nourish their *yin*, through sexual practices that essentially suck the life out of their partners. Su E is given in marriage to the son of Duke Ling of the neighboring state of Chen. In his mansion there is a bamboo grove named Zhulin where Su E sports with her young husband. Soon after she has borne him a son, her husband dies of exhaustion. On his deathbed, he entrusts his widow and infant son to the care of his friend, the minister Kong Ning. Su E establishes sexual relations with Kong and also with his friend, the minister Yixing. In order to safeguard his own position, Kong arranges a meeting between Su E and her father-in-law, Duke Ling. Thereafter, the Duke joins in the sexual orgies in the Bamboo Grove, in which the maid Hehua also takes an active part. Twenty years later, Su E and Hehua still look like young women but their three lovers have become old and weak. One day Su E's son, who has grown to be a strong warrior, overhears the Duke and his two ministers joking about which of the two fathered Su E's son. The young man rushes inside and kills the Duke. The two ministers escape and take refuge in the enemy state of Chu. The king of Chu had long planned an attack on Chen and now the murder of the Duke provides him with a good pretext. Su E's son is killed in battle and Su E herself taken captive. Kongning and Yixing plan for her to seduce the King of Chu but the ghost of Su E's son haunts them. Before they can carry out their plan Kong becomes insane. He kills his own wife and children and then himself. Yixing, in despair, ends his life by drowning.

At the court of Chu there is a minister named Wuchen, also an expert in the Daoist methods of strengthening the vital essence through sexual intercourse. He immediately recognizes in Su E a fellow-student and resolves to marry her so that they may practice this art together. The King, however has in the meantime given Su E in marriage to a common soldier. In the process, she has become separated from her maid, Hehua. An elaborate interstate intrigue follows which is described with considerable skill. In the end Wuchen becomes a minister of the state of Chin and is united with Su E and Hehua. These three experts in Daoist "sexual vampirism" need young victims to supply their vital essence. Wuchen seduces a young nobleman of Chin and gets him and his wife to join in their orgies. The Bamboo Grove is thus re-established in the state of Chin—this time with two men and three women. A servant betrays them and denounces them before the king, who has the mansion surrounded by his soldiers. The nobleman and his wife are arrested, but Su E, Hehua and Wuchen have already absorbed so much vital essence as to complete their "inner elixir." Transformed into Immortals, they disappear into the sky shrouded by a cloud of dust.

Though medical manuals and pamphlets of the Ming period seem to have been in general agreement, arguing against the possibility or advisability of prolonging life by nourishing the vital essence, the fact that they emphasized the inherent *danger* of sex, be it too much conservation or too much dissipation almost without exception is an important supplement to the preservation of sexual myths and metaphors in literature. The fact that medical manuals and pamphlets still addressed the supposedly outdated notion of nurturing the essence, even if only to debunk it, shows that the subtext of medical texts and that of erotic literature were essentially the same and that it was part of the popular imagination. Whether for procreation, life extension, or recreation, neither medical nor literary texts questioned the power and danger inherent in the sex act; a power and danger exacerbated by the concept of exchange.

This novel, though also obscene, is less coarse than the *Xiuta Yeshi* and has a carefully constructed plot. Nonetheless, it was also banned by name, twice listed as a forbidden book in the second half of the Qing Dynasty, in 1810 and 1868. Although neither *Zhulin Yeshi* or *Xiuta Yeshi* are illustrated, both novels seem to have been popular during the time of their authors and influenced by or exerting influence on, erotic picture albums, and the print culture of the late Ming dynasty.

Biography

The work is anonymous, supposedly of the early Qing period (mid-seventeenth century), although some believe that the author was a member of Lü Tiancheng's literary group.

ANDREW SCHONEBAUM

See also **Jin Ping Mei; Hong Lou Meng**

Editions and Translations

Zhulin Yeshi Shanghai Xiaoshuo Shepai yingben, in *Zhongguo gu yan xi pin cong kan. di 2 ji* reprint, Taipei, 1987.

Recommended Reading

Van Gulik, R.H. *Erotic Colour Prints of the Ming Period* Privately published in fifty copies in Tokyo 1951.
Van Gulik, R.H. *Sexual Life in Ancient China: A Preliminary Survey of Chinese sex and Society from ca. 1500 B.C. till 1644 A.D.,* Leiden: Brill 1961.

ZILLE, HEINRICH

1858–1929
German author and film maker

Today Heinrich Zille is best known for his humorous drawings of children and his portrayal of everyday life of working class people in Berlin at the turn of the century. Zille followed in the footsteps of his teacher, the renowned artist Theodor Hosemann, who is regarded as the father of typical Berlin humor. In his commentaries and short dialogues, which he added to his cartoon-like drawings, Zille used authentic Berlin slang. Although his drawings and sketches did not idealize Berlin and its population, he was very sympathetic towards the milieu he depicted. Zille's works, their amusing overtones notwithstanding, overtly criticize the horrific social standards of lower-class people. Unfortunately, Zille has not been properly appreciated for the sociocritical aspects of his oeuvre.

Aside from being a prolific draughtsman, Zille was also a gifted writer, who often made use of Berlin slang in his prose. In his *Zwanglose Geschichten und Bilder* [*Unconstrained Stories and Pictures*] (1919), he particularly emphasizes the utterly despicable living conditions in run-down tenement houses. In the story titled *Spezialitaten* [*Specialties*], Zille writes about Thusnelda, a young woman, who works as a performance artist before she becomes a singer in a cabaret. She lives with four other singers, who are rehearsing naked when a young mail boy delivers their mail. As in most of Zille's erotic pictures, the women are apparently overweight. Zille's fascination with buttocks is especially evident in his book *Die Landpartie*

[*A Country Outing*] of 1920. Here, on almost every picture, Zille's characters lie sleeping in their beds, covered except for their bare buttocks, with thick feather blankets. In his later works, Zille focused on depictions of oral sex and he also alluded to sodomy in his picture *In der Sommerfrische* [*During Summer Vacation*]. These aspects of his work, however, have rarely been mentioned by art critics.

In 1925, Zille's picture *Modelle im Atelier* [*Models in a Studio*] was heavily criticized by influential men in Stuttgart, who called the artist's work pornography. The case was brought to trial and although the defence relied on the testimonies of reputable expert witnesses, Zille was sentenced to a fine of 150 Reichsmarks. It is rather bewildering that despite widespread tolerant attitudes during the Weimar Republic the artist was indicted on grounds of one very harmless lithograph.

Hurengesprache

Aside from making a living as a draughtsman of humorous drawings for various Berlin magazines, Zille wanted to be appreciated as an original artist. Besides making lithographs, Zille created a series of etchings titled *Zwolf Kunstlerdrucke* [*Twelve Artistic Prints*] in 1905. In order to archive recognition from his colleagues at the Berlin Secession, he produced a number of highly crafted prints. His subsequent, extremely erotic lithographic series *Hurengesprache* [*Conversations among Prostitutes*] was particularly original. Zille published *Hurengesprache* in 1913 under the pseudonym W. Pfeifer, as he feared censorship. However, insiders of Berlin's artistic scene knew that the *Hurengesprache* were in fact Zille's work. Fairly recently discovered sketches of this particular series of lithographs demonstrate various stages in preparation of the book. Although the highly erotic pictures depict several prostitutes having intercourse with their customers, the book does not limit the reader's role to that of a mere voyeur. As the title suggests, eight prostitutes speak about their everyday lives and how they actually became prostitutes. Zille's talent as a socially critical writer is evident when one reads about the often times tragic life stories of his eight protagonists. While growing up, Pauline had sex repeatedly with her brother before she was raped by a neighbor. After her father abandoned Pauline and her family, they had to live on the streets of Berlin. In order to survive, Pauline became a prostitute. In her thick Berlin accent she wonders if her life would have been different had her parents not been as devastatingly poor. Rosa's first sexual relationship was also incestuous, as her father's sexual appetite did not decrease when her mother was incurably sick. As a child, Rosa was always in the same room when her parents had intercourse, as the family could not afford more than one room. Now the sick mother had to witness the incestuous encounters between her husband and her daughter. While Rosa gave birth in a delirious state, she unintentionally disclosed the name of her child's father. As a result, Rosa's father was brought to trial but he insisted that it was his paternal right to engage in a sexual relationship with his daughter. Zille, who was repeatedly involved with prostitutes, paints a vivid picture of the harsh lives of his protagonists. He does not condemn prostitution as morally wrong, nor does he depict prostitutes as nymphomaniac seductresses, who derive great pleasure from their overactive sex lives. Rather, in *Hurengesprache* he sympathetically portrays prostitutes as fairly ordinary women trying to make ends meet.

Biography

Born in Radeburg near Dresden, 10 January 1858. Educated at Hochschule fur Bildende Kunste, Berlin, main advisor Theodor Hosemann, 1872–1875; apprenticeship at printing company. First exhibition of drawings at the Berliner Secession, 1901; publications of drawings and lithographs in *Simplicissimus, Lustige Blatter,* and *Jugend: Illustrierte Wochenschrift fur Kunst und Leben.* Military service, 1880–1882. Married Hulda Frieske in 1883 (died 1919); three children. Worked for the Photographische Gesellschaft, 1877–1907. Founding member of the "Freie Secession," 1913; elected into the Preußische Akademie der Kunste, was awarded an honorary professorship, 1924. Directed various films, 1925–1929. Died in Berlin-Charlottenburg, 9 August 1929.

GREGOR THUSWALDNER

Selected Works

Das große Zille Album. Hannover: Fackeltrager, 1957.
Vater der Straße. Gerhard Függe, ed. Berlin: Das Neue Berlin, 1969.
300 Berliner BUder. "Mein Milljoh", Kinder der Straße, Rund ums Freibad. Hannover: Fackeltrager, 1977.
Die Landpartie. Zwanglose Geschichte und Bilder. Hannover: Fackeltrager, 1978.
Hurengesprache. Munich: Schirmer/Mosel, 1981.
Fotografien van Berlin urn 1900. Matthias Flugge, ed. Leipzig: VEB Fotokinoverlag, 1987.

Further Reading

Fischer, Lothar. *Heinrich Zille.* Reinbeck: Rowohlt, 1979.
Fuchs, Eduard. *Geschichte der erotischen Kunst. Erweiterung und Neubearbeitungdes Werkes. Das erotische Element in der Karikatur mit Einschluß der ernsten Kunst.* Munchen, Langen 1912.
Langemayer, Gerhard (ed. et al). *Bild als Waffe: Mittel und Motive der Karikatur in funf Jahrhunderten.* Munich: Prestel, 1984.
Nagel, Otto. *Heinrich Zille.* Berlin, Henschelverlag, 1961.
Puschel, Walter. *Mal'n Schluck in de Destille und een bißken kille kille...: Anekdoten von Heinrich Zille.* Berlin, Eulenspiegel, 2000.
Ranke, Winfried. *Heinrich Zille. Photographien Berlin 1890–1910.* Munich: Schirmer/Mosel, 1979.

ZINOV'EVA-ANNIBAL, LIDIIA DMITRIEVNA

1866–1907
Russian prose writer, dramatist, critic

Thirty Three Abominations
[Tridtsat' tri uroda]

Published in 1907, this novella is written as a diary of a young woman, and spans 4–5 months. The nameless protagonist is living with an older, famous dramatic actress named Vera. The diary entries reveal that underlying the relationship between the two women is Vera's worship of the protagonist's physical beauty. At the beginning of her diary the young woman is completely subsumed by Vera's personality, and Vera fashions her young lover into an orientalized ideal—the young woman's room is furnished with carpets and pillows, and Vera wraps her in beautiful cloth clasped at the shoulders and falling softly down to the ground.

As she writes her diary, the protagonist reflects back on her life. She has been raised by an authoritative grandmother, doesn't know her mother, and her presumed father is a homosexual dandy. She meets a young man who is willing to marry her despite her strange background. However, as she attends the theater on the night before her wedding, Vera, who sees her while acting on the stage, whisks her away from her family and fiancé, who was once Vera's lover, saying that they are not worthy of such beauty. Just as she earlier lived completely subsumed by her grandmother's will, the young woman starts living in Vera's house, subsumed by Vera's will and worship. Throughout the diary, the young protagonist sees her own beauty through Vera's eyes, and uses Vera's words to describe herself. Symbolically, the word *vera* means faith in Russian. Eventually, Vera, obsessed by her lover's beauty puts her on the stage, since she feels that she must share this beauty with the public. At the same time, Vera is jealously protective of the young woman, and initially refuses a famous painter's request to paint her portrait. In a show of will, the protagonist agrees on her own to pose for another painter. Jealous, Vera beats her lover. The protagonist feels she lives in a gilded cage and often fantasizes about her own and Vera's death. Eventually, Vera, realizing that she cannot keep this beauty all to herself, agrees to have members of the Association of Thirty Three Artists to paint her lover. Vera fears that she and her lover will succumb to old age and to ugliness, and she hopes that the portraits will preserve her lover's beauty. As Vera meditates on losing her lover to art and to public contemplation, she delves more and more into her theater work, becoming obsessed with her dramatic roles. Finally, the day of posing for the artists' association arrives, and the protagonist poses nude. Like Narcissus, she sees her body in the mirror and falls in love with it. She imagines herself as an undine. However, when she and Vera look at the completed paintings, they see thirty three fragments, thirty three abominations. The protagonist eventually realizes that these images are a part of her real self, and goes back to pose for the artists of her own volition. However, Vera can't get over the thirty three images, stops acting, and goes mad. The protagonist takes on a lover from among the thirty three artists, and her visits in the studio are described in hallucinogenic terms. She decides that she is reflected better in the paintings than in Vera's eyes. At the end of the diary, Vera commits suicide. The diary ends abruptly as the protagonist tries to understand what she is and how she would go on living without being reflected in Vera.

This novel, as well as Zinov'eva-Annibal's other writings, came out of her adherence to the Dyonisiac cult of the ecstatic co-existence of flesh and soul, which was the mainstay of the Tower literary salon. Zinov'eva-Annibal saw herself as sharing her husband and his art with others. To that extent, she also felt that their intimate life must be shared with others, particularly with the poet Sergei Gorodetskii and with the wife of the poet Maksimilian Voloshin, Margarita Sabashnikova. The practical failure of these ideas resonates in *Thirty Three Abominations*.

Critical reception of this story was negative and moralizing. The critic Amfiteatrov derided it as an anatomical lesson passing for a literary work, and Novopolin, in his study of the pornographic element in Russian literature, wrote that no female writer before Zinov'eva-Annibal fell so low as to exalt the supremacy of sexual perversion. Significantly, Novopolin refused to deal with the spiritual portions of the novel, concentrating instead on the erotic details, writing that they were scarce even in the works of the nineteenth-century sexologist Krafft-Ebing. Famous writers, like Andrei Bely and Valerii Bryusov, skewered Zinov'eva-Annibal for writing a piece of base erotica, and the writer Zinaida Gippius wrote in a review that she pitied Zinov'eva-Annibal," a simple and nice woman." Unlike Mikhail Kuzmin's novel of homosexuality, *Wings*, to which *Thirty Three Abominations* is often compared, and which is more optimistic in its sexual exuberance, *Thirty Three Abominations* explores the tragedy of love, beauty, art, guilt, and belief. Significantly, Zinov'eva-Annibal dedicated this story to her husband, Viacheslav Ivanov, and published it shortly before her own death. Later critics saw in it an acknowledgement of the tragedy of her own "giving" of the poet to others.

Late twentieth-century critics read *Thirty Three Abominations* from the perspective of Zinov'eva-Annibal's failed attempts to create a salon for women where they could transcend the mundane. As a critic herself, Zinov'eva-Annibal was particularly taken by the writings of the French actress and essayist Georgette Leblanc, from which she derived her idea of a women's collective intended to propagate corporeal beauty and freedom. *Thirty Three Abominations* and Zinov'eva-Annibal's other writings were finally republished in Russia in the 1990s, for the first time since the Bolshevik Revolution.

Biography

Lidiia Dmitrievna Zinov'eva-Annibal, born in Kopore in 1866, is famous in the literary history of the Russian Silver Age as a co-host of the symbolist literary salon The Tower with her husband Viacheslav Ivanov. She started publishing in 1889, mostly in literary periodicals, wrote several plays and stories, and died prematurely of scarlet fever in Zagor'e in 1907.

RUTH WALLACH

Editions

Tridtsat' tri uroda. S.-Peterburg: Izd-vo "Ory," 1907.
Trid't'sat' tri uroda. Moskva: Agraf, 1999.
"Thirty Three Abominations." In *The Silver Age of Russian Culture: An Anthology.* Ann Arbor, MI: Ardis, 1975.

Selected Works

Kol'tsa. 1904, 1971.
Tragicheskii zverinets. 1907, 1997.
Net! 1918.
The Tragic Menagerie. 1999.

Further Reading

Costlow, Jane. "Lidiia Zinov'eva-Annibal." In: Tomei, Christine D. (ed.). *Russian Women Writers, I–II.* Garland, New York, NY, 1999. Volume I, pp. 443–446.
Novopolin, Gr. *Pornograficheskii element v russkoi literature.* S.-Peterburg: M.M. Stasiulevich 1909.

ZOLA, ÉMILE

1840–1902
French novelist, dramatist, and journalist

Émile Zola (1840–1902) published 29 novels, several volumes of short stories, and a number of plays. He wrote countless, often polemical newspaper articles dealing with a wide range of subjects, from art to politics, and was the leading proponent of literary Naturalism. At the height of his career in the 1880s he was the most famous French novelist of his day. Zola's most important work is his twenty-volume novel cycle *Les Rougon-Macquart: histoire naturelle et sociale d'une famille sous le Second Empire* [*The Rougon-Macquart: the natural and social history of a family during the Second Empire*] in which he charts the lives of five generations of the Rougon-Macquart family. All his central protagonists descend from the family's founding matriarch, Tante Dide, and all inherit from her a kind of mental instability or *fêlure* [crack]. Although this instability manifests itself in different ways, it is frequently linked with excessive or perverse sexual desire. As well as Zola's most depraved heroine, Nana, Maxime in *La curée* [*The Kill*], Serge in *La faute de l'abbé Mouret* [*Father Mouret's Sin*], and Jacques in *La bête humaine* [*The Human Beast*] all engage in non-conventional sexual acts. For Zola, any preference for non-reproductive sex is an inherited flaw—failure to control these 'unnatural' (because non-reproductive) desires ultimately leads to the downfall of the character.

Although none of Zola's works can be described as erotic in the proper sense, his novels in particular deal often explicitly with human sexuality, which he considered—with money—to be the driving force behind society. Zola's treatment of human sexuality stems from his commitment to literary Naturalism. The primary aim of Zolian Naturalism,—a literary movement which had its roots in the Realism of Honoré de Balzac and Gustave Courbet—, was, according to Zola, to 'tout voir, tout savoir, tout dire' [see everything, know everything, say everything]. The novelist's quest to shed light even on the most troubling aspects of late nineteenth-century society was greeted with widespread condemnation. Even though, as Zola was at pains to demonstrate, all the details of his novels came from his observations of reality, he was considered by many to be both immoral and dangerous. His use of precise anatomical detail in descriptions of sex, and his unwillingness to avoid reference to taboo subjects, angered his critics who were uneasy about being presented with harsh truths whose existence they would rather ignore. They failed to see that it was the Second Empire society depicted by Zola, rather than the author himself, which should be condemned as immoral. Zola did not necessarily condone the behavior he described (indeed he often criticized it), but his aim was to force French society to confront its own, sordid, guilty, and hidden realities. It is not surprising then that Zola's novels contain many frank references to sex. As well as conventional heterosexual sex (on which the continuation of the family depends), and adultery (which is almost as common), he depicts rape (*La terre* [*The Earth*]), oral sex (*L'Argent* [*Money*]), lesbianism (*Pot-Bouille* [*Piping Hot*]), incest (*Le Docteur Pascal*), sadism (*Son excellence Eugène Rougon* [*His Excellency Eugène Rougon*]), castration (*Germinal*), sexually motivated murder (*Thérèse Raquin, La bête humaine*), and prostitution (*Nana*). Zola's most sexually active protagonists are ruled by their bodily urges: rather than acting on reflection, they act on impulse, being driven by their instincts, their passions, their appetites. An almost animalistic desire for sexual fulfilment is the motivating force behind the narratives of a number of novels, most notably *Thérèse Raquin, Nana*, and *La bête humaine*.

Although Zola was never tried for obscenity in France, the translator and publisher of a number of English translations, Henry Vizetelly, was twice prosecuted under the Obscene Publications Act. In October 1888, he was fined, and in May 1889, he was sentenced to three months imprisonment.

Thérèse Raquin

Thérèse Raquin was Zola's first overtly 'naturalist' novel, and his preface to the second edition can be read as something of a naturalist manifesto. *Thérèse Raquin* is the story of the eponymous heroine's sexual desire for her husband Camille's friend and colleague Laurent. Unable to ignore their mutual passion, Thérèse and Laurent engage in a lustful adulterous affair before plotting to kill Camille. After the murder, Thérèse and Laurent are eventually married. However their guilt at what they have done is so strong that soon any physical contact is repulsive to them. Their most erotic moments paradoxically become their most dreaded as the drowned corpse of Camille seems to lie between them in bed. Their increasingly violent and abusive relationship is symbolized by the scene in which Thérèse engineers a miscarriage by presenting her belly to Laurent as he beats her. The novel ends with a dramatic double-suicide in which the lovers kill themselves instead of killing each other.

Nana

Nana, the ninth novel in the *Rougon-Macquart* cycle, is arguably Zola's most erotic novel. The novel charts the life of the eponymous heroine from her strip-tease-like appearance (all-but-naked in the role of Venus) on stage at the *Variétés* Theatre, through her rise to infamy, to her death from smallpox. Nana, a working-class prostitute whose childhood is recounted in *L'Assommoir* [*The Dram Shop*], sees the wealthy men who desire her as a resource to be selfishly exploited. She takes no real pleasure with them, merely using them as a way of increasing her status. She has utter disrespect for their bourgeois values, and delights in exposing their hypocrisies and wrecking their marriages. All the men she encounters are in some way destroyed, either financially, physically, or emotionally, by the end of the novel. Zola describes Nana as a 'golden fly,' a filthy parasite who infests everyone she touches with the sordid dirt of her working-class existence. In one emblematic scene, Nana and her lesbian lover Satin delight in sullying their outwardly respectable companions with tales of their debauched childhood. The novel demonstrates above all the dangerous power of the female body, whose erotic charms can pose a threat to the very fabric of society by seducing and enthralling even the most morally upright of citizens.

Biography

Born in Paris, April 12, 1840, moved to Aix-en-Provence, 1843. Educated at the Pension de Notre-Dame, Aix, 1847–1852, the Collège Bourbon d'Aix-en-Provence, 1852–1858, and the Lycée Saint-Louis, Paris, 1858–1859, twice failed the *Baccalauréat*, 1859. Worked as a clerk in the Customs House in Paris, 1860–1862 and then as the director of publicity for the publisher Hachette, 1862–1866. Published his first collection of short stories in 1864. Left Hachette to become a freelance journalist, 1866. Married Gabrielle Alexandrine Meley in 1870. Moved from Paris to Médan, 1878. Began an affair with a young servant, Jeanne Rozerot, 1880; one son and one daughter. Elected President of the *Société des Gens de Lettres*, 1891. Awarded the rank of officer in the *Légion d'honneur*, 1893. Tried for slander and sentenced to a year's imprisonment after publication of *J'accuse*, 1898, and obliged to flee to London where he lived in exile, 1898–1899. Died from asphyxiation in his apartment in Paris on 29 September 1902. His remains were transferred to the Panthéon in 1908.

HANNAH THOMPSON

Selected Works

Thérèse Raquin. 1867; as *Thérèse Raquin*, translated by Andrew Rothwell. 1992.
La curée. 1871; as *The Kill*, translated by A. Teixeira de Mattos. 1954.
Nana. 1880; as *Nana*, translated by Douglas Parmee. 1992.
La bête humaine. 1890; as *La Bête humaine*, translated by Roger Pearson. 1996.

Further Reading

Borie, Jean. *Le Tyran timide: le naturalisme de la femme au dix-neuvième siècle*. Paris: Éditions Klincksieck, 1973.
Brooks, Peter. *Body Work: Objects of Desire in Modern Narrative*. Cambridge, MA: Harvard University Press, 1993.
Chitnis, Bernice. *Reflecting on 'Nana.'* London: Routledge, 1991.
Hemmings, F.W.J. *Émile Zola*. Oxford: Clarendon Press, 1966.

King, Graham. *Garden of Zola: Émile Zola and his Novels for English Readers*. London: Barrie and Jenkins, 1978.

Petrey, Sandy. 'Anna-Nana-Nana: identité sexuelle, écriture naturaliste, lectures lesbiennes.' *Cahiers Naturalistes*, 69 (1995): 69–80.

Schor, Naomi. *Zola's Crowds*. Baltimore, MD: John Hopkins University Press, 1978.

Vizetelly, Ernest A. *Émile Zola, Novelist and Reformer: An Account of his Life and Work*. London: John Lane, the Bodley Head, 1904.

White, Nicholas. *The Family in Crisis in Late Nineteenth-Century French Fiction*. Cambridge: Cambridge University Press, 1999.

INDEX

W